CHILD AND ADOLESCENT DEVELOPMENT

ANITA WOOLFOLK
THE OHIO STATE UNIVERSITY

NANCY E. PERRY
UNIVERSITY OF BRITISH COLUMBIA

PEARSON

Boston Columbus Indianapolis New York San Francisco Upper Saddle River
Amsterdam Cape Town Dubai London Madrid Milan Munich Paris Montreal Toronto
Delhi Mexico City Sao Paulo Sydney Hong Kong Seoul Singapore Taipei Tokyo

Vice President and Editor in Chief: Jeffery W. Johnston
Publisher: Kevin Davis
Executive Development Editor: Linda Ashe Bishop
Editorial Assistant: Lauren Carlson
Vice President, Director of Marketing: Margaret Waples
Marketing Manager: Joanna Sabella
Senior Managing Editor: Pamela D. Bennett
Senior Project Manager: Mary M. Irvin
Senior Operations Supervisor: Matt Ottenweller
Senior Art Director: Diane Lorenzo
Text Designer: Candace Rowley
Cover Designer: Diane Lorenzo
Permissions Administrator: Rebecca Savage
Cover Art: Jenny H., Age 5
Project Coordination: Kathy Smith
Photo Researcher: Lori Whitley
Composition: S4Carlisle Publishing Services
Printer/Binder: Courier/Kendallville
Cover Printer: Lehigh-Phoenix Color Corp.
Text Font: Garamond Book

Photo Credits appear on p. P-1, following the Subject Index.

Credits and acknowledgments borrowed from other sources and reproduced, with permission, in this textbook appear on appropriate pages within the text.

Library of Congress Cataloging-in-Publication Data

Hoy, Anita Woolfolk
Child and adolescent development/Anita E. Woolfolk, Nancy Perry.
p. cm.
Includes bibliographical references and index.
ISBN 978-0-13-702311-0
1. Child development. 2. Youth development. I. Perry, Nancy. II. Title.
HQ767.9.H69 2012
305.231–dc22

2010051009

10 9 8 7 6 5 4 3 2 1

www.pearsonhighered.com

ISBN-10: 0-13-702311-1
ISBN-13: 978-0-13-702311-0

TO AMAYA AND LUCY

the future . . .

ABOUT THE AUTHORS

Anita Woolfolk Hoy was born in Fort Worth, Texas, where her mother taught child development at TCU and her father was an early worker in the computer industry. She is a Texas Longhorn—all her degrees are from the University of Texas, Austin, the last one a Ph.D. After graduating, she was a psychologist working with children in elementary and secondary schools in 15 counties of central Texas. She began her career in higher education as a professor of educational psychology at Rutgers University, and then moved to The Ohio State University in 1994. Anita's research focuses on students' and teachers' sense of efficacy. She is the editor of *Theory Into Practice,* a journal that brings the best ideas from research to practicing educators. With students and colleagues, she has published over 70 book chapters and research articles. Anita has served as Vice-President for Division K (Teaching & Teacher Education) of the American Educational Research Association and President of Division 15 (Educational Psychology) of the American Psychological Association. Her textbook, *Educational Psychology,* is moving into its 12th edition and has been translated into over 10 different languages.

Nancy Perry worked as a classroom and resource teacher in school districts in British Columbia, Canada, before obtaining her Ph.D. from the University of Michigan. In 1996, she joined the Department of Educational and Counselling Psychology, and Special Education at the University of British Columbia (UBC). There she teaches courses across two program areas: Human Development, Learning, and Culture; and Special Education. She is a recipient of UBC's Killam Teaching Prize and Professor for the Struggling Youth Initiative. She is a Past President of the Canadian Association for Educational Psychology and has served on the Executive Boards of the Canadian Association for Studies in Education and Division 15 (Educational Psychology) of the American Psychological Association. Her research examines children's development of self-regulation and self-regulated learning. She has published widely in this area and worked extensively with teachers to develop practices that support self-regulated learning.

PREFACE

Welcome to the remarkable world of child and adolescent development. Many of you are reading this book because you plan to be teachers, counselors, speech therapists, recreational leaders, or medical practitioners. Some of you will be (or already are) parents. All of you are citizens who influence the lives of children through your knowledge, votes, and participation in communities. The material in this text should be of interest to everyone who is concerned about children and adolescents, from the library volunteer to the principal of a school for children facing the challenges of learning in a new language.

No background in human or developmental psychology is necessary to understand this material. We have avoided jargon and technical language whenever possible and focused on writing a clear, relevant, and interesting book on an exciting topic. We also have written this book with three features ever in mind:

- A chronological framework for discussing child development
- A commitment to clear explanations of theory coupled always with applications to practice
- A complete and thorough integration of diversity

Chronological Frame

As you glance at the table of contents for this book, you will notice that we examine three different *areas* of child development—physical, cognitive, and social emotional—during the specific *time periods* of infancy and toddlerhood, early childhood, middle childhood, and adolescence. Of course, these are not exact categories. Children develop continuously, not only across time periods, but also across areas—physical development is not separated from cognitive development, nor does emotional development proceed independently from social or physical development. Children are whole and so is their development. But you are likely to work with particular age groups, so it makes sense to consider all that is going on with those children during specific periods of their lives. By dealing separately with time periods and areas of development, we actually hope to paint a more complete and integrated picture that you can use as you interact with real children and adolescents.

Theory Into Practice

In the next few hundred pages you will explore the implications and applications of the best research on child development. Theory and practice are not separated in these pages; they are considered together. We show how information and ideas drawn from research in child development can be applied when working with, relating to, and supporting all children. To help you explore the connections between research and practice, you will encounter a wealth of examples, children's words and images, case studies, guidelines, and even tips from experienced practitioners. As you read this book, we believe you will see the immense value and usefulness of child development.

THE CASEBOOK

WHAT WOULD YOU DO?

ONLY CHILDREN AND IMAGINARY FRIENDS

Kayla has set her table again to make "tea" for Sassy. When her mother walks in and starts to sit down, Kayla protests, "No! that's Sassy's chair. You have to go, she is coming." Kayla's mother sighs, says, "OK, I'll leave," and returns to her desk to check her e-mail. In a few minutes she hears Kayla talking with Sassy, or at least she hears Kayla's side of the conversation. Sassy is not a real child but an imaginary friend that Kayla talks about and with often—she has for the past few years. When she is upset or has been scolded, Kayla threatens, "I'm going to run away and live with Sassy in China—she has a nice mommy!" But at other times, Kayla complains that Sassy has been mean to her and has spilled ice cream on her shirt. Her parents were not concerned at first about the invisible Sassy, but then they found out Kayla believes that Sassy is a giraffe who wears jeans and can make herself tiny to fit in Kayla's pocket when she goes to school. Her parents worry, what will the preschool teacher think? What will the other children think? Should we talk to someone about Kayla? Is it because she is lonely as an only child? Will Sassy keep Kayla from making real friends?

CRITICAL THINKING

- Did you or someone you know have an imaginary friend?
- What role could such a friend play for children?
- What else would you want to know about Kayla and her family to evaluate this situation?
- Should Kayla's parents be concerned?

One way we make theory into practice real is by starting every chapter with a vivid case situation, so we ask, **"What Would You Do?"** We end the chapter with ideas from experts about **"What Would They Do?"** As you read each chapter, the intricacies of the case may become more apparent and the answers of the experts more interesting. Do you agree with their suggestions?

As we take theory into practice, we challenge readers to avoid the trap of making "either/or" judgments and decisions. What matters more, nature or nurture? Who has greater influence, parents or peers? Which is more valid and reliable, the wisdom of practice or scientific research? Should we encourage stem cell research? Should we leave babies alone or pick them up every time they cry? Should children diagnosed with ADHD take pills? Do sex abstinence campaigns work? In every chapter we challenge critical thinking with a feature called **Point/ Counterpoint** on these and other controversial issues.

POINT/COUNTERPOINT: What Kind of Research Should Guide Social Policy?

For at least the past 30 years, debates have raged about the best kind of research to use in formulating policies for children, particularly in education. Should we rely only on scientific experiments or is that kind of work impossible in education? What are the arguments?

POINT

▶ **Social policy should be guided by scientific experiments—evidence-based research.** According to Grover Whitehurst, the director or the U.S. Office of Educational Research and Improvement, the best research to guide educational practice is randomized experiments. Robert Slavin (2002) paints a bright future for educational reform guided by scientifically based research:

> This process could create the kind of progressive, systematic improvement over time that has characterized successful parts of our economy and society throughout the 20th century, in fields such as medicine, agriculture, transportation, and technology. In each of these fields, processes of development, rigorous evaluation, and dissemination have produced a pace of innovation and improvement that is unprecedented in history. . . . Educational practice does change over time, but the change process more resembles the pendulum swings of taste characteristic of art or fashion (think hemlines) rather than the progressive improvements characteristic of science and technology. (p. 16)

The major reason for extraordinary advances in medicine and agriculture, according to Slavin, is that these fields base their practices on scientific evidence. Randomized clinical trials and replicated experiments are the sources of the evidence. The emphasis on evidence is not limited to education. Robert McCall and his colleagues note that "funders and policy makers at the national and local levels are insisting that new programs desiring funding must be essentially replications of service programs that research has already demonstrated to be effective" (McCall et al., 2004, p. 331).

COUNTERPOINT

▶ **Experiments are not the only or even the best source of evidence.** David Olson (2004) disagrees strongly with Slavin's position. He claims that we cannot use medicine as an analogy to education. "Treatments" in education are much more complex and unpredictable than administering one drug or another in medicine. In addition, every educational program is changed by classroom conditions and the way it is implemented. David Berliner (2002) makes a similar point:

> Doing science and implementing scientific findings are so difficult in education because humans in schools are embedded in complex and changing networks of social interaction. The participants in those networks have variable power to affect each other from day to day, and the ordinary events of life (a sick child, a messy divorce, a passionate love affair, migraine headaches, hot flashes, a birthday party, alcohol abuse, a new principal, a new child in the classroom, rain that keeps the children from a recess outside the school building) all affect doing science in school settings by limiting the generalizability of educational research findings.

Beware of Either/Or

Berliner concludes that a complex problem like education needs a whole range of methods for study—

> [E]thnographic research is crucial, as are case studies, survey research, time series, design experiments, action research, and other means to collect reliable evidence for engaging in unfettered argument about education issues. A single method is not what the government should be promoting for educational researchers. (Berliner, 2002, p. 20)

CONNECTING WITH CHILDREN

Guidelines for Teachers and Families: Scaffolding Children's Learning

Tailor scaffolding to the needs of each child.

Examples

1. Parent, teachers, and coaches, when students are beginning new tasks or topics, provide models, prompts, sentence starters, coaching, and feedback. As the children grow in competence, give less support and more opportunities for independent work.
2. Give children choices about the level of difficulty or degree of independence in reading books or projects; encourage them to challenge themselves but to seek help when they are really stuck.

Make sure children have access to powerful tools that support thinking.

Examples

1. Teach children to use learning and organizational strategies, research tools, language tools (dictionaries or computer searches), day planners, and word-processing programs.
2. Model the use of tools; show children how you use an appointment book or electronic notebook to make plans and manage time, for example.

Teachers, build on the students' cultural funds of knowledge (Moll et al., 1992)

Examples

1. Identify family knowledge by having students interview each other's families about their work and home knowledge (agriculture, economics, manufacturing, household management, medicine and illness, religion, child care, cooking, etc.).
2. Tie assignments to these funds of knowledge and use community experts to evaluate assignments.
3. Capitalize on dialogue and group learning by experimenting with peer tutoring; teach students how to ask good questions and give helpful explanations.

For more information about Vygotsky and his theories. see: http://tip.psychology.org/vygotsky.html

But don't worry. This is not another academic text that presents competing theories and nothing else. In every chapter, we also have several sections called **"Connecting with Children"** that provide guidelines and examples for teachers, parents, and other caregivers about how to support the physical, cognitive, emotional, and social development of children and adolescents.

DIVERSITY

Every person develops in context—in families, communities, countries, and cultures. Individuals develop first in the context of their mother's womb, but also in the context of their own unfolding and interacting genes. Every generation develops in a different context of history. Children learn one language or several languages. They learn in schools and in cliques, clubs, churches, and gangs. In every culture and across time, relationships with adults provide important guidance and support in the development of children and adolescents.

We honor this diversity by including research on many developmental pathways across a range of cultures. We are careful to note who are the participants in the research we describe and not to assume that what applies to one group applies to all. We sought out work on children with varying abilities and disabilities, children in different countries, children who do not speak English, and children who represent a range of poverty and privilege.

In every chapter we have a section called **Relating to Every Child** in which we go beyond acknowledging diversity to respecting and celebrating it. Some of the topics included are teaching bilingual children to read, building on children's funds of cultural knowledge, physical activity around the world, the impact of war on children's mental health, and cultural perspectives on decision making in adolescents.

RELATING TO EVERY CHILD

Different Parenting Styles in Different Cultures

NOT EVERY STUDY finds results consistent with Diane Baumrind's findings about the problems that accompany authoritarian styles in white, middle-class families. Other research indicates that higher control, more authoritarian parenting is linked to better grades for Asian and African American students (Glasgow, Dornbusch, Troyer, Steinberg, & Ritter, 1997). Parenting that is strict and directive, with clear rules and consequences, combined with high levels of warmth and emotional support, is associated with higher academic achievement and greater emotional maturity for inner-city children (Garner & Spears, 2000; Jarrett, 1995). Differences in cultural values and in the danger level of some urban neighborhoods may make tighter parental control appropriate, and even necessary (Smetana, 2000). In addition, in cultures that have a greater respect for elders and a more group-centered rather than individualistic philosophy, it may be a misreading of the parents' actions to perceive their demand for obedience as "authoritarian" (Lamb & Lewis, 2005; Nucci, 2001). In fact, research by Ruth Chao (2001; Chao & Tseng, 2002) has challenged Baumrind's conclusions for Asian families. Chao finds that an alternative parenting style of *chiao shun* (a Chinese term that Chao translates to mean "training") better characterizes parenting in Asian and Asian American families. Chao is also studying whether serving as a translator or "language broker" for parents who do not speak English has an impact on the child's psychological well-being and relationship with the parents.

Ruth Chao

Research with Latino parents also questions whether parenting styles studies based on European American families are helpful in understanding Latino families. Using a carefully designed observation system, Melanie Domenech Rodríguez and her colleagues included a third dimension of parenting—giving children more or less autonomy (freedom to make decisions). They found that almost all of the Latino parents they studied could be characterized as *protective* (high on warmth, high on control/demand, and low on granting autonomy) or *authoritative* (high on all three—warmth, control/ demand, and granting autonomy). Also, these Latino parents tended to be more demanding and less likely to grant autonomy to their female children (Domenech Rodríguez, Donovick, & Crowley, 2009).

We also honor the diverse talents of children by using children's art from around the world for the cover and the opening page of every chapter. Our "Flower" for the cover was painted by Jenny H., age 5, from the USA. Our chapter artists are:

Chapter	Artist	Age	Home Country
1	Chrissy C.	5	USA
2	Fatima Z.	8	Australia
3	Jenny I.	2	USA
4	Elaine Y.Y.	3	China
5	Nora Skalleova	9	Czech Republic
6	Jasmine T.	5	USA
7	Claudia Uno	8	Andorra
8	Trevor Yo Heng Ang	9	Singapore
9	Sisylia Octavia C.	12	Indonesia
10	Alannah H.	10	USA
11	Andrea Teresa Kurian	10	Botswana
12	Ganna Tarapygina	9	Ukraine
13	Soema Abdullaeva	12	Tajikistan

We hope you enjoy and marvel at their work as much as we have.

SUPPLEMENTS

This first edition of *Child and Adolescent Development* boasts of several useful and well-developed supplements. Pearson's MyEducationLab, an online and interactive resource, has been carefully designed to assist you with learning and teaching experiences that prepare you for teaching by using authentic classroom video footage and student artifacts. Also available are a number of ancillaries created for instructors to help maximize the time and opportunity needed to develop a syllabus and thoroughly prepare for course instruction.

PEARSON myeducationlab Prepare with the Power of Classroom Practice

In *Preparing Teachers for a Changing World,* Linda Darling Hammond and her colleagues point out that grounding teacher education in real classrooms—among real teachers and students and among actual examples of students' and teachers' work—is an important, and perhaps even an essential, part of training teachers for the complexities of teaching in today's classrooms. MyEducationLab is an online learning solution that provides contextualized interactive exercises, simulations, and other resources designed to help develop the knowledge and skills teachers need. All of the activities and exercises in MyEducationLab are built around essential learning outcomes for teachers and are mapped to professional teaching standards. Utilizing classroom video, authentic student and teacher artifacts, case studies, and other resources and assessments, the scaffolded learning experiences in MyEducationLab offer preservice teachers and those who teach them a unique and valuable education tool.

For each topic covered in the course you will find the following features and resources:

Connection to National Standards

Now it is easier than ever to see how coursework is connected to national standards. Each topic on MyEducationLab lists intended learning outcomes connected to the appropriate national standards. And all of the activities and exercises in MyEducationLab are mapped to the appropriate national standards and learning outcomes as well.

Assignments and Activities

Designed to enhance your understanding of concepts covered in class and save instructors preparation and grading time, these assignable exercises show concepts in action (through video, cases, and/or student and teacher artifacts). They will help you deepen your content knowledge and synthesize and apply concepts and strategies you read about in the book. (Correct answers for these assignments are available to the instructor only under the Instructor Resource tab.)

Building Teaching Skills and Dispositions

These learning units will help you practice and strengthen skills that are essential to quality teaching. After presenting the steps involved in a core teaching process, you are given an opportunity to practice applying this skill via videos, student and teacher artifacts, and/or case studies of authentic classrooms. Providing multiple opportunities to practice a single teaching concept, each activity encourages a deeper understanding and application of concepts, as well as the use of critical thinking skills.

IRIS Center Resources

The IRIS Center at Vanderbilt University (http://iris.peabody.vanderbilt.edu)—funded by the U.S. Department of Education's Office of Special Education Programs (OSEP) develops training enhancement materials for preservice and inservice teachers. The Center works with experts from across the country to create challenge-based interactive modules, case study units, and podcasts that provide research-validated information about working with students in inclusive settings. In your MyEducationLab course, we have integrated this content where appropriate.

Simulations in Classroom Management

One of the most difficult challenges facing teachers today is how to balance classroom instruction with classroom management. These interactive cases focus on the classroom management issues teachers most frequently encounter on a daily basis. Each simulation presents a challenge scenario at the beginning and then offers a series of choices to solve each challenge. Along the way you receive mentor feedback on your choices and have the opportunity to make better choices if necessary. Upon exiting each simulation you will have a clear understanding of how to address these common classroom management issues and will be better equipped to handle them in the classroom.

Study Plan Specific to Your Text

A MyEducationLab Study Plan is a multiple choice assessment tied to chapter objectives, supported by study material. A well-designed Study Plan offers multiple opportunities to fully master required course content as identified by the objectives in each chapter:

- **Chapter Objectives** identify the learning outcomes for the chapter and give you targets to shoot for as you read and study.
- **Multiple Choice Assessments** assess mastery of the content. These assessments are mapped to chapter objectives, and you can take the multiple choice quiz as many times as you want. Not only do these quizzes provide overall scores for each objective, but they also explain why responses to particular items are correct or incorrect.
- **Study Material: Review, Practice and Enrichment** give you a deeper understanding of what you do and do not know related to chapter content. This material includes text excerpts, activities that include hints and feedback, and interactive multimedia exercises built around videos, simulations, cases, or classroom artifacts.
- **Flashcards** help you study the definitions of the key terms within each chapter.

Course Resources

The Course Resources section on MyEducationLab is designed to help you put together an effective lesson plan, prepare for and begin your career, navigate your first year of teaching, and understand key educational standards, policies, and laws.

The Course Resources Tab includes the following:

- The **Lesson Plan Builder** is an effective and easy-to-use tool that you can use to create, update, and share quality lesson plans. The software also makes it easy to integrate state content standards into any lesson plan.
- The **Preparing a Portfolio** module provides guidelines for creating a high-quality teaching portfolio.
- **Beginning Your Career** offers tips, advice, and other valuable information on:
  - *Resume Writing and Interviewing:* Includes expert advice on how to write impressive resumes and prepare for job interviews.
  - *Your First Year of Teaching:* Provides practical tips to set up a first classroom, manage student behavior, and more easily organize for instruction and assessment.
  - *Law and Public Policies:* Details specific directives and requirements teachers need to understand under the No Child Left Behind Act and the Individuals with Disabilities Education Improvement Act of 2004.
- **Longman Dictionary of Contemporary English Online.** Make use of this online version of the CD-ROM of the *Longman Dictionary of Contemporary English*—the quickest and easiest way to look up any word while you are working on MyEducationLab.

Certification and Licensure

The Certification and Licensure section is designed to help you pass your licensure exam by giving you access to state test requirements, overviews of what tests cover, and sample test items.

The Certification and Licensure tab includes the following:

- **State Certification Test Requirements:** Here you can click on a state and will then be taken to a list of state certification tests.
  - Click on the **Licensure Exams** you need to take to find:
  - Basic information about each test
  - Descriptions of what is covered on each test
  - Sample test questions with explanations of correct answers
- **National Evaluation Series™** by Pearson: Here you can see the tests in the NES, learn what is covered on each exam, and access sample test items with descriptions and rationales of correct answers. You can also purchase interactive online tutorials developed by Pearson Evaluation Systems and the Pearson Teacher Education and Development group.
- **ETS Online Praxis Tutorials:** You can purchase interactive online tutorials developed by ETS and by the Pearson Teacher Education and Development group. Tutorials are available for the Praxis I exams and for select Praxis II exams.

Visit www.myeducationlab.com for a demonstration of this exciting new online teaching resource.

Additional Support for Instructors

The following resources are available for instructors to download from **www.pearsonhighered.com.** Enter the author, title of the text, or the ISBN number, then select this text, and click on the "Resources" tab. Download the supplement you need. If you require assistance in downloading any resources, contact your Pearson representative.

INSTRUCTOR'S MANUAL An Instructor's Manual, available electronically, includes guidelines for integrating the meaningful use of MyEducationLab into course work. The Instructor's Manual also provides ideas and strategies that explore core developmental themes, presents developmental characteristics and milestones, identifies the diversity in global, developmental perspectives, and offers critical discussion topics. This manual includes activities and strategies designed to help prospective teachers—and others seeking a career working with children or adolescents—to apply the developmental concepts and strategies they have learned.

POWERPOINT SLIDES PowerPoint slides include chapter objectives, key concepts, summaries of content, and graphic aids, each designed to support class lectures and help students organize, synthesize, and remember core content.

TEST BANK AND MYTEST Built from the course objectives, the test bank questions offer both lower-level questions that ask students to identify or explain concepts, principles, and theories about development and higher-level questions that will require students to apply concepts, principles, and theories to student behavior and teaching strategies. The test bank is available electronically in a secure online environment called PearsonMyTest. MyTest enables instructors to create and customize their exams. Please contact your local Pearson representative for log-in information to MyTest.

BLACKBOARD AND WEBCT COURSE CONTENT CARTRIDGES The course content cartridges contain the content of the Test Bank and are available for use on either Course Management system.

ACKNOWLEDGMENTS

During the years we worked on this book many people supported the project. Without their help, this text simply could not have been written.

Donna Wittmer, an expert on infancy, drafted Chapters 3 and 4. We appreciate her expertise and energy in providing that content. We are honored to have her knowledge reflected in our book.

As we developed and revised this book, we benefited from the ideas of professors around the country who took the time to complete surveys, review chapters, and answer questions. Thanks to:

Jennifer Betters-Bubon, University of Wisconsin, Madison; Gary Bingham, Georgia State University; Michael Block, Azusa Pacific University; Bill Fisk, Clemson University; Jenefer Husman, Arizona State University; Kathi Jensen, University of Redlands; Sue Offutt, University of North Dakota; Patricia Quijada, University of Texas, San Antonio; Ismael Ramos, The College of St. Rose; and Stacy Thompson, Southern Illinois University.

Child development professionals and teachers across the country and around the world contributed their experience, creativity, and expertise to the ***Casebook: What Would You Do?*** We have thoroughly enjoyed our association with these experts, and are grateful for the perspective they brought to the book.

Carol Apple, Staffing and Compliance Coordinator, Hillsborough County School District, Tampa, FL; Cathy Blanchfield, English/Language Arts teacher, Grades 10 and 12, Duncan Polytechnical High School, Fresno, CA; Elaine S. Boothby, AP Literature Teacher, Grade 12, South River High School, Edgewater, MD; Amanda Bosdeck, 8th Grade Math and Science teacher, West De Pere Middle School, De Pere, WI; Katie Burger, Kindergarten teacher, Washington Park Elementary School, Laurinburg, NC; Sarah Davlin, School Counselor, Wyandot Run Elementary School, Powell, OH; Karen E. Davies, Kindergarten teacher, North Royalton Early Childhood Center, Broadview Heights, OH; Lou De Lauro, 5th Grade Reading, Language Arts, and Social Studies teacher, John P. Faber School, Dunellen, NJ; Holly Fitchette, French teacher, Grades 9–11, Fleming Island High School, Fleming Island, FL; Chris Fraser, Behavioral Health Counselor in private practice, Columbus, OH; Shannon Gladieux, University of Toledo, Toledo, OH; Sarah Graff, California State University, Monterey Bay, Seaside, CA; Elizabeth Kennard, M.D., Director, Division of Reproductive Endocrinology and Infertility, Department of Obstetrics and Gynecology, The Ohio State University Medical Center, Columbus, OH; Jade Evette Muñoz, Texas A&M University, Corpus Christi, Corpus Christi, TX; Tracy L. MacDonald, School Counselor, Chesapeake Bay Middle School, Pasadena, MD; Jazmin Aguirre Moreno, The Ohio State University, Columbus, OH; Judy S. Pieper, Middle School Language Arts, Art, and Religion teacher, Holy Trinity Junior High, Newport, KY; Dr. D. Ray Reutzel, Endowed Chair and Director of Emma Eccles Early Childhood Center, Utah State University, Ogden, UT; Elizabeth Ruhl, California State University–Monterey Bay, Seaside, CA; Gina Stocks, Lecturer, Sul Ross State University Rio Grande College, Uvalde, TX; Jill Sullivan, Math teacher, Grades 9–11, Northside College Prep High School, Chicago, IL; Alyssa Vogt, University of Wisconsin, Madison, Madison, WI; Kami M. Wagner, School Counselor, Mt. Hebron High School, Ellicott City, MD; Judy Welch, M.D., Family Practitioner, Westbrook, ME; Debbie Wilson, School Nurse, St. Mary's Elementary School, St. Bernadette School, Lancaster City Schools, Lancaster, OH; Katherine A. Young, K–8 School Counselor, Montgomery County Intermediate Unit, Non-Public School Services Division, Norristown, PA; Dr. Vicky Zygouris-Coe, Researcher; Associate Professor of Education, University of Central Florida.

In a project of this size, so many people make essential contributions. Becky Savage, Permissions Coordinator, worked tirelessly to obtain permissions for the material reproduced in this text and the supplements. The text designer, Candace Rowley, and Senior Art Director, Diane Lorenzo, gave this book an international beauty. Lori Whitley searched relentlessly for photos from all over the world. Linda Bishop, Executive Development Editor, brought wisdom, expertise, tremendous organizational skills, a keen eye for good (and not so good) writing, and great humor to keep the entire project moving over several years. Kathy Smith, Project Coordinator, routinely performed minor miracles and held all aspects of the project in her wonderfully ordered and intelligent mind. She is a joy and a blessing as a colleague. Pam Bennett, Senior Managing Editor, and Mary Irvin, Senior Project Manager, coordinated all aspects of the project, with amazing skill and grace. Somehow they brought sanity to what could have been chaos and fun to what might have been drudgery. Now the book is in the capable hands of Joanna Sabella, Marketing Manager and Margaret Waples, Director of Marketing for Pearson Education. We can't wait to see what they are planning for us now! What a talented and creative group—we were honored to work with them all.

We were privileged to work with an outstanding editorial group. Nancy Forsyth, President of Pearson Teacher Education and Student Success, was with this project from the beginning and is the main reason it was launched. The book owes its completion to our editor, Kevin Davis, Publisher at Pearson. His enduring commitment to quality, unerring eye for design, and keen intellect made him the perfect guide for such an ambitious project. Lauren Carlson, Editorial Assistant, kept everything running smoothly and kept our fax machines and emails humming. In addition, we are grateful for the guidance of our early editors Karon Bowers, Susan Hartman, Christine Poolos, and Steven Frail, as well as development editors Cheryl de-Jong-Lambert, Lisa McLellan, and Sharon Geary for their work in the early stages of this project.

Also, we were fortunate to have excellent graduate assistants to dig up sources and resources, sometimes from the basements of libraries, create and adapt tables and figures, and compile the massive list of references. Thanks, in particular, to Michael Yough, Lynda Hutchinson, Silvia Mazebel Ortega, Cindy Lau, and Rebecca Collie.

Finally, we want to thank our family and friends for their kindness and support during the long days and nights that we worked on this book.

To Anita's family, Marion, Bob, Eric, Suzie, Liz, Wayne K., Marie, Kelly, and new baby Amaya—you are the greatest. And to Wayne Hoy, my friend, colleague, inspiration, passion, husband—you make every day a gift.

Thanks to Nancy's family, Elsie, Muriel, Doug, Corita, Gillian, Harv, and Lucy for your support and patience through all the weekends and holidays I was writing "the book." Most special thanks to Phil, my partner in life, who will no longer be a "textbook widow."

ANITA WOOLFOLK HOY, Columbus, Ohio
NANCY PERRY, Vancouver, Canada

BRIEF CONTENTS

CONTENTS

PART I UNDERSTANDING CHILDREN AND ADOLESCENTS

CHAPTER 1 INTRODUCTION: DIMENSIONS OF DEVELOPMENT 2

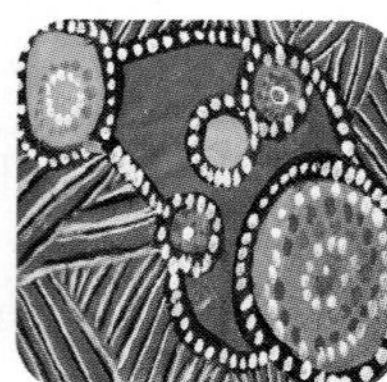

CHAPTER 2 THEORY AND RESEARCH IN CHILD DEVELOPMENT 28

PART II BIRTH, INFANCY, AND TODDLERHOOD

CHAPTER 3 GENETICS, PRENATAL DEVELOPMENT, AND BIRTH 76

CHAPTER 4

INFANCY AND TODDLERHOOD 116

CHAPTER 6 COGNITIVE DEVELOPMENT IN EARLY CHILDHOOD 196

CHAPTER 7 SOCIAL EMOTIONAL DEVELOPMENT IN EARLY CHILDHOOD 248

PART IV MIDDLE CHILDHOOD

CHAPTER 8 PHYSICAL DEVELOPMENT IN MIDDLE CHILDHOOD 298

CHAPTER 9

COGNITIVE DEVELOPMENT IN MIDDLE CHILDHOOD 330

CHAPTER 10 SOCIAL EMOTIONAL DEVELOPMENT IN MIDDLE CHILDHOOD 388

PART V ADOLESCENCE

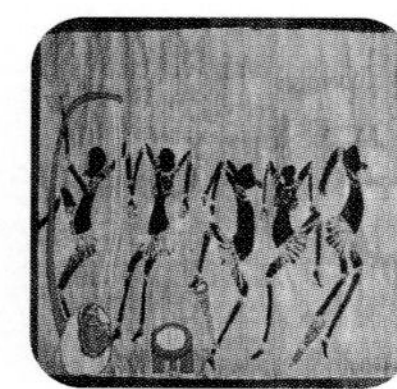

CHAPTER 11 PHYSICAL DEVELOPMENT IN ADOLESCENCE 442

CHAPTER 12

COGNITIVE DEVELOPMENT IN ADOLESCENCE 474

CHAPTER 13
SOCIAL EMOTIONAL DEVELOPMENT IN ADOLESCENCE 526

SPECIAL FEATURES

CASEBOOK: WHAT WOULD YOU DO?

CONNECTING WITH CHILDREN/ CONNECTING WITH ADOLESCENTS

POINT/COUNTERPOINT

RELATING TO EVERY CHILD/ RELATING TO EVERY ADOLESCENT

CHILD AND ADOLESCENT DEVELOPMENT

1

INTRODUCTION: DIMENSIONS OF DEVELOPMENT

THE CASEBOOK

WHAT WOULD YOU DO?

APPLYING YOUR KNOWLEDGE OF CHILD DEVELOPMENT

Every chapter in this text will begin with a case involving child development. The issues raised and problems posed will relate to the information in the chapter that follows. But in this chapter, the focus of the case is very specific: you. Why are you taking this class, and what will you do with the knowledge you gain? Do you plan a career in child development? Which one? How will you decide? Should you consider being a teacher, social worker, physician, child life specialist, speech therapist, psychologist, researcher, nutritionist, pediatric or neonatal nurse, recreational or camp director, children's minister, college professor, public policy analyst . . .? Are you now or will you ever be a parent, aunt, uncle, foster parent, guardian, voter . . .? If the answer to any of these questions is "yes" or even "maybe," then you need to think critically about what this class means for your future.

CRITICAL THINKING

- What experiences have you had with children?
- Which careers or roles involving children fit best with your talents, experiences, dispositions, and abilities?
- What is your final educational goal: Associate degree? Bachelor's degree? Master's? Doctorate?

Chrissy C., Age 5—USA

▶ OVERVIEW AND OBJECTIVES

Welcome to the remarkable world of children caught in the act of becoming. For the next several hundred pages, we will explore how children develop—and we will encounter some surprising situations.

- Ethan, a 3-year-old, confidently predicts that there will be "candy" in a big, red, heart-shaped candy box; when he sees that the box actually contains pencils, he claims that he always knew there were pencils in the box, and that his friend Jacob, who has never seen the candy box before, would also know this.
- A young girl who once said her *feet* hurt suddenly begins to refer to her *foots* hurting, and then describes her *footses* before she finally returns to talking about her *feet.*
- Elizabeth, a 4-year-old, watches as her mother flips through the channels on the TV. Elizabeth insists she wants to watch one channel on the TV, then another, then the first one, then the other—all at the same time.
- Leah, a 5-year-old, is certain that rolling out a ball of clay into a snake makes more clay.
- A 9-year-old child in Geneva, Switzerland is asked, "What is your nationality?"—*I am Swiss.*—"How come?"—*Because I live in Switzerland.*—"Are you also a Genevan?"—*No, that's not possible. I'm already Swiss, I can't also be Genevan.*
- Jamal, a very bright elementary school student, cannot answer the question, "How would life be different if there were no darkness at night?" because he insists, "It IS DARK at night!"
- A 2-year-old who brings his own mother to comfort a friend who is crying (even though the friend's mother is available too) becomes an adolescent who buys that friend a gift—a CD by a rapper he hates, but that his friend really likes.

What explanations are there for these interesting beliefs and behaviors? You will soon find out, because you also are entering the world of child development. By the time you finish this chapter you should be able to:

Objective 1.1 Describe the field of child development and compare it to the science of developmental psychology.

Objective 1.2 Explain four broad time periods in the development of children, including the social expectations about what children can do at each period.

Objective 1.3 Describe three broad areas of development during childhood and adolescence.

Objective 1.4 Discuss how family, ethnicity, social class, social policies, and historical time periods provide contexts for child development.

Objective 1.5 Discuss three key and constant questions in child development involving the shape, timing, and sources of development, and explain how these questions are answered today.

Objective 1.6 Decide how to apply the knowledge you have gained about child development.

What Is Child Development?

The term **development** in its most general sense refers to patterns of growth and change that occur in human beings (or animals) between conception and death. The patterns and change often involve greater complexity—the 3-month-old who stops following an object when it moves out of sight becomes an 8-year-old who can read a map and then a 16-year-old who can understand theories of geometry (Thelen & Corbetta, 2009; Thelen & Smith, 1998). Development is not applied to all changes, but rather to those that appear in orderly ways and remain for a reasonably long period of time. A temporary change caused by a brief illness, for example, is not considered a part of development. Even a more permanent change such as altering your appearance through plastic surgery is not development. A more technical definition is "a developmental theory describes changes over time in one or several areas of behavior or psychological activity such as thought, language, social behavior, or perception" (Miller, 2011, p. 8). So the study of child development is the study of predictable patterns of change in children over time.

Both the content of the change (for example, the child saying *feet,* then *foots,* then *footes,* then *feet* to refer to the plural of *foot*) and the processes (how children figure out the rules and exceptions in language) are part of the study of child development. Thus two important questions are: *What* changes? and *How* do the changes occur? A third important question is constancy: What does *not change,* and why? Miller's definition above tells us that the how and why questions about change are examined by considering biological and environmental factors *in continuous interaction.*

Now, let's get more specific. Developmental scientists approach the study of change/constancy and biology/environment in a systematic, scientific manner.

The Science of Child Development

Like so many other areas of study today, **child development** is a subfield of a larger category, **developmental science.** Developmental scientists are interested in human growth and change from conception until death, often called *lifespan development.* Those studying child development focus on the period from conception through adolescence, roughly the time from 0 to about 20 years old—the span covered by this book. Of course, people

OUTLINE ▼

The Casebook—Applying Your Knowledge of Child Development: What Would You Do?

Overview and Objectives

What Is Child Development?

Basic Themes and Debates in Development

What Are the Contexts for Development?

Why Study Development?

Summary and Key Terms

The Casebook—Applying Your Knowledge of Child Development: What Would They Do?

continue to develop after adolescence. The more we learn about adult development, the more we realize that it is impossible to disconnect child development from adult development. For example, abusive parents often were abused as children, and their children are more likely to continue the cycle of abuse. Still, our focus will be on the developing child, with attention to all the influences along the way, including adults.

People always have been interested in children. In the 1800s and 1900s, the systematic study of child development began with the "baby biographies." These biographies first appeared in Germany around the end of the 1700s. The author, usually a close relative, would keep a detailed journal, recording everything about the baby's growth and development. Often these baby biographies were written by mothers and published as guidance for parents and teachers. For example, in the United States, Dr. Milicent Washburn Shinn wrote four volumes, published between 1893 and 1898, called *Notes of the Development of a Child*. She condensed the four volumes into a popular version called *Biography of a Baby*, published in 1900. Dr. Shinn—quoted by David Noon (2004, p. 111)—believed that "It is hard to get statistics about babies, scattered as they are, one by one, in different homes, not massed in schoolrooms . . . the most fruitful method so far has been the biographical one—that of watching one baby's development, day by day, and recording it."

Most baby biographies lacked the more sophisticated research methods described in Chapter 2 of this book, and, of course, the authors were emotionally connected to their "subjects." But some of the early biographers were more systematic and scientific in their writings. For example, Charles Darwin (1877), the author of the theory of evolution, studied his own son's first two years of development with the care that he brought to his other scientific observations. Darwin thought that studying how an individual developed might provide insights about how a species develops. In fact, Darwin did use these observations to write a very important essay on the expression of emotions (Rochat, 2001).

As you can see, the *scientific study* of children is relatively recent—a bit over 100 years old (Cairns & Cairns, 2006). What is meant by scientific study? Volumes have been written on this question, but the simple answer is that scientific study involves asking carefully specified questions based on current understandings (theories); systematically gathering and analyzing of all kinds of information (data) about the questions; modifying and improving explanatory theories based on the results of those analyses; and then asking new questions based on the improved theories. We will examine this research cycle more closely in Chapter 2, because research in many different forms is the basis for our knowledge about how children develop.

Theory is very important in scientific study. It is both the *basis* for initial questions and the *outcome* of the questioning process—the beginning and the end of the research cycle. The common sense notion of *theory* (as in "Oh well, it was only a theory") is "a guess or hunch." But the scientific meaning of *theory* is quite different. "A **theory** in science is an interrelated set of concepts that is used to explain a body of data and to make predictions . . ." (Stanovich, 1992, p. 21). The overriding purpose of theories is to explain phenomena, to tell us why things happened and what will happen in the future (Green & Piel, 2010).

Developmental scientists have constructed explanations for the relationships among many variables and even whole systems of relationships. There are theories to explain how language develops, how differences in intelligence occur, and how people learn. There are *grand theories,* such as those of Piaget, Vygotsky, or Bronfenbrenner (see Chapter 2) that provide comprehensive explanations for many different aspects of a child's development—thinking, problem solving, language, social skills, and so on. There are smaller theories that focus on just one domain such as vocabulary development or self-concept. Today, because many different disciplines—from anthropology to zoology—are interested in understanding children, there are emerging theories that combine insights from many fields of research (Hartup, 2002; Salkind, 2004).

Science, then, is a process that allows us to gather and organize information into large and small theories to better understand the development of children. But few theories explain and predict perfectly. In this book, you will see many examples of people taking different theoretical positions and disagreeing on the overall explanations of such processes as the development of reasoning or the origins of self-concept. Because no one theory offers all the answers, it makes sense to consider what each has to offer.

In 1972, the United States Supreme Court ruled that the Older Order sects of the Amish were exempt from mandatory school attendance after grade 8, so Amish adolescents move to the world of work earlier than most other young people in America.

Periods of Development: Infancy, Childhood, and Adolescence

You may have noticed that this book is organized by periods of development—*beginnings* (which includes prenatal development, infants, and toddlers), *early childhood, middle childhood,* and *adolescence.* These time period segments are commonly used to organize discussions of child development because they tend to be characterized by particular patterns of limitations and growing capabilities. Also, each time period is associated with different *environments* for development and changing social *expectations.* For example, as infants mature and move into the period of early childhood, they often are in new environments outside their homes such as preschool or kindergarten, and they are expected to assume more and more responsibility for their own care—feeding themselves, toilet-learning, getting along with other children, and so on.

Before we examine these periods, a caveat is in order. These periods make some sense and are convenient organizers, but they do not represent some kind of biological imperative. Dividing the years from birth to adulthood into time periods is a **social construction**—a generally agreed upon set of categories based not so much on age but more on functional changes—what children can do and are expected to do. But all these periods have fuzzy boundaries and are affected by culture. In some cultures, for example, childhood ends much earlier as 12- or 13-year-olds work full time, marry, and start families. In the 1800s in many countries, including the United States and Canada, schooling ended and children entered the adult world before they were 13 years old, as they still do today in some cultures such as the Amish, who generally leave school after the 8th grade. So as we examine the periods, remember that these distinctions reflect **post-industrial,** technological cultural experiences and are not hard and fast categories. Here are the periods we will examine:

1. *Prenatal, Infancy, and Toddlerhood.* The **prenatal** period is the time between conception and birth, typically 38 weeks, though some children are born earlier and survive, as we will see in Chapter 3. In many ways, this is the time of greatest change. We go from being a single cell into a complex human being with ears, eyes, hands, feet, heart, lungs, digestive system, brain, and the capacity for lifelong development and learning. The first two years after birth also bring dramatic changes. Children progress from being infants who need care to survive to becoming toddlers who can crawl, then walk; babble, then talk; and interact with family to form social bonds. The new environment for the infant is the world outside the womb, but mostly the family. The new expectations are for gradually developing skills in the physical (particularly walking), cognitive (particularly language), and social/emotional arenas. We explore these accomplishments in Chapter 4.
2. *Early Childhood.* As children become fully able to form and use symbols such as language, they move to the next period of early childhood. The young child's physical and cognitive capabilities expand rapidly. At 2, children are walking, but by 6 most have added running, skipping, jumping, climbing, drawing, writing, and even swimming or other sports. Their vocabulary explodes from a few words to thousands. Their environments usually expand beyond family and home to include the neighborhood and caregivers outside the family such as nursery school, preschool, or kindergarten teachers. With growing physical and cognitive skills and new environments come new expectations for self-sufficiency and social competence. Children are expected to do many things for themselves and to get along with others—both children and adults—as you will see in Chapters 5, 6, and 7.
3. *Middle Childhood.* From ages 6 or 7 to 11 most children in post-industrial cultures are in the world of school. Their developing brains, language, and self-control allow them to learn reading,

writing, arithmetic, science, history, and many other subjects. They can play organized games and sports, form and abandon friendships, and understand more abstract concepts such as intention and morality. Standards for achievement both in school and outside escalate, and children are expected to be more independent, keeping up with schoolwork and perhaps even caring for younger members of their family. We meet children in the middle years in Chapters 8, 9, and 10.

4. *Adolescence.* The transition to adolescence is marked by the physical and psychosocial changes of puberty. Somewhere between ages 10 and 12 or so, most children in post-industrial countries experience the dramatic development of sexual maturity. Everything changes. In addition to physical changes, there are growing cognitive capabilities to think abstractly, leading to greater idealism and the ability to handle more advanced abstract learning. The new environment is the world of peers, high school, work, and even college for some, because adolescence continues until ages 18 to 22 years or so. Adolescents are expected to move toward an independent identity and deal with their changing bodies, particularly sexual development. As with all the periods of development described above, the edges of adolescence are fuzzy. Some adolescents have taken on adult responsibilities for work and family at 18; others will not do so for several more years, as you will see in Chapters 11, 12, and 13.

There are dramatic cultural differences in the meaning of adolescence, or even the existence of adolescence separate from adulthood. In most post-industrial cultures, adolescence continues until ages 18 to 22 years or so and marriage is delayed. But in many other cultures, children move directly to the world of adults, like this teenage girl in India being carried to her marriage ceremony.

Of course, as we mentioned earlier, development does not stop with adolescence. Today there is increased study of adults and an emphasis on lifespan development. But that is another story and another book.

What Develops? Domains of Development

Child development can be divided into a number of different aspects based on what is developing. **Physical development**, as you might guess, deals with changes in the body and brain. So the study of physical development includes such topics as health; growth and change in bones and muscles that affect size, movement, and strength; and changes in sensory capabilities such as seeing and hearing. **Cognitive development** refers to changes in problem solving, memory, language, reasoning, and other aspects of thinking. **Emotional/social development** is the term generally used for changes in the individual's feelings, personality, self-concept, and relations with other people. After we consider infancy and toddlerhood in Chapter 4, there is one chapter on each of these three domains for every period of development covered in this book—Early Childhood, Middle Childhood, and Adolescence. Table 1.1 on the next page lists the different periods of development along with example questions addressed in each domain of development for that period.

Another caveat is in order. We deal with physical, cognitive, and emotional/social development in separate chapters for each time period, but these domains are not separate in children. Having problems hearing (physical) will affect language development and reading (cognitive), as well as relationships with friends (social). So even though we discuss these domains of development separately, we know that development in one domain affects and is affected by development in the other two areas.

Many changes during development are strongly influenced by growth and **maturation.** Maturation refers to changes that occur naturally and spontaneously and that are, to a large extent, genetically based. Such changes emerge over time and are relatively unaffected by environment, except in cases of malnutrition or severe illness (Overton, 2006). Much of a person's physical development falls into this category.

TABLE 1.1 • **Periods and Domains of Development: Examples of Key Questions**

PERIODS OF DEVELOPMENT	PHYSICAL DOMAIN	COGNITIVE DOMAIN	EMOTIONAL/ SOCIAL
Prenatal (Conception to birth)	If a woman drinks coffee while she is pregnant, will it affect her baby? (Chapter 3)	Will playing music to babies before birth improve their cognitive abilities? (Chapter 3)	How does a mother's stress during pregnancy affect her baby? (Chapter 3)
Infancy (Birth to 2 years old)	If a baby is not walking at 18 months, is that a problem? (Chapter 4)	Can infants learn two languages? (Chapter 4)	If a child starts daycare at 3 months old, will that affect the emotional bonds between parents and the child? (Chapter 4)
Early Childhood (2 to 6 years old)	Is it a problem if a 5-year-old is "overweight"? (Chapter 5)	Should some children be "held back" in kindergarten? (Chapter 6)	Is it normal for a 5-year-old to be afraid of a Halloween mask? (Chapter 7)
Middle Childhood (6 to 11 years old)	What are the common diseases of childhood? (Chapter 8)	What does an IQ score tell you about a 7-year-old? (Chapter 9)	Why are some children victims and others bullies? (Chapter 10)
Adolescence (11 to 20+ years old)	What are the consequences of going through puberty late for boys? For girls? (Chapter 11)	Are there gender differences in mathematics abilities? (Chapter 12)	What factors influence racial identity? (Chapter 13)

So far, we have examined the periods and domains of development. There also are some fundamental themes and issues in explanations of development that will arise throughout this text. We turn to those now.

Basic Themes and Debates in Development

Along with the many different approaches to research and theory in child development, there are continuing debates about some key questions. After considering some early themes about children, we will look at three more current debates: What is the shape of development—is it continuous or are there leaps and distinct stages? How important is timing in development—are there critical periods when certain abilities must emerge or they will be forever lost? Which is the more influential source of development—personal characteristics or the environment? After considering these three issues, we will examine some emerging ideas in child development.

Early Themes

MINIATURE ADULTS? You may have read in other classes that during medieval times, children were viewed as miniature adults without special needs. One line of reasoning claims that as soon as they could walk, talk, and care for themselves (about age 8 or so), children were considered small adults. Children worked and dressed like their parents. If they broke the law, children could receive the same punishments as adults, including hanging (Jaffe, 1997). Evidence for this view of medieval childhood comes from paintings showing children dressed as adults.

But scholars studying the lives of medieval children have questioned these assumptions (Hanawalt, 1993; Orme, 2001). These historians believe that even though adolescence was not really recognized as a separate phase in medieval times, childhood was considered a special and vulnerable stage of life. For example, there were laws that protected children and medicines for children were different from those given to adults.

By the way, it has taken quite a while to provide full legal protection for children. For example, the United States tried several times during the early 1900s to limit the hours a young child could work, but it was 1938 before federal laws specified the minimum ages and maximum hours allowed. For current U.S. laws, see http://www.continuetolearn.uiowa.edu/laborctr/child_labor/about/us_laws.html.

Partly because artists in earlier centuries painted children to look like miniature adults and because many children did not survive the first few years of their lives, some scholars have assumed children were viewed simply as small adults, not as a separate and vulnerable group. These assumptions are questioned today.

INNATELY GOOD? ACTIVE OR PASSIVE? Following medieval times, conceptions of the nature of children continued to reflect religious and philosophical thinking. In the 1500s, the Puritans' idea of original sin assumed that children were born evil and should be educated and disciplined to overcome this perilous beginning. Training for some Puritan parents included harsh methods, but for others, persuasion and reason were the preferred approaches (Clarke-Stewart, 1998).

In the 1600s, John Locke, a British philosopher, presented a different idea. Rather than perceiving children as innately bad, Locke contended that they are blank slates (**tabula rasa** in Latin) on which the world "writes" knowledge and beliefs. Through education, nurture, training, correction, tutoring, and so on, the world molds the adult from the clay of childhood. Locke saw children as passive—neither evil nor active in shaping their own development (Locke, 1690/1892).

By the 1700s, a new idea emerged. Jean-Jacques Rousseau rejected the views of children as evil or as neutral blank slates. He proposed that children are inherently good—noble savages—who have a built-in sense of right and wrong. Rousseau believed that if children were left alone to develop without adult training they would naturally mature from infants to children to adolescents to adults (1762/1979).

Now we turn to the contemporary study of children. The first *Handbook of Child Psychology* was edited by Carl Murchison in 1991. Reflecting on all the *Handbook* editions since then in the preface of the 2006 edition, William Damon notes, "The perennial themes of the field were there from the start" (p. xiii). Damon goes on to describe debating nature versus nurture as the source of development, disagreeing about whether development unfolds similarly for all children or whether contexts are powerful influences, discussing continuity versus discontinuity in the shaping of development, and separating the analysis of development into different aspects (biological, cognitive, social, emotional) while insisting that these processes cannot be separated when it comes to the "dynamic mix of human development." Let's examine a few of these key themes.

What Is the Shape of Development? Continuity vs. Discontinuity

Is human development a continuous process of adding to and increasing abilities, or are there leaps or moves to new stages with completely new abilities? A **continuous** process would be like gradual improvement in your running endurance through systematic exercise. A **discontinuous** change would be like a tadpole becoming a frog—the frog developed from the tadpole, but the frog is not simply a bigger tadpole—not just "more of the same" tadpole. The tadpole-to-frog change has been called *qualitative* because the animal changes

FIGURE 1.1

CONTINUOUS AND DISCONTINUOUS CHANGE

Piaget's theory describing four qualitatively different stages of children's thinking is an example of discontinuous change.

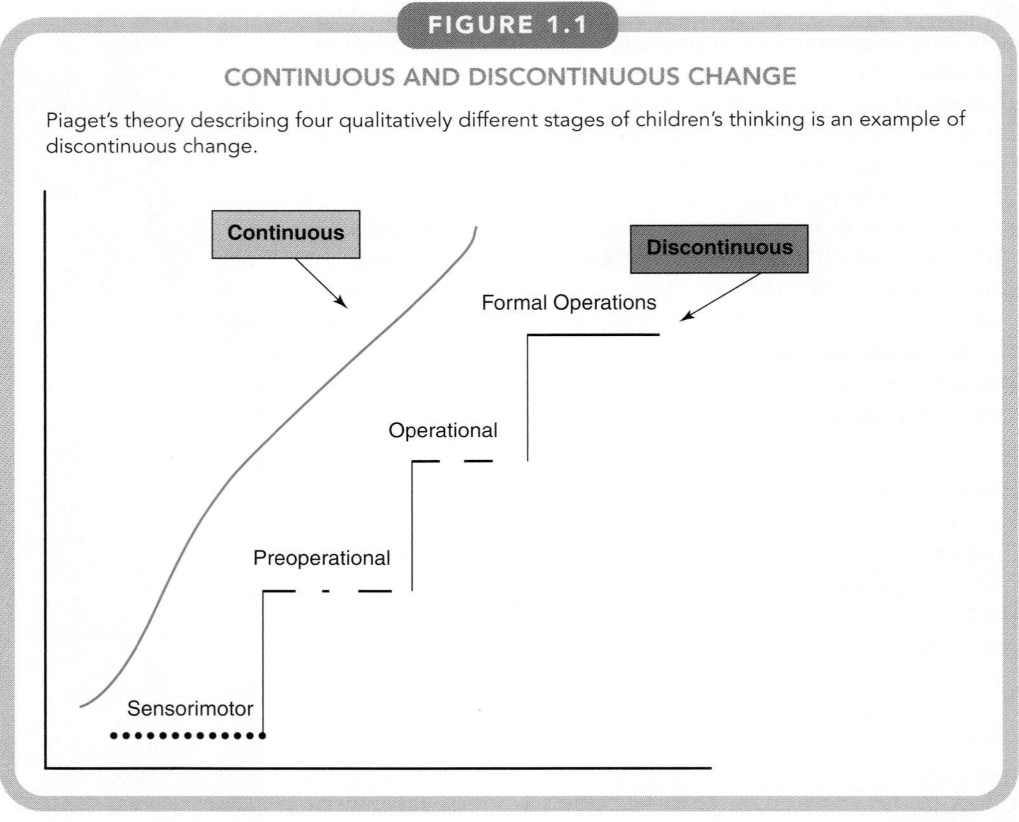

in its qualities (legs appear, for example). Qualitative changes are contrasted to purely *quantitative* change, such as the frog growing longer or heavier.

You can think of continuous or quantitative change like walking up a ramp to go higher and higher. Progress is steady, as you can see in Figure 1.1. A discontinuous or qualitative change is more like walking up stairs—there are level periods, then you move up to the next step all at once.

The best examples of discontinuous or qualitative change in child development are stage theories that describe qualitative changes in an aspect of development. In the next chapter we will look at several stage theories. One of the best known is Jean Piaget's theory describing four qualitatively different stages of cognitive development (Piaget, 1970, 1971). The four stages are:

Sensorimotor:	Children know the world through actions on the world—sucking, throwing, pounding, etc. They know what they can see. Objects out of sight are out of mind—they don't exist for the infant.
Preoperational:	Children can use symbols such as pretending and language, but thinking relies on appearances. At this stage, a child may think that five coins spread out are more coins than the same five pushed close together.
Operational:	Children can think about and reverse actions mentally, as long as they are thinking about objects they have experienced or dealt with personally, so they can mentally move the coins (or buttons, or blocks, etc.) apart and together to know that the quantity does not change just because the appearance changes.
Formal Operational:	Children can perform mental operations on abstract ideas and objects that are only imagined—objects or events they have never encountered personally.

From one stage to the next, the thinking of the child changes in ways that involve more than just the addition of knowledge and skills. Children at the preoperational stage may think, for example, that they will some day catch up to a sibling in age, or they may confuse the past and the future. But children at the next stage, operational, have no such confusions. According to Piaget's stage theory, all the explanation and practice in the world will not help a child functioning at one stage to understand the ways of thinking at a higher stage.

Besides continuous and discontinuous change, there is a third possibility. Changes may seem like discontinuous, qualitative leaps when we look across longer time periods. The adolescent contemplating possible utopian societies certainly is thinking differently than the 4-year-old who cannot reason about hypothetical, what-if situations, but maybe those changes developed continuously and gradually. If we watched a developing child very closely moment-to-moment or hour-to-hour, we might see the gradual, continuous changes. Rather than arising all at once, the knowledge that a hidden toy still exists may evolve gradually as children's memories develop. The longer you make the infants wait before searching—the longer you make them remember the object—the older they have to be to succeed, so there is some evidence for this third possibility of gradual evolution (Siegler & Alibali, 2005).

The opposite is also possible. Developments that seem quantitative may actually be based on qualitative changes. For example, when a 7-year-old can remember twice as many objects as a 4-year-old, that seems like a quantitative difference. But the 7-year-old may be using strategies to remember—a qualitatively different memory method than that employed by the 4-year-old, who likely is just "trying hard" to remember (Miller, 2011).

So change can be both continuous and discontinuous, as described by a branch of mathematics called *catastrophe theory*. Changes that appear suddenly, such as the collapse of a bridge, are preceded by many slowly developing changes such as gradual, continuous corrosion of the metal structures. Similarly, gradually developing changes in children, such as learning to use memory strategies, can lead to large changes in abilities that seem abrupt (Fischer & Pare-Blagoev, 2000; Siegler & Alibali, 2005).

Timing: Is It Too Late? Critical Periods and Earlier vs. Later Experiences

Are some experiences, such as exposure to toxic drugs or improved nutrition, more powerful at certain times than others? Are there **critical periods** when certain abilities, such as language, need to develop? If those opportunities are missed, can the child still "catch up"? These are questions about timing and development.

In answer to the first question, as you will see in Chapter 3, there are critical times in prenatal development when exposure to a toxin or a disease afflicting the mother, such as rubella, will cause damage to the developing fetus. But the same exposure earlier or later in the pregnancy would have minimal effects. So, what about developing abilities after the child is born? There appears to be a critical period for learning accurate language pronunciation. The earlier people learn a second language, the more their pronunciation is near-native. After adolescence it is difficult to learn a new language without speaking with an accent (Piske, MacKay, & Flege, 2001).

Does the critical period for developing near-native pronunciation extend to learning language itself? Years ago, Eric Lenneberg (1969) proposed that the time from infancy to puberty is the critical period for language development. If somehow a child were kept from developing language during that time, Lenneberg believed, then language would never develop. You can imagine that this is a difficult theory to test. It would be highly unethical, in fact criminal, to perform an experiment that would keep an infant from the chance to develop language. But in 1970, outside Los Angeles, authorities discovered a 13-year old-girl who had been kept in a tiny room, tied to a potty chair, and cut off from all human contact by her mentally ill father. She seemed to recognize her name, but did not speak. Would her experiences point to the existence of a critical period for language?

Funded by grants from the National Institute of Mental Health (NIMH), several researchers took over the care of "Genie," a name they gave her for reporting purposes. After a few years of intensive care and language teaching, Genie could use several words and say some simple sentences, but her language never became normal. When the funding ran out and Genie lived in a series of foster homes, she returned to complete silence. Genie's experiences seem to lend some support for the critical period theory. But it is also possible that the serious abuse she endured caused so much cognitive and emotional damage that language development was almost impossible.

Some critical periods for development appear to depend on the **plasticity** (adaptability or modifiability) of brain organization and structures. For example, we know that the left side of the brain is more involved in language processing for most people. But this specialization of the two sides of the brain takes a while to develop. Therefore, the brains of young children show more plasticity because they are not as specialized as the brains of older children and adults. Damage to the left side of a young child's brain can be somewhat overcome to allow language development to proceed. Other areas of the brain take over this task. But this compensation is less likely for older children and adults.

Many earlier developmental psychologists, particularly those influenced by Freud, believed that early childhood experiences were critical, especially for emotional/social and cognitive development. But does early "toilet teaching" really set all of us on a particular life path? Probably not. More recent research shows that later experiences are powerful, too, and can change the direction of development (Kagan & Herschkowitz, 2005). Most developmental psychologists today talk about **sensitive periods**—not critical periods. These are times when a person is especially ready for or responsive to certain experiences. Thus, although the best time to learn a second language on your own without direct instruction is childhood, adults can and do learn second languages all the time.

What Is the Source of Development? Nature vs. Nurture

Which is more important in development, the "nature" of an individual (heredity, genes, biological processes, maturation, etc.) or the "nurture" of environmental contexts (education, parenting, culture, social policies, etc.)? This debate has raged for at least 2,000 years and has had many labels along the way—"heredity versus environment," "nativism versus empiricism," "biology versus culture," "maturation versus learning," and "innate versus acquired abilities" (Cairns & Cairns, 2006; Miller, 2011). In earlier centuries, philosophers, poets, religious leaders, and politicians argued the question. Today scientists bring new tools to the discussion as they can map genes or trace the effects of drugs on brain activity, for example (Gottlieb, Wahlsten, & Lickliter, 2006).

If we look at the history of scientific explanations for development, we see that the pendulum has swung back and forth between nature and nurture (Cairns & Cairns, 2006; Lerner, Theokas, & Bobek, 2005). For an example of the differing views, see the ***Point/Counterpoint*** on the next page.

Today the environment is viewed as critical for development (more about this in the next section on contexts), but biological factors and individual differences are important, too. In fact, some scientists assert that behaviors are determined 100% by biology *and* 100% by environment—they can't be separated (Miller, 2011). Even with recent advances in mapping human genes, we still need to consider complex interactions with life experiences. Gilbert Gottlieb (2003) sums it up: "gene-environment coactions are the rule in developmental investigations" (p. 352).

Emerging Ideas

As you might imagine, the debates above proved too complicated to be settled by splitting alternatives into either/or possibilities (Griffins & Gray, 2005).

BEWARE OF EITHER/OR. Richard Lerner and his colleagues (2005) summed up the problems with either/or thinking:

> In human development, major instances of such splitting involved classic debates about nature versus nurture as "the" source of development, continuity versus discontinuity as an appropriate depiction of the character of the human development trajectory, and stability versus instability as an adequate means to describe

POINT/COUNTERPOINT: Are Numbers Innate or Learned?

Throughout this text we will be examining some debates in child development. We will look at the arguments for both sides, so this feature is called *Point/Counterpoint*. Here is the first one.

What seems like a simple notion, that 3 cups in a stack is the same number as 3 birds on a telephone wire, is not so simple. After all, the stacked cups and the lined-up birds look quite different. And what about counting? Different languages have very different ways of saying 17, for example. In English, 17 is "seventeen," but in French it is "dix-sept" or 10 - 7. Some psychologists claim that this whole process is easier because an understanding of number is innate—we are born with it. Others believe that we have to learn the meaning of numbers. Let's look at the arguments. After you read these positions, you might listen to a podcast on innate numbers from *Radiolab* (http://www.wnyc.org/shows/radiolab/episodes/2009/10/09/segments/137633).

POINT

We are born with a sense of numbers. The idea that people are predisposed to understand numbers comes mostly from work with babies. In the 1980s, Rochell Gelman and her student, Prentice Starkey, used a technique called *habituation* to study infants' understanding of number. In a typical experiment, babies are shown a series of 3 dots arranged in different ways—close together or farther apart. After a while, the babies usually habituate—their attention to the displays of dots decreases. But when a new display with just 2 dots appears, they look longer at it, indicating that the 2 dots is something new for them. This habituation to one number, then renewed attention to a new number doesn't work, however, with larger numbers, say 4 or above. Based on these studies and others like it, Gelman and her colleagues (Gelman & Gallistel, 1978; Starkey, Spelke, & Gelman, 1990) concluded that humans must be born with a sense that 2 is different from 3; that is, babies have "a clear understanding of the number continuum, which they can apply at first only to small numbers but extend to larger numbers as they grow older and their cognitive powers and memory capacities increase" (Bryant & Nunes, 2004, p. 414).

COUNTERPOINT

We need to learn about numbers. But are these experiments really about number? Other researchers claim that although these babies are detecting differences, they are not differences in number, just differences in the amount of "stuff" in the displays. To test this, researchers tried using 3 small dots in the first habituation phase, and then showed 3 larger dots in the checking phase. After habituating (growing uninterested) in the 3 dots, the babies increased their attention to the larger dots, even though the number was still 3. So it seemed that the babies were noticing greater size, not a change in number (Clearfield & Mix, 1999). Peter Bryant and Terezinha Nunes (2004) believe that basic mathematical ideas about numbers are not innate. "They are a source of genuine difficulty for children, and the idea that they come as an innate and universal gift is misguided and actually harmful, for it distracts us from giving help to children where they need it" (p. 349).

> development change. Today, most major developmental theories eschew such splits and use concepts drawn from developmental systems theories (e.g., Lerner, 2002; Overton, 1998, 2003). (p. 3)

Developmental systems theories are general perspectives on development, heredity, and evolution that emphasize the study of *interactions and coactions* among the many influences on development, without falling into the kinds of "which is more" debates described in the previous sections (Lerner, 2006). As you will see in the next chapter, these systems perspectives are leading explanations of development. So where does that leave us on the nature/nurture questions?

NATURE AND NURTURE TODAY. In Chapter 3 we examine heredity and environment closely, but for now we can say that current views emphasize complex **coactions** (joint actions) of nature and nurture. For example, a child born with a very easygoing, calm disposition will likely elicit different reactions from parents, playmates, and teachers compared to a child who is often upset and difficult to soothe, so individuals are active in constructing their own environments. But environments shape individuals as well—if not, what good would education be? So today, the either/or debates about nature and nurture are of less interest to developmental psychologists. The more exciting questions involve understanding how, as a pioneer in developmental psychology, James Mark Baldwin, said over 100 years ago, "both causes work together" (1895, p. 77). A recent special section in the journal *Developmental Psychology* on biology and environment (Diamond, 2009) included articles on how experience affects gene expression, how genes influence what effects environments have, and even how physical fitness affects cognition and the brain. The general public is beginning to understand that nature and nurture act together. A poll found that 90% of parents and teachers believed that genetics and environment are equally important factors for mental illness, intelligence, personality, and learning disabilities (Plomin, 2004).

Today, advanced research tools and technologies allow us to ask new questions about nature and nurture that reflect a developmental systems perspective, such as, "How do genes affect emotional development and how do those effects change over time?" An example is in the development of schizophrenia, a serious mental disorder that appears in adolescence. There is evidence that some genetic factors are involved in schizophrenia—it tends to run in families and an identical twin has about a 45% chance of having the disorder if the other twin has schizophrenia. But if genes are involved, why do the behaviors often observed, such as hearing voices or having paranoid delusions, not occur in childhood, before adolescence? One answer is that the brain may have to mature enough to be capable of abstract thought before genes that underlie schizophrenic behaviors will have the effects we associate with the disorder—voices and delusions (Plomin, 2004).

Another example involves intelligence as assessed by IQ tests (see Chapter 12 for more on these tests). We might guess that the effects of the environment on IQ would increase as we grow and have more different experiences, but that does not seem to be the case. Genetic influences on IQ increase from infancy to adulthood—the relationship between parents' IQs and their children's' IQs grows stronger over time—the opposite of what we might predict. One explanation is that as we go through life, we create environments, select experiences, and shape our contexts, so the environments we create are consistent with the genes and magnify the influence of the genes over time (Plomin, 2004).

The future of developmental research on the complex coactions of nature and nurture may well involve building on the work of the Human Genome Project that, in 2003, identified the 20,000 to 25,000 genes in human DNA and how these genes work collaboratively with other influences such as hormones to affect human development. As researchers understand gene-environment coactions to explain differences in development over time, we may be able to design more effective interventions for disorders such as schizophrenia or alcoholism.

A focus on coactions of biology and environment highlights the importance of contexts. No matter what, all scientists agree that the contexts in which children develop—their biological, physical, emotional, cultural, and social environments—are important considerations in development. We turn to those contexts next.

What Are the Contexts for Development?

Developmental researchers are increasingly interested in the role of **context.** Context is the total setting or situation that surrounds and interacts with a person or event. As we learn more about the biology of development, it is clear that there are contextual effects both internal and external to the developing individual. For example, the child's health is a context for developing organs, including the brain. In this book, however, we focus on the contexts outside the individual. These contexts may include family, neighborhood, school, economic conditions, cultural tools and traditions, social norms and processes, timing issues, architectural and environmental structures, emotional and physical climate, and historical factors—to name just a few (Lerner, Theokas, & Bobek, 2005). As we will see in the next chapter, Uri Bronfenbrenner's theory of development highlights these nested and interacting contexts for development.

Contexts affect how actions are interpreted. For example, when a stranger approaches a 7-month-old infant, the baby is likely to cry if the setting is unfamiliar, but not cry when the stranger approaches in the baby's home. Adults are more likely to help a stranger in need in small towns as opposed to larger cities (Kagan, & Herschkowitz, 2005). Here is another example: Standing on your seat and screaming means one thing at a football game and another on an airplane. Think about a ringing telephone. Is it 3:00 in the afternoon or 3:00 AM? Did you just call someone and leave a message asking for a return call? Has the phone been ringing off the hook, or is this the first call in days? Did you just sit down to dinner? Are you engrossed in a conversation or bored and looking for an excuse to exit the discussion? The meaning of the phone ringing and the feelings you have will vary, depending on the context. In making a case for greater attention to context in developmental research, Jerome Kagan (2004), director of Harvard University's Infant and Child Study Center said, "because humans evaluate every event with respect to the situation in which it normally occurs, every event must be conceptualized as an 'event in context'" (p. 293).

Contexts also influence the development of behaviors, beliefs, and knowledge by providing resources, supports, incentives and punishments, expectations, teachers, models, and tools—all the building blocks of development. Children do not develop in laboratories or isolation bubbles. They grow up in families and neighborhoods. They attend schools and are in classes, teams, or choirs. They are members of particular ethnic, religious, economic, and language communities. The social and educational programs and policies of their governments affect their lives. Moreover, the contexts in which we live and develop are incredibly diverse. For example, here are a few statistics about the United States and Canada (taken from Children's' Defense Fund, 2008; Dewan, 2010; Freisen, 2010; Meece & Kurtz-Costes, 2001; U.S. Census Bureau, 2010a):

- In 2003, 12% of the people living in the United States were born outside of the United States and 18% speak a language other than English at home—half of these families speak Spanish.
- Today 22% of children under the age of 18 are Latino. By 2050, Latinos will be about one quarter of the U.S. population (U.S. Census Bureau, 2010b).
- In Canada, projections are that by 2031, one in three Canadians will belong to a visible minority, with South Asians the largest group represented. About 17% of the population reported that their first language was not French or English, but instead one of over 100 languages.
- 1 in 5 American children lives in poverty and 1 in 12 lives in extreme poverty, defined in 2009 by the United States Department of Health and Human Services as an income of $22,050 for a family of four ($27,570 in Alaska and $25,360 in Hawaii). The numbers are very similar for Canada.
- In Georgia, Louisiana, Mississippi, and Texas, over half of the students live in low-income families.

In the next few pages we take a closer look at several influential interacting contexts for development.

These two children certainly are developing in different contexts. Can you identify all the differences in resources and supports available to each?

Family

The first context for development is the mother's womb. As research advances in biology, biochemistry, neuroscience, and other fields, we learn more about the effects of this first environment, as you will see in Chapter 3. You will learn about the influence of the expectant mother's level of stress, nutrition, smoking, alcohol and drug intake, exercise, general health, and even voice on her infant's development,. The influence of the family begins before birth. After the baby is born, new family influences are added.

FAMILY STRUCTURE. You may have grown up in a **nuclear family,** defined as a mother and father (or a single parent) along with biological, adopted, or stepchildren living in the same household. Sometimes this unit is called a *traditional family* when it includes both parents, but it is not the family configuration for everyone. Some children are being raised by same-sex parents in a nuclear family structure. These children may be the biological offspring of one of the parents or they may be adopted. Increasingly, children today may be part of **blended families,** with stepbrothers or stepsisters who move in and out of their lives. Some children live with an aunt, with grandparents, with one parent, in foster or adoptive homes, or with an older brother or sister. In some cultures such as Asian, Latin American, or African, children are more likely to grow up in **extended families,** with grandparents, aunts, uncles, and cousins living in the same household or at least in daily contact with them. Childcare and economic support often are shared among family members. Family structure is determined in part by cultural customs and in part by economics and mobility. For example, family groups that move to take advantage of economic opportunities tend to be smaller—more nuclear and less extended (Peterson, 1993).

PARENTING STYLES. The family context affects child development in many ways, but one of the most widely researched influences is parent discipline style. One well-known description of **parenting styles** is based on the research of Diane Baumrind (1991, 2005). Her early work focused on a careful longitudinal study of 100 (mostly European American, middle-class) preschool children. Through observation of children and parents and interviews with parents, Baumrind and the other researchers who built on her findings identified four styles based on the parents' high or low levels of *warmth* and *control* or *demandingness*. A general finding is that, at least in European American, middle-class families, children of authoritative (high warmth, high control/demand) parents are more likely to be happy with themselves and to relate well to others, whereas children of authoritarian parents (low warmth, high control/demand) are more likely to be guilty or depressed.

Cultures differ in parenting styles, as you can see in the **Relating to Every Child** discussion on the next page.

The research on parenting styles makes it clear that all families are part of a culture, and that culture is a powerful context for development.

Culture and Community

There are many definitions of **culture.** Most include the knowledge, skills, rules, traditions, beliefs, and values that guide behavior in a particular group of people, as well as the art and artifacts produced and passed down to the next generation (Betancourt & Lopez, 1993; Pai & Alder, 2001). The group creates a culture—a program for living—and communicates the program to members. Groups can be defined along regional, ethnic, religious, gender, social class, or other lines. Each of us—recent immigrant or longtime resident—is a member of many groups, so we all are influenced by many different cultures. Sometimes the influences are incompatible or even contradictory. For example, if you are a feminist but also a Roman Catholic, you may have trouble reconciling the two different cultures' beliefs about the ordination of women as priests. Your personal belief will be based, in part, on how strongly you identify with each group (Banks, 2002).

There are many different cultures, of course, within every modern country. In the United States, students growing up in a small rural town in the Great Plains are part of a cultural group that is very different from that of students from a large urban center or a Florida gated community. In Canada, students living in the suburbs of Toronto certainly differ in a number of ways from students growing up in a Vancouver high-rise apartment or on a farm in Quebec. Within

RELATING TO

EVERY CHILD

▸ Different Parenting Styles in Different Cultures

NOT EVERY STUDY finds results consistent with Diane Baumrind's findings about the problems that accompany authoritarian styles in white, middle-class families. Other research indicates that higher control, more authoritarian parenting is linked to better grades for Asian and African American students (Glasgow, Dornbusch, Troyer, Steinberg, & Ritter, 1997). Parenting that is strict and directive, with clear rules and consequences, combined with high levels of warmth and emotional support, is associated with higher academic achievement and greater emotional maturity for inner-city children (Garner & Spears, 2000; Jarrett, 1995). Differences in cultural values and in the danger level of some urban neighborhoods may make tighter parental control appropriate, and even necessary (Smetana, 2000). In addition, in cultures that have a greater respect for elders and a more group-centered rather than individualistic philosophy, it may be a misreading of the parents' actions to perceive their demand for obedience as "authoritarian" (Lamb & Lewis, 2005; Nucci, 2001). In fact, research by Ruth Chao (2001; Chao & Tseng, 2002) has challenged Baumrind's conclusions for Asian families. Chao finds that an alternative parenting style of *chiao shun* (a Chinese term that Chao translates to mean "training") better characterizes parenting in Asian and Asian American families. Chao is also studying whether serving as a translator or "language broker" for parents who do not speak English has an impact on the child's psychological well-being and relationship with the parents.

Ruth Chao

Research with Latino parents also questions whether parenting styles studies based on European American families are helpful in understanding Latino families. Using a carefully designed observation system, Melanie Domenech Rodríguez and her colleagues included a third dimension of parenting—giving children more or less autonomy (freedom to make decisions). They found that almost all of the Latino parents they studied could be characterized as *protective* (high on warmth, high on control/demand, and low on granting autonomy) or *authoritative* (high on all three—warmth, control/demand, and granting autonomy). Also, these Latino parents tended to be more demanding and less likely to grant autonomy to their female children (Domenech Rodríguez, Donovick, & Crowley, 2009).

those small towns in the Great Plains or Quebec, the child of a convenience store clerk grows up in a different culture from the child of the town doctor or dentist. Individuals of African, Asian, Hispanic, Native American, or European descent have distinctive histories and traditions.

The experiences of males and females are different in most ethnic and economic groups. Everyone living within a particular country shares many common experiences and values, especially because of the influence of the mass media. But other aspects of their lives are shaped by differing cultural backgrounds. For example, even symptoms of psychological disorders are affected by culture. In industrialized cultures where cleanliness is emphasized, people with obsessive-compulsive disorders often become obsessed with cleaning their hands, whereas in Bali, where social networks are emphasized, people with obsessive-compulsive disorders often become obsessed with knowing all the details about the lives of their friends and family—their social network (Lemelson, 2003). In fact, some cultures have mental health disorders not experienced in the Western countries. For example, in some Southeast Asian cultures men might experience *amok*—an episode of murderous rage followed by amnesia or *koro*—a terrible fear that their genitals are receding into their bodies (Watters, 2010).

The above examples are not meant to imply that there are no universals in child development. Jerome Kagan and Norbert Herschkowitz (2005) remind us that "over 90% of 1-year-olds in every village, town, and city across the world will smile at the approach of the caretaker, remember and reach toward a place where an adult hid a toy, cry occasionally to an approaching stranger, and imitate some parental behaviors" (p. 32). Throughout this book we will consider both universals and the influences of culture.

Ethnicity and race are two important elements of culture that influence individual development.

Ethnicity and Race

Since the beginning of the 20th century, scores of immigrants have entered the United Kingdom, Western Europe, Canada, Australia, the United States, and many other post-industrial countries. These immigrants bring with them their cultures and languages. By the year 2020, over 66% of all school-age children in the United States will be African American, Asian, Hispanic, or Native American—many the children of new immigrants. According to projections by the U.S. Census Bureau (2010a), the Hispanic and Asian populations will triple over the next half century and non-Hispanic whites will represent only about one-half of the total population by 2050.

Ethnicity usually refers to groups that share common cultural characteristics such as history, homeland, language, traditions, or religion. The word *ethnic* is from the Greek word for "nation" or "foreign people"—*ethnos*. We all have some ethnic heritage, whether our background is Italian, Ukrainian, Hmong, Chinese, Japanese, Navajo, Hawaiian, Puerto Rican, Cuban, Hungarian, German, African, or Irish—to name only a few.

Race, on the other hand, has been considered "a social category that is defined on the basis of physical characteristics" such as skin color or hair texture (Yetman, 1999, p. 3). In effect, race is a label people apply to themselves and to others based on appearances, ancestry, or history. There are no biologically pure races. In fact, for any two humans chosen at random, an average of only .01% (about one-hundredth of one percent) of the alphabetic sequence of their genetic codes is different due to race (Smedley & Smedley, 2005). Still, race is a powerful construct. At the individual level, race is part of our identity—how we understand ourselves and interact with others. At the group level, race is involved with economic and political structures (Omi & Winant, 1994).

Today many psychologists emphasize that ethnicity and race are socially constructed ideas. In an interview for the *Monitor on Psychology,* Helen Rose Markus, who studies identity, said that both race and ethnicity share a similar definition as "a dynamic set of historically derived and institutionalized ideas and practices that allow people to identify or be identified on the basis of commonalities including language, history, nation, customs, physical appearance and ancestry" (DeAngelis, 2008, p. 30).

Sociologists sometimes use the term **minority group** to refer to a group of people that have less power than the dominant group and receive unequal or discriminatory treatment. There was a time when the term indicated a numerical minority as well. But today, referring to particular racial or ethnic groups as "minorities" in the *numbers* sense is technically incorrect in many situations, because in certain places the "minority" group is actually the majority—for example, African Americans in Chicago or Mississippi. So minorities may not always be fewer in numbers, but they often have less political or economic power and experience discrimination.

There is another important contextual influence on children as they develop—social class.

Social Class and Socioeconomic Status

In modern societies, levels of wealth, power, and prestige are not always consistent. Some people—for instance, university professors—are members of professions that have a reasonably high social status, but provide little wealth or power (believe us). Other people have political power even though they are not wealthy or they may be members of the upper-class social register in a town, even though their family money is long gone. Most people are generally aware of their social class—that is, they perceive that some groups are above them in social class and some are below. They may even show a kind of "classism" (like racism or sexism); they believe they are "better" than members of lower social classes and avoid associating with them.

There is another way of thinking about class differences that is commonly used in research. Sociologists and psychologists combine variations in wealth, power, control over resources, and prestige into an index called **socioeconomic status,** or **SES.** In contrast to social class, most people are not conscious of their SES designation. SES is more ascribed to people by researchers; different formulas for determining SES might lead to different

TABLE 1.2 • **Selected Characteristics of Different Social Classes**

	UPPER CLASS	MIDDLE CLASS	WORKING CLASS	LOWER CLASS
Income	$200,000+	$110,000–$200,000 (1/2) $50,000–$110,000 (1/2)	$25,000–$50,000	Below $25,000
Occupation	Corporate, professional, family money	White-collar, skilled blue-collar	Blue-collar	Minimum wage, unskilled labor
Education	Prestigious colleges and graduate schools	High school, college, or professional school	High school	High school or less
Home ownership	At least one home	Usually own home	About half own a home	Uncommon
Health coverage	Full	Usually	Limited	Uncommon
Neighborhoods	Exclusive or comfortable	Comfortable	Modest	Deteriorating
Afford children's college	Easily	Usually	Seldom	Uncommon
Political power	National, state, local	State or local	Limited	No

Source: Information from Macionis, J. J. (2010). Sociology *(13th ed). Upper Saddle River, NJ: Pearson and Macionis, personal communication, 4/2/2010.*

assignments (Liu et al., 2004). No single variable, not even income, is an effective measure of SES. Most researchers identify four general levels of SES: upper, middle, working, and lower SES. The main characteristics of these four levels are summarized in Table 1.2.

Research in child development often examines variables such as race, SES, religion, ethnicity, or gender separately, because such research is easier to conduct and interpret. Of course, real children are not just African American or Buddhist or female; they are complex beings and members of many groups. Even though cultural and socioeconomic contexts are powerful influences on development, these influences are not consistent in their effects on every person, as James Banks cautions:

> Although membership in a gender, racial, ethnic, social-class, or religious group can provide us with important clues about an individual's behavior, it cannot enable us to predict behavior. *Membership in a particular group does not determine behavior but makes certain types of behavior more probable.* (1993, pp. 13–14, emphasis in original)

Another set of contextual influences comes from the larger society in which the individual develops and the policies of that society.

Society and Policy

As we were finishing this chapter, we noticed an article in the *New York Times*. Two studies summarized by Tara Parker-Pope (2010) reported the effects of Title XI, the regulation in the United States that required schools and colleges receiving federal money to provide the same opportunities in sports for girls as they do for boys. When the amendment passed in 1972, schools and colleges protested that they could not afford the increases in sports budgets, but the results of these two studies (Kaestner & Xu, 2010; Stevenson, 2010) show the money was well invested. For example, even after taking other important influences into account, Title XI explained about 20% of the increase in women's educational level and 40% of the rise in employment for 25- to 34-year-old women and a 7% decrease in obesity rates for the same age group. This federal policy has had dramatic effects for many women who attended high school after the early 1970s—maybe you are one of them.

Different societies and countries have different social and educational policies affecting development. What kind of prenatal care and education are available for expectant mothers? Are there national policies supporting maternity leave for new parents? What sort of childcare is provided for preschool age children? When do children begin school? Is there financial support available for higher education or job training? For example, as you will see in Chapter 6, there are great variations among countries in the childcare available to 4- and 5-year-olds. All 4-year-olds in Ireland and in the Netherlands are in school. All children in Belgium and France have access to preschool if their families want to send them. Most children in post-industrial societies attend at least a half-day kindergarten when they are 4 or 5. As you can see in Table 1.3, countries vary greatly in the amount of leave new parents are allowed when a baby is born. All these societal and policy differences can affect physical, cognitive, and emotional/social development. We will examine these contextual influences in the upcoming chapters.

Time and Place: Historical Contexts

Anita (one of your textbook authors) is a Baby Boomer—someone born between 1946 and 1964. She arrived after her father returned from World War II and started college under the GI bill, so her life was affected by a government policy that allowed her father to earn a

TABLE 1.3 • **A Few Examples of Policies Governing Leaves for Parents of New Babies in Different Countries**

COUNTRY	DURATION OF LEAVE	PERCENT OF WAGES REPLACED
Australia	1 year parental leave	Unpaid
Mexico	12 weeks maternity (6 weeks pre-birth)	100%
Switzerland	16 weeks maternity (8 weeks mandatory)	100%
Turkey	16 weeks maternity	66.7%
Canada	50 weeks (15 weeks maternity + 35 weeks parental leave shared with father)	55% up to $447/week
Italy	22 weeks (2 before birth)	80%
Greece	119 days	100%
Japan	14 weeks (6 pre- and 8 post-birth)	60%
Denmark	52 weeks: 18 to be taken by the mother, 2 weeks by the father, the rest as they see fit	100%
Unites States	12 weeks family leave, includes maternity	Unpaid

Source: Based on data from http://www.catalyst.org/publication/240/family-leave-us-canada-and-global; http://en.wikipedia.org/wiki/Parental_leave

degree. Nancy (your other textbook author) is also a Boomer, but born toward the end of that period and in Canada, so she experienced different events and different government policies growing up. Anita's children are all members of Generation X (1965–1981), so they have no memories of the Civil Rights Movement in the United States or the Vietnam War—experiences that defined Anita's high school and college years. Most undergraduates today are Millennials, sometimes called Generation Y, born between roughly1982 and 2002; you may be a member of that group yourself.

Millennial, Generation X, Baby Boomer—these names assigned by the media and popular culture refer to people born during certain time periods. According to popular wisdom, Baby Boomers are better educated and more individualistic than previous generations, more optimistic about money (they did not experience the Great Depression—until lately anyway), more comfortable with technology and less respectful of authority. For Generation Xers, racial segregation has always been illegal and the ability to walk on the moon is a given. Millennials are said to be more conforming and conventional and closer to their parents than Gen Xers (Howe & Strauss, 2000). Some people now identify a Generation Z, born in the 2000s. Others label these children the iGeneration (Rosen, 2010). So far the main characteristics highlighted for this group involve familiarity with and dependence on technology—IM, YouTube, cell phones, texting, the Internet, Twitter, Facebook. . . . Members of this generation sometimes are called "digital natives." These are not scientifically established groupings, but the designations let us consider the more scientific idea of cohorts.

A **cohort** is a group of people who share the same historical context because they were born during the same time period, during the presidential administration of Ronald Reagan, for example, or in the years right after the 9/11 destruction of the World Trade Center. A cohort can be narrowly defined, for instance—everyone born in 2000, or more broadly, such as the millions of Baby Boomers born during the post-World War II years. People in a cohort share many historical, economic, and social experiences, especially now that the media and Internet disseminate information so quickly and widely. For example, in the United States 200 years ago, close to 70% of children lived on farms with two parents and had little or no access to radio and travel, no access to television or the Internet. Today about 70% live with one parent or two working parents, not on farms, but with access to radio, television, travel, and the Internet (Kagan & Herschkowitz, 2005).

As we write this chapter, people around the world are dealing with the HIV virus and AIDS, a challenge not faced by children and adults before the 1980s. They also are worried about the increasingly destructive hurricanes, pandemics such as the H1N1 flu, ecology-destroying oil spills, and the financial crises that affect the entire world. Children growing up in many countries today must deal with violence and terrorism on a scale much greater

Can you match these pictures with the decades: 1950s, 1960s, 1970s, 1980s, 1990s, 2000s? What did you look at to decide?

than that faced by their parents or grandparents. So *when* you grow up—in what cohort—has a major impact on your development. It even has an impact on your name, as you can see if you go to http://www.ssa.gov/OACT/babynames/ and type in your birth year or any year back to 1880. For example, the most popular names in 1880 were John and Mary. By 1995 the top names were Michael and Jessica, and in 2009, the winners were Jacob and Isabella.

So, there is much to learn in the next years and much already known about the complexities of development. Why should you care?

Why Study Development?

You are beginning your investigation of child development, perhaps as a required course, perhaps as an elective. What can you hope to gain by studying this rapidly growing field? We turn to that question to end this first chapter.

Teaching

Many of you are planning to be teachers. What better foundation for quality teaching is there than an understanding of the people you will teach? In addition, teachers are a major force in children's development. Bridgett Hamre and Robert Pianta (2001) followed all the children in a small school district who entered kindergarten during one year and continued in that district through the eighth grade. The researchers found that the quality of the teacher–student relationship in kindergarten (defined in terms of level of conflict with the child, the child's dependency on the teacher, and the teacher's affection for the child) predicted a number of academic and behavioral outcomes through the eighth grade, particularly for students with high levels of behavior problems. Even when the gender, ethnicity, cognitive ability, and behavior ratings of the student were accounted for, the relationship with the teacher still predicted aspects of school success. Based on the results of this carefully conducted study, it appears that students with significant behavior problems in the early years are less likely to have problems later in school if their teachers are sensitive to their needs and provide frequent, consistent feedback.

So teaching is important in children's development. This leads to a question probably of interest to you: What is good teaching? Is it science or art, the application of research-based theories or the creative invention of specific practices? As we will say many times in this book, *beware of either/or choices*. Teachers must be both theoretically knowledgeable and inventive. They must be able to use a range of strategies, and they must also be able to invent new strategies. They must have some basic research-based routines for managing classes, but they must also be willing and able to break from the routine when the situation calls for change. They must know the research on children's development, "patterns common to particular ages, culture, social class, geography, and gender" (Ball, 1997, p. 773) and they also need to know their own particular students who are unique combinations of culture, gender, and geography. This book will help you understand development.

Other Careers

You may not be planning a career in teaching that requires knowledge of child development. But you may have worked as a camp counselor, nursery aide at your church, or volunteer in the pediatric wing of a hospital. Perhaps these experiences encouraged you to explore child development in college. Or maybe you don't even have a major yet and are open to many career possibilities. What are those possibilities?

Careers in child development might be in education, medicine, consultation and counseling, or research. Some careers require only a 2-year associate degree, others need a bachelor's or master's degree, and some require an advanced degree such as an M.D. or Ph.D. You may be familiar with some careers, such as kindergarten teacher or pediatrician. Other careers may be new to you. For example, today there are many people working in children's hospitals called Child Life Assistants or Child Life Specialists. These people have 2- or 4-year college degrees in child development or a related field. On their website, the Child Life Council describes the profession as:

> . . . trained professionals with expertise in helping children and their families overcome life's most challenging events. Armed with a strong background in child development and family systems, child life specialists promote effective coping through play, preparation, education, and self-expression activities. They provide emotional support for families, and encourage optimum development of children facing a broad range of challenging experiences, particularly those related to healthcare and hospitalization. (http://www.childlife.org/The Child Life Profession/)

Table 1.4 describes the possibilities for several example careers in education, medicine, and mental health areas that require different levels of education. The website associated with each career provides more information.

TABLE 1.4 • **Careers in Child Development**

EDUCATION	MEDICAL/NURSING	MENTAL HEALTH
2-YEAR PROGRAMS/ASSOCIATE DEGREE		
Park/Recreation Leader http://www.bls.gov/oco/ ocos058.htm *Childcare Worker* http://www.bls.gov/oco/ ocos170.htm	*Associate in Nursing* http://www.noadn.org/all.php *Hospital Child Life Assistant* http://www.childlife.org/	*Social & Human Services Assistant* http://www.bls.gov/oco/ ocos059.htm *Substance Abuse Counselor* http://www.flahec.org/ hlthcareers/SUBST.HTM
4-YEAR PROGRAMS/BACHELOR'S DEGREE		
Elementary/Secondary Teacher http://www.bls.gov/oco/ ocos069.htm *Children's Book Author or Illustrator* http://www.cbcbooks.org/ contacts/	*Pediatric Nurse* http://www.napnap.org/index_home.cfm *School Nurse* http://www.nasn.org/	*Child Welfare Worker* http://www.cwla.org/ default.htm *Art Therapist* http://www.arttherapy.org/
MASTER'S DEGREE		
School Principal http://www.naesp.org/ *Learning Disabilities Teacher* http://www.ldaamerica.org/	*Speech Therapist* http://www.asha.org/ *Genetic Counselor* http://www.nsgc.org/careers/ index.asp *Pediatric Occupational Therapist* http://www.pediatricoccupational therapist.net/	*School Psychologist* http://www.nasponline.org/ *Social Worker* http://www.naswdc.org/
DOCTORATE		
College Professor http://www.aera.net/ *Child Development Researcher* http://www.srcd.org/	*Pediatrician* http://www.aap.org/ *Child Psychiatrist* http://www.aacap.org/	*Parenting Coordinator in Divorces* http://www.apa.org/monitor/jan05/ niche.html *Family Therapist* http://www.ifta-familytherapy.org/ home.html

Parenting

Not all of you reading this book will select a career in child development, but many of you someday will have, or already do have, children. Take a moment now to type "parenting" into a search engine. Look at the hundreds of millions of resources and websites available. How will you evaluate this wealth of information? Surely knowledge of child development is useful for parents, but how do you select good information? Do parenting skills really matter? How much and for what outcomes?

If you become a parent, how will you know if your child's problems are fairly typical or deserve further attention? Early but appropriate intervention is important. Who could provide interventions if they are needed? How will you evaluate the claims of toy manufacturers, food companies, childcare facilities, or "how-to-parent" books and websites? The information in the next 12 chapters will help with all these challenges.

Relations between parents and their children change across time (Lamb & Lewis, 2005). In the early years, parents help their children learn that their behaviors have consequences. With parents' support, children also develop a sense of competence in their own growing abilities and appropriate trust in others. As children mature, parents help them develop self-control and self-regulation. In adolescence, parents are stable "targets" for their children's testing of limits and strivings for autonomy. But, of course, parents are not the only influence as children develop (Harris, 1998). "Certainly, researchers see parent-child relationships as dynamic systems that vary in quality depending on individual, familial, societal, and cultural circumstances" (Lamb & Lewis, 2005, p. 455). This book will help you make sense of all this information so you can be a better parent.

Policy

Some of you will work in child development careers, more of you will be parents, but all of you will be citizens and voters who can influence the public policies that affect children and families. What sort of work leave policies support families without harming businesses? Is full-day kindergarten better than half-day? For whom? Are government expenditures for early childhood education or children's television valuable? How much and what kind of achievement testing is useful in helping children learn? Are smaller classes worth the larger costs? How do we provide prenatal education and care for young women who cannot afford it? What will happen if we don't provide it? What are the implications of policy decisions for child development and how can you know? These are questions every citizen should be able to answer for the good of future generations (Groark & McCall, 2005). We hope this text will help.

▼ SUMMARY AND KEY TERMS

- **What Is Child Development?**

Developmental scientists study human growth and change from conception until death, often called *lifespan development*. Child development focuses on the time period from conception through adolescence, roughly the time from 0 to about 20 years old—the span covered by this book. The science of human development involves asking carefully specified questions based on current understandings (theories), systematically gathering and analyzing of all kinds of information (data) about the questions, modifying and improving explanatory theories based on the results of those analyses, and then asking new questions based on the improved theories.

- **Basic Themes and Debates in Development**

Three current debates in child development are: (1) Is human development a continuous process of adding to and increasing abilities, or are there leaps or moves to new stages when abilities actually change? Are changes continuous and quantitative (more of the same) or discontinuous, leading to qualitative differences? This may not be an either/or question because some changes that look discontinuous may be the result of very gradual changes over time and some changes that look continuous may result from using qualitatively different strategies. (2) Are there critical periods when certain abilities, such as language, need to develop? There are critical times in prenatal development when exposure to a toxin or a disease afflicting the mother, such as rubella, will cause damage to the developing fetus. There appears to be a critical period for learning accurate language pronunciation. Some critical periods for development appear to depend on the plasticity (adaptability or modifiability) of brain organization and structures. Most developmental psychologists today talk about sensitive periods—not critical periods. These are times when a person is especially ready for or responsive to certain experiences. (3) Which is more important in development, the "nature" of an individual (heredity, genes, biological processes, maturation, etc.) or the "nurture" of environmental contexts (education, parenting, culture, social policies, etc.)? This debate proved too complicated to be settled by splitting alternatives into either/or possibilities. Current views emphasize complex coactions (joint actions) of nature and nurture. Developmental systems theories are general perspectives on development, heredity, and evolution that emphasize the study of *interactions and coactions* between the many influences on development, without falling into the kinds of "which is more" debates.

- **What Are the Contexts for Development?**

Developmental scientists are increasingly interested in the role of context—the total setting or situation that surrounds and interacts with a person or event. Contexts also influence the development of behaviors, beliefs, and knowledge by providing resources, supports, incentives and punishments, expectations, teachers, models, tools—all the building blocks of development. Children grow up in families and neighborhoods. They attend schools and are in classes, teams, or choirs. They are members of particular ethnic, religious, economic, and language communities. The social and educational programs and policies of their governments affect their lives. Moreover, the contexts in which we live and develop are incredibly diverse. Family structures and parenting styles differ. Cultural rules and expectations differ. Resources, histories, and challenges for different ethnic, racial, geographic, religious, language, and SES groups differ. Finally, children develop in different historical times and under different societal policies and practices.

- **Why Study Development?**

We can't summarize this for you, but we can say that you will use knowledge of child development throughout your life—perhaps as a parent, aunt, uncle, teacher, medical worker, recreational leader, mental health worker, art therapist, speech therapist, social worker, school psychologist, or therapist. Enjoy the exploration.

▼ KEY TERMS

blended families (16)
child development (4)
coactions (13)
cognitive development (7)
cohort (21)
context (14)
continuous development (9)
critical periods (11)
culture (16)
development (4)
developmental science (4)
developmental systems theories (13)
discontinuous development (9)
emotional/social development (7)
ethnicity (18)
extended families (16)
maturation (7)
minority group (18)
nuclear family (16)
parenting styles (16)
physical development (7)
plasticity (12)
post-industrial (6)
prenatal (6)
race (18)
sensitive periods (12)
social construction (6)
socioeconomic status (SES) (18)
tabula rasa (9)
theory (5)

▼ THE CASEBOOK

APPLYING YOUR KNOWLEDGE OF CHILD DEVELOPMENT

Every chapter in this text will begin with a case involving child development. The issues raised and problems posed will relate to the information in the chapter that follows. But in this chapter, the focus of the case is very specific: you. Why are you taking this class, and what will you do with the knowledge you gain? Do you plan a career in child development? Which one? How will you decide? Should you consider being a teacher, social worker, physician, child life specialist, speech therapist, psychologist, researcher, nutritionist, pediatric or neonatal nurse, recreational or camp director, children's minister, college professor, public policy analyst . . .? Are you now or will you ever be a parent, aunt, uncle, foster parent, guardian, voter . . .? If the answer to any of these questions is "yes" or even "maybe," then you need to think critically about what this class means for your future.

WHAT WOULD THEY DO?

Here is how some students like you responded:

SARAH GRAFF—Junior, World Languages and Cultures/ Spanish Major
California State University–Monterey Bay, Monterey, California

For as long as I can remember I have enjoyed interacting with children. As a child, I attended an elementary school that strongly encouraged and facilitated cooperative learning and a sense of community. The classroom where I spent most of my elementary years was made up of students in kindergarten all the way to sixth grade. It was this early exposure to children of all ages and interacting and learning with them that initially directed me towards the path of babysitting throughout middle school, high school, and college, and now toward pursuing a career in child development.

Today I am a junior in college and after taking my first class in child development, I am adding a minor in Human Development. I hope to eventually receive my masters in Education and pursue a career as a Special Education or Spanish teacher.

Children have a curiosity and wonder to them that is difficult to find among adults. Working with children is not only rewarding for that reason; I want to continue to promote that curiosity and love of learning in the classroom. I hope to put my creativity and joy of working with children to use as a teacher. Understanding child development is critical to being a productive and positive teacher, but also knowledge I hope to use as a future aunt and mother.

SHANNON GLADIEUX—Early Childhood Education/ Mathematics Major
University of Toledo, Toledo, Ohio

Sometimes when I work with children I am amazed by how we as humans learn, develop, and process information. How does a child go from a crying, screaming, and completely dependent infant to a free thinking adult capable of complex, abstract and even profound thoughts? Watching a child's early language skills, spatial reasoning, and complex motor functioning develop can be an amazing experience giving you insight into the human condition or even your own self.

I personally am focusing my studies on early childhood education with a concentration in math. I am very intrigued by the ways in which we learn mathematics, on a fundamental level similar to the study of language literacy development. Piaget showed that all children construct logic and number concepts from within. I often ask myself how it is that children develop mathematics literacy and how educators can help to make mathematics deeply meaningful to a child, in the same way that a powerful piece of literature can deepen children's awareness of the written word and put them on the path to a truer understanding and interest in language and literacy. I am torn by a difficult life decision between working in a classroom setting exclusively or possibly pursuing a doctoral degree and continually doing research. Either way, I am convinced that children and their development will be a main focus of my life, and for that I am glad.

ELIZABETH RUHL—Social and Behavioral Sciences/ Psychology Major
California State University–Monterey Bay, Monterey, California

Working with children teaches important lessons for anyone who wishes to have a career involving social interactions. It teaches you patience, responsibility, and viewing the world in a different manner. I have worked with children on two separate occasions. The first was during my time volunteering at an in-patient pediatric ward. This was an interesting experience because I was able to witness how resilient children can be. The children could be battling diseases as serious as cancer, and yet they would still want to play board games or watch movies. I found this fascinating because most adults in their position would not have the positive energy that the children portrayed. Another opportunity I have had was spending a summer as a nanny. The children ranged from ages four to six. These ages were particularly intriguing to observe because the children were learning how to read. I was given the opportunity to help them sound out the tough words and form sentences. I was able to see how they viewed ethical decisions, such as sharing as well. These two experiences have definitely awakened my interest in child development.

A particular career involving children that would best fit my talents and experiences would a Psychologist. This would be interesting because the idea of using art therapy, which is often used while working with children, has always fascinated me. My final educational goal is to achieve my Ph.D. in Clinical or Counseling Psychology. I chose these two options because it leaves me with the widest range of opportunities whether I choose to counsel children or adults.

ALYSSA VOGT—Special Education Major
University of Wisconsin, Madison, Wisconsin

I have had many different meaningful experiences working with children, all of which have had an impact on preparing me to work with children in my future career. As a baby-sitter, I learned the necessary skills of how to care for the needs of children. I have tutored many different students at all grade levels in various subjects. As a tutor, I was a mentor to my students and developed a meaningful relationship with them.

One of the greatest experiences, though, was working as a counselor at a summer camp for individuals with disabilities. At this camp, I first discovered that becoming a special education teacher was my true calling in life. Now, I am majoring in Special Education with a concentration in working with individuals with cognitive disabilities. My child development courses as well as my years of working with children will help me to be successful in my future profession.

JAZMIN AGUIRRE MORENO—Human Development and Family Science (Family Studies) Major
The Ohio State University, Columbus, Ohio

Children have been a very important factor in my life. I grew up with two younger sisters, one who is two years younger and the other who is six years younger than I. The six year age difference allowed me to observe how my youngest sister developed through her childhood—from learning to walk and talk, to experiencing her first day of school, to watching her play on the junior varsity soccer team. Observing these changes sparked my interest in working with children. In high school, I became very involved in mentoring second and third grade students—helping them improve their reading and social skills through a program called Teen Trend Setters. I also volunteered at annual fundraisers held at local elementary schools and I started a small childcare and mentoring program at my own church, during high school, as well.

A career in family therapy would fit my personality well. I would enjoy working with a nonprofit organization possibly focusing on teen pregnancy prevention or working with children and teens at a young age to promote higher education. In college thus far, I have become a member of a few organizations that focus on children and young adults. It has sparked my desire to continue my path in higher education – I want to be the first in my family to receive not only a Bachelor's degree, but hopefully a Master's degree as well; one day I may even pursue a Doctoral degree. When I am much older, I would like to look back at my life and my experiences knowing that I helped educate children, teens, and their families, to help them make choices that will have a positive impact on their lives.

JADE EVETTE MUÑOZ

Texas A&M University Corpus Christi, Corpus Christi, Texas

I have had multiple rewarding experiences with children. My first experience was coaching and refereeing youth indoor soccer and basketball games, which I have done since the age of 14. I have also spent the past four summers as a camp assistant site coordinator working with more than 150 children a day from the ages of 7 to 14. During my time in Corpus Christi, I worked as a tutor and after school counselor at a local arts and education center and I am currently working at the early childhood development center at Texas A&M Corpus Christi, assisting in elementary school classes. I have a great passion for working with children. I know the kids feed off my passion and desire to see them succeed. After finishing my Bachelor's degree, my goal is to earn my Master's. I would like to further my education by learning more ideas and concepts that I will be able to use in the classroom.

PEARSON myeducationlab

Now go to MyEducationLab at **www.myeducationlab.com,** where you can:

- Find the instructional objectives for this chapter in the **Study Plan.**
- Take a quiz as a part of the **Study Plan** to self-assess your mastery of chapter content. The program generates an individualized Study Plan based upon your answers to the quiz.
- Complete **Activities and Applications** to assist you in deepening your understanding of important chapter concepts.
- Apply what you have learned through **Building Teaching Skills,** exercises that guide you in trying out skills and strategies you will use in professional practice.

2 THEORY AND RESEARCH IN CHILD DEVELOPMENT

THE CASEBOOK

WHAT WOULD YOU DO?

GIVING PERMISSION FOR CHILDREN TO PARTICIPATE IN RESEARCH

Today there are many procedures to protect children and adolescents when they participate in research. One of the most important is informed consent from parents or guardians. Here is a sample consent form Anita has used in research on middle school children's motivation to learn mathematics.

This is a parental permission form for research participation. It contains important information about this study and what to expect if you permit your child to participate. **Your child's participation is voluntary.**

Please consider the information carefully. Feel free to discuss the study with your friends and family and to ask questions before making your decision whether or not to permit your child to participate. If you permit your child to participate, you will be asked to sign this form and will receive a copy of the form.

Purpose: The purpose of this study is to examine the influence of perceived classroom psychological environment, personal beliefs, and feelings on middle school students' academic achievement and effort outcomes in mathematics.

Procedures/Tasks: Your child will be asked to respond to a self-report questionnaire in his/her classroom. Also your child's achievement test scores and grades in mathematics will be obtained from school records.

Duration: Survey administration will take approximately 15 to 25 minutes. Participation in the survey is completely voluntary and your child may leave the

Fatima Z., Age 8—Australia

study at any time. If you or your child decides to stop participation in the study, there will be no penalty and neither you nor your child will lose any benefits to which you are otherwise entitled. Your decision will not affect your future relationship with The Ohio State University. However, participation would be highly appreciated.

Risks and Benefits: There is no risk for your child to participate in this study. The results of this study will contribute to our understanding of the classroom psychological factors affecting early adolescents' motivational, emotional, and academic outcomes. Knowing students' individual perceptions will help us generate more effective middle school environments responsive to early adolescents' developmental needs. Efforts in this study are dedicated to contribute to the development of lifelong successful individuals. The findings of this study might be used in teacher preparation and school enhancement programs so that middle school students can study in classrooms where they can experience joy and success.

Confidentiality: Identifiable student data will not be shared with anyone, including school teachers, administrators, parents, and colleagues. In order to prevent any incidence of revealing students' data, students will be assigned participant numbers and a list of students' names and participant numbers will be kept separate from the data. All data will be de-identified by including participant numbers only. Efforts will be made to keep your child's study-related information confidential. However, there may be circumstances where this information must be released. For example, personal information regarding your child's participation in this study may be disclosed if required by state law. Also, your child's records may be reviewed by the following groups ________________________.

Incentives: Each participating student will have a chance to win one of the forty $10 gift cards determined through a drawing following the completion of the study in _____.

Participant Rights: You or your child may refuse to participate in this study without penalty or loss of benefits to which you are otherwise entitled. If you or your child is a student or employee at Ohio State, your decision will not affect your grades or employment status. If you and your child choose to participate in the study, you may discontinue participation at any time without penalty or loss of benefits. By signing this form, you do not give up any personal legal rights your child may have as a participant in this study. An Institutional Review Board responsible for human subjects research at The Ohio State University reviewed this research project and found it to be acceptable, according to applicable state and federal regulations and University policies designed to protect the rights and welfare of participants in research.

Contacts and Questions: For questions, concerns, or complaints about the study you may contact ________________

Signing the parental permission form I have read (or someone has read to me) this form and I am aware that I am being asked to provide permission for my child to participate in a research study. I have had the opportunity to ask questions and have had them answered to my satisfaction. I voluntarily agree to permit my child to participate in this study. I am not giving up any legal rights by signing this form. I will be given a copy of this form.

Parent or Guardian Signature______________________________

Date__________

CRITICAL THINKING

- If you were a parent reading this form, what would you think?
- Would you sign?
- How are children protected by this procedure?

OUTLINE ▼

▶ OVERVIEW AND OBJECTIVES

Several different fields are interested in the how and why of children's development, so we have many perspectives and theories to explore. In this chapter we preview the theories that will be important throughout our journey: ethology and sociobiology, Freud's psychoanalytic theory, Erikson's psychosocial theory, classical and operant conditioning, Bandura's cognitive learning theory, information processing theories, Piaget's cognitive developmental theory, Vygotsky's sociocultural theory, Bronfenbrenner's bioecological theory, and Thelen's dynamic systems theory. Then we ask where these theories came from and examine the process of research in child development. Along the way, we hope you will become more critical readers and thinkers about explanations of children's growth and development. By the time you finish this chapter you should be able to do the following:

Objective 2.1 Make the case that child development is a diverse field—multidisciplinary, multicultural, applying multiple methods, and producing multiple theories.

Objective 2.2 Summarize these developmental theories: ethology and sociobiology, Freud's psychoanalytic theory, Erikson's psychosocial theory, classical and operant conditioning, Bandura's cognitive learning theory, information processing theories, Piaget's cognitive developmental theory, Vygotsky's sociocultural theory, Bronfenbrenner's bioecological theory, and Thelen's dynamic systems theory.

Objective 2.3 Explain the research cycle in studying children's development, including methods for gathering information about development and different research designs (correlational, experimental, quantitative, and qualitative).

Objective 2.4 Describe key ethical considerations in research about children.

Objective 2.5 Compare and contrast basic, applied, and community-based research.

Objective 2.6 Explain some critical considerations about reliability, validity, and cultural sensitivity in research about children.

Objective 2.7 Evaluate sources of information about child development.

DIVERSITY IN THE STUDY OF DEVELOPMENT

People have been interested in children—especially the children in their families—since time began. But the science of child development is only about 100 years old. Who studies child development today? The theorists and researchers are from many different disciplines and cultures. They apply a range of methods and have created a wealth of theories.

Multidisciplinary

Many people are interested in the "what" and "why" questions of child development. What are the typical motor skills of a 5-year-old? Why do some children walk earlier or run faster than others? Why do some babies sleep through the night at 8 months while others are still waking every few hours at 18 months? What can be done to help the 18-month-old (and her parents) sleep more easily? Are there gender differences in math ability or in aggression? What explains the changes in memory abilities as children develop? Psychologists dominated the study of child development in earlier times, but today, questions of child development increasingly require multidisciplinary research along with the efforts of psychologists, educators, pediatricians, linguists, sociologists, and others using the tools and knowledge from their fields (Lerner, 2006; Salkind, 2004).

Multicultural

Understanding child development also requires a multicultural perspective. You saw in Chapter 1 that culture includes the knowledge, skills, traditions, beliefs, and values that guide behavior in a particular group of people as well as the art and artifacts produced and passed down to the next generation. Each of us is part of many different cultural groups, defined by our ethnicity, religion, race, geographic location, language, or other memberships. But diversity in cultures has not always been a major feature of research in child development. Carol Lee (2003) noted that the 1998 *Handbook of Child Psychology* (vol. 1) had only one chapter focused explicitly on African American or Latino populations. In other chapters, Lee claimed, European American middle-class norms and behaviors were used as the points of reference for all other groups. In addition, most of the primary authors of the chapters were European American.

Times are changing. In the sixth edition of the *Handbook of Child Psychology*, Lerner (2006, p. 7) proclaims, "diversity of person and context has moved into the foreground of the analysis of human development." Today, the Society for Research in Child Development (SRCD) has members from over 50 countries—20% of its membership is from outside the United States. On its website, the SRCD recognizes the value of diversity: "The Society fosters a commitment to research and training in diversity" (http://www.srcd.org/about.html).

Over the past decade, diversity has become a central concern in research and theory in child development. The role of culture in development is an important area of study. Psychologists today recognize that culture shapes development by determining what and how a child will learn about the world. For example, young Zinacanteco Indian girls of southern Mexico learn complicated ways of weaving cloth through informal teachings of adults in their communities. In Brazil, without going to school, children who sell candy on the streets learn sophisticated mathematics in order to buy from wholesalers, sell, barter, and make a profit. Cultures that prize cooperation and sharing teach these abilities early, whereas cultures that encourage competition nurture competitive skills in their children (Bakerman,

Culture affects development in every aspect of life. Both of the children above are learning mathematical concepts, but the processes and outcomes of learning vary. The Brazilian child selling candy can do many accurate mental calculations to buy candy wholesale and sell at a profit, but may have trouble with school paper-and-pencil tasks that require the same mathematical calculation. The opposite could be true of the Canadian child learning mathematics in a class. She might be able to do the paper-and-pencil work but have trouble applying the processes to real life.

Adamson, Koner, & Barr, 1990; Ceci & Roazzi, 1994). The stages observed by Piaget are not necessarily "natural" for all children because to some extent they reflect the expectations and activities of Western cultures (Kozulin, 2003; Rogoff, 2003).

Multiple Methods

With multiple disciplines and cultures come multiple methods for studying the "what" and "why" questions of child development. As you saw in Chapter 1, early baby biographies were based on careful, detailed (but often biased) observations of infants in their first few years. Today, careful observation is still an important method, but that observation is more systematic and scientific. It would be almost impossible to describe all the methods that might be applied in the multidisciplinary study of child development, because so many fields are involved—from sociology to medicine to linguistics. Even the methods used within a single discipline such as psychology or education can be quite varied, as you will see later in this chapter when we take a closer look at research methods for studying child development.

Multiple Theories

As we noted in Chapter 1, there are many theories in the field of child development. Some are all-encompassing, grand theories, such as those by Piaget or Erikson, which explain many aspects of cognitive, social, and personality development. Others focus on much more specific areas such as how children make moral judgments. Current emerging theories of development view the individual as embedded in multiple layers of interacting systems, from biological to societal and historical contexts (Bronfenbrenner & Morris, 2006; Thelen & Smith, 1998).

In the following section, we examine the major theories of development that will provide a frame to examine physical, cognitive, and emotional/social development in Chapters 3 through 13 of this text. After briefly noting early ideas about children, we examine six general perspectives or families of developmental theories: biological theories (ethology and sociobiology), psychoanalytic theories (Freud and Erikson), learning theories (classical and operant conditioning, social cognitive theory, and information processing), cognitive stages and structures (Piaget), contextual theories (Vygotsky and Bronfenbrenner), and dynamic systems theory (Thelen).

Explanations of Development

Early writings about children came from sacred books and the works of philosophers. For example, Plato, an ancient Greek philosopher, suggested that children should be taken from their families and brought up by "experts," because child rearing was too important for the future of society to be left to often-incompetent parents. The ancient Chinese philosopher Confucius is said to have cautioned, "The father who does not teach his son his duties is equally guilty with the son who neglects them." Passages from the Christian Bible make recommendations to parents about child rearing: "Train a child in the way he should go, and when he is old he will not turn from it" (Proverbs 22:6). In Judaism, childhood is considered a period of purity, joy, and beauty to be valued and cherished. The Talmud states "childhood is a garland of roses" (Babylonian Talmud, Shabbat 152,119a). In the Hindu religion, there are a number of ceremonies and rituals around pregnancy, birth, and childhood including Jatakarma to welcome the newborn into the world, Namkarma (the naming ceremony), and the Upanayana ceremony when the child reaches school age. A passage from the Koran states, "Money and children are the joys of this life, but the righteous works provide an eternal recompense from your Lord, and a far better hope." Clearly, many religions see children as valuable, but in need of training and guidance.

In the 1800s, the field of psychology was just emerging, and children's development was the focus of many early pioneers: in Great Britain, Charles Darwin's detailed observations of his own children; in the United States, G. Stanley Hall's child study movement and John Dewey's emphasis on child-centered education; in France, Alfred Binet's research on children's' mental abilities; and in Italy, Maria Montessori's schools.

The study of child development in the United States can be traced to societal and scientific concerns in the 1920s. John Dewey was studying and writing about the "whole child" in psychology and education. In addition, many young men being evaluated for military service in World War I were found either physically or cognitively unfit for service, so new organizations were funded with both public and private money to stimulate research on children's development. In 1924, the National Research Council founded the Committee on Child Development (CCD) and the 1920s was named "The Decade of the Child." Then, in 1933, CCD became the Society for Research in Child Development (SRCD), the most influential organization of child development researchers today (Cameron & Hagen, 2005).

Let's examine the major perspectives on child development that have emerged in the last 100 years.

Biological Perspectives: Ethology and Sociobiology

All theories of child development recognize that children are biological as well as psychological beings. But ethology focuses on biological processes in development. **Ethology** is the study of how behaviors adapt to support the survival of all animals, including humans. By carefully observing animals in their natural settings, ethologists try to understand and explain particular behavior patterns and instincts that allow the animals to adapt (Miller, 2011).

Charles Darwin's theory of evolution is a foundation of ethology, but the person most associated with ethology is Conrad Lorenz, a zoologist from Austria. You probably have seen pictures showing Lorenz swimming or walking with a gaggle of young geese. Lorenz's (1973/1977) best-known work was on **imprinting**, the tendency of some animals to attach to the first nurturing figure they observe after they are born. Lorenz demonstrated this process by guarding a group of geese as they hatched. After this imprinting experience, the goslings followed him everywhere. The explanation was that staying close to the mother has survival value for young animals, so imprinting and bonding are valuable processes.

Do human infants "imprint"? This general question led John Bowlby (1969/1982), a British psychoanalyst, to initiate a series of studies of *attachment* in humans. You will see in the upcoming chapters that research on attachment has flourished, but as you might imagine, attachment in humans is a more complex and lengthy process than it is for geese.

The discovery of imprinting just after birth led researchers to ask if there are other *critical periods* during which an organism is biologically primed to benefit from certain kinds of stimulation or input. You saw in Chapter 1 that, for the most part, humans have *sensitive periods* when they are particularly responsive to stimulation for certain kinds of development. We will encounter the ideas of critical and sensitive periods again in later chapters of this book.

Operation Migration has spearheaded an attempt by the U.S. Fish and Wildlife Service to reintroduce whooping cranes into eastern North America using the process of imprinting. The birds imprinted on an ultralight plane that led them to their new territory and taught them the migration route by leading them in flight—see http://www.operationmigration.org/index.html. A similar idea was the basis for the family film *Fly Away Home*.

Another area of ethology, **sociobiology**, examines the development of social behaviors that help the entire species survive. Instead of being concerned with how individuals develop across the lifespan, sociobiologists focus on the development of the species and how evolution selects genes that support the survival of the whole group (Green & Piel, 2010). Sociobiologists such as Edward O. Wilson (1975, 2006) study the adaptive value of other behavior patterns besides imprinting. For example, are certain mating rituals in animals and humans adaptive? When male mountain goats or lions battle for the right to mate with females, does this ensure that the stronger male is more likely to father strong offspring?

Do humans instinctively find certain aspects of babies' appearance (larger heads in relation to their bodies, short arms and legs, big round eyes) endearing so that they feel compelled to protect these helpless creatures? How does the attachment bond between infants and caregivers increase the infants' chances for survival? What is the biological basis of morality? Wilson has been awarded two Pulitzer prizes in literature for his sometimes-controversial writing about biodiversity and the implications of sociobiology.

Psychoanalytic Theories: Freud and Erikson

Sigmund Freud (1856–1939) was the oldest—and he believed, the most favored—of eight children. An avid reader in his youth, he even taught himself Spanish so he could read *Don Quixote* in the original. Freud entered medical school with the hope of becoming a research scientist, but had to leave for private practice because he needed the money and he realized that being Jewish would hinder his advancement in academia. His interest in neurology and treating nervous disorders led him to work with patients, mostly upper middle-class women with hysteria—a disorder characterized by numbness or paralysis with no known physical causes. By analyzing the dreams and childhood memories of his patients, Freud devised his approach to therapy, called **psychoanalysis**, that helped the patients discover, talk about, and understand emotional conflicts from childhood, buried in their unconscious, that were sources of their anxieties and problems as adults. At first, he was not recognized in Europe, but by the time he died in London in 1939 (he had fled from Vienna in 1937 to escape the Nazi takeover of Austria) he had written 23 volumes. His work has influenced literature, art, psychology, anthropology, religion, sociology, therapy, and history, to name only a few areas (Green & Piel, 2010; Miller, 2011).

FREUD: ELEMENTS OF PERSONALITY AND STAGES OF PSYCHOSEXUAL DEVELOPMENT. Freud believed that three elements of personality develop during childhood—the id, ego, and superego. The **id** is the screaming infant demanding immediate pleasure and gratification. But immediate gratification is not always possible, and the **ego** develops to deal with this reality, as the infant learns that she is separate from the world and cannot control her surroundings completely. The **superego** develops around age 6 and is the demanding conscience that dictates what "should" and "should not" be done. The ego tries to navigate how to satisfy the id without offending the superego. Freud suggested that all humans have inborn biological, sexual, and aggressive drives that have to be managed and redirected by the ego in order for us to live successfully in civilized societies. The way we learn to manage these conflicts, according to Freud, shapes our personalities and our typical ways of handling stresses and emotions as adults.

Further, Freud believed that these conflicts between inborn drives and the demands of society result in five stages of psychosexual development—the same five stages in the same order for all people. According to Freud, if the conflicts of one stage are not resolved, an individual can become fixated at that stage. When you hear a comedian refer to someone as an "anal personality," obsessed with order and control, for example, you are hearing the pop culture version of Freud's idea of fixation at the anal stage—the time when children are experiencing toilet training. Each stage is associated with a different area of the body that provides pleasure. Freud's stages and his assertions about them are:

1. *Oral* (first year of life). The mouth is the focus and pleasure comes from sucking, eating, biting, chewing, and so on. Too little oral gratification leads to anxiety and seeking oral gratification later in life (smoking, nail biting, etc.). Too much gratification may make it hard to move to the next stage.
2. *Anal* (ages about 1 to 3). The focus is the anus and pleasure comes from relieving tension by having bowel movements. Society (in the form of parents) insists that children learn to control their bowel movements. If toilet teaching is too harsh or too early, the child may become fixated at the anal stage, and be either very messy (anal expulsive) or very controlled and neat (anal retentive).
3. *Phallic* (ages about 3 to 5). Having solved the toilet learning challenge, boys move on, in Freud's view, to discover the pleasures of the penis. Girls are assumed to discover,

to their great sadness and envy, that they do not have a penis. Both boys and girls are attracted to their opposite sex parent (called the *Oedipal complex* for boys and the *Electra complex* for girls), but resolve this dilemma by identifying with and trying to become more like their same-sex parent. With the successful completion of the oral, anal, and phallic stages, Freud believed that personality was pretty much set.

4. *Latency* (ages about 5 to puberty). This is a time of calm. Sexual and aggressive energy flows into schoolwork, sports, clubs, and peer relations. Children tend to play with same-sex friends.
5. *Genital* (adolescence and adulthood). Sexual impulses return with a vengeance. The source of pleasure is in sexual relations, but in a more mature and appropriate way. People are ready for committed relationships with partners and families.

Freud was criticized on a number of fronts for overemphasizing sex and aggression; for basing his theories on the memories of wealthy European women with very specific mental problems; for creating stages of development in childhood without ever studying children; for collecting no experimental data that might support or refute his theories; and even for making up some data. But his concepts of unconscious motivation, the importance of early experiences, parent–child relationships, and psychosexual development have been powerful influences in the field.

As you may recall, the three themes we discussed in Chapter 1 were shape, timing, and source of development. Freud's stage theory puts him in the camp that believes the shape of development is discontinuous and qualitative—not continuous and quantitative. He clearly thought timing in terms of early experience was critical in shaping the developing child and, with his emphasis on both inborn drives and socialization practices, he had a place for nature and nurture as sources of development in his theory.

Freud also was an important influence on the life and work of Erik Erikson (1902–1994), as you will see next.

ERIKSON: STAGES OF PSYCHOSOCIAL DEVELOPMENT. Erikson also has a fascinating life story. He skipped college, traveled around Europe, and ended up teaching in Vienna. His students were mostly children of therapists learning psychoanalysis from Freud and children of patients who had come to be psychoanalyzed. In Vienna, Erikson not only studied psychoanalysis but also was analyzed by Anna Freud, daughter of Sigmund. Soon after completing his training, Erikson had to flee the terror of the Nazis. He was denied citizenship in Denmark, so he moved to his second choice—New York City. Even though he had never attended college, on the basis of his groundbreaking work he became a distinguished University Professor at Harvard. Later in his career he worked with the original Dr. Spock—Benjamin Spock, the widely read pediatrician whose books guided many baby boomers' parents, including Anita's (Green & Piel, 2010).

In his influential *Childhood and Society* (1963), Erikson offered a basic framework for understanding the needs of young people in relation to the society in which they grow, learn, and later make their contributions. His later books, *Identity, Youth, and Crisis* (1968) and *Identity and the Life Cycle* (1980), expanded on his ideas. Erikson's **psychosocial** theory emphasized the emergence of the self, the search for identity, the individual's relationships with others, and the role of culture throughout life. Perhaps his experiences traveling and living in so many different countries and cultures taught Erikson about the centrality of culture and society in human development.

Like Piaget (described later in this chapter) and Freud, Erikson saw development as a passage through a series of stages, each with its particular goals, concerns, accomplishments, and dangers. The stages are interdependent: Accomplishments at later stages depend on how conflicts are resolved in the earlier years. At each stage, Erikson suggests that the individual faces a **developmental crisis**. Each crisis can be resolved by embracing an extreme position or by the healthier and more productive stance of finding a balance between the extreme responses. The way in which the individual resolves each crisis will have a lasting effect on that person's self-image and view of society. We will look briefly at all eight stages in Erikson's theory. Table 2.1 presents the stages in summary form.

TABLE 2.1 • **Erikson's Eight Stages of Psychosocial Development**

AGE	PSYCHOSOCIAL CRISIS	SIGNIFICANT SOURCES OF PSYCHOSOCIAL CONFLICT
0–1	Trust versus mistrust	Mother
2–3	Autonomy versus shame and doubt	Both parents
3–6	Initiative versus guilt	Family members
7–12	Industry versus inferiority	Neighborhood and school
12–18	Identity versus role diffusion	Peer groups, out-groups, leadership models
20s	Intimacy and solidarity versus isolation	Cooperation with partner in friendship, recreation, production, sex
20s–50s	Generativity versus stagnation	Sharing child rearing, dividing labor, household responsibilities
50s and beyond	Integrity versus despair	Finding oneself within humanity, civilization, generations

Source: Green & Piel, Theories of Human Development, *Table 4.2, "Erikson's Eight Stages of Psychosocial Development," p. 93 © 2010. Reproduced by permission of Pearson Education, Inc.*

1. *Trust versus mistrust* is the basic conflict of infancy. According to Erikson, the infant will develop a sense of trust if its needs for food and care are met with comforting regularity and responsiveness from caregivers. In this first year, infants are just beginning to learn that they are separate from the world around them. This realization is part of what makes trust so important: Infants must trust the aspects of their world that are beyond their control but also learn that some situations should not be trusted, so they need a balance of being able to trust and mistrust appropriately—either extreme is dysfunctional (Isabella & Belsky, 1991; Posada et al., 2002).
2. *Autonomy versus shame and doubt* marks the beginning of self-control and self-confidence. Young children (about ages 2 to 3) begin to assume important responsibilities for self-care such as feeding, toileting, and dressing. During this period parents must tread a fine line; they must be protective—but not overprotective. If parents are not reassuring and fail to reinforce the child's efforts to master basic motor and cognitive skills, children may doubt their abilities to manage the world on their own terms and feel shame. Erikson believes that children who experience too much doubt at this stage will lack confidence in their own abilities throughout life. Of course, some doubt is appropriate if the task is too difficult or dangerous—again the need for balance.
3. *Initiative versus guilt* "adds to autonomy the quality of undertaking, planning, and attacking a task for the sake of being active and on the move" (Erikson, 1963, p. 255). The challenge of this period (from about ages 3 to 6) is to maintain a zest for activity and at the same time understand that not every impulse can be acted on. Again, adults must tread a fine line, this time in providing supervision without interference. If children are not allowed to do things on their own, a sense of guilt may develop; they may come to believe that what they want to do is always "wrong." The ***Connecting with Children*** suggestions on the next page provide ways of encouraging initiative.
4. *Industry versus inferiority* is the stage between the ages of 6 and 12. Cognitive development is proceeding rapidly. Children can process more information faster and their memory spans are increasing. They are beginning to see the relationship between perseverance and the pleasure of a job completed. In modern societies, the ability to move between the worlds of home, neighborhood, and school and to cope with academics, group activities, and friends will lead to a growing sense of competence in children. Difficulty with these challenges can result in feelings of inferiority. Children must master new skills and work toward new goals, while being compared to others and risking failure. As children deal with the challenge of industry versus

CONNECTING WITH CHILDREN

Guidelines for Teachers and Families: Encouraging Initiative and Industry in Children

Be tolerant of accidents and mistakes, especially when children are attempting to do something on their own.
Examples
1. Use cups and pitchers that make it easy to pour and hard to spill.
2. Recognize the attempt, even if the product is unsatisfactory.
3. If mistakes are made, show the child how to clean up, repair, or redo.

Encourage children to make and to act on choices.
Examples
1. Encourage children to select an activity or game.
2. As much as possible, avoid interrupting children who are very involved in what they are doing.
3. When children suggest an activity, try to follow their suggestions or incorporate their ideas into ongoing activities.
4. Offer positive choices: Instead of saying, "You can't have the cookies now," ask, "Would you like the cookies after lunch or after naptime?"

Make sure that young children have a chance to experience success.
Examples
1. In learning anything new, move in small steps.
2. Teachers, avoid competitive games when the range of abilities in the class is great.

Encourage make-believe with a wide variety of roles.
Examples
1. At home or in school, include costumes and props that go along with stories children enjoy. Encourage children to act out the stories or make up new adventures for favorite characters.
2. Teachers, monitor the children's play to be sure no one monopolizes playing "teacher," "Mommy," "Daddy," or other heroes.

Make sure that children have opportunities to set and work toward realistic goals.
Examples
1. In doing chores or homework, encourage children to set a goal for 10 minutes, then for longer and longer periods of time.
2. Praise children for doing their best, not for being perfect.

Give children a chance to show their independence and responsibility.
Examples
1. Tolerate honest mistakes.
2. Delegate tasks appropriate to the child's abilities such as watering plants, caring for pets, or cleaning up after dinner.
3. Don't compare children to their siblings or friends, but to their own improvement.

Teachers, provide support to students who seem discouraged.
Examples
1. Use individual charts and contracts that show student progress.
2. Keep samples of earlier work so students can see their improvement.
3. Give awards for most improved, most helpful, most hardworking.

---

inferiority, they must also reestablish Erikson's stages of psychosocial development in the unfamiliar school setting. They must learn which new adults they can *trust*, act *autonomously* in this more complex situation, and *initiate* actions in ways that fit the new rules of school. The ***Connecting with Children*** suggestions give some ideas.

5. *Identity versus role confusion* is the conflict for adolescents, from about ages 12 to 18. Cognitive processes are expanding as the young adolescents develop capabilities for abstract thinking and for understanding the perspectives of others. Even greater changes are taking place in their physical development as they approach puberty. So, along with their developing minds and bodies, adolescents must confront the central issue of developing an identity that will provide a firm basis for adulthood. The individual has been developing a sense of self since infancy. But adolescence marks the first time that a conscious effort is being made to answer the now pressing question, "Who am I?" Identity refers to the organization of the individual's drives, abilities, beliefs, and history into a consistent image of self. It involves deliberate choices and decisions, particularly about work, values, ideology, and commitments to people and

ideas (Green & Piel, 2010; Marcia, 1999). If adolescents fail to integrate all these aspects and choices, or if they feel unable to choose at all, role confusion threatens.

6. *Intimacy versus isolation,* like all the crises of Erikson's stages of adulthood, involves the quality of human relations. Intimacy in this sense refers to a willingness to relate to another person on a deep level, to have a relationship based on more than mutual need. Someone who has not achieved a sufficiently strong sense of identity tends to fear being overwhelmed or swallowed up by another person and may retreat into isolation. Of course, as with all the stages, a healthy resolution involves a balance—being capable of intimate relationships without being completely dependent on or lost in them.
7. *Generativity versus stagnation* is the challenge of the middle adult years. Generativity extends the ability to care for another person and involves caring and guidance for the next generation and for future generations. While generativity frequently refers to having and nurturing children, it has a broader meaning. Productivity and creativity are essential features.
8. *Integrity versus despair* is the last of Erikson's stages and involves coming to terms with death. Achieving integrity means consolidating your sense of self and fully accepting its unique and now unalterable history. Those unable to attain a feeling of fulfillment sink into despair.

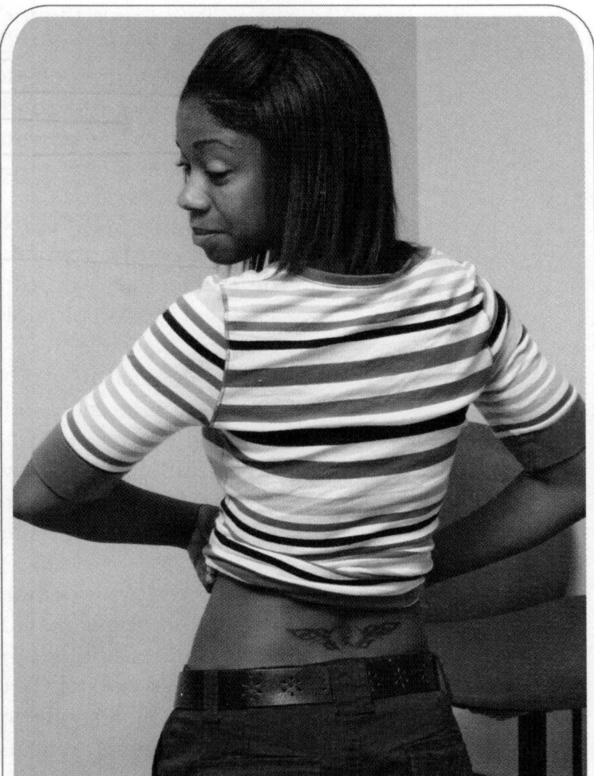
"Who am I?" Erikson suggests that it is valuable for adolescents to try on different identities in safe surroundings in order to establish a personal identity.

Erikson's work helped start the lifespan development approach, and his theories have been especially useful in understanding adolescence. But feminists have criticized his notion that identity precedes intimacy, because their research indicates that for women, identity achievement is fused with achieving intimacy. The theory, although creative and appealing, is based on observations, generalizations, and abstract theoretical claims, so it is virtually impossible to test. In addition, Erikson's theory is mostly descriptive—he describes what happens and the influences that are involved, but does not discuss how or why these factors effect change. If we don't know why failure to resolve a conflict at one stage causes problems at the other stages, we don't really know if the conflict-resolution model is valid. Maybe other factors are responsible and conflict resolution has nothing to do with the difficulties and accomplishments of later life (Miller, 2011). The results of research on infant attachment (Chapter 4) and on adolescents' identity statuses (Chapter 13) are consistent with Erikson's theory, however (Green & Piel, 2010).

In terms of the three themes in Chapter 1, shape, timing, source of development, Erikson tended to emphasize qualitative changes in development over time, the importance of timing in resolving the appropriate conflicts as they arose predictably throughout life, and nurture and socialization within the culture more than nature as the source of development.

Behavioral Learning Theories: Classical and Operant Conditioning

A fundamental idea behind many of the learning theories of development is that most of the changes in children's cognitive and emotional/social development, and even some physical changes, are consequences of learning: Nurture is more important than nature. Children learn language, problem solving, taking the perspective of others, and ways of coping with fears, for example. Learning theorists criticized Freud's ideas about unconscious motivations and fixations because these processes could not be observed and studied scientifically. The psychoanalytic explanations could not be proved wrong because they were just interesting stories about causes—and the stories couldn't be tested. Learning theories developed to take a more scientific look at change in something that *can* be observed—*behaviors*—so these theories are often classified under the general category of **behaviorism**.

Two major theories, classical conditioning and operant conditioning, explain how behaviors are learned. **Classical conditioning** focuses on the learning of often *involuntary* emotional or physiological responses such as fear, increased muscle tension, salivation, or sweating. **Operant conditioning** is the learning process involved in *intentional* behavior such as having a tantrum to get your way or improving your dancing through practice, so operant conditioning applies to many behaviors of interest in teaching.

CLASSICAL CONDITIONING. Through the process of classical conditioning, humans and animals can be trained to react to a stimulus that previously had no effect—or a very different effect—on them. Classical conditioning was discovered in the 1920s by Ivan Pavlov, a Russian physiologist who was trying to determine how long it took a dog to salivate (secrete digestive juices) after it had been fed. But the intervals of time kept changing. Pavlov decided to make a detour from his original experiments and examine these unexpected interferences in his work. In one of his first experiments, Pavlov began by sounding a tuning fork (a *neutral stimulus*) and recording a dog's response. As expected, there was no salivation. Then Pavlov fed the dog; the response was salivation. The food was an *unconditioned stimulus (US)* and the salivation was an *unconditioned response (UR),* because no prior training or "conditioning" was needed to establish the natural connection between food (US) and salivation (UR).

Then Pavlov demonstrated that a dog could be conditioned to salivate after hearing the tuning fork. He sounded the fork and then quickly fed the dog. After Pavlov repeated this several times, the dog began to salivate after hearing the sound but before receiving the food. The sound had become a *conditioned stimulus (CS)* that could bring forth salivation by itself. The response of salivating after the tone was now a *conditioned response (CR)*.

An early American behaviorist, John B. Watson, used Pavlov's ideas to develop a theory of child development. He believed that he could shape children by using classical conditioning techniques and even conditioned an 11-month-old boy, know as "Little Albert," to fear furry animals and some fur coats. The experiment has been widely condemned because Watson never even told Little Albert's mother what he was doing, nor did he try to "uncondition" the fear response. Nevertheless, Watson (1924) claimed:

> Give me a dozen healthy infants, well-formed, and my own specified world to bring them up in and I'll guarantee to take any one at random and train him to become any type of specialist I might select—doctor, lawyer, artist, merchant, chief, and yes, even beggar-man and thief—regardless of his talents, penchants, tendencies, abilities, vocations, and race of his ancestors. (p. 104)

But if you think that Pavlovian conditioning is of historical interest only, consider this excerpt from *USA Today* describing an advertising campaign for products aimed at "Gen Y"—young people born between 1977 and 1994:

> Mountain Dew executives have their own term for this [advertising strategy]: the Pavlovian connection. By handing out samples of the brand at surfing, skateboard and snowboard tournaments, "There's a Pavlovian connection between the brand and the exhilarating experience," says Dave Burwich, a top marketing executive at Pepsi, which makes Mountain Dew. (Horovitz, April 22, 2002, p. B2)

It is possible that many of our emotional reactions to various situations have been learned in part through classical conditioning. Physicians have a term, "white coat syndrome," that describes people whose blood pressure (an involuntary response) goes up when it is tested in the doctor's office, usually by someone in a white coat. Classical conditioning has implications for parents and teachers as well as marketing managers. Procedures based on classical conditioning also can be used to help people learn more adaptive emotional responses, as you will see in upcoming chapters when we discuss children's fears.

OPERANT CONDITIONING. Edward Thorndike and B. F. Skinner both played major roles in developing knowledge of operant conditioning. Thorndike's (1933) early work involved cats that he placed in problem boxes. To escape from the box and reach food outside, the cats had to pull out a bolt or perform some other task; they had to "operate" on their environment. During the frenzied movements that followed the closing of the box, the cats eventually made the correct movement to escape, usually by accident. After repeating the process several times, the cats learned to make the correct response almost immediately. Thorndike decided, on the basis of these experiments, that one important law of learning was the *law of effect*: Any act that produces a satisfying effect in a given situation will tend to be repeated in that situation. Because pulling out a bolt produced satisfaction (access to food), cats repeated that movement when they found themselves in the box again.

Thorndike thus established the basis for operant conditioning, but the person generally thought to be responsible for developing the concept is B. F. Skinner (1953). Like so many others, Skinner did not start out to be a psychologist. He majored in English and tried to write fiction, but gave that up in 1928 and enrolled in Harvard to study psychology. Skinner brought a combination of skills and abilities to his work. He was very organized in his life and in his thinking, as well as mechanically adept. He used these skills to design ingenious equipment to study learning in pigeons and rats (Green & Piel, 2010).

Skinner believed that classical conditioning accounts for only a small portion of learned behaviors; it is only relevant to how existing behaviors might be associated or paired with new stimuli. Classical conditioning does not explain how new operant behaviors (behaviors that *operate* on the environment) are acquired. According to Skinner's view, **consequences** determine to a great extent whether a person will repeat the behavior that led to the consequences. The type of consequences can strengthen or weaken behaviors. Consequences that strengthen are called *reinforcers* and consequences that weaken are called *punishers*.

Although a reinforcer is commonly understood to mean a "reward," this term has a particular meaning in psychology. A **reinforcer** is any consequence that strengthens the behavior it follows. Whenever you see a behavior persisting or increasing over time, you can assume the consequences of that behavior are reinforcers for the individual involved (Landrum & Kauffman, 2006). This process is called *reinforcement* and can be diagrammed as follows:

	CONSEQUENCE		EFFECT
Behavior ---➤	Reinforcer ---➤		Strengthened or repeated behavior

We can be fairly certain that food will be a reinforcer for a hungry animal, but what about people? There are many theories about why reinforcement works. For example, some psychologists suggest that reinforcers satisfy needs, whereas other psychologists believe that reinforcers reduce tension or stimulate a part of the brain (Rachlin, 1991). By the way, Skinner did not speculate about why reinforcers increase behavior. He believed that it was useless to talk about "imaginary constructs" such as meaning, needs, or tensions. Skinner simply described the tendency for a given behavior to increase after certain consequences (Skinner, 1953, 1989).

There are two types of reinforcement. When the consequence that strengthens a behavior is the *appearance (addition)* of a new stimulus, the situation is defined as ***positive* reinforcement.** Examples include pecking on the red key (producing food for a pigeon) or wearing a new outfit (producing many compliments for you). In contrast, when the consequence that strengthens a behavior is the *disappearance (subtraction)* of a stimulus, the process is called ***negative* reinforcement.** If a particular action leads to the disappearance of an **aversive** (unpleasant) situation, the action is likely to be repeated in a similar situation. A common example is the car seatbelt buzzer. As soon as you put on your seatbelt, the irritating buzzer stops. You are likely to repeat this behavior (putting on the seatbelt) in the future because the action made an aversive stimulus (buzzer) disappear. The "negative" in negative reinforcement does not imply that the behavior being reinforced is necessarily negative or that the consequence feels bad. The meaning is closer to that of "negative" numbers—something is subtracted. Associate *positive* and *negative* reinforcement with *adding* or *subtracting* something following a behavior that has the effect of reinforcing (strengthening) the behavior.

Negative reinforcement is often confused with punishment. The process of reinforcement (positive or negative) always involves strengthening behavior. **Punishment,** on the other hand, involves *decreasing* or *suppressing behavior.* A behavior followed by a punisher is *less* likely to be repeated in similar situations in the future. Again, it is the *effect* that defines a consequence as punishment, and different people have different perceptions of what is punishing. Some children may find being sent to their rooms punishing, whereas others wouldn't mind at all. The process of punishment is diagrammed as follows:

CONSEQUENCE EFFECT

Behavior ---→ Punisher ---→ Weakened or decreased behavior

Like reinforcement, punishment may take one of two forms. The first type has been called Type I punishment, but this name isn't very informative, so we use the term **presentation punishment.** It occurs when the appearance of a stimulus following the behavior suppresses or decreases the behavior. When parents scold children or when coaches make the team run extra laps because they broke the rules, they are using presentation punishment. We call the other type of punishment (Type II punishment) **removal punishment** because it involves removing a stimulus. When parents or teachers take away privileges (no TV, no driving, no recess) after a young person has behaved inappropriately, they are applying removal punishment. With both types, the effect is to decrease the behavior that led to the punishment. Figure 2.1 summarizes the two kinds of reinforcement and the two kinds of punishment.

Operant conditioning is the basis for many programs designed to teach or manage children at home or in classrooms and is especially prominent in special education (Alberto & Troutman, 2006; Canter & Canter, 1992; Foote, 2003; Lane, Falk, & Wehby, 2006; Patterson & Forgatch, 2005). We will look at some of these programs in the upcoming chapters.

FIGURE 2.1

TWO KINDS OF REINFORCEMENT AND TWO KINDS OF PUNISHMENT

Negative reinforcement and punishment are often confused. It may help you to remember that reinforcement is always associated with increases in behaviors, and punishment always involves decreasing or suppressing behavior.

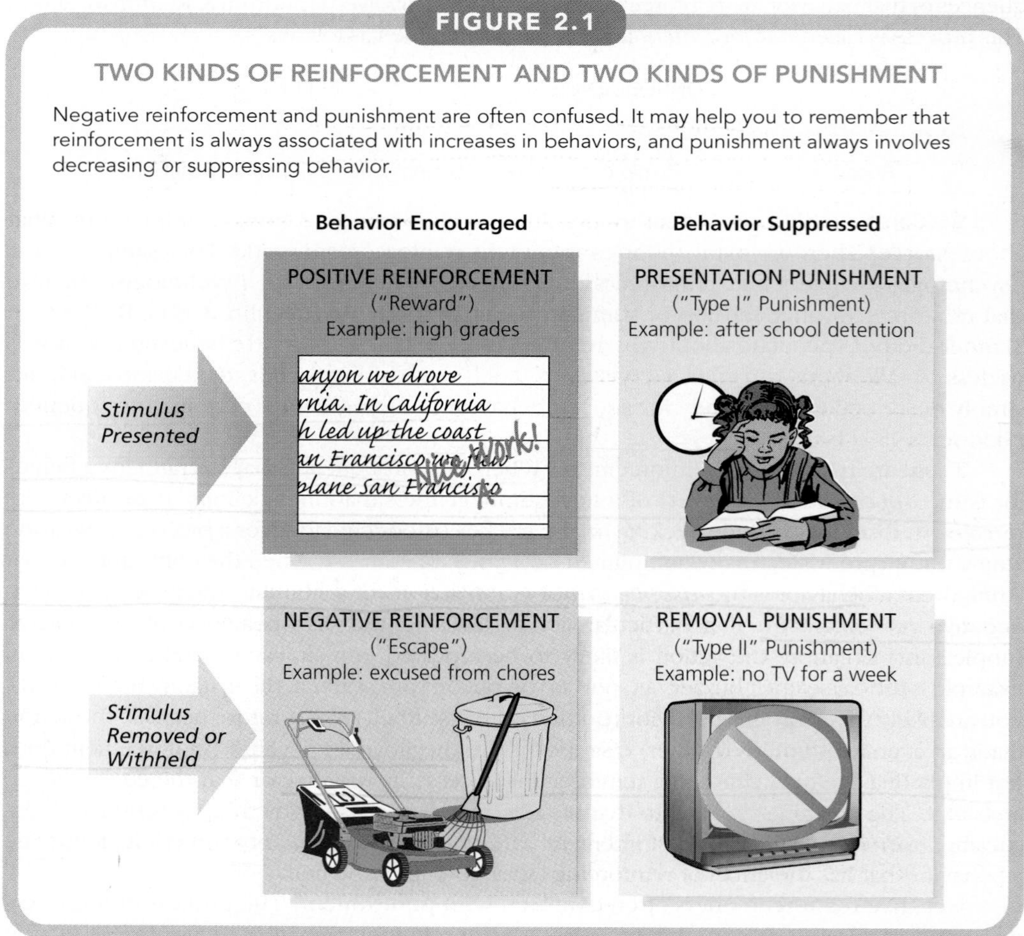

There are also some important cautions in using behavioral principles with children—we will consider these too in later chapters.

Bandura's Social Learning and Social Cognitive Theory

Albert Bandura's (1925—) life story should be a movie. You could say he lived the American dream, except that he is from Canada. His parents immigrated to farm the rugged land of northern Alberta. Bandura's parents never went to school, but they valued education. His father taught himself to read in three languages, giving young Albert a great model of self-regulated learning—a concept that figures prominently in social cognitive theory today. On the way to finishing high school, Bandura worked many jobs, including as a carpenter at a furniture factory and a road worker on the Alaska Highway in the Yukon. He finished his undergraduate degree at the University of British Columbia in three years, even though he had to cram all his classes into the morning to have time for his afternoon jobs. Because he needed a morning class to fill one time slot, he enrolled in introductory psychology and found his future profession (Bandura, 2006b, p. 46). Next was graduate school and then he joined the faculty at Stanford in 1953—at the age of 28. He is still at Stanford over 50 years later, but now some of his students are the children of his former students. You can read his autobiography at http://www.des.emory.edu/mfp/bandurabio.html.

SOCIAL LEARNING THEORY. Early in his career, Bandura noted that the traditional behavioral views of learning were accurate—but incomplete—because they gave only a partial explanation of learning and overlooked important elements, particularly social influences. His first work on learning was grounded in the behavioral principles of reinforcement and punishment, but he added a focus on *learning from observing others.* This expanded view was labeled **social learning theory**; it was considered a *neobehavioral* approach (Bandura, 1977; Zimmerman & Schunk, 2003).

To explain some limitations of the behavioral model, Bandura distinguished between the *acquisition of knowledge* (learning) and the *observable performance based on that knowledge* (behavior). In other words, Bandura suggested that we all might know more than we show. This was demonstrated in one of Bandura's early studies (1965). Preschool children saw a film of a model kicking and punching an inflatable "Bobo" doll. One group saw the model rewarded for the aggression, another group saw the model punished, and a third group saw no consequences. When they were moved to a room with the Bobo doll, the children who had seen the punching and kicking reinforced on the film were the most aggressive toward the doll. Those who had seen the attacks punished were the least aggressive. But when the children were promised rewards for imitating the model's aggression, all of them demonstrated that they had learned the behavior.

Bandura's "Bobo" doll study showed that young children could learn to behave aggressively by observing others.

Incentives can affect performance. Even though learning may have occurred, it may not be demonstrated until the situation is appropriate or there are incentives to perform, like those rewards promised to the preschool students for imitating the model in the Bobo doll study. This might explain why some adolescents don't perform "bad behaviors" such as swearing or smoking that they all see modeled by adults, peers, and the media. Personal consequences may discourage performing the behaviors. In other examples, children may have learned how to write the alphabet, but perform badly because their fine motor coordination is limited, or they may have learned how to simplify fractions, but perform badly on a test because they are anxious. In these cases, their performance is not an indication of their learning.

SOCIAL COGNITIVE THEORY. In his later work, Bandura has focused on cognitive factors such as beliefs, self-perceptions, and expectations, so his theory is now called a social cognitive theory (Bandura, 1986, 1997). **Social cognitive theory** distinguishes between enactive and vicarious learning. *Enactive learning* is learning by doing and experiencing the consequences of your actions. This may sound like operant conditioning all over again, but it is not, and the difference has to do with the role of consequences. Proponents of operant conditioning believe that consequences strengthen or weaken behavior. In enactive learning, however, consequences are seen as providing *information*. Our interpretations of the consequences create expectations, influence motivation, and shape beliefs about our own capabilities (Bandura, 2006; Schunk, 2004).

Vicarious learning is learning by observing others. People and animals can learn merely by observing another person or animal learn, and this fact challenges the behaviorist idea that cognitive factors are unnecessary in an explanation of learning. If people can learn by watching, they must be focusing their attention, constructing images, remembering, analyzing, and making decisions that affect learning. Thus, much is going on mentally before performance and reinforcement can even take place.

A key idea in social cognitive theory that you will encounter often in this book is self-efficacy—our beliefs about our personal competence or effectiveness *in a given area.* Albert Bandura (1997) defines **self-efficacy** as "beliefs in one's capabilities to organize and execute the courses of action required to produce given attainments" (p. 3). He suggests these predictions about possible outcomes of behavior are critical for learning because they affect motivation. Research in health and medicine, sports and exercise, nutrition, clinical psychology, counseling, educational psychology, child development, addictions, weight loss, and many other areas have identified self-efficacy beliefs as powerful elements of motivation.

Information Processing Perspectives

The behavioral views of learning were powerful forces in psychology during the 1940s and 1950s, but then the computer revolution, breakthroughs in understanding language development, and Piaget's work (discussed in the next section) all stimulated cognitive research. Evidence accumulated indicating that people plan their responses, use strategies to help themselves remember, and organize the materials they are learning in their own unique ways (Miller, Galanter, & Pribram, 1960), so the way people process and remember information became an important focus for research.

THE INFORMATION PROCESSING MODEL. Early **information processing** views of learning used the computer as a model. Like a computer, people take in information and organize it in relation to what they already know (*encoding*), store the information (*memory*), get the information when needed (*retrieval*), and guide all these information processing stages through *executive controls*. Also like a computer, the human mind is limited in the amount of information it can process and the speed of processing—the system has a *limited capacity*. It can deal with only so much information, especially new information, at one time. Computers can handle more information faster, but they are not as creative or flexible as the human mind (Atkinson & Shiffrin, 1968; Bjorklund, 2005; Neisser, 1976).

Figure 2.2 is a schematic representation of a typical information processing model of memory, derived from the ideas of several theorists (Atkinson & Shiffrin, 1968; Neisser, 1976; R. Gagné, 1985).

As you can see, **sensory memory** is the initial processing that transforms incoming stimuli (sights, sounds, smells, etc.) into information so we can make sense of them. We hold information, in the form of images or sounds or other codes, for only a very few seconds. **Attention** (maintaining cognitive focus on something and resisting distractions) is critical at this stage. What is not attended to is lost. This is actually useful because if every variation in color, movement, sound, smell, temperature, and so on ended up in memory, life would be impossible. But attention is *selective*. What we pay attention to is guided to a certain

FIGURE 2.2

AN INFORMATION PROCESSING MODEL

The Information Processing System

Information is encoded in sensory memory where perception and attention determine what will be held in working memory for further use. In working memory, new information connects with knowledge from long-term memory. Thoroughly processed and connected information becomes part of long-term memory, and can be activated to return to working memory. Implicit memories are formed without conscious effort.

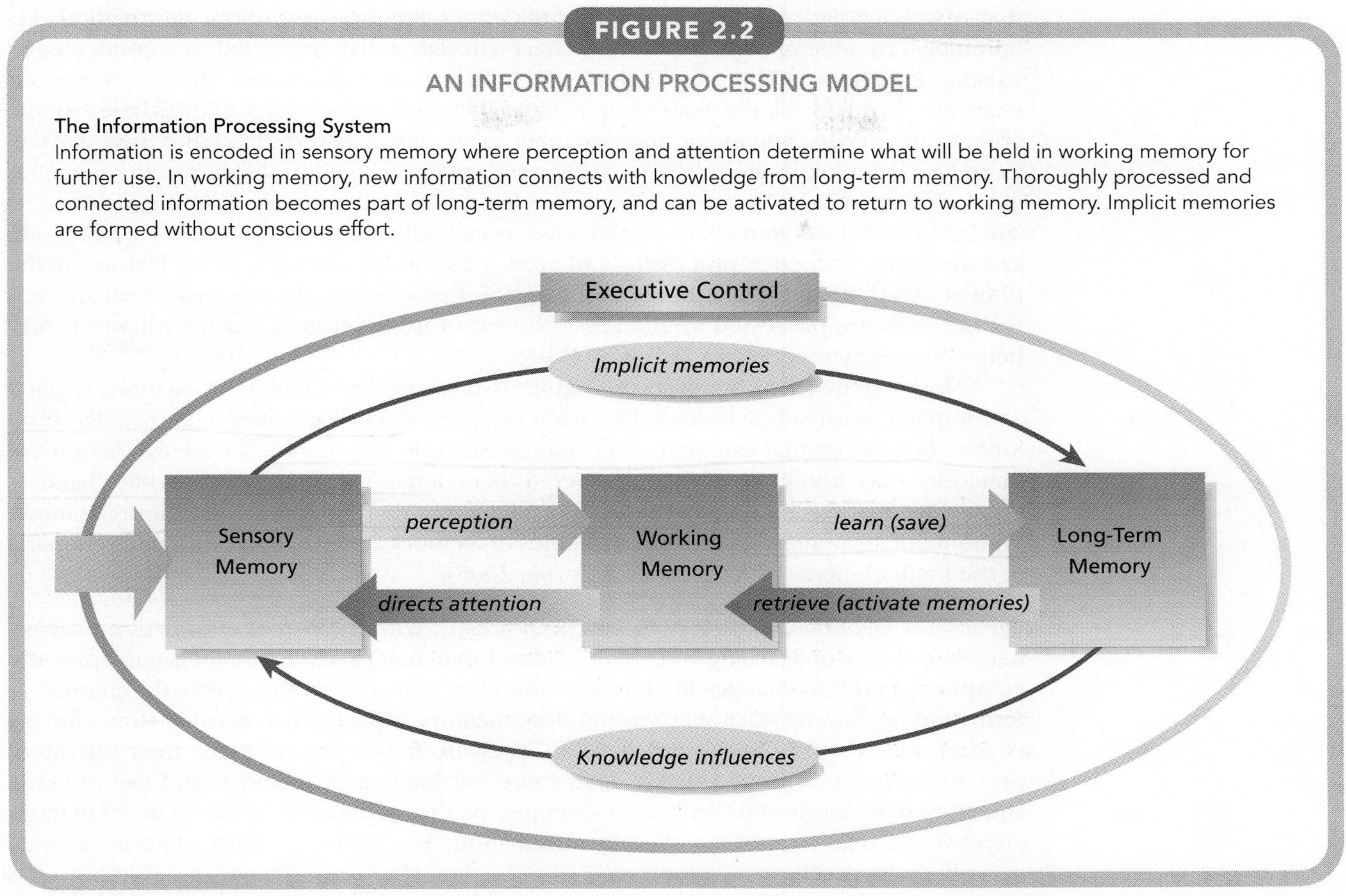

extent by what we already know and what we need to know, so attention is involved in and influenced by all three memory processes—sensory, working, and long-term—see Figure 2.2.

The working space of the memory system is called (surprise) **working memory.** It is the interface where new information is held temporarily (no more than 20 seconds or so) and combined with knowledge from long-term memory, to solve problems or comprehend a lecture, for example. Working memory "contains" what you are thinking about at the moment. You may have heard the term ***short-term memory.*** This is similar to working memory but refers only to the storage space available. Working memory includes both temporary storage and active processing—it is the process or stage in which active mental effort is applied to new and old information.

Because information in working memory is fragile and easily lost, it must be kept activated to be retained. To keep information activated in working memory for longer than 20 seconds, most people keep rehearsing the information mentally. There are two types of rehearsal (Craik & Lockhart, 1972). **Maintenance rehearsal** involves repeating the information in your mind. As long as you repeat the information, it can be maintained in working memory indefinitely. Maintenance rehearsal is useful for retaining something you plan to use and then forget, such as a phone number or a location on a map. **Elaborative rehearsal** involves connecting the information you are trying to remember with something you already know. For example, if you meet someone at a party whose name is the same as your brother's, you don't have to repeat the name to keep it in memory; you just have to make the connection. Rehearsal is one form of *executive control*—one of the processes that plans, monitors, and guides the flow of information throughout the whole information processing system. Selective attention is another executive control process.

Working memory holds the information that is currently activated, such as a telephone number you have just found and are about to dial. **Long-term memory** holds the information that is well learned, such as all the other telephone numbers you know. Information gets into long-term memory when it is well rehearsed, elaborated, organized, and connected to existing knowledge. The more completely information is processed, the better are our chances of remembering it. For example, if we ask you to sort pictures of dogs based on the color of their coats, you might not remember many of the pictures later. But if we ask you to rate each dog on how likely it is to chase you as you jog, you probably would remember more of the pictures. To rate the dogs, you must pay attention to details in the pictures, relate features of the dogs to characteristics associated with danger, and so on. This rating procedure requires "deeper" processing and more focus on the *meaning* of the features in the photos. Also, the dual-code theory of information processing suggests that visual and verbal materials are processed in different systems; so using imagery along with words may help you to remember (Clark & Paivio, 1991).

Most cognitive psychologists distinguish two categories of long-term memory, explicit and implicit, with subdivisions under each category. **Explicit memory** is knowledge from long-term memory that can be recalled and consciously considered. We are aware of these memories—we know we have remembered them. **Implicit memory**, on the other hand, is knowledge that we are not conscious of recalling, but that influences behavior or thought without our awareness. These different kinds of memory are associated with different parts of the brain (Ashcraft, 2006; Yeates & Enrile, 2005).

INFORMATION PROCESSING AND DEVELOPMENT. With the rise of information processing perspectives on learning and memory, developmental psychologists began to apply the computer model to changes in children's thinking, focusing on the child's developing information processing skills such as attention, memory capacity, and learning strategies. As children mature and their brains develop, they are better able to focus their attention, process information more quickly, hold more information in memory, and use thinking strategies more easily and flexibly, for example, As they grow older, children develop more effective strategies for remembering information. For example, most children spontaneously discover rehearsal around age 5 or 6. Siegler (1998) describes a 9-year-old boy who witnessed a robbery, then mentally repeated the license number of the getaway car until he could give the number to the police. Children are 10 to 11 years old before they have adult-like working memories.

Even though the range of developmental theories that emphasize learning is wide—from behaviorism to information processing—most learning theories of development share similar stances on the themes described in Chapter 1: shape, timing, and source of development. The shape of development is seen as quantitative and continuous because new learning expands development. Learning theories are less concerned about critical or sensitive periods for learning, except as sensitive periods for brain development (discussed in Chapters 5, 8, and 11) affect learning. Finally, the source of development is learning based on interactions with the environment, so nurture is very important. Both social cognitive theory and information processing theory see an important role for the individual's knowledge, but much of this has been learned over time. We turn next to a theory that takes a different stance on these issues—the work of Jean Piaget.

Cognitive Stages and Structures: Jean Piaget

Swiss psychologist Jean Piaget was a real prodigy. In fact, in his teens, he published so many scientific papers on mollusks (marine animals such as oysters, clams, octopuses, snails, and squid) that he was offered a job as the curator of the mollusk collection at the Museum of Natural History in Geneva. He told the museum officials that he wanted to finish high school first. For a while Piaget worked in Alfred Binet's laboratory in Paris, developing intelligence tests for children. There he became intrigued by children's wrong answers and wondered about the thinking behind the answers—a question that intrigued him his whole life (Green & Piel, 2010). During his long career, Piaget devised a model describing how humans go about making sense of their world by gathering and organizing information (Piaget, 1954, 1963, 1970a, b). We will examine Piaget's ideas closely, because they provide an explanation of the development of thinking from infancy to adulthood.

According to Piaget (1954), certain ways of thinking that are quite simple for an adult are not so simple for a child. For example, Piaget asked a 9-year-old:

> What is your nationality?—*I am Swiss.*—How come?—*Because I live in Switzerland.*—Are you also a Genevan?—*No, that's not possible I'm already Swiss, I can't also be Genevan.* (Piaget, 1965/1995, p. 252)

You encountered this question in Chapter 1. Imagine teaching this student geography. The student has trouble with classifying one concept (Geneva) as a subset of another (Switzerland). There are other differences between adult and child thinking. Let's examine why.

INFLUENCES ON DEVELOPMENT. Cognitive development is much more than the addition of new facts and ideas to an existing store of information. According to Piaget, our thinking processes change radically, although slowly, from birth to maturity because we constantly strive to make sense of the world. How do we do this? Piaget identified four factors—*biological maturation*, *activity*, *social experiences*, and *equilibration*—that interact to influence changes in thinking (Piaget, 1970a). Let's briefly examine the first three factors. We'll return to a discussion of equilibration in the next section.

One of the most important influences on the way we make sense of the world is *maturation,* the unfolding of the biological changes we experience. Parents have little impact on this aspect of cognitive development, except to be sure that children get the nourishment and care they need to be healthy.

Activity is another influence. With physical maturation comes the increasing ability to act on the environment and learn from it. When a young child's coordination is reasonably developed, for example, the child may discover principles about balance by experimenting with a seesaw. Thus, as we act on the environment—as we explore, test, observe, and eventually organize information—we are likely to alter our thinking processes at the same time.

As we develop, we are also interacting with the people around us. According to Piaget, our cognitive development is influenced by *social transmission,* or learning from others. Without social transmission, we would need to reinvent all the knowledge already offered by our culture. The amount people can learn from social transmission varies according to their stage of cognitive development.

Maturation, activity, and social transmission all work together to influence cognitive development. How do we respond to these influences?

BASIC TENDENCIES IN THINKING. As a result of his early research in biology, Piaget concluded that all species inherit two basic tendencies, or "invariant functions." The first of these tendencies is toward organization—the combining, arranging, recombining, and rearranging of behaviors and thoughts into coherent systems. The second tendency is toward adaptation, or adjusting to the environment.

People are born with a tendency to *organize* their thinking processes into psychological structures. These psychological structures are our systems for understanding and interacting with the world. Simple structures are continually combined and coordinated to become more sophisticated and thus more effective. Very young infants, for example, can either look at an object or grasp it when it comes in contact with their hands. They cannot coordinate looking and grasping at the same time. As they develop, however, infants organize these two separate behavioral structures into a coordinated higher-level structure of looking at, reaching for, and grasping the object. They can, of course, still use each structure separately (Piaget, 1970a, 1975/1985).

Piaget gave a special name to these structures: **schemes**. In his theory, schemes are organized patterns of behavior that can be repeated and generalized. Schemes may be very small and specific, for example, the sucking-through-a-straw scheme, or they may be larger and more general—the drinking scheme. As a person's actions become more organized and new schemes develop, behavior also becomes more sophisticated and better suited to the environment.

In addition to the tendency to organize their psychological structures, people also inherit the tendency to *adapt* to their environment. Two basic processes are involved in adaptation: assimilation and accommodation. **Assimilation** takes place when people use their existing schemes to make sense of events in their world. Assimilation involves trying to understand something new by fitting it into what we already know. At times, we may have to distort the new information to make it fit. For example, the first time many children see a skunk, they call it a "kitty." They try to match the new experience with an existing scheme for identifying animals (Piaget, 1978).

Accommodation occurs when a person must change existing schemes to respond to a new situation. If data cannot be made to fit any existing schemes, then more appropriate structures must be developed. We adjust our behavior to fit the new information, instead of adjusting the information to fit our behavior. Children demonstrate accommodation when they add the scheme for recognizing skunks to their other systems for identifying animals.

People adapt to their increasingly complex environments by using existing schemes whenever these schemes work (assimilation) and by modifying and adding to their schemes when something new is needed (accommodation). In fact, both processes are required most of the time. Even using an established pattern such as sucking through a straw may require some accommodation if the straw is of a different size or length than the type you are used to. If you have tried drinking juice from box packages, you know that you have to add a new skill to your sucking scheme—don't squeeze the box or you will shoot juice through the straw, straight up into the air and into your lap. Whenever new experiences are assimilated into an existing scheme, the scheme is enlarged and changed somewhat, so assimilation involves some accommodation.

There are also times when neither assimilation nor accommodation is used. If people encounter something that is too unfamiliar, they may ignore it. Experience is filtered to fit the kind of thinking a person is doing at a given time. For example, if you overhear a conversation in a foreign language, you probably will not try to make sense of the exchange unless you have some knowledge of the language.

EQUILIBRATION. According to Piaget, organizing, assimilating, and accommodating can be viewed as a kind of complex balancing act. In his theory, the actual changes in thinking take place through the process of **equilibration**—the act of searching for a balance. Piaget assumed that people continually test the adequacy of their thinking processes in order to achieve that balance. Briefly, the process of equilibration works like this: If we apply a particular scheme to an event or situation and the scheme works, then equilibrium exists. If the scheme does not produce a satisfying result, then **disequilibrium** exists, and we become uncomfortable. This motivates us to keep searching for a solution through assimilation and accommodation, and thus our thinking changes and moves ahead. Of course, the level of disequilibrium must be just right or optimal—too little and we aren't interested in changing, too much and we may be too anxious to change (Piaget, 1975/1985).

Children assimilate new information into current understandings. This girl assimilates "fleece" as "fleas," a word she already knew.

FOUR STAGES OF COGNITIVE DEVELOPMENT. Now we turn to the actual differences that Piaget hypothesized for children as they grow. Piaget believed that all people pass through the same four stages (sensorimotor, preoperational, concrete operational, and formal operational) in exactly the same order. These stages are generally associated with specific ages, as shown in Table 2.2, but these are only general guidelines, not labels for all children of a certain age. Piaget noted that individuals may go through long periods of transition between stages and that a person may show characteristics of one stage in one situation, but characteristics of a higher or lower stage in other situations. Therefore, knowing a student's age is never a guarantee that you know how the child will think (Orlando & Machado, 1996). We will look at each stage more fully in the upcoming Chapters 6, 9, and 12 on cognitive development.

TABLE 2.2 • **Piaget's Four Stages of Cognitive Development**

STAGE	APPROXIMATE AGE	CHARACTERISTICS
Sensorimotor	0–2 years	Begins to make use of imitation, memory, and thought. Begins to recognize that objects do not cease to exist when they are hidden. Moves from reflex actions to goal-directed activity.
Preoperational	2–7 years	Gradually develops use of language and ability to think in symbolic form. Able to think operations through logically in one direction. Has difficulties seeing another person's point of view.
Concrete Operational	7–11 years	Able to solve concrete (hands-on) problems in logical fashion. Understands laws of conservation and is able to classify and seriate. Understands reversibility.
Formal Operational	11–adult	Able to solve abstract problems in logical fashion. Becomes more scientific in thinking. Develops concerns about social issues, identity.

Source: From Wadsworth, Piaget's Theory of Cognitive and Affective Development, 5e. *"Piaget's Four Stages of Cognitive Development," p. 138.*

Some psychologists have pointed to research on the brain to support Piaget's stage model. Transition to the higher cognitive states in humans has also been related to changes in the brain, such as production of additional synaptic connections and changes in rates of growth in brain weight (Byrnes & Fox, 1998). Thus, there is some neurological support for stages, but the evidence is not strong at this point (Driscoll, 2005).

How would Piaget address the three themes in Chapter 1: shape, timing, and source of development? You know Piaget believed that the shape of development was in stages; he described qualitative changes in thinking. The notions of early experience and critical periods were not significant features of Piaget's theory; both nature (maturation and the "invariant functions" of organization and adaptation) and nurture (activity and social transmission) were essential sources of development in his theory.

LIMITATIONS OF PIAGET'S THEORY. Although most psychologists agree with Piaget's insightful descriptions of children's thinking, many disagree with his explanations of *how* thinking develops. Some psychologists have questioned the existence of four separate stages of thinking, even though they agree that children do go through the changes that Piaget described. One problem with the stage model is the lack of consistency in children's thinking. For example, children can conserve number (the number of blocks does not change when they are rearranged) a year or two before they can conserve weight (a ball of clay does not change volume when you flatten it). Why can't they use conservation consistently in every situation? In fairness, we should note that in his later work, even Piaget put less emphasis on *stages* of cognitive development and gave more attention to how thinking *changes* through equilibration (Piaget, 1975/1985).

As we will see in Chapter 4, Piaget seemed to underestimate the abilities of young children to understand the permanence of objects (Spelke & Newport, 1998), although this criticism also has been challenged (Bogartz, Shinskey, & Speaker, 1997). Piaget's theory does not explain how even young children can perform at an advanced level in certain areas in which they have highly developed knowledge and expertise. An expert 9-year-old chess player may think abstractly about chess moves, whereas a novice 20-year-old player may have to resort to more concrete strategies to plan and remember moves (Seigler & Alibali, 2005).

One final criticism of Piaget's theory is that it overlooks the important effects of the child's cultural and social group. Children in Western cultures may master scientific thinking and formal operations because this is the kind of thinking required in Western schools (Geary, 1998). Even concrete operations such as classification may develop differently in different cultures. For example, when individuals from the Kpelle people of Africa were asked to sort 20 objects, they created groups that made sense to them—a hoe with a potato, a knife with an orange. The experimenter could not get the Kpelle to change their categories; they said this is how a wise man would do it. Finally the experimenter asked in desperation, "Well, how would a fool do it?" Then the subjects promptly created the four neat classification piles the experimenter had expected—food, tools, and so on (Rogoff & Morelii, 1989). The ways that Piaget and others interviewed children and assessed cognitive development probably seemed unfamiliar and irrelevant to children in nontraditional cultures—and language could have been a problem as well (Owusu-Bempah & Howitt, 2000). We have to understand children's thinking in the context of their own culture so that we do not make the mistake of viewing cultural differences as deficits—remember the wisdom of the Kpelle and their knowledge of "how a fool would do it."

NEO-PIAGETIAN THEORIES. Some developmental psychologists have devised **neo-Piagetian** theories that retain Piaget's insights about children's construction of knowledge and the general trends in children's thinking, but add findings from information processing about the role of specific knowledge, attention, memory, strategies, and brain maturation (Kail, 2004). According to Robbie Case (1998), young children often use reasonable but incorrect strategies to solve problems because of their limited memories. They try to simplify the task by ignoring important information or skipping steps to reach a correct solution. This puts less strain on memory. For example, when comparing quantities, young children may consider only the height of the water in a glass, not the diameter of the glass, because this approach demands less of their memory. According to Case, this explains young children's inability to solve the classic Piagetian conservation problem of whether changes in appearance always signal changes in quantity.

Case (1992, 1998) devised an explanation of cognitive development suggesting that children develop in stages within specific domains such as numerical concepts, spatial concepts, social tasks, storytelling, reasoning about physical objects, and motor development. As children practice using the schemes in a particular domain (for example, using counting schemes in the number concept area), it takes less attention to accomplish the schemes; they become more automatic because the child does not have to "think so hard" about it. This frees up mental resources and memory to do more. The child now can combine simple schemes into more complex ones and invent new schemes when needed (assimilation and accommodation in action).

Within each domain, such as numerical concepts or social skills, children move from grasping simple schemes during the early preschool years to merging two schemes into a unit (between about ages 4 and 6), to coordinating these scheme units into larger combinations, and finally, by about ages 9 to 11, to forming complex relationships that can be applied to many problems. Children do progress through these qualitatively different stages within each domain, but Case argues that progress in one domain does not automatically affect movement in another. The child must have experience and involvement with the content and the ways of thinking within each domain in order to construct increasingly complex and useful schemes and coordinated conceptual understandings about the domain.

We now turn to several theories that are very prominent today—contextual and dynamic explanations of development.

Contextual and Dynamic Systems Theories

As you saw in Chapter 1, developmental theories today acknowledge the importance of context and the coaction of many factors in development: Questions about nature *or* nurture became nature *and* nurture acting together. In this section we examine the theories of Vygotsky, Bronfenbrenner, and Thelen.

Vygotsky: Sociocultural Theory

Lev Semenovich Vygotsky (1896–1934) was a Russian psychologist who emphasized context, history, and culture in his **sociocultural theory** (also called *sociohistoric*). Vygotsky was only 38 years old when he died of tuberculosis, but during his brief life he produced over 100 books and articles; many are now available in translation (1978, 1986, 1987, 1993, 1997). Vygotsky's work began when he was studying learning and development to improve his own teaching. He went on to write about language and thought, the psychology of art, learning and development, and educating students with special needs (Karpov, 2006; Kozulin, 2003; Wink & Putney, 2002).

Vygotsky believed that human activities take place in cultural settings and cannot be understood apart from these settings. One of his key ideas was that our specific mental structures and processes could be traced to our interactions with others. These social interactions are more than simple influences on cognitive development—they actually create our cognitive structures and thinking processes (Palincsar, 1998). In fact, "Vygotsky conceptualized development as the transformation of socially shared activities into internalized processes" (John-Steiner & Mahn, 1996, p. 192). We will examine three themes in Vygotsky's writings that explain how social processes form learning and thinking: the social sources of development; the role of tools in learning and development, especially the tool of language; and the zone of proximal development (Vygotsky, 1978, 1986, 1993; Wertsch & Tulviste, 1992).

THE SOCIAL SOURCES OF DEVELOPMENT. Vygotsky assumed that "every function in a child's cultural development appears twice: first, on the social level and later on the individual level; first between people (interpsychological) and then inside the child (intrapsychological)" (1978, p. 57). In other words, higher mental processes first are **co-constructed** during shared activities between the child and another person. Then the processes are internalized by the child and become part of that child's cognitive development. For example, children first use language in activities with others, to regulate the behavior of the others ("No nap!" or "I wanna cookie."). Later, however, the child can regulate her own behavior using private speech ("careful—don't spill"), as you will see in Chapter 6. So, for Vygotsky, social interaction was more than influence; it was the origin of higher mental processes such as problem solving. Consider this example:

> A six-year-old has lost a toy and asks her father for help. The father asks her where she last saw the toy; the child says, "I can't remember." He asks a series of questions—did you have it in your room? Outside? Next door? To each question, the child answers, "no." When he says "in the car?" she says, "I think so" and goes to retrieve the toy. (Tharp & Gallimore, 1988, p. 14)

Who remembered? The answer is really neither the father nor the daughter, but the two together. The remembering and problem solving were co-constructed—between people—in the interaction. But the child may have internalized strategies to use next time something is lost. At some point, the child will be able to function independently to solve this kind of problem. So, like the strategy for finding the toy, higher functions appear first between a child and a "teacher" before they exist within the individual child (Kozulin, 2003).

Both Piaget and Vygotsky emphasized the importance of social interactions in cognitive development, but Piaget saw a different role for interaction. He believed that interaction encouraged development by creating *disequilibrium*—cognitive conflict—that motivated change. Thus, Piaget believed that the most helpful interactions were those between peers, because peers are on an equal basis and can challenge each other's thinking. Vygotsky, on the other hand, suggested that children's cognitive development is fostered by interactions with people who are more capable or advanced in their thinking—people such as parents and teachers (Moshman, 1997; Palinscar, 1998). Of course, children can learn from both adults and peers.

CULTURAL TOOLS AND COGNITIVE DEVELOPMENT. Vygotsky believed that **cultural tools**, including material tools (such as printing presses, plows, rulers, abacuses—today, we would add cell phones, computers, the Internet) and psychological tools (signs and symbol systems such as numbers and mathematical systems, Braille and sign language, maps, works of art, codes, and language) play very important roles in cognitive development. All higher-order mental processes, such as reasoning and problem solving, are *mediated* by (accomplished through and with the help of) psychological tools, such as language and symbols. For example, as long as the culture provides only Roman numerals for representing quantity, certain ways of thinking mathematically—from long division to calculus—are difficult or impossible. But if a number system has a zero, fractions, positive and negative values, and an infinite number of numbers, then much more is possible. The number system is a

How many cultural tools are these young people using? How might these tools affect their understandings of the world?

psychological tool that supports learning and cognitive development—it changes the thinking process. This symbol system is passed from adult to child through formal and informal interactions and teachings (Goswami, 2008).

Thus, children's knowledge, ideas, attitudes, and values develop through **appropriating** or "taking for themselves" the ways of acting and thinking provided by their culture and by the more capable members of their group (Kozulin & Presseisen, 1995). In this exchange of signs and symbols and explanations, children begin to develop a "cultural tool kit" to make sense of and learn about their world (Wertsch, 1991). The kit is filled with physical tools such as pencils or rulers directed toward the external world and psychological tools such as concepts or problem-solving strategies for acting mentally. Children do not just receive the tools, however. They transform the tools as they construct their own representations, symbols, patterns, and understandings. As we learned from Piaget, children's constructions of meaning are not the same as those of adults. In the exchange of signs and symbols such as number systems and language, children create their own understandings (a skunk is a "kitty"). These understandings are gradually changed (a skunk is a skunk) as the children continue to engage in social activities and try to make sense of their world (John-Steiner & Mahn, 1996; Wertsch, 1991). This learning through exchange is most effective in the child's zone of proximal development, as you will see next.

THE ZONE OF PROXIMAL DEVELOPMENT AND SCAFFOLDING. According to Vygotsky, at any given point in development there are certain problems that a child can solve independently and others the child is on the verge of being able to solve. The child just needs some structure, clues, reminders, help with remembering details or steps, encouragement to keep trying, and so on. Some problems, of course, are beyond the child's capabilities, even if every step is clearly explained and supported. The **zone of proximal development (ZPD)** is the area between the child's current development level "as determined by independent problem solving" and the level of development that the child could achieve "through adult guidance or in collaboration with more capable peers" (Vygotsky, 1978, p. 86).

Vygotsky believed that the child is not alone in the world "discovering" the cognitive operations of conservation or classification. Rather, cognitive development occurs through the child's conversations and interactions with more capable members of the culture—adults or more able peers. These people serve as guides and teachers, providing the information and support necessary for the child to grow intellectually. Jerome Bruner called this adult assistance **scaffolding** (Wood, Bruner, & Ross, 1976). The father asking questions about where the toy was last seen in the earlier story was providing scaffolding for remembering. The term aptly suggests that children use this assistance for support while they build a firm understanding that will eventually allow them to solve the problems on their own. Most of this guidance is communicated through language, at least in Western cultures. In some cultures, observing a skilled performance, not talking about it, guides the child's learning (Rogoff, 1990). To give you a better sense of how scaffolding supports development, see the ***Connecting with Children*** suggestions.

Bronfenbrenner: Bioecological Model

Urie Bronfenbrenner (1917–2005) was born in Moscow, Russia, but moved with his family to the United States when he was 6. He completed a double major in psychology and music at Cornell in 1938 and a Ph.D. in psychology from Nancy's alma mater, the University of Michigan, in 1942. Over his long career in psychology he worked as a clinical psychologist

CONNECTING WITH CHILDREN

Guidelines for Teachers and Families: Scaffolding Children's Learning

Tailor scaffolding to the needs of each child.
Examples

1. Parent, teachers, and coaches, when students are beginning new tasks or topics, provide models, prompts, sentence starters, coaching, and feedback. As the children grow in competence, give less support and more opportunities for independent work.
2. Give children choices about the level of difficulty or degree of independence in reading books or projects; encourage them to challenge themselves but to seek help when they are really stuck.

Make sure children have access to powerful tools that support thinking.
Examples

1. Teach children to use learning and organizational strategies, research tools, language tools (dictionaries or computer searches), day planners, and word-processing programs.
2. Model the use of tools; show children how you use an appointment book or electronic notebook to make plans and manage time, for example.

Teachers, build on the students' cultural funds of knowledge (Moll et al., 1992)
Examples

1. Identify family knowledge by having students interview each other's families about their work and home knowledge (agriculture, economics, manufacturing, household management, medicine and illness, religion, child care, cooking, etc.).
2. Tie assignments to these funds of knowledge and use community experts to evaluate assignments.
3. Capitalize on dialogue and group learning by experimenting with peer tutoring; teach students how to ask good questions and give helpful explanations.

For more information about Vygotsky and his theories. see: http://tip.psychology.org/vygotsky.html

in the U.S. Army and as a professor at Michigan and at Cornell. He also helped to found the Head Start early childhood program.

Bronfenbrenner developed a frame to map the many interacting social contexts that affect development. His model actually served as an organizing frame for our look at the contexts of development in Chapter 1. Bronfenbrenner called his theory a **bioecological model** of development (Bronfenbrenner, 1979; Bronfenbrenner & Evans, 2000; Bronfenbrenner & Morris, 2006). The *bio* aspect of the model recognizes that people bring their biological selves to the developmental process. The *ecological* part recognizes that the social contexts in which we develop are ecosystems because they are in constant interaction with and exert influence on each other.

NESTED SYSTEMS. Look at Figure 2.3 on the next page. Every person lives within a *microsystem*, inside a *mesosystem*, embedded in an *exosystem*, all of which are a part of the *macrosystem* that occurs in time, the *chronosystem*—like a set of Russian painted dolls, one inside the other.

In the microsystem are the person's immediate relationships and activities. For a child it might be immediate family, friends, or teachers, and the activities of play and school. Relationships in the microsystem are reciprocal—they flow in both directions. The child affects the parent and the parent influences the child, for example. The mesosystem is the set of interactions and relationships among all the elements of the microsystem—the family members interacting with each other or with neighbors, doctors, or teachers, for example. Again, all relationships are reciprocal—the neighbor influences the parents and the parents affect the neighbor, and these interactions affect the child. The exosystem includes all the social settings that affect the child, even though the child is not a direct member of the systems. Examples are the parents' jobs; the community resources for health, employment, or recreation; or the family's religious affiliation. The macrosystem is the cultural and societal context with their laws, customs, rituals, resources, and cultural tools. All development occurs in and is influenced by the time period—the chronosystem.

FIGURE 2.3

URIE BRONFENBRENNER'S BIOECOLOGICAL MODEL OF HUMAN DEVELOPMENT

Every person develops within a *microsystem* (family, friends, classmates) inside a *mesosystem* (the interactions among all the microsystem elements), which is embedded in an *exosystem* (social settings that affect the child, even though the child is not a direct member—e.g., community resources, parents' workplace, etc.), all of which are part of the *macrosystem* (the larger society with its laws, customs, values, etc.). Running throughout the whole system is history or time—the *chronosystem* (not pictured but a part of all the other systems).

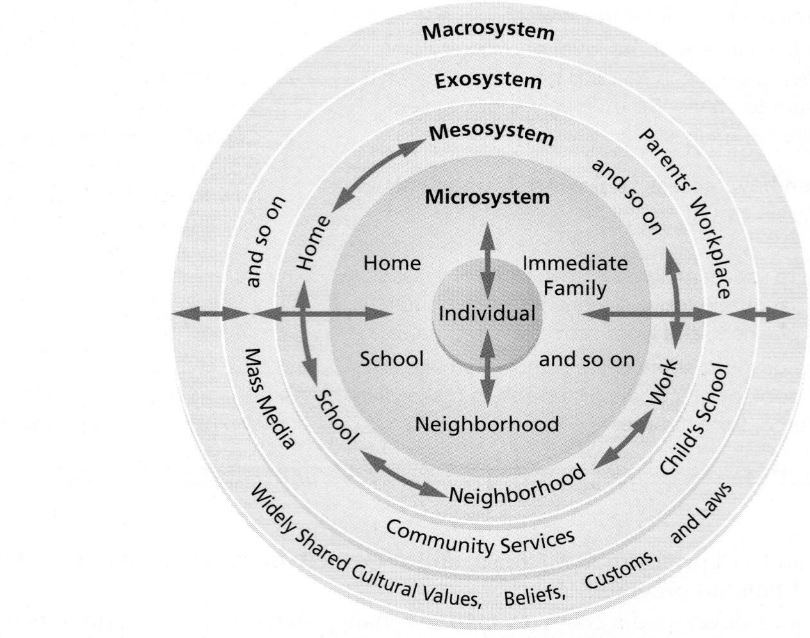

Note: Arrows across rings indicate reciprocal interactions at all levels.

ECOLOGY OF DEVELOPMENT. Bronfenbrenner's theory contains at least two lessons. First, influences in all social systems are reciprocal. Second, there are many dynamic forces that interact in a kind of ecological system for individual development. *Ecology* in this sense refers to the set of interacting and coacting contexts in which we all grow and change, from the inner biological structures and processes that influence development such as genes, cells, nutrition, and disease, to the external factors of families, neighborhoods, social relationships, educational and health institutions, public policies, time periods, historical events, and so on. So the effects of a childhood disease on the cognitive development of a child born in the 16th century to a poor family and treated by bloodletting or leeches will be quite different than the effect of the same disease on a child born in 2011 to a wealthy family and given the best treatment available for that time period.

DEVELOPMENTAL SYSTEMS. Urie Bronfenbrenner's bioecological model is an example of the developmental systems perspectives. Developmental systems explanations have four interrelated components. In fact, the components are so highly connected that they have been called "fused." The four components are:

1. *The focus of developmental study and understanding has to be change.* Change is possible across the entire lifespan and also across all the interacting contexts that make up the ecology of human development. Change isn't limitless, but it is possible. This means that well-designed interventions to improve children's development are worthwhile

and are never "too late." Early experiences are important, but later experiences are powerful too. Children can overcome the effects of negative early experiences, but also can lose the advantages of positive beginnings if later experiences are not supportive.

2. *The bases for change are the relations among all systems and levels of human life.* Relations are the units to study—simple explanations that focus on either-or distinctions are not useful. All levels of the individual and all levels of context—from cells to society—develop and change in relation to each other.
3. *All the systems that affect human development are embedded in history*—the most inclusive context of all. We all develop in a particular time, as you saw in our discussion of cohorts in Chapter 1. Because you were born in the 20th century, for example, you haven't had any experience with bloodletting or leeches as treatments for diseases—unless you traveled to Russia in the late 1990s where, according to an article in the *New York Times*, there is a resurgence of medical uses for leeches, including the treatment of migraines, hypertension, and stomachaches (Banerjee, 2000). This possible use of leeches in other cultures is also related to the last component of the developmental systems approach—the role of diversity.
4. *To understand development, we have to take into account diversity of people, relations, settings, and measurements.* So explanations of how children who speak Chinese come to understand addition in one historical period, using a particular way of assessing knowledge about addition, may not hold for other children in other cultures or time periods or alternative ways of assessing knowledge.

Let's look briefly at another developmental systems theory that emphasizes complex interactions—Thelen's dynamic systems perspective.

Thelen: Dynamic Self-Organizing Systems

The major challenge of developmental science, according to Ester Thelen and Linda Smith (2006), is to understand how new, more complex patterns of thought and behavior emerge: How does something completely novel arise? We have seen that some researchers point to individual biology (nature) and others to the environment (nurture) to explain the emergence of novel forms. In other words, some scientists, such as Konrad Lorenz, believe that the "instructions" for how to develop are mostly in the genes, whereas others, like B. F. Skinner, emphasize the "instructions" from the environment that guide development. But there is a third possibility, the coaction of nature and nurture, in the form of the individual ← → context relationships we saw in Chapter 1 (Lerner, 2006). Most developmental psychologists today support this third position.

One type *of* individual ← → context coaction is called **self-organization,** defined as patterns and orders that "*emerge from the interactions of the components in a complex system without explicit instructions,* either in the organism itself or from the environment" (Thelen & Smith, 2006, p. 259, italics in the original). With self-organization, children change themselves through their own activities. Thelen first proposed dynamic systems theory to understand perceptual motor development in infants and young children. Here is an example of self-organization in motor development. When an infant can hold up her head and look at a toy across the room, has enough strength and coordination in her arms and legs to assume an hands-and-knees crawling position, is on a surface that is not too soft or too uneven, and is motivated, she will crawl across the room to reach the toy. At first the crawling may be unsuccessful or awkward, but she corrects with feedback from senses and muscles to get better and better. The child has self-organized systems of perception, movement, and thinking to solve a problem (get that toy) with crawling. As she coordinates her actions in the environment, crawling gets faster and smoother, and is stable for several months. But when her balance, strength, and coordination improve, she will walk (or run) across the room to solve the "get me that toy" problem more efficiently.

Avoiding Either/Or

Vygotsky's sociocultural theory, Bronfenbrenner's bioecological model, and Thelen's dynamic systems theory avoid either/or splits and simple explanations. Humans develop in a complex, connected system of influences. These theories move beyond the either/or thinking of nature versus nurture, continuity versus discontinuity, or critical periods to unify many theories by examining dynamic interactions and coactions. Thelen and Smith (2006) summarize:

> What dynamic systems adds to this current landscape is both an emphasis on understanding development as a complex system of nested dynamics, and a complex system of self-organizing interactions at many levels of analysis, including those between the brain and the body and between the body and the world. (p. 307)

In the next chapter we will delve more deeply into these interactions between the brain, the body, and the world. Table 2.3 compares the five perspectives we have examined in terms of the focus, main theorist, and key concepts.

We have spent many pages discussing theories—the organized explanations of how children develop. The next section asks a very important question: Where do the theories come from? Current theories are not just speculations or opinions; they grow from the careful study of children—something you probably will do in your future as a teacher, medical or childcare worker, parent, or voter. One of our goals in this book is to give you tools for thinking clearly and wisely about your work with children. The basis for that kind of thinking is also the basis for theories—careful research.

TABLE 2.3 • **Perspectives on Development**

PERSPECTIVE	THEORY	THEORISTS	FOCUS	KEY CONCEPTS
Psychoanalytic Theories	Psychosexual	Freud	Stages of psychosexual development	Id, ego, superego Unconscious motivation
	Psychosocial	Erikson	Stages of psychosocial development	Identity Developmental crisis
Ethological	Biological/ Evolutionary	Lorenz, Wilson	Evolutionary changes, genetic inheritance, adaptation	Imprinting
Learning	Behavioral	Pavlov, Skinner, Watson	Formation of associations, observable behavior change	Classical and operant conditioning stimulus/ response, reinforcement/ punishment
	Social Learning Social Cognitive	Bandura	Role of observations and beliefs in learning and motivation	Enactive and vicarious learning, modeling, self-efficacy
	Information Processing	Anderson/ Siegler	How information processing changes over time	Attention; sensory, working, and long-term memory; kinds of knowledge; expertise
Cognitive Stages and Structures	Cognitive Constructivist	Piaget	Stages of cognitive development, structures of knowledge	Sensorimotor, preoperational, operational, and formal thinking, assimilation, accommodation, equilibration
Contextual/ Dynamic Systems	Sociocultural	Vygotsky	Role of history, culture, and more capable guides in learning and development	Cultural tools, social sources of individual thinking, zone of proximal development, assisted learning, apprenticeships
	Bioecological	Bronfenbrenner	Role of interacting and embedded contexts in development	Bioecological model including microsystem, mesosystem, exosystem, macrosystem
	Dynamic Systems	Thelen	Coaction of nature and nurture, development as a complex system of nested dynamics	Self-organization Individual ←→ context relations

WHERE DO THE THEORIES COME FROM? RESEARCH METHODS AND DESIGNS

Early theories of child development such as Freud's were not always based on research with children, but rather on logical or philosophical analyses. In the 1800s, Charles Darwin brought a scientist's eye to the process when he described the growth and development of his own son. But theories do more than describe—they explain and predict. Why do young children have a difficult time seeing the world from another person's point of view? How will new perspective-taking abilities unfold? Do boys and girls differ in their abilities to see another person's perspective? Why or why not? What would be the effects on children's relationships with their peers if they learned specific social skills? Questions like these require explanation and prediction—and theories provide the bases.

Theories of child development such as those of Piaget, Vygotsky, Bandura, or Thelen are based on systematic research. These theories are the beginning and ending points of the research cycle. In the beginning, theories provide the research **hypotheses** to be tested or the questions examined. A **hypothesis** is a prediction based on the theory. For example, two different theories might suggest two competing predictions that could be tested. Piaget's theory might suggest that instruction cannot teach preoperational thinkers to use concrete operational thinking, whereas Vygotsky's theory might suggest that teaching could help children learn to use concrete operations. Of course, at times, psychologists don't know enough to make predictions, so they just ask *research questions*. An example question might be, "Is there a difference in Internet usage for male and female adolescents from different ethnic groups?"

Research is a continuing cycle (see Figure 2.4) that involves:

- Clear specification of hypotheses or questions based on current understandings or theories,
- Systematic gathering and analyzing of all kinds of information (data) about the questions from well-chosen research participants,
- Modifying and improving explanatory theories based on the results of those analyses, and
- Asking new, better questions based on the improved theories . . . and on and on.

This empirical process of collecting data to test and improve theories is repeated over and over, as you can see in Figure 2.4. **Empirical** means based on data. When scientists say that identifying an effective antibiotic or choosing a successful way to teach reading is an

FIGURE 2.4

A RESEARCH CYCLE

Research begins with questions based on current understanding, followed by gathering, analyzing, and interpreting information to answer the questions. Using these findings, the current theories are refined and become the basis for new research questions.

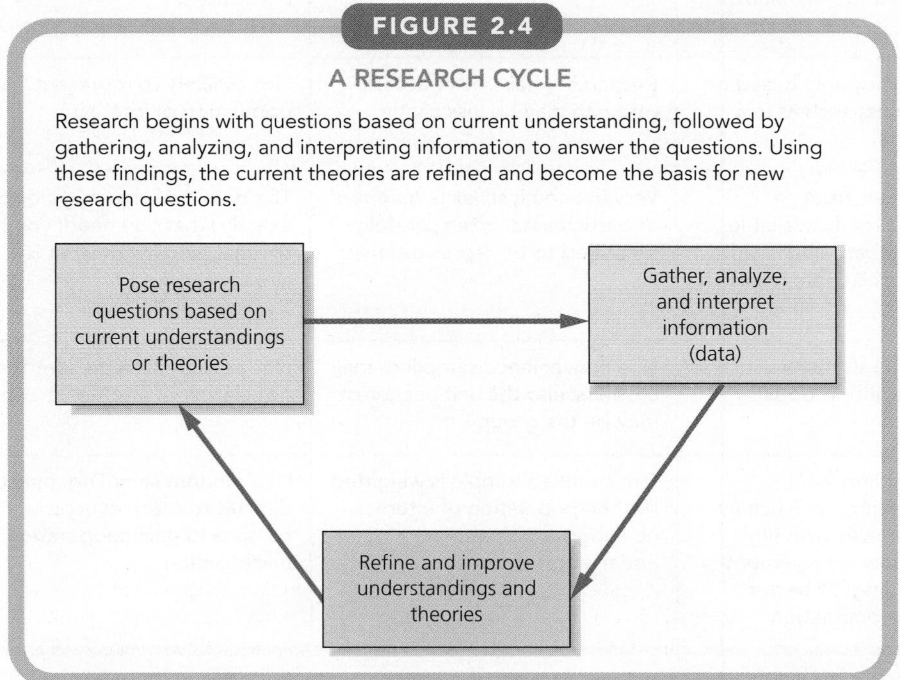

"empirical question," they mean that you need data and evidence to make the call. Basing decisions on empirical analyses protects scientists from developing theories based on personal biases, rumors, fears, faulty information, or preferences (Mertler & Charles, 2005). Answering questions with carefully gathered data means that science is self-correcting. If predictions do not play out or when answers to carefully asked questions do not support current best understandings (theories), the theories have to be changed. You can use the same kind of systematic and self-correcting thinking in your work with children.

In this section we look at the research methods that have been used to test hypotheses and examine questions about children. The major issues in such research are whom to study, how to study, and how to protect the rights of children in the process. So the first question is. . . .

Whom to Study? Samples and Participants

If we want to understand and explain the development of children or adolescents, whom do we study? The obvious answer is children or adolescents, but which ones? That depends on which children we want to make claims and predictions about. In other words, to whom do we want to *apply* the findings? This is a question about **generalizing** the results of the research to the appropriate children. A good start is to specify more clearly the age or grade, gender, SES level, race, language group, ethnicity, and so on of the target **population**—all the children we are interested in knowing about. For example, are we interested in children who attend day care centers, or children of single parents, or children who have younger siblings? Then we need to include those kinds of children in the research because they are the *target population*—the ones we are interested in. Let's assume researchers are interested in 3- to 4-year-old boys and girls who attend all-day preschools. Because they can't possibly study every child in that situation, they have to look at a **sample**—a smaller group that represents the whole population of children in all-day preschools. How do researchers find a representative sample? Table 2.4 summarizes several ways to identify participants through sampling.

TABLE 2.4 • **Types of Sampling Procedures**

TYPE OF SAMPLING	DEFINITION	ADVANTAGES	PROBLEMS
Random Sample	Selecting purely by chance; each participant has an equal chance of being selected—like names out of a hat	Best way to get an accurate representation	Difficult to reach everyone; may be hard to gain cooperation and participation
Convenience Sample	Selecting participants based on who is available, such as in a local preschool	Researcher has better access; research may be less costly	Not as likely to represent the population of interest
National Database Sample	Using responses from participants already available in a large database such as the **NICHD** Early Child Care Research Network	Very economical; large numbers of participants, often carefully identified to be representative	The data available may not be exactly what you need; you have to "make do" with what is already there
Cluster Sampling	Sampling natural clusters such as classes or neighborhoods	Like convenience sampling, may cost less; also the unit of interest may be the group	Not as likely to represent the population of interest
Stratified Sampling	Random sampling from subgroups of interest (such as males and females with high, middle, and low achievement scores in reading) to better represent the population	The stratified sample is weighted like the population of interest—no subgroup is over- or underrepresented	Like random sampling, may be difficult to reach everyone; may be hard to gain cooperation and participation

Research Designs: How to Study

A research design is an overall plan for the entire study. We will look at four basic designs—correlational, experimental, case studies, and ethnographies.

CORRELATIONAL STUDIES. Some research in child development is descriptive; that is, the purpose is simply to describe children, situations, relationships, and so on. Often the results of descriptive studies include reports of *correlations*. We will take a minute to examine this concept, because you will encounter many correlations in the coming chapters.

A **correlation** is a number that indicates both the strength and the direction of a relationship between two events or measurements. Correlations range from 1.00 to −1.00. The closer the correlation is to either 1.00 or −1.00, the stronger the relationship. For example, the correlation between height and weight is about .70 (a strong relationship); the correlation between height and number of languages spoken probably is about .00 (no linear relationship at all).

The sign of the correlation tells the direction of the relationship. A **positive correlation** indicates that the two factors increase or decrease together. As one gets larger, so does the other. Height and weight are positively correlated because greater height tends to be associated with greater weight. A **negative correlation** means that increases in one factor are related to decreases in the other. For example, the correlation between the gas mileage of a car and your monthly gas cost is negative—the lower the mileage, the higher the cost. Some correlations are not linear but **curvilinear**—the relationship changes at different points. For example, age and running speed would not appear to be correlated until you observed that people tend to run faster as they get older from toddlerhood to early adulthood, but then slower as they age—an upside down U-shaped curve.

It is important to note that correlations do not prove cause and effect, just co-occurrence (see Figure 2.5). Many people, especially politicians and others trying to make a point, mistakenly assume that correlation means causation. But if that were the case, looking at Figure 2.5, the way to raise test scores for failing schools would be to hire a lawn service for the neighborhoods around the schools—probably not a good plan.

With correlational studies, researchers can examine the relationships between variables such as hours of TV viewing and obesity in children or time spent in day care and aggressive play. Correlational studies can show that two things are related, but remember, they cannot say what is causing what. For example, amount of TV viewing is positively correlated with obesity, but does TV viewing cause obesity or does being obese cause children to

FIGURE 2.5

CORRELATIONS AND CAUSATION

Correlations Do Not Show Causation

When research shows that landscaped lawns and school achievement are correlated, it does not show causation. Community wealth, a third variable, may be the cause of both school achievement and landscaped lawns.

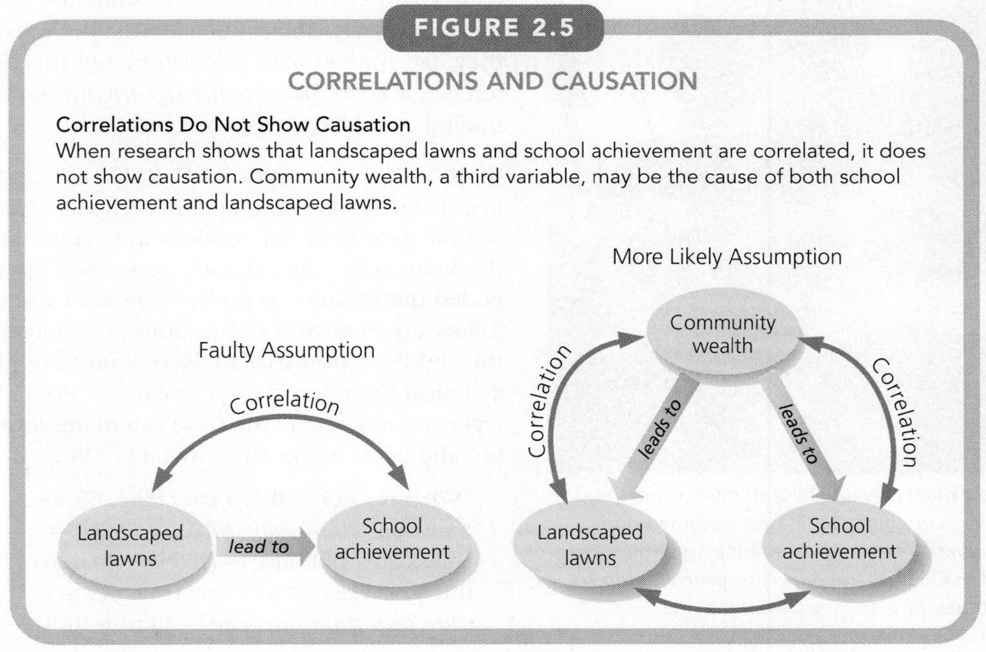

watch more TV because they don't enjoy playing outside? Does being in day care teach children to be more aggressive, or do parents leave their aggressive children in day care longer to get some peace at home? We can't tell based on correlations alone because—one more time—*correlation is not causation*. Keep this in mind in your observations of children.

EXPERIMENTAL STUDIES. A second type of research—**experimentation**—allows researchers to go beyond predictions to actually study causes and effects. Instead of just observing and describing an existing situation, the investigators introduce changes in some variables and note the effects on other variables. **Variables** are anything that can change or vary. The variables that are altered or manipulated are called **independent variables** and the resulting effects are noted in the **dependent variables**. The question in experimentation is, "Do changes in the independent variable (say, participation in a drug prevention program) cause changes in the dependent variable (decreased drug use for 14-year-olds)?" For example, Bethany Rittle-Johnson and Alexander Kmicikewycz (2008) conducted an experiment to determine whether studying arithmetic problems by figuring out the answers yourself led to higher test scores than studying the same problems using calculators to get the answers. Third-graders in two different schools were randomly assigned to one of the study methods, then tested two days later, and tested again two weeks after that. What do you suppose happened? Actually there were no significant differences in the average test scores of the "generate your own answer" group compared to the "use a calculator" group, but that is not the most interesting part. When the researchers considered the students' pretest scores, they found that students who began the experiment with less knowledge of arithmetic actually learned significantly more in the "generate your own answer" condition. So the effects of treatments are not always straightforward or simple.

In correlational and experimental research, statistical tests are used to analyze the data. When the relationship between two variables (correlation) or the difference between treatment groups (experiment) are described as **statistically significant**, it means that the relationship or the difference probably did not happen simply by chance. In studies you will see a notation indicating $p.<05$ or $p.<01$. This means statistical analyses indicate that the observed findings would happen by chance only 5 out of 100 times ($p.<05$) or 1 out of 100 times ($p.<01$). In other words, something besides chance or luck is probably operating in the situation. In the example above, students with *less* knowledge learned significantly more when they studied by figuring out the problems themselves. In contrast, students with *more* prior knowledge did better on the tests if they had studied with calculators, but this difference was *not statistically significant,* so the finding could have happened by chance.

While he was working with Albert Binet, giving children mental tests and asking questions for Binet's work on intelligence, Piaget became interested in the children's wrong answers—especially the thinking behind the answers. Later Piaget expanded the clinical interviews to probe children's thinking and understand their stages of cognitive development.

CLINICAL INTERVIEWS AND CASE STUDIES. Jean Piaget pioneered an approach called the **clinical interview** to understand children's thinking. The clinical interview uses open-ended questioning to probe responses and to follow up on answers. Questions go wherever the child's responses lead. Here is an example a clinical interview with a 7-year-old. Piaget is trying to understand the child's thinking about lies and truth, so he asks, "What is a lie?"

> "What is a lie?— *What isn't true. What they say that they haven't done.*— Guess how old I am. —*Twenty*. No, I'm thirty.—Was that a lie you told me? —*I didn't do it on purpose*. —I know. But

is it a lie all the same, or not?—*Yes, it is the same, because I didn't say how old you were.*—Is it a lie?—*Yes, because I didn't speak the truth.*—Ought you be punished?—*No.*—Was it naughty or not naughty?—*Not so naughty.*—Why?—*Because I spoke the truth afterwards*!" (Piaget, 1965, p. 144).

Researchers also may employ case studies. A **case study** investigates one person or situation in depth. For example, Benjamin Bloom and his colleagues conducted in-depth studies of highly accomplished concert pianists, sculptors, Olympic swimmers, tennis players, mathematicians, and neurologists to try to understand what factors supported the development of outstanding talent. The researchers interviewed family members, teachers, friends, and coaches to build an extensive case study of each of these highly accomplished individuals (Bloom, et al., 1985). Some educators recommend case study methods to identify students for gifted programs because the information gathered is richer than just test scores.

ETHNOGRAPHY. One descriptive approach, ethnography, is borrowed from anthropology. **Ethnographic methods** involve studying the naturally occurring events in the life of a group and trying to understand the meaning of these events to the people involved. In child development research, ethnographies might study how families, communities, or schools are organized to provide care for children and the effects of these organizational structures on the children. In some studies the researcher uses *participant observation*, actually participating in the group, to understand the actions from the perspectives of the people in the situation. Teachers can do their own informal ethnographies to understand life in their classrooms.

QUANTITATIVE VERSUS QUALITATIVE RESEARCH. There is a distinction that you will encounter in your journey through child development—the contrast between quantitative and qualitative research. These are large categories, and, like many categories, a bit fuzzy at the edges, but here are some simplified differences.

Quantitative research uses numbers, measurement, and statistics to assess levels or sizes of relationships among variables or differences between groups. Both correlational and experimental types of research generally are quantitative because measurements are taken and computations are made. Quantitative researchers try to be as objective as possible and remove their own biases from their results. One advantage of good quantitative research is that results from one study can be generalized or applied to other similar situations or people.

Qualitative research, on the other hand, uses words, dialogue, events, and images as data. Interviews and observations are key procedures. Case studies and ethnographies are examples of qualitative research. The goal is not to discover general principles, but rather to explore specific situations or people in depth and to understand the meaning of the events to the people involved in order to tell their story. Qualitative researchers assume that no process of understanding meaning can be completely objective. In fact, they are more interested in interpreting subjective, personal, or socially constructed meanings.

BEWARE OF EITHER/OR. *Qualitative* research tells us what specifically happened in one or a few situations. Conclusions can be applied deeply, but only to what was studied. *Quantitative* research can tell us what generally happens under certain conditions. Conclusions can be applied more broadly. Today many researchers are using mixed methods or complementary methods—both qualitative and quantitative—to study questions both broadly and deeply. In the final analysis, the methods used—quantitative, qualitative, or a mixture of both—should fit the questions asked.

TEACHERS AS RESEARCHERS. Research also can be a way to improve teaching in one classroom or one school. The same kind of careful observation, intervention, data gathering, and analysis that occurs in large research projects can be applied in any classroom to answer questions such as, "Which writing prompts seem to encourage the best descriptive writing in my class?" "When does Kenyon seem to have the greatest difficulty concentrating on academic tasks?" "Would assigning task roles in science project groups lead to more equitable participation of girls and boys in the work?" This kind of problem-solving investigation is called **action research.** By focusing on a specific problem and making careful observations, teachers can learn a great deal about both their teaching and their students.

How to Gather Information

Once you have a research design, you must decide what kind of information you need and how to get it. The researcher's toolkit is filled with different information-gathering methods. We will look at four basic tools in the researcher's methods kit: watching, asking, testing, and measuring. These same tools can help you as you think systematically about your work with children and adolescents or collect data for action research.

WATCHING: OBSERVATIONS. One way to gather information is to observe children and make careful notes. These observations could use running records (writing down everything that happens), checklists or structured observation guides, frequency counts or time records of certain behaviors, or any other way of systematically describing the observations. These days, the children might be recorded using video or audio technology to allow very careful, moment-by-moment observations. Children might be observed in naturally occurring situations such as restaurants, classrooms, grocery stores, or playgrounds as they interact with toys, school tasks, friends, strangers, teachers, or family members. When children are observed in their own real-life settings, the process is called **naturalistic observation**.

But what if researchers are interested in how children respond to a certain situation, such as seeing another child behave aggressively? If the researchers wait for every child in a preschool class to have such an experience, they may be in that class a long time. An alternative is to structure the situation so that children have the experiences that the researchers want them to have. This is called **laboratory** or **structured observation**. In this case, the researchers might show each child a video of a child punching or kicking a "Bobo doll" (a child-sized inflated toy), then see how the child responds to the same toy in real life, as Albert Bandura did (1965).

ASKING: SELF-REPORTS, SURVEYS, AND INTERVIEWS. By now you probably have completed a number of surveys, questionnaires, or interviews, so you know what this process is like. Questions for children have to be carefully designed so the children understand what is being asked and can respond in appropriate ways for their age and ability. There are many ways to gather self-report information. Older children and adults can keep diaries or journals. They can respond to *structured questions* (the same for everyone) or *open-ended questions* (following wherever the questions and answers lead). Older children and adults can take online surveys or complete printed mailed questionnaires.

One procedure often used to study infant development, called **habituation**, measures changes in the infant's responses to different stimulation. We can't ask babies to fill out questionnaires, but we can study changes in their breathing rate, direction of eye gaze, or length of time they look at something, as you will see in Chapter 4.

TESTS AND PERFORMANCES. Sometimes the best way to gather information about children's development is to test their abilities, ask them to perform an activity, solve a problem, read, write, draw, run, jump, resist the temptation of eating a piece of candy now with the promise of more candy later, or perform other tasks. For example, a common way of assessing cognitive development is to ask students to explain the meaning of words. The questions might move from simple and concrete words such as *apple* or *book*, to complex and abstract concepts such as *anthropomorphic* or *egotistical*. Today, in many countries, children undergo extensive testing, as you probably know well from your own experiences. We will explore the different kinds of cognitive tests—intelligence tests, standardized achievement tests, and diagnostic tests—in upcoming chapters of this text.

PSYCHOPHYSIOLOGICAL MEASURES. Today technology has advanced such that there are many ways to measure the biological processes that accompany different aspects of development. If researchers are interested in studying anxiety or fear in children, instead of just asking children how anxious they feel, the researchers might use measures of heart rate, blood pressure, dilation of the eyes, or stress hormone levels. Brain imaging techniques such as **functional magnetic resonance imaging (fMRI)** show how blood flows within the brain when children or adults do different cognitive tasks. In another technology, **positron emission tomography (PET)** scans can track brain activity under different conditions, as shown in Figure 2.6.

FIGURE 2.6

A PET SCAN

These positron emission tomography (PET) scans show that in one study, when compared with control subjects, adults with ADHD had lower levels of dopamine transporters (indicated by the red colors) in part of the brain's reward center.

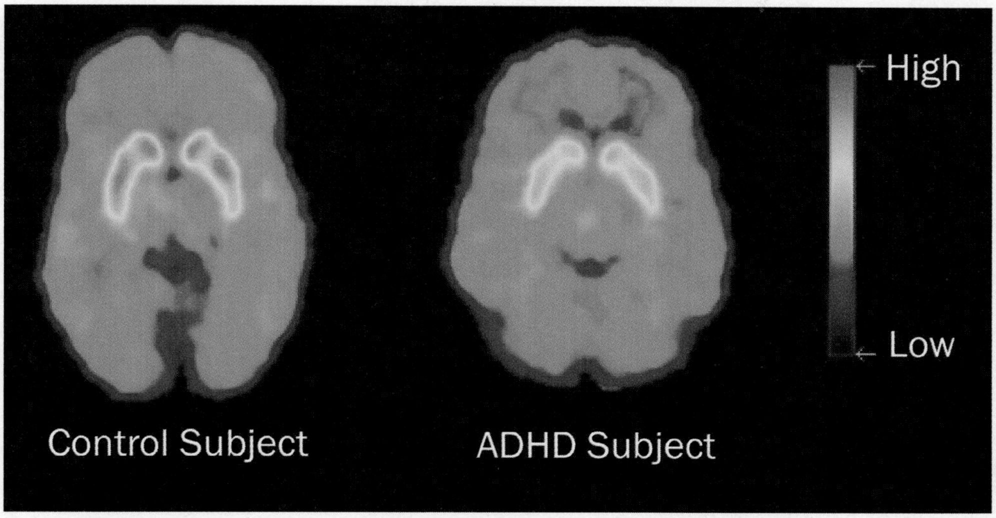

Source: Reprinted from Volkow, N. D. et al. (2007). Brain dopamine transporter levels in treatment and drug naïve adults with ADHD. Neuroimage, 34, 1182–1190 (p. 1184), *with permission from Elsevier.*

Even though these innovative technologies have created exciting possibilities for exploring connections between biological and neurological processes and behavior, there are limitations to these ways of gathering information. The equipment is very expensive, and interpreting results takes expert knowledge. Children may find the process frightening or very tiring. Their reactions may not reflect real-life responses. In many of the upcoming chapters, we will examine the uses of psychophysiological measures to gather data about child development.

Research requires good information, but gathering good information is not the end of the process. The information must be analyzed and interpreted in relation to the original research hypotheses or questions.

The Role of Time in Research

Another distinction is useful in understanding research—a distinction based on time. Many things that child development researchers want to study happen over several months or years. Time is a factor in longitudinal, cross-sectional, sequential, and microgenetic study designs.

LONGITUDINAL AND CROSS-SECTIONAL STUDIES. Ideally, researchers would study development by observing the same children over many years as changes occur. These are called **longitudinal studies** (see Figure 2.7 on the next page). For example, the NICHD Early Child Care Research Network (2005c) examined the connections between parenting and children's attention, memory, and planning skill development, while taking into account the effects of family income, mother's intelligence, and child's gender and ethnicity. They followed over 700 children from age 6 months to first grade. You will read about the results of this impressive longitudinal study in Chapter 6. We read in the newspaper this morning about plans for a massive study that will follow 100,000 children in 105 countries from before they are born to age 21 to learn about how environment, genes, and other factors affect children's health (Belluck, 2010). Longitudinal studies can be informative, but they are time-consuming, expensive (the prenatal to age 21 study is expected to cost almost $7 billion), and not always practical. Keeping up with subjects over the years as they grow up and move

FIGURE 2.7

CROSS-SECTIONAL AND LONGITUDINAL RESEARCH DESIGNS

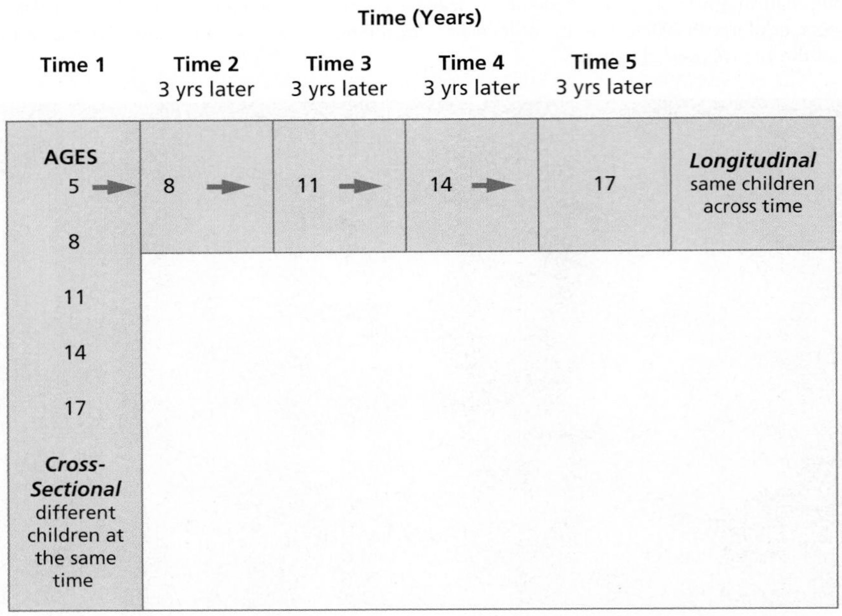

Time (Years)

Time 1	**Time 2** 3 yrs later	**Time 3** 3 yrs later	**Time 4** 3 yrs later	**Time 5** 3 yrs later	
AGES 5 →	8 →	11 →	14 →	17	***Longitudinal*** same children across time
8					
11					
14					
17					
Cross-Sectional different children at the same time					

can be impossible. As some participants drop out, disappear, or even die, the composition and nature of the group changes. Are the people who survive and stay in touch with the researcher different from those who drop out? Maybe.

Because longitudinal study is difficult and results take so long, much research in child development is **cross-sectional**, comparing groups of children at different ages. For example, to study how boys' and girls' self-concepts change from ages 5 to 17, researchers can interview children of several different ages, rather than following the same children for 12 years (see Figure 2.7). But there are disadvantages with cross-sectional designs. What if we compare the cognitive abilities of groups of children and adults ages 8, 12, 16, 20, 30, and 40? Some of the differences might be due to variations in nutrition or schooling for the different groups. The participants would be members of different historical cohorts (discussed in Chapter 1), so many of their life experiences would be different. For example, the 40-year-olds did not grow up with the same technology or even the same course requirements in high school as the others. Also, discovering differences between 8-year-olds and 40-year-olds does not reveal when or how the differences developed, just that the differences exist.

SEQUENTIAL STUDIES. One final design combines longitudinal and cross-sectional research by studying different age groups and then following those groups as they develop across time. So researchers might start with two groups (ages 2 and 6), then retest those groups every two years (at ages 4 and 8, then 6 and 10, then 8 and 12, then 10 and 14). Or the researchers might even add a new group every 2 years, and then keep following them too. These are called **sequential designs.**

MICROGENETIC STUDIES. The previous designs examine change over long periods of time. The goal of microgenetic research is to intensively study cognitive processes in the midst of change—as the change is actually happening. For example, researchers might analyze how children learn a particular strategy for adding two-digit numbers over the course of several weeks. The **microgenetic approach** has three basic characteristics: (a) researchers observe the entire period of the change—from when it starts to the time it is relatively stable; (b) many observations are made, often using videotape recordings, interviews, and transcriptions of the exact words of the individuals being studied; and (c) the behavior that is observed is "put under a microscope"—that is, examined moment by moment or trial by trial.

The goal is to explain the underlying mechanisms of change—for example, what new knowledge or skills are developing to allow change to take place (Siegler & Crowley, 1991). This kind of research is expensive and time-consuming, so often only one or a few children are studied.

Issues in Child Development Research

Here we examine three critical and interesting issues in research on child development. The first involves the ethical conduct of research with children. The second looks at the tension between basic and applied research as well as the emerging interest in community-based research. Finally, we explore the need to be a critical consumer of research in child development.

Ethics in Research with Children

The goal of research in child development is to *understand* the what, why, and how of development and also to use this increased knowledge to *improve* the lives of children and families. But research must be carefully designed and conducted so that the first goal of understanding is not reached at the expense of the second goal of improving the lives of the participants in the research. In other words, researchers must be careful to protect the children and families in their studies.

Not that long ago, scientists decided on their own if their research met ethical standards, but today special groups, called **Institutional Review Boards,** or **IRBs** evaluate every study involving human subjects conducted at universities and other research institutions such as hospitals or mental health agencies. The IRB reviews are based on guidelines established by the American Psychological Association (APA) and the Society for Research in Child Development (SRCD). Table 2.5 summarizes the main considerations from these two organizations.

TABLE 2.5 • **Ethical Considerations in Research with Children**

Protecting Children from Harm	Researchers should use no procedures that might harm the child physically or psychologically. When in doubt, consult with IRBs. If harm is possible, the researcher must find other ways to conduct the research. In all cases, the expected benefit must outweigh any potential harm to the participants.
Informed Consent	Research participants must give their informed consent to be a part of any study. Informed consent means that people have the right to an explanation about every part of a study that could affect their willingness to participate. Also, research participants must be able to withdraw consent and drop out of a study at any time they choose. Parents or guardians must give informed, preferably written, consent for children under 18. Other people involved in the study, such as teachers or therapists, have to give their consent too.
Incentives and Pressures	Incentives to participate in research must be consistent with what the children could expect in their own lives, so the incentives do not become pressures.
Confidentiality and Privacy	All information about individual participants is confidential. Names and other identifying information cannot be connected to the data. The information must be protected to prevent other people who are not involved in the research from getting access to the data.
Informing Participants	All research participants, including children, have the right to learn about the results of the study in language that they can understand. If there was deception involved, the researcher must explain what was done and why.
Cultural Sensitivity	The American Psychological Association asserts "psychologists are aware of and respect cultural, individual, and role differences, including those based on age, gender, gender identity, race, ethnicity, culture, national origin, religion, sexual orientation, disability, language, and socioeconomic status and consider these factors when working with members of such groups. Psychologists try to eliminate the effect on their work of biases based on those factors, and they do not knowingly participate in or condone activities of others based upon such prejudices." (http://www.apa.org/ethics/code2002.html)

Source: Adapted from the Ethical Standards for the Society for Research in Child Development (http://www.srcd.org/ethicalstandards.html) and from the Code of Ethics for the American Psychological Association. (http://www.apa.org/ethics/code2002.html)

PROTECTING CHILDREN FROM HARM. All research with human subjects and animals must be conducted ethically, but ethical considerations in research on children are especially important and complicated. Consider these situations:

- Middle school students are asked to list the names of the class members that they would most and least like to work with on a project.
- Children are given a puzzle that can't be solved, but are told that other children have solved it, to study reactions to failure.

One of the first standards that must be met by all research is that the *expected benefit must outweigh any potential harm* to the participants. Ideally, completing the research study will directly benefit each participant, but at the very least, the likely benefit to children in general must outweigh the possible harm to individuals in the study. Are these conditions met in the situations described above? You really don't have enough information to make this call, but just a quick analysis points to possible problems. In the first situation, rejected children might be even more rejected after they are identified as unwanted project partners by several of their peers. In the second situation, children could be frustrated, feel incompetent, or become distrustful of adults who misled them about the puzzles.

INFORMED CONSENT. Today all research participants must give their informed consent to be a part of any study. But children may not have the cognitive capability to understand the goals or procedures explained to them. So an adult—usually the parent or guardian—must give informed consent for children under 18 years old (remember the consent form at the beginning of this chapter). But what if children are abused or a parent does not have the child's best interests at heart? Determining who is allowed to give consent is an issue that IRBs evaluate.

INCENTIVES AND PRESSURES. Often children or parents are offered an incentive or "thank you gift" for participating in the research. Ethical guidelines require that these incentives be consistent with what the children could expect in their own lives, so the incentives do not become pressures. And keep in mind that concerned parents whose children have medical or psychological problems may feel pressed to consent to research participation just to have their child spend some time with a child development professional.

CONFIDENTIALITY. All information about individual participants is confidential. Names and other identifying information cannot be connected to the data. To protect the identity of participants, researchers often assign codes or pseudonyms in case studies. The only exception to not sharing any information with others is when researchers discover that a child may be in danger—in an abusive home or considering suicide, for example. Then there is a responsibility to act in the best interests of the child.

INFORMING PARTICIPANTS. All research participants, including children, have the right to learn about the results of the study in language that they can understand. If there was deception involved, the researcher must **debrief** the participants, that is, explain what was done and why. But children may have a hard time understanding why the adult "lied" to them, so deception with children is discouraged unless there is no other way to gather the necessary information.

Think for a moment—how will you protect the rights of children? How will these safeguards apply to your practice?

Basic and Applied Developmental Research

There were times in the history of child development when basic and applied research—the need for pure scientific knowledge versus the need for knowledge to guide public policy—were at odds. After World War II, the status of science around the world increased and the United States government set aside quite a bit of money for basic research in science. Cause-and-effect research and theory building were the most admired goals. "Practical" applied research was not as highly prized; those who did mostly practical work on university faculties were lower in status than their scientific colleagues (Groark & McCall, 2005).

But by the mid-1960s, the need for useful knowledge to guide public policy challenged earlier preferences for pure science. In 1969, George Miller gave his presidential address to the American Psychological Association and encouraged the APA members to "give psychology away" to policymakers, the public, and practitioners. Since that time, interest in and research funding for applied and policy-related research has grown. Today, there is a strong push from the United States government for *evidence-based social programs* in all areas—mental health, medicine, and education.

For example, in 2001 the landmark No Child Left Behind (NCLB) Act signed by United States President George W. Bush mandated that all educational programs and practices receiving federal money had to be consistent with "scientifically based research." The lawmakers believed that scientifically based research produced better knowledge because it was rigorous, systematic, and objective. In fact, the term "scientifically based research" appeared 110 times in the NCLB bill. Specifically, the No Child Left Behind Act stated that scientifically based research:

- Systematically uses observation or experiment to gather valid and reliable data
- Involves rigorous and appropriate procedures for analyzing the data
- Is evaluated using experimental or quasi-experimental designs, preferably with random assignment of participants to conditions
- Makes sure that experimental studies are carefully explained so other researchers can replicate the studies or build systematically on their findings
- Has been through a rigorous, objective, scientific review by a journal or a panel of independent experts

You can see that this description of scientifically based research fits the experimental approach described earlier better than other methods such as ethnographic research or case studies. So even with the renewed interest in policy and practice, the pendulum was swinging back to the research methods of the physical sciences. But not all psychologists or practitioners believe that the push for evidence-based programs is valuable, as you can see in the ***Point/Counterpoint*** on the next page.

Researchers in child development are comfortable using a range of methods, as you saw earlier in this chapter. Rather than debate about which methods are the best, Robert McCall and his colleagues (2004) argue that child development researchers should take advantage of the press for evidence-based social programs by working with practitioners and policymakers to design better research. One kind of partnership with practitioners is community-based research.

Community-Based Research

Community-based research is conducted by, with, and for communities. The goal is to develop and improve services for a specific community group, in contrast to pursuing scientific and academic communities' intellectual interests (Scolove, Scammell, & Holland, 1998). One example of community-based research is the Early Childhood Initiative in Pittsburgh. In 1994, the Heinz Endowments pulled together funding from other foundations, businesses, and social agencies to support several urban neighborhoods as they designed and expanded quality early childhood programs for children in poverty. Then in 1996, an interdisciplinary team began a longitudinal study of the different initiatives, applying authentic assessment procedures that:

- Used a collaborative research model with community partners for all phases of the research from beginning to end.
- Asked whether the program works in a natural setting rather than a laboratory setting.
- Applied the developmentally appropriate quality guidelines of the National Association for the Education of Young Children, the Division for Early Childhood, Council for Exceptional Children, and the Head Start Performance Standards (See Chapter 6).
- Relied on ongoing observations from consistent caregivers in the child's life.
- Offered ongoing feedback to teachers, parents, and the community about children's learning and needed program refinements.
- Operationalized a longitudinal repeated-measures design using sophisticated statistical techniques that could identify effects at different levels—teacher and school.

The results of the evaluations showed that the 1,350 students enrolled between 1997 and 2003 did learn the early skills needed for school success and their parents learned new ways of supporting their children's development (Bagnato, Grom, & Hayes, 2003).

POINT/COUNTERPOINT: What Kind of Research Should Guide Social Policy?

For at least the past 30 years, debates have raged about the best kind of research to use in formulating policies for children, particularly in education. Should we rely only on scientific experiments or is that kind of work impossible in education? What are the arguments?

POINT

Social policy should be guided by scientific experiments—evidence-based research. According to Grover Whitehurst, the director or the U.S. Office of Educational Research and Improvement, the best research to guide educational practice is randomized experiments. Robert Slavin (2002) paints a bright future for educational reform guided by scientifically based research:

> This process could create the kind of progressive, systematic improvement over time that has characterized successful parts of our economy and society throughout the 20th century, in fields such as medicine, agriculture, transportation, and technology. In each of these fields, processes of development, rigorous evaluation, and dissemination have produced a pace of innovation and improvement that is unprecedented in history. . . . Educational practice does change over time, but the change process more resembles the pendulum swings of taste characteristic of art or fashion (think hemlines) rather than the progressive improvements characteristic of science and technology. (p. 16)

The major reason for extraordinary advances in medicine and agriculture, according to Slavin, is that these fields base their practices on scientific evidence. Randomized clinical trials and replicated experiments are the sources of the evidence. The emphasis on evidence is not limited to education. Robert McCall and his colleagues note that "funders and policy makers at the national and local levels are insisting that new programs desiring funding must be essentially replications of service programs that research has already demonstrated to be effective" (McCall et al., 2004, p. 331).

COUNTERPOINT

Experiments are not the only or even the best source of evidence. David Olson (2004) disagrees strongly with Slavin's position. He claims that we cannot use medicine as an analogy to education. "Treatments" in education are much more complex and unpredictable than administering one drug or another in medicine. In addition, every educational program is changed by classroom conditions and the way it is implemented. David Berliner (2002) makes a similar point:

> Doing science and implementing scientific findings are so difficult in education because humans in schools are embedded in complex and changing networks of social interaction. The participants in those networks have variable power to affect each other from day to day, and the ordinary events of life (a sick child, a messy divorce, a passionate love affair, migraine headaches, hot flashes, a birthday party, alcohol abuse, a new principal, a new child in the classroom, rain that keeps the children from a recess outside the school building) all affect doing science in school settings by limiting the generalizability of educational research findings.

Beware of Either/Or

Berliner concludes that a complex problem like education needs a whole range of methods for study—

> [E]thnographic research is crucial, as are case studies, survey research, time series, design experiments, action research, and other means to collect reliable evidence for engaging in unfettered argument about education issues. A single method is not what the government should be promoting for educational researchers. (Berliner, 2002, p. 20)

Thinking Critically about Research

No matter what approach you use to research and no matter where you encounter claims and findings from studies, you have to be a critical consumer. Let's look first at some of the classic criteria for research, and then consider the special challenges presented today by the sea of information available through the media and technology.

RELIABILITY AND VALIDITY. We have talked quite a bit about evidence-based research. But the evidence from research is only as trustworthy as the information it is based on. No matter how the information was gathered—through observations, self-reports, surveys, tests, ethnographies, or physiological measures—the procedures used must be reliable and valid.

Reliability is the repeatability or stability of a measure: Would you get the same results if you used the procedure again? For example, a reliable scale gives you the same reading every time, as long as your weight stays the same. Quantitative researchers can calculate different statistics to assess measurement reliability. Qualitative researchers also have procedures for ensuring the dependability of their data. One way is called **triangulation** or seeking multiple perspectives, for example, by gathering data from multiple sources (observations, interviews, diaries, letters, etc.) or using multiple investigators to make interpretations and compare observations.

Validity is accuracy—assurance that the procedure measures what it was intended to measure. A reliable scale could give you the same reading every time, but still weigh you above or below your true weight—so reliability does not guarantee validity. A more precise definition of validity is that the judgments and decisions based on the procedures are appropriate and sound (Linn & Gronlund, 2000; Popham, 2005). Quantitative researchers have statistical ways to determine evidence of validity. Qualitative researchers also are interested in appropriate and sound judgments, but they are more likely to talk about the *trustworthiness* of the interpretations from the research.

GENERALIZATION AND APPLICATION. Another way to look at validity is to ask if the findings of the study will generalize to (apply to) people outside the participants in the study. If we set out to learn about the social development of 4-year-olds in all-day preschool, did we choose the sample, research methods, designs, and analyses well? Did we accomplish the study as planned without losing too many participants along the way? Will what we learned apply to other 4-year-olds in all-day preschool? This has been called **external validity:** Are the findings valid outside the original group studied? One threat to external validity occurs when the setting or situation of the research is so different from the participants' real lives that, in Urie Bronfenbrenner's (1979) words, the study just tells us about "the strange behavior of children in strange situations with strange adults" (p. 19). When the research situation is so "strange" compared to the child's usual world that generalization outside the study is unwarranted, we say that the study lacks **ecological validity.**

ABSENCE OF BIAS. Reliability and validity have long been criteria for judging assessments and research methods. But over the past 20 years, psychologists realized that another criterion should be added: absence of bias. **Assessment bias** "refers to qualities of an assessment instrument that offend or unfairly penalize a group of students because of the students' gender, ethnicity, socioeconomic status, religion, or other such group-defining characteristic" (Popham, 2005, p. 77). Biases are aspects of the test such as content, language, or examples that might distort the performance of a group—either for better or for worse. For example, if a reading test used passages that described boxing or football scenarios, we might expect—on average—males to do better than females.

As you encounter research in this book (or your own informal research and assessments in your work with children), think about how well the studies meet the standards of *reliability, validity, trustworthiness, absence of bias*, and *generalization*. But most of what you encounter about child development will be from sources other than this book. How will you think critically and evaluate these sources?

Cultural Sensitivity in Research

This chapter is about theory and research in child development, so it makes sense to ask how we can relate positively to all children in the research conducted in child development. This question has been studied, as you can see in ***Relating to Every Child*** feature on the next page.

Who Says? Evaluating Sources

It is likely that much of what you have learned about many topics, including child development, came from the media and the Internet. You are not alone.

MEDIA. Newspapers, magazines, and television are the "textbooks" for most adults after college. The media is a source of information for businesses, parents, and policymakers as well. But remember, there is a "middle person" between the researcher and the media story—the journalist, television producer, magazine editor, or blogger. To make the information from research more accessible and to fit the time or length requirements of the media, research results are shortened, summarized, and simplified (Albee, 2002; Groark & McCall, 2005).

RELATING TO

EVERY CHILD

Cultural Sensitivity in Child Development Research

IN 2001, the American Psychological Association, the National Institute of Mental Health, and the Fordham University Center for Ethics Education held a conference on research ethics involving ethnic minority children and youth. They identified 32 key issues in research organized around four critical dimensions of research that support ethical behavior: "a) applying a cultural perspective to the evaluation of research risks and benefits; b) developing and implementing respectful informed consent procedures; c) constructing confidentially and disclosure policies sensitive to cultural values; and d) engaging in community and participant consultation" (Fisher et al., 2002, p. 1025). Table 2.6 gives some examples of each dimension. Community-based research, discussed earlier in this chapter, is an example of culturally sensitive research that attempts to understand and honor the culture of the participants.

TABLE 2.6 • **Cultural Sensitivity in Research with Ethnic Minority Children and Youths**

DIMENSION	EXAMPLE ISSUES AND GUIDELINES
Cultural perspective in evaluating research risks and benefits	• Take care in defining race, ethnicity, and culture—avoid overgeneralizations. • Select assessment instruments with norms that fit the groups being studied. • Examine the roles of prejudice and discrimination in development. • Study resilience as well as vulnerability in ethnic minority children. • Make sure research teams have appropriate cultural knowledge and awareness of their own biases.
Respectful informed consent procedures	• Use community organizations to educate prospective participants about the research. • Use language understood by the participants and their families. • Be sensitive to concerns about signed forms and to children's cultural expectations about authority. • Select fair and noncoercive compensation for research participation—consult with community leaders to be sure. • Explain to participants recruited from community services that refusing to participate in the research will not limit access to the service.
Culturally sensitive confidentiality and disclosure policies	• Take extra precautions to protect privacy of participants from small towns or rural setting were everyone knows everyone. • Be sensitive to cultural expectations and values about confidentiality.
Community and participant consultation	• Maintain an ongoing dialogue with community members about the goals of the research. • Be prepared to modify research based on community input. • All researchers on the team, not just those who are members of the same ethnic group as the participants, should be aware of community concerns. • Include a description of the community consultation procedures in the research report.

Adapted from Fisher, C. B. et al. (2002). Research ethics for mental health science involving ethnic minority children and youths. American Psychologist, 57, *1024–1040.*

TABLE 2.7 • **What It Takes to "Make News"**

Recency	Something is not news unless it just happened. So journalists tend to get their social science news in the form of one new study at time from conferences or news releases. Because the journalists do not wait for studies to be replicated and for evidence to build up, the public may get the impression that research in behavioral science is inconsistent and unreliable—each new study seems to disagree a bit with the last "new" one.
New information	Something is news if it was not known before or if it contradicts earlier "news." So summaries of whole programs of work or literature reviews are "old news" even though they provide the most accurate and stable information.
The unusual	The more counterintuitive, surprising, or unexpected, the more likely it is news.
Controversy	Scholars are not good debaters. Some journalists believe researchers have too many hands ("on one hand, but on the other hand. . ."), so they are inconclusive. The scholar's claims that "there is no evidence for that statement" seem feeble and whiny.
Public interest	To be news, research must be interesting and relevant to large numbers of readers or viewers, so new weight-loss programs are news, but a new method for assessing social perspective-taking in young children is not.
The famous	Some people's opinions, activities, childcare choices, and so on are news because they are celebrities, even if they know less than you about the topic.

Source: Developmental Science: An Advanced Textbook *by C. J. Gorak & R. B. McCall. Copyright 2005 by Taylor & Francis Group LLC Books. Reproduced with permission of Taylor & Francis Group LLC--Books in formats Textbook and other Book via Copyright Clearance Center.*

Most of the errors in media coverage of research are errors of omission, not errors of commission. In other words, what is reported and the quotes from scientists tend to be accurate—as far as they go. But details of methods and qualifications about the findings (for example, under what conditions they might not apply, limitations on generalization beyond the sample, etc.) are not covered (Albee, 2002; McCall, 1987). Table 2.7 describes the criteria for what makes "news." Keep these criteria in mind when you read about child development studies in the media. What you read could be fairly accurate, but much information is not available because it is not considered "news."

JOURNALS. There are a number of excellent journals in child development published by professional organizations, as you can see in Table 2.8 on the next page. These are but a few of the journals that publish research on child and adolescent development. If you read articles from these journals, you will get complete information, but be prepared for academic writing that generally is quite technical. The articles in scholarly journals do not exactly read like novels.

You can have confidence in the information from research journals such as those in Table 2.8 because there is a rigorous evaluation process, called **peer review**, for all the articles. Several scholars who are experts in the area review every manuscript sent to a research journal. Your challenge in reading these articles will be to decide if the studies and findings apply to the children you are interested in. Look to the description of the sample and to the discussion of limitations to think critically about these questions.

THE INTERNET. It is impossible to estimate how much information about child development is available on the Internet—try any search engine. All of the child development societies and organizations in Table 2.8 have websites with information. Any topic has resources on the Internet. The challenge is thinking critically about what is available. One guide for evaluating websites from the Ithaca College Library (Ithaca, New York) gives these tips: Make sure you are in the right place. When in doubt, doubt. Consider the source.

Know what is happening. Look at details. Distinguish Web pages from pages (in books, magazines, newspapers, or journals) that can be found on the Web. To be more specific, the library recommends asking these questions:

- *Authority:* Who are the authors of the Web page, or who is responsible for it? What gives them the authority or expertise to write?
- *Accuracy:* Do you have good reason to believe that the information on the site is accurate? Do the authors provide any supportive evidence for their conclusions?
- *Objectivity:* What is the author's point of view? What is the purpose of the site? Is this a commercial, governmental, professional, personal, or academic website?
- *Details:* Are there misspelled words or examples of poor grammar? Do the links work? Has the site been kept up-to-date? Is the site well organized? Was this page designed for the Web, or is it something else, such as a government document or a journal article, that happens to be available through the Web?
- *Value:* Does this site address the topic you are researching? Was the page worth visiting? Does the site offer anything informative, unique, or insightful? (http://www.ithaca.edu/library/training/think.html)

TABLE 2.8 • **Examples of Journals in Child Development**

JOURNAL	ORGANIZATION/PUBLISHER	WEBSITE
Child Development	Society for Research in Child Development	http://www.srcd.org/
Developmental Psychology	American Psychological Association	http://www.apa.org/
Journal of Applied Developmental Psychology	Elsevier	http://www.elsevier.com/
Developmental Review	Elsevier	http://www.elsevier.com/
Journal of Experimental Child Psychology	Elsevier	http://www.elsevier.com/
Merrill Palmer Quarterly	Wayne State University	http://www.asu.edu/clas/ssfd/mpq/
Cognitive Development	Jean Piaget Society	http://www.piaget.org/
British Journal of Developmental Psychology	British Psychological Society	http://www.bps.org.uk/
Journal of Adolescence	Elsevier	http://www.elsevier.com/
Journal of Child Language	Cambridge University Press	http://www.cambridge.org/journals/
Early Childhood Research Quarterly	National Association for the Education of Young Children (NAEYC).	http://www.naeyc.org/
Journal of Abnormal Child Psychology	International Society for Research in Child and Adolescent Psychopathology	http://devepi.mc.duke.edu/isrcap/
Infant Behavior and Development	Elsevier	http://www.elsevier.com/
Childhood: A Global Journal of Child Research	Norwegian Centre for Child Research (NOSEB)	http://www.svt.ntnu.no/noseb/english/

▼ SUMMARY AND KEY TERMS

• Diversity in the Study of Development

Questions of child development increasingly require multidisciplinary research and the efforts of psychologists, educators, pediatricians, linguists, sociologists, and others using the tools and knowledge from their fields. All children develop in cultural contexts, so diversity and multicultural resources are integral to research in the field. With multiple disciplines and cultures come multiple methods for studying the "what" and "why" questions of child development. This research has led to multiple theories of development—some all-encompassing, grand theories and others more specific.

• Explanations of Development

Ethology is the study of how behaviors adapt to support the survival of all animals, including humans. Imprinting and attachment are two key concepts. Sociobiologists study the adaptive value of other behavior patterns besides imprinting.

Freud believed that the conflicts between inborn drives and the demands of society resulted in five stages of psychosexual development—oral, anal, phallic, latency, and genital. If the conflicts of one stage are not resolved, Freud suggested that the individual could become fixated at that stage. Erikson's psychosocial theory emphasized the emergence of the self, the search for identity, the individual's relationships with others, and the role of culture throughout life. At eight different stages between infancy and adulthood, Erikson suggested that the individual faces a developmental crisis that can be resolved by embracing an extreme position or by the healthier stance of finding a balance.

Classical and operant conditioning explain how associations and consequences shape behaviors for humans and animals. Consequences that increase behaviors are called *reinforcers* and consequences that decrease behaviors are called *punishers*. Bandura's social learning theory adds an element to reinforcement and punishment—people can learn by observing others, not just by experiencing consequences themselves. Social cognitive theory also includes learning from observing, but adds cognitive factors such as beliefs, self-perceptions, and expectations. Self-efficacy is a key concept in social cognitive theory. Information processing theories are concerned with how attention, working memory, long-term memory, prior knowledge, and executive control develop and affect development.

Piaget's theory of cognitive development focuses on changes in children's thinking over time and the processes that move thinking forward—equilibration (that balances assimilation and accommodation), activity, maturation, and social transmission. Piaget believed that all children move through four stages in the same order as their thinking develops—sensorimotor, preoperational, operational, and formal operational. Neo-Piagetian theories add knowledge from information processing about the development of memory and attention to Piaget's insights about different thinking abilities to explain how children develop in stages within specific domains such as numerical concepts, spatial concepts, social tasks, storytelling, reasoning about physical objects, or motor development.

• Contextual and Dynamic Systems Theories

Vygotsky believed that human activities take place in cultural settings and cannot be understood apart from these settings. One of his key ideas was that our specific mental structures and processes could be traced to our interactions with others as we co-construct understandings. Vygotsky believed that all higher-order mental processes, such as reasoning and problem solving, are *mediated* psychological tools, such as language. The zone of proximal development (ZPD) is the area between the child's current development level of independent problem solving and the level of development that the child could achieve with scaffolding from adults or more capable peers.

Bronfenbrenner created a developmental systems theory to map the many interacting social contexts that affect development. He suggested that every person lives within a *microsystem* (immediate relationships and activities), inside a *mesosystem* (interactions and relationships among all the elements of the microsystem), embedded in an *exosystem* (all the social settings that affect the child), all of which are a part of the *macrosystem* (cultural and societal laws, customs, rituals, resources, and cultural tools) that occurs in time, the *chronosystem*. Influences in all social systems are reciprocal. Thelen's theory is also a developmental systems approach that emphasizes the coaction of nature and nurture, in the form of the individual ←→ context relationships. The theories of Vygotsky, Bronfenbrenner, and Thelen avoid either/or splits and simple explanations. Humans develop in a complex, connected system of influences.

• Where Do the Theories Come From? Research Methods and Designs

In the beginning, theories provide the research hypotheses to be tested or the questions examined. Then researchers identify a sample that represents the children they want to learn about; select a research design (correlational, experimental, clinical interview, case study, or ethnography); gather data by observing, asking questions, assessing tests or performances, or using psychophysiological measures; then analyze data with appropriate methods. If participants are studied over time, the research is called longitudinal. If researchers intensively study cognitive processes in the midst of change—as the change is actually happening—over several sessions or weeks, then the research is microgenetic.

• Issues in Child Development Research

The goal of research in child development is to *understand* development and also to use this knowledge to *improve* the lives of children and families. To protect the second goal, Institutional Review Boards, or IRBs, evaluate every study involving human subjects conducted at universities and other research institutions such as hospitals or mental health agencies.

The goal of basic research is pure scientific knowledge. The goal of applied research is knowledge to guide public policy. Today, there is a strong push from the United States government for *evidence-based social programs* in all areas—mental health, medicine, and education. So even with the renewed interest in policy and practice, the pendulum is swinging back to the research methods of the physical sciences. The goal of community-based research is to develop and improve services for a specific community group, in contrast to pursuing scientific and academic communities' intellectual interests.

To be a critical consumer of research, readers should consider reliability, validity, generalizability, and absence of bias. Reliability is the repeatability or stability of a measure. Validity means the judgments and decisions based on the procedures are appropriate and sound. External validity means the findings are valid outside the original group studied. Ecological validity means that the results have meaning for children in real situations in the real world. Cultural sensitivity involves (a) use of a cultural perspective, (b) respectful informed consent procedures, (c) confidentiality and disclosure policies sensitive to cultural values, and (d) community and participant consultation.

Most of the errors in media coverage of research are errors of omission, not errors of commission. Details of methods and qualifications about the findings may not be covered. You can have confidence in the information in the child development research journals listed in this chapter because there is a rigorous evaluation process, called peer review, for all the articles. To evaluate Web pages, make sure you are in the right place. When in doubt, doubt. Consider the source. Know what is happening. Look at details.

▼ KEY TERMS

accommodation (48)
action research (61)
appropriating (52)
assessment bias (69)
assimilation (47)
attention (44)
autonomy (37)
aversive (41)
behaviorism (39)
bioecological model (53)
case study (61)
classical conditioning (40)
clinical interview (60)
co-constructed process (51)
community-based research (67)
consequences (41)
correlations (59)
cross-sectional studies (64)
cultural tools (51)
curvilinear (59)
debrief (66)
dependent variable (60)
developmental crisis (36)
disequilibrium (48)
ecological validity (69)
elaborative rehearsal (45)
empirical (57)
equilibration (48)
ethnographic methods (61)
ethology (34)
experimentation (60)
explicit memory (46)
external validity (69)
functional magnetic resonance imaging (fMRI) (62)
generalizing (58)
generativity (39)
habituation (62)
hypothesis/hypotheses (57)
id, ego, and superego (35)
identity (38)
implicit memory (46)
imprinting (34)
independent variable (60)
industry (37)
information processing (44)
initiative (37)
institutional review boards, or IRBs (65)
integrity (39)
intimacy (39)
laboratory/structured observation (62)
longitudinal studies (63)
long-term memory (45)
maintenance rehearsal (45)
microgenetic approach (64)
naturalistic observation (62)
negative correlation (59)
negative reinforcement (41)
neo-Piagetian theories (50)
operant conditioning (40)
peer review (71)
population (58)
positive correlation (59)
positive reinforcement (41)
positron emission tomography (PET) (62)
presentation punishment (42)
psychoanalysis (35)
psychosocial (36)
punishment (41)
reinforcer (41)
reliability (68)
removal punishment (42)
sample (58)
scaffolding (52)
schemes (47)
self-efficacy (44)
self-organization (55)
sensory memory (44)
sequential studies (64)
short-term memory (45)
social cognitive theory (44)
social learning theory (43)
sociobiology (34)
sociocultural theory (50)
statistically significant (60)
triangulation (68)
validity (69)
variable (60)
working memory (45)
zone of proximal development (ZPD) (52)

▼ THE CASEBOOK

GIVING PERMISSION FOR CHILDREN TO PARTICIPATE IN RESEARCH

Today there are many procedures to protect children and adolescents when they participate in research. One of the most important is informed consent from parents or guardians. (See the permission form at the beginning of this chapter.)

WHAT WOULD THEY DO?

Here is how some professionals from several fields responded:

CAROL APPLE—Staffing and Compliance Coordinator
Hillsborough County School District, Tampa, Florida

As a parent evaluating this permission document, it appears to adequately cover most initial concerns of purpose, procedures, confidentiality, and granting informed consent. However, the document does lack specific examples of the types of survey questions the students will be asked to respond to which could be of concern to parents.

The risks (or lack thereof) and benefits are clearly outlined and appear to follow the U.S. Department of Health and Human Services protocol for involving children in research:

- Present minimal risk to the child—the child will be participating in a survey that has confidentiality safeguards in place
- Project has direct benefits for the child (or related group of children)—the study will determine effective academic environments for teaching math
- Provide for parent permission—right to refuse or discontinue without penalty

One additional area that could have been addressed, considering that middle school age children are the subject of the study, is gaining their "assent" to participate. In other words, provide an opportunity to the child to express *her or his* willingness to participate in the study with fidelity. Having these concerns adequately addressed, consent could be given without hesitation.

VICKY ZYGOURIS-COE—Researcher;
Associate Professor of Education
University of Central Florida

Yes, I would sign the consent form. As a parent, I would think that the researchers focused on protecting the rights of minors. They adhered to research guidelines and they informed parents of the purpose of the study, procedures, and anticipated risks involved. I particularly liked the fact that participation is voluntary and the participants can withdraw from the study without any penalty or risk involved. After reading this form, I also learned more about what is involved in research; as a parent, I would feel educated and informed about research study participation and potential benefits of this research. The fact that I know who will be conducting the study, how the study will take place and for how long, what will be involved with this study and what will happen to the student data the researchers collect makes me feel comfortable with the entire process.

Participants in the study will be protected as follows: (a) participation is voluntary; (b) the study meets ethical treatment of minors guidelines as specified by the Institutional Review Board; (c) there are no anticipated risks involved; (d) student data will be treated with confidentiality; and (e) participants can withdraw from the study at any point without any penalty or risk involved.

GINA STOCKS—Lecturer
Sul Ross State University–Rio Grande College, Uvalde, Texas

My perspective on research involving students is twofold. I am a parent of two children attending public school, and I am an educator myself. As an educator, I understand the importance of credible, valid research and its potential influence for improving conditions within our schools. My familiarity with the research process is what allows me to be in favor of my children participating in such an activity. That said, educational documents themselves can be very intimidating. The formal nature of an informed consent document such as this can easily result in a parent feeling guarded. Terminology common to these documents *(tasks, risks, confidentiality, legal rights)* might raise a sense of caution unless the process is thoroughly discussed. As a parent I would appreciate this being explained in an informal parent meeting, school assembly, or conference session rather than receiving it in the mail or via my child.

The informed consent procedure ensures the safety of students by explaining in detail what procedures will be followed as well as allowing for refusal to participate with no obligation. I believe the process of receiving informed consent is clearly stating that my child's well-being is more important than any outcomes that might be a result of the research being conducted.

PEARSON **myeducationlab**

Now go to MyEducationLab at **www.myeducationlab.com**, where you can:

- Find the instructional objectives for this chapter in the **Study Plan.**
- Take a quiz as a part of the **Study Plan** to self-assess your mastery of chapter content. The program generates an individualized Study Plan based upon your answers to the quiz.
- Complete **Activities and Applications** to assist you in deepening your understanding of important chapter concepts.
- Apply what you have learned through **Building Teaching Skills,** exercises that guide you in trying out skills and strategies you will use in professional practice.

3 GENETICS, PRENATAL DEVELOPMENT, AND BIRTH

THE CASEBOOK

WHAT WOULD YOU DO?
FAMILY BALANCING

Imagine that you have been newly hired to provide child development guidance at your community child development center. Yesterday, some parents approached you for advice on *family balancing*, a term that refers to the methods used to choose the gender of a child through techniques such as sperm sorting and diagnosis of embryos before implantation. The couple has been thinking about expanding their family, but they have three sons already and would really prefer at this point in their lives to have a daughter. You have heard of "family balancing," but until now had not been asked to comment on it. These parents know of several clinics in the region that specialize in family balancing, and they wonder if you approve of the practice. You know this is the family's decision to make in consultation with their physician, but what aspects of this dilemma could you discuss with them?

CRITICAL THINKING

- What are the implications, if any, of the widespread practice of family balancing?
- What issues would you discuss with this couple or a new couple just starting a family who wanted to plan the sex of their children, beginning with their first child?
- What might happen if parents use a procedure to allow them to make a reproductive choice and the procedure fails? Would the parents' disappointment result in resentment toward the child?
- What other medical or ethical issues should parents consider?

Jenny I., Age 2—USA

▶ OVERVIEW AND OBJECTIVES

Have you ever wondered why you look like you do? Do you see a resemblance between yourself and your mother, father, or siblings? Even as you share some traits with others in your family, you also have characteristics like no one else in the family, in fact, like no one else in the universe. Each of you develops along a path that is completely unique from other humans, while sharing biological events that are similar for all human beings. This chapter explores those similar events and the issues that surround them.

The first section of this chapter covers **genetics**, the exciting study of heredity—how human beings inherit traits from their ancestors. The section describes genetic abnormalities and explores the benefits of genetic counseling for future parents. The next section on reproductive technology identifies the process of becoming pregnant, the frequency and causes of miscarriages, and reproduction technology. Both cloning and stem cell research are discussed. The following section on prenatal development illuminates the remarkable growth of an embryo and fetus, describes critical diagnostic tests of fetal development, and presents useful information on prenatal intervention. During these discussions, we highlight the context in which pregnancy occurs—including the role of the father, the family's culture, and relationships among family members—and their effects on the health of the mother, child, and the mother–child relationship. The chapter ends with a discussion of birth, the beginning of life outside the womb, including the physical and emotional aspects of birth, prematurity, multiples, and delivery complications. By the time you finish this chapter, you should be able to:

Objective 3.1 Explain how genes are inherited, how genes are expressed, and why genetic beginnings are important for teachers and other professionals to know.

Objective 3.2	Summarize the research on and implications of reproductive challenges, technologies, and cloning as well as the arguments for and against stem cell research.
Objective 3.3	Describe the stages of prenatal development, testing during pregnancy, and the contextual factors that influence prenatal growth.
Objective 3.4	Explain the stages of labor, delivery methods, and delivery complications.
Objective 3.5	Elaborate on ways that professionals can support families and siblings both before and after the birth of a baby, especially when the new addition includes twins or other multiple births.

GENETICS

Is there anything more remarkable than the prenatal development and birth of a baby? You emerged from a single cell to grow into trillions of cells that differentiated themselves into skin, organs, brain, and many other types of cells. You and all other human beings are alike in some ways, but very different in other ways. How did this happen? For us to comprehend this process, we need to know and appreciate genetics. **Genetics** is the study of how humans and other species (plant and animal) inherit the characteristics that make them unique and how the interactions between heritability and the environment influence development. An appreciation of genetics begins with understanding the terms *cells, chromosomes, DNA,* and *genes.*

Genetic Beginnings

Cells, chromosomes, DNA, and *genes* seem like complex terms, but they are simply the body and beginnings of life. A cell is the smallest living organism or unit of life. Cells grow, differentiate, communicate, and die, but the cells of the human body cannot live alone; they must live within a body. The human body has approximately 60 trillion cells and approximately 200 different types of cells (hair shaft cells, oral cavity cells, esophagus cells, muscle cells, etc.). As Watson and Crick first discovered in 1953, the major components of a cell are the cell membrane, cytoplasm, and nucleus that contain the chromosomes, DNA, and genes (see Figure 3.1). To see parts of a cell in action go to website http://learn.genetics.utah.edu.

In each cell in a human body, there are 46 **chromosomes**—44 autosomes and 2 sex chromosomes. Chromosomes exist within the nucleus of cells and consist of 23 pairs of elongated bodies, each consisting of thousands of chemical segments. These chemical segments are our DNA (deoxyribonucleic acid). **DNA** consists of two strands of sugar and phosphate molecules that twist around each other in a "double helix" shape that looks something like a spiral staircase (see Figure 3.2). The "steps" that connect the two strands of the double helix are made of four different varieties of molecules called adenine, thymine, guanine, and cytosine. Instances of these molecules appear as pairs to form the complete DNA strand (see Figure 3.2). Within the 46 chromosomes of each human cell, there are approximately 3 billion pairs of such molecules (Human Genome Project Information, 2001). The specific sequence of the molecule pairs makes up our genetic code. Interestingly, only about 10% of the molecule pairs actually provide active instructions. Some of the inactive sequences play a role in cell division, but scientists do not yet know the function of many of the remaining sequences of DNA.

You've read about DNA testing, a procedure developed in 1985 by Sir Alec Jeffreys. Although much of our DNA is exactly like other human beings' DNA, each individual's DNA has a unique composition that contributes to a DNA fingerprint. DNA testing identifies patterns within DNA that are unique to an individual. By matching DNA from hair, blood, and saliva samples, forensic scientists can use evidence at a crime scene to match these samples to a criminal's DNA as well as identify bodies. DNA testing can also determine who is the father or mother of a child.

OUTLINE ▼

FIGURE 3.1

COMPONENTS OF A CELL

The major components of a cell are the cell membrane, cytoplasm, and nucleus that contain the chromosomes, DNA, and genes. For an interactive description of a cell and its membrane go to http://learn.genetics.utah.edu/content/begin/cells/insideacell/

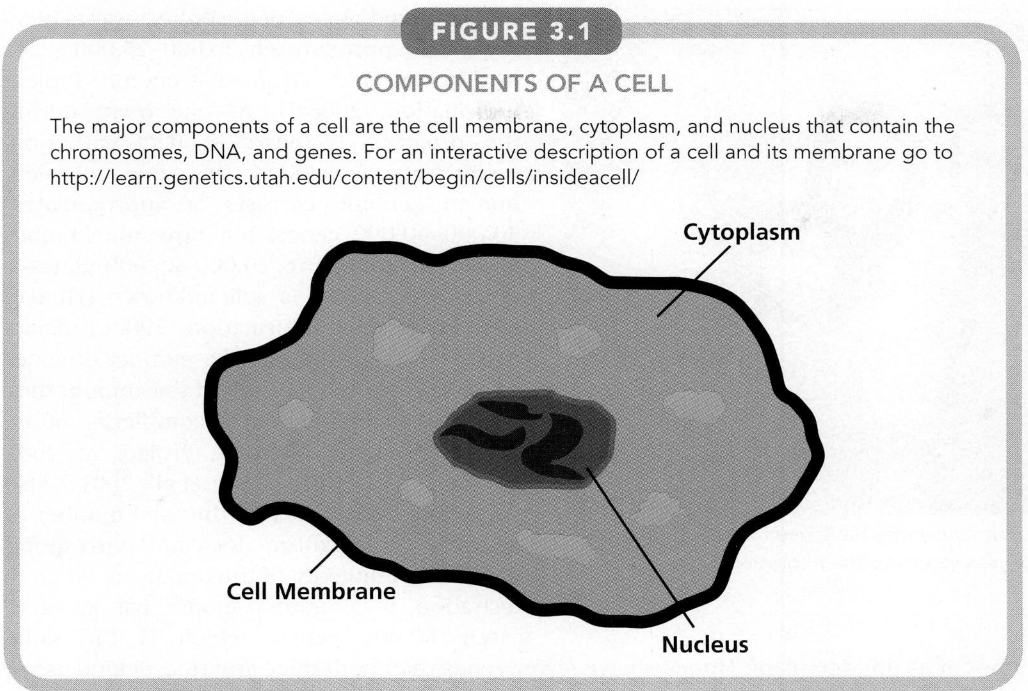

FIGURE 3.2

DNA STRAND

DNA consists of two strands of sugar and phosphate molecules that twist around each other in a "double helix" shape that looks something like a spiral staircase.

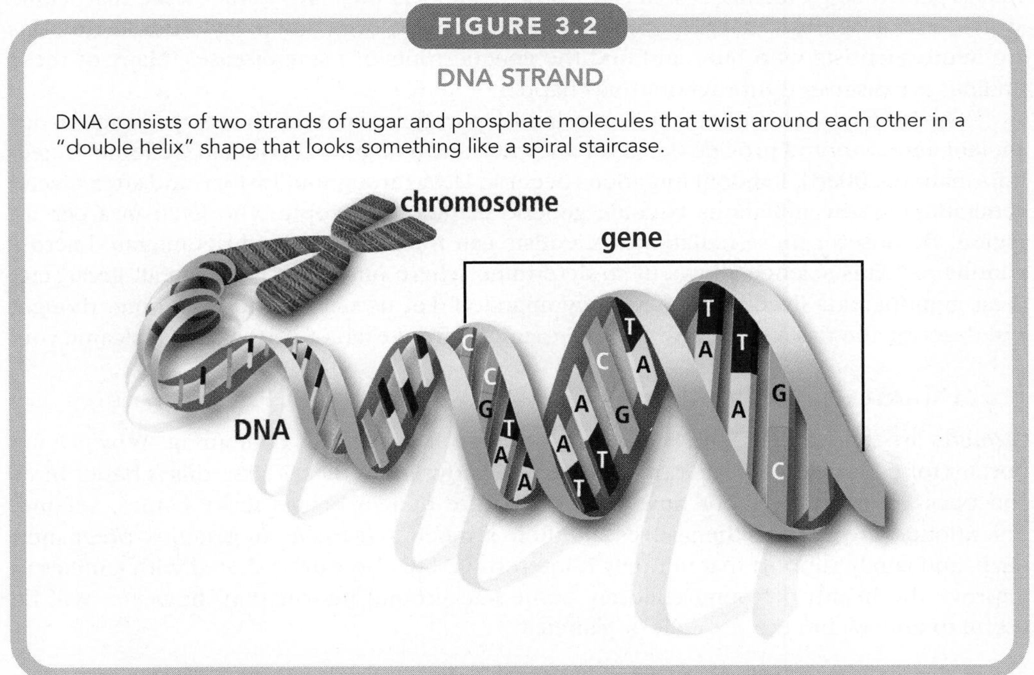

Source: Image courtesy U.S. Department of Energy Human Genome Program.

Within DNA are **genes** that tell cells which proteins to make. Genes influence the color of a person's hair, how the nose is shaped, the color of the eyes, and possibly aspects of a person's personality. Scientists call genes the blueprints of life. Just as a contractor needs a blueprint from an architect to create a building according to certain specifications, the cells need genes to tell them when and where to make proteins. The Human Genome Project started in 1990 and continues today as scientists analyze the immense amount of

Everyone in this three-generation family may have been born in the same geographic area, but DNA analyses can trace the migration patterns of their ancestors across time.

data collected. A goal of the project was to identify all the approximately 20,000–25,000 genes in human DNA (Human Genome Project Information, 2008a.). At one point during the project's 13 years of data gathering, researchers concluded that the complete human genome consists of approximately 30,000–40,000 genes, but now the number has been reduced to 20,000–25,000 genes—the exact number is still unknown (Human Genome Project Information, 2008c). Scientists were surprised that the number of genes represents about one-third of the amount they expected to find before the completion of the Human Genome Mapping Project in 2001 (Lander, et al., 2001; Venter et al., 2001). Also surprising is the fact that the total number of genes in an organism does not correspond with the complexity of the organism. As an illustration, a laboratory mouse has approximately 50,000 genes, which is the same amount as the rice plant. Humans have fewer genes than both mice and rice. Scientists are discovering new information about genes at a rate that is nothing short of astonishing—how genes express themselves, the origin of diseases and conditions such as alcoholism, as well as gene therapy techniques. In fact, "gene hunters" at the Mayo Clinic (www.mayoclinic.org), Johns Hopkins University (www.hopkinsmedicine.org), and many other institutions are neuroscientists who hunt and find the genetic roots of many diseases. Many of these findings are discussed throughout this chapter.

The Human Genome Project researchers report that genes tell the story of each of our ancient ancestors and provide details of ancient human migration (Human Genome Project Information, 2008d). Random mutations occur in DNA throughout history, and after several generations, these mutations become genetic markers of people who lived in a certain region. Because of these mutations, scientists can track how individuals migrated across continents. This science allows us to determine where our great, great, great, great, etc. great grandparents lived and where they migrated. Let us start at the beginning, though, and describe the process of how one cell (gamete) from each of your parents became you.

From Gametes to Zygotes

Gametes are the sex cells, and the *zygote* is the result of sex cells combining. Why is it important for educators and other practitioners to know about these? First, this is basic "birds and bees" information about how sexually mature human beings make babies. Second, practitioners are learners themselves and there is much to learn about genetics, pregnancy, birth, and family support that not only is interesting, but also can be shared with families to improve the health of young children. Some background information, however, will be useful to understand the sex cells or gametes.

DEVELOPMENT OF THE SEX CELLS *(GAMETES)*. Male sperm cells (the **male gametes**) are dormant in the testicles until puberty, at which time they begin to mature through a process called **spermatogenesis.** Remarkably, the male body requires just 48 hours to complete spermatogenesis in the two testes located in the scrotum. Each microscopic **sperm** cell is composed of a head, a flagellum (tail), and a cap containing enzymes that facilitate infiltration into the egg (see Figure 3.3). Men produce 500 million sperm every 48 hours until they are in their 70s or 80s. Altogether, the average male produces some 500 billion sperm during his reproductive lifetime—enough to populate the entire planet!

Female egg cells (**ova** or gametes) form in females while their mothers are still pregnant with them. By birth, all of the ova that a female will have in her life have formed. Eggs

FIGURE 3.3

SPERM FERTILIZING AN OVUM

At the moment of penetration by a fertilizing sperm, the zona pellucida undergoes a reaction that prevents any additional sperm from entering a single ovum. This cellular change is mediated by the release of materials from the cortical granules and is called the cortical reaction.

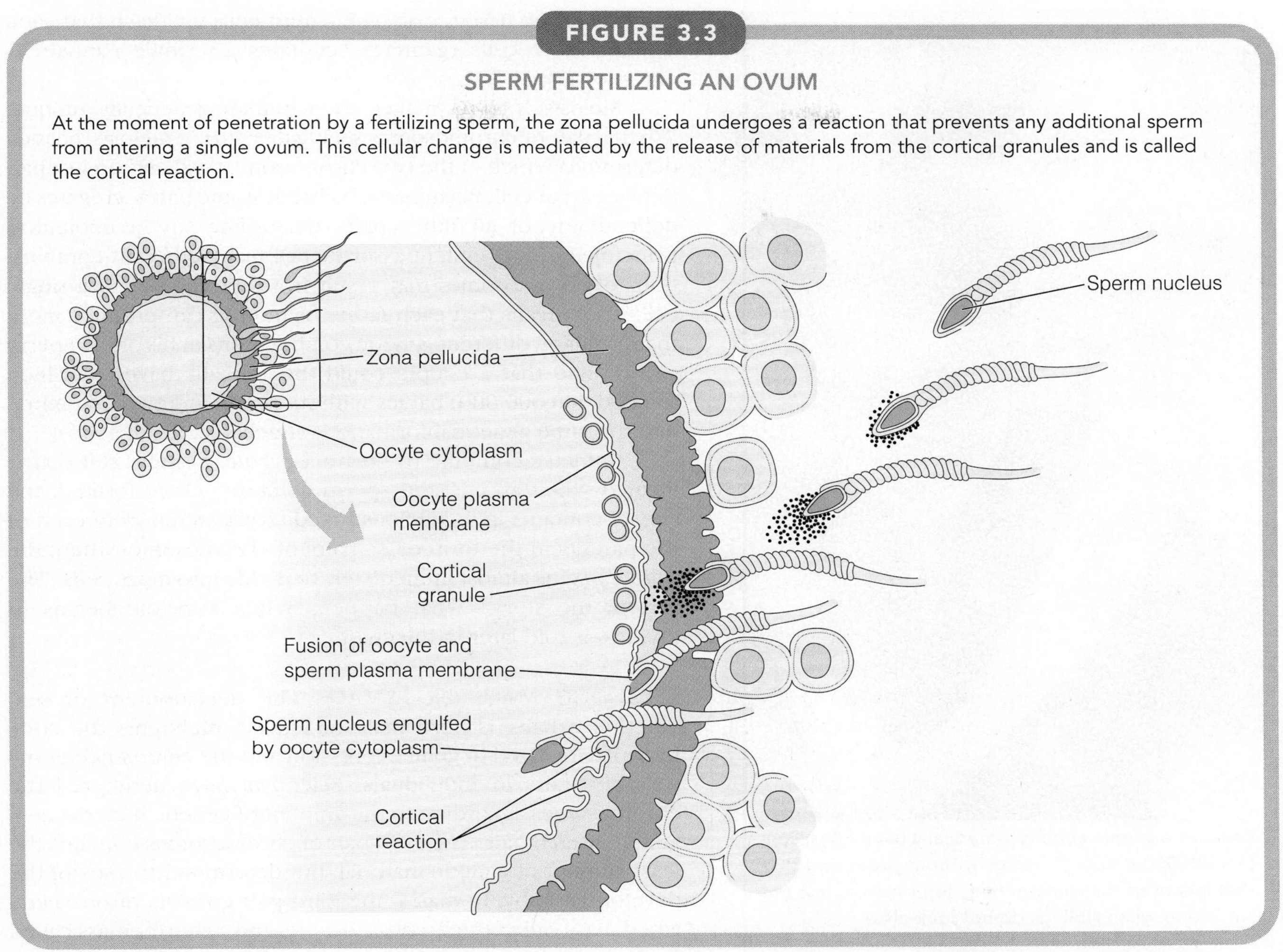

Source: Ladewig, Patricia W., London, Marcia L., Davidson, Michele R. Contemporary Maternal-Newborn Nursing, *7th edition, © 2010. Printed and Electronically reproduced by permission of Pearson Education, Inc. Upper Saddle River, New Jersey.*

are stored in the pair of almond-shaped structures called the *ovaries* that sit astride, but do not connect to the fallopian tubes. Each fallopian tube attaches to either side of the top of the uterus, or womb. At the base of the pear-sized uterus is the cervix, which serves as the gateway to the vagina. Of approximately 40,000 ova present at puberty, only about 400 will ever reach maturity. During a woman's reproductive lifetime and via the process known as the *menstrual cycle,* those eggs mature in follicles on the ovaries at a rate of about one every 28 days. Compared to the tiny sperm cell, each individual ovum is massive, abundant with cytoplasm, and immobile.

Sperm and ova, the human reproductive cells, are the only cells in the body that contain 23 chromosomes (all other cells contain 46). This means that each healthy sperm or ovum contains *half* the genetic complement needed to produce a fertilized egg. Each month an egg (or in some cases, several eggs) travels down the fallopian tube. When a man deposits semen in a woman's vagina, many sperm attempt to penetrate the egg that is generally still in the fallopian tube. Once a sperm does penetrate the egg, the egg repels any additional sperm through a process called *polarization*.

How is the information from genes imparted to the egg and sperm cells? Most cells in the human body are created via **mitosis,** a process in which two identical cells are produced by one cell that has divided. But gametes are different. They are created via **meiosis,** a form of cell production in which the new cells receive only half of the original chromosomal

Because a couple could theoretically have 64 trillion (64,000,000,000,000) babies without producing two that inherited the same genetic information, it is not surprising when siblings do not look alike.

material of the parent cell. The parent cells divide so that each of their new cells (gametes) contains 23 single (unpaired) chromosomes.

Meiosis is what makes each human genetically unique. When a pair of chromosomes segregates during meiosis, chance determines which of the two chromosomes will end up in a particular parent cell. Because each chromosome pair segregates independently of all other pairs (according to the biological principle of independent assortment), many different combinations of chromosomes may result from the meiosis of a single cell. That means that each father or mother can produce more than 8 million different genetic combinations in his or her sperm or ova, and that a couple could theoretically have 64 trillion (64,000,000,000,000) babies without producing two that inherited the same genetic information (Strachan & Read, 1996)!

Gametes combine to create a *zygote,* a single cell that is formed when an egg and sperm combine. Once formed, the zygote contains in its nucleus hereditary material from each of the parents in the form of 23 pairs of chromosomes; then, the zygote begins almost immediately to divide into more cells. The rest of the story—what happens when a zygote begins to divide—is told later in the chapter.

BECOMING MALE OR FEMALE. The development of sex, whether a baby is born male or female, highlights the complexities involved in gene expression and the emergence of observable traits in individuals. Scientists have numbered the chromosomes according to the amount of genetic material contained in each pair. The 23rd pair of chromosomes contains the least amount of genetic material, but determines the sex of the developing baby. In males, the 23rd pair consists of one elongated mass called the *X chromosome,* and a shorter mass called the *Y chromosome*. In females, both chromosomes are Xs. The chromosome pair that the zygote receives depends upon the particular sperm cell that fertilizes the egg, meaning that the father's sperm sets off a series of complex events leading the embryo to develop into a certain sex. More specifically, when the sex chromosome of a male (genetically XY) segregates into gametes during meiosis, half of the sperm produced will contain an X chromosome (which can create a female) and half will contain a Y chromosome (which can create a male). There is a single gene located on the Y chromosome that contributes to the development of testes-determining factor, a protein that creates the testes in XY embryos by two months gestation (Milunsky, 1992). The absence of testes-determining factor permits the development of ovaries.

MULTIPLE BIRTHS. **Multiples** is the term used to refer to more than one developing fetus in a given pregnancy. The natural occurrence of twins is rare, and of triplets even more so (1 out of 8,000 births). The Center for the Evaluation of Risks to Human Reproduction (CERHR, 2010) reports that since 1980, the number of multiple births has increased for several reasons: more women are becoming pregnant when they are over the age of 30, there is an increase in the use of fertility-stimulating drugs, and there are a number of assisted reproductive techniques now being used. How do multiple births occur?

You may be a twin or have seen fraternal and identical twins. **Fraternal twins (*dizygotic twins*)** occur when two sperm fertilize two ova. Each fetus has its own placenta. This means that the twins are no more genetically similar to one another than typical siblings separated by years of birth. Fraternal twins simply share a birth date. **Identical twins (*monozygotic twins*)** occur when a single fertilized ovum splits during the first two weeks after conception, resulting in two zygotes. In a report summarizing the research on monozygotic births,

Zach, Arun, Pramanik, and Ford (2007) state that whether there is one placenta or more, however, depends on when the fertilized ovum splits. If it splits within two days of conception, there can be two separate placentas that are separate or fused (see Figure 3.4A.). Approximately 30% of monozygotic twins have two placentas. If the ovum splits between three and eight days, then there is one placenta (see Figure 3.4B). Approximately 70% of monozygotic twins experience this type of prenatal environment. Only about 1% of monozygotic twins share a common placenta that has vascular communication between the two fetuses. This can occur when splitting occurs 9–12 days after conception. When the ovum splits more than 12 days after conception, then the result is conjoined twins.

Identical twins occur at a rate of about once in every 250 births in the United States. The frequency of multiple fetuses varies significantly among different races. Twins occur in 1 out of every 100 pregnancies in Caucasian women compared to 1 out of every 79 pregnancies in African American women. Certain areas of Africa have a high frequency of twins. In some places, twins occur once in every 20 births! The occurrence of twins among Asians

FIGURE 3.4

FORMATION OF TWINS

Figure A shows the formation of fraternal twins (note separate placentas). Figure B shows the formation of identical twins.

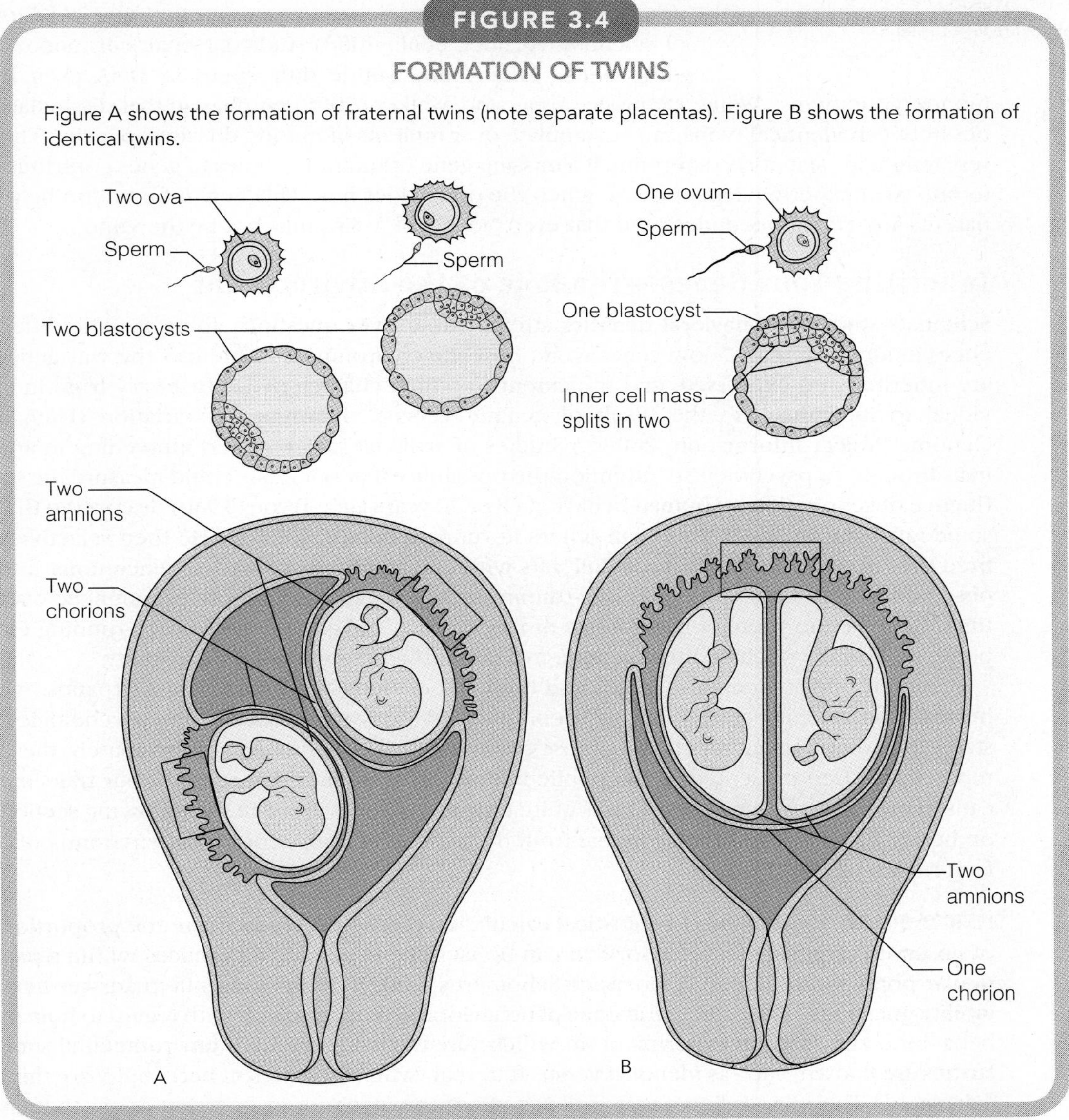

Source: Ladewig, Patricia W., London, Marcia L., Davidson, Michele R. Contemporary Maternal-Newborn Nursing, *7th edition, © 2010. Printed and Electronically reproduced by permission of Pearson Education, Inc. Upper Saddle River, New Jersey.*

There can be subtle differences in DNA even in monozygotic (identical) twins like these.

is less common: about 1 in every 150 births. In the past 20 years, there have been dramatic increases in the incidence of multiples due to increased maternal age (associated with a higher incidence of multiples) and assisted reproductive technologies (Wen, Demissie, Yang, & Walker, 2004). Women who are younger than 20 years old have twins at a rate of 3 per 1,000 births, whereas women older than 35 to 40 have twins at a rate of 14 per 1,000 births (Zach, Arun, Pramanik, & Ford, (2007). Triplets occur once per 7,000 to 10,000 births in the United States. Triplets may occur from the splitting of one ovum (monozygotic) or two ova (dizygotic), or from three ova (trizygotic).

Until recently, scientists and parents were mystified by an interesting phenomenon—that one identical twin could have a disease while the other did not. How could this happen, if the twins were genetically identical? With new genetic research comes fascinating information on monozygotic twins. A team of scientists (Bruder, et al., 2008) studied 19 pairs of monozygotic twins. They found subtle differences in DNA even in monozygotic twins. Wong, Demissie, Yang, and Walker (2005) emphasize that dissimilarities between identical twins can accumulate over millions of mitotic divisions of cells. This research helps scientists determine if a missing gene or multiple copies of genes contribute to one twin experiencing a disease when the other does not. This new information helps parents and educators understand that even "identical" twins may not be the same.

Inheriting Your Genes—The Role of the Environment

Scientists studying **behavioral genetics** attempt to answer questions about genetic differences in identical twins, how genes work, how the environment influences the way genes are inherited and expressed, and the extent to which characteristics that vary from individual to individual are the result of genetic versus environmental variation (Human Genome Project Information, 2008b.) Studies of artificial selection and inbreeding in animals brought to psychologists' attention the possibility that scientists could measure the influence of gene action on human behavior. Over 70 years ago, Tryon (1940) discovered that some rats have an easier time than others in running complex mazes. He then selectively bred the "maze bright" and "maze dull" rats with one another over several generations, and observed that the differences in maze-running ability became even more pronounced over time. Because the younger generations of rats had not had any previous maze running experience, Tryon concluded that genetic makeup influences maze-learning ability.

As our understanding of genes and their association with human traits expands, we hear of discoveries of genes "for" many complicated illnesses, behaviors, and psychological states including cancer, memory, homosexuality, aggression, and love. Unfortunately, these reports are often presented to the public in a way that implies that some of our traits are caused primarily by our genes. This is quite untrue. As you will see in the following section on heritability, all of our traits emerge from the activity of both genetic and environmental factors (Moore, 2001).

HERITABILITY. **Heritability** is a statistical calculation that is used to estimate the proportion of observed variance of a behavior that can be ascribed to genetic differences within a particular population (Plomin & Koeppen-Schomerus, 2002). Twin studies help answer heritability questions. The principal avenue of behavioral genetic research with regard to human behavior is the "natural experiment" in which variations of genetic or environmental similarities are known, such as identical versus fraternal twins. Estimates of heritability are then calculated. The logic follows that if genes affect the attribute in question (even though changes can occur during meiosis), identical twins should be more similar on that trait, because they have 100% of their genes in common (kinship = 1.00), whereas fraternal twins should be less alike since they share only 50% (kinship = .50) of their genetic endowment in common. Because of this, researchers are studying twins all over the world. There is even a journal for researchers to publish their findings—*Twin Research and Human Genetics.*

Wong, Gottesman, and Petronis (2005) summarized research on the heritability of different factors. *Concordance rates* define the probability of two people having the same trait. In Figure 3.5 the concordance rates between monozygotic (identical) twins is greater than dyzygotic twins, who have traits similar to what siblings would have. The rates for reading disability, autism, major affective disorders, and alcoholism are 60% or higher between monozygotic twins, indicating a genetic basis for these disorders, but because the concordance rates are not 99%, environment plays a part, too.

The results of twin studies demonstrate that there is a complex interaction between genes and the environment. The most famous twin studies were conducted at the University of Minnesota on data collected from 1979 to 1999. These studies focused on twins reared together and twins reared apart from each other (Bouchard, Lykken, McGue, Segal, & Tellegen, 1990; Bouchard & McGue, 2003; Segal, 2005). The researchers asked how much genes and/or environment influence "falling in love, divorce, aging, personality development, vocational choices, talents and abilities, attitudes, body characteristics, health, migraines, temperament, coping with stress, and brain waves and other physiological responses." Although they found strong heritability, the authors concluded that this "does not detract from the value or importance of parenting, education, and other

FIGURE 3.5

HERITABILITY

Wong, Gottesman, and Petronis (2005) summarized research on the heritability of different factors. The concordance rate for monozyotic twins (identical) is greater than that of dyzygotic twins whose concordance rate is similar to other siblings. Review the graphs to see concordance rates for (A) some common behavioral occurrences and (B) medical disorders. The concordance rates (%) shown are an approximate mid-range value derived from multiple reported figures.

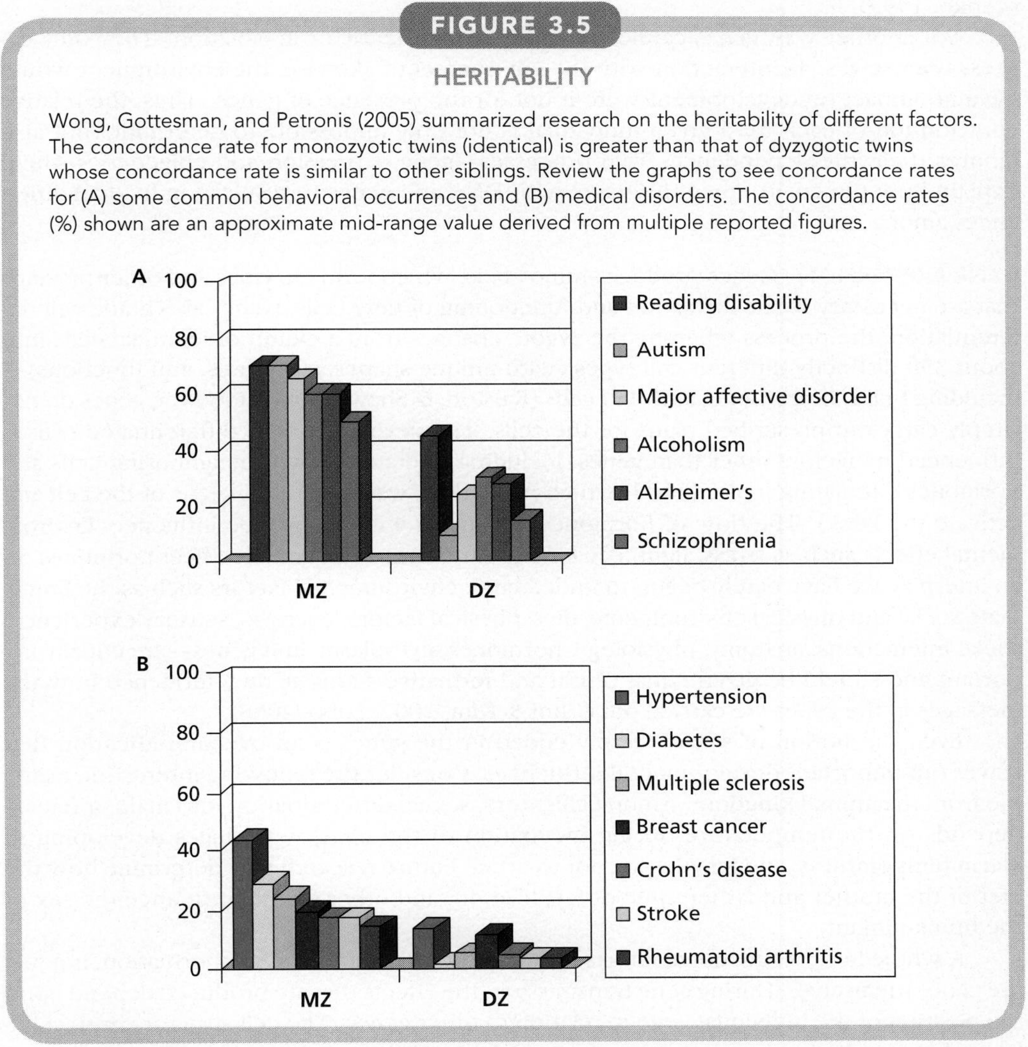

Source: Albert H.C. Wong, et al., Human Molecular Genetics,14 *(Review Issue 1), p. R 12, (2005). Used by permission of Oxford University Press.*

propaedeutic interventions" (Bouchard et al., 1990, p. 223). Researchers involved in The Harvard Twin Study of Substance Abuse (Tsuang, Bar, Harley, & Lyons, 2001), a study of 8,000 male twins who served in the U.S. military between 1965 and 1975, concluded that there is a complex pattern of genetics and environmental influences on substance use and abuse.

At first glance, it seems that heritability coefficients can tell us whether an individual has inherited a trait, whether an individual in a variety of situations will develop that trait, or whether clearly heritable traits are immune to the effects of the environment. In fact, heritability coefficients cannot tell us any of those things. *Genes do not ever directly map on to behavior*. That is, "the things that people do hardly ever arise directly from the promptings of their DNA" (Benderly, 2000, p.1). In fact, it is critical that we realize that "heritable" does not mean "inherited" or "unchangeable." For example, if a behavioral trait has a heritability statistic of 70%, we can't say that the development of the trait in an individual is 70% genetic (Sternberg, Grigorenko & Kidd, 2005). Furthermore, heritability coefficients are not at all informative about the *development* of that characteristic in any *individual*. There is no way of estimating heritability for an individual, nor is the concept meaningful for individuals, because variation between individuals cannot be applied to variation within individuals (Molenaar, Huizinga, & Nesselroade, 2003). Each individual develops along a path that is exclusively his or her own. And, it is impossible to ascertain the relative importance of genetics and environment on any trait's final appearance (Moore, 2001; Sternberg & Grigorenko, 1999).

Put another way, genes cannot operate independently or in isolation. They only express themselves via interaction with the environment. Likewise, the environment would have no impact on development were it not for the presence of genes. Thus, the relative contribution of each for a given individual is not only impossible to determine, but also ignores their interdependence. Two processes—gene expression and epigenetics—help explain how the environment interacts with DNA and genes to result in individual differences among us.

GENE EXPRESSION. Genes produce amino acids, which form enzymes and other proteins that are necessary in the formation and functioning of new cells. Genes also guide cell differentiation, the process whereby the zygote changes from a clump of identical cells into about 350 distinctly different cell types (with unique shapes, structures, and functions)—including brain, heart, bone, and skin cells (Ralston, & Shaw, 2008). However, genes do not simply carry out prescribed plans for the cells. The development of differentiated cells is influenced by factors other than genes, including interactions with neighboring cells and hormones circulating in the blood (which make their way into the nucleus of the cell and activate the DNA). The flow of hormones is also not without outside influence. Environmental effects such as stress, light, day length, nutrition, and behavior affect hormones. In an interplay we have barely begun to understand, environmental factors such as the immediate social and physical environments, diet, physical factors, exercise, sensory experience, social interactions, anatomy, physiology, hormones, cytoplasm, and genes—are equally important and should be given equal causal and formative status as they influence how the messages in the genes are carried out (Choi & Kim, 2007; Lobo, 2008).

Even the notion of sex as simply coded in the genes is an oversimplification that leaves out important developmental influences. Consider the following interesting example from the animal kingdom: Among alligators, sexual differentiation into male or female depends on the temperature during incubation of the eggs, with males developing in warm temperatures, and females in cool weather. Future research may determine how the diet of the mother and father, time of fertilization, and other factors influence the sex of the human infant.

A whole host of situational effects influences the transmission of information, not just the genes themselves. During gene transmission, the effects that are produced depend upon the position of the individual gene in relation to other genes. The cell structure, intracellular and extracellular chemicals, the extracellular environment, the parental reproductive system (physiological and behavioral), self-stimulation by the organism, the immediate physical environment, climate, food sources, exposure to toxins, and the external environment all influence the communication among genes (Oyama, 2000).

For example, rat pups will only exhibit certain "innate" (instinctual) behaviors if the odor of their own nesting material is present. If scientists move the pups to other nests, they will not show species-typical learning and behavior, including grooming and the discrimination of stimuli. However, in the typical course of the rat's development, the nest and its odors are reliably present, as is the olfactory system with which the rat senses them (Oyama, 2000). In rats, there is also a species-characteristic fearful response to novel environments. This is the result of natural selection (i.e., a change in the gene frequency in the population of rats). However, if rats are weaned early or handled when they are pups, the amount of fearfulness exhibited is dramatically changed. Thus, the amount of fearfulness a rat exhibits in response to a novel environment is mediated by its early maternal treatment.

In another elegant series of experiments on the role of experience in early development, Gottlieb (1997) discovered that maternal call recognition in mallard ducklings (always thought to be innate) actually results from experience with their own vocalizations 2–3 days prior to hatching. When Gottlieb and his colleagues muted the embryonic ducklings (i.e., stopped them from peeping in the egg before they had hatched) by anesthetizing their vocal cords, their response to their species-typical maternal call was disorganized or nonexistent, and clearly not hard-wired.

These examples of nonobvious experiential influences on development show how inadequate it is to regard the developmental environment as supportive rather than formative. Scientists do not deny the important role that genes play in development. However, once we recognize how intricately and complexly behavior patterns are constructed, the notion that a trait could be reduced to a simple sum of genes and the environment is not viable. Such a view misses all of the complexity that makes development interesting. Epigenetics helps us understand just how complex our inheritance of genes really is.

EPIGENETICS—THE INTERPLAY OF HEREDITY AND ENVIRONMENT. Individual development works by way of **epigenesis,** the creation of new forms. Epigenesis is a molecular mechanism that describes how the environment affects the way genes express themselves. Researchers have recently discovered that in addition to inheriting your genes, you also inherited methyls (small chemical groups) that latch on to the DNA strands and switch genes on or off (Jablonka & Raz, 2009). This process causes certain changes in an organism due to environmental conditions—for example, exposure to chemicals or changes in temperature—to be passed on to future generations. In one study conducted with flies, researchers found if the temperature surrounding certain fly embryos was increased, the flies were born with red eyes rather than white. This trait was then passed on to their offspring for several generations, even though the temperature for the new embryos was reduced to previous levels. Jablonka and Raz (2009) discovered that when fruit flies were exposed to certain chemicals, then 13 generations of descendants were born with bristly outgrowths on their eyes. Thus, **phenotypic characteristics** (observable traits) are influenced by conditions present in the environment, both before and after birth, which influence cell division and activation. It seems that histones activate or deactivate certain genes—directing how genes will express themselves (Jablonka & Raz, 2009; Jaenisch & Bird, 2003). These histones are then inherited even though the DNA stays the same; thus certain characteristics, influenced by the environment, are passed on to offspring. Thus phenotypes develop out of the epigenetic interplay between genetic information and environmental information at every level of function.

DOMINANT-RECESSIVE INHERITANCE. There are human characteristics, however, that develop out of the influence of a single gene pair: one from the mother and one from the father (plus, of course, the influence of the environment at all levels). This is known as simple **dominant-recessive inheritance.** A 19th century Austrian monk named Gregor Mendel conducted seminal studies on simple dominant-recessive inheritance by crossbreeding peas. Mendel discovered that certain characteristics of the initial peas appeared more often in later generations than other seemingly opposite traits. He called the traits that more

TABLE 3.1 • **Dominant and Recessive Traits**

	DOMINANT TRAITS	DOMINANT OVER	RECESSIVE TRAITS
Eye coloring	Brown eyes But gray, green, hazel And blue	→ → →	Gray, green, hazel, blue eyes Blue Albino (pink)
Hair	Dark hair Non-red hair (blonde, brunette) Curly hair But wavy hair Widow's peak hairline	→ → → → →	Blonde hair, light hair Red hair Wavy hair Straight hair Normal hairline
Facial features/ Tongue	Dimples in cheek Unattached ear lobes Freckles Chin cleft present Broad lips Roller tongue	→ → → → → →	No dimples Attached ear lobes No freckles No chin cleft Thin lips Non roller tongue
Appendages	Hair on fingers' second joint Last joint of little finger bent toward 4th finger When clasping hands, left thumb fits naturally on top of right	→ → →	No hair on fingers' second joint Little finger straight When clasping hands, right thumb fits naturally on top of left

Source: Based on Nagle, J.J. (1983). Heredity and human affairs. *St. Louis, MO: Mosby.; Griffiths, A.J. F., Miller, J.H. Suzuki, D.T., Lewontin, R.C., & Gelbart, W.M. (2000).* An introduction to genetic analysis. *(7th ed.). New York, NY: W.H. Freeman.*

commonly appeared "dominant," and the lesser-expressed traits "recessive." Common dominant traits in humans include dark hair (as opposed to light hair), a full head of hair (as opposed to pattern baldness), curly hair (as opposed to straight hair), facial dimples (as opposed to no dimples), and pigmented skin (as opposed to albinism). See Table 3.1. for a list of dominant and recessive traits.

Some genes produce a phenotype that is a compromise between the two genes (plus the environment), rather than reflecting dominant over recessive characteristics. More specifically, **co-dominance** occurs when the alleles of the gene (the members of a pair or series of genes that occupy a specific position on a specific chromosome) are expressed equally, or when one is stronger yet does not mask the effects of the other. An example of a phenotype created by co-dominance is the sickle cell. The recessive sickle cell allele (which about 8% of African Americans carry) can cause some of the recipient's red blood cells to assume a rounded "sickle" shape. These blood cells tend to cluster together more than normal, distributing less oxygen throughout the circulatory system. If an offspring inherits two recessive sickle cell genes, co-dominance creates **sickle cell anemia,** a severe blood disorder in which there is a chronic deficiency in distribution of oxygen in the blood (Learning about Sickle Cell Disease, 2009).

SEX-LINKED INHERITANCE. Certain genetic effects are linked to particular genes that are located on the sex chromosomes. This situation is termed **sex-linked inheritance.** Most sex-linked phenotypes are produced by recessive genes, which are located on the X chromosome. Interestingly, females are less likely to develop sex-linked genetic effects because they have corresponding genes on their second X chromosome that can counteract the affected allele. Males, whose Y chromosome may lack corresponding counteracting genes, more commonly develop the sex-linked effect. Examples of sex-linked genetic disorders that most often occur in males include color blindness, hemophilia, muscular dystrophy, and degeneration of the optic nerve.

POLYGENIC INHERITANCE. Although the genetic effects just described are caused by the interaction of the environment and the expression of a single gene, most physical traits are **polygenetic,** that is, produced by multiple gene actions (e.g., height, weight, and skin color). Scientists do not yet know how many pairs of alleles influence these characteristics because such a wide range of individual differences of the phenotypes can be observed. Virtually all *behavioral* traits such as intelligence, aggression, shyness, and alcoholism are polygenetic (and of course highly influenced by environmental factors at every level of analysis). Although attempts have been made to establish genes for intelligence (Plomin, 1997; Plomin & Spinath, 2004), none are conclusively identified. Furthermore, every attempt to study genes related to behavioral traits has been indirect, via studies of heritability.

Genetic Abnormalities

In contrast to the way traits are expressed based on a given genetic inheritance from one or both parents, genetic abnormalities can be the result of **mutations:** random changes in the chemical structure of one or more genes that lead to the production of a different phenotype and may or may not be harmful. Spontaneous mutations can be caused by environmental hazards such as toxic waste and agricultural chemicals that enter the food supply (including heavy metals found in fish), as well as additives and preservatives in processed foods.

When cell division occurs via meiosis, the distribution of the 46 chromosomes within the resultant sperm or egg is sometimes uneven. That is, one of the gametes may have too many chromosomes while the other has too few. In the vast majority of such cases the embryo fails to develop and is spontaneously aborted (i.e., the mother miscarries the embryo). Some do develop (approximately 1 child out of every 150) and are born with either one chromosome too many or one chromosome too few (March of Dimes, 2010b).

SEX-CHROMOSOME ABNORMALITIES. Many chromosomal abnormalities involve the 23rd pair of chromosomes: the sex chromosomes. A female who is conceived with only one X chromosome rather than two (which occurs in approximately 1 in 2,500 female births) develops **Turner's syndrome,** which is characterized by a small stature, a broad chest with underdeveloped breasts, a webbed neck, and shortened fingers and toes. Individuals with Turner's syndrome are infertile and score below average on tests of spatial reasoning. See http://www.turnersyndrome.org/ for more information. If a female is conceived with more than two X chromosomes (1 in 1,000 female births), she will develop **Poly-X syndrome,** which is characterized by normal appearance and fertility, but developmental delays, deficits in verbal reasoning, and below average intelligence. Likewise, a male who is conceived with more than one X chromosome in addition to his Y chromosome (1 in 750 male births are XXY) will develop **Klinefelter's syndrome,** a disease in which the phenotypical male develops enlargement of the hips and breasts at puberty ("Klinefelter's syndrome," 2008). Individuals with Klinefelter's syndrome are also taller than normal, are sterile, and score below normal on tests of verbal intelligence.

Recall from our discussion above that sex-linked traits show inheritance patterns that differ from autosomal traits. They occur because males only have one copy of the X chromosome (plus their Y chromosome), whereas females have two X chromosomes. As a result, males and females show different patterns of inheritance and severity of manifestation. Also called **X-linked diseases,** they produce single gene disorders that reflect the presence of defective genes on the X chromosome. Although there are both dominant and recessive X-linked diseases, some characteristics are common to X-linked disorders in general. For example, sex-linked genes are never passed from father to son because the Y chromosome is the only sex chromosome that passes from father to son. Furthermore, males are never merely carriers—if they have a mutated gene on the X chromosome, this gene is expressed in their phenotype. The inheritance patterns of X-linked diseases in families over several generations are complicated by the fact that males always pass their X chromosome to their daughters only, whereas females pass their X chromosomes to daughters and sons with equal frequency.

X-linked *dominant* diseases are those that are expressed in females when only a single copy of the mutated gene is present. Very few X-linked dominant diseases have been identified (e.g. hypophosphatemic rickets and Rett syndrome). An affected male with an X-linked dominant disease only has one X chromosome to pass on to his daughters, all of whom are affected because dominant disorders are expressed when only one copy of a mutation is present. Affected females, on the other hand, produce 50% unaffected and 50% affected offspring (whether sons or daughters). Still, males are usually more severely affected than females, and some X-linked dominant traits may even be lethal to males. These differences arise because males do not have a normal copy of the gene to balance the effects of the mutation on their single X chromosome.

X-linked *recessive* diseases are those in which a female must have two copies of the mutant gene in order for the mutant phenotype to develop. Many X-linked recessive disorders are well known, including color blindness, hemophilia, and Duchenne muscular dystrophy. Males are much more likely to be affected because they only need one copy of the mutant gene to express the phenotype. Because affected males carry only the defective gene, all of their daughters are carriers. Sons of mothers who have one affected and one unaffected gene have a 50% chance of inheriting the mutation.

Queen Victoria, ruler of England from 1837–1901, was a carrier of the gene for hemophilia, a disease in which a deficiency in one of several blood-clotting factors causes uncontrollable bleeding. She passed the harmful allele for this X-linked recessive trait on to one of her four sons and at least two of her five daughters. Her son Leopold had the disease and died at age 30, while her daughters were only carriers. By marrying into other European royal families, princesses Alice and Beatrice spread hemophilia to Russia, Germany, and Spain. By the early 20th century, ten of Victoria's male descendents had hemophilia. (See Figure 3.6 for Principles of Sex-Linked Inheritance.) For more information on hemophilia go to http://www.nlm.nih.gov/medlineplus/hemophilia.html.

FIGURE 3.6

PRINCIPLES OF SEX-LINKED INHERITANCE

Queen Victoria of England, ruler of England from 1837–1901, was a carrier of the gene for hemophilia, a disease in which a deficiency in one of several blood-clotting factors causes uncontrollable bleeding. She passed the harmful allele for this X-linked recessive trait on to one of her four sons and at least two of her five daughters.

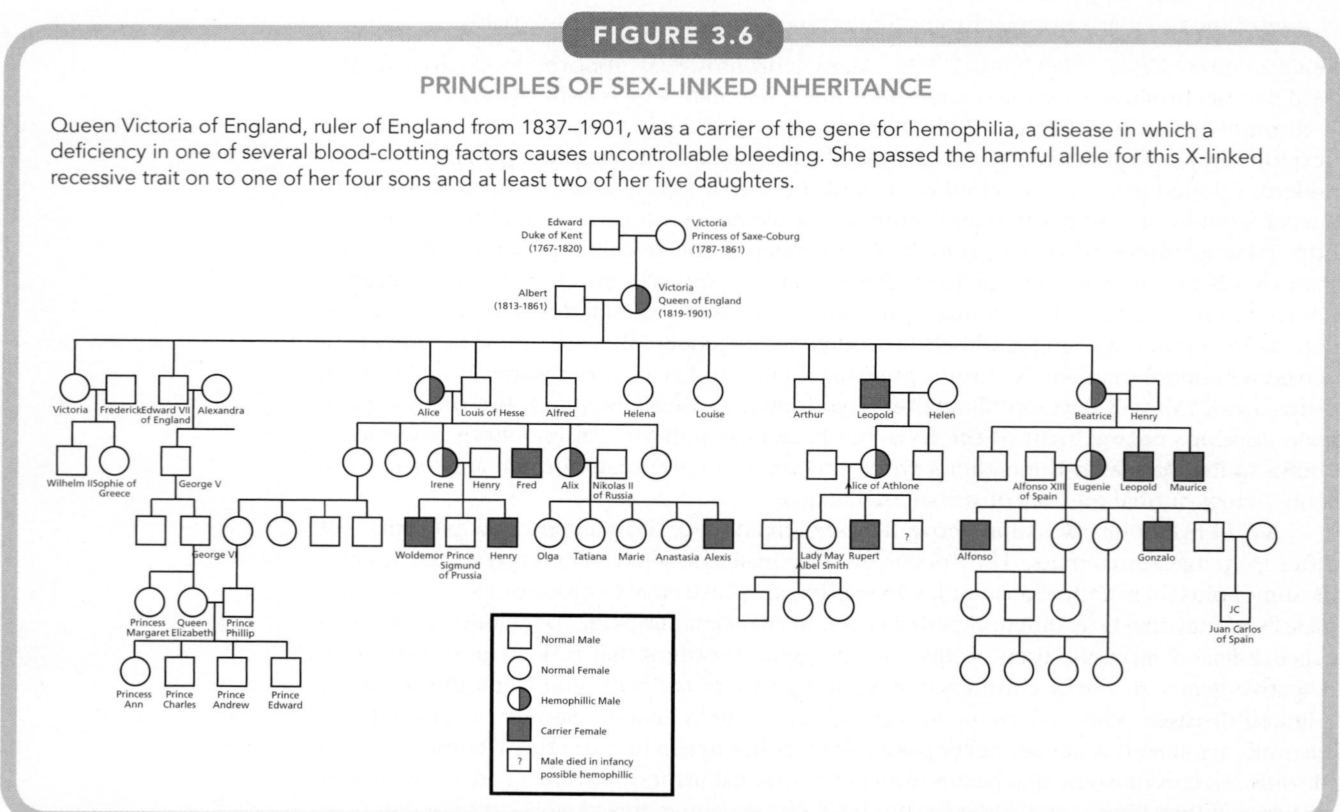

Source: From "Hemophilia: 'The Royal Disease'" by Yelena Aronova-Tiuntseva and Clyde Freeman Herreid, University at Buffalo, State University of New York. Copyright held by the National Center for Case Study Teaching in Science (NCCSTS), University at Buffalo, State University of New York. Used with permission.

GENE THERAPY. Gene therapy may prove especially helpful in treating sex-linked disorders because a single gene produces so many of the disorders. Gene therapy involves the treatment of a genetic defect either by directly correcting the affected gene or by inserting the correct gene alongside it in every cell that would normally manufacture the product of that gene. It is, then, theoretically possible to alter either **germ cells** (cells involved in reproduction, that is, ova, sperm, or their precursors) or **somatic cells** (any other cells in the body). There is general agreement among researchers and members of the medical profession that the alteration of germ cells should be undertaken with extreme caution until we have more knowledge of the potential benefits and risks of a treatment whose effects may be passed on from generation to generation. However, somatic therapy is limited to the individual concerned, and should therefore be subject to the same constraints as any other experimental therapy. Somatic gene therapy has already been successfully carried out for Severe Combined Immunodeficiency Disease, a rare genetic disorder affecting about 40 children each year worldwide.

There has also been considerable progress in treating a much more common genetic disease—cystic fibrosis (CF), a life-shortening disease of the respiratory and digestive systems. A missing protein in the genes of a person with cystic fibrosis prevents the body from processing salt correctly, resulting in a sticky mucous affecting the lungs and digestive system. Since 1990, scientists have experimented with different methods of gene therapy and prevention of infections in persons with cystic fibrosis. The Genetic Science Learning Center at the University of Utah describes why cystic fibrosis is a good candidate for gene therapy (Learn.Genetics, 2009). They ask: (1) Does the condition result from mutation in one or more genes? (yes) (2) Which genes are involved? (gene on Chromosome 7) (3) What do you know about the biology of the disorder? and (4) Will adding a normal copy of the gene fix the problem in the affected tissue? (yes) Question number 5 asks: Is it feasible to deliver the gene to cells of the affected tissue? The answer to this question requires more information. Fifteen years ago, all that doctors could do to treat cystic fibrosis was to administer antibiotics to lessen discomfort. Since the gene for CF was located in 1989, experimental gene replacement therapies have shown promise (Griesenbach, Geddes, & Alton, 2004; Mitomo, et al., 2010). See http://learn.genetics.utah.edu/content/tech/genetherapy/cysticfibrosis/candidate.html.

This disease provides a great example of how researchers are discovering new means each day for treating different diseases with gene therapy. Fears that gene therapy may lead to the treatment of "conditions" that are actually personality traits seem unfounded, because these qualities are not attributable to a single gene, but rather to a combination of the effects of several genes (Jacoby, 2004).

AUTOSOMOSAL ABNORMALITIES. The most commonly observed chromosomal abnormalities are called *autosomal abnormalities,* in which a sperm or egg carrying an extra autosome (i.e., non-sex-linked chromosome) combines with a normal gamete to produce a zygote with 47 chromosomes. Often referred to as *trisomy,* the extra chromosome appears in one of the 22 pairs of autosomes to yield 3 chromosomes of that type. The most frequently occurring form of trisomy (1 in 800 live births) is **Down syndrome** (or "trisomy 21"), in which the child inherits all or part of an extra 21st chromosome. People with Down syndrome have distinctive physical features characterized by a protruding tongue, sloped forehead, a slightly flat nose, shorter than usual limbs and elongated eyes, delayed milestones such as walking, and reduced cognitive functioning. They may also have congenital heart, ear, and eye defects. Environment plays an important part in supporting how children with Down syndrome progress developmentally. Researchers Ulrich, Ulrich, Angulo-Kinzler, and Yun (2001) developed a mini treadmill for children with Down syndrome who could sit for 30 seconds or more. When the children in the experimental group used the treadmill (with adult support) for five days a week (eight minutes a day), they walked significantly sooner than the control group did. Both groups received physical therapy every other week.

The likelihood that an infant will be born with a chromosomal abnormality increases dramatically among older mothers. There are several potential causes of this increase. One hypothesis is that the mother's egg cells have deteriorated due to age. Recall that sexually

CONNECTING WITH CHILDREN

Guidelines for Teachers: Teaching Genetics to Children

Identify reliable sources of information.
Examples
1. Consult universities such as University of Kansas Medical Center's Genetics Education Website: http://www.kumc.edu/gec/
2. Visit the Human Genome Research Institute at http://www.genome.gov/
3. See the National Center for Biotechnology Information http://www.ncbi.nlm.nih.gov/

Connect to art projects.
Examples
1. DNA Helix at the Lawrence Hall of Science http://www.eyeondna.com/2007/04/28/dna-helix-at-the-lawrence-hall-of-science/
2. Genome quilts at http://www.genomequilts.com/
3. DNA art http://www.eyeondna.com/2007/05/01/dna-art/

Use museum and virtual museum resources.
Examples
1. American Natural History Museum http://www.eyeondna.com/2007/05/01/dna-art/
2. Museum of Science and Industry Chicago http://www.msichicago.org/whats-here/exhibits/genetics/resources/
3. The Tech Museum, Stanford School of Medicine http://www.thetech.org/genetics/

Know your terms.
Examples
1. University of Kansas Medical Center glossary http://www.kumc.edu/gec/glossnew.html
2. GeneReview Illustrated Glossary http://www.ncbi.nlm.nih.gov/bookshelf/br.fcgi?book=gene&part=glossary

mature males continue to produce sperm throughout their lives, whereas females are born with all of their eggs already present in their ovaries. Exposure to environmental hazards (e.g., radiation, toxic chemicals) and poor nutrition are linked to chromosomal abnormality. Women who have a common medical condition in which they cannot metabolize folic acid (a B vitamin found in green vegetables, beans, fish, and eggs) show an elevated risk of having Down syndrome babies (James et al., 2000). When children are born healthy, however, the increased age of the mother relates to children's higher scores on cognitive tests (Cannon, 2009).

Research now indicates that the elevated risk of chromosomal abnormality is linked to *paternal* age as well (Fisch et al., 2003). Also, a risk of chromosomal abnormality increases if the father smokes, drinks heavily, or is exposed to radiation or toxic chemicals (Merewood, 2000). Recent research demonstrated that the older the father, the more likely the child will have decreased intelligence (Saha et al., 2009) and an increased risk of bipolar disorder (Dalman, 2009; Frans et al., 2008). Researchers think that perhaps a combination of genetic and social factors operates in males to increase the incidence of mutations as they age. However, scientists must complete more research to study how social and environmental factors influence the outcomes of children of older men. Scientists are also studying how chromosomal anomalies can be prevented.

Genetic Counseling

As our understanding of genetic disorders has increased, so has our ability to respond to them. **Genetic counseling** is a forum for helping prospective parents assess the likelihood of their children developing hereditary defects. This type of counseling is especially helpful for individuals who have genetic diseases in their family histories. Typically, the couple under genetic counseling will begin by learning as much as possible about their family histories in order to identify relatives who have had genetic disorders. The genetic counselor can then assess the likelihood that these parents' offspring will be born with genetic abnormalities. In addition to examining family history, genetic counselors will often conduct blood and DNA analyses to determine whether parents carry genes for hereditary disorders.

Think for a moment about your first exposure to genetics. For many, the concepts of DNA, chromosomes, and heritability were introduced in a high school biology class. Unbelievably, some first and second grade teachers are being asked to teach genetics to their

6- and 7-year-old pupils! The Genetics Education Center at the University of Kansas (http://www.kumc.edu/gec/) is among a growing list of resources available to educators. Offering lesson plans, interactive activities, and support, these facilities not only provide help to teachers, but also are instrumental in promoting awareness of genetics-related careers and opportunities for tomorrow's graduates. The ***Connecting with Children*** guidelines offer suggestions about teaching genetics to children.

Reproduction Challenges, Technologies, and Controversies

Reproductive Challenges

Kianne and her husband wanted children, but after two years of trying, they wondered if it would ever happen. There are three broad categories of infertility, each of which accounts for one-third of all cases such as Kianne's: *male factor infertility, female factor infertility,* and *unexplained infertility*. Two female conditions that interfere with reproduction are **Polycystic Ovary Syndrome (PCOS)** and repeated miscarriages. PCOS is "a condition in which women have high levels of certain hormones, may be infertile, and may have cysts on their ovaries" (NICHD, 2008). There are now reproductive technologies that are helping women like Kianne and her husband to have children.

Reproductive Technologies

The Centers for Disease Control define *infertility* as not being able to get pregnant after trying for one year (CDC, 2009a). Increasingly, women are achieving pregnancy as a result of Assisted Reproductive Technologies (ART) designed to aid fertilization or implantation, determine the sex of their baby (see the Casebook: *What Would You Do: Family Balancing*), or treat forms of infertility associated with advancing age. For example, young women undergoing radiation therapy for the treatment of cancer are advised that doing so will result in sterility, or the inability to reproduce. New technologies, however, now allow for the possibility of conceiving by cryogenically preserving (freezing) portions of the affected woman's ovaries for later use (Donnez et al., 2006) or by freezing fertilized ovum prior to radiation therapy or chemotherapy. Most often, ART is sought because one or both partners wishing to conceive has a history of infertility of at least one year or more duration. The CDC (2009a) reports that the term ART is used only if doctors handle both the woman's eggs and the man's sperm. The American Society of Reproductive Medicine (ASRM, 2009) reports that between 1985 and 2006, approximately 500,000 babies were born as a result of ART; however, ART is used in less than 3% of infertility services. Most infertility services include surgery or medication, rather than ART.

ART METHODS. ART methods range from the relatively inexpensive use of fertility-enhancing medications to the increasingly more costly procedures known as intrauterine insemination (IUI), *in vitro* fertilization (IVF), gamete intrafallopian transfer (GIFT), and zygote intrafallopian transfer (ZIFT). IUI involves a physician placing sperm provided by the intended father or a sperm bank directly into the uterus so that the likelihood of sperm meeting an egg is increased. IVF, ZIFT, and GIFT all rely on some form of fertilization of the egg outside the fallopian tube in a laboratory setting. At a given point following conception, and depending on the particular procedure, the zygote is placed in the uterus or fallopian tube prior to implantation.

With IVF, one or more blastocysts are placed directly into the uterus. Because implantation rates increase when more than one blastocyst is present, physicians used to routinely insert as many as five of them. However, given the increased risk of miscarriage associated with multiple pregnancies, researchers have challenged this practice and many doctors now deposit no more than one or two blastocysts. With ZIFT, the egg is fertilized in the laboratory and then placed in the fallopian tube, whereas GIFT involves placing sperm and eggs directly in the fallopian tube to fertilize on their own. These procedures typically cost approximately $12,000, with many couples electing to undergo several cycles of treatment.

In 1997 the world met Dolly, a Dorset ewe produced from the single cell of another sheep by Scottish scientists at the Roslin Institute. Prior to her birth, scientists thought mammals could not be successfully cloned, let alone survive for any length of time. The next year Dolly gave birth to a daughter named "Bonnie."

Although most U.S. insurance companies do not cover IVF, GIFT, or ZIFT, a few do to varying degrees.

It is important to keep in mind that ART does not ensure pregnancy. It is estimated that over 600,000 IUIs are performed in the United States each year, with just a 20–25% success rate. All together, approximately 25,000 IVF, GIFT, and ZIFT interventions are performed, with success rates ranging from 23–28%. This rate sounds low; however, the success rate each month for couples trying to conceive on their own is close to 20% (ASRM, 2009).

CLONING. In 1997, the possibility of human cloning moved out of the realm of science fiction when Scottish scientists at the Roslin Institute introduced us to "Dolly," a Dorset ewe produced from the single cell of another sheep. Prior to her birth scientists thought mammals could not be successfully cloned let alone survive for any length of time. The next year Dolly gave birth to a daughter named "Bonnie." This birth proved that Dolly was not only a successful living clone when she was born, but that she could thrive by growing, maturing to adulthood, and reproducing.

Cloning denotes the production of genetically identical organisms or cells. The term covers a range of techniques. Bacterial cloning has been carried out for some years with little controversy. At the other end of the spectrum, reproductive cloning of human beings has now become a realistic possibility and has consequently attracted considerable publicity. Scientists make a distinction between reproductive cloning, which produces genetically identical individuals, and techniques such as stem cell research that do not have this result but may have therapeutic benefits.

The issues concerning cloning are complex, but there has been a surprising degree of agreement across the medical, political, and religious spectrums. In general, we should use cloning techniques with caution. When sheep and other mammals are cloned, malformed embryos are produced and a high proportion of the offspring die within a few days of birth (there are only about 1 or 2 viable offspring for every 100 experiments). The same may apply in human cloning, where such a cost would be unacceptable. Physicians from the American Medical Association and scientists with the American Association for the Advancement of Science have both issued formal public statements advising against human reproductive cloning. Due to the inefficiency and lack of understanding about reproductive cloning, many experts believe that it would be unethical to attempt to clone humans. In addition, scientists do not know how cloning could affect the cloned person's mental development. Although factors such as intellect and mood may not be important for a cow or a mouse (though they could be), they are crucial for the development of healthy humans. With so many unknowns concerning reproductive cloning, most scientists consider the attempt to clone humans at this time potentially dangerous and ethically irresponsible.

STEM CELLS. One of the great advances in knowledge has also been a source of great controversy. Stem cells are cells that are able to differentiate into many types of cells, for example, muscle or brain cells, or more stem cells. Stem cells may originate as embryonic stem cells, non-embryonic stem cells, or induced pluripotent stem cells (iPSCs) (National Institute of Health Stem Cell Institute, 2009). See the ***Point/Counterpoint*** on stem cell research for an explanation of these differences and a discussion of the process.

Family Balancing

For centuries, females were believed to determine a baby's sex. In one of the most famous cases of false blame, the 16th century King Henry VIII of Britain annulled his marriage to Catherine of Aragon for her failure to produce a male heir. Later, another wife, Anne Boleyn,

POINT/COUNTERPOINT: How Should Stem Cell Research Be Conducted?

POINT

Embryonic stem cells are essential for research and advancing medicine. Embryonic stem cells are derived from embryos developed during *in vitro* fertilization that were not implanted, and were then donated to research. Undifferentiated embryonic "stem" cells are triggered to multiply indefinitely, and can be used to grow healthy tissues to replace damaged or diseased tissue. The National Institutes of Health Stem Cell Institute (2009) reports that "Diseases that might be treated by transplanting cells generated from human embryonic stem cells include Parkinson's disease, diabetes, traumatic spinal cord injury, Duchenne's muscular dystrophy, heart disease, and vision and hearing loss" (online).

According to the National Institutes of Health Stem Cell Institute, the development of stem cell lines that can produce many tissues of the human body is an important scientific breakthrough and has the potential to revolutionize the practice of medicine and improve the quality and length of life for many. *In vitro* fertilizations produce thousand of embryos that are not used, and, as a consequence, destroyed. These embryos could be used to advance medicine and save lives. In addition, embryonic stem cells divide more rapidly than adult stem cells, so they could potentially treat more diseases, and they don't contain the toxins sometimes found in adult cells (Scott, 2006).

COUNTERPOINT

Other kinds of cells can be used for research and advancing medicine. Those who argue against using embryonic stem cells believe that embryos are lives that are inherently valuable. They argue that destroying embryos to harvest the cells violates the sanctity of life. In addition, they suggest that money should be spent on research perfecting the use of non-embryonic adult stem cells (Genetic engineering, 2002-2010). A **non-embryonic adult stem cell** is a cell that can grow into different types of cells. Researchers are now finding these cells in many parts of the adult body; however, they are difficult to reproduce in the number needed for repairing damaged tissue in humans. Scientists produce **pluripotent stem cells** (iPSCs) by programming adult cells to an embryonic state. These cells have the potential to repair damaged tissues in a person without rejection when the pluripotent stem cells are retrieved from that person. These types of cells also could provide information on what drugs counteract particular diseases.

What do you think about stem-cell research? Conduct your own research on stem-cell research and discuss your findings with others. What are the moral issues? What are the potential benefits of stem-cell research?

was executed for the same reason. With consequences like these, it is perhaps not surprising that women sought to determine and predict the sex of their baby well in advance of birth! Commonly touted methods of sex selection included using particular positions during intercourse, bathing the vagina with vinegar or other agents, and ingesting a variety of herbal or medicinal products.

With the advent of scientific breakthroughs over the last century, we now know that *fathers,* not mothers, determine the sex of their offspring by supplying either an X or a Y chromosome to the developing zygote. In cultures such as the United States, China, and India, where gender-typing (categorizing people's life roles, career choices, behaviors, etc., according to their sex) is prevalent or one-child family planning policies exist, tales still abound regarding how to "naturally" produce a son or daughter that aren't that much different from those used in ancient times. Questions about family balancing are not as rare as you might think. One Internet site (GenSelect.com, 2004) offers guaranteed gender selection for $199 plus shipping. It features boy and girl "kits" containing ovulation detectors, a thermometer, special douches, and "gender specific" herbal supplements. Despite its claims, such home-use products are generally agreed by experts to be bogus, with no more likelihood of success than chance (CBSNews.com, 2004). In fact, two methods have been proven effective at sex selection, but both require medical intervention to sort sperm into X- or Y-bearing groups.

Family balancing is a medical form of sex selection that has become an increasingly viable and successful option for families who can afford its several thousand-dollar price tag. Families with an abundance of children of one sex may seek help to increase their chance of having a baby of the other sex. So, a couple with three boys, like the one referred to in the casebook, may decide to use family balancing to have a baby girl. Perhaps reflecting society's approval of the practice, ads for family balancing are appearing in publication outlets like the *New York Times* and on the Internet with greater frequency (Darnovsky, 2003).

Although family balancing may have its merits, the outcry against the practice of sex selection has been loud. In 2003, the United Kingdom's reproduction watchdog, the Human Fertilization and Embryology Authority, advised its government to ban the practice of sex selection, saying that the public was steadfastly against it (Kmietowicz, 2003). Even fertility specialists disagree over whether family balancing in particular, and sex selection in general, are acceptable (Kalb, 2004). The major objection to sex selection appears to lie in its potential for producing unwanted embryos that are rejected solely on the basis of their sex. In countries such as India and China where cultural practices favor boys, activists document that female infanticide is murderous, inhumane, "playing God," and will result in a disproportionate number of males in the general population. Indeed, there is evidence that this has happened in parts of North Africa (Amartya, 2003), China (Zhu, Lu, & Hesketh, 2009) and India (Sharma, 2003). For example, Zhu et al. reported that in China in 2005, there were 32 million more boys than girls under the age of 20.

Prenatal Development

In this section we examine the very beginnings of human development. As we explore all that happens to develop a fetus over the course of a nine-month pregnancy, we will also pay special attention to the interaction between events inside and outside the womb. For example, we will look at the role of experience on fetal learning and the impact of prenatal care on the emergent newborn. We hope this section will challenge your awareness and appreciation of the complexities involved in this first stage of life.

> Most of us count the length of our lives beginning with the day we were born. Indeed, the traditional practice in human development has been to treat birth as the beginning of experience. However, activities such as perceiving, growing, behaving and learning begin far before that day. Newborns have a history of months of experience, which shapes who they are and what they bring to their new situation. Birth gives the fetus a change in climate and scenery—and provides observers with an unprecedented opportunity to see and hear it—but this event is not the beginning of the infant's life. (Locke, 1993, p. 3)

Prior to birth, then, the seeds of development can be traced back to before the moment of conception with the formation of the sex cells: sperm and ova.

The Stages of Prenatal Development

One popular method of describing pregnancy divides it into three equal trimesters of 13 weeks, but those who study development prefer to divide prenatal growth according to an alternate set of sequential stages known as the *germinal stage* (fertilization to two weeks), the *embryonic stage* (two weeks to eight weeks), and the *fetal stage* (nine weeks to birth).

THE GERMINAL STAGE: FERTILIZATION TO TWO WEEKS. The average pregnancy lasts 40 weeks, based on the first day of a woman's last menstrual cycle. The first phase is known as the *germinal stage* and lasts around two weeks.

Although it takes just a few minutes for sperm to reach the spaghetti-thin fallopian tubes, they must first swim through the uterus, a journey of three to four inches. Furthermore, because of the acidic environment of the vagina, approximately 20% of sperm die immediately after ejaculation. Another 25% are deformed or immobile in the average male. Some sperm try to fertilize ordinary body cells before they ever reach the fallopian tubes, and half will swim up the wrong tube! Their numbers are reduced further by the tendency of the female's immune system to attack sperm. Taken together, these factors mean that only a few hundred sperm cells, out of all those millions that are released from the testes, reach the egg.

It takes the action of many sperm (more specifically, the release of enzymes from the sperm) to allow one to break through the outer layer of the ovum. When the head of a single sperm makes its way into the opening that has been forged, an immediate chemical reaction occurs that makes the egg impenetrable to any other sperm. The male and female cell nuclei approach each other, lose their nuclear membranes, and fuse to form a diploid cell with 46 chromosomes, a **zygote.** From this moment of conception, it will take about 266 days for the single-celled zygote to become a 200 billion-celled fetus ready to be born.

Fertilization takes up to 24 hours to complete. Approximately 12 hours later, the first cell division begins. Within 24 hours, the zygote also begins to move down the fallopian tube to the uterus. It develops a cleavage and begins rapid mitotic division (first into 2 cells, then 4 cells, then 8 cells and so on) for days until it reaches about 60 to 80 cells. These cell divisions take place every 12–15 hours, but the zygote does not begin to enlarge until it leaves the fallopian tube. The ball of cells, now called a **blastocyst,** compresses into compact layers. Three to four days after conception, the blastocyst enters the uterus, where it remains for another several days prior to implantation. The blastocyst forms a hollow, fluid-filled center. The inner cells form the embryonic disk, which will become the embryo, while the outer cells eventually form the **placenta,** the sac that nourishes and protects the embryo.

Six to ten days after fertilization, small tendrils emerge from the surface of the blastocyst and attach to the endometrial tissue lining of the uterus via the erosion of maternal vessels, glands, and tissue in a process known as **implantation.** Blood from the mother seeps directly into the blastocyst. Only approximately half of fertilized eggs will firmly implant; of those that do, typically another 50% will fail because of genetic abnormality or instability in the uterine environment and will be miscarried (Moore & Persaud, 2003). When this happens, the pregnancy ends in a spontaneous miscarriage, meaning that there is a natural end to the pregnancy well before a woman's due date. In fact, because the signs and symptoms of pregnancy typically do not appear until two weeks after fertilization, many women may miscarry never having known they were pregnant. They simply interpret the bleeding associated with miscarriage as a menstrual period. When this happens during the first trimester, the cause is widely believed to be the result of chromosomal abnormalities stemming from early cell division. Remarkably, only about 25% of zygotes complete the initial phase of prenatal development.

By the end of the germinal period, human cells have already begun to differentiate, that is, to assume specialized roles depending on their location. The zygote is now referred to as an **embryo** and the embryonic stage begins.

THE EMBRYONIC STAGE: TWO WEEKS TO EIGHT WEEKS. The embryonic stage lasts from the second through the eighth week of pregnancy and coincides with the implantation of the blastocyst into the uterus of the mother (see Figure 3.7 on the next page). The window of uterine receptivity to embryo implantation is just a few days, and implantation itself involves a series of complex interactions between the lining of the uterus and the embryo.

At about this time the mother's cervix forms a cervical plug that will protect the growing baby from foreign substances, and her breasts begin to enlarge to prepare for lactation (milk production). Other signs of pregnancy in the woman include a missed period, an unusual or abnormal period, soreness of breasts, and increased need to urinate.

As the embryo grows and develops a vascular system (blood supply), it establishes a more efficient means of obtaining nutrients and eliminating waste products via the interface of the placenta. The placenta is a remarkable organ. A completely self-contained package creates itself out of the combination of two individuals (the fetus and the mother), sustains itself, and discards itself with no adverse effects when its job is done. The usual full-term placenta weighs approximately one pound. During the nine-month period of **gestation** (pregnancy), it provides nutrition, gas exchange, waste removal, hormones, and immune support for the developing embryo/fetus. It is a living organ that has to be fed, just like the embryo/fetus, and it burns glucose to provide energy for its daily activities. Blood vessels connect to the placenta from both the mother and the embryo or fetus, but its hair-like villi prevent these two bloodstreams from mixing. The placental barrier is semi-permeable, meaning that it allows some substances to pass through but not others. Gases such as oxygen and carbon dioxide, salts, sugars, proteins, and fats are small enough to cross this barrier, but blood cells are too large to pass. The mother's blood flowing into the placenta delivers oxygen and nutrients into the embryo's bloodstream via the **umbilical cord,** which connects the embryo to the placenta. In addition to its primary goal of

FIGURE 3.7

AN IMPLANTED BLASTOCYST (EMBRYO)

Once the ovum is fertilized, it takes about five days for human embryos to reach the blastocyst stage. An inner cell mass of the blastocyst becomes the fetus; the outer layer of cells contributes to the development of the placenta. This photo illustrates an implanted blastocyst cultured for *in vitro* fertilization.

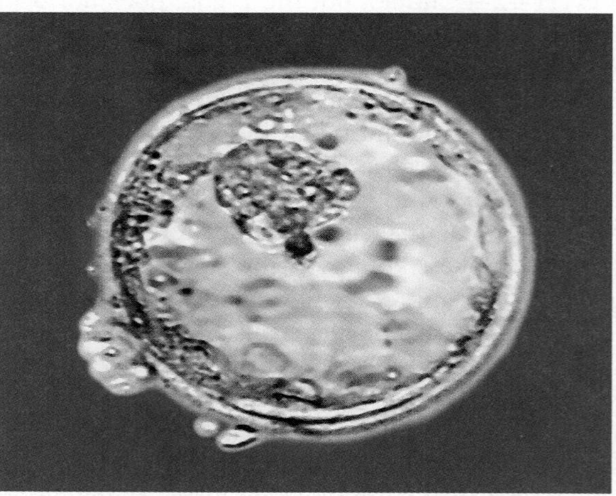

facilitating transport between mother and fetus, the placenta is also a major endocrine organ. In all mammals, the placenta synthesizes and secretes steroid hormones—progestins and estrogens.

During the brief period of embryonic development, and with the help of the placenta, virtually all of the future baby's body structures (respiratory, cardiovascular, gastrointestinal, and so forth) are formed (Moore & Persaud, 2003). In a process that scientists do not understand well, each embryonic cell becomes specialized to perform a particular function. For example, some cells become devoted to the respiratory system, serving as lung tissue or air ventricles, whereas others might develop into cells that make up muscle tissue. This process is called **differentiation.** Before differentiation, embryonic cells have the potential to become any type of tissue.

As the embryo produces more and more cells, these cells migrate toward their destination and the flat embryonic disc begins to change shape. The lengthwise growth of the embryo produces a head fold and a tail fold. Growth along the sides forms into a tube with a strong curvature that differentiates into three layers of cells: **endoderm,** which will become the internal glands, digestive tract, lungs, urinary tract, pancreas, and liver; **mesoderm,** which will become the muscles, bones, circulatory system, heart, blood, gonads, muscles, and skeleton; and **ectoderm,** which will become the nervous system, skin, teeth, and hair.

Of particular importance to ectoderm development is the formation of the **neural tube.** This precursor to the brain and spinal cord forms at about 21 days after conception—well before many women suspect they are pregnant. At three to four weeks' gestation, a linear heaping up of cells in the ectoderm proliferates and migrates into the center of the embryo. This bulge elongates as cells push out toward the ends, and the cells form a bulbous mass at one end, known as the *primitive node*. The primitive node develops into the *neural plate,* which folds and fuses to become the closed neural tube by the end of the fourth week. In a short time the neural tube will differentiate into the spinal cord and the brain.

By the end of the fourth week the heart tube forms and begins to force blood (of its own blood type) to circulate through the blood vessels of the embryonic disk (see Figure 3.8). The eyes, ears, nose, and mouth have begun to form and buds that will become the arms and legs appear. One month after conception the embryo is only about one-fourth inch long, but it is already 10,000 times the size it was as a zygote. The embryo is strangely proportioned,

FIGURE 3.8

A 4-WEEK-OLD HUMAN EMBRYO

By four weeks, the embryo has a head, tail, backbone, and limb buds, which will eventually become arms and legs. The beginnings of ears and eyes are also visible. Its heart is already beating, and the other organs are forming fast. An umbilical cord starts to grow between the embryo and the placenta. During this time, the embryo is especially sensitive to any drugs or infections capable of crossing the placenta from the mother.

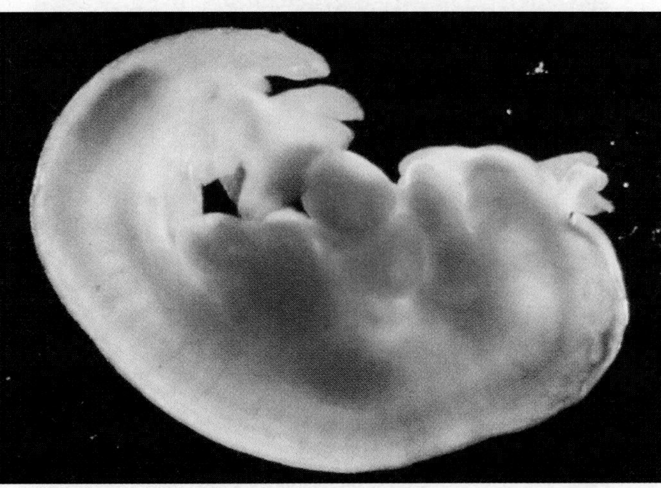

about the size of a raisin with the head constituting almost half of the entire length. But the embryo is quite functional in many domains. The embryonic stomach produces digestive juices, its kidneys filter blood, and its heart beats. In the second month, the embryo becomes more humanlike in appearance. A primitive tail is enclosed with tissue and becomes the tailbone or coccyx at the base of the spine. Facial features are visible, including a mouth and a tongue. The eyes have corneas and lenses.

In the seventh week, the ears are well formed and the embryo has a rudimentary skeleton. The brain also develops rapidly during this time and it directs the first muscular contractions. During the seventh and eighth weeks of gestation, sexual development begins with the appearance of a primordial genital ridge. Altogether, the process of sexual differentiation takes several weeks to complete and it is not until the 16th week that an ultrasound performed on the mother might clearly identify the fetus as a girl or boy.

In summary, by the end of the embryonic period, the organism has a distinctly human appearance, but it is just an inch in length and weighs less than an ounce! Furthermore, although all organ systems exist by the end of this embryonic period, the functions of these systems are limited.

THE FETAL STAGE: WEEKS NINE TO BIRTH. In humans, the embryo is called a **fetus** after all the body's structures have begun to form. The fetal period is the longest of the three developmental phases and lasts from the ninth week of pregnancy through birth in the fortieth week. Sometimes referred to as "the growth and finishing stage," the period of the fetus is primarily associated with the laying down of bone, rapid growth, and body system integration. Let's examine some of those developments a bit more closely.

During the first part of this period, the size of the fetus's body catches up with the outsized head, making it look more human, although the legs are still slightly short. Protected by the amniotic fluid, the fetus can move around and flex its limbs. By 12 weeks, the fetus can hear sounds, and its skin is sensitive to touch (see Figure 3.9).

In the third month of gestation, the organ systems become coordinated: The nervous and muscular systems begin working together to allow the fetus to stretch, kick, and leap around the womb; the digestive and excretory systems begin working together to allow the

FIGURE 3.9

A 10–12 WEEK-OLD FETUS

From week 9 (the 11th week of pregnancy) the developing embryo is called a fetus. The size of its body catches up with the outsized head, making it look more human, although the legs are still slightly short. Protected by the amniotic fluid, the fetus can move around and flex its limbs. By 12 weeks, it can hear sounds, and its skin is sensitive to touch.

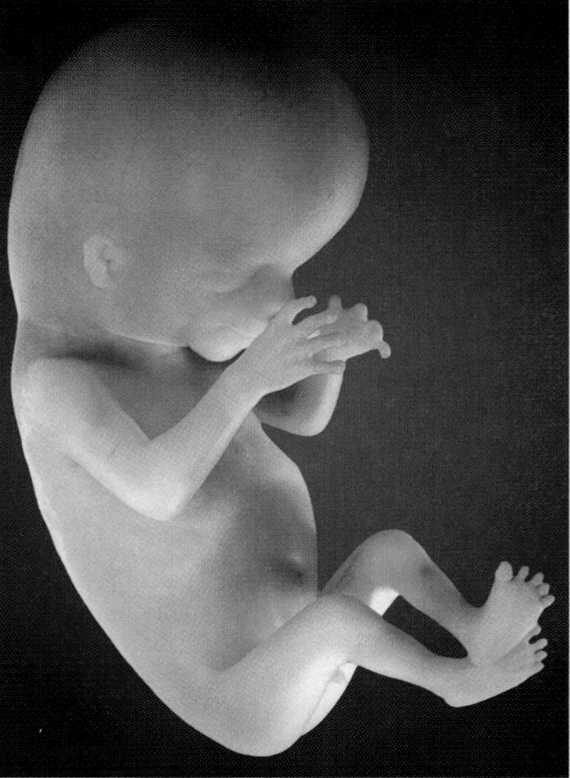

fetus to swallow, digest nutrients, and urinate. By the end of the third month, the fetus's reproductive system already contains immature ova or sperm cells, even though it is still only about 2 inches long and weighs less than an ounce. Additionally, by the fifth and sixth months, the fetus's fingernails harden, its skin thickens, its sweat glands are functioning, and eyebrows, eyelashes, and scalp hair have appeared. The fetus is covered by a white cheesy substance called **vernix,** which protects the skin from chapping during the long time it will live in fluid, and by a fine layer of body hair called *lanugo* (which helps the vernix stick to the skin).

Fetal actions such as thumb sucking and kicking become increasingly refined by the second trimester. Nerve cell clusters fire spontaneously and cyclically without practice or environmental stimulation, and fetal movement plays an important part in neuromuscular development. For example, movement of the limbs helps to sculpt the joints. At this time bones and muscles continue development, and movement of the arms, legs, fingers, and toes is common.

Fetal taste buds are present by 7 to 9 weeks' gestation. By 12 weeks, the taste buds contain pores with a direct channel to the oral environment. Fetuses first become sensitive to sweet tastes, then bitter ones, and finally to salt. If the amniotic fluid is sweetened, fetuses will ingest more of it; if it contains alcohol, they will ingest less. Likewise, the fetal sense of smell is active by 28 weeks. By 8 to 9 weeks, the cochlea of the inner ear has completed its turns and the hair cells of the ear have differentiated. (See Figure 3.10 for drawings of the sequence of embryo and fetal development from week 3-1/2 to 32 weeks.)

FIGURE 3.10

DEVELOPMENT OF THE EMBRYO AND THE FETUS

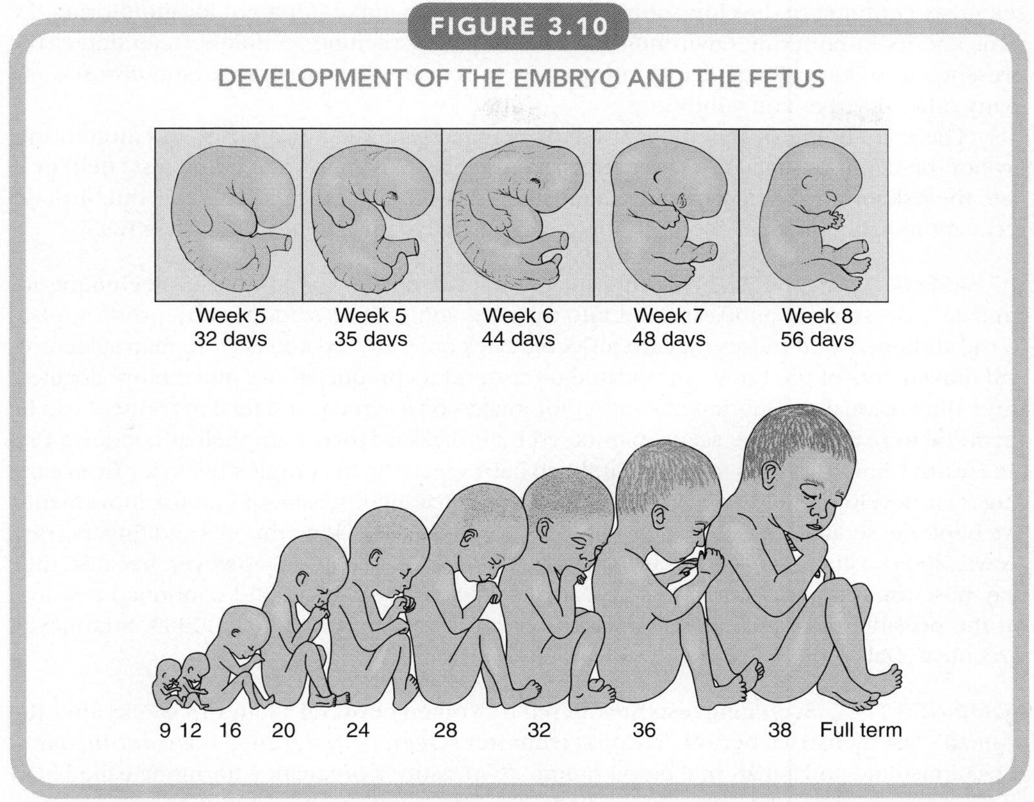

By the third trimester the fetus has reached the age of viability, meaning that it can survive outside of the womb (Moore & Persaud, 2003). Organ systems mature rapidly during this time as 28- to 32-week-old fetuses suddenly begin to show organized and predictable cycles of heart rate activity, gross motor activity, and sleepiness/wakefulness—the nervous system organization required for survival. However, fetuses born this young still require oxygen assistance. This is largely because the pulmonary alveoli (air sacs) in the lungs are too immature to inflate and exchange oxygen for carbon dioxide on their own (Moore & Persaud, 2003). By the middle of the ninth month, less room in the uterus means the fetus is less active and sleeps more (Tsiaras & Werth, 2002).

Late in pregnancy the fetal cells begin to produce increasing amounts of **oxytocin,** a powerful smooth muscle stimulant hormone that causes receptors in the uterus to respond and contract. High estrogen levels stimulate the placenta to make prostaglandins, which also stimulate contractions. These irregular contractions promote the toning of the uterine muscles and the dilation of the cervix, and help position the head of the fetus into the gap between the pelvic bones through which it will be pushed. As delivery nears, most fetuses assume an upside-down position—another factor that limits movement. At birth, the average fetus is 18–20 inches long and weighs 6-1/2–7-1/2 pounds. There is much more to know about prenatal development.

Prenatal Testing and Fetal Monitoring

During the course of prenatal development, screening and diagnostic procedures to determine the health and development of the zygote, embryo, or fetus are performed on mothers who seek prenatal care. Prenatal testing and fetal monitoring, while frightening because the outcomes are unknown, have the benefit of allowing parents to make informed decisions rather than reactive ones. The detection of problems before birth allows parents to seek possible intervention or treatment, including medical therapy, gene therapy, and prenatal surgery. It also can help parents to make difficult moral and ethical choices concerning the termination of a pregnancy, or make preparations for raising a child with disabilities or a disease. There are many medical technologies available to assess prenatal health, and scientists continue to develop sophisticated techniques and equipment for monitoring the fetus and its intrauterine environment. Today's fetal screening techniques can detect the presence of sickle cell anemia, Huntington's chorea, Down syndrome, cystic fibrosis, and many other diseases and conditions.

There are numerous methods used for prenatal screening, diagnosis, and monitoring. Five of the major prenatal tests are discussed in more detail here. Screening tests help evaluate the risk for birth defects while diagnostic tests accurately diagnose or rule out birth defects. Monitoring includes methods for "keeping an eye on" the health of the fetus.

ULTRASOUND IMAGING. Ultrasound imaging is the most commonly used technique for prenatal assessment. Sounds are sent into the pregnant woman's body from a probe applied to the abdomen, and pulses that are reflected back are analyzed and used to map structures and movements of the body. An updated ultrasound technique shows much more detailed, three-dimensional or four-dimensional color images on a screen, and fetal movement can be recorded in real time. The scans, pioneered by Professor Stuart Campbell at London's Create Health Clinic, allow us to see the unborn baby engaging in complex behavior from early stages of development. Such movements include making coordinated motor movements, eye blinking, scratching, smiling, crying, hiccupping, and sucking thumbs and fingers (BBC News, 2004). Ultrasounds seem to have no ill effects on the fetus; however, because they may raise the temperature of the fetus, medical scientists recommend continued research on the possible biological effects of this procedure (Abramowicz et al., 2009; Stratmeyer, Greenleaf, Dalecki, & Salvesen, 2008).

COMBINED TEST. Screening tests are offered to women between 11 and 13 weeks after the woman's last menstrual period. The first trimester screening test, called the *combined test,* uses ultrasound and a maternal blood sample to measure a pregnancy hormone called hCG and pregnancy-associated protein A (PAPP-A). The hormone hCG tends to increase and PAPP-A decreases when the woman is carrying a fetus with Down syndrome. The specialized ultrasound exam measures the back of the fetus's neck, which has increased thickness in cases of Down syndrome. The lab determines the woman's risk for chromosomal abnormalities using the blood tests.

ALPHA-FETOPROTEIN TEST (AFP). Another screening test is conducted in the second trimester approximately 17–20 weeks after the woman's last menstrual period. The March of Dimes (2010c) reports that this test, which used to be called the *alpha-fetoprotein (AFP) test,* is now called by various names including the *maternal serum screening test*, the *multiple marker screening,* the *triple screen,* or the *quad screen*. Abnormalities are detected by testing the mother's blood for the presence of AFP—a protein produced by the fetus's liver—hormones estriol and hCG, and often inhibin A. These combined screens are useful in detecting Down syndrome and neural tube defects such as spina bifida and anencephaly. Abnormal results are often verified by more sensitive tests such as amniocentesis. Often, women have both the Combined Test and the Alpha-Fetoprotein Test (AFP) (Malone et al., 2005).

AMNIOCENTESIS. As noted above, when the mother's age increases, so does the risk of abnormality in the fetus. For this reason, mothers over 35 routinely are advised to undergo prenatal screening. Amniocentesis is a prenatal diagnostic test in which a sample of the amniotic fluid, which surrounds the fetus, is withdrawn via a large hollow needle in the mother's abdomen. The chromosomes within fetal cells found in the fluid are examined to determine the sex of the fetus and/or the presence of chromosomal abnormalities such as Down syndrome. Amniotic fluid can also be used to detect the presence of more than 100 genetic disorders, including Tay-Sachs disease, cystic fibrosis, sickle cell anemia, and hemophilia. Amniocentesis does carry a small risk of miscarriage (approximately 1 case in 300 to 1 in 500) (March of Dimes, 2010a.).

CHORIONIC VILLUS SAMPLING (CVS). In this diagnostic technique, cells that contain fetal tissue are collected from the villi (hair-like protrusions) of the chorion, the membrane that surrounds the fetus. CVS can be done sooner than amniocentesis (as early as the 10th–12th week of gestation). However, both can be used to diagnose chromosomal, metabolic, and blood-borne conditions; identify congenital defects (like muscular dystrophy); assess levels of alpha-fetoprotein that indicate neural tube deficits; and screen DNA. CVS is performed either by inserting a catheter into the mother's vagina (transcervical CVS) or by inserting a needle in her abdomen though the chorion (transabdominal CVS). Fetal cells are extracted and tested for hereditary abnormalities, with the results available in as few as 24 hours. However, because CVS has a greater chance of inducing miscarriage (approximately 1 in 100 cases) than amniocentesis (MayoClinic.com, 2010), it is used only if there is a concern after a screening test, a family history of chromosomal abnormalities, or maternal age over 35. Even so, all women have the option of having CVS and an amniocentesis.

Early Interventions and Ethical Questions

Medical and technological advances have made it possible to treat many hereditary disorders detected by prenatal or early postnatal screening. For example, until recent years babies born with **phenylketonuria (PKU),** a genetic disorder characterized by a lack of ability to produce the enzyme that allows metabolism of phenylalanine (which is found in many foods including milk), suffered from microencephaly (abnormal smallness of the brain), congenital heart disease, and severe mental retardation. In babies with PKU, phenylalanine accumulates in the body and is converted to a harmful substance that attacks the nervous system. A simple blood test for newborn infants now allows doctors to determine if an infant has PKU within a few days after birth. If so, the infant is placed on a low-phenylalanine diet and suffers few, if any, of the harmful consequences. Furthermore, recent evidence has shown that putting a pregnant mother who is a carrier of PKU on a low-phenylalanine diet reduces the incidence of microencephaly and congenital heart disease in her unborn child (Matalon, Acosta & Azen, 2003).

Potentially devastating effects of other hereditary diseases can be minimized or controlled if detected early. In fact, medical and surgical techniques are now commonly performed on fetuses in the womb (Cortes & Farmer, 2004). For example, tumor-like masses on the lungs of the fetus are nearly 100% fatal after birth, but can be successfully removed *in utero* (Adzick & Kitano, 2003). Necessary drugs or hormones can also be administered to the developing fetus (Hunter & Yankowitz, 1996), bone marrow transplants can be conducted, and genetically transmitted defects of the heart, neural tube, urinary tract, and respiratory system can be surgically repaired *in utero* (Yankowitz, 1996). Fetuses who test positive for Turner's or Klinefelter's Syndrome can be placed on hormone therapy; diabetes can be treated prenatally by a low-sugar maternal diet and periodic doses of insulin. See http://fetus.ucsfmedicalcenter.org/our_team/research.asp to view videos of prenatal surgery.

Prenatal interventions have associated risks. Fetal surgical procedures have a high rate of miscarriage associated with them. For example, the risk of fetal death during urinary tract surgery (which is one of the safest procedures) is 5–10% from the surgery itself, with another 20% suffering serious complications.

Prenatal Growth in Context

Context includes the environment, situation, circumstances, and conditions in which the pregnancy exists. It also includes how the fetus influences its own development.

FETAL PRACTICING, LEARNING, AND EXPERIENCING. Much of prenatal research focuses on the study of fetal motor, sensory, perceptual, and learning capabilities, and how they contribute to the development of new structure and function. Recent "evidence of fetal learning has been used to suggest that you may be able to teach the fetus, enroll it in a prenatal University and produce superbabies" (Fetal Behaviour Research Center, 2009). While we hope that this is a "tongue in cheek" suggestion, increased understanding of prenatal learning will allow physicians to detect abnormalities during the prenatal period and determine the effects of maternal nutrition and exposure to toxins, in addition to helping us understand fetal learning.

Innovative research completed in the 1980s and 1990s opened our eyes to the capabilities of infants to pay attention to, learn, and remember particular *speech* sounds that they hear in the womb. See the ***Relating to Every Child*** discussion (next page) for some examples.

RELATING TO

EVERY CHILD

▸ Communicating Before Birth

IT NOW APPEARS that parents can begin "relating" to their child even before birth. In one study, fetuses of 26–34 weeks' gestation exhibited marked differences in heart rate in response to the presentation of vowel sounds (Fifer & Moon, 1994). Further evidence for prenatal learning comes from the fact that prenatal language experience affects the responsiveness of the infant after birth. Newborns exhibit behavioral preferences for sounds they have perceived *in utero*, including, for instance, their mother's voice (DeCasper & Fifer, 1980) and a melodic story (*The Cat in the Hat*) read aloud by their mother (Panneton, 1985, cited in Cooper, 1997).

Research that is more recent has confirmed the ability of fetuses to hear during the last trimester (James, Spencer, & Stepsis, 2002) and remember for short periods. Dirix, Nijhuis, Jongsma, and Hornstra (2009) tested fetuses' memory at 30, 32, 34, 36, and 38 weeks by exposing them to stimulation and viewing through ultrasonography how they responded and when they stopped responding (habituated). If the fetuses remembered, then the next time they were exposed to that stimuli they would stop responding sooner than they had during a previous session. Thirty-week-old fetuses remembered for 10 minutes and 34-week-old fetuses remembered the stimuli four weeks later.

Around the world, fetuses have even learned the characteristics of their native language. In one well-known study, Moon, Cooper and Fifer (1993) presented 2-day-old infants of English- and Spanish-speaking parents with both languages and discovered that the newborns preferred a native language recording to a foreign language recording. In other experiments, French 4-day-olds could distinguish changes among syllables (the elementary unit of French), but they could not discriminate between morae (the elemental unit of Japanese). French 4-day-olds could also discriminate French from Russian speech, even when the infants only heard the melody of the speech, not the speech sounds (Mehler, Dupoux, Nazzi & Dehaene-Lambertz, 1996; Mehler et al., 1988).

There are additional factors that affect prenatal development, including the role of the mother's relationship with her developing fetus, maternal nutrition, and maternal stress.

PREGNANCY AS RELATIONSHIP. The mother and fetus not only respond physically to one another, they also respond socially to their shared experience of embodiment. For example, when the baby presses on the mother's bladder, she may respond by making another trip to the bathroom; but she also responds socially, with amusement, irritation, anger, sometimes even with pleasure at the apparent liveliness of the baby. In ways like this, social and emotional overlays give meaning to the experience. As the fetus takes up more space in the mother's body and becomes more capable of responding to its environment, mother and fetus must come to a shared cycle. Negotiating sleep during pregnancy is another example. Mothers need to find ways of soothing fetuses to sleep when they want to sleep; they must learn when to lie down and ease the fetus into quiet or when to give up and get out of bed for a while (Katz, 2000).

In the beginning of pregnancy, the embryo/fetus does not have sleep-wake cycles that scientists recognize. However, by 33 weeks (about two months before birth) fetuses have developed both **Rapid Eye Movement (REM) sleep,** during which dreams take place, and deep non-REM sleep. Gingras, Mitchell, and Grattan (2005) discovered that the fetus experiences four behavioral states that are comparable to those of the neonate: 1F (quiet sleep), 2F (active state), 3F (quiet awake), and 4F (active awake). These researchers note that State 5, or crying, has been "observed on ultrasound, and has been captured on video recordings and include: an initial exhalation movement associated with mouth opening and tongue depression, followed by a series of three augmented breaths, the last breath ending in an inspiratory pause followed by an expiration and settling."

When, from birth, babies sleep by their mother's side throughout the night (as is the case throughout most of the world), the transition from inside to outside is part of a continuum (Katz, 2000). The sleep-wake cycle of the mother and baby can stay synchronized. In American society, mothers and babies often sleep separately and new parenthood is sometimes experienced as an exercise in sleep deprivation. This is not a biological fact of life, but a cultural creation.

MATERNAL NUTRITION. Researchers Morgane, Mokler, and Galler (2002) describe two conditions that represent problems with maternal nutrition. The term *undernutrition* is used if all the nutrients required by the species are available in the diet, but the amount ingested is insufficient. The term *malnutrition* is used if one or more of the essential nutrients is missing or if the nutrients are present but in the wrong proportions. Either one contributes to cognitive and behavioral challenges in the child. Morgane and colleagues (2002) emphasize that "Malnutrition is a worldwide problem affecting millions of unborn and young children during the most vulnerable stages of their brain development. As such it alters various maturational events in the brain resulting in behavioral abnormalities, altered cognitive functioning, and disturbances in learning and memory" (p. 471). Other studies also demonstrate problems for the fetus and newborn related to the type of diet of the mother; for example, maternal high-fat diets contribute to the development of nonalcoholic fatty liver disease in the fetus and newborn of both lean and obese primates (McCurdy et al., 2009).

Expectant mothers who have plenty to eat must also vigilantly add certain vitamins, minerals, and other nutrients to their diets for optimal care of their fetuses. Women especially need diets rich in protein to ensure healthy brain functioning in the baby (Morgane, Mokler, & Galler, 2002). The March of Dimes ("Folic Acid," 2010), an organization whose mission is to improve the health of babies by preventing birth defects, premature birth, and infant mortality, emphasizes that folic acid is *critical* for women of child-bearing age and pregnant women to help prevent neural tube defects in the fetus. Folic acid is a B-complex vitamin found in vitamins, fresh fruits and green vegetables, dried beans, orange juice, and fortified cereals. Programs such as the Special Supplemental Nutrition Program for Women, Infants and Children (WIC) help to increase the birth weight of babies of low-income women by providing the mothers with the nutritional foods they need during pregnancy (Reichman & Teitler, 2003).

MATERNAL STRESS. When a mother is emotionally aroused, her body produces powerful hormones such as cortisol and adrenaline. These can cross the placental barrier, enter the fetus's bloodstream, and increase its motor activity. The good news is that low to moderate levels of stress are unlikely to cause problems in pregnancy for most women. The bad news is that very prolonged and severe emotional stress and anxiety have been associated with risk for spontaneous abortion, preterm labor, preeclampsia, reduced birth weight, and reduced head circumference (Mulder et al., 2002). There is no objective measure of stress, however, for each woman responds differently to stressors (e.g., divorce, death of a family member, anxiety-producing job).

THE IMPORTANCE OF SOCIAL SUPPORT. *Social support* refers to all those individuals, institutions, and resources that are available to women that enhance and contribute to a positive pregnancy experience. A pregnant woman's spouse, friends, and family members serve as social supports when they act as advocates on her behalf, serve as caregivers to children she already has while she attends a prenatal appointment, remind her to take her prenatal vitamins, or support her decisions—for example, to breastfeed when the baby is born. Individuals make strong social supports, then, when they provide reassurance, give practical support (like transportation to and from prenatal appointments), act as role models, and share in the joys and burdens of pregnancy. Other sources of social support include childbirth education classes, patient-centered health care centers, support groups, and media geared toward helping with the pregnancy experience.

Teratology

A discussion of teratogens is so important to the health and well-being of the embryo/fetus that it deserves recognition apart from those elements of prenatal development that were discussed earlier in this chapter. A **teratogen** is any disease, drug, or other environmental agent that can harm a developing embryo or fetus. Before considering the effects of teratogens, we need to remember that 96–97% of infants are considered perfectly healthy and normal (Children's Hospital Boston, 2005–2009). Not surprisingly, the effects of a teratogen on a body part or organ system are worst during the period when that structure is forming and growing most rapidly (during so-called "sensitive periods"). Not all embryos or fetuses are equally affected by a particular teratogen; susceptibility to harm is influenced by both the unborn child's and the mother's constitutions and the quality of the prenatal environment. In the same vein, similar effects can be caused by different teratogens. Furthermore, the longer the exposure or the higher the dose, the more likely that serious harm will be done. An embryo or fetus can be affected by its father's as well as its mother's exposure to some teratogens. The long-term effects of a teratogen often depend on the quality of the postnatal environment.

In sum, then, to aid our understanding of the consequences of teratogens, there are three things to know about the exposure: its timing (when during prenatal development the exposure occurred), duration, and amount. Coverage of specific teratogens is divided below according to whether they fall under the category of diseases or drugs.

MATERNAL DISEASES. Maternal diseases frequently do more harm to the developing fetus than they do to the mother, because the fetus has an immature immune system that often cannot produce enough antibodies to combat infection effectively. For example, maternal rubella (German measles) has been correlated with a number of birth defects including blindness, deafness, cardiac abnormalities, and mental retardation. As another example, toxoplasmosis is a disease caused by a parasite found in many animals. Expectant mothers can acquire this parasite by eating undercooked meat or by handling the feces of an infected family cat. Although toxoplasmosis causes only mild cold-like symptoms in adults, it can cause severe eye and brain damage if transmitted to the fetus during the first trimester, and can cause miscarriage later in pregnancy (CDC, 2008).

Sexually transmitted diseases are also particularly common and hazardous to prenatal development. The CDC's 2006 *Guidelines for Treatment of Sexually Transmitted Diseases* (CDC, 2009b) recommends that on their first prenatal visit pregnant women be screened for STDs, which may include chlamydia, gonorrhea, hepatitis B, HIV, and syphilis. Mothers with genital herpes infections are advised to deliver through caesarean section to avoid infecting their babies.

Human immunodeficiency virus (HIV), which causes Acquired Immunodeficiency Syndrome (AIDS), can be transmitted through the placenta, during birth (where there may be an exchange of blood between the mother and child as the umbilical cord separates from the placenta), or after birth through the mother's breast milk (CDC, 2006). "The number of children reported with AIDS attributed to perinatal HIV transmission peaked at 945 in 1992 and declined 95% to 48 in 2004 (*1*), primarily because of the identification of HIV-infected pregnant women and the effectiveness of antiretroviral prophylaxis in reducing mother-to-child transmission of HIV (*2*)" (CDC, 2006). Again, early screening before becoming pregnant or causing a pregnancy is critically important, especially for adolescents and young women. Nearly half of HIV-positive U.S. adolescents and young adults are unaware of their infection, and only 22% of sexually active high school students are tested for HIV (Reuters, June 25, 2009).

DRUGS. Substances that are perfectly safe for adult humans to ingest can be toxic for developing embryos and fetuses. Heavy caffeine use has been linked to miscarriage, low birth weight, and higher neonatal heart rates during both quiet and active sleep (Schuetze & Zeskind, 1998). The results of recent research on the effects of caffeine on fetal death are mixed, however. A study of 88,482 pregnant women found that the consumption of coffee during pregnancy was associated with fetal death, especially after 20 weeks gestation (Bech, Nohr, Vaeth, Henriksen, & Olsen, 2005), whereas a more recent study of 2,407 pregnancies indicates that there is little risk of miscarriage from typical use of caffeine (Savitz, Chan, Herring, Howards, & Hartmann, 2008). Women who take psychotropic medications (e.g., antidepressants) prior to their pregnancy should discuss with their physicians *if* they should stop taking their medications and if so, *how*, as abrupt discontinuation is not recommended (Einarson, Selby, & Koren, 2001). We emphasize that pregnant women and women considering

The symptoms associated with mothers' consumption of alcohol vary along a full spectrum from milder to more severe, but even social drinking has been linked to some problems.

pregnancy should always consult with their physician about updated research on the effects of caffeine and medications during pregnancy and breastfeeding.

Alcohol easily crosses the placenta and affects fetal cells and tissues (Zhang, Sliwowska, & Weinberg, 2005). In addition, alcohol changes the hormone system of the mother, which has a continuing negative effect on the fetus (Weinberg, Sliwowska, Lan, & Hellemans, 2008). The symptoms associated with alcohol exposure in fetuses clearly increase as the dose increases, but even social drinking (1 to 3 ounces per day) has been linked to **fetal alcohol spectrum disorder (FASD)** with symptoms of poor motor skills, attention problems, and below normal intellectual performance.

Babies with **fetal alcohol syndrome (FAS),** the most severe type of FASD, are likely to display excessive irritability, hyperactivity, seizures, and tremors. They are smaller and lighter than normal age-mates; score well below average in intelligence tests throughout childhood and adolescence; and have a variety of attention problems including distractibility (Lee, Mattson, & Riley, 2004). Many children of alcoholic mothers suffer from microencephaly (small head) and malformations of the heart, limbs, joints, and face. In fact, of the causes that are understood, FAS is the *leading* cause of mental retardation (Connor, Sampson, Bookstein, Barr & Streissguth, 2001).

In 1981 (updated and reissued in 2005), the United States Surgeon General concluded that no amount of alcohol consumption is entirely safe and urged women not to drink at all during pregnancy. Yet, in a summary of research on the effects of alcohol, Spong (2006) reported that 50% of women of childbearing age consume alcohol, 15–20% of women continue to drink when they are pregnant, and 1 in 25 pregnant women reported binge drinking. These numbers reinforce the need for continued educational initiatives about the dangers of drinking alcohol during pregnancy.

Nicotine is believed to constrict placental blood vessels, temporarily deprive the fetal brain of oxygen, stimulate the cardiovascular system, and depress the respiratory system. High maternal smoking rates have been consistently associated with low birth weight and spontaneous abortion. The data on long-term developmental and behavioral effects are still controversial, but disturbances in neuronal pathways and abnormalities in cell proliferation and differentiation have been reported in animal studies of *in utero* exposure to nicotine. Prenatal exposure to nicotine may also put humans at higher risk for psychiatric problems, including substance abuse (Ernst, Moolchan, & Robinson, 2001). A recent study by Shaw and colleagues (2009) measured a nicotine metabolite (cotinine) in the blood of pregnant women rather than relying on women's self-reporting of how much they smoked during pregnancy. Increased cotinine relates to the number of babies born with orofacial clefts and neural tube defects. Obviously, maternal smoking during pregnancy increases the chances

of babies born with birth defects. The research implications are clear. Women should make strong efforts to quit or reduce their smoking and physicians and clinicians should educate women on the dangers of smoking during pregnancy and after (Nichter, Adrian, Goldade, Tesler, & Muramato, 2008).

Each year in the United States, there are as many as 700,000 infants who have had prenatal exposure to marijuana, cocaine, and heroin. Marijuana is the most frequently used illicit drug. One study found that prenatal exposure to marijuana was negatively associated with tasks that required visual memory, analysis, and integration (Fried, Watkinson & Gray, 2003). Heroin, methadone, and other narcotic drugs have been linked to miscarriage, premature delivery, and fetus/infant death. Approximately 60–80% of babies exposed to narcotics are born addicted to the drug, and in the first month display such withdrawal symptoms as vomiting, dehydration, convulsions, irritability, and high pitched crying.

Cocaine exposure also inhibits the uptake and metabolism of neurotransmitters such as dopamine, norepinephrine, and serotonin, thereby increasing their levels in the infant's brain. The Miami Prenatal Cocaine Study, one of the nation's largest single-site studies, followed 200 African American children exposed to cocaine prenatally compared to 176 noncocaine-exposed children for seven years. This study sought to determine whether there was a relationship between the severity of prenatal cocaine exposure and problems in language development in the children from 3 to 7 years of age. The researchers (Bandstra, Vogel, Morrow, Xue, & Anthony, 2004) concluded that there is a modest cocaine-associated deficit in young children's language competence, with greater severity of cocaine exposure related to increased deficits in language functioning. The authors stated that although the differences between cocaine-exposed and noncocaine-exposed children's language functioning is subtle; these subtle differences can affect children's academic and social functioning. They recommend that cocaine-exposed children receive periodic assessments and then intervention if warranted. Intervention can make a difference. Children of cocaine-using mothers who received case management services had higher verbal scores at 36 months than children whose mothers received standard management.

Eiden (2009) studied how 7-month-old infants responded to stress and how many strategies the infants used to cope with stress. In a laboratory setting, after the infant played with a toy for 30 seconds, the mother prevented her child from reaching a toy. This sequence was repeated twice to study the effects of increased stress on the infants. Infants exposed to cocaine prenatally showed more anger and sadness than nonexposed infants did, and, as stress increased, these infants reacted more quickly. The cocaine-exposed infants also had fewer strategies to regulate their emotional reactions when stress increased. The noncocaine-exposed infants used self-regulating, calming strategies such as looking away from the toy, sucking, moving their arms and legs, and looking to the mother. How an infant handles stress can influence the quality of the parent–child interactions. Infants who are more reactive and have fewer self-regulatory strategies are more difficult to soothe.

PROTECTIVE FACTORS. Fortunately, when pregnant women and others make an effort to learn about fetal development and pregnancy, the chances that teratogens will impact embryonic growth are reduced. In particular, three broad protective factors have been identified that diminish the impact of teratogens on women and their babies and reduce the likelihood of a negative developmental outcome. Two of these, maternal nutrition and social support, were discussed above. For example, researchers found that social support may inspire healthier behaviors and lifestyles in pregnant women, discouraging such behaviors as smoking, substance use, and poor nutritional intake. The third protective factor, prenatal care, is essential to mitigating the impact of teratogenic exposure.

Prenatal care that is comprehensive, begins in the first trimester, and includes basic screening tests is one of the best predictors of a healthy pregnancy, an easy birth, and a normal newborn. When a screening test indicates that further diagnostic testing is warranted, doing so allows parents to make informed choices about the care of their child (Hamamy & Dahoun, 2004). Thus, they may:

- Pursue potential interventions (i.e., fetal surgery or medication)
- Plan for a child with special needs

CONNECTING WITH CHILDREN

Guidelines for Teachers: Supporting Families during Their Prenatal Period

Practitioners who work with infants, toddlers, and preschool children in childcare and education programs are often in an excellent position to support families when they are experiencing pregnancy and newborns. Programs that provide family support can make literature, DVDs, and other materials available to families that include the following:

- The importance of early prenatal visits
- Ideas concerning the prevention of the mother's exposure to teratogens and effects on the fetus
- The importance of and ideas for reducing the incidence of premature and low birth-weight babies
- Information on breast feeding
- The importance of father involvement (if possible)
- Characteristics of newborns
- Community resources available for the families experiencing pregnancy and newborns
- Cultural variations in parenting styles

Programs that provide a mental health component may use home visits or invite parents to meetings to address the anxieties of parents about pregnancy, how to address the reactions of family members, and how best to support the siblings of the new baby.

- Address anticipated lifestyle changes
- Identify support groups and resources
- Make a decision about carrying the embryo or fetus to term

The ***Connecting with Children*** guidelines provide ideas about what teachers and other professionals can do to support families before a new baby is born.

BIRTH

At some time around the fortieth week of pregnancy, expectant mothers begin the process of birth. Ninety-five percent of all babies are born within two weeks of their due date, but just 5% of all babies are born exactly on the day expected. This section describes the stages of birth and concludes with a discussion of some of the more common delivery complications, including multiple births.

The Stages of Labor

Even though there are atypical experiences, usually two to four weeks before labor begins, the head of the fetus "drops" into the pelvic cavity. Other symptoms signal prelabor as well: a pink vaginal discharge caused by the loss of the cervical plug, lower back pain, and 2- to 5-pound weight loss.

The process of giving birth traditionally is divided into three stages called dilation, expulsion, and afterbirth. **Dilation** begins when the mother experiences uterine contractions at 10- to 15-minute intervals, and ends when the cervix is fully dilated (10 cm or about 4 inches) so that the fetus's head can pass through it. The dilation stage typically lasts from 6 to 18 hours for women delivering their first baby and from 2 to 6 hours for subsequent deliveries. This stage is divided into three phases. The first phase is the *latent phase* and is characterized by mild uterine contractions that are long and infrequent: they occur about 5 to 8 minutes apart and last for about 30 seconds. The mother enters the *active phase* when the cervix reaches 3 to 4 cm of dilation. During this phase the time between contractions is shorter (about 3–5 minutes) and the contractions last longer (about 45–60 seconds). The spontaneous rupture of the fetal membranes (sometimes called the "water breaking") most often occurs during this phase. The average amount of time that women spend in this phase is 4 hours for a first birth and 2 hours for subsequent deliveries. The following websites provide additional resources on the topic of childbirth: <http://www.babycenter.com/childbirth-images-gallery.htm> <http://www.babycenter.com/303_week-1_1615724.bc> <http://pregnancy.about.com/od/pregnancyphotos/Pregnancy_Labor_Birth_and_Baby_Photos.htm>

The most difficult and painful phase of dilation is called *transition*. During this time, the cervix dilates to a full 8 to 10 centimeters. Uterine contractions become stronger, closer together, and longer lasting (approximately 80 seconds). The mother may feel a strong desire to push with her diaphragm and abdominal muscles, and will be encouraged to do so. She may also feel a sense of panic, irritability, discouragement, or loss of control accompanied by the physical symptoms of hot and cold flashes, nausea, and disorientation. The transition phase lasts between 30 and 60 minutes for first deliveries and 20 to 30 minutes for subsequent births.

The second stage of labor is called **expulsion**, an interesting term used to portray a baby's entry into the world. It begins as the fetus's head passes through the cervix into the vagina and ends when the baby emerges from the mother's body. Again, the mother will likely be told to push with the contractions to assist the baby through the birth canal. If the baby is positioned head first, the head will advance through the birth canal with each contraction and recede slightly as the uterus relaxes. The head must rotate in order to move through the mother's pelvic structure. The term "crowning" is used when the top of the baby's head is visible at the vaginal opening and does not recede between contractions. Once the baby's head has crowned and moved out of the birth canal, it must rotate again to become aligned with the shoulders. The shoulders must also rotate to fit out of the birth canal. First one shoulder emerges, then the other, followed by the buttocks and lower limbs. The baby arrives with the umbilical cord still attached to the placenta. The cord is clamped in two places and cut.

As the fetus is squeezed down the birth canal and into the outside world, it experiences a good deal of stress. For several hours, its head sustains pressure and it is intermittently deprived of oxygen due to compression of the placenta and umbilical cord during contractions. In response, the fetal endocrine system releases unusually high levels of the stress hormones adrenaline and noradrenaline (higher levels than women in labor or people experiencing heart attacks!). But, this surge of hormones is adaptive in that it helps the newborn make the transition to its new environment. More specifically, the surge of hormones clears the lungs and helps the newborn manage oxygen deprivation by increasing its heart rate and the flow of oxygenated blood to the brain (Nelson, 1995). Birth stress also ensures that babies are awake and ready to breathe by the time they emerge from the birth canal.

Most women report that labor is painful; however, there is both nonpharmacologic pain relief and pharmacologic pain relief (Leeman, Fontaine, King, Klein, & Ratcliffe, 2003a, 2003b). Nonpharmacologic relief includes continuous labor support; intradermal water blocks; warm water baths; sterile-water injections; and positions, touch, and massage (Simkin & O'Hara, 2002). *Continuous* (not intermittent) labor support provided by a **doula**—a person trained in labor support—has been found to consistently decrease the use of caesarean deliveries and requests for pain medication (Hodnett, Gates, Hofmeyr, & Sakala, 2003; Leeman, et al., 2003a.).

Finally, following the birth of the baby, the third stage of delivery is the afterbirth stage, in which uterine contractions stop for a few minutes before starting again to expel the placenta. Because the uterus immediately shrinks following expulsion of the baby, the placenta usually peels off the uterine wall with ease. This last stage typically takes about 10–20 minutes to complete.

Birth Alternatives

In most Western countries, pregnancy, labor, and birth are often treated as if they were symptoms of an illness, characterized by visits to doctors and hospitals. This attitude is contrasted with that of cultures in which birth is seen as an everyday occurrence and a ritual that young girls and women witness and assist with throughout their lives. In the middle of the last century, a movement called "natural" or "prepared" childbirth began to gain popularity in the Western world. This movement arose out of the work of many obstetricians and midwives and was based on the philosophy that childbirth is a normal and natural part of life rather than a disease or medical event. Proponents of natural childbirth believe that most women can give birth comfortably and without medication by learning exercises, breathing methods, and relaxation techniques (Dick-Read, 1933/1972; Lamaze, 1958).

The first birthing center opened in 1974 to offer women and their partners and/or families a comfortable, homey environment with close proximity to a hospital in case of complications. Birthing centers usually have fewer restrictions and guidelines for families to follow than traditional hospitals, and they may allow for more freedom in making laboring decisions. Birthing centers are often recommended for pregnancies that are considered low risk.

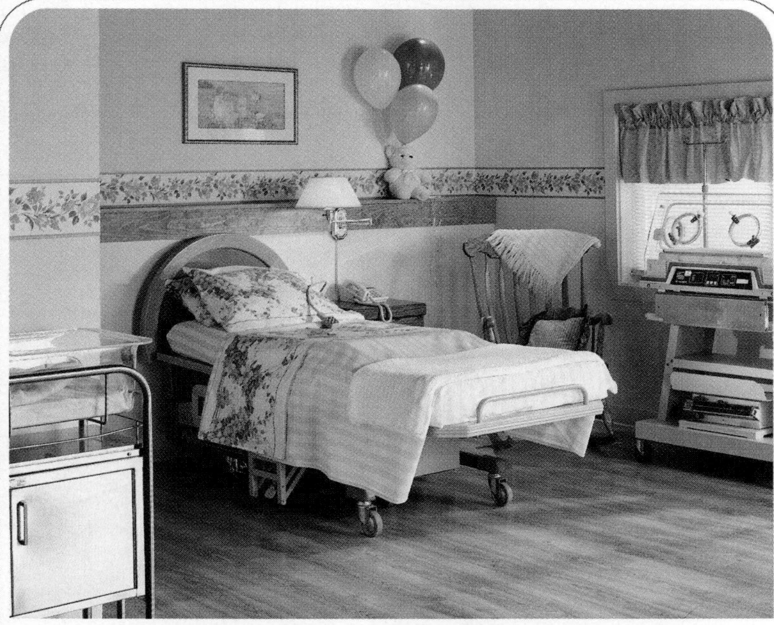

New birthing centers are designed to meet the needs of mothers from their active labor through their stages of delivery and into recovery.

The popularity of the birthing center environment is reflected in the move many hospitals made in the 1990s to establish centers of their own and in the way that they market their facilities to families now. Whereas women previously labored in one room, delivered in another, and recovered in yet a third location when delivering in a hospital, they are now likely to do all three in one cozily furnished room equipped with the latest technology. Billboards and brochures speak to the stiff competition between birthing centers and hospitals, with some offering steak dinners and other incentives in an effort to lure expectant parents to them.

Birth experiences have definitely changed for fathers. Fathers now are generally present at the journey of their baby down the birth canal and are important members of the team, but this was not always the case.

> Men's involvement in pregnancy and birth and their participation in the early years of their child/children's lives has changed dramatically over the past 25 years. In 1965, about 5% of fathers attended the birth of their child. In 1989, almost 95% of fathers were present at childbirth. Men are clearly asking for more participation in the childbirth process. It is also interesting to note how, in a recent survey on men and work, 75% of the men would accept slower career advancement if they could have a job that would let them arrange their work schedule to have more time with their families. (Linton, 2009, online)

Delivery Complications

Sometimes birth cannot proceed according to nature's plan. There are a number of events that would cause a physician to intercede in the birthing process: if the fetus is lying in an unusual position in the womb (feet or buttocks down), if the fetus is more than two weeks past its due date (and the placenta begins to calcify), if the mother's or baby's health is in danger, if the delivery is commencing too slowly, or if the baby's head is too large to pass through the mother's cervix. In such cases, doctors often elect to perform a **caesarean section,** in which the infant is surgically removed from the uterus. Rates of caesarean deliveries have skyrocketed in the United States. In 2007, according to the National Center for Health Statistics (Hamilton, Martin, & Ventura, 2009), almost one-third of births in the United States were caesarean section (see Figure 3.11). Critics claim that caesarean section procedures are sometimes done for unjustifiable reasons such as lengthy labors and the increased money that doctors receive for performing surgery (Savage, 2000).

One of the most common birth complications is a lack of oxygen to the fetus called **anoxia.** As previously mentioned, some deprivation of oxygen is normal (and even

FIGURE 3.11

CAESAREAN DELIVERY RATES

Total caesarean delivery rate: United States, final 1989–2006 and preliminary 2007

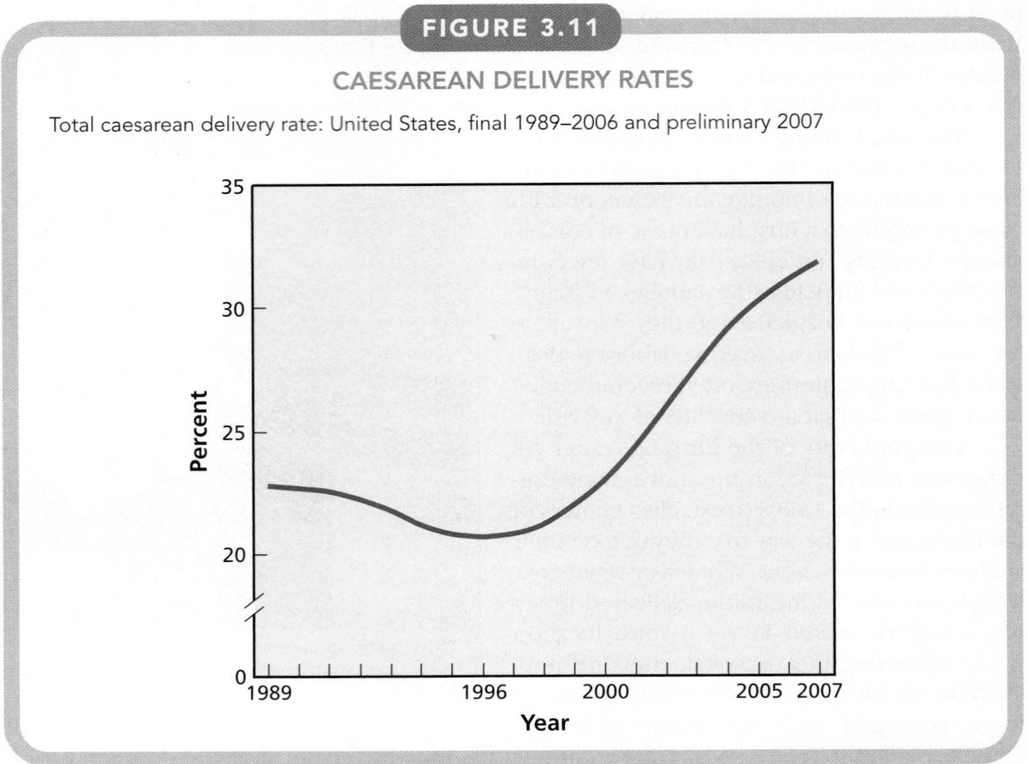

Source: National Vital Statistics Reports, Volume 57, Number 12, March 18, 2009, 1-23 (p. 3). Retrieved September 14, 2009 from http://www.cdc.gov/nchs/data/nvsr/nvsr57/nvsr57_12.pdf

adaptive) as the baby travels down the birth canal. Mild anoxia does not seem to have lasting effects on children's motor skills or intellectual development (Behrman & Kliegman, 2002), but permanent brain damage can result if the breathing is delayed more than 3 to 4 minutes. Prolonged anoxia can occur if the umbilical cord has been blocked or tangled during childbirth or if the infant is in the breech position (feet or buttocks down). Anoxia can also occur if the placenta separates from the uterus prematurely (blocking the transmission of nutrients and oxygen from the mother's body), sedatives given to the mother cross the placental boundary and interfere with breathing, mucus ingested during childbirth is lodged in baby's throat, or there is a genetic incompatibility between the mother's and the fetus's blood types. More specifically, if the fetus has a protein called RH factor in its blood that the mother lacks, the RH-negative mother's body may build up antibodies that attack the red blood cells of the fetus, depleting oxygen and leading to possible brain damage. Problems stemming from RH incompatibility are now treated with rhogam, a vaccine that prevents the RH-negative mother from forming the antibodies. Prematurity and low birth weight, increasing problems in the United States, will be discussed in Chapter 4.

The Birthing of Multiples

How does the presence of more than one fetus affect birthing? One of the biggest problems with multiple pregnancies is premature delivery. As the number of fetuses increases, the length of gestation and the birth weight decrease, although this is not true in every case. Being pregnant with multiples does increase the risk of prenatal death and the likelihood of long-term health effects. Research has consistently shown that twins and triplets show some physical and mental delays compared to single-borns. Fortunately, about half of those babies who demonstrate delays will catch up to their single-born peers within one year of birth (Sasaki, Sasaki, Takahashi, Nakajo, & Kyono, 2004). In certain cases, to counteract some of the delays described, healthcare providers may delay the birth of a second-born twin, if possible. In cases of premature delivery of the first-born twin, where additional time in the womb might lead to increases in development and weight gain for the second-born, a delay in delivery of several days to several months might be sought. Recent research has shown higher survival rates in such second-born twins (Zhang, Hamilton, Martin, & Trumble, 2004).

▼ SUMMARY AND KEY TERMS

• Genetics

Genetics is the study of how humans and other species (plant and animal) inherit the characteristics that make them unique, and how the interactions between heritability and the environment influence development. *Cells*, *chromosomes*, *genes*, and *DNA* are the body and beginnings of life. The information on The Human Genome Project that started in 1990 and continues today helps educators and other professionals understand the remarkable discoveries related to genes and their effect on the development of the child. A brief description of the development of sex cells (gametes) into zygotes as well as the process of mitosis and meiosis allows professionals to understand the "basic birds and bees" as they work with families. Information on multiple births, heritability, and epigenetic factors help behavioral geneticists understand the extent to which characteristics that vary from individual to individual are the result of genetic versus environmental variation. The section on dominant-recessive inheritance, co-dominance, sex-linked inheritance, and polygenic inheritance explained how traits are a product of the interaction of genetics and the environment. Readers learned how genetic abnormalities develop, which brings them up to date on children with special needs, the benefits of genetic counseling for future parents, and the relatively new field of gene therapy.

• Reproduction Challenges, Technologies, and Controversies

Much is known today about the process of becoming pregnant, the frequency and causes of miscarriages, and reproduction technology. Assisted Reproductive Technologies (ART) aid fertilization or implantation, determine the sex of a baby, and treat forms of infertility associated with advancing age. Both cloning and stem cell research are important and controversial topics today.

• Prenatal Development

The development of an embryo and fetus is remarkable—a miracle in many ways. This section described in detail the stages of prenatal development, discussed critical diagnostic tests of fetal development, and presented useful information on prenatal intervention. The context in which pregnancy occurs and its effects on the health of the mother, child, and the mother-child relationship was emphasized.

• Birth

Birth is the beginning of life outside the womb, even though infants have been responding to some stimulation from the outside world before birth. This section describes the amazing process of birth, including the physical and emotional aspects of birth, prematurity, multiples, and possible delivery complications.

▼ KEY TERMS

anoxia (111)
behavioral genetics (84)
blastocyst (97)
caesarean section (111)
chromosomes (78)
co-dominance (88)
differentiation (98)
dilation (109)
DNA (78)
dominant-recessive inheritance (87)
doula (110)
Down syndrome (trisomy 21) (91)
ectoderm (98)
embryo (97)
embryonic stem cells (95)
endoderm (98)
epigenesis (87)
expulsion (110)
fetal alcohol spectrum disorder (FASD) (107)
fetal alcohol syndrome (FAS) (107)
fetus (99)
fraternal twins (dizygotic twins) (82)
genes (79)
genetic counseling (92)
genetics (78)
germ cells (91)
gestation (97)
heritability (84)
identical twins (monozygotic twins) (82)
implantation (97)
Klinefelter's syndrome (89)
male gametes (80)
meiosis (81)
mesoderm (98)
mitosis (81)
multiples (82)
mutations (89)
neural tube (98)
non-embryonic adult stem cells (95)
ova (80)
oxytocin (101)
phenotypic characteristics (87)
phenylketonuria (103)
placenta (97)
pluripotent stem cells (95)
Poly-X syndrome (89)
polycystic ovary syndrome (PCOS) (93)
polygenetic (89)
rapid eye movement (REM) sleep (104)
sex-linked inheritance (88)
sickle cell anemia (88)
somatic cells (91)
sperm (80)
spermatogenesis (80)
teratogen (105)
Turner's syndrome (89)
umbilical cord (97)
vernix (100)
X-linked diseases (89)
zygote (97)

▼ CASEBOOK

FAMILY BALANCING

Imagine that you have been newly hired to provide child development guidance at your community child development center. Yesterday, some parents approached you for advice on *family balancing*, a term that refers to the methods used to choose the gender of a child through techniques such as sperm sorting and diagnosis of embryos before implantation. The couple has been thinking about expanding their family, but they have three sons already and would really prefer at this point in their lives to have a daughter. You have heard of "family balancing," but until now had not been asked to comment on it. These parents know of several clinics in the region that specialize in family balancing, and they wonder if you approve of the practice. You know this is the family's decision to make in consultation with their physician, but what aspects of this dilemma could you discuss with them?

WHAT WOULD THEY DO?

Here is how two professionals responded:

JUDY WELCH, M.D.—Family Practitioner, Westbrook, Maine

The implications of widespread family balancing without restrictions would create much the same issues that the Far East countries of India and China are experiencing—an imbalance in the natural selection of gender, for example, a male-to-female ratio of 130:100 versus 104:107 in the natural selection process. This creates demographic changes associated with problems involving crime, violence, emigration, and selling of brides in these countries. Other ethical and medical issues that arise are the risk of discrimination in the unselected group.

For the couple trying to select the sex of their first child, you would almost expect disappointment. The first hurdle to overcome is the odds of having the sex they select. According to my research, the procedure that is most commonly used is sperm sorting and the odds are 80% to 90% success if you are trying for a female and 60% to 70% if you are trying for a male—certainly not a guarantee! Expectations for firstborns already are high, and if the baby's sex does not meet the parents' expectations, there is another reason for disappointment.

If the procedure fails, there is a risk that the parents would be resentful of the child and could even go to the extreme of sex-determined abortion, offering for adoption, or child abandonment. Abandonment and infanticide are illegal in most countries, as is sex-related abortion. However, some of these practices still occur, especially in the countries where there is a one-child policy.

In the United States the main purpose of selection is the reduction of birth defects. If the procedure went unchecked, then we may actually see propagation of those sex-linked diseases, which would cause more disappointment in those families. Selecting the sex of the child fills some desires of the parents but could create a lack of respect for the child as a person.

ELIZABETH KENNARD, M.D—Director, Division of Reproductive Endocrinology and Infertility, Department of Obstetrics and Gynecology
The Ohio State University

Although it may seem simply obvious for families to have a preference for one gender or another, the ethical issues in this case are complex. Unfortunately, widespread gender selection might lead to an imbalance of the sexes, as it already has in countries such as China. Its opponents argue that supporting gender selection endorses the idea that children of one sex are more inherently valuable than children of another sex. Although these procedures are legal in the United States, several organizations, including the United Nations, the International Federation of Gynecology and Obstetrics, and the American College of Obstetrics and Gynecology are opposed to its use except in the case of sex-linked disease prevention.

Gender selection techniques include sperm sorting to try to enrich the sperm for the desired gender, and embryo biopsy to determine gender prior to implantation. However, usually those asking for gender selection are unaware of the difficulty, success rates, costs, and risks of the procedures. Once they are counseled about the techniques available, most couples do not proceed any further. The sperm sorting procedure typically costs several thousand dollars and improves chances—but is not perfect; also, several attempts at insemination may be required prior to successfully achieving a pregnancy. *In addition, the procedure has currently been suspended by the Food and Drug administration until sufficient follow-up of families has established no harm from the process.* The preimplantation procedure is more accurate at providing the desired gender but involves using *in vitro* fertilization to obtain embryos for biopsy and implantation. There are many cultures and religions for whom IVF is unacceptable, and this procedure can easily cost more than $15,000. Success rates with IVF procedures are usually less than 50% per cycle.

If a couple continues to express interest in sex selection then I recommend counseling to explore several issues. In addition to the possibility of not achieving any pregnancy, they could deliver a child of the "non-preferred" gender. They need to decide whether to disclose their gender selection procedure and preference to friends and family who would have contact with the resultant child. They should carefully examine their motives for this request and any harm the process might do themselves, their child, or their family.

myeducationlab

Now go to MyEducationLab at *www.myeducationlab.com,* where you can:

- Find the instructional objectives for this chapter in the **Study Plan.**
- Take a quiz as a part of the **Study Plan** to self-assess your mastery of chapter content. The program generates an individualized Study Plan based upon your answers to the quiz.
- Complete **Activities and Applications** to assist you in deepening your understanding of important chapter concepts.
- Apply what you have learned through **Building Teaching Skills,** exercises that guide you in trying out skills and strategies you will use in professional practice.

4

INFANCY AND TODDLERHOOD

THE CASEBOOK

WHAT WOULD YOU DO?

PICKING UP A CRYING BABY

Dom's parents didn't know what to do about his crying. Dom's mother, Robin, read in her new book on infant care that parents should respond to their baby's cries, comfort them, and help them become calm again. There was a chapter on how important a secure attachment is for the child and that parents' responding to crying helps the child feel safe, learn to trust in his parents' availability, and have a sense of self-worth. Yet Dom's grandmother, Fara, let Robin and her husband know her beliefs about picking up crying children. Fara felt strongly that picking up a crying baby would spoil the child rotten and the baby would just become more demanding. What should Robin and her husband do?

CRITICAL THINKING

- Does Fara value interdependence or independence in children?
- How might families from different cultures solve this problem?
- What does the research conclude about comforting crying infants and toddlers?

Elaine Y.Y., Age 3—China

▶ OVERVIEW AND OBJECTIVES

This chapter examines the significance of the first three years of life for young children. New information on brain development and neurobiology explains why the quality of young children's experiences is so important to optimal development. At first glance, newborns may seem limited in their skills, but novel and exciting research has uncovered endless surprises that now help us see newborn babies differently. Topics of interest in this chapter include newborns' capabilities, vulnerabilities, and physical health, along with neurobehavioral assessments and screenings that identify health conditions. Having an understanding of infants' reflexes and physical states can enhance an adult's responsive nurturing of children at this stage.

A discussion of the principles of development sets the stage for more detailed information on the health, physical growth, and nutrition of infants and toddlers. You will read how perception involving the senses of vision, hearing, taste, smell, and touch develops in the context of environments and relationships. Then we delve into each aspect of child development—cognitive, emotional, social, language, and motor development, as well as conditions of delay and disability. At the end of the chapter, you will read about the importance of families and family support for the well-being of infants and toddlers. The influence of culture is emphasized throughout the chapter. By the time you finish this chapter you should be able to do the following:

Objective 4.1 Describe the scientific evidence, including brain development, for why the first three years of life are important and list five ways to support infant development.

Objective 4.2 Identify characteristics of newborn infants' capabilities, vulnerabilities, and health issues, including prematurity, and discuss screenings and assessments, reflexes, and states.

Objective 4.3 Identify components of health, physical growth, and nutrition of the infant and toddler.

Objective 4.4 Explain how infants and toddlers develop and learn in each of the following domains: sensory/perceptual development, cognitive development, emotional development, social development, language and communication, and motor development.

Objective 4.5 Describe at least five critical components of the Early Intervention System for infants and toddlers with developmental challenges and their families.

The Meaning and Significance of Infancy

Who Are Infants and Toddlers?

Watching an infant or toddler brings endless delight to an admiring observer who marvels that children who are so little can do so many things, communicate their needs, and practice new skills tirelessly. Infants and toddlers desire to learn, experiment, and explore. They practice persistence at batting a rattle to make a sound, stacking blocks into towers, or nesting small boxes within bigger boxes. And infants who are learning to walk will toddle as far as 37 football fields a day, falling an average of 15 times an hour (Adolph, 2009). "Babies are no longer thought of as vegetables—carrots that can cry" (Gopnik, et al., 1999, p. 143). Rather, infants and toddlers think, feel, and actively attempt to understand themselves, others, and the world around them.

Newborns, infancy, infants, babies, and *toddlers*—these are terms used to describe stages of development in children from birth to 3 years of age. In this chapter, the terms *newborns* or *neonates* refer to the period from birth to 4 months. The terms *infants* and *babies* refer to children from birth to 12 months, and the term *toddlers* applies to children from 12 to 24 months of age. We use the term *twos* to refer to children from 24 to 36 months, and the more general term *infancy* covers the whole early period of growth and development from birth to 36 months. The purpose of this chapter is to describe development in newborns, infants, toddlers, and twos, and to illustrate how families, teachers, and early childhood programs can sustain young children who are both vulnerable and competent.

OUTLINE ▼

Infants and Toddlers Live in Families and Depend on Responsive Adults to Care for Them

Young children are dependent on adults to take care of them, and because of this, we cannot consider an infant, toddler, or 2-year-old without considering the context in which the child lives—their families and for some children some of the time, their childcare and education providers. There are many different family structures—two parents, single mother or father, grandparent, foster parents, multiple generations—and there are many types of childcare and education programs. However, neither the kind of family structure nor the type of childcare or early education program is as important as the emotional experiences of the infants, toddlers, or 2-year-olds during their first three years of life.

Infants and toddlers in all cultures have emotional needs for safety, a sense of security, affection (Gerhardt, 2004), support in regulating intense negative emotions, reciprocal interactions, language interactions, and beneficial social experiences. They need positive emotional and social experiences to build a sense of self-worth and efficacy—a sense that they have some control that makes a difference in their lives and the lives of others (Bandura, 1997). Or, as Bronfenbrenner (1970) stated, "All children need someone who is just crazy about them." Research on risk and resiliency factors has concluded that if children have someone who believes in them and forms a special connection with them, that connection counters many risk factors for later developmental challenges (Werner, 1989).

Social support and social networks (Lamb, 2005; Lewis, 2005) are critically important for families to reduce the negative effects of risk factors such as poverty, alcoholism or drug use, and mental illness in the family. As you read the remainder of the chapter, you will find information on how families can be supported and on the elements of quality childcare providers and programs. Teachers of infants and toddlers in childcare and education programs as well as family childcare providers will find guidance about how to improve their practice and share with families about the importance of the early years.

First time parents are joyful when their infants are born, but often are naïve to the responsibilities infant care requires.

The Importance of the First Three Years of Life

Prior to the 19th century, the dominant view was that children were essentially "defective adults" (Gopnik et al., 1999, p. 12). Now, however, there is strong scientific evidence for the importance of the first 36 months of life for children's long-term development. The landmark book, *Neurons to Neighborhoods* (Shonkoff & Phillips, 2000), inspired a fervent and renewed interest in infant and toddler development. In their detailed research, Shonkoff and Phillips provide testimony about how children learn and develop, uncovering the significance of children's first three years of life. Highlighted is how responsive adult–child interactions are essential to a young child's development and how the sensitivity, emotional availability, and positive guidance of caring adults is critical for infants' and toddlers' **well-being**—their happiness, health, comfort, and security. Shonkoff and Phillips further explain that

1. all children are born wired for feelings and ready to learn;
2. early environments matter, and nurturing relationships are essential;
3. society is changing, and the needs of young children are not being addressed; and
4. interactions among early childhood science, policy, and practice are problematic and demand dramatic rethinking (p. 4).

In the past, survival of the infant required parents' full attention (and still does in many cultures). So, when did scientists begin to see the period from birth to 3 as critical for optimal emotional, social, language, cognitive, and motor development?

Many researchers and theorists were influential in identifying the first three years as an important time of life. René Spitz (1945, 1946), a Hungarian psychiatrist and psychoanalyst, influenced thinking about infant and toddler development with his landmark studies of infants in foundling homes and other institutional settings. Dr. Spitz's videos of infants rocking back and forth on their backs in their cribs looking emaciated and forlorn made a lasting impression on everyone who saw them. He emphasized that although the children were adequately nourished, they languished without continual nurturing interactions with dependable adults. Erik Erikson (1950, 1968), a theorist discussed in Chapter 2 and in the chapters on social-emotional development, also helped us think about infants' psychological well-being as well as their physical development. Erikson described the first stage of life as one in which the infant learns to trust and the second stage of life as important for the development of autonomy. Bowlby's (1960a, 1960b, 1961) work on attachment and separation helped adults understand that infants and toddlers need a strong, secure attachment—an emotional connection—to primary caregivers, grieve when separated from familiar caregivers, and become detached and defensive if they are not reunited with an attachment figure. In addition, we cannot forget how Piaget (1952, 1954, 1962) demonstrated that infants

are powerful learners and that Vygotsky (1987) established the importance of adults, peers, and culture for enhancing young children's learning.

Results from early intervention programs in the 1960s and 1970s also influenced our thinking about the experiences that children need to thrive. Researchers such as Honig (2002) and Lally (2006) moved the interest in infancy forward with their work on improving childcare for infants and toddlers and supporting intimate adult-child responsive interactions in homes and in programs. Most recently, Nugent, Petrauskas, and Brazelton (2009) edited the book *The Newborn as a Person: Enabling Healthy Development Worldwide*, emphasizing the global perspective that infants are beings who deserve our best care. There is strong research evidence that the quality of children's relationships and the environment children experience in the first three years of life influence who they are and who they will become.

The research on brain development is another factor that moves the field of infancy forward as it identifies what is important for children's optimal brain development. The information on brain development provides a scientific basis for what parents, infant development pioneers, and professionals have intuitively known about the importance of the first three years.

Brain Development and Neurological Development

Knowledge of infant, toddler, and twos' brain development has sparked educators to examine the way they and family members interact with young children, the experiences that young children need, and the policies and practices that lead to young children's optimal brain development (*Better Brains for Babies*, 2006; Education Commission of the States, 2006; Spelke, 2002).

DEVELOPMENT OF THE BRAIN. Recent technology, including brain-imaging techniques, now permits neuroscientists to observe specific areas and functions of the brain (see Figure 4.1).

As discussed in Chapter 3, the **neural tube**—the beginning of the brain and spinal cord—develops at approximately 3 weeks prenatally, and becomes the brain and spinal cord. During prenatal development, different parts of the brain take on different functions. The brain, which has grown exponentially during pregnancy, continues to grow at a rapid pace during the child's first three years of life. "A newborn's brain is about 25 percent of its approximate adult weight. Although brain development continues throughout our lifetime, by age 3, the brain has grown dramatically by producing billions of cells and hundreds of trillions of connections, or synapses, between these cells" (ZERO TO THREE, 2009, paragraph 1).

How do a young child's experiences shape the brain? The synaptic connections from neuron to neuron continue to develop quickly over the first two years. Synapses are overproduced in the cerebral cortex and then **pruned**—mechanisms by which the brain becomes more finely tuned and functional (Thomas & Johnson, 2008)—based on the experiences that the infant or toddler has. Erica Lurie-Hurvitz (2009, p. 1) emphasizes that "Early experiences can and do influence the physical architecture of the brain, literally shaping the neural connections in an infant's developing mind." As an event occurs and reoccurs, the synapses storing information about the event become reactivated, thicker, and stronger. For example, synapses for language become more frequent and stronger when infants and toddlers hear and use language. The synapses for emotional development strengthen as parents comfort babies and use the language of emotions—words such as *sad, happy, angry,* or *frustrated.* While the used synapses are strengthened, neurons and synapses that are not exercised are pruned or deleted to make room for those connections that are utilized the most. The concepts of plasticity and sensitive periods help explain this phenomenon of pruning.

PLASTICITY AND SENSITIVE PERIODS. The term ***plasticity*** refers to how the brain can reorganize in response to environmental stimuli and experience. "The brain possesses the ability to modify neural connections to better cope with new circumstances" (Society for Neuroscience, 2009, p. 4). About half of the neurons created during infant development survive to function in adults (Society for Neuroscience, 2009). **Sensitive periods** are those times when certain types of plasticity are dominant in the brain. "These are windows of time

FIGURE 4.1

PARTS OF THE BRAIN AND THEIR FUNCTIONS

The brain—the body's nervous and communication center—is responsible for managing differing body functions. The frontal lobe is associated with reasoning, planning, organizing parts of speech, behavior, emotions: most of the body's higher cognitive functions. In addition, the frontal lobe is involved in premotor and motor areas that produce and modify movement. The parietal lobe manages information processing, spatial orientation, movement, perception of stimuli including pain and touch sensations, and an understanding of written and spoken language. The occipital lobe is responsible for visual reception and processing. The temporal lobe is associated with perception and recognition of auditory stimuli, visual and verbal memory, and speech. In addition, the cerebellum assists in muscle coordination and balance. The brainstem is necessary for survival including breathing, digestion, heart rate, blood pressure, being awake and alert.

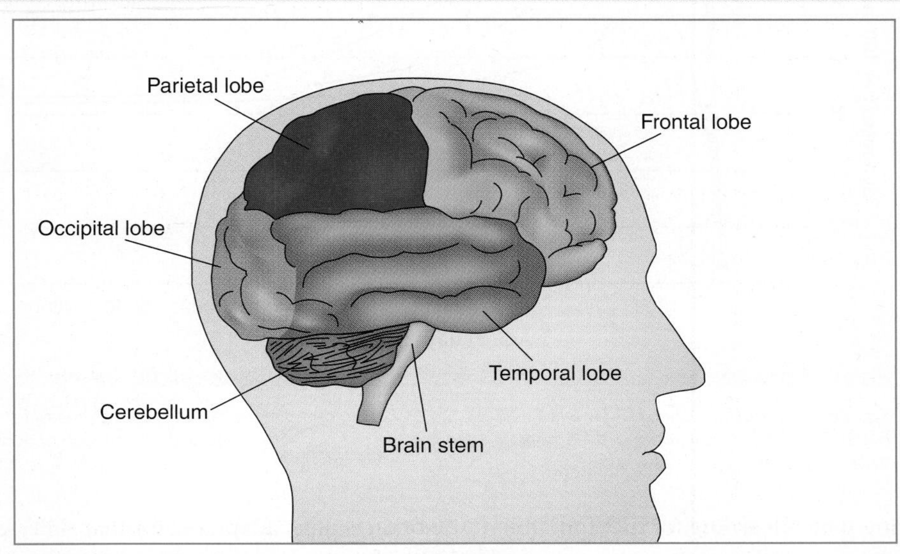

Frontal lobe

- Emotions
- Expressive language
- Word associations
- Memory for habits and motor activities
- Problem solving
- Reasoning

Parietal lobe

- Integration of different senses
- Location for visual attention
- Location for touch perception
- Manipulation of objects

Occipital lobe

- Vision

Cerebellum

- Balance and equilibrium
- Some memory for reflex motor acts

Brain stem

- Regulates body functions (e.g., breathing, heart rate, swallowing)
- Reflexes to seeing and hearing (e.g., startle response)
- Controls autonomic nervous system (e.g., sweating, blood pressure, digestion, internal temperature)
- Affects level of alertness

Temporal lobe

- Hearing
- Speech
- Memory acquisition
- Categorization of objects

Source: Heward, W., Exceptional Children, Figure 12.2 "Parts of the brain and some of their functions" p. 461, © 2009 Pearson Education, Inc. Reproduced by permission of Pearson Education, Inc.

during development when the nervous system must obtain certain critical experiences, such as sensory, movement, or emotional input, to develop properly" (Society for Neuroscience, 2009, p. 14). Thomas and Johnson (2008), in an article titled "New Advances in Understanding Sensitive Periods in Brain Development," created a chart that demonstrates how the number of synapses peak and then begin to decrease for different functions of the brain (see Figure 4.2). These peak periods—and instances prior to the peaks—are sensitive periods

FIGURE 4.2

SYNAPSES DURING AGE IN DAYS FROM CONCEPTION

Synaptic density in different brain areas across the lifespan. Synapses, the structures through which neurons communicate, are initially overproduced in the brain, and the environment selects which ones are retained to support function. The density of synapses may be viewed as one measure of the plasticity of the system—the potential to alter connection strengths to reflect experience (Huttenlocher, 2002).

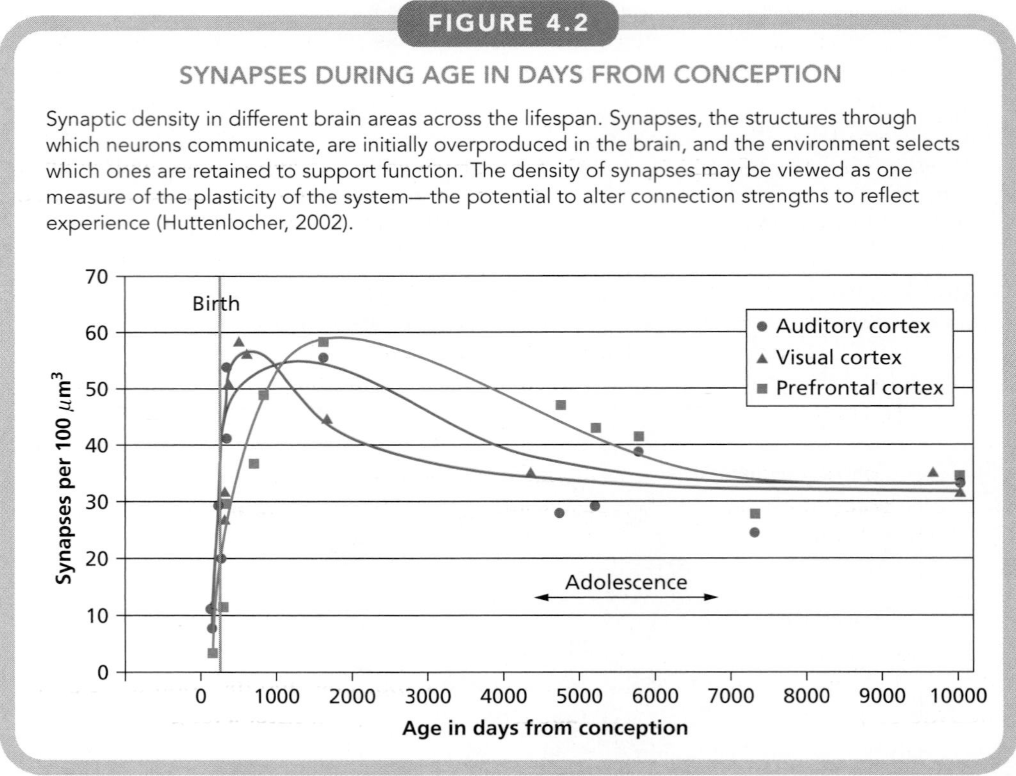

Source: From Huttenlocher, P. R., & Dabholkar, A. S. (1997). Regional differences in synaptogenesis in human cerebral cortex. Journal of Comparative Neurology, 387, 167–187. Used with permission of John Wiley and Sons.

during which learning for that function of the brain is most adaptable for that skill. After this sensitive period, connections are less likely to change. However, the ones remaining are more specific, defined, precise, and stable. You can observe in Figure 4.2 how plasticity for the auditory, visual, and prefrontal functions of the brain begins to decrease after three years of age, although most functions do not stabilize until after adolescence. You also can see that the child's first 1,000 days are critical for brain development!

WHAT IS REQUIRED FOR OPTIMAL DEVELOPMENT? A broad range of factors influences brain development, with both physical maturation and experience playing important roles. Even though the baby is born with a genetic predisposition for vision and hearing, specific abilities arise because of experience. In other words, most infants can see, but what they prefer to look at and are able to distinguish develops because of their experiences. Halfon, Shulman, and Hochstein (2001) concluded that (1) a child's brain is immature at birth; (2) it is changed by experience; (3) the timing of experience can be important; and (4) relationships influence a child's social and emotional functioning. As these four facts indicate, the importance of the child's relationships and other experiences cannot be underestimated. Several experiential factors contribute positively or negatively to infants' and toddlers' brain development, including relationships and responsive interactions, adults' responses to children's stress, and encouragement for exploration and play.

Infants' relationships with the important adults in their lives influence not only what young children learn, but also *how* they learn. In 2004, the National Scientific Council on the Developing Child (2004b) documented what science tells us about the importance of nurturing and stable relationships to early brain development. Friedman (2005) emphasized that early experiences, "shape the developing brain's architecture and profoundly influence who we become" and that "nurturing, positive interactions release chemicals in a child's brain that promote its growth and development, while negative interactions produce chemicals that weaken its architecture" (p. 1).

Sensitivity to young children's *distress* (McElwain & Booth-LaForce, 2006; McElwain, Cox, Burchinal, & Macfie, 2003), *affective mutuality* (McElwain, Booth-LaForce, Lansford, Wu, & Dyer, 2008), *emotional availability*, and *responsiveness* are key terms that describe the care that infants and toddlers need from adults (Biringen, 2000). Adults are "coping resources" (Nachmias & Gunnar, 1996) for young children who are just learning how to regulate their emotions and behavior. Sensitivity to infant cues such as crying and cooing, with adults responding by picking up or talking with children, leads to young children's increased language and cognitive development. In fact, the level of responsiveness of mothers to their children who have disabilities (in early intervention programs) was the only factor that was positively associated with children's outcomes (Mahoney, Boyce, Fewell, Spiker, & Wheeden, 1998).

Time and encouragement for exploration and play are critical elements. During play, infants and toddlers experiment by using all of their senses. They are truly sensory beings who learn by actively trying out different strategies to make things work. Repetition of activities plays a part in developing the connections in the brain. Parents or teachers who have read *Pat the Bunny* 100 times may tire of reading this story, but if during this reading the adult–child interaction is responsive, the infant or toddler learns something new each time the book is read, and synapses involved in listening, comprehending, and relationship building are strengthened.

The Newborn (Neonate)

Serena and Matt had been waiting for this day for 8 months—since they first found out that Serena was pregnant. Labor pains started early in the morning, and the soon to be parents timed the contractions until they were about 10 minutes apart. After a long labor, the baby emerged into the world. She was now a newborn—a neonate—their baby. They were surprised that the baby looked nothing like the archetypical chubby babies they were used to seeing. She was wrinkled, red skinned, and covered with *vernix,* a waxy substance. She appeared bluish in color due to normal oxygen deprivation during the birth process. Her passage through the narrow cervix and birth canal led to a flattened nose, misshaped head and forehead, and bumps and bruises. However, in the eyes of the parents, this child was a beautiful miracle. They named the baby Rose. As Matt and Serena soon discovered, their newborn had the ability to communicate her needs from the moment she was born. She could tell them when she was hungry, contented, or ready for them to talk to her with soft sounds.

The Capabilities and Vulnerabilities of Newborns

Newborns emerge from the womb ready to relate and learn. They arrive with the ability to woo and engage their family members to take care of them. They have emotional and physical needs that adults in their lives meet when they care for them in responsive and sensitive ways. They are newly born, but they have untaught skills that they practiced in the womb and their systems are ready to survive and relate.

You may recall from Chapter 3 that infants are eavesdropping on their world from the uterine environment during the third trimester. The music and the voices that infants hear *in utero* are what they now prefer as newborns. Later in the chapter we discuss *habituation*, which means that when babies first hear, see, feel, or smell information available to their senses, their interest is often sparked, but if the stimuli continues, they become less attentive—they habituate. Scientists use this well-known fact about babies to assess what their interests and capabilities are. For example, when a nipple is placed in an infant's mouth while a picture is shown to the infant, the infant sucks fast as if this is an interesting phenomenon, but slows down as his or her interest wanes. Using this technique, researchers found that newborns prefer to listen to a story that their mother read to them prior to birth (DeCasper & Spence, 1986) rather than a story they had not heard prenatally.

The newborn's sensory systems are surprisingly ready to process information. Their sense of smell is so acute that they turn their heads to smell the breast-pad (a cloth that fits over the nipple to reduce leaking of milk) of their mother rather than a stranger's breast-pad. Their sense of touch requires that their primary caregivers hold them skin to skin, massage them, and carry them snugly. As caregivers know, newborns feel pain. Note however, that physicians did not always realize that this was the case. Before 1987, doctors performed male **circumcision**—a medical procedure that removes the foreskin on the penis—without pain medication. The use of anesthesia for neonatal circumcision is now considered crucial for pain relief.

Newborns use behaviors such as making eye contact, crying, wriggling, moving hands and feet, and arching away to communicate their needs to ready observers. They can stick out their tongue in imitation and take cooing turns with a responsive caregiver (Meltzoff & Moore, 1983). Newborns are truly ready to learn and relate. Recognizing how they accomplish this can perhaps best be understood by first learning about the physical nature of newborns. The physical health of newborns is a topic of discussion and research for world leaders, scientists, educators, and parents alike.

HEALTHY NEWBORNS. Healthy newborns weigh between 5-1/2 and 10 pounds and average 20 inches long. During their first few days, they typically lose 5–7% of their body weight, although in a study of 812 newborns in Canada, exclusively and partially breast-fed babies lost more than babies fed with formula (Martens & Romphf, 2007). You may think, then, that formula feeding is best. Losing weight during the first three days of life, however, is normal because of meconium loss (anal excretions) and little fluid intake. These researchers expressed concern that newborns who were formula fed might actually be overfed babies.

Many parents do not know what to expect with a newborn; thus the U.S. Department of Agriculture, U.S. Department of Education, & U.S. Department of Health and Human Services (2002) created a booklet available online to prepare parents and other caregivers. Following are a few of the facts that parents appreciate knowing.

- Newborns have a "soft spot" in the center of their head (bones not fused together) that allows their heads to be flexible during birth. The skull bones grow together by the age of 2.
- Babies differ in the amount of hair that they have. Most of the hair that babies are born with often rubs off.
- The umbilical cord stump drops off in 5 to 10 days. A physician will tell you how to treat the umbilical cord.
- Baby girls sometimes bleed from the vagina, and sometimes both boys and girls will have swollen breasts.
- Babies have special reflexes. (These will be described later in this chapter.)
- Newborns eat often—every 90 minutes to two hours—and will eat different amounts at each feeding.

Figure 4.3 describes what newborns need from the perspective of the baby. While most babies are born healthy, in the United States and worldwide, prematurity contributes to many challenges for babies and their families.

FIGURE 4.3

WHAT IT'S LIKE TO BE A NEWBORN

- I need others to take care of me.
- I can't decide things for myself.
- I need someone to love, feed, hold and play with me.
- I like to feel warm, and I don't like lots of noise.
- I like to be held very gently and very close.
- My face may be wrinkled, puffy or red, and I may have a large head, but I'm normal.
- I like to sleep a lot.
- I am hungry every few hours.
- I may be fussy and cry a lot.
- I need my diapers changed as soon as they are wet or soiled.

Source: U.S. Department of Agriculture, U.S. Department of Education, and U.S. Department of Health and Human Services (2002). Healthy start, grow smart, your newborn. Washington, D.C., 2002.

Prematurity and Low-Birth Weight Newborns

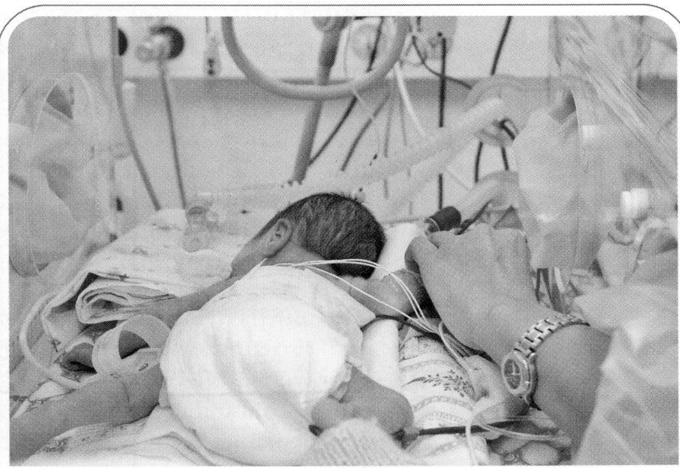

Premature babies need extensive monitoring and care—and the newborn diapers are often as big as the baby.

Angelia could not believe that her baby was born at 32 weeks. Her little girl was in the Neonatal Intensive Care Unit (NICU) at her local hospital, and Angelia and her mother knew nothing about premature babies. Would her baby live? What physical and emotional hurdles would the baby, mother, and grandmother face in the days to come? All Angelia knew was that she wanted to hold her baby in her arms and tell her how much she loved her.

A typical **full-term** infant is born about 40 weeks after the mother's last menstrual period. Approximately 12.8% of infants are born **prematurely** (before 37 weeks' gestational age) (March of Dimes, 2009b). Two percent of live births are born prior to 32 weeks. According to Kramer and Hogue (2009), delivering a baby preterm is the leading cause of infant mortality and morbidity in the United States. The most serious difficulty for premature infants is breathing. Preterm infants have little of a substance called **surfactin** that normally coats the lungs during the last 3 to 4 weeks of pregnancy to prevent the lungs from collapsing. Deficiencies in surfactin cause irregular breathing and can result in respiratory distress syndrome. Out of necessity, preterm infants often spend the first few weeks of their postnatal life in an isolette or ventilator, which maintains their body temperature and protects them from infection.

WHAT CAUSES PREMATURITY? A number of factors are related to premature births. Mothers may have toxemia or high blood pressure caused by pregnancy, infections, or abnormal structure of the uterus or an inability of the cervix to stay closed during pregnancy; mothers also may be drug users. There may be problems with the pregnancy including premature ruptures of the amniotic sac or abnormal placentas. Multiples (twins, triplets, and more) are likely to be born premature. For reasons not completely understood, African American women have a two- to threefold risk compared to Caucasian women of delivering a baby before 32 weeks, although Kramer and Hogue (2009) stress that both biological and social causes also must be considered. Causes for babies to be born before 28 weeks of gestation include inflammation of the uterus and aberrations of the placenta (McElrath et al., 2008).

WHY IS PREMATURITY A CONCERN? Prematurity increases the chances of birth defects, a health condition, or disability in a newborn. Researchers who conducted an analysis of live births from 24–44 weeks gestational age in 13 states concluded that birth defects were more than twice as common among preterm births (24–36 weeks) compared with term births (37–41 weeks gestation) and approximately 8% of preterm babies had a birth defect. Sixteen percent of very preterm babies (24–31 weeks gestation) had a birth defect, including central nervous system defects and cardiovascular defects (Honein et al., 2009).

The tiny babies born below 5-1/2 pounds may have organs that are not fully developed and have difficulty breathing and regulating their body temperature due to less body fat. Several conditions are of most concern.

- **Hyaline membrane disease,** also called respiratory distress syndrome, occurs when the air sacs of the lungs cannot stay open due to lack of surfactant in the lungs.
- **Chronic lung disease,** also called *bronchopulmonary dyspasia,* includes injury to lung tissue, contributing to long-term respiratory problems.
- **Apnea** (stopping breathing), sometimes causing heart and blood conditions, as well as feeding/digestion problems.
- **Necrotizing enterocolitis (NEC),** a serious disease of the intestines.
- **Intraventricular hemorrhage,** bleeding in the brain.
- **Retinopathy of prematurity,** where blood vessels grow abnormally in the eye.

LATE-PRETERM INFANTS. Staying in the womb until 39–40 weeks after the woman's last menstrual period is important for an infant's health. **Late-preterm** babies are those born between 34 and 36 weeks gestation (Kramer, 2008). These babies account for 70% of premature babies (March of Dimes, 2009b). There has been an increase in the number of late-preterm babies, and physicians now are realizing the risks of developmental delay and cognitive challenges for babies who are born even three to six weeks early (Kramer, 2009; Petrini et al., 2009). Michael S. Kramer, an expert on preterm births, emphasizes that the developmental problems of the babies may not stem from the early delivery itself, but from other fetal or maternal conditions that lead to early delivery.

LOW BIRTH WEIGHT, VERY LOW BIRTH WEIGHT, AND SMALL FOR GESTATIONAL AGE BABIES. Babies are considered **low birth weight** if they weigh below 5-1/2 pounds. **Very low birth weight (VLBW)** babies are born below 1,500 grams or approximately 3.3 pounds or below. Cole and colleagues and (2002) analyzed 178 English language research articles concerning babies weighing below 1,500 grams at birth. The authors conclude that the lower the birth weight of a baby, the more likely that baby is to have cerebral palsy, major neurological challenges, speech and language delays, cognitive delays, and/or hearing and vision loss. **Small-for-gestational-age (SGA)** babies are born too small (under 5-1/2 pounds) due to slow growth as fetuses, even though they are delivered close to their due date. Small-for-gestational-age infants who experience **intrauterine growth restriction** (poor growth in the uterus) are more likely than babies with an appropriate weight at birth to experience learning difficulties and behavior problems at school (Rogers & Piecuch, 2009).

In summary, both babies born before 37 weeks (or 38 in some research studies) and below 5-1/2 pounds are at risk for illness and future developmental challenges. We need to ask, "What can prevent these births?" and "What can be done to lessen the developmental and physical risks of these babies?" Innovative prevention programs, medical interventions, and social interaction therapies prevent premature births and improve outcomes for premature infants. Prevention of preterm births is critically important; research has shown that prenatal care decreases the number of these births (Leveno et al., 2009). Medical interventions are improving each day. For example, while doctors recommend that women who want to become pregnant and who are pregnant forgo caffeinated drinks, researchers are finding that caffeine may help premature babies after they are born. Professionals who teach family members how to be responsive to their infants through social interaction therapies make a difference as well.

Low birth weight infants are reported to be less irritable and more responsive, and to show quicker neurological and mental development if they are rocked, massaged, or soothed with the mother's voice. An experiment by Tiffany Field and her colleagues at the Touch Research Institute of the University of Miami School of Medicine examined the effects of 5 days of massage therapy on the weight gain and sleep/wake behavior of hospitalized preterm infants. Results indicated that the massage group averaged 53% greater daily weight gain, and spent less time sleeping at the end of 5 treatment days than the control group (Dieter, Field, Hernandex-Reif, Emory, & Redzepi, 2003). Linda Franck, from the Institute of Child Health in London, emphasizes that "This study suggests that, even for the very youngest premature babies, skin to skin contact can reduce the stress response" (BBC, 2008). As with other developmental challenges, the long-term consequences of low birth weight depend on the quality of postnatal nutrition (Rao et al., 2009) and the caregiving environment.

Neurobehavioral Assessment and Screening of Newborn Health and Vitality

The assessment of a newborn's health and behaviors provides important information for treatment and prevention of physical and developmental challenges. The *APGAR* and the *Neonatal Behavior Assessment Scale* are two assessments that professionals use.

APGAR. Most infants experience uneventful births; however, approximately 10% will require some medical intervention. The **APGAR** is a rating system developed by Virginia Apgar in 1952 to provide a way to determine the level of intervention that an infant might

TABLE 4.1 • **Apgar Scoring Scale**

The total APGAR score is the sum of the scores for the five signs.

	INFANT SCREENING FACTORS				
SCORE	HEART RATE	RESPIRATORY EFFORT	MUSCLE TONE	REFLEX RESPONSE	SKIN COLORATION
2	Normal (more than 100 beats per minute)	Normal rate and effort with a good cry	Active; flexed arms and legs	Pulls away, sneezes, or coughs if stimulated	Pink all over
1	Less than 100 beats per minute	Slow or irregular breathing with a weak cry	Arms and legs extended only; little movement	Facial movement only; facial grimace if stimulated	Pink body but hands and feet are bluish
0	Absent (no pulse)	Absent (no breathing)	No movement	Absent; no response to stimulation	Bluish gray or pale all over

Source: Based on "A Proposal for a New Method of Evaluation of the Newborn Infant" by Virginia Apgar, Current Researches in Anesthesia and Analgesia—July-August 1953.

need and the infant's response to intervention (Apgar, 1953). The APGAR has helped physicians see the newborn in a new way, as this scoring system advanced the attention paid by medical personnel to the condition of the newborn baby (Casey, McIntire, & Leveno, 2001) and provided a common language that improved communication among the medical staff.

Just after birth, medical personnel assess the infant's global physical condition by observing five characteristics: heart rate, respiratory effect, muscle tone, color, and reflex irritability. Each characteristic is given a score between 0 and 2 and the score is totaled. A neonate's score on the APGAR test can range from 0 to 10, with a higher score indicating a better condition. The APGAR test is repeated a second time after 5 minutes to measure improvements. Scores of 7 or higher indicate good physical condition and scores of 4 or lower indicate the need for immediate medical attention. This test is very helpful in assessing gross physical or neurological irregularities in the newborn. (See Table 4.1 for how to score an APGAR.)

Fox (1993) emphasized that "We must focus on what the APGAR score is and what it is not. The low APGAR score is not synonymous with perinatal asphyxia or neurologic handicap, and the high APGAR score is not a guarantee of health, ultimate quality of survival, or superior intelligence. We must keep the APGAR score in perspective. It is a descriptor of the baby's condition at specified times" (p. 1). In addition, with regard to preterm infants, the American Academy of Pediatrics, Committee on Fetus and Newborn (American Academy of Pediatrics, 2006) states, "There are no consistent data on the significance of the APGAR score in preterm infants" (p. 1444).

NEONATAL BEHAVIOR ASSESSMENT SCALE. In addition to the APGAR, medical or specially trained personnel assess newborns with the **Neonatal Behavioral Assessment Scale (NBAS),** a more subtle and specific measure of the neonate's health, neurological well-being, and behavior than the APGAR test (Brazelton & Nugent, 1995). Trained professionals administer the NBAS a few days after birth, ideally with the parents present. The NBAS measures 28 behaviors and 18 inborn reflexes (reactions to stimuli) that include how babies (1) regulate their breathing, their temperature, and other aspects of their autonomic system; (2) control their motor system; (3) manage "state" (levels of consciousness such as sleep, active awake, or quiet alert states); and (4) interact socially.

The NBAS items demonstrate how capable babies are, and what each unique baby might need to interact and develop successfully. By creating this assessment, Brazelton and his colleagues (2008) helped change the view of babies as helpless and knowing nothing to the view that infants are "highly capable when they are born." The NBAS items reveal that infants communicate by responding to cues; they like the sound of their parents' voices; they cry and make other sounds that enable adults to understand how they are feeling; and their movements have meaning.

The NBAS examines a baby's strengths as well as his or her vulnerabilities. "The Scale gives us the chance to see what the baby's behavior will tell us," and "[i]t gives us a window into what it will take to nurture the baby" (Brazelton Institute, 2008). Each infant is unique; for example, some are more sensitive to light and sounds, whereas others are not. While the baby is asleep, the examiner briefly shines a light in her eyes. You can predict that a baby will blink and squirm, indicating irritation. However, when the examiner repeats the process several times, the infant's ability to ignore the stimulation allows her to conserve energy. If the baby has difficulty blocking the stimulation, then the examiner discusses with the parents how they can support their child by their sensitivity to her responses to light and sound and by exposing her to stimulation gradually. As parents observe a specialist administering the NBAS, they are in awe of the capabilities of newborns whose eyes follow a ball from one side of their body to another, and who turn to the sound of the parent's voice. They begin to understand their baby's individual preferences and ways of handling stress. A positive parent–child relationship begins, and this, is after all, the ultimate goal of the NBAS.

SCREENING FOR PHYSICAL DISORDERS. An important component of public health is newborn screening for genetic, metabolic, hormonal, and functional disorders via blood samples. The March of Dimes (2009a) reports that often these birth defects are not visible at birth, but if not detected early, they may cause physical problems, intellectual challenges, and in some cases, death. Newborn screening began in the United States in the 1960s and now is practiced throughout the world, although there are great differences among states in the United States and across countries concerning how many newborns are screened (coverage), the genetic conditions that are screened, and the technologies used for screening. For example, some countries strive for universal coverage (100% of newborns screened), but others do not. Some countries screen for only one disorder, whereas others screen for all of the 29 core conditions identified by the American College of Medical Genetics that are treatable. The 29 core conditions can be divided into five major categories (March of Dimes, 2009a):

- Amino acid metabolism disorders
- Organic acid metabolism disorders
- Fatty acid oxidation disorders
- Hemoglobinopathies
- Others

Typically, the government or a Minister of Health mandates screening programs in a country and the public funds the screening program, although in some countries, screening is voluntary and parental permission is required before screening occurs. Common disorders that are screened are discussed below.

Phenylketonuria (PKU) and congenital hypothyroidism (CH) are the conditions most frequently screened. In Europe, for instance, all member states of the European Union are required to provide newborn screening. Infants with PKU cannot process a part of protein called phenylalanine, which is found in most foods. Phenylalanine builds up in the bloodstream, causing brain damage; however, if it is detected early, parents prevent their children's intellectual challenges by giving their babies a low-phenylalanine diet, which children generally follow throughout life. Congenital hypothyroidism (CH) affects at least one baby in 5,000 (March of Dimes, 2009a.). This thyroid hormone deficiency retards growth and brain development, but when physicians treat the baby with oral doses of thyroid hormone, normal development occurs.

HEARING SCREENING. Determining hearing problems early is vitally important. When hearing loss is detected before 2 months of age, the outcomes for language development are significantly better (Yoshinaga-Itano & Apuzzo, 1998; Yoshinaga-Itano, Sedey, Coulter, & Mehl, 1998) than if children's hearing challenges are discovered after that time. Without

TABLE 4.2 • **Misconceptions about Children's Hearing Loss**

MISCONCEPTION	CLINICAL FACT
Parents will know if their child has a hearing loss by the time their child is 2–3 months of age.	Prior to the universal screening, the average age at which children were found to have a hearing loss is 2–3 years. Children with mild-to-moderate hearing loss were often not identified until 4 years of age.
Parents can identify a hearing loss by clapping their hands behind the child's head.	Children can compensate for a hearing loss. They use visual cues, such as shadows or parental expressions and reactions, or they may feel the breeze caused by the motion of the hands.
The HRR* is all that is needed to identify children with hearing loss.	The HRR misses approximately 50% of all children with hearing loss.
Hearing loss does not occur often enough to justify the use of universal screening programs.	Hearing loss affects approximately 2–4 per 1000 live births, and it has been estimated to be one of the most common congenital anomalies.
Tests are not reliable and cause too many infants to be referred to specialists.	Referral rates are as low as 5–7%.
There is no rush to identify a hearing loss. The loss does not need to be identified until a child is aged 2–3 years.	Children identified when they are older than 6 months can have speech and language delays. Children identified when they are younger than 6 months do not have these delays and are equal to their hearing peers in terms of speech and language.
Children younger than 12 months cannot be fitted with hearing aids.	Children as young as 1 month of age can be fit with and benefit from hearing aids.

*HRR: High Risk Register
Source: De Michele, A. M., & Ruth, R. A. (2008), Newborn Hearing Screening. http://emedicine.medscape.com. Table used with permission from EMEDICINE.com.

hearing screening for newborns, the average age that physicians and/or parents discover children's hearing challenges is at 2–3 years of age, long after the optimal period for language development. You may legitimately ask why there are states that do not provide universal screening for hearing loss with all newborns. De Michele and Ruth (2008) state that this lack of universal screening may be the result of many misconceptions about hearing loss. Their clinical findings that contradict these misconceptions are found in Table 4.2.

The American Speech-Language-Hearing Association (ASHA, 2010) reports that the screening of newborns and infants involves the use of noninvasive, objective physiologic measures that include otoacoustic emissions (OAEs) and/or auditory brainstem response (ABR). Both procedures are painless and professionals conduct them while the infant is resting quietly. Kibby, Mersch, Bredenkamp, and Shiel (2009) describe the OAE and ABR tests as follows. In an OAE test, the clinician inserts a small microphone and speaker (on a probe) into the infant's ear, generates sounds through the probe, measures the emission or sound that bounces back from the inner ear or cochlea, and determines which sounds emitted a response. An ABR measures the electrical impulses that nerves transmit from the ears to the brainstem at the base of the brain. The clinician places on the infant's head four or five electrodes that capture the firing of nerves as sounds, which are presented through small earphones to the infant and travel from the ear to the brainstem. Clinicians can view the nerve firings represented as waveforms on a computer screen. Parents of infants who fail these tests are referred to an audiologist for further evaluation of their children's hearing.

VISION SCREENING. Newborn and first year vision screenings are important, as well. Neurological and central nervous system injuries are the leading causes of vision impairment in children in Western countries (Good, 2007). Good recommends that the term *impairment* be used in these cases of neurological injury because virtually all of these children are not blind, but have some preservation of vision. Vision exams should be conducted at birth and at 6 to 8 weeks to determine either vision impairment or the presence of cataracts, as they cloud the eye lens; dense cataracts must be removed by 3 months of age to prevent blindness. A study done in Britain showed that although eye exams are required at birth, ophthalmologists saw only 57% of the children with cataracts by the age of 3 months (Rahi & Dezateux, 1999). This meant that 43% of the infants with cataracts were at risk for vision impairment or blindness. In addition, in the case of vascular birthmarks (hemangiomas) on the upper or lower eyelids, physicians should conduct vision tests immediately to determine if the birthmarks were interfering with vision and creating amblyopia (weaker vision in one eye) or permanent reductions in vision. New visual acuity tests allow physicians to detect "amblyopia-like effects" in children with eyelid hemangiomas (Good, 1997).

Vaccinations

Most physicians and health providers consider vaccinations to be children's best defense again infectious diseases. For a schedule of recommended vaccinations, see the following website: http://www.cdc.gov/vaccines/recs/schedules/downloads/child/2009/09_0-6yrs_schedule_pr.pdf During the last 10 years, controversy has swirled about the possible contribution of vaccines to children's development of **autism** (a disorder of communication and perception identified before age 3). A number of parents who have children with autism are convinced that their children's behavior changed after receiving vaccinations. Well-constructed research does not support the claim that vaccines (too many at one time, harmful ingredients, etc.) cause autism (Gerber & Offit, 2009). However, while it fully recommends that all children receive vaccinations, the CDC (2009d) states that our bodies react differently to vaccines and that a very small proportion of children may have side effects or may not be totally protected after receiving vaccines. They recommend that parents talk with a trusted physician about any concerns that they may have, but the best evidence to date indicates the benefits of vaccination to individuals and society far outweigh the risks.

Newborns' Reflexes and States Promote Survival and Relationships

Infant Reflexes

Understanding the reflexes of infants leads to better parent– or teacher–child relationships. **Reflexes** are involuntary movements of infants that support their survival. **Survival reflexes**, such as the breathing, rooting, sucking and swallowing, and eye blink reflexes ensure that neonates will be able to breathe, find the nipple, eat by sucking, and protect their eyes. **Primitive reflexes** have developed in humans over many thousands of years and include the grasping, moro, babinski, and tonic-neck reflexes (see Table 4.3). These ancient reflexes serve to protect infants. With the moro and babinski reflexes, infants are better able to grab on to the parent's body, grasping the parent's hair as he or she is moving. While these reflexes may have limited value today when parents carry their babies or push them in a stroller, they continue to exist and serve as a form of communication to sensitive parents. When a neonate startles and throws her arms out with hands wide open, her parents know that they need to hold her or swaddle her to facilitate her becoming calm again.

Reflexes provide a means for physicians to determine the neurological development of infants. Most reflexes disappear during the first year of life. Table 4.3 provides information on when each reflex typically disappears. Reflexes that are not present at birth or that do not disappear at a typical age may indicate problems with the infants' neurological system.

Infant States

States are cyclic periods of arousal, activity, and sleep. Table 4.4 on page 132 provides a list of nine different states of arousal in infants. When parents, teachers, and other adults who interact with babies know about states, this provides a new level of understanding of infant behavior, needs, and communication and enables the adults to build responsive

TABLE 4.3 • **Major Reflexes Present in Infancy**

SURVIVAL REFLEXES	
Breathing reflex	Inhales/exhales, oxygenating the red blood cells and expelling carbon dioxide.
Rooting reflex	Turns in the direction of a touch on the cheek as though searching for a nipple. Serves to orient the infant to the breast or the bottle.
Sucking and swallowing reflex	Stimulated by a nipple placed in the mouth; allows the infant to take in nourishment.
Eyeblink and pupillary reflex	Eyes close or blink; pupils dilate or constrict to protect the eyes.
PRIMITIVE REFLEXES	
Grasping reflex	Holds firmly to an object touching the palm of the hand. Disappearance around the 4th month signals advancing neurological development.
Moro reflex	Often referred to as the *startle reflex*; a loud noise or sudden jolt causes the arms to thrust outward, then return to an embrace-like position. Disappearance around the 4th or 6th month signals advancing neurological development.
Babinski reflex	Toes fan outward, then curl when the bottom of the foot is stroked. Disappearance by the end of the 1st year signals advancing neurological development.
Tonic neck reflex	A "fencing pose," often assumed when sleeping—head turned to one side, arm extended on the same side, and opposite arm and leg flexed at the elbow and knee. Disappearance around 7 months signals advancing neurological development.

Source: Puckett, et al., The Young Child, Table 5.2 "Major Reflexes Present in Infancy" p. 124, © 2009. Reproduced by permission of Pearson Education, Inc.

relationships with infants to help them feel understood and able to communicate. We may think that we would have noticed these states in babies, and many adults do respond sensitively without knowing the names of the states. However, knowledge often helps us "see" and understand the importance of these behaviors.

"Reading" the state of the child is an important aspect of responsive caregiving. When an adult tries to interact with a drowsy baby, both the caregiver and the baby may feel frustrated. Drowsy time is an ideal time to support the infant in falling sleep. Further, when a caregiver plays with an alert baby, he is taking advantage of an ideal time for building relationships. In this way, adults' familiarity with the different infant "states" is another key to building optimal relationships.

Crying-Soothing

Crying is one of the nine states that infants and toddlers experience. Researchers conclude that infants can have different types of cries—their own distinctive signatures—and even if the cries are similar to typical children's cries, adults may interpret the cries of infants in unique ways based on their culture, social experiences, and emotional states. A mother who experiences post-partum depression may interpret normal crying as annoying, whereas a parent or teacher who has much support from loved ones may understand that an infant's cries are normal and meaningful.

Crying is the baby's way to communicate his needs to adults when, for example, the tummy rumbles with hunger or pain courses through the infant's body. Yet, parents are unsure about whether they should comfort their crying baby during the infants' first 12 weeks of life (Queensland University of Technology, 2006). Researchers Dowd, Thorpe, and Halle interviewed first time and experienced parents, and discovered that 20% of first time parents and 30% of experienced parents were uncertain about picking up their very young baby for fear of "spoiling them." The researchers assured parents that during the first

TABLE 4.4 • **Nine Infant States of Arousal**

STATES	CHARACTERISTICS
Awake	
Alert	Eyes open, bright, and attentively scanning
Nonalert waking	Eyes open but dull and unfocused. Motor activity often high; isolated fussing is possible
Fuss	Continuous or intermittent low intensity fussing
Cry	Intense vocalizations, singly or in succession
Transition States Between Sleep and Waking	
Drowse	Eyes either open or opening and closing slowly; usually little motor activity
Sleep-wake transition	Usually generalized motor activity; eyes may be closed or open and close rapidly. Isolated fusses may occur. This state usually occurs when the baby is awakening.
Sleep States	
Active sleep	Eyes closed, uneven respiration, and low muscle tone despite sporadic movement. Rapid eye movements (REMs) occur intermittently, as do smiles, frowns, grimaces, sighs, grunts, cries, mouthing, and sucking.
Quiet sleep	Eyes closed, respiration slow, regular, and deep. Tonic motor tone but limited motor activity, especially in preterm infants.
Transition Sleep State	
Active-quiet transition	Typically occurs between periods of active and quiet sleep; eyes closed and sleep. Little motor activity. Respiration pattern is intermediate between that of quiet and active sleep.

Source: Adapted from Lamb, M.E., Bornstein, M.H., & Teti, D.M. (2002). Development in infancy. (4th Ed.). Mahwah, NJ: Lawrence Erlbaum Associates (p. 135). Originally adapted from data provided by Thoman, E.B., & Whitney, M.P. (1990). Behavioral states in infants: Individual differences and individual analyses. In J. Colombo & J. Fagen (Eds.), Individual differences in infancy: Reliability, stability, prediction (pp 113–136). Hillsdale, NJ: Lawrence Erlbaum Associates. Reproduced with permission of Taylor & Francis Group LLC - Books in the formats Textbook and Other Book via Copyright Clearance Center.

12 weeks of their lives, babies need highly responsive parents to help them become calm and gain trust. In an interview, Dr. Dominique Cousineau explained:

> In the first few months of life, the mother and the child are one. Holding babies and responding quickly to their cries helps develop their sense of security and plays an important role in developing the attachment relationship. It also fosters cerebral growth. Parents are teaching their baby that there is a consistent response to their actions, and this helps the brain organize and structure itself. (Krakow, 2007, p. 5)

Responsiveness to crying helps babies regulate their physiological and emotional responses. This in turn, influences long-term infant responses to distress. Almost 40 years ago, Bell and Ainsworth (1972) found that parental responsiveness to young infants' distress led to less crying and higher levels of other forms of communication at 1 year of age. More recently, Jalromi and Stifter (2007) found similar results after observing specific maternal regulatory behaviors in direct response to infant distress in 128 mother-infant dyads during the infants' inoculations at 2 and 6 months. The researchers found that mother's affection, touching, and vocalizing at 2 months predicted reduced lengths of infants' crying at 6 months of age—although not the intensity of crying. Infants were still surprised at the intruding needle and probably gave an intense burst of crying, but were able to calm down more quickly than did infants of mothers who used fewer of the soothing behaviors at 2 months. From a relationship-based perspective, responding to infants' cries as communication led to infants' higher levels of regulation later.

Periodic crying is normal, and knowing this fact may help parents control any anger and frustration they have toward their baby and gather their energy for experimenting with different ways to comfort an inconsolable baby. The quantity of crying typically increases during the first few months (the babies' crying—not the parents' crying) with a peak around 6 to 8 weeks of age. Many parents do not know this fact and think that their poor parenting skills are contributing to the infant's increased crying.

There are infants who cry excessively and/or persistently, taxing parents', teachers', or other professionals' coping skills. Krakow (2007) reports on work by Dr. Cynthia Stifter, who defines two types of excessive crying. Ten percent of infants may have persistent crying in the first 3 months of life that Dr. Stifter calls "colic." Other infants who are continuously difficult to soothe may have a "difficult temperament" (discussed later in the chapter). Prolonged crying after 3 months of age that is not colic may be related to cognitive challenges at age 5 (Rao, Brenner, Schisterman, Vik, & Mills, 2004); however, the way caregivers respond to the crying and neurological reasons may also contribute to excessive crying. For example, infants with a genetic condition called *Cri-du-chat syndrome* have a high-pitched cry that resembles a cat's vocalization.

Unfortunately, crying babies are one of the leading causes of SBS/AHT (Shaken Baby Syndrome/Abusive Head Trauma)—a constellation of symptoms resulting from violent shaking and/or impacting of the head. See Figure 4.4 for a description of what happens in a baby's brain when he or she is shaken.

The immediate consequences include compromised breathing, irritability, limp arms or legs, vomiting or poor feeding, decreased levels of consciousness, inability to suck or swallow, heart stopping, or death. Long-term consequences include learning, physical, visual, hearing, speech, cognitive, and/or behavior disabilities; cerebral palsy; seizures; and death (National Center on Shaken Baby Syndrome, nd). Intervention materials can help parents to NEVER shake a crying baby or hit the baby.

The National Center on Shaken Baby Syndrome has developed intervention materials called *The Period of PURPLE Crying*: **P** for crying peak; **U** for unexpected; **R** for resistance to soothing; **P** for pain-like face (even when the infant is not in pain); **L** for long crying bouts;

FIGURE 4.4

WHAT HAPPENS TO THE BRAIN WHEN A BABY IS SHAKEN

When babies are shaken, the child's head swings back and forth which causes bleeding in the brain, bleeding in the retina, and damage to the spinal cord and neck; it also may fracture ribs and bones.

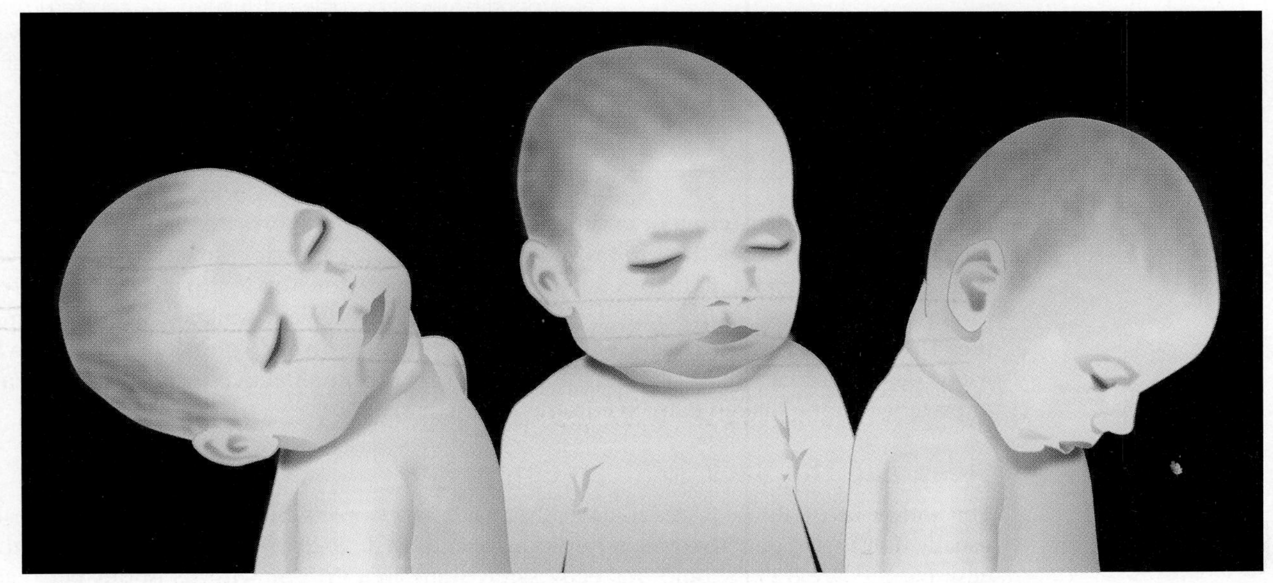

POINT/COUNTERPOINT: Should Babies Sleep with Their Parents?

Co-sleeping occurs when the parent(s) sleep with the baby in the family bed. With solitary sleeping, babies sleep in a crib, often in another room. The U.S. Consumer Product Safety Commission (CPSC) and the American Academy of Pediatrics recommend that infants **not** sleep with their parents (AAP, 2005a.), stating that the practice puts babies at risk of suffocation and strangulation. Even so, co-sleeping occurs in most cultures in the world (Oskar & O'Connor, 2005; Small, 1998). Is a baby sleeping with his/her parents in the family bed a good idea?

POINT

Yes, it just makes sense. The KidsHealth Web Site (http://kidshealth.org/parent/general/sleep/cosleeping.html#) emphasizes that "cosleeping supporters believe—and some studies support their beliefs—that cosleeping:

- encourages breastfeeding by making nighttime breastfeeding more convenient
- makes it easier for a nursing mother to get her sleep cycle in sync with her baby's
- helps babies fall asleep more easily, especially during their first few months and when they wake up in the middle of the night
- helps babies get more nighttime sleep (because they awaken more frequently with shorter duration of feeds, which can add up to a greater amount of sleep throughout the night)
- helps parents who are separated from their babies during the day regain the closeness with their infant that they feel they missed"

Ball (2002) emphasizes that with an increase in breastfeeding, there is a corresponding increase in co-sleeping.

COUNTERPOINT

No, co-sleeping never makes sense—Babies should sleep in their own beds. As mentioned above, the U.S. Consumer Product Safety Commission (CPSC) and the American Academy of Pediatrics state that co-sleeping puts babies at risk of suffocation and strangulation. While co-sleeping is prevalent in many countries, parents in these countries generally sleep on firmer surfaces than parents do in the United States.

The KidsHealth website (http://kidshealth.org/parent/general/sleep/cosleeping.html#) cites CPSC data concerning more than 100 infant deaths between January 1999 and December 2001 attributable to hidden hazards for babies on adult beds, including:

- suffocation when an infant gets trapped or wedged between a mattress and headboard, wall, or other object
- suffocation resulting from a baby being face-down on a waterbed, a regular mattress, or on soft bedding such as pillows, blankets, or quilts
- strangulation in a bed frame that allows part of an infant's body to pass through an area while trapping the baby's head

Beware of Either/Or

Whether a parent should sleep with an infant is a complex question. As always, multiple variables influence the outcomes of co-sleeping for the parent and child. Sudden infant death syndrome occurs in higher rates among co-sleepers in poverty environments, when a mother smokes, when bedding is soft, and when the baby is in a prone (face down) position (McKenna & McDade, 2005). In an article titled, "Why Babies Should Never Sleep Alone: A Review of the Co-sleeping Controversy in Relation to SIDS, Bedsharing and Breast Feeding," McKenna and McDade (2005) emphasized that there are many kinds of co-sleeping, including babies sleeping in the same room, but not in the same bed as parents. For more information on the culture of sleep and how infants', toddlers', and twos' teachers can support families from different cultures and children in early care and education programs, go to: http://www.ehsnrc.org/Publications/nycu_archive/nycu_sleep.htm to see a publication of the Early Childhood Resource Center.

and **E** for evening clustering of crying. Eva Krakow (2007) reports that "caregivers are encouraged to take three actions to prevent SBS: First, increase their contact, carry, walk, and talk responses, which will help reduce crying, although not stop it altogether. Secondly, if the crying becomes too frustrating, put the baby in the crib and walk away for a few minutes to calm themselves. Finally, never shake or hurt their baby" (p. 4). Researchers who used these materials in a class situation found them to be effective in changing parents' knowledge about Shaken Baby Syndrome (Barr et al., 2009).

Sleep and the Back to Sleep Campaign

The author Leo J. Burke is said to have observed that people who say they sleep like a baby usually don't have one. Two main questions asked by sleep-deprived new parents to other new parents are: (1) "Should our baby sleep alone in a crib or with us in our bed?" and

(2) "How much does your baby sleep?" (See the ***Point/Counterpoint*** for information on whether infants should sleep in the family bed.) A discussion of the second question follows. Few topics are more important to parents, and yet research studies on how much and when infants sleep are rare.

HOURS OF SLEEP. Iglowstein, Jenni,, Molinari, and Largo (2003) studied children from Zurich, Switzerland. Parents were asked to complete structured sleep-related questionnaires when their children were 1, 3, 6, 9, 12, 18, and 24 months old and then at annual intervals until 16 years of age. Total sleep duration averaged 14.2 hours at 6 months of age and 12.5 at three years of age. The total hours of sleep decreased by approximately two hours from 6 months to 3 years of age. Hours of nighttime sleep did not change much from 6 months of age (an average of 11 hours) to 3 years of age (an average of 11.4 hours).

PREVENTING SIDS—SAFE SLEEPING: BABIES MUST SLEEP ON THEIR BACKS. In 1992, the American Academy of Pediatrics published guidelines for infants to be placed on their backs to sleep in order to prevent Sudden Infant Death Syndrome—the death of an infant that is unexplained. In 2005, the AAP (2005a) recommended that to reduce the risk of SIDS, babies must be placed to sleep on their backs and not on their sides or stomachs. Blankets, pillows, quilts, or any other soft or loose bedding should not be used. (See Figure 4.5 for a listing of safe sleeping practices for infants.) Even so, parents are receiving the wrong message in popular women's magazines. Researchers Joyner, Gill-Bailey, and Moon (2009) analyzed 329 unique pictures found in 24 magazines with

FIGURE 4.5

THE TOP 10 SAFE SLEEPING PRACTICES FOR INFANTS

1. **Always place your baby on his or her back to sleep, for naps and at night.** The back sleep position is the safest, and every sleep time counts.
2. **Place your baby on a firm sleep surface, such as on a safety-approved crib mattress, covered by a fitted sheet.** Never place your baby to sleep on pillows, quilts, sheepskins, or other soft surfaces.
3. **Keep soft objects, toys, and loose bedding out of your baby's sleep area.** Don't use pillows, blankets, quilts, sheepskins, or pillow-like crib bumpers in your baby's sleep area, and keep all objects away from your baby's face.
4. **Do not allow smoking around your baby.** Don't smoke before or after the birth of your baby, and don't let others smoke around your baby.
5. **Keep your baby's sleep area close to, but separate from, where you and others sleep.** Your baby should not sleep in a bed or on a couch or armchair with adults or other children, but he or she can sleep in the same room as you. If you bring your baby into bed with you to breastfeed, put him or her back in a separate sleep area, such as a bassinet, crib, cradle, or a bedside cosleeper (infant bed that attaches to an adult bed) when finished.
6. **Think about using a clean, dry pacifier when placing the infant down to sleep, but don't force the baby to take it.** (If you are breastfeeding your baby, wait until your child is 1 month old or is used to breastfeeding before using a pacifier.)
7. **Do not let your baby overheat during sleep.** Dress your baby in light sleep clothing, and keep the room at a temperature that is comfortable for an adult.
8. **Avoid products that claim to reduce the risk of SIDS** because most have not been tested for effectiveness or safety.
9. **Do not use home monitors to reduce the risk of SIDS.** If you have questions about using monitors for other conditions talk to your health care provider.
10. **Reduce the chance that flat spots will develop on your baby's head:** provide "Tummy Time" when your baby is awake and someone is watching; change the direction that your baby lies in the crib from one week to the next; and avoid too much time in car seats, carriers and bouncers.

Source: Eunice Kennedy Shriver National Institute of Child Health and Human Development, NIH, DHHS. (2005). Safe Sleep for Your Baby: What Does a Safe Sleep Environment Look Like? (05-5759). Washington, DC: U.S. Government Printing Office.

wide circulation to parenting-aged women. They concluded that, "16 years after the initial AAP recommendations to place infants in a nonprone position, more than one third of pictures of sleeping infants in magazines geared toward childbearing women demonstrated infants in an inappropriate sleep position and two thirds of pictures of the infant sleep environment were not consistent with AAP recommendations" (e 419). These researchers' findings are alarming. Based on the pictures in the 24 magazines, only 57 pictures (64%) portraying sleeping infants not being held by an adult showed the infants in the supine position, 32 (36%) of the infants were in the side or prone (on the tummy) position, and 18 infants (4.8%) were portrayed as sleeping with another person. Of the 99 pictures of infant sleep environments that did not show the infant present, only 36 pictures (36.4%) of infant sleep environments portrayed a safe sleep environment as recommended by the AAP.

In 1986, the U.S. Consumer Product Safety Commission (2001) required that full-size infant cribs have slats that are less than or equal to 2-3/8 inches apart to prevent infants from wedging their heads through the bars. Cribs do not need bumper pads (a continuous pad tied to the inside frame of the crib) to be safe for infants. In fact, even firm bumper pads contribute to a risk of suffocation, and the ties of bumper pads can strangle infants (Thach, Rutherford, & Harris, 2007). The AAP recommends that if parents or day care teachers do place bumper pads around the inside of the crib, they must be firm, well secured, and not pillow-like. The U.S. Consumer Product Safety Commission (2010) reports on recalls of cribs with drop-down sides because of sides breaking or detaching, causing infant suffocation. The website http://www.cpsc.gov/ is a good one to check periodically for recalls of equipment and toys for safety reasons.

Excessive sitting or sleeping in car seats, swings, carriers, and bouncy seats contributes to an increase in head deformities among infants because of the constant pressure on the backs of their heads (Littlefield, Kelly, Reiff, & Pomatto, 2003) (see photo). Although many infants may enjoy sleeping or sitting in these devices, parents, teachers, or other professionals must be aware of the potential for cranial distortions for infants. Children in childcare and other programs should not sit in car seats—they should be in the arms of caregivers, playing on the floor, or sleeping in their cribs.

Without good health, a child's development is impeded and the child and family's well-being is hampered. Healthy growth and development also depend on good nutrition.

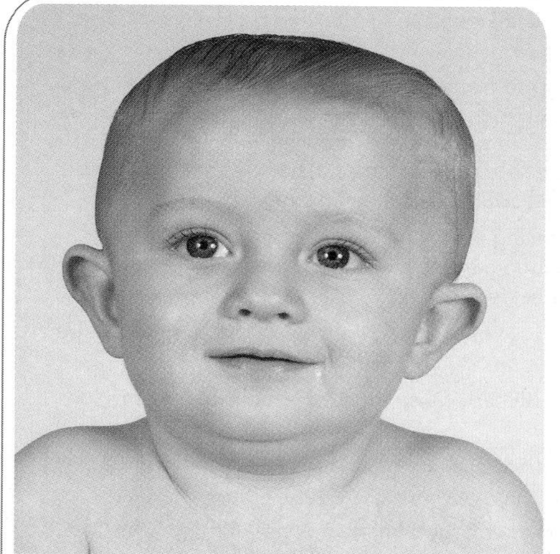

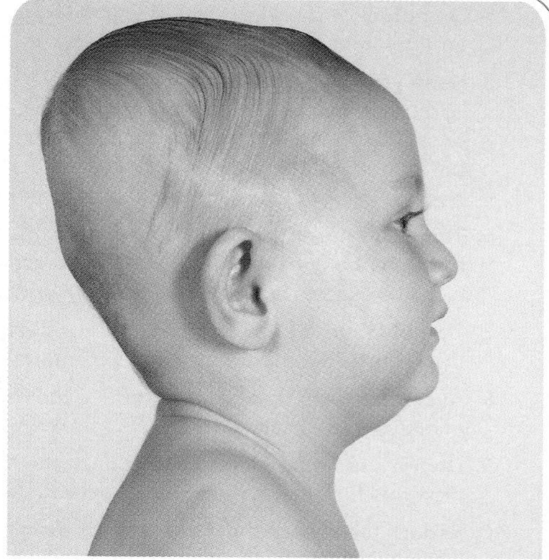

This 9-month-old child routinely spent 10 hours a day in a car seat, bouncy chair, or swing. Note the cranial distortion in the second photo. ("Images provided courtesy of Cranial Technologies, Inc." From Littlefield, T.R., Kelly K.M., Reiff J.L., Pomatto J.K., *Journal of Prothestics and Orthotics* July 2003; 15:3; 102-106.)

Physical Growth and Nutrition of the Infant and Toddler

Physical Growth

As any parent or teacher of infants and toddlers knows, it sometimes seems as if an infant grew during the middle of the night. We now know that it is a true phenomenon and not a figment of the parent's imagination. Infants and toddlers seem to grow in spurts—growing for several days (often at night) and then resting (Lampl. Veldhuis, & Johnson, 1992; Noonan et al., 2004). Because girls grow at a different pace than boys, the CDC developed two different charts that highlight typical growth. You can find these growth charts (2000 revision) at the following websites:

Boys 0–36 months
http://www.cdc.gov/growthcharts/data/set1clinical/Cj41cs017c.pdf
Girls 0–36 months:
http://www.cdc.gov/growthcharts/data/set1clinical/Cj41cs018c.pdf

Nutrition

The United States Department of Agriculture (2010) provides the most recent information and resources on infant and toddler nutrition. Breastfeeding is highly recommended, as is not introducing solid foods until after 4–6 months.

BREASTFEEDING. Human breast milk is ideal for infants. It is composed of lactose—a sugar that provides energy—and lipids—healthy fats. The mother's colostrum—a thick, yellowish first milk secreted in the first few days after birth—prepares infants' intestines for food (Marchbank, Weaver, Nilsen-Hamilton, & Playford, 2009) and is full of antibodies. Proteins in breast milk remove bacteria, viruses, and other dangerous pathogens from infants' gastrointestinal tracts (Wilson et al., 2008). The American Academy of Pediatrics policy statement on breastfeeding (2005b) cites strong evidence that infants who are breastfed have less diarrhea, fewer infectious diseases, fewer cases of otitis media (ear infections), fewer urinary tract infections, lower obesity rates, and decreases in the rates of sudden infant death syndrome in the first year of life. However, is breastfeeding good for high-risk infants who are born small for gestational age?

The AAP (2005b) highly recommends that premature and high-risk infants also receive breast milk by direct breastfeeding or with mother's expressed milk, although expressed human milk for very low birth weight babies may need to be fortified. Infants born small for gestational age do benefit greatly from breastfeeding. A research study conducted with 550 European children found that when babies who were small for gestational age were breastfed, they had higher intelligence levels at 3-1/2 years of age (Slykerman et al., 2005). Another study with Norwegian and Swedish infants found that babies born small for gestational age who were breastfed for 24 weeks as opposed to 12 weeks were predicted to have an 11-point IQ advantage at age 5 (Rao, Hediger, Levine, Naficy, & Vik, 2002).

There are benefits to breastfeeding mothers as well as their babies. The American Academy of Pediatrics (2005b) states that mothers experience the following:

- decreased postpartum bleeding and more rapid uterine involution
- decreased menstrual blood loss and increased child spacing (lactational amenorrhea)
- earlier return to prepregnancy weight
- decreased risk of breast and ovarian cancers

INTRODUCTION OF SOLID FOODS. When introducing solid foods, talk with a physician about when and what to feed the infant and consider the recommendations in Figure 4.6.

Obesity—a condition of being extremely overweight— is now a national health concern. Physicians recommend that parents and day care teachers focus on feeding children healthy foods, decreasing sweet foods, and offering many opportunities for active play. We talk about childhood nutrition in greater detail in Chapter 8.

FIGURE 4.6

NUTRITION FOR INFANTS AND TODDLERS

Some things to watch for:

- Make sure your child gets enough iron.
- Toddlers between 1 and 3 need 500 milligrams of calcium each day.
- Dietary fiber is important after age 3 because it might prevent diseases later on.
- Don't feed your baby eggs, citrus fruits and juices, cow's milk or honey until after his or her first birthday.
- Don't feed your child seafood, peanuts or tree nuts before age 2 or 3.

Source: http://www.nlm.nih.gov/medlineplus/infantandtoddlernutrition.html

Infant and Toddler Development and Learning

Infants and toddlers develop and learn in six domains—sensory and perceptual, cognitive, emotional, social, language, and motor—in the context of their culture and family. We have discussed how infants and toddlers communicate their needs, but in this section of the chapter, you will learn what they know and how they learn. Let's start with a discussion of five topics to explain development and learning. As you read, remember that a complex interaction between nature (genes) and nurture (the environment) explains how infants and toddlers develop and learn. After the discussion of these five topics, the six domains of development and learning are discussed in detail.

1. You might ask, "Is there such a thing as a 'normal' infant or toddler or family context?" The simple answer is "yes" in a broad sense. Piaget's stage theory supports the idea of universal, biological, "normal" synchrony of development with stages of growth that are distinct from each other and similar across individuals and cultures. If development is synchronous, then all aspects of mental or motor development emerge at the same age. In a stage theory model, development is considered discontinuous because in each stage of development the child thinks differently than in the previous and forthcoming stage. As a counterargument to "stage" theory, Fischer and Silvern (1985) propose that development is sequential and continuous, that each child develops differently from others, and that different aspects of development emerge at different times within an individual child. Motor development, for example, may exceed language development, and even within a domain such as cognitive development, different skills emerge based on the child's experience and environment (i.e., knowing about cause/effect or the permanence of objects). Information processing theory emphasizes that development is continuous, with one skill building on previous ones. Lamb, Bornstein, and Teti (2002) sum up this topic in the following way: "It thus seems inappropriate to talk about cohesive 'stages' of cognitive development in infancy, or even later. Stage implies synchrony of development, and synchrony may occur less frequently than the term stage connotes" (p. 215). Other theorists and researchers emphasize the role of dynamic systems theory and culture in children's development and learning.
2. A dynamic systems theory (Thelan & Smith, 1998), discussed briefly in Chapter 2, emphasizes that competencies in all domains of development emerge from experience rather than from maturation alone and that many systems, including perception, cognition, motor, and emotional development, work together as a child learns to roll over, crawl, and move in many ways. Adolph, Karasik, and Tamis-LeMonda (2010) use motor development to explain dynamic systems theory. They emphasize that infant and toddler development is not just a result of skills learned in sequence and at a universally, biologically set timetable. These authors propose that child rearing practices and other contextual factors alter the course of motor development. In fact, researchers summarizing Adolph's work conclude that motor development involves "complex reciprocal relations among maturation,

perception, and experience" (Lamb, Bornstein, & Teti, 2002, p. 129). Adolph, Karasik, and Tamis-LeMonda (2009), reporting on cultural differences, state the following:

> In Jamaica, for example, 29% of infants skipped crawling, and the remaining infants began crawling at the same age as they began walking—10.1 months and 10.0 months for crawling and walking, respectively (Hopkins & Westra, 1989, 1990). The surprise is that crawling—a skill featured on the Gesell and Bayley scales as a major milestone en route to walking—could be entirely missing from the repertoire of healthy infants, or misplaced in the normative sequence. Indeed, up to 17% of British infants skip crawling (10% hitch in a sitting position, and 7% simply stand up and walk), providing further evidence that crawling is not an obligatory milestone (Robson, 1984). One hundred years ago, 40% of American infants skipped crawling (Trettien, 1900). Instead, they hitched, crabbed on their backs, or log-rolled, perhaps to avoid catching their knees and feet at the edge of their long gowns (Hrdlicka, 1928). Moreover, modern American infants display skills such as rolling, sitting, crawling, cruising, walking, and stair ascent and descent in a staggering variety of orders, rather than in the invariant sequence suggested by ordering average onset ages in normative data. (Berger, Theuring, & Adolph, 2007)

3. The effects of the quality of one relationship on the quality and dimensions of other relationships impact development. As emphasized throughout this chapter, infants, toddlers, and twos do not develop in isolation. Young children are completely dependent on adults to care for them, even as they develop their independent personalities, interests, and desires. The relationships that they experience are complex, with effects of relationships on relationships (Emde, 1988). For example, the strength of the marital relationship influences how parents will interact with their child (Brook, Zheng, Whiteman, & Brook, 2001), and the health of the child, for example, influences how the parents and the child interact with each other. Sameroff and Feise (2000), in their discussion of transactional theory, identify the interaction interplay between child characteristics/behavior and adult characteristics/behavior over time (see Figure 4.7).

4. There is clearly a social and emotional basis for learning. Rochat (2007) argues that the ability to focus during learning develops during the first face-to-face responsive and sensitive emotional interactions between adults and infants. The emotions of others influence

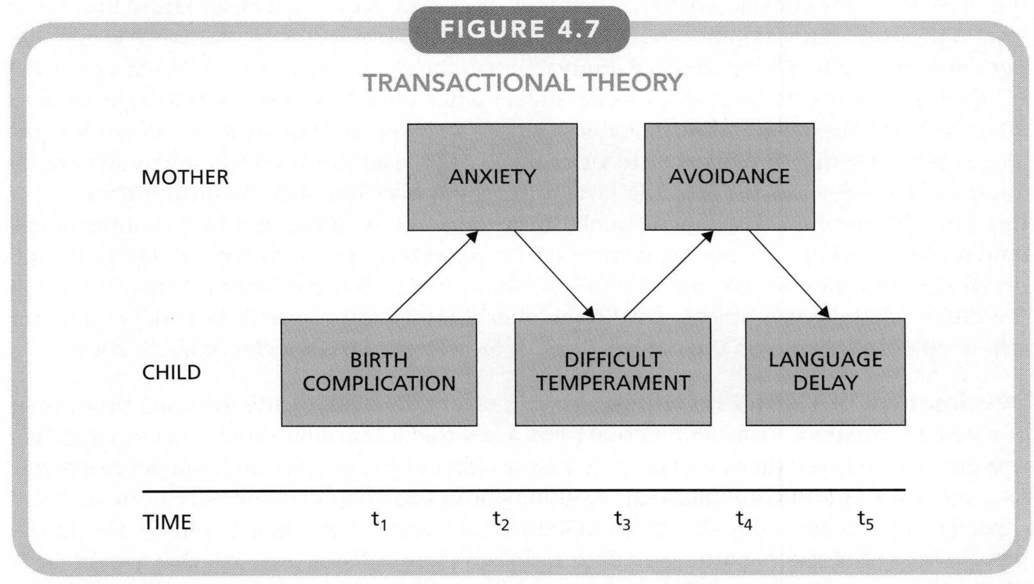

Source: Sameroff, A. J., & Feise, B. H. (2000). Transactional regulation: The development ecology of early intervention. In J. P. Shonkoff & S. J. Meisels (Eds.), Handbook of early childhood intervention (2nd ed., 135–159). New York: Cambridge University Press.

children's ability to learn. It is difficult for infants to focus on learning if there is a fearful adult face present, as it draws their attention. Children's ability to control and channel intense emotions predicts school success, and children's ability to socialize successfully does as well (National Scientific Council on the Developing Child, 2004).

5. Finally, there are individual differences in children and families that are the result of the interaction between genetics and environment. These individual differences in vulnerability, temperament, gender, and experiences not only have a transactional effect (mutual influence on others' behavior), but also have an individual effect on how the child reacts to, say, parental behavior or nutritional differences. For example, a study completed in the United States concluded that if an infant begins with an irritable temperament, then that child is more likely to be influenced negatively by a mother's negative guidance strategies (Shaw & Vondra, 1995). Irritable children seem to need adults who are more sensitive and flexible with them.

The power of development, children's responses to cultural and environmental influences, the effect of relationships on relationships, a social and emotional basis for learning, and children's individual characteristics all are a product of the interaction of nature and nurture or genes and environment. These five factors and a continuous interaction between genetic influences and environmental factors also influence sensory and perceptual development.

The Sensory and Perceptual Development of the Infant and Toddler

Perceptual development includes both experiencing and interpreting the world through the senses. It includes the acuity or sharpness of the senses as well as the discrimination, memory, and insight gained from sight, hearing, taste, smell, and touch. The biological aspects of vision and hearing are discussed first; then perception based on an interaction between biology and experiences (including cultural influences and relationships); and last, the individual variation and developmental challenges that can occur.

VISION. Vision includes not only the biological apparatus that supports our ability to see, but also the ability to interpret and react to what we see.

Biological Aspects of Vision. One-fourth of the brain is devoted to vision (Society for Neuroscience, 2009). When they are born, infants have all of the necessary eye structures, but these structures develop over the first few years of life. Slater, Field, and Hernandez-Reif (2007) propose that vision may be the least developed sense at birth because of lack of experience prenatally. The term **visual acuity** refers to the sharpness of vision. Visual acuity develops from about 20/400 (babies see at 20 feet what adults can see at 400 feet) at birth to 20/25 at 6 months of age. At birth, babies can see well objects that are approximately eight inches away, just the right distance to view the face of the adult who is feeding them or holding them, but they are just learning how to use both eyes together. At birth, the cones of the retina are not fully developed (Lamb, Bornstein, & Teti, 2002), but by 3 months of age (and possibly earlier), infants can distinguish between blue, green, yellow, and red (the colors of the rainbow). In two recent studies, 7-month-olds, but not 6-month-olds, could tell the difference between objects (and remember the location of the colors) depending on where colors appeared on the objects (Oakes, Messenger, Ross-Sheehy, & Luck, 2009).

Development of Visual Perception. **Visual perception** includes attention and processing of visual information. Visual perception plays a key role in learning about objects, language, and the emotions of others, and there is a clear effect of experience on brain development. As discussed in the section on brain development in this chapter, babies are born with the capacity to perceive subtle differences (Kelly et al., 2009). But what do infants like to observe? One entity that is particularly interesting to them is faces. At birth they prefer faces that are oriented correctly rather than upside down (Leo & Simion, 2009), which indicates that they are visually sensitive to spatial information at a young age. By 3 months, infants can distinguish between persons of different genders (Quinn, Yahr, Kuhn, Slater, & Pascalis,

2002) and different races (Sangrigoli & de Schonen, 2004a, 2004b). In a review of research on face and race recognition, Kelly and colleagues (2009) summarized research that demonstrates that babies from Western cultures focus on the eyes and mouth region of faces, and babies from Eastern cultures focus more on the nose region. These authors hypothesized that the strategy used by babies from Western cultures is consistent with an analytical style and the strategy used by babies from Eastern cultures represents a more holistic processing style.

Can infants distinguish the differences between faces in all ethnic groups, even the ones that they do not see on a regular basis? In a study of babies' ability to distinguish between faces, 3-month-old infants could identify the differences in faces within four ethnic groups; at 6 months, they could identify two ethnic groups; and at 9 months, they could only identify their own ethnic group. This ability of infants to distinguish only faces of races that are in their own visual environment is called the **other race effect (ORE).** Authors Kelly and colleagues (2009) state that the visual system of infants, "becomes 'tuned' in to process the category of faces that are most prevalent in the infant's visual environment" (p. 106), a process called "perceptual narrowing" by Nelson (2001).

Through vision, infants can read the emotions of others by means of a process called *emotional face processing*. For example, 7-month-olds have a difficult time disengaging from looking at a fearful face—the sticky fixation phenomenon (Hood, 1995). This ability to respond differently to fearful faces protects the child, as he "freezes" and doesn't move forward. However, when adults have fearful expressions, for example, when they overreact immediately after a child's fall, it could limit the exploration and learning of the child.

The quote "The eye sees only what the mind is prepared to comprehend" (Henri Bergson) takes on additional meaning when applied to infants, who by 10 or 11 months of age show that they understand that an adult's gaze on an object communicates his interest (Brooks & Meltzoff, 2005). Researchers had infants watch as an adult turned her head toward a target with either open or closed eyes. Nine-month-olds did not respond differently based on the adult's eyes, but 10- and 11-month-old children did. The older infants recognized the turning of the head and open eyes looking toward a target as a form of communication and, as the authors state, "visually connected" to the world. Twelve-, 14-, and 18-month-old infants also looked at the target of the adult's gaze when the adult's eyes were open rather than closed, and when the adult wore a headband as opposed to a blindfold (Meltzoff & Brooks, 2007). This research demonstrated that toddlers were recognizing that the adult's eyes, and not just the adult's turning his head toward the object, communicated interest.

Throughout their first year of life, infants also learn about the meaning of the orientation of an object. Technology allows researchers to track an infant's eye movements by placing on the infant's head a cap containing magnets that follow an infrared camera while the infant sits in his mother's lap. Aslin and McMurray (2004) found that infants could learn to look one way for a video when they saw the shape of a cross and another way when they saw the shape of a square. Even when the researchers presented the infants with the shape in a different color, they looked in the right direction to see the video. These infants could place objects in categories based on their shape. However, when a shape was rotated, the infants could no longer do the task.

Gaze following by 1-year-old infants. Infants selectively look with eyes open vs. eyes closed, showing they take into account the status of the adult's eyes, not just the gross direction of head movement (Metzoff, 2005, p. 68).

Developmental Challenges in Vision. Vision screening is imperative to detect visual impairments. The USAID for the American People, an independent federal government agency, estimates that approximately 1.4 million children in the world are blind (USAID, 2009) and that three times that many children have serious vision challenges. Corneal scarring from vitamin A deficiency, measles, conjunctivitis, and harmful traditional eye treatments, such as using urine to treat eye infections, may cause blindness and serious vision impairment.

As mentioned earlier in this chapter, cataracts cause about half of the cases of blindness in developing countries (USAID, 2009). Congenital cataracts, a clouding of the eye's natural lens, occur in about 0.4% of all births and contribute to cloudy vision. Many cataracts require surgery between 6 weeks and 3 months following birth to prevent vision loss. After cataract surgery, the infant will need a surgically implanted lens, contact lens, or eyeglasses. Treatment for amblyopia, a condition in which one eye is weaker than the other, is more effective if the problem is detected before age 2 (All About Vision, 2010). Information about preventing blindness can be obtained at http://www.preventblindness.org/ We expand on the topic of visual impairment in Chapter 8.

HEARING. Hearing is the ability to perceive sound through the auditory system. The ear detects vibrations that are changed into nerve impulses that the brain perceives as sound.

The Development of Hearing. As you can see in Figure 4.8, the ear is made up of the outer, middle, and inner ear. The outer ear captures and funnels sound vibrations to the middle ear. The auditory bones in the middle ear consist of the anvil, hammer, and stapes. The middle ear sends sound vibrations on to the inner ear or cochlea, which converts those vibrations into nerve pulses that the brain interprets as sound.

The development of the ear and hearing begins early during the gestational period. By five months, fetuses turn toward the source of a sound. At 38–39 weeks gestation, brain-imaging techniques detect significant activation in the cortical auditory section of the fetal brain when mothers read nursery rhymes (Lecanuet & Schaal, 2002). Very loud noises cause

FIGURE 4.8

THE EAR

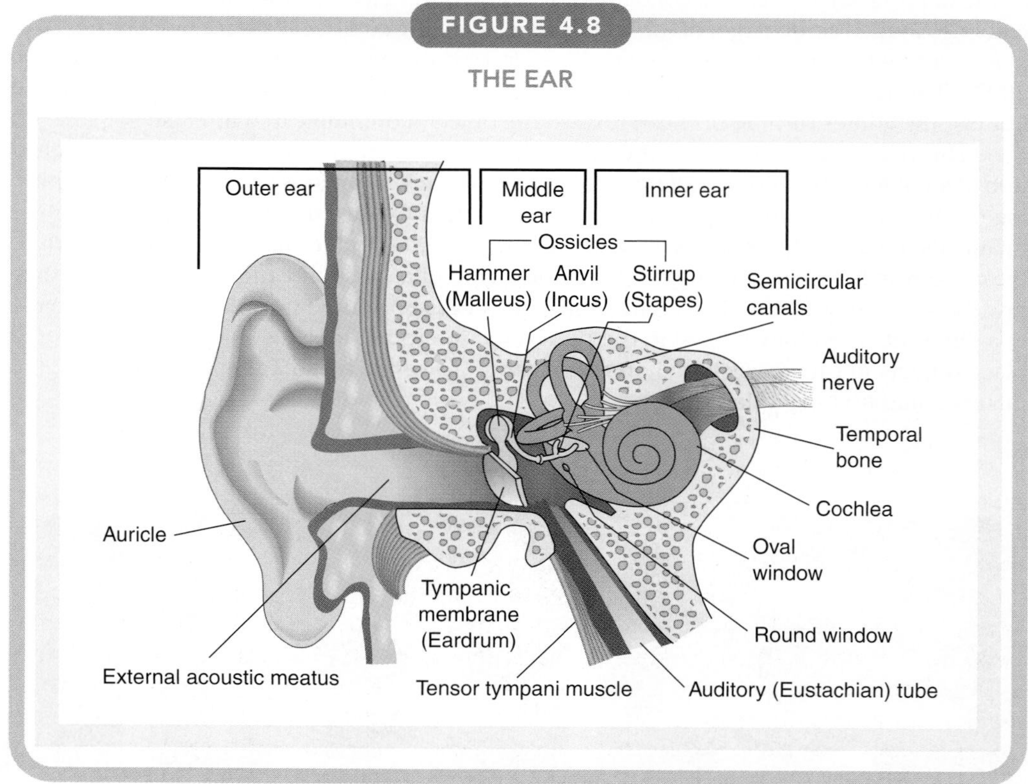

Source: Heward, W., Exceptional Children, Figure 9.1 "Basic anatomy of the human ear" p. 335, © 2009 Pearson Education, Inc. Reproduced by permission of Pearson Education, Inc.

an increase in movement in fetuses for approximately 30 minutes after they hear the sound (Lecanuet & Schaal, 2002). Researchers have detected amazing auditory discrimination skills in healthy preterm babies born between 30 and 35 weeks after conception. These babies could discriminate the differences in words that were repeated with only a change in a vowel—words such as *pat, pot, pit* (Cheour-Luhtanen et al., 2009). In another study, researchers demonstrated that newborns could distinguish between the voice of their mother and that of a stranger. At birth, researchers played a two-minute audiotape of their mother's voice to 30 newborns and an audiotape of a stranger's voice to 30 different newborns. The heart rate of those babies who heard their mother's voice accelerated while the heart rate of the newborns who heard a stranger's voice decelerated (Kisilevsky et al., 2003). These newborn infants demonstrated auditory perceptual skills when they distinguished between their mother's voice and a stranger's voice.

Development of Auditory Perception. Infants are quite capable discriminators of sounds in language. In a novel study, researchers found that at the age of 1 month, infants could hear the differences between "ba" and "pa" (Eimas, Sigueland, Jusczyk, & Vigorito, 1971). The development of auditory perception also follows the "perceptual narrowing" experience discussed under visual processing above. Infants are born with the ability to hear the differences between all of the sounds of all languages, but by 8 months of age, they begin to lose this ability as they focus on the sounds of the language spoken to them (Kuhl, 2000). As in the development of vision, infants who are exposed to the sounds of another language (with human interaction) between 8 and 12 months are able to hear the differences between sounds in those languages. More research on auditory perception as it relates to language development is discussed later in this chapter.

Individual Variation and Developmental Challenges in Hearing. Early Hearing Detection and Intervention (EHDI) programs identify children with hearing challenges and provide services to the children and their families in Early Intervention (EI) settings that may include the children's homes or childcare programs. Infants and toddlers with hearing challenges may need hearing aids (HA) or cochlear implants (CI) (Robinson, 2009). A CI is a small electronic device that helps hard-of-hearing children and adults sense sound. Part of it sits behind the ear and the other part is placed under the skin. A CI includes a microphone, a speech processor, a transmitter and receiver/stimulator, and an electrode array that sends impulses to different regions of the auditory nerve (NIDCD, 2009). We return to the topic of hearing impairment and cochlear implants in Chapter 8.

TASTE AND SMELL. "The gustatory [taste] and olfactory [smell] sensory systems . . . have extraordinary sensitivity" (Lamb, Bornstein, & Teti, 2002, p. 163). We know how important the senses of taste and smell are to us as adults, but did you know that tasting and smelling play an important part in infants' and toddlers' prenatal development as well as during the first three years of life? According to the Society for Neuroscience, "Although different, the two sensory experiences of taste and smell are intimately entwined. They are separate senses with their own receptor organs. These two senses act together allowing us to distinguish thousands of different flavors" (SFN, 2009, p. 18).

Taste is both innate and acquired. Lamb and colleagues (2002) report that by 12 weeks gestation, taste buds form. Newborns prefer the smell of chocolate over rotten eggs (imagine that smelly research project!), indicating that infants' sense of smell is highly developed at birth (Pomares, Schirrer, & Abadie, 2002). Newborns can distinguish between four different tastes—sucrose (sweet), salty, sour, and bitter (Rosenstein & Oster, 1988). Researchers Beauchamp and Mennella (2009) added umami (savory) flavors to the original four tastes. These authors concluded that sweet, umami, and salty flavors are innately preferred while infants reject bitter and sour substances. They also emphasize that infants' preferences for certain flavors are influenced by what the pregnant and breastfeeding mother eats. For example, newborns whose mothers ate anise (used in licorice) during pregnancy showed a stable preference for the anise odor whereas newborns whose mothers did not eat anise rejected or were neutral when exposed to the anise smell (Schaal, Marlier, & Sourssignan, 2009). (It is not recommended that high levels of licorice be eaten during pregnancy.)

TOUCH. Muir (2002) emphasizes that touch is the forgotten sense and that adults should make use of the largest organ, the skin, to communicate and soothe infants and toddlers. Premature and high-risk newborns gain more weight when their parents carry them skin to skin next to their chest in a way called "Kangaroo Care." This has been found to be true in recent studies in India (Suman, Udani, & Nanavati, 2008) and Ethiopia (Worku & Kassie, 2005).

Just as we find massage to be relaxing, so do preterm infants during their stay in the NICU. Infants who received three 15-minute massages each day for five consecutive days showed few stress behaviors (Hernandez-Reif, Diego, & Field, 2007). Increased weight gain is another benefit of massage for preterm neonates (Diego, Field, & Hernandez-Reif, 2005).

INTEGRATION OF THE SENSES—AMODAL LEARNING. Infants and toddlers do not just focus on one sense at a time, although it may seem like it when a toddler, who is focusing intensely on a toy, does not pay attention when you tell him it may be time to change his diaper. From early in infancy, however, infants demonstrate **cross-modal abilities**—the coordination of two or more senses. More than 30 years ago, Meltzoff and Moore (1977) learned that infants could transfer information from one sense to another. After giving babies a bumpy or smooth nipple to suck on, babies looked longer at a picture that matched the texture they were sucking.

It seems that infants expect coherent information. Vision and hearing are two other senses that are coordinated early in children's lives. Infants just 18- to 20-weeks-old, who are cooing (vowel sounds) and babbling (consonant and vowel sounds together) but not yet saying words, attended to a face articulating possible sounds but not to a face articulating impossible sounds (Meltzoff & Kuhl, 1989).

Infant and Toddler Cognitive Development, Thinking, and Learning

The term *cognitive* refers to the act of knowing. In the study of child development, the term refers to the way that children come to know through developing, thinking, and learning. The following discussion identifies important ways that infants and toddlers gain and apply knowledge. "We are born with the ability to discover the secrets of the universe and of our own minds, and with the drive to explore and experiment until we do." (Gopnik, Meltzoff, & Kuhl, 1999, p. 3)

Kai, 18 months old, held his spoon at the very end with his fingers, but soon found it difficult to scoop up his applesauce that way. His fingers moved down the spoon until he was holding it in a hammer grip at the base of the spoon. Soon he managed to maneuver a big, sloppy spoonful of applesauce into his waiting open mouth. Infants and toddlers, like Kai, are continuously learning, but how do they learn?

INFANTS AND TODDLERS ARE MOTIVATED TO LEARN AND GENERALLY LEARN QUICKLY. Stand back and watch an infant or toddler. Unless that child has been discouraged from and punished for exploration, you will see a child eager to learn. A 9-month-old infant given a ball might taste it, feel it with his hands, turn it over and look at the other side, and drop it to see what will happen. An example from exciting research on children's visual perception highlights how quickly an infant can learn. Scott Johnson and colleagues (2003) studied what 6-month-olds and 4-month-olds knew about **object permanence**—whether an object continues to exist when out of sight—by tracking their eye movements as a ball on a screen traveled behind a barrier and then out again. Those older and wiser 6-month-olds (remember they are barely sitting independently at this time) anticipated that the ball would come out on the other side of the barrier much more reliably than did the 4-month-olds (who are not sitting independently yet and may have just learned to roll over). However, after showing 4-month-olds the ball moving through space without the barrier in the picture, the 4-month-olds anticipated the ball appearing on the other side of the barrier after disappearing; they did this as well as the 6-month-olds. Those 4-month-olds learned, within a two-minute session, about trajectories and that balls do not just disappear as they travel through space.

INFANTS AND TODDLERS ATTEND, HABITUATE, AND REMEMBER. **Attention** is the awareness of and interest in phenomena and **habituation** is the tendency of young children to tire of information they have mastered and to seek novel information. Attention is necessary, although not sufficient, to move information from the senses to memory (see the section on information processing theory in Chapter 2). In many of the research studies cited in this chapter, researchers use infants' and toddlers' abilities to attend and habituate to assess their perception, knowledge, and skills. Parents and other caregivers who are "tuned" in to infants and toddlers also know that they are always attending (except perhaps when they are asleep) and that they enjoy new information and challenges that are slightly above their present developmental level.

INFANTS AND TODDLERS ARE GOAL ORIENTED AND UNDERSTAND INTENTION. Infants are goal oriented (Tomasello, 1998) and understand others' intentions quite early during infancy. At 2 months, infants kick to make a mobile move, and at 5 months, they reach to obtain a toy. Toddlers turn a small raisin box upside-down, shake it, and turn it over in an attempt to get the last sticky raisin out. Their recognition that they can cause certain effects to happen and can learn different strategies to achieve goals develops during the first three years.

When do infants or toddlers begin to understand that others have intentions? Do they understand, for example, that when an adult picks up a cup, he intends to take a drink? When do young children learn that another person has intentions even if he tries, but does not achieve his goal (Brandone & Wellman, 2009)? Johnson, Booth, and O'Hearn (2001) found that 15-month-olds seemed to understand that a robot was trying to complete a task, even though the inept robot could not complete it. Although these toddlers didn't see the completed goal to imitate it, they completed the goal when it was their turn. Meltzoff (1995) showed that 18-month-olds who watched an adult try to pull apart two halves of a dumbbell imitated the action, even when the adult was not successful. These toddlers seemed to know that the adult's goal was to pull the dumbbell apart, so they did not just imitate the adult's hands slipping off the ends.

An interesting research study by Carpenter, Akhtar, and Tomasello (1998) assessed whether toddlers from 14 to 18 months of age would imitate a mistaken action or the intention of an adult. The researchers had toddlers, sitting on their parents' laps, watch a female adult say, "There!" as she spun a wheel deliberately. She then exclaimed, "Woops!" as she accidently activated a set of lights by placing her hand on a lever. When the toddlers were given a turn, you might think they would touch the lever to see the eye-catching lights, but instead, they spun the wheel. These young children determined that the goal of the adult's actions was to spin the wheel, not push the lever, and so they imitated the intended act, not the accidental one.

Research that is more recent shows that infants and toddlers seem to understand another person's intentional behavior by 9 months of age. In a very clever study, Behne, Carpenter, Call, and Tomasello (2005) set up an experience for 6-, 9-, 12-, and 18-month-olds. A female researcher sat across a platform from the infant and either (1) teased the infant with the toy, refused to give the toy, or was distracted from giving the toy to the infant, or (2) "couldn't" give the toy to the infant because she dropped it or could not get the lid off a container. In the teased, refused, or distracted condition, the researcher held the ball forward, looking at the infant, but when the infant reached for the ball, she pulled it back in a teasing way. In the second condition, the experimenter repeatedly held forward a ball, looking at the infant. When the infant reached for the ball, the experimenter "accidentally" dropped it, and the ball rolled down the ramp toward the "surprised" or "frustrated" experimenter.

Infants and toddlers of all ages, except 6-month-olds, were more impatient when the researcher would not give them the toy than when the researcher dropped it or tried, but could not retrieve the toy. The authors state that

> "[I]infants did not just discriminate the two types of adult actions but they interpreted each in its own way and reacted appropriately: They showed impatience when the adult was unwilling to give them a toy (by reaching and/or looking away), but they showed patience (less reaching and looking away) when the adult was unable to give them the toy. They appeared to know that in the unwilling condition the adult was doing just what she wanted to do (retaining the object was part of her goal), whereas in the unable condition she was not achieving what she wanted to (because giving the toy was her goal)." (p. 333)

The authors concluded that understanding the goal-directed behavior of others begins at around 9 months. It would be a mistake, however, to think that infants cry because they want to irritate their parents. They are goal oriented, but as the research shows, although they begin to understand that others have intentions during infancy, they have a difficult time taking the perspective of another person until about 18 months of age. You will read about when children learn the difference between self and other as separate beings later in this chapter in the emotional development section.

INFANTS AND TODDLERS OBSERVE AND IMITATE. Social cognitive/learning theory (Bandura, 1997) describes how young children learn by observing, imitating, and cognitively processing information. "Social cognitive theory suggests that behavior is influenced by direct experience, as well as by observation of others, and that individuals are able to learn about expected outcomes or consequences of certain behaviors from different aspects of their social environment and to use those expectations in selecting their own behavior" (Joyner, Gill-Bailey, & Moon, 2009, e416).

Think about the times that an infant or toddler has imitated your action. One teacher of a 2-year-old squatted down to look into the toddler's eyes. Immediately, the toddler squatted down too, imitating the teacher, making it difficult, once again, for the teacher to gaze into the child's eyes. Ryalls, Gul, and Ryalls (2000), in a summary of the literature on imitation, noted that children as young as 9 months can learn from adults through imitation in a variety of circumstances. However, are infants and toddlers capable of **deferred imitation,** the ability to remember and imitate after a period of time? Meltozff (1985) concluded that 14-month-olds and 24-month-olds could imitate immediately and after 24 hours; however, Klein and Meltzoff (1999) found that 12-month-olds remember how to manipulate unusual toys after four weeks and in a different context. For example, infants were able to manipulate a toy in a special way after seeing the experimenter at home and then four weeks later in a laboratory setting. These toys were *unusual* and created by the inventive researchers, so the infants could not have practiced at home. One toy was dumbbell shaped, made out of blocks, and had a tube extending from it. The experimenter demonstrated, but did not allow the infant to manipulate the blocks in such a way as to pull them apart. Yet, these 1-year-old infants were able to remember how to manipulate the toy after one month. These studies indicate that infants are "born to learn" and "learn from watching us" (Meltzoff, 1999, p. 1).

Do toddlers imitate peers, too? It seems that peers do attract their age-mates' attention. In a study of 30 infants between the ages of 14 and 18 months, Ryalls and colleagues (2000) found that the toddlers who watched a peer outperformed the adult-modeled group. You may have seen 15-month-old toddlers playing a game in which one toddler imitates the other. Toddlers' nonverbal imitations of each other lead to reciprocal imitation games such as "you follow me and then I'll follow you" (Eckerman & Didow, 1996; Eckerman & Whitehead, 1999). However, infants do not just learn through imitation. They think: they categorize, sort, classify, and generalize.

INFANTS AND TODDLERS HAVE THE ABILITY TO CATEGORIZE, SORT, CLASSIFY, AND GENERALIZE. As humans, we classify, order, and organize information to make sense of the world. This ability is activated long before infants can talk. Quinn (2002) found that during their first few months, infants classify classes of objects such as animals and furniture based on the perceptual similarity of these objects. Infants as early as 7 months of age expect previously active objects to start moving again. Pauen and Träuble (2009) discovered that the appearance of an object or animal, for example, leads to the activation in the infants' brain of other aspects of the object or animal, such as whether it moves independently. These scientists summarize research that demonstrates that young infants treat highly different-looking animals (e.g., a giraffe, a crocodile, a bird, and a fish) as members of the same category (alive), which they discriminate from other broad classes of inanimates, such as vehicles or furniture. They report that infants consider static attributes such as facial features, leg-like appendages, body configuration, and surface information as relevant for identifying animates. Remarkably, infants who are barely able to sit are making assumptions based on their systematic sorting of information that they perceive—identify and remember.

A more challenging task is for toddlers to sort objects by invisible information—for example, the function of items. If you watched someone pretend to give a toy dog a drink from a cup and then you were given three toys—a cup, a bird, and an airplane—how would you use the cup? Would you offer a drink to the bird or the airplane? Fourteen-month-old toddlers offered the cup to the bird, but not the airplane. They seemed to be developing concepts or abstract ideas about which entities would drink (Mandler & McDonough, 1996).

INFANTS AND TODDLERS UNDERSTAND AND GENERATE SYMBOLS.

> We are the symbolic species. There's really nothing that distinguishes us more from other creatures than our very flexible, creative use of different kinds of symbols and it's also what underlies our enormous cognitive power, because we're not limited to just learning about the world through direct experience with the world. We can learn about it through what somebody else tells us, through pictures, through maps, through videos, through a whole host of different kinds of symbolic representations. So what we know is just hugely expanded by the fact that we can use different kinds of symbols, so this is clearly a very important aspect of the development of any human child. (DeLoache, Uttal, & Rosengren, 2004, p. 1027)

Over the first three years, infants and toddlers begin to understand that symbols and signs represent real objects or feelings—that one thing can represent another. They learn that a picture of a cat is a symbol for a real cat and that carrying a matchbox car in his pocket (a gift from his father) helps a boy feel emotionally closer to his father.

Westby (2000) identified different levels of symbolic play in very young children. *Autosymbolic schemes* emerge around 17–19 months and include children's pretend play aimed at themselves, such as using a toy brush to brush their own hair or pretending to snore as they are feigning sleep, especially when the adult playing with them says in a playful voice, "I'm going to sleep now, I hope you don't snore." *Decentered symbolic play* occurs around 19–22 months and entails the use of pretend actions with a toy, such as moving a toy truck and trying to make the sound that trucks make. *Sequencing pretend actions* occur around 20–25 months and include a sequence of pretend actions such as stirring a toy pot to make cookies, then eating them, and then putting the pot away. *Internally directed symbolic play* occurs around 24–30 months and includes pretending that an object has intention. One 27-month-old pretended that a flower was a cat that wanted to go for a ride in his toy truck. *Behavioral role-play* occurs around 30–36 months and includes the child pretending to be someone or something else. Play often centers on familiar roles such as mother, father, doctor, and dog. A higher level of play includes children using an object that does not look like the real object to pretend, as seen in the example of the child using a flower to represent a cat.

INFANTS ARE PROBLEM SOLVERS AND DEVELOP SCHEMAS. Problem solving is an aspect of goal-directed behavior. Infants will try different strategies and develop hypotheses about how the world works. As you watch a young toddler try to open the lid of a box, you will see him use his fingers to pry open the lid. If that doesn't work, the toddler might shake the box, turn it over as if to see if there is another opening, and then bang on the box as he has seen adults do to an obstinate door. They are true problem solvers using the schemas that Piaget (1954) first noted that young children use. **Schemas** are ideas and actions that infants develop to learn and explore. As the young toddler tried to open the box, he first used his most recently developed schema—opening the lid with his fingers. Then he used past schemas that worked for him—shaking, turning an object over, and banging it. Obviously, this toddler had an interest in learning about how the world works. The research described above opens our eyes to how much infants and toddlers are learning in the first three years of life and how they actively seek and organize information.

Quality childcare is related to infants' and toddlers' cognitive and language development. Clarke-Stewart and colleagues (2002) summarized data from the NICHD Study of Early Child Care on features of childcare homes that contributed to 15-, 24-, and 36-month-olds'

CONNECTING WITH CHILDREN

Guidelines for Teachers and Families: Supporting Cognitive Development

Use turn-taking reciprocal interactions with the child through emotional expressions, language, and motor actions.

- A 4-month-old cooed soft sounds while gazing intently into her teacher's eyes. Her teacher delightedly cooed back and then waited for the baby to take her turn in the cooing conversation.
- An 18-month-old played with sand in a large container outside. He looked up at his teacher and shouted, "ook (look), sand." His teacher looked at the sand and then at the toddler and in an engaging voice, said, "yes, wet sand."

Encourage and support play as one of the primary ways that infants and toddlers learn.

- The infant teacher supported play by offering a variety of rich materials. When the babies weren't being fed or sleeping, they were playing.
- The toddler teacher knew that children need long periods of time to choose their own activity from the choices of materials, toys, equipment, and people offered to them.

Provide many opportunities for infants and toddlers to explore their world. When infants and toddlers explore objects, they learn about cause/effect, means/ends relationships, and spatial and number concepts, etc.

- The infant teacher watched as an 8-month-old picked up a toy, turned it over (spatial concept) and banged it on the floor and then the carpet while intently listening to the different sounds the toys made on different surfaces (cause-effect).
- A toddler pulled a toy by pulling the short handle (means-ends relationships).

Follow infants' and toddlers' lead during play rather than trying to direct the play. Observe infants' and toddlers' goals, strategies, and ideas about the world.

- The infant teacher observed that an 11-month-old kept trying to fit a block into a small plastic container by turning the block different ways. When the child succeeded the teacher found more blocks and placed them by her side.
- A toddler teacher sat on the floor while toddlers played around her. One toddler brought a book to her to read.

Use language to describe what the child is doing or to encourage problem-solving.

- An infant teacher watched a child who was trying to push large buttons on a toy to make sounds. The teacher said, "Hmm, I wonder how that works."
- While reading a book to two toddlers, the teacher asked them, "What do you think the bear will do next?"

When a child becomes frustrated while trying to accomplish a task, such as eat with a spoon or take off a jacket, help just enough so that the child learns strategies to complete the task.

- After noticing that an infant became frustrated while trying to turn the knob on a musical toy, the teacher asked, "Do you need help?" The infant teacher took the child's hand and placed it over the knob and lightly helped her turn it.
- A toddler became frustrated while putting together a 4-piece puzzle. The teacher helped the child turn a piece to fit (thus helping the child learn a strategy).

---

cognitive development. The factors that contributed to richer learning environments and more positive caregiving (warmer and more sensitive caregiving) were the following:

1. Caregivers' higher educational level
2. More recent and higher levels of training
3. More child-centered beliefs about how to handle children
4. Smaller groups

Factors that contributed to children's performance on tests of cognitive and language development were the following:

1. Caregivers' higher educational and training levels
2. Higher quality care that included attentive, responsive, and emotionally supportive caregivers

There has always been a question, though, about how adults can use *specific* strategies to support cognitive development, including the curiosity, motivation, imagination, imitation, and problem-solving capabilities of young children. These "learning to learn" skills and attitudes support lifelong learning. Research recommends the strategies summarized in the ***Connecting with Children*** guidelines.

Infant Emotional Development

Emotional development is the growth of children's ability to express and regulate their feelings, and emotional learning encompasses the mechanisms by which children learn *which* feelings to express and *how* to express them. Emotions, both those experienced internally and those observed externally in others, motivate young children to behave in certain ways. A 7-month-old who experiences anger will usually show that anger by crying and possibly flailing arms. Emotions also communicate, and an astute adult reads the infant's behavior as anger rather than sadness and responds differently to the child based on the emotion expressed. Emotional development as a motivator of behavior and as communication is an important aspect of development (Emde, 1998).

EMOTIONAL DEVELOPMENT. Infants and toddlers use all of the cognitive processes to learn about emotions. Although there are universal emotions expressed by all infants, the frequency and use of these emotions are influenced by the quality of adult-child interactions, culture, and the context in which they are expressed or suppressed. Emde (1998) provides a list and timetable for infants' and toddlers' emotional expressions; however, he emphasizes that this timetable is for white, middle-class children from Denver, Colorado, and could vary depending on culture.

One marker of emotional development is the infants' ability to use social referencing—the ability to search for and use the emotional signals of others to guide their behavior in new situations. Not only does this mean that infants are paying attention to others' emotions, but they are using them to guide their own behavior. An infant, for example, may begin to crawl toward a toy if the mother smiles, but not if the mother shows a fearful face after looking at the toy. We could also call this ability *emotional referencing*, as the infant responds to the emotions of the adult or others. Infants at 7 months react to fearful faces, as discussed earlier in this chapter, and researchers found that it was not just the eyes of the other person, but rather the whole fearful face (Peltola, Leppänen, Vogel-Farley Hietanen, & Nelson, 2009). Infants responded to fearful faces more than angry faces (Kobiella, Grossmann, Reid, & Striano, 2008). Why do you think this might occur?

Although the research literature generally emphasized that social referencing occurs around 7 months of age, new technology may change our understanding about when social referencing develops. Researchers using brain technology found that 3-month-olds showed increased brain activity and looked more at objects that adults had responded to with a fearful face (Hoehl, Wiese, & Striano, 2008). The authors of the research conclude that 3-month-old infants use social cues to process information about objects.

Researchers and practitioners consider several other constructs as aspects of emotional development—temperament and emotional affect, self-regulation, and attachment. Following is a brief discussion of these constructs.

New research indicates that infants as young as three months respond to the emotional expressions of adults, changing our understanding of when social referencing occurs. (Hoehl, Wiese, & Striano, 2008).

TEMPERAMENT. The term **temperament** refers to the unique personality and characteristics of a child that influences how the child reacts to environmental stimuli and includes the dimensions of emotionality, sociability, and activity level. Wittmer and Petersen (2009) give an example of three children who differ in temperament.

> On entering the toddler room in the morning, Kevin sobs as though his heart is broken as his father leaves. After a moment of comforting, and full of energy, he enthusiastically plays with the rocking horse, leaps off, and runs to the easel. Faron enters the room quietly, kisses her mother good-bye, and settles into the housekeeping area. Terra clings to her mother's skirt, preventing her from leaving in

> the morning. When her mother finally is able to leave, Terra hangs back and watches the other children play while she sucks her thumb and holds her teddy bear. (p. 114)

Although cultural practices may contribute to Kevin's, Faron's, and Terra's behavior, temperament may also play a part. Some infants gulp their milk as if there won't be any more tomorrow, whereas others leisurely graze at the bottle, taking time to look into the caregiver's eyes. An infant or toddler needs adults who recognize that each child has a unique personality—that some are more peaceful and others are feisty, some get irritated more easily and others aren't bothered by much, and some really like being with a lot of people and others like to be with fewer people. These are the infants' temperaments, a concept discussed by Thomas, Chess, and Birch (1970). The researchers described some infants as easy, others as difficult, and still others as slow to warm.

Thomas, Chess, Birch, Hertzig, and Korn (1963) introduced the nine dimensions of temperament shown in Table 4.5.

TABLE 4.5 • **The Nine Dimensions of Temperament**

- *Activity level:* Amount of physical movement
- *Biological rhythms:* Regularity of eating, sleeping, elimination
- *Approach/withdrawal:* Comfort in new situations
- *Mood:* Amount of time in pleasant, cheerful mood as opposed to fussing, crying, or resisting others
- *Intensity of reaction:* Energy level of emotional expressions
- *Sensitivity:* Response to sensory information, including light, sounds, textures, smells, tastes
- *Adaptability:* Ability to manage changes in routine or recover from being upset
- *Distractibility:* How easily the child's attention is distracted
- *Persistence:* How long a child will stay with a difficult activity before giving up

Source: Based on Thomas, Chess, Birch, Hertzig, and Korn (1963).

The authors then divided these nine temperament traits into temperament types—easy, difficult, and slow to warm. Based on the nine traits, the "easy" or flexible children, like Faron in the vignette above, have a moderate activity level; have regular biological rhythms; seem fairly comfortable in new situations; are in a pleasant, cheerful mood much of the time; aren't too sensitive to light, sounds, textures, smells, and tastes; recover fairly quickly from being upset; and are moderately distractible and persistent. Slow-to-warm children, like Kevin above tend to need time to feel comfortable in new situations and demonstrate less intensity of reaction. Difficult or feisty children such as Terra experience more intense moods and reactions, have more negative moods, are quite persistent and difficult to distract, and often are sensitive to sensory information. With these children the term *persistence*, often thought to be an attribute that contributes to the child's learning, is challenging because it is difficult to distract the child to make transitions, such as going from playing to eating.

The term ***goodness of fit*** is used to describe how well the caregiver's temperament matches the child's temperament or how well caregivers understand, accept, and work with the child's temperament (Thomas, Chess, & Birch, 1970). For example, difficult/feisty children may often experience intense emotions, but if these children are seen as having *emotional vitality* (Robinson & Acevedo, 2001) and are recognized for their engaging nature, then caregivers appreciate the child and help the child express emotions in culturally acceptable ways.

ARE THESE TRAITS INHERITED OR ARE THEY A RESULT OF THE CHILD'S EXPERIENCE? There seems to be a complex interaction, as usual, between nature (heredity) and nurture (the child's experiences). There is a strong genetic component, but adults can help children who have irritable or difficult temperaments deal with their sensitivity. One prevailing opinion is that "temperament should be considered, not as a fixed characteristic, but as the emotional organization which can be influenced by the environment" (Balleyguier, 1991, p. 641). Research supports this statement. Warren and Simmens (2005) found that if mothers were rated as more sensitive to their children, then irritable infants at 1 and 6 months of age were less anxious or depressed at age 2. The following quote from a recent national study of over 1,000 children summarized their findings:

> Not all difficult infants evidence behavior problems in the preschool years, and there are often complex interactions between child characteristics and aspects of parental behavior that together predict which difficult children will and will not show problem behavior at later ages. (NICHD Early Child Care Research Network, 2004b, p. 45)

Again, our awareness of children's individual differences and our reactions to them is key to supporting infants' and toddlers' emotional development. Other researchers consider the reactivity and regulation of the child to be the two major components of infant and toddler temperament (Zeanah & Fox, 2004).

THE DEVELOPMENT OF SELF-WORTH AND REGULATION. Self-awareness and awareness of others begins early in life. **Theory of mind** is a term used to describe the process of young children realizing that others have feelings and intentions that may be different from their own.

Self-regulation refers to the ability of the child to regulate emotions and behavior; however the construct involves more than just controlling emotions—it also refers to the ability to attend. Infants' and toddlers' ability to self-regulate commences in the first reciprocal and sensitive interactions between adults and children (Rochat, 2007). A 7-week-old infant who engages in soft cooing sounds with an enthralled adult is learning self-regulation as she waits expectantly for the adult to take a turn. An 8-month-old child who sits on an adult's lap and listens to the adult excitedly name the pictures in a book demonstrates behavioral regulation and focus of attention. A 3-year-old who can say, "I'm so mad" instead of hitting a playmate is showing how he can regulate his emotions. It is easy to see that self-regulation is a cornerstone of social success and achievement in school.

Self-regulation develops over a young child's life; in fact, as adults, we are still trying to regulate how much we eat, control our physical movements, and monitor our emotional reactions. Raikes and colleagues (2007) concluded that among 2,441 low-income children ages 14–36 months, self-regulation increased with age, although there was great individual variation. How do young children regulate their emotions and behavior?

Infants will suck their thumbs and twirl the corner of a favorite blanket to feel regulated. You may see a toddler hold his hands behind his back to help himself not touch a forbidden item. There are many ways that young children soothe themselves. They also count on adults to help them become calm again when they are distressed and to learn how to express emotions in culturally acceptable ways. Unfortunately, not all young children receive this kind of empathetic support. Young, maltreated children may have a difficult time modulating their emotions and behavior (Van der Kolk & Fisler, 1994). In an attempt to control their intense feelings, they may use aggression and other maladaptive and socially challenging behaviors against others. Adults' awareness of these behaviors will help them to use strategies that acknowledge children's intense negative feelings and teach them how to manage those difficult feelings.

CHARACTERISTICS OF ATTACHMENT. Bowlby (1988) summarized the need that humans have for relationships and attachment when he said, "The propensity to make strong emotional bonds to particular individuals [is] a basic component of human nature" (p. 3). **Attachment** is a term that describes the emotional bond between infants/toddlers and the adults who care for them. The following section on attachment is adapted from Wittmer (2009).

Studies on attachment have focused on the behavior of infants or toddlers as they attempt to elicit caregiving and protection from, seek proximity to, and stay in contact with an adult or adults who care for them (Ainsworth, Blehar, Waters, & Wall, 1978; Bowlby, 1969/1982, 1988; Main & Solomon, 1990). Based on research and theory, Edwards (2002) defined the attachment relationship as follows:

> Bowlby (1979) and Ainsworth et al. (1978) defined attachment as a special type of affectional bond between individuals. An affectional bond: (1) is persistent; (2) involves a specific person who is not interchangeable with anyone else; (3) is emotionally significant; (4) produces a desire to maintain proximity; and (5) results

> in distress from involuntary separation. An attachment bond involves all five of these criteria, and involves seeking security and comfort in the relationship with that person (Ainsworth, 1989; Bowlby, 1969/1982). (p. 390)

An important aspect of the attachment relationship is the child's ability to explore his or her environment (as soon as he is capable of doing so) while feeling safe in the presence of the attachment figure (Bowlby, 1979). The adult provides a secure base from which the child feels safe to explore. Bowlby believed that there are four distinguishing characteristics of attachment related to the two dimensions of attachment—proximity and exploration.

1. *Proximity Maintenance.* The desire to be near the people we are attached to.
2. *Safe Haven.* Returning to the attachment figure for comfort and safety in the face of a fear or threat.
3. *Secure Base.* The attachment figure acts as a base of security from which the child can explore the surrounding environment.
4. *Separation Distress.* Anxiety that occurs in the absence of the attachment figure.

The quality of the child's attachment is generally observed with the mother in a protocol called the Strange Situation, but has also been observed with fathers and care teachers in childcare programs. Through a series of observations of the young child responding to the stress of a parent leaving the room, a stranger entering, and the parent returning, researchers have observed how the child responds to separation and reunion with the parent. Researchers then describe the attachment relationship as secure or insecure (anxious-resistant, avoidant, or disorganized).

Securely Attached. These children seem to feel secure and protected by their parents, seek the parent after separation, are comforted by the parent, feel safe to explore as toddlers, and are more socially competent as preschoolers (Braungart-Rieker, Garwood, Powers, & Wang, 2001; McElwain, Cox, Burchinal, & Macfie, 2003). They know what it is like to feel genuine affection for another and enjoy human interaction (McElwain, 2006). They learn to self-regulate with caring adults and expect that others have good intentions and can be trusted to treat them kindly.

> Their [securely attached children] openness to their own emotions and to the overtures of others is thought to help them regulate their emotions and emotional responsiveness and adapt creatively and successfully to changing circumstances and new challenges. (NICHD Early Child Care Research Network, 2004, pp. 38–39)

Parents of securely attached children encourage reciprocity and cooperativeness (Russell, Pettit, & Mize, 1998), are more sensitive (Braungart-Rieker et al., 2001), and help infants manage difficult feelings (NICHD Early Child Care Research Network, 2004). The parents read their children's communication cues and respond accordingly (Emde & Robinson, 2000; McElwain et al., 2003), are more emotionally available (Aviezar, Sagi, Joels, & Ziv, 1999), and are more empathic (Weil, 1992). "Mothers of secure infants have been observed to be more reliable, consistent, sensitive, and accepting of their infants than mothers of insecurely attached infants" (Braungart-Rieker et al., p. 252).

Insecurely Attached: Anxious–Resistant. Children who are identified as ambivalent or resistant increase their efforts to stay close to their caregiver because of the inconsistency of the adult's responses to the child's distress. Harel and Scher (2003) wrote about insufficient responsiveness of adults with ambivalently attached children. The children feel ambivalent about the relationship, wanting to be near the adult but unable to feel satisfied in the relationship (NICHD Early Child Care Research Network, 2006). They stay close to the adult to feel protected, and "as a result of the infant's heightened vigilance of the caregiver's whereabouts, exploration of the environment may become limited" (McElwain et al., 2003, p. 139). The resistantly attached child's competence is compromised if parents are intrusive, interfere with the child's explorations, and are negatively controlling (Rubin, 2002). Children may also feel incompetent because of the caregivers' tendency to obstruct the infants' explorations and play (McElwain et al., 2003, p. 139).

Mothers of ambivalently attached children, however, seem to be feeling stressed as well. Scher and Mayseless (2000) found that mothers of ambivalent infants have higher separation anxiety and stress than do mothers of children classified as securely attached. Perhaps their ambivalence about their child's exploration contributes to their children's ambivalent feelings about the parents' ability to protect them.

Insecurely Attached: Avoidant. Children identified as avoidantly attached experience "a chronic failure of communication" (Edwards, 2002, p. 391). In an attempt to defend themselves and to self-regulate, they avoid the adult (e.g., tune out, look away, arch their backs) and turn to the environment rather than to others as a source of interest and comfort. They have been found to be able to persist with toys better than other children, but at a cost to relationship building. They see their caregivers as unavailable, and they learn to suppress their negative emotions of distress and anger (NICHD Early Child Care Research Network, 2006). They may demonstrate these feelings inappropriately with other adults and peers (Carlson & Sroufe, 1995). Mothers of avoidantly attached children have been found to be particularly sensitive to distress; however, they then withdraw from the child rather than take "effective emotional action" (Mills-Koonce et al., 2007).

Insecurely Attached: Disorganized–Disoriented. Researchers have classified children who seem dazed and confused when they are with their primary caregiver as having disorganized attachments. This can be a result of abuse and mistreatment or of a parent's unresolved experience of emotional abuse as a child.

Are there long-term effects of the child's experience of attachment? Do the relationships during the first three years influence how children view all subsequent relationships? Bowlby used the term "working model of relationships" to describe the child's thinking about how to relate to others that develops in the child's first relationships with adults. In these relationships, infants and toddlers learn what to expect from themselves and others during interactions. The term "working model of relationships" was used because the way children feel and behave in relationships is open to change. The attachment classifications can change when the relational environment changes for the infant/toddler; for example, if an insecure toddler's parents become more sensitive, the toddlers may become more secure. However, a child's *continuous* experience of an avoidant attachment relationship can lead to a pattern of behavior and beliefs about self and others, and, as you read earlier in the chapter, this can actually influence brain development. The ***Connecting with Children*** guidelines on the next page give ideas for supporting infants' and toddlers' emotional development.

Infant Social Development and Learning

SOCIAL DEVELOPMENT. Infants and toddlers are sociable with peers earlier than many of us think (Wittmer, 2008). Most show interest and engagement, are prosocial, develop friendships, and engage in conflict during the first three years of life. Social experience is one of the most important aspects of human development, and there seem to be universal human motives for belonging (Galardini & Giovannini, 2001) and connecting with others (Emde & Cyman, 1997). The early years are an important time to develop social competence, as socially successful toddlers are more competent as preschoolers and less aggressive as 9-year-olds (Howes & Phillipsen, 1998). Toddlers who are aggressive, withdrawn, or the target of rejection by peers (Hay, Payne, & Chadwick, 2004; Rubin & Coplan, 2004), and who are without support will continue these behaviors into the elementary years (Tremblay et al., 2004). These children and their families/teachers need ongoing support to develop more socially successful ways of interacting.

INTEREST. When we focus on and read about infant and toddler peer interactions and relationships, we begin to see young children's curiosity, interest, and peer potential (Wittmer, 2008). Again, they use all of the cognitive processes we have described to learn how to be social with peers. Studies have found that infants who were just 6 and 9 months old preferred to look at babies their same age (Sanefuji, Ohgami, & Hashiya, 2006); at 10–14 months of age, they even preferred to look at infants of their own gender (Kujawski & Bower, 1993). More research will need to be completed to find out exactly what interests babies have in each other.

CONNECTING WITH CHILDREN

Guidelines for Teachers and Families: Supporting Emotional Development

Following are strategies to support emotional development that are individually, developmentally, and culturally appropriate.

Recognize that all humans experience anger, disappointment, sadness, and fear and that it is important to label these feelings and help infants/toddlers find culturally appropriate ways to express them.

- An infant teacher soothed a crying infant by quietly saying, "Oh, I know you are hungry."
- A toddler teacher stated emphatically to a tantruming toddler, "You can tell me, 'I'm angry.'"

Appreciate cultural differences in children's emotional expression. Culture influences how emotions are expressed and regulated. Some cultures endorse anger while others feel shame (Cole, Bruschi, & Tamang, 2002).

- An infant teacher recognized that one infant expressed her sadness by crying and another child by whimpering.
- A toddler teacher noticed that one child withdrew from peers when angry and another yelled loudly when angry.

Provide a safe (holding) physical and emotional environment for the infant and toddler. Rather than worrying about spoiling a child, focus on relationship-building and empathy.

- When an 8-month-old cried, the teacher said, "You seem sad." When the infant lifted her hands up, the teacher picked her up.
- A toddler teacher held a toddler who had fallen and hit his head, saying, "I know that hurt"; the child quickly calmed down.

Understand that attachment reflects how the adult and child are handling both positive and negative emotions (affect regulation) that influence how safe and supported the child feels in the relationship and the strategies that a child learns to handle difficult emotions.

- An infant, who was very cautious of strangers, crawled to her favorite welcoming teacher when another child's parent came in the room.
- A toddler began to feel ambivalent about his teacher, when she sometimes helped him and at other times scolded him.

Support the child's value of self and the child's self-efficacy. There is a human need to be competent and adults must constantly explore ways for all children to be successful.

- The infant teacher placed sturdy, safe furniture in the room so infants could safely pull to stand. Several infants who did beamed at their accomplishments.
- A toddler teacher exclaimed to a toddler who looked up to see if the teacher was watching him play in the sand. The teacher smiled and said, "You are digging in the sand."
- Support the child's self-regulation by responding to infants' and toddlers' cries to help them calm down. As children develop, encourage them to use sounds, words, and short sentences to express feelings.

Support families to help them reduce negative emotions and maternal depression.

- A teacher talked with the parent of an infant who cried most of the day to figure out with her whether she wanted additional support from a social worker.
- A teacher greeted and stayed with a toddler who cried with abandon each morning after the father left.

Provide quality education and care programs that include relationship-based care (Wittmer & Petersen, 2009)—sensitive and responsive care teachers, primary care, and continuity of care.

- The infant teachers in the Heart Room explained to parents that primary care involves infants being cared for by primarily one person, but she was not the only person.
- The teachers in the "Wee Care" program provided continuity of care. The program moved at least one teacher "up" with a group of children to a new room, rather than asking children to move, often one by one, to a new room with all new teachers and often new peers as well.

Do infants and toddlers prefer to spend time with each other or with adults? There are two different conclusions, and the answers seem to depend on context. Children 10–12, 16–18, and 22–24 months of age in an unfamiliar setting with their mothers preferred to smile, vocalize, and imitate each other rather than spend much time with their mothers. In a child-care setting in the Netherlands, however, 15-month-olds had twice as many interactions with caregivers as peers (Deynoot-Schaub & Riksen-Walraven, 2006). From what we know about the importance of a secure base from which to explore, perhaps toddlers who were in a smaller setting with their mothers present felt safer to spend time with peers. In addition, during a long day in childcare, perhaps toddlers need additional attention from caregivers.

After watching toddlers together, you may see many types of play themes and imitation. Researchers in 1982 discovered twelve shared play themes in 1,200 minutes of observation among six toddler boys ages 12–18 months. These included toddlers talking with each other (vocal prosocial), sharing laughter and other emotions (positive affect as a meaning sharer), and imitating each other's vocalizations and motor actions (vocal and motor copy). These toddlers played run and chase games (run-chase or run-follow and curtain running), peek-a-boo games, object exchange, struggle over objects, aggression, rough-tumble play, and shared referencing such as pointing at or naming people or objects. We know that toddlers imitate each other and that they imitate peer behaviors later (deferred imitation) even after not seeing the behavior for a period of time. Deferred imitation has positive and negative aspects. Toddlers can imitate both how to play with toys *and* how to bite or hit another person.

Infants and toddlers not only show interest and play themes with their peers, but also are capable of being cooperative and prosocial with them. Does this mean that we expect them to be kind, helping, and cooperative at all times with peers? No! However, they are capable of being prosocial, and this behavior must be noticed and supported.

PROSOCIAL DEVELOPMENT. **Prosocial** is a term that is used to describe helping, being cooperative, comforting, responding to peer cries, and displaying empathy behaviors. While toddlers have been called "the terrible twos," we could call them the *prosocial twos* because of their capacity to care for others. In fact, during the second and third year, prosocial behaviors develop quickly when parents and teachers are supportive.

Toddlers can comfort others in distress. You may have seen 2-year-olds, as Lois Murphy did in 1936, comfort others with pats, hugs, and kisses; help another child; or protect a peer. Children younger than 2 years old are capable of comforting or giving objects to peers and adults in response to their sadness and other emotions. Even though many (87%) children tried at some point to help the distressed person by providing something that would comfort themselves rather than something that might comfort the other person, they were trying to help and comfort them. Eighty-one percent at one point provided instrumental help, for example, bringing a Kleenex to a grandmother. Toddlers are still learning how to respond to others' distress, and many also can be ambivalent to others' distress at times.

Toddlers can be quite empathetic, as well. Quann and Wien (2006) observed 20–23-month-olds and discovered three types of empathic behaviors. **Proximal empathy** includes those times when a child doesn't cause a second child's distress, but helps the peer. One girl (20 months old) comforted another girl (23 months old) when the older girl hurt her finger. **Altruistic empathy** tales place when a child stops her own activity to help a distressed child who is farther away. One child brought toys to a child who was distressed that his mother had left. **Self-corrective empathy** occurs when one child causes another child distress and then tries to help, seemingly to make amends, or at least to comfort the other child.

Of course, there are conflicts between toddlers! Toddlers might protest, resist another child entering their play, or even retaliate. Conflicts are relational, as are friendships. They occur between some children and not others. Conflict, as difficult as it is for parents and teachers, is a valuable experience for young children. It provides opportunities for children to learn that other children have different perspectives and that they can negotiate and communicate with peers. Conflicts also can provide opportunities for adults to help children restore relationships (Singer & Hannikainen, 2002). The ***Connecting with Children*** guidelines on the next page give more suggestions for supporting social development.

Almost 90% of toddlers will try to help or comfort someone in distress, even if the help they offer is what they would want, not necessarily what the distressed person might want. This boy's rough hug may not be that comforting to the sad little girl, but he is trying.

CONNECTING WITH CHILDREN

Guidelines for Teachers and Families: Supporting Social Development with Peers

Provide opportunities for peers to play together. Play is the way that young children learn.

- An infant teacher found that infants show great interest in each other, especially if she places them side by side on their backs; when they are able to sit, she places them close together.
- A toddler teacher provided a cozy corner for two or three toddlers to play with soft toys.

Encourage relationship building as a part of conflict resolution. Teach them what you want them to learn.

- Recognize that sharing is difficult, but turn-taking is easier for toddlers and twos. There will be conflicts, but this is how toddlers and twos learn to negotiate, cooperate, and take turns.
- A toddler teacher helped toddlers ask when they want a toy from another child even though the first child could say, "No." Usually the toddler with the toy soon stopped playing with it so the second child could have it.
- A toddler teacher helped the children in her group to take the perspective of the other child by saying, "Look, he's crying. He's sad. How can we help him?"

Recognize, encourage, and label prosocial behavior. Ask young children to help each other. Model for them how to be kind with pats and hugs.

- The toddler teacher created opportunities for peer "glee"—laughing, dancing around, showing delight, and experiencing joy and hilarity.
- The toddler teacher recognized motor behavior and interactions as a precursor to verbal interactions and imitation as a form of peer conversations—a kinesthetic (motor) dance (Capatides, Colins, & Bennett, 1996), so she encouraged two toddlers who loudly imitated each other's sounds.

Provide quality childcare. Childcare quality with low teacher-child ratios, small group size, and responsive caregivers predicts 36-month-old children's social skills.

- The infant teacher knew that state licensing requirements allowed for only three infants with one teacher.
- The two toddler teachers knew that when they had eight children in their group, the children were happier and played together better than when there were more children.

Infant Language and Communication

One of the most important things that an infant has to do is learn to communicate with others. Language competence is the ability of a person to communicate to make meaning. Communication includes children's use of sign language, gestures, body movements, and/or adaptive equipment. The study of infant/toddler language learning is one of the most exciting fields of research in infancy.

LISTENING AND LEARNING. During infancy, young children are learning about language long before they can talk. When they are born, newborns can discriminate speech sounds and attentively listen to adults' sounds, words, and the rhythms of language. We now know how important children's early language experience is to their learning how to listen and communicate.

Language processing begins early in a child's life. As noted earlier, infants prefer to hear their mother's voice over a stranger's voice at birth, indicating that they have been listening prior to birth (DeCasper, & Fifer, 1980). It has been said that "when two pregnant mothers, close to their delivery date, are talking, there are four people listening" (source unknown). Children's receptive language (listening and processing) is quite remarkable during the first year. Stanislas Dehaene, a French neurobiologist, recorded the brain activity of 2- and 3-month-old infants using a functional magnetic resonance imaging (fMRI) machine to detect brain flow to certain areas of the brain when French was read backward or forward to them. The same areas in the brain that adults use to process language was much more active when babies listened to forward speech rather than backward speech. These babies were discerning patterns in language. In fact, the language learning powers of infants and toddlers are amazing, as you can see in the ***Relating to Every Child*** feature.

RELATING TO

EVERY CHILD

▸ Universal Language Learning

IT SEEMS THAT INFANTS are **universal language learners**; they are "citizens of the world" (Kuhl et al., 2006) born ready to learn languages. Six-month-old infants learning English, for example, can discriminate speech-sound differences in languages other than the one they are learning, but by 12 months, they have lost the ability to discriminate the sounds in, for example, Hindu. This seems to be because by 7–12 months of age, they are focusing on and practicing the sounds in the language that they hear and they lose the ability to distinguish all sounds in all languages (Kuhl et al., 2006; Rivera-Gaxiola, Silvia-Pereyra, & Kuhl, 2008). This perceptual narrowing, you may remember, occurs in visual processing as well and is a neural language learning mechanism that facilitates infants learning the language spoken to them (Rivera-Gaxiola, et al., 2008). Researchers Kuhl, Tsao, and Liu (2003) made a remarkable discovery, however. After only five hours of hearing another language (Mandarin) at 8 to 10 months of age, infants retained their ability to hear the differences in the sounds of that non-native language. Listening to someone speak the non-native language on TV or through other media did not help the children learn; the language exposure had to be while interacting with a real person speaking the other language and reading stories.

Alsin emphasizes that infants are "statistical language learners." By 8 months, infants learn the forms for words, such as which sounds are more likely to follow other sounds. Infants' own names seem to help them recognize that speech is made up of words strung together; thus, saying a child's name helps that child learn where words begin and end in sentences (Bortfeld, Morgan, Golinkoff, & Rathbun, 2005).

Eight-month-old infants learn words for objects that interest them, not ones that interest the speaker. When researchers introduced new words while playing with infants, they attached the new word to an object that the infants focused on, not to an object the adult labeled. However, by 18 months of age, infants learn words differently—by focusing on the object of interest of the speaker (Pruden, Hirsh-Pasek, Golinkoff, & Hennon, 2006). This research tells us that adults should name the objects that are the focus of the infants' attention when infants are younger.

By 12 months, infants understand that when an adult points at an object, they are supposed to look at it (Woodward & Guadjardo, 2002). They learn the names of objects at 13 and 18 months after hearing the name of the object just 9 times within 5 minutes, and they still remember the names of the objects after 24 hours (Woodward, Markman, & Fitzsimmons, 1994). It is clear that long before infants speak or use sign language, they are busy processing language. The information on the development of receptive language helps adults understand how important their reciprocal, turn-taking, responsive language interactions are with very young children. Infants also begin expressing themselves long before their first words.

EXPRESSIVE LANGUAGE. Infants begin with "cooing" sounds, soft vowel (a, e, i, o, u) sounds and progress to babbling around 5 months of age, first babbling consonant and vowel sounds together that may sound like "da" or "ma." While these babbling sounds are not used by the child to specifically name her mother or father, parents may excitedly share the news that the infant called them by name. Babbling increases to include repetitions of sounds, such as "da-da," and includes "well-formed syllables required for meaningful speech" (Oller, Eilers, Neal, & Cobo-Lewis, 1998). Babies babble whether they are learning a vocal or sign language.

Since eye-hand coordination develops before the acquisition of verbal skills, some parents teach their infants and toddlers sign language, allowing the child to communicate certain needs in lieu of crying.

Infants learning sign language babble with their fingers and hands—approximating the correct sign modeled for them (Petitto & Marentette 1991). By 9 months of age, infants may call dad, "da-da" or mom, "ma-ma," if these are sounds the parents call each other.

Late syllabic babbling (i.e., "ma-ma, pa-pa, ba-ba") after 11 months of age among 1,536 high-risk infants was associated with language delays or disabilities (Oller, et al., 1998); thus it is important for parents and teachers to listen to, imitate, and encourage babbling.

Toddlers' rapid learning of words between 12 and 18 months is referred to as a **language explosion** (Woodward, Markman, & Fitzsimmons, 1994). Another term that is used is **fast mapping** as toddlers map labels to objects (Gershkoff-Stowe & Hahn, 2007). Infants learn language best when an adult talks directly to them (Thiessen, 2005), but by 18 months, they also learn language by overhearing adults talk (Floor & Akhtar, 2006). Eighteen-month-olds have a vocabulary of over 50 words, with some toddlers naming more objects and others using more socially expressive words. After 50 words, toddlers generally combine two words with the use of an open-pivot strategy; for example, they might say, "no kitty," "no eat" using the word, "no" as the pivot word and other words as the open words. Toddlers also use telegraphic speech—talk that uses nouns and verbs as in a telegram; for example, a 2-year-old learning English might say, "Daddy go?" (noun-verb) or "want juice" (verb-noun). They may overgeneralize when they use a name, such as "cats" for all animals with four legs, and undergeneralize when they use the word *cat* for only the black cat that is a family pet, but not for the neighbor's cat.

Two-year-olds continue to add words to their vocabularies and sentences; by age 3, they are saying an average of three words per utterance. By 2 to 3, you will hear children use possessives ("Mommy's coat"), plurals ("Grandma's coats"), "ing" at the end of words ("Me jumping"), the word "and" ("Papa and Daddy have white cars" or "Baby Ayla have a crib and I have a crib") and the ending "ed" (I breaked it"). When 2-year-olds add "ed" to the end of a word such as *break* ("breaked") and *find* ("finded"), rejoice, because they are applying a rule that they learned by listening to adults and peers. They are demonstrating that they are learning the structure of language! They will soon learn the exceptions to the rule. See the ***Connecting with Children*** *guidelines* for ideas about supporting language development.

Infant Motor Development and Learning

When you watch an infant as she learns to crawl, or a toddler as he practices walking up and down steps, you may wonder why these young children practice continuously until they can perform these motor actions with ease. You will see that each child is not just imitating how an older sibling or a parent performs these motor actions. Rather, the infant or toddler is continually adapting her motor actions to her constantly changing skills and the terrain of the environment.

Motor development in infancy, just as in other developmental domains, involves the child constantly thinking and experimenting with actions that result in various effects. "Motor skill in the natural environment involves knowing which actions are possible for the given situation. It requires a continual, online decision-making process because the everyday environment and one's physical capabilities are continually changing. Both factors (i.e., properties of the environment and physical abilities of the individual) must be considered together in a relationship that is dynamic rather than fixed" (Adolph & Eppler, 2002, pp. 121–122). Motor skills become more complex during the first three years as infants and toddlers adapt to different environmental conditions. Strategies that educators and parents can use to support motor development should include both fine motor and large/gross motor development activities.

CONNECTING WITH CHILDREN

Guidelines for Teachers and Families: Supporting Language Development

We must talk *with* children, not at children, *before* they can talk, in fact, from the moment they are born. Use infant-directed speech (IDS) with young infants.

- "You are on *top* of the climber" the infant teacher said when an infant looked back at her from the top of a very short climber.
- The infant teacher said to two infants outside, "Look, a dog—a brown dog."

Point to objects, label them, and expand on the sounds and words infants make once they are 9 months or older.

- Most adults, no matter where they live in the world, say things like, "Oh, that's a kitty. See the kitty. She's a pretty kitty" (in their own language) with a higher pitch, probably emphasizing the word, "Kitty" and pointing to it each time they say the word.
- A 15 month-old mobile infant looked to the sky and loudly yelled, "airplane." The teacher responded by saying, "An airplane—up in the sky."

Use reciprocal, turn-taking strategies to help children feel heard and learn how to participate in conversations. Respond by staying on topic, imitating the child's sounds and words, and using language that is slightly more advanced.

- The parent of a 1-year-old sat watching the street from a park. The parent described what he saw by saying, "That's a truck. It's big. That's a car. Ooh, here comes a firetruck."
- An infant babbled, "Da-da, Ma-ma." The father said, "I'm dada," while pointing to himself. "There is mama," pointing to the child's mother.

Use joint-attention strategies.

- The teacher and infant sat while both looked at a toy that moved up and down. The teacher pointed to it and said, "The toy is jumping."
- "Look," the infant teacher said while pointing to a worm on the ground. The teacher waited until both infants looked to where she was pointing and said, "It's a worm."

Identify language delay early.

- An infant teacher noticed that a girl in her room was not cooing at 5 months of age. The teacher talked with the parent and discovered that the girl made no sounds at home. The parent talked with the girl's pediatrician.
- A toddler with a hearing challenge used the sign for "eat," "drink," "tree," and "more." The teacher asked the parent to teach her other signs that were used at home.

FINE MOTOR DEVELOPMENT. Fine motor activities are more finely tuned movements that include grasping, reaching, and bilateral coordination—the use of both hands together. Newborns can grasp an adult's finger because of the grasping reflex. As the reflex disappears, new grasping skills appear (see Table 4.6 on the next page), and although these skills are presented in sequence, infants may use different types of grasping behavior from previous stages as needed for different tasks (Lee, Liu, & Newel, 2006). Reaching abilities also improve during the first year (Spencer, Vereijken, Diedrich, & Thelen, 2000). In one study, 9-week-old infants did not reach, but all ten of the study infants reached for objects by about 17 weeks (Lee, Liu, & Newel, 2006). Researchers Rocha, Silva, and Tudella (2006), using a motion capture filming system, found that from 4 to 6 months of age, the ability to reach—including frequency, speed, straightness of reaching, and the ability to reach for small objects—improved. There is evidence that by 10 months, infants have sophisticated motor planning strategies. Claxton and colleagues (2003) found that infants reach for a ball faster if they are going to throw it than if they are placing the ball into a tube.

LARGE MOTOR DEVELOPMENT. Have you noticed that infant or toddler walkers are constantly adjusting to different kinds of floors (carpeted, hardwood, tile) and terrains outdoors? They might walk fast on a familiar carpeted floor, but walk cautiously on slippery floors. As they grow, they also have to adapt to changes in their body structure (Adolph & Avolio, 2000), and they are constantly organizing and adapting their movements to accomplish their goals (Thelen & Corbetta, 1996). For example, toddlers who are 16 months old and walk well

TABLE 4.6 • **Fine and Large Motor Development of Infants and Toddlers**

	DEVELOPMENT	EXAMPLE
Motor 0–4 Months	Infants • lift head when held at shoulder. • hold head steady and erect. • turn head toward a familiar voice. • hold body still to pay attention; wiggle and move to encourage continued interaction. • on back, thrust arms and legs in play. • hold finger, lift toy with reflexive grasp. • suck on own fingers and hands, objects. By 3-4 months, infants • when on their tummies, can lift their head and shoulders off the ground. • turn from side to back. • hold a toy in hand.	Isabella held her head up and looked around at the other children as Mrs. Jackson held her against her shoulder. Jahmonte, sat on his tummy on a blanket, lifted his head to see himself in the mirror mounted at floor level on the wall. Jennifer held a rattle placed in her hand, but seemed unaware it was there. Filipe brought his fingers to his mouth and sucked on them, while looking intently at the toddlers.
Motor 4–8 Months	Infants • turn from back to side, later roll from back to front. • sit first with support but steady alone by the end of this period. • reach with one arm. • use raking grasp. • creep on tummy and may crawl on hands and knees by the end of the period. • shake, bang, hold, let go of objects. • move objects from hand to hand. • hold their own bottle. • bring objects to their mouth.	Abha rolls from his back to his tummy to reach a toy, then rolls back over to play with it. Abigail, sitting steadily alone, loves using both hands to pick up objects and study them. Diego loves being held while he has his bottle, but he insists on holding it himself.
Motor 8–12 Months	Mobile infants • pull to stand. • cruise. • stand alone. • walk with help and then alone. • sit in a short chair. • finger-feed. • use spoon, sippy cup.	Thuc crawls to his teacher's side, then holds her leg as he pulls up to stand. Fatina sits at the lunch table, alternating between using her spoon and her fingers to enjoy her meal.
Motor 12–18 Months	Mobile infants • stack and line up blocks. • can put arm into sleeve, foot into shoe. • can walk. • walk while carrying objects in each hand. • climb stairs often by placing first one foot and then the other on one step. • try to use a spoon, but awkwardly	Ethan stood at the table, carefully using both hands to build a tower with colored blocks. Conisha toddled across the room, with her teddy bear in one hand and her blanket in the other.
Motor 18–24 Months	Toddlers • point to objects to communicate. • make marks on paper. • pound, shape clay. • run. • sit on and get up from small chairs alone.	Toshiko rolled the dough with her hands, then used tools to make designs. Kavon sat down at the table to eat, then took his dirty dishes to the tub.
Motor 24–36 Months	Toddlers • thread beads, use scissors, paint with fingers or brushes, & do simple puzzles. • throw and kick a ball. • stand on one foot. • stand and walk on tiptoes. • climb stairs with one foot on each step. • climb, slide, and jump. • eat with spoon and fork. • can pour milk from a small pitcher.	Pablo doesn't even have to think about his body as he runs to greet his dad at the end of the day. Two toddlers make a game out of imitating each other's tiptoe steps, postures, and gestures. Eliana and Eva use the dress-up clothes for their game, struggling to pull on some of the easier pieces.

Source: Adapted from Wittmer & Petersen, Infant and Toddler Development and Responsive Program Planning, "Developmental Trends and Responsive Interactions" from pp. 238–240, © 2010 by Pearson Education, Inc. Reproduced by permission of Pearson Education, Inc.

CONNECTING WITH CHILDREN

Guidelines for Families, Teachers, and Other Professionals: Supporting Motor Development

Create an environment for children's explorations. Infants and toddlers do not need adults to tell them, "get up and walk"; rather they need supportive adults who create an environment conducive to walking and who admire their efforts.

- The infant teacher provided a place for infants to crawl up two steps, pull to stand on sturdy furniture and a bar attached to the wall.
- The toddler teacher provided a climber with three steps going up and a slide going down.

Provide a variety of materials and toys for children to grasp, put in and out of containers, carry, and problem-solve how to work.

- The infant teacher noticed that one infant loved taking blocks out of a box and then putting them in again.
- The toddler teacher provided a play cash register that the children could open by pushing the red button first and then the blue button.

Provide opportunities for children to balance, such as when sitting, reaching, walking, and running.

- The teacher placed a small basket of toys by a sitting infant who reached with one hand to get a toy.
- The toddler teacher provided a "trail" through one side of the room with masking tape and watched as the toddlers joyfully tried to walk within the lines.

Remember that the sequence and timing of children's motor development varies by culture.

- The infant teacher was not concerned when one mother often carried her child on her back in a sling made out of a large scarf. The child often crawled while in the program even though her mother carried her frequently.
- A toddler teacher noticed that one toddler often ate with a spoon, while another toddler generally ate by picking up food in her hands, just like the adults in their cultures.

---

will walk from one platform to another on wider bridges without handrails, but not narrower bridges, and they will walk more frequently on narrower bridges if there is a sturdy handrail available rather than a foam one (Berger, Adolph, & Lobo, 2005). A general sequence of large motor development appears in Table 4.6, although, as noted in dynamic systems theory, children may skip stages or revert to using previously developed skills to accomplish tasks.

Each new ability brings with it new understanding of cognitive concepts such as "near," "far," "size," "shape," and "depth perception." New skills also bring new social understanding and opportunities for adult–child relationship realignments. For example, when an infant begins to crawl on hands and knees, parents begin to see their child as an explorer with a will of his own as he decides where and when to crawl. Infants' ability to "socially reference" adults for emotional cues of danger increases around 7 months of age as infants move from rolling and sitting to moving by creeping or crawling. It is no wonder that the ability to understand others' intentions increases around 9 months as the crawling and sometimes walking infant learns that he can have goals and achieve them. The ***Connecting with Children*** guidelines have some specific suggestions about how to support motor development.

Although cultural differences do exist, if a delay or disability is suspected, the child has a right to a free evaluation from a professional team, as described in the next section on children's developmental and health challenges.

The Early Intervention System for Children with Developmental Challenges

Carlina was born with spina bifida, a birth defect that occurs when the neural tube does not close entirely while forming prenatally. Her young parents were in shock after the doctor revealed the surprising news. They felt isolated, confused, and very concerned about the future of their baby girl. Soon, however, the hospital, in collaboration with the state's Early Intervention System, provided Carlina's parents with information on the services and supports that Carlina and the family had a right to expect.

Developmental challenges in young children with special needs include physical and mental health challenges, sensory impairments, developmental delays, and conditions that place children at risk for developmental delay, including cerebral palsy, autism, Down syndrome, and spina bifida. The Early Intervention System in each state provides supports and services for children with identified disabilities and their families.

Federal law, specifically the Individuals with Disabilities Act (IDEA), requires that each state provide an Early Intervention System. This system provides free assessments to determine if a child has or is at risk of developing a disability, as well as services/supports provided to families by a multidisciplinary team that often includes an early childhood special educator, a physical or occupational therapist, a speech/language therapist, and/or psychologist. Part C of IDEA is the infant/toddler piece of the law that requires that each state have:

- a rigorous definition of developmental delay
- appropriate early intervention services based on scientifically based research
- timely and comprehensive evaluations
- public awareness programs to inform families of the services/supports available
- policies and procedures for safeguarding the rights of families
- personnel standards and policies that ensure that early intervention services are provided, as much as possible, in natural environments—in the home and community where children without disabilities participate in family and community life

States receive money from the federal government to implement the Part C legislation, and each state names its lead agency to ensure that all of the policies and procedures are enacted. Examples of lead agencies include the following: Department of Health (Florida), Department of Health and Human Services (Colorado), Rehabilitation Services (Alabama), Economic Security (Arizona), Developmental Services (California), Department of Education (Iowa), or a collaboration of state agencies (Minnesota) (NECTAC, 2009). Each state creates its own definition of *developmental delay*. In Florida, for example, eligibility criteria requires that infants and toddlers show a 25% or greater delay in one or more of the developmental domains. Idaho requires that children demonstrate significant delay in one domain or delay in two or more domains. The federal agency IDEA (2006) recommends, however, that a well-developed definition should include:

- Children with a physical or sensory impairment who, without assistance, would be unlikely to achieve their full potential
- Children with a learning disability, who again would not achieve their full potential without assistance from agencies outside the family
- Children with emotional, behavioral, or mental health problems.

Each state gives its Early Intervention System different names; for example, Minnesota's system is named "Help Me Grow." Although the family has a right to self-refer, usually hospital personnel, physicians, or educators help families gain information about the Early Intervention System if a child is suspected of having delays.

A critical piece of Part C is the **Individualized Family Service Plan (IFSP),** a document the family and professionals develop together. This plan includes the goals for the child's development and the supports/services that the child and family need to achieve them. This family-centered document ensures that families' rights are protected and that their priorities and goals are central to the supports/services provided. More information and resources are available concerning IDEA, Part C, and each state's early intervention system at http://www.nectac.org. The National Early Childhood Technical Assistance Center (NECTAC, 2009) is a nationally funded center that provides extensive resources for families and professionals seeking information on the U.S. Department of Education's Office of Special Education Programs, including more information on Early Intervention Systems.

For more information on specific types of delays and disabilities, see CDC's website at http://www.cdc.gov (2009e.). Many of the children with these conditions receive ongoing medical care and are eligible for early intervention services if they are delayed in one or more domains or at risk of developmental delay. Other children may receive services/supports only through the medical system. Remember that children (and adults) who have a disability are referred to as "children with a disability," rather than, for example, "a Down's child." **Person-first language** is used because children are individuals first and the disability is just a part of who they are.

▼ SUMMARY AND KEY TERMS

• The Meaning and Significance of Infancy

The amount of growth, development, and learning that infants, toddlers, and twos accomplish is amazing. There is strong scientific evidence for the importance of the first 36 months of life for children's long-term development. Many researchers and theorists, including René Spitz, Erik Erikson, Piaget, Vygotsky, Bowlby, Honig, and Lally were influential in identifying the first three years as an important time of life.

A child's brain develops at a rapid pace during the first three years: (1) a child's brain is immature at birth; (2) it is changed by experience; (3) the timing of experience can be important; and (4) relationships influence a child's social and emotional functioning.

Infants' relationships with the important adults in their lives influence not only what young children learn, but also *how* they learn. Early experiences with adults who are sensitive to young children's distress, provide emotional availability, are responsive, and encourage children's play and exploration profoundly influence the architecture of the brain.

• The Newborn (Neonate)

Newborns are both capable and vulnerable. The newborn's sensory systems are ready to process information and use many behaviors to communicate their needs to responsive adults. Healthy newborns weigh from 5-1/2 to 10 pounds and average 20 inches long. Losing weight during the first three days of life is normal because of meconium loss (anal excretions) and little fluid intake.

Parents and other caregivers need information on characteristics of newborns so that strong relationships between caring adults and newborns develop early. Prematurity and low birth weight in newborns are of critical concern to the adults who care for the newborns, health care providers, and the society as these conditions relate to developmental concerns among newborns. Babies born below 5-1/2 pounds may experience hyaline membrane disease, chronic lung disease, apnea, necrotizing enterocolitis, intraventricular hemorrhage, and/or retinopathy of prematurity.

Prevention of prematurity and low birth weight is critically important, and medical interventions and social interaction interventions are improving to both prevent these conditions and support infants and their families. Massage of hospitalized preterm infants works to increase weight gain. The outcomes for premature and low birth weight newborns depend on the quality of postnatal nutrition and the caregiving environment.

Neurobehavioral assessments and screenings for newborns' health and vitality increase the opportunities for early interventions that improve children's physical and emotional health and foster quality relationships between them and the important adults in their lives. The APGAR, Neonatal Behavior Assessment Scale, and screenings for physical disorders such as phenylketonuria, hypothyroidism, hearing impairments, and vision impairments are key assessments that occur at birth or shortly after.

• Newborns' Reflexes and States Promote Survival and Relationships

When adults understand newborns' reflexes and states, they are more likely to provide optimal care, be sensitive and responsive to infants' cues, and identify early developmental challenges. Crying is an infant "state" that causes concern for families and teachers; a case study presented at the beginning of the chapter and discussed at the end provides key points on the importance of and methods for soothing infants. The "Never Shake a Baby" campaign emphasizes that when babies are shaken, the brain rotates within the skull cavity, severely injuring the child's brain and leading to death or disabilities. Sleep is another "state" that is often of concern to families and teachers. A Point/Counterpoint discussion highlights the debate about whether infants should sleep in the family bed with one or more family members. Infants must be placed on their backs (supine) to sleep to prevent Sudden Infant Death Syndrome. Excessive sitting or sleeping in car seats, swings, carriers, and bouncy seats contributes to an increase in head deformities among infants because of the constant pressure on the backs of their heads.

• Physical Growth and Nutrition of the Infant and Toddler

Without good health, the child's development is impeded and the children's and families' well-being is hampered. In this section, readers will find information on physical growth and nutrition, the importance of breastfeeding, introduction of solid food, and obesity.

• Infant and Toddler Development and Learning

Infants and toddlers develop and learn in six domains—sensory and perceptual, cognitive, emotional, social, language, and motor—in the context of their culture and family. Competencies in all domains of development emerge from experience rather than from maturation alone and many systems, including perception, cognition, motor, and emotional development, work together as a child learns. The power of development, children's responses to cultural and environmental influences, the effect of relationships on relationships, a social and emotional basis for learning, and children's individual characteristics all are a product of the interaction of nature and nurture or genes and environment. These five factors and a continuous interaction between genetic influences and environmental factors also influence sensory and perceptual development.

It seems that infants expect coherent information. Vision and hearing are two other senses that are coordinated early in children's lives. Infants and toddlers are motivated to learn and generally learn quickly; they can focus attention and remember. They are goal oriented and understand intentions. Modeling and observations as well as categorizing, classifying, sorting, generalizing, and using symbols are processes infants and toddlers use to learn.

Emotional development is the growth of children's ability to express and regulate their feelings, and emotional learning encompasses the mechanisms by which children learn *which* feelings to express and *how* to express them. Children have characteristic temperaments; goodness of fit describes how well the caregiver's temperament matches the child's temperament or how well caregivers understand, accept, and work with the child's temperament. Secure attachments with caregivers allow the child to explore his environment (as soon as he is capable of doing so) while feeling safe in the presence of the attachment figure. Infants and toddlers show interest in other people, are prosocial, develop friendships, and engage in conflict during the first three years of life. Social experience is one of the most important aspects of human development, and there seem to be universal human motives for belonging. Toddlers can comfort others in distress and can express empathy.

One of the most important things that an infant has to do is learn to communicate with others. By 8 months, infants learn the forms for words, such as which sounds are more likely to follow other sounds. Infants' own names seem to help them recognize that speech is made up of words strung together. It is clear that long before infants speak or use sign language, they are busy processing language. Toddlers' rapid learning of words between 12 and 18 months is referred to as a language explosion. Motor development in infancy, just as in other developmental domains, involves the child constantly thinking and experimenting with actions that result in various effects. Motor skills become more complex during the first three years as infants and toddlers adapt to different environmental conditions.

• The Early Intervention System for Children with Developmental Challenges

Developmental challenges in young children with special needs include physical and mental health challenges, sensory impairments, developmental delays, and conditions that place the children at risk for developmental delay, including cerebral palsy, autism, Down syndrome, and spina bifida. The Early Intervention System in each state (required by IDEA) provides supports and services for children with identified disabilities and their families. Each state creates its own definition of *developmental delay*. The Individualized Family Service Plan (IFSP), a document the family and professionals develop together, includes the goals for the child's development and the supports/services that the child and family need to achieve them. This family-centered document ensures that families' rights are protected and that their priorities and goals are central to the supports/services provided.

▼ KEY TERMS

altruistic empathy (155)
APGAR (126)
attachment (151)
attention (144)
autism (130)
circumcision (124)
cross-modal abilities (144)
deferred imitation (146)
fast mapping (158)
full-term (125)
goodness of fit (150)
habituation (144)
Individualized Family Service Plan (IFSP) (162)
infant-directed speech (159)
intrauterine growth restriction (126)
language explosion (158)
late-preterm (126)
low birth weight (126)
Neonatal Behavioral Assessment Scale (NBAS) (127)
neural tube (120)
object permanence (144)
other race effect (141)
person-first language (162)
plasticity (120)
premature (125)
primitive reflexes (130)
prosocial (155)
proximal empathy (155)
pruned (120)
reflexes (130)
schemas (147)
self-corrective empathy (155)
self-regulation (151)
sensitive periods (120)
small-for-gestational-age (SGA) (126)
states (130)
surfactin (125)
survival reflexes (130)
temperament (149)
theory of mind (151)
universal language learner (157)
very low birth weight (126)
visual acuity (140)
visual perception (140)
well-being (119)

▼ THE CASEBOOK

PICKING UP A CRYING BABY

Dom's parents didn't know what to do about his crying. Dom's mother, Robin, read in her new book on infant care that parents should respond to their baby's cries, comfort them, and help them become calm again. There was a chapter on how important a secure attachment is for the child and that parents' responding to crying helps the child feel safe, learn to trust in his parents' availability, and have a sense of self-worth. Yet Dom's grandmother, Fara, let Robin and her husband know her beliefs about picking up crying children. Fara felt strongly that picking up a crying baby would spoil the child rotten and the baby would just become more demanding. What should Robin and her husband do?

WHAT WOULD THEY DO?

Here is how some professionals responded:

JUDY WELCH, M.D.—Family Practitioner, Westbrook, Maine

Grandmother Fara appears to value independence for her grandchild. A newborn baby by nature is dependent, so expecting independence at too early an age can cause development problems in this child. Normal development usually moves from dependence to independence in the second year of life. The next phase, possibly the most important, is the interdependent phase in which the child interacts with the parent to complete a task more successfully than if the child were acting independently. An example is the 2-year-old who wants to do tasks by himself (independent), developing to become the 3- to 5-year-old who asks for assistance with the more difficult task, and works together with the parent to accomplish the task.

Different cultures place different emphasis on these values. In the United States, as with this grandmother, independence is favored. In one study of Japanese preschool teachers, the observers were made uncomfortable by the degree of independence that the children were allowed to demonstrate. The teachers encouraged self-reliance and let the children solve their own social issues. Australian Indigenous cultures demonstrated interdependence. (Warrki Jarrinjaku Abouriginal Child Rearing Strategy Project Team, 2002). Interdependence has also been demonstrated in various non-Western cultures. These included Marquesas Islanders, Mexican and Guatemalan Mayans, and Euro-American children. There is a definite intertwining of the two principles of interdependence and independence, and to the casual observer, an act that looks independent could actually be interdependent if it fits into greater tribe or social group needs.

The current research (MayoClinic.com and other websites) concur that the average time that a newborn infant will cry is 2–3 hours per day. Babies cry as a means to communicate a need to the caregiver. That need may be an alert that they are hungry, wet, tired, bored, or uncomfortable. They may be sick or in pain. Researchers recommend that the parent/caregiver interpret the cry and address the need of the infant. Crying is the infant's only way to communicate distress in this dependent phase of development; meeting the needs of the infant will help it develop into the independent and the interdependent stages of development. The grandmother need not fear; baby will not be "spoiled" at this age.

CHRIS FRASER, MSW, LISW

Behavioral Health Counselor in Private Practice, Columbus, Ohio

Robin and her husband should thank Fara for her input on how to best parent their child. They might admit to Fara their uncertainty on what the best practice would be for dealing with a crying infant. Additionally, they could invite Fara to a consultation with a child and family therapist who can inform them of evidence-based best parenting practices for dealing with a crying infant.

A skilled child and family therapist can intervene in a positive way in which the grandmother's perspective is not discounted, but honored while at the same time educating both the parents and the grandmother about the research regarding childhood attachment and resiliency.

Bringing in a skillful child and family therapist can prevent unhelpful power struggles and hurt feelings between the parents and grandmother. It is preferable to research a child and family therapist who has competency in working with families from that specific culture.

Research has shown that when parents consistently respond to an infant's crying, it fosters a sense of unconditional love. Unconditional love is the hallmark of what creates resiliency in later years. Responding to crying infants provides the children with a sense that they are safe and that they can get their fundamental needs met. Responding to an infant's cries also fosters language development, emotional intelligence, self-confidence, and overall brain development.

PEARSON **myeducationlab**

Now go to MyEducationLab at ***www.myeducationlab.com,*** where you can:

- Find the instructional objectives for this chapter in the **Study Plan**.
- Take a quiz as a part of the **Study Plan** to self-assess your mastery of chapter content. The program generates an individualized Study Plan based upon your answers to the quiz.
- Complete **Activities and Applications** to assist you in deepening your understanding of important chapter concepts.
- Apply what you have learned through **Building Teaching Skills,** exercises that guide you in trying out skills and strategies you will use in professional practice.

5 PHYSICAL DEVELOPMENT IN EARLY CHILDHOOD

THE CASEBOOK

WHAT WOULD YOU DO?
CHILDHOOD OVERWEIGHT AND OBESITY

Near the end of every school year, Susan makes a point of meeting with the families of each child in her preschool class to review what she's observed in terms of physical, cognitive, and social emotional development. One child in particular is extremely overweight for her age and height—an increasing problem among preschoolers. Susan struggled with how to broach this very sensitive subject. She tried very hard not to sound judgmental—just concerned—when speaking with Laura's mom about her diet and activity level. After all, Laura is just 4 years old, but if the issue is not addressed now, she could struggle with overweight and health issues throughout her life. Laura's mom reasoned that it was very difficult to deny Laura the foods many of her friends are allowed to eat. But Laura doesn't want to participate in games or other activities that would burn off calories because the kids in the neighborhood tease her about the way she looks and moves. Susan struggled with how to impress upon this mother and her young daughter her concerns about the grave risks to health and well-being that stem from being overweight. And this risk will only get more serious as Laura "grows." How can Susan help them understand?

CRITICAL THINKING

- As a medical professional, teacher, family member, or friend, how would you broach this issue with Laura's parents?
- How might some reasonable goals for diet and exercise be set?

Nora Skalleova, Age 9—Czech Republic

- How would you speak to Laura about the consequences of being overweight?
- How would you help her to cope with the peer rejection and humiliation she is experiencing?
- What should schools and teachers be doing to educate children and families about health and nutrition, as well as the causes and long-term consequences of being overweight?

▶ OVERVIEW AND OBJECTIVES

As children develop, they experience numerous and dramatic physical changes. For example, birth weight tends to triple from birth to age 1, and quadruple by 30 months of age. Similarly, most humans increase their height by 50% in their first year of life. Body growth presents the most obvious changes, but developing bodies also undergo profound changes in the brain and other internal systems. The three chapters on physical development in this text consider changes in children's bodies and brains from early childhood through adolescence. In this chapter, we focus specifically on physical development in the early years (ages 2 through 6) and how physical changes influence and are influenced by children's overall health and well-being. Also, we examine some special physical needs that arise from chronic illnesses and cancer. Finally, we will look at how parents, educators, and other professionals can support healthy development in all children, especially children with special physical needs. By the time you finish this chapter you should be able to do the following:

Objective 5.1 Describe some significant physical changes in children from ages 2 through 6.
Objective 5.2 Explain the implications of myelination and lateralization for young children's thinking and functioning.
Objective 5.3 Provide examples of major milestones in gross and fine motor development during the early years.
Objective 5.4 Summarize the risks for and implications of overweight and obesity in early childhood.
Objective 5.5 Identify common sleep problems in young children and present some evidence-based solutions.
Objective 5.6 Summarize advances in research on childhood cancer as well as challenges that require further study.
Objective 5.7 Describe common environmental hazards and discuss their implications for children.

BODY GROWTH

Compared to other species, humans experience a prolonged period of physical growth and development. On average, humans' bodies continue to grow for 20% of their lifespan, compared with mice's bodies, which grow for 2% of their lifespan, and other primates (e.g., chimpanzees), whose physical development lasts for 16% of their lifespan. In most children, growth follows a typical trajectory, or growth curve, which is shown in Figure 5.1. During infancy, growth is very rapid! On average, infants increase their height by 50% during their first year and by 75% by the time they are 2 years old. Infants' weight shows a similar increase over the first two years of life. This rapid rate of growth slows during the preschool and middle childhood years, but accelerates again in adolescence.

From ages 2 through 6, young children lose their babyish appearance. Their body fat decreases and their signature "pot-bellies" flatten as the muscles in their stomachs gain strength. Also, whereas babies' heads appear large in proportion to the rest of their bodies, young children's bodies appear appropriately sized relative to their heads. Finally, as young children grow and develop, they become stronger and more coordinated. We will examine these developments in the section on motor development below.

Different systems in the body grow at different rates. For example, just as infants' heads appear large compared to their bodies (at birth their heads are 25% of their total length at two months of age), adolescents' hands and feet often appear large relative to their total body size, giving them a "gawky" appearance. Figure 5.2 on page 170 shows these changes. Internal systems grow at different rates as well. For example, the lymphoid system, which includes tonsils and lymph nodes, grows rapidly in the early years, building children's immunity to the many infectious diseases they come in contact with as they begin to socialize more outside their homes. Recall from Chapter 4 that breastfeeding boosts the immune system and is believed to protect against developing allergies. In contrast, reproductive organs grow slowly until adolescence, when they grow rapidly.

Boys and girls are similar in their patterns of growth during the early years. Girls tend to have more body fat and boys more muscle mass throughout the lifespan. In general, the proportion of body fat is highest during infancy. It slowly declines during the early and middle childhood years. In adolescence, body fat increases in girls and decreases in boys. Muscle mass, in contrast, increases from early childhood through adolescence for both sexes. However, boys have a greater increase in muscle mass during adolescence than girls, giving them the edge in many physical activities.

OUTLINE ▼

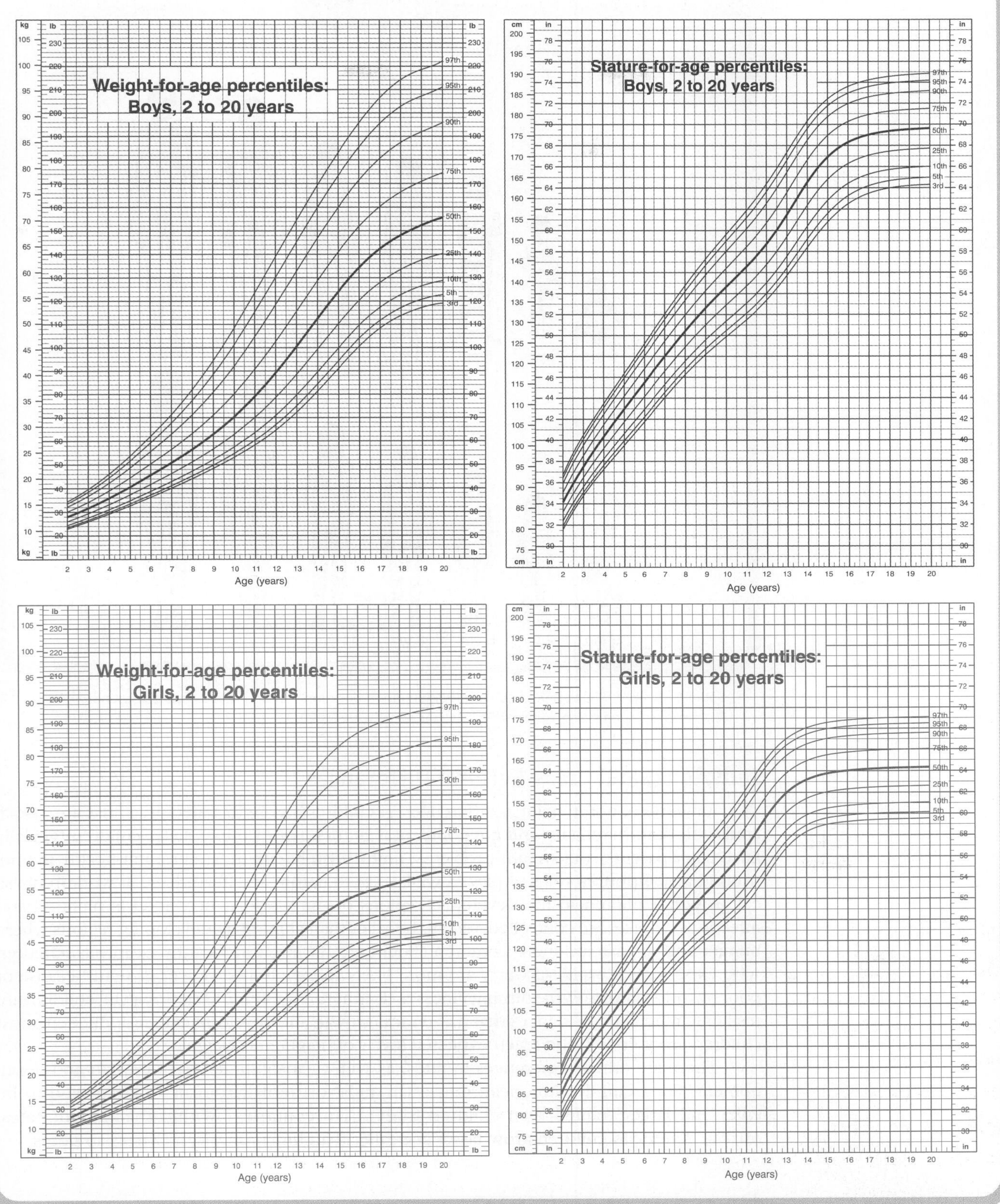

Source: Adapted from Vital and Health Statistics. (2002). 2000 CDC growth charts for the United States: Methods and development *(DHHS Publication No. PHS 2002-1696). Maryland, MD: Department of Health and Human Services, Centers for Disease Control and Prevention, and National Center of Health Statistics. Used courtesy of Centers for Disease Control and Prevention, www.cdc.gov*

FIGURE 5.2

CHANGES IN DIFFERENT BODY SYSTEMS

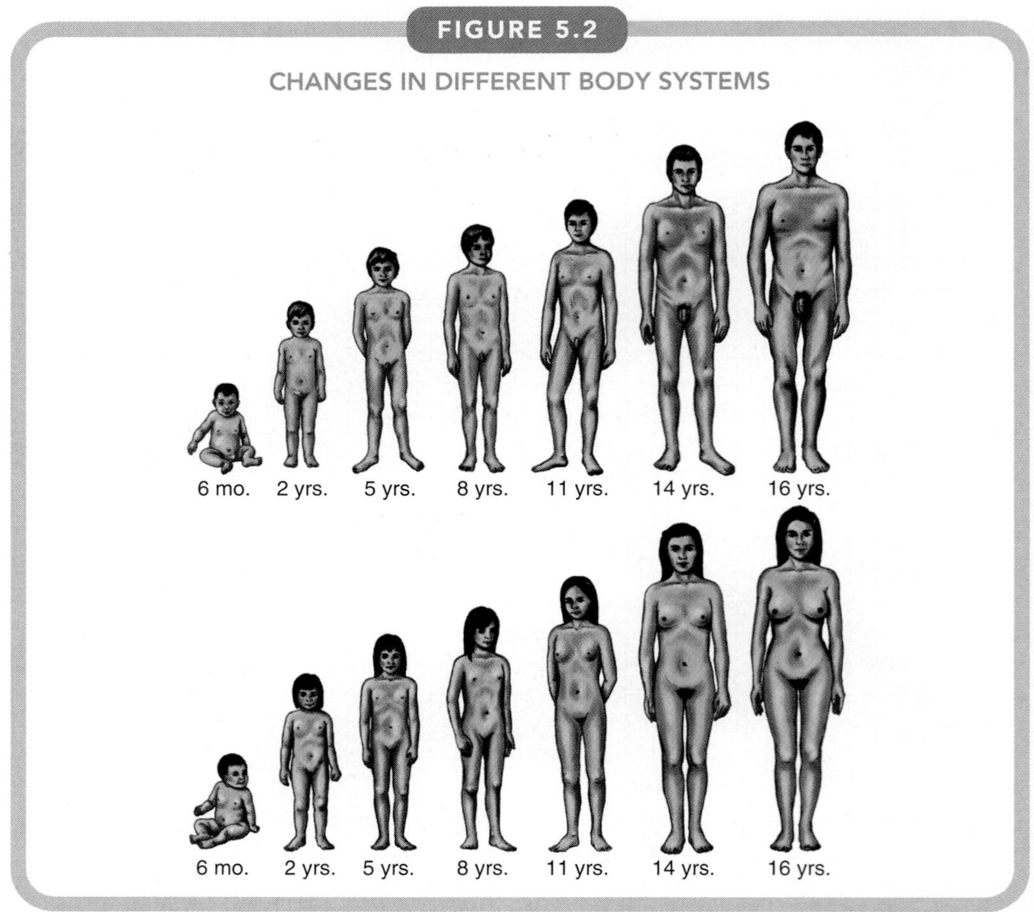

Source: McDevitt & Ormrod, Child Development and Education, *"Changes in different body systems" p. 146, © 2010. Reproduced by permission of Pearson Education, Inc.*

Individual and Cross-Cultural Differences

Of course, there are individual differences in children's growth trajectories that are associated with both hereditary and environmental factors. For example, taller children typically have taller parents, and weight problems, unfortunately, run in families. But health and nutrition have important roles to play as well, so both nature and nurture are at work in physical growth. Children in the developed regions of the world, where food is plentiful and infectious diseases are controlled, tend to be taller than children in developing regions where hunger and disease are more common (Bogin, 2001). Even in wealthy countries, children who experience chronic poverty are more likely to experience slower growth because of poor nutrition and growth-stunting illnesses (Leathers & Foster, 2004). However, children are resilient. When circumstances that halt typical growth and development are addressed, most children grow rapidly and reach expected levels of height and weight.

There are ethnic differences in rates, as well as absolute levels of growth and development. For example, American Caucasian and Northern European children tend to be taller and larger framed than children from Asian countries. Within the United States, African American children grow faster and taller than their American Caucasian peers.

Brain Development

One of the most important areas of physical development during early childhood is brain development. The brain continues to grow more rapidly than other parts of the body during early childhood, such that children's brains reach 75% of their adult size by the time they are 3 and 90% by the time they are 5. In comparison, children's bodies continue growing in the middle childhood years and undergo another growth spurt in adolescence. More importantly, between the ages of about 2 and 6, changes in children's brains both support and reflect impressive cognitive developments.

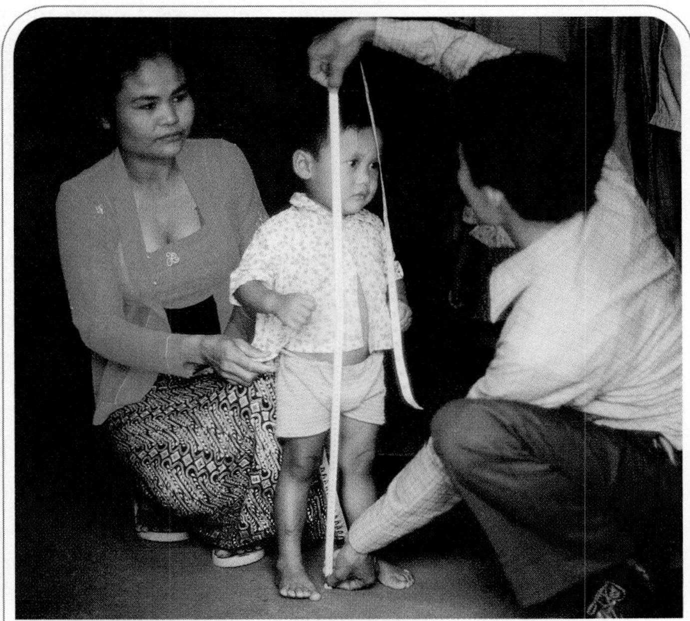
Children in developed countries, where food is plentiful and diseases are controlled, tend to be taller than children in developing countries.

The production and pruning of brain synapses that takes place in the first two years continues during the early childhood years. But the number of synapses pruned in early childhood is more than the number of new synapses formed, so the circuits that experience has made useful and adaptive are strengthened while less adaptive circuits are pruned away (Kagan & Herschkowitz, 2005). Growth of neural fibers and the coating of the fibers with fatty myelin—a process called **myelination**—increase brain efficiency, particularly in the parts of the brain involved with memory. Young children are able to think faster and to hold more thoughts in mind, so they can make sense of increasingly complex sequences of words or actions. They can remember what comes next when doing an activity (Sampaio & Truwit, 2001). With this capacity for faster thought and the ability to make sense of longer sequences of words and ideas, young children are ready to learn—language, concepts about other people, simple games, and other cultural tools.

The process of myelination is also responsible for the rapid growth in brain size we mentioned above, from an average weight of about 1,000 to 1,100 grams at 2 years old to an average of 1,200 to 1,300 grams by 5 years old (boys tend to have larger brains than girls). But these developing brains are doing more than growing in size. The two hemispheres of the brain are specializing—called **lateralization.** By about age 3, most children (around 90%) favor the left hemisphere of the brain for language processing and logical, step-by-step reasoning. The right hemisphere handles much of the spatial-visual information and such nonverbal tasks as appreciation of art or music and emotions. For some left-handed people, the relationship may be reversed, but for most left-handers, and for females on average, there is less hemispheric specialization altogether (O'Boyle & Gill, 1998).

These differences in performance by the brain's hemispheres, however, are more relative than absolute; one hemisphere is just more efficient than the other in performing certain functions. Nearly any task, but particularly complex skills and abilities, requires participation of many different areas of the brain in constant communication with each other. You may also remember from Chapter 4 that the *corpus callosum* is made up of a thick band of nerve fibers that connects the two hemispheres and coordinates this constant communication between the two sides of the brain. During the early childhood years, this area of the brain develops rapidly, increasing in size and becoming more myelinated. As a result, the young child's coordination improves for complex tasks that require both sides of the brain. For example, the right side of the brain is better at figuring out the whole meaning of a story, but the left side is the region where grammar and syntax are understood, so both sides of the brain have to work together in understanding stories.

Before lateralization takes place, damage to one part of the cortex often can be overcome as other parts of the cortex take over the function of the damaged area. For example, when young children experience damage to the left side of their brains, their right hemispheres can take over language processing fairly well. But after lateralization, the brain is less able to compensate, so damage to an adult's left brain hemisphere is likely to cause greater language problems (Stiles, Reilly, Paul, & Moses, 2005).

Another development in the brain during the early years involves the prefrontal cortex—the area of the brain related to planning, decision making, risk taking, and managing impulsive behaviors. Getting angry or wanting revenge when we are insulted or hurt are common human emotions. It is the job of the prefrontal cortex to control these impulses through reason, planning, or delay of gratification. But the impulse-inhibiting capacities of the brain are not present at birth (as all new parents quickly discover). An immature prefrontal cortex explains some of the impulsiveness and temper tantrums of 2-year-olds. Many studies show advances in the prefrontal cortex around 3 to 4 years old. This means 3- to 5-year-olds become increasingly able to control their emotions and impulses, and to focus attention. But, as we will see when we look at adolescent brain development in Chapter 11, it takes at least two decades for the biological processes of brain development to produce a fully functional prefrontal cortex (Kagan & Herschkowitz, 2005).

With slimmer, stronger bodies and the increased control and coordination that come from brain development, children are able to move more quickly and gracefully.

Motor Development

Motor development is a hallmark of early childhood, and young children thrive on physical activity. In fact, the early years constitute the most active time in children's lives. During this time, children experience dramatic advances in both gross and fine motor development.

Gross Motor Development

Gross motor skills involve movement of the large muscle groups, and advances in gross motor skills are associated with brain development, especially enhanced myelination of neuron connections in areas of the brain that are responsible for balance and coordination. Changes in body size and proportions also contribute to advances in gross motor skills. As indicated above, preschool children's bodies are leaner and stronger than when they were toddlers; they are less top-heavy, and their center of gravity shifts to the center of their bodies. This leads to improvements in balance. Vision also improves, which allows for better eye-hand coordination.

Table 5.1 lists some of the movement milestones from ages 2 to 6. By age 2, most children stop "toddling." Their awkward, wide-legged gait becomes smooth and rhythmic—they have perfected walking. During their third year, most children learn to run, throw, and jump, but these activities are not well controlled until children are 4 or 5 years old. For example, when children first attempt running, they find it difficult to lift both legs off the ground and to start and stop quickly. Similarly, their first attempts at throwing a ball look very rigid because they throw using only their arms. By age 4 or 5, children learn to use their whole bodies—shoulders, torso, trunk, and legs—in a more flexible motion that lets a ball travel farther and faster. In general, motor developments are cumulative and sequential: They occur as a consequence of children bootstrapping previously learned skills into increasingly complex and dynamic systems (Thelen, 1995; Thelen & Jensen, 1990).

In addition to simple maturation (i.e., body growth and brain development), a number of factors are associated with children's gross motor development, including practice, temperament, genes, parental and cultural norms, and children's sex. Because of their high energy and activity levels, young children spend a lot of time practicing gross motor movements; running, jumping, and climbing are often part of children's play. Of course, levels of activity vary among children, as do differences in gross motor development. For example, infants characterized as unusually active typically continue to be active during the preschool years. Children with African origins tend to be more advanced in their motor development than children of European descent (Cratty, 1986). Genetics has much to do with this difference (e.g., the lengths and proportions of arms and legs), but activity levels and gross motor development also are associated with parental and cultural norms concerning how much and what kinds of physical activities are appropriate. Some cultures expect and encourage high levels of physical activity in young children, whereas others are more restrictive.

In general, boys are more physically active than girls, and stronger (Pelligrini & Smith, 1998). Typically, they can throw a ball farther and jump higher. However, girls often outperform boys on tasks that involve the coordination of arms and legs. By age 5,

TABLE 5.1 • **Gross and Fine Motor Development of Children Ages 2–6**

AGE	GROSS MOTOR SKILLS	FINE MOTOR SKILLS
TWENTY-FOUR TO THIRTY-SIX MONTHS (2–3 YEARS OLD):		
	Hops on one foot Walks up stairs alternating feet Walks down stairs alternating feet Walks backward Balances on one foot briefly Throws overhand at a target Catches a rolled ball Throws a small ball 2 feet Rides a tricycle using pedals	Turns pages one at a time Builds a 9 block tower Strings small 1/2 inch beads Unscrews lid of a jar Imitates horizontal line, cross, circle Holds pencil in hand instead of fist Makes snips with scissors Unbuttons Places pegs in a pegboard
THIRTY-SIX TO FORTY-EIGHT MONTHS (3–4 YEARS OLD):		
	Throws ball overhand with accuracy Catches large ball from 5 feet Hops on one foot 2 or more times Balances on one foot briefly	Builds 9 block tower Cuts with scissors Holds pencil like an adult (static) Copies a circle/cross
FORTY-EIGHT TO SIXTY MONTHS (4–5 YEARS OLD):		
	Catches ball with hands only Bounces and catches a ball Throws a ball in the air and catches Balances on one foot for 4-5 seconds Walks on a line heel to toe	Screws together a threaded object Tripod grasp on a pencil Builds 10 block tower Cuts fairly accurately with scissors
SIXTY TO SEVENTY-TWO MONTHS (5–6 YEARS OLD):		
	Jumps rope by self Kicks a rolling ball Rides a bicycle Dribbles a ball Throws a ball with good accuracy	Copies triangle/square Cuts on a straight/curved line Ties shoes/zips Completes a lacing card Attempts to stay in lines when coloring

Source: Suba, R. (n.d.) Stages of motor development in infants/young children: An informative guide for parents *(lecture notes). Developed from various sources by Rae Suba, OTR/L for Child's Play Clinic. Reprinted by permission.*

girls typically are better than boys at balancing on one foot or performing a set of jumping jacks. In Chapter 7, we discuss the ways parents and society influence children's views about what activities are appropriate for boys and girls, respectively. If children interpret that games and activities that involve gross motor movement are more appropriate for boys than girls, boys probably will engage in these activities more than girls, thus increasing their opportunities to practice and develop skills in this area (Golombok & Fivush, 1994; Yee & Brown, 1994).

Finally, some children experience greater difficulty with respect to gross motor development than others, including children with physical disabilities, such as cerebral palsy (Beckung, Carlsson, Carlsdotter, & Uvebrant, 2007); children with hearing and visual impairments (Fazzi et al., 2002; Rine et al., 2000); and children with developmental disabilities such as autism (Ozonoff et al., 2008).

At the same time that young children are developing gross motor skills, they also are making significant advances in the development of fine motor skills.

Fine Motor Development

Fine motor skills involve small muscle movements that are more limited and controlled (e.g., eating with a fork or spoon, tying shoelaces, or cutting with a pair of scissors). As was true for the development of gross motor skills, fine motor skills follow a developmental progression from less to more differentiation, coordination, and control (see Table 5.1 on the previous page). In addition, fine motor skills require a good deal of practice, as anyone who has observed a 2-year-old struggle to put on a pair of shoes or awkwardly grasp a crayon and scribble a picture can attest. By age 3 or 4, children can do much more. They can put on and take off articles of clothing, although they may need help with buttons and zippers. Also, they can hold and manipulate crayons and pencils to draw shapes and people. Like gross motor skills, many fine motor skills are acquired early and are perfected over time, as children gain experience through practice, but also as their brains develop and visual systems and eye-hand coordination improve.

Large variations in children's fine motor skills are not uncommon. Opportunities and interests have much to do with individual differences. For example, your text author Nancy has a niece, Lucy, the child painting below. Lucy is less than 2 at the writing of this chapter, yet her mother has already created a space in her playroom where she can draw and paint. In addition, Lucy and her mother attend the Strong Start program in a neighborhood school, where trained early childhood educators create opportunities for children to engage in a wide range of literacy, art, and play activities, many of which support fine motor development (Human Early Learning Partnership, 2008). Lucy loves to turn pages and point to objects in books and "draw" with crayons. Often the first words she says in the morning are "Read, read." Some children have fewer opportunities to practice these skills and others have less interest in them. Boys tend to have less interest in such activities early on, and some research indicates girls acquire fine motor skills sooner and more easily than boys (Cohen, 1997). Children with disabilities often develop fine motor skills more slowly.

DRAWING AS A FORM OF FINE MOTOR DEVELOPMENT. Children's developmental changes in drawing have been studied quite extensively. Kellog (1970) proposed a sequence of developmental stages to describe how children's drawing progresses from scribbles to pictures. He and later researchers (e.g., Gardner, 1989; Golomb, 2003) have argued that children's *scribbles*, which correspond to *Stage 1* in the progression, are not random and may contain the building blocks for more sophisticated forms they will produce later. Kellog identified 20 distinct types of scribbles (e.g., horizontal lines and zig-zags) that are characteristic of children's first attempts at drawing. Most children begin to scribble at around 18 months. By age 3, they reach *Stage 2*, and their drawings contain clear *shapes*, such as squares and circles. They may also draw familiar symbols, such as X's and plus signs. During this stage, children make their first attempts at drawing people—"tadpole" people. Typically, these people have stick arms and legs growing out of a circle that is the head and body. Eyes, noses, and mouths are typically included in these renderings, and often belly buttons. By age 5, however, children's drawings of people have more realistic proportions.

Young children's scribbles are not random. They may be limited, but they are controlled.

Stage 3 is referred to as the *design* stage, in which children can combine more than one shape to create a more complex representation. Finally, children enter *Stage 4*, the *pictorial* stage, and we can recognize objects in them (e.g., people, the sun). Children typically reach the pictorial stage by age 4 or 5. Figure 5.3 shows children's progression through these stages.

HANDEDNESS. The term **handedness** is used to describe each person's preference for using one hand or another to perform one-handed tasks (Cavill & Bryden, 2003). Approximately 90% of the population shows a preference for using their right hand—they are right-handed. More boys than girls are left-handed, and a small but indeterminate number of people are

FIGURE 5.3

CHILDREN'S PROGRESSION THROUGH THE STAGES OF DRAWING

Lucy scribbles at 18 and 20 months

Rowen draws mommy's face and Ashley signs her name at 3 years

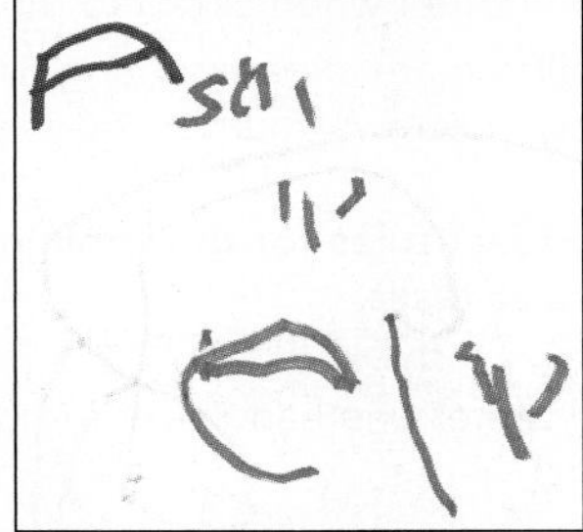

Andrew draws people at ages 4 and 5, respectively

Savannah draws a picture at age 4

CONNECTING WITH CHILDREN

Guidelines for Families, Teachers, and Other Professionals: Attending to Children's Hand Preferences

Watch for signs of hand (and foot) preference.
Examples

1. Observe which hand children use to reach for toys and other objects that are put directly in front of them.
2. Note which hand they use to feed themselves.
3. Notice whether children prefer the left or right when they are standing on one leg. Do they consistently lead with one foot or the other when asked to move?
4. Observe when children are experimenting with toys, to see if they turn lids or screws counterclockwise.

There are no hard and fast rules for determining hand preference for particular tasks.
Examples

1. Most children will prefer one hand over the other for delicate work.
2. Some left-handed children prefer the left eye when looking through telescopes or the lens of a camera.
3. Preferences may be less strong for gross motor activities or tasks requiring less precision.

For left-handed children, get equipment that reflects their hand preferences.
Examples

1. Purchase left-handed scissors and rulers, as well as smudge-free pens and pencils.
2. Switch the settings on computers to make using the mouse or cursor more "lefty" friendly.
3. Buy left-handed baseball mitts and other sports equipment.
4. See "Anything Left-handed" for access to all sorts of tools and equipment for lefties: http://www.anythingleft-handed.co.uk/

Learn about teaching children who are left-handed.
Examples

1. Sit across from children for demonstrations, rather than beside or behind them. This way, they can watch your hand movements. Left-handed movements are mirror images of right-handed movements, so be the children's mirror.
2. Watch the "How to Tie Your Shoes" demonstration on YouTube: http://www.youtube.com/watch?v=lc4H6goKFB0&feature=PlayList&p=FC32D5CF567EAAF2&playnext_from=PL&index=0&playnext=4 to learn how to model teaching left-handed children how to tie shoes.
3. Ask family and friends who are left-handed to be models for left-handed children.

Create a physical environment that is lefty friendly.
Examples

1. Seat left-handed children with left-handed children at tables (or lefties on the left), to avoid knocking elbows.
2. Seat left-handed children on the right side of the classroom, so they can clearly see the main writing board without twisting their bodies.

---

ambidextrous—these individuals may prefer different hands, depending on what task they need to complete, or switch hands, even when completing the same task, but at different times (Porac, Coren, & Searlman, 1986). Infants typically do not show hand preferences; however, most children show a clear hand preference by the time they are 3 to 4 years of age (Cavell & Bryden, 2003; Coren, 1993).

Handedness is more influenced by genetics than the environment (Beaton, 2003; Hill & Khanem, 2009). However, in the past, parents and educators tried to influence and change children's handedness, believing there was something wrong with a child who was left-handed. Now we understand that hand preferences are linked to brain development and the way the brain is organized, but not necessarily in a bad way. For example, children who are right-handed tend to have stronger brain lateralization (i.e., their left hemisphere is dominant for language processing and their right hemisphere dominates for spatial tasks). In contrast, some (not all) children who are left-handed show less specialization in brain function.

There are some challenges associated with being left-handed. Many everyday objects, such as scissors and soup ladles, are designed for right-handed people. Handedness also presents challenges for playing sports—left-handed baseball mitts and golf clubs are more difficult to find. Finally, left-handed models are less available, so children who are left-handed often have to learn from parents, teachers, and peers who are right-handed. Try tying your shoes while looking in the mirror to experience some of what these children face. The ***Connecting with Children*** guidelines offer some suggestions for supporting young children's development of handedness, especially left-handedness.

Health and Well-Being

Children's physical, cognitive, and social emotional development depend on their overall health and well-being. Good nutrition and eating habits and adequate rest and exercise are important throughout the lifespan. We focus on exercise in Chapter 8. In this chapter, we focus on nutrition and sleep, although both continue to be important for healthy development in middle childhood and adolescence. When children do not eat well or sleep well, they are at risk for a number of health-related problems and they can have difficulty learning (Rosales, Reznick, & Zeisel, 2009; Wagner, Meusel, & Kirch, 2005).

Nutritional Needs and Eating Habits

What is a healthy diet in the early years? Young children need fewer calories than infants and toddlers because their brains and bodies are growing more slowly. As a result, appetite typically decreases from ages 2 to 6, which causes some parents concern. However, as long as children are growing and gaining weight, concern is likely unwarranted. The American Heart Association (AHA, 2010) provides estimates of how many calories children should consume each day according to their age. Table 5.2 shows these figures, along with guidelines about how much and what types of foods children should be eating. Keep in mind that

TABLE 5.2 • **Estimated Calories, Recommended Servings, and Guidelines for Healthy Eating**

	1 YEAR	2–3 YEARS	4–8 YEARS	9–13 YEARS	14–18 YEARS	EXAMPLES
Calories	900 kcal	1000 kcal				
Female			1200 kcal	1600 kcal	1800 kcal	
Male			1400 kcal	1800 kcal	2200 kcal	
Fat	30–40% kcal	30–35% kcal	25–35% kcal	25–35% kcal	25–35% kcal	
Milk/Dairy	2 cups	2 cups	2 cups	3 cups	3 cups	Lowfat and fat-free milk, milk products
Lean meat/ Beans	1.5 oz	2 oz		5 oz		Fish, nuts, liquid oils (corn, soybean, canola, olive)
Female			3 oz		5 oz	
Male			4 oz		6 oz	
Fruits	1 cup	1 cup	1.5 cups	1.5 cups		Eat fresh, frozen, canned, dried, or even fruit juice
Female					1.5 cups	
Male					2 cups	
Vegetables	3/4 cup	1 cup				Spinach, broccoli, carrots, and sweet potatoes
Female			1 cup	2 cups	2.5 cups	
Male			1.5 cups	2.5 cups	3 cups	
Grains	2 oz	3 oz				Whole-wheat bread, oatmeal, brown rice, lowfat popcorn
Female			4 oz	5 oz	6 oz	
Male			5 oz	6 oz	7 oz	

Source: Dietary Recommendations for Children. *(2010). Retrieved from American Heart Association: http://www.americanheart.org/presenter.jhtml?identifier=3033999*
MyPyramid for Preschoolers. *(2009, September 4). Retrieved from United States Department of Agriculture: http://www.mypyramid.gov/preschoolers/index.html*

CONNECTING WITH CHILDREN

Guidelines for Families, Teachers, and Other Professionals: Promoting Healthy Eating Habits in Young Children

Take children food shopping and involve them in making healthy choices for healthy eating.
Examples

1. Fill your cart with fresh produce and cut down on processed foods that often contain a lot of fat and salt and/or sugar.
2. Make a game out of picking many colors of fruits and vegetables.
3. Think about the meals you can make in the coming week (e.g., stir fries can include green broccoli, yellow and red peppers, and orange carrots).

Invite children to participate in the food preparation.
Examples

1. Ask children to help by washing vegetables and tearing up lettuce.
2. Have them set the table and put bread in a basket.
3. Help them to measure and mix ingredients.

Don't stress about how much your children eat.
Examples

1. Do not worry when young children finish everything on their plate and ask for more on one day, and then eat two peas and declare they are done the next day.
2. Offer smaller portions with the option of seconds if, once finished, they are still hungry.

Encourage smart snacking.
Examples

1. Avoid sugary snacks, such as candy, cookies, juice, and soft drinks.
2. Stay away from high fat junk foods, such as chips and cheese puffs.
3. Promote snacks that contain some protein, such as peanut butter or low-fat cheese, because they will be satisfying.
4. Try to avoid snacking close to mealtime, or offer something light and healthy, such as fresh fruit or cut-up vegetables, that won't interfere with appetite.

Don't ban junk food.
Examples

1. Let children indulge in some candy or chocolate every once in a while—forbidding these foods can create an unhealthy relationship with food and result in children scarfing down all the sugar or fat or salt they can find when they eat out.
2. Keep the portions small.
3. Steer children who clamor for sweet treats toward raisins and other healthier choices most of the time.

Adapted from: Lee, K. (nd). Best ways to build healthy food habits. Retrieved from http://childparenting.about.com/od/nutrition/tp/healthyfoodhabits.htm.

these are just estimates for "average" children and there is a range of normal in every age group. Also, children differ in their activity levels—the more physically active they are, the more calories they will require.

There is general consensus among health professionals (American Academy of Pediatrics, 2003; American Dietetic Association, 2008; AHA, 2010) that between the ages of 2 and 5, children should gradually reduce their intake of fat from a recommended 30–40% of calories consumed to 25–35% of calories consumed. Moreover, calories from saturated fats should be limited to 10% of the total calories consumed each day. Finally, these health professionals recommend that juice (and sugar generally) be restricted to 4–6 ounces per day. Whole fruits should be promoted over juice and 100% juice is preferable to mixed beverages. According to the American Dietetic Association (ADA, 2010), a balanced diet for most children includes 2½ cups of vegetables and 1½ cups of fruit each day, 2–3 ounces of lean meat or the equivalent of ½ cup of beans at each meal; in addition, half the grains consumed should be whole grains. For lunch and dinner, they recommend drawing an imaginary line across a plate and filling half with fruit and vegetables. Then divide the remaining space in half again. Fill one of these halves with grains and the other with protein. Also, they recommend children drink milk with meals and water with snacks, which amounts to three 8-ounce glasses of milk and two 8-ounce glasses of water each day. For most children, this will be all the liquid they need to stay well hydrated and meet their calcium needs. Finally, the ADA emphasizes that "no one food group provides all the nutrients growing bodies need for good health." Therefore, the best way to meet children's nutritional needs each day is to provide access to a variety of foods from all the food groups.

What about children's food preferences? Young children can be finicky eaters. They may want macaroni and cheese for every meal and turn their noses up at anything green. How can parents promote healthy eating habits and avoid unpleasant food fights? The ***Connecting with Children*** guidelines provide tips on how to accomplish this. One overarching principle is to offer children a variety of healthy choices and allow them to regulate how much they eat. You will learn throughout this text that self-regulation is involved in all domains of development (physical, cognitive, social emotional), including energy intake, which should be guided by feelings of hunger and satiety. The development of self-regulation for eating can be derailed if parents coax too hard or are overly restrictive about eating. If children turn their noses up at a healthy choice, don't give up, but don't bribe them either. Reintroduce the food in the future. Similarly, don't deny children sweet and salty treats. Fisher and Birch (2003) studied the effects of limiting access to palatable foods on children's food preferences and behaviors and found that it does not teach children to moderate their intake of less healthy foods and may, in the long run, encourage consumption of sweet and salty foods. A second principle is to communicate a consistent message about health and nutrition in the family. Parents should model good eating habits; they should not have different sets of rules about food for different members of the family; and they should promote physical activity as a complement to good eating habits.

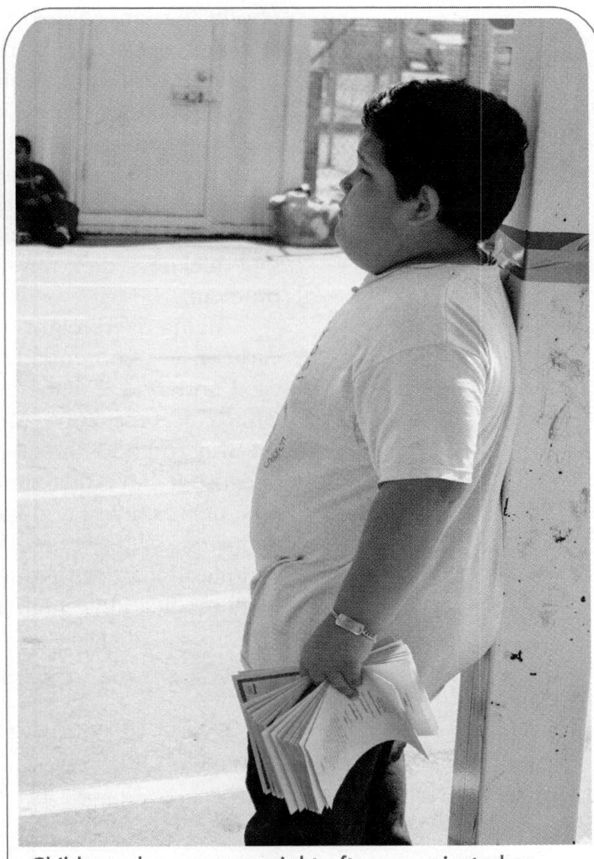

Children who are overweight often are rejected or teased by peers.

CHILDHOOD OVERWEIGHT AND OBESITY. According to the Centers for Disease Control (2009g), the incidence of childhood obesity has more than doubled in all age groups, from ages 2 to 19, since 1971 (see Figure 5.4). The CDC (2009g) defines childhood

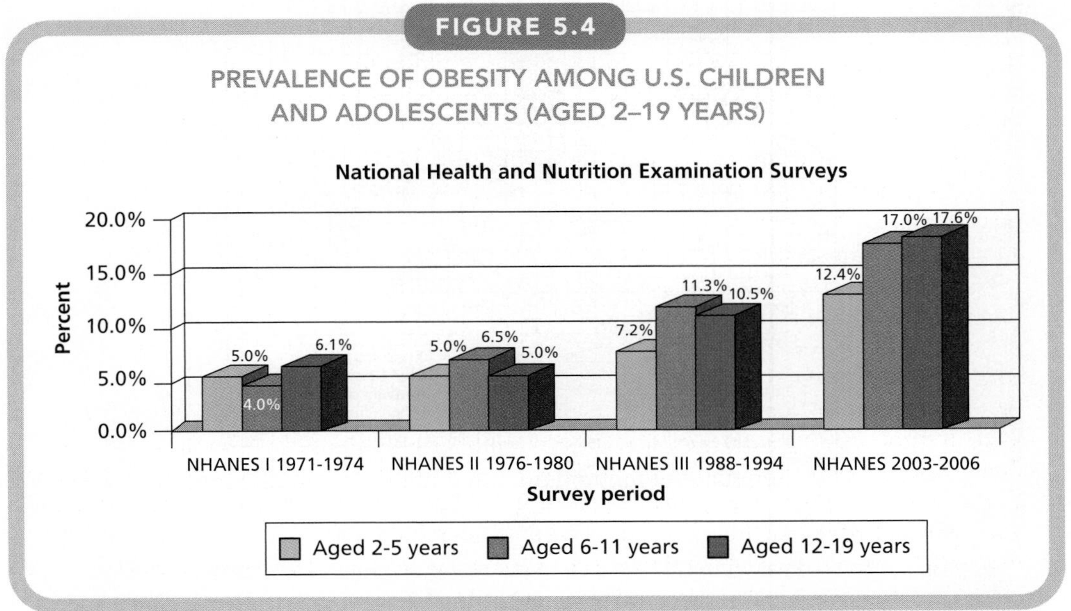

Source: Adapted from: Centers for Disease Control and Prevention (2009, November 17). Overweight and obesity. *Retrieved from http://www.cdc.gov/obesity/childhood/prevalence.html. Used courtesy of Centers for Disease Control, www.cdc.gov*

obesity in terms of children's **body mass index (BMI)** plotted on the CDC growth charts for boys and girls, respectively. An example is shown in Figure 5.5. BMI measures weight in relation to height and can be calculated using either English or metric units. Children are classified as *overweight* when their BMI is at or above the 85th percentile (i.e., 85% of children the same age and sex weigh less than they do) and below the 95th percentile. Children are classified as *obese* when their BMI is at or above the 95th percentile. The BMI provides a good screen for overweight and obesity, but other factors need to be considered, too. Children with BMIs at the 85th percentile or higher should see a healthcare provider who will assess other factors, such as skinfold thickness, diet, physical activity, and family history, to determine whether excess fat is a problem.

Being overweight or obese is a serious health concern for children. It is linked to the early onset of potentially life-threatening diseases, such as hypertension, cardiovascular disease, and Type 2 diabetes, previously associated with overweight and aging adults (Dubois, Girard, & Kent, 2006; Mei et al., 1998). **Type 2 diabetes** is a chronic condition that affects the way the body metabolizes sugar (glucose). This condition needs to be taken seriously because it can affect almost every major organ in the body, including the heart, blood vessels, nerves, eyes, and kidneys (Mayo Clinic, 2009). For most children, this disease can be managed, or prevented all together, by eating healthy foods, being physically active, and maintaining a healthy body weight. When diet and exercise are not enough, children will need medications, such as insulin, to manage their blood sugar.

FIGURE 5.5

BOYS' AND GIRLS' AVERAGE BMI BY AGE (BMI)

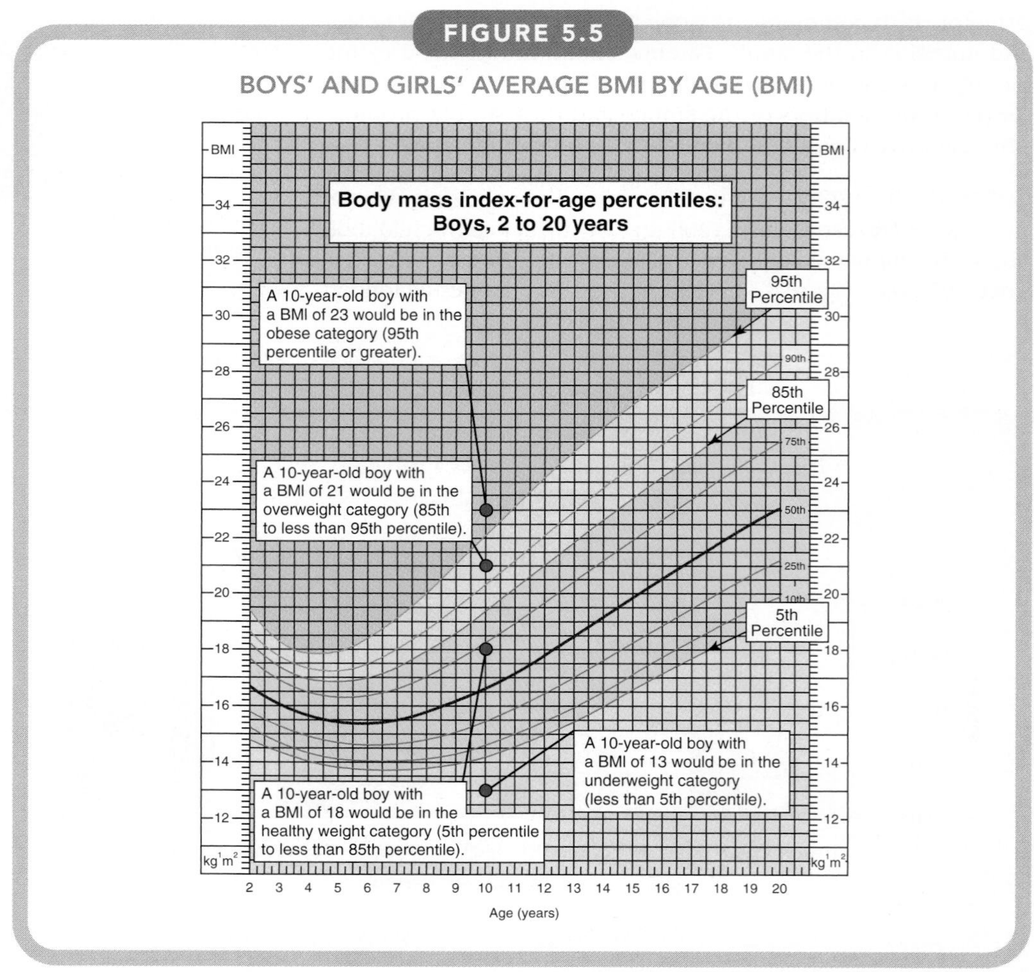

Source: Adapted from: Centers for Disease Control and Prevention (2009, January, 27). About BMI for children and teens. *Retrieved from http://www.cdc.gov/healthyweight/assessing/bmi/childrens_bmi/about_childrens_bmi.html. Used courtesy of Centers for Disease Control, www.cdc.gov*

Other health concerns, such as asthma, also are more common in children who are overweight or obese. Some research indicates that children's academic achievement goes down as weight goes up, although it's not clear why (Guillaume & Lissau, 2002). Importantly, being overweight or obese is associated with social and emotional problems (Allen, Byrne, Blair, & Davis, 2006; Hill & Lissau, 2002). Children who are overweight tend to have more negative body images than children who are a healthy weight, and often they are teased and/or rejected by peers. Over the long term, self-esteem can suffer (Friedlander, Larkin, Rosen, Palermo, & Redline, 2003; Mustillo et al., 2003).

The causes of overweight and obesity in children are many and varied. Some are controllable and others are not. Heredity is implicated. Genes affect children's activity levels, food preferences, body types, and metabolic rates, and children whose biological parents are overweight are more likely to be overweight themselves. Also, some ethnic groups appear more predisposed to overweight and obesity than others. Wang and Beydoun (2007) examined National Health and Nutrition Examination Survey data for disparities in rates of obesity among ethnic/racial groups within the United States. Their findings indicate racial/ethnic disparities emerge at very young ages and are present even in homogeneous SES groups. Cultural eating habits and food preferences may contribute to these differences, as can **food security**—consistent access to sufficient quantities of food. Kaiser and colleagues (2002) studied the relationship between food insecurity and nutrition and overweight in a group of Mexican American families ($N = 211$). Their findings indicate children in food-insecure households were less likely to meet nutritional guidelines, such as those promoted in the government's *Food Guide Pyramid*. Also, children in these families had higher weight for height ratios than children living in households where food insecurity was not an issue. Many North American children live with food insecurity issues. In a national study of Canadian food banks, findings indicated 39% of users were children (Langlois, 2006). Food insecurity is associated with poor nutrition, which can lead to overweight and obesity as well as undernutrition, which is discussed below.

Lifestyle is likely the most important contributor to overweight and obesity. As a society, we have come to rely more on prepared and fast foods that accommodate our busy lifestyles. Unfortunately, these foods tend to have more calories and higher fat, salt, and sugar content than foods we prepare from scratch. Table 5.3 displays nutritional information for some fast foods that are popular with children. As you can see from the calorie count, it is possible for children to consume most of their daily allotment of calories in one meal at McDonald's or Burger King. In addition, soft drink consumption, which rose from ninety 8-ounce servings per capita per year in the United States in 1942 to 600 servings per capita per year in 2000, has been linked to overweight and obesity, as well as to increased risk for diabetes (Vartanian, Schwartz, & Brownell, 2007). These drinks have been banned from schools in Britain and France and from some school districts in the United States. To counter,

TABLE 5.3 • **Nutritional Information for Fast Foods That Are Most Popular with Children**

FOOD	CALORIES	FAT (GMS)	CARBS (GMS)
A&W Cheeseburger, kids fries, and small root beer	1000	37	142
Burger King Chicken Whopper Junior and medium fries (salted)	770	44	81
McDonalds Chicken McNuggets (6 pieces), small fries, and small soft drink	610	27	75
Pizza Hut Pepperoni Pan pizza (each slice)	353	14	44
Kentucky Fried Chicken one piece of drumstick and one piece of breast	630	40	19

Source: Retrieved from http://www.shapefit.com/burgerking.html. Used with permission from ShapeFit.com.

the American Beverage Association argues that the research linking soft drink consumption to negative health outcomes is flawed or insufficient. However, in a meta-analysis of 88 studies, Vartanian and colleagues concluded, "Recommendations to reduce population soft drink consumption are strongly supported by the available science" (p. 667). Their research provided support for the negative outcomes associated with soft drink consumption. Furthermore, their findings indicated that higher levels of soft drink consumption are associated with lower consumption of milk, calcium, and other nutrients.

Children lead more sedentary lives today than they did 50, or even 20 years ago. For example, children spend less time playing outside than they did in the past. Some people blame television, video games, computers, and unsafe neighborhoods for this. When they reach school age, fewer children walk to school. Parents are more likely to drive their children to school and extracurricular activities. In school, less time is devoted to recess and physical education in favor of boosting academic performance (Graber, Locke, Lambdin, & Solmon, 2008; Graham, 2008). Inactivity is a topic we return to in Chapter 8.

Finally, overweight and obesity in North American children have been linked to SES (Dubois et al., 2006; Mei et al., 1998). Lean cuts of meat and fish are more expensive than those containing more fat. Similarly, fresh fruit and vegetables can be expensive, especially when they are out of season (e.g., in winter) in some regions of the country. Families with fewer resources may not be able to afford the healthy choices. Moreover, children in low-SES communities are more likely to miss breakfast, which doubles their risk of overweight and obesity (Dubois et al., 2006).

Given the risks of overweight and obesity to children's health and general well-being, how can we help children (like Laura in our casebook) to lose weight? Attending to energy intake and physical activity in overweight and obese children is important, but successful weight loss for individuals usually requires family-wide changes, too. It is important to send a consistent message about health and nutrition within families and, later, within schools (see Chapter 8). Also, it is important that programs for weight loss not be perceived as punitive. The ***Connecting with Children*** guidelines offer some ideas about how to accomplish these goals.

UNDERWEIGHT AND MALNOURISHMENT. Children in developed countries may consume more than enough calories, but still not get adequate nutrients for their bodies and brains to grow and develop. For example, it is not uncommon for young children to have **iron deficiency anemia**, which is a decrease in the number of red blood cells caused by a lack of iron (Medline Plus, 2008; University of Maryland Medical Center, 2009). The most common cause of iron deficiency is an iron-poor diet. Iron-rich foods include red meat, legumes, nuts, and dark green vegetables. When children do not get enough of these foods, their iron levels can be low. Also, children who drink too much cow's milk (more than 2 cups per day) may have iron deficiency: Milk is a poor source of iron and actually prevents the absorption of iron from other foods. Finally, lead exposure can also cause iron deficiency anemia. Signs of iron deficiency anemia include chronic fatigue, decreased appetite, poor concentration, irritability, and poor growth and development. Children with iron deficiency anemia can suffer physical, cognitive, and social delays and are more likely to become ill because their immune system is weakened. Calcium and zinc are other nutrients that are commonly deficient in children.

Children from low-income families are most at risk for poor nutrition (Hampton, 2007; Yu, Lombe, & Nebbitt, 2010). In developed countries, persistent hunger is typically not due to lack of food or food programs, but may be due to the stigma associated with using them. For example, in the United States, only 60% of those who qualify for food stamps and other programs actually utilize them (Share Our Strength, retrieved 2010, Yu et al., 2010). Children who are chronically hungry are at a disadvantage when it comes to learning and development.

> A child who is hungry has difficulty concentrating, is more easily distracted, and may exhibit behavior problems. A hungry or undernourished child cannot take full advantage of educational opportunities and may disrupt other children from learning as well. (Langlois, 2006, p. 8)

CONNECTING WITH CHILDREN

Guidelines for Families, Teachers, and Other Professionals: Helping Children Lose Weight

Set realistic goals.
Examples

1. Begin with a modest goal of not gaining weight. Since children are growing, they will naturally become thinner if they don't gain weight.
2. Set a new goal of losing a pound a week once children have reached the goal of not gaining weight.

Encourage exercise.
Examples

1. Promote any type of aerobic activity, including walking, running, and bike-riding. These burn calories, and burning calories through physical activity reduces the number of calories that need to be removed from the diet.
2. Involve children in preschool programs that include physical activities.
3. Make equipment for physical activity available at home (e.g., balls, hula hoops, jump ropes).
4. Stay active with children—use stairs instead of elevators, walk to friends' houses and on local errands instead of taking the car.

Encourage healthy eating and a healthy weight rather than pushing diets on children.
Examples

1. Encourage children to eat three small meals and two snacks, so they don't go for long periods without food and start feeling hungry.
2. Provide snacks of fruits and vegetables, and encourage children to drink water instead of juice.
3. Make available popcorn, pretzels, and whole wheat crackers; these are better choices than chips, cakes, and cookies.
4. Encourage children to eat only when they are hungry and only enough to fill the void.

Change your family's eating habits.
Examples

1. Stock the house with healthy food choices and make the menu the same for everyone.
2. Turn off the TV and remove other distractions during mealtime. If children eat while watching TV, they may not be aware of how much food they are consuming.
3. Keep a diary that records general trends in your family's eating habits (e.g., which foods are popular, which are not, what schedule works best for meals and snacks).

Adapted from: Iannelli, V. (2008). Weight loss goals for kids: Childhood obesity basics. Retrieved from http://pediatrics.about.com/od/obesity/a/0707_wt_loss_gl.htm. Lee, K. (No Date). Best ways to build healthy food habits. Retrieved from http://childparenting.about.com/od/nutrition/tp/healthyfoodhabits.htm. Trachtenberg, J. (No Date). Weight management: 7 ways to help your child lose weight. Retrieved from http:// parenting.ivillage.com/gs/gshealth/0,,n9k5,00.html.

Around the world, child hunger is a powerful predictor of population health. The ***Relating to Every Child*** feature on the next page examines the implications of feeding the world's children.

Sleep

In addition to getting adequate nutrition, children need sufficient amounts of good quality sleep to function well. Newborn infants divide their sleep time equally between day and night. Gradually, over the first three years of life, children consolidate sleep at night into one long block—they sleep through the night—and the amount of time they spend sleeping during the day decreases. By age 4 or 5, most children no longer nap during the day and by age 15 or 16, their sleep patterns are similar to those of adults. Figure 5.6 on page 185 shows these sleep patterns across childhood. It's important to note that these data reflect parents' reports of average times children spend sleeping, not scientific studies of absolute requirements for sleeping. However, the numbers are remarkably consistent across time and countries. For example, the data in Figure 5.6 are from an American sample that was first reported in Ferber (1986/2006), but results from a more recent study of children in Switzerland (Iglowstein, Jenni, Molinari, & Largo, 2003) are almost the same. Also, research indicates that children who get less sleep than what is reported here suffer a wide range of difficulties relating to cognition, learning, behavior, social and emotional well-being, and health (Buckhalt, Wolfson, & El-Sheikh, 2009; Iglowstein et al., 2003; Sadeh, 2007).

RELATING TO

EVERY CHILD

▸ Feeding the World's Children

CHILDREN who live with chronic hunger are likely to suffer extreme malnourishment, which puts them at higher risk for illness and is associated with more than half of childhood deaths (WHO, 2003). The vast majority of children at risk for or living with extreme malnutrition live in just 10 countries in the world: India, Nigeria, China, Bangladesh, Ethiopia, Indonesia, Pakistan, Democratic Republic of Congo, Uganda, and Tanzania (Irwin, Siddiqi, & Hertzman, 2007). These children account for 145 million (66%) of 219 million children living in extreme poverty in the developing world. As a result of their circumstances, many of these children will never attend school (UNESCO, 2007); they will subsequently have low earning potential as adults but high fertility, and will provide poor nutrition, health care, and stimulation to their own children, continuing the cycle (Irwin et al., 2007).

Economists argue investments in early childhood are the most powerful investment countries can make (Irwin et al., 2007). Research indicates that societies—rich and poor—that invest in children and families in the early years have the most literate and numerate populations. They also have the best health status and health equality in the world. And, as a proportion of GDP, these countries spend only 1.5–2% on policies and programs for early childhood development. Estimates are that $1 spent to help a child to thrive and reach school age will generate up to $17 in benefits to society over the following four decades, even after controlling for inflation (Schweinhart, 2004; Schweinhart, Barnes, & Weikart, 1993, cited in Irwin et al., 2007). Therefore, according to Irwin and colleagues, investing in early childhood development is a productive strategy that should be adopted by governments, international agencies, and civil society partners. Giving children a healthy start in life not only allows children to thrive, but also supports the prosperity—economically and socially—of communities and countries.

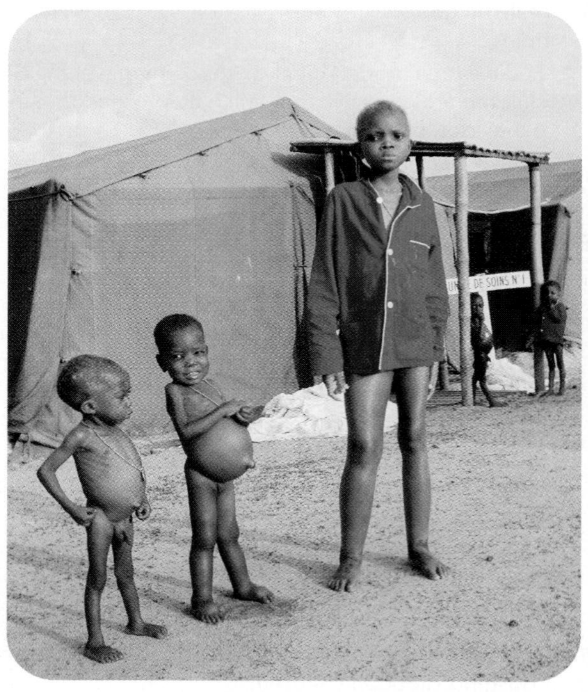

The vast majority of children living with extreme hunger live in just 10 countries in the world.

Shortened sleep time, erratic sleep/wake schedules, late bedtimes, and poor sleep quality are linked to problems with cognitive functions (e.g., attention, self-regulation) and learning (Sadeh, 2007). Sleep is believed to play an active role in brain maturation, information processing, memory consolidation, and affect regulation. When children get insufficient amounts or a poor quality of sleep, especially rapid eye movement (REM) sleep, the brain activity required for these functions to develop is reduced. Similarly, sleep plays a reinvigorating role, so insufficient or disrupted sleep at night leaves children feeling sleepy and less alert during the day. Daytime sleepiness is associated with learning and behavior difficulties (Fallone, Owens, & Deane, 2002; Sadeh, 2007; Sadeh, Gruber, & Raviv, 2002). Children who are tired are more irritable and less able to control their emotions. Also, they are more prone to accidents (Valent, Brusaferro, & Barbone, 2001). In general, sleep deprivation and disruptions negatively affect children's daytime behavior as well as family functioning.

Although most complaints about children's sleeping patterns are about not getting enough sleep (Ferber, 2006), getting too much sleep can also be a problem. If the time

FIGURE 5.6

TYPICAL SLEEP REQUIREMENTS IN CHILDHOOD

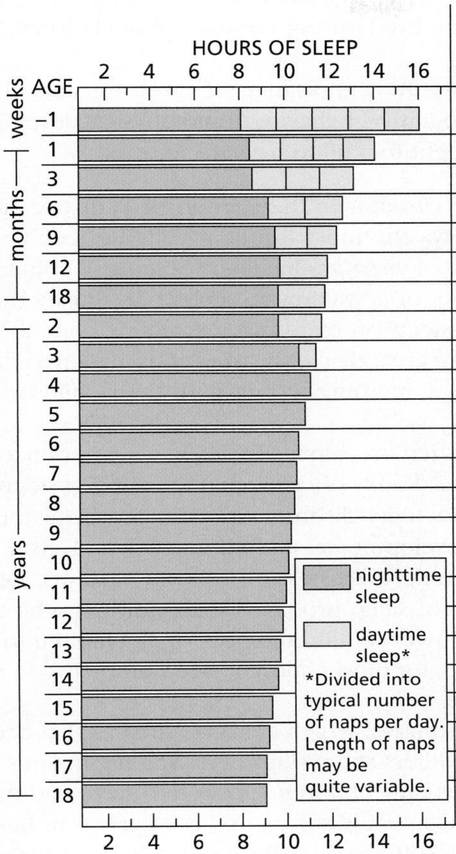

HOURS OF SLEEP

2 4 6 8 10 12 14 16

nighttime sleep

daytime sleep*

*Divided into typical number of naps per day. Length of naps may be quite variable.

AGE		Total Hours of Sleep	Typical Range
weeks	–1	16	14 –18
	1	14	12 1/2–15 1/2
months	3	13	12 –14
	6	12 1/2	11 1/2–13 1/2
	9	12 1/4	11 1/4–13 1/4
	12	11 3/4	11 –12 1/2
	18	11 5/8	11 –12 1/4
years	2	11 1/2	11 –12
	3	11 1/4	10 3/4–11 3/4
	4	11	10 1/2–11 1/2
	5	10 3/4	10 1/4–11 1/4
	6	10 1/2	10 –11
	7	10 3/8	9 7/8 –10 7/8
	8	10 1/4	9 3/4 –10 3/4
	9	10 1/8	9 5/8 –10 5/8
	10	10	9 1/2 –10 1/2
	11	9 7/8	9 3/8 –10 3/8
	12	9 3/4	9 1/4 –10 1/4
	13	9 5/8	9 1/8 –10 1/8
	14	9 1/2	9 –10
	15	9 1/4	8 3/4 –9 3/4
	16	9 1/8	8 5/8 –9 5/8
	17	9	8 1/2 –9 1/2
	18	9	8 1/2 –9 1/2

AGE		Total Hours of Sleep	Night Sleep	Day Sleep	No. of Naps (1/2–1 Hrs)
weeks	–1	16	Varied	Varied	Varied
	1	14	Varied	Varied	Varied
months	3	13	8 1/2	4 1/2	3–4
	6	12 1/2	9 1/4	3 1/4	2–3
	9	12 1/4	9 1/2	2 3/4	2
	12	11 3/4	9 1/4–10 1/4	1 1/2–2 1/2	1–2
	18	11 5/8	9 5/8	2	1
years	2	11 1/2	9 5/8	1 7/8	1
	3	11 1/4	9 3/4–11 1/4	0 –1 1/2	0–1
	4	11	10 –11	0 –1	0–1
	5	10 3/4	10 3/4	0	0
	6	10 1/2	10 1/2	0	0
	7	10 3/8	10 3/8	0	0
	8	10 1/4	10 1/4	0	0
	9	10 1/8	10 1/8	0	0
	10	10	10	0	0
	11	9 7/8	9 7/8	0	0
	12	9 3/4	9 3/4	0	0
	13	9 5/8	9 5/8	0	0
	14	9 1/2	9 1/2	0	0
	15	9 1/4	9 1/4	0	0
	16	9 1/8	9 1/8	0	0
	17	9	9	0	0
	18	9	9	0	0

Source: Reprinted with the permission of Touchstone, a Division of Simon & Schuster, Inc., from Solve Your Child's Sleep Problems *by Richard Ferber, M. D. Copyright © 1985, 2006 by Richard Ferber, M. D. All rights reserved.*

children spend in bed exceeds their actual sleep need, they can have difficulty falling asleep or they may awaken during the night or very early in the morning (Iglowstein et al., 2003). According to Iglowstein and colleagues, sleep duration is an indicator of sleep need, so one way to manage bedtime and sleeping problems is to monitor children's sleep duration and adjust bedtime schedules accordingly.

SLEEP AND OBESITY. There is growing evidence that persistent short sleep latencies are associated with obesity. One cross-sectional study of 5,358 Turkish children ages 6 to 17 found that as children's sleep duration increased, their BMI decreased (Ozturk et al., 2009). This was the case for both boys and girls. In fact, boys who slept less than 8 hours at night were more than twice as likely to be overweight or obese. Similarly, a longitudinal study that followed Canadian children from ages 2-1/2 to 6 found four patterns of sleep duration in children: short persistent, short increasing, 10-hour persistent, and 11-hour persistent (Touchette et al., 2007). Findings indicated the risk for overweight and obesity was 4.2 times greater for short persistent sleepers than for 11-hour persistent sleepers. The causal relationship between sleep and weight remains unclear, but experts believe short sleep may result in metabolic changes that affect growth and appetite (Cappuccio et al., 2008; Ozturk et al., 2009; Touchette et al., 2007). One hypothesis is that shorter sleep leads to the secretion of hormones that increase appetite. Alternatively, longer sleep may increase the secretion of the growth hormone, thereby reducing the risk of overweight and obesity. Both of these may be true. Also, length of sleep likely affects energy intake and expenditure: Children who are awake more hours in the day have more time to consume calories, whereas children who are tired during the day are likely to engage in less physical activity.

Taken together, research points to the importance of ensuring that children get adequate amounts of sleep for optimal cognitive, behavioral, and physical development. On average, this means 10–11 hours each night for children ages 2 to 6.

SLEEP PROBLEMS. Dr. Richard Ferber, Director in the Center for Pediatric Sleep Disorders at Boston's Children's Hospital, says the most frequent calls he receives are from parents whose children ages 5 months to 4 years are having problems sleeping. Typically, the child is having difficulty falling asleep or is waking up repeatedly during the night, or both. According to Dr. Ferber (2006), sleep problems are extremely common in young children, but they are also the source of a great deal of distress at home—parents get tired and frustrated. They wonder if there is something wrong with their child or with their parenting.

It is true that some groups of children are especially likely to experience problems sleeping. For example, there is a substantial body of research documenting sleep problems in children with attention deficit/hyperactivity disorder (ADHD) and behavior disorders (Buckhalt et al., 2009). Children with developmental disabilities such as autism, or mental or chronic health concerns such as anxiety, depression, obesity, asthma, or migraine headaches, also experience higher rates of sleep problems than children who don't have these disabilities and health concerns. However, it is common for all children to have difficulty sleeping at one time or another and, for most children, sleep problems do not persist or reflect more serious underlying issues.

Almost all children experience **nightmares,** which are scary dreams that occur during REM sleep (Ferber, 2006). Infants and toddlers show signs of having nightmares (e.g., they may wake up crying and upset), but certainly children ages 3 to 6 have bad dreams that involve some threat to their well-being (e.g., being separated from parents or being chased by an animal). Nightmares can be quite upsetting and make it difficult for children to return to sleep without some soothing and reassurance from parents or other caregivers. They need to know the adults in their lives are in control and will keep them safe. When children are old enough (age 3 or 4), discussing the substance of the nightmare and the feelings associated with it usually serves to calm their fears and help them to return to their normal sleep routine.

Night terrors are associated with partial arousal from the deepest phase of non-REM sleep and higher levels of physiological response than nightmares (e.g., rapid heart rate and breathing, perspiration, thrashing). During night terrors, children are not fully awake: They may not recognize an adult who approaches and tries to comfort them. After the event, they may not remember yelling or thrashing or what it was that scared them. Once awake, the signs of fear subside and children often return to sleep easily. In the morning, many children do not remember or only vaguely remember the event and, therefore, are not afraid to go to sleep on subsequent nights. Night terrors are less common than nightmares, but are not usually a serious problem (Thiedke, 2001). They are more likely associated with situational stress and fatigue, lasting only a short period of time. Table 5.4 shows the differences between nightmares and night terrors.

SOLUTIONS. Bedtime resistance, waking during the night, and difficulties falling and/or returning to sleep are the most common sleep problems in young children (Buckhalt et al., 2009). Behavioral strategies have proven effective for addressing these problems, and most parents and clinicians find them more acceptable than pharmacological remedies. One strategy is to develop a **positive bedtime routine,** which includes familiar and relaxing activities that children come to associate with bedtime. The ***Connecting with Children*** guidelines provide tips on how to quiet children and get them ready for bed. Once bedtime routines are established, major disruptions at bedtime are rare.

TABLE 5.4 • **Guidelines for Distinguishing Nightmares and Night Terrors**

NIGHTMARES	NIGHT TERRORS
Child has frightening dreams that occur during the REM sleep stage.	Child experiences frightening episodes that happen during a partial awakening from a deep, non-REM sleep stage.
These dreams typically occur during the latter half of a night's sleep.	These events usually occur in the first half of a night's sleep—1–4 hours after falling asleep.
Child is comforted by the presence of one or both parents.	Child does not notice if a parent is present and resists any effort of comfort or reassurance.
Child remembers the nightmare.	Child has no memory of the event.
The dream may interfere with child's ability to return to sleep or go to sleep in the future.	Child returns to sleep easily once the event is over.

Source: Based on Ferber, R. (2006). Solve your child's sleep problems *(pp. 343–344). New York: Simon & Schuster.*

If difficulties with settling or returning to sleep once wakened in the night are attributable to **sleep associations**—conditions children have come to connect with falling asleep (e.g., rocking or nursing until asleep)—changes may be needed. Initiating change may be met with resistance at first. Extinction is a well-established, but somewhat controversial strategy for addressing settling and night waking problems in children. The ***Point/ Counterpoint*** discusses the advantages and disadvantages of this strategy.

CONNECTING WITH CHILDREN

Guidelines for Families and Professionals: Establishing Positive Bedtime Routines

Engage in bedtime hygiene.
Examples
1. Start with a warm, soothing bath.
2. Put on pajamas.
3. Brush teeth.

Spend time unwinding with quiet activities before bedtime.
Examples
1. Spend time assembling puzzles or drawing and coloring.
2. Curl up with a basket of books.
3. Don't tease or read scary stories that tend to excite children.
4. Save wrestling and other active forms of play for a different time in the day.

Help children anticipate sleep as part of their routine.
Examples
1. Tell children how much longer they have before it will be time to go to sleep—"Just one more story" or "Just 2–3 more pages."
2. Tuck children into bed, perhaps with a favorite toy, kiss and hug good night, and provide assurances about where you are and how you will know they are all right (e.g., listening through a monitor, checking on them before you go to bed).
3. Turn the lights out and leave the room while children are still awake, so they learn to settle and soothe themselves to sleep.

Follow the routine as consistently as you can.
Examples
1. Choose a routine that suits your family—if you are uncomfortable with the routine, sticking with it will be difficult.
2. Avoid frequent interruptions to the routine. Make sure other caregivers know and follow the routine when you are out. Excuse yourself to follow the routine when you have guests in the evening.
3. Put one parent in charge of the routine; this can help with consistency.

POINT/COUNTERPOINT: Using Extinction to Solve Children's Sleep Problems

Night settling and night waking problems are the most common sleep problems reported for young children. Approximately 20% of typically developing children experience these problems and this rate more than doubles for groups of children with developmental disabilities. Treatment approaches are controversial. Parents are reluctant to use medications and some behavioral approaches, although they have proven effective, can be difficult for parents to implement. Extinction is one of those strategies.

POINT ▶ **Standard extinction** involves putting children to bed and then ignoring disruptions (e.g., not attending to their crying, tantrums, calls to parents) until, eventually, they fall asleep on their own. If children get out of bed, parents lead them back without talking or making eye contact. Extinction is well researched and has a high success rate. Improvements are typically observed within a few days and maintain over the long term (Buckhalt et al., 2009; Thackeray & Richdale, 2002). Also, extinction has proven effective with special populations of children, including children with ADHD and developmental disabilities such as autism.

COUNTERPOINT ▶ Extinction's effectiveness hinges on parents' ability to comply with the requirement to ignore children and outlast their emotional and behavioral outbursts. This has proven stressful for many parents and children. However, when parents are not consistent in their implementation of an extinction protocol (e.g., they allow children to cry sometimes, but not others, or they give in to children's crying after an amount of time has passed), they may actually exacerbate the problem (positively reinforce the behavior they want to extinguish). Moreover, extinction may not be appropriate for all children and all sleep problems. For example, sleep problems that are associated with separation anxiety or nighttime fears will not be solved by leaving children alone. Similarly, it is not safe to ignore children who engage in self-injurious behavior when they become upset. Before initiating any strategy for solving sleep problems, it is important to ask, "What's the source of the problem?"

A modified version of extinction—**graduated extinction**—is extinction with parental presence. Parents can remain in children's bedrooms until they fall asleep, but still ignore their bedtime-resistant behavior. Alternatively, parents can engage in a process of "progressive waiting." Rather than ignoring children completely, this process allows parents to check on children according to a schedule of gradually decreasing frequency. Parents can go to children briefly, reassure them and ensure their safety, and then leave again, so that the children learn to soothe and settle themselves. Numerous studies and meta-analyses indicate that graduated extinction and standard extinction are similarly effective (Buckhalt et al., 2009; Mindell, 2005; Owens, Palermo, & Rosen, 2002), and it seems a good compromise for parents. Graduated extinction may take a bit longer to achieve the desired result, but is less stressful for parents. Parents' "buy-in" leads to more consistent implementation, which is associated with greater success.

Special Physical Needs

Some children have special physical needs. In this chapter, we focus on how illness and environmental hazards can affect children's growth and development.

Most children living in resource-rich nations experience good health, thanks in large measure to medical advances and schedules of immunization that can control or eradicate diseases that once were life-threatening (e.g., influenza, measles, polio). In developing nations, where vaccines are not so readily available, these diseases continue to pose significant threats to public health. Not all children in the United States get vaccinated. For example, families in low-SES communities may not have medical insurance to cover the cost of children's vaccinations. Alternatively, as we read in Chapter 4, some parents choose not to vaccinate their children for fear of negative consequences (e.g., they are concerned about possible side effects and links between vaccines and other disabling conditions, such as autism, which have been largely disproven). However, the preponderance of the evidence indicates vaccines are safe and they are an important safety measure to protect individual children and the general public from the reemergence of serious diseases.

Chronic Illness

Unfortunately, some children still experience serious, chronic illnesses. In this chapter we focus on asthma and cancer.

ASTHMA. **Asthma** affects people of all ages, but the onset of symptoms typically begins during childhood (Department of Health and Human Services [DHHS], 2008). It is one of the most common chronic childhood diseases, affecting more than 22 million people in the United States, nearly 6 million of them children. Asthma causes an inflammation of the airways—the tubes that carry air in and out of the lungs—and interferes with breathing (Medline Plus, 2010). Children have smaller airways than adults, making asthma a particularly serious condition for them. Children who have asthma can experience wheezing, coughing, chest tightness, and trouble breathing, especially early in the morning or at night.

The exact cause of asthma is unknown, but researchers attribute the disease to both genetic and environmental factors (DHHS, 2008). Children whose parents have asthma and children with an inherited tendency to develop allergies are more likely to develop the disease. Asthma is also linked to certain respiratory infections during childhood and exposure to irritants, such as mold, pollen, animal dander, air pollution, and cigarette smoke. In one study, researchers found that 20% of children living in homes where there was cigarette smoke had asthma compared with 15% of children living in smoke-free homes (MacDonald, Pertowski, & Jackson, 1996). We talk more about the negative impact exposure to second-hand smoke has on children's health below.

Since there is no cure for asthma, the goal is to manage the disease (DHHS, 2008; Medline Plus, 2010). The most common treatments include long-term medicines that reduce inflammation in airways and prevent asthma symptoms, and quick-relief, or "rescue," medicines, such as inhalers, that relieve asthma symptoms when they flare up. Importantly, parents and caregivers need to help children avoid what "triggers" their asthma symptoms. If pollens or air pollution make asthma worse, limit children's time outdoors when levels of these substances are high. Air conditioning prevents outdoor allergens from getting inside during the spring and summer. If animal dander is a problem, keep animals with fur outside, or at least out of children's bedrooms. There are dogs without dander (e.g., poodles and wheaten terriers) that make better choices for family pets when children have allergies or asthma. Limit or eliminate children's exposure to second-hand smoke. Finally, since young children may not be able to monitor their asthma symptoms, parents, teachers, and other caregivers need to work together to watch for signs and symptoms that might lead to an asthma attack. Figure 5.7 on the next page shows the common signs and symptoms of asthma.

CANCER. Childhood cancer is a rare but very serious disease. In the United States, 1–2 children in 10,000 (.0001%) develop cancer each year (Daly, Kral, & Brown, 2008). However, this still represents more than 10,000 new cases of pediatric cancer in children 0 to 14 years of age each year (National Cancer Institute [NCI], 2009). The most common forms of childhood cancers are **leukemias,** which are blood cell cancers, and brain and central nervous system tumors. Together, these forms of cancer account for more than 50% of new cases. Leukemia causes the production of abnormal numbers of early stage white blood cells, which eventually block the production of normal white blood cells; this compromises the body's ability to fight infections. The most common cancer in children in the United States is a specific form of leukemia, *Acute Lymphoblastic Leukemia* (ALL), which peaks in incidence in children 4 to 5 years of age (Daly et al., 2008).

Fortunately, there have been dramatic improvements in early detection and treatment of childhood cancers. Today, the 5-year survival rate exceeds 80%, compared with less than 50% in the 1970s (Daly et al., 2008; NCI, 2009). Unfortunately, therapies used to treat these cancers (e.g., chemotherapy and radiation) often have negative long-term effects that have implications for development and learning. Cancer treatments are designed to kill cells that grow quickly, but in children, healthy cells in their brains, bones, and other organs also are

FIGURE 5.7

COMMON SIGNS AND SYMPTOMS OF ASTHMA

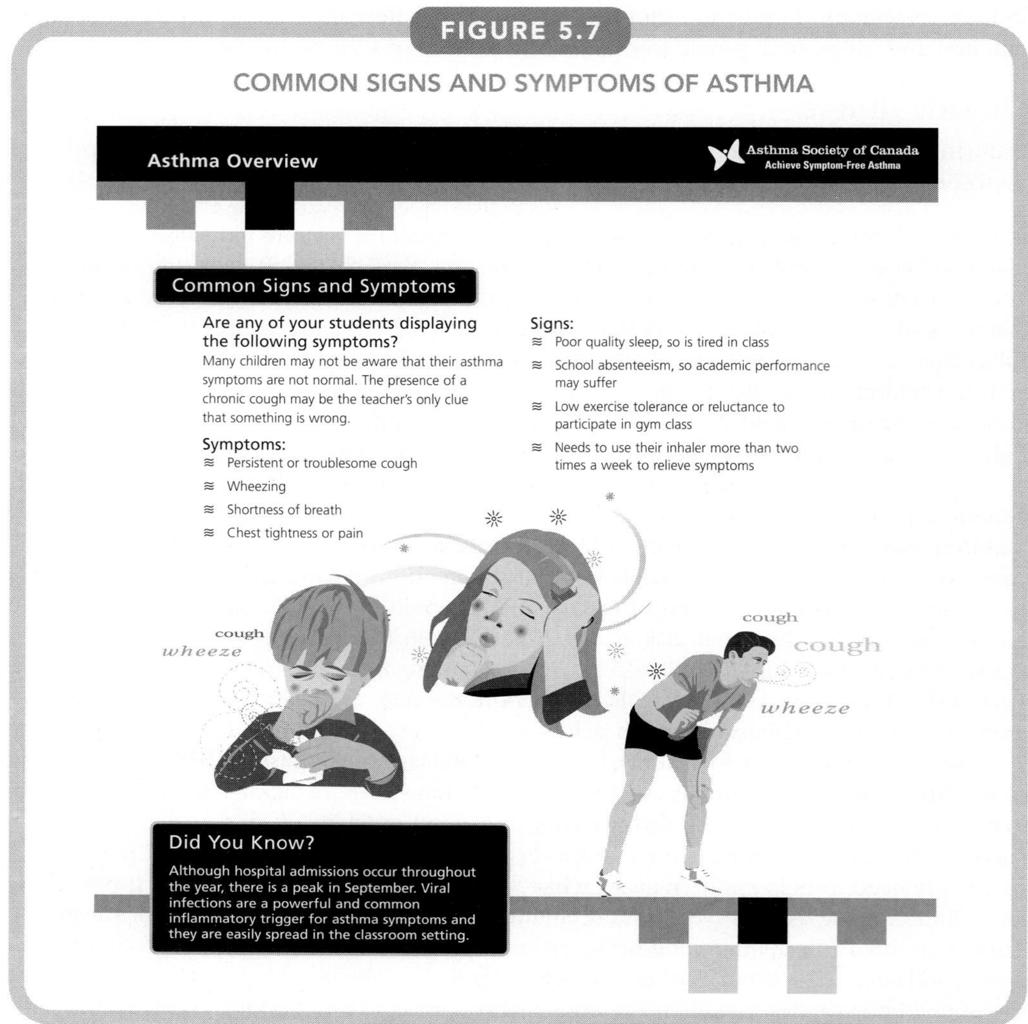

Source: From Asthma Society of Canada. Asthma Kit for Canadian Schools. *Retrieved from www .Asthma-Kids.ca. Used with permission.*

growing fast. Cancer treatments can damage these cells and keep them from growing the way they should. Children who receive cranial radiation therapy, especially to their head and neck, are at risk of developing cognitive impairments that result in academic difficulties when they go to school. Similarly, children who receive CNS chemotherapy are at risk of developing learning disabilities post-treatment.

These treatment effects, referred to as **late effects,** may not show up until months or even years after treatment and range from mild to severe. For this reason, long-term follow-up care that focuses on children's development and learning, as well as their health and emotional well-being, is receiving more attention from researchers and caregivers (Butler & Haser, 2006; Daly et al., 2008). Research goals include understanding the specific deficits that result from disease and treatment, and developing interventions that ameliorate these deficits. Early intervention is critical but receiving treatment at an early age is associated with higher risks for late effects. However, attention also needs to be paid to school reentry for children who may experience gaps in learning due to long absences in addition to late effects that are a consequence of having cancer and treatment.

Environmental Hazards

Young children are exposed to many toxins in their environments, and these put their health at risk. Fortunately, as a consequence of widespread efforts at public education, mandated use of child-resistant safety caps, availability of poison control centers, and advances in medical care, deaths from accidental poisonings are far less common than they were 50 years ago (AAP Committee on Injury, Violence, and Poison Prevention, 2003). Still, more than 2 million poisonings are reported to poison control centers across the United States each year, and more than half occur in children under age 6 (Liller, 2007). Kitchens, bathrooms, and garages are the most common sites of accidental poisoning in homes. Parents and caregivers need to remain vigilant about keeping harmful substances, including cleaners and medications, out of the reach of young children.

Exposure to lead is a serious health issue for children (CDC, 2009b). Lead is present in many substances, including paint, window frames, dust, gasoline, foods, and toys. It gets into children's bloodstreams when they eat food or drink water that is contaminated with lead, put their fingers in their mouths after touching lead, or inhale dust from lead-based paint (Gulson et al., 2004; McLaughlin et al., 2004). Lead-based paint in older homes is the most common cause of lead poisoning, so children who live in older homes, especially if the paint is deteriorating, are most at risk, as are children who live in areas of substantial air pollution from automobile traffic. Not surprisingly, children in low-SES communities are more at risk for lead poisoning than children in higher income communities. Even small amounts of lead poisoning can have negative consequences (Kaneshiro, 2009, writing for Medline). For example, a single exposure can cause symptoms requiring a visit to the emergency room. However, it is more common for lead to build up over time and from repeated exposure. Exposure to lead is associated with a myriad of negative outcomes, including slowed body growth, hearing impairment, kidney damage, lower intelligence, delayed development and low achievement in school, attention problems, hyperactivity, and aggression. The CDC (2009b) emphasizes that lead poisoning is preventable and advises that the key to prevention is stopping children from coming into contact with lead and treating children who have been poisoned by lead.

Second-hand smoke is another toxin with which children's contact is entirely preventable, yet a recent report from the Surgeon General (CDC, 2007) indicates that 60% of American children ages 3 to 11 are exposed to second-hand smoke, about 22% in their homes and family vehicles. Similarly, data collected by Health Canada (Canadian Lung Association, 2007) indicated that 7% of children under the age of 12 were regularly exposed to second-hand smoke in their homes, whereas 16% of 12-year-olds were exposed to second-hand smoke in public spaces and in private vehicles. Because second-hand smoke permeates an environment and lingers long after a cigarette has been extinguished, smoking inside, even at certain times or near a fan or a window, is not safe (CDC, 2009). Furthermore, evidence about the effects of second-hand smoke is clear—children exposed to high levels of second-hand smoke are more susceptible to ear and respiratory infections, such as bronchitis and pneumonia, than children who live in smoke-free environments. Also, children who already have asthma experience more frequent and severe attacks when they are exposed to second-hand smoke. Finally, children exposed to second-hand smoke on a regular basis have higher levels of cotinine—the major metabolite (breakdown) product of nicotine—in their systems than children who live in homes where smoking is not allowed (CDC, 2009).

Young children are powerless to protect themselves from toxins in their environment. They depend on the adults in their lives to be responsible. Recommendations about how adults can protect children from accidental poisoning and environmental hazards are provided in the ***Connecting with Children*** guidelines on the next page.

Lead-based paint in older homes is the most common cause of lead poisoning, so children who live in older homes, especially if the paint is deteriorating, are most at risk. Children in low-SES communities are more at risk for lead poisoning than children in higher income communities.

CONNECTING WITH CHILDREN

Guidelines for Families, Teachers, and Other Professionals: Protecting Children from Toxic Substances

Increase awareness of substances in and around your home that can be poisonous when children inhale or ingest them.

Examples

1. Identify common household substances that are highly toxic (e.g., charcoal, lighter fluid, paint thinner and remover, antifreeze, turpentine, pesticides, and cleaning products).
2. Teach children to recognize these substances as things they should not touch.
3. Obtain "Mr. Yuk" stickers from local poison control centers and place them on poisonous substances to warn children to stay away from them.

Store harmful products, including cleaners, paints, medicines, and even vitamins and minerals, safely.

Examples

1. Store harmful products on shelves that are out of the reach of children or, better yet, in locked cabinets—use childproof locks.
2. Store harmful products in their original containers—labels on the original containers typically provide information about what to do in the event of accidental ingestion.
3. Never store toxic substances in containers that can be mistaken for food and drink (e.g., old soda bottles or ice cream buckets).
4. Seek out child-resistant packaging when purchasing medications and other potentially poisonous substances.
5. Make sure that other homes where your children spend time (e.g., grandparents) are childproofed too.

Prevent children's exposure to lead.

Examples

1. Test paint and dust in older homes (built before 1978) for lead.
2. Make sure pregnant women and young children are not present in older homes or schools during renovations.
3. Avoid having children play on older playground equipment, especially if paint is chipped, as it could contain lead.
4. Teach children not to suck on toys or playground equipment that may be covered in lead-based paint.
5. Wash children's hands and toys regularly—both can be contaminated by household dust or exterior soil, which can contain lead.

Protect children from secondhand smoke.

Examples

1. Make your home and vehicles 100% smoke-free at all times.
2. Make sure your children's daycare centers and schools also are smoke free.
3. Choose smoke-free restaurants.
4. Insist that no one smokes around your children.

Adapted from: CDC. (2007). Children and secondhand smoke exposure. Retrieved from http://www.cdc.gov/features/childrenandsmoke/. CDC. (2009). Prevention tips. Retrieved from http://www.cdc.gov/nceh/Lead/tips.htm. Optum Health. (2008). Accidental poisoning in children. Retrieved from http://www.myoptumhealth.com/portal/Information/item/Accidental+Poisoning+in+Children?archiveChannel=Home%2FArticle&clicked=true

▼ SUMMARY AND KEY TERMS

• Body Growth

Compared to other species, humans experience a prolonged period of growth and development—we continue to grow during 20% of our lifespan. The rate of growth during the early years is not as fast as it was during infancy, but some significant changes take place. From ages 2 through 6, children lose their babyish appearance. Specifically, their body fat decreases and their bodies appear more appropriately proportioned relative to the size of their heads.

Different body systems grow at different rates. For example, the lymphoid system, which includes tonsils and lymph nodes, grows rapidly during the early years, building children's immunity to the many infections and diseases they come in contact with as they socialize more outside their homes. In contrast, the reproductive system grows slowly until adolescence.

Boys and girls have similar growth patterns during the early years, but girls tend to have more body fat and boys more muscle mass throughout the lifespan. This gives boys the edge in many physical activities. Hereditary and environmental factors also influence children's growth trajectories. For example, children who have tall parents tend to be tall themselves, and weight problems often run in families. Children who are under- or malnourished don't grow as fast or as tall as children who have adequate food and a healthy diet. Finally, there are ethnic differences in rates and absolute levels of growth and development, too (e.g., Northern European children tend to be larger than their Asian peers).

• Brain Development

Children's brains continue to grow more rapidly than other parts of the body during early childhood. In addition, changes are taking place in children's brains that both support and reflect impressive cognitive developments. For example, the process of myelination increases the brain's efficiency. Children can think faster, remember better, and make sense of increasingly complex sequences of words and actions. These enhancements help children learn language and complex concepts. Similarly, the two hemispheres of the brain undergo a process of lateralization, or specialization. By age 3, in most children, the left hemisphere dominates for language processing and logical reasoning, whereas the right hemisphere is primarily responsible for visual-spatial information and controlling emotions. For some left-handed individuals, this relationship may be reversed, but for most left-handers and girls, there is less hemispheric specialization altogether.

Differences in hemispheric function are more relative than absolute. Nearly all tasks, particularly complex tasks, require participation from many parts of the brain. During the early years, the corpus callosum, which is responsible for communication and coordination between the two sides of the brain, develops rapidly. Before lateralization, damage to one part of the brain often can be overcome because other parts of the brain take over that function. After lateralization, the brain is less able to compensate.

Finally, advances in the development of the prefrontal cortex between ages 3 and 4 lead to increases in children's ability to control emotions and impulses and to focus attention. Children become less impulsive and have fewer temper tantrums than they did at age 2.

• Motor Development

Advances in gross motor development are associated with brain development, particularly myelination of neuron connections that are responsible for balance and coordination. Changes in body size and proportions also contribute to gross motor development. By age 2, most children have perfected walking and, in their third year, most children learn to run, throw, and jump. However, these activities are not well controlled until children are 4 or 5 years old. In general, motor developments are cumulative and sequential—new skills develop from previously learned skills. However, a number of factors other than maturation are associated with children's gross motor development, including practice, temperament, genes, cultural norms, and sex.

Finally, some groups of children experience particular difficulties with respect to gross motor development (e.g., children with physical disabilities, children with hearing or visual impairments, and children with developmental disabilities such as autism). Like gross motor development, fine motor development follows a progression from less to more differentiation, coordination, and control. By age 3 or 4, children can put on and take off articles of clothing they might have struggled with at age 2, and they can hold and manipulate crayons to draw. Fine motor skills, such as putting on a pair of shoes or grasping a crayon, develop over time, with practice, and as children's brains develop and their visual systems and eye-hand coordination improves.

• Health and Well-Being

Developing good nutrition and eating habits in early childhood can make a difference to an individual's overall health and well-being throughout the lifespan. Children need fewer calories, especially calories from fat, than infants and toddlers because their brains and bodies are growing more slowly. A healthy and balanced diet for most children includes mainly fruits and vegetables, lean proteins, and whole grains. Juice should be restricted to 4–6 ounces per day. It's healthier for children to drink milk with meals and water with snacks.

Children can be finicky eaters. The best way to promote healthy eating is to provide access to a variety of foods from all food groups and then allow children to regulate how much they eat. Don't coax too hard when children refuse a healthy choice or indicate they're "all done." Also, don't deny children sweet and salty treats. Rather, communicate a consistent message about health and nutrition in the family; model good eating habits and encourage physical activity as a complement to good eating habits.

The incidence of childhood obesity has more than doubled since 1976. Children's body mass index (BMI)—a ratio of weight to height—is a common measure of overweight and obesity. Other indices, such as skinfold thickness, diet, physical activity, and family history also can be used. Being overweight is linked to a wide range of health concerns for children, including early onset of diabetes and heart disease. Also, being overweight is associated with lower academic achievement, social and emotional problems, negative body image, and low self-esteem. Causes of overweight and obesity include heredity, ethnicity, poverty, and lifestyle. In particular, contemporary society's reliance on processed foods, along with our sedentary lifestyle are often blamed for the rising incidence of childhood overweight and obesity.

Some children eat more than enough calories, but still don't get sufficient nutrients. For example, iron deficiency anemia occurs when children don't eat sufficient quantities of iron-rich foods or are exposed to substances that interfere with iron absorption. Calcium and zinc are other nutrients that are commonly deficient in children. Around the world, childhood hunger and malnutrition are a powerful predictor of population health. Children who are hungry are at a disadvantage for learning and development, which limits their later earning potential and ability to provide for their own families.

In addition to getting adequate amounts of nutrition, children need sufficient amounts of good quality sleep. Those who get less sleep than they need suffer a wide range of difficulties relating to cognition, learning, behavior, social and emotional well-being, and health (e.g., getting too little sleep has been linked to obesity). Getting too much sleep can also be a problem—children who get too much sleep can have difficulty falling asleep or awaken during the night or early in the morning.

The most common sleep problems for children include bedtime resistance, waking during the night, and difficulties falling and/or returning to sleep once awake. Nightmares and night terrors are also common problems. Some groups of children are more likely to experience sleep problems (e.g., children with ADHD or behavior disorders, children with developmental disabilities, children with chronic health concerns). Establishing positive bedtime routines and graduated extinction are two established strategies for addressing children's sleep problems.

• Special Physical Needs

Children can experience a wide range of chronic illnesses that affect development and learning. Asthma is one of the most common childhood diseases. It causes inflammation of the airways and interferes with breathing. Children with asthma may experience wheezing, coughing, chest tightness, and trouble breathing. The exact cause of asthma is not known, but researchers attribute it to both genetic and environmental factors (e.g., mold, pollen, animal dander, and air pollution). There is no cure for asthma, so treatments are designed to manage the disease. Common treatments include medicines that reduce inflammation and prevent asthma symptoms, as well as inhalers that relieve asthma symptoms when they flare up. It's important for children with asthma to avoid whatever triggers their symptoms (e.g., stay indoors when pollens and air pollution are high and choose pets with hair, not fur, to reduce exposure to dander).

Childhood cancer is a rare but very serious disease. The most common forms of cancer are leukemias and brain and central nervous system tumors. Today, the 5-year survival rate for children with cancer is 80%, up from less than 50% in the 1970s. Unfortunately, the therapies used to treat cancer can have negative effects that may not show up until months, or even years after treatment. Therefore, long-term follow-up care is essential and needs to focus on children's development and learning as well as their health and emotional well-being.

Exposure to toxins is a serious health concern for children. Parents and caregivers need to work hard to keep harmful substances, such as household cleaners and medications, out of children's reach. Lead is present in many substances, including paint, window frames, dust, foods, and toys. Children may ingest it or inhale it. Over time, it can build up in their bodies and cause a myriad of negative outcomes (e.g., slowed growth, hearing impairment, kidney damage, lower intelligence, low achievement, attention and behavior problems). Children in low-SES communities tend to be exposed to higher levels of lead than other children.

Lead poisoning is preventable, as is children's exposure to second-hand smoke. Evidence is clear that children exposed to high levels of second-hand smoke are more likely to acquire ear and respiratory infections than children who live in smoke-free environments. Also, children who have asthma experience more frequent and severe attacks when they are exposed to second-hand smoke.

▼ KEY TERMS

asthma (189)
body mass index (BMI) (180)
fine motor skills (174)
food security (181)
graduated extinction (188)
gross motor skills (172)
handedness (174)
iron deficiency anemia (182)
late effects (190)
lateralization (171)
leukemias (189)
myelination (171)
night terrors (186)
nightmares (186)
positive bedtime routine (186)
sleep associations (187)
standard extinction (188)
Type 2 diabetes (180)

▼ CASEBOOK

CHILDHOOD OVERWEIGHT AND OBESITY

Near the end of every school year, Susan makes a point of meeting with the families of each child in her preschool class to review what she's observed in terms of physical, cognitive, and social emotional development. One child in particular is extremely overweight for her age and height—an increasing problem among preschoolers. Susan struggled with how to broach this very sensitive subject. She tried very hard not to sound judgmental—just concerned—when speaking with Laura's mom about her diet and activity level. After all, Laura is just 4 years old, but if the issue is not addressed now, she could struggle with overweight and health issues throughout her life. Laura's mom reasoned that it was very difficult to deny Laura the foods many of her friends are allowed to eat. But Laura doesn't want to participate in games or other activities that would burn off calories because the kids in the neighborhood tease her about the way she looks and moves. Susan struggled with how to impress upon this mother and her young daughter her concerns about the grave risks to health and well-being that stem from being overweight. And this risk will only get more serious as Laura "grows." How can Susan help them understand?

WHAT WOULD THEY DO?

Here is how some professionals in several fields responded:

KATHERINE A. YOUNG—K–8 School Counselor
Montgomery County Intermediate Unit, Non-Public School Services Division, Norristown, PA

To help with a situation involving an overweight child, I would first schedule the conference with the parents for a time when the school nurse is available to offer insights from a medical professional. To begin, I would share some of the wonderful strengths that the child possesses. Then, I would express my concerns that the implications of being overweight have not only on a child's health and mental well-being, but on his or her social development as well. Resources for the parents may include referral to the pediatrician, parenting classes, and websites and support groups dedicated to children's health issues. Since children learn by example, I would encourage the parents to lead by example. When they prepare a healthy snack or meal for their child, they should eat the same thing. Also, I would suggest to limit time spent on the computer or in front of the television and to start making plans to do activities outdoors as a family. I would gather resources for teachers to learn how to incorporate nutrition and physical activity into their lesson plans. Above all, it is important for parents and schools to work together to help children develop healthy habits that will provide life-long benefits.

KAREN E. DAVIES—Kindergarten Teacher
North Royalton Early Childhood Center, Broadview Heights, Ohio

I would not wait until the end of the school year to meet with each child's parents. Early and frequent communication is essential for building trust with parents. A call to introduce oneself, or to communicate good news of the day goes a long way to building a good rapport. With a connection established early, it is much easier to discuss difficult topics, such as a preschooler's weight.

I would begin by discussing the school curriculum with the parents, explaining that we have been learning about healthy eating. I would explain to the parents that these lessons have been difficult for Laura and she seemed to be bothered by them. I would also tell Laura's parents that she was hesitant to participate in our classroom physical activities. I would ask if she is bothered by playmates teasing her about her size or coordination, and then ask her parents about her activities outside of school. As a teacher, I would explain my concerns for her health and social development, citing examples from the classroom, as well as medical research. As a result of this discussion, I would offer some suggestions about cutting quantities of food, rather than eliminating favorite foods. I would also include some fun ideas for movement that Laura could do alone or with her parents, (hula hoop, hopscotch, etc.) to build her confidence and coordination. Finally, I would tell Laura's parents that I will keep them informed of her progress at school and ask them to do the same from home. I would tell Laura that her parents and I will be communicating about her progress and I will be glad to talk with her any time.

SARAH DAVLIN—Elementary School Counselor (K–5)
Wyandot Run Elementary School, Olentangy Local Schools, Powell, Ohio

With the obesity and weight epidemic within our country, we, as educators, face a very difficult question: Do we dare tackle this incredibly sensitive issue with the children and families that face it *or* do we look away, too afraid to "step on toes" or broach a matter that we possibly struggle with ourselves? The reality is many of us ignore obesity and weight problems within our students because we are not sure how to approach them constructively. The reality is also that we can make a significant difference if we are willing to attempt to help.

When addressing childhood obesity, we must recognize that our impact will be minimal, at best, if we do not take the plunge and involve a child's family. We can assist families by pointing them toward useful school and community resources. The school counselor can explore the possibility of underlying emotional causes and consequences and give referrals to community counselors if necessary.

Finally, we can help prevent and end childhood obesity through our honesty and openness with children. When we are willing to serve as role models by sharing our personal fitness and nutrition goals, we communicate the value of a healthy lifestyle and our belief that change is possible. We can further demonstrate healthy living by "taking the long way" when we walk students through the building or by playing jump rope or basketball during the occasional recess.

DEBBIE WILSON, RN—School Nurse
St. Mary's Elementary School; St. Bernadette School; Lancaster City Schools, Lancaster, Ohio

I would try to be positive and honest with Laura's mother. I would probably begin the conversation by pointing to Laura's strengths (e.g., "She is smart, sweet spirited, eager to learn and please teachers and peers"). Also, I would affirm that her parents want only the best for her—health, happiness, and success.

I would then broach the subject of weight. "She does seem to shy away from games that involve physical activity and I was wondering how we can help Laura join in the fun!" It takes everybody working together, parents, teachers, and school nurses. I would suggest it might be helpful to have Laura's pediatrician involved with the diet and exercise plan. Perhaps the doctor would include a dietician. Many local services are available to teach children and parents healthy eating strategies that benefit the entire family so that the child doesn't feel like the "target." "Let's all do this together." Many local parks and recreation centers as well as hospitals have exercise programs that are geared toward children and make exercise fun.

Goals should be attainable. Make a chart with healthy choices for meals and snacks. Laura can help make the chart by cutting pictures of fruits, vegetables, and whole grains out of magazines and planning family meals. Teach about portions (e.g., a fist-sized serving of chicken, beef, or pork is about 3 oz.). I would talk about the benefits of increasing the amount of water she drinks while cutting back on soda and sugary juices. Let her pick out a cute reusable water bottle. You can purchase some flavor packets to add to water that are non-calorie. I really believe at age 4 you could make this fun for Laura and the whole family. I would suggest family activities—take a walk together, go to the park, walk the dog, take a bike ride together. Turn off the TV! Again, challenge Laura to suggest activities for the family—a weekend hike, a scavenger hunt that involves school or neighborhood friends.

To help Laura cope with peer rejection and humiliation, again I would stress the positive "fun, sweet, caring, loyal child." Don't make the issue become "the world is against me." Rather continue to stress the positives of personal choices and how good choices can keep us healthy and feeling good so that we can feel like joining in with others in group activities. The goal is to make healthy diet choices and exercise choices a fun game for Laura and her whole family so it's not always, "No, we can't have pizza and movie night." Let pizza and movie night become a VERY special reward for an accomplished goal.

PEARSON **myeducationlab**

Now go to MyEducationLab at ***www.myeducationlab.com***, where you can:

- Find the instructional objectives for this chapter in the **Study Plan**.
- Take a quiz as a part of the **Study Plan** to self-assess your mastery of chapter content. The program generates an individualized Study Plan based upon your answers to the quiz.
- Complete **Activities and Applications** to assist you in deepening your understanding of important chapter concepts.
- Apply what you have learned through **Building Teaching Skills**, exercises that guide you in trying out skills and strategies you will use in professional practice.

6

COGNITIVE DEVELOPMENT IN EARLY CHILDHOOD

THE CASEBOOK

WHAT WOULD YOU DO?

ONLY CHILDREN AND IMAGINARY FRIENDS

Kayla has set her table again to make "tea" for Sassy. When her mother walks in and starts to sit down, Kayla protests, "No! that's Sassy's chair. You have to go, she is coming." Kayla's mother sighs, says, "OK, I'll leave," and returns to her desk to check her e-mail. In a few minutes she hears Kayla talking with Sassy, or at least she hears Kayla's side of the conversation. Sassy is not a real child but an imaginary friend that Kayla talks about and with often—she has for the past few years. When she is upset or has been scolded, Kayla threatens, "I'm going to run away and live with Sassy in China—she has a nice mommy!" But at other times, Kayla complains that Sassy has been mean to her and has spilled ice cream on her shirt. Her parents were not concerned at first about the invisible Sassy, but then they found out Kayla believes that Sassy is a giraffe who wears jeans and can make herself tiny to fit in Kayla's pocket when she goes to school. Her parents worry, what will the preschool teacher think? What will the other children think? Should we talk to someone about Kayla? Is it because she is lonely as an only child? Will Sassy keep Kayla from making real friends?

CRITICAL THINKING

- Did you or someone you know have an imaginary friend?
- What role could such a friend play for children?
- What else would you want to know about Kayla and her family to evaluate this situation?
- Should Kayla's parents be concerned?

Jasmine T., Age 5—USA

▶ OVERVIEW AND OBJECTIVES

The years from ages 2 to 7 are filled with remarkable cognitive accomplishments. All over the world, children learn the language(s) of their families. Some even learn two or more languages at once. They go from using fewer than 500 words at age 3 to using over 2,500 words and understanding over 20,000 at age 6. They learn the grammar and syntax of their languages. By age 5 or 6 many can read. Language development reflects the changes in thinking and reasoning during the early years. In this chapter we will look at the perspectives of Piaget, Vygotsky, and the information processing theorists on thinking, self-regulation, attention, memory, knowledge, problem-solving strategies, and theory of mind. Next we move outside the child to explore contexts for development—the family, home, school, and the digital world. By the time you finish this chapter you should be able to:

Objective 6.1 Identify five cognitive abilities that appear and increase from ages 2 to 7.

Objective 6.2 Describe the development of language during the early years, including the role of culture in language, dual language development, and what can be done to support emergent literacy in the early years.

Objective 6.3 Explain the differences between and the implications of Piaget's and Vygotsky's theories for parents, teachers, and other professionals working with young children.

Objective 6.4 Distinguish and describe changes in children's knowledge of numbers, attention, memory, problem-solving strategies, and theory of mind during the early years.

Objective 6.5 Summarize the research on the impact of home environments and early childhood education on children's cognitive development during the early years.

Objective 6.6 Choose developmentally appropriate uses of television and computers during the early years.

New Cognitive Possibilities for a Developing Brain

For centuries, the period from about ages 2 to 6 has been viewed as a time of great growth in cognitive abilities. Even if they were unsure of their child's exact age, medieval European parents first assigned chores to their children around age 6, the time considered the end of infancy (Orme, 2001). During these years of early childhood, most 2-year-olds who know several hundred words become 6-year-olds with a vocabulary of about 20,000 words. Children who at age 2 believed that everyone shared their thoughts and feelings realize at age 6 that different people have different minds, and thus different thoughts and beliefs. Three-year-olds who count, "one, two, three, seven, five, ten," can do simple addition by age 6. And most children have a preference for using their right or left hand by age 5 or 6. Kagan and Herschkowitz (2005) summarize five cognitive abilities that appear and increase during these years in Western cultures:

- *Integrating the present with the past.* Children can connect an experience in the present with an event in the past. For example, beginning around age 4, a child greeting a parent returning from the store with a grocery bag might retrieve the knowledge that the parent left earlier to buy ice cream and ask, "What ice cream did you get?' A younger child is less likely to integrate the parent's present return with the past event of leaving to buy ice cream.
- *Anticipating the future.* Children develop a better sense of what is "sooner" and what is "later." For example, 7-year-olds, but not most 3- or 4-year-olds can differentiate events close in time (a birthday next week, an upcoming holiday) from events that are farther away (summer vacation, Halloween next year).
- *Appreciating causality.* Even though younger children can make causal connections, "I got medicine because it makes my fever go away" (Hickling & Wellman, 2001; McCormack & Hoeri, 2005), they are less likely to reflect on situations and search for causes. If something unfamiliar happens, however, 7-year-olds are likely to try to understand why.
- *Relying on semantic categories.* As children develop during this time, they increasingly use words and networks of meaning (semantic categories) to represent and remember experiences. For example, ask a 4- or 5-year-old "What is the first word that comes to mind when you say *sun*?" and you might get a response of *shine* or *burn*—simple word associations. But ask a 6- or 7-year-old the same question and the response might be other objects in the semantic category such as *moon, earth,* or *planet*. Being able to use meaningful categories allows children to think more logically and to expand their knowledge of the world by adding new information to categories and building hierarchies such as dog is a pet, is a animal, is a living thing . . .
- *Detecting relationships between events and concepts.* During this period, children are increasingly able to understand abstract relationships such as *larger, smaller, shorter,* and *taller* and to apply these flexibly, so they know, for example, that a child can be the shortest in one group but the tallest in another group.

Underlying these accomplishments are several brain developments that allow maturing children to focus attention, inhibit impulses, think faster, and follow longer, more complex sequences of actions and ideas. With these growing capacities, young children are ready to expand their language. Language plays an important role in the five cognitive abilities described above because it provides a means for expressing ideas and asking questions, the categories and concepts for thinking, and the links between the past and the future. Language frees us from the immediate situation to think about what was and what might be (Das, 1995; Driscoll, 2005).

OUTLINE ▼

Language in the Preschool Years: Amazing Developments

All children in every culture master the complicated system of their native language, unless severe deprivation or physical problems interfere. This knowledge is remarkable. Sounds, meanings, words and sequences of words, volume, voice tone, inflection, and turn-taking rules must all be coordinated just to have a conversation. Yet, by about age 4, most children have a vocabulary of thousands of words and knowledge of both rules of grammar and rules of conversations. They have "basically all that is needed for communication in face-to-face contexts with friends and family" (Colledge et al., 2002).

What Develops: Language and Cultural Diversity

There are over 6,000 natural languages in the world (Tomasello, 2006). In general, cultures develop words for the concepts that are important to them. For example: How many different shades of green can you name—mint, olive, emerald, teal, sea foam, chromium, turquoise, chartreuse, lime, apple? An oil painting artist can add cobalt, titanate green, cinnabar green, phthalo yellow green, viridian green, and many others. Google a few of your favorite clothing stores. What colors do they offer for T-shirts? A quick check on one popular site revealed burnished olive, seashore green, wild mushroom, dark pewter, sand dune, light pineapple, faded mango, and light maritime. English-speaking countries have over 3,000 words for colors. Such words are important in our lives for fashion and home design, artistic expression, films and television, and T-shirt choices—to name only a few areas. In contrast, the Himba people of Namibia and a tribe of hunter-gather people in Papua New Guinea who speak Berinmo have five words for colors, even though they can recognize many color variations. But whether there are few or many color terms, children gradually acquire the color categories that are appropriate for their culture (Roberson, Davidoff, Davies, & Shapiro, 2004).

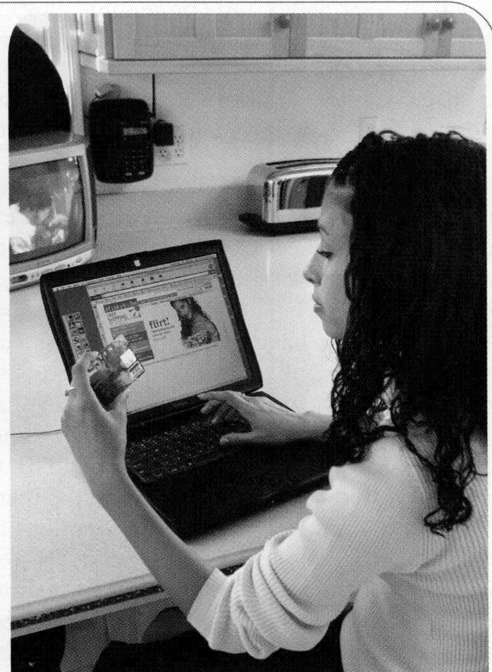

The words that children learn are shaped by the values and needs of the culture. Eskimos really don't have hundreds of words for snow, but the Ulgunigamiut Eskimo do have more that 160 words for ice, because they have to recognize ice at different stages of freezing to hunt and live safely in their environment. Industrialized cultures have many words for communications technologies. In the picture here you see a telephone, television, computer, and even a credit card number that "communicates" to the online seller that the buyer can pay.

Languages change over time to reflect changing cultural needs and values. The Shoshoni Native Americans have one word that means, "to make a crunching sound walking on the sand." This word was valuable in the past to communicate about hunting, but today new words describing technical tools have been added to the Shoshoni language, as the emphasis of life moves away from nomadic hunting. To hear hundreds of new 21st century tool words, listen to techies talk about computers and apps (Price & Crapo, 2002).

Diversity in Language Development

Some children learn two or more languages growing up. In fact, about half the children in the world live in environments where two or more languages are spoken (Hoff, 2006). In 2003, approximately 15% of school-age children in the United States spoke a language other than English at home. The number grows each year. For example, by 2025, the number of Spanish-speaking Latinos in the United States is projected to reach 40.2 million, up from 28 million today. By 2050, Latinos are projected to represent about one-fourth of the U.S. population. Today three out of four Latino children age 8 and younger live in homes where some Spanish is regularly spoken (Garcia & Jensen, 2009; Roslow, 2005; SRCD, 2009).

We call people who speak two or more languages *bilingual*—but this is not a simple idea. There are disagreements about the meaning of the term **bilingualism.** Some definitions focus exclusively on a language-based meaning: Bilingual people, or bilinguals, speak two languages. But most bilingual individuals also must be able to move back and forth between two cultures while still maintaining a sense of identity. Being bilingual and bicultural means mastering the knowledge necessary to communicate in two cultures as well as dealing with potential discrimination.

Do you speak two or more languages? If you mastered your own first language, then added a second or third language, you are an example of *additive* bilingualism—you kept your first language and added another. But if you lost your first language when you added a second one, you experienced *subtractive* bilingualism (Norbert, 2005). If children's first language is valued by their family and community, they are more likely to keep the first language when they add a second one. But if they experience discrimination against their use of the first language, they may be at greater risk of leaving the first language behind as they learn a new language (Hamers & Blanc, 2000). Immigrants are more likely to experience discrimination and therefore "subtract" their first language, at least in interactions outside the family.

DUAL LANGUAGE DEVELOPMENT. Are children at a disadvantage if they are learning two languages at once? That depends. Children exposed to two languages from birth reach the language milestones in both languages on the same schedule as *monolingual* children (children who are learning only one language). Initially, bilingual children may have a larger vocabulary in the language that they are learning from the person with whom they spend the most time or have the closest bond, so a child who stays home all day with a French-speaking parent will likely use more French words. But over time, these children "can and do become fully and equally bilingual if dual language exposure occurs (a) early in life, (b) consistently and in a sustained manner, and (c) across a wide and rich range of contexts" (Petitto & Kovelman, 2003). One general finding is that children will not develop a second language if that language constitutes less than 25% of the language input they receive, but if adequate input is available and continues over time in both first and second languages, children can become **balanced bilinguals**—equally fluent in both languages (Hoff, 2006; Petitto & Kovelman, 2003). Simply put, learning two languages simultaneously is not detrimental to language growth in either of the languages (Brice & Brice, 2009). Even balanced bilingual children may mix vocabularies of the two languages when they speak, but this is not a sign that they are confused because their bilingual parents often intentionally mix vocabularies as well, selecting the word that best expresses their intent. So with consistent and sustained engagement in two languages, children can become fully bilingual.

BENEFITS OF BILINGUALISM. There is no cognitive penalty for children who learn and speak two languages. In fact, there are benefits. Higher degrees of bilingualism are correlated with increased cognitive abilities in such areas as concept formation, creativity, theory of mind, cognitive flexibility, and understanding that printed words are symbols for language. In addition, these children have more advanced metalinguistic awareness (awareness of the forms and structures of language); for example, they are more likely to notice grammar errors. These findings seem to hold as long as there is no stigma attached to being bilingual and as long as children are not expected to abandon their first language to learn the second (Bialystok, 2001; Bialystok, Majumder, & Martin, 2003; Hamers & Blanc, 2000). Laura Petitto and Ioulia Kovelman (2003) suggest that perhaps humans evolved to speak multiple languages because this would have survival value, so maybe the "contemporary pockets of civilization where one language is spoken are the aberrant deviation; in other words, perhaps our brains were neurologically set to be multilingual" (p. 14). In addition, fluency in two or more languages is an asset when graduates enter the business world (Mears, 1998).

How and When Does Language Develop?

It is likely that many factors—biological, cultural, and experiential—play a role in language development. To master a language, children must (a) read the intentions of others to acquire the words, phrases, and concepts of their language and also (b) find patterns in the ways other people use these linguistic symbols to construct the grammar of their language (Tomasello, 2006). There are individual differences in language development. One conclusion of years of research is that children in social environments with "more adult-produced, child-directed speech—particularly speech that uses rich vocabulary and complex structure—acquire language more rapidly" (Hoff, 2006).

The important point is that children develop language as they develop other cognitive abilities by actively trying to make sense of what they hear and by looking for patterns and making up rules to put together the jigsaw puzzle of language. In this process, humans may have built-in biases, rules, and constraints about language that restrict the number of possibilities considered. Another built-in bias leads children to assume that the label refers to a class of similar objects. So the child learning about the rabbit is equipped naturally to assume that *rabbit* refers to the whole animal (not just its ears) and that other similar-looking animals are also rabbits (Jaswal & Markman, 2001; Markman, 1992). Reward and correction play a role in helping children learn correct language use, but the child's thinking in putting together the parts of this complicated system is very important (Waxman & Lidz, 2006). Table 6.1 on the next page shows the milestones of language development, ages 1 to 6, in Western cultures, along with ideas for encouraging language development.

SOUNDS AND PRONUNCIATION. **Phonology** is the study of how sounds function in a language system. A *phoneme* is the smallest unit of sound that can affect meaning: For example, in English, the *k* sound can change *at* to *cat*. By about age 5, most children have mastered the sounds of their native language, but a few may remain unconquered. In English, generally the *j* and *v* sounds and the consonant clusters of *th, zh, str, sl,* and *dr* are the last to develop (Owens, 2008). Young children may understand and be able to use many words, but they prefer to use the words they can pronounce easily.

As young children learn to hear differences in the sounds of language, they enjoy rhymes, songs, and general sound silliness. Young children like stories by Dr. Seuss partly because of the sounds, as is evident by the book titles—*All Aboard the Circus McGurkus* or *Wet Pet, Dry Pet, Your Pet, My Pet*. The young son of a friend of ours wanted to name his new baby sister *Brontosaurus* "just because it's fun to say."

VOCABULARY AND MEANING. As you can see in Table 6.1, children between ages 2 and 3 can *use* about 450 words (**expressive vocabulary**) even though they can *understand* many more (**receptive vocabulary**). By age 6, children's expressive vocabularies will grow to about 2,600 words and their receptive vocabulary will be an impressive 20,000 plus words (Otto, 2010). Children who are learning two languages at once tend to have smaller vocabularies in each language compared to children learning only one, at least in during childhood, but these size differences depend on the bilingual children's exposure to each language—more exposure, larger vocabulary (Hoff, 2006). In addition, the vocabulary of bilingual children is linked to the context in which they use each language, so children are more likely to

TABLE 6.1 • **Milestones in Language in the First 6 Years and Ways to Encourage Development**

AGE RANGE	MILESTONE	STRATEGIES TO ENCOURAGE DEVELOPMENT
By age 1	Says 1–2 words; responds to name; imitates familiar sounds; can follow simple instructions	• Respond to sounds and babbles • Sing songs and repeat nursery rhymes • Teach the names of familiar items and people • Play "peek-a-boo," "I spy with my little eye," and other simple games
Between 1 and 2	Uses 5–20 words, including names, says 2-word sentences; vocabulary is growing; gestures "bye-bye"; makes familiar "animal sounds"; can express wishes by saying words like "more" or "up"; understands "no"	• Acknowledge and encourage all efforts to use new words • Talk about everything you're doing while you're with the child • Use simple, clear language and speak slowly • Maintain eye contact when the child talks to you • Describe the world around the child—what he or she is seeing, hearing, or doing • Let the child listen to children's audio recordings.
Between 2 and 3	Can point to body parts; calls self "me" instead of name; combines nouns and verbs; vocabulary is about 450 words; uses short sentences; can identify 3–4 colors, knows *big* and *little*; enjoys hearing the same story over and over; can use some simple plurals; answers "where" questions	• Help the child listen and follow instructions by playing simple games • Repeat new words; use them over and over • Describe your actions, thoughts, and feelings • Give the child simple messages to communicate to others • Let the child know you understand by responding, smiling, and nodding your head • Expand what the child says. Child: "no nap!" You say, "Amaya does not want to take a nap."
Between 3 and 4	Sentences are about 4–5 words and vocabulary of about 1,000 words; knows last name, name of street, several nursery rhymes; tells a simple story	• Describe similarities and differences in objects • Support child's story telling with pictures and books • Encourage play with other children • Talk about trips, visits, outings, etc.
Between 4 and 5	Sentence length of 4–5 words; uses past tense; vocabulary of about 1,500 words; identifies colors, shapes; asks many questions like "why?" and "who?"	• Help the child create and use categories—food, pets, friends, colors, etc. • Teach the child how to use the telephone and how to call for help • Involve the child when you plan activities and encourage the child to make some plans • Use the child's interests as a focus of conversations • Encourage storytelling and listen to the stories
Between 5 and 6	Sentence length of 5–6 words and expressive vocabulary of about 2,600 words; defines objects by their use; knows spatial relations (like "on top" and "far") and opposites; knows address; understands same and different; uses all types of sentences	• Encourage children when they talk about feelings, thoughts, hopes, fears • Sing songs, rhymes • Talk with them as you would an adult
At every age		• Listen and show your pleasure when the child talks to you • Carry on conversations with the child • Ask questions to get the child to think and talk • Read books to the child every day, increasing in length as the child develops

Source: Based on: http://www.ldonline.org/ld_indepth/speech-language/lda_milestones.html
http://www.med.umich.edu/1libr/yourchild/devmile.htm

know more academic words in the language they use in school. If you combine vocabulary knowledge for bilingual children—the total number of concepts that they have words for from both languages—vocabulary size likely is the same for bilingual and monolingual children (Pearson, Fernandez, Lewedeg, & Oller, 1997).

By some estimates, children learn about 10 words a day between the ages of 1 and 18 (Bloom, 2002). How is this incredible rate of learning possible? Researchers describe a process called **fast-mapping**—children hear a word once and quickly locate the meaning on their mental map of the language, based on what they already know or what is "close by" on the map. So if they already know that *blue* is a color, they can map the meaning of *turquoise* quickly when they are told it is a color. This fast-mapping is amazingly, well, fast. One study showed that children as young as 2 could fast-map a new word after only a 3-second exposure (Halberda, 2003a). Children can fast-map nouns and adjectives, map several words at a time, and can even map from television. But the learning may be a rough estimate of the exact meaning—*turquoise* is some kind of color, for example. Refining the precise meaning takes a bit more time and experience with different color concepts (Flavell, Miller, & Miller, 2002). More accurate fast-mapping is supported when adults provide more cues as part of extended and rich conversations (Mintz, 2005).

Children generally fast-map concrete nouns and action verbs that can be pointed to or demonstrated before mapping more abstract words that denote relations or comparisons (*big—little* or *tall—short*). But even when they learn the meaning of a relational word such as *big* or *tall*, children may have very specific meanings for these words—the meanings they first mapped. So a child may insist that a tall glass can't be tall because it is not as high as a tree that his parents called "tall."

Another process in learning words is **mutual exclusivity**—the assumption that each object in the world belongs in just one category, so it has just one category label (Markman, 1992; Markman, Wasow, & Hansen, 2003). Imagine this situation. Brian, a 4-year-old boy, is shown two objects—a key (he knows the word *key*)—and a soda bottle vacuum stopper he has never seen. An adult asks Brian to give him the *blicket*. Like most children, Brian selects the soda bottle vacuum stopper as the *blicket* because he knows the key is not a *blicket*. So without being told that the unknown object was a blicket, Brian learned the name indirectly by comparing it to a known object. In one study, six different familiar and unfamiliar pairs of objects were used (a key and a soda bottle vacuum stopper, a spoon and a honey dipper, etc.), and the adult actually pointed to the familiar object while asking, "Can you give me the blicket?" Still, the children in the study selected the unfamiliar object as the blicket (in spite of the pointing) over 87% of the time (Jaswal & Hansen, 2006).

Young children begin to elaborate on their simple language by adding plurals; endings for verbs such as *-ed* and *-ing*; small words such as *and, but,* and *in*; and articles (*a, the*); and by using possessives (the *girl's* hair). A classic study by Jean Berko (1958) demonstrated that children could even apply these rules for making plurals, possessives, or past tense verbs to words that they had never encountered. For example, when shown a picture of a single "wug" (see Figure 6.1 on the next page), the preschool children in the study could answer correctly "wugs" when the researcher said, "Now there is another one. There are two of them. There are two ______."

In the process of figuring out the rules governing these aspects of language, children make some very interesting mistakes.

LEARNING GRAMMAR AND SYNTAX. For a brief time, children may use irregular forms of particular words properly, as if they are saying what they have heard. Then, as they begin to learn rules, they **overregularize** words by applying the rules to everything. Children who once said "Our car is broken" begin to insist, "Our car is broked." A child who once talked about her *feet* may discover the "*s*" for plurals and refer to her *foots* or *feets,* then learn about *-es* for plurals (*horses, kisses*) and describe her *footses,* before she finally returns to talking about her *feet* (Flavell, Miller, & Miller, 2002). Parents often wonder why their child seems to be "regressing." Actually, these "mistakes" show how logical and rational children can be as they try to assimilate new words into existing schemes (review Piaget's theory in Chapter 2 for a discussion of *assimilation* and *schemes*). Apparently these overregularizations

FIGURE 6.1

BERKO'S WUG TEST

Jean Berko (1958) used these pictures and questions to study preschool children's understanding of English language rules for making plurals, possessives, present tense, and past tense.

This is a wug.

Now there is another one.
There are two of them.
There are two ________

This is a man who knows how to rick.
He is ricking. He did the same thing yesterday. What did he do yesterday?
Yesterday he ________________

Source: From The child's learning of English morphology in Word, *14 by Jean Berko, ©1958, pp. 150–177. Used with permission of the International Linguistic Association.*

happen in all languages, including American Sign Language. Because most languages have many irregular words, *accommodation* (Piaget's term) is necessary in mastering language. One interesting finding was that girls tend to overregularize verb tenses more than boys, so they are more likely to say "holded" instead of "held." Joshua Hartshore and Michael Ullman (2006) speculate that because girls may have better memory for words, they have better access to similar words (*folded, molded, scolded*) and generalize to "holded"; thus, "girls' hypothesized superior lexical memory abilities may lead to more rather than fewer over-regularizations, thanks to their memorization and associative generalization of regular past-tense forms" (p. 31).

Copyright © 2000 Sidney Harris. Reprinted with permission of Sidney Harris. ScienceCartoonsPlus.com.

Children master the basics of word order, or **syntax,** in their native language early. Another aspect of overregularizing language involves syntax. Because the usual order in English is subject-verb-object, preschoolers just mastering the rules of language have trouble with sentences in any different order. For example, if 4-year-old Justin hears a statement in the passive voice, such as "The truck was bumped by the car," he probably thinks the truck did the bumping to the car because "truck" came first in the sentence. Interestingly, however, in languages where the passive voice is more important, such as the South African language Sesotho, children use this construction much earlier, as young as 3 or 4 (Demuth, 1990). So in talking with young children, in English at least, it is generally better to use direct language—not passive. If you use passive constructions, immediately rephrase in active language. By early elementary school, many children can understand the meaning of passive sentences, but they do not use such constructions in their normal conversations, unless the passive construction is common in their culture.

PRAGMATICS: USING LANGUAGE IN SOCIAL SITUATIONS. **Pragmatics** involves the appropriate use of language to communicate in social situations—how to enter a conversation, tell a joke, interrupt, keep a conversation going, or adjust your language for the listener. For instance, children must learn the rules of turn-taking in conversation. Young children may appear to take turns in conversations, but if you listen in, you realize that they are not exchanging information, only talk time. Even so, they are learning and practicing the pragmatics of conversations.

Children show an understanding of pragmatics when they talk in simpler sentences to younger children or command their pets to "Come here!" in louder, deeper voices (Rice, 1984). Children as young as 2 provide more details in their descriptions of a situation to a parent who was not there than they do in descriptions they give to a parent who had experienced the situation with them. So even young children seem quite able to fit their language to the situation, at least with familiar people (Flavell, Miller, & Miller, 2002).

There are cultural differences in pragmatics, even within the same spoken language. For example, Shirley Brice Heath (1989) spent many hours observing White middle-class parents and African American families who were poor. She found that the adults asked different kinds of questions and encouraged different kinds of "talk." White parents asked test-like questions with right answers, such as "How many cars are there?" or "Which car is bigger?" These questions seem odd to African American children, whose families don't ask about what they already know. The African American child might wonder, "Why would my aunt ask me how many cars? She can see there are 3." Instead, Heath found that African American families encourage rich storytelling and also teasing that hones their children's quick wit and assertive responses.

Emergent Literacy

Today, in most languages, reading is a cornerstone of learning, and the foundation for reading is built in early childhood. But young children vary greatly in their knowledge and skills related to reading, so research has expanded to study what supports these emerging literacy skills. **Emergent literacy** is made up of the skills, knowledge, and attitudes that develop along the way as children learn to read and write, as well as the environments and contexts that support these developments (Whitehurst & Lonigan, 1998). Look at the picture of a 4-year-old's story and grocery list to see some emerging literacy skills.

What are the most important skills that help literacy emerge? Here, the answers are not certain, but research has identified two broad categories of skills that are important for later reading: (1) skills related to understanding sounds and codes such as knowing that letters have names, that sounds are associated with letters, and that words are made up of sounds in a sequence (this last skill often is called **phonemic awareness**), and (2) oral language skills such as expressive and receptive vocabulary, knowledge of syntax, and the ability to understand and tell stories (Dickinson, McCabe, Anastopoulos, Peisner-Feinberg, & Poe, 2003; Storch & Whitehurst, 2002). Some educators have emphasized code skills and others oral language, but a study by the National Institute of Child Health and Human Development Early Childhood Research Network (2005a) that followed over 1,000 children from age 3 through third grade found that oral language skills at age 4½ predicted word decoding in first grade and reading comprehension in third grade. The NICHD researchers concluded, "most recent investigations find that preschool oral language skills [for example, size of vocabulary, ability to use syntax, ability to understand and tell stories] play an important role alongside code skills in predicting reading in the transition to school" (p. 439).

This child knows quite a bit about reading and writing—letters have different forms, letters make words that communicate meaning, writing goes from left to right and lists go down the page, and stories look different than shopping lists.

The relationships found were more than simple correlations, so there is evidence that both code and oral language skills are necessary for later literacy. In fact, these sets of skills probably support each other in the process of learning to read and write.

One way to think about emergent literacy that captures both code and oral language skills for emergent literacy is the notion of **inside-out skills** and **outside-in skills** and processes, described in Table 6.2. This model, developed by Grover Whitehurst and Christopher Lonigan (1998), includes two interdependent sets of skills and processes.

> A reader must decode units of print into units of sound and units of sound into units of language. This is an inside-out process. However, being able to say a written word or series of written words is only a part of reading. The fluent reader must understand those auditory derivations, which involves placing them in the correct conceptual and contextual framework. This is an outside-in process. (p. 855)

For example, to understand even a simple sentence in print, such as "She ordered a camera from Amazon?" the reader must know about letters, sounds, grammar, and punctuation. The reader also has to remember the first words as he is reading the last ones. But these inside-out skills are not enough. To understand, the reader needs to have conceptual knowledge—what is a camera? What does it mean to order? Is this the Amazon River or Amazon online? Why the question mark? Who is asking? How does this sentence fit in the context of the story? Answering these questions takes outside-in skills and knowledge.

TABLE 6.2 • **Components of Emergent Literacy**

COMPONENT	BRIEF DEFINITION	EXAMPLE
OUTSIDE-IN PROCESSES		
Language	Semantic, syntactic, and conceptual knowledge	A child reads the word "bat" and connects the meaning to knowledge of baseball or flying mammals.
Narrative	Understanding and producing narrative	A child can tell a story; understands that books have stories.
Conventions of print	Knowledge of standard print formats	The child understands that print is read from left-to-right and front-to-back in English; understands the difference between pictures and print or the cover and the inside of the book.
Emergent reading	Pretending to read	Child takes a favorite book and retells the "story," often by using pictures as cues.
INSIDE-OUT PROCESSES		
Knowledge of graphemes	Letter-name knowledge	A child can recognize letters and name letters.
Phonological awareness	Detection of rhyme; manipulation of syllables; manipulation of individual phonemes	A child can tell you words that rhyme with "hat." A child can clap as she says sounds in a word *cat*: /k/ /ă/ /t/.
Syntactic awareness	Repair grammatical errors	A child says, "No! you say I *went* to the zoo, not I *goed* to the zoo."
Phoneme-grapheme correspondence	Letter-sound knowledge	The child can answer the question, "What sounds do these letters make?"
Emergent writing	Phonetic spelling	The child writes "eenuf," or ""hambrgr."
Other Factors	Emergent literacy also depends on other factors such as short-term memory for sounds and sequences, the ability to recognize and name lists of letters, motivation, and interest.	

Source: Adapted from G. J. Whitehurst & C. J. Lonigan (1998). Child development and emergent literacy. Child Development, 69, p. 850. Reprinted with permission of John Wiley & Sons, Inc.

BUILDING A FOUNDATION. What builds this foundation of emergent literacy skills? Two related activities are critical: (1) conversations with adults that develop knowledge about language and (2) joint reading, using books as supports for talk about letters, sounds, words, pictures, and concepts (NIL, 2008; Whitehurst & Lonigan, 1998). Especially in the early years, children's home experiences are central in the development of language and literacy (Burgess, Hecht & Lonigan, 2002; Sénéchal & LeFevre, 2002). In homes that promote literacy, parents and other adults value reading as a source of pleasure, and there are books and other printed materials everywhere. Parents read to their children (even a few minutes a day is helpful), take them to bookstores and libraries, limit the amount of television everyone watches, and encourage literacy-related play such as setting up a pretend school or writing "letters" (Pressley, 1996; Snow, 1993; Zeece, 2008). For all children, teachers and childcare workers can help, as you can see in the ***Connecting with Children*** suggestions.

CONNECTING WITH CHILDREN

Guidelines for Teachers and Families: Supporting Language and Emergent Literacy

FAMILIES

Read with your children.

Examples

1. Help children understand that books contain stories, they can visit the stories as often as the like, the pictures in the books go along with the story meaning, and the words are always the same when they visit the story—that's reading! (Hulit, Howard, & Fahey, 2011)
2. Have a nighttime reading ritual.

Choose appropriate books and stories.

Examples

1. Books should have simple plots and clear illustrations.
2. Illustrations should precede the text related to the illustration. This helps children learn to predict what is coming next.
3. Language should be repetitive, rhythmic, and natural.

Use stories as a springboard for conversations.

Examples

1. Retell stories you have read with your child.
2. Talk about the words, activities, and objects in the books. Do you have anything like these in your home?

CHILDCARE WORKERS AND TEACHERS

Communicate with families about the goals and activities of your program.

Examples

1. Have someone from the school, the community, or even an older student translate anything you plan to send home into the language of the family that will be reading the material.
2. Send home a newsletter giving suggestions for home activities that support emergent literacy.

Involve families in decisions about literacy activities.

Examples

1. Have planning workshops at times family members can attend—provide child care for younger siblings, but let children and families work together on projects.
2. Invite parents to come to class to read to children, take dictation of stories, tell stories, record or bind books, and demonstrate skills.

Identify and build on strengths the families already have (Delpit, 2003).

Examples

1. Find out about the histories, stories, and skills of family members. Children can draw or write about these.
2. Show respect for the student's language by celebrating poets or songs from the language.

Provide home activities to be shared with family members.

Examples

1. Encourage family members to work with children to read and follow simple recipes, play language games, keep diaries or journals for the family, and visit the library. Get feedback from families or children about the activities.
2. Provide lists of good children's literature available locally—work with libraries, clubs, and churches to identify sources.
3. Encourage families to use wordless books and have their children dictate stories to fit the pictures—write the story together (Jalongo, Dragich, Conrad, & Zhang, 2002).

For more information on Family Literacy Partnerships, see: http://www.famlit.org/

Source: From Born to talk: An introduction to speech and language development *(5th ed.) by L. M. Hulit, M. R. Howard., & K. R. Fahey. Published by Allyn & Bacon, Boston, MA. Copyright © 2011 by Pearson Education. Reprinted by permission of the publisher.*

RELATING TO EVERY CHILD

▸Teaching Bilingual Students to Read

MANY YOUNG CHILDREN begin school knowing one language—the language of their parents. Some children, however, are bilingual—they begin school already speaking two languages. No matter what the child's language or languages, emergent literacy skills are critical for school readiness (Hammer, Farkas, & Maczuga, 2010).

Most school programs expect all children to learn to read in English. According to new research, this emphasis on reading only in English may not be necessary. In fact, one key factor may facilitate literacy development—growth in receptive language. *Receptive* language is made up of the words and language structures you understand, even if you do not use them in your *expressive* language, the words and structures you actually use when you talk. For example, by age 6, even though children's expressive vocabularies include about 2,600 words, their receptive vocabularies are much larger—about 20,000 plus words (Otto, 2010).

Carol Hammer and her colleagues have done extensive research on literacy development for bilingual students. In one study, they followed 88 children for two years in a Head Start program (Hammer, Lawrence, & Miccio, 2007). The mothers of all the children spoke the Puerto Rican dialect of Spanish. There actually were two groups of students—those who had been expected to speak both English and Spanish from birth and those who were not expected to learn English until they started Head Start at age 3. The researchers found that it was not a particular score on any test, but *growth in receptive language* in general during the program that predicated early reading outcomes—and it did not matter if the students spoke English and Spanish from birth or if they just started speaking English in school.

The researchers concluded "that growth in children's English receptive language abilities during Head Start, as opposed to the level of English they had achieved by the end of Head Start, positively predicted the children's emergent reading abilities in English and the children's ability to identify letters and words in English. This was the case regardless of the level of the children's prior exposure to English" (p. 243). In addition, growth in Spanish language abilities predicted reading performance in Spanish. One implication is that teachers and parents should focus on continuing language development and not worry about rushing children into speaking English exclusively. As Hammer and her colleagues note, "if bilingual children's language growth is progressing well in either Spanish or English during the preschool years, positive early English and Spanish reading outcomes result in kindergarten" (p. 244). These findings are consistent with the recommendations of the Society for Research in Child Development: "Investing in dual-language instead of English-only programs and encouraging pre-kindergarten attendance can improve learning opportunities for Hispanic children and increase their chances of success" (SRCD, 2009, p. 1). See the ***Connecting with Children*** guidelines for ideas.

Growth in receptive language in general during Head Start predicated early reading outcomes—both for students who spoke English and Spanish from birth and for those who just started speaking English in school.

EMERGENT LITERACY AND BILINGUAL CHILDREN. Parent involvement and quality preschools support emergent literacy in both English and Spanish. When Spanish-speaking and bilingual parents are more involved with their young children in literacy activities, the children's oral language improves in both English and in Spanish (Farver, 2007). In addition, preschool children who participated in an English-only preschool literacy program improved in their English skills, but the preschoolers who began the program in Spanish and transitioned to English improved both their English and their Spanish literacy skills (Farver, Lonigan, & Eppe, 2009). See ***Relating to Every Child*** for an example of research in this area.

PIAGET AND VYGOTSKY

Language is a major cognitive accomplishment of early childhood. In fact, when children have difficulties in their language development, it often is because they have problems in cognitive abilities (Colledge et al., 2002). Two early theorists provided insight into cognitive abilities: Jean Piaget and Lev Vygotsky.

Preoperational Thinking: Piaget

By the end of the sensorimotor stage, at about age 2, the child can use many goal-directed action schemes—searching for a lost toy, for example, or throwing a spoon to the floor in a game of "how many times will you pick this up?" with parents. As long as these schemes remain tied to physical actions, however, they are of no use in recalling the past, keeping track of information, or planning. For this, children need what Piaget called **operations,** or actions that are carried out and reversed mentally rather than physically, such as mentally pouring the water from the thin tall glass back into the short fat glass to confirm that the amount of water stays the same. The stage after the sensorimotor period is called **preoperational** (roughly ages 2 to 7), because the child has not yet mastered these mental operations, but is moving toward mastery. During this time, children are developing important abilities to represent actions internally—to "think" about actions (Piaget, 1970a, 1971).

ADVANCES IN THE PREOPERATIONAL STAGE. According to Piaget, the first type of thinking that is separate from action involves making action schemes symbolic. *Symbols* are representations that look similar to what they stand for—a picture of a tree symbolizing a tree, for example, or a child pretending to drink from a cup. *Signs* are more arbitrary; like alphabets or numbers, they represent things or ideas without necessarily looking like them. The ability to form and use signs and symbols—words, gestures, images, sounds, and so on—is a major accomplishment of the preoperational period and moves children closer to mastering the mental operations of the next stage.

This ability to work with signs and symbols, such as using the word "horse" or a picture of a horse or even pretending to ride a horse to represent a real horse that is not actually present, is called the **semiotic function.** In fact, the child's earliest use of symbols is in pretending. Children who are not yet able to talk will often use action symbols—pretending to stir food in an empty bowl cup or touching a toothbrush to their teeth, showing that they know what each object is for. This behavior also shows that their schemes are becoming more general and less tied to specific actions. The eating scheme, for example, may be used in playing house.

There is an order to the development of the semiotic function. Young children are first able to use *deferred imagination*—to imitate actions or sounds of objects or people not present. For example, a child may scold the dog with words and a voice tone he heard his older sister use earlier. Then comes *symbolic play*—the child uses a piece of wood as a boat or a house. Next to develop is *drawing* that moves from scribbles to drawings that represent something, although that something may be obvious only to the child artist. Finally, children are able to create *mental images* of objects or people—they have a "picture in their minds" of things that are not moving like their pet dog or a cartoon character. Mental images in motion take longer to develop (Wadsworth, 2004).

Of course, as we saw earlier, during the preoperational stage, we also see the rapid development of that very important symbol system, *language*. Between the ages of 2 and 6, most children enlarge their vocabulary from about 200 to 20,000 words. The development of the semiotic system of language opens many more possibilities for thinking, remembering, planning, and problem solving.

Even though young children know a great deal, they still have limited understandings about their world and they lack key cognitive operations.

LIMITATIONS OF THE PREOPERATIONAL STAGE. As the child moves through the preoperational stage, the developing ability to think about objects in symbolic form remains somewhat limited to thinking in one direction only, or using *one-way logic*. It is very difficult for the child to "think backwards," or imagine how to reverse the steps in a task. Remember Justin's difficulties with the passive voice? In order to make sense of the sentence "The truck was bumped by the car," Justin must mentally undo and then redo the sequence by translating from the passive voice "was bumped" to the active voice, "The car bumped the truck." This translation requires **reversible thinking**—mentally undoing and redoing an event, and preschool children have not yet mastered this ability (Davies, 2004; Piaget, 1970a, 1974). Reversible thinking is involved in many other tasks that are difficult for the preoperational child, such as conservation. What is conservation? Read on.

Conservation is the principle that the amount or number of something remains the same even if the arrangement or appearance is changed, as long as nothing is added and nothing is taken away. You know that if you tear a piece of paper into several pieces, you will still have the same amount of paper. To prove this, you know that you can reverse the process by taping the pieces back together; however, this kind of thinking is difficult for young children. The principle of conservation applies in several areas—number, area, volume, mass, and weight. The ability to conserve in these different areas develops slowly between ages 6 and 7, but conservation of weight takes a few years longer. A classic example of difficulty with conservation is found in the preoperational child's response to the following Piagetian task, described in Figure 6.2.

Piaget's explanation for Amaya's answer is that she is focusing, or centering, attention on the dimension of height. She has difficulty considering more than one aspect of the situation at a time, or **decentering.** The preoperational child cannot understand that decreased diameter compensates for increased height because this would require taking into account two dimensions at once. Thus, children at the preoperational stage have trouble

FIGURE 6.2

EXAMPLE OF CONSERVATION OF LIQUID

In a test of conservation, Amaya is shown two short, fat glasses filled with the same amount of colored liquid. She agrees the amounts are "the same." Then the experimenter pours one of the glasses into a tall, narrower glass and asks, "Now, does one glass have more water, or are they the same?" Amaya responds that the tall glass has more because "It goes up more here" (she points to a higher level on the taller glass).

freeing themselves from their own immediate perceptions of how the world appears. At the beginning of this chapter we described five basic cognitive abilities that develop during the preschool years. As Amaya improves in two of those abilities, integrating the past with the present and reflecting on the causes of changes, she will be able to understand that the current situation (taller glass of water) is still connected to the past situation (shorter, wider glass of water) and the change in glass shape may have caused the water to go higher (Bruner & Herschkowitz, 2005).

This brings us to another important characteristic of the preoperational stage. Preoperational children, according to Piaget, have a tendency to be **egocentric,** that is, they see the world and the experiences of others from their own viewpoint. *Egocentric,* as Piaget intended it, does not mean selfish; it simply means that children often assume everyone else shares their feelings, reactions, and perspectives. For example, if a little boy at this stage is afraid of dogs, he may assume that all children share this fear. Very young children center on their own perceptions and on the way the situation appears to them. This is one reason it is difficult for preoperational children to understand that your right hand is not on the same side as theirs when you are facing them.

Egocentrism is also evident in the child's language. You may have seen young children happily talking about what they are doing even though no one is listening. This can happen when the child is alone or, even more often, in a group of children: Each child talks enthusiastically, without any real interaction or conversation. Piaget called this the **collective monologue.**

Research has shown that young children are not totally egocentric in every situation, however. Young children do seem quite able to take the needs and different perspectives of others into account, at least in certain situations. For example, when asked by a researcher, 3- and 4-year-olds can place objects where another person or doll would be able to either see the object or not see it, so they can take the visual perspective of another into account (Harris, 2006; Newcombe & Huttenlocher, 1993). In fairness to young children, even adults can make assumptions that others feel or think like they do. For example, have you ever gotten a gift that the giver loved but was clearly inappropriate for you?

Piaget has taught us that we can learn a great deal about how children think by listening carefully, by paying close attention to their ways of solving problems. If we understand children's thinking, we will be better able to match educational experiences to children's current knowledge and abilities. In the early childhood years, activity and play are important educational experiences. The ***Connecting with Children*** guidelines on the next page give suggestions about the care of preoperational thinkers.

LIMITATIONS OF PIAGET'S THEORIES. Piaget taught us that children do not think like adults. His influence on developmental psychology and education has been enormous, even though recent research has not supported all of his ideas. It now appears that Piaget underestimated the cognitive abilities of young children. The problems he gave them may have been too difficult and the directions too confusing. His subjects may have understood more than they could show on these problems. For example, work by Gelman and her colleagues (Gelman, 2000; Gelman & Cordes, 2001) shows that preschool children know much more about the concept of number than Piaget thought, even if they sometimes make mistakes or get confused. As long as preschoolers work with only three or four objects at a time, they can tell that the number remains the same, even if the objects are spread far apart or clumped close together. So, we may be born with a greater store of cognitive tools than Piaget suggested.

Research across different cultures has generally confirmed that Piaget was accurate in the characteristic ways of thinking and the sequence of the stages he described, but age ranges for the stages vary. Western children typically move to the next stage about 2 to 3 years earlier than children in non-Western societies. But careful research has shown that these differences across cultures depend on the subject or domain tested and how much the culture values and teaches knowledge in that domain. For example, children in Brazil who

CONNECTING WITH CHILDREN

Guidelines for Teachers and Families: Caring for the Preoperational Child

Use concrete props and visual aids whenever possible.
Examples
1. When you discuss concepts such as "part," "whole," or "one-half," use shapes on a felt board or cardboard "pizzas" to demonstrate.
2. Let children add and subtract with sticks, rocks, or colored chips. This technique also is helpful for early concrete-operational children.

Make instructions relatively short—not too many steps at once. Use actions as well as words.
Examples
1. When giving instructions about how to enter the room after recess and prepare for social studies, ask a child to demonstrate the procedure for the rest of the class by walking in quietly, going straight to his or her seat, and placing the text, paper, and a pencil on his or her desk.
2. Explain a game by acting out one of the parts.
3. Show children what their finished papers should look like. Use an overhead projector or display examples where children can see them easily.

Help children develop their ability to see the world from someone else's point of view.
Examples
1. Discuss how characters in books, siblings, or playmates might feel when something happens.
2. Avoid long lectures on "sharing" or being "nice." Instead, be clear about rules for sharing or use of material.
3. Help children understand the value of the rules and develop empathy by asking them to think about how they would like to be treated.

Be sensitive to the possibility that children may have different meanings for the same word or different words for the same meaning. Children may also expect everyone to understand words they have invented.
Examples
1. If a child protests, "I won't take a nap. I'll just rest!" when she is away from home, be aware that a nap may mean something such as "having my stuffed animals and being in my bed at home."
2. Ask children to explain the meanings of their invented words.

Give children a great deal of hands-on practice with the skills that serve as building blocks for more complex skills such as reading comprehension or collaboration.
Examples
1. Provide cut-out letters to build words.
2. Include the child in cooking, building projects, or dividing a batch of popcorn equally for the family or class.
3. Allow children to clip from used magazines pictures of people collaborating—families, workers, educators, children all helping each other.

Provide a wide range of experiences in order to build a foundation for concept learning and language.
Examples
1. Take trips to zoos, gardens, theaters, and concerts; make sure to talk about the experiences later.
2. Give children words to describe what they are doing, hearing, seeing, touching, tasting, and smelling.

For ideas about and connections between Piaget and the Reggio Emilia approach, see http://www.aquinas.edu/education/ece/reggio.html

sell candy in the streets instead of attending school appear to fail a certain kind of Piagetian task—class inclusion (*Are there more daisies, more tulips, or more flowers in the picture?*). But when the tasks are phrased in concepts they understand—selling candy—then these children perform better that Brazilian children the same age who attend school (Saxe, 1999). So cultural differences and the type of tasks used affect children's performances on Piaget's assessments.

One theory that includes culture as a major component of children's cognitive development was proposed by Lev Vygotsky, described next.

Vygotsky: The Beginning of Self-Regulation

At the beginning of the chapter we described five general abilities that develop during the preschool years. Two of the abilities, anticipating the future and appreciating causality, are involved in regulating your own thinking and actions. Language plays an important role in developing self-regulation as well.

THE ROLE OF LANGUAGE AND PRIVATE SPEECH. Vygotsky believed that **cultural tools,** including material tools (pencils, computers, and so on) and psychological tools (signs and symbol systems such as numbers, maps, and language) play very important roles in cognitive development.

In Vygotsky's theory, language is the most important symbol system in the cultural tool kit, and it is the one that helps to fill the kit with other tools. Vygotsky placed more emphasis than Piaget on the role of language in cognitive development. He believed that "thinking depends on speech, on the means of thinking, and on the child's socio-cultural experience" (1987, p. 120). In fact, Vygotsky believed that language in the form of private speech (talking to yourself) guides cognitive development. If you have spent much time around young children, you know that they often talk to themselves as they play. Vygotsky suggested that these mutterings, called **private speech,** play an important role in cognitive development by moving children toward **self-regulation,** the ability to anticipate the future, and to plan, monitor, and guide one's own thinking and problem solving.

This child is learning to use an important cultural tool—a computer—and the "teacher" is a more expert peer.

Vygotsky explained that self-regulation developed in a series of stages. First, the child's behavior is regulated by others using language and other signs such as gestures. For example, the parent says, "No!" when the child reaches toward a candle flame. Next, the child learns to regulate the behavior of others using the same language tools. The child says, "No!" to another child who is trying to take away a toy, often even imitating the parent's voice tone. The child also begins to use private speech to regulate her own behavior, saying "no" quietly to herself, as she is tempted to touch the flame. Finally, the child learns to regulate her own behavior by using silent inner speech (Karpov & Haywood, 1998). The use of private speech peaks at around 9 years and then decreases, although one study found that some children from ages 11 to 17 still spontaneously muttered to themselves during problem solving (McCafferty, 2004; Winsler, Carlton, & Barry, 2000; Winsler & Naglieri, 2003).

This series of steps from spoken words to silent inner speech is another example of how higher mental functions appear first between people as they communicate and regulate each other's behavior, and then emerge again within the individual as cognitive processes. Through this fundamental process the child is using language to accomplish important cognitive activities such as directing attention, solving problems, planning, forming concepts, and gaining self-control. Research supports Vygotsky's ideas (Berk & Spuhl, 1995; Emerson & Miyake, 2003). Children and adults tend to use more private speech when they are confused, having difficulties, or making mistakes (Duncan & Cheyne, 1999). Inner speech not only helps us solve problems but also allows us to regulate our behavior. Have you ever thought to yourself something like, "Let's see, the first step is" or "Where did I use my glasses last?" or "If I work to the end of this page, then I can . . ."? You were using inner speech to remind, cue, encourage, or guide yourself. In a really tough situation, such as taking an important test, you might even find that you return to muttering out loud.

Because private speech helps children to regulate their thinking, it makes sense to allow, and even encourage, children to use private speech at home and in school. Insisting on total silence when young children are working on difficult problems may make the work even harder for them. One approach, called *cognitive self-instruction,* teaches children to use self-talk to guide learning. For example, children learn to give themselves reminders to go slowly and carefully.

LIMITATIONS OF VYGOTSKY'S THEORIES. Vygotsky added important considerations by highlighting the role of culture and social processes in cognitive development, but he may have gone too far. As we have seen in this chapter, we may be born with a greater store of cognitive tools than either Piaget or Vygotsky suggested. Some basic understandings, such as the idea that adding increases quantity, may be part of our biological predispositions, ready for use to guide our cognitive development. Young children appear to figure out a great deal about the world before they have the chance to learn from their culture or more capable adults and peers (Schunk, 2004). Also, Vygotsky did not detail the cognitive processes underlying developmental changes: Which cognitive processes allow children to engage in more advanced and independent participation in social activities? The major limitation of Vygotsky's theory, however, is that it consists mostly of general ideas; Vygotsky died before he could expand and elaborate his ideas and pursue his research. His students continued to investigate his ideas, but much of that work was suppressed until the 1950s and 1960s by Josef Stalin's dictatorial regime that stifled scientific development and the free flow of ideas in the Soviet Union (Gredler, 2005; Kozulin, 2003; Kozulin & Presseisen, 1995). A final limitation might be that Vygotsky did not have time to detail the applications of his theories. As a result, others have created most of the applications described today—and we don't know if Vygotsky would have agreed with them.

Comparing Piaget and Vygotsky

SELF-TALK. Piaget called children's self-directed talk "egocentric speech." He assumed that this egocentric speech is another indication that young children can't see the world through the eyes of others. They talk about what matters to them, without taking into account the needs or interests of their listeners. As they mature, and especially as they have disagreements with peers, Piaget believed, children develop socialized speech. They learn to listen and exchange (or argue about) ideas. As you saw above, Vygotsky had very different ideas about young children's private speech. Rather than being a sign of cognitive immaturity, it is a necessary stage in the development of self-regulation. Table 6.3 contrasts Piaget's and Vygotsky's theories of private speech. We should note that Piaget came to accept many of Vygotsky's arguments and agreed that language could be used in both egocentric and problem-solving ways (Piaget, 1962).

LEARNING AND DEVELOPMENT. Piaget defined *development* as the active construction of knowledge and *learning* as the passive formation of associations (Siegler, 2000). He was interested in knowledge construction and believed that cognitive development has to

TABLE 6.3 • **Differences between Piaget's and Vygotsky's Theories of Egocentric or Private Speech**

	PIAGET	VYGOTSKY
Developmental Significance	Represents an inability to take the perspective of another and engage in reciprocal communication.	Represents externalized thought; its function is to communicate with the self for the purpose of self-guidance and self-direction.
Course of Development	Declines with age.	Increases at younger ages and then gradually loses its audible quality to become internal verbal thought.
Relationship to Social Speech	Negative; least socially and cognitively mature children use more egocentric speech.	Positive; private speech develops out of social interaction with others.
Relationship to Environmental Contexts	—	Increases with task difficulty. Private speech serves a helpful self-guiding function in situations where more cognitive effort is needed to reach a solution.

come before learning: The child had to be cognitively "ready" to learn. He said that "learning is subordinated to development and not vice-versa" (Piaget, 1964, p. 17). Children can memorize, for example, that Geneva is in Switzerland, but still insist that they cannot be Genevan and Swiss at the same time. True understanding will happen only when the child has developed the operation of *class inclusion*—that one category can be included in another.

In contrast, Vygotsky believed that learning was an active process that does not have to wait for readiness. In fact, "properly organized learning results in mental development and sets in motion a variety of developmental processes that would be impossible apart from *learning*" (Vygotsky, 1978, p. 90). He saw learning as a tool in development—learning pulls development up to higher levels and social interaction is a key in learning (Glassman, 2001; Wink & Putney, 2002). Vygotsky's belief that learning pulls development to higher levels means that other people, including family members and teachers, play significant roles in cognitive development.

Piaget and Vygotsky: Implications for Early Childhood Education

Piaget was more interested in understanding children's thinking than in guiding educators. He did express some general ideas about educational philosophy, however. He believed that the main goal of education should be to help children learn how to learn (Piaget, 1969). Even though he did not design programs of education based on his ideas, many other people have. For example, the National Association for the Education of Young Children has guidelines for developmentally appropriate education that incorporate Piaget's findings (Copple & Bredekamp, 2009). Some of these guidelines are in Table 6.7 on page 234.

PIAGET: THE VALUE OF ACTIVITY AND PLAY. We saw in Chapter 5 that the brain develops with stimulation, and activity provides some of that stimulation at every age. Babies in the sensorimotor stage learn by exploring, sucking, pounding, shaking, throwing—acting on their environments. Preoperational preschoolers love pretend play and through pretending form symbols, use language, and interact with others. They are beginning to play simple games with predictable rules.

As with so many other topics, there are cultural differences in play (as Vygotsky probably would emphasize). In some cultures, such as American or Turkish, adults, particularly mothers, often are play partners with their children. But in other cultures such as East Indian, Indonesian, or Mayan, adults are not seen as appropriate play partners for children; siblings and peers are the ones who teach younger children to how to participate in play activities (Gaskins, 1996, 2000; Vandermass-Peler, 2002). In some families and cultures, children spend more time helping with chores and less time in solitary or group play. Different materials and "toys" are used as available—everything from expensive video games to sticks, rocks, and banana leaves. Children use what their culture provides to play.

VYGOTSKY: THE VALUE OF ASSISTED LEARNING AND CULTURAL TOOLS. Vygotsky's theory suggests that teachers need to do more than just arrange the environment so that children can discover on their own. Children cannot and should not be expected to reinvent or rediscover knowledge and tools already available in their cultures. Rather, they should be guided and assisted in their learning—so Vygotsky saw teachers, parents, and other adults as central to the child's learning and development (Karpov & Haywood, 1998). **Assisted learning,** or **guided participation,** requires support and scaffolding—giving information, prompts, reminders, and encouragement at the right time and in the right amounts, and then gradually allowing the children to do more and more on their own. But assisted learning does not mean interrupting children who are engaged. Rather, adults are encouraged to provide the level of scaffolding needed. When children are in meaningful interactions with activities or each other, leave them alone. On the other hand, when children are frustrated or troubled—the puzzle has too many pieces or a fight is about to break out—then some assistance makes sense.

Here is an example of a teacher providing scaffolding. Two children are playing in the music center and one gets stuck trying to create a song: "A man fell . . . um . . . down a tree, down a tree . . . I don't know . . ." Frustration ensues as one child strums an autoharp and insists that the other keep making up the song. The would-be singer protests, "But I can't think of the rest." The teacher steps in:

Teacher: I like the first part. "A man fell down a tree." That's a good start to a song.
Singer: Yeah, but I don't know any more words to sing.
Teacher: Well, what else could the man do besides fall down a tree?
Autoharp player: (Stops playing the autoharp) I know. He could go up the tree. (Laughs)
Singer: OK. Play it. . . . A man fell down the tree, up the tree, up the tree. A man fell down and up and down . . . and . . . Wait. What can he do next?
Teacher: You could sing what happens to him when he falls down.
Singer: Oh . . . A man fell up and down and up and down and fell to the dirty floor.
Teacher: Wonderful. Now what will be your second verse?

Discussion, playing, and singing continue and the teacher moves on (Frost, Wortham, & Reifel, 2005, p. 240)

LEARNING AND THE "ZPD." Both Piaget and Vygotsky probably would agree that children need to be taught in the place where the learning challenge *matches* their current abilities (Hunt, 1961)—where they are neither bored nor frustrated. Piaget might emphasize matching children's current thinking abilities, but Vygotsky probably would recommend providing support to extend and grow current thinking. Vygotsky called the place where this growth is possible the **zone of proximal development (ZPD),** defined as the area between the child's current development level "as determined by independent problem solving" and the level of development that the child could achieve "through adult guidance or in collaboration with more capable peers" (Vygotsky, 1978, p. 86). This is the area where instruction can succeed, because real learning is possible. Children should be put in situations where they have to reach to understand, but where support and teaching are also available. Sometimes the best teacher is another child who has just figured out how to solve the problem, because this child is probably operating in the learner's *zone of proximal development.* Having a child interact with someone who is just a bit better at the activity is a good idea—both children benefit in the exchange of explanations, elaborations, and questions. In addition, children should be encouraged to use language to organize their thinking and to talk about what they are trying to accomplish. Dialogue and discussion are important avenues to learning (Karpov & Bransford, 1995; Kozulin & Presseisen, 1995; Wink & Putney, 2002).

One explanation for the significant changes in cognitive development and languages in the early years is that the capacities for attention and memory are rapidly increasing. There are a number of theories describing attention and memory, but the most common are the information processing explanations (Ashcraft & Radvansky, 2009; Sternberg, 1999).

Information Processing: Knowing and Remembering

There are several information processing theories of cognitive development, but all share some basic assumptions:

- Thinking is processing information.
- Information is represented in different ways in order to be remembered.
- Cognitive processes vary in how much attention and effort they require.
- What we already know plays a major role in information processing.
- Children become better information processors as they develop—they become faster and more efficient thinkers. (Bjorklund, 2005; Munakata, 2006)

Most information processing theories also assume that there are different kinds of memory, including **short-term/working memory** (what we are currently thinking about and can hold briefly in memory) and **long-term memory,** where all that we know is stored. What do information processing theories tell us about young children's cognitive development? We start with knowledge.

The Importance of Knowledge

Information processing theories suggest that one of the most important elements in cognitive development is what the individual brings to the situation. What we already know is the foundation and frame for constructing all future learning—because what we already know determines to a great extent what we will pay attention to, perceive, learn, remember, and forget (Alexander, 1996; Bransford, Brown, & Cocking, 2000).

Earlier information processing approaches emphasized domain-general abilities—general cognitive abilities such as processing speed that explain performance on all cognitive tasks. Today, many information processing theories are **domain-specific,** meaning the theories apply to specific cognitive abilities (e.g., the *domain* of visual perception, language, or spatial reasoning) or particular area of knowledge (e.g., the *domain* of number, physics, or biology). Research on children's knowledge in different domains has helped us understand their cognitive development. In fact, David Bjorklund, who has done extensive research on children's developing knowledge, notes that in the research on cognitive development, one of the most consistent findings in the last 30 years has been that children's thinking is domain-specific. As Bjorklund notes, "There are many examples in the literature of children performing one cognitive task like a champ while performing other seemingly similar tasks like a chump" (2005, p. 140). Children's thinking develops in specific domains of knowledge—and number is one important domain.

YOUNG CHILDREN'S UNDERSTANDING OF NUMBER. An understanding of number develops during the early childhood period. An essential step is learning the *number words* for your culture. In European languages and those derived from them such as English, the numbers 1 to 10 are fairly easy to learn, but after 10 there are numbers that don't match a base-10 pattern, like 11 12, 13, 14, and so on. In contrast, the words for numbers in East Asian languages match the base-10 number system—for example, the Chinese word for 12 is translated, "ten two." So Chinese children do not have to learn special words for numbers like 11, 12, 13, and 14. Another advantage in Chinese is that the word for 12 immediately tells you that 12 is made up of one tens-value and two units-values. There is evidence that this difference in counting words from 10 to 100 is one of the reasons that East Asian children generally are better than English speakers in some arithmetic procedures (Geary, 2006; Geary, Bow-Thomas, Liu, & Siegler, 1996).

PRINCIPLES OF COUNTING. Knowing the number words is just one part of learning to count. Piaget, one of the first psychologists to carefully study children's understanding of number, noted that children can say the number names, and even apply the names to a sequence of objects, years before they count accurately or even understand that they are determining quantity. So 3-year-old Emily might count her books—"one, two, three, ten, seven, eleven-teen, three-teen, sixteen!" When asked how many books, Emily is likely to announce, "sixteen." Years ago, Gelman and Gallistel (1978) identified five counting principles. Which ones does Emily seem to know?

How to Count

One-to-one principle: Each thing counted is assigned to one and only one number name (1, 2, 3, . . .).

Stable order principle: Number names have to be said in the same order every time (1, 2, 3, 4 . . . not 1, 3, 4, 2 . . .).

Cardinal principle: The last number said is the cardinal value (quantity) of the things counted (1, 2, 3, 4 . . . there are 4 books!).

What to Count

Abstraction principle: Any entity (alive or not, concrete or abstract) can be counted.

Which Way to Count

Order-irrelevance principle: You can count things in any order (top to bottom, left to right, middle to ends), but as long as you count each object only once, the number you get will be the same.

It looks as though Emily knows the first three principles, but we would have to watch her count more than once to be sure. She does use one number name for each book and knows that the last number name said (sixteen) is the number in the set, even though she is wrong on the count. She may always count in a stable order ("one, two, three, ten, seven, eleven-teen, three-teen . . ."), but we don't know for sure.

Children between ages 2 and 4 seem to grasp the how-to-count principles as long as the number counted is small, under five or six (Gallistel & Gelman, 1992; Gelman & Gallistel, 1978). For example, 4-year-old Brennan and his grandfather are playing catch. They agree that each will take nine steps backward before beginning the game. Brendan confidently takes "one, two, three, four, five" steps back, calling out the number each time. But after five, the numbers come more slowly and Brendan loses the one-to-one correspondence between the called out count and the steps. By "nine" he had taken over a dozen steps backwards (Bjorklund, 2005, p. 406).

The *abstraction* principle is more advanced, but seems to be understood by many 5-year-olds, at least implicitly. The *order-irrelevance principle* may not be fully understood until age 11 or older (Flavell, Miller, & Miller, 2002; Kamawar et al., 2010). For years, psychologists believed that children needed to understand these principles before they could count, but evidence suggests that children construct an understanding of these principles through their experiences in counting (Bryant & Nunes, 2004; Siegler, 1998). For example, children may discover the order-irrelevance principle after counting many sets of objects in different orders and still reaching the same final answer. So, as Piaget would recommend, lots of activities with numbers and counting can be valuable experiences for young children.

With the five principles listed above, children can do a good job of counting, but they still do not fully understand numbers. They also need to know about relations among sets. They need to know, for example, that two sets with the same number in them have the same quantity in them—that is, there is a one-to-one correspondence between sets as well (Bryant & Nunes, 2004). They also need to reason about numbers: What happens when you add an object to a set or take objects away? Does changing the appearance of something change the number? How can you determine if two sets are equal? Can a number be larger than one quantity and smaller than another? In other words, can a number be big and little at the same time?

Understanding numbers may seem rather simple and basic. In fact, some researchers have suggested that a sense of number may be part of our evolutionary equipment (Geary & Bjorklund, 2000; Gelman, 2000; Gelman, & Cordes, 2001), but others disagree and make the case that a full understanding of number requires learning (Bryant & Nunes, 2004). It is true that young children are ready and motivated to learn about numbers, but teaching and experience play roles as well. One study by Raquel Klibanoff and her colleagues found that when preschool teachers incorporate "math talk" into the daily routine—for example, saying "You two get your coats" instead of "You guys get your coats" or asking students to figure out how many students in a 21-member class were present if one was absent that day—the children performed better on math assessments at the end of the year, compared to students in classrooms with less math talk (Klibanoff, Levine, Huttenlocher, Vasilyeva, & Hedges, 2006).

Information Processing Improves with Development

Typically, as they grow older, children become better at processing information—that is, better at encoding, memory, retrieval, and executive control. As children become more sophisticated and effective in processing information, they are active in advancing their own development; they are constructing, organizing, and improving their own knowledge and strategies. Information processing theories are concerned about children's successes as well as their errors as they accomplish particular tasks and solve problems, because these outcomes reveal the child's developing knowledge and strategies (Siegler & Alibali, 2005).

Let's examine three important aspects of children's developing information processing systems—attention, memory, and problem solving.

YOUNG CHILDREN'S ATTENTION. Attention takes effort and is a limited resource. By now in this chapter, you probably have to work a bit to pay attention to these words about attention! For younger children, mental operations require a good amount of effort and attention. But with time and practice, some processes can become automatic (called **automaticity**). This is true for all of us at the beginning of learning something new. For example, when you were learning to drive, you probably couldn't listen to the radio and drive at the same time. After some practice, you could listen, but had to turn the radio off when traffic was heavy. After years of practice, you can plan a party, listen to the radio, and carry on a conversation as you drive. Like driving or searching for a toy, processes that initially require attention and concentration become automatic with practice. Actually, automaticity probably is a matter of degree; we are not completely automatic, but rather more or less automatic in our performances depending on how much practice we have had and the situation. For example, even experienced drivers might become very attentive and focused during a blinding blizzard (Anderson, 1995).

As the driving example demonstrates, we can pay attention to only one cognitively demanding task at a time (Ashcraft & Radvansky, 2009). The ability to regulate attention is a critical skill—one that children need to develop. In order to regulate attention, children need to focus on relevant information, ignore irrelevant information, sustain attention over time, and control impulsive responses to distractions. In fact, a study that followed over 1,000 children from birth to age 4-1/2 found that the ability to control attention was related to several positive outcomes in language and social skills (NICHD Early Child Care Network Research, 2005c).

Young children are not aware that they need to focus and sustain their attention. They think of their mind as being like a lamp that "lights" everything equally. But attention is more like a flashlight that focuses selectively (Flavell, Miller, & Miller, 2002). Over 25 years ago, John Flavell (1985) described four aspects of attention that seem to develop as children mature, including the growing knowledge that attention shines its selective flashlight on some things and not others:

1. As children grow older, they are more able to *control their attention*. Older children not only have longer attention spans; they also focus more accurately on what is important while ignoring irrelevant details. In addition, they can simultaneously pay attention to more than one dimension of a situation, which may explain why they develop conservation in the Piagetian sense. They can focus on both the width and the height of the liquid in a glass, for example.
2. As children develop, they become better at *fitting their attention to the task*. Older children, for example, know that they should focus their attention on the items they keep missing when they are trying to learn a list of words or pictures. Children below second or third grade are more likely to keep studying all the words or pictures.
3. Children improve in their ability to *plan how to direct their attention*. Younger children have a hard time redirecting attention and changing plans. For example, when asked to sort pictures based on one dimension such a color, 3-year-olds in a

It appears that this child is becoming more able to focus attention and resist distraction. Between the ages of about 2 and 3-1/2, there is a sharp increase in the length of time that children can sustain their attention to an appropriate toy and resist distractions such as images or sounds (NICHD Early Child Care Network Research, 2005c; Ruff & Capozzoli, 2003).

study by Zelazo, Frye, and Rapus (1996) had no trouble. But when asked to re-sort the pictures by shape, the children kept returning to the previous way of sorting by color. They could not change strategies and inhibit the previous way of sorting. This difficulty changing sorting criteria shows up in research on 3-year-olds around the world, but older children are able to change plans and redirect their attention to new sorting criteria (Diamond & Kirkham, 2005).

4. Children improve their abilities to *monitor their attention*, to decide if they are using the right plan, and to change approaches when necessary to follow a complicated series of events.

Some of these improvements in attention stem from the rapid growth of the frontal lobes of the brain's cerebral cortex during the preschool years, described in Chapter 5. Also, as their brains develop, young children are more able to inhibit impulsive responses (such as sorting based on a previous rule, described above) as well as resist distractions that interfere with the task at hand. Other factors include improved language that allows children to benefit from the scaffolding of parents and teachers who help the children plan their next steps, maintain focus, solve distracting problems, and reach goals through sustained attention (Bono & Stifter, 2003; Gauvain, 2004). But there are individual as well as developmental differences in attention. Children can vary greatly in their ability to attend selectively to information in their environment. In fact, many children diagnosed as having learning disabilities actually have attention disorders (Hallahan, Kauffman, & Pullen, 2009), particularly with long tasks. As we will see later in the chapter, the development of attentional skills is related to quality characteristics of children's environments such as their mother's or primary caretaker's responsiveness and the cognitive stimulation available in their homes (NICHD Early Child Care Research Network, 2003, 2005c).

YOUNG CHILDREN'S MEMORIES. Before age 4, children think remembering means what they see or know now and forgetting means not knowing, but by age 4, children begin to understand that "remembering" means recalling something from the past (Perner, 2000). Working memory plays a role in many cognitive abilities, including performance on vocabulary and addition tasks for 4- and 5-year-olds in one study (Noël, 2009). There are three basic aspects of memory: *memory span* or the amount of information that can be held in short-term/working memory, *memory processing efficiency*, and *speed of processing*. These three basic capacities act together and influence each other; more efficient processing allows greater amounts to be held in memory, for example (Demetriou, Christou, Spanoudis, & Platsidou, 2002). You can experience this effect of efficient processing by trying to hold these letters in memory:

HMOBFFMTVATMSUV

Now try these:

HMO BFF MTV ATM SUV

You just used a **strategy**—a general plan or set of plans to achieve a goal (Pressley & Hilden, 2006)—to group the string of letters into memorable (and meaningful) chunks, and you could hold more in memory: Your more efficient and faster processing expanded your memory span. Also, you brought your knowledge of the world to bear on the memory task. Young children have fewer strategies and less knowledge, so they have more trouble with memorizing a longer series.

As children grow older, they develop more effective strategies for remembering information. Most children spontaneously discover rehearsal around age 5 or 6 and continue to use it. In a series of studies that followed children from ages 4 to 18 (a difficult process, so there are few studies like this), Beate Sodian and Wolfgang Schneider (1999) found that as soon as most (81%) of the children discovered the memory strategy of clustering items in categories, they used it from then on. So some strategies can develop very quickly, but teaching strategies to very young children is not always effective. Children younger than 5 or so can be taught to use clustering or rehearsal strategies, and will use the strategies effectively as long as they are reminded. But they will not apply the strategies spontaneously.

Young children have very limited working memory spans, but they improve with age. It is not clear whether these differences are the result of changes in memory *capacity* or improvements in *strategy* use, but probably both are involved. As the brain and neurological system of the child mature and myelinization makes processing faster and more efficient, more working-memory space is available (Bransford, Brown, & Cocking, 2000). Changes in the brain that support memory affect how efficiently memories can be encoded, consolidated, stored, and then retrieved (Bauer, 2006). In terms of strategies, for young children, using a new strategy or operation—such as reaching for a toy, counting, or finding a word—takes up a large portion of their working memory. Once an operation is mastered and becomes more automatic, however, there is more working memory available for short-term storage of new information (Johnson, 2003). So, through changes in the brain, faster processing of information, the development and automating of strategies, and added knowledge, working memory increases in capacity from ages 4 through adolescence (Alloway, Gathercole, & Pickering, 2006; Gathercole, Pickering, Ambridge, & Wearing, 2004). Children are 10 to 11 years old before they have adult-like memories (Bauer, 2006).

CHILDREN'S MEMORIES FOR EVENTS. Research has shown that preschool children can and do remember events in their lives, even events that happened before they were 2 or 3 years old, and they can accurately describe something about these events more than a year later, but very few memories for events that occurred before 1 or 2 years old persist into adulthood (Fivush & Nelson, 2004; Peterson, 2002). Do children's memories for events in their lives improve with age? Generally speaking, the answer is yes, but there is some evidence that the type of event matters. Memory for positive events seems fairly accurate, as long as the child was at least 3 years old at the time of the event. For example, when adults were asked about the birth of a sibling, it did not matter if the adults were 3, 17, or any age in between—the number of questions they could answer about the birth was the same. But if the event was negative, such as a painful medical procedure or a fire alarm that the child did not understand at the time, children below age about 5 did not have a clear memory of the event (Bauer, 2006; Pipe, Lamb, Orbach, & Esplin, 2004). Other age differences involve *cues*, *content*, and *quantity* of reported memories. Compared to older children, younger children need more cues and prompts to remember, the content of their memories includes more common or routine parts of the experience ("we went hiking and had lunch" versus "we went hiking and I found an arrowhead"), and they report less information; for example, they use fewer connections and qualifiers such as *then, before, after, because, so,* and so on (Fivush & Haden, 1997; Fivush & Hamond, 1990; Fivush, Hazzard, Sales, Sarfrati, & Brown, 2003).

There are individual differences in forming autobiographical memories. Children who engage in more elaborated discussions with adults about shared experiences, who talk about the emotions involved ("Were you scared when you saw the spider?"), and who reminisce about details of the experiences can recount more coherent and complete narratives by the end of the preschool years. Adults provide scaffolding and guide talking about past, present, and future, so memories are socially constructed, as Vygotsky would say. This social construction leads to gender and cultural differences in early memories. As adults, women have earlier, longer, and more detailed first memories than men, and individuals from Western cultures have earlier, longer, and more detailed first memories than people from Asian cultures. One reason suggested by Fivush and Nelson (2004) is that young children's discussions about the past with adults in Western cultures tend to focus on the child's actions (for boys and girls) and feelings (more for girls), whereas Asian parents are less likely to talk about the child separate from the group and tend to downplay emotions such as anger that would interfere with group membership. So when Asian parents reminisce with their children, they tend not to scaffold early memories of the child separate from the group.

During the preschool years, children develop an autobiographical or personal memory for the events in their own lives. Their memories begin to include what happened to them and how they felt; for example, "I fell down and *was so embarrassed* because everyone was watching me" (Bauer, 2006, p. 398, emphasis in the original). There are more time markers such as "last summer" or "at Thanksgiving" (Nelson & Fivush, 2004). There is more detail and description, and maybe even quoted dialogue—"And then I said . . . and then Jamal said . . ." So children develop richer narratives—stories—about their own lives during their preschool years (Bauer, 2006). As these narratives grow, children begin to realize that they might have experienced the past events differently—remember different details or have different feelings—compared to others who were there. As they sort out these differences, children are developing their *theory of mind*—the realization that others have different minds, thoughts, feelings, and beliefs (Fivush & Nelson, 2004). We will look more closely at theory of mind later in this chapter.

SCRIPTS. One kind of memory involves repeated events in our lives, such as getting ready for bed or going to a grocery store. The memories for these common recurring events are sometimes called **scripts.** We all have scripts for events like ordering food in restaurants and these scripts differ depending on whether the restaurant is a four-star bistro or a fast-food drive through. Even young children have scripts for how to behave during snack time at preschool or at a friend's birthday party, as you can see in Figure 6.3 In fact, scripts seem to help very young children to organize and remember the predictable aspects of their world. Having a script for visiting a fast-food restaurant is useful in predicting what will happen when you walk in and in knowing how to behave. This frees up some working memory to learn new things and recognize when something is out of place in the situation. In terms of human survival, it probably is useful to remember what is likely to keep happening and to notice when something is out of place (Nelson, 2004).

FIGURE 6.3

A CHILD'S SCRIPT FOR A FAST FOOD RESTAURANT

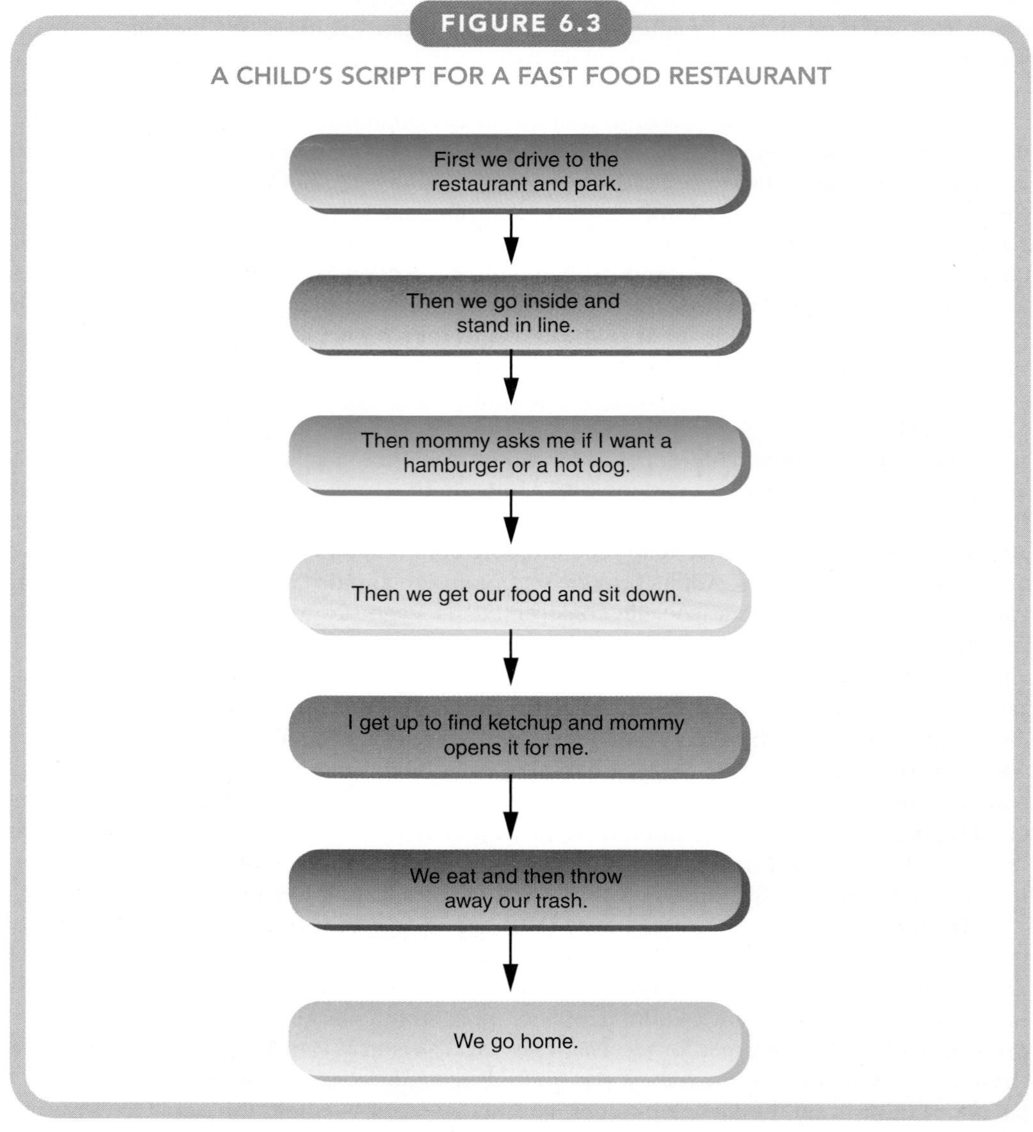

ACCURACY OF CHILDREN'S EYEWITNESS MEMORIES. Often children are asked about their memories of something they witnessed. Can we rely on young children's memories in these situations? The answer appears to be, it depends: "when interviewed appropriately, preschoolers can exhibit reliable long-term recall" (Peterson, 2002, p. 395).

Young children can give accurate testimony, if the adults working with them do not ask leading or suggestive questions.

Children's eyewitness memories are usually studied by showing children a video, having them observe something in school, or having them participate in an activity. Then, after a few minutes, hours, days, or even weeks, they are asked a *free recall question* ("Tell me what happened in the video you saw"), a *cued recall question* ("What did the man who came into your class yesterday morning do?"), or a *recognition question* ("Was the bicycle in the video red?"). As you might expect, the older the child, the more accurate are the memories. In free recall situations, young children don't recall much about the details of the event, but what they do recall is usually about the core happening and is generally accurate. For example, after viewing a video of someone stealing a bicycle, a young child probably would recall that the bike was stolen, but not remember much about who did it or how. If asked specific questions such as "Who took the bicycle?" young children will remember more accurate, but also *inaccurate* information. The longer the time that passes between the remembering of inaccurate information and a retest of recall, the more likely the child will recall the inaccurate version of the memory and the more those inaccurate versions will resist forgetting (Bjorklund, 2005; Gordon, Baker-Ward, & Ornstein, 2001).

The real problem with memory accuracy occurs for young children when *suggestive questions* are asked, such as, "Did the girl in the red shirt steal the bicycle?" or "Was the monkey wearing a collar or a leash?" (Bruck, Ceci, & Hembrooke, 2002). Compared to older children and adults, young children are more likely to be influenced by leading questions and false suggestions, in part because young children have trouble with **source monitoring** or remembering where they encountered the information. Was it something they really experienced, or did they see it on TV, or did the event happen to a friend, not to them (Gordon, Baker-Ward, & Ornstein, 2001)? Also, when questions are suggestive, repeated, and high pressure ("the other children said yes!"), then young children are more likely to recall inaccurate memories (Finnila, Mahlberga, Santtilaa, & Niemib, 2003). Of course, adults also are affected by the questions asked and the way they are interviewed (Wells, Memon, & Penrod, 2006).

Unfortunately, when children are interviewed by attorneys or police, questions are likely to be suggestive. For example, Livia Gilstrap (2004) studied 80 interviews of children (ages 3 to 7 years) conducted by 41 male and female British police officers who specialized in child protection interviews. One month before the study, two events were staged in the children's schools. The police officers were asked to question the children about these events, following their usual procedures for child interviews, and were told only that one event involved a magician visiting the class and the other, a worker. Gilstrap found that from 20–28% of the questions asked were suggestive leading questions ("I think the magician was wearing a black hat, was he?"), the kind that tend to distort the memories of young children. About one-third of these leading questions introduced inaccurate information. So, leading questions probably are used with children in real-life settings and can lead to inaccurate memories. If one of your children or students is interviewed by an adult, be sure that person is well qualified. ***Connecting with Children*** on the next page gives just a few example guidelines for talking with young children about events in their lives.

CONNECTING WITH CHILDREN

Guidelines for Teachers and Other Professionals: Interviewing Children and Eyewitness Testimony

Plan the interview to make the most of the child's memory.
Examples

1. Interview the child as soon as possible after the event.
2. Have the interview in a simply furnished room with child-friendly furniture and not too many toys—these could suggest make-believe play.

Establish rapport.
Examples

1. Be friendly; avoid titles like "Doctor," or "Officer."
2. Make sure the child knows it is OK to say, "I don't remember," "I don't know," or "I don't understand." Practice answering made up questions this way. For example, ask, "What did your mommy say the day you were born?"
3. Tell the child you have no information about the event and the child should just report what he or she remembers because you were not there.

Do not use suggestive techniques.
Examples

1. Avoid leading questions such as, "What happened after he hit you?" Ask open-ended and free recall questions such as, "Tell me what happened yesterday on the playground," or "Is there anything else you can tell me?"
2. Be careful not to praise some answers while ignoring others. Don't promise the child a reward for talking to you.
3. Avoid repeating questions—children might think you did not believe their first answer or that you thought it was wrong.

Encourage children to monitor the source of their information.
Examples

1. Ask the child to think carefully about where the information came from.
2. Ask if the child heard from others about the event.

Respect the child's wishes.
Examples

1. If the child does not want to talk about a topic, don't press.
2. If the child wants to end the interview, say, "OK, we can talk again another time."
3. End the interview with a thank you and then discuss something neutral such as what the child is doing after the interview.

Learn more about interviewing.
Examples

1. See: http://www.ipt-forensics.com/journal/volume6/j6_3_2.htm, taken from the journal, *Issues in Child Abuse Accusations*.
2. See UNICEF: Principles of Ethical Reporting on Children http://www.unicef.org/media/media_tools_guidelines.html
3. See the journal, *Law and Contemporary Problems* http://www.law.duke.edu/journals/lcp/articles/lcp65dWinter2002p149.htm
4. Read, *Investigative Interviews of Children: A Guide for Helping Professionals*, by Debra A. Poole and Michael E. Lamb, published by the American Psychological Association, 2003.

USING STRATEGIES AND SOLVING PROBLEMS. You saw in the previous section that memory capacity and speed of processing affect the strategies children can use to solve problems, such as the water-poured-into-a-taller-glass problem. You also saw that having effective strategies could improve memory capacity. In this section we look more deeply at how young children develop problem-solving strategies and explore the role played by instruction or demonstration.

Young children may be able to use a strategy, but they might not employ it when they should. This is called a **production deficiency**—failing to produce a strategy when it would be useful, even though you know the strategy. Children can learn to apply more effective strategies to solve problems, either through instruction or by discovery. Instruction often is more efficient, but many strategies are discovered and improved over time (Pressley & Hilden, 2006).

By using microgenetic methods (discussed in Chapter 2) to examine very tiny, subtle changes in children's thinking, Robert Siegler (Shrager & Siegler, 1998; Siegler, 2000, 2004) has developed a model of how problem-solving strategies are discovered and developed over time. For example, there are several strategies for adding two numbers. One of the first that children use is the *count* strategy. If you have two numbers to add, say 2 + 4, you can count: 1, 2, (pause and go to the next set) 3, 4, 5, **6**! So 2 + 4 is 6. A bit more sophisticated is the *min* strategy: Start with the larger number and keep counting. So a child might say 4, then keep counting 5, 6—the answer is 6. An even more advanced strategy is *fact retrieval*, simply remembering the memorized fact that 2 + 4 is 6. Prior to Siegler's microgenetic studies, most psychologists had concluded that children always solve simple addition problems using the *min* strategy. Siegler contended that this was wrong. It only appeared that the *min* strategy predominated because the researchers were averaging data across time instead of carefully observing how individual children's problem solving varied over time. In fact, children often use several of these strategies at once, depending on the type of problem and the context. David Bjorklund and Kristina Rosenblum (2002) asked kindergarten children to add pairs of numbers between 1 and 6, either by adding the numbers from a roll of two dice to determine their moves in the game, *Chutes and Ladders*, or by just doing addition problems like in school ("What is 2 plus 4?"). First of all, the children used an average of 2 to 3 strategies in both situations, so *count*, *min*, and *fact retrieval* all were used. The actual problem mattered: Children used *fact retrieval* to add identical pairs (5 + 5; 3 + 3, etc.). The situation mattered as well: Children used the *count* strategy most in the game and least in the "school" context. But older children were likely to just use the *fact retrieval* (more efficient) strategy in both situations and for all problems; retrieving addition facts had become more automatic for them.

A clear finding from this research is that there are few "aha" moments. Young children will try an effective strategy, then an ineffective one, then another ineffective one, then move to a more effective one—back and forth. This pattern has been called the **overlapping wave theory** of adaptive strategy choice and is shown in Figure 6.4.

FIGURE 6.4

OVERLAPPING WAVE MODEL OF COGNITIVE DEVELOPMENT

As children try strategies to solve problems, they may try an effective strategy, then an ineffective one, then another ineffective one, then move to a more effective one—back and forth. Even after they discover the most effective strategy, they do not use it exclusively. But gradually over time, they let go of less effective strategies and focus on the one that works.

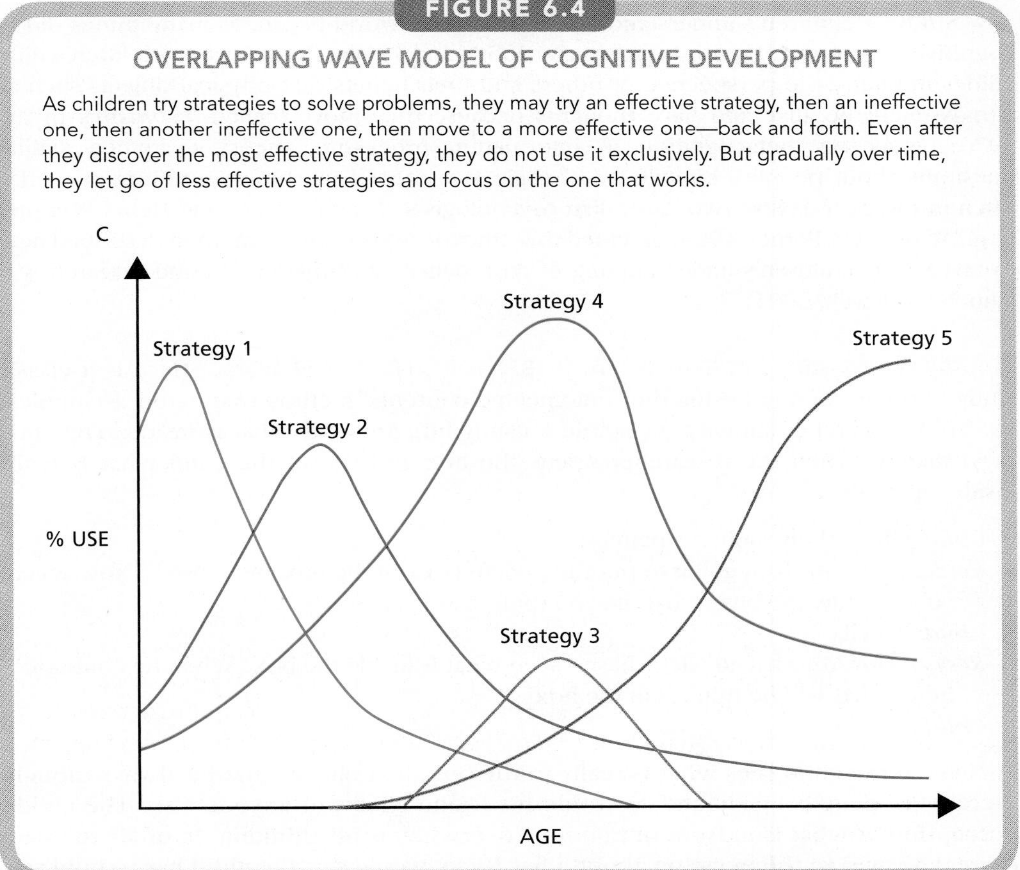

Source: Adapted from Siegler, R. S. (2006). Microgenetic analyses of learning. In D. Kuhn & R. S. Siegler (Eds.), Handbook of Child Psychology: Cognition, Perception & Language, *(6e, Vol. 2, p. 479). New York: John Wiley & Sons. Used with permission.*

Look back at Figure 6.4. You can see that children may begin using a less effective strategy (Strategy 1) most of the time, but every now and then apply other, often better strategies (2, 3, and 4) before settling on a final successful strategy (5). At any given time, one strategy may dominate efforts, but others are part of the repertoire as well. As you can see in the graph, even when strategy 5 is used most often, strategy 4 is still used sometimes, and strategy 2 once in a while (don't you still count on your fingers some of the time—be honest!).

Theory of Mind

Do you remember how much trouble 3-year-olds have changing the way they sort objects, switching from color to shape, for example (Diamond & Kirkham, 2005)? One reason this switch is difficult may have to do with children's **theory of mind,** an understanding of how mental processes work. A theory of mind is not a formal scientific theory, but is more like an everyday, common sense understanding (Wellman, 2004). John Flavell defines theory of mind as "our understanding of the mental world—the inner world inhabited by beliefs, desires, emotions, thoughts, perceptions, intentions, and other mental states" (2004, p. 274). Basically, a theory of mind allows children to understand that thought and reality are not always the same—people can believe things that are not true and they can be deceived. Children need a theory of mind to understand that other people have their own minds, thoughts, dreams, feelings, beliefs, desires, and perceptions (Harris, 2006). Children need a theory of mind to make sense of other peoples' behavior. Why is Sarah crying? Does she feel sad because no one will play with her? Children also probably need a theory of mind to understand that they can "change their minds" and plan a new sorting strategy, switching from color to shape, for example.

Study of children's understanding of the mental world began, as many things did in cognitive development, with Piaget in the 1950s and 1960s. He described children's difficulties in taking the perspective of others and their beliefs that physical objects such as clouds might be alive and have thoughts because they move (called *animism*). In the 1970s, work on metacognition in information processing theory examined similar questions about people's knowledge of their own mental machinery and how it works. Then in the early 1980s, two Australian psychologists, Joseph Perner and Heinz Wimmer (e.g., Wimmer & Perner, 1983) invented the "unexpected contents" method described next to test young children's understanding of false beliefs, and theory of mind research was launched (Flavell, 2004).

APPEARANCES ARE DECEIVING: FALSE BELIEFS AND DECEPTIONS. Here is a classic study of theory of mind using the "unexpected contents" method (Astington & Gopnick, 1988). A researcher shows a 3-year-old a candy box and asks what is inside. The child says, "candy." Then the researcher opens the box and shows the child what is really inside—pencils:

Child: Oh . . . holy moly . . . pencils!
Researcher: OK, I am going to put the pencils back in the box and close it. Now when you first saw the box, what did you think was inside?
Child: Pencils.
Researcher: Your friend Nicky hasn't seen what is inside the box. When he comes in here, what will he think is in the box?
Child: Pencils.

Once the child sees what is really in the box, he believes that he always thought there were pencils inside and so would his friend Nicky, or anyone else. The child's perception of what is in front of him now overwhelms his thinking. In order to give a correct answer to the question about what Nicky would say, the child has to hold two ideas in his mind at the same time—what Nicky would *expect* to be in a candy box and what *actually is* in the box. The child also would need to understand that people could have *false beliefs*. Much of the research on theory of mind uses this kind of false belief task.

Around the world, most 3-year-old children do not have a theory of mind (unless their language is very advanced); at 4 the understanding is growing; and by 5 it is in place (Harris, 2006). Some researchers suggest that this almost universal timing indicates brain maturation plays a big role in developing a theory of mind. Language is important, too. Children with advanced language develop this understanding sooner and deaf children who do not learn sign language develop the understanding much later. When parents talk to their children about thoughts and beliefs and encourage them to imagine what others might think, then the children develop a theory of mind sooner (Lockl & Schneider, 2007; Ruffman, Slade, & Crowe, 2002; Symons, 2004). Children with older siblings develop a theory of mind sooner, perhaps because siblings argue, negotiate, cooperate, and try to trick each other, so these children learn earlier that other people have their own thoughts and beliefs (Perner, 2000; Wellman, 2004).

What advances come with an advancing theory of mind? Flavell summarizes the understandings that develop and those that take longer, as you can see in Table 6.4.

Theory of mind figures prominently in current explanations for the disorder of autism.

AUTISM SPECTRUM DISORDERS. One current explanation for autism spectrum disorders is that children with these disorders have an underdeveloped theory of mind. Autism is diagnosed using three criteria: (a) significant, persistent deficits in social communication and interactions, (b) restricted, repetitive patterns of behavior, interests, and activities, and (c) symptoms must be present in early childhood (DSM-5 proposed revisions, 2010). About 1 in every 150 children is born with autism. We have used the term preferred by professionals in the field, **autism spectrum disorders** to emphasize that autism includes a range of disorders from mild to major. In fact, as the American Psychiatric Association (2010) plans the fifth edition of the *Diagnostic and Statistical Manual of Mental Disorders (DSM-5)*, recommendations being considered would fold autism, Asperger syndrome, and some other disorders into the one category of autism spectrum disorders.

Children with autism spectrum disorders have difficulties in at least three other areas associated with theory of mind: joint attention (focusing attention with another person on some object), pretend play, and empathy for the distress of others. Thus, children with autism are deficient or delayed in developing some of the components of theory of mind (Harris, 2006). They have difficulty explaining their own behaviors, appreciating that other people might have different feelings, and predicting how behaviors might affect emotions. So, for example, a student with autism may not understand why classmates are bored by his constant repetition of stories or obscure facts about topics he finds fascinating. The student

TABLE 6.4 • **Understandings Related to a Developing Theory of Mind in the Early Childhood Years**

Following are some examples of understandings about mental life that develop between ages 3 to 5 and some understandings that usually don't develop until the early or middle elementary school years.

UNDERSTANDINGS THAT DEVELOP (AGES 3–5)	UNDERSTANDINGS THAT TAKE MORE TIME
• Attention is selective; different people can pay attention to different things. • People have different emotions. • Emotions and desires are connected. People are happy when they get what they want, for example. • Thinking is an internal activity.	• People do not always feel the way they look—they can be unhappy without showing it, for example. • People's interpretation of an event can be influenced by biases and previous experiences. • You did not always know what you know now. • You need information to make a judgment and sometimes you don't have enough; for example, you can't tell what an object is if you see only a small part. • People can be actively thinking, even when they are sitting quietly, not moving.

may stand too close or too far away when interacting, not realizing that he is making other people uncomfortable (Friend, 2011).

Early on, children with autism spectrum disorders may have difficulties in social relations. They do not form connections with others, they avoid eye contact, and they don't share feelings such as enjoyment or interest with others. Communication is impaired. About half of these students are nonverbal; they have no or very few language skills. Others make up their own language. They may obsessively insist on regularity and sameness in their environments—change is very disturbing. They may repeat behaviors and have restricted interests, watching the same DVD over and over for example. They may be very sensitive to light, sound, touch, or other sensory information—sounds may be painful, for example, or the slight flickering of fluorescent lights may seem like constant bursts, causing severe headaches. They may be able to memorize words or steps in problem solving, but not use them appropriately or be very confused when the situation changes or questions are asked in a different way (Franklin, 2007; Friend, 2011; Matson, Matson, & Rivet, 2007).

Asperger syndrome is one of the disabilities included in the autism spectrum. These children have many of the characteristics described above, but they have the greatest trouble with social relations. Language is less affected. Their speech may be fluent but unusual, mixing up pronouns of "I" and "you," for example (Friend, 2011). Many students with autism also have moderate to severe intellectual disabilities, but those with Asperger syndrome usually have average to above average intelligence.

Early and intense interventions that focus on communications and social relations are particularly important for children with autism spectrum disorders. Without interventions, behaviors such as poor eye contact and odd-seeming mannerisms tend to increase over time (Matson, Matson, & Rivet, 2007). As they move into elementary school, some of these students will be in inclusive settings, others in specialized classes, and many in some combination of these two. Collaboration among teachers and the family is particularly important. Strategies such as smaller classes, structured environments, finding a class "buddy" to give support, providing a safe "home base" for times of stress, consistency in instruction and transition routines, assistive technologies, and the use of visuals may be part of intervention plans (Harrower & Dunlap, 2001; Smith & Tyler, 2010).

WHAT IS REAL? PRETENDING, FANTASIES, AND IMAGINARY FRIENDS. Imagination and pretending play important roles in cognitive development. We saw earlier that one of the child's earliest uses of symbols is in pretending—using a block as a car, zoom, zoom—for example. The child is able to separate the object from its meaning. This ability is a preparation for later abstract thought and may provide the basis for higher-order thinking such as hypothetical "what if" reasoning (Garner, Curenton, & Taylor, 2005). By age 3 at the latest, most children know the difference between "trying" and "pretending" (Rakoczy, Tomasello, & Striano, 2004). Some researchers describe different levels of play, with symbolic or dramatic pretend play as one important level. For example, Vygotsky (1978) describes constructive play as playing with objects toward a goal such as building a tower. Next comes symbolic or fantasy play that begins with simple substitutions of one object for another—a plastic bowl for a hat, for example. But this fantasy play becomes more complex as children create fantasy characters and rules, for example, rules about how to bow to and obey the "Queen of everything." Finally children move to more complex real games that involve turns, spinners, and dice or sports. Vygotsky believed that making and following rules in imaginary play enabled children to later follow rules for real games.

But what about imaginary friends like Sassy, the invisible shrinking giraffe that kept Kayla company at the beginning of this chapter? Is this carrying imagination too far? Actually, the phenomenon is pretty widespread. Between 60% and 70% of children under the age of 7 have played with imaginary companions, with first-born and only children more likely to have these invisible friends. One study found that 28% of children ages 5 to 12 had imaginary friends (Taylor, Carlson, Maring, Gerow, & Charley, 2004). For younger children, imaginary companions can be toys or other objects on which children bestow special powers or personalities (a magic stuffed tiger), animals, or different versions of real people (your author's daughter had "another mother in China" who was more understanding of some misbehaviors). For the children under age 7 in the Taylor study above, about half of the imaginary companions were invisible and the other half were based on toys. Here are a few companions of children in their study:

"Rose," an invisible female squirrel, 9-years-old, lived in a tree in the yard.

"Skateboard guy," an invisible 11-year-old boy who wore cool shirts, had a fancy skateboard, lived in the pocket of a 7-year-old boy, and liked to see the boy run fast.

"Fake Rachel," an alternative version of a real friend named Rachel. Fake Rachel lived under the child's bed.

"Elephant," a 7-inch-high invisible female elephant that wore shorts and a tank top and was mean at times.

The results of the Taylor study and others indicated that by and large, preschool girls create imaginary companions more often than boys, but boys are more likely than girls to pretend to be an imaginary character, like Spiderman or a monster dinosaur. This may be related to an interesting gender difference. Boys create characters they can enact alone, but girls' pretending tends to be more about relationships, so other players are needed in girls' pretending. By age 7, as many girls as boys have played with imaginary companions. Imaginary companions who were left behind by age 7 were given up gradually with little trouble or drama (Carlson & Taylor, 2005; Gleason, Sebanc, & Hartup, 2000; Taylor & Carlson, 1997; Taylor et al., 2004).

There appear to be some benefits to having imaginary companions. These pretend creations help children deal with fears, such as facing the first day of preschool. Children can practice conflict resolution when two imaginary companions are fighting or when the imaginary friend disagrees with the child. Children with imaginary friends perform better on theory of mind tests, so they are actually better at distinguishing reality from fantasy. Stephanie Carlson, who has interviewed many children about their imaginary companions, said in an interview that some of the children started to worry about the researcher's grasp on reality and pulled her aside to say, "You know this is just pretend, right?" Finally, often children with imaginary companions are more cooperative in playing, have no shortage of real friends, are more imaginative and curious in their play, and have more advanced language (Carlson & Taylor, 2005; Singer & Singer, 1990; Taylor & Carlson, 1997; Taylor et al., 2004). So children's imaginary companions should not worry parents or teachers, unless the children seem depressed, have no real friends, or claim to be controlled by the invisible companion and forced to do things they do not want to do.

INTENTIONS. Between the ages of 18 months and 2 years, children start to use *want, wish, hope*, and other desire terms, and between 24 and 30 months, they can distinguish between what they want and what they will get: "I want a dog, but I can't have one" (Bartsch & Wellman, 1995). So by about age 2, children have a sense of *intention,* at least of their own intentions. As children develop a theory of mind, they also are able to understand that other people have intentions of their own. Older preschoolers who get along well with their peers are able to separate intentional from unintentional actions and react accordingly. For example, they will not get angry when another child accidentally knocks over their block tower. But aggressive children have more trouble assessing intention. They are likely to attack anyone who topples their tower, even accidentally (Dodge & Pettit, 2003). As children mature, they are more able to assess and consider the intentions of others.

Contexts for Development: Family and Home

Many of you reading these pages are now or some day will be parents. We have spent much of this chapter exploring young children's developing language, cognitive operations, use of cultural tools, self-regulation, domain-specific knowledge, attention, memory, and theory of mind. Now we turn to the world outside the child. What roles do families, peers, siblings, and teachers play in cognitive development in these early years? There are two useful sources of information on this question. The first is research on home environments using the *Home Observation for Measurement of the Environment* or *HOME.* The second is a longitudinal study by the NICHD Early Child Care Research Network. (2005c).

Assessing Home Care

The *Home Observation for Measurement of the Environment* or *HOME* has been used for over 30 years to study the relationship between different aspects of the home environment and children's cognitive and social emotional development (Bakermans-Kraneburg, van Ijzendoorn, & Bradley, 2005; Caldwell & Bradley, 1984, 1994). A consistent finding is that the quality of the home environment and interactions with mothers assessed by the HOME are related to children's cognitive development from infancy through adolescence (Bjorklund, 2005). The scales have been refined and used with five different national data sets that followed over 10,000 children from ages 3 to 5 (Leventhal, Martin, & Brooks-Gunn, 2004; Linver, Brooks-Gunn, & Cabrera, 2004). What did they find?

First, the scales on the HOME that were the most reliable and predictive of children's development at age 5 were Learning Stimulation, Access to Reading, Parental Warmth, Parent Lack of Hostility, and Interior of Home. Look at Table 6.5 to see the kinds of items on these scales. Scores on these subscales were related to U.S. children's scores on widely used measures of cognitive abilities such as subtests of the Stanford-Binet, Wechsler, Woodcock-Johnson, or Peabody Picture Vocabulary test.

Second, after controlling for such background factors as mother's socioeconomic status (SES), race, ethnicity, and education, the two scales that were most predictive of cognitive ability were Learning Stimulation and Access to Reading. So homes where children have toys, games, or puzzles that teach concepts such as color, size, shape, number, animal names, and so on; homes where children are encouraged to learn songs, rhymes, letters, new words, numbers, and spatial relations; and homes where there are books and family members who read to children are those where children score higher on cognitive abilities tests. In addition, these characteristics were also more predictive of children's social competence: The greater the learning stimulation and access to reading during the preschool years, the fewer behavioral problems were reported at age 5.

Margaret Caughy (1996) examined the importance of supportive home environments for children with biological risks such as low birth weight or hospitalization before age 1. She found that both increased biological risks and lower scores on the HOME assessment were related to lower math and reading readiness scores at ages 5 and 6, but the home environment was more important. The children who suffered the most adverse effects had both early health problems *and* unsupportive home environments.

TABLE 6.5 • **Example Items from the HOME Scale**

Items such as these below assess the quality of the home environment for young children.

SCALE	EXAMPLE ITEMS
Learning Stimulation	Child has toys that teach color, size, shape. Child has three or more puzzles.
Access to Reading	At least 10 books are visible in the apartment. Child is encouraged to learn the alphabet.
Parental Warmth	Parent encourages child to talk and takes time to listen. Parent's voice conveys positive feeling to child.
Parental Lack of Hostility	No more than one instance of physical punishment during the last week. Parent does not shout at child during visit.
Interior of Home	Building appears safe. House is reasonably clean and minimally cluttered.

Source: From Leventhal, T., Martin, A., & Brooks-Gunn, J. (2004). The EC-HOME across five national datasets in the third to fifth year of life. Parenting: Science and Practice *4(2–3), Table 2, 171–177. Reprinted by permission of the publisher, Taylor & Francis Group, http://www.informaworld.com.*

NICHD Early Child Care Research Network

One of the questions asked by researchers in the NICHD Early Child Care Research Network (2005b) was, "how do experiences at home and in preschools affect the development of the critical cognitive processes of attention, memory, and planning?" As we have seen, these cognitive processes develop gradually over time, with important advances happening during early childhood, along with changes in the frontal lobes of the brain (Welsh, 2002). Quite a bit of correlational evidence links parents' behaviors to their children's memory and planning skills (Gauvain, 2004; Ornstein & Haden, 2001), but we know that correlation is not cause. Often other characteristics such as family wealth or education are involved in these correlational relationships.

The NICHD Early Child Care Research Network researchers examined the connections between parenting and children's cognitive skill development, while controlling the effects of family income, mother's intelligence, and child's gender and ethnicity. They followed over 700 children from age 6 months to first grade. Researchers assessed the quality of the home environment using the HOME instrument (see Table 6.5 for example items) and also the mother's sensitivity to her child's needs as they played together while being videotaped. Raters watching the videotapes noted how the mother assisted her child when the task was too difficult—what kind of scaffolding (in the Vygotskian sense) did she provide?

The quality of childcare *outside* the home was assessed through observations of how much the caregivers seemed to like the child, respond to the child's needs, and stimulate the child's development. The quality of first grade classroom environments was also assessed through observations of the child-centered behavior of the teachers and the way the teachers supported the child's developing cognitive skills in teacher-student conversations. The study used a sophisticated statistical analysis called *structural equation modeling* that allows the researchers to test relationships among variables, so the relationships found were more than simple correlations. What did the researchers learn?

- The first conclusion was that most of the variations among individual children in their attention and memory abilities in first grade could be traced to the differences in the quality of the child's *family environment*. Surprisingly, the quality of the childcare, preschool, or first grade environments had little connection to the development of attention or memory.
- Second, differences in planning abilities were not related to home or school environment, perhaps because children under age 6 are not ready to benefit from supports for developing the more complex skills of planning.
- Family environment quality was important for attention and memory skill development during both the child's first three years and second three years. The early ages—6 months to 3 years old—were no more or less important than the later ages of 3 to 5-1/2 years old. So children need both early and continuing supportive and responsive environments for development (Bjorklund, 2005).

Does this mean that early childhood education programs have no effect? Not at all. The cognitive skills assessed in the NICHD study were very specific—attention, memory, and planning. The next section looks more broadly at the many possible effects of early childhood education—beyond attention and memory.

Early Childhood Education

In the 1840s in Germany, Friedrich Froebel decided that young children needed a place to be nurtured, and the kindergarten (or children's garden) was born. The focus was on all the child's needs—physical, emotional, cognitive, and social—and on the process of learning by doing (Frost, Wortham, & Reifel, 2005). But even though the concept of kindergarten was developed over 160 years ago, it is only in the last 50 years or so that preschools, nursery schools, play schools, day care, childcare, pre-primary schools, pre-kindergartens, and kindergartens have come to serve a large number of young children. The more parents learned about the important cognitive developments happening between ages 3 and 5, the more they wanted educational opportunities that would enrich the learning and development of their young children. In addition, because many parents work outside the home, **childcare** or **day care** is necessary. In the United States and Canada, between 60 and 70% of mothers with children under 6 years old work outside the home. In the United States, about 59% of White and 62% of African American women with children under age 6 are working (United States Bureau of Labor, 2009; United States Census, 2006).

Early childhood education programs are provided for all children in some countries. For example, all 4-year-olds attend school in Ireland and the Netherlands. All children in Belgium and France have access to preschool if their families choose to send them. Most children in developed countries attend at least a half-day kindergarten when they are 4 or 5. Table 6.6 shows the children enrolled in *early childhood education* in several countries. *Center-based* means children in groups in organized programs such as daycare centers, nursery schools, or preschools. The United States and Canada fall below these other countries in enrollment. In Great Britain, all children must be enrolled in formal schooling at age 5.

Learning from the Italians

Two early childhood approaches that originated in Italy, the Montessori Method and Reggio Emilia, have influenced programs in many other countries.

THE MONTESSORI METHOD. In the early 1900s, Italian physician Maria Montessori developed a method of teaching young children that has become a widely used educational approach. She worked first with children who had intellectual impairments and then opened a school for poor children in Rome. In each case, her methods were successful in helping the children learn to read and write. Montessori believed that "the hand leads the mind" (Lillard, 2004, p. 200); that is, children learn from self-chosen activities and games that give them a sense of accomplishment and responsibility.

TABLE 6.6 • **Percentage of Children Ages 3 to 4 Enrolled in Full-time or Part-time Education in 12 Countries in 2007**

COUNTRY	PERCENT 3–4 YEAR-OLDS
Australia	32
Belgium	100
Czech Republic	80
France	100
Greece	28
Italy	100
Japan	84
Korea	27
Spain	100
Turkey	7
United Kingdom	90
United States	50

Source: Adapted from OECD (2009). http://www.oecd.org/dataoecd/35/11/43619343.pdf

Teachers in a Montessori classroom might demonstrate how to use manipulative objects such as Cuisenaire rods (see the picture), but then provide more guidance only if the child asks. Children are encouraged to be responsible—they put away their toys or games and help clean the room. Social interaction with the teacher and other children, as well as pretend play, are less important than individual exploration. Children are more likely to trace letters, do puzzles, or look at books than play in a pretend kitchen or act out stories (Edwards, 2002; Lillard, 2005).

REGGIO EMILIA. Reggio Emilia is a city in northern Italy that has pioneered its own early childhood schools. As in Montessori schools, children in Reggio Emilia select their own projects and learn by doing, but in Reggio Emilia, the children are more likely to work together. Teachers are facilitators, but the children identify and design their own projects, often involving dance, music, costumes, puppets, painting, photography, or construction. The arts and imaginative play are more important than in the Montessori method. Reggio Emilia schools have an abundance of resources—space, materials, teachers, and other adults from the community. Demand for enrollment is high in the community and all children can participate, with the costs adjusted to the resources of the family. It is not clear yet if the approach will work as well in communities that do not devote the extensive human and material resources required to sustain the school. Even so, there is quite a bit of interest in Reggio Emilia in countries outside Italy. For example, Howard Gardner and his Project Zero worked with the Reggio Emilia schools to publish *Making Learning Visible: Children as Individual and Group Learners* (2001).

This child is learning number concepts working with Cuisenaire rods. Each different color is a different length—white is 1 centimeter, red is 2, light green is 3, purple is 4, and so on. Children can manipulate the rods and discover that 2 red rods equal 1 white and 1 light green rod, but 4 whites work too. You can see all the possibilities, not just for addition or subtraction, but also other concepts such as volume.

Types of Programs: Different Schools for Different Goals

There are many ways to characterize early childhood programs (Morrison, 2011). Some educators distinguish between child-centered and teacher-centered programs (or play-centered versus academic programs). Others add the category of intervention or compensatory programs, such as Head Start, aimed at closing the gap between children placed at risk and children from more privileged backgrounds. As you will see, the different goals of these programs lead to different experiences and activities for the children in them.

LET THE CHILDREN PLAY: CHILD-CENTERED PROGRAMS. Maria Montessori once noted, "Play is children's work." Froebel and Piaget both would agree. Programs such as Montessori, Reggio Emilia, and many kindergartens often are called *child-centered* because their physical and social environments are based on the developmental needs of the whole child. Many early childhood educators emphasize the value of **developmentally appropriate practices (DAP)** that avoid pressures to master academic subjects. Programs that agree with this philosophy encourage the child's self-paced exploration, discovery, pretend play, artistic expression, and knowledge construction. Usually there are no formal lessons in math or reading, but teachers are alert to times in which number or word knowledge can be developed through talking about the daily calendar or singing songs about sounds, for example. The National Association for the Education of Young Children (NAEYC) has created a set of guidelines for developmentally appropriate practice, as you can see in Table 6.7 on the next page.

TABLE 6.7 • **Guidelines for Developmentally Appropriate Practice (DAP)**

1. KNOWLEDGE IN THREE AREAS MUST INFORM DECISION MAKING

- **What is known about child development and learning**—research-based knowledge of age-related characteristics that permits general predictions about what experiences are likely to best promote children's learning and development.
- **What is known about each child as an individual**—what educators learn about the specific child that has implications for how best to adapt and be responsive to that individual variation.
- **What is known about the social and cultural contexts in which children live**—educators must strive to understand the values, expectations, and behavioral and linguistic conventions that shape each of the children's lives at home and in their communities in order to ensure that learning experiences in the program or school are meaningful, relevant, and respectful for each child and family.

2. GOALS MUST BE CHALLENGING *AND* ACHIEVABLE

- **Meeting children where they are is essential, but no good teacher simply leaves them there.** Keeping in mind desired outcomes and what is known about those children as a group and individually, the teacher plans experiences to promote the children's learning and development.
- **Learning and development are most likely to occur when new experiences build on what a child already knows and is able to do** and when those experiences also entail the child stretching a reasonable amount in acquiring new skills, abilities, or knowledge. After the child reaches that new level of mastery in skill or understanding, the effective teacher reflects on what goals should come next; and the cycle continues, advancing the child's learning in a developmentally appropriate way.

3. TEACHING MUST BE INTENTIONAL TO BE EFFECTIVE

- **Creating a Caring Community of Learners:** In DAP, practitioners create and foster a "community of learners" that supports *all* children to develop and learn. The role of the community is to provide a physical, emotional, and cognitive environment conducive to that development and learning.
- **Teaching to Enhance Development and Learning:** DAP provides an optimal balance of adult-guided and child-guided experiences. *Adult-guided* experience proceeds primarily along the lines of the teacher's goals, but is also shaped by the children's active engagement; *child-guided* experience proceeds primarily along the lines of children's interests and actions, with strategic teacher support.
- **Planning Curriculum to Achieve Important Goals:** In developmentally appropriate practice, the curriculum helps young children achieve goals that are developmentally and educationally significant. The curriculum does this through learning experiences (including play, small group, large group, interest centers, and routines) that reflect what is known about young children in general and about these children in particular, as well as about the sequences in which children acquire specific concepts, skills, and abilities, building on prior experiences.
- **Assessing Children's Development and Learning:** In developmentally appropriate practice, the experiences and the assessments are linked (the experiences are developing what is being assessed, and vice versa); both are aligned with the program's desired outcomes or goals for children.
- **Establishing Reciprocal Relationships with Families:** Developmentally appropriate practices derive from deep knowledge of child development principles and of the program's children in particular, as well as the context within which each of them is living. The younger the child, the more necessary it is for practitioners to acquire this particular knowledge through relationships with children's families.

Source: National Association for the Education of Young Children. Available online at http://www.naeyc.org/files/naeyc/file/positions/PSDAP.pdf. Downloaded on February 25, 2010

TEACH THE CHILDREN WELL: ACADEMIC PROGRAMS. With the No Child Left Behind legislation in the United States, and more recently the Race to the Top, there is increasing pressure to focus on academics and readiness for school, even in programs for young children. Some countries such as China have expected preschools to focus on academics for quite a while, but the emphasis is more recent in the United States and Canada. In academic preschools, children spend time doing teacher-led activities such as counting, practicing letters, learning shapes, studying word sounds, and even reviewing homework. Increasingly, individual states have created learning standards for young children, describing what they should know and be able to (Kagan & Scott-Little, 2004).

Because American schools are held accountable for the test scores of their elementary school students, they are eager to begin preparation for good test performance earlier and earlier. Parents do not want their children "left behind," so they may select preschools with an academic emphasis. Also, many of the government-funded intervention programs such as Head Start stress academic preparation for children from low-income families who tend to enter first grade with fewer basic skills than their more privileged peers.

"Is there too much focus on academics for young children?"

© United Feature Syndicate, Inc.

HEAD START AND OTHER INTERVENTION PROGRAMS. Before the 1960s, it was common for children from low-income homes to encounter school for the very first time in first grade, whereas children from middle and upper classes were more likely to have attended preschools and kindergartens, or to have had other educational experiences that prepared them for formal schooling. As a consequence, even though both groups of children made progress in school, many economically disadvantaged children remained behind because they started behind and just did not catch up (Stipek & Ryan, 1997).

In 1965, President Lyndon Johnson signed the legislation that created Head Start, one of the many initiatives of the War on Poverty. The idea was to provide educational experiences to better prepare children from low-income homes for school. In addition to education, children got medical and dental care, some meals, and family social services. As you can imagine, when the Head Start program began, there were many different types of approaches, some better than others. Your author, Anita taught in a 3-month Head Start program in Texas for children about to enter first grade that fall—a really limited experience for the participants (most programs today are at least a half-day for 32 weeks). Around the United States, some Head Start programs were more academic, others more child-centered.

Were these Head Start programs effective? Early research called *Project Follow Through* examined variations in Head Start approaches to track their effects through the early grades. Some programs included enrichments that followed the Head Start students through third grade. Reviewing the results of Project Follow Through, Jane Stallings (1975) concluded that different designs and emphases had different outcomes. Children who had participated in programs that emphasized self-esteem and social emotional development were absent less and were more able to work independently on tasks than students who had not participated in the programs. Students from the academic Head Start programs were more persistent and scored higher on achievement tests. But for all groups, the initial increases in IQ test scores that appeared right after the program had disappeared by third grade. Were the programs a waste?

More recent research findings would say no! Children who participate in Head Start are less likely to repeat a grade or be placed in special education. They also are more likely to finish high school. But quality matters. The longer a child participates in a high-quality program, the better the outcomes—both social and cognitive (Brooks-Gunn, 2003). In fact, when programs such as Early Head Start begin by providing services for women during their pregnancy and continue through the child's first three years, the children benefit in terms of language development and the parents provide more of the quality care assessed by the HOME items in Table 6.5 on page 230 (Head Start Bureau, 2001). Three examples of excellent Head Start programs are High/Scope Perry Preschool Project of Ypsilanti, Michigan; the Abecedarian program in North Carolina; and the Child-Parent Centers in Chicago (Campbell, Pungello, Miller-Johnson, Burchinal, & Ramey, 2001; Reynolds, Temple, Robertson, & Mann, 2001). Let's look at the Perry Preschool, a 2-year program that has been following its graduates for over 40 years (Schweinhart, 2005). The curriculum combines weekly home visits; direct teaching of academic readiness skills; and child-centered exploration, play, and responsiveness to individual children's needs. As middle-aged adults, compared to adults with similar backgrounds who did not attend the school, the Perry graduates are less likely to have been assigned to special education, experienced teenage pregnancy, needed welfare, or accumulated criminal records. Other differences are evident in Figure 6.5 on the next page.

FIGURE 6.5

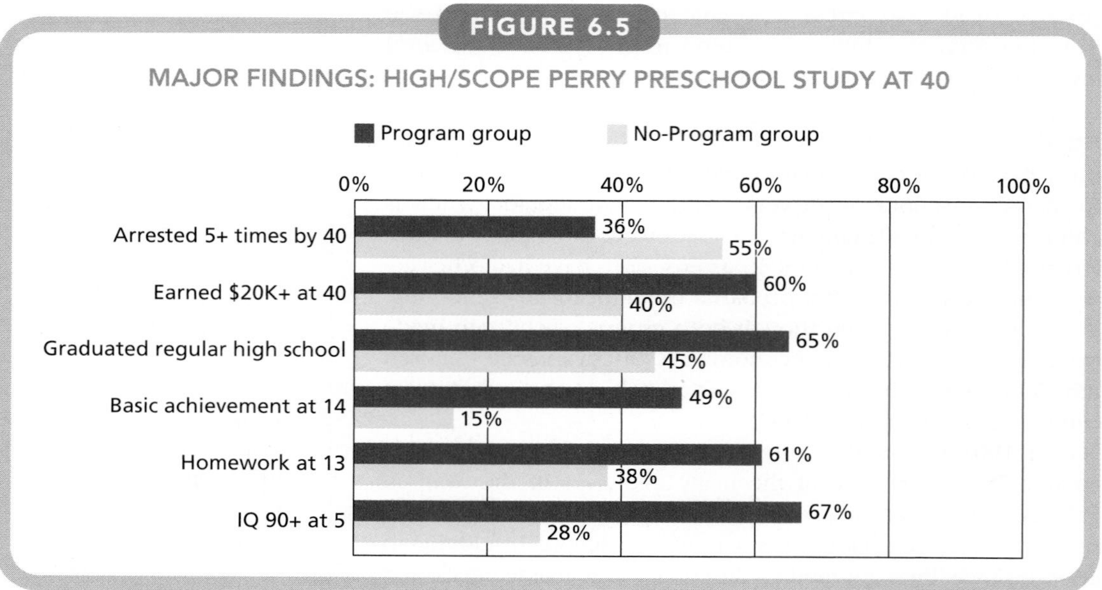

From The High/Scope Perry Preschool Study through Age 40: Summary, Conclusions, and Frequently Asked Questions, *p. 2, by L. J. Schweinhart (Ed.), (2005), Ypsilanti, MI: HighScope Press. Copyright © 2005 by the HighScope Educational Research Foundation. Reprinted with permission.*

Although the cost of good quality preschools such as these seems high (about $15,000 per year in 2009 dollars), several economic studies have shown that these investments are more than repaid in decreased costs to society for special education, welfare, and jail time as well as by increased revenue from the taxes paid by fully employed citizens.

EARLY CHILDHOOD CARE CONCLUSIONS. Deborah Vandell (2004) has summarized the last 25 years of research on early childcare. Luckily, there has been great progress in answering some important questions about the effects of childcare because researchers have examined large, diverse samples over time using reliable and valid measures and sophisticated statistical techniques that can control for other influences such as SES. What can we conclude?

First, children score higher on cognitive outcomes if they attend childcare facilities where the ratio of adults to children is high and adults have a college degree with more early childhood training. Also, it is important that the adults like the children and are responsive to their needs. In effective programs, language fills the rooms as children talk, listen, and are listened to. The space, materials, toys, activities, and equipment support learning. There are many opportunities for art, blocks, and dramatic play. Parents are involved. Finally, children do better in programs that meet more of the American Public Health Association standards for childcare centers. Unfortunately, perhaps as few as 20% of all early childhood programs are truly high quality (Vandell, 2004). See Figure 6.6 on the next page for a checklist that can be used to evaluate preschool environments.

BEWARE OF "MAGICAL THINKING." High-quality programs are especially valuable for the most vulnerable children—those whose families have the least education and resources. The power of these programs increases if there is good follow-up, that is, if graduates of high-quality programs receive continuing support into elementary school. Too often, voters and government representatives hope for a magic bullet—a year of Head Start that changes children forever. But Jeanne Brooks-Gunn, testifying before the U.S. House of Representatives Committee on Ways and Means, cautioned: "It is unrealistic, given our knowledge of development, to expect short-term early interventions to last indefinitely, especially if children end up attending poor quality schools. It is magical thinking to expect that if we intervene in the early years, no further help will be needed by children in the elementary

FIGURE 6.6

CHOICES: RATING CHILDCARE ENVIRONMENTS

Think about (and look at) your environment and rate the following areas, indicating **S** for Satisfactory, **N** for Needs Improvement, and **NI** for Needs IMMEDIATE Improvement. Remember, you're not looking at how much space you have but how well you use it!

The arrival and entrance area

____ adequate parking for parents
____ safe, well-lit entrance to home (e.g. snow cleared, path to door and steps in good repair)
____ entrance area is warm and welcoming
____ adequate space for adults and children
____ washable door mat
____ place for shoes and boots
____ place for the children's outdoor clothes
____ place for each child's personal belongings
____ bulletin board for menu, parent info, pictures, etc.

The eating area:

____ is cheerful and comfortable
____ table and chairs
____ any required booster seats, high chairs/infant chairs
____ child-friendly dishes, cutlery, and cups
____ washable table, chairs, and floor surface
____ convenient sink

The personal care area:

____ is functional and bright
____ adequate space for adult and child(ren)
____ toilet, potty seat or chair
____ sink
____ soap dispenser
____ non-slip stool for access to sink
____ shelves for supplies
____ cleaning supplies (stored out of reach)
____ hooks/hangers/shelves for children's personal care supplies (face cloths, towels, toothbrushes, combs, etc.)
____ accessible diapering facilities (change table, necessary supplies/equipment.

The sleeping area:

____ is quiet and pleasant
____ comfortable mats, cots, or beds
____ individual bedding
____ cribs or playpens for infants/toddlers
____ window coverings to reduce brightness

Play areas:

____ are bright, cheerful and provide adequate space for intended use
____ child-sized table and chairs
____ adequate and accessible shelving and storage for toys, books, materials, and equipment
____ shelves, tables or other furniture used to divide and organize areas for different kinds of play
____ comfortable rugs where appropriate
____ washable floors where appropriate
____ children's artwork, posters, and decorations

Space, equipment, and supplies for:

____ creative play
____ block/building play
____ manipulative/cognitive play
____ dramatic play
____ language/reading activities
____ active play (indoors and outdoors)

Other areas:

Immediate Improvement: ____________________

Satisfactory: ____________________

Needs Improvement: ____________________

Source: Illinois Early Learning Project http://www.illinoisearlylearning.org/tipsheets/preschoolchoice.htm and Canadian Child Care Federation: http://www.cccf-fcsge.ca/subsites/familytp/english/resourcesh1a_en.htm.

school years and beyond" (Brooks-Gunn, 2003, p. 1). Recommendations in the ***Connecting with Children*** guidelines on the next page may help.

Transition to Kindergarten

More and more often, children are attending kindergarten classes before entering first grade. In fact, with the increasing emphasis on testing and accountability in U.S. and Canadian schools, state-funded kindergartens are becoming more like first grades. The kindergarten teachers we work with say that many children come to their classes already able to read a few words, count to 20, and write their names. But other children are far behind. They have limited vocabularies, little exposure to books and reading, and minimal

CONNECTING WITH CHILDREN

Guidelines for Families: Making Childcare and Preschool Choices

Check to see if the program is accredited by the state or province or by the National Association for the Education of Young Children (NAEYC—rhymes with "Gracie").
Examples

1. Go online to find centers in your area accredited by NAEYC: http://www.naeyc.org/accreditation/search/
2. Ask at the center for evidence of accreditation.

Ask about the teachers.
Examples

1. What educational backgrounds do they have? Are they trained to work with this age group and diverse groups of students?
2. Is the staff stable, or does it change constantly?
3. How many children are there for each teacher?
4. Is my child's cultural background represented in the instructional materials used?

Ask about the program.
Examples

1. Are children involved in enjoyable as well as intellectually stimulating individual and group activities using a variety of materials?
2. Is there time for outdoor as well as indoor play?
3. Are children involved and absorbed in interesting activities much of the time, and not sitting still listening to a teacher for long periods?

Look at the classroom.
Examples

1. Are all areas—indoors and outdoors—clearly safe?
2. Are there distinct areas for reading, playing, and participating in group activities with blocks, toys, props for pretend play, puzzles, and games? Does the room look inviting?
3. Is the noise level generally pleasing?
4. Is there a comfortable, enclosed space where a child can calm down away from the crowd?

Observe the children.
Examples

1. Do most of the children seem happy and truly absorbed in their activities most of the time?
2. Are the classroom rules fair and consistently applied? Does the teacher help misbehaving children reflect on how to act next time, saying clearly what behavior she expects?
3. Listen for positive discipline words. "Remember to walk in our classroom" rather than "Stop running!" "I want you to use your indoor voices" rather than "Stop shouting!"

Find out whether the school encourages parent involvement.
Examples

1. Does the teacher discuss the child's progress with parents at scheduled times as well as informal times?
2. Listen for such statements as "Here's a book we read today that your son really enjoyed. Would you like to take it home to read with him?"

Sources: 10 Signs of a Great Preschool http://www.naeyc.org/resources/eyly/1996/01.htm; What Is a Quality Preschool Program? http://www.parentingweb .com/dev_edu/qualitypresch.htm

understanding of numbers. What does it mean to be ready to learn? One early answer was that children needed to score well on school readiness tests. Let's look critically at this definition of readiness.

THE IDEA OF "READINESS." In the late 1980s, many states required paper-and-pencil tests for admission to kindergarten. Public outcry led to modifications of the policy and spurred many educators to reform the **readiness testing** process. Critics of readiness tests (Linn & Gronlund, 2000) believe:

1. Group-administered paper-and-pencil tests are inappropriate for preschool children and thus should not be the basis for decisions about school entry. Readiness tests do not have sufficient predictive validity to be used alone to make screening or placement decisions.
2. The use of readiness tests narrows the preschool curriculum, making it more academic and less developmentally appropriate.
3. The evidence shows that delaying entry into first grade or retaining children in kindergarten is not effective. Children who are retained do no better than similar children who are not held back. See the ***Point/Counterpoint*** for a discussion of holding children back.

For the last 100 years, parents and educators have debated about the value of retention versus social promotion (passing students on to the next grade with their peers). One study in North Carolina found that kindergarten retention had more than doubled from 1992 to 2002, with over 6% of students retained in 2002. Almost 20% of seniors have repeated at least one grade since kindergarten, usually in the earlier grades (Kelly, 1999). Retained children are more likely to be male, members of minority groups, living in poverty, and younger, and less likely to have participated in early childhood programs (Beebe-Frankenberger, Berger, Bovina, Macmillan, & Gresham, 2004; Hong & Raudenbush, 2005). Is retention a good policy? What does the evidence say? What are the arguments?

POINT

Yes, it just makes sense. Retention in kindergarten for children considered "not ready" for first grade is a common practice. In fact, some parents hold their son or daughter back to give the child an edge over peers in each grade thereafter or because the child was born late in the year—a practice sometimes called "academic red-shirting." In the mid-1960s, 96% of 6-year-olds were enrolled in first grade in the United States. By 2008, the number was 84% (Barnard-Brak, 2008). With the increased emphasis on high standards and accountability, the idea of social promotion has come under fire and retention is seen as the better way. Schoolteachers and administrators often argue that instruction is more effective when all the students in a class are at roughly the same achievement level and ready to benefit from teaching. Ganglier Hong and Stephen Raudenbush (2005) summarize this and other arguments that have been made in favor of retention:

> A widely endorsed argument is that, when low-achieving students are retained in a grade, the academic status of children in a classroom will become more homogeneous, easing the teacher's task of managing instructional activities (Byrnes, 1989; also see Shepard & Smith, 1988, for a review). In particular, retaining some children in kindergarten may allow the first-grade teacher to teach at a higher level, benefiting those who would be promoted under the policy. Meanwhile, children who view grade retention as a punishment may study harder to avoid being retained in the future. Some have argued that, in comparison with the social promotion policy, repeating a grade is perhaps developmentally more appropriate and may make learning more meaningful for children who are struggling (Plummer & Graziano, 1987; Smith & Shepard, 1988). If these arguments are correct, adopting a policy of grade retention will benefit those promoted and those retained, thus boosting achievement overall. (p. 206)

COUNTERPOINT

No, Retention in Not Effective. After summarizing the arguments in favor of kindergarten retention, Hong and Raudenbush (2005) review the findings of almost a century of research. They note that even though there are a small number of studies that support the value of retention, the weight of the evidence indicates that it is not helpful and may be harmful. Most research finds that grade retention is associated with poor long-term outcomes such as dropping out of school, higher arrest rates, fewer job opportunities, lower self-esteem (Jimerson, Anderson, & Whipple, 2002; Shepard, 1989). For example, in a longitudinal study of 29 retained and 50 low-achieving but promoted students, Shane Jimerson (1999) found that years later, the retained students had poorer educational and employment outcomes than the promoted students. The retained children dropped out more often, had lower-paying jobs, and received lower competence ratings from employers. In addition, the low-achieving but promoted students were comparable to a control group in all employment outcomes at age 20.

The study by Hong and Raudenbush (2005) examined data on 11,843 kindergarten students who participated in a longitudinal study that followed them to the end of first grade. The researchers were able to compare retained and promoted students from schools that practice retention as well as promoted students from schools that practice social promotion. They found no evidence that retention improved either reading or mathematics achievement. In addition, retention did not seem to improve instruction in the first grade by making the class more similar in academic ability. After one year, the retained students were an average of one year behind, and evidence indicated that these children would have done better if promoted. The researchers concluded that retention "seemed to have constrained the learning potential for all but the highest-risk children" (p. 220).

The results on academic red-shirting are mixed. Some studies have found benefits for students held back by their parents, but other studies have found no benefits. Lucy Barnard-Brak (2008) identified 986 children from the national Early Childhood Longitudinal Study-Kindergarten who had been identified as having learning disabilities. She concluded, "delayed kindergarten entrance was not associated with better academic achievement for children with learning disabilities across time" (P. 50).

Beware of Either/Or: Using Research for Children

No matter what, children who are having trouble should get help, whether they are promoted or retained. However, just covering the same material again in the same way won't solve the children's academic or social problems. As Jeannie Oakes (1999) has said, "No sensible person advocates social promotion as it is currently framed—simply passing incompetent children on to the next grade" (p. 8). The best approach may be to promote the children along with their peers, but to give them special remediation during the summer or the next year (Mantzicopoulos & Morrison, 1992; Shepard & Smith, 1988). In addition, because the inability to focus attention and self-regulate is an important aspect of readiness to learn (Blair, 2002), help should also focus on these skills as well. An even better approach would be to prevent the problems before they occur by providing extra resources (McCoy & Reynolds, 1999).

Another answer suggested in the last decade was that cognitive and emergent literacy skills are important foundations for later achievement, so children need these to be ready to learn in school (Kauerz, 2002). It appears that children who have expressive and particularly receptive language difficulties right before starting school have lower performance on many kindergarten academic and social outcomes (Justice, Bowles, Turnbull, & Skibbe, 2009). In addition to having adequate language skills, being physically healthy, well rested, and well nourished; being able to communicate needs and thoughts; being enthusiastic and curious; and being able to focus attention, self-regulate, and especially control negative emotions are better indicators of readiness than paper-and pencil testing, according to kindergarten teachers (Blair, 2002; Lewit & Baker, 1995).

How about success after kindergarten? One large national study added social/emotional and health measures to the usual cognitive and language measures. Elizabeth Hair and her colleagues (2006) clustered a representative sample of over 17,000 first-time kindergarten students into four groups: students with positive development in all areas—cognitive, language, social/emotional, and health (30%), students with social/emotional and health strengths (34%), students at risk for social/emotional problems (13%), and students with health risks (23%). Children in the two risk groups performed the worst in the early elementary grades, whereas children with positive development in all areas performed the best. The researchers summarize:

> [L]anguage and cognitive skills, although important components of school readiness, are not the only relevant factors that predict later school success. Below-average language and cognition skills *in combination with* severely poor health or a lack of social skills at the beginning of kindergarten predicts the lowest scores on math and reading assessments at the end of first grade. Furthermore, below-average language and cognition skills *in combination with* severely limited social/emotional skills at the beginning of kindergarten predict the lowest ratings on self-control and classroom motivation at the end of first grade. (p. 450)

The children in this study who were in the two high-risk groups were more likely to have other risk factors in their background—poverty, single and/or teen parent, low birth weight—pointing to the importance of early health and educational interventions, support, and parent education.

Young Children in a Digital World

It seems that computers, cell phones, iPods, iPads, iPhones, Kindles, video games, Nooks, BlackBerries, and other digital media have changed life for everyone. But what about young children? How is their cognitive development affected? Think about it—young children today have never known a world without the Internet and cell phones. Some people have even suggested that we call this the *iGeneration* (Rosen, 2010).

Until the 21st century, very little was known about the impact of electronic media on children's development. In 2003, a group of researchers surveyed a random sample of 1,000 parents of children from ages 6 months to 6 years and analyzed the results (Rideout, Vandewater, & Wartella, 2003; Vandewater et al., 2005). They concluded, "Children's homes are packed with media options, including TVs, computers, DVD players and video game consoles" (Rideout et al., 2003, p. 4). Television is everywhere. What is the effect of all this TV exposure on young children?

Television

Because most children spend more time watching television than they do in any other activity except sleep, the possible influence of television is a real concern. In their survey, Rideout and her colleagues (2003) found that almost all (99%) of children lived in a home with a television and 36% of these children had a television *in their own bedroom*. More recent research found that 35% of children *ages 6 months to 3 years* had a TV in their own bedroom, so the percentage for all children is probably higher now (Rosen, 2010). Rideout's research found DVD players in 95% of the homes, and 27% of the children had a DVD player in their bedrooms. The television is on an average of 6 hours a day. In fact, Vandewater and colleagues (2005) found that the TV was on all day or most of the day in 35% of the homes they studied.

Television viewing is related to a number of problematic physical and social outcomes such as increased childhood obesity, eyestrain, aggressive behaviors, acceptance of violence to solve problems, lack of empathy for victims of violence, and some childhood anxieties. In terms of cognitive outcomes, viewing more hours of television tends to have negative effects on young children's creativity, language development, and achievement in school (Frost, Wortham, & Reifel, 2005). In the study of homes with the TV on most of the time described above, parents read less to their children and the children were less likely to be able to read (Vandewater et al., 2005). See the ***Connecting with Children*** on page 243 for guidelines about television viewing.

Clearly, just spending hours in front of a TV is not helpful for children, but can television be a positive force for young children? Yes. In fact, television has been used to improve emergent literacy skills of young children. For example, Linebarger and her colleagues (2004) used 17 episodes of the educational television program *Between the Lions* with kindergarten and first grade children. The program focuses on whole language processes such as different contexts for reading and writing as well as specific skills such as letter-sound correspondences and the alphabet. All the children who viewed the program improved in word recognition and reading test scores, but the ones who improved the most were the kindergarten students who were at no risk or moderate risk for developing reading problems. Kindergartners at greatest risk and first graders did not benefit as much—which indicates the importance of the lessons fitting the needs and abilities of the child. Too advanced or too easy won't be as helpful—as Vygotsky would remind us.

Young Children and Computers

Before about age 3, children learn best by being active. They are in the sensorimotor stage and need to use their hands, mouths, ears, eyes, arms, and legs to act on their environments. Sitting in front of computers or standing too still for anything will not support their development (Hohman, 1998). But digital media are appealing (Rosen, 2010). Rideout and colleagues (2003) found that nearly half of the children under 6 that they studied had used computers and 30% had played video games. Every day, 27% of the 4- to 6-year-olds in the study used a computer. Rosen's (2010) more recent research found that 10% of children ages 4–8 had a computer in *their own bedroom*. Joe Frost and his colleagues (2005) note that "Computers, the Internet, video games, and electronic toys are the new electric playgrounds for children, combining three forms of games: practice, symbolic, and rule governed" (p. 77). These games provide challenge that requires *practice*, fantasy worlds that allow "as-if" and *symbolic* play, and *rules* that often must be discovered to allow control. According to Malone and Lepper (1987) the features of challenge, fantasy, and control greatly increase motivation and may explain some of the appeal of computer and video games.

Are these digital experiences appropriate for preschool children? This is a hotly debated issue. Much of the research on the effects of computer usage on cognitive skills such as spatial representation or the ability to divide visual attention have been conducted with school age children and college undergraduates (Subrahmanyam, Greenfield, Kraut, & Gross, 2001). The Alliance for Children (2000) argues that we should stop using computers in early childhood education until we learn more about their effects. These researchers believe that computers take children away from the physical activities and social interactions they require for their development. Children in front of a computer playing alone are not having conversations with adults about a story or cooperating with peers to build with blocks. They may be exposed to violence and sexual content that is completely inappropriate. But it is likely that digital media are here to stay and will only expand in the future (Rosen, 2010), so are there appropriate uses with young children?

Developmentally Appropriate Computer Activities

Computers should not be used to do solitary drill and practice activities. Developmentally appropriate ways to use computers with 3- and 4-year-olds are different from the ways we use computers in kindergarten and the primary grades (http://www.kidsource.com/education/computers.children.html). With developmentally appropriate computer activities, young children can benefit cognitively without sustaining losses in creativity (Haugland & Wright, 1997). Developmentally appropriate software for children should include simple spoken directions. The computer activities should be open-ended and encourage discovery, exploration, problem solving, and understanding of cause and effect. Children should be able to remain in control of the activities through a variety of responses. Finally, the content should be appropriate for and respectful of diverse cultures, ages, and abilities (Fischer & Gillespie, 2003; Frost, Wortham, & Reifel, 2005). Linda Tsantis and her colleagues suggest that you ask this question about any program you are considering: "Does this software program help create learning opportunities that did not exist without it?" (Tsantis, Berwick, & Thouvenelle, 2003).

There is another important consideration—do the material's multimedia features (e.g., embedded videos, zoom-ins, music, added sounds, images) add to learning or take away from it? One danger is that programs will include attractive visuals or sound effects interruptions that actually interfere with the development of important concepts. For example, describing a Peter Rabbit storytelling program that includes the sound effects of a buzz saw and the thud of a tree falling, Tsantis and colleagues (2003) caution:

> How do these cute asides fit into a child's construction of the notion of story sequence and plot? Perhaps these digressions foster lack of focus and distractibility for youngsters who already have such tendencies. Further, how does this interruption affect the comprehension of the plot, action, and characters? (p. 6)

Dealing with all of this stimulation might make children better at multitasking, but also worse at deeper thought processes such as developing perspective-taking skills and understanding the plot, theme, and sequence of the story. So children learn to do several things at once, but have a superficial understanding of what they are doing (Carpenter, 2000).

Research in the Netherlands, however, demonstrated that multimedia storybooks can provide support for understanding stories and remembering linguistic information for kindergarten students from families with low educational levels who are behind in language and literacy skills (Verhallen, Bus, & de Jong, 2006). The difference in this study seemed to be that the multimedia features of the story supported understanding and memory by providing multiple pathways to meaning, giving visual and verbal representations of key story elements, focusing attention on important information, and reinforcing key ideas. This extra scaffolding may be especially important for students with limited language and literacy skills. So the bottom line is that multimedia elements should focus on meaning and not just provide attractive "bells and whistles." The ***Connecting with Children*** guidelines summarize ideas for developmentally appropriate uses of technology with young children.

CONNECTING WITH CHILDREN

Guidelines for Families and Teachers: Using Technology

TELEVISION

Limit television-viewing time in keeping with the child's age.

Examples

1. Children under the age of 2 generally should not watch television.
2. Children older than 2 should watch TV no more than 10 hours per week or about 1 to 2 hours per day.
3. Do not put a television in a child's bedroom.

Involve children in decisions about television choices, but maintain adult control and monitor viewing.

Examples

1. Offer young children a limited number of appropriate choices between programs.
2. Watch programs with your child and talk about what is happening in the program.
3. Use filtering software to protect children from inappropriate programs.

Use the TV programs as springboards for conversations with your child.

Examples

1. Discuss alternative solutions to the problems presented—What else could the character do to solve the problem?
2. Discuss the difference between make believe and real life.
3. Stress that the violent acts on TV are not real, but are created by special effects and stunts; and there are better ways to resolve conflicts—these are the ways most real people use to solve their problems (Huesmann et al., 2003).
4. Avoid using TV viewing as a reward or punishment—that makes television even more attractive and important to children (Slaby et al., 1995).

COMPUTERS AND THE INTERNET

Select developmentally appropriate programs that encourage learning, creativity, and social interaction.

Examples

1. Encourage two children to work together rather than having children work alone.
2. Check the implicit messages in programs. For example, some drawing programs allow children to "blow up" their projects if they don't like them, so instead of solving a problem they just destroy it. Tsantis et al. (2003) recommend a "recycle" metaphor instead of a "blow it up" option.
3. Look for programs that encourage discovery, exploration, problem solving, and multiple responses.

Monitor children as they work at computers.

Examples

1. Make sure computers are in areas where adults can see them.
2. Discuss with children why some programs or websites are off limits.
3. Watch what children eat while they are using computers—replace junk food with healthy snacks.
4. Balance computer time with active play such as hands-on projects, blocks, sand, water, and art.

Keep children safe as they work at computers.

Examples

1. Teach children to shield their identity on the Internet and monitor any "friends" they may be communicating with.
2. Install filtering software to protect children from inappropriate content.

Suggestions are taken from Frost, J. L., Wortham, S. C., & Reifel, S. (2005). Play and child development *(2nd ed.). Upper Saddle River, NJ: Prentice-Hall, pp. 76–80 and Tsantis, L. A., Bewick, C. J., & Thouvenelle, S. (2003, November). Examining some common myths about computer use in the early years.* Beyond the Journal: Young Children on the Web. *(pp. 1–9).*

SUMMARY AND KEY TERMS

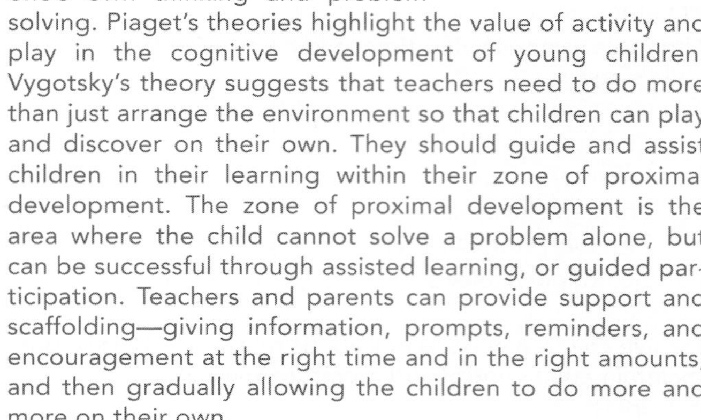

- **New Cognitive Possibilities for a Developing Brain**

In the early years, children develop the abilities to integrate the present with past experiences, anticipate what might happen in the future, think about and understand causality, use semantic (meaning) categories and concepts to organize their thinking and express ideas, and detect relationships between concepts such as *larger* and *smaller*.

- **Language in the Preschool Years: Amazing Developments**

In general, cultures develop words for the concepts that are important to them. Languages change over time to indicate changing cultural needs and values. About half the children in the world live in environments where two or more languages are spoken. If adequate input is available and continues over time in both the first and second languages, children can become balanced bilinguals—equally fluent in both languages. Higher degrees of bilingualism are correlated with increased cognitive abilities, creativity, theory of mind development, cognitive flexibility, and metalinguistic awareness.

Children in social environments with more adult-produced, child-directed speech—particularly speech that uses rich vocabulary and complex structure—acquire language more rapidly. In learning language, humans may have built-in biases, rules, and constraints about language that restrict the number of possibilities considered. Areas of language development in the early years are sounds, pronunciation, and vocabulary. Fast-mapping can add as many as 10 words a day. At this time, young children learn grammar and syntax, often by overregularizing grammar rules. Young children also begin to master pragmatics—knowing how to use language appropriately in social situations.

Emergent literacy is made up of the skills, knowledge, and attitudes that develop along the way as children learn to read and write, as well as the environments and contexts that support these developments. Two broad categories of skills that are important for later reading are: (1) skills related to understanding sounds and codes, such as knowing that letters have names, that sounds are associated with letters, and that words are made up of sounds in a sequence (phonemic awareness), and (2) oral language skills, such as expressive and receptive vocabulary, knowledge of syntax, and the ability to understand and tell stories. In homes that promote literacy, parents and other adults value reading as a source of pleasure, and there are books and other printed materials everywhere. Parents read to their children, take them to bookstores and libraries, limit the amount of television everyone watches, and encourage literacy-related play. Parent involvement and quality preschools support emergent literacy in both English and Spanish.

- **Piaget and Vygotsky**

Piaget called children's self-directed talk "egocentric speech," but Vygotsky believed children's self-directed talk—private speech—played an important role in guiding and monitoring thinking and problem solving, in addition to moving children toward self-regulation, the ability to anticipate the future, and to plan, monitor, and guide one's own thinking and problem solving. Piaget's theories highlight the value of activity and play in the cognitive development of young children. Vygotsky's theory suggests that teachers need to do more than just arrange the environment so that children can play and discover on their own. They should guide and assist children in their learning within their zone of proximal development. The zone of proximal development is the area where the child cannot solve a problem alone, but can be successful through assisted learning, or guided participation. Teachers and parents can provide support and scaffolding—giving information, prompts, reminders, and encouragement at the right time and in the right amounts, and then gradually allowing the children to do more and more on their own.

- **Information Processing: Knowing and Remembering**

Information processing theories suggest that one of the most important elements in cognitive development is that person's knowledge, particularly domain-specific knowledge. For example, between the ages of 2 and 6, children seem to grasp how-to-count principles. Some researchers have suggested that a sense of number may be part of our evolutionary equipment, but others disagree and make the case that a full understanding of number requires learning. Many activities with numbers and counting can be valuable experiences for young children.

In order to regulate attention, a critical skill, children need to focus on relevant information, ignore irrelevant information, sustain attention over time, and control impulsive responses to distractions. There are three basic aspects of memory: *memory span,* or the amount of information that can be held in short-term/working memory; *memory processing efficiency*; and *speed of processing*. These three basic capacities act together and influence each other. As children grow older, they develop more effective strategies for remembering information. During the preschool years, children develop an autobiographical or personal memory for the events in their own lives that improves with age and may be affected by cultural differences. One kind of personal memory, called scripts, involves repeated events in our lives, such as getting ready for bed. Young children also can report accurate eyewitness memories if they do not have to wait too long to report and are not asked leading questions.

Children can learn to apply more effective strategies to solve problems, either through instruction or by discovery. Even if they have been taught or have discovered more effective strategies, young children may not use them unless cued. Effective strategies may develop in waves, as more effective strategies gradually replace less effective ones. One kind of knowledge to develop in the early years is a theory of mind, an understanding of the nature of thinking and mental states. One current explanation for autism spectrum disorders is that children with these disorders have an underdeveloped theory of mind.

Between 60% and 70% of children under the age of 7 have played with imaginary companions. These pretend creations can help children deal with fears and practice conflict resolution. Compared with children who do not have imaginary friends, children with imaginary companions perform better on theory of mind tests, so they are actually better at distinguishing reality from fantasy.

• Contexts for Cognitive Development: Family and Home

The quality of the home environment and interactions with mothers assessed by the *HOME scale* are related to children's cognitive development from infancy through adolescence. The two scales that were most predictive of cognitive ability are Learning Stimulation and Access to Reading. The NICHD Early Child Care Research Network researchers concluded that most of the variations among individual children in their attention and memory abilities in first grade could be traced to the differences in the quality of the child's family environment.

• Early Childhood Education

Today, many young children around the world are in early childhood education programs of various kinds. Italy has given us the Montessori Method and the Reggio Emilia model; both support and encourage cognitive development through creative play. Many early childhood educators emphasize the value of developmentally appropriate practices (DAP) that avoid pressures to master academic subjects, but today there is increasing pressure to focus on academics and readiness for school, even in programs for young children.

The goal of Head Start, an initiative begun in 1965, was to provide educational experiences to better prepare children from low-income homes for school. Children who participate in Head Start are less likely to repeat a grade or be placed in special education and are more likely to finish high school. The longer a child participates in a high-quality program, the better the outcomes—both social and cognitive.

Children score higher on cognitive outcomes if they attend childcare facilities where the ratio of adults to children is high; adults have a college degree with more early childhood training; adults like the children and are responsive to their needs; language fills the rooms; parents are involved; and the space, materials, toys, activities, and equipment support learning. Children who have expressive and particularly receptive language difficulties right before starting school have lower performance on many kindergarten academic and social outcomes. In addition to language, the ability to focus attention, self-regulate, and especially control negative emotions is a better indicator of readiness than paper-and-pencil testing.

• Young Children in a Digital World

In terms of cognitive outcomes, viewing more hours of television tends to have negative effects on young children's creativity, language development, and achievement in school. But television also has been used to improve emergent literacy skills of young children. Similarly, computers can be used appropriately. Developmentally appropriate software for children should include simple spoken directions. The computer activities should be open-ended and encourage discovery, exploration, problem solving, and understanding of cause and effect. Children should be able to remain in control of the activities through a variety of responses. Finally, the content should be appropriate for and respectful of diverse cultures, ages, and abilities. Multimedia elements should focus on meaning, not just provide attractive "bells and whistles."

▾ KEY TERMS

assisted learning/guided participation (215)
autism spectrum disorders (227)
automaticity (219)
balanced bilingualism (200)
bilingualism (200)
childcare/day care (232)
collective monologue (211)
conservation (210)
cultural tools (213)
decentering (210)
developmentally appropriate practices (DAP) (233)
domain-specific knowledge (217)
egocentric (211)
emergent literacy (205)
expressive vocabulary (201)
fast-mapping (203)
inside-out skills (206)
long-term memory (217)
mutual exclusivity (203)
operations (207)
outside-in skills (206)
overlapping wave theory (225)
overregularize (203)
phonemic awareness (205)
phonology (201)
pragmatics (205)
preoperational (207)
private speech (213)
production deficiency (224)
readiness testing (238)
receptive vocabulary (201)
reversible thinking (210)
script (222)
self-regulation (213)
semiotic function (207)
short-term memory (216)
source monitoring (223)
strategy (220)
syntax (204)
theory of mind (226)
working memory (216)
zone of proximal development (ZPD) (216)

▼ THE CASEBOOK

ONLY CHILDREN AND IMAGINARY FRIENDS

Kayla has set her table again to make "tea" for Sassy. When her mother walks in and starts to sit down, Kayla protests, "No! that's Sassy's chair. You have to go, she is coming." Kayla's mother sighs, says, "OK, I'll leave," and returns to her desk to check her e-mail. In a few minutes she hears Kayla talking with Sassy, or at least she hears Kayla's side of the conversation. Sassy is not a real child but an imaginary friend that Kayla talks about and with often—she has for the past few years. When she is upset or has been scolded, Kayla threatens, "I'm going to run away and live with Sassy in China—she has a nice mommy!" But at other times, Kayla complains that Sassy has been mean to her and has spilled ice cream on her shirt. Her parents were not concerned at first about the invisible Sassy, but then they found out Kayla believes that Sassy is a giraffe who wears jeans and can make herself tiny to fit in Kayla's pocket when she goes to school. Her parents worry, what will the preschool teacher think? What will the other children think? Should we talk to someone about Kayla? Is it because she is lonely as an only child? Will Sassy keep Kayla from making real friends?

WHAT WOULD THEY DO?

Here is how some professionals in several fields responded:

KATHERINE A. YOUNG—K–8 School Counselor
Montgomery County Intermediate Unit, Non-Public School Services Division, Norristown, Pennsylvania

Imaginary friends can hold a special role in a child's life. Having an imaginary friend can help a child build the skills to make friends and work out problems. When meeting with Kayla's parents, I would share with them some of the information that I've learned about imaginary friends. It is typically not something parents need to be concerned about, and parents should hold a neutral attitude, neither encouraging nor discouraging the child's interaction with the imaginary friend. Parents should not interact with the imaginary friend, if possible. The imaginary friend may be helping Kayla to build confidence in social situations or work on feelings of insecurity. I would be interested in finding out if there have been or will be any changes in the family. If a new baby is on the way or another major change has left Kayla with less attention from her parents, she could be using "Sassy" as a way to seek attention. Once Kayla starts preschool, her parents and teachers should monitor her play. If she seems to prefer playing with her imaginary friend instead of real children, she may need some help with social skills. If she is able to develop friendships with the other children in her class, her parents have no reason to be concerned.

KATIE BURGER—Kindergarten Teacher
Washington Park Elementary, Laurinburg, North Carolina

It is likely that Kayla has found a playmate because she did not have one. This is very common for only-children or children who do not have anyone else to play with. She finds comfort knowing she will always have someone there for her, just like having a brother or sister around. She probably pretends to fight and argue with her because that is what she has observed from other children or people around her.

I would ask the parents if Kayla has ever had a play date with someone her age or if she has neighbors or family members that she has played with. Does she always play by herself? When other children approach her, does she try to play or remain alone? As a teacher, I would not be concerned because an imaginary friend is common for children to have. However, if the imaginary friend is making the child withdrawn from interactions with other children, I would want to look into the situation more closely.

SARAH DAVLIN—Elementary School Counselor (K–5)
Wyandot Run Elementary School, Olentangy Local Schools, Powell, Ohio

Although the presence of an imaginary friend may be disconcerting to parents, as professionals, we can alleviate stress on the home front by reminding parents that fantasy friends are well within the "normal" range of child development. Old school thinking tells us imaginary friends are usually invented by only children as a means to compensate for a lack of companionship or socialization, but our new understanding indicates many children have make-believe friends at some point during their younger years. We can comfort families by helping them recognize the active, healthy imagination within their child.

Although imaginary friends are well within the parameters of "typical development," we can still help parents connect with their child on a deeper level by exploring the "function" of the behavior. By tuning into common themes among imaginary playmates, we can speculate the meaning of the fantasy friend in the child's life. Is the purpose of the friend to explore new things or bring entertainment? It is possible the friend is a means to satisfy loneliness, cope with change, or express frustration? If one of latter is the case, we can work with parents to develop a plan to further address the specific child's needs.

Finally we can provide parents a few quick tips for dealing with imaginary friends, such as: stay positive and try not to show disapproval, take cues from your child to determine how to interact with the make-believe friend, and calmly inform your child there is "guilt by association" if there is an attempt to blame misbehaviors on the imaginary friend.

To hear a podcast by Australian researcher Dr. Evan Kidd on children's imaginary friends, click: http://www.latrobe.edu.au/marketing/assets/podcasts/2009/jun1909-evan-kidd.mp3

PEARSON **myeducationlab**

Now go to MyEducationLab **at www.myeducationlab.com,** where you can:

- Find the instructional objectives for this chapter in the **Study Plan.**
- Take a quiz as a part of the **Study Plan** to self-assess your mastery of chapter content. The program generates an individualized Study Plan based upon your answers to the quiz.
- Complete **Activities and Applications** to assist you in deepening your understanding of important chapter concepts.
- Apply what you have learned through **Building Teaching Skills,** exercises that guide you in trying out skills and strategies you will use in professional practice.

7

SOCIAL EMOTIONAL DEVELOPMENT IN EARLY CHILDHOOD

THE CASEBOOK

WHAT WOULD YOU DO?

WHY NOT SAY WHAT YOU REALLY MEAN?

It crosses Tara's mind that the party has gone very well . . . so far. Daughter Katie is having her first birthday party. She turns three today and so she and five "friends" have gathered at her home, with parents in tow, to celebrate. The weather is good, which allowed for games in the back yard and a barbeque. The piñata was a great success and the children have had their fill of cake. Now it's time to open the gifts. Katie is the center of attention. As parents and children gather around to watch, hoping their gifts are met with approval, Tara is mortified by the words that come out of Katie's mouth. "I don't want this. It's dumb," she says about one gift. "I already have one of these," she says about another. Tara exchanges looks with her husband, David, recognizing his sense of helplessness. As she scans the faces of Katie's guests, she sees hurt and disappointment on the faces of the children who gave the gifts. Some parents are silent, others laugh awkwardly. One child chimes in, "I don't have one. I want it." Tara wonders: "What should I say? Should I intervene? How? Is there any way to salvage what remains of the party and future friendships for Katie?"

CRITICAL THINKING

- How would you explain Katie's behavior to her mom and, perhaps, to the other parents?
- What characteristics of preschool children do you observe in this scenario and how would you expect this behavior to change over time?
- How could Katie's mom intervene in this situation to address Katie's behavior and the feelings of her guests?

Claudia Uno, Age 8—Andorra

▶ OVERVIEW AND OBJECTIVES

This chapter tracks the development of preschool children from egocentric toddlers with limited understandings of self and others into school-age children who have more self-awareness and self-control, along with greater compassion for the needs and concerns of others. During this period, children gradually relinquish their self-centered view of the world and come to realize that many events happen in the world that don't have a direct reference to them: "You mean it's not all about me?!" In this chapter, we will chronicle children's growing awareness of self and understanding of others. We will see how they develop skills for empathizing, perspective-taking, negotiating, and cooperating through interactions with peers and first friendships. We will examine the central role of play in preschool children's lives. Through play, young children develop both cognitive and social skills, explore alternative realities, and face fears. Also, we will study the nature and significance of children's attachments to parents and examine different parenting styles and approaches to discipline. Finally, we will look at the cumulative and transactional effect of various risk and protective factors on children's adjustment and resiliency. By the time you finish this chapter you should be able to:

Objective 7.1 Explain how self-concept, self-esteem, and self-regulation are related to children's social and emotional functioning.

Objective 7.2 Distinguish three forms of aggression and describe differences in the way they are manifested depending on children's age and sex.

Objective 7.3 Synthesize theory and research about how children develop gendered beliefs and behaviors.

Objective 7.4 Characterize children's first friendships and explain how advances in peer sociability and cultural differences affect these relationships.

Objective 7.5 Describe dimensions of play and explain how they contribute to children's cognitive and social development.

Objective 7.6 Compare and contrast different styles of parenting in terms of their positive and negative consequences for children's development.

Objective 7.7 Explain the role of inductive discipline in children's development of effective emotion control and prosocial behavior.

Objective 7.8 Define child maltreatment and describe its short- and long-term consequences.

Testing the Limits

According to Erikson (1950), once children have attained a certain level of autonomy (i.e., control over basic bodily and psychosocial functions), they become eager to try new tasks and activities, interact with peers, and see what they can do on their own as well as with the help of an adult. Parents become familiar with the phrase, "I can do it," or "Let me do it myself." Preschool children are continually increasing their abilities to carry out complex actions on their own, and their actions and activities are characterized by a sense of purpose and planning that is not as evident in the behavior of toddlers.

The conflict for preschool children is their emerging recognition that not all of the things they want to do will meet with the approval of the significant people in their lives. Children are developing a conscience. Erikson referred to this conflict as one of *initiative vs. guilt*. Initiative is important for children's movement away from dependency on caregivers and toward the ability to satisfy their own personal needs (Salkind, 2004). Guilt can be instrumental in children's decisions about how to behave, but relying too much on guilt to promote moral behavior can lead to high levels of self-blame, which then interfere with the internalization of moral behavior (we discuss this further in the section on moral development). In general, when children are supported and encouraged for their efforts, they are gratified and develop a strong sense of initiative. They need opportunities to test and explore the limits of their capabilities. Caregivers must strike a delicate balance during this time. They need to be protective, but not overprotective. They need to provide guidance and supervision without interfering.

When children resolve the conflict of initiative vs. guilt in Erikson's third stage, they emerge with a positive self-image, increased control of emotions, new social skills, and positive peer relations. We look next at children's developing sense of self in the preschool years.

OUTLINE ▼

Who Am I, and How Am I Different from Others?

As adults, it is difficult to conceive of life without a sense of "self." However, this integrated and multifaceted perception of "me" at the center of all of life's experiences emerges gradually over the course of our lifetimes (Thompson & Goodvin, 2005). During the preschool years, children develop multiple ways of understanding and representing themselves, both to others and to themselves.

Multiple Selves

Our most basic sense of self is our *subjective self-awareness*, or our sense of self as an individual apart from other individuals (Thompson & Goodvin, 2005). It involves understanding that, as an individual, I have my own unique thoughts, emotions, and experiences. Moreover, it includes the knowledge that my actions and emotions can affect others around me. This understanding is associated with children's developing sense of *personal agency,* which is associated with self-efficacy and self-regulation (described below). William James (1890) referred to this subjective and uniquely personal perception as the "I-self" and distinguished it from the "me-self"—the recognition that I have characteristics that others can objectively know about me (e.g., "My hair is curly." "My eyes are blue."). Most experts agree infants are born without a sense that they are individuals, separate from other people. However, children emerge from toddlerhood with a clear sense of their I-self, and preschool children, with their increased facility for representing and talking about phenomena, are better able to reflect on several aspects of self, including their me-self—how others might see them.

Before they are 2, children recognize themselves when they look in a mirror, and by age 3, they can offer simple descriptions of themselves (e.g., "I am a girl." "I have brown eyes."), and their emotions ("I am mad." "I feel sad"). Physical and psychological forms of *self-representation* lead to children's gaining perceptions of similarities and differences between self and others, applying social schemas (such as gender schemas) to the self, understanding the causes or motives for one's behavior, and creating a self-concept (Thompson & Goodvin, 2005, p. 411). Children's self-representations expand and become more differentiated as they develop and their self-awareness increases. By the age of 4, children remark about differences related to skin color and identify themselves as members of particular ethnic groups (Davies, 2004).

Before they are 2, children recognize themselves when they look in a mirror. Physical and psychological forms of self-representation lead to perceptions of similarities and differences between self and others.

What is your first memory of an event involving yourself? How old were you when the event took place? One of your author Nancy's "oldest" memories is falling down a staircase just after her family moved to a new home. She was 3 at the time. This is typical. Children's autobiographical memories start to emerge at about age 3 and begin to form the *autobiographical personal narrative*, their stories (Nelson & Fivush, 2004). Autobiographical memories are different from general event recall in that a person's sense of self gives meaning to and organizes the events that are remembered. Parents and other adults play an important role in children's development of a personal narrative, as they talk with children about their experiences and provide elaboration. So for example, Nancy may remember details about falling down the stairs because her mom talked with her about the fall later.

Self-evaluations guide perceptions that certain personal characteristics (or our whole person) are good or bad, as well as perceptions about strengths or weaknesses and benefits or liabilities (Cole et al., 2001; Harter, 1999; Thompson & Goodvin, 2005). In part, we derive our self-evaluations from the evaluations of others, but they also arise from our general sense of self-regard and self-understanding (Stipek, 1995). Self- and others' evaluations are central to the formation of self-esteem, as we will see in another section of this chapter.

Finally, the *social self* refers to the ways in which we orient to and are regarded in social contexts (Thompson & Goodvin, 2005). At about age 2, children begin to be concerned with how others (primarily parents and other caregivers) perceive their behavior, but in the years that follow, feedback from social interactions and social comparisons become important facets of self-evaluation (Frey & Ruble, 1990). Children and adolescents grow concerned with managing their self-presentation, and adolescents realize they need to present themselves differently depending on the demands and expectations of various social situations. Social situations also prompt distinctions between "possible" and "real" selves (Markus & Nurius, 1986)—the distinction between our actual self and the self we could become for better or for worse.

These facets of self are not independent; rather, they are mutually influential throughout development. Moreover, the development of self is an extremely complex and extended process. Our sense of self is qualitatively different when we are infants and young children than when we are adolescents, young adults, and older adults. Changes in

Cultural views of self are socialized and develop early.

self-representation, autobiographical personal narrative, self-evaluations, and social selves occur over time. Finally, aspects of self develop in the context of social and cultural experiences. Although all children distinguish themselves from others and use similar categories to describe themselves, the specific characteristics and qualities they reference and, often, what they value or don't value about themselves depends on the cultural context in which they live.

One dimension of the self that varies across cultures is individualism versus collectivism (Triandis, 1989), or independence versus interdependence (Markus & Kitayama, 1991). In cultures characterized as interdependent, it is more important to connect with others than to distinguish yourself; the salience of one's own thoughts and feelings is less important than being able to perceive the thoughts and feelings of others; and there is less emphasis on a core self that is stable across settings and situations than on understanding the self in relation to others in specific situations. These cultural views of self are socialized and develop early (Thompson & Goodvin, 2005). For example, in the United States, mothers emphasize their preschool children's autonomy much more than mothers in Japan (Dennis, Cole, Zahn-Waxler, & Mizuta, 2002; Wiley, Rose, Burger, & Miller, 1998), and these socialization influences are evident in the self-representations and autobiographical narratives of children from independent and interdependent cultures (Wang, 2004). However, some research indicates that emphasis on independence and interdependence may differ within ethnic groups as a consequence of sociodemographic variables. For example, Suizzo and colleagues (2008) studied parents' socialization practices across African American, Asian, European American, and Latino groups within the United States. They found that parents' level of education (often a proxy for SES), in addition to ethnicity, predicted their value of conformity. In their study, mothers with higher education valued conformity less.

Our integrated view of the attributes, abilities, and attitudes that make us who we are is our **self-concept.** This is the mental picture we have of ourselves. Let's examine the emergence of self-concept in preschool children.

Self-Concept

Very young children tend to describe themselves in concrete terms, relying on features that are readily observable (e.g., "I have blue eyes." "My hair is short."). Often their descriptions are tied to specific behaviors (e.g., "I can run fast."), or to preferences (e.g., "I like chocolate ice cream.") and possessions ("I have a puppy and a blue bike."). However, by age 3-1/2, children also can use psychological terms, such as *happy, sad, good,* and *bad,* to describe themselves and how they are feeling (Eder, 1989; Harter, 1999; 2006). Even though these descriptions lack the depth of meaning older children and adults attach to them and they do not generalize to higher order categories of self-concept, such as being generally optimistic or depressed, they suggest a budding understanding of one's physical characteristics and psychological states.

Because young children's self-descriptions focus on particular attributes, emotions, and behaviors, their self-concepts can appear disjointed. In fact, young children find it very difficult to integrate their compartmentalized representations of self (Harter, 2006). They also find it hard to reconcile attributes and emotions that are opposites. They have trouble believing and therefore acknowledging that people can be both good and bad or feel both happy and sad, especially at the same time. This has been referred to as *all-or-none* thinking and reflects beliefs on the part of young children that they are "always good" and "always happy" (Harter, 2006; Ruble & Dweck, 1995). Finally, young children's descriptions of self are characterized by instability. In contrast to older children and adults, whose descriptions include higher order characteristics that remain stable over time, young children's descriptions reference characteristics and behaviors that change over time, depending on the contexts in which they find themselves and their present focus (Harter, 1999).

Young children's self-concepts tend to include inflated, perhaps unrealistic, perceptions of strengths and abilities. They believe they are capable of many things and can easily overcome failures, and they hold optimistic views for the future. What accounts for these sunny dispositions? Young children have difficulty distinguishing between their desired level of competence and their actual performance; they have yet to formulate a concept of their *ideal self* that is separate from their *real self* (Harter, 2006). Also, they rarely engage in social comparisons to evaluate their performance. They don't compare themselves to peers; rather, they compare their current skill level to what they could do at a previous point in time (Frey & Ruble, 1990). These cognitive limitations may actually serve a protective function. Maintaining a positive self-view may be what drives young children's initiative. It may motivate children to persist on challenging tasks, while instilling confidence and repelling perceptions of inadequacy and the potential for failure. According to Harter (2006, p. 518), "such liabilities may represent critical strengths at this developmental level."

For this reason, it is important for parents, teachers, and other caregivers to recognize that such optimistic distortions in self-concept are normative in young children, more likely reflecting their desire for increased competence than a conscious effort to deceive listeners (Davies, 2004; Harter, 2006). Also, by about age 4-1/2, young children are able to use comparative information to evaluate themselves when that information is made salient (Butler, 1998; Thompson & Goodvin, 2005). At this time, young children are becoming vulnerable to factors that lead to negative self-evaluations and lower self-esteem, the topic we turn to now.

Self-Esteem

Whereas *self-concept* refers to the mental picture we have of ourselves, *self-esteem* refers to the value we attach to that picture. **Self-esteem** is the self-evaluative part of the self-concept—the judgment children make about their overall self-worth. Often these judgments derive from the internalization of feedback from others, but they also arise from children's developing capacities for self-understanding (Thompson & Goodvin, 2005). Both self-esteem and self-concept can vary by domain/activity. Moreover, self-esteem also can differ from self-concept in a given domain. For example, a child may realistically assess she is not good at sports (perhaps she is small for her age and uncoordinated) without experiencing low self-esteem about it. Alternatively, a child with low self-esteem may make unrealistically low judgments about her skills and abilities, demonstrating an inaccurate self-concept. Judgments about self-esteem are associated with the value placed on particular characteristics, skills, and activities. If, for example, a child perceives he is not athletic, but does not particularly value athletic prowess, he may not suffer low self-esteem associated with his lack of skill in this area. Also, if he has talents in other areas (e.g., he is artistic or does well academically), these may compensate for the difficulties he has playing sports.

Young children typically have high self-esteem. Their positive self-regard is likely the result of the cognitive liabilities we mentioned earlier and the encouragement and support they receive from caregivers and on-lookers as they accomplish new tasks. However, children's perceptions of self are strongly influenced by the way they perceive the significant people in their lives regard them. Exposure to inappropriate expectations, belittling comments, and impatience can result in negative self-regard, shame, and avoidance even before children have mastered the linguistic capabilities to express self-regard (Harter, 2006; Kelley & Brownell, 2000; Thompson & Goodvin, 2005). Harter's research (1990, 1999) indicates that parents and teachers should look for children's expressions of self-esteem in their

TABLE 7.1 • **Teachers Recognize Behaviors Associated with High and Low Self-Esteem in Preschool Children**

INDICES OF HIGH SELF-ESTEEM	INDICES OF LOW SELF-ESTEEM
Displays confidence, curiosity, initiative, and independence	Does not display confidence, curiosity, initiative, or independence
Approaches challenging tasks and activities	Doesn't approach challenge
Sets goals independently	Doesn't trust his or her own ideas
Explores, asks questions, and is eager to try new things	Doesn't explore, hangs back, watches only May withdraw and sit apart
Describes self in positive terms	Describes self in negative terms
Shows pride in work	Doesn't show pride in work
Is able to adjust to changes	Has difficulty adjusting to change or stress
Is comfortable with transitions	Gives up easily when frustrated
Tolerates stress and frustration	Reacts inappropriately or immaturely to stress or accidents
Is persistent	
Handles criticism and teasing well	

Source: Harter, S. (1990; 2006)

behavior. Table 7.1 shows how experienced nursery school and kindergarten teachers distinguished behaviors that characterize children with high and low self-esteem. Of particular interest to Harter was the fact that teachers did not associate displays of competence with self-esteem. At this age, it appears confidence is not associated with skill level, which may, in part, account for young children's resilience in the face of challenging tasks. In Chapter 10, we will see how confidence and competence become more tightly linked during the elementary school years.

What can parents and other caregivers do to foster a healthy self-image early in children's lives? The ***Connecting with Children*** guidelines offer some ideas.

Self-Regulation

Self-regulation refers to our ability to voluntarily control our thoughts and actions to achieve personal goals and respond to environmental contingencies (Zimmerman, 2008). Individuals who are effectively self-regulating can inhibit automatic or more favored responses that won't serve them well in particular situations. They can resist distractions and persist when tasks are difficult but seen as necessary or worthwhile, and they can delay immediate gratification in favor of meeting a more important long-term goal. Sticking with a diet and quitting smoking are adult examples of tasks that require self-regulation, as are controlling your temper when you are frustrated and studying for an exam when you'd rather be watching TV (for many ages).

According to Eisenberg and colleagues (2004, p. 279), "optimally regulated" individuals are not overly controlled or under-controlled. They respond appropriately and flexibly to the demands of a wide range of contexts. Children who are well regulated are flexible in their use of regulatory behaviors, not overly inhibited or impulsive. These children are characterized as being well adjusted, socially competent, and resilient (Eisenberg et al., 2007; Spinrad et al., 2006).

Researchers have studied self-regulation across the lifespan and in relation to a wide range of behaviors, including those associated with health and nutrition, athleticism, writing and other intellectual/academic pursuits, and social interactions. In general, self-regulation is associated with numerous positive outcomes. For example, children who

CONNECTING WITH CHILDREN

Guidelines for Families, Teachers, and Other Professionals: Fostering a Healthy Self-Image Early in Children's Lives

Be unconditional.
Examples
1. Let children know you accept them for who they are, regardless of their strengths, difficulties, temperament, or abilities.
2. When correcting children, make it clear that it's their behavior and not them that is unacceptable.
3. Avoid comparisons.

Help children to believe that they are capable, valued, and worthwhile.
Examples
1. Pay attention, listen well, and make eye contact with them when they need to talk to you.
2. Build their self-pride and self-respect by letting them know their thoughts, feelings, desires, and opinions are valuable and they can express them.
3. Take some time daily to emphasize the positive things you observe about them.
4. Encourage children by acknowledging their progress and not just rewarding achievement.

Mistakes are valuable lessons; let them happen.
Examples
1. Let children know we all have strengths and weaknesses, and that they don't have to be perfect to feel good about themselves.
2. If children make mistakes, encourage them to think about what they would do differently next time.
3. Teach children that failure is an opportunity to learn.
4. Acknowledge and recover from your own mistakes.
5. Keep criticism constructive and celebrate the positive.

Encourage healthy risks.
Examples
1. Help children to explore new experiences and let them safely experiment.
2. Resist the urge to intervene (even if children are showing mild frustration).
3. Balance your need to protect them with their need to tackle new tasks.
4. Encourage them to be as independent as their skill level permits.

Source: Adapted from Kaltman, G. S. (2005). More help! for teachers of young children: 99 tips to promote intellectual development and creativity. *California: Corwin Press.*
http://hindumommy.wordpress.com/2006/07/07/10-ways-to-increase-your-preschoolers-self-esteem/
http://life.familyeducation.com/self-esteem

effectively regulate their emotions and behavior receive high ratings on social skills inventories and are more popular with peers (Bronson, 2000; Fabes et al., 1999; Gilliom, Shaw, Beck, Schonberg, & Lukon, 2002). Also, self-regulated learning is associated with success in school (Linnenbrink & Pintrich, 2003; Perry, VandeKamp, Mercer, & Nordby, 2002). In contrast, poor self-regulation is associated with maladaptive behavior, such as noncompliance and negative emotionality (Eisenberg et al., 2004; Stifter, Spinrad, and Braungart-Rieker, 1999; Tice, Baumeister, & Zhang, 2004).

WHEN DOES SELF-REGULATION FIRST APPEAR? Aspects of self-regulation appear very early in life, and emotional and behavioral self-regulation, as we shall see, are pivotal achievements in early social and emotional development (Eisenberg et al., 2004; Thompson, 1994). **Emotional self-regulation** involves effortful, voluntary control of emotions, attention, and behavior (Eisenberg & Spinrad, 2004; Spinrad, Eisenberg, & Gaertner, 2007). Developing strategies for regulating emotions enhances our ability to feel and think better in stressful situations, act courageously, seek support, and support others by showing sympathy or empathy (Thompson & Goodvin, 2005). Children with poor emotion control tend to get irritable or angry in stressful situations; they are more likely to respond aggressively when they become frustrated; and they have difficulty adjusting to new routines (Denham, Blair, Schmidt, & DeMulder, 2002; Shields et al., 2001).

There is general agreement that newborn infants do not consciously regulate their emotions and behavior. However, within the first few months of life, babies will avoid or control exposure to loud sounds or scary images by turning their heads in another direction. Such re-orienting and self-distracting behaviors are interpreted as early efforts to regulate or reduce negative affect (Calkins & Johnson, 1998; Eisenberg et al., 2004). Toddlers engage in more self-distracting/coping behaviors than infants and can voluntarily initiate, maintain, and stop behavior, especially when they are interacting with a caregiver who models or provides guidance about self-regulatory strategies (Calkins & Johnson, 1998).

During the preschool years, children's control over their emotions and behavior increases significantly. This is due to general increases in self-awareness and to the development of key cognitive capacities for attending to environmental demands, anticipating consequences for actions, inhibiting inappropriate responses, and initiating appropriate tactics and strategies to achieve goals (Bronson, 2000). Moreover, children's vocabulary and working memory are expanding, which enables them to talk about and reflect on their emotions. Beyond experiencing the basic emotions—happiness, anger, sadness, and fear—children at this age begin to experience **self-conscious emotions,** such as pride, envy, guilt, and shame, that are linked to evaluation by others and self-evaluation. These higher order feelings depend on not only self-awareness but also an appreciation of standards—often referred to as **display rules**—for conduct and the appropriate expression of emotions (Thompson & Goodvin, 2005; Thompson, Meyer, & McGinley, 2006, pp. 267–297). Display rules dictate when and how to mask true emotions with more appropriate emotions to protect one's own self-esteem or preserve relationships with others. Katie, in our casebook example, has not mastered a display rule that directs people to look pleased when they receive a disappointing gift. Carolyn Saarni (1984) conducted a now classic study concerning this display rule that indicates children may not adjust their behavior in this way until they are 6 years of age or older. In her study, first, third, and fifth graders were led to anticipate an appealing gift, but instead they received a toy that was for children much younger then they were—"a baby toy." The youngest children (especially boys) were more likely to demonstrate negative emotionality in this situation, but the older children were able to maintain their composure and respond positively to the gift.

Opportunities to prompt children's emotional understanding and self-regulation often occur in everyday conversations. In such conversations, adults can enhance children's emotional knowledge, convey expectations for appropriate behavior, and explain potential consequences of inappropriate emotional displays.

HOW DOES SELF-REGULATION DEVELOP? Self-regulation is influenced by characteristics that are internal to children, such as their cognitive capacities and temperament, but it also develops along a continuum from *other*-regulation to *self*-regulation. At first, parents and caregivers regulate the emotions of their newborn infants by soothing them when they cry and reassuring them when they are afraid. Later, parents and caregivers model appropriate emotional responses and guide their young children's affect and behavior in particular circumstances. Opportunities to prompt children's emotional understanding and self-regulation often occur in everyday conversations. For example, it would be appropriate for Katie's parents to take her aside at her party and explain how what she said could hurt the feelings of another child. They also could ask her to apologize. In such conversations, parents can enhance children's emotional knowledge, convey expectations for appropriate behavior, and explain potential consequences of inappropriate emotional displays (Thompson & Goodvin, 2005; Thompson, Laible, & Ontai, 2003).

Dale Schunk and Barry Zimmerman (1997) proposed a four-phase model to describe how self-regulation develops through observation, imitation, self-control, and self-regulation. Consistent with this model, young children observe how others (e.g., parents, older siblings, teachers) regulate their emotions and behavior. Then they begin to imitate them and gradually increase self-control of their emotions and behavior. One way young children cope with challenging problems is to engage in self-talk. Often, they talk their way through a new or difficult process (e.g., they may verbalize the steps involved in tying their shoes). Finally, when they have full control of their emotions and behavior, they internalize both speech and strategies and can modify and adapt their actions and reactions to suit a variety of situations. For example, in any preschool room you might hear 4- or 5-year-olds saying, "No, it won't fit. Try it here. Turn. Turn. Maybe this one!" while they do puzzles. As these children mature, their self-talk goes underground, changing from spoken to whispered speech and then to silent lip movements. Finally, the children just "think" the guiding words.

The importance of adult mediation for developing self-regulation is highlighted in Vygotsky's sociocultural theory of development (1978). This theory was described in Chapter 2. Of course, children's development of effective emotional and behavior control strategies depends on having good modeling, guidance, and feedback from the adults in their lives. For example, studies indicate that infants and toddlers whose parents are supportive without being controlling or overprotective during periods of distress or frustration use constructive coping strategies (e.g., shifting attention), and are able to regulate emotional arousal in social contexts (Calkins & Johnson, 1998; Eisenberg et al., 2004; Gilliom, Shaw, Beck, Schonberg, & Lukon, 2002). Later, supportive parenting is associated with high ratings of social competence and the ability to get along with peers. In contrast, children whose parents are overly protective and intervene to solve problems for them, rather than allowing them to first try on their own, tend to be less skilled socially and emotionally. Therefore, adults should model and guide children's use of effective problem-solving strategies, model positive forms of emotion expression (i.e., show children how and when to express emotions, so they can do so appropriately), and talk with children about emotions and emotion control. All of these actions are associated with high ratings of emotional awareness, social competence, social status, and self-esteem (Eisenberg et al., 2004). We talk more about what parents can do to support children's development of emotion and behavior regulation in Chapter 10.

INDIVIDUAL DIFFERENCES IN SELF-REGULATION. Some children are impulsive or easily frustrated and have difficulty inhibiting inappropriate behavior. Other children are fearful or overly inhibited. They are anxious and have difficulty adjusting to new situations. Adults may struggle to be supportive under these circumstances and this can result in ineffective caregiving (Chang, Schwartz, Dodge, & McBride, 2003). In fact, parents' self-reports of nonsupportive practices often are associated with perceptions that their children are emotionally intense or vulnerable and prone to negative emotionality (Eisenberg et al., 2004; Jones, Eisenberg, Fabes, & MacKinnon, 2002). Parents may find themselves snapping at children who are whiny or emotionally demanding (e.g., "Stop whining!") instead of prompting a more appropriate tone or behavior. Finally, children with specific disabilities, such as learning disabilities, ADHD, developmental disabilities, or conduct disorders, have deficits in self-regulation (Lewis & Sullivan, 1996; Siegel, 1999). Often these children need very explicit and intensive interventions to master skills for regulating emotions and behavior.

Positive behavior support (PBS) is one such strategy that has proved effective for helping children to control their emotions and behavior (Lucyshyn et al., 2007; Turnbull, Taylor, Erwin, & Soodak, 2005). An example of a PBS plan is shown in Table 7.2 on the next page. This plan was developed to support Katherine, a child with autism and severe problem behaviors, including screaming and screeching, physical resistance to parental assistance, throwing objects, kicking walls and doors, and physical aggression toward others (hitting, kicking, biting). The strategies in Katherine's PBS plan were designed to remedy these problem behaviors and increase her participation in family routines, such as mealtime and preparing for bed. Following the implementation of this plan, Katherine's problem behaviors decreased to near-zero levels and her appropriate participation in family routines increased proportionately. Moreover, these changes were maintained across seven years of follow-up interventions and were associated with improvements in

TABLE 7.2 • **Katherine's Positive Behavior Support Plan**

SETTING EVENT STRATEGIES	ANTECEDENT STRATEGIES	TEACHING STRATEGIES	CONSEQUENCES STRATEGIES
1. Make sure tasks and activities are meaningful and rewarding.	1. Give Katherine information about tasks, changes, transitions, and being alone to reduce her anxiety.	1. Teach Katherine to use language (i.e., verbal or through pictures) to communicate her wants and needs: (a) assess her wants and needs, (b) prompt or model language, (c) support attempts to communicate.	1. Simultaneously praise adequate behaviors, including use of language, progress toward independence, calmly waiting, and acceptance of changes in routine.
2. Help her predict daily activities and transitions with visuals (e.g., picture schedules, board).	2. Use natural rewarding events to motivate cooperation.	2. Teach Katherine to (a) participate in group activities, (b) wait or accept a delay, and (c) comply with "stop" and "come here" cues.	2. Deliver what she wants or needs at the same time she uses language, but not with a problem behavior.
3. Enhance friendships with non-disabled peers.	3. Use preferred objects, activities, or interactions to mediate a delay or wait.		3. Minimize support of escape-motivated behavior: (a) actively ignore low-intensity problem behaviors, stop it once, and prompt language or use of safety signal; (b) actively ignore moderate and high-intensity behaviors, stop it twice or three times, and prompt language or use safety signal.
4. When Katherine is ill, decrease demands and increase rewarding events.	4. Enhance task success by giving Katherine instruction that matches her learning style. For example: Physically assist her with new tasks and gradually fade assistance, give her enough time to answer when prompted verbally.		4. Minimize support for get-item and activity-motivated behavior: (a) actively ignore low-intensity behavior, assess want, prompt language use, and honor, use safety signal, or provide information or reassurance as appropriate for the situation; (b) for moderate to high-intensity behavior, say, "When you're calm, we'll talk," do not deliver what she wants, redirect her to a less preferred alternative or a familiar or easy task.
	5. When Katherine appears tired or agitated during a task, use a "safety signal" that predicts a break.		5. Minimize support for attention-motivated behavior: (a) actively ignore low-intensity behaviors, prompt language use, and honor or use safety signal; (b) for screaming, throwing, or pounding, say, " When you're calm, we'll talk," prompt language use, honor or use safety signal; (c) for running away, command, "stop, come here"; if she returns, redirect to task; if she doesn't, block forward motion, redirect for 10–15 seconds; remind to use language.

Source: Adapted from Lucyshyn, J. M., Albin, R. W., Horner, R. H., Mann, J. C., Mann, J. A., & Wadsworth, G. (2007). Family implementation of positive behavior support for a child with autism: Longitudinal, single-case, experimental, and descriptive replication and extension. Journal of Positive Behavior Interventions, *9, p. 138. Reprinted by permission of SAGE publications.*

both Katherine's and her family's quality of life. Positive behavior support also is being applied in classrooms and schools to address problem behavior in typically as well as atypically developing learners. The principles are the same whether the plan is for an individual, a class, or a whole school: Understand why children are misbehaving, teach them alternative behaviors to meet a desired goal, and reward them for engaging in those behaviors (Osher, Bear, Sprague, & Doyle, 2010).

In general, children are more compliant and more likely to initiate positive, self-regulated behaviors when they understand how or why a behavior will be beneficial. Kochanska, Coy, and Murray (2001) found this to be the case in their study of young children's compliance with their mothers' requests to either stop playing with toys (inhibit a pleasant behavior: "You need to put that toy away now.") or keep working on a puzzle (persist at a behavior that may be perceived as unpleasant: "You've almost got it. Give it one more try."). Helping children to understand when and why certain behaviors are more appropriate than others requires more time and effort in the short term, but is more likely to promote internalization and self-regulation of such behaviors over the long term.

CULTURAL DIFFERENCES IN EMOTION EXPRESSION AND CONTROL. Children's understanding and expression of emotions are influenced by their cultural experiences, too. Cultural groups differ in terms of the significance placed on particular kinds of emotional events and the expectations for how to respond to them. Some cultures encourage children to express negative emotions, such as anger, whereas others believe it is important to mask such emotions to preserve harmony in one's family or social group. Pamela Cole and her colleagues (Cole, Brushchi, & Tamang, 2002; Cole & Tamang, 1998; Cole, Tamang, & Shrestha, 2006) have studied Nepalese children's responses to emotionally charged situations. What is interesting about this research is that it reveals differences among subcultures in Nepal as well as between children in Nepal and children in the United States. In Nepal, the Tamang culture emphasizes equality among people and values tolerance and harmony. Consistent with their Buddhist religious principles, the Tamang avoid the expression of strong emotions, especially anger, because such expressions cause others to suffer. In contrast, the Chhetri-Brahmin culture, influenced by Hinduism, is organized around a hierarchical social order with strict expectations concerning conduct according to place in the hierarchy. Chhetri-Brahmin children also are expected to exercise self-control concerning the expression of emotions, but the caste system in which they live appears to promote greater awareness of self, differences between self and others, and self-regulatory strategies than the social order of the Tamang people.

In their studies, Cole and colleagues found that Chhetri-Brahmin children were more likely to acknowledge experiencing negative emotions and to describe ways of masking them than the Tamang children, who interpreted events such that they didn't experience strong emotions. Like the Chhetri-Brahmin children, American children acknowledged their negative emotions, but were more likely to describe how they would act on those emotions, rather than masking them. Age was related to Nepalese and American children's reports of emotion regulation and decisions about whether and how to communicate emotions to others. To summarize, it appears children's emotion awareness and control develop with age, but also from their experiences in a wide range of social groups: familial, cultural, and religious.

Understanding Intentions

In addition to a growing awareness of their own thinking and feeling, preschool children are increasingly able to assess and respond to what they perceive are the thoughts and feelings of others. Around this time, they are developing a **theory of mind**—an understanding that other people are distinct from them and may have thoughts and feelings that are different from their own (Astington & Dack, 2008; Flavell, 2004; Flavell, Miller, & Miller, 2002). Children need a theory of mind to interpret other people's actions and intentions. For example, children who can distinguish intentions from actions understand that a child who bumps into them during a game of musical chairs may have done so accidentally. Children who get along well with their peers are able to distinguish intentional from unintentional behavior and to respond appropriately. They are more likely to overlook a bump during a game or accept an apology, if one is forthcoming. Children who have difficulty making such distinctions are likely to interpret such actions as threatening or hostile and to respond aggressively (Crick, Grotpeter, & Bigbee, 2002; Dodge & Pettit, 2003).

Children have a clear sense of their own intentions around the age of 2. If they are scolded for bumping into a playmate, they might defend themselves by explaining, "I didn't do it on purpose," or "It was an accident." Around the age of 3, this understanding of intentions extends to others and becomes more sophisticated in older children. Children come to understand that other people have different feelings and experiences and, as a result, they may also have different points of view or perspectives. **Perspective-taking ability,** or the ability to imagine what other people are thinking or feeling, continues to develop throughout childhood and adolescence, and even early adulthood, and is associated with overall positive, prosocial behavior (Gehlbach, 2004; Woolfolk, 2010).

Empathy and Sympathy

One form of perspective-taking that is beginning to develop in the preschool years is **empathy,** which involves the ability to understand what another person is feeling and, as a consequence, experience the same or similar emotions. Empathy often leads to **sympathy,** which involves feeling sorry or concerned for another person because he or she is experiencing negative emotions. Empathy and sympathy have been linked to prosocial behavior in studies in the United States and around the world—in countries such as Germany, Japan, and Brazil (Eisenberg, Fabes, & Spinrad, 1998; Eisenberg, Zhou, & Koller, 2001).

There is evidence that infants perceive and respond to others' emotions (e.g., infants may cry when they hear another infant crying), but it is doubtful these reactions are truly empathic because babies cannot comprehend the circumstances that provoked the emotion (Eisenberg, Fabes, & Spinrad, 2006; Thompson & Goodvin, 2005). However, scholars agree the rapid growth in emotional understanding that takes place in early childhood leads to true demonstrations of empathy by age 2 or 3. Toddlers respond with concerned attention to signs their mother is distressed and express more joy when their mother is perceived to be happy (Eisenberg et al., 2006; Zahn-Waxler, 2000). Three-year-old children are likely to respond to Mom's distress with prosocial or helping behavior. At this age, children's attempts at helping may be egocentric—they understand the distress and want to help, but often help in the way they would like to be helped (e.g., offering to share their favorite toy with Mom). They may not understand that other people experience the same emotions they do, but have different needs for coping. Later, when children can take the perspective of another person, they are able to assess the needs of that person and respond appropriately.

Three-year old children—they understand the distress and want to help, but often help in the way they would like to be helped. They may not understand that other people experience the same emotions they do, but have different ways of coping.

Young children's empathic responding is limited to familiar people and situations (Szagun, 1992), whereas older children experience empathy for a broader range of situations and people they don't know personally (e.g., homeless children in their communities or people in war-torn or poverty-stricken countries) (Hart & Damon, 1988; Hoffman, 2000). How does empathy develop? Temperament plays a role in whether empathy leads to sympathy and helping behaviors or to personal distress. Children who are sociable, assertive, and have good emotion control are more likely to show sympathy and helping behaviors for someone in distress than children who are poor emotion regulators (Eisenberg et al., 1996, 2006). For example, children who are aggressive or impulsive tend to have a reduced capacity for taking other people's perspective, so they are less likely to respond with empathy and sympathy. In fact, aggressive children tend to show a decline, rather than the typical increase, in empathy and sympathy over time. Children who are shy often feel anxious themselves when others are distressed, which inhibits empathic and sympathetic responding.

Parenting also influences children's empathy and sympathy. Parents who are warm, talk with their children about emotions, and model concern for others are likely to have children who respond empathically to other people (Denham & Kochanoff, 2002; Eisenberg & McNally, 1993; Strayer & Roberts, 2004). Parents can intervene to correct children's inappropriate responding and to prompt consideration of other people's feelings (e.g., "Why is he angry?" "What is making her sad?" "What could you do to help?"). Research indicates that when parents intervene in disputes among children, especially sibling disputes, children become more sensitive to the feelings of siblings and friends and more skilled at avoiding or resolving conflict (Eisenberg, 2003; Perlman & Ross, 1997). In general, children who have knowledge about emotions and who show empathy and sympathy have better relationships with peers.

We discuss first friendships later in this chapter. Right now, we turn to a discussion of children's emerging morality, which also extends from children's understanding of self and other.

Developing Morality

Morality refers to standards that guide people's judgments about what is right and wrong, and about justice (Damon, 1988). It involves cognition, affect, and behavior, and it is fundamental and important in our relationships with others. Children's understanding of and concern for moral issues emerge early, as you will see in the following section.

Young Children's Capacity for Moral Reasoning

As early as age 2, children have a sense of right and wrong and label their own and other children's actions as being "good" or "bad." At age 3, they begin to be concerned with matters of justice or fairness (e.g., claiming, "It's my turn," or "Sally got more than me") and can experience guilt and shame when their words or actions cause hurt feelings or physical harm for someone else. All theories of moral development agree that preschool children are developing a conscience. However, as was the case for developing self-regulation, children's morality appears at first to be externally controlled. Typically, parents and other adults communicate standards of behavior for their group and/or society to children, who gradually internalize these norms and make them the standards for their own behavior. At first, children's compliance with group standards or rules may be self-serving—to get what they want or to avoid the negative consequences associated with behaving badly. In time, most children engage in moral behavior because they agree with a principle or out of a sense of genuine concern for others.

Children who are 3 and 4 years old understand there are degrees of good and bad, and they make moral judgments based on what they perceive is fair. For example, preschool children judge that knocking a playmate off a swing intentionally is worse than doing so accidentally (Yuill & Perner, 1988). Also, they distinguish between **moral imperatives** that are intended to protect people's rights and welfare and **social conventions** that reflect generally understood rules about how one should act. Social conventions are more likely to reflect cultural norms (e.g., don't talk with your mouth full, or cover your mouth when you cough), whereas moral imperatives (don't steal or intentionally harm someone) tend to be universally accepted and apply to behavior even when authority figures aren't present to punish misbehavior and laws don't exist to prohibit it (Nucci, 2001; Turiel, 1998, 2002). By age 3, children judge moral transgressions more harshly than violations of social conventions. Finally, children at this age understand that some decisions about behavior are a matter of personal choice, which is evident when a young child announces, "I'm wearing the red shirt!" As children get older and more independent, matters of personal choice that do not offend or violate the rights of other people become topics of negotiation between parents/adults and children/youth.

Despite their ability to make these distinctions, young children still reason fairly rigidly about moral issues. Often they perceive that rules are unchangeable and should be adhered to strictly. They believe, for example, that there is only one set of rules for every game and that lying and stealing are wrong no matter what the circumstances or how morally sound a person's reasons are for engaging in such behavior. Piaget (1932, 1965) referred to this kind of moral reasoning as **heteronomous,** and it corresponds to Kohlberg's (1963) preconventional level of moral development. We discuss these cognitive-developmental theories of moral development in greater detail in Chapter 10. In this chapter we focus on social learning theory, which describes how young children internalize standards for moral reasoning and moral behavior.

Social-Contextual Influences on Moral Development

Social learning theorists believe children's moral development occurs as a consequence of observing others (Bandura, 1986, 2006). Adults, older siblings, and even peers serve as models of moral behavior. Often, when children adopt moral behaviors, adults praise them (e.g., "That was a nice thing to do."). This reinforces the good behavior and increases the likelihood children will behave similarly in the future (Mills & Grusec, 1989). In addition, siblings and peers respond more favorably to moral versus immoral actions, thus making moral behavior more rewarding.

Studies have shown that certain characteristics of models are attractive and therefore encourage imitation. For example, children are more likely to imitate models they perceive are warm and responsive than those they believe are cold and distant (Yarrow, Scott, & Waxler, 1973). Also, children admire models they perceive are competent and powerful (Bandura, 1977). This may be the reason they are particularly inclined to copy adults and older siblings or peers. Finally, children are more inclined to do what you do, versus what you say to do, so consistency between moral assertions and actions is important (Mischel & Leibert, 1966).

The Role of Discipline

Discipline can be an effective tool for teaching moral lessons. In particular, *inductive discipline* supports moral development because it involves correction plus explanation. Parents and teachers who engage in inductive discipline not only intervene to stop misbehavior, they also help children to understand why their actions are hurtful or unfair. In our casebook example, Katie's mother might explain, "You hurt people's feelings when you say you don't want their presents. How would you feel if your friend said he didn't like your present?" Children who experience inductive discipline are more likely to feel empathy and sympathy for victims of misdeeds, and more likely to experience guilt when they are the source of someone else's distress (Krevans & Gibbs, 1996). Guilt that is induced through empathy is associated with stopping the harmful behavior, making amends, and engaging in prosocial behavior in the future (Baumeister, 1998; Kerr, Lopez, Olson, & Sameroff, 2004).

Guilt can be a powerful motivator for moral behavior, but relying on guilt to promote moral behavior can also backfire. For example, guilt can lead to high levels of self-blame, which interfere with the internalization of moral behavior. Moreover, if parents or teachers emphasize disappointment or withhold love when children misbehave without explaining why they disapprove or what children can do to rectify the situation, children may avoid feelings of guilt and shame by denying both these feelings and their immoral behavior. Alternatively, they may try to justify their actions with explanations such as "He hit me first," or "She didn't ask me to share." Punishment, too, has a limited effect on moral development. Although it may be justified when immediate compliance is needed (e.g., when a child is behaving in a way that puts himself or others in danger), most caregivers and teachers recognize that punishment in the form of scolding, threats, or harsh physical control does not produce lasting changes in children's thinking and behavior. In fact, over the long term, punishment without induction can lead to weak internalization of moral values and increased antisocial and aggressive behavior (Gershoff, 2002; Kochanska, Aksan, & Nichols, 2003).

Discipline is discussed in more detail later in this chapter, in the section on parenting. Regarding moral development, parents and caregivers are well advised to focus on inductive approaches to discipline and to limit their use of guilt-inducing and punishing tactics, which may actually model aggression.

The Role of Personal and Biological Factors

Clearly, many social and contextual factors influence young children's emerging morality. However, children are individuals with unique characteristics that affect their interactions with the world around them and contribute to their moral development.

TEMPERAMENT. The majority of young children are eager to please parents and caregivers and respond well to inductive forms of discipline most of the time. For children who are anxious and fearful, especially, patience and mild forms of correction (e.g., explanations and suggestions) are enough to cause a guilt reaction and gain compliance (Kochanska, Gross, Lin, & Nichols (2002). For children who are fearless and impulsive, however, inductive forms of discipline may have little, or perhaps no effect on their behavior. Unfortunately, these children may not respond to punishment either. According to Fowles and Kochanska (2000), parents and other adults should build a positive relationship with such children—a secure attachment that makes them want to comply—and then combine firm, consistent correction with inductive discipline to foster their moral development.

BRAIN BIOLOGY. There is evidence that moral behaviors have a biological basis and may not be unique to humans. For example, Russell Church's research (1959) offered evidence of rats interrupting their lever pressing behavior, for which they were rewarded, when they became aware that rats in the cages beside them were in distress (these rats were receiving shocks from the electrified floor of their cages). Were the rats expressing concern for the other rats, or were they simply afraid something similar was about to happen to them? This early research did not provide definitive evidence to answer that question. However, more recent studies indicate that mice witnessing other mice in pain are more sensitive to pain themselves and show more apparent empathy for mates who are familiar to them (de Waal, 2007/08).

In humans, research involving brain scanners reveals interesting patterns of brain activity when people witness others in pain or distress (de Waal, 2007/08). In particular, there is evidence that the ventromedial area of the cerebral cortex—located just behind the bridge of the nose—is implicated in our empathic and sympathetic responding and in our guilt reactions to our own misdeeds (Barrash, Tranel, & Anderson, 2000). Compared to the general population, adults with damage to this part of the brain respond less negatively when they witness other people being harmed and are less concerned about adhering to social norms. In children, damage to this area of the brain is associated with disruptions in social learning resulting in extreme antisocial behavior (Anderson, Bechara, Damasio, Tranel, & Damasio, 1999).

GENDER. Some research indicates girls are more likely than boys to experience emotions associated with moral reasoning and behavior, including guilt, shame, and empathy (Alessandri & Lewis, 1993; Zahn-Waxler & Robinson, 1995). Also, they are more likely than boys to take responsibility for their misdeeds. However, the preponderance of the research on gender and morality indicates the extent of the differences is small and may be more an artifact of the way gender and morality have been studied (Eisenberg, Martin, & Fabes, 1996; Jaffee & Hyde, 2000). We address this topic again in Chapter 10 when we describe the strengths and limitations of cognitive developmental theories of moral development.

Now we turn to the opposite of moral behavior, the emergence of aggressive behavior.

Aggression in Young Children

According to Eleanor Maccoby (1980), before children's behavior can be considered aggressive, they must first understand that other people can feel distress and pain and then intentionally engage in behaviors to cause such discomfort. From this point of view, infants are not aggressive, since they lack such understanding. However, by age 2, children are capable of acting aggressively. In fact, aggression among preschool children (e.g., hitting, kicking, throwing or breaking toys) is quite common, but it should not be ignored.

Typically, preschool children act aggressively to gain or regain objects of desire (e.g., grabbing a favorite toy from another child) or to usurp popular spaces (e.g., pushing a peer out of the way to take the place next to a parent or teacher). In these instances, the aggression is inadvertent—more likely the result of having a specific goal and poor self-control than having malicious intent—and may not target a particular person. Anyone unlucky enough to be in the way could be on the receiving end of these behaviors. This type of aggression is referred to as **instrumental aggression** and, in most children, it declines over the preschool years as children learn to control their emotions and behaviors; acquire language to express their wants and needs; and develop empathy, care, and concern for those around them (Anderson et al., 2003; Eisenberg & Zhou, 2000; Philippot & Feldman, 2004).

Hostile aggression involves behaviors intended to harm another person. It can include physical or verbal assaults and it can be direct (e.g., hitting a person or calling them names in a face-to-face confrontation) or indirect (e.g., destroying someone's property or saying mean things about them to other children). **Relational aggression** has as its goal damaging a peer's social status and/or relationships. Insults, gossip, and exclusionary tactics are all examples of relational aggression. Hostile and relational aggression are more common in interactions among older children and youth, so we will examine these forms of aggression in greater detail in Chapters 10 and 13, but researchers also have found evidence of hostile and relational aggression in interactions among 3-year-olds (Dodge, Coie, Lynam, 2006). The early emergence of hostile and relational aggression should be particularly troubling to adult caregivers, because young children rated high on indices of physical or relational aggression tend to remain so over time (Tremblay, 2000; Vaillancourt, Hymel, & McDougall, 2003), and early onset of aggression is associated with adjustment problems and antisocial behavior in late childhood and adolescence (Dodge et al., 2006).

GENDER DIFFERENCES IN YOUNG CHILDREN'S AGGRESSION. In general, research finds that boys are more physically aggressive than girls, and this finding is consistent across age groups and cultures (Dodge et al., 2006). From infancy, boys are more likely to grab objects and, once they can talk, less likely to use language to solve problems (Coie & Dodge, 1998). Also, "play aggression" (Eisenberg, Martin, & Fabes, 1996) is more typical in boys than girls. Boys engage in more rough-and-tumble play and more frequently engage in play fighting and dominance-related behaviors that can turn into aggression under certain circumstances. In most boys, however, these forms of play aggression are not directly associated with hostile aggression (Meaney, Stewart, & Beatty, 1985). Girls are more likely to engage in social and relational aggression than physical aggression (Dodge et al., 2006).

In preschool, girls tend to engage in direct forms of relational aggression (e.g., face-to-face insults or name-calling), whereas older girls use more subtle and sophisticated forms of relational aggression (e.g., spreading rumors or finding ways to exclude someone from social groups). Research about whether girls engage in more relational aggression than boys has produced mixed results. Some research indicates this is the case (Crick & Zahn-Waxler, 2003), but other studies indicate boys and girls engage in similar rates of relational aggression (Underwood, 2003). Girls may appear more relationally aggressive because they rely on relational tactics almost exclusively. Boys, on the other hand, use a variety of tactics, both physical and relational.

The origins of sex differences in aggression are likely biological and environmental. There is some evidence that male sex hormones, or androgens, are associated with aggression in animals (Dodge et al., 2006; Eisenberg et al., 1996), but this link is less clear in humans. However, it is possible that differences in strength, reactivity to pain, and temperamental characteristics, such as activity level, account for some observed sex differences in aggression. Environmental variables are believed to play an important role, too. For example, boys have access to more physical aggression in their peer groups than girls, and adults may communicate tacit approval for boys' aggressive or dominant behavior by not intervening or by encouraging boys to be "competitive" in sports or to play with toys that provoke aggressive role-playing (e.g., toy guns, some action figures, and video games). In contrast, adults' emphasis on "ladylike" behavior may counteract physical aggression in girls. Whatever the reason, research indicates that as soon as children realize boys and girls are expected to behave differently (by age 2 or 3), there is a sharp decline in physical aggression among girls (Eisenberg et al., 1996; Fagot & Leinbach, 1989).

It is important to put these differences into perspective. Overall, the difference in the amount of aggression observed between boys and girls is small (Eisenberg et al., 1996; Underwood, Galen, & Paquette, 2001; Willoughby, Kupersmidt, & Bryant, 2001), especially when relational aggression is taken into account. As indicated above, girls may be just as aggressive as boys, but they rely almost exclusively on relational tactics, and adults may overlook or underemphasize the harm these approaches can do (see Chapters 10 and 13).

OTHER SOURCES OF AGGRESSIVE BEHAVIOR. Research studies involving large cross-national samples and samples of twins and adoptees offer strong evidence that aggression is heritable (Arseneault et al., 2003; Dodge et al., 2006; Moffitt, 2005; Rhee & Waldman, 2002). No single gene has been identified to predict aggressive or antisocial behavior, but there is clear evidence that person-specific characteristics are reliably associated with it. For example, parents and teachers more often rate children with difficult temperaments (e.g., children who are fearless and children who are easily frustrated or upset) and children with low self-control (e.g., difficulties sustaining attention and inhibiting inappropriate responses to provocation) as aggressive compared with children characterized as easy-going and well-regulated (Dodge et al., 2006; Eisenberg et al., 2001; Rothbart, Ahadi, & Evans, 2000; Shaw, Gilliom, Ingoldsby, & Nagin, 2003). Prenatal and perinatal complications, such as exposure to toxins, also are associated with higher rates of aggression (Dodge et al., 2006), as are deficits in verbal ability. However, these person-specific characteristics don't tell the whole story. Social experiences also can contribute to children's development of aggression.

According to social learning theories, children can learn to be aggressive through direct reinforcement or modeling. For example, children who are not disciplined when they push peers out of the way to ensure their seat next to the teacher are being reinforced to believe they can get what they want by overpowering others, and they are likely to continue to act aggressively in the future. Similarly, children can learn to be aggressive by witnessing the aggressive acts of others (e.g., among family members or on TV). In a now seminal study of preschool children, Albert Bandura and his colleagues (Bandura, Ross, & Ross, 1963) arranged for one group of children to watch a film in which an adult interacted aggressively with a Bobo doll—an inflatable doll that the adult used as a punching bag—while another group of children (the control group) watched an adult playing appropriately with a set of Tinkertoys. After they watched the film, children in both groups were allowed to play with toys, including the Bobo doll and the Tinkertoys, but first they were denied the opportunity to play with their favorite toy. Researchers observed that the preschool children who had observed the aggressive adult model interacted with the Bobo doll more aggressively than their peers who had observed the adult playing more appropriately. Photos from the study are shown in Figure 7.1 on the next page. This and subsequent studies support the contention of social learning theorists that children learn to behave aggressively based on what they see and experience in their environment.

Finally, cognitive developmental theories stress the importance of understanding how children interpret and respond to other children's behavior and the social context in which the behavior occurs. Figure 7.2 on page 267 presents a model of six cognitive

FIGURE 7.1

THE BOBO DOLL STUDY

Source: Bandura, A. Ross, D., & Ross, S. A. (1963). Imitation of film-mediated aggressive models. Journal of Abnormal and Social Psychology, *66, 3-11.*

processes believed to influence children's aggressive or nonaggressive response to social events (Arsenio & Lemerise, 2004). According to the model, children first (a) encode and then (b) interpret the social cues that are present in an event—they attempt to understand what happened and why. Arsenio and Lemerise (p. 989) use the example of one child tripping over another's feet. First, he thinks about what happened ("I tripped on his feet."). Then, he considers why it happened ("He tripped me," or "It was an accident."). Next, the child (c) clarifies a set of goals for the situation ("I'm going to show that kid he can't do that to me," or "I'm going to ignore it and go about my business."). Based on his goals, the child will (d) generate and (e) evaluate a set of possible responses to the situation. A good evaluation will take into account the likely success and consequences of a response. Finally, the child will (f) enact a response. Arsenio and Lemerise admit that in a heightened state of arousal, children may move fairly directly from the first two steps in their model to the last.

There is research showing that some children are particularly prone to interpret the actions of others as intentional and hostile (Arsenio & Lemerise, 2004; Dodge et al., 2006; Dodge & Pettit, 2003). According to Dodge and colleagues (2006), aggressive children are less able than nonaggressive children to recall relevant social cues, they are more likely to focus on aggressive social cues, and they have difficulty diverting attention away from aggressive social cues. Moreover, these children are more likely to generate aggressive responses to events and have difficulty inhibiting aggressive responses. It appears they are programmed to respond aggressively.

How can adults help? See some suggestions in the ***Connecting with Children*** guidelines.

FIGURE 7.2

SIX COGNITIVE PROCESSES THAT INFLUENCE CHILDREN'S AGGRESSIVE OR NON-AGGRESSIVE RESPONSE TO SOCIAL EVENTS

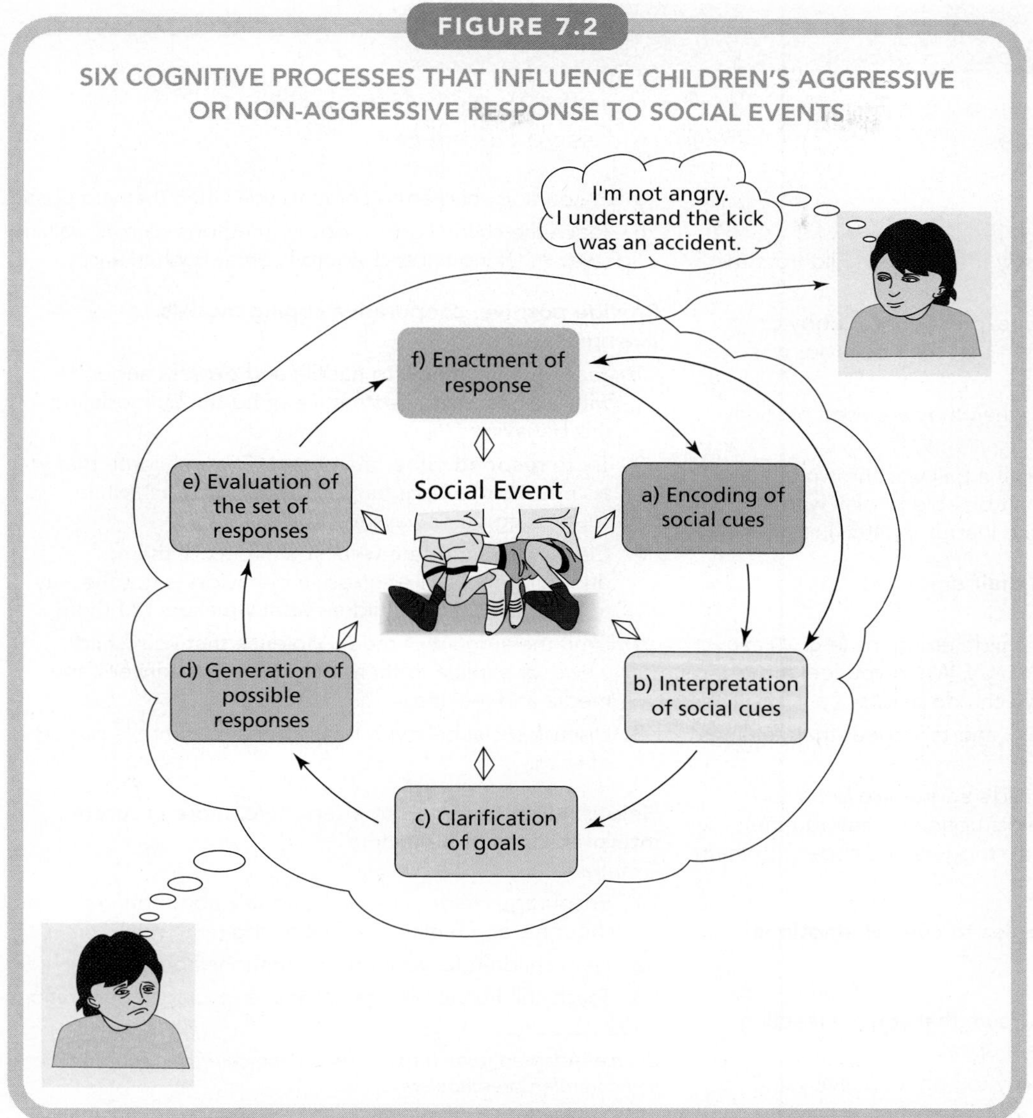

Source: Adapted from Arsenio, W. E. & Lemerise, E. A. (2004). Aggressive and moral development: Integrating social information processing and moral domain models. Child Development, *75, 987–1002.*

Gender Development

An important part of children's development involves their knowing that they are a boy or a girl and understanding what it means to be a boy or girl.

The Emergence of Gender Identity

By the age of 2, most toddlers can tell you if they are a boy or a girl, and they can label other people—children and adults—as male or female (Campbell, Shirley, & Caygill, 2002; Ruble et al., 2006). Gender labeling is the first indication of **gender identity**—the sense of self as male or female as well as the beliefs one has about gender roles and attributes (e.g., boys play rough and boys don't mind getting dirty when they play). Gender identity is an important part of children's self-concept and a powerful source of self-esteem (Powlishta, 2004). Once children are aware of their gender, they tend to identify with and imitate the behavior of their same-sex parents and siblings; develop expectations about the kinds of

CONNECTING WITH CHILDREN

Guidelines for Families, Teachers, and Other Professionals: Addressing Young Children's Aggressive Behavior

Don't ignore aggression!
Examples

1. Intervene quickly and calmly remove the child from the aggressive situation.
2. Communicate (using facial expressions, or body or verbal language) to children that their behavior was inappropriate.
3. Time-outs can be helpful when they are used properly and sparingly.
4. Use logical consequences (if a ball was thrown at a friend's face, the child won't be able to play with it for a while because it was used inappropriately).

Help children to understand their emotions.
Examples

1. Use words to refer to the child's emotions (e.g., "I can see you are feeling really angry. When you feel more calm we'll see how else we can do this.")
2. Encourage children to think and talk about their feelings with other people.
3. Learn what triggers the child's aggressive behavior (e.g., tiredness, hunger, a disruption in their routine) and help them to recognize triggers and cope with them appropriately.

Help them to develop strategies to control emotions and behaviors.
Examples

1. Be a good example. Make sure that you are reacting appropriately when you are upset.
2. Show the child the right way to behave socially and praise positive behaviors such as sharing and using words instead of actions to express anger.
3. Give the child clear, firm, and consistent limits to help him/her learn to manage out-of-control emotions.
4. Give the child different opportunities to release energy (e.g., running, pounding play dough, or hammering on the workbench).
5. Encourage children to come to you when they are upset.
6. Teach the child "cooling-down" methods such as walking away or taking full and vigorous breaths when angry.

Provide positive, cooperative coping models.
Examples

1. Teach the child how to handle and express anger without becoming destructive or hurtful by modeling this behavior.
2. Try to **respond** rather than **react.** Show children that you accept their feelings (anger, frustration, etc.), while suggesting other ways to express them.
3. Clearly communicate what you expect of them; punishing for their aggressive behaviors is not the way to communicate to children what we expect of them.
4. Limit the amount of media violence that your child views, or explain to them the difference between the media and real life.
5. Discuss social behavior rules after a reasonable period of calm.

Help children to generate alternative, more accurate interpretations of behaviors.
Examples

1. Encourage children to think and talk about others' thoughts and feelings before acting (empathy).
2. Help children to distinguish intentions from actions.
3. Teach children to play games that encourage cooperation.

Source: Adapted from: http://www.webmd.com/hw-popup/promote-self-control-in-preschoolers
http://www.babycenter.com/404_how-can-i-teach-my-preschooler-to-stop-hitting-his-playmates_70222.bc
http://fatherhood.about.com/od/discipliningfordads/a/childaggression.htm
http://parenting.families.com/blog/10-ways-to-prevent-aggression-in-toddlers
http://www.mindpub.com/art455.htm
http://www.consistent-parenting-advice.com/toddler-behavior.html

objects and activities that are typically associated with and appropriate for boys and girls; and begin to express preferences for playing with same-sex peers and gender stereotypic toys (Davies, 2004; Martin & Ruble, 2004).

One study of 18-month-olds found they looked longer at a doll than a toy truck after being presented with a series of female faces and longer at the toy truck than the doll after being habituated to a series of male faces (Serbin, Poulin-Dubois, Colburne, Sen, & Eichstedt, 2001). Similarly, in preschool classrooms boys are more often observed playing with blocks and toy vehicles, whereas girls more often choose to play dress-up and house (Maccoby, 1998). Observations in preschools indicate boys and girls do play together and the roles they take sometimes blend stereotypically masculine and feminine characteristics (e.g., girls may pretend they have superpowers and boys sometimes care for babies), but the majority of preschool children's playtime (approximately two-thirds) involves interactions among same-sex peers (Davies, 2004) and this preference for same-sex playmates and gender segregation increases from preschool to elementary school.

As children internalize gender roles and stereotypes, they become less tolerant of children whose appearance and/or behavior does not conform to what they have come to expect of boys or girls. In general, boys are more insistent than girls about maintaining gender-stereotyped play themes and avoiding toys that are associated with girls, and girls and adults are less forgiving of boys who engage in cross-gendered behavior than they are of girls who violate gender-role norms (Davies, 2004; Knafo, Iervolino, & Plomin, 2005; Ruble et al., 2006).

These biases are remarkably consistent across cultures (Aydt & Corsaro, 2003; Ruble et al., 2006; Whiting & Edwards, 1988). Figure 7.3 shows the results of a study of children in four non-Western societies (Munroe & Romney, 2006) that indicates preference for engaging in activities with same-sex peers increased from preschool (ages 3 to 5) to the early school years (ages 7 to 9) in all four societies, and this preference was stronger in males than in females. Look at the photos in Figure 7.4 from a study of children's preferences for play spaces in a Slovakian preschool (Gmitrova, Podhajecká, & Gmitrov, 2007). The Slovakian children's preferences reflected gender stereotypes much like their North American peers. The girls chose to play in the "flower shop" more than boys, who preferred building with Legos™. There was one space that attracted both boys and girls, however—the medical center.

Gender constancy—understanding the biologically based permanence of gender—combines understandings of three core concepts: gender labeling, gender stability, and gender consistency (Ruble et al., 2006). Kohlberg (1966) proposed a three-stage developmental

FIGURE 7.3

PREFERENCE FOR SAME-SEX PLAY AMONG YOUNGER AND OLDER CHILDREN ACROSS FOUR CULTURES

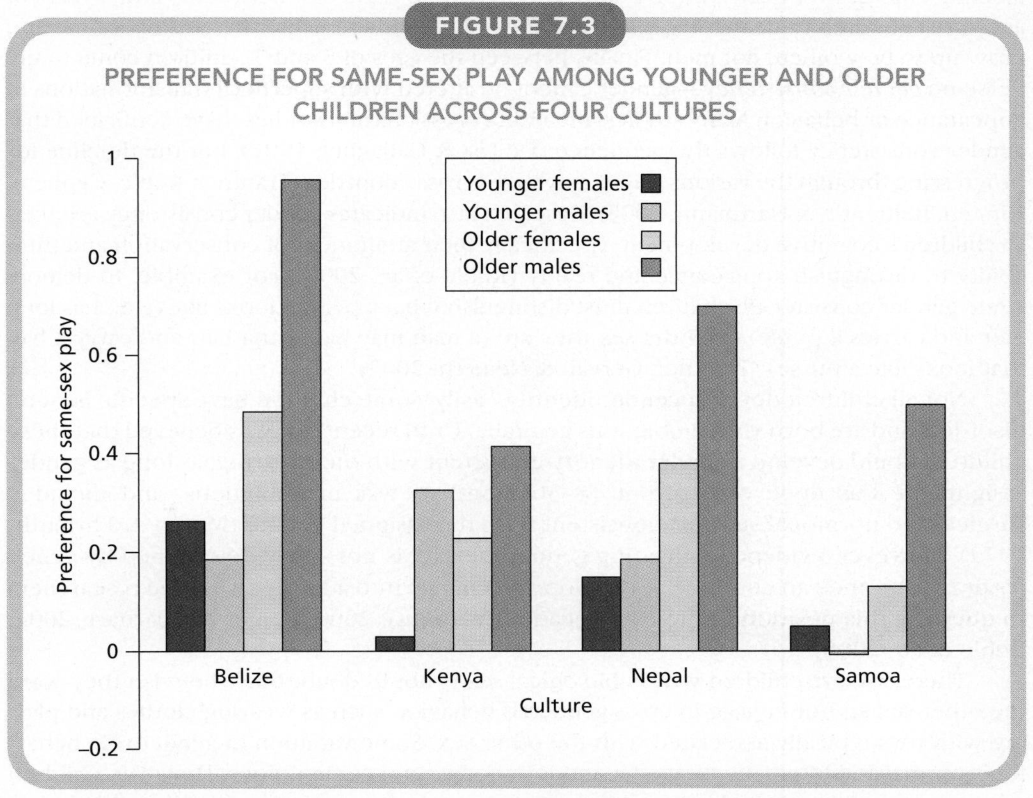

Source: From Munroe, R. L. & Romney, A. K. (2006). Gender and age differeces in same-sex aggregation and social behavior. A four-culture study. Journal of Cross-Cultural Psychology, 37, p. 11. Reprinted by permission of Sage publications.

FIGURE 7.4

CHILDREN'S PREFERENCES FOR PLAY SPACES IN A SLOVAKIAN PRESCHOOL

In a Slovakian preschool the girls (left) preferred to play "Flower Shop" and the boys preferred Legos, but both played in the "Medical Center."

Source: Gmitrova, *V., Podhajecká, M., &* Gmitrov, *J. (2007). Children's play preferences: implications for the preschool education.* Early child Development and Care, *1–14.*

model to explain how children acquire these understandings. As described above, gender labeling emerges very early, often before children are 2 years old. Between 3 and 5 years of age, most children understand *gender stability*—little girls remain little girls over time and grow up to be women, not men. Finally, between the ages of 5 and 7, children come to understand *gender consistency*—gender cannot be altered with superficial transformations in appearance or behavior. Many studies, including cross-cultural studies, have confirmed that gender consistency follows this sequence (De Lisi & Gallagher, 1991), but the timeline for progressing through the various stages may vary across countries (Trautner, Ruble, Cyphers, Kirsten, Behrendt, & Hartmann, 2005). Research also indicates gender consistency is linked to children's cognitive development, specifically their attainment of conservation and their ability to distinguish appearance and reality (Ruble et al., 2006). For example, to demonstrate gender consistency, children must distinguish what a person looks like (e.g., has long hair and carries a purse) from the sex they are (a man may have long hair and carry a bag that looks like a purse) (Trautner, Gervai, & Nemeth, 2003).

Not all children develop gender identity easily. Some children have specific genetic disorders and are born with ambiguous genitalia. Until recently, it was believed that these children would develop a gender identity consistent with their rearing, as long as gender assignment was done early (from 18–30 months), was unambiguous, and included surgical and hormonal support consistent with the assigned gender (Money & Ehrhardt, 1972). However, evidence indicating gender identity is not solely determined by genetics or rearing and can continue to develop and change into adulthood has led researchers to question this position in the past decade (Colapinto, 2000; Reiner & Gearhart, 2004; Ruble et al., 2006).

There also are children whose biological sex is not in doubt but who wish they were the other sex and/or engage in cross-gendered behavior, such as wearing clothes and playing with toys typically associated with the other sex. Some variation in gender role behavior is normal and often encouraged in modern homes and communities. However, children whose preferences and behaviors are viewed as atypical or extreme are still at risk for experiencing a variety of negative social and psychological outcomes. Parents, peers, and even teachers continue to reward gender-typical behavior and to criticize or punish cross-gender behavior, especially in boys (Knafo et al., 2005), and children's perceived gender typicality is associated with their global self-worth, perceptions of social competence, and parent–child relationship quality (Carver, Yunger, & Perry, 2003). Also, recalled childhood gender nonconformity is associated with adult body dissatisfaction in both homosexual and heterosexual men (Strong, Singh, & Randall, 2000), and loneliness, depression, and suicidal ideation, especially in men (Harry, 1983; Knafo et al., 2005). Findings such as these point to the significance of children's gender development.

In the social sciences, we typically use the term **sex** to refer to the biological differences between boys and girls and men and women, and the term **gender** to refer to the social and psychological dimensions of being male or female. However, as is true for most nature-nurture distinctions, there is a great deal of interaction between our biological and psychosocial selves. Let's examine some theories of and influences on gender development.

Influences on Gender Development

What factors are responsible for children's gender development? Some evidence points to biological differences between males and females, including differences in hormones and brain structures. Other evidence points to social experiential factors, and still more evidence highlights the role of cognitive development in gender development. It is likely that gender development depends on complex interactions among biological, social, and cognitive factors.

BIOLOGICAL INFLUENCES. Some researchers who emphasize the role of biology in observed differences between males and females point to the adaptive function these differences play in both human and nonhuman evolution. For example, males show some advantage over females in spatial reasoning and rapid responding. These abilities benefit males of a species who often are responsible for hunting prey, perhaps over long distances (Geary, 2005). Also, males' propensity to behave aggressively is believed to afford some advantage in competing for resources and attracting mates (Geary, 2005). In contrast, females of a species often are more nurturing and self-sacrificing than males. This is an advantage in their role as caregivers to offspring and increases the likelihood of the offspring's survival (Geary, 1998; Miller, Putcha-Bhagavatula, & Pederson, 2002). Sex differences such as these are observed in 97% of mammalian species (de Waal & Johanowicz, 1993), and are evident in the play behavior of human boys and girls as well as primates (Geary, 2005). Earlier in this chapter we described how boys engage in more rough-and-tumble play and demonstrate higher levels of physical aggression than girls. Boys also spend more time jockeying for position and playing games of one-upmanship in their interactions with one another (Davies, 2004; Geary, 2005). Most girls want to form more intimate bonds with their friends and avoid conflict in these relationships. They also engage in more pretend parenting than boys do. According to Geary (1999, 2005), these differences in play behaviors may reflect an evolutionary tendency to practice competencies associated with historical male and female roles.

Hormones are another sex-related biological characteristic found to affect gender-based behavior. In particular, research has shown the effects of androgens (male hormones) on boys' and girls' developing bodies (Ruble et al., 2006). In boys, these hormones are associated with rough-and-tumble play and physical aggression. When girls' adrenal systems secrete abnormally high levels of androgens, a disorder known as *congenital adrenal hyperplasia* (CAH), they can be born with external genitalia, masculinized to varying degrees, and often are behaviorally more masculine and less feminine than girls without CAH. Most girls with CAH are diagnosed at birth; they are treated with cortisol to reduce the secretion of excess androgens and have surgery to feminize their genitalia—these girls have ovaries and a uterus and are fertile. Behaviorally, girls with CAH often are characterized as "tomboys." They have higher activity levels than most other girls and male gender stereotypic preferences; for example, they prefer playing with toy vehicles and blocks than with dolls, choose male over female playmates, and are more interested in male-oriented careers, such as driving trucks or serving in the military (Hines, Brook, & Conway, 2004; Ruble et al., 2006).

There is increasing evidence that male and female brains have structural differences (Cahill, 2005). For example, on average, male brains are larger than female brains, a difference consistent with males' typically larger body mass. Also, there is evidence that male brains have a higher proportion of cortical gray matter, whereas female brains have more white matter. Whether or how these differences affect cognitive abilities is not clear (Gur et al., 1999); however, other variations in brain structure have been associated with differences in cognitive processing. The corpus callosum, which is the bundle of nerves that connects the two hemispheres of the brain, tends to be larger and to include more dense nerve bundles in female than male brains. Differences in hemispheric specialization have been attributed to this difference. For example, when engaging in cognitive tasks, male brain activation tends to be limited to one hemisphere or the other, whereas female brain activation often is spread across both hemispheres (Shaywitz et al., 1995). This difference doesn't appear to provide a performance advantage, but other differences do. Females have more dense nerve connections in areas associated with linguistic processing and, in fact, research indicates girls have a slight advantage over males on tasks requiring skill with language (Witelson, Glezer, & Kigar, 1995). We have already indicated that boys are typically better at spatial reasoning tasks, and research has found that the area in the brain associated with spatial reasoning is larger in males than in females.

Some research indicates observed differences in brain structure may be the result of hormonal influence (Cahill, 2005; Gron, Wunderlich, Spitzer, Tomczak, & Riepe, 2000). For example, the area of the brain associated with spatial processing has high numbers of sex-hormone receptors. It is possible that higher levels of male sex hormones in this area are linked to males' greater proficiency with spatial reasoning. Alternatively, male–female differences in brain structure may reflect evolutionary transformations. In prehistoric times, women stayed home together and, as a consequence, engaged in more social interaction, while men went out alone to hunt. The result may be that female brains evolved for greater language proficiency (Gleason & Ely, 2002).

Although the evidence for biological influences on gender development is convincing, it does not tell the whole story. It's also important to consider social influences.

SOCIAL INFLUENCES. There is an extensive body of research showing how social and contextual factors influence children's gender development. According to social learning theories, children gather information about gender and what is considered appropriate behavior for their own sex by observing and interacting with others, including parents, siblings, peers, and cultural models in advertising, toys, TV, and films.

In Western cultures, boys' and girls' experiences in their home environments are different from infancy. Many parents decorate their children's bedrooms with gender-related colors and themes, and dress their boys and girls in gender-typical clothing (Kane, 2006; Sutfin, Fulcher, Bowles, & Patterson, 2008). Also, parents tend to encourage and reward what they consider to be "gender-appropriate" behavior and provide their children with gender-typed toys (Leaper 1994, 2002). Consistent with these beliefs, boys often are presented with toys that stress action and competition, such as tools, weaponry, and sports equipment, whereas girls receive toys that emphasize caregiving, cooperation, and physical appearance, such as dolls, kitchen sets, and jewelry. Furthermore, parents tend to feel more protective of their daughters and often place greater restrictions on their activities and where they can go (Brody, 1999; Morrow, 2006), which may narrow their range of activities and independence.

Even though the gendered roles in modern families are more blurred than they used to be (with many mothers working outside the home and some fathers working from home and taking more responsibility for childcare and cooking), it is still the case that most parents' tolerance for children's gender nonconformity is limited (Gleason, 2005; Kane, 2006; Ruble et al., 2006). In Kane's study, 42 parents with children ages 3 to 5 were interviewed about their children's current toys, activities, and clothes; how they felt about their children's interests and behaviors in relation to gendered expectations; and the desirability and feasibility of gender neutrality in childhood. In general, mothers and fathers in the study supported some cross-gender activity. Especially for girls, parents expressed pleasure at seeing their daughters engaged in activities more strongly associated with boys (e.g., playing soccer or building things) and reported encouraging them to consider traditionally male occupations. Similarly, parents said they wanted their sons to develop domestic skills and nurturing, nonviolent, and empathic behaviors. Also, they reported encouraging their sons to play with dolls and other toys traditionally associated with girls. However, parents did temper their support for gender neutrality with a concern that it not go too far in the opposite direction. This concern appeared greater for boys than girls and was more often expressed by fathers than mothers. For example, one father commented, "I wouldn't want her to be too boyish, because she's a girl," and another father expressed relief that his son was more interested in the Ken doll than Barbie. Other fathers indicated they would be concerned if their sons played with dolls and other "icons of femininity" much beyond the preschool years. These findings are consistent with previous research indicating parents are much more tolerant of gender nonconformity in girls than in boys (Ruble et al., 2006; Sandnabba & Ahlberg, 1999).

In general, children are influenced by the extent of gender stereotyping they experience, and parents differ in the extent to which they model and promote gender-stereotypic beliefs and behaviors. For example, African American parents, especially mothers, often reject traditional gender divisions (Kane, 2000), whereas Latin cultures have more strongly marked gender-role divisions (Raffaelli & Ontai, 2004). Also, studies indicate children raised by single parents and lesbian parents show less gender stereotypic preferences than children raised by two-parent and heterosexual couples (Ruble et al., 2006; Sutfin et al., 2008). Sutfin and colleagues compared lesbian parents and their children (ages 3 to 6) with heterosexual parents and their children in terms of their attitudes toward gender roles. In addition, they compared children's bedrooms across the two types of family to determine the extent to which these environments were "gendered." In general, lesbian parents' attitudes about gender roles were more liberal than those of their heterosexual peers. Similarly, children of lesbian couples reported more liberal attitudes toward gender roles and their bedrooms were more gender neutral than those of children with heterosexual parents. Across both groups, however, mothers were more liberal than fathers, girls were more liberal than boys, and boys' bedrooms tended to be more stereotypical than those of girls.

What about siblings? How do they influence gender development? Research indicates the sibling relationship is complex in this regard and depends on birth order, age, how many, and whether siblings are the same or different sexes (McHale, Crouter, & Whiteman, 2003). It appears that younger siblings have little influence over older siblings' gender typing, but older siblings serve as powerful models of gendered behavior for younger siblings. Also, some research indicates children with same-sex siblings are more stereotyped than only children and children with no siblings are more gender typed than children with older other-sex siblings (Rust et al., & the ALSPAC Study Team, 2000). However, other research contradicts these findings, indicating that children with same-sex siblings are less stereotyped than children with other-sex siblings (Grotevant, 1978). There is some evidence that siblings strive to differentiate themselves from one another. This may lead one sister to develop artistic talents whereas the other follows a more athletic path. Also, children in all-girl or all-boy families may be called upon for more cross-gendered chores. These opportunities enable them to try out a greater variety of roles. In general, it appears there are some sibling effects, which likely are mediated by features of the family context.

We have already described how gender segregation among same-age peers begins very early, peaks in the early school years, and then declines as children move toward adolescence. The finding that by the age of 3 or 4, children prefer to play with same-sex peers has been replicated in many societies around the world (Gmitrova et al., 2007; Munroe & Romney, 2006). This may reflect children's natural inclination to seek play partners who have interests in common with them, but it also exposes children to more same-sex than other-sex behaviors and interaction styles (Ruble et al., 2006). A preponderance of practice with gender-typed toys and activities may facilitate interactions with same-sex peers, but it narrows children's behavioral repertoire and limits interactions with the opposite sex. That is what Martin and Fabes (2001) found when they studied preschool children across a school year. Children who played more with same-sex peers early in the year demonstrated higher

CONNECTING WITH CHILDREN

Guidelines for Families, Teachers, and Other Professionals: Encouraging More Gender-Neutral Beliefs and Behaviors

Encourage children to engage in a broad range of activities without associating them with gender.
Examples

1. Model gender-neutral beliefs and behaviors through a non-gendered distribution of house chores (both boys and girls can do yard work, shovel snow, take out the garbage, clean the house, wash dishes, cook, and babysit). Children will learn more from your attitude and actions than from anything else.
2. Encourage children to play games, use toys, and engage in activities regardless of gender roles. Both girls and boys should be encouraged to invent, explore, compete, and problem-solve as well as be creative, assertive, nurturing, active/passive, and emotionally expressive.
3. Develop children's interest in performing activities commonly assigned to the opposite sex if they like and enjoy them.
4. Create a learning environment that is free of sex stereotyping in instructional organization, interactions, materials, and activities.
5. Expose children to gender-equitable literature and media.

Avoid gender bias in your interactions with children.
Examples

1. Make it clear that conventions belong to particular times/places to show children that gender roles are not fixed. Use sentences such as: "In our culture, we . . ." "Today it is the custom to . . ." "Years ago people thought . . . but now we think. . . ."
2. Use non-gendered language; avoid generalizations such as "Boys don't cry and girls don't fight."
3. Support behaviors that defy gender stereotypes (e.g., allow boys to play girls and vice versa in skits, support children who prefer wearing gender-atypical clothing or colors, respect children's preferences for gender-variant interests).
4. Promote mixed-sex groups and avoid putting the boys against the girls when forming teams for classroom contests and projects.

Let children be themselves and express their emotions.
Examples

1. Allow children to fully express their emotions, hopes, desires, needs, and interests, regardless of their gender.
2. Learn about the person that your child already is—not who you want him/her to become.
3. Examine your own gendered behavior. What messages are you sending your children about masculinity and femininity?

Source: Adapted from http://www.associatedcontent.com/article/225115/helping_children_understand_gender.html?cat=47 http://www.associatedcontent.com/article/10340/a_lesson_in_gender_equality_for_parents.html?cat=25 http://edchange.org/multicultural/papers/genderbias.html http://www.blnz.com/news/2008/04/23/Gender_Bias_Classroom_Current_Controversies_2969.html

levels of gender-typed behaviors later in the school year than children who played in mixed or other-sex groups. Boys who played together increased their rough-and-tumble play, aggression, and gender-typed play, and played farther away from teachers. In contrast, girls who played together decreased their level of activity and aggression and increased gender-typed behavior and proximity to teachers.

It also appears children "police" one another's gendered behavior. Children praise one another for gender-appropriate play and tease or criticize peers who engage in gender-inconsistent behavior (Davies, 2004; Ruble et al., 2006). Boys are more insistent than girls about following gender-consistent play themes and avoiding toys that are "for girls." Also, like adults, children are particularly intolerant of boys who cross gender lines, and boys who do this regularly may find they are ignored and excluded by their peers, even if they also engage in "masculine" activities.

Preschool teachers and adults who supervise organized activities (e.g., in childcare settings, sports, and clubs) reinforce children's gendered beliefs and behaviors when they group children by sex ("I'd like all the girls to line up here.") or compare the behavior of one sex to that of the other ("Look how quietly the girls are sitting waiting for the story."). Comments such as these communicate that girls are quiet and obedient, but it also can reinforce conformity and a lack of assertiveness in groups. Another powerful influence on children's gender development is the media. Toys are marketed specifically to boys or girls, and characters in books, television shows, and computer environments often are strongly gender typed (Morrow, 2006; Ruble et al., 2006). Socializing gender roles through popular culture and the media begins very early and continues—in fact it becomes more potent—throughout childhood and adolescence, as we will see in Chapters 10 and 13. The ***Connecting with Children*** guidelines offer some ideas for encouraging more flexibility in children's gendered beliefs and behaviors.

COGNITIVE INFLUENCES. Earlier in this section on gender development, we described Kohlberg's (1966) three-stage theory of how children come to understand gender constancy. This is a cognitive theory because it emphasizes how children's thinking about what it means to be male or female or masculine or feminine develops, and how their thinking shapes their preferences and behavior. Cognitive theorists also refer to schema theory to explain how children construct mental representations of gender based on their experiences with males and females, as well as the gender-related messages they receive either directly from parents and peers or indirectly through the media.

Gender schema theory is based on the assumption that as children interact with the world, they form organized cognitive structures, or *schemas* (see Chapter 2) that include gender-related information and these schemas influence how they think and behave (Martin & Halverson, 1981; Martin & Ruble, 2004). Martin and Halverson proposed that two types of gender schemas guide behavior. The first is a general *in-group/out-group schema* that includes information children need to categorize objects, behavior, traits, and roles as being for males or females. The second, referred to as an *own-sex schema,* includes more detailed and specific information about objects, behaviors, traits, and roles that characterize their own sex. Figure 7.5 shows how a young girl might use this information to think about the appropriateness of playing with a doll or a truck. In this example, the girl's gender schema places toy trucks in a category for boys. Given that she is not a boy, she may decide this toy is not for her and choose not to play with it. Dolls, on the other hand, are in a category for girls, so she is likely to decide this is an appropriate toy for her.

In general, children's early learning of gender categories and associated attributes results in schemas that are very rigid (e.g., that only boys or only girls can do or be something). However, as children mature and acquire more gender-related information, their gender-related schemas become more flexible and realistic (e.g., that either boys or girls can do most anything) (Martin & Ruble, 2004, p. 68). One longitudinal study that questioned children yearly about their gender concepts found gender rigidity peaked around age 5 or 6 and then showed a marked increase in flexibility by age 7 or 8 (Trautner et al.,

FIGURE 7.5

SCHEMATIC-PROCESSING MODEL OF SEX ROLE STEREOTYPING

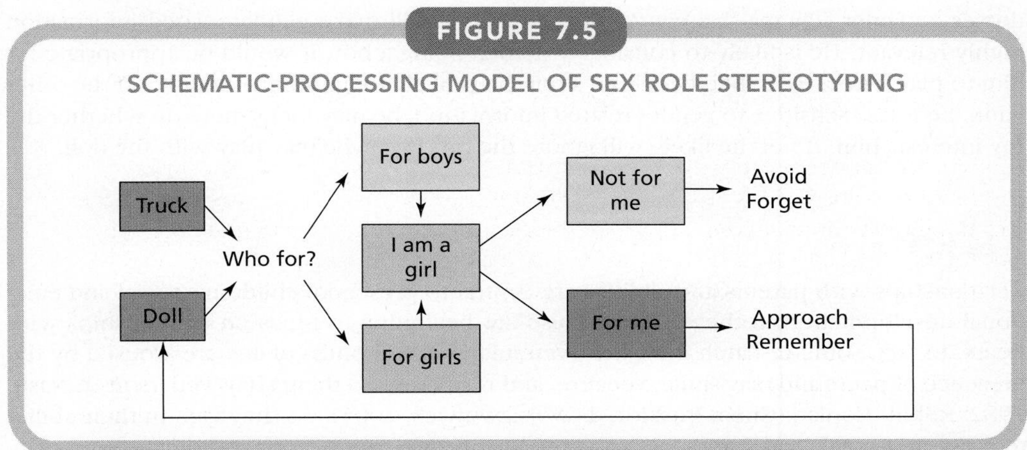

Source: Adapted from Martin, C. L., & Halverson, C. F. Jr. (1981). A schematic -processing model of sex typing and stereotyping in children. Child Development, 52. *1119–1134.*

FIGURE 7.6

EXAMPLE OF THE GENDER SCHEME THEORY

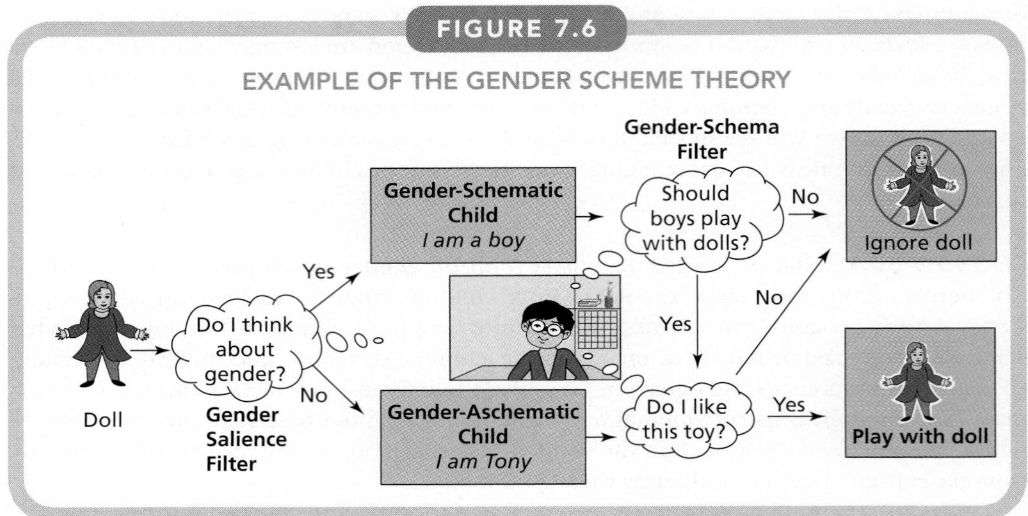

Source: Adapted from Liben, L. S., & Bigler, R. S. (2002). The developmental course of gender differentiation: Conceptualizing, measuring, and evaluating constructs and pathways. Monographs of the Society for Research in Child Development, *67(2), 1–187.*

2005). This finding is consistent with other cross-sectional research indicating that children's gender rigidity remains strong up to age 8 and then declines as children move toward adolescence and become romantically interested in the other sex (Maccoby & Jacklin, 1987; Ruble et al., 2007).

Cognitive theorists attribute the biases in children's processing and remembering information to their typically rigid gender schemas. Recall that infants looked longer at toy trucks after being habituated to a male face (Serbin et al., 2001). Similarly, children tend to remember what they observe members of their own sex doing better than they recall what they see members of the opposite sex doing (Signorella, Bigler, & Liben, 1997), and they more accurately recall the actions of individuals who behave in gender-consistent ways than the actions of those whose behavior would be considered gender atypical (Liben & Signorella, 1993).

However, there are individual differences in children's levels of gender rigidity (Golombok et al., 2008; Martin & Ruble, 2004) and there is some evidence that gender schemas can be modified through explicit instruction (Bigler & Liben, 2002; Liben & Bigler, 2002). Figure 7.6 shows how children may differ in the extent to which they endorse gender-specific schemas. Consider a young boy who is presented with a doll. If he strongly endorses a gender schema, his *gender salience filter* will make gender-related information highly relevant. He is likely to consider whether, being a boy, it would be appropriate for him to play with a doll. If he decides it's not, he is likely to ignore the doll. If, on the other hand, he is less sensitive to gender-related information, he may focus more on whether the toy interests him. If not, he likely will ignore the toy. If yes, he may play with the doll.

PEER RELATIONSHIPS

Relationships with parents and siblings are central to preschool children's social and emotional development, but these children also are beginning to focus on relationships with peers. In fact, some research indicates even infants 0–6 months of age are aroused by the presence of peers and may smile, vocalize, and reach toward them (Hay, Pederson, & Nash, 1982; Rubin, Coplan, Chen, Buskirk, & Wojslawowicz, 2005). As they gain in their ability to move and speak, toddlers' social interactions become much more coordinated and complex, involving simple games (e.g., imitating one another) and turn taking. Between 2 and 4 years of age, children begin to share symbolic meanings with one another (e.g., they agree to adopt imaginary roles in pretend play). Social interactions among older preschoolers are lengthier and more complex than those of toddlers; they involve longer sequences, more turn taking, and more complex coordination among partners of roles, rules, and themes (Rubin et al., 2005). Also, in contrast to toddlers, who seek attention from adults more than peers in social situations (e.g., in daycare, on play dates), children ages 3 to 5 seek out friends to play with and share information of significance to them ("I have new shoes.") (Davies, 2004). This shift in focus likely reflects advances in both social and cognitive development that enable the development of "first friendships."

Advances in Peer Sociability

Preschool children are less egocentric and more prosocial (Davies, 2004; Rubin et al., 2005). They are more aware of and interested in the needs of others—they want to be liked. Also, they are more willing and able to consider other children's ideas and opinions during play and to avoid conflict. As a result, sharing, helping, comforting, and control over anger and aggression increase. In addition, as children's facility with language increases, so too does their communicative competence (Rubin et al., 2005). They learn to direct speech to their partner and to use more indirect interrogatives or inferred requests (e.g., "Could I play with that truck now?") versus direct imperatives (e.g., "Give me that truck now!"). This is not to say preschool children's interactions are free of conflict—quite the contrary. Observations of typical preschool children reveal frequent disagreements, aggressive actions, falling-outs, and disruptions in cooperative play (Davies, 2004). However, for typical preschool children, disagreements and conflict create opportunities to develop skills in social problem solving.

In contrast, preschool children who are aggressive or impulsive show higher rates of aggression during pretend play, are more often engaged in conflict with peers (e.g., teasing, bullying, and physical aggression), and are more often rejected by peers than typical preschoolers (Davies, 2004; Gleason, Gower, Hohmann, & Gleason, 2005; Ladd & Troop-Gordon, 2003). These children show relatively low levels of empathy and self-control, and they often misinterpret the actions of others, perceiving aggression when none was intended. These characteristics put them at a significant social disadvantage. Often these children continue to be rejected and friendless through school and are at risk for developing maladjustment problems, such as internalizing (self-blame or self-hate) and/or externalizing problems (e.g., aggression toward others), because positive peer relationships become an important source of perceived competence and self-esteem through middle childhood and adolescence.

Research indicates a number of links between the quality of children's early relationships with parents and their subsequent relationships with peers. For example, preschool children who have secure and satisfying relationships with parents approach interactions with peers more confidently and expect these interactions will be enjoyable (Davies, 2004; Hartup, 1992; Rubin et al., 2005). This orientation results in opportunities for peer interaction and play, which in turn creates opportunities to develop skills that are essential for establishing and maintaining positive peer relationships. Alternatively, children who have experienced relationships with parents that are rejecting or neglectful are more likely than their securely attached peers to respond to peers aggressively or to withdraw from interactions with peers altogether. Either way, they lose the benefits of peer interactions for developing social skills.

Parents also can influence the quality of their children's relationships with peers through their own characteristics and behaviors. Parents who are warm and positive when communicating with their children (e.g., they praise, encourage, demonstrate affection and approval), yet consistent in their enforcement of rules and expectations, tend to have children who are popular and socially competent (Rubin et al., 2005). In contrast, parents characterized as cold, punitive, or overly permissive tend to have children who are aggressive and/or rejected by peers. Moreover, controlling and overprotective parenting behaviors are associated with children's social withdrawal. According to Rubin and colleagues, parents can support their children's development of positive peer relationships by (a) providing numerous and varied opportunities for them to interact with peers, (b) monitoring these encounters as necessary, (c) coaching them to interact positively with peers and solve social problems, and (d) disciplining unacceptable or maladaptive peer-directed behaviors. We discuss positive

CONNECTING WITH CHILDREN

Guidelines for Families, Teachers, and Other Professionals: Coaching Children's Peer Relationships

Nurture your child's social skills.
Examples

1. Teach your child about emotions and feelings and how to regulate them. The better children understand emotions and feelings, the more they are liked by peers and can engage in positive social interactions.
2. Develop a secure attachment with your child. Children whose parents are responsive to them have more empathy for others and adapt more easily to new social situations.
3. Help children to develop prosocial behaviors such as helping, sharing, and showing concern for others.
4. Practice inductive discipline (explaining the reasons for rules and the consequences of bad behavior) to help children show more self-control and cooperation with peers.

Become familiar with your child's social world.
Examples

1. Discuss your child's experiences with peers in a pleasant, conversational way.
2. Encourage children to have a positive and constructive attitude toward social difficulties; let them know that everybody gets rebuffed and rejected sometimes.
3. Suggest socially "generous" reasons for social rejection such as "Maybe she's just shy," or "Maybe he just wants to play on his own for a while." Help children brainstorm solutions and predict how different social strategies may work.
4. Watch for peer rejection and bullying and act wisely by protecting and validating your child's perceptions. Bringing the issue to the problematic setting, discuss your concerns with other adults and look for realistic solutions.

Understand social developmental trends.
Examples

1. Sharing is difficult for preschoolers. When you encourage it, try to make it as comfortable as possible and be patient (e.g., before friends visit, put favorite or new toys away to avoid conflicts).
2. Preschoolers often make rude or hurtful comments; don't take them personally, but don't ignore them. Explain how words can hurt feelings.
3. Gradually disengage from involvement in young children's play with peers; intervene when necessary, but allow them to solve conflicts on their own.

Provide children with opportunities to play.
Examples

1. Enrolling children in community center or neighborhood activities assures stable interactions with peers. Children benefit when they can develop long-lasting relationships.
2. Engage in pretend play with your child. Role-play tactics and strategies for forming and maintaining friendships.
3. Promote your child's developing ability to be well attuned to the social context (e.g., recognize other children's preferences, frame of reference, behavior, and interests).

Source: Adapted from http://www.parentingscience.com/preschool-social-skills.html
Mize, J., & Abell, E. (1996). Encouraging social skills in young children: Tips teachers can share with parents. Dimensions of Early Childhood, 24*(3). Retrieved from http://www.humsci.auburn.edu/parent/socialskills.html*

disciplinary tactics later, in the section on parenting. For ideas about how parents and other caregivers can coach children's peer relationships, see the ***Connecting with Children*** guidelines.

Teachers also can make a difference. In a 5-year longitudinal study, Carollee Howes (2000) examined the influence of the social emotional climate of preschool classrooms, children's early relationships with teachers, and behavior problems on children's social competence with peers in grade 2. In fact, the social emotional classroom climate (operationalized as the number of behavior problems, time spent with peers, and time spent in pretend play) and children's relationships with their preschool teacher did predict their social competence with peers in grade 2. In particular, time spent interacting with peers, low levels of behavior problems, and high levels of child–teacher closeness were associated with prosocial behavior ratings. Teacher–child conflict was negatively correlated with prosocial behavior and positively correlated with aggressive and disruptive behavior. These findings remind us that relationships are constructed in particular contexts and, as adults and caregivers, we need to do our best to create supportive contexts for children's development of positive peer relationships.

First Friendships

Toddlers show preferences for playing with some peers and not others, but preschool children begin to label peers as friends (Davies, 2004; Hartup, 1992). Very young children describe friends as people to play with, but by age 4 or 5, children begin to express affection for friends, concern for their feelings, and a desire to win their approval. These "first friendships" are good practice for having a "best friend," which is common in middle childhood (see Chapter 10). In addition, these first friendships provide contexts for children to develop and practice prosocial behavior (Avgitidou, 2001; Davies, 2004). Specifically, making and maintaining friends depends on children's ability to demonstrate good social skills: Friendships require cooperation, negotiation, compromise, and the desire and skill to resolve conflicts when they arise.

Researchers define friendships as close, mutual, and voluntary relationships (Gleason & Hohmann, 2006; Rubin et al., 2005). Reciprocity and equality are key features of friendships (Fujisawa, Kutsukake, & Hasagawa, 2008), as are empathy and perspective-taking (Rubin et al., 2005). Best friendships are characterized by greater intimacy and exclusivity than other friendships; preschool children typically don't have best friends, and girls are more likely than boys to have best friends (Sebanc, Kearns, Hernandez, & Galvin, 2007).

What attracts children to one another? From an early age, children are attracted to and choose friends who look like them (e.g., children who are the same age and sex, who share a similar racial and ethnic history), and friends with similar interests, behaviors, and activity levels (Gleason et al., 2005; Rubin et al., 2005). Unfortunately, this means that children who engage in antisocial behavior are attracted to one another (Haselager, Cillissen, Lieshout, Riksen-Walraven, & Hartup, 2002). Friends spend more time with one another than with non-friends; they talk more to each other, are more cooperative, and engage in more sophisticated forms of play (Rubin et al., 2005). Research indicates children, especially girls, as young as ages 3 to 5 recognize the benefits of friendship and distinguish between reciprocal and unilateral (one-sided) friendships based on the social provisions (companionship, intimacy, affection, enhancement of self-worth) available in these relationships (Gleason & Hohmann, 2006).

Research also indicates friends have more conflicts than non-friends (Davies, 2004), perhaps because they spend more time together. However, friends are more committed than non-friends to resolving conflicts and, because they know one another's interests and preferences, they know what to do to restore harmony in their relationships. For young children, friendships enhance excitement and amusement levels during play (Parker & Gottman, 1989). In general, friendships provide children with emotional security, support for self-esteem, intimacy and affection, instrumental assistance, and a context in which to develop interpersonal sensitivity (Rubin et al., 2005). Children with friends cope better with stressful events and situations (Davies, 2004), and children who enter kindergarten with friends or make friends early in the school year adjust better to this transition, have better attitudes toward school, and better academic outcomes than children who have difficulty forming friendships (Ladd, 1999). Moreover, research indicates early friendships are instrumental to children's developing representations of friendship, which influence their subsequent friendships in school (Dunn, Cutting, & Fisher, 2002).

Culture and Peer Relationships

Most of the research about children's peer relationships has been conducted in North America and Western Europe, so we know very little about the development and significance of peer relationships and friendships in non-Western cultures (Rubin et al., 2005). Rubin and colleagues assert that children's interactions with peers likely are culture bound because they are directed by cultural conventions and values that are experienced in interactions with family members, teachers, and other cultural role models. For example, cultures may differentially endorse or constrain behaviors associated with cooperation, compliance, or emotional expressivity. This was certainly true for the Tamang and Chhetri-Brahmin cultures in Nepal (Cole et al., 2002; Cole et al., 2006). Recall how Tamang children were raised in a culture that stressed equality among people and valued tolerance and harmony, whereas children in

First friendships are good practice for best friendships, which commonly develop in middle childhood.

the Chhetri-Brahmin culture were encouraged to develop awareness of self and differences between self and others. Cultural differences such as these often are observed between collectivist and individualist cultures. Medina and colleagues (2001) compared children' interactions during play in preschools in Andalusa, Spain, and the Netherlands. In particular, they focused on children's interactions when conflicts arose. Consistent with other research on collectivist cultures, their findings indicate Andalusian children were more likely to put aside personal objectives to maintain a positive interaction than were Dutch children. Consistent with cultures characterized as individualistic, Dutch children were more interested in getting their point of view across to others, even if it disrupted an activity.

Other research indicates cultural value systems may influence standards for peer acceptance and rejection. For example, in Western cultures, shy or inhibited behavior is associated with social incompetence or immaturity, whereas in traditional Chinese cultures, such behavior is highly valued (Rubin et al., 2005). In Canada and the United States, shy and inhibited children are likely to experience peer rejection and loneliness, whereas Chinese children who are shy are generally accepted by peers (Chen, Rubin, Li, & Li, 1999). In an observational study, DeSouza and Chen (2002) found that when shy and inhibited children made overtures to peers, they were encouraged and supported in China, but rejected in Canada. Moreover, Chinese peers were more likely to initiate prosocial interactions, such as sharing and helping, with shy children than with Canadian peers. These findings emphasize the important role of cultural norms in children's development of peer relationships.

Play

Play is both universal and adaptable. It is a common experience among children all over the world; children invent games whether they live in small, sometimes primitive, villages or large urban centers, whether they have few material resources or all the toys that money can buy. The ***Relating to Every Child*** feature makes this point by describing children's play in India. Children are highly motivated to play and will sustain activities they consider play for long periods of time without any extrinsic reward (Elkind, 2007). However, play is more than fun and games. It contributes importantly to children's physical, cognitive, and social development. Play stimulates the senses and offers opportunities to develop hand-eye as well as gross and fine motor coordination. Through play, preschool children increase their understanding of cause-and-effect relationships and enhance their language, problem-solving, and perspective-taking skills (Davies, 2004; Singer, 1994; Singer & Singer, 1990). Also, because play provides opportunities for children to practice skills they are acquiring (e.g., sorting and counting blocks to build things, practicing emergent literacy skills while playing post office), it is associated with success on academic tasks in school (Katz, 2001; Russ, 2006).

In particular, **pretend play,** which involves using objects and toys symbolically and integrating them in imaginary scenarios, promotes abstract and creative thinking. Through pretend play, children test roles and behaviors that are unfamiliar to them. Some research indicates preschoolers with strong imaginations have a better grip on reality than peers with less active fantasy lives (Dunn & Cutting, 1999). These children tend to be better at interpreting the emotions, actions, and intentions of others and can take a more objective and comprehensive view of their experiences, both positive and negative (Davies, 2004). It appears, therefore, that parents, teachers, and other caregivers should provide ample time and space for children to play.

Researchers characterize children's play in terms of its content (what children are doing while they play; what purpose play serves) and social dimensions (whether children play alone or with others). Children begin playing as infants, but play changes dramatically

RELATING TO

EVERY CHILD

▸ Play in India

OKE AND COLLEAGUES (Oke, Khattar, Pant, & Saraswathi, 1999) studied children playing in the cities of Mumbai and Vadodara in India. Specifically, they observed 451 episodes of children playing in both high and low SES neighborhoods and then characterized the form and content of their play. The games children played in these communities had much in common with the games children play in the Western world. For example, they observed children playing a game like "tag" (*pakda-pakdi*) in which one child was "it" and had to catch all the players. The last child to be caught was the winner. They also played "quick tag," a modified version of tag in which the child who was it caught one child who caught another and so the game continued and every child got to play all the time. For variations of tag as well as games that involve jumping rope (skipping) or using marbles and balls that children play in countries all over the world, see http://www.topics-mag.com/edition11/games-section.htm.

In India, Oke et al. (1999) observed that children in high SES communities had many of the same resources as children in the developed world (e.g., they played on playground equipment in parks designed for children). In poor neighborhoods, however, children seldom had access to materials designed specifically for children's play, but their play was more imaginative. They made toys from materials they found in their community (e.g., plastic bags, scraps of paper, empty tins and boxes). Often these children combined play with the work they did for their family. For example, Oke et al. described girls, with siblings strapped to their hips, coming down a slide at a public park, and "rag pickers" chasing one another in the streets as they picked rags. Also, not all of the places where these children played were safe. Often children played in heavily trafficked streets, areas where they were exposed to garbage and sewage, or near construction sites containing materials that put them at risk for injury or worse.

Organizations, such as the International Playground Association (2009) are making it their purpose to "protect, preserve, and promote the child's right to play." They have active groups in close to 50 countries in the world, including India, and are working with governments to initiate projects that are increasing children's access to safe, fun, and appropriate play spaces and equipment.

between the ages of 2 and 6. We will examine this developmental trajectory as we look at the different types of play.

Cognitive Dimensions of Play

Infants and toddlers are interested in the properties and functions of objects (Davies, 2004). Therefore, they are drawn to toys on the basis of how they look or what noises they make and play with them to find out what they do and how they work. Piaget (1951) labeled this "experimentation" with toys *sensorimotor play,* but it is also referred to in the literature as **functional play,** or practice play. Functional play involves simple repetitive actions with objects or physical movements such as jumping or rolling. Continuously pressing a stuffed cow to hear it "moo-oo-oo" or repeatedly stacking Mom's pots and pans are examples of functional play.

Constructive play is more goal-oriented than functional play and emerges after children figure out how things work and understand the effects of their actions (Davies, 2004). They learn to manipulate objects to produce something. Stacking blocks to make a tower or putting a puzzle together are examples of constructive play. This form of play is especially common in children ages 3 to 6 (Rubin, Fein, & Vandenberg, 1983).

Finally, pretend play—also referred to as dramatic or imaginative play—is based on make-believe, even fantastical, scenarios. In pretend play, children use objects symbolically or make believe they are someone or something they are not. Often, pretend play has a narrative quality and emerges about the same time as language is developing (between 2 and 3 years of age). However, language development often lags behind other forms of representation, so observing children at play can be a good way to gain insight into what they are thinking and feeling that they may not be able to communicate with words (Davies, 2004).

Children's engagement in pretend play increases during the preschool years, peaks around 6 or 7, and then declines during the school years as children become more involved in formal games with rules and procedures (Pellegrini & Smith, 1998). At first, children's pretend play is self-referenced and generally reflects a familiar routine (e.g., pretending to drink from a cup or take a nap). As children become less egocentric, their pretend play has a more social focus and the roles they assume are less familiar and more abstract (e.g., pretending to have superhuman powers or imagining what it would be like to be a bear) (Cohen, 2006).

Social Dimensions of Play

In a now classic study, Mildred Parten (1932) studied 42 children (from less than 2 years old to 4) in a nursery school at the University of Minnesota from October through June, 1926, and observed six forms of play in relation to children's level of involvement with peers. Her categories and observations, summarized in Table 7.3, characterize play on a continuum

TABLE 7.3 • **Parten's Six Forms of Play**

FORMS OF PLAY	OPERATIONAL DEFINITION	EXAMPLE
Unoccupied	The child does not appear to be playing, just observing anything that is of momentary interest.	This can include observing others in the environment, climbing on the furniture, or sitting in one spot glancing around the room.
Onlooker	The child observes other children playing, but does not overtly enter into the play activity. The child may interact with the group of children he is observing.	As an onlooker, the child hovers at the periphery of a playgroup—typically near enough to hear and speak with children in the group he is observing. He may ask questions, or make suggestions, but does not participate in the play.
Solitary independent play	The child plays alone, even if there are other children in the room. He is not interested in or distracted by the activities of the other children.	The child plays independently with dolls or trucks or building blocks. Some card and computer games are intended for solitary play.
Parallel group activity	The child plays the same game in the same space as other children, but she plays *beside* rather than *with* the other children.	The child is part of a group in a sandbox. The children in the group have their own cups and fill them with sand without considering what the other children are doing. There is very little conversation about the activity. Children come and go all the time, but those remaining at the sandbox pay no attention to the movements of others; they are absorbed in their own activities.
Associative group play	The child plays with other children and the interaction concerns a common activity. They may share play material and may attempt to control who may or may not play in the group. All the members engage in similar if not identical activity, but there is no division of labor, and no organization of the activity of several individuals around any material goal or product. Leadership has not been established; instead each child acts as she wishes.	In the sandbox example above, children begin to borrow one another's cups. They engage in conversation about the shared activity (they communicate their needs and are aware of other's needs). They invite other children to the sandbox, and ask those present to make room for her. The others may or may not move over, depending upon their wishes.
Cooperative group play	Children play with one another in a group that is organized for the purpose of making some material product, or of attaining a competitive goal, or of dramatizing situations of adult and group life, or of playing formal games. There is a marked sense of belonging or of not belonging to the group. Elements of division of labor, group censorship, leadership, and the subordination of individual desire to that of the group are observed.	While in the sandbox, one child suggests that they are all making supper. Then, the family roles are assigned or adopted and the children speak about their roles in preparing the meal. Leadership or domination by one or more of the children occurs, one child being informed that he can't cook because he's the baby. They are not permitted to leave the sandbox unless it is known what they are going to do next.

Source: Parten, M. B. (1932). Social participation among preschool children. Journal of Abnormal and Social Psychology, 29, *pp. 243–269. Reprinted with permission from the American Psychological Association.*

from uninvolved or passive onlooker to increasingly interactive and cooperative. Some researchers criticize Parten's work because she sampled a relatively small number of children in a unique environment (see, for example, Rubin et al., 2005). They advise researchers and practitioners to use caution and not overgeneralize Parten's findings to all children. However, a close reading of Parten's study reveals a careful methodology. She made many observations of the same children over a long period of time and correlated her observations with their teachers' assessments. Regardless, her findings and social participation scale continue to influence assessments of children's social interactions.

It is important not to think about Parten's six categories as developmental stages. Although it's true that children's play becomes increasingly social and cooperative during the preschool years, Parten observed some toddlers engaging in associative and cooperative play, and older preschoolers engaging in solitary play and onlooker behaviors (see Figure 7.7). Also, it's important not to interpret older children's solitary or onlooker behavior as a sign of immaturity or social problems, or to assume all children will enjoy similar amounts of social interaction during play. Some children prefer to play alone—they may be more focused on objects or tasks than people (Henderson, Marshall, Fox, & Rubin, 2004). Moreover, some research indicates that children who enjoy solitary play have longer attention spans and more placid personalities (Coplan, Prakash, O'Neil, & Armer, 2004), and onlooker behaviors have been characterized as adaptive strategies for learning about toys or becoming part of a group (Hughs, 1995; Lindsey & Colwell, 2003). However, solitary play in some children can indicate shyness, fearfulness, or social rejection (Coplan et al., 2004; Henderson et al., 2004), so it is important for parents and teachers to consider other indicators of maladjustment in children who often play alone. More research is needed to distinguish between adaptive and maladaptive solitary play.

Gender and Play

Earlier in this chapter we described how play becomes more gender segregated through the preschool years. Boys tend to be more physically active than girls and enjoy "rough-and-tumble" play in large groups. Girls enjoy quieter, more cooperative forms of play with one or a few play partners. And boys are more likely than girls to choose outside spaces to play, and are more likely to roam or play away from adult supervision, a finding replicated in both Western and non-Western countries (Morrow, 2006; Munroe & Romney, 2006). Holmes and Procaccino (2008) observed preschool children's preferences for outdoor play spaces. Boys' favorite spaces were the jungle gym, a wheeled vehicle area, and open spaces, whereas girls preferred the sandboxes. In general, girls tend to choose more structured

FIGURE 7.7

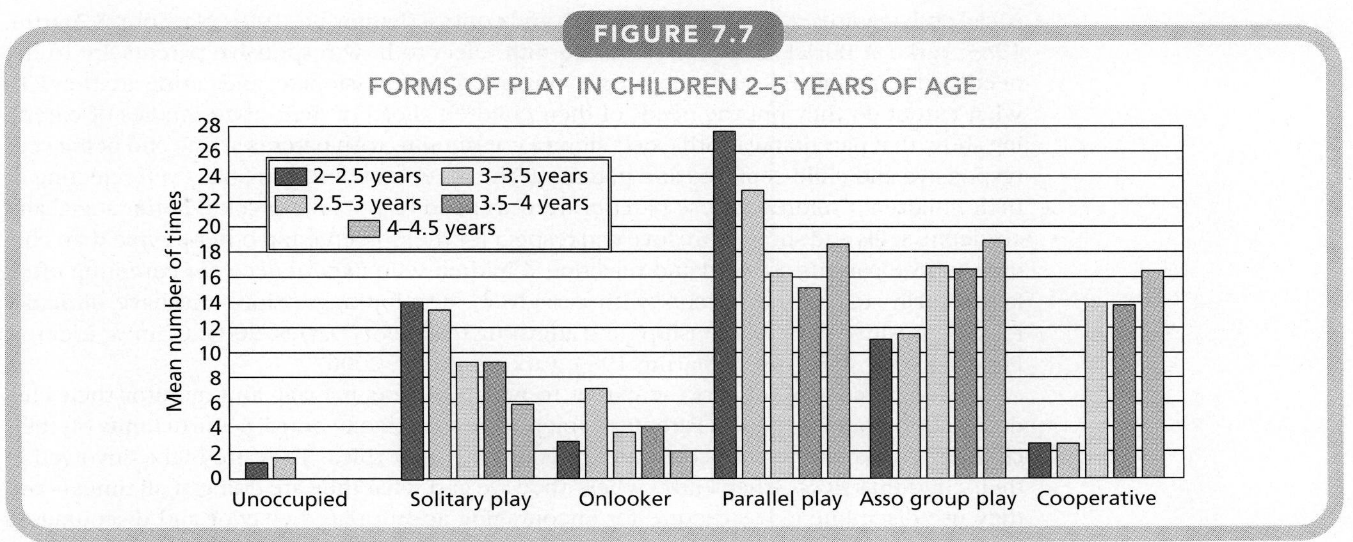

Source: Parten, M. B. (1932). Social participation among preschool children. Journal of Abnormal and Social Psychology, *29, p. 260. Reprinted with permission from the American Psychological Association.*

environments in proximity to adults, perhaps as a response to parents' tendency to be more protective of girls and more restrictive about where they play (Morrow, 2006).

Girls engage in more pretend play than boys, and the themes in children's imaginary scenarios appear to differ by gender (Gmitrova et al., 2007). Themes for boys tend to revolve around competition and danger or discord (e.g., war games). In contrast, girls tend to focus more on intimate and orderly relationships and themes (e.g., playing house or school). Also, girls are more likely than boys to have imaginary friends (discussed in Chapter 6), but boys are more likely than girls to impersonate characters (Gleason, 2005). When boys and girls play together, masculine themes tend to predominate (Fabes, Hanish, & Martin, 2003). These differences may reflect children's socialization—recall parents are more comfortable when girls cross gender boundaries than when boys try out roles or activities that are considered more typical for girls.

Although there is widespread agreement about the important role for play in children's social emotional development (Cheng & Johnson, 2010; Roskos & Christie, 2007), research about play has been relatively sparse. Cheng and Johnson's search for "play" in key early childhood journals in the years 2005–2007 found only 57 of 1,000 articles with play in the title, abstract, or list of keywords. More concerning is the trend toward standards-based education and the emphasis on skill development in early childhood education programs, which has reduced the attention and status given to play (Roskos & Christie, 2007).

Parent–Child Relationships in Early Childhood

In Chapter 4, we discussed the importance of forming a secure attachment in infancy as a foundation for healthy parent–child relationships and social emotional adjustment (Wittmer, 2009). From infancy, children's dependence on parents for basic childcare as well as emotion and behavior regulation declines progressively. As they become more independent and more involved in relationships outside their families, children also recognize that the plans and preferences their parents have for them can differ from their own. They may try to challenge parents to change their rules and plans. Research indicates parent–child attachment histories and the way parents and caregivers respond to these challenges will influence the extent to which children adopt parents' values and adhere to the limits they set (Davies, 2004; Kochanska, 2002).

Dimensions of Parenting

As you saw in Chapter 1, decades of research on parenting indicate two dimensions of parents' interactions with their children are particularly important for the development of both social and cognitive competence: warmth and control (Baumrind, 1991; Maccoby & Martin, 1983; Parke & Buriel, 2006). **Parental warmth** refers to how responsive parents are to the needs of their children. How supportive, nurturing, compassionate, and caring are they? To what extent do they put the needs of their children ahead of their own? Studies of parenting show that parental warmth exists along a continuum, with parents at one end being very responsive and child-centered and parents at the other end unresponsive, even rejecting of their children. Children whose parents are warm and responsive develop better social and academic skills and show more love and respect for their parents and other people than children whose parents are cold and rejecting. Children who experience *cold* parenting often fail to form secure attachments with caregivers, develop aggression, and have difficulty forming positive peer relationships and adjusting to school (Davies, 2005; Grimes, Klein, & Putallaz, 2004; Maccoby & Martin, 1983; Parke & Buriel, 2006).

Parental control reflects the extent to which parents manage and monitor their children's actions and activities. Parents characterized as high on control set firm limits on their children's behavior and are consistent in enforcing their rules. They are highly involved in their children's lives—they know where they are and what they are doing at all times—and they use discipline as a structure for encouraging appropriate behavior and discouraging inappropriate behavior. In contrast, parents characterized as low in control tend to be permissive and uninvolved in their children's lives. Like warmth, parental control exists along a continuum, with some parents being high and others being low. Researchers have distinguished between appropriate forms of behavioral control and inappropriate forms of psychological control, such as using guilt or withholding love to get children to comply with rules. Whereas appropriate behavioral control is associated with positive outcomes, psychological control is associated with a higher incidence of depression, drug use, and delinquency when children become adolescents (Barber, 2002; Galambos, Barker, & Almeida, 2003). Another recent distinction in types of parental control is between trying to control the child's behavior versus attempts to control the child's thoughts and feelings. You will see in Chapter 13 that trying to control thoughts and feelings is more intrusive and is associated with behavior problems for adolescents (Smetana et al., 2006).

Much of the research on parenting has examined the combined effects of the warmth and control dimensions. We discuss this research next.

Parenting Styles

Diane Baumrind's program of research, beginning in the mid-1960s, has had a strong influence on how we think about parenting today, especially in Western, European American cultures. Her research, and the research of Maccoby and Martin (1983) that followed, identified four distinct styles of parenting that reflect different combinations of high and low parental warmth and high and low parental control (see Figure 7.8).

According to Baumrind's model (1966, 1971), **authoritative parents** are high in warmth, but they also exert firm control. They monitor their children closely, set clear standards, and have high expectations for behavior. They are firm, but not harsh or unreasonable. Authoritative parents are rational and supportive in their approach to discipline. They allow for give and take in disciplinary matters. For example, in response to a child who is resisting leaving the park or a play date, an authoritative parent would listen to the child's complaint and then explain why the child needs to come now (e.g., "We need to pick up your brother from school."), or engage in age-appropriate negotiation to come to a resolution about the reasonableness of staying longer at the park ("We can stay for 10 more minutes, but then we need to hurry to pick up your brother from school. He will be waiting for us."). Preschool children raised by authoritative parents tend to be friendly, cooperative, socially competent, and independent (Mattanah, Pratt, Cowan, & Cowan, 2005). In later

FIGURE 7.8

PARENTING STYLES

	Accepting Responsive Child-centered	*Rejecting Unresponsive Parent-centered*
Demanding, controlling	Authoritative-reciprocal High in bidirectional communication	Authoritarian Power assertive
Undemanding, low in control attempts	Indulgent	Neglecting, ignoring, indifferent, uninvolved

Source: Macoby, E. E. & Martin, J. A. (1983). Socialization in the context of family: Parent-child interaction in E. M. Hetherington, Handbook of Child Psychology, Vol. 4, Socialization, Personality, and Social Development, *4e. Reproduced with permission of John Wiley & Sons, Inc.*

years, these children tend to be more successful in school, both socially and academically, and to have better relationships with parents than children who experience the other styles of parenting (Baumrind, 1971, 1991; Knafo & Schwartz, 2003; Parke & Buriel, 2006).

In contrast to authoritative parents, **authoritarian parents** tend to be high in control and low in warmth and responsiveness. They set firm limits and expect children will follow orders, because they say so, often without explanation or negotiation. Their approach to discipline may be harsh and punitive; the reciprocity or verbal give and take that characterizes authoritative approaches to parenting is not present in relationships between authoritarian parents and their children. On average, children raised by authoritarian parents perform less well in school, are more hostile and less popular with peers, and have lower levels of self-control and independence than children raised in authoritative contexts (Baumrind, 1971; Thompson, Hollis, & Richards, 2003). However, research has found different outcomes for children raised by authoritarian parents that relate to differences in SES, culture, and religion. We discuss these differences in more detail below.

Permissive parents are characterized as being warm, but having little control. They fail to set standards or enforce rules for their children and avoid conflict and confrontation. Rather than actively trying to shape their children's behavior, these parents view themselves as resources for their children to use as they wish. Children raised by permissive parents tend to be immature and demanding. Also, these children tend to be more impulsive, rebellious, and aggressive than children raised by authoritative parents, as well as less socially competent and confident (Baumrind, 1971; Parke & Buriel, 2006).

Finally, Maccoby and Martin (1983) identified the fourth style of parenting. **Uninvolved parents** are neither warm nor in control. They put little effort into parenting, and often are more focused on their own needs than the needs of their children. At the extreme, uninvolved parents may neglect or reject their children (e.g., failing to set schedules for sleeping and eating; reacting harshly to children's advances or requests for attention). Often, these parents are dealing with significant problems of their own that limit or inhibit their ability to place the needs of their children ahead of their own. Instead of being child-centered, they are "self-centered." Parents who are depressed or who have drug or alcohol problems may neglect or reject their children. Not surprisingly, children raised by uninvolved parents fare worst of all. They tend to be insecure in their attachments to others, noncompliant, aggressive, and withdrawn (Baumrind, 1991; Parke & Buriel, 2006). In adolescence, these children are more likely to engage in risky and delinquent behavior, suffer disruptions in social and cognitive development, and perform poorly in school (Hetherington & Clingempeel, 1992; Parke & Buriel, 2006).

Why do children of authoritative parents fare best? Steinberg and Silk (2002) suggest there are at least three reasons. First, authoritative parents appear to strike the right balance between support for autonomy and control. They balance warmth and responsiveness with appropriate restrictions, creating opportunities for children to develop self-reliance while providing the limits and guidance they need. Second, the verbal give and take that characterizes relationships between authoritative parents and their children promotes cognitive development that is linked to social competence and good decision making (e.g., reasoning abilities, role taking, moral judgment, and empathy). Finally, the high levels of nurturance and involvement that characterize authoritative parenting styles are linked to close, positive relationships with children. The result is that children are more receptive to parents' influence.

Critiques of the Research on Parenting Styles

The research on parenting styles is extensive and has intuitive appeal, particularly in North American and Western European cultures. Most of us recognize aspects of one or more of the styles from experiences with our own parents or as parents ourselves, and it makes sense that parenting that is firm, but not harsh, and responsive to children's needs promotes healthy development. However, for several reasons described next, it is important not to overinterpret or overgeneralize the research results.

First, most of the research on parenting styles is correlational. Therefore, we cannot be sure that authoritative styles are causing positive outcomes for children. We know that certain characteristics of children also influence how parents respond to them. For example, when children are easy-going and responsive, parents may be more inclined to be flexible and to give them choices, which are practices associated with authoritative parenting. Alternatively, parents whose children have difficult temperaments may find that their first attempts at explanation and negotiation are ineffective and, as a consequence, become more rigid and restrictive, more authoritarian, in their parenting.

Second, the differences reported among styles of parenting, although statistically significant, often are small. For example, one study (Lamborn, Mounts, Steinberg, & Dornbusch, 1991) assigned youth (ages 14 to 18) to one of four groups (authoritative, authoritarian, indulgent, and neglectful) on the basis of their ratings of the parenting they received. Then, they compared outcomes for these youth, including psychosocial development, school achievement, internalized stress, and problem behavior. Overall, their findings support the previous research on parenting styles. However, these researchers emphasized that although many of the contrasts were statistically significant, the magnitude of the effects for some contrasts was small. Specifically, the largest effects were observed between youth raised in authoritative versus neglectful contexts, whereas the size of the effects associated with the other comparisons was much smaller.

Third, many research findings concerning parenting styles are not universal. In particular, findings concerning outcomes for children raised by so-called authoritarian parents vary across SES, cultural, and religious communities. Even Baumrind's data (1972) revealed differences in outcomes for African American children and European American children in relation to parenting styles. By far, the majority of participants in Baumrind's research were white, European American, and middle class. However, for a small subsample of African American families, authoritarian parenting practices appeared to have some benefits, especially for daughters. Specifically, Baumrind observed that African American girls raised by authoritarian parents were more at ease and more independent than their white, European American peers in preschool. In addition, she characterized these girls as being more socially mature and adaptive in contexts that were unfamiliar to them. Baumrind emphasized, however, that the restrictive disciplinary style of the African American parents was not accompanied by the dogmatic or intolerant attitudes and emotional coldness she observed in the majority of [White] parents she characterized as authoritarian in her study. She interpreted that "the black parents were not so much rejecting the child as training her to take care of herself from an early age" (Baumrind, 1972, p. 266). You may remember from Chapter 1 that the notion of firm control as "training" is consistent with Ruth Chao's (2001, 2002) research on Asian parenting styles.

Since Baumrind's original research, numerous studies involving minority families and families living in low SES communities in the United States indicate parents can be authoritarian without being overly harsh and rejecting (Fagan, 2000; McWayne, Owsianik, Green, & Fantuzzo, 2008; Varela, Vernberg, Sanchez-Sosa, Riveros, Mitchell, & Mashunkashey, 2004). Similarly, studies involving Asian cultures in the United States and abroad find parents characterized as authoritarian often are highly involved in their children's lives and have relationships characterized by physical and emotional closeness (Chao, 1994; 2001). In low SES communities, authoritarian approaches to parenting may reflect caregivers' adaptation to contextual factors that threaten children's safety and success (Furstenberg, Cook, Eccles, Elder, & Sameroff, 1999). In such circumstances, research has linked the use of authoritarian strategies to positive outcomes for children (Baldwin, Baldwin, & Cole, 1990; Parke & Buriel, 2006).

Finally, what happens when parents are inconsistent? How many parents are warm and supportive all of the time? Even Baumrind found one-third of the parents in her studies did not conform to one pure style of parenting. And parents who are warm and supportive most of the time may be rigid and restrictive on some issues (e.g., choosing peers, having pets, or bedtimes). Also, parents may disagree with one another, or may give more freedom to one child than another within the family. More research is needed on issues of inconsistency and co-parenting, especially comparing parenting across intact and non-intact families and in nontraditional families (e.g., in gay and lesbian families; in families where grandparents have a large role in child-rearing). Not surprisingly, warm and consistent co-parenting (presenting a united front) is associated with positive outcomes for children, including prosocial behavior and positive peer relationships (McHale et al., 2002). Also not surprisingly, research indicates young children who are exposed to hostile and competitive co-parenting, largely inconsistent co-parenting, and problematic family alliances are at higher risk for developing aggression, insecure attachment, anxiety, and other clinical symptoms (McHale & Rasmussen, 1998; McHale, Lauretti, Talbot, & Pouquette, 2002; Parke & Buriel, 2006).

Clearly, parenting is fraught with many complexities. One of the most challenging tasks for parents is how to discipline their children appropriately. Ideally, parents anticipate their children's misbehavior and intervene to encourage a more positive or prosocial act. However, children of even the wisest and most vigilant parents are bound to misbehave, so sometimes discipline is necessary.

Approaches to Discipline

The term *discipline* often is associated with punishment, but in fact it means much more than this. **Discipline** refers to any attempts parents make to change the behavior or attitudes of their children to conform to what they and society deem appropriate. Before children reach the age of 2, parents rarely discipline them. However, from ages 2 through 6, disciplinary encounters dominate parent–child interactions (Minton, Kagan, & Levine, 1971), and parents increasingly expect children to comply with their rules. The goal of discipline is to increase desirable behavior and decrease undesirable behavior. Over time, parents want children to internalize the values promoted in their families and communities and to exercise self-discipline—to self-regulate their actions so that parental discipline is not necessary.

Most approaches to disciplinary practices can be characterized in three categories. We have already described **inductive discipline,** which emphasizes positive, prosocial behavior and involves strategies such as reasoning, negotiating, explaining, and even eliciting input from children. It also involves setting limits and demonstrating logical consequences. This approach to discipline is consistent with authoritative approaches to parenting and is believed to be highly effective because it helps children to understand why their behavior was wrong or offensive and fosters empathy for their victims and remorse for their actions.

Withdrawal of love occurs when parents attempt to gain compliance from children by withholding affection or ignoring or rejecting them (e.g., isolating them or showing dislike). In the short term, this approach to discipline may be effective, especially with young children because they don't want to lose their parents' approval and affection. However, over the long term, it is associated with fear of rejection and abandonment in children (Elliot & Thrash, 2004; Magai, Hunziker, Mesias, & Culver, 2000). Therefore, parents need to be judicious in their use of withdrawal of love.

Finally, **power assertion** refers to parents' attempts to stop behavior by making demands or threats, or by withdrawing privileges. It also includes physical forms of punishment, such as spanking, slapping, and shaking. However, the use of physical, or corporal punishment is very controversial. Read the ***Point/Counterpoint*** for a more detailed discussion of this debate. Some forms of power assertion may be necessary and appropriate when children are at risk of injuring themselves or others, or when children engage in intentional acts of defiance (e.g., stealing; destroying property). In these instances, however, the punishment should be delivered immediately and consistently, it should be logically tied to the offense, and it should be administered calmly—in private, if possible—and accompanied by an explanation.

Opinions about what behavior should be punished and approaches to discipline vary by culture. For example, African American parents report using power assertive techniques more than Caucasian American parents, but without the negative consequences typically associated with such practices (Dodge, McLoyd, & Lansford, 2005). In contrast, Japanese mothers use induction and expressions of disappointment more than U.S. mothers to control children's behavior (Rothbaum, Pott, Azuma, Miyake, & Weisz, 2000; Zahn-Waxler, Friedman, Cole, Mizuta, & Hiruma, 1996). These approaches are believed to be highly effective in cultures such as Japan where the mother–child bond is particularly valued.

POINT/COUNTERPOINT: Using Corporal Punishment to Promote Prosocial Behavior

Whether corporal, or physical, punishment can be justified as a means of promoting good and controlling bad behavior in children is a controversial issue around the world (Gershoff & Bitensky, 2007; Knox, 2010). Many countries have an all out ban on parents' use of all forms of corporal punishment (including spanking) to discipline their children (e.g., Sweden, Finland, Norway, Spain, Portugal, Chile, Croatia, Bulgaria, Greece). In the academic community, the debate concerning corporal punishment reflects two views. One view is that corporal punishment can be effective and may at times be necessary to discipline children (e.g., Larzelere, 2000). The opposing view is that research offers little evidence that corporal punishment is beneficial (at least over and above other tactics) and may, in fact, harm children (e.g., Gershoff, 2002).

POINT ▶ Those who argue against the use of corporal punishment cite research indicating it doesn't accomplish the disciplinary goals most parents have for their children. For example, most parents enact disciplinary strategies they believe promote good and discourage, or extinguish, bad behaviors. Gershoff (2002) conducted a meta-analysis of research studies to examine the efficacy of corporal punishment in this regard and concluded spanking and other forms of physical punishment may gain immediate compliance from children, but seldom promote children's long-term compliance or their internalization of the reasons for behaving in a certain way. Moreover, she pointed to studies linking corporal punishment to higher levels of aggression and anti-social behavior in children, and increases in anxiety, depression, alcohol and drug use, and general maladjustment. Each of these outcomes is typically counter to parents' goals. Finally, a big concern for opponents of corporal punishment is the risk for physical punishment to escalate to child maltreatment. They view physical punishment on a continuum that could result in harm or abuse—the challenge in real life may be to draw a line between non-abusive physical punishment and abuse.

COUNTERPOINT ▶ Larzelere (2000) and others (e.g., Baumrind, 2002) believe the scientific evidence does not warrant a total ban on physical punishment (typically they refer to spanking). They argue there may be an appropriate but limited role for physical punishment in parent discipline. They point to limitations in the research that has been done on corporal punishment to date. First, most of the research is correlational and cross-sectional, which precludes determinations of cause and effect. Second, many studies don't distinguish between the effects of more and less severe forms of physical punishment. Also, the research relies predominantly on parents self-reporting using corporal punishment and these are at odds with children's reports of experiencing physical forms of punishment by age 12 (Barkin, Scheindlin, Ip, Richardson, & Finch, 2007). Barkin et al. suggest this discrepancy may reflect parents' perception that reporting using physical punishment is not a "desirable" response. Finally, those who see a place for physical punishment in parent discipline argue the need to consider children's age and temperament, as well as a wide range of cultural and contextual factors (e.g., frequency and severity of the punishment, reasons for use, other strategies used, and overall discipline/parenting style).

In general, the researchers we cite above agree other strategies, such as time-outs, inductive discipline, withholding privileges, and reinforcing prosocial behavior, can be as or more effective than physical forms of punishment, and have less potential to harm children. Also, parents need support to learn about these alternatives—in one survey, 94% of parents perceived they had significant unmet needs for parenting (Bethell, Reuland, Halfon & Schor, 2004). According to Baumrind (2002), all forms of punishment should be used sparingly and only after other tactics have been tried. Also, parents should implement the mildest form of punishment they believe will be effective and reserve firmer tactics for times when children are noncompliant about an issue that is nonnegotiable. Finally, she emphasizes that parents should focus on the child's needs and welfare—try to be instrumental, not impulsive.

Approaches to discipline also are linked to SES communities, although stress appears to be a significant factor in these research findings (McLoyd, Aikens, & Burton, 2006; Parke et al., 2004). Stress in any family, regardless of their financial situation, can undermine the quality of parenting, but families living in low SES communities are known to face a number of significant stressors (e.g., finding adequate housing and employment, buying food and other necessities, living in neighborhoods that are unsafe). Parenting children alone (i.e., single parenting) is another known stress factor (Magnuson & Duncan, 2004). Such stressors diminish parents' psychological well-being and are associated with higher levels of physical and mental health problems. Adults suffering such difficulties understandably struggle to parent patiently and supportively. However, it's also important to note that many

CONNECTING WITH CHILDREN

Guidelines for Teachers and Families: Disciplining Preschool Children

Be aware of your emotions and behavior.
Examples

1. Avoid losing your control by not reacting out of anger, fatigue, or other emotions.
2. If you lose control, regain your composure, keep your voice at a normal volume level; accept your inappropriate behavior and comfort your child by admitting your mistake, expressing your love, and by asking permission to hug him/her.
3. Be a good behavioral role model; respond positively with approval and praise for good behavior.
4. Know what to ignore.

Promote self-discipline at home.
Examples

1. Make sure to tell children what is acceptable and what is not and why, use explanation and reasoning.
2. Agree on logical consequences for when, not if, the rules are broken. Use clear consequences and consistent enforcement that match the age of the child (e.g., if your child throws food on the floor, make sure she helps you clean up the mess; once the mess is cleaned up, the consequence is over).
3. When a child breaks a rule, give her a chance to do it right before you apply a consequence, but be consistent.
4. If punishment is needed, deliver it immediately and consistently, and accompany it with an explanation. When there is not a clear consequence, remove privileges and use timeouts.
5. Encourage problem-solving by allowing your child to help find a solution to misbehavior.

Tailor your discipline practices to the child, his or her characteristics, and the situation.
Examples

1. Make rules and expectations clear and reasonable (for the child's age, stage of development, personality, and needs). Rules should tell children what to do rather than what not to do.
2. Set up routines clearly (e.g., mealtime, bath, and bedtime) and avoid discussion over them, but supervise children when they are following directions.
3. Prevent challenging behaviors (e.g., childproof your home, put temptation out of reach, reduce misbehavior triggers such as hunger or tiredness).
4. Redirect their attention to activities other than the problematic one.
5. Make activities and situations predictable so they know what to expect (e.g., plan transitions from one activity to the next; talk to your child about them).

Source: Adapted from *http://www.drheller.com/tbppangr.html*
http://www.lfcc.on.ca/HCT_SWASM_pages60-61.pdf
http://www.publichealthgreybruce.on.ca/Family/Preschool/BehaviourAndDiscipline.htm
http://www.caringforkids.cps.ca/behaviour&parenting/Misbehaves.htm

parents living in stressful circumstances are responsive to the needs of their children and do an excellent job of protecting them from potentially negative outcomes (Epps & Huston, 2007; Raikes & Thompson, 2005).

Recently, researchers have expanded their assessments of people's stress levels to include physiological measures, such as heart rate and changes in hormone levels. Martorell and Bugental (2006) studied a group of mothers living in stressful circumstances and examined the extent to which strong physiological reactions to stress—demonstrated by elevated cortisol (hormone) levels in their saliva—were associated with harsh parenting practices. In their study, stronger physiological reactions to stress were associated with increased use of harsh discipline practices. In addition, their findings linked elevations in mothers' cortisol levels to having children with difficult temperaments and feeling powerless as a caregiver. These findings suggest it is important to consider not only *that* parents are under stress, but also *how* they react to stress and how best to help. In a related study (Bugental et al., 2002), a program of home visitations that focused on strategies to increase mothers' perceived efficacy for parenting difficult children was successful in reducing instances of harsh or abusive parenting.

In general, punishment that is overly harsh and exhibits lack of control on the parents' part is not effective. It has been linked to higher levels of aggression and lower levels of moral behavior and mental health among children (Gershoff, 2002). Also, it can instill fear and anger in children, which can lead to passivity, helplessness, or avoidance, which undermines parents' ability to influence behavior. When do overly harsh disciplinary practices become abusive? For sure, physical punishment is abusive when it injures the child, but what about verbal or psychological abuse, including yelling and swearing at children, threatening to hit them or send them away, or accusing them of being stupid or lazy? According to a nationally representative sample of parents in the United States (Straus & Field, 2003), these forms of punishment are very common. In fact, 98% of the parents surveyed indicated they had used some form of psychological punishment with their children by the time they reached 5 years of age. Perhaps this finding signals how difficult it is to parent—to keep your cool 100% of the time.

Losing control occasionally is nothing to be proud of, but it likely won't cause lasting and irreparable harm. Children interpret discipline in the context of their ongoing relationships with parents and patterns (styles) of parenting are more important than specific and isolated practices (Parke & Buriel, 2006). The ***Connecting with Children*** guidelines offer tips about how to control emotions or how to recover lost control when disciplining children.

Challenges for Children: Child Abuse

Child abuse is a serious public health issue that results in significant short- and long-term costs to both the individuals who are the victims of the abuse and society as a whole. It is difficult to get accurate information about the number of abused children in North America. Experts agree that large numbers of cases go unreported. However, in 2006, an estimated 905,000 children (0 to 17 years of age) in the United States were determined to be victims of child maltreatment, a rate of 12.1 per 1,000 children in the general population (Department of Health & Human Services, 2006). In Canada, the rate in 2003 was higher. According to the Public Health Agency of Canada (2005), reports of maltreatment in children (0 to 15 years of age) in 2003 were substantiated in 18.67 investigations out of 1,000. The predominant categories of child abuse or maltreatment in both nations are shown in Table 7.4 on the next page, along with their definitions and examples of abusive behaviors. They include physical and sexual abuse, extreme neglect, emotional abuse, and exposure to family violence. The most common forms of maltreatment are neglect and exposure to family violence, accounting for well over half of the substantiated cases of child abuse in the United States and Canada. Physical abuse is the next most common form of abuse, followed by sexual abuse and emotional harm.

Who are the victims? Figure 7.9 on page 293 shows the victimization rates by age group in the United States, but the trends are similar in Canada. It is clear to see that infants and very young children are most at risk for maltreatment. In general, girls tend to be the victims of abuse more than boys, except between the ages of 8 and 11, when more boys than girls experience physical abuse. In the United States, victimization also varied by ethnicity, with the highest rates found in the African American population (19.8 per 1,000 children) and the lowest rates found in the Asian population (2.5 per 1,000 children). The rates for Caucasian and Hispanic children were 10.7 and 10.8 per 1,000 children, respectively. In nearly 83% of cases, children were abused or maltreated by a parent acting alone or with another person, and approximately 40% of cases involved a mother acting alone. In cases of sexual abuse (approximately 9% of all substantiated cases), a parent or relative was responsible for the abuse more than 50% of the time. About half of all abusive parents could change their destructive behavior patterns if they received help and support. Without assistance, however, only about 5% of abusing parents improve (Starr, 1979).

The consequences are devastating. Children who are physically or sexually abused evidence serious adjustment problems, such as depression and, over the long term, symptoms of post-traumatic stress disorder (Teicher, 2000). In adolescence, these children are more likely to abuse alcohol and drugs and attempt suicide. In addition, individuals who experience abuse as children often get involved in unhealthy relationships as adults; they may have

TABLE 7.4 • **Types of Child Maltreatment and Examples of Abusive Behaviors**

CATEGORY	DEFINITIONS	EXAMPLE OF ABUSIVE BEHAVIOURS
1. Physical abuse (assault)	The application of unreasonable force by an adult or youth to any part of a child's body	Harsh physical discipline, forceful shaking, pushing, grabbing, throwing, hitting with a hand, punching, kicking, biting, hitting with an object, choking, strangling, stabbing, burning, shooting, poisoning and the excessive use of restraints
2. Sexual abuse	Involvement of a child, by an adult or youth, in an act of sexual gratification, or exposure of a child to sexual contact, activity or behaviour	Penetration, attempted penetration, oral sex, fondling, sex talk, voyeurism and sexual exploitation
3. Neglect	Failure by a parent or caregiver to provide the physical or psychological necessities of life to a child	Failure to supervise, leading to physical harm or to sexual harm; permitting criminal behaviour; physical neglect; medical neglect; failure to provide psychological treatment; abandonment; and educational neglect
4. Emotional harm	Adult behaviour that harms a child psychologically, emotionally or spiritually	Hostile or unreasonable and abusive treatment, frequent or extreme verbal abuse (that may include threatening and demeaning or insulting behaviours), causing non-organic failure to thrive*, emotional neglect, and direct exposure to violence between adults others than primary caregivers
5. Exposure to family violence	Circumstances that allow a child to be aware of violence occurring between a caregiver and his/her partner or between other family members	Allowing a child to see, hear or otherwise be exposed to signs of the violence (e.g., to see bruises or physical injuries on the caregiver or to overhear violent episodes)

*"Non-organic failure to thrive" is a diagnostic term applied in cases of children less then age three years who have suffered a slowing or cessation of growth for which no physical or physiological causes can be identified.

Source: Government of Canada. (2003). Child maltreatment in Canada. National Clearing House on Family Violence. This is a copy of an official work that is published by the Government of Canada. Reproduction has not been produced in affiliation with, or with the endorsement of the Government of Canada. Used with permission.

partners who abuse them and their children. Approximately one-third of these individuals will go on to abuse or neglect their own children (National Clearinghouse on Child Abuse and Neglect Information, 2005). In this way, the cycle of abuse continues.

Although parents are the most likely perpetrators of physical and sexual abuse against children, they are not the only people guilty of these crimes. Siblings, other relatives, teachers, and coaches have been responsible for physically and sexually abusing children. Today, there is another way for adults who want to abuse children to reach them—the Internet. Typically, abusers are people that children know and trust. We have all heard reports of predators approaching children and youth through social networking on the Internet and gaining their trust. Caregivers need to be vigilant about children's interactions in this medium.

If you work with children and suspect abuse, you must report it. In all 50 states, the District of Columbia, and the U.S. territories, professionals, including teachers, principals, school psychologists, social workers, medical professionals, and all other childcare workers, are required by law to report suspected cases of child abuse. Moreover, many states have broadened the legal definition of abuse to include neglect and failure to provide adequate care and supervision. Make sure you understand the laws in your state concerning this important issue, and consider your moral responsibility. Also, be aware of signs that can

FIGURE 7.9

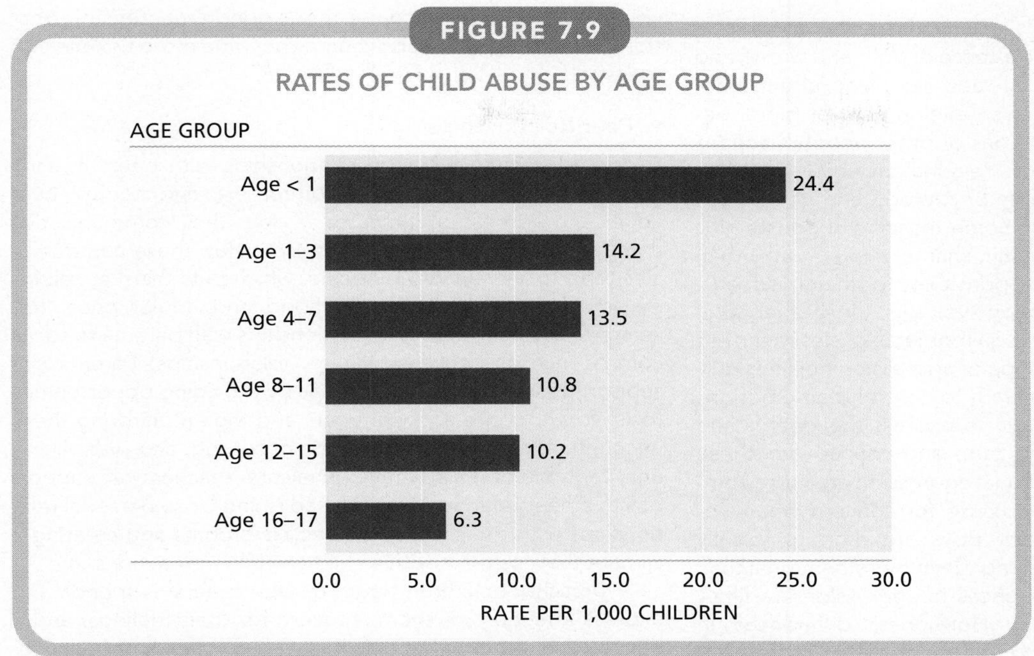

Source: U.S. Department of Health and Human Services, Administration on Children, Youth and Families. Child Maltreatment 2006 (Washington, DC: U.S. Government Printing Office, 2008).

indicate abuse, such as childhood depression, low self-esteem, mistrust of adults, anger and hostility, generalized fear, and developmentally advanced and inappropriate sexual knowledge and behavior. Each year thousands of children die because of abuse or neglect, in many cases because no one would "get involved" (Department of Health & Human Services, 2006; Thompson & Wyatt, 1999).

▼ SUMMARY AND KEY TERMS

- **Testing the Limits**

Throughout the early years, children are eager to try new tasks and activities on their own. At the same time, they recognize that not everything they want to do will meet with the approval of the significant people in their lives. Erikson referred to this conflict as one of *initiative vs. guilt*, and when children resolve it, they develop a positive self-image, can control emotions, and demonstrate social competence and positive peer relations.

- **Who Am I, and How Am I Different from Others?**

Preschool children are able to reflect on several aspects of self, including objective characteristics, such as the length of their hair and the color of their eyes, and subjective characteristics that reflect values and comparisons with standards (e.g., "I am good." "I am bad."). Objective understandings about self are linked with self-concept, whereas evaluative judgments about self are linked to self-esteem. Young children tend to have inflated self-concepts and high self-esteem. However, young children can experience low self-esteem if comparisons are made salient by parents and other significant people in their lives. Moreover, self-concept and self-esteem can vary by domain and within domains, so it is possible for children to accurately perceive they are not good in sports without experiencing low self-esteem.

Self-regulation is associated with a wide range of positive outcomes, and emotion and behavior regulation are pivotal achievements in early childhood. Children's development of self-regulation is influenced by internal characteristics, such as cognitive capacities and temperament, but typically develops along a continuum from other regulation to self-regulation. In addition to a growing awareness of their own thinking and feeling, preschool children are increasingly able to assess and respond to the thoughts and feelings of others. Perspective-taking ability continues to develop throughout childhood and is associated with positive, prosocial behaviors, such as empathy and sympathy.

• Developing Morality

As early as age 2, children have a sense of right and wrong and by ages 3 and 4 can distinguish degrees of good and bad. Many factors influence children's development of moral behavior, including their observations of other people's actions and the discipline they receive. Personal and biological factors, such as temperament, brain physiology, and gender can influence moral behavior, too. Some research suggests girls are more likely to experience guilt, shame, and empathy than boys, and more likely to take responsibility for their misdeeds.

Young children's aggression typically is instrumental in nature—they use it to gain or regain objects of desire, not to harm another individual. This type of aggression declines during the early years as children learn to control their emotions and behaviors; acquire language to express their wants and needs; and develop empathy, care, and concern for those around them. Hostile and relational aggression are more common in older children and are cause for concern when observed in very young children. Boys are more physically aggressive than girls, and girls engage in more relational than physical aggression. Sex differences in aggression are likely biological and environmental. Hormones, differences in strength, reactivity to pain, and temperamental characteristics may account for some differences, but environmental factors likely are implicated as well. Modeling and reinforcing aggressive behavior increases the likelihood it will occur. Finally, some children are more likely to interpret the actions of others as intentional and hostile. These children may not attend to relevant social cues (e.g., cues indicating an action was actually an accident), which prompts aggressive responses.

• Gender Development

Gender identity is an important part of children's self-concept and a powerful source of self-esteem. Once children are aware of their gender, they tend to identify with and imitate behavior of same-sex parents and siblings; develop expectations about objects and activities typically associated with and appropriate for boys and girls; and express preferences for playing with same-sex peers and gender stereotypic toys. Boys are generally more insistent than girls about maintaining gender stereotypes; girls and adults are less forgiving of boys who engage in cross-gendered behavior; and these biases are remarkably consistent across cultures. However, not all children develop gender identity easily.

Biological, social, and cognitive factors are believed to influence gender development. Some differences between males and females are believed to be to the result of evolutionary adaptations (e.g., men's greater physical strength helped them to hunt and travel over long distances), hormonal secretions, and structural differences between male and female brains.

Children also learn about gender and gender-appropriate behavior by observing and interacting with parents, siblings, peers, teachers, and cultural models. As children interact with the world, they form organized cognitive structures, or *schemas,* that include gender-related information and these schemas influence how they think and behave. In general, children's early learning of gender categories and associated attributes results in schemas that are very rigid, but as children mature and acquire more gender-related information, their gender-related schemas become more flexible and realistic.

• Peer Relationships

Children begin to focus on relationships with peers in early childhood. Sharing, helping, comforting, and control over anger and aggression increase, as does their communicative competence. Children who do not develop these competencies tend to be rejected by peers, which puts them at risk for maladjustment in middle childhood and adolescence. Research links positive, secure relationships with parents to social competence and successful peer relationships. Parents can support positive peer relationships by providing opportunities for children to interact with peers and then monitoring these encounters, coaching social problem-solving, and disciplining unacceptable or maladaptive behaviors. Teachers can support positive peer relationships by establishing close personal relationships with the children in their classrooms and creating a climate that fosters positive child-to-child interactions.

Preschool children begin to label peers as friends and express affection for them, concern for their feelings, and a desire to win their approval. Friendships offer emotional security, support for self-esteem, intimacy and affection, instrumental assistance, and a context in which to develop interpersonal sensitivity. Young children with friends cope better with stressful events and situations, and adjust better to school. More research is needed about the significance of children's peer relationships and friendships in non-Western cultures. Likely, cultures differentially endorse behaviors associated with cooperation, compliance, or emotional expressivity, which may influence standards for peer acceptance and rejection.

• Play

Play contributes importantly to children's physical, cognitive, and social development. The content and function of play change across the early years. Infants and toddlers engage in functional play—they are drawn to toys on the basis of how they look and what they do. Play for them involves simple repetitive actions with objects or physical movements such as jumping or rolling. For children 3 to 6 years old, play is more goal-oriented and constructive—they manipulate objects to produce something. Pretend play emerges about the time children are learning language (ages 2 to 3), increases across the early years (to ages 6 or 7), and then declines during the school years. At first, children's pretend play is self-referenced, but increases in its social focus as they become less egocentric. Pretend play, in particular, promotes abstract and creative thinking, and research indicates children with active imaginations are better at interpreting the emotions, actions, and intentions of others, and view of their experiences more objectively and comprehensively.

Girls and boys have different interests in play. Boys tend to enjoy physical activities, outdoor spaces, and are more willing to play away from adult supervision. Girls engage in more pretend play than boys and are more likely to have an imaginary friend. When boys and girls play together, masculine themes predominate.

• Parent–Child Relationships in Early Childhood

Parental warmth and control are important for children's cognitive and social development. Four parenting styles reflect different combinations of high and low warmth and high and low control. Authoritative parents are high on warmth and control. They are responsive, but set firm limits on behavior and enforce rules consistently. Authoritarian parents are high on control, but tend to be low on warmth. Their discipline practices may be harsh or undemocratic. Permissive parents are warm, but have little control, and uninvolved parents are neither warm nor in control. On average, children raised by authoritative parents have the most positive outcomes, but there are exceptions. Parents in some ethnic groups and low SES communities are sometimes authoritarian without being overly harsh and rejecting. This combination has been shown to benefit children growing up in adverse, perhaps dangerous, conditions. Consistent co-parenting also is associated with positive outcomes for children.

From ages 2 through 6, disciplinary encounters dominate parent–child interactions. The goal is to increase desirable behavior and decrease undesirable behavior so that, over time, children internalize the values promoted in their families and communities and exercise self-discipline. Inductive discipline is consistent with authoritative parenting and appears most effective for meeting this goal. Withdrawing love and power assertion should be used sparingly—they are not highly effective over the long term. Power assertion may be necessary when children are at risk for injuring themselves or others, or engage in intentional acts of defiance, but it should be appropriate for the offense and administered calmly, in private, if possible, and include an explanation. Opinions about what should be punished and approaches to discipline vary by culture. Stressors, such as financial difficulties and parenting alone, also can be a factor. Stress affects parents' psychological well-being and adults suffering such difficulties understandably may struggle to parent effectively.

• Challenges for Children: Child Abuse

The most common forms of child abuse or maltreatment are neglect and exposure to family violence. Physical abuse is the next most common form of abuse, followed by sexual abuse and emotional harm. Infants and young children are most at risk for maltreatment. Girls are more likely to be abused than boys and some ethnic groups are particularly vulnerable. Often perpetrators are people children know and trust. Parents are the most likely perpetrators, but siblings, teachers, and other people in positions of trust also may abuse children. Today, caregivers need to be vigilant about children's interactions on the Internet as predators can use social networking software to approach children and gain their trust. Children who are physically or sexually abused evidence serious adjustment problems and, over the long term, symptoms of post-traumatic stress disorder. Laws in all 50 states are such that, if you suspect abuse, you must report it.

▼ KEY TERMS

authoritarian parents (286)
authoritative parents (285)
constructive play (281)
discipline (288)
display rules (256)
emotional self-regulation (255)
empathy (260)
functional play (281)
gender (271)
gender constancy (269)
gender identity (267)
gender schema theory (275)
heteronomous (262)
hostile aggression (264)
inductive discipline (288)
instrumental aggression (264)
moral imperatives (261)
parental control (284)
parental warmth (284)
permissive parents (286)
perspective-taking ability (260)
power assertion (288)
pretend play (280)
relational aggression (264)
self-concept (252)
self-conscious emotions (256)
self-esteem (253)
self-regulation (254)
sex (271)
social conventions (261)
sympathy (260)
theory of mind (259)
uninvolved parents (286)
withdrawal of love (288)

▼ THE CASEBOOK

WHY NOT SAY WHAT YOU REALLY MEAN?

It crosses Tara's mind that the party has gone very well . . . so far. Daughter Katie is having her first birthday party. She turns three today and so she and five "friends" have gathered at her home, with parents in tow, to celebrate. The weather is good, which allowed for games in the back yard and a barbeque. The piñata was a great success and the children have had their fill of cake. Now it's time to open the gifts. Katie is the center of attention. As parents and children gather around to watch, hoping their gifts are met with approval, Tara is mortified by the words that come out of Katie's mouth. "I don't want this. It's dumb," she says about one gift. "I already have one of these," she says about another. Tara exchanges looks with her husband, David, recognizing his sense of helplessness. As she scans the faces of Katie's guests, she sees hurt and disappointment on the faces of the children who gave the gifts. Some parents are silent, others laugh awkwardly. One child chimes in, "I don't have one. I want it." Tara wonders: "What should I say? Should I intervene? How? Is there any way to salvage what remains of the party and future friendships for Katie?"

WHAT WOULD THEY DO?

Here is how some professionals in several fields responded:

SARAH DAVLIN—Elementary School Counselor (K–5)
Wyandot Run Elementary School: Olentangy Local Schools, Powell, Ohio

As educators, we have all been victim to the unbridled candor of children at one time or another. "What's that red spot on your face?" "Is your hair supposed to look that way?" "This is boring." How do we teach children to respect the feelings of others without losing the precious gift of their honesty? The unfortunate reality is that, in our quest to teach proper manners, we often inadvertently encourage children to avoid or sugarcoat the truth and remain quiet when, perhaps, it is important to speak up.

Rather than focusing on what *not* to say or what *not* to do, we can impart better manners in children through discussion and role-playing of basic social skills (i.e., what *to* do). For example, practicing strategies such as "Feelings Talk" (I Feel when; I want) teaches children "tact" and a means to politely communicate upset feelings. We can also encourage children to "filter" their words by reflecting on whether or not their comments were necessary or helpful in a given situation.

Finally, when we implement character education initiatives within our school community, we directly impact the way students communicate. For instance, as we discuss the meaning of *empathy* with children and encourage them to "put themselves in someone else's shoes" or "imagine how another person might feel," children are significantly more likely to make their own attempts to filter their words and use tactful speech.

KATHERINE A. YOUNG—K–8 School Counselor
Montgomery County Intermediate Unit, Non-Public School Services Division, Norristown, Pennsylvania

When explaining the behavior to Katie's mom, I would describe it as a preschooler being brutally honest. Young children often say how they feel without thinking about how it may make another person feel. Teaching children in advance how to act in situations like this one gives them a framework of appropriate behavior. It is also important to build empathy in young children. By asking questions like, "How would you feel if you gave someone a present and she called it dumb?" parents can help their children begin to develop empathy. I would suggest that before a party or another social situation where good manners are expected, parents should review what to say if something doesn't go the way the child would have liked. For the example above, before the next party, Katie's parents may give her examples of what to say when she gets a present that she wants as well as what to say if she gets a present that she doesn't like. It is important for parents to give children the words that they need to still be honest, but not hurtful. Parents may want to consider holding off on opening gifts until after the party is over. Then, parents can help their children write polite thank-you notes to each gift giver.

KAREN E. DAVIES—Kindergarten Teacher
North Royalton Early Childhood Center, Broadview Heights, Ohio

I am sure that it would be difficult for a parent to share this story with a teacher, but it would also indicate that the parent really wanted suggestions about how to solve this problem. Children are always told to tell the truth, so this is not even an obvious blunder to Katie. Adults must exhibit correct behavior to children and explain why they are acting in a particular manner, as children this age must learn behaviors. They do not automatically know how to behave in new situations. Katie's parents should discuss her friends' feelings and how she would feel in their place. I would suggest to the parents that Katie dictate thank you notes to each of her friends, explaining that she was sorry for what she said. This might be a good opportunity to discuss wants versus needs and people who are less fortunate, perhaps donating some of the gifts to a charity, if appropriate. I would encourage Katie's parents to continue to model appropriate behavior (especially right before an event of this type) and then to compliment Katie's appropriate behaviors. Katie's behavior should improve as she sees the rewards (friendship) and approval that come with her kind words.

KATIE BURGER—Kindergarten Teacher
Washington Park Elementary, Laurinburg, North Carolina

Children at this age don't understand what it means to be gracious in opening gifts. When they don't like something, they will likely let you know. Honesty is the one of the most endearing traits in children, most of the time. Katie's parents are embarrassed by their child's rude behavior, but if the children at the party are around the same age as Katie, they probably do not understand how rude she is acting.

In the future, Katie's mom may want to pull her aside and let her child know that it hurts people's feelings when she says out loud that she does not like a gift. Children will not understand that they are doing anything wrong until it is explained to them.

PEARSON myeducationlab

Now go to MyEducationLab at *www.myeducationlab.com*, where you can:

- Find the instructional objectives for this chapter in the **Study Plan.**
- Take a quiz as a part of the **Study Plan** to self-assess your mastery of chapter content. The program generates an individualized Study Plan based upon your answers to the quiz.
- Complete **Activities and Applications** to assist you in deepening your understanding of important chapter concepts.
- Apply what you have learned through **Building Teaching Skills,** exercises that guide you in trying out skills and strategies you will use in professional practice.

8 PHYSICAL DEVELOPMENT IN MIDDLE CHILDHOOD

THE CASEBOOK

WHAT WOULD YOU DO?

MEETING THE CHALLENGE OF INCLUSION

As the director of Tall Trees Camp, David is preparing for the onslaught of campers who will begin arriving on July 5th, just two weeks away. In particular, he is mulling over ways to include one camper, 10-year-old Jason, who uses a wheelchair. All of the cabins and communal buildings are wheelchair accessible, but most of the grounds surrounding the camp are pretty uneven and the trails are fairly inhospitable to all but those traveling on foot. David is determined, however. The camp prides itself on being inclusive, and inclusion to David means *everyone*. So . . . his job is to figure out how to include a child in a wheelchair in the physical activities of the camp. Soccer and swimming aren't so hard, actually. But hiking and beachcombing, given the rocky shore, will present a bit of a challenge. And what about the overnight hiking and camping trip?

CRITICAL THINKING

- Does inclusion mean everyone in every event?
- How would you handle this challenge?
- What factors should be considered when designing physical/recreational activities (including field trips/excursions from school) to accommodate children with a wide range of physical and/or sensorial differences and disabilities?

Trevor Yo Heng Ang, Age 9—Singapore

▶ OVERVIEW AND OBJECTIVES

Physical development in middle childhood is characterized by slow and steady growth. Children's bodies continue to grow and develop, but not at the same rapid pace as in the early years. Some experts refer to this period as the calm before the storm, referring to the growth spurt that characterizes adolescents' physical development. In this chapter, we describe body growth, brain development, and motor development in the middle years. In particular, we will examine children's participation in more organized physical activities and how involvement in these activities can lead to accidents and injuries, with a focus on prevention. Finally, we will consider some special physical needs in children at this age; specifically, we will look at children who have physical disabilities and sensory impairments. By the time you finish this chapter you should be able to:

Objective 8.1	Provide examples of steps to be taken throughout childhood to ensure good bone and oral health across the lifespan.
Objective 8.2	Describe advances in higher order cognitive processes during middle childhood and explain how they impact children's thinking and learning.
Objective 8.3	Summarize the reasons for and risks associated with declining levels of children's involvement in physical activity.
Objective 8.4	Identify several physical, cognitive, and social and emotional benefits of physical activity for all children, including children with disabilities.
Objective 8.5	Summarize the leading causes of accidents and injuries during childhood and identify actions that can minimize their negative consequences.
Objective 8.6	Describe special considerations for preventing injury and illness in child athletes.

Objective 8.7 Provide examples of how to accommodate and include children with physical disabilities and/or sensory impairments in activities with their same-age, typically developing peers.

Body Growth

Typical growth and development in the middle years is characterized by slow and steady gains in height and weight without dramatic alterations in basic body structures—proportions change less in middle childhood than they do in infancy and early childhood. Table 8.1 shows the average height and weight of children ages 5 to 12. As we indicated in Chapter 5, girls ages 10 to 12 tend to be taller than boys their age. This results from girls' tendency to mature faster and experience their adolescent growth spurt before boys. Weight gains follow a similar pattern. However, the weight is distributed differently. Before they reach the middle years, children lose their baby fat and their bodies become more muscular. It is important to remember, however, that averages can disguise individual differences, which can be substantial at this age.

TABLE 8.1 • **Average Height and Weight of Children Ages 5–12**

AGE	AVERAGE WEIGHT (IN POUNDS)		AVERAGE HEIGHT (IN INCHES)	
	MALE	FEMALE	MALE	FEMALE
5	46.9	45.3	44.5	44.3
6	51.7	49.2	46.9	46.1
7	59.8	56.9	49.7	49
8	72	70.1	52.2	51.5
9	79.2	78	54.4	53.9
10	84.9	87.9	55.7	56.4
11	96.2	105.4	58.5	59.6
12	110.9	114.3	60.9	61.4

Source: Ogden, C. L., Fryar, C. D., Carroll, M. D., Flegal, K. M., & Division of Health and Nutrition Examination Surveys (October 27, 2004). Mean body weight, height, and body mass index, United States 1960–2002. Retrieved from http://www.cdc.gov/nchs/data/ad/ad347.pdf

The slower rate of growth at this age enables gains in motor control and coordination (Gallahue & Ozmun, 1995). These developments are evidenced in activities such as running, jumping, kicking, and throwing. At this age, children often become involved in organized sports. We will return to this topic later in the chapter when we discuss motor development.

Bone Health

Building bone mass, or density, during childhood has important implications for lifelong health, especially for preventing **osteoporosis,** a disease that involves serious loss of bone density and leaves bones fragile and at risk for breaking. Bone mass peaks during the mid-20s. Boys

OUTLINE ▼

typically have greater bone mass than girls and African American girls have higher bone density than Caucasian girls. However, bone mass also depends to a great extent on diet and exercise. Calcium in the diet is especially important, as are weight-bearing exercises such as running, walking, dancing, and jumping. Weight training also prevents bone loss as we age. The more we use our bones, the stronger they become. This is one reason physical education is an important aspect of school curricula. We examine this issue in the section on motor development.

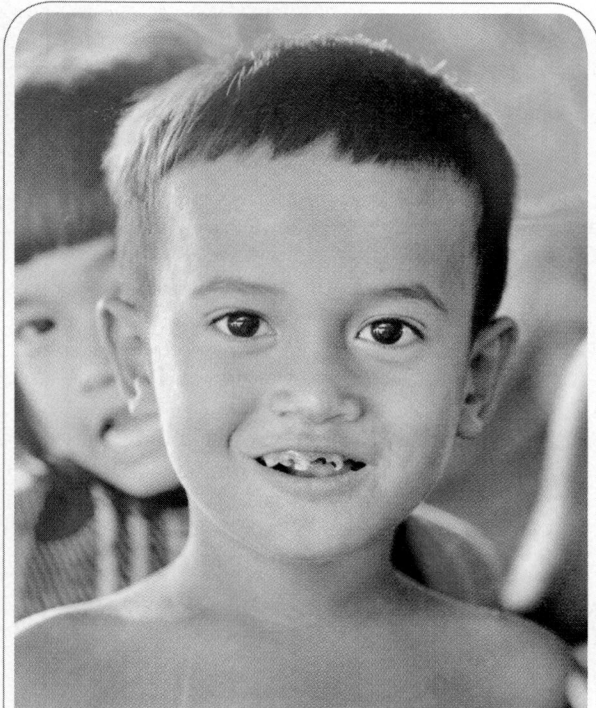

Children who live in poverty and whose families cannot afford medical insurance are most at risk for experiencing oral disease. Some ethnic minority populations have higher rates of tooth problems and decay.

Tooth Development and Oral Health

Between the ages of 5 and 7, most children's baby teeth are lost and replaced by a set of permanent teeth. Healthy teeth and gums are extremely important. They help children chew food, speak clearly, and they give shape to their faces. Moreover, tooth decay is associated with problems eating and speaking, school absences, learning difficulties, and even serious illness (U.S. Department of Health and Human Services, 2005). Children who live in poverty and whose families cannot afford medical insurance are most at risk for experiencing oral disease. Also, children with disabilities and some ethnic minority populations have higher rates of tooth problems and decay. The best way for children to prevent tooth decay is to floss and brush their teeth regularly and avoid foods that are high in sugar content. Fruit juices and sugary sodas are particularly problematic in this regard (American Academy of Pediatrics, 2003). Like bone health, oral health deserves attention from the early years as it has implications for health and well-being across the lifespan. The ***Connecting with Children*** guidelines on the next page offer ideas about maintaining good oral hygiene.

Brain Development

During the middle years, the brain continues to grow and change, but the changes are not as dramatic as in infancy and the early years. The brain continues to add cells and connections, at least in some areas such as the hippocampus, and functioning improves (Black, 1998). For example, increased myelination of the nerve fibers and increased lateralization of the two hemispheres result in information being processed more efficiently. In particular, the myelination that occurs in the prefrontal cortex during this period is believed to promote higher cognitive functions such as planning, goal setting, and inhibiting inappropriate behavior. Children become more able to integrate past and present experiences and information in order to select an appropriate response from several alternatives. Whereas an infant or a toddler reacts impulsively, the 9-year-old can now remember and reflect. Self-regulation is enhanced through analysis, control, abstraction, memory space, speed of processing, and the integration of information (Kagan & Herschkowitz, 2005). Moreover, neural connections continue to be pruned, especially in areas of the brain that involve higher order thinking. The brain becomes increasingly more organized, which may account for improvements in problem-solving, memory, and language comprehension that occur in the middle years and in adolescence (Blair, 2002; Case, 1992; Diamond, 2000).

Learning is affected by these changes. Clearly the child's brain is involved whenever learning takes place. As Blakemore and Firth (2005) note in their book on lessons for education from research in neuroscience: "We start with the idea that the brain has evolved to educate and be educated, often instinctively and effortlessly" (p. 459). The brain shapes and is shaped by the child's cognitive processing activities. Because the brain continues to change, children with learning disabilities such as dyslexia can be taught strategies to compensate using other areas

CONNECTING WITH CHILDREN

Guidelines for Families, Teachers, and Other Professionals: Practicing Good Oral Hygiene

Begin flossing and brushing early, and make these activities part of children's regular routines.
Examples

1. Have children begin brushing their teeth as soon as the teeth break through their gums.
2. Have children brush their teeth two times each day for two minutes each time. Morning and bedtime are good times to brush teeth.
3. Assist and supervise teeth brushing until children are 7 or 8 years of age. Teach them to brush using a gentle circular motion.
4. Once all primary (baby) teeth have erupted through the gums, have children begin flossing once each day.

Make sure children have the right equipment to care for teeth effectively.
Examples

1. Choose brushes according to children's ages.
2. Choose brushes with small heads for young children. For all children, choose brushes with soft bristles.
3. Replace toothbrushes every three months.
4. Use toothpaste that contains fluoride to strengthen tooth enamel and prevent decay, but use toothpaste sparingly, an amount about the size of a small pea is sufficient.

Establish a positive relationship with a dentist and schedule regular dental appointments.
Examples

1. Schedule children for their first dental appointment around their first birthday per American Dental Association recommendations.
2. Take young children with you when you go to the dentist. This way, children and dentists can get to know each other. Perhaps the dentist will look in children's mouths informally and show them what will happen when they come for an appointment.
3. Schedule children's dental visits often. Children typically need to see dentists more often than adults. Primary teeth are smaller and have thinner enamel than permanent teeth, so decay can spread quickly.
4. Get X-ray images so the dentist can check for decay.

Teach children how to care for their teeth when toothbrushes and toothpaste are not available.
Examples

1. Have them chew on a piece of sugar-free gum to help remove pieces of food and sugar substances on the teeth.
2. Have them eat high fiber foods, which increase saliva in the mouth; this has a rinsing effect for teeth.
3. Limit sugary snacks and drinks. Encourage children to drink water.

Children like to imitate adults, so model good oral hygiene.
Examples

1. Floss and brush with young children.
2. Make dental appointments a family priority.
3. Model eating habits that are good for teeth.

Sources: Bupa. (2009). Caring for your child's teeth. Retrieved from http://hcd2.bupa.co.uk/fact_sheets/html/child_dental.html. Leeds, Grenville, & Lanark District Health Unit. Oral hygiene for children. Retrieved from http://www.healthunit.org/dental/children_oral/hygienechild.htm.

of the brain (Blakemore & Firth, 2005). In children with hearing impairments, the areas of the brain that ordinarily would process auditory stimulation change over time to process visual information and the opposite is true for children with visual impairments. The areas of the brain that usually would process visual stimuli process auditory information (Neville, 2007). Even at the level of synapse formation, 15 minutes after a child is unsuccessful at processing information, new synapses are formed. As Siegler (2004) notes, "the key factor is the unsuccessful processing activity in particular areas of the brain. Neural development does not just happen; it reflects in large part the organism's past processing activity" (p. 473).

Motor Development

Children's gross motor skills are typically well developed by the beginning of the school years, but they continue to improve throughout middle childhood (Davies, 2004). One reason for these improvements may be the slowing of body growth, which gives children time to adjust to their bodies and learn to use them more effectively. Children's fine motor skills also develop during middle childhood. Hand-eye coordination is necessary for writing and drawing and improves during the early school years such that by the time children reach

FIGURE 8.1

TIMELINES FOR DEVELOPMENT OF MOTOR SKILLS IN MIDDLE CHILDHOOD

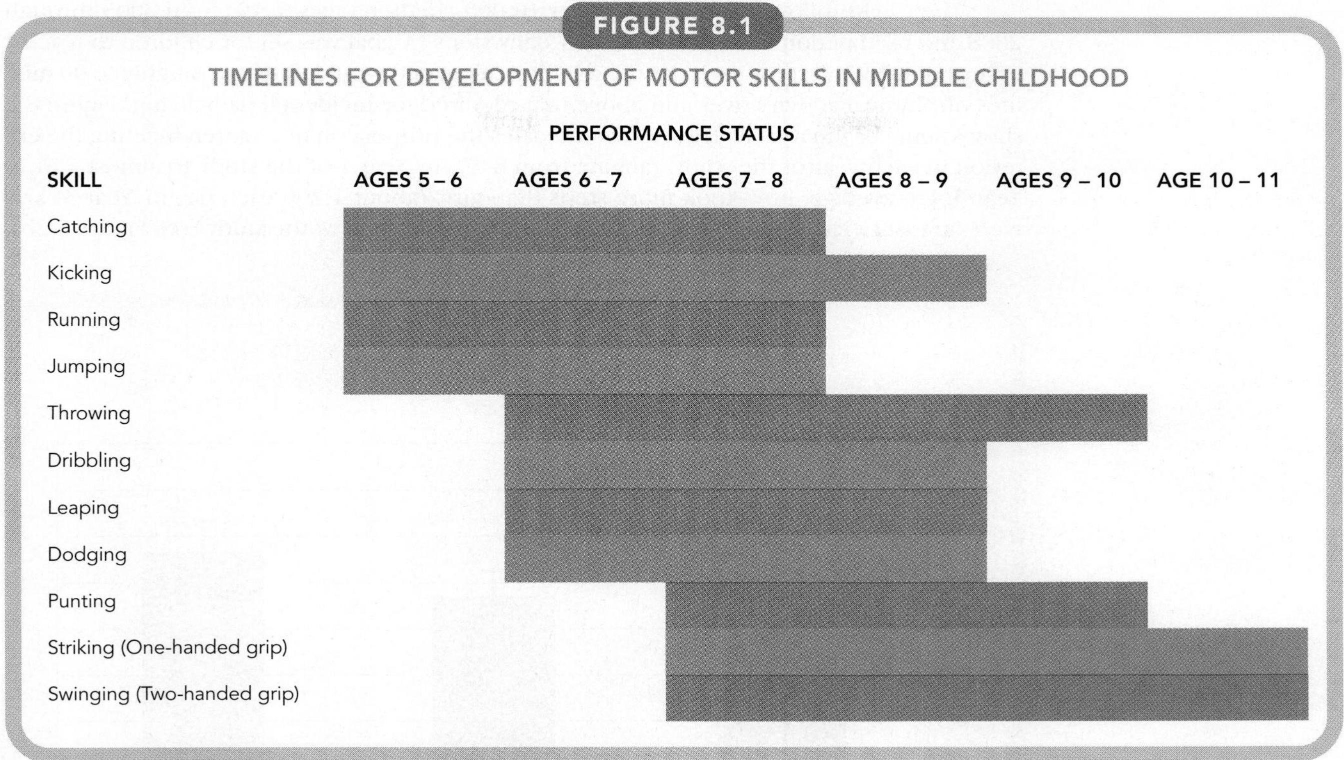

Source: Based on data from Department of Education. (2009). Fundamental motor skills: A manual for classroom teachers. Melbourne, Victoria, Australia: Community Information Service.

the third and fourth grades, most can write rapidly and automatically (Davies, 2004). Fine motor difficulties are associated with learning disabilities and problems in school during the early elementary grades (Hooper, Schwartz, Wakely, DeKruif, & Montgomery, 2002). Figure 8.1 shows developments in motor skills throughout the middle years.

School-age boys and girls have similar levels of motor skills, but there are some differences. Boys tend to have more upper body strength, which gives them an advantage for some activities (e.g., throwing a ball farther and faster). Girls typically are more agile, which gives them an advantage for activities involving flexibility (e.g., gymnastics and dance). Historically, boys' leisure activities have involved higher levels of physical activity, giving them more time to practice physical skills, but girls in contemporary society may be closing this gap.

Individual differences in motor development are important to children during the middle years. Physical and athletic abilities become a measure of competence in children during the middle years, in both their own eyes and those of their peers (Davies, 2004). Children put a great deal of effort into acquiring skills for individual and team sports and those children with poor gross motor skills or physical disabilities may be teased and suffer social rejection.

Physical Activity

The evidence is overwhelming that regular physical activity is critical for overall health and well-being during childhood and throughout our lives (AAP, 2006; Canadian Fitness and Lifestyle Research Institute, 2008). Activity helps to control weight gain, blood pressure, and cholesterol levels, and it reduces the risk of diabetes and some kinds of cancer. Exercise is associated with psychosocial well-being, too. For example, physically active children report higher levels of confidence and self-esteem than their inactive peers (Findlay & Coplan, 2008). However, studies indicate more than 50% of American children are not getting the recommended 60 minutes per day of moderate to vigorous exercise (Centers for Disease Control and Prevention, 2003). In Canada, health authorities recommend 90 minutes of moderate to vigorous physical activity each day for children, but the Canadian Fitness and Lifestyle Research Institute (CFLRI) reports that only about 23% are reaching this benchmark (CFLRI, 2008).

The CFLRI followed a sample of over 10,000 children (ages 5–19) from 2005 through 2008 and used pedometers to count their daily steps. A goal was set for children to reach a criterion of 16,500 steps each day, which they calculated would translate roughly to 90 minutes of physical activity over and above that required for incidental daily living. Figure 8.2 shows some of the results. Figure 8.2a indicates the proportion of children meeting the criterion in each year of the study, ranging from 8–9% in Year 1 of the study to almost 14% in Year 3. On average, boys took more steps than girls (about 1,200 each day in Year 3) and were almost twice as likely to meet the criterion in each year of the study (see Figure 8.2b).

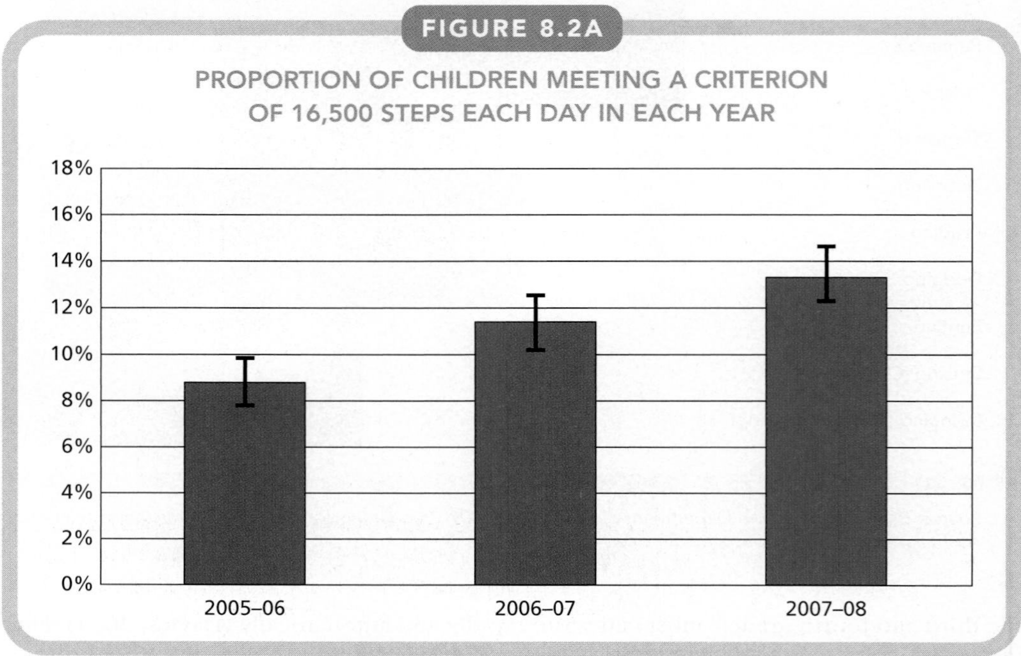

Source: 2005-2008 CANPLAY Study, CFLRI. Used with permission of Canadian Fitness and Lifestyle Research Institute.

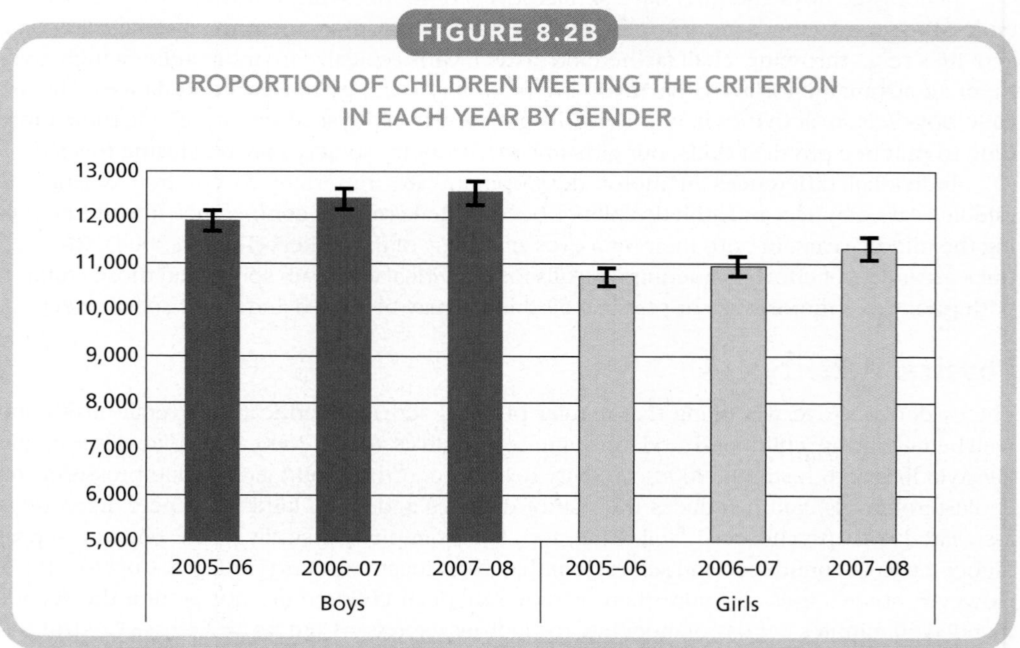

Source: 2005-2008 CANPLAY study, CFLRI. Used with permission of Canadian Fitness and Lifestyle Research Institute.

The proportion of children meeting the criterion declined in older age groups, with almost twice as many 5- to 10-year-olds meeting the criterion as 15- to 19-yearolds. The CFLRI study also found differences across regions of the country, with amounts of physical activity increasing from east to west, and differences among SES groups, with children in higher SES communities engaging in more physical activity than children living in low SES communities.

Given the clear links between physical activity and people's health and well-being across the lifespan, these findings suggest that several challenges should be addressed. First, the reasons modern children are leading such sedentary lives must be explored. Increases in television viewing and time spent playing video games or surfing the Internet are often blamed. Children should be encouraged to be more physically active. Unfortunately, many children live in urban settings where adults perceive it is unsafe for them to play outdoors unsupervised or where space for physical activities is limited. Second, it appears some groups of children are particularly vulnerable (e.g., girls, adolescents, children with disabilities, and children in low SES communities). These children need opportunities and encouragement to increase their levels of physical activity.

This issue of childhood inactivity is gaining attention around the world, so much so that the World Health Organization (WHO) has adopted a "Global Strategy on Diet, Physical Activity, and Health" (2004) and is currently working with member states and a wide range of national and international partners to develop and implement strategies that support health through physical activity. The ***Relating to Every Child*** feature on the next page describes the WHO's strategy and how it is being applied in developing countries.

Physical education and organized sports are two contexts in which modern-day children can engage in physical activities. We examine the opportunities in these contexts next.

Participation in Physical Education

Physical Education (PE) became a firmly established part of the elementary school curriculum during the twentieth century (Graber, Locke, Lambdin, & Solmon, 2008). The goals of PE include teaching children basic motor skills, engaging them in regular vigorous physical activity, and encouraging them to adopt and then maintain a physically active lifestyle. In recent years, concerns about how high rates of inactivity and obesity lead to early onset of chronic diseases such as diabetes have led to compelling arguments in favor of requiring at least 150 minutes of PE in school each week (National Association for Sport and Physical Education, [NASPE], 2006). Certainly, following these guidelines would go a long way toward helping children to meet the goal of participating in 60 minutes of moderate to vigorous physical activity every day (as indicated above). In addition, schools can promote physical activity by encouraging children to get up and get active at recess; providing opportunities for participation in a wide range of physical and sports-related activities commensurate with children's interests through extracurricular offerings; and promoting the use of "active transportation," such as walking or riding bikes to get to school (McKenzie & Kahan, 2008; Shephard & Trudeau, 2008).

Positive experiences in PE are associated with a wide range of positive outcomes. For example, research links children's attitudes about PE to their physical activity outside of school (Cox, Smith, & Williams, 2008). However, attitudes about PE are linked to many factors, including curriculum and pedagogy (how PE is taught), perceived ability, gender, race and ethnicity, and SES (Graham, 2008; Solmon & Lee, 2008). According to Harrison and Belcher (2006), children may resist participating in activities they perceive are inconsistent with aspects of their identity. African American children, for example, have been shown to seek out activities that, in their view, fit with their "Black" identity (e.g., football and basketball) and avoid activities they consider more consistent with a "White" identity (golf and hockey). Teachers should be aware of these sensitivities and support students' preferences, but also be careful not to communicate implicit messages about student characteristics that may undermine their confidence and limit their willingness to participate in activities (Solmon & Lee, 2008).

Exercise has been shown to stimulate physiological development, enhance motor abilities, and organize the brain for social, emotional, and academic learning (Coe, Pivarnik, Womack, Reeves, & Malina, 2006; Graber et al., 2008; Stork & Sanders, 2008). In one study

RELATING TO

EVERY CHILD

Promoting Physical Activity in Developing Countries

PHYSICAL INACTIVITY and other lifestyle factors (e.g., unhealthy diet, tobacco use, and alcohol consumption) are increasingly associated with health problems in developing countries, especially those experiencing rapid economic and social development, urbanization, and industrialization (Bauman, Schoeppe, & Lewicka, 2005). The prevalence of overweight and associated noncommunicable diseases (NCDs) such as cardiovascular disease, diabetes, and cancer are on the rise in these transitional countries (Bauman et al., 2005; Katzmarzyk et al., 2008). The importance of physical activity as a means of preventing and controlling NCDs is recognized, as is the need for programs, policies, and guidelines that are suited to the unique needs of communities.

In response, the World Health Organization (WHO, 2004) has proposed a "Global Strategy on Diet, Physical Activity, and Health" with four main objectives:

1. reducing NCD risk factors stemming from unhealthy diets and physical inactivity;
2. increasing overall awareness and understanding of (a) the influences of diet and physical activity on health and (b) the positive impact of preventative interventions;
3. encouraging the development and implementation of global, regional, national, and community policies and action plans . . . that are comprehensive, sustainable, engage all population groups, and use multisectoral approaches; and
4. monitoring progress (p. 3–4).

While the main focus of this initiative is on interventions supported by ministries of health, sport, and education that are conducted on a large scale, implementation depends on involvement at the local level (i.e., community groups, schools, and the workplace). One example is the NEWSTART program developed to address obesity through physical activity in one school in the Cook Islands (see Bauman et al. 2005 for a complete description). This program was a collaboration between educators and health professionals. Its goal was to develop long-term plans for health and physical education. In addition to skill development, it focused on enjoyment, confidence building, and full participation. Children (ages 5 to 16) received instruction about health and three physical education sessions each week all year—two lessons on skill development and one on sports—plus daily 15-minute fitness sessions right before lunch.

Teachers were involved in lesson planning and curriculum development with the Ministry of Health and the Ministry of Education. They were provided resources to purchase physical education and cooking equipment and opportunities for professional development that also included teachers from other community schools. Special care was taken to tailor the program to the unique context in which they were teaching (e.g., attending to religious beliefs and issues related to addressing obesity in the Cook Islands). Anecdotal evidence indicates physical activity levels increased in the school as a result of NEWSTART and these changes were sustained after the program was completed. A more formal evaluation of the children's overall health status, activity levels, diet, and attitudes to healthy choices is an ongoing collaboration between the school and the Ministries of Health and Education.

Ministries of health, sport, and education in developing countries are collaborating to promote health and physical education. Their goals, in addition to skill building, are to foster enjoyment, confidence and full participation in physical activities.

(Chomitz et al., 2009), researchers found the more physical fitness tests children passed, the better they did on academic tests. In another study (Barros, Silver, & Stein, 2009), researchers examined the effects of having or not having recess on children's behavior in school. They compared children 8 to 9 years of age who did and did not receive recess on

African American children have been shown to seek out activities that, in their view, fit with their "black" identity (e.g., football and basketball) and avoid activities they consider more consistent with a "white" identity (golf and hockey).

a daily basis and found that those who had more than 15 minutes of recess each day behaved better in class, according to teacher ratings, and were more successful academically. Dr. Barros is quoted in the *New York Times* (Parker-Pope, 2009) as saying, "We should understand that kids need that break because the brain needs that break."

However, even with evidence that physical activity is good for learning, growing concerns about inactivity and obesity in children, and positive public and parent perceptions of PE as part of the school curriculum (81% of adults surveyed agreed, "Daily physical education should be mandatory in schools" [NASPE, 2000]), elementary and middle school teachers are typically allocating *less* time to PE in their schedules. According to a NASPE survey (2006, cited in Graber et al., 2008), only 22% of states (11) require a minimum number of minutes of PE in elementary schools each week, only 8% require daily PE, and only two states require the recommended 30 minutes each day.

What accounts for the decline? Teachers and administrators feel pressured to increase time spent on academic subjects to improve students' scores on standardized tests (Graham, 2008). Often, they perceive a need to take time away from physical activities, such as PE and recess, to meet their academic goals. Moreover, budget cuts have resulted in fewer resources to hire specialist teachers to provide instruction in this subject area. In elementary schools in particular, classroom teachers typically teach PE, and most of these teachers are not prepared to provide high quality, developmentally appropriate physical education. Teacher preparation programs offer very little in the way of substantive training in PE—perhaps one course (Graber et al., 2008; Locke & Graber, 2008). This leaves teachers and administrators concerned about providing safe and appropriate programs for children with increasingly complex health profiles.

In response to these concerns, the National Association for Sport and Physical Education (NASPE) created a task force of experts and charged them with identifying a set of standards for physical education. The standards (NASPE, 2004) describe what children should know and be able to do by the end of grades 2, 5, 8, and high school. Table 8.2 on the next page shows the standards, along with examples of safe and developmentally appropriate activities that will support children to meet them.

Outside of school, children can meet requirements for physical activity through participation in organized sports.

Participation in Organized Sports

Theokas (2009) characterized organized youth sports as structured activities with certain rules for engagement. Events can be individual or team-oriented and require different skills and abilities (e.g., strength, speed, agility). Generally, there is a coach—someone skilled in the sport—who is "in charge" and takes responsibility for managing the game and

TABLE 8.2 • **Participation in Physical Education**
NASPE standards with examples of what children can do to meet them.

STANDARDS	EXAMPLES
1. Demonstrates competency in motor skills and movement patterns needed to perform a variety of physical activities.	• Demonstrates ways to send, project, and receive an object with control, individually and with others, using a variety of body parts and implements • Aims and projects an object at a target with increasing accuracy
2. Demonstrates understanding of movement concepts, principles, strategies, and tactics as they apply to the learning and performance of physical activities.	• Selects and performs simple movement sequences using elements of body awareness, space awareness, qualities, and relationships • Uses critical-thinking and problem-solving skills to create competitive and co-operative games
3. Participates regularly in physical activity.	• Engages in physical education at least 150 minutes per week. • Engages in extracurricular and informal physical activity regularly.
4. Achieves and maintains a health-enhancing level of physical fitness.	• Demonstrates and describes ways to achieve a personal functional level of physical fitness • Describes the importance of exercise and its effect on the body
5. Exhibits responsible personal and social behavior that respects self and others in physical activity settings.	• Identifies and follows rules, routines, and procedures of safety in a variety of activities from all movement categories • Identifies and demonstrates positive behaviors that show respect for individuals' potential, interests, and cultural backgrounds
6. Values physical activity for health, enjoyment, challenge, self-expression, and/or social interaction.	• Identifies and describes positive benefits gained from physical activity in a natural setting • Describes the importance of exercise and its effect on the body

Source: NASPE. National Standards for Physical Education. Retrieved from http://www.aahperd.org/naspe/standards/nationalStandards/ PEstandards .cfm. British Columbia Ministry of Education (1995). Physical education K to 7. Retrieved from http://www.bced.gov.bc.ca/irp/pek7/petoc.htm

teaching/training the players. Participants follow directions and execute skills as needed for competition. Finally, participation in youth sports requires commitment because it is voluntary. However, voluntary participation is associated with higher levels of motivation and cognitive engagement (Csikszentmihalyi & Larson, 1984; Larson, Hansen & Moneta, 2006).

Involvement in organized sports is associated with numerous physical, psychological, and social benefits. For example, children who are involved in sports generally are more physically active than their uninvolved peers; they develop physical skills associated with the sport they play; and they establish habits that sustain health and well-being across the lifespan (CFLRI, 2008; Theokas, 2009). Moreover, sports have long been considered a medium through which other life skills, such as persistence, teamwork, humility and self-control, can be taught and learned (Baron, 2007; Theokas, 2009; Weiss, 2004). Participation in sports has been linked to the development of social skills and social competence, popularity with peers, and increased self-confidence and self-esteem associated with physical appearance and physical ability (Coatsworth & Conroy, 2009; Findlay & Coplan, 2008).

Findlay and Coplan (2008) examined relationships between sports participation and various indices of positive adjustment in children who are shy. Participants in their study were 355 children in grades 4 and 5 (M_{age} = 10.1 years). Their parents rated their social skills and the children were asked to answer questions about their level of shyness, social anxiety, aggressiveness, self-concept in the physical and social domains, general perceptions of well-being, and participation in sports. The results indicated children who are shy were less likely to participate in organized sports. However, those who did participate reported higher levels of self-esteem and decreased levels of social anxiety over time. Findlay and Coplan concluded that sport participation may play a protective role against some of the negative outcomes associated with shyness. In their words, children who are shy should be encouraged to "come out and play."

Theokas (2009, p. 304) aptly cautions that "mere participation [in sports] does not confer benefits; it is the quality and implementation of sport programs that are likely causal mechanisms for enjoyment and development." In recent years, youth sports have been criticized for being excessively competitive. Some participants, including parents and coaches, view winning at all costs as the sole goal of sports. Others perceive that youth sports have become increasingly professionalized, emphasizing year-round training, early specialization and ranking, and a focus on success—defined as winning—rather than the educational and developmental goals we listed above (Gould & Carson, 2004; Theokas, 2009). Moreover, violence in youth sports appears to be increasing and is too often ignored or treated as a "side effect" of the game (e.g., "It's a contact sport. . . . Emotions run high."). When competition and winning at all costs become the focus of sports, enjoyment of the game can be diminished, especially for children who are not naturally athletic and cannot "win" on the basis of their physical performance (Weber, 2009).

The pressure to perform in sports is especially strong for boys (Bowkers, Gabdois, & Cornrock, 2003; Findlay & Coplan, 2008; Kanters & Casper, 2008). Although societal norms are changing and girls' participation in sports is more frequent and more highly valued, there remains a bias that boys should be able to perform well in the physical domain. Boys perceived as big, strong, and physically competent are more desirable than boys with slight builds who are not athletic. In contrast, the standards for physical success for women are less demanding; in fact, physical prowess is admired less in women than in men throughout the lifespan, particularly in some events (e.g., body building, hockey). These norms may influence children's attitudes toward and participation in various sports.

Some groups of children are underrepresented in youth sports. For example, children from ethnic minority groups and children from low SES communities are less likely to participate in organized sports, as are children with disabilities and children who are overweight or obese (Deforche, Bourdeaudhuij, & Tanghe, 2006; Murphy, Carbone, & the Council on Children with Disabilities, 2008; Solmon & Lee, 2008). Deforche and colleagues investigated differences in rates of participation and attitudes toward physical activity in normal weight, overweight, and obese youth (ages 13–15). They found higher rates of participation among youth with normal weight compared with those who were either overweight or obese. The three groups did not differ in terms of their perceived benefits of physical activity, but children in the overweight and obese groups perceived more barriers to participating in sports and reported liking physical activity less than children in the normal weight group. Specifically, they reported physical complaints, such as feeling exhausted, finding it difficult to breathe, and experiencing stitches or muscle pain, as well as feeling insecure about their appearance and worrying about not being good at sports. Also, they didn't enjoy physical activity as much as their normal weight peers. Deforche and colleagues emphasized the need to increase participation in sports among children and youth who are overweight by targeting activities that are fun and attractive to them.

Adults can influence children's attitudes toward and enjoyment of sport participation. Coatsworth and Conroy (2009) examined relationships between coaching behaviors and developmental outcomes for children and youth. Participants in their study were 117 children (77 girls, 40 boys), ages 10 to 17, who were participating in a community-directed summer swim league. In their study, coaching behaviors characterized as supportive, nurturing, encouraging, and non-hostile were associated with positive outcomes for the swimmers, including positive self-evaluations of swimming, self-esteem, initiative, and identity reflection and exploration (e.g., trying new things). Similarly, Gano-Overway and colleagues (2009) found children's perceptions of a caring context for sport participation were associated with positive outcomes in their study of children and youth ages 9 to 16 who were attending a federally funded summer program, the National Youth Sports Program. The program sought to increase opportunities for underserved youth to participate in sports and other

The National Youth Sports Program sought to increase opportunities for underserved youth to participate in sport and other physical activities, involving children primarily from ethnic minority groups.

physical activities. Gano-Overway and colleagues' sample was approximately 50% boys and primarily children from ethnic minority groups (e.g., 61% African American, 26% Hispanic Americans). Their findings indicate children's perceptions of caring contexts were associated with prosocial behavior and higher levels of self-efficacy.

Finally, Kanters and Casper (2008) studied how parental attitudes and behavior influenced young hockey players' self-assessment of hockey ability and enjoyment of the game. Participants in their study were all boys 9 to 11 years old. Consistent with the other studies, these researchers found that children who perceive parental support as encouraging and facilitative (i.e., paying registration fees, purchasing equipment, providing transportation, and attending games) had more positive attitudes toward participating and higher levels of perceived competence for the sport than children who perceived parental involvement negatively (e.g., perceived parental pressure).

In summary, youth sports can engage families and communities in activities that are healthy, mutually entertaining, and fun. The focus of participation in sports and other physical activities should be on developing physical skills; maintaining health and fitness; and developing positive self-perceptions and prosocial attitudes and behavior. The ***Connecting with Children*** guidelines offer some tips on how adults can support children's positive participation in sports and physical activity.

CONNECTING WITH CHILDREN

Guidelines for Families, Teachers, and Other Professionals: Encouraging Physical Activity

Increase physical activity by reducing sedentary activity.
Examples
1. Limit children's TV viewing, time on the computer, and talking on the phone.
2. Encourage and facilitate outdoor play.
3. Go for a walk around the neighborhood instead of watching TV after dinner or before settling into homework. Everyone will feel refreshed and energized.

Incorporate physical activity into daily routines.
Examples
1. Walk or ride a bike to school.
2. Take the stairs instead of the elevator.
3. Build in "fitness breaks." Teachers can do this to transition between lessons. Sing an action song or get up and stretch.

Make physical activity fun.
Examples
1. Give children choices about the activities in which they engage.
2. Create opportunities for children to participate in a wide variety of activities—variety is the spice of life.
3. Give non-competitive choices for activities. Participating in non-competitive sports can be fun for children who aren't particularly athletic or just don't want the pressure of competitive sports.

Exercise indoors when the weather is poor.
Examples
1. Put on some music and groove.
2. Pop in an exercise video.
3. Do some yoga.

See http://kidshealth.org/parent/nutrition_fit/fitness/exercise.html for ideas about a wide range of aerobic, strength and endurance promoting activities that are fun.

Sources: KidsHealth. (2009). Kids and exercise. Retrieved from http://kidshealth.org/parent/nutrition_fit/fitness/exercise.html#.

Stewart, C. (2007). Physical activity in children: Tips to help parents encourage exercise in kids. Retrieved from http://earlychildhood.suite101.com/article.cfm/your_childs_fitness

Including Children with Disabilities in Sports and Physical Activities

Approximately 18% of children and adolescents in the United States have a chronic condition or disability with implications for participating in sports and other physical activities (Murphy, Carbone, & the Council on Children with Disabilities, 2008). However, regular physical activity for children with disabilities is associated with numerous benefits, including controlling or slowing the progression of disease and disability, improving overall health and function, and mediating the psychosocial impact of having a disability (for both children and their families). For example, participation in sports provides opportunities for children with disabilities to form friendships, express creativity, develop positive self-concepts and self-esteem, and cultivate meaning and purpose in their lives (Dykens, Rosner, & Butterbaugh, 1998; Murphy et al., 2008).

The Paralympics and Special Olympics are good examples of what is possible for individuals with disabilities in terms of physical activity and athletic ability. The Special Olympics is the largest recreational program for children with intellectual disabilities, with a presence in more than 200 countries. The Paralympic Games, for athletes with physical and visual disabilities, are held every four years, following the Olympic Games; they are governed by the International Paralympic Committee (IPC). Many of the events parallel those in the Olympic Games (e.g., archery, track and field, cycling, power lifting, swimming, volleyball, and basketball). You can find out more about these organizations by visiting their websites: specialolympics.org and paralympic.org.

Unfortunately, for many children with disabilities, there are many barriers to participation in sports, most of which have nothing to do with their physical ability. In addition to functional limitations, frequently cited barriers to participation include high costs for specialized programs and equipment, lack of nearby facilities and programs, and lack of awareness about what is possible or available for children with disabilities. Their participation in sports and other physical activities requires a good deal of support from their families, schools, and communities. In general, families who are physically active tend to also promote physical activity in children with physical disabilities (American Academy of Pediatrics, Council on Sports Medicine and Fitness, and Council on School Health, 2006; King et al., 2003, Murphy et al., 2008). Unfortunately, inactive role models, competing demands and time pressures, unsafe environments, lack of adequate facilities, insufficient funds, and insufficient access to high quality daily physical education are more common for children with special physical needs than for other populations. Finally, many adults believe children with disabilities are more susceptible to injury from sport participation than other groups of children. This is not the case.

Table 8.3 on the next page, prepared by the American Academy of Orthopedic Surgeons, shows the range of individual and team sports recommended for individuals with disabilities. Notice that very few activities in the table are marked with an X; that is, there are very few activities not recommended for individuals with disabilities. Of course, many activities need to be adapted or individualized in accordance with particular physical needs. For example, "goalball" is a team sport played by individuals who are blind or who have visual impairments. Two teams, each with three players, try to roll a 3-pound ball past the opposing team players and into their goal. The court on

Goalball is a team sport played by individuals who are blind or who have visual impairments.

TABLE 8.3 • Including Children with Disabilities in Sport and Physical Activities

Individual and team sports recommended for individuals with disabilities by the American Academy of Orthopedic Surgeons

CONDITIONS	INDIVIDUAL SPORTS																								
	ARCHERY	BICYCLING	TRICYCLING	BOWLING	CANOEING/KAYAKING	DIVING	FENCING	FIELD EVENTS*	FISHING	GOLF	HORSEBACK RIDING	RIFLE SHOOTING	SAILING	SCUBA DIVING	SKATING: ROLLER & ICE	SKIING: DOWNHILL	SKIING: CROSS-COUNTRY	SWIMMING	TABLE TENNIS	TENNIS	TENNIS: WHEELCHAIR	TRACK	TRACK: WHEELCHAIR	WEIGHT LIFTING	WHEELCHAIR POLING
Amputations																									
Upper extremity	RA	R	R	R	RA	R	R	R	R	RA	R	RA	R	R	R	R	R	R	R	R	–	R	–	R	–
Lower extremity																									
Above knee	R	R	R	R	R	R	I	R	R	R	R	R	R	R	I	RA	RA	R	R	I	R	–	R	R	R
Below knee	R	R	R	R	R	R	R	R	R	R	R	R	R	R	R	R	R	R	R	R	I	R	I	R	I
Cerebral palsy																									
Ambulatory	R	R	R	R	R	R	I	R	R	R	R	R	R	I	R	RA	RA	R	R	R	–	R	–	R	–
Wheelchair	R	I	I	R	R	I	I	I	R	I	I	R	R	–	–	–	–	I	R	–	R	–	R	R	R
Spinal cord disruption																									
Cervical	RA	–	RA	RA	IA	–	–	I	R	–	X	RA	R	–	–	IA	IA	R	RA	–	IA	–	R	–	I
High thoracic: T1-T5	R	–	R	R	R	–	RA	R	R	RA	I	R	R	R	–	IA	IA	R	R	–	R	–	R	R	R
Low thoracolumbar: T6-L3	R	–	R	R	R	–	RA	R	R	RA	R	R	R	R	–	RA	RA	R	R	–	R	–	R	R	R
Lumbosacral: L4-sacral	R	R	R	R	R	R	R	R	R	R	R	R	R	I	R	R	R	R	R	R	–	R	–	R	–
Neuromuscular disorders																									
Muscular dystrophy	RA	I	R	R	I	I	–	R	R	R	I	RA	R	I	I	I	I	R	R	I	I	I	I	–	R
Spinal muscular atrophy	RA	I	R	R	I	I	–	R	R	R	I	RA	R	I	I	I	I	R	R	I	I	I	I	–	R
Charcot-Marie-Tooth syndrome	R	R	R	R	R	R	R	R	R	R	R	R	R	R	R	R	R	R	R	R	–	R	–	R	–
Ataxias	R	I	I	R	I	I	–	R	R	I	I	R	R	I	I	I	R	R	R	R	R	I	R	I	R
Others																									
Osteogenesis imperfecta	R	I	R	R	R	I	R	R	R	I	I	R	R	I	I	I	R	R	R	R	R	R	R	I	R
Arthrogryposis	R	I	I	R	R	I	I	R	R	I	R	R	R	I	I	I	R	R	R	R	–	R	X	I	X
Juvenile rheumatoid arthritis	RA	I	I	RA	R	I	I	I	R	I	I	R	R	I	I	I	I	R	R	I	I	I	I	I	I
Hemophilia	RA	R	R	R	R	R	R	R	R	R	R	R	R	R	I	I	R	R	R	I	–	R	–	I	–
Skeletal dysplasias	R	R	R	R	R	R	R	R	R	R	R	R	R	R	R	RA	R	R	R	R	–	R	–	I	–

R = recommended, X = not recommended, A = adapted, I = individualized, – = no information or not applicable.

*Clubthrow, discus, javelin, shot put.

Source: From Chang, F. M., The disabled athlete (pp. 48–76) published in Pediatric and Adolescent Sports Medicine, Vol. 3, *by Stanitski, C. L., DeLee, J. C., Drez, Jr., D. Copyright Elservier, 1994. Used with permission.*

TABLE 8.3 • **(Continued)**

CONDITIONS	TEAM SPORTS											
	BASEBALL	SOFTBALL	BASKETBALL	BASKETBALL: WHEELCHAIR	FOOTBALL: TACKLE	FOOTBALL: TOUCH	FOOTBALL: WHEELCHAIR	ICE HOCKEY	SLEDGE HOCKEY	SOCCER	SOCCER: WHEELCHAIR	VOLLEYBALL
Amputations												
Upper extremity	R	R	R	–	R	R	–	R	–	R	–	R
Lower extremity												
Above knee	RA	RA	–	R	I	I	R	–	R	I	R	R
Below knee	R	R	R	I	R	R	I	I	I	R	I	R
Cerebral palsy												
Ambulatory	R	R	I	–	I	I	–	I	–	R	–	R
Wheelchair	I	I	–	R	–	–	R	–	I	–	R	I
Spinal cord disruption												
Cervical	–	–	–	I	–	–	I	–	I	–	–	IA
High thoracic: T1-T5	RA	RA	–	R	–	–	R	–	R	–	R	RA
Low thoracolumbar: T6-L3	RA	RA	–	R	–	–	R	–	R	–	R	RA
Lumbosacral: L4-Sacral	R	R	R	I	I	R	I	I	–	R	–	R
Neuromuscular disorders												
Muscular dystrophy	I	I	I	I	–	–	I	I	I	I	I	I
Spinal muscular atrophy	I	I	I	I	–	–	I	I	I	I	I	I
Charcot-Marie-Tooth syndrome	R	R	R	–	R	R	–	I	–	R	–	R
Ataxias	I	I	I	R	–	I	I	I	I	I	R	I
Others												
Osteogenesis imperfecta	I	I	I	R	X	I	I	X	X	X	R	I
Arthrogryposis	R	R	R	–	X	R	I	I	–	I	–	R
Juvenile rheumatoid arthritis	I	I	I	I	I	I	I	I	I	I	I	I
Hemophilia	I	R	R	–	X	I	–	X	–	I	–	R
Skeletal dysplasias	R	R	R	–	I	R	–	R	–	R	–	R

which the game is played is approximately the same size as a volleyball court. You may wonder how individuals who cannot see can guide a ball down the court, past their opponents, and into a goal. Similarly, how does the opposing team stop goals from being scored? The ball has bells in it. Players learn to judge the position and movement of the ball in relation to the sound of the bell, often getting low on the floor to enhance their ability to follow the sounds. Goalball is played all over the world. It originated in Austria, but if you Google "goalball," you will find organizing bodies for the sport in many countries, including the United States, Australia, and the United Kingdom. In fact, goalball has been a Paralympic sport since 1976, when the games were held in Toronto, Canada.

Experts agree that children with physical disabilities can and should participate in a variety of physical activities (Wind, Schwend, & Larson, 2004) with guidance and support from a multidisciplinary team, which could include, among others, physicians, therapists, counselors, and special education teachers. The goal should be to include children with disabilities in appropriate activities as long as they show interest and have the ability to participate. "It is important that children are empowered with an 'I can do' attitude rather than discouraged by the message 'you can't do that'" (Murphy et al., 2008, p. 1058).

Recommendations for including children with physical disabilities in sports and other physical activities are provided in the ***Connecting with Children*** guidelines.

CONNECTING WITH CHILDREN

Guidelines for Families, Teachers, and Other Professionals: Including Children with Disabilities in Sports and Other Physical Activities

Perform a pre-participation evaluation (PPE) in collaboration with children and their families, pediatric specialists, therapists, coaches, and other relevant professionals.

Examples

1. Obtain a medical history that includes functional, cardiorespiratory, and fitness assessments.
2. Consider children's interests and talents.
3. Direct children with disabilities into the most appropriate activities. Do not exclude them from activities automatically.
4. Work with a multidisciplinary team to identify and address implications of children's disability for participation.

Identify strategies to minimize the risk of illness and injury related to participation. Make appropriate accommodations and take safety precautions.

Examples

1. Plan programs that are longer in duration, greater in frequency, but lower in intensity than those designed for typically developing children.
2. Attend to disability-specific needs for training, hydration, clothing, and equipment.
3. Attend to motor and mechanical characteristics that predispose some children to injuries and overuse syndromes. Consult sports-specific and condition-specific guidelines for participation.

Recognize and reduce child, family, and societal barriers to participation.

Examples

1. Note that activities for children with disabilities, to a large extent, continue to be socially segregated. Participating with other children in the community can reduce societal stereotypes and barriers for children with disabilities.
2. Don't allow fear of injury to be a barrier to participation. The actual rates of injury in children with disabilities are similar to those of their typically developing peers.

Increase awareness of the resources available locally.

Examples

1. Seek out people, facilities, and programs that can support children with disabilities to participate with peers in their schools and communities.
2. See the National Center of Medical Home Initiatives for Children with Special Needs for information and resources: www.medicalhomeinfo.org/health/recreation.html).

Sources: Murphy et al. (2008). Promoting the participation of children with disabilities in sports, recreation, and physical activities. Pediatrics, *121, 1057–1061.*

Wind et al. (2004). Sports for the physically challenged child. Journal of the American Academy of Orthopaedic Surgeons, 12, 126–137.

Health and Well-Being

Nutrition

Because children's bodies and brains are continuing to grow and develop during middle childhood, maintaining good eating habits and a balanced diet are important. Children this age will need more calories than they did during the early years, but the absolute number of calories to consume will depend on their level of physical activity and metabolism. Recommendations and guidelines concerning healthy eating that were introduced in Chapter 5 are relevant for children in their middle years, too.

Although what children eat remains the primary responsibility of parents during the middle years, it is more difficult to monitor (Langlois, 2006). Children begin to eat more meals outside of the home (e.g., at school, with friends) and have more opportunities to exercise personal choice. Also, they are exposed to more diverse messages about food, not all of them healthy, through television, peers, and school curriculum. As a result, children want to try new foods and exert pressure within the family to modify food choices based on outside influences.

Schools can be instrumental in helping children to eat well and be healthy. Most public elementary schools (94%) serve meals or have food and drinks available for purchase (Parsad & Lewis, 2006). Increasingly, they are coming under fire to exclude unhealthy foods and drinks (e.g., foods high in saturated or trans fats, soft drinks) in favor of more healthy options (e.g., filling vending machines with milk, 100% fruit juice, and water). Some schools and districts are taking this challenge to heart, developing programs and policies that promote good eating habits and an active lifestyle. Foster and colleagues (2008) describe a multicomponent initiative developed and implemented in 10 schools in a school district in Philadelphia. The schools enrolled students in kindergarten through eighth grade in communities where more than 50% of students were eligible for free or reduced price meals. The initiative included five components: school self-assessment, nutrition education, nutrition policy, social marketing, and family outreach. A brief description of each component is provided in Table 8.4.

TABLE 8.4 • **A Multicomponent School Nutrition Policy Initiative**

COMPONENT	DESCRIPTION
School Self-assessment	Schools formed advisory groups that included administrators, teachers, nurses, coaches, and parents. Advisory groups conducted self-assessments of their schools in terms of healthy eating and physical activities and set goals for change (e.g., limiting the use of foods as rewards, promoting active recess).
Nutrition Education	Nutrition education was provided to teachers through 10 hours of professional development each year. Teachers then provided 50 hours of nutrition development to students each year. Instruction was designed to be integrative and interdisciplinary. • Nutrition was integrated into various classroom subjects. • The goal was to show how food choices and physical activity are tied to personal behavior, individual health, and the environment.
Nutrition Policy	Foods sold in the schools were changed to meet the following nutritional standards: • Beverages were limited to 100% juice (6-ounce serving size), water, and milk (8-ounce serving size. • Snacks contained ≤ 7 g of total fat, 2 g of saturated fat, 360 mg of sodium, and 15 g of sugar per serving.
Social Marketing	Schools promoted the slogan, "Want strength? Eat healthy foods." Incentives were offered for participating in healthy meals and buying healthy snacks, or bringing healthy snacks from home.
Family Outreach	Nutrition education was provided to families at home-school association meetings, report card nights, parent education meetings, and weekly nutrition workshops. Parents and students were encouraged to purchase healthy snacks and be more active and reduce time spent in sedentary activities. Healthy foods were sold at parent fundraisers. Parents were discouraged from sending sweets to teachers at holiday times.

Source: Foster, G. D., Sherman, S., Borradaile, K. E. et al. (2008). A policy-based school intervention to prevent overweight and obesity. Pediatrics, 128, 794–802.

Foster and colleagues (2008) studied the effects of the initiative on children in grades 4 through 6 over a two-year period. Specifically, the researchers measured children's height and weight annually and plotted their BMI scores and percentiles according to their age and gender. Then children were classified as underweight, normal weight, overweight, and obese according to the CDC growth charts (recall from Chapter 5). In addition, children completed self-report questionnaires about their eating habits, including their consumption of fatty foods, fruits and vegetables, and physical and sedentary activities, including time spent watching television. After two years, there was a substantial (50%) and statistically significant reduction in the incidence of overweight in schools participating in the initiative. The initiative was particularly effective for reducing the incidence of overweight in African American children. Children reported decreases in both overall food consumption and consumption of fatty foods, as well as decreases in time spent in sedentary activities, but also decreases in physical activity. The researchers emphasized that self-report data need to be interpreted cautiously and that initiatives such as this one should target children before they get to grade 4 and be studied over a longer period of time (i.e., school-wide and family-wide changes, such as those strived for with this initiative, take time to achieve). Importantly, there was no evidence to suggest children's body images were more negative as a consequence of participating in the initiative, nor was there any increase in underweight. Therefore, the researchers concluded the multicomponent school-based initiative was effective in curbing overweight in children and promoting the adoption of healthy lifestyles.

Accidents and Injuries

When children are physically active, they are bound to suffer accidents and injuries. Most of the time these mishaps are minor, but accidents result in more serious harm, even death, for a significant minority of children and youth. In the United States, approximately 12,000 children (ages 1–19) die as a result of an unintentional injury each year (CDC, 2008). This number accounts for 44% of all deaths in this age group. An additional 9.2 million nonfatal injuries are treated in emergency rooms. This translates into an annual nonfatal injury rate of 11,272 per 100,000 children, or just over 10% of the population.

DEADLY INJURIES. Figure 8.3 shows the leading causes of death resulting from an unintentional injury by age group. Motor vehicle and transportation-related (MVT-related) accidents and injuries are by far the leading cause of death for all age groups except infants, who are at greater risk of dying from suffocation (this relates to the SID syndrome described in Chapter 4). Adolescents ages 15 to 19 are particularly at risk for dying in a car accident, and boys are more at risk in this regard than girls, perhaps because of their inexperience and propensity for engaging in high-risk behavior (see Chapter 13). Children ages 1 to 14 are at particular risk of being struck by cars. Lack of experience may cause children to misjudge the distance between themselves and cars or to underestimate the time it takes for cars to stop. Bicycle accidents also present a risk as children venture onto busy streets. Drowning, injuries from fires and burns, poisoning, and falls are other common causes of injury and death during childhood.

Males have higher rates of injury and death in all age groups and almost every category of injury (see Figures 8.4 and 8.5), likely resulting from their higher activity levels and participation in more risky activities (e.g., rough-and-tumble play in the early years, contact sports in middle childhood). This sex difference maintains across ethnic groups within the United States (see Figure 8.6) and in countries all over the world (WHO, 2008). Within the United States, Native American and Alaska Native children are more likely to die from unintentional injuries than African American or Caucasian children, and boys in these groups are particularly at risk. The burden of injury is unequal across SES communities, too. Children in poorer countries and children from poorer families in better-off countries are more vulnerable than children in high-income countries and communities, respectively. In fact, more than 95% of all injury-related deaths in children worldwide occur in low- and middle-income countries (WHO, 2008). Finally, children characterized as risk takers and children

FIGURE 8.3

ACCIDENTS AND INJURIES

Leading causes of death resulting from an unintentional injury by age group from 2000–2005

	Age Group in Years				
Rank	Less than 1 (n = 5,883)	1 to 4 (n = 10,203)	5 to 9 (n = 7,144)	10 to 14 (n = 9,088)	15 to 19 (n = 40,734)
1	Suffocation 66%	MVT-related 31%	MVT-related 53%	MVT-related 58%	MVT-related 76%
2	MVT-related 14%	Drowning 27%	Other Injuries 15%	Other Injuries 18%	Other Injuries 9%
3	Drowning 7%	Other Injuries 15%	Fires or Burns 13%	Drowning 10%	Poisoning 7%
4	Other Injuries 6%	Fires or Burns 14%	Drowning 13%	Fires or Burns 6%	Drowning 5%
5	Fires or Burns 4%	Suffocation 8%	Suffocation 4%	Suffocation 4%	Falls 1%
6	Poisoning 2%	Falls 2%	Falls 1%	Poisoning 2%	Fires or Burns 1%
7	Falls 2%	Poisoning 2%	Poisoning 1%	Falls 2%	Suffocation 1%

Source: Borse, N. N., Gilchrist, J., Dellinger, A. M., Rudd, R. A., Ballesteros, M. F., & Sleet, D. A. (2008). CDC Childhood injury report: Patterns of unintentional injuries among 0–19 year olds in the United States, 2000–2006. Atlanta, GA: Centers for Disease Control and Prevention, National Center for Injury Prevention and Control.

FIGURE 8.4

INJURY DEATH RATES IN CHILDREN 0–19 YEARS, BY AGE AND SEX

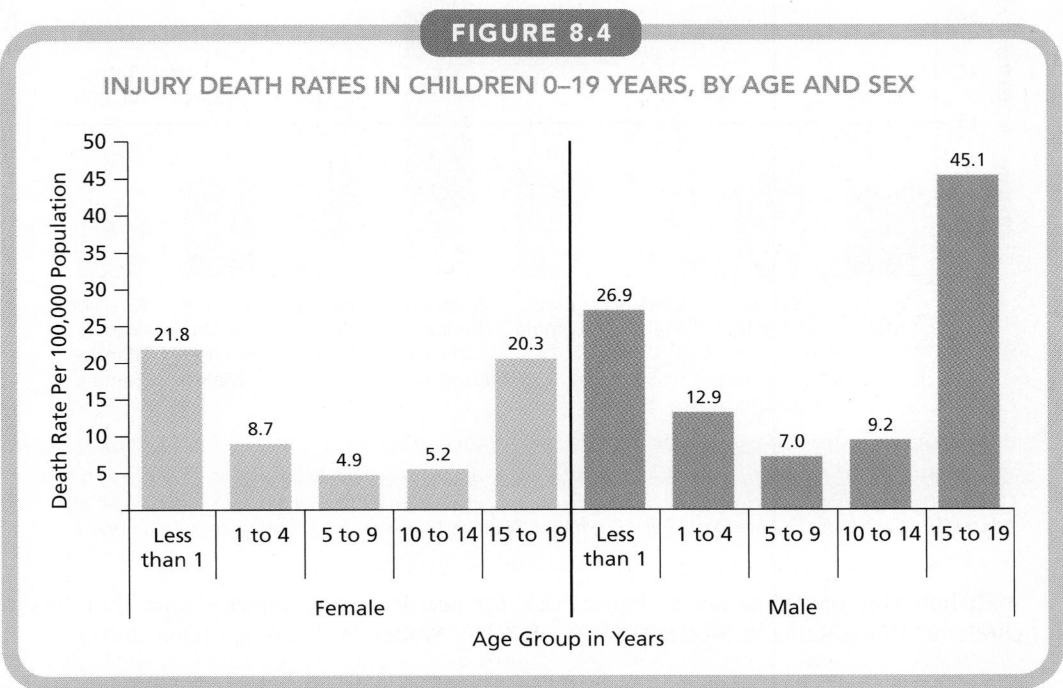

Source: CDC/NCHS. National Vital Statistics System

FIGURE 8.5

INJURY DEATH RATES AMONG CHILDREN 0–19 YEARS BY SEX AND CAUSE

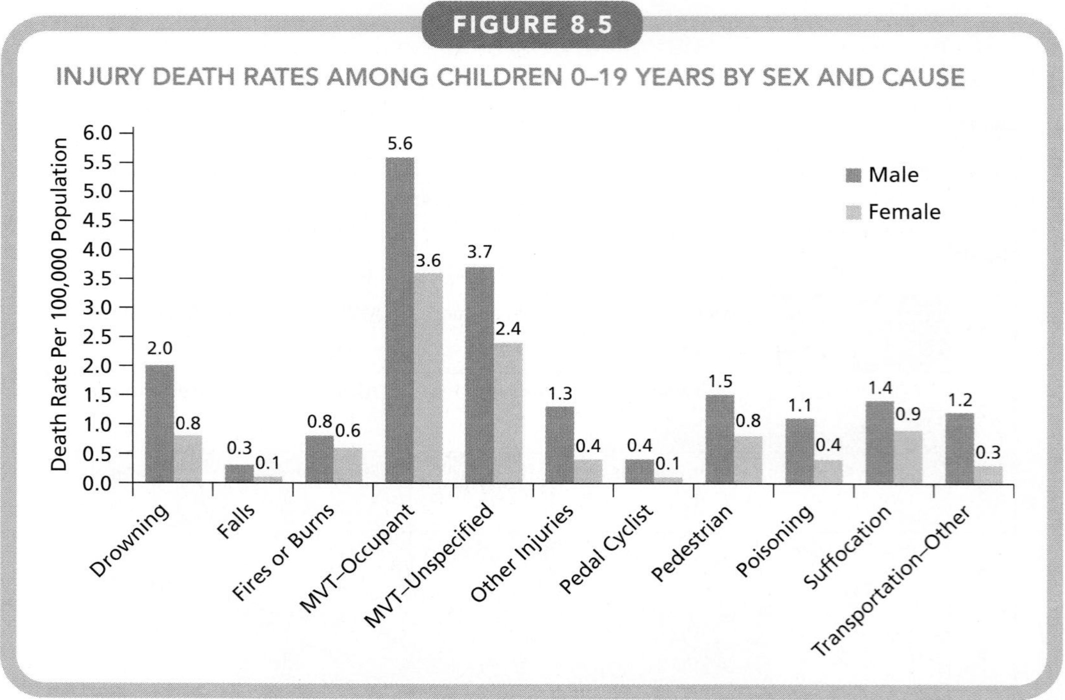

Source: CDC/NCHS. National Vital Statistics System

FIGURE 8.6

INJURY DEATH RATES AMONG CHILDREN 0–19 YEARS BY RACE AND SEX

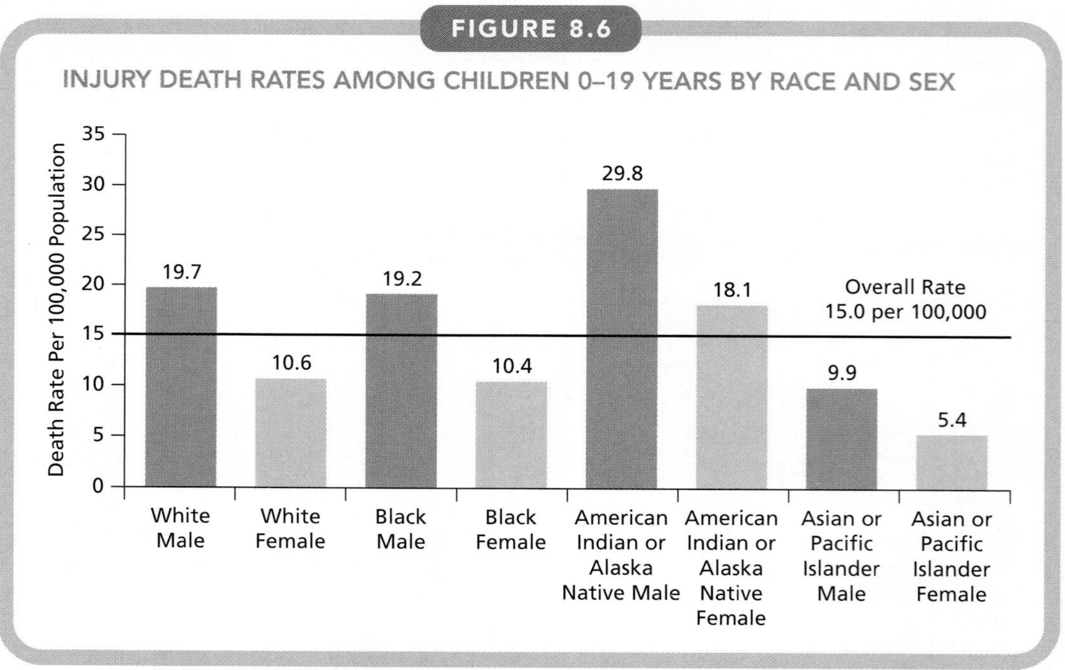

Source: Borse, N. N., Gilchrist, J., Dellinger, A. M., Rudd, R. A., Ballesteros, M. F., & Sleet, D. A. (2008). CDC Childhood injury report: Patterns of unintentional injuries among 0–19 year olds in the United States, 2000–2006. Atlanta, GA: Centers for Disease Control and Prevention, National Center for Injury Prevention and Control.

with behavior problems are at higher risk for accidents and injuries than their peers (Brehaut, Miller, Raina, & McGrail, 2003; Hoffrage, Weber, Hertwig, & Chase, 2003).

INJURIES IN AND AROUND THE HOME. Most non-vehicle-related accidents occur in or around children's homes. We've all read tragic reports of young children drowning in bathtubs and swimming pools, ingesting poisons, falling from bicycles and other play equipment, or being burned in a fire in their own homes. Injuries also commonly occur on playgrounds, especially in school-age children (Phelan, Khoury, Kalkwarf, & Lanphear, 2001). According to the National Program for Playground Safety (2006), injuries on playgrounds often are the result of inadequate adult supervision, children playing on equipment that is unsafe or not age appropriate, and lack of safe surfaces for falling (i.e., impact-absorbing surfaces, such as pea gravel or sand). Accidents also tend to be more serious when children do not wear protective clothing and safety equipment, such as helmets and protective padding.

TRAMPOLINES: SPECIAL CONCERNS. Trampolines are a popular piece of play equipment that has proven very dangerous. In 1996, more than 83,000 trampoline-related injuries were reported in the United States (AAP, 1999). By 2004, this figure had jumped to 111,000 (Brayden, 2008). Most trampoline injuries are sustained at home, and two-thirds occur in children under the age of 14, with the highest rate of injury in children under age 6. Serious injuries occur in all parts of the body, including arms, legs, face, neck, spine, and head. Adult supervision is not a guarantee that children will be safe on trampolines. More than half of trampoline accidents occur when adults are watching children. Having spotters around the trampoline can reduce the risk somewhat, but spotters need to be large and strong enough to protect the jumper if he or she gets too close to the edge. For all these reasons, the American Academy of Pediatrics Committee on Injury and Poison Prevention and Committee on Sports Medicine and Fitness recommends, "trampolines should never be used in the home environment, in routine physical education classes, or in outdoor playgrounds" (AAP, 1999, p. 1053). Furthermore, the AAP endorses a set of very specific design and behavioral recommendations for limited use of trampolines in "supervised training programs." These recommendations are summarized in Table 8.5.

SPORTS INJURIES. With approximately 35–40 million youth ages 6 to 18 participating in some form of athletic activity, it is hardly surprising that sports-related injuries are on the rise in children and youth. In fact, almost one-third of all childhood injuries occur while they are participating in sports activities (Children's Hospital Boston and Harvard Medical Center, 2005–2007). Some sports are more dangerous than others. For example, injuries

TABLE 8.5 • **Recommendations for the Safe Use of Trampolines**

DESIGN RECOMMENDATIONS	BEHAVIORAL RECOMMENDATIONS
Cover the trampoline frame with padding, and ensure the surface surrounding the trampoline is covered with an impact-absorbing safety material.	Allow only one child on the trampoline at a time.
Make sure the trampoline is in good condition (e.g., no tears or equipment detachments).	Ensure that adults who are trained in trampoline safety and competent spotters are present whenever the trampoline is in use.
Use safety harnesses and spotting belts for protection when children are learning or practicing more challenging skills.	Ensure the child on the trampoline remains in the center of the mat and is performing routines that are appropriate for his/her capability or training.
Consider placing the trampoline away from other play structures and immersing it in a pit so the mat is at ground level.	Ensure the trampoline is secured and not accessible when it not in use.
Prevent young children from accessing the trampoline, especially when adults are not available to supervise. Don't use ladders.	Even in supervised training programs, don't allow children younger than 6 years of age to use full-size trampolines.

Source: Based on American Academy of Pediatrics: Committee on Injury and Poison Prevention and Committee on Sports Medicine and Fitness. (1999). Trampolines at home, school, and recreational centers. Pediatrics, 103, 1053–1056. *U. S. Consumer Product Safety Commission. Trampoline Safety Alert. Retrieved from http://www.cpsc.gov/cpscpub/pubs/085.html.*

occur more frequently in contact sports such as football than in non-contact sports such as swimming. Weight-bearing exercises such as running also place participants at higher risk for injury. However, it is possible to get injured from participating in all kinds of sports, and injuries can result from a single traumatic event, as occurs when a sudden direct force is applied to bones or joints (e.g., being tackled in football), or from repetitive stress to bones, muscles, and tendons without allowing sufficient time to heal (Brenner & Council on Sports Medicine and Fitness, 2007; Kerssmakers, Fotiadou, de Jonge, Karantanas, & Maas, 2009).

Injuries due to overuse are a growing phenomenon, at least in the United States. According to Brenner and colleagues (2007), they account for half of all injuries treated at pediatric sports medicine clinics. These injuries can be serious and, if not accurately diagnosed and appropriately treated, they can lead to permanent disability. Experts agree that special consideration needs to be given for injuries that occur in a child's growing skeleton (Kerssemakers et al., 2009): "The growing bones of the young athlete cannot handle as much stress as the mature bones of adults" (Brenner et al., 2007, p. 1243). Overtraining is one way in which overuse injuries occur, so training and competitive programs need to be adapted for pediatric and adolescent populations (Kerssemakers et al., 2009). The AAP Committee on Sports Medicine and Fitness (2000) recommends children limit participation in any single sporting event to five days per week, with at least one day each week to rest from all organized physical activity.

Similarly, children and youth are more vulnerable to the risks associated with exercising in extreme heat; they sweat less, create more body heat per body mass, and acclimatize more slowly to hot weather and climates (AAP Committee on Sports Medicine and Fitness, 2000). Finally, some evidence indicates child and youth athletes can experience "burnout," or overtraining syndrome, as a result of physical and emotional stress, missed social and educational opportunities, and disruptions to family life (AAP, 2000; Brenner et al., 2007). Indications of burnout can include chronic muscle or joint pain, personality changes, decreased enthusiasm for practice and competition, and difficulty completing usual routines.

All of the sources cited here emphasize the importance of parents and trainers maintaining realistic expectations and carefully monitoring children's physical and psychosocial responses to pressure. This presents a challenge for some parents whose ambitions for their children can be one source of the problem. Mark Hyman (2009), writing on this topic in an issue of *Sports Illustrated,* recounts a doctor's story of a mother becoming enraged with him when he recommended that her daughter take a six-month break from tennis because she had a acquired a potentially serious injury that could affect the normal growth of her shoulder. The mother accused him of being overly cautious and insisted the injury could be treated equally well in physiotherapy. Hopefully, the attitudes of this parent reflect only a small minority of those whose children are involved in sports.

As indicated previously in this chapter, the main goal of participating in sports should be to promote lifelong physical activity that leads to overall health and well-being. Brenner and colleagues (2007) suggest educating parents, athletes, and coaches that sports should be part of a plan to promote fun, skill development, and success for each athlete. Moreover, research indicates that, on average, children are more consistent performers, have fewer injuries, and persist in sports longer when they engage in a variety of sports during early childhood, specialize only after reaching the age of puberty, take time to rest and recover from sports activities, and participate in other activities (AAP Committee on Sports Medicine and Fitness, 2000; Brenner et al., 2007).

HEAD INJURIES. Head injuries are the most common and potentially serious injuries children suffer (WHO, 2008). In the United States, approximately 475,000 children ages 0 to 14 sustain head injuries from playground falls, bicycle accidents, and other mishaps each year (Langlois, Rutland-Brown, & Thomas, 2004). About 20% of head injuries are attributed to sports participation. Depending on the location and severity of the injury, children can experience temporary or lasting effects on physical functions and psychological processes.

Research indicates children who sustain moderate to severe brain injuries can experience persistent difficulties in emotional, behavioral, and adaptive domains as well as cognitive deficits that interfere with learning (Conklin, Salorio, & Slomine, 2008; Fay et al., 2009). Recent research also indicates that early trauma may increase particular vulnerabilities more than was previously presumed, especially when injuries are diffuse, as is the case with concussion (Conklin et al., 2008; Yee, 2007). Specifically, earlier age-at-injury has been associated with greater deficits in overall cognitive functioning, attention, and executive functioning, which may not reveal themselves until long after the injury was sustained (e.g., when children fail to meet increased age-related expectations). However, the early years also are associated with brain plasticity, so there is evidence for recovery over time as well.

Concussion is the most common type of head injury, especially in child and adolescent athletes. The American Academy of Neurology defines **concussion** as "a trauma-induced alteration in mental status that may or may not involve a loss of consciousness" (AAN Report of the Quality Standards Subcommittee, 1997). In the majority of concussion cases (90%), there is no documented loss of consciousness. More likely, people experience a transient period of post-trauma amnesia or loss of mental alertness—they are unable to maintain a cogent stream of thought or carry out a sequence of tasks (Yee, 2007). Other common symptoms of concussion include headache, dizziness or balance problems, nausea and vomiting, a foggy or dazed sensation, vision and hearing difficulties, emotional lability (strong emotions with mood swings), and fatigue (Yee, 2007).

Table 8.6 outlines criteria used to characterize concussions as simple or complex, along with "return-to-play" parameters—also referred to as the Prague guidelines—created by experts at the 2nd International Conference on Concussion in Sport (McCrory et al., 2005). Children who suffer simple concussions can recover in a relatively short period of time, with rest, and then return to their normal activities without a recurrence of any symptoms. In the case of complex concussions, symptoms persist and more extensive intervention is needed to address specific concerns. The key is allowing for full recovery before returning to sports, and this can take time. One case study followed an 8-year-old girl who sustained a concussion while playing soccer (Boutin, Lassonde, Robert, Vanassing, & Ellemberg, 2008). At the time of injury, the child did not lose consciousness, but suffered a brief period (5 minutes) of amnesia. Assessments were conducted at 24 hours and then 7, 22, 32, and 55 weeks post-injury. Cognitive impairments, mainly relating to attention, were resolved by 22 weeks. However, brain impairments remained up to one year post-injury, affecting vigilance, attention, and performance in school.

Of concern is the fact that young athletes may not be waiting for full recovery before resuming their sport and other physically demanding activities. Yard and Comstock (2009) studied athletes in 100 nationally representative high schools in the United States. They observed 15% of high school athletes returning to play prematurely according to the Prague guidelines. In football, they observed 15.8% of players who sustained concussions resulting

TABLE 8.6 • **Head Injuries**
Simple and complex concussions and "return to play" parameters

CONCUSSIONS	RETURN-TO-PLAY
SIMPLE	
• Symptoms resolve within 7–10 days • No further symptoms • No follow-up and further intervention required	• No play on the same day and rest until symptoms resolve • Should not be left alone; monitoring for deterioration is necessary • Medical evaluation is required before return to play • Player should train progressively and no resistance training
COMPLEX	
• Symptoms are persistent • Loss of consciousness at time of injury over one minute • Prolonged cognitive impairment • Player suffered multiple concussions or repetitive concussions since original injury • Symptom recurrence with activity • Subspecialty consultation with more extensive testing	• Rehabilitation will be more prolonged • Complex cases should be managed by experienced doctors

Source: Adapted from: Yard, E. D. & Comstock, R. D. (2009). Compliance with return to play guidelines following concussion in US high school athletes, 2005–2008. Brain Injury, 23, 888–898.

CONNECTING WITH CHILDREN

Guidelines for Families, Teachers, and Other Professionals: Preventing Accidents and Injuries

Adult supervision is essential.
Examples

1. Ensure children use age-appropriate equipment and that children ages 2 to 5 and 5 to 12 can play separately.
2. Enforce safety rules, such as no pushing, shoving, or crowding, or inappropriate use of playground equipment.
3. Ensure articles of clothing and accessories that are not safe, such as hood and neck strings, necklaces, purses, and scarves, are removed around playground equipment.

Ensure play environments and equipment are safe.
Examples

1. Check to make sure equipment is well maintained and in good working order.
2. Is equipment anchored safely to the ground?
3. Is there a soft surface for falling? Recommended surface materials include sand, pea gravel, wood chips, mulch, shredded rubber, and rubber mats.

Ensure children wear sport-specific protective gear.
Examples

1. Make sure children wear helmets to protect against head injuries.
2. Use knee and elbow pads to protect limbs.
3. Make sure protective gear is sport-specific and fits properly.

Ensure children are prepared for the demands of playing a sport.
Examples

1. Administer a Pre-participation Exam (PPE) to all children before enrolling them in any sport.
2. Provide children with the proper aerobic conditioning and skill building when they are learning a new sport.
3. Ensure children drink adequate amounts of liquid before and during physical activities.
4. Provide frequent rest periods, especially during hot weather. Refer to the Safe Kids web site for excellent tips on keeping children safe and physically active: www.safekids.org.

Sources: National Program for Playground Safety. Safety tips. Retrieved from http://www.playgroundsafety.org April 26, 2010.

Safe Kids. Preventing injuries at home, at play, and on the way. Retrieved from http://www.safekids.org.

in lost of consciousness returning to play on the same day. Boys were more likely than girls to return to play 1 to 2 days after sustaining a concussion. According to these researchers, "Too many adolescent athletes are failing to comply with recommended return to play guidelines" (p. 888). They recommend sports medicine professionals, parents, coaches, and sports administrators work together to ensure athletes fully recover before returning to play. Those who return prematurely are at risk for the "second impact syndrome," in which athletes sustain a second concussion before the first is healed (Yee, 2007). Secondary injuries can lead to permanent brain injury or fatal brain swelling, even after an apparently minor head trauma.

PREVENTION. Fortunately, many accidents and injuries can be prevented and the potential for seriously negative outcomes diminished. The ***Connecting with Children*** guidelines offer suggestions about ways to increase children's safety and reduce their risk of sustaining serious and permanent injuries, so they can enjoy the benefits of physical activity.

Special Physical Needs

Some children are born with or develop special physical needs. In this chapter we discuss physical disabilities and sensory impairments. Although we introduce these disabilities here, we recognize that these challenges can affect development and learning in the cognitive and social emotional domains as well.

Physical Disabilities

Physical disabilities include orthopedic disorders, such as cerebral palsy and muscular dystrophy, as well as chronic ailments, such as congenital heart disease. Children with physical disabilities have the same basic physical needs as other children (i.e., good nutrition, regular physical activity, and adequate rest). However, they may need special equipment and adaptations to activities and the environment to participate meaningfully and safely with other children.

Adaptations and accommodations should focus on providing necessary support that enables successful participation. However, human development involves a progression from dependence on others to self-care and self-determination, so the goal should be to support children with disabilities toward independence (Robinson & Lieberman, 2004). Parents and adults tend to overprotect children with disabilities, particularly when they perceive participation in activities poses a risk to safety. However, limiting children's opportunities to participate in activities, such as physical education, sports, and recreation, contribute to low societal expectations for individuals with disabilities and the social isolation they often experience. According to Robinson and Lieberman, parents, teachers, and other adults in supervisory roles should allow children to take [calculated] risks and encourage independent choice-making, problem-solving, and goal-setting, which are associated with the development of skills that are critical for leading successful, high-quality lives (see also Deci, Vallerand, Pelletier, & Ryan, 1991).

Children with physical disabilities can have **orthopedic impairments,** which involve the skeletal system (bones, joints, and associated muscles), or **neuromotor impairments,** which involve the central nervous system. In this chapter we focus on orthopedic impairments, specifically cerebral palsy, because these are the most common physical disabilities in children.

Cerebral palsy (CP) is a disorder that affects muscle tone, movement, and motor skills; children with CP have difficulty moving in a coordinated way (KidsHealth, 2009). Other vital functions that also involve motor skills and muscles may be involved with and cause difficulty breathing, controlling bladder and bowel functioning, and eating. The most common cause of CP is lack of oxygen causing brain damage at or before birth. However, CP also can develop during the first 3 to 5 years of a child's life if, for example, a child contracts meningitis or viral encephalitis (American Academy of Family Physicians, 2009). CP can be mild or severe. For example, a child with mild CP may have awkward movements but require very little in the way of adaptations and accommodations. A child who has severe CP may not be able to walk or may have trouble speaking. Some children with CP will require lifelong care and assistance. CP is not degenerative; that is, it does not get worse over time.

There are three types of cerebral palsy:

- **Spastic CP,** the most common type, causes muscles to stiffen and makes movement difficult. It can affect just one side of the body, both legs, or both arms and legs.
- **Athetotic CP** causes uncontrolled, slow body movements and affects the entire body.
- **Ataxic CP** is the least common form and affects balance and coordination.

Some children have what is referred to as a mixed form of CP. They show signs of more than one type.

Often children with CP have additional disabilities, including vision or hearing impairments, speech problems, or developmental or learning disabilities. In school and in other settings, these secondary disabilities may be the greatest cause for concern. However, specialized equipment, such as computers, speech and voice synthesizers, communication boards, and page turners can help children do their work. Exercise and muscle training are critical for these children. Physical and occupational therapy may be part of individualized family or education plans for these children. Crutches, braces, splints, and wheelchairs can help them to move independently. Doctors can prescribe medications to ease muscle stiffness and, in some instances, surgery may be recommended to increase range of motion in arms and legs when muscles or tendons are very stiff. A multidisciplinary team and a coordinated plan can provide a wide range of resources leading to positive development and learning in children with CP and other physical disabilities.

Sensory Impairments

Sensory impairments refer to disabilities involving hearing and vision.

VISUAL IMPAIRMENTS. Most serious vision problems are identified early, but some problems emerge gradually as children develop and experience physiological changes in their eyes. Parents and teachers should attend to signals that children may be having problems seeing. Children who have difficulty seeing often hold books and other objects either very close to or very far from their eyes. They may squint, rub their eyes frequently, or complain that their eyes burn or itch. Their eyes may actually appear swollen or irritated. Children with vision problems may misread material at a distance, describe their vision as being blurred, be very sensitive to light, or hold their heads at an odd angle. They may become irritable when they have to work at a desk or lose interest if they have to follow an activity happening at some distance (Hunt & Marshall, 2002). Adults who notice any of these signals should make a referral to an appropriate professional so that vision can be assessed.

Mild vision problems can be overcome with corrective lenses. However, children with more significant visual impairments probably require special materials and equipment to function optimally. Most of these students have partial or **low vision;** that is, they have some useful vision between 20/70 and 20/200 (on the Snellen scale, where 20/20 is considered normal). For example, a person with 20/70 vision sees at 20 feet (6 meters) what individuals with normal vision see at 70 feet (21.3 meters). An individual with 20/200 vision is considered legally and **educationally blind.** Approximately 1 in 1,000 children in North America are classified as visually impaired (Hutchinson, 2009). About 1 in 3,000 are educationally blind.

In school, special materials and equipment can help students who are visually impaired to learn. For example, large-print books, software that converts printed material to speech or to Braille, personal organizers that have talking appointment books, and variable-speed tape recorders (which allow teachers to make time-compressed tape recordings that can be sped up in a way that changes the rate of speech without changing the voice pitch) can support reading, writing, and learning of content. Special calculators, the abacus, and special measuring devices provide support for carrying out mathematical tasks. The majority of children who are visually impaired are print users. For these children, the quality of the print is often more important than the size, so materials that use distinctive fonts and sharp contrasts (e.g., black text on a white page, matte and not glossy paper) are helpful. Children who are educationally blind may also rely on other senses, such as hearing and touch, to compensate for their disability (Friend & Bursuck, 2009).

Special materials and equipment can help students who have visual impairments to learn. Children with visual impairments may receive instruction about orientation and mobility from a trained teacher as part of their expanded core curriculum.

The arrangement of the physical environment is also an issue for these children. Children with low vision or blindness need to know where things are, so consistency matters. Leave plenty of space for moving around rooms, and make sure to monitor possible obstacles and safety hazards, such as toys in unexpected places and open cabinet doors. If you rearrange a room, give children with visual impairments a chance to learn the new layout and make sure they know what to do in case of fire or other emergencies (Friend & Bursuck, 2009). In school, children with visual impairments may receive instruction about orientation and mobility from a trained teacher as part of their **expanded core curriculum,** which is a body of knowledge and skills that addresses these individuals' unique disability-specific needs (American Foundation for the Blind, 2010). The term **orientation** refers to people's ability to establish their position in relation to their environment. **Mobility** refers to people's ability to move safely and efficiently in their environment. Children with visual impairments may learn to use their residual vision to move around, but other senses, such as touch and feeling, are useful, too. Most likely, children will learn to use a human guide, and some move around with the assistance of a guide dog.

HEARING IMPAIRMENTS. You will hear the term *hearing impaired* used to describe students who have difficulties hearing.

The Deaf community and researchers prefer the terms *deaf* and *hard of hearing*. The incidence of hearing impairment has been declining over the past three decades, but between one and three of every 1,000 children in North America will be born with hearing loss (BC Early Hearing Program, 2008; National Institute on Deafness and Communication Disorders, 2001). When the problem does occur, the consequences for language development and learning can be serious (Hunt & Marshall, 2002). For this reason, many states have implemented newborn screening programs—infants are screened before they even leave the hospital so that hearing impairments can be detected early. Similarly, in British Columbia, Canada, the Provincial Health Services Authority provides for universal hearing screening of infants in their first month. Their goal is to detect problems in babies' first three months and provide amplification to infants who need it. Intervention to support hearing and language development begins by six months. A recent report on the first three years of the program's implementation indicates this agenda is positively influencing the development of children with hearing loss (BC Early Hearing Program, 2008).

Signs of hearing problems are turning one ear toward the speaker, favoring one ear in conversation, or misunderstanding conversation when the speaker's face cannot be seen. Other indications include inability to follow directions, seeming distracted or confused at times, frequently asking people to repeat what they have said, mispronouncing new words or names, and being reluctant to participate in discussions. Take note particularly of children who have frequent earaches, sinus infections, or allergies, as these are associated with hearing loss.

Intervention approaches for children with hearing impairments fall into two categories. Oral approaches involve **speech reading** (also called lip reading) and teaching students to use whatever limited hearing they may have. Manual approaches involve teaching children to communicate using visual languages, such as **sign language or signed English.** Research indicates that children who learn some manual method of communicating perform better in academic subjects and are more socially mature than students who are exposed only to oral methods. Today, the trend is to combine both approaches (Hallahan, Kauffman, & Pullen, 2008).

A third option available to children today is a surgically implanted electronic device called a **cochlear implant** that provides them with a sense of sound. Children with severe to profound sensorineural hearing loss and a functioning auditory nerve are ideal candidates for implantation (Kim, Jeong, Lee, & Kim, 2009). However, implantation is a controversial issue in the Deaf community, whose perspective on hearing impairment is that it is not an impairment at all. From this perspective, people who are deaf are part of a different culture with a different language and the goal should be to help deaf children become bilingual and bicultural, to be able to function effectively in both cultures. You can read more about this interesting debate in the ***Point/Counterpoint*** on the next page.

In the opening casebook for this chapter, we considered the challenges of including a child who moves around in a wheelchair in hiking and other activities at a camp. This is a common challenge for teachers as well as camp directors: How can children with physical disabilities be included in field trips and other outdoor/off site activities? Table 8.7 provides a list of organizations and resources to consult for help with planning such activities. Also, review the ***Connecting with Children*** guidelines in the earlier section on including children with disabilities in sports and other physical activities.

TABLE 8.7 • **Organizations and Resources to Consult for Help with Planning Activities with Children with Physical Disabilities**

http://www.mysummercamps.com/camps/Special_Needs_Camps/Physical_Disabilities/index.html
http://www.familyvillage.wisc.edu/Leisure/camps.html
http://www.campresource.com/summer-camps/special-needs-camps.cfm/physical-disabilitites-camps
http://www.usatechguide.org/techguide.php?vmode=1&catid=405

POINT/COUNTERPOINT: The Controversy over Cochlear Implants

People with moderate to severe hearing loss have been receiving cochlear implants for approximately 30 years. During that time, the technology has improved such that those receiving them typically hear 70–90% of the words spoken to them (Gantz & Tyler, 2010). For those in the hearing world, the controversy over cochlear implants is difficult to understand: How could a device that allows severe and profoundly deaf people to hear sounds be a bad thing? And why wouldn't parents want to give their deaf children the opportunity to live and communicate easily in the hearing world?

POINT ▶ From the perspective of the Deaf community, the focus on cochlear implants as a possible "cure" for deafness is part of a more pervasive problem of viewing deafness as a deficit and something that needs to be fixed when, in fact, many individuals who are deaf or hard of hearing lead very successful and satisfying lives without the benefit of hearing aids or cochlear implants. In particular, the Deaf community cautions parents, who typically make the choice about cochlear implantation for their children. Although they recognize cochlear implants as one technology that can assist hearing, they emphasize that cochlear implants are not a cure for deafness. Cochlear implants won't impart the ability to understand spoken language or guarantee typical speech development. In fact, in pre-lingual children, the concern is that language development will be delayed if children who are deaf do not also have access to a visual language, such as American Sign Language (ASL). The Deaf community asks that parents of deaf children consider a wide range of options, including supporting children's identification with and involvement in the Deaf community, and adopting ASL as a language of communication in their homes.

COCHLEAR IMPLANT

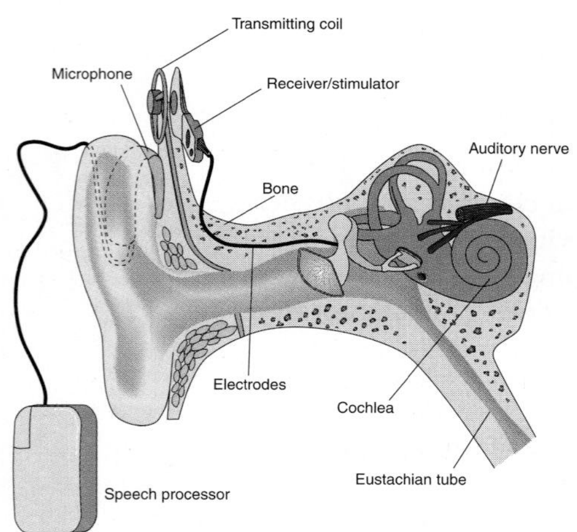

Source: Heyward, Exceptional Children, Figure 9.5 "Internal and external components of the cochlear implant" p. 247, © 2009 Pearson Education, Inc. Reproduced by permission of Pearson Education, Inc.

COUNTERPOINT ▶ Proponents of cochlear implants point out that approximately 90% of children who are deaf have hearing parents who want their children to hear sounds and communicate with them in words. In recent years, research has shown good potential for these outcomes, but only when children receive cochlear implants at an early age (ideally before age 2). Nicholas and Geers (2006) studied the language development of 76 children who received cochlear implants between the ages of 12 and 38 months. They found a positive, statistically significant relationship between early implantation and language proficiency at age 3.5 years—earlier implantation was associated with greater language proficiency. A similar study (Kim et al., 2010) found that children who received cochlear implantation before age 2 reached developmental milestones at ages equivalent to hearing peers and had a higher chance of being successful in inclusive educational settings. Likely, these particularly positive outcomes for young children are due to the plasticity that characterizes brain development at this age and the fact that early childhood is a particularly sensitive period for language development. Therefore, proponents of cochlear implants perceive a need to identify hearing problems and to intervene early with children who are deaf or hard of hearing.

Beyond Either/Or

More and more, the two sides of this issue are finding middle ground. The Deaf community has softened its stance on cochlear implants. The science behind cochlear implants is hard to ignore, but research also supports the value of a cultural connection and learning sign language as an additional language. Today, children who are deaf have an opportunity to belong to both Deaf and hearing communities. Jesse, who chose to have a cochlear implant at age 20, told KPBS reporter, Maureen Cavanaugh, "I am very active in the Deaf community but at the same time, in my [work], I'm very involved in the hearing world, and I'm really thankful to my cochlear implant for that."

Sources: Canadian Association of the Deaf. Position statement on cochlear implants. Retrieved from http://www.cad.ca/en/issues/cochlear_implants.asp.

Cavanaugh, M. & Walsh, N. (2009, November). How the Deaf community is dealing with cochlear implants. Retrieved from http://www.kpbs.org/news/2009/nov/03/how-deaf-community-dealing-cochlear-implants/.

National Association of the Deaf. Position statement on cochlear implants. Retrieved from http://www.nad.org/issues/technology/assistive-listening/cochlear-implants.

▼ SUMMARY AND KEY TERMS

• Body Growth

Children's rate of growth slows during the middle years, and changes in body structures are less dramatic. This slower rate of growth enables gains in motor control and coordination. Building bone density during childhood has important implications for lifelong health, especially for preventing osteoporosis. Bone mass is influenced by heredity, gender, and ethnicity, but diet and exercise are important, too. Calcium is particularly important, as are weight-bearing exercises such as running, walking, dancing, and jumping.

Baby teeth are lost and replaced by a permanent set during the middle years. Like bone health, good oral hygiene deserves attention because it has implications for general health across the lifespan. Children who live in poverty and whose families cannot afford medical/dental insurance are most at risk for experiencing oral diseases. The best way to prevent tooth decay is to floss and brush teeth regularly and to avoid foods that are high in sugar content.

• Brain Development

The brain continues to grow and change during the middle years, but the changes are less dramatic than they were during infancy and the early years. Particularly noteworthy are changes in higher cognitive functions that lead to enhanced self-regulation, including planning, goal-setting, and behavior control. The brain becomes increasingly more organized, leading to improvements in problem-solving, memory, and language comprehension. These changes affect learning. Because the brain shapes and is shaped by cognitive processing activities, children with learning disabilities can learn strategies to help them to compensate for their core processing problems and children with hearing disabilities can learn to process visual information in areas of their brains that typically are responsible for processing auditory stimulation.

• Motor Development

Children's gross and fine motor skills continue to develop during middle childhood. Boys' upper body strength gives them an advantage in activities that involve throwing or lifting, and girls typically are more agile. Physical and athletic abilities become a measure of competence during middle childhood, and are associated with positive self-esteem. Physical activity is critical for good health during childhood and throughout the lifespan. Unfortunately, many children are not active enough to realize these benefits. This is particularly true of girls, adolescents, children with disabilities, children living in urban environments, and children living in low SES communities.

Physical education (PE) is one context in which children engage in physical activities. Positive experiences in PE are associated with increased physical activity outside of school and favorable effects on learning and behavior in school. However, budget cuts and increased pressures to focus on academics have resulted in schools reducing PE schedules and hiring fewer specialist PE teachers. Another way to promote physical activity is through organized sports. Participation in sports can promote persistence, teamwork, humility, and self-control; it also has been linked to the development of social skills and social competence, popularity with peers, and increased self-confidence and self-esteem. Unfortunately, youth sports have become increasingly competitive in recent years, emphasizing year-round training, early specialization, and focusing on winning rather than education and development and having fun.

Children with disabilities are one group that is underrepresented in organized sports and other physical activities, and there continue to be barriers to their participation that have little to do with their disabilities. Experts agree children with disabilities can and should participate in appropriate physical activities. Multidisciplinary teams can support teachers and families to make accommodations to activities to make them safe and enjoyable for these children.

• Health and Well-Being

Good eating habits remain important during middle childhood because children's bodies and brains are continuing to grow. Although parents are primarily responsible for what children eat, children's diets become increasingly difficult to monitor. Children have more opportunities to exercise personal choice as they begin to eat meals outside their homes (e.g., with friends or at school), and they are exposed to more diverse messages about food, not all of them healthy (e.g., through the media). Schools can help children eat well and be healthy by removing foods that are high in fat and sugar from their cafeterias and vending machines and replacing them with healthy choices. Also, they can implement programs and policies that promote healthy eating and an active lifestyle.

Accidents and injuries pose a significant threat to children's health and well-being. Overall, the most common cause of death or serious injury during childhood is involvement in motor vehicle accidents: as a passenger, pedestrian, or adolescent driver. Other common causes of injury and death in children are drowning, injuries from fires and burns, poisoning, and falls. Boys have higher rates of injury and death than girls, a finding that maintains across age groups and ethnicities, in North America and around the world. The burden of injury is unequal across SES, too, with children in poor countries and communities being the most vulnerable.

Most non-vehicle accidents occur in or around children's homes (e.g., at local playgrounds). Often they result from inadequate adult supervision or equipment that is unsafe (e.g., trampolines), not age appropriate, or surfaces are unsafe for falling.

Sports injuries are a growing phenomenon for children and they can lead to serious and permanent disabilities. Overuse and overtraining are two ways in which injuries occur. Experts caution that growing skeletons cannot withstand as much stress as the mature bones of adults. Also, children are more vulnerable to the risks associated with exercising in excessive heat because they sweat less, create more body heat, and acclimatize more slowly to hot weather and climates than adults do. Children engaged in overtraining may experience burnout as a result of physical and emotional stress, missed social opportunities, and disruptions to family life. For these reasons, parents and trainers should maintain realistic expectations and focus on enjoyment and long-term health as reasons for participating in sports. Children should be encouraged to try out a variety of sports in early and middle childhood, specialize only after reaching puberty, and take time to rest and recover from activities.

Head injuries are the most common and potentially serious injuries children suffer. About 20% of head injuries occur during sports participation. Depending on the location and severity of the injury, effects can be temporary or lasting and can impact emotional, behavioral, and cognitive processes as well as physical functioning. Concussions are the most common type of head injury, especially in child and adolescent athletes. They can be simple or complex. The key is allowing for full recovery before allowing children to return to sports and other physical activities. Those who return prematurely are at risk for experiencing second impact syndrome, which can lead to permanent brain injury or fatal brain swelling.

• Special Physical Needs

Children with physical disabilities may need special equipment or adaptations to activities or the environment to participate meaningfully and safely with other children. Adaptations and accommodations should focus on providing necessary supports to ensure successful participation while enabling children to progress from reliance on others to reliance on themselves. Children with disabilities should be encouraged to take risks in supportive environments, so they develop skills that are critical for leading independent and successful lives.

Cerebral palsy (CP) affects muscle tone, movement, and motor skills. It can be mild or severe. Often children with CP have additional disabilities, including sensory impairments and developmental or learning disabilities, which can actually be the primary source of their difficulties in school and other settings. Specialized equipment, such as computers and speech and voice synthesizers can help, and physical and occupational therapy may be part of their individualized family or education plans. Medication and surgery also are options. Ideally, a multidisciplinary team and coordinated plan provide a wide range of resources to support these children's development and learning.

Sensory impairments refer to disabilities involving hearing and vision. Most vision problems are identified early, but problems can emerge as children develop and experience physiological changes in their eyes. Mild vision problems can be overcome with corrective lenses, whereas more significant visual impairments probably will require special materials, equipment, and instruction to function optimally. Efforts are being made to identify children with hearing impairments early. Once children are identified, early intervention is key to supporting language development and learning. Cochlear implants that can help with hearing sounds have been controversial within the Deaf community. Their view is that people who are deaf are part of a unique culture. Today, many individuals who are deaf or hard of hearing participate in both Deaf and hearing communities using assistive technologies as desired and appropriate.

▼ KEY TERMS

ataxic CP (323)
athetotic CP (323)
cerebral palsy (CP) (323)
cochlear implant (325)
concussion (321)
educationally blind (324)
expanded core curriculum (324)
low vision (324)
mobility (324)
neuromotor impairments (323)
orientation (324)
orthopedic impairments (323)
osteoporosis (300)
sign language and signed English (325)
spastic CP (323)
speech reading (325)

▼ THE CASEBOOK

MEETING THE CHALLENGE OF INCLUSION

As the director of Tall Trees Camp, David is preparing for the onslaught of campers who will begin arriving on July 5th, just two weeks away. In particular, he is mulling over ways to include one camper, 10-year-old Jason, who uses a wheelchair. All of the cabins and communal buildings are wheelchair accessible, but most of the grounds surrounding the camp are pretty uneven and the trails are fairly inhospitable to all but those traveling on foot. David is determined, however. The camp prides itself on being inclusive, and inclusion to David means *everyone*. So . . . his job is to figure out how to include a child in a wheelchair in the physical activities of the camp. Soccer and swimming aren't so hard, actually. But hiking and beachcombing, given the rocky shore, will present a bit of a challenge. And what about the overnight hiking and camping trip?

WHAT WOULD THEY DO?

Here is how some professionals in several fields responded:

TRACY MACDONALD—School Counselor
Chesapeake Bay Middle School, Pasadena, Maryland

Collaborating with the family is important and will ensure that Jason has a positive camp experience. The camp director should prepare for this meeting by consulting with other camp directors who have experience working with children in wheelchairs so that he can make practical activity and accommodation suggestions to the family. There should be a discussion of Jason and the family's expectations and the kind of camp experience they desire. It is important for the camp director to get to know the family and how they view Jason's disability. Jason should be given an opportunity to express the kind of camp activities he is looking forward to and what new skills he would like to learn.

The number one concern for any camp director should be safety. The camp director should be focused on providing the least restrictive environment for Jason while taking precautions to keep him safe. Jason should be placed into a camp group that includes children without disabilities so they can learn how to value human differences and have respect for diversity in a recreational setting. Jason's assigned camp counselor should be someone with a compassionate disposition who has experience working with children with disabilities.

AMANDA BOSDECK—8th Grade Math and Science
West De Pere Middle School, De Pere, Wisconsin

Inclusion means everyone in every event. If the camp prides itself on being inclusive, then the first part is to begin renovations on the area. Having wheelchair accessible buildings is not enough; a person like Jason must be able to maneuver in between them to be part of the camp experience. For all of the activities that a person cannot be a part of in the traditional sense due to immobility, adaptations need to be created. For instance, when beachcombing, place planks down that would allow Jason to be in the area and provide him with adjustable tools so he can participate. David should not take activities away from the other campers; rather he should add more variety in order to properly include Jason. If a wheelchair path could not be built in time for Jason this year, then David could use technology to help create a simulated experience of the hiking trail. Campers could be involved in creating streaming videos for these areas and explaining it to Jason as he views them. When designing activities for recreational programs, one should look at how children with different types of disabilities can participate and create a list of ideas on what accommodations need to be made for these children.

JUDY S. PIEPER—Language Arts, Art, and Religion; Grades 6–8
Holy Trinity Junior High, Newport, Kentucky

Parents of children with physical and sensorial differences and disabilities are aware of the limitations to their child regarding access to and participation in planned activities. What inclusion offers is the willingness to identify ways and means to have a child with special needs successfully interact with the class, teacher, or instructor and experience the lesson or event in a positive way to the best of his or her capability. To assist with inclusion, I always rely on the peer buddy system. For example, on a field trip that would include a creek walk or rocky shoreline, the student with the disability can go as far as safely feasible, and the buddy student can bring the activity back to him or her via predetermined tools and supplies. The buddy may scoop up a sample of sand, rock or water in a pail and spend time poring over it with the other student. I have found a protectiveness and willingness among students to help each other, and using peer pairs for inclusion is a natural extension of this altruistic characteristic.

Another inclusion method useful in physically limiting situations is the employment of digital video cameras linked to a monitor with the child who has physical limitations. Technology enables the child to "be there" for the entire visual and audio experience with his or her buddy running the camera for them. When one of his or her classmates or instructors slips and falls with a huge splash, the entire class or group will surely be laughing and will remember that event with many retellings. Not only will the child have experienced the fun, but the event will also be recorded for posterity on the video!

myeducationlab

Now go to MyEducationLab at *www.myeducationlab.com*, where you can:

- Find the instructional objectives for this chapter in the **Study Plan**.
- Take a quiz as a part of the **Study Plan** to self-assess your mastery of chapter content. The program generates an individualized Study Plan based upon your answers to the quiz.
- Complete **Activities and Applications** to assist you in deepening your understanding of important chapter concepts.
- Apply what you have learned through **Building Teaching Skills**, exercises that guide you in trying out skills and strategies you will use in professional practice.

9 COGNITIVE DEVELOPMENT IN MIDDLE CHILDHOOD

THE CASEBOOK

WHAT WOULD YOU DO?

DECISIONS ABOUT INTELLIGENCE TESTING

This is not your favorite time of year. As the only counselor in the middle school, you have come to almost dread the arrival of "the scores." Last week, the school sent out results of the placement test that determines who is eligible for the highly regarded, but selective, gifted and talented program. All students in the school had taken the standardized, paper-and-pencil, group-administered test to determine if they met the selection criteria of an IQ score of 130 or higher. Again this year, the calls, e-mails, and notes are flooding in. Some parents want to meet with you to talk about their child's scores, and especially, as one father put it, "To tell you how smart Jason really is." One mother is incensed because the school cut back on the music program. She had read an article claiming that music lessons raise IQ scores and now is sure that her daughter would have scored better on the test (and been selected for the gifted program) if she had continued in music class. Several other parents have found an online IQ test, given it to their child, and now want the school to admit their children to the gifted program based on the higher online test results. A few of the wealthier parents have hired a psychologist to administer an individual test and want those results used for the admission requirement. Also troubling is your meeting with a girl who was selected for the program, but refuses to be a part of it because her best friends were not selected, and she says, "I'm not really that smart." And

Sisylia Octavia C., Age 12—Indonesia

today, another possible problem caught your eye. As you look down the list, there are very few students of color and virtually no children of recent immigrants. Maybe this whole process is flawed, but the gifted program is admired all over the district. You look at phone messages and e-mails and wonder where to start.

CRITICAL THINKING

- What does an IQ score of 130 mean? Is it a good guide for identifying students for a gifted program? Should other factors besides IQ be considered?
- Does it matter that the test was a paper-and-pencil test administered to the whole group at once, as opposed to an individually administered test?
- Are such tests appropriate for primary grade students? For students whose home language is not the language of the test? For students who live in poverty?
- What is intelligence anyway? What factors influence its development?
- Why might a child ask to be left out of a gifted program?
- Are online tests a good measure of intelligence? Why or why not?

▶ OVERVIEW AND OBJECTIVES

By about age 7, most children can connect an experience in the past with something that is happening to them now, anticipate the future, appreciate causality, use semantic categories, and understand abstract relationships such as *larger, smaller, shorter,* and *taller.* Because of the continuing development of the brain described in the previous chapter, particularly the maturing prefrontal cortex, children become more able to integrate information in order to select an appropriate response. An infant or a toddler reacts impulsively, but the 9-year-old can now remember and reflect. In this chapter we continue the journey. We explore language development, the theories of Piaget, Vygotsky, and the information processing perspective on cognitive development. Next, we look critically at the important concept of intelligence: What is intelligence? How is it assessed? and What influences intelligence? Most children in the middle childhood years are in school, so we consider what is known about the effects of schooling on children's cognitive development. Finally, we examine the child in the digital age: What are the new opportunities and dangers of the Internet world? We will begin with language. By the time you finish this chapter you should be able to:

Objective 9.1 Summarize changes in language development in the middle childhood years, including the roles of social and cultural contexts and how second languages and signed languages develop during this time.

Objective 9.2 Compare and contrast the implications of Piaget's and Vygotsky's theories for cognitive development in the middle childhood years.

Objective 9.3 Examine changes in children's attention, working memory, long-term memory, and metacognition during the middle childhood years.

Objective 9.4 Explain intelligence, how it is measured, what shapes it, and how differences in abilities can be handled productively in schools.

Objective 9.5 Evaluate factors that influence achievement in schools, including how ADHD, learning disabilities, and cultural differences affect children in the middle years, and explore what can to done to help all children achieve.

Objective 9.6 List some possible contributions of digital media to children's cognitive development in the middle years.

OUTLINE ▼

CONTINUING LANGUAGE DEVELOPMENT

Before we explore language development in middle childhood, let's remember what has developed so far. Of course, every child is unique, and different languages vary in their patterns of development, but there are some universals.

Development So Far

In the relatively safe, predictable, and supportive environment of home, the young child usually interacted one-to-one, often with a more competent communicator. The language-learning context had lots of nonverbal cues and the communication partners generally encouraged, corrected, and extended the child's language development (Hulit, Howard, & Fahey, 2011). So, by about age 5 or 6, the majority of children have mastered the basics of their native language. In fact, by the end of kindergarten, healthy children without major language challenges will understand and use most of the essential words in their language, even if they are not accurate about the meanings of some words. In addition, they can create complete sentences and turn statements into questions or into the negative form. For example, they can say:

"I'm going to play with Josh today."
"Am I going to play with Josh today?"
"I'm not playing with Josh today."

But the more complicated forms, such as the passive voice ("The girl was bitten by mosquitoes"), take longer to master. Five-year-olds may still think the girl did the biting because "girl" came first in the sentence; they have not yet mastered the reversible thinking needed to translate from passive to active voice (Piaget, 1970b, 1974).

Children beginning school can talk about the past and the future, as long as the events are fairly recent and concrete, but they lack the cognitive capability to consider hypothetical futures ("What would it be like if you moved to a new town when you started high school?"). If their caregivers have read to them, taught them songs and nursery rhymes, and had conversations about books and pictures, then the children are ready for learning in school. They will understand that speaking, writing, and drawing all are ways to communicate and that symbols on a page are related to sounds, and sounds make up words (Hulit, Howard, & Fahey, 2011).

What remains for the child to accomplish? Well, when the child enters school, the world changes. Not only are there more people but also there are new expectations and opportunities to challenge and support the child's developing cognitive capabilities. In fact, language development is more rapid when children attend school (Hoff, 2006). Let's see what develops now.

Semantics, Vocabulary, Syntax, and Grammar

School-age children continue to learn words and phrases by fast mapping. So when they hear "She text-messaged him the directions," they can quickly figure out that this means something like "She GAVE him directions using a text message" (Casenhiser & Goldberg, 2005). Another way that children's language develops is through discovering new meanings for words they already know, such as learning that a "party" can be an event (a birthday party), a political group (the Green party), or a participant (a party in a legal action). The average 6-year-old has an expressive vocabulary of about 2,600 words and a receptive vocabulary of 20,000 words, counting the multiple meanings of words such as *party*. This number grows to about 50,000 by age 11 (Brice & Brice, 2009). By some estimates, children learn about 10 words a day between the ages of 1 and 18 (Bloom, 2002).

In the early elementary years, some children may have trouble with abstract words such as *justice* or *economy*. They also may not understand the subjunctive case ("If you were a butterfly") because they lack the cognitive ability to reason about things that are not true ("But I'm not a butterfly!"). They may interpret all statements literally and thus misunderstand sarcasm or metaphor. For example, fables are understood concretely—simply as stories instead of as moral lessons. Many children are in their preadolescent years before they are able to distinguish being kidded from being taunted, or before they know that a sarcastic remark is not meant to be taken literally (Anglin, 1993; Bloom, 1998).

HOW DOES VOCABULARY GROW? By using context clues and word knowledge, children figure out what new, unfamiliar words might mean. So, for example, when 9-year-old Valencia encounters the word *wholeheartedly*, she might use her knowledge of the word parts—*heart* is like *spirit* or *enthusiasm* ("put your heart into it"). *Whole* means all, so *wholehearted* is like, "with all your enthusiasm or spirit." And *-ly* makes the word an adverb, so *wholeheartedly* is acting with your whole heart or whole spirit (Anglin, 1993; Hulit et al., 2011). Obviously, the more words children know, the better they are at figuring out new words. In addition, as children develop the cognitive abilities to think abstractly, they can move beyond figuring out the meaning of a word in narrow terms based on a single sentence (about age 5) to abstracting and synthesizing a broader meaning based on many experiences, by about age 11 (Owens, 2008).

Reading is a pathway to learning the meanings of words, and vocabulary development is a foundation for deeper understanding and continued learning. The setting can invite enjoyable reading, as it seems to for these children.

This shift from concrete and personal to abstract and socially shared is apparent in children's definitions of words as well. Young children's definitions often reflect their personal experiences, so 5-year-old Jasmine might tell you that "A bus goes to the store!" Definitions for most words are functional—they describe what the word does: "A dog barks." The definition is concrete and tied to action. Around second grade, children begin to give longer definitions that describe complex relationships: "A bus is big and carries lots of people." As children mature, they give more dictionary-like definitions that include the general category of the word. So by about age 10, children can tell you, "A dog is an animal." By early adolescence, they can add specific characteristics to their definitions ("A dog is a four-legged animal and is a pet"). Here, the child has linked the concept of "dog" to another concept—"pet." Children can define base words like "dog" or "heart" before they can define derived words like "dogged" or "wholeheartedly" (Johnson & Anglin, 1995; Nippold, Hegel, Sohlberg, & Schwarz, 1999).

Children learn new words in their homes, communities, or churches, and from their peers or the media—television, magazines, games, the Internet, and films. Before a child enters school, the major influences on language development are talk, conversation, songs, rhymes, and other forms of spoken language. With school come powerful new influences—direct teaching of vocabulary and the written word. Children who read often and are skillful readers have larger vocabularies than children who are poorer readers. And children who have larger vocabularies are better at reading comprehension, so reading and vocabulary development are closely tied. The more words children know and the earlier they know them, the better they are at learning more words and learning from reading (Hirsh, Morrison, Gaset, & Carnicer, 2003).

At every age, children from lower SES families tend to hear fewer words at home and they know fewer words than children of the same age from higher SES families—only half as many words by some accounts (Hart & Risley, 1995; Hoff, 2006). So children in poverty are disadvantaged both in learning *to read* and in learning *from reading*. Direct teaching can make a difference. Isabel Beck and Margaret McKeown (2007) used extensive instruction and practice to teach sophisticated words to kindergarten and first grade students from low-income families. By reading stories that included the words, using context, defining the words, having students practice using the words, assessing, and reteaching, the teachers helped these young students learn words like *feast, exhausted, cautiously, menacing, exquisite*, and *argumentative*.

ORGANIZING ALL THOSE WORDS. With increased cognitive development, children not only learn and remember more words but also apply their increasing abilities to organize the words they know. They learn that words can be organized in sequences (*one, two, three*) and in hierarchies (*big, bigger, biggest*), for example. Two main strategies help with this organization: chunking and the syntagmatic-paradigmatic shift.

Children organize their words into categories or chunks. The process is cleverly called *chunking*. For young children, these chunks can be large and undifferentiated, so the *food* category might include fried chicken, pizza, ice cream, oatmeal, popcorn, M&Ms, apples, and so on. As children develop cognitively, these large categories are divided into subcategories: meats, desserts, fruits, breakfast foods, and so on. Chunking also helps children make sense of words that sound alike such as *not* and *knot*. *Knot* gets chunked with nouns and *not* is organized with other negating words such as *none* or *never* (Hulit et al., 2011).

A second strategy involves organizing words based on associations or connections. If you ask preschool children what comes to mind when you say "baby," they might say "cries" or "bottle"—words that come next in a sentence. So the association or connection is syntactic (*syntagmatic*)—having to do with the order of words. Ask an older child what comes to mind when you say "baby" and you are more likely to get connections based on semantics or meanings such as "infant," "child," "adult," or "family." The shift to meaning-based categories is a shift to *paradigmatic* (category) associations. Organizing words around meanings reflects the developing child's ability to think abstractly (Owens, 2008). This change from organizing words by what might come next (syntagmatic associations) to organizing by meaning (paradigmatic associations) is called the **syntagmatic-paradigmatic shift.**

As language develops and children expand their vocabularies, finding a word when they need it becomes a more complex task. Organization helps here, too. If words are organized into chunks, these categories can be used to find the needed word, so if Shannon is trying to remember the word for *asparagus*, searching the *vegetables* category may help. Also, as they develop cognitively, children are more able to use strategies, such as auditory or visual cues to retrieve words (Owens, 2008).

HAVING FUN WITH WORDS. The language of young children can be funny and seem playful, as when one researcher's 4-year-old daughter ran outside naked and proclaimed, "Look, Daddy, my bottom is barefootin!" The girl was not trying to use creative, metaphorical language; she was simply using the language she had to describe the situation (Hulit et al., 2011, p. 249). But as language and knowledge of word meanings develop, children begin to intentionally play with language. By kindergarten, about one-fourth of children's language involves playing with words (Ely & McCabe, 1994). Early playfulness often involves the sounds of words, so you might hear a young child proclaim that okra is, "Icky, sticky, yicky!" but by ages 6 or 7, children's word play is more likely to involve word meanings, puns, and double meanings. Children in the middle years enjoy language games and jokes that play on words. With an appreciation of double meanings, especially the multiple meanings of words that sound alike, children can laugh at riddles:

What is black and white and red (read) all over? A newspaper.
What house has the least weight? A lighthouse.
Why is a river so rich? Because it has two banks.
How many bees are there in a hive? None, the letter "b" is not in the word "hive."

During the middle years, another kind of playful language usage develops: Children learn to use figurative language such as similes ("he's as strong as a horse"), metaphors ("he's a horse"), and idioms ("I'm so hungry, I could eat a horse"). As with many aspects of language, children can *understand* the meaning of the metaphor or the idiom before they will *use* these language forms, and children who are better readers will learn idioms faster (Nippold, Moran, & Schwartz, 2001). Understanding idioms is one of the things that makes learning a second language more difficult. For example, consider what you would think about these idioms if you were just learning the English language:

Does the cat have your tongue?	Eat your heart out!
I cross my heart and hope to die.	You are really a bookworm.

Here are some Spanish idioms and the English idioms that are similar:

Tener más lana que un borrego. *Translation*: *To have more wool than a lamb*. English idiom: To have money to burn.
Por un pelito de rana. *Translation*: *By a little hair of the frog*. English idiom: It was a close shave.

GRAMMAR AND SYNTAX. Early on, children master the basics of syntax (word order) in their native language. But some syntactical structures take time to learn. For example, Carol

Chomsky (1969) found that most preschool children think these two sentences mean the same thing: "Jose promised Alfonzo to clean the house" and "Jose told Alfonzo to clean the house." Younger children think Alfonzo is the one doing the cleaning in both cases—the name closer to the verb is assumed to do the action. As children develop cognitively, by about age 8, they can hold the entire sentence in memory and focus on meaning, not just the order of the words, so they understand who is actually doing the cleaning in these sentences. Other accomplishments during elementary school include first understanding and then using complex grammatical structures such as extra clauses, qualifiers, and conjunctions (Owens, 2008).

Pragmatics and Metalinguistic Development

Pragmatics involves the appropriate use of language to communicate. During the middle years, children show dramatic changes in their pragmatic skills, having conversations, telling stories, and generally fitting their language to each situation. These accomplishments require adjusting word choice or sentence complexity to match the listener's abilities (speaking in short, simple statements to a young child, for example), repairing breakdowns in communications, and comprehending subtle nonverbal or intonational cues to "hear" what someone is trying to say. One capability that supports these accomplishments is the child's developing social perspective-taking ability, described in Chapters 7 and 10. Children who can view things through another person's perspective are better at having conversations and telling stories.

CONVERSATIONS. To use language appropriately, children must learn the rules of turn taking in conversation. In later elementary school, children's communications start to sound like conversations. Contributions are usually relevant and on the same topic. Children listen to each other, so arguments become possible. As they mature, older children are more able to judge if their communications are clear to their audience. They learn how to diagnose why there was a breakdown and they have more ways to repair the conversation. The topics of conversations can be more abstract as children's cognitive capabilities develop, so they can discuss fairness and justice, obligations, or preferences.

By age 6 or so, children understand and use *now, so*, and *then* (called **conjunctives** because they are usually followed by information that is consistent with the overall message), but they are about 12 before they can use *however, therefore, although*, or *anyway*. These are **disjunctives**—they prepare the listener for information that is inconsistent or out of keeping with previous statements. Disjunctives are a more complex form than conjunctives. Also, by middle childhood, students understand that an observation also can be a hint or a command, as in "I see you have not eaten your broccoli yet." By later childhood, they become very adept at varying their language style to fit the situation. So they can talk to their peers in a form of slang that makes little sense to adults, but that marks the children as members of a group. Yet these same students can speak politely to adults (especially when making requests) and write persuasively about a topic in history. Interactions with adults, and especially with peers who challenge unclear messages, help develop these skills (Hulit et al., 2011).

NARRATIVES. Narratives are stories, often about personal experiences from the past. Whereas 2-year-olds may tell a story as a single statement or as a set of unrelated sentences called *heaps* (piles of words and clauses), a 4-year-old's story is longer, but it often jumps from one topic to another, so it is called a *leapfrog narrative* (Peterson & McCabe, 1983). These narratives tend to focus on the child's immediate situation—so the language is *contextualized*—supported by the people, places, and events in the child's life. To tell more mature stories about other people or places requires *decontextualized language*—talk about people, events, concepts, and other things that are not part of the person's immediate context (Snow, 1991). Generally, the people listening to the story were not participants in the events of the story, so the child must take the listeners' knowledge and perspective into account. In addition, these more mature stories require organization. Rather than the *heaps* or *leaps* of preschoolers' statements, the narratives of middle childhood have main characters, settings, and plots. As children mature cognitively, plots become more defined, the problems presented are clearer, and the details given are not superfluous, but are important for the resolution of the problem. Stories begin to include characters' thoughts, feelings, and motivations, as well as depictions of psychological and physical causes for the events and outcomes described. All of these changes in narratives require increased cognitive development and social perspective-taking skills (Owens, 2008).

Narratives, particularly personal chronicles about the life experiences of children, are dependent on culture. For example, Japanese children tell haiku-like stories, connected by a theme and not necessarily in time order. The stories of some African American children are similar in that they connect several different events around a common theme. Latino/Latina children's stories often center on social relationships, particularly about their families (Ely, 1997; McCabe, 1996; Minami, 2001). Caregivers and teachers need to be aware of these cultural differences in narrative style. For example, a study done years ago found that the home conversation style of Hawaiian children is to chime in with contributions to a story. In school, however, this overlapping style was viewed as "interrupting." When the teachers in one school learned about these differences and made reading groups more like the students' home conversation groups, the young Hawaiian children improved in reading (Au, 1980; Tharp, 1989).

METALINGUISTIC AWARENESS. Around the age of 5, children begin to develop **metalinguistic awareness.** This means their understanding about language and how it works becomes explicit: They can use language to describe language because they have knowledge about language itself. As young children, they used language to communicate; their focus was on the content or meaning of language, not on the process of language. As they mature cognitively, children are able to consider two things at once, both the meaning they are trying to convey and the correctness of the language form. Is the verb tense right? Should the subject of the sentence be plural or singular (Purcell-Gates, 2001)? Now the children are ready to study and extend the rules that have been implicit—understood but not consciously expressed. For children in countries with public educational systems, metalinguistic awareness increases because language is a subject of study in schools.

Children and adults in every culture tell stories about personal life events, but the structure of the stories and even the way the listeners engage varies. In some cultures such as the native Hawaiian, listeners chime in to add to the story and elaborate.

Difference and Diversity in Language Development

Language develops in social and cultural contexts, so there are many individual and group differences (Hoff, 2006). Here, we will examine variety in spoken language in the form of dialects and genderlects, as well as in speaking different languages—bilingualism and signed languages.

DIALECTS. When you ask for a carbonated beverage, do you request *a soft drink, soda, coke*, or *pop*? When your textbook author, Anita, moved from New Jersey to Ohio, a colleague who had grown up in Columbus, Ohio said, "You are going to have to learn to speak Midwestern and ask for a "*bottlapop*." Different regions have different ways of speaking—both in their accents and in their word usage.

Eugene Garcia (2002) defines a **dialect** as "a regional variation of language characterized by distinct grammar, vocabulary, and pronunciation" (p. 218). The dialect is part of the group's collective identity. Actually, every person reading this book speaks at least one dialect, maybe more. The English language has several dialects, for example Australian, Canadian, British, and American. Within each of these dialects are variations. A few examples for American English are Southern, Bostonian, Cajun, and African American English (Garcia, 2002).

Dialects differ in their rules about pronunciation, grammar, and vocabulary, but it is important to remember that these differences are not errors. Each dialect is logical, complex, and rule-governed. An example of this is the use of the double negative (Brice & Brice, 2009). In many versions of American English, the double negative construction, such as "I don't have no more," is incorrect. But in many dialects such as some varieties of African American English and in other languages (for instance, Russian, French, Spanish, and Hungarian), the double negative is part of the grammatical rules. To say "I don't want anything" in Spanish, you must literally say, "I don't want nothing," or "No quiero nada." Table 9.1 gives some other examples of dialect differences.

DIALECTS AND CARING FOR CHILDREN. What does all of this mean for adults working with children? How can they cope with dialect differences? First, they can be sensitive to their own possible negative stereotypes about children who speak a different dialect; remember, dialects are differences, not deficits. Second, adults can ensure comprehension by repeating instructions using different words. Teachers can ask other students to paraphrase instructions or give examples. The best teaching approach seems to be to focus on understanding the children and accepting their language as a valid and correct system, but to teach the formal form of the language that is used in work settings and writing so that the students will have access to a range of opportunities. Lisa Delpit (1995) describes Martha Demientieff, a Native Alaskan teacher of Athabaskan children in a small village. The teacher's goal is for her students to become fluent in both their dialect, which she calls "Heritage English," and the "Formal English" of employers and others outside the village. She explains to her students that people outside the village will judge them by the way they talk and write. She goes on to say:

> We're going to learn two ways to say things. One will be our Heritage way. The other will be Formal English. Then when we go to get jobs, we'll be able to talk like those people who only know and can only listen to one way. Maybe after we get the jobs we can help them to learn how it feels to have another language, like ours, that feels so good. (p. 41)

Moving between two speech forms is called **code-switching**—something we all have learned to do. Sometimes the code is formal speech for professional communication. Or the code is informal for talk among friends and family. At other times, the codes are different dialects. Even young children recognize variations in codes. Lisa Delpit (1995) describes the reaction of one of her first grade students to her very first reading lesson. After she carefully recited the memorized introduction from the teacher's manual, a student raised his hand and asked, "Teacher, how come you talkin' like a white person? You talkin' just like my momma talk when she get on the phone."

Learning the alternative version of a language is easy for most children, as long as they have good models, clear instruction, and opportunities for authentic practice.

TABLE 9.1 • **A Few Examples of Dialect Differences in African American English and Spanish Influenced English**

AREA OF LANGUAGE	STANDARD ENGLISH	AFRICAN AMERICAN ENGLISH
Sounds: Final consonants dropped	hand, picked	han, pick
Noun plurals	Two puppies	Two puppy
Noun possessives	Mama's house	Mama house
Past tense	John came.	John come.
Use of *being* verb	John is sick.	John sick.
Use of *bin* for remote past	She has been running for a long time.	She bin running.
Multiple negation	I don't ever have any problems.	I don't never have no problems.
AREA OF LANGUAGE	**STANDARD ENGLISH**	**SPANISH INFLUENCED ENGLISH**
Sounds: Alternate *ch* and *sh* sounds	Chair, show	Share, chow
Sounds: Final consonants dropped	Start, least	Star, leas
Reflexive pronouns	Himself, themselves	Hisself, theirselves
Borrow for *lend*	Lend me a pencil.	Borrow me a pencil.
Barely for *recently*	They recently graduated from high school.	They barely graduated from high school.
Multiple negation	I don't have any pain.	I don't have no pain.
Using words from Spanish	15-year-old girl's coming out party	quinceñera

Source: Adapted from Brice, A. E., & Brice, R. G. (2009). Language development: Monolingual and bilingual acquisitions, *pp. 317–319. Reproduced by permission of Pearson Education, Inc.*

GENDERLECTS. If you had to guess what **genderlects** are, based on what you know about dia*lects*, you probably would figure out that genderlects are different ways of talking for males and females. There are some small differences between boys and girls—girls tend to be slightly more talkative and affiliative in their speech (*affiliative speech* is talk intended to establish and maintain relationships). But much of the research has been conducted with white, middle-class children and results do not necessarily hold for other groups and cultures (Leaper & Smith, 2004). For example, some research reports that girls are more likely to cooperate and to talk about caring, whereas boys are more competitive and talk about rights and justice. But Leaper & Smith (2004) found that African American girls were just as likely as African American boys to compete and talk about their rights in conversations.

As with most aspects of language, there are cultural differences in genderlects. Interrupting is a good example. In America, boys interrupt more often than girls, but in Africa, the Caribbean, South America, and Eastern Europe, females interrupt males much more often than they do in America. And in Thailand, Hawaii, Japan, and Antigua, the style of speaking for boys and girls is overlapping—these are not interruptions but cooperative turn taking (Owens, 2008).

BILINGUALISM IN THE MIDDLE YEARS. You may remember from previous chapters that in some states almost one-fourth of all students speak a first language other than English—usually Spanish (Gersten, 1996). Ironically, by the time many of these children have mastered a new language and let their home language deteriorate, they reach secondary school and are encouraged to "learn a second language." Perhaps the goals of the educational system should be the development of *all students* as balanced bilinguals. The United States is "one of the few countries in the world that takes pride in the fact that we speak only one language" (Noguera, 2005, p. 13). There are a number of misconceptions about becoming bilingual. Table 9.2 summarizes a few of these taken from Brice (2002).

Proficiency in a second language has two separate aspects: face-to-face communication (known as basic or *contextualized* language) and academic uses of language such as reading texts and doing grammar exercises (known as *academic language*) (Filmore & Snow, 2000; Garcia, 2002). It takes children about two to three years in a good-quality program for **English Language Learners (ELLs)** to be able to communicate face to face in a second language, but mastering academic language skills such as reading texts in the new language takes five to seven years. So children who seem to "know" a second language in conversations may still have great difficulty with complex schoolwork in that language (Bialystok, 2001).

Even though the advantages of bilingualism described in Chapter 6 seem clear (increased cognitive abilities in concept formation, creativity, theory of mind, cognitive flexibility, and metalinguistic awareness), many children and adults are losing their **heritage language:** They experience *subtractive bilingualism.* In a large survey of eighth and ninth grade first- and second-generation immigrant students in Miami and San Diego, Portes and Hao (1998) found that only 16% had retained the ability to speak their heritage language well. And 72% said they preferred to speak English. The languages of Native Americans are disappearing as well. Only about one-third still exist, and 9 out of 10 of those are no longer spoken by the children (Krauss, 1992).

TABLE 9.2 • **Myths and Misconceptions about Being Bilingual**

In the following table, L1 means the original language and L2 means the second language.

MYTH	TRUTH
Learning a second language (L2) takes little time and effort.	Learning English as a second language takes 2–3 years for oral and 5–7 years for academic language use.
All language skills (listening, speaking, reading, writing) transfer from L1 to L2.	Reading is the skill that transfers most readily.
Code-switching is an indication of a language disorder.	Code-switching indicates high-level language skills in both L1 and L2.
All bilinguals easily maintain both languages.	It takes great effort and attention to maintain high-level skills in both languages.
Children do not lose their first language.	Loss of L1 and underdevelopment of L2 are problems for second language learners (semilingual in L1 and L2).
Exposure to English is sufficient for L2 learning.	To learn L2, students need to have a reason to communicate, access to English speakers, interaction, support, feedback, and time.
To learn English, students' parents need to speak only English at home.	Children need to use both languages in many contexts.
Reading in L1 is detrimental to learning English.	Literacy-rich environments in either L1 or L2 support development of necessary prereading skills.
Language disorders must be identified by tests in English.	Children must be tested in both L1 and L2 to determine language disorders.

Source: Brice, The Hispanic Child, *Table 4.3 "Myths About Bilingual Students" pp. 45–46, 2002. Reproduced by permission of Pearson Education, Inc.*

SECOND LANGUAGE LEARNING. What if you didn't learn two languages as you were growing up? When and how should you learn a second language? It is a misconception that young children learn a second language faster than adolescents or adults. In fact, older children go through the stages of language learning faster than young children. Adults have more learning strategies and greater knowledge of language in general to bring to bear in mastering a second language (Brice & Brice, 2009; Diaz-Rico & Weed, 2002). Age is a factor in learning language, but "not because of any critical period that limits the possibility of language learning by adults" (Marinova-Todd, Marshall, & Snow, 2000, p. 28).

There appears, however, to be a critical period for learning accurate language *pronunciation*. The earlier people learn a second language, the more their pronunciation is near-native. After adolescence it is difficult to learn a new language without speaking with an accent (Brice & Brice, 2009). Even overhearing a language as a child, without actually learning the language, can improve later learning. After studying college students who were learning Spanish, Terry Au and colleagues concluded that "Although waiting until adulthood to learn a language almost guarantees a bad accent, having overheard the target language during childhood seems to lessen this predicament substantially" (Au, Knightly, Jun, & Oh, 2002, p. 242). So the best time to teach a second language probably is during early or middle childhood, but the best time to acquire two languages on your own through exposure (and to learn native pronunciation for both languages) is early childhood.

SIGNED LANGUAGES. There are a number of parallels between spoken languages and the many signed languages used around the world, such as American Sign Language (ASL), Signed English (USA, Ireland, New Zealand, Australia, Great Britain), Lingua de Signos Nicaraguense (Nicaraguan Sign Language), Warlpiri Sign Language (Australia Aboriginal), and Langue des Signes Quebecoise (LSQ) or Quebec Sign Language. Each of these languages is distinct and not simply a derived version of a spoken language. For example, people using Quebec Sign Language and French Sign Language cannot understand each other, even though the French spoken language is common to both countries.

Both spoken and signed languages have large vocabularies and complex grammars. Laura Ann Petitto and Iugio Kovelman (2003) suggest that the same mechanisms for language acquisition are used for both spoken and signed languages. In addition, the milestones for signed language are the same as for spoken language. For example, children "say" their first words at about the same time, around 12 months, with both spoken and signed languages (Bloom, 2002). In fact, research with children learning a signed and a spoken language from infancy demonstrates that "being exposed to two languages from birth—and, in particular, being exposed to a signed and a spoken language from birth—does not cause a child to be language delayed or confused" (Petittto & Kovelman, 2003, p. 16). As with two spoken languages, children can become balanced bilinguals in a spoken and a signed language.

In the 1970s when Nicaragua established its first school for the deaf, the students invented their own sign language to communicate. Today that language has developed to become Lingua de Signos Nicaraguense (Nicaraguan Sign Language).

In the 1970s, language researchers were able to study the birth of a new socially shared signed language when Nicaragua established its first school for the deaf. The students came using their own unique invented sign languages. Over the years, a new language emerged that was based on the students' own sign languages. As the children developed the new Lingua de Signos Nicaraguense (Nicaraguan Sign Language), it became more systematic. The vocabulary expanded and the grammar grew more complex. New students learned the developing Nicaraguan Sign Language as their native language (Hoff, 2006; Senghaus & Coppola, 2001).

Language development in the school years reflects and supports the cognitive changes that are taking place. We turn to those changes now.

PIAGET AND VYGOTSKY

During the middle years, children add to their conceptual tool kit. They are more able to think logically and connect present to past and future. Piaget and Vygotsky explain these developments.

Piaget's Concrete Operational Stage

You may remember 5-year-old Amaya in Chapter 6, who thought that when water was poured from a short, fat glass into a tall, thin glass the quantity of water was greater in the tall glass because it reached a higher level. She was fooled by appearances and had difficulty taking several variables into account at the same time. Children like Amaya (roughly ages 2 to 6 or 7) are considered *preoperational* because they lack cognitive *operations*—actions that are carried out and reversed mentally. But as Amaya is able to integrate the past with the present, over time, all the assimilations and accommodations she has made in thinking in specific situations will be generalized into a shift that emphasizes deeper, more enduring qualities over surface appearances, and she will master **concrete operations** (Kagan & Herschkowitz, 2005; Siegler & Alibali, 2005).

The basic characteristics of this stage are the recognition of the logical stability of the physical world, the realization that elements can be changed or transformed and still conserve many of their original characteristics, and the understanding that these changes can be reversed. We will examine several accomplishments of this period, including conservation, classification, and seriation.

CONSERVATION. Look at Figure 9.1 to see examples of the different tasks given to children to assess conservation and the approximate age ranges at which most children can solve these problems. **Conservation** is the understanding that quantities such as number, weight, volume, or area stay the same even when their appearances change. According to Piaget, the ability to solve conservation problems depends on an understanding of three basic aspects of reasoning: identity, compensation, and reversibility. With a complete mastery of **identity,** the child knows that if nothing is added or taken away, the material remains the same. With an understanding of **compensation,** the child knows that an apparent change in one direction can be compensated for by a change in another direction. That is, if the glass is narrower, the liquid will rise higher in the glass. And with an understanding of **reversibility,** the child can mentally cancel out the change that has been made. With the ability to conserve, the child is able to mentally represent and reverse transformations. The preoperational child could mentally represent static states, but not changing states. By the way, Amaya apparently knew it was the same water, so she demonstrated identity, but she lacked compensation and reversibility, thus at age 5 she was moving toward, but not yet grasping, conservation.

Another important operation mastered at this stage is **classification.** Classification depends on a child's abilities to focus on a single characteristic of objects in a set (for example, color) and group the objects according to that characteristic. More advanced classification at this stage involves recognizing that one class fits into another. A city can be in a particular state or province and also in a particular country. As children apply this advanced classification to locations, they often become fascinated with "complete" addresses, similar to the line from the Thornton Wilder play, *Our Town*: "Jane Crofut; The Crofut Farm; Grover's Corners; Sutton County; New Hampshire; United States of America; Continent of North America; Western Hemisphere; the Earth; the Solar System; the Universe; the Mind of God."

Classification is also related to *reversibility*. The ability to reverse a process mentally allows the concrete operational child to see that there is more than one way to classify a group of objects. The child understands, for example, that coins can be classified by date, then reclassified by value, or by the country of origin; or buttons can be sorted into the

FIGURE 9.1

DIFFERENT TASKS USED TO ASSESS CONSERVATION IN CHILDREN

	Suppose you start with this	➡	Then you change the situation to this	➡	The question you would ask a child is
(a) conservation of mass	A B	Roll out clay ball B	A B		Which is bigger, A or B?
(b) conservation of weight	A B	Roll out clay ball B	A B		Which will weigh more, A or B?
(c) conservation of volume	A B	Take clay ball out of water and roll out clay ball B	A B		When I put the clay back into the water beakers, in which beaker will the water be higher?
(d) conservation of continuous quantity	A B C	Pour water in beaker A into beaker C	A B C		Which beaker has more liquid, B or C?
(e) conservation of number	A B	Break candy bar B into pieces	A B		Which is more candy? A or B

round red ones, round white ones, and square white ones—using two characteristics at once to classify. With classification and reversibility, children can organize and reorganize their collections of coins, insects, trading cards, fossils, music, or comic books.

Seriation is the process of making an orderly arrangement from large to small or vice versa. Preoperational thinking might seriate through trial and error, but concrete operational thinking can mentally plan the series. This understanding of sequential relationships permits a student to construct a logical series in which $A < B < C$ (A is less than B is less than C) and so on. Around age 7, as long as they are handling concrete objects such as sticks or blocks, children understand the principle of *transitivity*—if stick A is shorter than stick B and B is shorter than C, then A must be shorter than C too. With an understanding of transitivity, a child can grasp the notion that B can be *longer* than A, but still *shorter* than C. Preoperational children cannot detect and explain these relationships and patterns: How can stick B be longer and shorter at the same time? But ask a hypothetical question, "If Juan is shorter than Jacob, and Jacob is shorter than Luis, who is the shortest?" and concrete thinkers might have trouble—especially if they know a tall person named Juan.

CONNECTING WITH CHILDREN

Guidelines for Teachers: Fostering Concrete Operational Thinking

Use concrete props and visual aids, especially when dealing with sophisticated material.

Examples

1. Use time lines in history and three-dimensional models in science.
2. Use diagrams to illustrate hierarchical relationships such as branches of government and the agencies under each branch.

Continue to give students a chance to manipulate and test objects.

Examples

1. Set up simple scientific experiments such as the following involving the relationship between fire and oxygen. What happens to a flame when you blow on it from a distance? (If you don't blow it out, the flame gets larger briefly, because it has more oxygen to burn.) What happens when you cover the flame with a jar?
2. Have students make candles by dipping wicks in wax, weave cloth on a simple loom, bake bread, set type by hand, or do other craft work that illustrates the daily occupations of people in the colonial period.
3. Give students slips of paper with individual sentences written on each paper and ask the students to group the sentences into paragraphs.

Use familiar examples to explain more complex ideas.

Examples

1. Compare children's lives with those of characters in a story. After reading *Island of the Blue Dolphins* (the true story of a girl who grew up alone on a deserted island), ask "Have you ever had to stay alone for a long time? How did you feel?"
2. Explain the concept of area by having children measure two rooms in the house that are different sizes.
3. Compare the systems of the human body to other kinds of systems: the brain to a computer, the heart to a pump.

With the abilities to handle operations such as conservation, classification, seriation, and transitivity, the child at the concrete operational stage has finally developed a complete and very logical system of thinking—one that can represent changes and transformations. This system of thinking, however, is still tied to experiences and physical reality. The logic is based on *concrete* situations that can be organized, classified, or manipulated. Thus, children at this stage can imagine several different arrangements for the furniture in their rooms before they act. They do not have to solve the problem strictly through trial and error by actually moving the furniture.

In caring for children, knowledge of concrete operational thinking will be helpful (see the ***Connecting with Children*** guidelines for teachers).

LIMITATIONS OF CONCRETE OPERATIONAL THINKING. Even though it is logical, concrete operational thinking is not very good for reasoning about hypothetical problems that involve the coordination of many factors at once, such as how many different combinations are possible in a set or how variables might interact in a scientific experiment. Children who think at the concrete operational level also have difficulties with hypothetical and counter-to-reality thinking, such as "How would your life be different if there were only 2 hours of dark at night?" Thinking about hypotheticals and multiple variables is difficult for children at the concrete operational stage.

LIMITATIONS OF PIAGET'S THEORIES. As we saw in Chapter 6, some researchers believe Piaget's theory underestimates children's abilities. The theory does not explain how children in the middle years can perform at an advanced level in certain areas in which they have highly developed knowledge and expertise. An expert 9-year-old chess player may think hypothetically about chess moves, whereas a novice 20-year-old player may have to resort to more concrete strategies to plan and remember moves (Siegler, 1998). Children have the ability to think abstractly in areas in which they have extensive knowledge.

In addition, Piaget's theory overlooks the influence of the task itself and the cultural context in which the task is accomplished (Meadows, 2006). For example, children who seem to lack the concrete operational thinking necessary to conserve liquids when asked in the usual Piagetian way demonstrate they can conserve when the task is explicit and fits their cultural experience. Working with children in Brazil, Roazzi and Bryant (1997) found that many 5-, 6-, 7-, and 8-year-olds could answer conservation of liquid questions correctly if the tasks were in the context of selling lemonade and *measuring* out equal amounts. Children in the study could "sell" 4 ladles full of lemonade to the experimenter and to a friend and know that the amounts and the costs should be the same, regardless of the size or shape of the glasses. Roazzi and Bryant suggest that children may answer the usual conservation questions wrong because they assume that the experimenters expect a different answer—why else would the experimenter pour the liquid into a different glass and ask, "Are the amounts the same now?" But when the experimenter is explicit about getting the quantities the same, and has children measure out, then the children know the amount is the same in the different shaped glasses.

When a culture or context emphasizes a cognitive ability, children growing up in that culture tend to acquire the ability sooner. In another example that compared Chinese first, third, and fifth grade students with American students in the same grades, the Chinese students mastered a Piagetian task that involved distance, time, and speed relationships about two years ahead of American students. The Chinese education system puts more emphasis on math and science in the early grades (Zhou, Peverly, Beohm, & Chongde, 2001).

As we have seen in previous chapters, Vygotsky's theory places the developing child in cultural and historic contexts.

Vygotsky: Contexts for Learning and Development

You may remember from previous chapters that Vygotsky believed cognitive development occurs through the child's conversations and interactions with more capable members of the culture—adults or more able peers. Children need to grapple with problems in their **zone of proximal development,** the area between their current development level—where the child can solve problems independently—and the level of development that the child could achieve with support from others. As they grapple with problems, children need the *scaffolding* provided by interaction with adults such as teachers or more capable peers. Here is a good definition of scaffolding in teaching that emphasizes the knowledge that both teacher and child bring—both are experts on something: "Scaffolding is a powerful conception of teaching and learning in which teachers and students create meaningful connections between teachers' cultural knowledge and the everyday experience and knowledge of the student"(McCaslin & Hickey, 2001, p. 137). In Western cultures, this guidance tends to use language, but in some cultures, observing a skilled performance with little talk guides the child's learning (Rogoff, 1990).

There are several applications of Vygotsky's theory with children in the middle years. We will look at assisted learning, instructional conversations, and building on the child's funds of cultural knowledge.

ASSISTED LEARNING. Assisted learning, or guided participation, requires the scaffolding described above—giving information, prompts, reminders, and encouragement at the right time and in the right amounts, and then gradually allowing the children to do more and more on their own. In schools, teachers can assist learning by adapting materials or problems to students' current levels; demonstrating skills or thought processes; walking students through the steps of a complicated problem; doing part of the problem (for example, in algebra, the students set up the equation and the teacher does the calculations or vice versa); giving detailed feedback and allowing revisions; or asking questions that refocus students' attention (Rosenshine & Meister, 1992). Look at Table 9.3 on the next page for examples of strategies that can be used in any class.

INSTRUCTIONAL CONVERSATIONS. Here is a segment of an **instructional conversation** from a literature group in a bilingual third grade classroom (Moll & Whitmore, 1993). The example is *instructional* because it is designed to promote learning, but it is a *conversation,* not a lecture or traditional discussion. The conversation shows how the participants mediate each other's learning through dialogue about a shared experience.

TABLE 9.3 • **Assisted Learning: Strategies to Scaffold Complex Learning**

• **Procedural facilitators.** These provide a "scaffold" to help students learn implicit skills. For example, a teacher might encourage students to use "signal words" such as *who, what, where, when, why,* and *how* to generate questions after reading a passage.
• **Modeling use of facilitators.** The teacher in the above example might model the generation of questions about the reading.
• **Thinking out loud.** This models the teacher's expert thought processes, showing students the revisions and choices the learner makes in using procedural facilitators to work on problems.
• **Anticipating difficult areas.** During the modeling and presentations phase of instructions, for example, the teacher anticipates and discusses potential student errors.
• **Providing prompt or cue cards.** Procedural facilitators are written on "prompt cards" that students keep for reference as they work. As students practice, the cards gradually become unnecessary. Think of these like the "quick reference cards" that came with your computer or fax machine.
• **Regulating the difficulty.** Tasks involving implicit skills are introduced by beginning with simpler problems, providing for student practice after each stage, and gradually increasing the complexity of the task.
• **Providing half-done examples.** Giving students half-done examples of problems and having them work out the conclusions can be an effective way to teach students how to ultimately solve problems on their own.
• **Reciprocal teaching.** Having the teacher and students rotate the role of teacher. The teacher provides support to students as they learn to lead discussions and ask their own questions.
• **Providing checklists.** Students can be taught self-checking procedures to help them regulate the quality of their responses.

Source: "Effective Teaching Redux," by John O'Neil. In the 1990 issue of ASCD Update, *32(6), p. 5. © 1990 by ASCD. Used with permission. Learn more about ASCD at www.ascd.org.*

T: Sylvester and the Magic Pebble. What did you think about this story?
Rita: I think they cared a lot for him.
T: What do you mean? You mean his parents?
Rita: Yes.
T: What made you think that when you read the story?
Rita: Because they really worried about him.
T: Who else wants to share something? I'd like to hear everybody's ideas. Then we can decide what we want to talk about. Sarah?
Sarah: I think he got the idea of it when he was little, or maybe one of his friends got lost or something?
T: What do you mean, he got the idea?
Sarah: He got the idea for his parents to think that Sylvester got lost.
T: You're talking about where William Steig might have gotten his ideas.
Sarah: Yes.
T: That maybe something like this happened to him or someone he knew. A lot of times authors get their ideas from real life things, don't they? Jon, what did you think about this story?
Jon: It was like a moral story. It's like you can't wish for everything. But, in a sense, everything happened to him when he was panicking.
T: When did you think he panicked?
Jon: Well, when he saw the lion, he started to panic.
Richard: And he turned himself into a rock.
Jon: Yeah. He said, "I wish I were a rock."
T: Right. And it happened, didn't it?
Richard: It was stupid of him.
T: So maybe he wasn't thinking far enough ahead? What would you have wished for instead of a rock? (pp. 24–25)

The conversation continues as the students contribute different levels of interpretation of the story. The teacher notes these interpretations in her summary: "Look at all the different kinds of things you had to say. Rita talked about the characters in the story and what they must be feeling. Sarah took the author's point of view. And you saw it as a particular kind of story, Jon, a moral story."

In instructional conversations, the goal is to keep everyone cognitively engaged in a substantive discussion. In the preceding conversation, the teacher takes almost every other turn. As the students become more familiar with this learning approach, we would expect them to talk more among themselves with less teacher talk. These conversations do not have to be long and they can occur anywhere. For example, a trip to the grocery store with a parent provides aisle after aisle of instructional conversation opportunities. Table 9.4 summarizes the elements of productive instructional conversations.

TABLE 9.4 • **Productive Instructional Conversations**

Good instructional conversations must have elements of both instruction and conversation.

INSTRUCTION	CONVERSATION
• *Thematic focus.* Teacher selects a theme on which to focus the discussion and has a general plan for how the theme will unfold, including how to "chunk" the text to permit optimal exploration of the theme. • *Activation and use of background knowledge.* Teacher either "hooks into" or provides students with pertinent background knowledge necessary for understanding a text, weaving the information into the discussion. • *Direct teaching.* When necessary, teacher provides direct teaching of a skill or concept. • *Promotion of more complex language and expression.* Teacher elicits more extended student contributions by using a variety of elicitation techniques: invitation to expand, questions, restatements, and pauses. • *Promotion of bases for statements or positions.* Teacher promotes students' use of text, pictures, and reasoning to support an argument or position, by gently probing: "What makes you think that?" or "Show us where it says______."	• *Fewer "known-answer" questions.* Much of the discussion centers on questions for which there might be more than one correct answer. • *Responsiveness to student contributions.* While having an initial plan and maintaining the focus and coherence of the discussion, teacher is also responsive to students' statements and the opportunities they provide. • *Connected discourse.* The discussion is characterized by multiple, interactive, connected turns; succeeding utterances build on and extend previous ones. • *Challenging, but non-threatening, atmosphere.* Teacher creates a challenging atmosphere that is balanced by a positive affective climate. Teacher is more collaborator than evaluator and students are challenged to negotiate and construct the meaning of the text. • *General participation, including self-selected turns.* Teacher does not hold exclusive right to determine who talks; students are encouraged to volunteer or otherwise influence the selection of speaking turns.

Source: From Elements of the instructional conversation by Claude Goldenberg in The Reading Teacher. *Copyright 1993 by International Reading Association. Reproduced with permission of International Reading Association in the formats textbook and other book via Copyright Clearance Center.*

USING THE TOOLS OF THE CULTURE. Luis Moll and his colleagues wanted a better way to teach the children of working-class Mexican American families in the barrio schools of Tucson, Arizona (Moll et al., 1992). Rather than adopt a model of remediation, Moll decided to identify and build on strengths—the cultural tools and funds of knowledge of these families. **Funds of knowledge** are the understandings and skills developed over generations that families need to function. By interviewing the families, the researchers identified extensive knowledge about ranching, farming, soils and irrigation systems, hunting, renting and selling, loans, consumer knowledge, appliance and car repairs, construction, carpentry, first aid, modern and folk medicines, cooking, and bible studies, to name only a few. When teachers based their assignments on this fund of knowledge, students were more engaged and they learned. See

RELATING TO

EVERY CHILD

▸ Cultural Perspectives on Funds of Knowledge

MARY MCCASLIN AND DANIEL HICKEY (2001) defined *scaffolding* as "a powerful conception of teaching and learning in which teachers and students create meaningful connections between teachers' cultural knowledge and the everyday experience and knowledge of the student" (p. 137). Luis Moll's research has inspired teachers to discover and connect with the funds of knowledge of working-class Mexican American families in the barrio schools of Tucson, Arizona (Moll et al., 1992).

Hilda Angiulo is an example of one teacher who worked with Moll to achieve dramatic results with her sixth grade bilingual class. Hilda's approach of using basal readers supplemented with novels, newspapers, and magazines was not working, so she researched her students' funds of cultural knowledge. Using the results, she developed an instructional unit around a topic of interest to them: building and construction, something she knew nothing about—but many of her students and their families were experts.

> First, Hilda asked students to do library research on building, using books and magazines. She also brought into the classroom a series of books on the subject. Then she directed the students to build model buildings for their homework project. They also wrote short essays in either English or Spanish explaining their research, ideas, and conclusions.
>
> Hilda invited parents and other community members who worked in construction to share their expertise with the children. Some parents talked about their tools and explained how they used numbers and measurements in their work. Others spoke about their work methods and told how they solved problems.
>
> Eventually, the students took the models that they had built and used them as the basis for constructing a model community with streets, parks, and other structures. The follow-up project required additional research, which the students undertook enthusiastically.
>
> Students continued to write up their research and give oral reports to the class. Peer editing groups helped with the process of English and Spanish writing. By the end of the semester, 20 parents and community people had visited Hilda's class and shared their knowledge with her students. By then, the students had successfully completed extensive reading and writing activities. (Gonzales, Greenberg, & Velez, 1994)

Students learned a great deal, and Hilda did, too—she learned about the valuable cognitive resources in the community and her respect for her students' and their families' knowledge increased.

the ***Relating to Every Child*** feature for an example of a teacher using funds of knowledge to connect with her students.

Knowledge also is central in the next topic we consider—information processing.

Information Processing and Memory: Developing Cognitive Processes

As you saw in Chapter 2, information processing theories assume that human thinking *is* processing information. Now we are ready to look at how the main components of the information processing system—attention, memory, processing speed, control processes, and strategies—develop during the middle years. Changes in these processes allow children to become better problem solvers and to add greatly to their knowledge of the world.

Attention

During the middle years, children continue to develop in their abilities to focus attention selectively on relevant information, ignore irrelevant information, and use strategies to plan the best use of attention (Barrouillet, Bernardin, & Camos, 2004; Engle, Tuholski, Laughlin, & Conway, 1999). In one study, Miller and Seier (1994) presented children between the ages of 3 and 8 with a challenge: to remember where pictures of different animals were hidden behind doors in two rows of boxes, as shown in Figure 9.2. Some of the boxes (those with

FIGURE 9.2

A STUDY ON FOCUSING ATTENTION

The boxes with a picture of a cage on the front have drawings of different animals behind the doors. If you were asked to memorize the location of every animal and given a limited time to do it, you would know to focus your attention on the doors with a cage drawing and not bother to look behind the doors with a house drawing. Older children use this strategy, but younger ones might open every door, or open some house doors, as they try to memorize the locations of the animals.

Source: Sigler & Alibali, Children's Thinking, "A Study on Focusing Attention" from p. 249, © 2005 by Prentice-Hall Inc. Reproduced by permission of Pearson Education, Inc.

a drawing of a house on the cover) had pictures of household objects behind the doors. The animal pictures were behind the doors with cage drawings. Children were told to memorize where each animal picture was and were given time to open any of the doors. The most efficient strategy would be to open only the cage doors to study the location of the animals. The youngest children opened all the doors; many older preschool children looked behind the cage doors more often, but sometimes they looked behind the house doors, too. Older children looked only behind the cage doors; they used better strategies to plan and focus their attention and remembered the locations of more animals.

It is usually in elementary school, around age 8, when **attention disorders** are identified (Sonuga-Barke, Auerbach, Campbell, Daley, & Thompson, 2005). Often these children are called *hyperactive*. The notion is a modern one; there were no "hyperactive" children 50 to 60 years ago. Such children, like Mark Twain's Huckleberry Finn, were seen as rebellious, lazy, or "fidgety" (Nylund, 2000). Actually, hyperactivity is not one particular condition, but two kinds of problems that may or may not occur together—attention disorders and **impulsive-hyperactivity disorders,** usually called **ADHD.** The most common estimate is that 3–7% of the elementary school population in the United States, Japan, China, and New Zealand has attention deficit or hyperactive disorders, with over half of these students having the combined attention and hyperactivity conditions. The number identified is actually larger in some countries—up to 18% in Germany and 20% in Ukraine (Smith & Tyler, 2010).

About 3 to 4 times more boys than girls are identified as hyperactive, but the gap appears to be narrowing (Hallahan, Lloyd, Kauffman, Weiss, & Martinez, 2005). Just a few years ago, most psychologists thought that ADHD diminished as children entered adolescence, but now there are some researchers who believe that the problems can persist into adulthood (Barkley, 2006). Even if the primary symptoms of difficulty focusing attention or hyperactivity diminish in older children, academic problems persist (Bailey, Lorch, Milich, & Charnigo, 2009). We will look at treatments for ADHD later in this chapter.

Memory

The development of memory is a major change in childhood. Do you remember the different kinds of memory we discussed in Chapter 2? *Working memory* is the workspace of the memory system where new information is combined with existing knowledge. Working memory involves the ability to hold and work with information over a brief time period (Best, Miller, & Jones, 2009). *Long-term memory* is where well-learned knowledge is stored more permanently. There are two distinct memory systems—explicit and implicit. To retrieve *explicit* memories we have to search intentionally, as in when you try to remember an acquaintance's name while she walks up to you. Explicit memories can be about meaning and knowledge (*semantic*) or about specific events (*episodic*). Other memories are out of awareness or *implicit*; we just use them without trying to remember, such as most of the words we use every day, the names of close friends and family, or how to ride a bicycle. We don't have to intentionally search for these memories as long as we use them often. All of these kinds of memories develop during childhood, but research suggests that the implicit memory system is fully developed earlier in childhood than the explicit memory system (Schneider, 2004).

WORKING MEMORY. To form explicit memories, you must pay attention to information, form representations, and make connections—so working memory processes are key. If information never gets "worked with," it is not likely to be remembered (Siegler, 2004). Working memory is made up of a **phonological loop** for verbal/sound information, a **visual sketchpad** for visual/spatial information, and a **central executive** "worker" that oversees processing. These different aspects of working memory are assessed with tasks such as recalling words and numbers (phonological), remembering block designs and mazes (visual/spatial), and counting backwards (central executive). All of the components of working memory are in place by about age 4. Performance on working memory tasks improves steadily over the elementary and secondary school years, but visual/spatial memory appears to develop earlier (Alloway, Gathercole, & Pickering, 2006; Schneider, 2004).

So how does working memory improve? Some researchers have suggested working memory improves with age because processing speed increases—processing speed is the time it takes to accomplish a mental act such as recognizing a face or a word. As they get older, children can process many different kinds of information—verbal, visual, mathematical, etc.—faster, so increased speed of processing seems to be a general factor. In addition, the increase in speed with age is the same for American and Korean children, so increasing processing speed with age may be universal (Kail, 2000; Kail & Park, 1994).

But speed is not the whole story. With age comes an increase in storage capacity, too. These increases may be due to brain development or to more efficient use of strategies, or both. Remember that as children become more automatic in using strategies, more memory space is freed up to handle new information (Case, 1985; Johnson, 2003). So, through changes in the brain, faster processing of information, the development and automating of strategies, increased storage, and added knowledge, working memory improves from ages 4 through adolescence (Gathercole, Pickering, Ambridge, & Wearing, 2004). Moreover, these changes are very important for higher-level thinking (Bayliss, Jarrold, Baddeley, Gunn, & Leigh, 2005).

Quite a bit of research on children's memories has focused on working memory, partly because working memory capacity is a good predictor of a range of cognitive skills including language understanding, reading and mathematics abilities, and fluid intelligence—discussed in the next section (Bayliss et al., 2005). In addition, research indicates that children who have learning disabilities in reading and mathematics problem solving have considerable difficulties with working memory (Siegel, 2003; Swanson & Saez, 2003). Specifically, some research shows that children with learning disabilities have problems in using the *phonological loop* of working memory—the system that holds verbal and auditory information while you work with it. Because children with learning disabilities have trouble holding on to words and sounds, it is difficult for them to comprehend the meaning of a sentence or figure out what a math story problem is really asking.

An even more serious problem may be difficulties retrieving needed information from long-term memory (described below), so it is hard for children with learning disabilities to simultaneously hold on to information (such as the amount carried or borrowed in an arithmetic problem) while they have to transform new incoming information, such as the next number to add. Important bits of information keep getting lost. Finally, children with learning disabilities in arithmetic and problem solving seem to have problems holding visual-spatial information such as number lines or quantity comparisons in working memory, so creating mental representations of "less than" and "greater than" problems is challenging (D'Amico & Guarnera, 2005).

LONG-TERM MEMORY. Earlier work (1970s–1990s) on the long-term memory of school-age children often focused on memory strategies that were relevant for school (Bjorklund, 2004). These strategies were based on focusing attention, rehearsing (repeating), elaborating (making connections with existing knowledge), organizing, and using imagery (Derry, 1989; Pressley & Hilden, 2006). These processes move information from working memory into long-term memory.

There are several developmental differences in the way students use organization, elaboration, and knowledge to process information. Around age 6, most children discover the value of using organizational strategies, and by 9 or 10, they use these strategies spontaneously. So, given the following words to learn:

couch, orange, rat, lamp, pear, sheep, banana, rug, pineapple, horse, table, dog

an older child might organize the words into three short lists of furniture, fruit, and animals. Younger children can be taught to use organization to improve memory, but they probably won't apply the strategy unless they are reminded. Children become more able to use elaboration strategies (connecting to existing knowledge) as they mature, but these strategies, along with creating images or stories to remember ideas, are developed late in childhood. In general, older children benefit more from strategy training than younger children, but there also are individual differences—some young children benefit more from coaching and strategy training than others, regardless of age (Schwenck, Bjorklund, & Schneider, 2009; Siegler, 1998).

MEMORY STRATEGIES. **Mnemonics** are systematic procedures for improving memory (Atkinson et al., 1999; Levin, 1994; Rummel, Levin, & Woodward, 2003). When information has little inherent meaning, mnemonic strategies build in meaning by connecting what you are trying to remember with established words or images. An *acronym* is a word formed from the first letter of each word in a phrase; for example, use HOMES to remember the Great Lakes (Huron, Ontario, Michigan, Erie, Superior). Chain mnemonics connect the first item to be memorized with the second, the second item with the third, and so on. In one type of chain method, all the items to be memorized are incorporated into a jingle such as "i before e except after c."

The **keyword method** is the most well researched mnemonic strategy. Joel Levin and his colleagues used a mnemonic (the *3 Rs*) to teach the keyword mnemonic method:

recode the to-be-learned vocabulary item as a more familiar, concrete word—this is the keyword;
relate the keyword clue to the vocabulary item's definition through a sentence;
retrieve the desired definition.

For example, to remember that the English word *carlin* means *old woman,* you might recode *carlin* as the more familiar keyword *car.* Then, make up a sentence such as *The old woman was driving a car.* When you are asked for the meaning of the word *carlin,* you think of the keyword *car,* which triggers the sentence about the car and the *old woman,* the meaning (Jones, Levin, Levin, & Beitzel, 2000). The keyword method has been used extensively in foreign language learning. Figure 9.3 on the next page is an example of using mnemonic pictures as aids in learning complicated science concepts (Carney & Levin, 2002).

One problem is that vocabulary learned with keywords may be easily forgotten if students are given keywords and images instead of being asked to supply their own. When someone else provides the memory links, these associations may not fit the child's existing knowledge and may be forgotten or confused later, so remembering suffers (Wang & Thomas, 1995; Wang, Thomas, & Ouelette, 1992).

What was learned in the decades of research on memory strategies? First, like preschool children, children in the middle years can learn and apply strategies when coached, but they might not use the strategies spontaneously; this is called a *production deficiency*. All children, but particularly children with learning disabilities, need instruction and practice in the *what, when*, and *why* of using memory strategies. They need to learn to do the

FIGURE 9.3

USING MNEMONICS OF PROMOTE LEARNING COMPLEX CONCEPTS

The illustration tells a story that provides a frame for remembering and pegs for hanging the concept names in the biological subdivision of angiospersms.

To remember that the subdivision **angiosperms** includes the class **dicotyledons,** which in turn includes the three orders **rubales, sapindales,** and **rosales,** study the picture of the angel with the pet **dinosaur** that is walking up the **Rubik's cubes** so that he can lick the sweet **sap** that drips down from the **rose** tree.

Source: American Educational Research Journal *by Levin, M. E. & Levin, J. R.. Copyright 1990 by Sage Publications Inc. Journals. Reproduced with permission of Sage Publications Inc. Journals in the format Textbook via Copyright Clearance Center.*

strategy (what), recognize situations that require the strategy (when), and be motivated to apply the strategy to improve learning and remembering (why). Based on over 40 years of research on strategy instruction, Michael Pressley, who did much of this work himself, concluded:

> [T]he most effective strategies instruction includes direct explanation and modeling, provision of metacognitive information, opportunities to discover strategies during practice, efforts to motivate strategy use by assuring students experience benefits for strategy use, and emphasis on the mixture of strategy use and prior knowledge in solving problems, reading, and writing. (Pressley & Hilden, 2006, p. 545)

There are cultural differences in strategic memory. In cultures where parents and teachers emphasize strategies, children are better at using them. For example, compared to Americans, German children tend to perform better on strategic memory tasks, probably because German teachers and parents teach strategies directly and monitor strategy use in homework. Parents even buy games for their children that require strategic thinking, so the effective elements of direct teaching, modeling, practice, and monitoring of strategies described by Pressley are more common in homes and schools in Germany—children learn what they live (Carr, Kurtz, Schneider, Turner, & Borkowski, 1989; Kurz, Schneider, Carr, Borkowski, & Rellinger, 1990).

MEMORY FOR ACTUAL EVENTS. As with younger children, much of the recent research on the development of long-term memory in older children has focused on memory for actual events. This research has implications for children in many cultures and contexts because children in every culture spontaneously develop memories for events, whereas development of memory strategies depends mostly on formal schooling. Remembering events essentially is storytelling, and parents in every culture teach their children to tell stories to recount the experiences in their lives. Event memory through stories and narratives is an example of Vygotsky's social constructivist theory—stories of events are socially constructed with family and friends and then remembered (Roebers, Bjorklund, & Schneider, 2002).

Recent research on event memory with older children has focused on eyewitness testimony and children's suggestibility (Bjorklund, Brown, & Bjorklund, 2002). Like young children, children in the middle years tend to be more accurate when they are interviewed in unbiased ways without suggestive questions. In addition, older children are better than younger children at identifying the source of a memory, so they can separate what happened in a specific situation, such as a particular birthday party, from what generally happens in similar situations (Odegard, Cooper, Lampinen, Reyna, & Brainerd, 2009).

Children can be accurate in giving eyewitness testimony if they are not asked suggestive or leading questions. Interviewers should be well trained to be unbiased.

There are cultural differences in eyewitness memories, too. Roebers and her colleagues (2002) showed German and American kindergartners, second graders, fourth graders, and college adults a brief video that involved a theft. She interviewed them a week later using free recall questions, and then either a misleading question or unbiased questions, and finally recognition questions. Compared to Americans, German children and adults had more accurate memories using free recall and misleading question formats. American adults and fourth graders were more accurate than their German counterparts when questions were unbiased.

Metacognition

Metacognition is knowing about how your own cognitive processes work and using that knowledge to reach your goals. Using memory strategies, such as mnemonics (described earlier), is a metacognitive skill. There are many metacognitive processes, including judging if you have the right knowledge to solve a problem, deciding where to focus attention, determining if you understood what you just read, devising a plan, revising the plan as you proceed, determining if you have studied enough to pass a test, evaluating a problem solution, deciding to get help, and generally orchestrating your cognitive powers to reach a goal (Meadows, 2006; Schneider, 2004).

KINDS OF METACOGNITION. Psychologists make two (and sometimes three) distinctions between different kinds of metacognition. *Declarative metacognition* is explicit, conscious, and factual knowledge about your cognitive abilities and the skills, strategies, and resources needed to perform a task—knowing *what* to do. *Procedural metacognition* is knowing *how*—how to use the strategies, focus attention, and generally enact the plans you make. This procedural metacognitive knowledge often is implicit and unconscious—you just do it when you need to. For example, better readers slow down and reread as they come to more difficult passages, without consciously "deciding" to slow down (Siegler & Alibali, 2005). Some psychologists add a third category, *conditional metacognition*—knowing *when* and *why* to apply the procedures and strategies (Paris & Cunningham, 1996). Metacognition is the strategic orchestration of declarative, procedural, and conditional (sometimes called *conceptual* or *self-regulatory*) knowledge to accomplish goals and solve problems (Schneider, 1998; Schneider & Lockl, 2002; Schunk, 2004).

Many researchers trace some of the problems of children with learning disabilities to procedural deficits in metacognitive knowledge. Even if they learn new procedures and strategies, these children often lack conditional metacognition—knowing *when* and *why* to focus on the relevant information, get organized, apply learning strategies and study skills, change strategies when one isn't working, or evaluate their learning in order to apply the learning procedures and strategies (Paris & Cunningham, 1996). They tend to be passive learners, in part because they don't know how to learn. Working independently is especially trying, so homework and seatwork are often left incomplete (Hallahan & Kauffman, 2006; Hallahan, Kauffman, & Pullen, 2009). We will look at strategies for teaching children with learning disabilities later in the chapter.

DEVELOPING METACOGNITION. Of course, we don't have to be metacognitive all the time. Some actions become routine. Metacognition is most useful when tasks are challenging, but not too difficult. As we develop procedural and conditional metacognitive knowledge, we may use these skills automatically without being aware of our efforts (Perner, 2000). Experts in a field—even child experts—may plan, monitor, and evaluate as second nature; however, they may have difficulty describing their metacognitive knowledge and skills (Bargh & Chartrand, 1999; Reder, 1996).

Every cognitive process has its own metaprocess, so knowing how your attention works is called metaattention, knowing how your memory works is metamemory, knowing about strategies is metastrategic knowledge, and knowing how you comprehend is metacomprehension (Bjorklund, 2005; Schneider & Lockl, 2002). Metacognition in all these areas improves during the childhood years, as you can see in Table 9.5.

TABLE 9.5 • **The Development of Metacognition in the Middle Childhood Years**

PROCESS	CHANGES	EXAMPLE STUDY
Metaattention	Beginning around ages 6–7, children understand that they must focus attention selectively to understand and remember.	Flavell, Green, & Flavell (1995) 6- and 8-year-old children but not 4-year-olds understood that a woman selecting a gift would be paying attention to the gift options.
Metamemory	Compared to preschool children, by age 9 or 10, children better understand the connection between using learning strategies and performance. Children understand that related and meaningful items are easier to remember than unrelated items and that it is easier to summarize the meaning of a passage than remember it word for word. Children are better predictors of how well they will perform a memory task and better judges of how well they actually performed after the task.	Kreutzer, Leonard, & Flavell (1975) Compared to kindergarten and first grade children, older children knew that they might forget a phone number if they did not call right away after looking it up and that it would be harder to memorize unrelated word pairs than opposites.
Metastrategies	By about age 9 or 10, children use rehearsal and organizing strategies more often and more effectively to remember.	Coyle & Bjorklund (1997) Third and fourth grade children used more strategies than second graders to remember word lists; children who used more strategies remembered more, but even young children used several strategies some of the time.
Metacomprehension	Older children are better able to determine if they have understood what they read.	Lovett & Flavell (1990) 6- to 7-year-olds showed no understanding of the comprehension-memory distinction; they were not able to distinguish between strategies/variables that were relevant to comprehension and strategies/variables that were relevant to memorization; 8- to 9-year-olds were beginning to distinguish between these kinds of strategies, and undergraduates knew the difference.

INDIVIDUAL DIFFERENCES IN METACOGNITION. Some differences in metacognitive abilities are the result of development, as you saw in Table 9.5. Younger children, for example, may not be aware of the purpose of a lesson—they may think the point is simply to finish. They also may not be good at gauging the difficulty of a task—they may think that reading for fun and reading a science book are the same (Gredler, 2005). Metacognitive abilities begin to develop around ages 5 to 7 and improve throughout school (Flavell, Green, & Flavell, 1995; Garner, 1990). In her work with first and second graders, Nancy, one of your textbook authors, found that asking children two questions helped them become more metacognitive in school. The questions were "What did you learn about yourself as a reader/writer today?" and "What did you learn that you can do again and again and again?" When teachers asked these questions regularly during class, even young children demonstrated fairly sophisticated levels of metacognitive understanding and action (Perry, Phillips, & Dowler, 2004).

Not all differences in metacognitive abilities have to do with age or maturation. There are strong relationships between the development of language abilities and metamemory, for example (Lockl & Schneider, 2007). There is great variability even among students of the same developmental level, but these differences do not appear to be related to intellectual abilities. In fact, superior metacognitive skills can compensate for lower levels of ability, so these metacognitive skills can be especially important for students who often have trouble in school (Schunk, 2004). And some individual differences in metacognitive abilities are probably caused by biological differences or by variations in learning experiences. For example, children can vary greatly in their ability to control and direct their attention.

METACOGNITION AND PERFORMANCE. One question that has prompted quite a bit of research is a kind of "chicken and egg" question: Does developing metacognition improve cognitive performance or do we develop metacognitive knowledge as we learn from our improvements in performances? As usual, it probably works both ways. Metamemory has been the focus of quite a bit of research on this question. Schneider, Schlagmüller, and Visé (1998) used sophisticated statistical techniques to examine the relationships among verbal intelligence, memory span, metamemory, and performance on memory tasks for third and fourth grade children. Verbal IQ and memory span had moderate effects on metamemory, but metamemory had a stronger impact on memory strategy use. In addition, metamemory had a strong influence on recall, mostly because children with better metamemory knowledge and skills used more and better memory strategies. So, a large portion of the differences among children on memory recall probably is explained by differences in their metamemories (Schneider, 2004).

METACOGNITION AND THEORY OF MIND. There is less research today on children's metacognition, partly because the issues and questions from this line of work have been folded into the research on children's theory of mind, discussed later. Some psychologists believe theory of mind is a more general area than metacognition because theory of mind researchers are interested in children's knowledge about mental life, emotions, beliefs, and intentions, so metacognition (knowledge of your own cognitive processes) can be viewed a one aspect of children's theory of mind (Schneider, 2004). Other psychologists suggest that metacognition is the larger category that includes theory of mind (Flavell, 2004).

Even though they may be part of the same family of study, there are some contrasts between work on metacognition and research on theory of mind. Research on metacognition has focused mostly on school-age children's knowledge about their own mental processes involved in accomplishing tasks, especially school tasks. Theory of mind researchers have focused on infants' and younger children's beginning knowledge about other people's thoughts, desires, beliefs, and intentions (Lockl & Schneider, 2007; Schneider & Lockl, 2002).

The research on metacognition helped to identify another important influence on thinking and memory: content knowledge. We turn to that now.

Conceptual Development and Domains of Knowledge

One of the major cognitive developments during the school years is the growth of knowledge about the world. As we have said before (and will probably say again), knowledge—what we already know—is the foundation and frame for constructing all future learning. Knowledge determines to a great extent what we will pay attention to, perceive, learn, remember, and forget (Alexander, 1996; Bransford, Brown, & Cocking, 2000). Older children remember more than younger children, in part because they know more about the world, and this knowledge scaffolds remembering. In fact, children with extensive knowledge outperform adults with limited knowledge on many tasks ranging from memory for pieces on a chessboard to recalling titles of children's television programs (Schneider & Bjorklund, 1998, 2003). So, children's advantages in content knowledge can trump adults' advantages in memory abilities (if you have content knowledge of bridge and other card games, you know that *trump* means "outweighs" or "overtakes"—nothing to do with "the Donald").

An extensive base of knowledge even compensates for lower overall intelligence, as long as the task is in the area of the child's expertise (Schneider, 2004). Schneider, Korkel, and Weinert (1989) tested German children's memory for a story about a young soccer player and his big game. The children varied in knowledge of soccer and in IQ. Compared to children with less soccer knowledge, the children who knew more about soccer, no matter what their IQ, remembered more about the story, noticed more mistakes, and made more accurate inferences.

A great deal of research on children's knowledge development has focused on mathematics and science.

MATHEMATICS. By the time they enter school, most children have developed a sense of numbers, order, and quantity—6 is more than 5 and 6 is always the same number. They can use number words to count and know what counting means, and they can solve simple addition and subtraction problems using concrete objects. Geary (2006) calls these *biologically primary mathematical abilities* because he believes they were selected during the evolutionary process as our early ancestors solved problems of survival. But there is much more to develop in mathematical understanding, and most of these abilities emerge in cultural contexts such as schools and families. Geary calls these *biologically secondary abilities*. Table 9.6 describes development of conceptual knowledge, arithmetic operations, and problem solving during the school years.

There has been quite a bit or research on what children know in mathematics and when they know it, but less on what helps the knowledge to develop. Some recent research has identified a few principles in learning arithmetic operations (Prather & Alibali, 2009).

- *Density of relevant experiences:* When children have many experiences close together with the same type of problem, they show greater learning than if they deal with several problem types at once.
- *Problem sequencing:* Problem sequencing can help children learn. For example, instead of presenting 3 + 6 followed by 9 + 4, 7 + 2, . . . then finally 3 + 6, present 3 + 6 followed immediately by 6 + 3. This sequence helps children "discover" commutativity—order doesn't not matter in adding numbers.
- *Exposure to principle violations:* Show children equations that are consistent with principles they are learning and also equations that violate the principles—examples and nonexamples.

Let's look at the last development in Table 9.6, *problem solving*. You see that at least two abilities are necessary for word problem solving: understanding the meaning of the words and sentences and then understanding the whole problem (Mayer, 1992). Sometimes children have been taught to search for key words (*more, less, greater,* etc.), pick a strategy or formula based on the key words (*more* means "add," *less* means "subtract"), and apply the formula. But this actually gets in the way of forming a conceptual understanding of the whole problem. To be successful, children need to understand what the problem is *really* asking (Fuchs et al., 2006; Jonassen, 2003). For example, consider this problem:

Question: Joan has 15 bonus points and Louise has 24. How many more does Louise have?
Child's answer: More means add, so 15 + 24 = 39.

This child saw two numbers and the word *more,* so he applied the *add to get more* procedure. When children use the wrong schema, they overlook necessary information, use irrelevant information, and may even misread or misremember critical information so that

TABLE 9.6 • **The Development of Mathematical Understandings in the Middle Childhood Years**

Conceptual Knowledge	*Properties of Arithmetic*	By about second grade, most children have an implicit understanding that the order in which 2 numbers are added or multiplied doesn't change the result. $3 + 5 = 5 + 3$ $3 \times 5 = 5 \times 3$ It takes longer to understand that order doesn't matter with more numbers. $(5 + 3) + 4 = 5 + (3 + 4)$ $(5 \times 3) \times 4 = 5 \times (3 \times 4)$
	Base-10	Many elementary school age children do not fully understand place value in the base-10 system; i.e., 23 is 2 tens and 3 ones, but 2 can also mean ones, as in 22. East Asian children understand place value earlier, perhaps because their language is consistent and transparent with base-10. For example, the number 23 is said "two ten three."
	Fractions	Children's conceptual understanding of part/whole relations (fractions) and the procedures to add, subtract, multiply, and divide fractions emerge slowly during elementary school and may not be complete for some children until late adolescence.
	Estimation	The ability to estimate mathematical calculations is difficult for children and some adults. Formal schooling is key. Children can estimate in a zone of problems just a bit more advanced than their current computational skills.
Arithmetic Operations	*Addition and Subtraction*	To add and subtract, children begin with simple counting strategies, counting all the elements or starting with one number and then counting up for addition ($9 + 4 = 9, \ldots 10, 11, 12, 13$) or down for subtraction ($23 - 4 = 22, 21, 20, 19$). Older children and adults simply retrieve the solutions from memory. For more complicated problems, many strategies including regrouping ($23 + 45 = 20 + 40 + 3 + 5$), and carrying are taught in school. The load on working memory grows with more complicated problems.
	Multiplication and Division	Some early strategies include repeated adding for multiplication and solving division problems based on knowledge of multiplication or addition facts. These are expanded by strategies taught in school.
Problem Solving	*Problem Schema*	Children develop increasingly complex ways to represent word problems (schemas), from simple schemas such as *change* (Alicia has 2 pens. Carey gave her 3 more. How many does Alicia have now?); *combine* (Alicia has 2 pens. Carey has 3 pens. How many do they have altogether?); *compare* (Alicia has two pens. She has 3 less than Carey. How many pens does Carey have?); *equalize* (Alicia has 4 pens and Carey has 1. How many does Carey need to have as many pens as Alicia?). By the time they reach middle school and take algebra, many more schemas are needed to make sense of word problems.
	Problem Solving Processes	As problems grow more complex, children must not only understand the meaning of the words in the problem, they also must understand the whole problem and not be fooled by words such as *more* in a subtraction problem, or by information that is irrelevant to the problem solution.

Source: Adapted from Geary, D. C. (2006). Development of mathematical understanding. In D. Kuhn & R. S. Siegler (Eds.), Handbook of child psychology (Vol. 2, Cognition, perception, and language, pp. 777-810). New York: Wiley.

it fits the schema. But when children use the proper schema to represent a problem, they are less likely to be confused by irrelevant information or tricky wording, such as *more* in a problem that really requires *subtraction* (Kalyuga, Chandler, Tuovinen, & Sweller, 2001).

SCIENCE. During the school years, children develop their understanding of scientific concepts. Physics provides good examples (Wilkening & Huber, 2004). Many children approach physics with a great deal of misinformation, partly because a number of their intuitive ideas about the physical world are wrong. For example, most elementary school children believe that light helps us see by brightening the area around objects. They do not realize that we see an object because the light is reflected by the object to our eyes. This concept does not fit with the everyday experience of turning on a light and "brightening" the dark area.

CONNECTING WITH CHILDREN

Guidelines for Teachers: Encouraging Conceptual Change

Encourage students to make their ideas explicit.

Examples

1. Ask children to make predictions that might contradict their naïve conceptions.
2. Ask children to state their ideas in their own words, including the attractions and limitations of the ideas for them.
3. Have children explain their ideas using physical models or illustrations.

Help students see the differences among ideas.

Examples

1. Have children summarize or paraphrase each other's ideas.
2. Encourage comparing ideas by presenting and comparing evidence.

Encourage metacognition.

Examples

1. Give a pretest before starting a unit; then have children discuss their own responses to the pretest. Group similar pretest responses together and ask children to discover what is a more general concept underlying the responses.
2. Ask children at the end of lessons: "What did you learn?" "What do you understand?" "What do you believe about the lesson?" "How have your ideas changed?"

Explore the status of ideas. Status is an indication of how much students know and accept ideas and find them useful.

Examples

1. Ask direct questions about how intelligible, plausible, and fruitful an idea is. That is, do you know what the idea means, do you believe it, and can you achieve some valuable outcome using the idea?
2. Teach children to use terms such as *logical, consistent, inconsistent,* and *coherent* in giving justifications.
3. Ask children to share and analyze each other's justifications.

For more information see, http://www.physics.ohio-state.edu/~jossem/ICPE/C5.html

One key to understanding in science is for children to directly examine their own theories and confront the shortcomings they find (Hewson, Beeth, & Thorley, 1998). For this *conceptual change* to take place, children must go through six stages: initial discomfort with their own ideas and beliefs, attempts to explain away inconsistencies between their theories and evidence presented to them, attempts to adjust measurements or observations to fit personal theories, doubt, vacillation, and finally conceptual change (Carey, 1999; Nissani & Hoefler-Nissani, 1992). You can see Piaget's notions of assimilation, disequilibrium, and accommodation operating here. Children try to make new information fit existing ideas (assimilation), but when the fit simply won't work and disequilibrium occurs, then accommodation or changes in cognitive structures follow. The ***Connecting with Children*** guidelines for teachers, adapted from Hewson, Beeth, and Thorley (1998), give some ideas for teaching for conceptual change.

Theory of Mind and Conceptions of Intelligence

Theory of mind, you may recall, is an understanding of our own and other people's mental life—beliefs, desires, emotions, intentions, thoughts, plans, and so on. Much of the research on theory of mind focuses on infants and children, but conceptions of mental life such as the following emerge from ages 6 to 8 and beyond (Wellman, 2004).

- People do not always feel the way they look—they can be unhappy without showing it, for example.
- People's interpretation of an event can be influenced by biases and previous experiences.
- You did not always know what you know now.
- You need information to make a judgment and sometimes you don't have enough; for example, you can't tell what an object is if you see only a small part.
- People can be actively thinking, even when they are sitting quietly, not moving.

In later elementary school, particularly in postindustrial societies, children begin to understand the mind as an active constructor of knowledge. Older children see that they can be agents in their own learning and actively use their metacognitive knowledge and skills. They are more accurate in judging what they know and what they don't know and can tell you where they learned what they know (called *source monitoring*). Older children also come to understand that different people may have different interpretations of the same event (Wellman, 2004).

One belief about mental processes has important implications for children's cognitive development and motivation—their implicit theories of intelligence. In fact, some of the most powerful beliefs affecting motivation are beliefs about *ability*. Before we examine this topic, rate the following statements taken from Dweck (2000) on a scale from 1 (Strongly Agree) to 6 (Strongly Disagree).

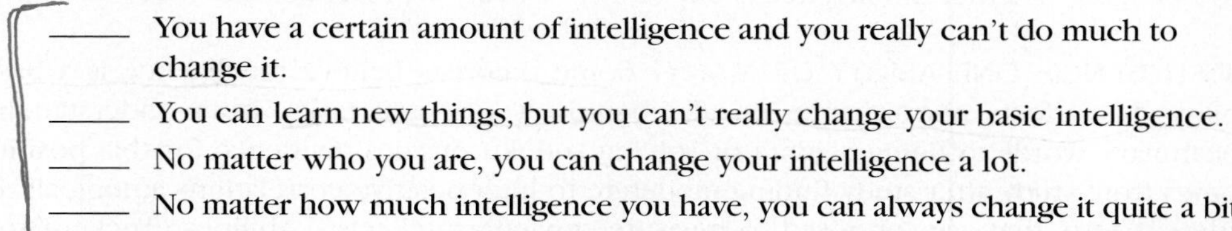

_____ You have a certain amount of intelligence and you really can't do much to change it.

_____ You can learn new things, but you can't really change your basic intelligence.

_____ No matter who you are, you can change your intelligence a lot.

_____ No matter how much intelligence you have, you can always change it quite a bit.

Adults use two basic concepts of ability (Dweck, 1999, 2002). An **entity view of ability** assumes that ability is an *uncontrollable* trait—a characteristic of the individual that cannot be changed. Some people have more ability than others, but the amount each person has is set. An **incremental view of ability,** on the other hand, suggests that ability is controllable and potentially always expanding. By hard work, study, or practice, knowledge can be increased and thus ability can be improved. What is your view of ability? Look back at your answers to the questions above to see.

Young children tend to hold an exclusively incremental view of ability. Through the early elementary grades, most students believe that effort is the same as intelligence. Smart people try hard, and trying hard makes you smart. If you fail, you aren't smart and you didn't try hard (Dweck, 2000; Stipek, 2002). Children are age 11 or 12 before they can differentiate among effort, ability, and performance. About this time, they come to believe that someone who succeeds without working at all must be *really* smart. This is when beliefs about ability begin to influence motivation (Anderman & Maehr, 1994).

Children who hold an entity (unchangeable) view of intelligence tend to want to avoid looking bad in the eyes of others. They seek situations where they can look smart and protect their self-esteem, so they generally keep doing what they can do well without expending too much effort or risking failure, because either one—working hard or failing—indicates (to them) low ability. To work hard but still fail would be devastating. Children with learning disabilities are more likely to hold an entity view. Teachers who hold entity views are quicker to form judgments about students and slower to modify their opinions when confronted with contradictory evidence (Stipek, 2002).

Incremental theorists, in contrast, tend to set goals and seek situations in which they can improve their skills, because improvement means getting smarter. Failure is not devastating; it simply indicates more work is needed. Ability is not threatened. Incremental theorists tend to set moderately difficult goals, the kinds that are the most motivating.

This discussion of beliefs about intelligence brings us to a critical aspect of cognitive development in the middle years—the development of intelligence and intelligence testing—issues very much involved in our opening case about the guidance counselor and the gifted program.

Intelligence and Intelligence Testing

The idea that people vary in what we call **intelligence** has been with us for a long time. Plato discussed similar variations over 2,000 years ago. Most early theories about the nature of intelligence involved one or more of the following three themes: (1) the capacity to learn; (2) the total knowledge a person has acquired; and (3) the ability to adapt successfully to new situations and to the environment in general. What does current research tell us about intelligence?

What Does Intelligence Mean?

In 2006, a discussion on intelligence appeared in the journal *Behavioral and Brain Sciences* (vol. 29). In that discussion, 37 psychologists, neurobiologists, and sociologists debated the roles in intelligence of working memory, executive control processes, the ability to sustain and shift attention, emotional regulation, stress, inhibitory control, aging, and underlying brain structures and neurological processes. Many of these researchers agreed that one concept, fluid cognition, is an important element in intelligence, no matter what you think intelligence is. **Fluid cognition** is defined as all-purpose cognitive processing that involves holding and working with verbal and visual information in working memory in order to plan and move toward goals. In spite of this agreement, the authors of the special issue did not agree whether intelligence is one ability or many separate abilities (Blair, 2006).

INTELLIGENCE: ONE ABILITY OR MANY? Some theorists believe intelligence is a basic ability that affects performance on all cognitively oriented tasks, from understanding vocabulary words to doing algebra or solving sudoku puzzles. Evidence for this position comes from study after study finding moderate to high positive correlations among all the different tests that are supposed to measure separate intellectual abilities (Tucker-Drob, 2009; van der Mass et al., 2006). What could explain these results? Charles Spearman (1927) suggested mental energy, which he called ***g*** or **general intelligence,** was used to perform any mental test, but each test also requires some specific abilities in addition to *g*. Today, psychologists generally agree that *g* exists as a mathematically derived concept, but it isn't much help in understanding human abilities; the notion of *g* does not have much explanatory power (Blair, 2006).

Raymond Cattell and John Horn proposed a theory of fluid and crystallized intelligence that is more helpful in providing explanations (Cattell, 1963, 1998; Horn, 1998). Sometimes people assume that fluid intelligence is process—the ability to learn—and crystallized intelligence is content—what you have learned. But, of course, it isn't quite that simple. **Fluid intelligence** is mental efficiency and reasoning ability. The neurophysiological underpinnings of fluid intelligence may be related to changes in brain volume, myelinization (coating of neural fibers that makes processing faster), the density of dopamine receptors, or processing abilities in the prefrontal lobe of the brain such as selective attention and working memory. This aspect of intelligence increases until late adolescence (about age 22) because it is grounded in brain development, and then declines gradually with age. Fluid intelligence is sensitive to injuries and diseases.

In contrast, **crystallized intelligence** is the ability to apply the problem-solving methods appropriate in your cultural context, so processes are involved here too. Crystallized intelligence can increase throughout the lifespan because it includes the learned skills and knowledge such as reading, facts, and how to hail a cab, make a quilt, locate a good place to fish, or study in college. By *investing fluid intelligence* in solving problems, we *develop our crystallized intelligence,* but many tasks in life such as mathematical reasoning draw on both fluid and crystallized intelligence (Ferrer & McArdle, 2004; Finkel, Reynolds, McArdle, Gatz, & Peterson, 2003; Hunt, 2000).

THE MANY FACETS OF INTELLIGENCE. A widely accepted view is that intelligence has many facets and is a hierarchy of abilities, with general ability at the top and more specific abilities at lower levels of the hierarchy (Carroll, 1997; Tucker-Drob, 2009). Earl Hunt (2000) summarized the current thinking about the structure of intelligence this way:

> After almost a century of such research, that structure is pretty well-established. There is considerable agreement for the bottom two levels of a three-tiered lattice model of intelligence. At the bottom are elementary information-processing actions, and immediately above them are eight or so secondary abilities. These are more broadly defined capabilities, such as holding and accessing information in short- and long-term memory and, most importantly, the trio of 'intellectual' abilities: crystallized intelligence, fluid intelligence, and visual-spatial reasoning ability [which] may be just the most visible of several abilities to manipulate information coded in a particular sensory modality. (p. 123)

FIGURE 9.4

A HIERARCHICAL MODEL OF INTELLIGENCE

The specific abilities at the third level are just some of the possibilities. Carroll identified over 70 specific abilities.

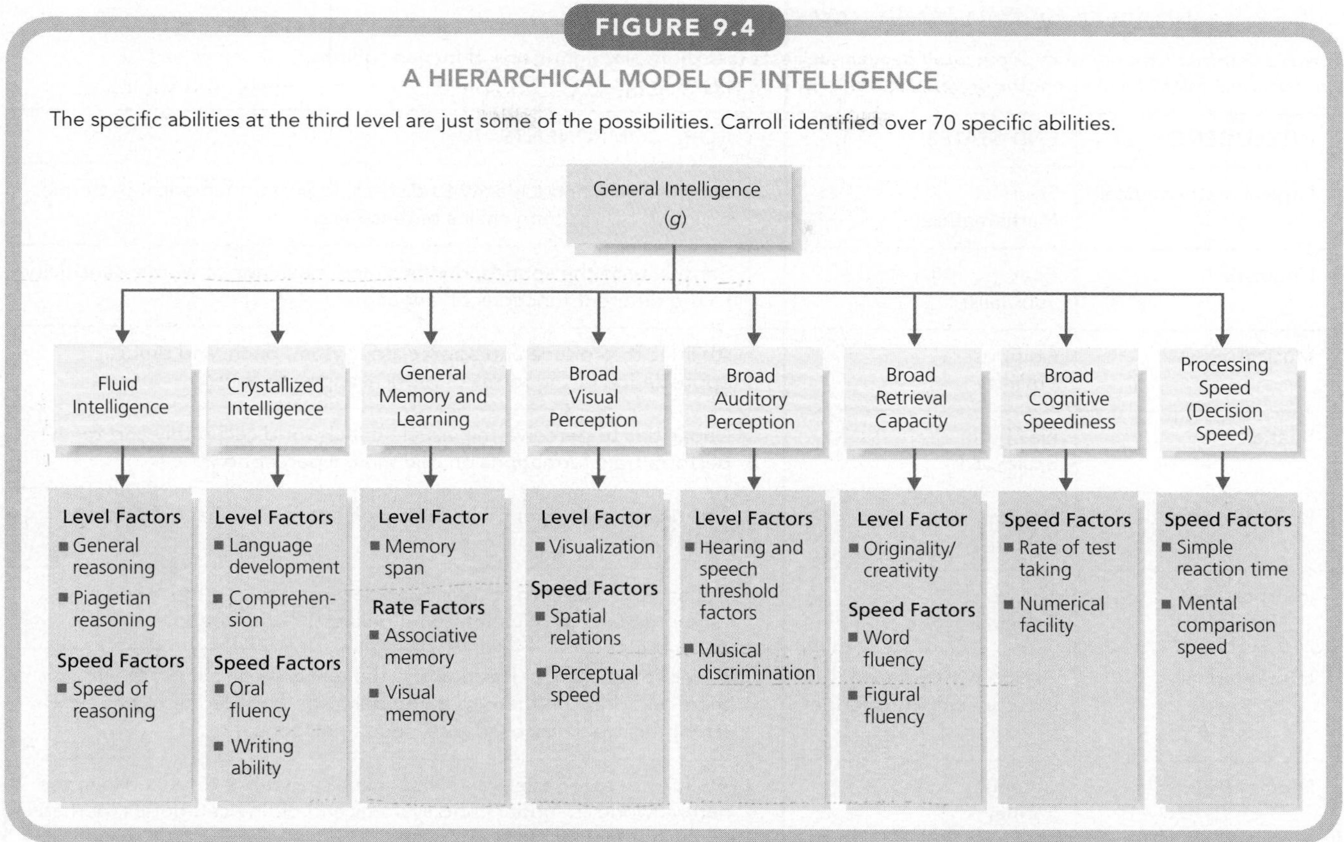

Source: Contemporary intellectual assessment: Theories, tests, and issues by Carroll, J. B., Copyright 1996 by Guilford Publications, Inc. Reproduced with permission of Guilford Publications, Inc in the formats Textbook and Other Book via Copyright Clearance Center.

A current version of this hierarchical view of intelligence often is called the Catttell/Horn/Carroll or CHC model, shown in Figure 9.4 above.

Research on intelligence has produced thousands of volumes, but we still do not know much about the forms of intelligence that are harder to measure, such as creativity, wisdom, social and emotional skills, practical knowledge, and so on (Neisser et al., 1996). Other approaches look at multiple forms of intelligence.

Multiple Intelligences

In spite of the correlations among the various tests of different abilities, some psychologists insist that there are several separate mental abilities (Gardner, 1983; Guilford, 1988). According to Gardner's (1983, 2003) **theory of multiple intelligences,** there are at least eight separate intelligences: linguistic (verbal), musical, spatial, logical-mathematical, bodily-kinesthetic (movement), interpersonal (understanding others), intrapersonal (understanding self), and naturalist (observing and understanding natural and human-made patterns and systems) (see Table 9.7 on the next page). Gardner stresses that there may be more kinds of intelligence—eight is not a magic number. He has speculated that there may be a ninth existential intelligence or the ability to contemplate big questions about the meaning of life (Gardner, 2009). Gardner bases his notion of separate abilities on evidence that brain damage (from a stroke, for example) often interferes with functioning in one area, such as language, but does not affect functioning in other areas. Also, individuals may excel in one of these eight areas but have no remarkable abilities in the other seven.

Gardner (2009) contends that an intelligence is "a biopsychological potential to process information in certain ways in order to solve problems or create products that are valued in at least one culture or community" (p. 5). Various cultures and eras in history place different values on the different intelligences. A naturalist intelligence is critical in farming cultures, whereas verbal and mathematical intelligences are important in technological cultures.

TABLE 9.7 • **Gardner's Multiple Intelligences**

Howard Gardner's theory of multiple intelligences suggests that there are eight kinds of human abilities. An individual might have strengths or weaknesses in one or several areas.

INTELLIGENCE	END STATES	CORE COMPONENTS
Logical-mathematical	Scientist Mathematician	Sensitivity to, and capacity to discern, logical or numerical patterns; ability to handle long chains of reasoning.
Linguistic	Poet Journalist	Sensitivity to the sounds, rhythms, and meanings of words; sensitivity to the different functions of language.
Musical	Composer Violinist	Abilities to produce and appreciate rhythm, pitch, and timbre; appreciation of the forms of musical expressiveness.
Spatial	Navigator Sculptor	Capacities to perceive the visual-spatial world accurately and to perform transformations on one's initial perceptions.
Bodily-kinesthetic	Dancer Athlete	Abilities to control one's body movements and to handle objects skillfully.
Interpersonal	Therapist Salesman	Capacities to discern and respond appropriately to the moods, temperaments, motivations, and desires of other people.
Intrapersonal	Person with detailed, accurate self-knowledge	Access to one's own feelings and the ability to discriminate among them and draw on them to guide behavior; knowledge of one's own strengths, weaknesses. desires, and intelligence.
Naturalist	Botanist Farmer Hunter	Abilities to recognize plants and animals, to make distinctions in the natural world, to understand systems and define categories (perhaps even categories of intelligence).

Source: Educational Research: *Official Newsletter of the American Educational Research Association by H. Gardner & T. Hatch. Copyright 1989 by Sage Publications Inc. Journals. Reproduced with permission of Sage Publications Inc. Journals in the formats Textbook and Other Book via Copyright Clearance Center.*

Gardner's multiple intelligences theory has not received wide acceptance in the scientific community, even though it has been embraced by many educators. Some critics suggest that several of the intelligences are really talents (bodily-kinesthetic skill, musical ability) or personality traits (interpersonal ability). Other "intelligences" are not new at all. Many researchers have identified verbal and spatial abilities as elements of intelligence. In addition, the eight intelligences are not independent; there are correlations among the abilities (Sattler, 2008). So, these "separate abilities" may not be so separate after all. Evidence linking musical and spatial abilities has prompted Gardner to consider that there may be connections among the intelligences (Gardner, 1998). Stay tuned for more developments.

Gardner (2003, 2009) has responded to critics by identifying a number of myths and misconceptions about multiple intelligences theory and schooling. One is that intelligences are the same as learning styles. Gardner doesn't believe that people actually have consistent learning styles. Another misconception is that multiple intelligences theory disproves the idea of *g*. Gardner does not deny the existence of a general ability, but does question how useful *g* is as an explanation for human achievements.

Intelligence as Information Processing

As you can see, the theories of Spearman, Cattell and Horn, and Gardner tend to describe how individuals differ in the *structure* of intelligence—different abilities and factors. Work in cognitive psychology has emphasized instead the information processing that is common to all people. How do humans gather and use information to solve problems and behave intelligently? New views of intelligence are growing out of this work. For example, the debates in the 2006 issue of *Behavioral and Brain Sciences* emphasized working memory capacity, executive control processes such as the abilities to focus attention and inhibit impulses, and emotional self-regulation as aspects of fluid cognitive abilities.

Robert Sternberg's (2004) **triarchic theory of successful intelligence** is a cognitive process approach to understanding intelligence. Successful intelligence includes "the skills and knowledge needed for success in life, according to one's own definition of success, within one's own sociocultural context" (p. 326). As you might guess from the name, this triarchic theory has three parts—analytic, creative, and practical.

Analytical intelligence results when we apply our information processing abilities to abstract, but familiar problems such as reading about a subject we know. *Creative intelligence* involves applying the abilities to new experiences using (1) **insight,** or dealing effectively with novel situations, and (2) **automaticity**—becoming efficient and automatic in thinking and problem solving. Thus creative intelligence involves solving new problems, and then quickly turning these new solutions into routine processes that can be applied without much cognitive effort. *Practical intelligence* results when we select, shape, and adapt to everyday situations in our lives. Here, culture is a major factor in defining successful choice, adaptation, and shaping. For example, abilities that make a person successful in a rural farm community may be useless in the inner city or at a country club in the suburbs. People who are successful often seek situations in which their abilities will be valuable; thus, intelligence in this third sense involves practical matters such as career choice.

In some ways, these three kinds of intelligence are like the three themes described at the beginning of this section: (1) the capacity to learn—analytic intelligence; (2) the total knowledge a person has acquired—practical intelligence; and (3) the ability to adapt successfully to new situations and to the environment in general—creative intelligence.

An emerging challenge to all the theories of intelligence comes from dynamic theories of development. One model, called **mutualism,** suggests that in the beginning of cognitive development, humans have many unrelated cognitive processes such as short-term memory or reaction time. Over time, these processes work together to the mutual benefit of each other and enhance the problem-solving capabilities of the developing individual. For example, in the beginning, simple reaction time and reasoning as measured by a test might not be related, but speed of reaction helps reasoning develop, so the two processes become related. As all the processes work together to process information and solve problems, elementary processes that are uncorrelated initially become correlated during development (van der Maas et al., 2006). Stay tuned to research on cognitive development to see if dynamic theories take over as the main explanations of intelligence.

How Is Intelligence Measured?

Even though psychologists do not agree about what intelligence is, they do agree that intelligence, as measured by standard tests, is related to learning in school. In fact, some psychologists believe that the most common intelligence tests are best at assessing academic intelligence. Why is this so? It has to do in part with the way intelligence tests were first developed.

BINET'S DILEMMA. Alfred Binet was a political activist, concerned with the rights of children. He believed that having an objective measure of learning ability, not just achievement, could protect students who came from poor families from being forced to leave school because teachers assumed they were slow learners. After trying many different tests and eliminating items that did not predict achievement in school, Binet and his collaborator Theodore Simon finally identified 58 tests, several for each age group from 3 to 13, that allowed the examiner to determine the child's *mental age*. A child who succeeded on the items passed by most 6-year-olds, for example, was considered to have a mental age of 6, whether the child was actually 4, 6, or 8 years old.

The concept of *intelligence quotient,* or *IQ,* was added after Binet's test was brought to the United States and revised at Stanford University to give us the Stanford-Binet test. The formula was

$$\text{Intelligence Quotient} = \text{Mental Age}/\text{Chronological Age} + 100$$

The practice of computing a mental age proved to be problematic because IQ scores calculated on the basis of mental age do not have the same meaning as children get older. So the formula on the previous page was replaced with a **deviation IQ** score—a number that tells exactly how much above or below the average a person scored on the test, compared to others in the same age group. Notice—this is not an absolute score such as weight or height; IQ simply ranks people in relation to each other (Lichten, 2004).

The early *Stanford-Binet test* has been revised five times, most recently in 2003 (Roid, 2003, Roid, Shaughnessy, & Greathouse, 2005). This version of the Stanford-Binet is consistent with the CHC hierarchical model of intelligence, with a general factor on the top and five cognitive factors below: fluid reasoning, knowledge (crystallized ability), quantitative reasoning, visual-spatial ability, and working memory. But psychologists are encouraged to pay more attention to a child's performance on the separate cognitive abilities than to the total general score.

The *Wechsler Intelligence Scale for Children IV (WISC-IV)* is another commonly used individual intelligence test for children. Scores from different kinds of questions about concepts, vocabulary, puzzles, number sequences, general knowledge, arithmetic, symbol sequences, and pictures are used to assess the child in four areas: Verbal Comprehension, Perceptual Reasoning, Working Memory, and Processing Speed. You can compute a total score too, but the test developers believe that the child's performance in the four specific areas is more useful and revealing. (See the WISC-IV Report Form on page 365.) The latest version of the WISC was designed to be consistent with the multi-faceted Catttell/Horn/Carroll or CHC model in Figure 9.4 (on page 361). So even though the Stanford-Binet and the WISC-IV were not originally designed with the CHC model in mind, both tests have been revised lately to better match that model.

KAUFFMAN ASSESSMENT BATTERY FOR CHILDREN II. The *Kauffman Assessment Battery for Children II (KABC-II)* actually was designed based on the CHC model of intelligence and on information processing research (Kaufman & Kaufman, 2003). Areas assessed include visual processing, short-term memory, fluid reasoning, long-term storage and retrieval, and crystallized ability. One advantage of the KABC-II is that it was developed using a sample of children from many different backgrounds and with a range of learning challenges. The children in the sample were closely matched to the 2001 United States census data in terms of race, ethnicity, geography, gender, and socioeconomic status. The authors attempted to limit the cultural content of the items, so there are smaller score differences among children from various ethnic backgrounds. One feature of the KABC-II allows the examiner to teach children how to do a test if they fail early because they are unfamiliar with the format or type of item; examiners can provide scaffolding. The idea is to assess the underlying ability, not just test familiarity.

GROUP VERSUS INDIVIDUAL IQ TESTS. The WISC IV, the Stanford-Binet, and the Kauffman Assessment Battery for Children II are individual intelligence tests. They have to be administered to one child at a time by a trained psychologist, and they take about one to two hours. Most of the questions are asked orally and do not require reading or writing. A child usually pays closer attention and is more motivated to do well when working directly with an adult.

Psychologists also have developed group tests that can be given to whole groups, classes, or schools, like the one probably used in the opening case of this chapter. Compared to an individual test, a group test is much less likely to yield an accurate picture of any one person's abilities. When students take tests in a group, they may do poorly because they do not understand the instructions, because they have trouble reading, because their pencils break or they lose their place on the answer sheet, because other students distract them, or because the answer format confuses them (Sattler, 2008). As a parent or teacher, you should be very wary of IQ scores based on group tests.

WHAT DOES AN IQ SCORE MEAN? Most intelligence tests are designed so that they have certain statistical characteristics. For example, the average score is 100; 50% of the people from the general population who take the tests will score 100 or above, and 50% will score below 100. About 68% of the general population will earn IQ scores between 85 and 115.

WISC-IV

WECHSLER INTELLIGENCE SCALE FOR CHILDREN®– FOURTH EDITION

Record Form

Child's Name ____________________

Examiner's Name ____________________

Calculation of Child's Age

	Year	Month	Day
Date of Testing			
Date of Birth			
Age at Testing			

Total Raw Score to Scaled Score Conversions

Subtest	Raw Score	Scaled Scores				
		Verbal Comp.	Perc. Rsng.	Work. Mem.	Proc. Speed	Full Scale
Block Design						
Similarities						
Digit Span						
Picture Concepts						
Coding						
Vocabulary						
Letter–Number Seq.						
Matrix Reasoning						
Comprehension						
Symbol Search						
(Picture Completion)			( )			( )
(Cancellation)					( )	( )
(Information)		( )				( )
(Arithmetic)				( )		( )
(Word Reasoning)		( )				( )
Sums of Scaled Scores						

Subtest Scaled Score Profile

	Verbal Comprehension					Perceptual Reasoning				Working Memory			Processing Speed		
	SI	VC	CO	(IN)	(WR)	BD	PCn	MR	(PCm)	DS	LN	(AR)	CD	SS	(CA)
19															
18															
17															
16															
15															
14															
13															
12															
11															
10															
9															
8															
7															
6															
5															
4															
3															
2															
1															

Composite Score Profile

	VCI	PRI	WMI	PSI	FSIQ
160					
150					
140					
130					
120					
110					
100					
90					
80					
70					
60					
50					
40					

Sum of Scaled Scores to Composite Score Conversions

Scale	Sum of Scaled Scores	Composite Score	Percentile Rank	___% Confidence Interval
Verbal Comprehension		VCI		
Perceptual Reasoning		PRI		
Working Memory		WMI		
Processing Speed		PSI		
Full Scale		FSIQ		

Ψ PsychCorp™

To reorder WISC–IV Record Forms, call 1-800-211-8378

1 2 3 4 5 6 7 8 9 10 11 12 A B C D E

The WISC-IV (the 4th revision of the *Wechsler Intelligence Scale for Children* first published in 1949) includes a record form like this one for reporting scores on 15 subtests (Block Design, Similarities, Digit span, etc.) and converts those scores into four subscales (Verbal Comprehension, Perceptual Reasoning, Working Memory, and Processing Speed). Teachers and parents may not see this form but might get a written report based on this information.

Source: Simulated items similar to those found in the Wechsler Intelligence Scale for Children, Fourth Edition (WISC-IV). Copyright © 2003 NCS Pearson, Inc. Reproduced with permission. All rights reserved. "Weschler Intelligence Scale for Children" and "WISC" are trademarks, in the US and/or other countries, of Pearson Education, Inc. or its affiliates.

Only about 16% will receive scores below 85, and only 16% will score above 115. Only about 2% score 130 or above and only 2% score 70 or below. Note, however, that these figures hold true for White, native-born Americans whose first language is Standard English. Whether IQ tests should even be used with ethnic minority-group students is hotly debated.

BIAS IN IQ TESTING. **Assessment biases** are aspects of the test such as content, language, or examples that might distort the performance of a group—either for better or for worse. For example, if a reading test used passages that described farming scenarios, we might expect rural students on average to do better than city kids. Two forms of assessment bias are unfair penalization and offensiveness. The reading assessment with heavy farming content is an example of *unfair penalization:* Urban students may be penalized for their lack of farming knowledge. *Offensiveness* occurs when a particular group might be insulted by the content of the assessment. Offended, angry students do not perform at their best.

Are tests such as the individual measures of intelligence fair assessments for minority-group students? This is a complex question. Research on test bias shows that most standardized tests predict school achievement equally well across all groups of students. Items that might on the surface appear to be biased against minority-group students are not necessarily more difficult for them to answer correctly (Sattler, 2008). But even though standardized aptitude and achievement tests are not biased in predicting school performance, many people believe that the tests still can be unfair to some groups. Tests may not have *procedural fairness;* that is, some groups may not have an equal opportunity to show what they know on the test. Here are a few examples:

1. The language of the test and the tester is often different from the languages of the students.
2. Answers that support middle-class values are often rewarded with more points.
3. On individually administered intelligence tests, being very verbal and talking a lot is rewarded. This favors students who feel comfortable in that particular situation.

Also, tests may not be fair because different groups have had different *opportunities to learn* the material tested. The questions asked tend to center on experiences and facts more familiar to the dominant culture than to minority-group students. Consider this test item for fourth graders described by Popham (2005, p. 336):

My uncle's *field* is computer programming.

Look at the sentences below. In which sentence does the word *field* mean the same as in the boxed sentence above?

A. The softball pitcher knew how to *field* her position.
B. They prepared the *field* by spraying and plowing it.
C. I know the *field* I plan to enter when I finish college.
D. The doctor used a wall chart to examine my *field* of vision.

Items like this are found on most standardized tests. But not all families describe their work as a *field* of employment. If your parents work in professions such as computers, medicine, law, or education, the item would make sense, but what if your parents worked at a grocery store or a car repair shop? Are these fields? Life outside class has prepared some students, but not others for this item.

Concern about cultural bias in testing has led some psychologists to try to develop **culture-fair or culture-free tests.** These efforts have not been very successful. When you think about it, how can you separate culture from cognition? Every student's learning is embedded in his or her culture and every test question stems from some kind of cultural knowledge (Sattler, 2008). The ***Connecting with Children*** guidelines will help you interpret IQ scores realistically.

Influences on Intelligence

What influences intelligence? What does intelligence influence? As you can imagine, with such a complex concept, there are many possible answers. We will look critically at several possible influences on intelligence: heredity, race, family, schooling, culture, and time period.

INTELLIGENCE: HEREDITY OR ENVIRONMENT? Nowhere has the nature-versus-nurture debate raged so hard as in the area of intelligence. Should intelligence be viewed as a potential, limited by our genetic makeup? Or does intelligence simply refer to an individual's

CONNECTING WITH CHILDREN

Guidelines for Teachers and Families: Interpreting IQ Scores

Check to see if the score is based on an individual or a group test. Be wary of group test scores.

Examples

1. Individual tests include the Wechsler Scales (WPPSI, WISC-IV, WAIS-III, WAIS Abbreviated), the Stanford-Binet 5th ed., the McCarthy Scales of Children's Abilities, the Woodcock-Johnson III, the Kaufman Assessment Battery for Children II (KABC-II), the Kaufman Adolescent and Adult Intelligence Test (KAIT), and the Das-Naglieri Cognitive Assessment System (CAS).
2. Group tests include the Cognitive Abilities Test (CogAT—formerly the Lorge-Thorndike Intelligence Tests), the Analysis of Learning Potential, the Kuhlman-Anderson Intelligence Tests, the Otis-Lennon School Ability Test (OLSAT), (formerly the Otis-Lennon Intelligence Test), and the School and College Ability Tests (SCAT).

Remember that IQ tests are only estimates of general aptitude for learning.

Examples

1. Ignore small differences in scores among children.
2. Bear in mind that even an individual child's scores may change over time for many reasons, including measurement error.
3. Be aware that a total score is usually an average of scores on several kinds of questions. A score in the middle or average range may mean that the child performed at the average on every kind of question or that the child did quite well in some areas (for example, on verbal tasks) and rather poorly in other areas (for example, on quantitative tasks).

Remember that IQ scores reflect a child's past experiences and learning.

Examples

1. Consider these scores to be predictors of school abilities, not measures of innate intellectual abilities.
2. If a child is doing well in school and at home, do not change your opinion or lower your expectations just because one score seems low.
3. Be wary of IQ scores for children of color, children in poverty, and for children whose first language is not English. Even scores on "culture-free" tests are lower for children placed at risk.
4. Remember that both adaptive skills and scores on IQ tests are used to determine intellectual abilities and disabilities.

For more about interpreting IQ scores, see: http://www.wilderdom.com/personality/L2-1UnderstandingIQ.html

---

current level of intellectual functioning, as influenced by experience and education? In fact, it is almost impossible to separate nature and nurture in intelligence. "As a result, few contemporary scientists seriously engage in nature *versus* nurture debates or dispute the overwhelming finding that cognitive ability involves both genetic and environmental influences" (Petrill et al., 2004, p. 805) with genetic influences accounting for about 20% of the variation among children to about 80% among adults. So, the impact of genetic differences appears to increase with age, and research has not determined why (Petrill et al., 2004). It may be that people make choices that are consistent with their genetic makeup—for example, people with higher IQ scores may choose to stay in school longer—so the genetic influences are magnified by life choices.

But no matter what the cause, it is clear that genes do not determine intelligence. David Bjorklund (2004) sums up a fundamental change in thinking in the developmental sciences:

> Social and biological influences are no longer viewed as competing world views of development, as seen in the false nature versus nurture dichotomy of earlier eras, but are conceived as bidirectionally and fundamentally interactive at all levels of organization; cognitive development is embedded within both the child's emerging biological system and the social environment in which he or she lives. (p. 344)

RACE AND INTELLIGENCE. In 1969, Arthur Jensen published an article claiming that there were significant differences in intelligence by race and that those differences were due mostly to genetics. A firestorm of controversy ensued. Twenty-five years later, a book called *The Bell Curve* (Herrnstein & Murray, 1994) set off another round of debate by making similar claims. In response, the Board of Scientific Affairs of the American Psychological Association established a task force of respected researchers, headed by Uric Neisser, to examine the issues. The conclusion of the task force was that there is a difference between African American and White average IQ scores of about 15 points, but the gap has been decreasing lately. There is no evidence, however, that this difference is due to genetics and "at present, no one knows what causes this differential" (Neisser et al., 1996, p. 97).

One reason that claims about race and IQ cannot be supported is that race is not biologically based; rather, it is a social construct. Race is mostly a label we give to others or to ourselves. For example, the label, "Hispanic" has been used for diverse populations in Cuba, Puerto Rico, Costa Rica, Spain, Mexico, Argentina, and many other countries. But the ancestry of people in these countries varies from entirely African, entirely Native American, or entirely European to mixtures of all these (Sternberg, Grigorenko, & Kidd, 2005). As the study of genetics advances, the findings reveal many more similarities than differences among the "races." All humans are 99.9% alike; there is a very minute amount of genetic differences among the races—about .01% (Smedley & Smedley, 2005). In fact, Smedley and Smedley assert, "From its inception, race was a folk idea, a culturally invented conception about human differences. It became an important mechanism for limiting and restricting access to privilege, power, and wealth" (p. 22).

Another reason that it is difficult to link genetic differences to intelligence is that genetic differences are expressed in environments and shaped by them. For example, when nutrition and health are good, differences in adult height are associated with genetic differences. But when children are constantly sick and starving growing up, they will be short and genes will have little to do with their adult height (Moore, 2001). All genetic effects on observable human traits can be modified by influences from the environment. Further, all environmental effects involve genes or structures influenced by genes—and round and round it goes (Neisser et al., 1996). So, we can look to the environment to understand apparent racial differences in IQ scores. Test bias, poverty, poorer schools and teachers, tracking, and other causes have been suggested as influences that may play a role.

FAMILIES AND NEIGHBORHOODS. It is clear that severe deprivation, neglect, and abuse have negative effects on intellectual development, but what about more typical variations in families? Studies of twins who grew up in the same home compared to twins separated and growing up in different homes, as well as studies of biological and adopted siblings in the same household indicate that family environment is a powerful influence during early childhood, but its effects decrease as children grow older. Neisser and colleagues (1996) concluded that although the lifestyles of families are important for many aspects of children's lives, they "make little long term difference for the skills measured by intelligence tests" (p. 88). There is one problem with these findings, however. Most of the participants in the studies were middle-class White families, so we do not have good information about the connection between family environment and measured IQ for other groups.

There are toxins and other biological agents that can affect measured intelligence. Prolonged exposure to lead, which is present in many older homes and buildings in inner cities, is associated with lower scores on IQ tests (Baghurst et al., 1992). Very poor nutrition during childhood can lead to lower IQ scores, and there is some evidence that improved nutrition for undernourished children can raise scores over time. But it is not clear that more typical variations in nutrition will influence measured intelligence (Neisser et al., 1996).

SCHOOLS AND INTERVENTIONS. It is difficult to separate the effects of schools on intelligence from the effects of intelligence on school achievement. Intelligence test scores predict achievement in schools quite well, at least for large groups. For example, intelligence scores correlate about .5 with school grades. Correlations between intelligence test scores and standardized achievement test scores are higher. This isn't surprising because, remember, Binet threw out test items that did not predict achievement. Intelligence also correlates about .55 with number of years of school completed (Neisser et al., 1996). And staying in school actually elevates IQ scores, so schooling and IQ are interrelated—people with higher IQs tend to stay in school longer and the longer you stay in school, the more your intelligence is elevated (or at least maintained) (Ceci & Williams, 1997).

Even though staying in school longer appears to increase IQ scores (or at least prevent declines), it has been difficult to identify educational interventions that permanently increase IQ for children who are at risk of failing. Often an early gain in IQ for preschool children seems to vanish by elementary school (Ceci & Williams, 1997). But there are exceptions. As you saw in Chapter 6, intensive and continuing programs that work in the home with parents and also provide good daycare and other support services have the best results. One example is the Carolina Abecedarian program in North Carolina (Campbell et al., 2001; Reynolds, Temple, Robertson, & Mann, 2001). Children in the Abecedarian project already scored higher than a control group by age 2, and were still 5 points higher on IQ measure and ahead in academic achievement by age 12, which was seven years after the program ended. In order to be effective, early intervention programs need to be high quality and continue into elementary school. It is not surprising that the children who benefit the most are from families with little money or education (Brooks-Gunn, 2003).

CULTURAL DIFFERENCES. The discussion so far has been very "Western," focusing on intelligence as it is conceived in North American and European cultures. Studies of Americans' implicit notions of intelligence show the "person on the street's" idea of intelligence includes (a) practical problem solving, (b) verbal ability, and (c) social competence—much broader than the psychometric view of fluid and crystallized abilities (Sternberg, 2004). How do these conceptions compare with views of intelligence in other cultures? As Robert Sternberg said in his presidential address to the American Psychological Association in 2004, "Behavior that in one cultural context is smart may be, in another cultural context, stupid" (p. 325). Sternberg went on to describe cultural differences in conceptions about intelligence. Some of these differences are shown in Table 9.8.

Cultural differences in intelligence are evident in another way. The tests and items that are appropriate for one culture are unlikely to be appropriate for another. For example, when Serpell (1997) asked English and Zambian children to do tasks that required perceptual abilities, the English children performed better on a drawing task, whereas the Zambian children were superior on a wire-shaping task. Members of each group could best apply their perceptual abilities to familiar materials for their culture. In a similar example, Moroccans are better than North Americans at remembering patterns in rugs, but worse at remembering pictures of everyday objects (Nunes & Roazzi, 1999; Saxe, 1999). When your text author, Anita gave intelligence tests to children in Texas, she found that a question about "coal" often brought blank stares. But the same question about charcoal almost always got a right answer. There were more barbeque pits than coal furnaces in Austin.

TIME AND THE FLYNN EFFECT: ARE WE GETTING SMARTER? Ever since IQ tests were introduced in the early 1900s, scores in 20 different industrialized countries and some more traditional cultures have been rising (Daley, Whaley, Sigman, Espinosa, & Neumann,

TABLE 9.8 • **Cultural Differences in Conceptions of Intelligence**

These are some aspects of intelligence emphasized by adults in their everyday notions of intelligence.

CULTURAL GROUP	VIEWS OF INTELLIGENCE
Taiwanese Chinese	General intelligence (*g*), inter- and intrapersonal intelligence, social competence, confidence with humility about intellectual matters
Zambia	Cooperation, being social, responsible in family and community
Zimbabwe	Prudence and caution in social relationships
Kenya	Knowledge and skill, respect, handling real-world problems, initiative
Latino American	Social competence
United States	Verbal ability, practical problem solving, social competence

2003). In fact, in a generation, the average score goes up about 18 points on standardized IQ tests—maybe you really are smarter than your parents! This is called the **Flynn effect** after James Flynn, a political scientist who documented the phenomenon, beginning in the 1980s (Flynn, 1984). Some explanations include better nutrition and medical care for children and parents, increasing complexity in the environment that stimulates thinking, smaller families who give more attention to their children, increased literacy of parents, more and better schooling, and better preparation for taking tests. One result of the Flynn effect is the standards used to determine scores have to be continually revised. In other words, to keep a score of 100 as the average, the test questions have to be made more difficult. This increasing difficulty has implications for any program that uses IQ scores as part of its entrance requirements. For example, students who were not identified as having intellectual disabilities a generation ago might be identified as disabled now because the test questions are harder (Kanaya, Scullin, & Ceci, 2003).

For adults caring for children—parents, teachers, counselors, medical workers—it is especially important to realize that cognitive skills, like any other skills, are always improvable. *Intelligence is a current state of affairs,* affected by past experiences and open to future changes, as the Flynn effect demonstrates. Even if intelligence is a limited potential, the potential is still quite large.

Extreme Differences in Measured IQ

As you saw earlier, only about 2% of the population will score below 70 or above 130 on an individual IQ test. Let's look at these two extremes.

CHILDREN WITH INTELLECTUAL DISABILITIES. **Intellectual disability** is a more current name for what was once called *mental retardation*. As defined by the American Association on Intellectual and Developmental Disabilities (AAIDD, 2010), "Intellectual disability is a disability characterized by significant limitations both in intellectual functioning and in adaptive behavior, which covers many everyday social and practical skills. This disability originates before the age of 18."

Intellectual function is usually measured by IQ tests, with a cutoff score of 70 as one indicator of intellectual disability. But an IQ score below the 70 range is *not* enough to diagnose a child as having intellectual disabilities. There must also be problems with adaptive behavior, day-to-day independent living, and social functioning. This caution is especially important when interpreting the scores of students from different cultures. Defining intellectual disabilities based on test scores alone can falsely label students who are perceived as disabled only for the part of the day they attend school, but function well in their homes and neighborhoods. Only about 1% of the population fits the AAIDD's definition of having disabilities in both intellectual functioning and adaptive behavior.

For many students with intellectual disabilities who are between the ages of 9 and 13, learning goals include basic reading, writing, arithmetic, learning about the local environment, social behavior, and personal interests. In middle and high school, the emphasis is on vocational and domestic skills, literacy for living (using money; reading signs, labels, and newspaper ads; completing a job application), job-related behaviors such as punctuality or taking messages and notes; health self-care; and citizenship skills. Today there is a growing emphasis on **transition and functional skills**—preparing the student to live and work in the community (Smith & Tyler, 2010).

CHILDREN WHO ARE GIFTED AND TALENTED. Consider this situation, a true story:

> Latoya was already an advanced reader when she entered first grade in a large urban school district. Her teacher noticed the challenging chapter books Latoya brought to school and read with little effort. After administering a reading assessment, the school's reading consultant confirmed that Latoya was reading at

> the fifth-grade level. Latoya's parents reported with pride that she had started to read independently when she was three years old and "had read every book she could get her hands on." (Reis et al., 2002)

In her struggling urban school, Latoya received no particular accommodations, and by fifth grade she was still reading at just above the fifth-grade level. Her teacher had no idea that Latoya had ever been an advanced reader. Latoya is not alone. A national survey found that more than one-half of all **gifted children** do not achieve in school at a level equal to their ability (Tomlinson-Keasey, 1990).

Who is gifted and talented? There are many definitions of gifted because individuals can have many different gifts. Remember that Gardner (2009) identified eight separate "intelligences" and Sternberg (1997) suggests a triarchic model. Renzulli and Reis (2003) have a different three-part conception of giftedness: above-average general ability, a high level of creativity, and a high level of task commitment or motivation to achieve. Truly gifted children are not the ones who learn quickly with little effort. The work of gifted children is original, extremely advanced for their age, and potentially of lasting importance. They may play a musical instrument like a skillful adult, turn a visit to the grocery store into a mathematical puzzle, and become fascinated with algebra when their friends are having trouble carrying in addition (Winner, 2000). Recent conceptions widen the view of giftedness to include attention to the children's culture, language, and exceptionalities (NAGC, 2010). Some students with intellectual gifts and talents also have learning problems such as difficulties hearing, learning disabilities, or attention deficit disorders, so their talents will be missed without careful assessment. And like the girl mentioned in the chapter opening case, older students may actually try to hide their abilities from their friends and teachers.

The best single predictor of academic giftedness is the individual IQ test; often a cutoff score of 130 is used (two standard deviations above the mean or the upper 2%). But these tests are costly and time-consuming, and far from perfect. Group achievement and intelligence tests tend to underestimate the IQs of very bright children. Group tests may be appropriate for screening, but they are not appropriate for making placement decisions. One answer is a case study approach: gathering many kinds of information, test scores, grades, examples of work, projects and portfolios, letters or ratings from teachers, self-ratings, and so on (Renzulli & Reis, 2003). Especially for recognizing artistic talent, experts in the field can be called in to judge the merits of a child's creations. Creativity tests may identify some children not picked up by other measures, particularly minority students who may be at a disadvantage on the other types of tests.

TEACHING GIFTED CHILDREN. Teaching methods for gifted students should encourage abstract thinking, creativity, and independence, not just the learning of greater quantities of facts. In working with gifted and talented students, adults must be imaginative, flexible, and unthreatened by their capabilities. What does this child need most? What is she or he ready to learn? Who can help me to help this child? Answers might come from faculty members at nearby colleges, retired professionals, books, museums, or older peers. Strategies might be as simple as letting the child do math with the next grade. Increasingly, more flexible programs are being devised for gifted children: summer institutes; courses at nearby colleges; classes with local artists, musicians, or dancers; independent research projects; selected classes in high school for younger students; honors classes; and special-interest clubs.

As the guidance counselor realized in the opening case, there are three groups of students who are underrepresented in gifted education programs: women, students with learning disabilities, and students living in poverty, often children of color (Stormont, Stebbins, & Holliday, 2001). The ***Connecting with Children*** guidelines on the next page provide suggestions.

Because school is such an important context for development, at least in cultures where children attend school, let's look at this world more closely.

CONNECTING WITH CHILDREN

Guidelines for Teachers: Teaching Underrepresented Gifted Students

GIRLS

"As they grow older, girls may hide their abilities or even deliberately score lower on standardized tests and take fewer challenging courses" (Stormont et al., 2001).

Notice when girls' test scores seem to decline or when they are hiding good grade reports.

Examples

1. Look back at test scores from previous years, especially if students seem very capable in class, but average on tests.
2. Notice when able girls select easy tasks or books and ask why.

Encourage assertiveness, achievement, high goals, and demanding work from all students.

Examples

1. Provide models of achievement through speakers, internships, or readings.
2. Look for and support gifts in arenas other than academic achievement.

GIFTED STUDENTS WITH LEARNING DISABILITIES: TWICE-EXCEPTIONAL

Learning problems may be subtle and the child is fine through elementary school, but begins to have problems as academic work gets harder in the later grades, or the child's gifts may be used to compensate for learning disabilities, so the student seems just average to teachers (McCoach, Kehle, Bray, & Siegle, 2001).

Understand that these children may be more angry and frustrated than others by the problems that they encounter.

Examples

1. See the emotions as possible diagnostics—why is the child angry and frustrated?
2. Provide emotional support—important for all children, but especially for this group.
3. Identify these children by looking longitudinally at achievement: Who was a high achiever in elementary school, but began having trouble as more and more reading was required in later grades?

Address both learning problems and gifts.

Examples

1. Remediate skill deficits but also identify and develop talents and strengths.
2. Help children learn to compensate directly for their learning problems and help them "tune in" to their own strengths and difficulties.

GIFTED CHILDREN WHO LIVE IN POVERTY

Health problems, lack of resources, homelessness, fears about safety and survival, frequent moves, responsibilities for the care of other family members—all make achievement in school more difficult.

Identify students with gifts who live in poverty or who are ethnic minority students.

Examples

1. Use alternative assessment, teacher nomination, or creativity tests.
2. Look for children who are expressive, good storytellers, or able to improvise when they have limited materials. Try dynamic assessments that give students clues and observe how they solve problems using the clues.

Be sensitive to cultural differences in values about cooperative or solitary achievement (Ford, 2000).

Examples

1. Focus on development of racial identities and be aware of your own racial or ethnic identity.
2. Explore culturally relevant pedagogy. Use multicultural strategies to encourage achievement.

The Child in School

In postindustrial societies, children between the ages of 6 and 11 years are in school, so teachers, peers, curriculum materials, assessments, and school policies provide a context for cognitive development.

International Comparisons and Their Effects

Different countries have different kinds of schooling, with different effects on learning and probably on cognitive development,

CULTURAL DIFFERENCES IN SCHOOL ACHIEVEMENT. The *Trends in International Mathematics and Science Study* (TIMSS) and the *Program for International Student Assessment* (PISA) are two international assessment programs. The TIMSS is the source used in the United States for international comparisons of student achievement in mathematics and science at the fourth and eighth grades. The PISA is the U.S. and Canadian source for comparisons of students' mathematical and scientific literacy at age 15, at or near the end of compulsory schooling for most of the countries assessed. Four TIMSS studies have been conducted, 1995, 1999, 2003, and 2007. Another is planned for 2011. In the fourth grade, a total of 37 countries participated in the 2007 administration of the TIMSS tests, with 27 testing at both the fourth and eighth grade levels. The results of the mathematics tests are in Table 9.9.

The math superiority of the Asian countries of Hong Kong, Singapore, Korea, Chinese Taipei, and Japan is clear in Table 9.9. In addition, many students in these Asian countries reached the Advanced International Benchmark for mathematics that indicates ability to deal with the most complex topics and superior reasoning skills (Mullis, Martin, & Foy, 2009). Why are Asian children superior in mathematics? Is it nature or nurture? By now, we know better than to ask such either/or questions, but in this case nurture appears to play a large role. This superiority in math probably is related to differences in the way mathematics is taught and studied and to the self-motivation skills of many Asian students (Baron, 1998; Stevenson & Stigler, 1992). Also, students who spoke the same language at home and in school, more common in many Asian countries, scored higher on the tests (Mullis et al., 2009).

In terms of gender differences, at the fourth grade, there were no differences in mathematics achievement on average across the TIMSS 2007 countries. In approximately half the countries, the difference in average achievement between boys and girls was close to zero.

TABLE 9.9 • **Mathematics Achievement Results of the 2003 Trends in International Mathematics and Science Study (TIMSS) for Countries That Took Both the Fourth and Eighth Grade Tests (Average score is 500)**

FOURTH GRADE		RANK	EIGHTH GRADE	
COUNTRY	AVERAGE SCALED SCORE		COUNTRY	AVERAGE SCALED SCORE
Hong Kong	607	1	Chinese Taipei	598
Singapore	599	2	Korea	597
Chinese Taipei	576	3	Singapore	593
Japan	568	4	Hong Kong	572
Kazakhstan	549	5	Japan	570
Russian Federation	544	6	Hungary	517
England	541	7	England	513
Latvia	537	8	Russian Federation	512
Netherlands	535	9	United States	508
Lithuania	530	10	Lithuania	506
United States	529	11	Czech Republic	504
Germany	525	12	Slovenia	501
Denmark	523	13	Armenia	499
Australia	516	14	Australia	496
Hungary	510	15	Sweden	491

In 2007, the Pan-Canadian Assessment Program (PCAP) began testing. Factors that were associated with higher scores included having more books at home, mothers reading to their children, parents and teachers helping children with reading, teachers assigning reading outside class, students reading for meaning and reading outside class, having reading routines, and enjoying reading.

Girls had higher mathematics achievement than boys in 8 countries and boys had higher achievement than girls in 12 countries. At the eighth grade, on average, girls had higher achievement than boys.

Let's examine responses to international comparisons around the world, in Canada, and in the United States.

EFFECTS AROUND THE WORLD. The international comparisons of student achievement appear to be useful in many countries, particularly those without a history of gathering this type of information. Because they are highly visible, the findings of these comparisons are valued by policymakers in the participating countries. The results help educators in the countries better understand how the teaching methods and curriculum materials used contribute to student achievement. In addition, these increased understandings motivate reforms in educational programs and promote more research on student learning (Gilmore, 2005).

CANADA: PROVINCIAL TESTING. Partly in response to international comparisons like the TIMSS and PISA, in 2003, a new assessment approach, the Pan-Canadian Assessment Program (PCAP) was approved and administered for the first time in spring, 2007. The PCAP also measures student achievement (at ages 13 and 15) in mathematics, reading and writing, and science, with the option to add more subjects later. The intent of the PCAP was to provide information on achievement levels, so a random sample of 13- and 15-year-olds is tested in English and French. Results so far for reading indicate that factors such as being female, having more books at home, mothers reading to their children, parents and teachers helping children with reading, teachers assigning reading outside class, students reading for meaning and reading outside class, having reading routines, and enjoying reading are associated with higher achievement, whereas reading by decoding, being absent from school, and being male are associated with lower achievement on the PCAP (CMCE, 2009).

THE UNITED STATES: ACCOUNTABILITY. One of the outcomes of the TIMSS and earlier international comparisons has been federally mandated accountability in the United States. On January 8, 2002, then President George W. Bush signed into law the No Child Left Behind (NCLB) Act. In a nutshell, the NCLB Act requires that *all* students in grades 3 through 8 take standardized achievement tests in reading and mathematics every year; in addition, one more exam is required in high school. In 2007, a science test was added—one test a year in each of three grade spans (3–5, 6–9, 10–12). Based on these test scores, schools are judged to determine if their students are making *Adequate Yearly Progress (AYP)* toward becoming proficient in the subjects tested. Regardless of how states define AYP standards, the NCLB Act requires that all students in the schools reach proficiency by the end of the 2013–2014 school year. In addition, schools must develop AYP goals and report scores separately for several groups, including racial and ethnic minority students, students with disabilities, students whose first language is not English, and students from low-income homes.

As we write this page, there is heated discussion about the upcoming reauthorization of NCLB. The greatest concern focuses on improving the way AYP is determined. One suggestion is to focus on growth, not just target scores and to allow greater flexibility for students with disabilities and English language learners. Other recommendations emphasize alternative assessments or strengthening standards to reflect a broader curriculum that connects with the demands of college and work (ECS, 2010).

In response to international and local achievement test results, everyone has a favorite answer to improving schools—back to basics, more accountability, smaller classes, charter schools, better teachers, parent involvement . . . the list goes on. But as a parent, teacher, or voting citizen, or person concerned about children's development, you must ask, "What does the research tell us about the influences on children's achievement in school?" We turn to that question now.

Influences on School Achievement

In this section we take an approach consistent with Bronfenbrenner's bioecological theory of development; that is, we begin with the child and move outward to the many other contexts that influence cognitive development in school.

CHILDREN'S COMPETENCIES AND RESILIENCE. We saw in the section on intelligence that IQ, as assessed by standardized tests (particularly individually administered tests), predicts achievement in school. No surprises there—Binet's goal was to do just that when he developed the first tests of intelligence. What other individual abilities or characteristics are associated with school achievement? Children's achievement patterns that develop in the first few years of school are remarkably stable across their years of education (Alexander & Entwisle, 1998). In a study of children in Head Start programs, McWayne, Fantuzzo, and McDermott (2004) identified teachable competencies and skills that uniquely contribute to early academic success and resilience: literacy and number skills, motor and social skills, persistence, attention, motivation, positive responses to instruction, and cooperative interactions with peers. Children who developed these competencies were in a position to respond with resilience to the challenges of school. So it makes sense to focus on these competencies in the early years of schooling. In Chapter 10 you will learn about how schools can foster social emotional skills and resilience.

PARENTING. It makes sense that parental behaviors supporting the development of children's social skills and emotional self-regulation would prepare the children for success in school. Parents who are reassuring and supportive but also encourage the child's autonomy will help their children handle the frustrations, delays, and tensions that are bound to come with schooling (Grossman et al., 2002).

A longitudinal study of children's adjustment to school by the National Institute of Child Health and Human Development Early Child Care Research Network found support for these ideas. The researchers concluded that "the most competent and least problematic children from the teachers' perspectives are those whose fathers are sensitive and supportive of their children's autonomy, whose mothers' parenting beliefs support self-directed child behavior, and whose parents maintain an emotionally intimate relationship" (NICHD, 2004b, p. 628). In addition, other research has found that when parents have more education themselves and higher expectations for their children's education, they structure the home environment and their own interactions with their children to support the child's achievement in school (Davis-Kean, 2005).

FAMILY AND NEIGHBORHOOD INFLUENCES. Children from higher socioeconomic (SES) families show higher average levels of achievement on test scores and stay in school longer than children from lower SES families (Boyle, Georgiades, Mustard, & Racine, 2007; Gutman, Sameroff, & Cole, 2003), but the relationship between SES and school achievement appears to be weaker for minority-group students (Sirin, 2005). Poor children are at least twice as likely as non-poor children to be kept back in school. The longer the child is in poverty, the stronger the impact on achievement. For example, even when we take into account parents' education, the chance that children will be retained in grades or placed in special education increases by 2–3% for every year the children live in poverty (Ackerman & Brown, 2006; Bronfenbrenner, McClelland, Wethington, Moen, & Ceci, 1996; Sherman, 1994). About 1 in 6 American children lives in poverty and 1 in 14 lives in extreme poverty, defined in 2009 by the United States Department of Health and Human Services as an income of $22,050 for a family of four ($27,570 in Alaska and $25,360 in Hawaii). The numbers are very similar for Canada.

What are the effects of poverty that might explain the lower school achievement of these students? Research suggests that it is not low income itself, but the material hardships that come with poverty that lead to greater parental stress and fewer resources for children's achievement (Gershoff, Aber, Raver, & Lennon, 2007). Material hardships include poor health care for the family; dangerous, unhealthy, or unstable housing; insecurity about getting enough food;

and general financial trouble—too many bills and not enough money. Other factors that follow are family stress and instability, interruptions in schooling, overcrowding, homelessness, discrimination, tracking in school, lower quality school resources—all of which can lead to school failures. Poor children have less access to books, computers, high-quality day care, libraries, trips, and museums (Evans, 2004). Home and neighborhood resources seem to have the greatest impact on children's achievement when school is not in session—during the summer or before children enter school. For example, Entwisle, Alexander, and Olson (1997) found that low-SES and high-SES students made comparable gains in reading and math when schools were open, but the low-SES students lost ground during the summer while the high-SES students continued to improve academically, probably because the high-SES children had access to such enrichments as camps, clubs, books, special tutoring, and travel.

Of course, not all low-income families lack resources. Many of these families provide rich learning environments for their children. In fact, "most disadvantaged children grow up in relatively stable and secure environments" (Ackerman & Brown, 2006, p. 92), the kind of environments we have seen teach children how to handle school. Relationships with teachers also contribute to a stable environment.

TEACHERS. Do teachers make a difference? In one large study, researchers examined how students are affected by having several effective or ineffective teachers in a row (Sanders & Rivers, 1996). They looked at fifth graders in two large metropolitan school systems in Tennessee. Students who had highly effective teachers for third, fourth, and fifth grades scored an average of 83rd percentile on a standardized mathematics achievement test in one district and 96th percentile in the other (99th percentile is the highest possible score). In contrast, students who had the least effective teachers three years in a row averaged 29th percentile in math achievement in one district and 44th percentile in the other—a difference of over 50 percentile points in both cases! Students with average teachers or with a mixture of low, average, and high effectiveness teachers for the three years had math scores between these extremes. Sanders and Rivers concluded that the best teachers encouraged good to excellent gains in achievement for all students, but lower achieving students were the first to benefit from good teaching. The effects of teaching were cumulative and residual—that is, better teaching in a later grade could make up *in part* for less effective teaching in earlier grades, but could not erase all the deficits. In fact, one study found that at least 7% of the differences in test score gains for students could be traced to their teachers (Rivkin, Hanushek, & Kain, 2001).

What do effective teachers know and do that supports students' learning? This is an important question; researchers have been asking it for years. You will learn about the importance of teachers and their social emotional relationships with students in Chapter 10. Here we look simply at cognitive characteristics—their educational qualifications and knowledge of the subjects they teach.

Using data from a 50-state survey of policies, state case study analyses, the Schools and Staffing Surveys, and the National Assessment of Educational Progress (NAEP), Linda Darling-Hammond (2000) examined the ways in which teacher qualifications are related to student achievement across states. Her findings indicated that the quality of teachers—as measured by whether the teachers were fully certified and had a major in their teaching field—was related to student performance. In fact, measures of teacher preparation and certification were by far the strongest predictors of student achievement in reading and mathematics, both before and after controlling for student poverty and English language proficiency (Darling-Hammond & Youngs, 2002).

Children with Learning Challenges

It is beyond this book to discuss all the challenges children face, so we will focus on two common cognitive problems: attention deficit disorder and learning disabilities. You will learn about social emotional and behavioral challenges such as autism spectrum disorders in other chapters.

HYPERACTIVITY AND ATTENTION DISORDERS. You have probably heard and may even have used the term *hyperactivity.* Children with ADHD (defined on page 349) may be more physically active and inattentive than other children, but not necessarily. They often have difficulty responding appropriately and working steadily toward goals (even their own goals), and they

POINT/COUNTERPOINT: Pills or Skills for Children with ADHD?

This morning we opened the newspaper to a headline, "ADHD diagnoses soar in 4 years." The Centers for Disease Control now puts the number of children diagnosed with ADHD as 1 in 10 in the U.S. (Wechsler, 2010). A report from the 2nd International Congress on ADHD (Thome & Reddy, 2009) noted, "There is increasing evidence that ADHD is a worldwide transcultural phenomenon and exhibits striking and consistent characteristics which seem to be independent of cultural background" (p. 163). The rates in different countries vary from 4% to 10% worldwide (Fabiano et al., 2009; Gerwe et al., 2009). Today, there is an increasing reliance on drug therapy for ADHD. Almost 3% of school-age children (ages 6 to 18) take some kind of medication for ADHD. Should children with ADHD be given drugs?

POINT

Yes, drugs are helpful in ADHD. Ritalin and other prescribed drugs such as Adderall, Focalin, Dexadrine, Vyvanse, and Cylert are stimulants, but in particular dosages, they tend to have paradoxical effects on many children with ADHD. Short-term effects include possible improvements in social behaviors such as cooperation, attention, and compliance. Research suggests that about 70–80% of children with ADHD are more manageable and better able to benefit from educational and social interventions when on medication (Hutchinson, 2007). In fact, both stimulants such as Adderall and Ritalin and nonstimulant treatments such as Strattera appear to have some helpful effects for many children and adolescents with ADHD (Kratchovil, 2009). Positive results also have been reported with Buspar, generally used to treat anxiety, and even some supplements such as pycnogenol (Trebaticka et al., 2009). There is also some evidence that Strattera might have positive effects on working memory, planning, and inhibition—at least for the Chinese children studied (Yang et al., 2009). German researchers studying the effects of longer-acting once-a-day Concerta concluded that the transition from short-acting stimulants to Concerta was "associated with significant improvements in daily functioning in several areas of life, severity of disease, and in quality of life" (Gerwe et al., 2009, p. 185).

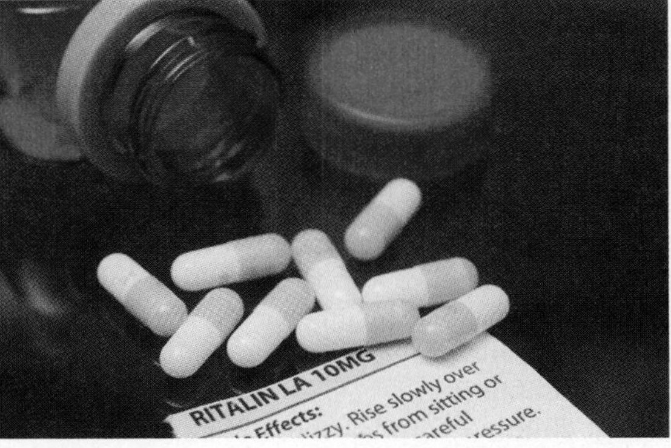

COUNTERPOINT

NO, drugs should not be the first treatment tried with ADHD. For many children there are negative side effects of these drugs, such as increased heart rate and higher blood pressure, interference with growth rate, insomnia, weight loss, and nausea (Smith & Tyler, 2010). For most children, these side effects are mild and can be controlled by adjusting the dosage. However, little is known about the long-term effects of drug therapy. A new drug called Strattera is not a stimulant, but may lead to increased thoughts of suicide. As a parent or teacher, you need to keep up with the research on treatments for ADHD.

Gregory A. Fabiano and his colleagues (2009) identified 174 studies with almost 3,000 participants in behavioral treatments for ADHD conducted between 1967 and 2006 that met rigorous standards of quality research. Behavioral treatments involve the application of methods derived from behavioral learning theories such as contingency management, time-out, shaping, self-regulation, and modeling (see Chapter 2). The researchers compared treated with untreated groups or individuals before and after one or more different kinds of treatments. Their conclusion? Findings were clear and impressive. "Based on these results, there is strong and consistent evidence that behavioral treatments are effective for treating ADHD" (p. 129). In an interview, Gregory Fabiano said, "Our results suggest that efforts should be redirected from debating the effectiveness of behavioral interventions to dissemination, enhancing and improving the use of these programs in community, school and mental health settings" (http://www.physorg.com/news158342976.html).

Beware of Either/Or

Many studies have concluded that the improvements in behavior from the drugs seldom lead to improvements in academic learning or peer relationships, two areas where children with ADHD have great problems. Because children appear to improve dramatically in their behavior, parents and teachers, relieved to see change, may assume the problem has been cured. It hasn't. The children still need special help in learning, especially interventions focused on how to make *connections* among elements in readings or presentations in order to build coherent, accurate representations of the information (Bailey et al., 2009; Doggett, 2004; Purdie, Hattie, & Caroll, 2002).

The bottom line is that even if students in your class are on medication, it is critical that they also learn the academic and social skills they will need to succeed. They need to learn how and when to apply learning strategies and study skills. Also, they need to be encouraged to persist when challenged by difficult tasks and to see themselves as having control over their learning and behavior. Medication alone will not make this happen, but it may help. For learning to occur, medication needs to be paired with other effective interventions.

may be impulsive and unable to control their behavior on command, even for a brief period. A particular difficulty involves inhibitions. They have problems delaying actions to think about them, and instead, they just act (Barkley, 2006). The problem behaviors are generally evident in all situations and with every teacher in school. One common treatment involves drugs, but there is controversy about this approach, as you can see in the ***Point/Counterpoint*** on page 377.

David Nylund (2000) asked his ADHD clients what would help them gain control of their attention in school. Here is their list:

These are also good suggestions for children with learning disabilities, discussed next.

- Use lots of pictures (visual clues) to help me learn.
- Offer us choices.
- Recognize cultural and racial identity.
- Realize that I am intelligent.
- Don't just lecture—it's boring!
- Let me walk around the classroom.
- Know when to bend the rules.
- Don't give tons of homework.
- Notice when I am doing well.
- More recess!
- Be patient.
- Don't tell the other kids that I am taking Ritalin.

LEARNING DISABILITIES. How do you explain what is wrong with a child who does not have intellectual or emotional disabilities or lack education; who has normal vision, hearing, and language capabilities; and who still cannot learn to read, write, or compute? One explanation is that the child has a **learning disability.** There is no fully accepted definition, but most agree that children with learning disabilities perform significantly below what would be expected, given their other abilities. The National Institutes of Health, National Institute of Neurological Disorders and Stroke (NINDS, 2009) gives the following definition:

> Learning disabilities are disorders that affect the ability to understand or use spoken or written language, do mathematical calculations, coordinate movements, or direct attention. Although learning disabilities occur in very young children, the disorders usually are not recognized until the child reaches school age. Research shows that 8 to 10 percent of American children under 18 years of age have some type of learning disability.

Some educators and psychologists believe the learning disability label is overused and abused. But there is evidence from brain imaging studies that at least some specific reading disabilities, including dyslexia—phonological processing problems with breaking words into letters and corresponding sounds—are neurobiological in origin (Shaywitz & Shaywitz, 2005).

Children with learning disabilities are not all alike. The most common characteristics are specific difficulties in one or more academic areas; poor fine motor coordination; problems paying attention; hyperactivity and impulsivity; problems organizing and interpreting visual and auditory information; disorders of thinking, memory, speech, and hearing; and difficulties making and keeping friends (Hallahan, Lloyd, Kauffman, Weiss, & Martinez, 2005; Smith & Tyler, 2010). The writing of some children with learning disabilities is virtually unreadable, and their spoken language can be halting and disorganized. As you can see, many students with other disabilities (such as attention deficit disorder) and many normal students may have some of the same characteristics. To complicate the situation even more, these students may be well below average in some academic areas, but average or strong in others.

Table 9.10 lists some of the most common problems and characteristics, although these problems are not always signs of learning disabilities. Most students with learning disabilities have difficulties reading. These difficulties appear to be due to problems with relating sounds to letters that make up words, making spelling hard as well (Stanovich, 1994; Willicut et al., 2001). Math, both computation and problem solving, is the second most common problem for children with learning disabilities.

Early diagnosis is important so that children with learning disabilities do not become terribly frustrated and discouraged or develop bad habits in an attempt to compensate. The children themselves do not understand why they are having such trouble, and they may become victims of **learned helplessness** (Seligman, 1975), in which they come to believe that they cannot control or improve their own learning. This is a powerful belief. The children never exert the effort to discover that they can make a difference in their own learning, so they remain passive and helpless.

There is controversy over how best to help these students. In teaching reading, a combination of teaching letter-sound (phonological) knowledge and word identification strategies appears to be effective. Maureen Lovett and her colleagues (2000) in Canada taught students with severe reading disabilities to use the four different word identification strategies: (1) word identification by analogy, (2) seeking the part of the word that you know, (3) attempting different vowel pronunciations, and (4) "peeling off" prefixes and suffixes in a multisyllabic word. Teachers worked one on one with the students so they could learn and practice these four strategies; analyze word sounds; and blend sounds into words (phonological knowledge). Direct teaching of skills and strategies is especially important for students with reading disabilities. See the ***Connecting with Children*** guidelines for some suggestions.

TABLE 9.10 • **Common Characteristics of Learning Disabilities**

ACADEMIC	SOCIAL	BEHAVIORAL STYLE
Unexpected underachievement	Immature	Inattentive
Resistant to treatment	Socially unacceptable	Distractible
Difficult to teach	Misinterprets social an nonverbal cues	Hyperactive
Inability to solve problems	Makes poor decisions	Impulsive
Uneven academic abilities	Victimized	Poorly coordinated
Inactive learning style	Unable to predict social consequences	Disorganized
Poor basic language skills	Unable to follow social conventions (manners)	Unmotivated
Poor basic reading and decoding skills	Rejected	Dependent
Inefficient information processing abilities	Naive	
Inability to generalize	Shy, withdrawn, insecure	

Source: Smith & Tyler, Introduction to Special Education, Table 5.2 "Characteristics of Learning Disabilities" p. 163, © 2010 by Pearson Education, Inc. Reproduced by permission of Pearson Education, Inc.

CONNECTING WITH CHILDREN

Guidelines for Teachers: Teaching Children with Learning Disabilities

Provide structure and a standard set of expectations.
Examples
1. Establish schedules and rules for academic and social activities and tasks—be consistent.
2. Help students develop and practice organizational skills—assignment and "to do" lists, dividers for folders, color-coding, etc.

Adjust instructional materials and activities.
Examples
1. Match assignments and materials to students' reading levels—supplement with learning aids such as computer resources.
2. Break larger tasks into smaller chunks.
3. Give support—assign a tutor or allow more time or a different format on tests.

Give plenty of feedback and reinforcement for success.
Examples
1. Catch the student being good or productive—say something positive.
2. Focus on improvement and personal best.

Make tasks more interesting.
Examples
1. Incorporate novelty and stimulate curiosity—use different formats and types of materials.
2. Encourage students to work together.

Source: Adapted from D. D. Smith & N. C. Tyler (2010). Introduction to special education: Making a difference. Columbus, OH: Merrill. p. 180.

Culturally Relevant Pedagogy

Several researchers have focused on teachers who are especially successful with students of color and students in poverty (Delpit, 1995; Ladson-Billings, 1994, 1995; Moll, Amanti, Neff, & Gonzalez, 1992; Pressley, Raphael, Gallagher, & DiBella, 2004; Siddle Walker, 2001). The work of Gloria Ladson-Billings (1992, 1995) is a good example. For three years, she studied excellent teachers in a California school district that served an African American community. In order to select the teachers, she asked parents and principals for nominations, then examined in depth 8 of the 9 teachers who were nominated by *both* parents and principals.

Based on her research, Ladson-Billings developed a conception of teaching excellence. She uses the term **culturally relevant pedagogy** to describe teaching that rests on three propositions.

STUDENTS MUST EXPERIENCE ACADEMIC SUCCESS. No matter what the barriers, students must develop academic skills because "all students need literacy, numeracy, technological, social, and political skills in order to be active participants in a democracy" (Ladson-Billings, 1995, p. 160).

STUDENTS MUST DEVELOP/MAINTAIN THEIR CULTURAL COMPETENCE. As they become more academically skilled, students still retain their cultural competence. "Culturally relevant teachers utilize students' culture as a vehicle for learning" (Ladson-Billings, 1995, p. 161). For example, one teacher brought in a community expert known for her sweet potato pies to work with students. Follow-up lessons included investigations of George Washington Carver's sweet potato research, numerical analyses of taste tests, marketing plans for selling pies, and research on the educational preparation needed to become a chef.

STUDENTS MUST DEVELOP A CRITICAL CONSCIOUSNESS TO CHALLENGE THE STATUS QUO. In addition to developing academic skills while retaining cultural competence, excellent teachers help students "critique the social norms, values, mores, and institutions that produce and maintain social inequities" (Ladson-Billings, 1995, p. 162). For example, in one school students were upset that their textbooks were out of date. They mobilized to investigate the funding formulas that allowed middle-class students to have newer books, wrote letters to the newspaper editor to challenge these inequities, and updated their texts with current information from other sources.

Lisa Delpit (2003) describes three steps for teaching students of color that are consistent with culturally relevant pedagogy: (1) Teachers must be convinced of the inherent intellectual capability, humanity, and spiritual character of their students—they must believe in the children. When scores are low, the fault is not in the students but in their education. (2) Teachers must fight the foolishness that test scores or scripted lessons make for good learning. Successful instruction is "constant, rigorous, integrated across disciplines, connected to students' lived cultures, connected to their intellectual legacies, engaging, and designed for critical thinking and problem solving that is useful beyond the classroom" (p. 18). (3) Teachers must learn who their children are and the legacies they bring. Then students can explore their own intellectual legacies and understand the important reasons for academic, social, physical, and moral excellence—not just to "get a job" but also "for our community, for your ancestors, for your descendents" (p. 19). When Pressley and colleagues (2004) did a case study of a very successful K–12 school for African American children, they found similar characteristics of schools and teachers, as you can see in Table 9.11 on the next page.

Children in a Digital World

When children enter school, they may encounter a new world of digital technology, or they may simply find much of the same technology they grew up with at home. As we saw in Chapter 6, televisions can be found in almost every home and cell phones are common, but what about computers and Internet access? Even though access to computers and the Internet is increasing every year, people who are younger, have high incomes, are Asians and Whites, highly educated, and employed tend to have higher rates of broadband use at home. People with low incomes, seniors, minorities, the less-educated, and the unemployed tend to lag behind other groups in home broadband use. In fact, over 35% of the people living in the United States do not use the Internet at home and 30% don't use it anywhere (Strickling & Gomez,

TABLE 9.11 • **Research-Based Characteristics of Schools and Teachers Associated with Academic Achievement for African American Students**

CHARACTERISTICS OF SCHOOLS	CHARACTERISTICS OF EFFECTIVE TEACHING	OTHER CHARACTERISTICS
Strong administrative leadership	Dedicated teachers who are accountable to produce results	Much total academic time: A very long functional school day/week, including before-school-hours to after-school-hours interactions and tutoring, good use of almost every minute of every class hour, and summer school for students who need it
Frequent evaluation of student progress	Much teacher scaffolding, encouraging student self-regulation	Students who help one another with academics
Emphasis on academics	Curriculum and instruction emphasizing understanding	Strong family–school connections
Safe and orderly environment	Mentoring, especially with regard to college admissions	Donors and visibly supportive, successful alumni
High expectations for student achievement including selective recruitment/retention of students, with the school weeding out students who are not using the opportunity well in favor of students who will (i.e., weeding out misbehaving students, students not meeting academic standards)	Intentional, massive, and frequent attempts to motivate students, including use of the following mechanisms: Positive expectations Visible care by teachers and administrators Praise of specific accomplishments Generally positive atmosphere Encouragement of effort attributions Cooperative learning experiences Tangible rewards for achievements	Motivational mechanisms not often encountered in schools: Extreme community celebrations of academic achievements Encouragement of a possible self as college graduate and successful professional, discouragement of negative possible selves Development of informed pride in African American heritage and life
Excellent classroom management in most classrooms, resulting in a high proportion of academic time on task	Teachers who provide strong instructional supports for academic achievement (e.g., study guides, test expectations made apparent, informative, feedback on homework and before exams)	Many extracurricular and curricular-enrichment activities—almost all academically oriented or intended to increase commitment to academic pursuits
		An attractive school building loaded with resources to support academic pursuits

Source: Adapted from Pressley, Rahael, DiBella, & Gallagher, 2004, pp. 234–235.

2010), as you can see in Figure 9.5 on page 382. This split in access to technology has been called the **digital divide.** Let's examine the effects of technology use at home and in school on cognitive development during middle childhood, with the digital divide in mind.

HomeNetToo was a longitudinal study that addressed the digital divide and examined the effects of home Internet use on children in low-income families in the United States (Jackson et al., 2006). The participants—mostly African American boys, ages 10–18, in single-parent homes—got a computer, Internet access, and in-home technical support for 16 months. Their computer use was monitored, and all participants completed surveys and interviews along the way. The families got to keep the computers after the project and the researchers helped them find low-cost Internet service. Compared to children who used the Internet less, participants who used it more had higher school GPAs and higher scores on standardized reading tests at the end of the project.

Learning and Computers

Does computer use support academic learning? The answer is complex and even surprising. One review concluded that using computer tutorial programs appeared to improve achievement

FIGURE 9.5

PERCENT OF PEOPLE OVER 3 USING BROADBAND IN THEIR HOMES

Family income still is a major factor in computer and broadband access in the United States.

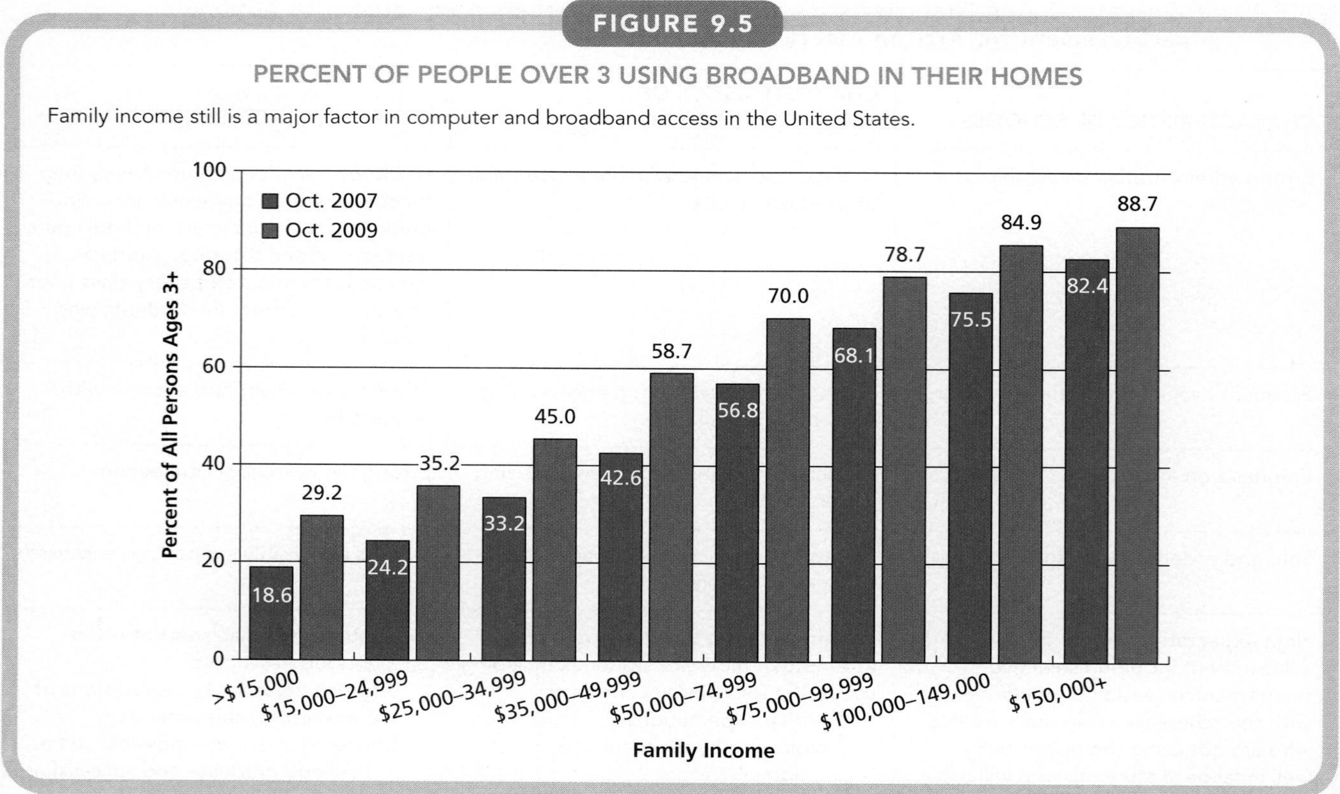

Source: Strickling, L. E., & Gomez, A. (2010). Digital nation: 21st century America's progress toward universal broadband Internet access. *Washington, DC: U.S. Department of Commerce National Telecommunications and Information Administration, p. 5.*

test scores for K–12 students, but simulations and enrichment programs had few effects—perhaps another example that when you teach and test specific skills, children learn the skills. Computers are more likely to increase achievement if they support the basic processes that lead to learning: active engagement, frequent interaction with feedback, authenticity and real world connection, and productive group work (Jackson et al., 2006; Roschelle, Pea, Hoadley, Gordon, & Means, 2000). Like any teaching tool, computers can be effective if used well, but just being on a computer will not automatically increase academic achievement.

Government and international surveys have found that home computer availability is a strong predictor of academic achievement in math and science, but these studies have not separated home computer usage from socioeconomic status, so it is difficult to say if computers alone make a difference. Many other resources come with higher SES (Jackson et al., 2006; Mullis, Martin, & Foy, 2009; TIMSS, 2008). In terms of reading, home computer access is associated with higher achievement, even when family income is taken in to account (Atwell, 2000). Some of the advantage for reading, at least for children with Internet access, may be the result of the reading practice that comes with using the Web—skills that are practiced generally improve and using the Internet requires reading. In the homes with Internet access, children's usage estimates vary from one hour a day to only about 3 hours per week. The most common use of the Internet appears to be searching for information for school projects, followed by communication with friends (girls tend to communicate with friends more than boys), but these numbers generally are based on self-report. We are not sure exactly how children are using the Internet (Jackson et al., 2006).

Children's Understandings of Computers and the Internet

As relatively recent, complex technologies, computers and the Internet present challenges to children's understanding. Unlike most of the hands-on toys and tools in a child's world, these technologies are more virtual than visible. But to use the Internet for school research or to protect themselves from child predators, children must understand something about the technical features of the Internet (keywords for searches, bookmaking, judging quality of sites, etc.) and the complex openness of the social networks (bad people can pretend, lie, and intercept messages; not all e-mails are safe, etc.) (Yan, 2006).

To study understanding of the technical complexity of the Internet, Yan (2006) asked children in grades 4 through 8 questions such as: What is the Internet? How big is it? How many computers are on it? How do you know that? If you stood a long distance from the Internet, what would it look like? To explore their understanding of social complexity, Yan asked: What kinds of things can you do on the Internet? What good things can happen when you use e-mail? When you visit websites? What bad things can happen? Do you have to be careful when you e-mail or visit websites?

Yan concluded that children's understandings of the technical and social complexity of the Internet increased with age, but social understanding lagged behind technical comprehension. By grades 5 or 6, children had an adult level of understanding of Internet technical complexity. This understanding moved from the younger children's concrete sense based on appearances (see drawing (a) in Figure 9.6) to a conceptualization that matches the scientific picture of interconnected computers (drawing (d) in Figure 9.6). For social complexity, it was not until the seventh or eighth grade that children's understandings matched those of adults. In fact, children seemed to need a better understanding of the technical complexity of the Internet before they could grasp the many good and bad social connections that could take place. Age, not attending classes or hours of computer use, was associated with technical understanding of the Internet, but classes did help children cope with social dangers on the Web.

FIGURE 9.6

HOW CHILDREN OF DIFFERENT AGES UNDERSTAND THE INTERNET

Four student's drawings of the Internet from Yan (2006) that show (a) a minimal level of understanding of the technical complexity of the Internet, (b) a partial level of understanding of the technical complexity of the Internet, (c) a sophisticated level of understanding of the technical complexity of the Internet, and (d) a scientific level of understanding of the technical complexity of the Internet.

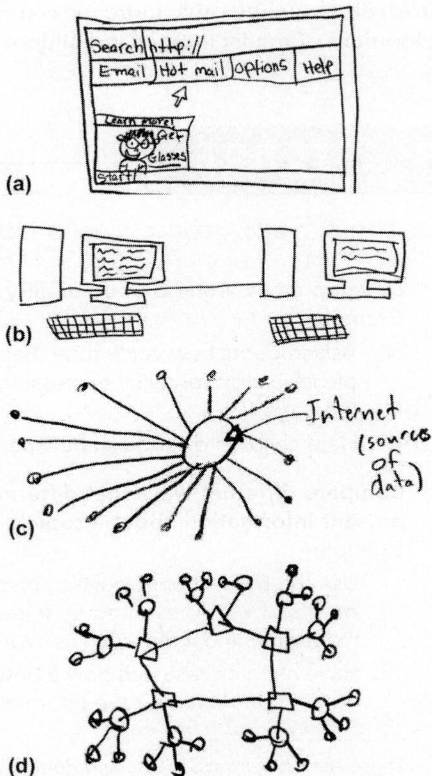

Source: From What Influences Children's and Adolescents' Understanding of the Complexity of the Internet? by Zheng Yan. Developmental Psychology, 42(3), pp. 418–428. Copyright 2006 by the American Psychological Association. Reprinted with permission.

Media/Digital Literacy

With the advent of digital media comes a new concern with literacy—media or digital literacy. Today, to be literate—that is to be able to read, write, and communicate—children have to read and write in many media, not just printed words. Media literacy generally is defined as the ability to access, analyze, evaluate, and communicate messages in many different modes of media. Films, videos, DVDs, computers, games, Web pages, photographs, artwork, magazines, music, television, billboards, and more communicate with images and sounds. How do children read these messages? This is an emerging area of research and application in developmental psychology (Hobbs, 2004).

As an example of practice, consider *Project Look Sharp* at Ithaca College, directed by Cynthia Scheibe, a developmental psychologist (http://www.ithaca.edu/looksharp/). The goal of the project is to provide materials, training, and support as teachers integrate media literacy and critical thinking about media into their class lessons. Teachers participating in the project help their students become critical readers of media. One group of elementary school students studied ants in science, then viewed the animated film, *Antz*. In the discussion after the movie, students were challenged to describe what was accurate and inaccurate in the film's portrayal of ants. What were the messages of the film? How was product placement (e.g., an ant drinking a bottle of Pepsi) used? Tests immediately and 6 months later indicated that the children performed best on the questions related to the discussion about the accuracy of the film (Scheibe, 2004). *Project Look Sharp* suggests the following questions to guide discussion of media:

1. Who made—and who sponsored—this message, and what is their purpose?
2. Who is the target audience, and how is the message specifically tailored to that audience?
3. What are the different techniques used to inform, persuade, entertain, and attract attention?
4. What messages are communicated (and/or implied) about certain people, places, events, behaviors, lifestyles, and so forth?
5. How current, accurate, and credible is the information in this message?
6. What is left out of the message that might be good to know? (p. 63)

The ***Connecting with Children*** guidelines give more ideas from Scheibe and Rogow (2004) for supporting the development of media literacy in children.

CONNECTING WITH CHILDREN

Guidelines for Families and Teachers: Supporting Media Literacy

Identity erroneous beliefs about a topic fostered by media content.
Examples

1. Ask if tarantulas are deadly. Where did that idea come from?
2. Question how statistics are used. Are the sources presented? Are charts drawn to make the results look more dramatic?

Use media to practice general observation skills
Examples

1. Have children watch advertisements on television and ask them to identify characteristics of the spokesperson that are meant to persuade or impress (e.g., the cool Mac guy and the nerdy PC guy; the well dressed cell-phone users, the beautiful car owners).
2. Ask children to look for specific details when they watch a movie or video, and then talk about them afterward.

Develop an awareness of credibility and bias in media.
Examples

1. Ask students how voice tone, background music, editing of video clips, or facial expressions are used to bias a message.
2. Help children distinguish between fiction and nonfiction.

Compare different ways that different media sources present information about a topic.
Examples

1. Use the 6 questions above to discuss a story about the events of 9-11 presented by television news, a news magazine, and a film such as *World Trade Center*.
2. Have children research how a news story is covered in other countries using the Internet.

These are taken from Scheibe and Rogow, 2004. For more ideas, see: http://www.ithaca.edu/looksharp/resources_12principles.php

▼ SUMMARY AND KEY TERMS

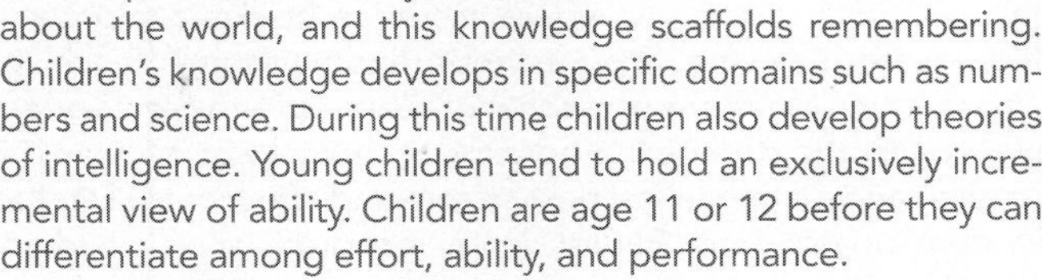

- **Continuing Language Development**

By the end of kindergarten, healthy children without major language challenges will understand and use most of the essential words in their language. But the more complicated forms such as the passive voice take longer to master. School-age children continue to learn words and phrases by fast mapping, about 10 words a day between the ages of 1 and 18. With school come powerful new influences—direct teaching of vocabulary and the written word. But at every age, children from lower SES homes tend to know only half as many words as children of the same age from higher SES homes. Children organize words by chunking and the syntagmatic-paradigmatic shift. During the middle years, children show dramatic changes in their pragmatic skills, having conversations, telling stories, and generally fitting their language to the situation. The narratives of middle childhood have main characters, settings, and plots. Around the age of 5, children begin to develop metalinguistic awareness. Many children in the middle years speak a dialect, second language in addition to their heritage language, or a signed language. All of these language variations are complex and rule governed.

- **Piaget and Vygotsky**

The basic characteristics of Piaget's stage of concrete operations are the recognition of the logical stability of the physical world, the realization that elements can be changed or transformed and still conserve many of their original characteristics, and the understanding that these changes can be reversed. Children are able to reason using identity, compensation, reversibility, classification, and seriation, but reasoning using hypothetical thinking is still difficult. Vygotsky believed that development and learning progress when children grapple with problems in their zone of proximal development, the area between their current development level—where the child can solve problems independently—and the level of development that the child could achieve with support from others. In this zone, assisted learning, instructional conversations, and building on children's funds of knowledge move thinking forward.

- **Information Processing and Memory: Developing Cognitive Processes**

During the middle years, children continue to develop in their abilities to focus attention selectively on relevant information, ignore irrelevant information, and use strategies to plan the best use of attention. In the middle years, some children are diagnosed with attention deficit disorders. Working memory expands with age because of increases in processing speed, metacognition, and improvements of strategy use. Around age 6, most children discover the value of using organizational strategies to remember, and by 9 or 10, they use these strategies spontaneously. Like young children, children in the middle years tend to be more accurate when they are interviewed in unbiased ways without suggestive questions. In addition, older children are better than younger children at identifying the source of a memory, so they can separate what happened in a specific situation from what generally happens in similar situations. In the middle years, metacognition improves cognitive performance and metacognition also is improved as we learn from our cognitive performances. One of the major cognitive developments during the school years is the growth of knowledge about the world. Older children remember more than younger children in part because they know more about the world, and this knowledge scaffolds remembering. Children's knowledge develops in specific domains such as numbers and science. During this time children also develop theories of intelligence. Young children tend to hold an exclusively incremental view of ability. Children are age 11 or 12 before they can differentiate among effort, ability, and performance.

- **Intelligence and Intelligence Testing**

Fluid cognition, all-purpose cognitive processing that involves holding and working with verbal and visual information in working memory in order to plan and move toward goals, is an important aspect of intelligence. But psychologists disagree whether intelligence is one ability or several. Two key abilities are fluid intelligence (mental efficiency and reasoning ability) and crystallized intelligence (the ability to apply the problem-solving methods appropriate in your cultural context). A widely accepted view is that intelligence has many facets and is a hierarchy of abilities, with general ability at the top and more specific abilities at lower levels of the hierarchy. According to Gardner's theory of multiple intelligences, there are at least eight separate intelligences: linguistic (verbal), musical, spatial, logical-mathematical, bodily-kinesthetic (movement), interpersonal (understanding others), intrapersonal (understanding self), and naturalist (observing and understanding natural and human-made patterns and systems). Sternberg defines successful intelligence as the skills and knowledge needed for success in life. Intelligence is measured with individual tests such as the Stanford-Binet, WISC-IV, and KABC-II. Individual tests are more valid and reliable than group tests. In interpreting IQ test scores, we need to be cautious that there are no assessment biases and that tests are appropriate for the language and culture of the test takers. Many factors influence performance on intelligence tests: genetics interacting with environment, family and neighborhood factors, schooling, and the culture's definition of intelligence. In addition, IQ scores have been increasing over the past several generations. Children with intellectual disabilities and children with intellectual gifts and talents both require supportive and appropriate teaching.

- **The Child in School**

Recent international comparisons of achievement around the world have caused many countries, including the United States and Canada, to increase accountability testing in their schools. Many factors affect children's performance in school including literacy and number skills, motor and social skills, persistence, attention, motivation, positive responses to instruction, and cooperative interactions with peers. Children who developed these competencies are in a position to respond with resilience to the challenges of school. When parents have more education themselves and higher expectations for their children's education, they structure the home environment and their own interactions with their children to support the child's achievement in school. Children from higher socioeconomic (SES) families show higher average levels of achievement on test scores and stay in school longer than children from lower SES families. Material hardships; dangerous, unhealthy, or unstable housing; insecurity about getting enough food; general financial trouble; family stress and instability; interruptions in schooling; overcrowding; homelessness; discrimination and tracking in school; and lower quality school resources can lead to school failures. Poor children have less access to books, computers, high-quality day care, libraries, trips, and museums. Teaching also matters. Measures of teacher preparation and certification were by far the strongest predictors of student achievement in reading and mathematics, both before and after controlling for student poverty and English language proficiency. Children with ADHD and/or learning disabilities require careful diagnosis and appropriate teaching. Research also has identified effective ways of teaching students from different ethnic and cultural groups—called culturally relevant pedagogy.

- **Children in a Digital World**

When children enter school, they may encounter a new world of digital technology, or they may simply find much of the same technology they grew up with at home. People with low incomes, seniors, minorities, the less-educated, and the unemployed tend to lag behind other groups in home broadband use. Like any teaching tool, computers can be effective if used well, but just being on a computer will not automatically increase academic achievement. Government and international surveys have found that home computer availability is a strong predictor of academic achievement in math and science, but these studies have not separated home computer usage from socioeconomic status, so it is difficult to say if computers alone make a difference. Children's understandings of the technical and social complexity of the Internet increased with age, but social understanding lagged behind technical comprehension. By grades 5 or 6, children had an adult level of understanding of Internet technical complexity. With the advent of digital media comes a new concern with literacy—media or digital literacy. Today, to be literate—that is, to be able to read, write, and communicate—children have to read and write in many media, not just printed words. Today children need to learn to be safe and savvy when using technology.

▼ KEY TERMS

assessment bias (366)
attention-deficit hyperactivity disorder (ADHD) (349)
automaticity (363)
central executive (350)
classification (342)
code-switching (338)
compensation (342)
concrete operations (342)
conjunctives (336)
conservation (342)
crystallized intelligence (360)
culturally relevant pedagogy (380)
culture-fair/culture-free test (366)
deviation IQ (364)
dialect (338)
digital divide (381)
disjunctives (336)
English Language Learners (ELLs) (340)
entity view of ability (359)
fluid cognition (360)
fluid intelligence (360)
Flynn effect (370)
funds of knowledge (347)
***g* (general intelligence)** (360)
genderlects (339)
gifted children (371)
heritage language (340)
identity (342)
incremental view of ability (359)
insight (363)
instructional conversation (345)
intellectual disabilities (370)
intelligence (359)
keyword method (351)
learned helplessness (378)
learning disability (378)
metacognition (353)
metalinguistic awareness (337)
mnemonics (351)
mutualism (363)
phonological loop (350)
pragmatics (336)
reversibility (342)
seriation (343)
syntagmatic-paradigmatic shift (335)
theory of multiple intelligences (361)
transition and functional skills (370)
triarchic theory of successful intelligence (363)
visual sketchpad (350)
zone of proximal development (345)

▼ THE CASEBOOK

DECISIONS ABOUT INTELLIGENCE TESTING

This is not your favorite time of year. As the only counselor in the middle school, you have come to almost dread the arrival of "the scores." Last week, the school sent out results of the placement test that determines who is eligible for the highly regarded, but selective, gifted and talented program. All students in the school had taken the standardized, paper-and-pencil, group-administered test to determine if they met the selection criteria of an IQ score of 130 or higher. Again this year, the calls, e-mails, and notes are flooding in. Some parents want to meet with you to talk about their child's scores, and especially, as one father put it, "To tell you how smart Jason really is." One mother is incensed because the school cut back on the music program. She had read an article claiming that music lessons raise IQ scores and now is sure that her daughter would have scored better on the test (and been selected for the gifted program) if she had continued in music class. Several other parents have found an online IQ test, given it to their child, and now want the school to admit their children to the gifted program based on the higher online test results. A few of the wealthier parents have hired a psychologist to administer an individual test and want those results used for the admission requirement. Also troubling is your meeting with a girl who was selected for the program, but refuses to be a part of it because her best friends were not selected, and she says, "I'm not really that smart." And today, another possible problem caught your eye. As you look down the list, there are very few students of color and virtually no children of recent immigrants. Maybe this whole process is flawed, but the gifted program is admired all over the district. You look at phone messages and e-mails and wonder where to start.

WHAT WOULD THEY DO?

Here is how some professionals in several fields responded:

TRACY MACDONALD—School Counselor
Chesapeake Bay Middle School, Pasadena, Maryland

Hosting a parent night, prior to the administration of the test, would provide an opportunity for parents to see a presentation that explains the kinds of questions on the test and how the test is scored. Further, breaking down all of the numbers and using common language helps parents understand those results in a meaningful way. It is also important to effectively communicate to the teachers who make these recommendations that a single test score should never be used as the sole criterion to make decisions that affect a child's education. In addition to test scores, grades, academic attitude, and teacher/parent observations should all be evaluated before making recommendations to any program.

Intelligence is more than just one test score on an IQ exam. There are multiple forms of intelligence and multiple ways of determining if a student has potential. As a leader in the school, the school counselor should voice concerns to the administration and teachers about the underrepresentation of minority students on the Gifted and Talented recommendation list. The school counselor should advocate on behalf of all the students and request that the teachers take a second look at the lists to identify students of color to be added. Teachers should be encouraged to go back and evaluate each student using the multiple forms of data to make sure they are extending opportunities to students with culturally diverse backgrounds.

JUDY S. PIEPER—Language Arts, Art, and Religion; Grades 6–8
Holy Trinity Junior High, Newport, Kentucky

As a nonsupporter of "standardized" testing in its current formats, I have been grieving over the present educational focus on scores. There are so many variables to consider with formal testing, that it should NEVER be the basis for stereotyping or placing students. Classroom interaction and observation remain the best weight for assessing a child's ability and his or her willingness to capitalize on it. A school that offers a gifted "program" creates labels for both students and parents to quarrel over, and may exclude those with disabilities, ethnic, cultural or religious traditions not evidenced in a paper and pencil test.

The best way for a school to offer ALL students the opportunity to use their individual talents, which are unique "gifts," is to stop the sorting and offer a variety of interesting programs and extracurriculars such as academic teams, choir, playing an instrument at an assembly or religious ceremony; making posters, murals and banners for the school; reading to or tutoring a younger student; preparing and publishing a school or class newspaper; creating a yearbook or photo memory book; playing a sport; preparing an entry for a community poster or art contest; making a slide show or PowerPoint for video CDs or DVDs; performing in a play or skit; assisting in school and community service projects; participating in science fairs; performing storytelling; presenting oral speeches or giving a class presentation; making a creative depiction about a book; participating in an after school reading or chess club, or leading through student councils and committees. The list of possibilities can be as expansive as are the students' desires. I have been to schools that have bug clubs, fishing clubs, cave clubs, language clubs, and even video game clubs. The bottom line is the more ways a school can offer EVERY child a chance to experience and find his or her niche, the better that school's enrollment will be.

AMANDA BOSDECK—8th Grade Math and Science
West De Pere Middle School, De Pere, Wisconsin

Intelligence testing seems to provoke some controversy, especially among typically sensitive parents. Students may be gifted in a specific area that would contribute to a high IQ score, but may have scored much lower in another area. Some can even test at genius level, but would be unable to apply their knowledge to real-life situations. One single test is not enough to measure a student's overall ability. Standardized testing is great in theory, but because schools are diverse, there are other factors that can skew the scores. Some students perform better while having tests read to them, whereas others might perform better being in a room alone, etc. Children may ask to be left out of a gifted program because their friends will not be part of the class or they do not want a label of the "smart" kid. Kids can develop low self-esteem when labeled and that can contribute to a lack of confidence in their abilities. Various measurements such as utilizing a combination of computer tests, standard written tests, and teacher observations would be appropriate for determining placement in such programs. Using multiple resources for placement could in effect alleviate some of the issues the counselor is facing and more thoroughly assess the intelligence of each individual student.

LOU DE LAURO—5th Grade Reading, Language Arts, and Social Studies
John P. Faber School, Dunellen, New Jersey

As a former gifted and talented specialist, I feel strongly that first students should be self-selected for gifted programs. Surveys should be given to students to determine their interest in a gifted and talented program and to see if they feel they have a special gift. Questions might ask students if they seek more challenges in school or about their specific areas of expertise. Then self-selected students might qualify with a test score or a recommendation by a teacher. Once students express interest, only then I would use criteria for placement into the program.

Do I feel one IQ test can determine who is selected and who is overlooked? No. In my opinion schools should consider self-selection, then consider IQ tests, other standardized tests, teacher recommendation, and prodigal talent. All of this information will need to be charted and explained to parents who have complaints.

These complaining parents who are seeking a spot in the gifted program for their child will need to accept the selection process. They can petition to change the process for the following year, if they feel strongly that their child was overlooked, but they will have to respect whatever criteria is in place.

myeducationlab

Now go to MyEducationLab at ***www.myeducationlab.com,*** where you can:

- Find the instructional objectives for this chapter in the **Study Plan**.
- Take a quiz as a part of the **Study Plan** to self-assess your mastery of chapter content. The program generates an individualized Study Plan based upon your answers to the quiz.
- Complete **Activities and Applications** to assist you in deepening your understanding of important chapter concepts.
- Apply what you have learned through **Building Teaching Skills**, exercises that guide you in trying out skills and strategies you will use in professional practice.

10

SOCIAL EMOTIONAL DEVELOPMENT IN MIDDLE CHILDHOOD

THE CASEBOOK

WHAT WOULD YOU DO?

COACHING CHILDREN—AND PARENTS—ON THE SOCCER FIELD

Jeanie pulled into a parking space at the local soccer field and reached for her latte. It was Saturday morning and she wished she could say she was looking forward to meeting her commitment to the community—she had signed on as director of recreation for children and youth in the small town where she grew up. She had such fond memories of playing baseball and soccer when she was a kid, but things were quite different now. The coaches and parents took the whole thing so seriously. They put so much pressure on the kids to win, yelling at them from the sidelines, reprimanding them when they came off the field. It was becoming difficult to find referees because the parents and coaches harassed them so much about their calls. It was embarrassing to watch; and of greater concern was seeing how it affected the children. Some claimed they were "no good" at soccer. Others were beginning to bully teammates who never scored a goal. "They're only eight years old," thought Jeanie. "Shouldn't the focus be on fun, learning some skills (e.g., being a team player), and doing the best you can?" Jeanie wondered how she should handle this problem. As she walked onto the field, she wondered if anyone had written a book on the etiquette of watching from the sidelines.

Alannah H., Age 10—USA

CRITICAL THINKING

- How would you respond to Jeanie's query about how an overly competitive context could affect school-age children, both in the short and the long term?
- What is the role of a recreation director in this situation? How might people in leadership roles approach parents, coaches, and players to change the overall tone of the game?

▶ OVERVIEW AND OBJECTIVES

During middle childhood, when children are 6 to 12 years old, their social worlds expand beyond family and immediate caregivers to include teachers, coaches, club leaders, peers, and friends. They begin to direct their energies toward accomplishing a wide variety of goals—some they set for themselves, others are valued and imposed by society and caregivers. Historically and cross-culturally, the period when children are 5 to 7 or 8 years old has been considered a turning point. Children are given more responsibility at this time, and they begin acquiring work habits and social skills that will help them function successfully throughout their lives (Davies, 2004). At the same time, children are learning to reason about and perceive themselves and their world more realistically. In this chapter we will examine how these changes affect children's self and moral development. Also, we will look at how children's friendships and relationships with family change as they enter school and engage with more people in activities outside the home. Finally, we will examine some challenges for children in their middle years. By the time you finish this chapter you should be able to:

Objective 10.1 Distinguish self-esteem from self-concept and describe some major sources of influence on children's development of self-esteem in middle childhood.

Objective 10.2	Summarize some major changes in children's moral reasoning during middle childhood.
Objective 10.3	Provide examples of different types of aggression and list steps adults can take to curb aggression and bullying in schools and communities.
Objective 10.4	Explain how parents' and teachers' interactions with boys and girls might influence their gender identity and self-esteem.
Objective 10.5	Describe the role of peers and friends in children's lives during the middle years.
Objective 10.6	Explain how children's relationships with parents and siblings change from early to middle childhood.
Objective 10.7	Provide examples of how teacher–student relationships can affect children's school adjustment and academic success.
Objective 10.8	Describe the impact fear and stress can have on children's lives.

MOVING BEYOND BASIC NEEDS

Erikson (1950) claimed the personality changes observed during middle childhood reflect the latency stage in Freud's psychoanalytic theory. This stage is characterized by children's focus on pursuing knowledge and other intellectual and social exercises rather than meeting basic biological needs (Salkind, 2004). At this age, cultural expectations take precedence over other needs, and the ability to master certain skills is paramount. Children are becoming aware of their capacity to work and learn skills by practicing. Also, their perceptions of competence and self-worth are developing through comparisons with peers (Davies, 2004; Stone, Barber, & Eccles, 2008).

Erikson referred to this drive for mastery as the period of **industry.** Children who successfully master valued skills are industrious, and industriousness leads to feelings of competence and self-satisfaction (Salkind, 2004). However, the conflict at this age is one of *industry versus inferiority*. When children struggle to master valued skills, or are unsuccessful, they are at risk for developing feelings of inferiority and low self-worth. In general, when conditions surrounding children support their development of needed skills (e.g., good relationships with parents and teachers, adequate resources at home and school), they are likely to develop the industriousness that leads to competence and feelings of self-worth. When children's early years are filled with positive, supportive, and successful experiences, they are ready to meet the challenges of middle childhood. They are ready to learn, make friends, and participate safely and appropriately in their social world more independently than was previously possible. In contrast, social conditions that fail to support children's acquisition of skills that are valued and necessary encourage feelings of inferiority and diminish children's confidence in their ability to do anything well (Davies, 2004; Salkind, 2004).

Industry, as Erikson framed it, reflects developments in self-concept, self-esteem, and self-regulation during middle childhood. Let's look at how these aspects of self develop during these years.

OUTLINE ▼

MY PEERS AND ME

During middle childhood, the psychological self becomes more complex and differentiated than it was in the early years. Children describe themselves using more abstract, psychological terms (e.g., *smart, well-behaved, friendly*); they are more aware of how they compare to others like them (their peers); and they begin to speculate about the causes of those differences and about their personal strengths and weaknesses.

Self-Concept

In Chapter 7, we described **self-concept** as a composite of the beliefs and attitudes we have about ourselves. In Piaget's terms, self-concept is a scheme that organizes what we know and feel about ourselves (e.g., "I am a good student." "I am popular." "I am not very athletic."). This scheme or model of self is malleable; our self-concept can vary from situation to situation and from one phase of our lives to another.

During middle childhood, children's self-perceptions become much more refined and realistic than they were in the early years. Whereas very young children tend to rate themselves highly regardless of the task or their actual performance on it, school-age children begin to recognize and acknowledge their strengths and limitations in relation to the standards set for particular tasks and domains of activity, and in comparison to others who engage in the same tasks and activities. In this way, children's self-concepts become more balanced and realistic. They are beginning to distinguish between their *ideal* and *real* selves. Also, compared to very young children who describe themselves in very concrete, often physical, terms (e.g., "I am a girl." "I have red hair and blue eyes."), school-age children begin to include more abstract, psychological dimensions in their self-descriptions (e.g., "I am kind." "I try to be honest.").

What accounts for these changes? Some are due to cognitive development (Harter, 1998, 1999, 2006). Just as school-age children reason better about their physical world, they also reason better about social phenomena. Furthermore, school-age children are exposed to a greater range of experiences and reference points, which they can relate to themselves. For example, they often belong to various social groups and describe themselves according to these associations (e.g., "I'm a Boy Scout," or "I play in a children's orchestra."). They receive feedback from a wider network of individuals and, at the same time, have increased capacity to imagine what others think of them. George Herbert Mead (1934) described the self as a "blend of what important people in our lives think of us." The opinions of significant adults still mean a great deal to school-age children, but feedback from friends becomes more influential in their perceptions of self, especially as they move closer to adolescence.

Much of what we know about the developing self-concept is based on research conducted in North America and Western Europe, and it is important to note that self-concept does not follow the same developmental path in all societies. Whereas Western and European parents want their children to develop a strong sense of self and a spirit of independence, Asian parents want their children to develop a strong sense of interdependence and to define themselves in relation to the significant people in their lives (their family, their community/culture) (Markus & Kitayama, 1991; Peterson, Cobas, Bush, Supple, & Wilson, 2004). Similarly, not all sub-cultures within Western societies emphasize independence to the same extent. Many ethnic groups value family or group interdependence over independence. For example, Latino children are taught that their personal identities are inseparable from the identity of their families, and Native American families, even in urban areas, often live with or near relatives and operate like a communal village (Parke & Buriel, 2006).

Latino children are taught that their personal identities are inseparable from the identify of their families, and Native American families, even in urban areas, often live with or near relatives and operate like a communal village.

Self-Esteem

Recall from Chapter 7 that **self-esteem** refers to the self-evaluative part of the self-concept and that self-evaluations often are based on feedback from others, including parents, teachers, and peers. Also recall that preschool children typically have high self-esteem, perhaps because much of the feedback they receive is positive and encouraging. In middle childhood, children's self-esteem becomes more differentiated as they experience success and failure in a variety of domains (e.g., academic, athletic, social) and in comparison to peers (e.g., some children learn to read more easily than others; some children are more musical or more athletic than others their age). Some skills and abilities are weighted more heavily in self- and others' assessments and, therefore, have more influence on children's sense of self-worth. For example, having difficulty learning to read is associated with low self-esteem because of the importance individuals and society place on developing skills for literacy.

How consistent is self-esteem over time? Is a child with low self-esteem in middle childhood doomed to experience feelings of low self-worth throughout her life? In general, self-esteem is quite high in early childhood, drops during the school years, rises gradually during adulthood, and declines again when people become older. Interestingly, despite these changes across the lifespan, most individuals maintain their level of self-esteem relative to one another (Robins & Trzesniewski, 2005). This suggests that children who have a healthy sense of self at age 7 or 8 will likely continue to have high self-esteem at age 9 or 10, and on into adulthood. However, it is possible for children to experience different levels of self-esteem over time and for relatively low self-esteem to persist throughout the lifespan.

Researchers who study children's declining self-esteem during middle childhood agree that while it's true that children become more self-conscious and self-critical during this period, the extent of the decline is small for most children and reflects their more realistic assessment of their competence in particular areas (Merrell & Gimpel, 1998; Robins & Trzesniewski, 2005; Wigfield & Eccles, 2002; Wigfield et al., 1997). In fact, a drop in self-esteem may lead to increased effort to improve competence. However, when self-esteem is associated with feedback that is unconstructively critical or other stresses (e.g., peer rejection or a specific learning disability), it can lead to emotional uncertainty and psychic stress that negatively impacts emotional development.

WHAT ARE THE SOURCES OF DIFFERENCES IN SELF-ESTEEM? According to Harter (1987, 1990, 2006), a prominent researcher in this field, self-esteem is the product of two internal judgments: mental comparisons of our ideal selves with actual experiences and the support we receive from significant others in our lives. Our mental comparisons often are prompted by direct experience with success and failure in different domains and tempered by the value attached to particular characteristics, skills, and activities. For example, compared to a child who doesn't value sports as much, a child who would like to be a basketball star would likely experience lower self-esteem if she did not score in several games. The discrepancy between what we desire and what we perceive we have achieved or can achieve, therefore, is key in judgments about self-esteem. But so is the support we receive from significant others in our lives. Are we liked and accepted by our family and friends? Do we have stable relationships with others who share our interests and are similarly skilled? Such supports can go a long way toward ameliorating the disappointment in realizing we may have an unrealistic goal.

Harter's (1987) research offers evidence of the combined influence of our mental comparisons and social supports. She asked children in elementary and middle school to rate both the personal importance of doing well in each of five domains and how well they thought they actually did in each one. The discrepancy between these ratings was interpreted as a reflection of the extent to which children believed they were doing well in areas that mattered to them. In addition, Harter asked children to rate the extent to which they believed significant others (parents and friends) supported them in these areas (e.g., accepted them as they were, treated them humanely, and thought they were important). The results of this study are shown in Figure 10.1.

For these children, it appears that self-esteem was equally influenced by a low discrepancy between their ideal selves and actual experiences and the amount of social support they saw themselves receiving from significant others. These findings have been supported in subsequent research (Bouchey & Harter, 2005; Wigfield & Eccles, 2002), including studies of African American children (Luster & McAdoo, 1995).

CULTURE INFLUENCES SELF-ESTEEM. Self-esteem is influenced by both individual qualities and characteristics of the groups to which we belong—we have both individual and **collective self-esteem** (Wright & Taylor, 1995). Furthermore, not all cultures engage in social comparison to the same extent, or value individual achievement and competition. For

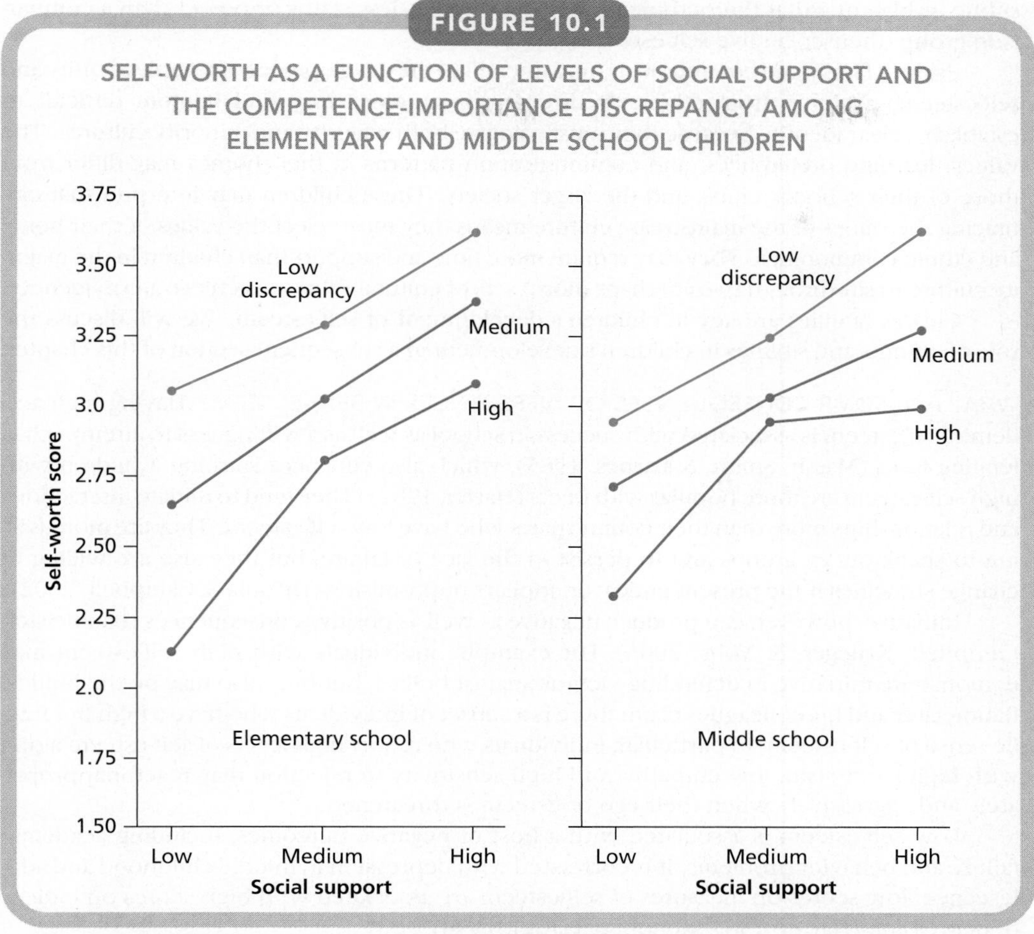

Source: Harter, S. (1987). The determinations and mediational role of global self-worth in children. In N. Eisenberg (Ed.), Contemporary Topics in Developmental Psychology *(pp. 219–242). New York: Wiley-Interscience. Used with permission.*

example, Damon and Hart (1988) studied Puerto Rican children living in a fishing village and found that these children almost never compared themselves to others. In contrast, social comparisons are prominent in American culture. Asian cultures are interesting in that they place high emphasis on doing well, but they also value modesty and social harmony. Therefore, children in these cultures tend to be reserved about judging themselves positively, but offer high praise to others (Falbo, Poston, Triscari, & Zhang, 1997; Heine & Lehman, 1995). Also, these children tend to rate themselves lower on measures of self-esteem than children in the United States (Hawkins, 1994).

Children become more aware of their racial and ethnic identity during the elementary school years (Davies, 2004), and although children tend to choose peers with whom they identify, there is some evidence that prejudice based on stereotypes declines in middle childhood, as children learn to differentiate between learned stereotypes and personal experience. This is particularly true for children who attend multicultural schools and camps. These children are more likely to interact with peers across ethnic lines and to form friendships based on personal liking (Moore, 2002).

It is true that minority children show greater awareness of race and ethnicity than children who identify with the majority group (Verkuyten & Thijs, 2001). Also, it seems these children can develop a positive regard for White cultural symbols and attitudes because they realize these symbols are associated with status and power (Cross, 1987). This interest may reflect efforts on the part of minority families to socialize their children to develop "bicultural competence" so they can function in both the majority and minority cultures (McAdoo, 2001). However, when children are faced with daily reminders—which can be subtle or blatant—that their ethnic or family group has less status or power than a comparison group, their collective self-esteem may suffer.

Pride in family and community is fundamental to the development of a stable identity and self-esteem. Children from ethnically diverse communities may find it more difficult to establish a clear identity because they must navigate both majority and minority cultures. The values, learning preferences, and communication patterns in their homes may differ from those of their schools, clubs, and the larger society. These children may interpret that embracing the values of the mainstream culture means they must reject the values of their home and ethnic communities. They may require more time and support than children in the majority culture to sift through two (perhaps more) sets of cultural values to achieve a firm identity.

Clearly, families are key in children's development of self-esteem. We will discuss the role of parents and siblings in children's development in a subsequent section of this chapter.

WHAT ARE SOME CONSEQUENCES OF DIFFERENCES IN SELF-ESTEEM? Having high academic self-esteem is associated with success in school as well as a willingness to attempt challenging tasks (Marsh, Smith, & Barnes, 1985), which also enhances learning. Children with high self-esteem are more popular with peers (Harter, 1982). They tend to initiate interactions and relationships more than their counterparts who have low self-esteem. They are more willing to speak out in groups and to persist in the face of failure, but they also are willing to change strategies if the present endeavor appears unpromising (DiPaula & Campbell, 2002).

Initiative, however, can produce negative as well as positive consequences (Baumeister, Campbell, Krueger, & Vohs, 2003). For example, individuals with high self-esteem may demonstrate initiative in defending victims against bullies, but they also may be the bullies. Baumeister and his colleagues claim there is a subset of individuals who have a high but fragile sense of self-esteem. In particular, individuals who report high levels of self-esteem along with high narcissism, low empathy, and high sensitivity to rejection may react inappropriately and aggressively when their ego or esteem is threatened.

Low self-esteem is associated with a host of negative outcomes, including academic failure and behavior problems. It is correlated with depression in middle childhood and adolescence; low scores on measures of self-esteem are associated with high scores on indices of depression (Harter, 1987; Renouf & Harter, 1990).

Clearly, self-esteem is associated with a number of significant outcomes for children. Therefore, it is not surprising that researchers, teachers, parents, and other caregivers are intensely interested in determining what causes self-esteem to be high for some children and low for others. If we can find ways to improve children's perceived self-worth, other aspects of their development might be enhanced as well. See the ***Connecting with Children*** guidelines for some ideas about building children's self-esteem.

Self-Regulation

Achieving self-regulation (also discussed in Chapter 7) and self-control are important milestones in children's development and are linked to successful outcomes across the lifespan, including success in school (Linnenbrink & Pintrich, 2003; Perry, VandeKamp, Mercer, & Nordby, 2002) and popularity with peers (Fabes et al., 1999; Gilliom, Shaw, Beck, Schonberg, & Lukon, 2002). In this section, we focus on children's advances in **emotional self-regulation** during middle childhood. Emotion regulation is a special aspect of self-regulation that enables individuals to remain focused on goals, even in the face of difficult and stressful circumstances (Patterson, 1982; Tice, Baumeister, & Zhang, 2004). Emotional regulation involves effortful, voluntary control of emotions, attention, and behavior (Eisenberg et al., 2004; Eisenberg & Spinrad; 2004). Along with the successful acquisition of emotion control strategies comes a sense of *emotional self-efficacy,* in which children believe they are in control of their emotional experiences (Saarni, 1999). Children who have low emotional control evidence outbursts of anger and/or frustration, whereas children with moderate to high emotion control can suppress emotional displays that are inappropriate in a given situation.

Children are less at the mercy of strong emotions during middle childhood than they were in the early years. If they perceive it is in their best interest to suppress their feelings, they can do so (e.g., they can hide anger if they perceive that emotion will lead to punishment, and they

CONNECTING WITH CHILDREN

Guidelines for Families, Teachers, and Other Professionals: Building Self-Esteem

Identify potential sources of low self-esteem.

Examples

1. Be aware of your biases and expectations, and try not to let these color your interactions with children.
2. Create a climate that is physically and psychologically safe for children.
3. Avoid comparisons and competition among children. Instead, encourage children to compete with their prior levels of achievement.

Let children know you accept and support them.

Examples

1. Show your approval for children's attempts as well as their achievements.
2. Highlight the value of individual differences in ethnicity and ability.
3. Let children know you accept them, even when you are unhappy about a particular behavior or outcome.

Help children to achieve.

Examples

1. Focus on children's talents and abilities. Make sure they have lots of opportunities to pursue their interests.
2. Make expectations or standards clear for children, and help them to understand how they can meet them (e.g., brainstorm a list of resources they might use to reach their goals).
3. Provide feedback that is positive and informative; emphasize progress and accomplishment; and provide concrete suggestions for areas that need improvement.

Help children to develop coping skills.

Examples

1. Encourage children to take responsibility for their reactions to events and to understand they have choices in how to respond.
2. Set up support groups or "study buddies," and teach children how to encourage one another.
3. Model appropriate self-criticism, setting clear and reasonable goals, and initiating self-rewards.

Create adult partnerships that support children.

Examples

1. Teachers, coaches, counselors . . . should keep in regular contact with parents. Make communication positive, but also keep parents apprised of problems.
2. Work with parents to design celebrations of children's efforts and accomplishments.
3. Encourage parent involvement in school and community activities.

Source: Canfield, J. (1990). Improving children's self-esteem. Educational Leadership, *48(1), 48-50; Kash, M. M. & Borich, G. (1978).* Teacher behavior and student self-concept. *Menlo Park, CA: Addison-Wesley; Marshall, H. H. (1989. The development of self-concept.* Young Children, *44(5), 44-51; Fantuzzo, J., Davis, G., & Ginsburg, M. (1995). Effects of parent involvement in isolation or in combination with peer tutoring on student self-concept and mathematics achievement.* Journal of Educational Psychology, *87, 272-281.*

can rationalize disappointment or combine disappointment with denial—"I don't care about not making the basketball team. I have too many after-school activities already." (Davies, 2004, p. 369). Similarly, school-age children don't rely on parents and other caregivers to monitor and guide their reactions to emotional events to the extent that preschool children do.

Adults can help children to develop emotion control, empathy, and prosocial behavior by acknowledging their feelings of distress and helping them develop coping strategies. Parents who respond with disapproval or punishment may intensify children's anger and fear and inhibit their emotional adjustment (Fabes, Leonard, Kupanoff, & Martin, 2001). Alternatively, children may become secretive and anxious about negative emotions. In the longer term, parental intolerance for negative emotions may intensify parent–child conflict during adolescence (Eisenberg et al., 1999).

We have also emphasized that self-regulation needs to be understood in a sociocultural context (see Chapter 7). Children learn that there are social and cultural rules concerning the expression of emotions (Cole, Bruschi, & Tamang, 2002). Toddlers and preschoolers learn these rules by receiving feedback from parents and others in their communities. By middle childhood, they implicitly know what kinds of emotional displays are expected or permitted in particular situations and relationships (Davies, 2004, p. 373). They have internalized rules or schemas for expressing or suppressing feelings, or adapting them to suit particular social situations (Raver, 2004; Saarni, 1999).

The rules concerning emotional expression can vary across cultures. For example, Asian cultures generally value an expressive style that emphasizes emotional restraint and a calm demeanor (Bond, 1993; Eisenberg, Liew, & Pidada, 2001). In these cultures, adults are likely to interpret boisterous behavior and impulsivity as poor self-regulation. In contrast, in North American cultures, children know that adults generally accept expressions of excitement. However, even within American cultures, different groups have different rules about displaying emotions. African American children may talk more loudly or excitedly in peer groups than White children do. Rather than interpreting their behavior as appropriate in this cultural context, White teachers or clinicians may judge they have poor self-control.

Finally, children who experience higher levels of risk factors (e.g., personal maltreatment and/or exposure to interadult violence) are more likely to experience problems in the area of emotional self-regulation (Raver, 2004). These children can develop either undercontrolled or overcontrolled, hypervigilant, regulatory profiles. In addition, children who witness violence in their neighborhoods or who live in crowded, lower quality residences are at higher risk for exhibiting lower levels of self-control. However, most children who receive competent caregiving develop effective self-regulatory skills, even those who live in dangerous neighborhoods and conditions of poverty. We discuss parenting styles that are associated with higher levels of self-regulation later in this chapter.

Emotion control can be linked to temperament, but it generally increases with age. Also, as children get older and become more aware of other people's feelings, they can empathize, or take the perspective of others, and they can respond to others in emotional distress.

Perspective-Taking

Perspective-taking, or the ability to imagine what other people are thinking and feeling, develops gradually as children become less egocentric and more able to recognize and coordinate multiple dimensions of interpersonal experiences (Burack et al., 2006). Whereas preschool children have limited understandings of other people's thoughts and feelings, school-age children come to understand that others may not interpret or respond to a situation in the same way they do. They can imagine how another person is feeling, or "put themselves in [someone else's] shoes." Perspective-taking skills continue to develop through adolescence and into early adulthood. For example, early adolescents develop the ability to take the role of an objective bystander and to analyze the perspectives of several people involved in a situation, and older adolescents and adults can imagine how different social and cultural factors can influence the perception of the bystander. According to Burack and her colleagues, developing age-appropriate social perspective-taking skills is fundamental for understanding self and navigating relationships with peers, parents, and other authority figures.

Selman (1980) proposed a five-stage model to describe the development of perspective-taking skills (see Table 10.1). In this model, qualitative changes in children's perspective-taking abilities and interpersonal understanding reflect their increasing ability to both differentiate and integrate the points of view of self and others. As children advance to higher levels of perspective-taking, they adopt increasingly sophisticated strategies for interacting interpersonally and resolving interpersonal problems. According to Selman, the highest levels of perspective-taking are not reached until well into adolescence, and some individuals never reach these levels. Consistent with this claim, developmental models of social information processing agree that the way children understand and interpret (or misunderstand and misinterpret) the behaviors and motives of others influences their immediate response as well as their long-term moral and aggressive patterns of responding (Arsenio & Lemerise, 2004, p. 987).

In a study of children's perspective-taking, Fitzgerald and White (2003) found that children's perspective-taking was positively related to prosocial behavior and negatively related to aggression. Other researchers also have reported associations between deficits in reading social cues and aggressive or antisocial behavior in children (Arsenio & Fleiss, 1996; Schonert-Reichl & Scott, 2009 Warden & MacKinnon, 2003). Fortunately, parents and other adults can foster age-appropriate perspective-taking by prompting children to consider the perspectives of others. For example, Fitzgerald and White (2003) found that children's aggression was

TABLE 10.1 • **Selman's Five Stages of Perspective-Taking**

Stage 0 Egocentric Viewpoint (Age Range 3–6)	Child has a sense of differentiation of self and other but fails to distinguish between the social perspective (thoughts, feelings) of other and self. Child can label other's overt feelings but does not see the cause-and-effect relation of reasons to social actions.
Stage 1 Social-Informational Role Taking (Age Range 6–8)	Child is aware that other has a social perspective based on other's own reasoning, which may or may not be similar to child's. However, child tends to focus on one perspective rather than coordinating viewpoints.
Stage 2 Self-Reflective Role Taking (Age Range 8–10)	Child is conscious that each individual is aware of the other's perspective and that this awareness influences self and other's view of each other. Putting self in other's place is a way of judging his intentions, purposes, and actions. Child can form a coordinated chain of perspectives, but cannot yet abstract from this process to the level of simultaneous mutuality.
Stage 3 Mutual Role Taking (Age Range 10–12)	Child realizes that both self and other can view each other mutually and simultaneously as subjects. Child can step outside the two-person dyad and view the interaction from a third-person perspective.
Stage 4 Social and Conventional System Role-Taking (Age Range 12–15+)	Person realizes mutual perspective-taking does not always lead to complete understanding. Social conventions are seen as necessary because they are understood by all members of the group (the generalized other) regardless of their position, role, or experience.

Source: Adapted from Selman, R. L. (1976). Social-cognitive understanding: A guide to educational and clinical practice. In T. Lickona (ed.), Moral Development and Behavior: Theory, Research, and Social Issues *(pp. 299–316). New York: Holt, Rinehart, & Winston. Used with permission.*

inhibited when parents engaged in victim-centered discipline—encouraged children to consider how their words or deeds might harm another person. Also, school-based interventions that provide children with coaching and practice in perspective-taking can help to reduce antisocial behavior and increase empathy and prosocial responding. Promoting Alternative Thinking Strategies (PATHS) and The Roots of Empathy (ROE) are two such school programs.

The ROE program is unique in its approach to fostering empathy, emotional understanding, and concern for others. Classrooms that adopt the program also adopt an infant for the school year. The infant and his/her mother visit the class once each month during the school year and provide the focus for discussions about how to interpret nonverbal communication and respond to the needs of others. In 1996, Mary Gordon piloted the program in two classrooms in Toronto, Ontario. Currently, the program is being implemented in over 500 classrooms across Canada (Gordon, 2005). Evaluations of the program show its success in increasing children's understandings of the needs and emotions of infants, translating into more prosocial and less aggressive behavior with peers (Schonert-Reichl, et al., in press). For more information about these programs, go to: www.colorado.edu/cspv/blueprints/model/programs/PATHS.html and www.rootsofempathy.org. Clearly, the ability to empathize, or take the perspective of others, is implicated in children's moral development.

Knowing and Doing the Right Thing

Morality involves both thought and behavior, assessing what is right and wrong in a particular situation and then acting in accord with that assessment. Morality also elicits an emotional response, as most people feel good when they "do the right thing," and guilty or ashamed when they behave in ways that are considered immoral. In this section, we focus on the development of moral reasoning and moral behavior during middle childhood.

Moral Reasoning

Moral reasoning involves making judgments about the rightness or wrongness of certain acts. Children's ability to think about moral issues expands tremendously during middle childhood. In part, this is attributable to the general expansion of their reasoning and perspective-taking capacities, and to their expanding social worlds.

TABLE 10.2 • **Damon's Sequence for Reasoning about Distributive Justice**

BASIS FOR REASONING	AGE (YEARS)	DESCRIPTION
Equality	5–6	Children believe that fairness requires that everyone be treated equally—the same.
Merit	6–7	Children recognize that some people deserve to be treated differently because they have worked extra hard or done something special—meritorious.
Benevolence	8	Children are able to consider the needs of others and recognize that some people require more attention or more resources because they have special needs.

Source: Based on Damon, W. (1977). The social world of the child. *San Francisco: Jossey-Bass. Damon, W. (1988).* The moral child. *New York: Free Press.*

Some of the earliest moral decisions in which children are involved concern how to distribute or share materials fairly. Damon (1977, 1988) examined changes in children's beliefs about **distributive justice** through middle childhood. As shown in Table 10.2, very young children (ages 5 to 6) believe fair distribution requires *equality*. When your text author Nancy was very young, for example, she felt it was unfair that her brother Doug was allowed to stay up later on Saturday evenings to watch *The Honeymooners* television show with mom, even though he was two years older. At 6 or 7 years of age, children recognize that some people should be treated differently on the basis of *merit* (e.g., they've worked especially hard or they're old enough for some extra rights and responsibilities). Finally, around age 8, when children are able to consider the needs of other individuals, they understand that sometimes, fair distribution of resources requires *benevolence* (e.g., some children require more of a parent's or teacher's time because they have exceptional needs).

Adults can promote children's understanding of distributive justice, but interactions with peers are especially important. Having disagreements with peers and resolving them requires that children consider the issues involved in distributing justice. They must consider peers' perspectives and come up with a fair solution that will satisfy everyone involved. Children who demonstrate advanced reasoning about distributive justice also demonstrate effective social problem-solving skills and a willingness to help and share with others (Blotner & Bearison, 1984; McNamee & Peterson, 1986).

PIAGET. Piaget studied moral development by observing children playing games and then asking them questions about the rules. Based on their answers, he proposed a two-stage theory of moral development (Piaget, 1932). In Piaget's first stage, which he called **moral realism,** children ages 5 or 6 believe that rules are absolute—they cannot be changed because they come from authorities, such as parents, teachers, government officials, or religious officials. Children at this age also believe that if a rule is broken, the punishment should be determined by how much damage is done, not by the intention of the rule breaker. According to this reasoning, a child who accidentally breaks three cups should receive a harsher punishment than a child who intentionally breaks one cup.

After age 8, children move into the stage Piaget referred to as **moral relativism.** Children understand that people can agree to change rules if they want to and they realize what is important is that all participants in an activity understand and operate according to the same set of rules. Children ages 8 to 12 also understand that you don't get punished for breaking rules unless you get caught and that intentions, as well as the damage done, are considerations in determining a just punishment.

KOHLBERG. Building on Piaget's ideas, Lawrence Kohlberg (1963, 1975, 1981) divided moral development into three levels: preconventional, where judgment is based solely on a person's own needs and perceptions; conventional, where the expectations of informal and formal groups, society, and law are taken into account; and postconventional, where judgments are based on more generalizable universal principles that are personally held and not necessarily based on society's laws. Look at Table 10.3 to see how these levels are further divided into six stages.

TABLE 10.3 • **The Six Moral Stages**

	CONTENT OF STAGE		
LEVEL AND STAGE	WHAT IS RIGHT	REASONS FOR DOING RIGHT	SOCIAL PERSPECTIVE OF STAGE
Level I. Preconventional **Stage 1:** Heteronomous morality	To avoid breaking rules backed by punishment, obedience for its own sake, and avoiding physical damage to persons and property.	Avoidance of punishment and the superior power of authorities.	Egocentric point of view. Doesn't consider the interests of others or recognize that they differ from the actor's; doesn't relate two points of view. Actions are considered physically rather than in terms of psychological interests of others. Confusion of authority's perspective with one's own.
Stage 2: Individualism, instrumental purpose, and exchange	Following rules only when it is to someone's immediate interest; acting to meet one's own interests and needs and letting others do the same. Right is also what's fair, what's an equal exchange, a deal, an agreement.	To serve one's own needs or interests in a world where you have to recognize that other people have their interests, too.	Concrete individualistic perspective. Aware that everybody has his or her own exchange interest to pursue and that these interests conflict, so that right is relative (in the concrete individualistic sense).
Level II. Conventional **Stage 3:** Mutual interpersonal expectations, relationships, and interpersonal conformity	Living up to what is expected by people close to you or what people generally expect of your role as son, brother, friend, etc. "Being good" is important and means having good motives, showing concern about others. It also means keeping mutual relationships, such as trust, loyalty, respect, and gratitude.	The need to be a good person in your own eyes and those of others. Your caring for others. Belief in the Golden Rule. Desire to maintain rules and authority, which support stereotypical good behavior.	Individualistic perspective in relationships with other individuals. Aware of shared feelings, agreements, and expectations, which take primacy over individual interests. Relates points of view through the concrete Golden Rule, putting oneself in the other person's shoes. Does not yet consider generalized system perspective.
Stage 4: Social system and conscience	Fulfilling the actual duties to which you have agreed. Laws are to be upheld except in extreme cases where they conflict with other fixed social duties. Right is also contributing to society, the group, or institution.	To keep the institution going as a whole, to avoid the "if everyone did it," or the imperative of conscience to meet one's defined obligations (easily confused with stage 3 belief in rules and authority).	Differentiates societal point of view from interpersonal agreement or motives. Takes the point of view of the system that defines roles and rules. Considers individual relations in terms of place in the system.
Level III. Postconventional **Stage 5:** Social contract or utility and individual rights	Being aware that people hold a variety of values and opinions, that most values and rules are relative to your group. These relative rules should usually be upheld, however, in the interest of impartiality and because they are the social contract. Some nonrelative values and rights like *life* and *liberty*, however, must be upheld in any society and regardless of majority opinion.	A sense of obligation to law because of one's social contract to make and abide by laws for the welfare of all and for the protection of all people's rights. A feeling of contractual commitment, freely entered upon, to family, friendship, trust, and work obligations. Concern that laws and duties be based on rational calculation of overall utility, "the greatest good for the greatest number."	Perspective independent of formal rules. Perspective of a rational individual aware of values and rights (such as fairness) prior to social attachments and legal contracts. Integrates perspectives by formal mechanisms of agreement, legal contract, objective impartiality, and due process. Considers moral and legal points of view; recognizes that these sometimes conflict and finds it difficult to integrate them.

(*Continued*)

TABLE 10.3 • **(Continued)**

CONTENT OF STAGE			
LEVEL AND STAGE	WHAT IS RIGHT	REASONS FOR DOING RIGHT	SOCIAL PERSPECTIVE OF STAGE
Stage 6: Universal ethical principles	Following self-chosen ethical principles. Particular laws or social agreements are usually valid because they rest upon such principles. When laws violate these principles, one acts in accordance with the principle. Principles are universal principles of justice; the equality of human rights and respect for the dignity of human beings as individual persons.	The belief as a rational person in the validity of universal moral principles, and a sense of personal commitment to them.	Perspective of a moral point of view from which social arrangements derive. Perspective is that of any rational individual recognizing the nature of morality or the fact that persons are ends in themselves and must be treated as such.

Source: The Six Moral Stages from The Psychology of Moral Development by Lawrence Kohlberg, © 1984, Table 2.1, pp. 174–175. Used with permission of The Estate of Lawrence Kohlberg.

Kohlberg pioneered the practice of assessing people's moral reasoning by presenting them with a series of dilemmas in story form. **Moral dilemmas** are hypothetical situations that ask people to make difficult decisions and then justify them. Perhaps the most widely used example of Kohlberg's dilemmas is about Heinz, a man whose wife is dying. There is one drug that can save her, but it is very expensive and the druggist who invented the medicine will not sell it at a price Heinz can afford. Heinz must choose between stealing the drug or letting his wife die. Participants in Kohlberg's studies were asked what they would do if they found themselves in such a dilemma and why they made their particular decision.

At level 1 (preconventional), a child might answer, "It's wrong to steal because you might get caught." This answer reflects the child's focus on what might happen to him—I might get caught and punished—and whether the outcome is likely to bring pleasure or pain. At level 2 (conventional), responses move beyond a strict focus on self to include some consideration of the views and approval of others. Laws, religious or civil, are very important and are considered absolute and unalterable. An answer that stresses adherence to rules could be, "It is wrong to steal because it is against the law." Another answer, placing high value on loyalty to family and loved ones but still respecting the law, is, "It's right to steal because the man means well—he's trying to help his wife. But he will still have to pay the druggist when he can or accept the penalty for breaking the law." Finally, at level 3 (postconventional), responses reflect the underlying values that might be involved in the decision, and rules are replaced by principles or principled moral operations, such as the Golden Rule, or what Kohlberg called "moral musical chairs" in which everyone in the dilemma decides what is right to do after considering the decisions from the perspectives of all others in the dilemma or affected by the decision. A person reasoning on this level understands that what is considered right by the majority of people most of the time may not be considered right according to the moral values and principles that underlie and inform conventional reasoning. An answer might be, "It is not wrong to steal because human life must be preserved. The worth of a human life is greater than, and supersedes, the worth of property."

Colby, Kohlberg, Gibbs, and Lieberman (1983) conducted a 20-year longitudinal study with Kohlberg's original sample. The results, shown in Figure 10.2, indicate the expected sequence of development from Stages 1 to 5, with no evidence that people skipped stages or fell back to lower stages once a higher stage had been reached. The correlation between age and stage was .78, indicating a strong positive relationship between people's age and stage of moral development.

More recently, Ty Binfet (1995, 2004), who taught sixth and seventh grades in Richmond, British Columbia, adapted Kohlberg's research protocol to engage his students

FIGURE 10.2

RESULTS FROM COLBY ET AL.'S LONGITUDINAL STUDY OF MORAL JUDGMENT

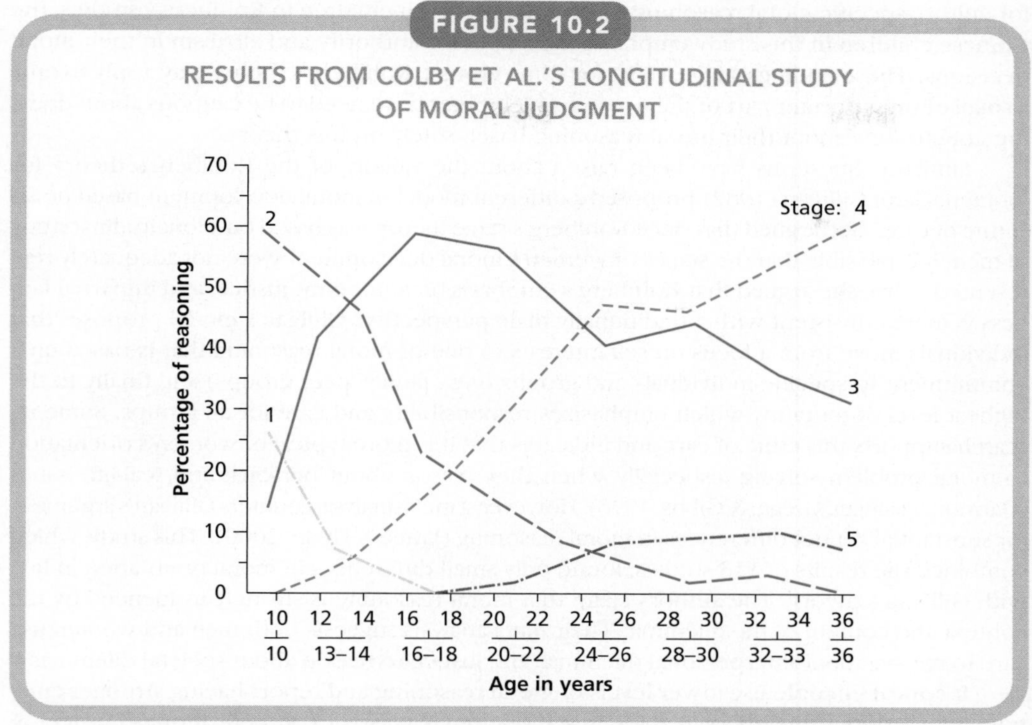

Source: Colby, A., Kohlberg, L., Gibbs, J. C., & Lieberman, M. (1983). A longitudinal study of moral judgment. Monographs of the Society for Research in Child Development, *48 (1-2, Serial No. 200).*

in *moral dilemma discussions*. His goal was to enhance students' ability to reason about moral issues. Students sat in a circle and listened as he read a dilemma. Then students began their discussion by formulating a *should* question (e.g., "How should . . . ?" "What should . . . ?"). The rules for participation included taking turns, not engaging in side conversations, justifying opinions, and respecting the opinions of others. Binfet facilitated the discussion by asking questions designed to elicit, paraphrase, clarify, and check students' understanding. According to Binfet, finding a solution is not the goal of these discussions. Rather, the focus is on the process of moral reasoning and learning to consider other people's points of view. What did his students think? In the words of one student:

> [Moral dilemma discussions are] a good and fun way of learning . . . you learn how to speak clearly and have a good conversation with people. If you get into a problem, you might think back to the discussion to do what's best. (Binfet, 1995, p. 4)

Binfet's teacher-initiated approach to moral education exemplifies the way social responsibility is promoted in North American schools. In some countries (e.g., China and Korea), national curricula are being developed in an effort to teach children to reason morally about everyday events (Baek, 2002; Jie & Desheng, 2004).

ALTERNATIVES TO KOHLBERG'S THEORY. Although numerous studies support Kohlberg's stage theory of moral development, some important questions have been raised about it as well. For example, although cross-cultural studies generally support Kohlberg's sequence of stages, they also find that people in less technologically advanced societies move through the stages more slowly and achieve a lower end stage than people in more advanced societies (Snarey, 1995). This has led to the criticism that the theory is biased in favor of Western cultures that value individualism. Some cultures value community more than autonomy and, for them, the highest moral value may involve putting the opinions of the group above decisions based on individual conscience (Shweder, Much, Mahapatra, & Park, 1997). This was the finding in a developmental study of children in Mainland China (Fang et al., 2003). Although the findings supported Kohlberg's stage-like progression, there also was evidence for culture-specific moral reasoning. In comparison with children in Kohlberg's studies, the Chinese children in this study emphasized respect for authority and altruism in their moral decisions. These findings suggest that for some groups, Kohlberg's theory may apply to only a small or unimportant part of their moral development; we need to be cautious about drawing conclusions about their moral reasoning based solely on this theory.

Similarly, questions have been raised about the validity of the Kohlberg's theory for women. Carol Gilligan (1982) proposed a different model of moral development based on an "ethic of care." She argued that since Kohlberg's stage theory was based on a longitudinal study of men, it is possible that the stages of women's moral development were not adequately represented. Also, she argued that Kohlberg's emphasis on autonomy, justice, and impartial fairness is more consistent with a traditionally male perspective. Gilligan's model proposes that individuals move from a focus on self-interests to one of moral reasoning that is based on a commitment to specific individuals and groups (e.g., family, peer groups) and finally to the highest level of morality, which emphasizes responsibility and care for all groups. Some research supports this ethic of care and indicates that it is more typical of women's orientation to moral problem solving, especially when they reason about personal and real-life issues (Garmon, Basinger, Gregg, & Gibbs, 1996). However, a meta-analysis counters Gilligan's argument for substantial gender differences in moral reasoning (Jaffee & Hyde, 2000). This study, which combined the results of 113 studies, found only small differences in moral orientation in line with Gilligan's theory. The authors claim that moral reasoning is strongly influenced by the context and content of the dilemma. Their meta-analysis suggests both men and women use care to reason about interpersonal dilemmas and justice to reason about societal dilemmas.

It appears people use lower levels of moral reasoning and report having stronger emotions when they think about real-life moral dilemmas versus hypothetical ones (Walker & Hennig, 1997; Walker, Pitts, Hennig, & Matsuba, 1995). And even young children (age 3) can distinguish between social conventions and moral imperatives. They know, for example, that being noisy in school would be fine if there were no rule requiring quiet, but hitting another child is wrong even if there is no rule against it.

In his later work, Kohlberg said that some aspects of moral development are universal, whereas others reflect elements of the social context in which individuals find themselves. Also, he acknowledged that few people actually reach Stage 6 in their moral development. However, he also speculated that there could be a Stage 7 representing an ethical orientation that arises from religious or existential experiences and thinking rather than from moral experience alone (Kohlberg & Power, 1981, p. 354).

Moral Behavior

Does moral reasoning lead to moral behavior? There is research to suggest it does and that children who lack empathy or who reason ineffectually about moral issues are more likely to engage in immoral or antisocial behavior (Dodge, Coie, & Lynam, 2006; Fitzgerald & White, 2003; Schonert-Reichl, Smith, & Zaidman-Zait, in press). In this section, we examine both prosocial and antisocial or aggressive behavior, and several sources of influence on these behaviors.

PROSOCIAL BEHAVIOR. The term **prosocial behavior** is used to describe voluntary behavior intended to benefit other people. Prosocial behaviors are evident in the actions of very young children (e.g., when they share a toy or try to help their parents). However, young children's prosocial behavior is most likely to occur in situations that involve little self-sacrifice or when adults actively encourage it (Hay, Caplan, Castle, & Stimson, 1991). Prosocial behavior, such as sharing, helping, and cooperating on projects, tends to increase during the elementary school years and, ideally, it becomes more altruistic—motivated by care and concern for others, rather than by self-serving interests or in compliance with the requests of authority figures. Prosocial behavior is associated with moral and prosocial reasoning, perspective-taking, empathy and sympathy, self-regulation, and self-esteem. In general, children with higher, more other-oriented levels of moral reasoning and higher levels of self-regulation, self-esteem, and perspective-taking engage in more prosocial behavior and are motivated to do so by more altruistic concerns (Eisenberg & Morris, 2004; Eisenberg, Fabes, & Spinrad, 2006).

In addition, prosocial behavior is influenced by specific cultural and familial practices (Cole et al., 2002; Walker, Hennig, & Krettenauer, 2000). In general, children demonstrate higher levels of prosocial behavior when they live in cultures that stress cooperation and the importance of contributing to the welfare of the group (Wentzel, 2002). Researchers have consistently found that children from traditional rural and semi-agricultural communities are more cooperative than children from urban and "Westernized" cultures (Eisenberg et al., 2006). Similarly, studies comparing Asian and Caucasian children report higher levels of prosocial behavior among Asian children (Rao & Stewart, 1999; Stewart & McBride-Chang, 2000).

When children are regularly expected to perform tasks that benefit their family or other children in their classroom at school, prosocial behavior is promoted. Most theories of moral development assume parents and other adults initially control young children's moral behavior through direct instruction, supervision, and correction. In fact, the development of prosocial behavior is enhanced when children feel connected to others, are exposed to parental warmth and adult guidance, and have opportunities to participate in prosocial activities (Eisenberg et al., 2006; Osher et al., 2010). In time, children **internalize** the moral rules and principles of the authority figures guiding them; that is, children adopt the external standards as their own. When adults use **inductive discipline,** they give children reasons why their behavior is wrong, with explanations they can understand and that highlight the effects of their actions on others. Recall from Chapter 7 that children who receive this form of discipline are more likely to internalize moral principles and behave prosocially even when "no one is watching" (Hoffman, 2000).

As we have seen in previous chapters, observation is a powerful form of learning. Models of moral behavior can be real people (e.g., parents, siblings, and peers) or characters children observe on TV, in books, or even video games. In general, models who are emotionally warm and responsive, who are perceived as competent, and who behave [morally] in a way that is consistent with what they say children should do have a positive influence on children's prosocial development (Bandura, 1977; Eisenberg & Fabes, 1998; Eisenberg et al., 2001). In contrast, children learn aggressive behaviors when their models are verbally and physically aggressive.

AGGRESSIVE BEHAVIOR. Antisocial or **aggressive behavior** is intended to hurt others or to damage property. It should not be confused with assertiveness, which means affirming or maintaining a legitimate right. As Helen Bee (1981) explains, "A child who says, 'That's my toy!' is showing assertiveness. If he bashes his playmate over the head to reclaim it, he has shown aggression" (p. 350). We described several forms of aggressive behavior in Chapter 7, including instrumental aggression, hostile aggression, and retaliatory aggression.

All children show aggression sometimes, particularly in the early childhood years. In fact, both physical and relational forms of aggression can be reliably detected in interactions among 3-year-old children (Dodge, Coie, & Lynam, 2006). However, as children mature, most gain control over their emotions, can delay gratification, and can express their needs and concerns verbally. Therefore, the overall rate at which children respond to problem situations with overt physical aggression declines through the preschool and elementary school years, and most children who act aggressively in the early years do not grow into aggressive teens and adults (Anderson et al., 2003). Unfortunately, the aggression that does occur among school-age children becomes increasingly more hostile, person-directed, and relational (Craig & Pepler, 2003; Dodge et al., 2006; Pepler & Sedighdeilami, 1998; Tremblay, Boulerice et al., 1996; Tremblay, Nagin et al., 2004).

Insults, gossip, exclusion, and taunts are all examples of hostile but indirect and relational aggression.

Often, it is during the elementary school years that children with more serious conduct problems are identified. However, the problems these children experience typically are behaviors they have not outgrown from their early years—not new ones (Petitclerc, Boivin, Dionne, Zoccolillo & Tremblay, 2009). When these problems are not addressed (e.g., adults don't intervene to correct the aggressive behavior), it is quite possible that these children will continue to be aggressive into adolescence and adulthood and that their aggressive and antisocial behaviors will expand to include criminal activity. In fact, aggressive behavior that is not successfully extinguished in childhood is the best predictor of aggressive and violent behavior in adolescence and adulthood (Anderson et al., 2003). Huesmann, Eron, Lefkowitz, and Walder's now seminal longitudinal study (1984) indicated that children who were rated high on aggression at age 8 were significantly more likely to be convicted of criminal offenses and serious offenses by age 30 (see Figure 10.3), and more likely to engage in spousal and/or child abuse as adults.

FIGURE 10.3

RELATIONSHIP BETWEEN CHILDREN'S AGGRESSIVE BEHAVIOR AND CRIMINALITY IN LATER LIFE

Mean criminal justice convictions and mean seriousness of crimes up to age 30 according to a subject's peer-nominated aggression score at age 8. The group differences are significant for males, $F(2, 319) = 4.87$, $p < .01$ and $F(2, 319) = 4.13$, $p < .02$.

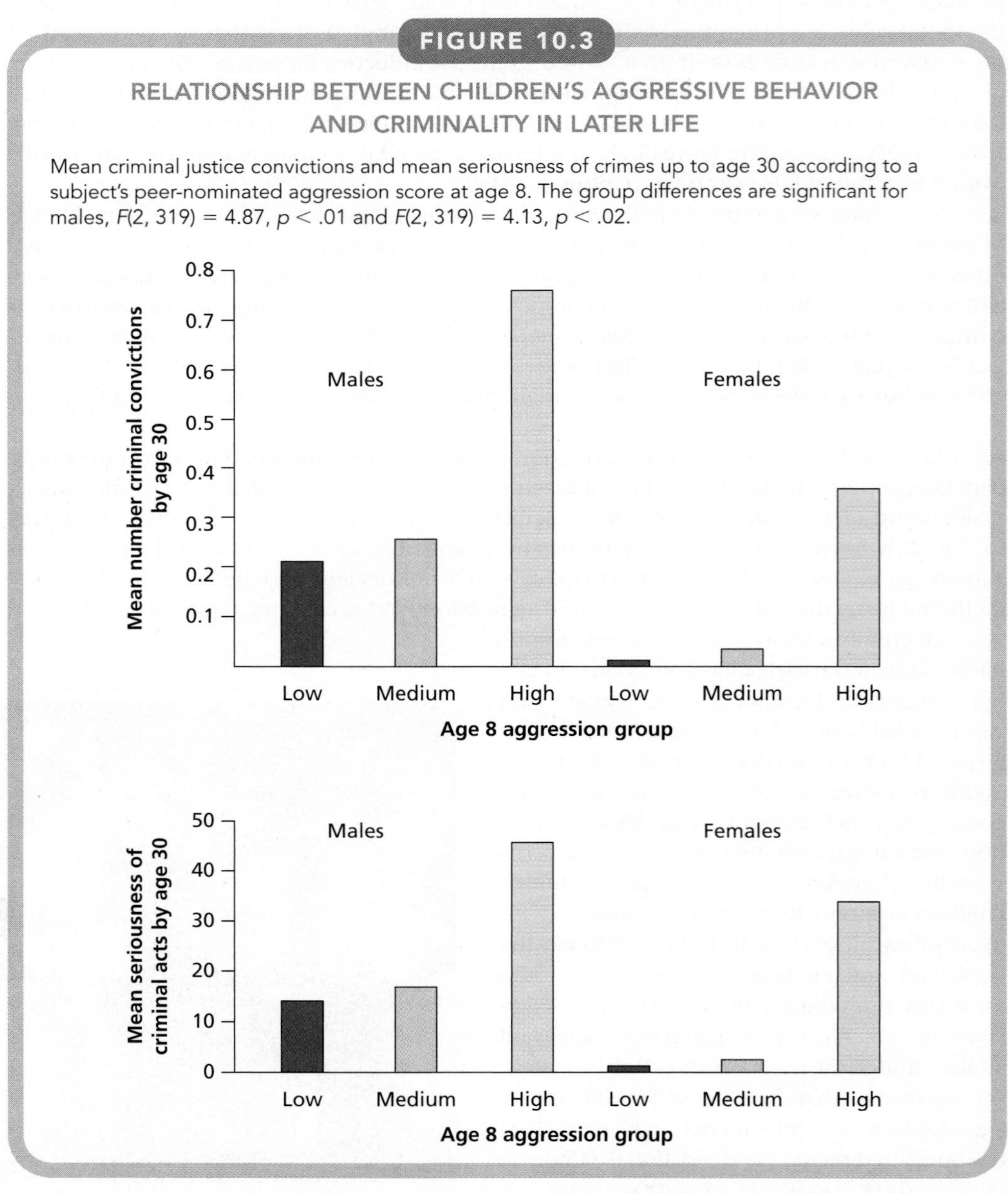

Source: Huesmann, L. R., Eron, L. D., Lefkowitz, M. M., & Walder, L. O. (1984). Stability of aggression over time and generations. Developmental Psychology, 20, *pp. 1120–1134. Reprinted with permission from the American Psychological Association.*

Gender differences in aggression emerge early (in 3-year-olds), and appear to be stable through adolescence and across countries/cultures (Dodge, Coie, & Lynam, 2006). In particular, the rate and intensity of physical aggression is higher for boys than girls. Broidy and his colleagues (2003) examined data from 6 longitudinal studies in the United States, New Zealand, and Canada, and found that girls consistently exhibited lower mean levels of physical aggression than boys. Even girls characterized as chronically physically aggressive had lower mean levels of physical aggression than boys with the same designation. Similarly, Stanger, Achenback, and Verhulst (1997) found boys were more physically aggressive than girls at every age from 4 to 18 in their sample of over 2,000 Dutch children. The evidence concerning social or relational aggression is more mixed, however. Some research findings suggest boys and girls engage in relational aggression at similar rates (Underwood, 2003). Other findings indicate that girls engage in this form of aggression more than boys (Crick & Zahn-Waxler, 2003). There is general agreement that girls are more likely to engage in relational than physical forms of aggression (Dodge et al., 2006). Also, research indicates girls are more distressed by interpersonal problems and relational slights, and are more likely than boys to incorporate information gained from such interactions into their "self-views" (Crick et al, 2001, p. 203).

Some evidence points to a biological basis for aggressive behavior. Studies of twins suggest a genetic predisposition toward aggressive behavior (Plomin, 1990). Pre- and perinatal complications, *in utero* exposure to nicotine, and low levels of certain neurotransmitters also have been linked to aggressive and antisocial behavior (Dodge et al., 2006). Other research links aggression with psychological factors, such as low levels of perspective-taking, moral reasoning, self-control, and sympathy relative to peers (Boldizar, Perry, & Perry, 1989; Dodge et al., 2006; Gregg, Gibbs, & Basinger, 1994). Finally, research indicates the important role ecological factors play in behavioral outcomes. We turn now to evidence that aggressive behavior can be learned in families, from television and other media, and from societal influences generally.

FAMILY ENVIRONMENT. Modeling plays an important role in the expression of aggression (Bandura, Ross, & Ross, 1963) and families may play a key role. According to the National Longitudinal Survey of Children and Youth (NLSCY) in Canada (Craig, Peters, & Konarski, 1998; Tremblay et al., 1996), there is a strong relationship between family membership and family functioning and aggressive behavior. Data from the survey indicate that children who are aggressive tend to have aggressive siblings and parents who, perhaps inadvertently, reinforce aggressive interactions between or among siblings (e.g., by not consistently praising prosocial behavior and punishing antisocial behavior). Furthermore, research indicates that children who grow up in coercive home environments—homes filled with harsh and inconsistent punishment and daily interactions within the family that can be characterized as aggressive—are more likely to use aggression to solve their own problems (Craig et al., 1998; Dodge et al., 2006). They learn to use aggression to get what they want.

MEDIA VIOLENCE. Another source of aggressive models is media entertainment. Today, children interact with video games and the Internet in addition to television and the print media. Almost every home in North America has a television and, estimates are that, on average, by the time children reach the age of 18 they will have witnessed over 200,000 acts of violence on TV (National Center for Children Exposed to Violence, 2003). Particularly disturbing is the fact that much of the violence they observe goes unpunished. Again, children see that violence is rewarded and may come to believe that violent retaliation is acceptable: "It's OK to shove people when you're mad" (Egan, Monson, & Perry, 1998). Whether and to what extent TV promotes aggressive behavior in children has been a matter for debate for some time. We examine this issue in the ***Point/Counterpoint*** on the next page.

Films and video games also contain violence, which is often perpetrated by the hero. Similarly, newspapers and magazines are filled with stories of murders, rapes, and robberies. In a review of children's books (Entenman, Murnen, & Hendricks, 2005), researchers found evidence of physical and relational aggression and characters that modeled behaviors associated with being either a bully or a bystander. On a positive note, these researchers describe how some of this literature can be used by parents and teachers to help children

POINT/COUNTERPOINT: What Are Children Learning from Television?

Televisions are found in 98% of North American homes, and children spend an average of four hours each day watching television or sitting in front of a computer screen (Nielsen Media Research, 2005). What children are watching and what they are learning are questions researchers have investigated over a number of years. Researchers have been particularly interested in whether watching television programs that contain violence increases children's propensity to engage in aggressive or violent acts in real life.

POINT

▶ **Television fosters aggression and violence in children.** There is general agreement among experts that viewing violence on TV and in other media "can lead to aggressive attitudes, values, and behaviors" (Anderson et al., 2003, p. 82). Numerous studies have demonstrated that viewing violence on TV is associated with increases in aggressive and antisocial behavior (Huesmann & Miller, 1994; Huesmann, Moise, & Podolski, 1997; Huesmann, Moise-Titus, Podolski, & Eron, 2003). Unfortunately, many programs produced for children contain high rates of violence. One study of Sunday morning cartoons recorded violent acts occurring approximately 20–25 times each hour, compared with a rate of 5 or 6 times each hour during prime time programs (Donnerstein, Slaby, & Eron, 1994). In fact, these researchers found the highest rates of violence in programs aired during hours when children are likely to be watching. What is the effect? Experimental studies in which some children view moderately violent TV programs and others view more neutral content indicate children who are exposed to the more violent content are more likely to engage in aggressive or violent acts, at least in the short term (Paik & Comstock, 1994). Also, studies of the absolute amount of television viewed by children indicate that those who watch more TV are more aggressive. Finally, longitudinal studies have linked aggressiveness at age 19 and criminal behavior by age 30 in males with the amount of violence they viewed on television at age 8 (Eron, 1987). Furthermore, some research indicates that viewing violence repeatedly on TV leads to desensitization toward violence in real life and the belief that violence can be a good strategy for accomplishing goals—getting what you want (Anderson et al., 2003; Huesmann et al., 2003).

COUNTERPOINT

▶ **Not all children respond to violence with violence.** Experts also agree that not all children who view violence on television will behave aggressively or violently in response (Anderson et al., 2003). It seems the relationship between TV viewing and increased aggression is complex. Some research indicates children who are more aggressive to begin with watch more TV and choose more violent shows on TV. A number of studies support this interpretation of the data. In Eron's (1987) study, the 8-year-old boys who watched a lot of violence on TV already tended to be more aggressive with their peers. In addition, of these already aggressive youngsters, those who watched the most violence on TV were the most aggressive and delinquent as teenagers and adults. Similarly, a more recent study found that viewing aggression on TV led to increased aggression in children with behavior problems, but not in children who didn't exhibit aggressive behavior prior to watching TV (CBC Segment A, March, 2006). It seems that viewing violence on TV will not turn all children into hardened criminals. However, there is good evidence to indicate that habitual exposure to violence on TV, identification with same-sex aggressive characters, and strong beliefs that violent shows are a realistic portrayal of real life can increase aggressive behavior in children (both males and females) in the short and long term (Huesmann et al., 2003).

Of course, an argument can be made for the positive effects of television on children's social and cognitive development (see Linebarger & Wainwright, 2007). Programs designed to be educational have demonstrated positive effects, such as increasing viewers' vocabulary and general knowledge, particularly when viewers are preschoolers or English language learners (CBC Segment B, March, 2006; Neuman & Koskinen, 1992). Programs that target disadvantaged children, such as *Sesame Street* and *Reading Rainbow*, are credited with preparing them for school by increasing their knowledge of letter names and sounds, sight words, and vocabulary, and by improving their general knowledge and reading comprehension skills so they can acquire new concepts (Fowles-Mates & Strommen, 1996; Leitner, 1991). And children who watch programs that emphasize prosocial behavior are more kind and helpful (Murray, 1980).

Beware of Either/Or views of television and aggression

Clearly, television is a teacher, but parents can influence what children learn by monitoring what they watch and controlling the hours they spend in front of the television set. Even violence on television can be used for positive purposes. Adults can talk with children about what they see, distinguish between fiction and reality, and generate nonviolent alternatives for coping with problems.

understand issues related to violence and the impact it has on individuals and society as a whole. According to Entenman et al., "In the right hands of the right teacher at the right moment, a children's book can be a powerful tool for engaging students in dialogue that either ends the [aggression] or gives victims and bystanders the knowledge and confidence to face it" (2005, p. 362). The key is for teachers to be aware of what is happening among their students, not just in their classrooms, but also on the playground, on the bus, and in their neighborhoods after school. In addition, they need to make themselves aware of children's books and how they deal with aggression, and be prepared to use them as teaching tools when issues of aggression arise in their classrooms.

ECOLOGICAL AND SOCIOCULTURAL INFLUENCES. Finally, just as cultural conditions can foster prosocial behavior, they also can encourage aggressive behavior. In particular, cultural norms and public policies can influence the extent to which aggressive behavior is tolerated within communities. In the United States, for example, rates of homicide involving firearms, including rates for children, are 12 to 16 times higher than the average of 25 other industrialized countries, including Canada, perhaps because of different laws that allow for gun ownership (Dodge et al., 2006). Many children witness violence associated with drugs and guns in their neighborhood every day. They may observe that often, there are no consequences for such illegal and antisocial behavior. Similarly, schools have been criticized for ineffective policies concerning antisocial behavior and lax discipline practices. Finally, marital conflict and the breakdown of the family have been suggested as possible sources of aggression in children and youth. In particular, poverty is associated with increased family stress, discipline practices that model aggression, less effective parental monitoring, lower quality of education, and greater likelihood of associating with aggressive peers (Raver, 2004; Tremblay et al., 1996).

It is important to bear in mind that violence is seldom the result of exposure to one kind of model. More typically, it results from a convergence of multiple factors over time (Anderson et al., 2003). Therefore, the influence of the mass media is best viewed as one of many factors that shape behavior.

One form of aggression among children and youth that is receiving a lot of attention is bullying.

How Big a Problem Is Bullying?

Bullying is "a willful act of aggression or manipulation by one or more people against another person or people" (Enteman et al., 2005, p. 352). It involves sustained verbal or physical mistreatment in which there is an imbalance of power and a desire on the part of the bully to intimidate or dominate a victim, as in the case of an older or bigger child picking on a younger or smaller peer (Merrell, Gueldner, Ross, & Isava, 2008). Bullying also is a game of one-upmanship. Bullies get satisfaction from winning while someone else loses (Lingren, 1997).

Research around the world indicates that bullying is a serious problem for school-age children (Hara, 2002; Hawkins, Pepler, & Craig, 2001; Kanetsuna & Smith, 2002; Swearer, Expelage, Vaillancourt, & Hymel, 2010). In international surveys involving more than 36 countries around the world, between 10% and 23% of school-age children report being involved in bullying incidents, as either the bully or the victim (Hawkins et al., 2001; Nansel et al., 2001), and students in North America reported some of the highest rates of bullying (Craig & Pepler, 2003). One problem with the research on bullying is that it depends almost entirely on student self-reports or reports about others. If students over- or underreport incidents of bullying (e.g., girls tend not to view their exclusionary behaviors as bullying [Craig & Pepler, 2003]), estimates of its prevalence may not be accurate. In a seminal study, Craig and Pepler (1998) observed 65 elementary school children playing in the schoolyard at recess and lunch. During 48 hours of observations, they witnessed a total of 314 bullying episodes, approximately 6.5 episodes every hour. They rated 84% of the episodes they observed as overt and occurring when peers and/or adults were present. Most surprising was that according to their ratings, school staff intervened in only 25% of the episodes in which they were proximal. These findings and those of subsequent observation studies (Craig & Harel, 2004) indicate bullying presents a significant challenge for at least a sizeable minority of school-age children.

BULLIES. Contrary to what is widely believed, bullies may have high self-esteem and suffer less anxiety and insecurity than peers (Enteman et al., 2005; Kriedler, 1996; Olweus, 1991). Also, contrary to the image of a bully who is failing and frustrated in school, many bullies do quite well academically. Often peers perceive them as attractive and popular leaders in their schools (Swearer et al., 2010). They don't feel empathy for their victims and often see themselves in a positive light. In fact, they may perceive they are the victims and rationalize their aggressive behavior on the basis of a need to "get them before they get me" (Kriedler, 1996, p. 71).

Sullivan (2000) identified three types of bullies. As we have described, there are *confident bullies* who have high self-esteem, are reasonably popular, and are physically strong. But there also are *anxious bullies* who are weak academically and who are less popular and secure. Finally, there are *bully/victims*. These children are bullies in some situations and victims in others (e.g., children who are bullied by siblings or receive harsh, often physical, punishment from parents). Bully/victims tend to be the most troubled psychologically, compared with children who are either just bullies or just victims (Juvonen, Graham, & Schuster, 2003). These children have the highest levels of conduct, school, and peer relationship problems.

Girls bully nearly as often as boys, but they use less physical forms of bullying (Werner & Crick, 2004). And, whereas much of boys' bullying is done one on one, girls tend to bully in groups (Kriedler, 1996). Bullies tend to have more family problems than their peers (DeHaan, 1997; Enteman et al., 2005). Often, they come from families in which there is little warmth or affection, and communication among members is generally poor. These children are frequently the recipients of harsh punishment, even emotional and physical abuse. These factors may explain why bullies are rarely capable of maintaining close friendships and are more likely to engage in delinquent acts or to abuse drugs and alcohol during adolescence unless they experience some kind of intervention (DeHaan, 1997; Werner & Crick, 2004).

VICTIMS. Sullivan (2000) also identified three types of victims. *Passive victims* are anxious, have low self-esteem, and are physically weak and unpopular. Often, these children do nothing to provoke attacks and do little to defend themselves against bullies. *Provocative victims* tend to have their own set of problems that draws negative attention to them. They tend to be physically stronger than passive victims and more actively engaged in incidents that lead to bullying. *Bully/victims* provoke bullying in others and initiate aggressive acts. Some groups of children are more likely to be bullied than others, including children who are obese, children who don't belong to a peer group, children in remedial education, and children with disabilities (Swearer et al., 2010).

There are short- and long-term consequences to being a victim (DeHaan, 1997; Enteman et al., 2005; Swearer et al., 2010). In the short term, children who are victims may develop a strong dislike for going to school or participating in gym. They may distrust peers and have difficulty making friends. The long-term effects of being bullied can be anxiety, embarrassment, guilt, loneliness, and loss of self-esteem. Some individuals experience sleep, speech, and dissociative disorders; panic attacks; paranoia; obsessive compulsive disorder; self-mutilation; and delays in mental, social emotional, and physical development. Some children who are severely bullied develop Post-Traumatic Stress Disorder. However, most victims, especially if they receive support from significant adults, survive bullying without long-term effects.

A bystander is a child who witnesses bullying behavior and may or may not do anything about it.

BYSTANDERS. A bystander is a child who witnesses bullying behavior and may or may not do anything about it (Enteman et al., 2005, p. 355). In a recent study of over 2,000 children in the United Kingdom (Rivers, Voret, Pote, & Ashurst, 2009), 63% reported having witnessed bullying within the current school term. Bystanders may unwittingly encourage bullying by watching and not helping the victim. Or they may take a more active role, following the lead of the bully and laughing and harassing the victim. Either way, bystanders play an important role in the bully–victim dynamic. In a continuation of Craig and Pepler's (1998) observational study, Hawkins and her colleagues (2001) observed peer interventions in bullying incidents. Their data indicate that peers were present at 85% of 306 bullying incidents, but intervened in only 19%. Most interventions targeted the bully, and boys intervened more often than girls. However, boys were more likely than girls to use aggression. In general, bystanders may not know what to do or whom to tell. They may fear reprisals from the bully or blame the victim for provoking an attack. Observing bullying is associated with risks to mental health, including elevated levels of anxiety, depression, and substance use (Bonnano & Hymel, 2006; Rivers et al., 2010).

Clearly, bullying is a big problem for children, with wide-ranging consequences for everyone involved. In Chapter 13, we will revisit this issue and see how technology is being used as a medium for bullying. What can adults do to address the problem of bullying? Some suggestions are presented in the ***Connecting with Children*** guidelines.

Experts are recommending approaches to discipline in schools that address schoolwide, classroom, and individual student needs through broad prevention, targeted intervention, and development of self-discipline (Osher, Bear, Sprague, & Doyle, 2010). Swearer

CONNECTING WITH CHILDREN

Guidelines for Families, Teachers, and Other Professionals: What Can Adults Do about Bullying and Aggression?

Don't just stand there!

Examples

1. Have clear and consistent consequences for aggressive behavior (e.g., remove privileges or institute a timeout). In particular, don't ignore relational aggression, which can be just as damaging as overt aggression over the long term.
2. Explain clearly and specifically what behavior was aggressive. Help children to consider and plan how they will respond to similar events in the future.
3. Be present and supervise in situations where children may be vulnerable to aggression (e.g., schoolyards and hallways, playgrounds, sports arenas).

Draw attention to good behavior.

Examples

1. Catch children being good and comment on it (e.g., "I like the way you controlled your anger in that situation.").
2. Point to the helping behaviors of children and comment on how good it feels to help one another.
3. Reward helping behavior with praise and affection or a special treat for the group (e.g., "You worked so well together on your homework. Now let's take a break and play a game.").

Monitor television and other sources of modeling.

Examples

1. Be aware of what children are watching on TV, and limit the amount of aggression and violence they see, even in programs produced for their age group. Parents should be aware of the V-chip that can be inserted in TV sets and used to block access to certain programs.
2. Monitor aggressive content in video and computer games, and in children's literature.
3. Talk about the violence children do see. Use the examples to open discussion about more appropriate ways to solve problems and what victims and bystanders can do if they experience violence.

Be a good example.

Examples

1. Use nonaggressive methods to solve your problems. Model positive coping strategies, such as taking a walk or talking to a friend.
2. Make nonviolence a clear and consistent family, classroom, team value.
3. Show and tell children how you help others when you can, and tell children how good it makes you and the other people feel.

Foster empathy and perspective-taking.

Examples

1. Encourage children to think about how their actions and words affect others. Engaging in role-playing (e.g., "Pretend the kids in your class called you names. How did that make you feel?").
2. When a child has hurt someone else, encourage him/her to consider how the other child must feel. Ask him/her to think of a way to make up for the hurt (e.g., apologizing, sharing a toy) and to follow through on some of the ideas.
3. When a child gets hurt by someone else, ask him/her to consider whether the hurt was intentional or just an accident.

Source: Adapted from Enteman, J., Murnen, T. J., & Hendricks, C. (2005). Victims, bullies, and bystanders in K-3 literature. The Reading Teacher, *59, 352-364.*

and her colleagues (2010) argue that a social-ecological framework is particularly useful for understanding the problem of bullying in schools. Such a framework considers all systems that directly affect students, including families, peer groups, teacher–student relationships, parent–school relationships, neighborhoods, and cultural expectations. Considering these factors helps teachers design meaningful activities and create positive classroom climates that foster healthy development and enhance student cooperation, motivation, and learning. These approaches contrast punitive and exclusionary approaches such as zero-tolerance, which have exacerbated problems in many cases (e.g., increased antisocial behavior and contributed to school disengagement, loss of opportunities to learn, and school dropout—see Chapter 12). In addition, Osher and his colleagues advocate the development of school-wide positive behavior supports (SWPBS) and social emotional learning. SWPBS are school-wide systems that teach rules and reward students for following them. Misbehavior is analyzed from a functional perspective (e.g., what purpose does the behavior serve—attention, power, avoidance), and interventions address the root of the problem. Social Emotional Learning (SEL) emphasizes self-awareness, self-control, social awareness, relationship skills, and responsible decision-making.

Gender Development

In this section, we focus on children's increasing awareness of gender roles in middle childhood, how some of those understandings are stereotyped, and the relationship between gender and self-esteem. We also look at precursors to the development of sexual orientation, which some evidence suggests are evident in pre- and early adolescence.

Thinking and Acting Like Boys and Girls

As children enter middle childhood (ages 6 or 7), they increasingly adopt gender-specific behavior (as defined by their cultures) and avoid behavior associated with the opposite sex (Davies, 2004; Ruble, Martin, & Berenbaum, 2006). About this time, children also become aware of **gender constancy**—the fact that gender cannot be changed. Kohlberg (1966) believed this developing sense of gender permanence is critical for organizing and motivating children to learn gender concepts and behaviors. Apparently, the implicit awareness of "being a girl" leads to an insistence on "behaving like a girl, not like a boy" (Davies, 2004, p. 308). As we discussed earlier, families have a primary role in socializing gendered behavior in early childhood. In middle childhood, role models also include older and same-age, same-sex peers, relatives, and other adults, including media celebrities. Observing these role models leads children to form impressions about what girls and boys are like, what they like to do, and how they behave in particular situations.

On average, boys are stronger and more physically active than girls, a difference that is noted from infancy. In middle childhood, boys are more likely to choose outdoor activities and rough activities, compared with girls, who tend to choose quieter activities that involve more conversation and fine motor coordination (Blatchford, Baines, & Pellegrini, 2003; Eaton & Enns, 1986; Fabes, Martin, & Hanish, 2004; Maccoby, 1998; Ruble et al., 2006). Boys show more physical aggression and higher levels of assertiveness than girls, but girls are more likely to seek and receive help than boys (Coie & Dodge, 1998; Eisenberg & Fabes, 1998). When interacting with one another, girls are more agreeable than boys and more likely to engage in turn-taking during conversations (Davies, 2004; O'Brien, 1992; Ruble et al., 2006). Boys, on the other hand, interrupt one another, make demands and then refuse to comply with the demands of others, tell jokes and stories, and compete with one another for attention. Finally, girls and boys differ according to the themes that motivate their reading, writing, and drawing. For example, boys like to read science fiction, sports, and war stories, whereas girls prefer adventures, ghost, animal, and relationship/romance stories (Coles & Hall, 2002; Ruble et al., 2006). Similarly, girls tend to develop stories with affectionate themes, whereas boys' stories contain more violence.

These gendered interests and styles of interacting reinforce **gender segregation,** or the preference for playing with children of the same sex. Gender segregation increases during middle childhood and remains strong to adolescence (Maccoby, 1998). Both boys and girls prefer same-sex peers. They expect to have more fun with them and, on the whole, have more positive interactions with them (Strough & Covatto, 2002; Vaughn, 2001). Of course, some children develop friendships with other-sex peers, but these friendships often go underground during school hours (Ruble et al., 2006). In fact, children who engage in behaviors typically associated with the opposite sex, or who prefer playing with children of the opposite sex, may be stigmatized for it. This is especially true for boys.

Gender-Role Stereotyping

Different treatment of boys and girls persists in middle childhood. Parents continue to emphasize independence and industry more in boys than in girls, and gender biases are promoted in schools as well. Schools provide gender-related information through the roles adult men and women play in these contexts. Men are disproportionately represented in positions of leadership within the school system, and most elementary school teachers are women. Parents and teachers are well advised to review textbooks and other materials and to consider how boys and girls, men and women are portrayed. Are they in stereotypical roles and activities? Although progress has been made, content analyses indicate males occur more often in book titles and pictures and girls are more often depicted as dependent and needing help (Ruble et al., 2006). Interestingly, female characters are more likely than male characters to cross gender roles and become more active and assertive, but male characters seldom show feminine, expressive traits (Brannon, 2002; Evans & Davies, 2000). These findings apply to other media, such as video games, educational software, and testing materials as well (Meece, 2002).

There is quite a bit of research about how teachers treat boys and girls; one consistent finding is that teachers interact more with boys than with girls. They ask more questions of boys, wait longer for them to respond, and provide them with more detailed feedback (Meece, 2002). These findings vary by grade, subject area, and sex of the teacher. For example, teachers of elementary students showed more sex-differentiated responses than did high school teachers (Ruble et al., 2006), and female math and language teachers interacted more with their male students than with their female students (Duffy, Warren, & Walsh, 2002). Also, there is evidence that teachers judge boys' and girls' behavior differently. In one study, teachers judged that lying and cheating were less desirable in girls than in boys and quarreling was more serious for boys than for girls (Borg, 1998). Two cautions are relevant to interpreting these research findings, however. First, much of this research has involved predominantly White students, and the findings may not hold for other populations. There is evidence, for example, that White high-achieving males receive more of their teachers' attention than males from minority groups; however, high-achieving girls get the least amount of teacher attention (Woolfolk, 2010). Second, some research indicates that although teachers interact more with boys than girls, their interactions with girls are not less positive than their interactions with boys, just less frequent (Jones & Dindia, 2004). Moreover, the impact of such differential treatment on children's gender concepts is not clear from the research that has been done. Effects may be small but enduring and more pronounced for some students than others. For this reason, teachers, as well as parents and other adults who work with children, should be mindful of their differential treatment of girls and boys.

One other source of gender stereotyping and gender bias is television. Females are generally underrepresented on television. Males appear more often in commercials, and their voices are used more often to narrate commercials (Brannon, 2002). In children's programs—even those characterized as educational—males outnumber females as much as four or five to one (Signorielli, 2001). Moreover, although there have been improvements in the past two decades, the sexes continue to be portrayed in stereotypic ways in terms of occupations, personality characteristics, social relationships, appearance, and dress styles (Ruble et al., 2006).

Fortunately, children's views about what it means to be male or female become more flexible at age 7 or 8, when they begin to realize that most gender norms for behavior, activities, and occupations are more culturally determined than absolute (Blakemore, 2003; Brannon, 2002). However, this flexibility seems to reach a ceiling in the mid-elementary grades. Also, there is some evidence that gender stereotypes develop earlier and are more rigid for boys than for girls, and this applies across cultures (Ruble et al., 2006). Both boys and girls respond negatively when boys engage in cross-gendered behavior or have a cross-gendered appearance. Similarly, parents and other adults are more accepting of girls and women in cross-gendered roles than they are of boys and men in these roles. These findings suggest girls may have more room to explore interests and activities that are not traditionally associated with their sex.

Gender and Self-Esteem

Recall that children's development of self-esteem in particular domains derives from two evaluative judgments: one about their competence in the domain and another about the extent to which being competent in the domain is something they value. Researchers have studied differences in boys' and girls' perceptions of competence across a variety of domains and have found some fairly consistent differences, especially in gender-stereotyped domains. On average, boys have higher competence beliefs than girls in sports and math, and girls have higher competence beliefs than boys in reading, English, and social activities (Wigfield & Eccles, 2001). These differences emerge very early and are fairly stable over time. Wigfield and his colleagues (1997) conducted a longitudinal study of children's competence beliefs and values in sports, music, math, and reading. When the study began, the children were in first, second, and fourth grades. The researchers followed them for three years. Their findings were consistent with those outlined above—boys had higher competence beliefs in sports and math and girls felt stronger in reading—even in first grade, and these gender differences did not change over the course of their study. However, in a follow-up study, Jacobs and her colleagues (2002) followed the same students through high school and documented changes in their competence beliefs in the different domains from first through twelfth grade. The results, shown in Figure 10.4, indicate there is a general decline in perceived competence across the school years in all domains for both boys and girls. By high school, boys and girls were similar in reported levels of math competence, but girls continued to have higher levels of perceived competence in English and boys continued to hold higher competence beliefs in sports.

Children's beliefs about which sex is likely to be more talented in a given domain predicts the likelihood their competence judgments and expectations will be distorted in a gender-stereotypic direction (Wigfield & Eccles, 2001). For example, boys who believe that boys are generally better than girls in math tend to report more positive competence beliefs in math. Similarly, children's values for particular activities often reflect their beliefs about what is appropriate for boys and girls to do. One reason differences in beliefs about competence and values are important is that they influence the choices children make concerning their engagement in tasks and activities, which in turn influence the choices available to them as they move through school and out into the workforce (Eccles, 2007; Frome, Alfeld, Eccles, & Barber, 2006). Beliefs and values that conflict with interests and abilities may cause gender-role conflict for children who have interests and talents not typically associated their sex. This point has been well illustrated in research on gifted girls. Bell (1989) conducted a now-classic ethnographic study of a group of gifted third through sixth grade girls in an urban, multiethnic school. In interviews, the girls revealed they were often conflicted between doing their best and trying to appear feminine and caring. Specifically, they expressed concerns about hurting other people's feelings by winning achievement contests, appearing to be a braggart if they expressed pride in their achievements, and not wanting to appear overly aggressive in their efforts to get teachers' attention. A decade later, Lupart and Barva (1998) reported similar results from their study of a national sample of gifted girls in Canada.

Although we have focused on the differences between boys and girls in this section, it is important to emphasize that although these differences are important, they tend to be small. As is true for comparisons of many groups, there is a great deal of overlap (similarities, not differences) between groups of boys and girls and a great deal of variation within groups of girls and boys.

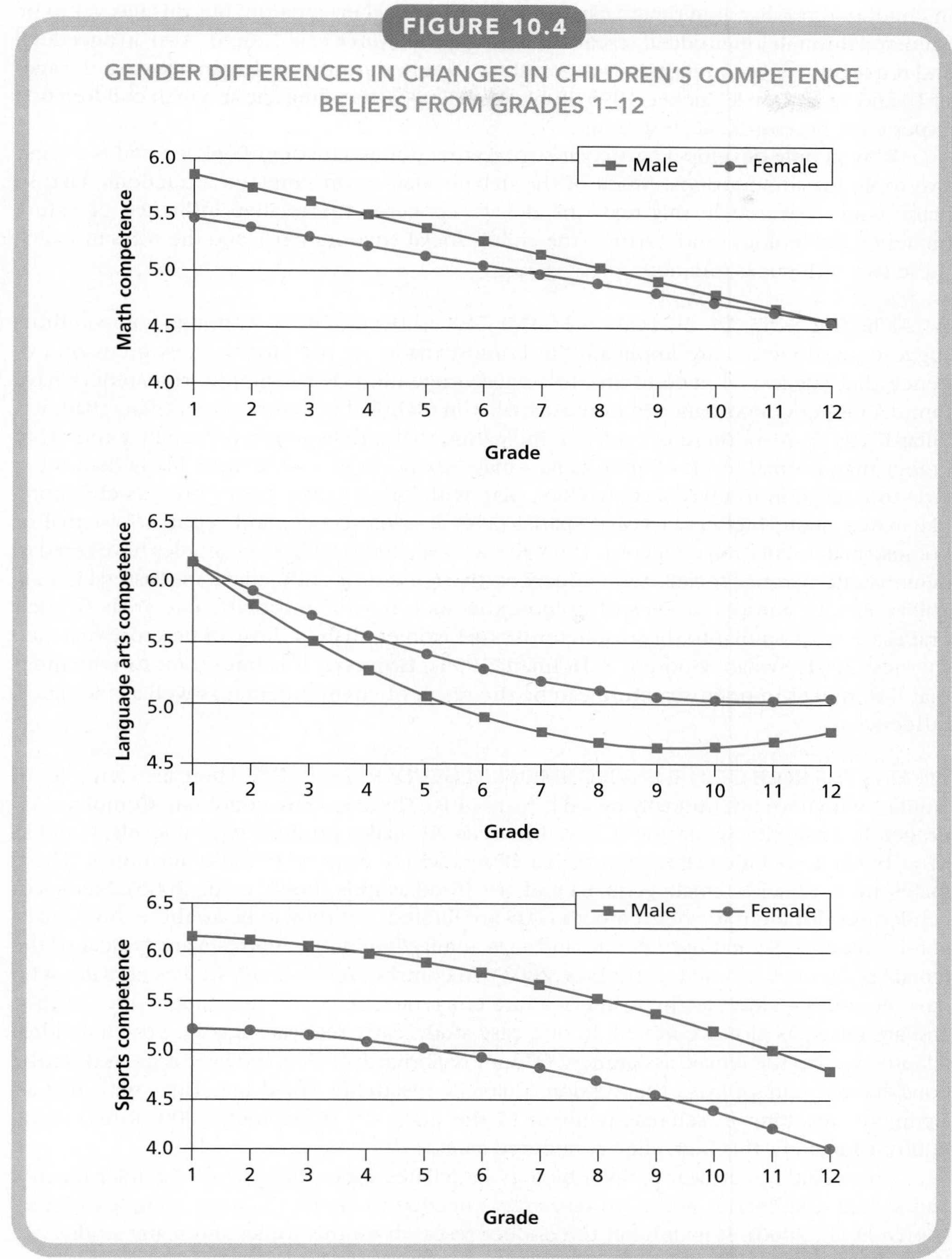

Source: Jacobs, J. E., Lanza, S., Osgood, D. W., Eccles, J. S. & Wigfield, A. (2002). Changes in children's self-competence and values: Gender and domain differences across grades 1 and 12. Child Development, 73, 509–527. Used with permission of John Wiles & Sons, Inc.

Developing Sexual Orientation

Most children begin experiencing feelings of sexual attraction during late childhood, but sexual orientation does not appear with any clarity until adolescence. **Sexual orientation** refers to a person's tendency to be attracted to members of the same sex, the opposite sex, or both sexes. It has been hypothesized that vague discomfort with one's gender, interest in opposite-gender activities, and the emergence of sexual questioning or same-sex attractions in childhood predict an ultimate gay, lesbian, or bisexual orientation, but this has yet to be validated through longitudinal research (Davies, 2004; Ruble et al., 2006). Also, in anecdotal and retrospective accounts, adults report their same-sex attractions began between the ages of 10 and 12 (Bailey & Zucker, 1995; Ruble et al., 2006), the same age at which children first experience heterosexual attractions.

Why people develop a particular sexual attraction is a matter of debate, and is a sensitive topic for some groups. Much of the debate focuses on same-sex attractions. Like so many issues covered in this text, the debate concerns the relative influence of nature (genetics and biology) and nurture (the child's social environment), and the ways in which these two influences interact.

WHAT IS THE ROLE OF BIOLOGY IN SAME-SEX ATTRACTIONS? Although some authors suggest social factors are implicated in homosexuality or bisexuality, most focus on evidence that suggests a genetic link to sexual orientation. For example, researchers have found a higher concordance in homosexuality in identical versus fraternal twins (Bailey & Pillard, 1991). Also, there is evidence indicating that girls who are prenatally exposed to higher than normal levels of androgens—male sex hormones—are more likely than other girls to engage in tomboyish behaviors, play with "boys'" toys, prefer boys as childhood playmates, score higher on visual spatial tasks at adolescence, and report a bisexual or homosexual orientation (Maccoby, 1998; Ruble et al., 2006). Moreover, studies have failed to demonstrate parents' socialization effects on these interests and behaviors (Pasterski et al., 2005). Finally, autopsy studies of homosexual men have found that some areas of their brains are more similar to those of heterosexual women than to those of heterosexual men (Byrnes, 2001; Swaab, Gooren, & Hofman, 1995). However, it is important to remember that differences in brain structure can be the result of environmental as well as biological influences.

WHAT IS THE ROLE OF THE ENVIRONMENT IN GENDER IDENTITY? There are examples of families who have intentionally raised boys as girls. There is a rare condition, Complete Androgen Insensitivity Syndrome (CAIS), in which XY males produce typical levels of androgens, but lack specific cell receptors that allow them to respond to these hormones. These males are born with female genitalia and are raised as girls (Ruble et al., 2006). Studies of gender development in children with CAIS are limited, but they indicate these individuals' gender identity, sexual orientation, and masculinity/femininity interests are typical of the female sex (Hines, Ahmed, & Hughes, 2003). In contrast, results from studies of males who have no penis—either as the result of a rare congenital defect or an accident after birth—and are raised as girls are mixed. In one case study, early reports suggested the individual adapted well to the female assignment (Money & Ehrhardt, 1972), but later reports describe considerable unhappiness (depression, financial instability, failed marriage) with this assignment, resulting in self-reassignment to the male sex (Colapinto, 2000; Ruble et al., 2006). Ultimately, this individual committed suicide.

These findings appear to favor biology in debates about the origins of gender identity and sexual orientation, but more research is needed to clarify this very complex picture (Ruble et al., 2006). It is difficult to conduct research on this topic, and many studies are limited by methods that don't allow researchers to make causal claims. Moreover, it is possible that socialization effects are subtle and that parents respond to their children's physical appearance, interests, and behaviors and treat them accordingly.

Peer Relationships

Relationships with peers and friends are central to children's development. In fact, many researchers argue that positive peer relationships are responsible for a significant amount of adaptive development and that maladaptive development occurs when children are rejected by peers or have difficulty forming and maintaining friendships. In this section, we examine the nature and significance of peer relationships and friendships in middle childhood.

Peer Groups

Although young children may play in groups, they do not form **peer groups**—that is, social groups that form on the basis of shared interests and values and typically are composed of children of the same age, sex, race/ethnicity, and other commonalities (e.g., achievement levels, popularity, athleticism). Rubin and his colleagues (2005) distinguish between two kinds of peer groups: cliques and crowds. *Cliques* are relatively smaller friendship-based groups (typically between 3 and a dozen children). These groups predominate in middle childhood, whereas affiliation with larger crowds becomes salient during adolescence. *Crowds* are less intimate, more loosely organized groups in which members may or may not interact with one another. Affiliation with such crowds provides adolescents with an identity within a larger social structure (e.g., John's a jock, Joan's a brain). Peer group ties can be formal, as is the case with organizations such as Girl Scouts, after-school clubs, and church groups, or informal, as is the case with friendships.

Participation in peer groups is associated with both positive and negative consequences for children (Berndt, 2004; Leets & Sunwolf, 2005). Peer groups teach children a variety of valuable social skills, including how to: (a) engage in cooperative activities aimed at collective versus individual goals; (b) effectively lead and follow others; and (c) control hostile impulses directed at other members (Fine, 1987; Rubin et al., 2005). Moreover, peer groups can provide support that helps children to cope with stress in their lives. However, peer groups also can become exclusive societies that rebuff children who don't conform to certain dress codes and behavior (Leets & Sunwolf, 2005). Interestingly, the time at which children begin to form peer groups is also the time during which relational aggression rises among girls and overt aggression increases among boys (Crick & Grotpeter, 1995). Sometimes, peer groups turn on their own members, casting out individuals who are no longer respected according to some group criteria. In short, peer groups are powerful forces for socialization and, depending on the social character of the group, can influence behavior in both positive and negative ways.

PEER ACCEPTANCE AND REJECTION. Researchers have assessed children's popularity, or the extent to which they are liked by others in their peer group, in a variety of ways (e.g., with teacher and parent ratings or through direct observation), but peer assessments are most often used in contemporary research (Rubin et al., 2005). This methodology uses peers as informants to answer two main questions: Is the child liked? and What is the child like? These sociometric techniques yield four categories of peer acceptance, which are detailed in Table 10.4 on the next page.

Popular children are rated highly by their peers and may achieve their social status by engaging in either prosocial or antisocial behavior. **Rejected children** are actively disliked by their peers. They may be aggressive, immature, socially unskilled, or socially wary and withdrawn. **Controversial children** get mixed reviews from peers because they display a mix of positive and negative social behaviors. Finally, **neglected children** receive few peer nominations of any kind. These children interact less with peers and this "lack of noticeability" makes it very difficult to obtain good peer assessments of their behavior (Rubin et al., 2005, p. 488). However, there is no consistent evidence that these children experience the social anxiety and extreme social wariness that characterizes socially withdrawn children.

WHY SOME KIDS ARE POPULAR. Peer acceptance is positively associated with academic achievement and attractive physical appearance and negatively associated with having an uncommon name (Coie & Krehbiehl, 1984; Hartup, 1981; Langlois & Stephan, 1981). However, social behavior and ways of thinking about social phenomena are the variables most highly associated with status in a peer group (Rubin et al., 2005). For example, children who are sociometrically popular—who receive high ratings on peer assessment measures—are characterized as cooperative, friendly, sociable, and sensitive. These children are skilled at maintaining qualitatively positive relationships. They speak clearly and respond appropriately when others speak to them. When faced with conflict, they use negotiation and compromise, believing they can get what they want and preserve positive relationships. Finally, children who are popular with peers tend to have higher perceived social competence and social efficacy (Harter, 1998; Wheeler & Ladd, 1982).

TABLE 10.4 • **Categories of Peer Acceptance**

POPULAR CHILDREN Popular prosocial children: These children are both academically and socially competent. They do well in school and communicate well with peers. When they disagree with other children, they respond appropriately and have effective strategies for working things out. Popular antisocial children: This subgroup of children often includes boys who are aggressive. They may be athletic and other children tend to think they are "cool" in the ways they bully other children and defy adult authority.
REJECTED CHILDREN Rejected aggressive children: High rates of conflict and hyperactivity/impulsivity characterize the behaviors of this subgroup. These children have poor perspective-taking skills and self-control. They often misunderstand the intentions of others, assign blame, and act aggressively on their angry or hurt feelings. Rejected withdrawn children: These children are timid and withdrawn, often the targets of bullies. They are often socially awkward and withdraw from social interactions to avoid being scorned or attacked.
CONTROVERSIAL CHILDREN As the descriptor implies, these children have both positive and negative social qualities and, as a result, their social status can change over time. They can be hostile and disruptive in some situations and then engage in positive prosocial behaviors in others. These children have friends and are generally happy with their peer relationships.
NEGLECTED CHILDREN Perhaps surprisingly, most of these children are well adjusted and they are not less socially competent than other children. Peers tend to view them as shy, but they don't report being lonely or unhappy about their social lives. Apparently they don't experience the extreme social anxiety and wariness that withdrawn children do.

Research has linked parent–child relationships and parenting behavior to children's peer acceptance. For example, several studies indicate that children who have a secure, positive attachment to their parents (mothers) are more popular and socially competent than children whose relationship to parents is less secure (Granot & Mayseless, 2001; Rose-Krasnor, Rubin, Booth, & Coplan, 1996). Also, children whose parents scaffold their interactions with peers (e.g., monitor child–peer interactions and coach them through conflicts) tend to be more popular with peers and are rated more socially competent by other adults (McDowell, Parke, & Wang, 2003). Finally, popular children tend to have parents who use more feelings-oriented reasoning, warm control, and more positive communication in their parent–child interactions (Mize & Pettit, 1997; Rubin et al., 2005). In contrast, punitive, rejecting, cold, and overly permissive parenting behaviors are associated with childhood aggression, which is associated with peer rejection (Rubin et al., 2005).

CONSEQUENCES OF PEER REJECTION. Peer rejection is associated with academic difficulties as well as problems relating to psychosocial adjustment and functioning (McDougall, Hymel, Vaillancourt, & Mercer, 2001). For example, results of longitudinal studies indicate that peer rejection in childhood predicts a wide range of externalizing problems in adolescence, including delinquency, conduct disorder, attention problems, and substance abuse (Kupersmidt & Coie, 1990; Rubin et al., 2005). Also, peer rejection is associated with internalizing problems, such as loneliness, low self-esteem, and depression. Apparently, children's perception of rejection—their belief that they are being rejected—may influence whether and to what extent they develop externalizing or internalizing problems related to psychosocial adjustment (Rubin et al., 2005). Having at least one good friend may protect children from developing negative feelings about their social lives.

Friendships

Friends are people with whom we share a close, mutual, and dyadic relationship. Reciprocity and equality are key features of friendship. Typically, school-age children choose friends who are like them in age, sex, ethnicity, and interests. Also, friendships deepen across middle childhood as children's conceptions of what it means to be and have a friend evolve (Davies, 2004). Young children's (ages 6 to 8) conception of friendship relates to their social

context and concrete activities ("John is my friend because he lives near me and we lik ride bikes."). For older children, friends are people who share common values, commitmen loyalty, mutual support, and responsibility (Davies, 2004; Rubin, Bukowski, & Parker, 199

Friends serve a number of functions in middle childhood (Davies, 2004; Rubin et a. 2005). For example, they help children acquire knowledge of behavioral norms and lear skills for interacting successfully with peers. They provide children with people to identify with who are like themselves, as opposed to adults or older siblings whose abilities are typically far beyond those of the school-age child. Friends provide support for important transitions or family disruptions (e.g., separation and divorce). Finally, resolving conflicts with friends provides practice for solving conflicts with others (e.g., co-workers, spouses) in later life. Childhood friends have frequent falling outs, but often are motivated to resolve their differences to preserve the friendship. Therefore, in their quarrels, they make more use of negotiation and disengagement, and are more likely than non-friends to reach an equitable agreement (Rubin et al., 2005).

Most middle years children (75–80%) have a **mutual best friend**—a child who reciprocates a "best" friend nomination—and, once formed, these friendships show remarkable stability over time (Rubin et al., 2005). This is not always positive. Since children choose friends who are like them, they may choose friends who reinforce their antisocial or aggressive tendencies, or share their shyness and internalized distress. Berndt, Hawkins, and Jiao (1999) found that behavior problems increased for only those children in their sample who had stable friendships with other children with behavior problems. It seems, therefore, that the positive effects of friendship on children's psychosocial adjustment may be determined by the characteristics of the friend. Interestingly, boys are more likely than girls to maintain mutual friendships. Hardy, Bukowski, and Sippola (2002) found this was the case when children transitioned from elementary to middle school (grades 6 to 7). Through the transition, girls experienced more instability in friendships than did boys and were more likely to form new friendships in the fall of seventh grade.

HOW DO FRIENDSHIPS DIFFER FOR BOYS AND GIRLS? Both boys and girls depend on friends for company, approval, and support (Craft, 1994). However, boys and girls differ in their answers to questions concerning their expectations of friends (Rubin et al., 2005). For example, girls tend to focus on what they receive from friends, whereas boys emphasize reciprocity. Girls describe their same-sex friends with adjectives (e.g., she is nice), but boys tend to describe their friends' interests (e.g., sports). Also, girls report more intimate exchanges in their friendships than do boys. Finally, girls report more relational victimization in their friendships (e.g., "My friend ignores me when she's mad at me."). Boys report more physical victimizations in their altercations with friends.

WHAT HAPPENS TO CHILDREN WHO DON'T HAVE FRIENDS? Children without mutual friendships report more loneliness, and being friendless in childhood is associated with lower self-worth in adulthood (Rubin et al., 2005). It is important to note that not all rejected children are friendless and not all children who are generally accepted by peers have close mutual friendships. The significance of friendships, over and above peer acceptance, is evident in research that shows children who are victimized by peers may only be at risk of developing maladaptive externalizing and internalizing behaviors when they do not have friends (Hodges, Boivin, Vitaro, & Bukowski, 1999). Apparently, having a close friend can alleviate the negative effects of being disliked and rejected by peers.

FAMILIES

Even though peers and friends have increasing significance in children's development during middle childhood, families are important, too. This section examines children's relationships with parents and siblings and how these relationships influence other aspects of development, such as social relationships and self-regulation. Also, we will see that families come in all shapes and sizes these days, and they face a number of difficult challenges.

Parent–Child Relationships in Middle Childhood

Parents continue to play an important role in children's lives throughout middle childhood, but their relationship changes to accommodate children's expanding social world and their increased competencies. Bryant (1985) asked children 7 to 10 years of age to identify the 10 most important people in their lives. A significant proportion of children (approximately 80%) included their moms and dads on this list. However, unrelated peers also were included 72% of the time, and 23% of children identified an unrelated adult as one of the most important people in their lives.

As children move through middle childhood, they spend less time with their parents, and parents spend less time supervising their activities (Davies, 2004; Lamb & Lewis, 2005). Children spend less time at home and, when they are at home, they spend less time interacting directly with parents. Time at home is often spent doing homework, watching TV, doing chores, playing independently, or playing with siblings. In many non-Western societies, children in late-middle childhood enter the workforce or begin to contribute to the sustainability of the family in other ways (e.g., tending crops or looking after younger siblings). Even in Western societies, many mothers return to working part or full time. Children have less time with mothers and often are expected to take on more responsibility in the family. We discuss the impact of mothers and parents working on children's development in a subsequent section.

APPROACHES TO PARENTING. In Chapter 7 we highlighted the work of Diana Baumrind (1973, 1991) that characterizes effective parents as supportive, caring, and child-centered in their approach to parenting; their primary concern is meeting the needs of their children, rather than meeting their own needs or convenience. In addition, these parents exercise firm behavioral control. They monitor their children's activities closely, hold high but age-appropriate expectations for behavior, and apply inductive versus punitive approaches to discipline when problems arise. Baumrind referred to such approaches to parenting as authoritative. Authoritative approaches to parenting are associated with better peer relationships (as indicated in the previous section) and academic outcomes for school-age children, and greater demonstrations of love and respect for parents and other people. In contrast, children who experience what Baumrind referred to as cold and authoritarian parenting tend to be more aggressive, less popular with peers, and less successful in school. Also, children raised by authoritarian parents tend to be less independent than children raised by authoritative parents.

Children whose parents are, in Baumrind's terms, either permissive or rejecting/neglecting are most at risk for poor outcomes. For example, children from permissive homes tend to do less well in school and to be less independent and self-assured than children who are raised by authoritative parents. This is particularly true for children whose parents are not only permissive but also indulgent. Children whose parents reject or neglect them often do poorly in school and show other disruptions in peer relationships and cognitive development (Parke & Buriel, 2006). Also, these children evidence higher rates of delinquency, alcohol and drug abuse, and early sexual behavior.

Although there is general support for Baumrind's characterizations of effective parenting, especially in Western societies among middle-class communities of European descent, effective parenting, and the constructs associated with it, may be viewed differently by different cultures. For example, authoritarian characterizations of parenting do not elicit the negative associations in Arab and Asian cultures that they do in North American and many European cultures (Chao & Sue, 1996; Dwairy et al., 2006; Rudy & Grusec, 2006), nor are they associated with negative outcomes for children (e.g., low self-esteem). Even within societies, both Western and non-Western, there is considerable variation in both parenting practices and their efficacy for children's development (Dwairy et al., 2006; Leyendecker et al., 2002). In the following section, we describe how different parenting practices can achieve the same goal of promoting self-regulation.

Of primary importance across cultures is that children do best when their relationships with parents are characterized as warm and loving and when their parents are actively engaged in helping them to learn appropriate behavior and make good choices.

PARENTS PROMOTING SELF-REGULATION. Several parenting variables are believed to contribute to the development of self-regulation. Parents' own ability to self-regulate is important, as they serve as good or poor models of self-regulation (Prinstein & La Greca, 1999). Also, parents' high expectations concerning self-regulation, as well as the monitoring that ensures those expectations are met, are associated with greater self-regulatory competence on the part of children (Rodrigo, Janssen, & Ceballos, 1999). Finally, what we have described as authoritative approaches to parenting are associated with greater independence and self-regulation (Lamb & Lewis, 2005).

Why might this be? Authoritative parents recognize that as children grow and develop, they will need to monitor their actions and activities from a distance. They understand the need to give children a reasonable amount of freedom and set and enforce limits in ways that teach children to be responsible. These parents don't set and enforce rules arbitrarily or unilaterally. They explain *why* rules are in place, typically for children's safety and well-being, and they work with children to set rules that are reasonable and age-appropriate. When children object to rules, authoritative parents are willing to listen to their points of view and to negotiate a compromise. In this way, parents and children in authoritative families *co-regulate* behavior. Over time, authoritative parents expect children to develop the ability to regulate their own behavior. These parents recognize that as children spend more and more time away from home, they need to be effectively self-regulating to make good choices, be liked, and withstand peer and societal pressures.

However, there is some evidence to suggest that authoritarian approaches to parenting can produce some of the same positive results that are observed when parenting is authoritative. For example, Baumrind (1973) found that African American daughters raised by authoritarian parents were exceptionally independent and at ease. In fact, stricter disciplinary practices are characteristic of many minority groups, especially those living in poor and dangerous neighborhoods (Parke & Buriel, 2006). It is possible that parents in these communities use more authoritarian discipline approaches both to protect their children from becoming victims or perpetrators of violence and to ensure success in school and a better life in the future. However, stricter discipline in these communities often is coupled with a strong system of interdependence among family and extended family members, and it is balanced by warm and caring interactions most of the time. It seems that strict and directive parenting combined with high levels of warmth and emotional support is linked to higher levels of academic achievement and emotional maturity for inner-city children (Garner & Spears, 2000; Jarrett, 1995). Perhaps children interpret this as caring and commitment on their parents' part (Stewart & Bond, 2002). This combination of parenting styles also is characteristic of Chinese and immigrant Chinese families (Lim & Lim, 2003; Peterson, Cobas, Bush, Supple, & Wilson, 2004).

COOPERATION AND CONSISTENCY. One other important feature of successful parenting is cooperation and consistency between parents. This can be difficult to achieve in contemporary families in which both parents work outside the home and, often, have little time to interact and check with one another about the decisions they make for their children. Also, parents can disagree or have different styles of parenting. Children quickly learn who is more permissive and thus is likely to give them what they want. Even when parents don't live together, they should communicate and cooperate on matters that concern their children.

Sibling Relationships

Those of us who have siblings likely can relate to this comment: "[I]t is our brothers and sisters who see us as no one else does, who are experts at how to both please and annoy us, and who bring out the best and the worst in us" (Kramer & Bank, 2005, p. 483). Surprisingly, sibling relationships have received relatively little consideration in research about families when compared, for example, to the attention given to parent–child and marital relationships and their impact on children's well-being and family functioning (Kramer & Bank, 2005). Interactions with siblings provide a context for children to learn and practice a range of positive prosocial skills, including perspective-taking, sharing, and caring effectively for others (Eisenberg et al., 2006; Parke & Buriel, 2006). Also, because sibling relationships typically involve some conflict, they present opportunities for children to practice controlling their emotions and behaviors and to develop strategies for solving interpersonal problems (Brody, 2004). Of course, sibling relationships also can have a negative impact on children's social and emotional development. Older siblings can model and encourage behavior that is harmful or antisocial (e.g., smoking cigarettes), and children who grow up with older siblings who are aggressive are at increased risk for developing behavior problems, relationship difficulties, and trouble in school (Brody, 2004; Kramer & Bank, 2005). Finally, sibling relationships can provide a buffer from other stressors in children's lives. For example, older siblings may provide emotional support and protection to younger siblings when there is family turmoil (e.g., parental conflict), or victimization by peers (Brody, 2004; Lamarche & Brendgen, 2006; Parke & Buriel, 2006).

In general, sibling relationships in middle childhood are characterized by declines in both warmth and conflict (Parke & Buriel, 2006; Slomkowski & Manke, 2004). Perhaps this is due to children's broadening interests and friendships outside the home. Still, siblings are an important source of companionship, emotional support, and care for many school-age children, and sisters, in particular, continue to report feelings of warmth and closeness during this time (Slomkowski & Manke, 2004). Considerable proportions of children who have siblings share a bedroom, do chores with them, and play together on a regular basis (Bryant, 1982). This is particularly true when siblings are close in age and are the same sex. Where there is an age difference, older siblings often comfort, support, and care for younger children (Eisenberg et al., 2006). This is particularly true in large families and non-industrialized societies where there is a strong sense of interdependence among family members (Maynard, 2002; Weisner, 1993), and in families where both parents work and are often unavailable (Eisenberg et al., 2006). However, at least in North America, the care and support children receive from siblings does not match the richness and complexity of care they typically receive from parents (Bryant, 1992). For example, when children seek help with complex and emotionally stressful problems, parents offer more coping strategies than siblings; the comfort and support provided by siblings in these instances do not match the level of care parents typically provide.

There also is the issue of sibling rivalry, which tends to increase in intensity during middle childhood. It is natural for children to compare themselves to siblings and to learn about themselves and how they differ from one another through these comparisons (Updegraff & Obeidallah, 1999). It also is typical for parents to compare siblings in terms of their traits and accomplishments, and to form expectations for younger children based on experiences with their older siblings, especially when the siblings are close in age and the same sex. Such comparisons, and even differential treatment from parents, don't necessarily lead to poor outcomes for children who compare less favorably to siblings or who spend less time with or receive less positive attention from parents (Brody, 2004). What matters is the quality of children's individual relationships with parents. When those are positive, and when children understand the rationale for parents' treating siblings differently (e.g., parents may need to attend more to siblings who are younger or who have a disability), children can tolerate comparisons and differential treatment. However, when comparisons or differential treatment lead children to perceive that they receive less warmth and more negative

Siblings are an important source of companionship and emotional support for many school-age children. They can help one another learn and practice a range of positive prosocial skills, including perspective-taking, sharing, and caring effectively for others.

treatment from parents, or that one or another sibling is the favorite and unfairly receives more attention, approval, or material resources, resentment and quarrelling may ensue (Reiss, Neiderhiser, Hetherington, & Plomin, 2000). Parents can reduce these antagonisms by acknowledging the unique characteristics of each child and supporting each child in developing his or her particular interests and talents.

What about only children? Do children who don't have siblings suffer any ill effects in terms of their cognitive and social development? The preponderance of the research on this topic indicates that only children are just as well adjusted as other children, and they also have some advantages. On average, only children score higher on measures of self-esteem and motivation for learning than children with siblings, and they are just as likely to be resourceful, popular, independent, and successful in relationships (Blake, 1989; Dawson, 1991; Polit & Falbo, 1987). Also, these children tend to have closer relationships with parents (Falbo & Polit, 1986).

What about children with step-siblings and half-siblings? In the section that follows, we describe the many different family configurations that exist in our society today. Different sibling relationships arise out of different family configurations. Edward Anderson (1999) examined differences in qualities of relationships among full biological siblings, half-siblings, and unrelated step-siblings. At the time of his study, participants were pairs of same-sex siblings ages 12 to 15. His findings indicate that, in general, relationships between female siblings were more positive than relationships between male siblings. Specifically, girls' relationships involved more communication and support. They also involved more directivity: one sibling telling the other sibling what to do. Step-sibling relationships were characterized as less negative than other sibling relationships. They involved less aggression, rivalry, and avoidance. Finally, positive relationships among siblings in all three groups were associated with lower levels of externalizing behavior and depressive symptoms, and higher levels of social responsibility, cognitive agency, sociability, autonomy, and self-worth, and this was true for both older and younger siblings.

Family Portraits

Perhaps the most appropriate expectation to have about children's families is no expectation all. Today, many children have only one sibling or no siblings at all. They may be part of blended families and have "step" siblings who move in and out of their lives. They may receive care from extended family members—perhaps living with an aunt or grandparents—they may have two moms or two dads, or they may live with adoptive or foster families. In fact, fully intact families—consisting of married couples living just with their biological children—represented just under 25% of U.S. households in 1990 (U.S. Census Bureau, 2000). In this section we consider several of the many family structures and their implications for children.

NEVER-MARRIED AND SINGLE-PARENT FAMILIES. According to the U.S. Census Bureau (2000), approximately 10% of children have parents who never married, and most of these children (89%) live with their mothers. Rates of childbearing outside of marriage vary greatly by ethnic group, with African American women delaying marriage more and childbirth less than any other ethnic group (Glick, 1997). Perhaps this is the result of the persistent difficulties Black men in poor neighborhoods have had in providing for their families, as well as the common practice in African American communities of involving extended family members, primarily grandmothers, in caring for children. Regardless, African American women have children out of wedlock at a rate of 70% compared with 41% of Hispanic mothers and 26% of White, non-Hispanic mothers (Ventura, Peters, Martin, & Maurer, 1997).

Historically, research has indicated that children in never-married families are at risk for experiencing some of the same poor outcomes as children whose parents have divorced; in some instances, their level of risk is higher (McLanahan, 1999). For example, children who live in never-married families are more likely to drop out of school and to become parents in their teen years than children whose parents are divorced. Both these groups are more than twice as likely to experience these outcomes as children in two-parent families or families

According to 2000 Census data, just under 25% of U.S. households consisted of married couples living with only their biological children. There are many family structures, and each has implications for the children. Within this variety of structures, children may have only one sibling, no siblings, or step-siblings; they may live with grandparents or other extended family members; they may live in adoptive or foster families; they may live with one parent; or they may have two moms or two dads. Perhaps the most appropriate expectation to have about children's families is to have no expectation at all.

where one parent is widowed. Often, however, these outcomes are associated with a family's financial security. Most of the research on single parents focuses on mothers who have low incomes and may not receive adequate child support from fathers, particularly if they never married their children's fathers (Meyer, 1999). Lower family income has important consequences for children's development. It places extra stress on families, which can lead to less effective parenting and fewer opportunities for children to engage in the kinds of activities that distract from problem behaviors and lead to success both in and beyond school.

More and more, however, women-headed families are not poor. Many women who are well educated and financially secure are having children out of wedlock by choice. Rosana Hertz (2006), a professor of women's studies and sociology, writes about these women in her book titled "Single by Chance, Mothers by Choice." Most of these women are more mature than the stereotypic unwed mother and have established themselves in their careers. Certainly, they are able to provide their children with all they need in the way of material resources, but what else might children miss from living without a father? Some research indicates that fathers' active engagement has positive effects on children's overall health and their degree of behavioral and psychological problems (Lamb, 1999; McLanahan, 1997; 1999). However, in her book, "Raising Boys Without Men," Peggy Drexler (2005) argues that boys raised by mothers become socially savvy, generous, caring communicators while remaining extremely boyish. She compared outcomes for boys who were raised in female-headed households with those of boys raised in traditional mom and dad families, and her in-depth interviews refute many of the previous stereotypes. More research is needed about how this group of children fares compared to children of other never-married parents. Similarly, we need more research about how children fare when their primary caregiver is their father.

BLENDED FAMILIES. Many benefits accrue from the successful blending of families. Often, when mothers remarry, their financial circumstances improve, and this leads to increased services and educational opportunities for their children. For boys in particular, living with a stepfather increases their chances of finishing high school, attending and graduating from college, and being successful in the job market. Moreover, when blended families stay together for many years, they serve as positive role models for children's future intimate relationships. Finally, if both biological parents are involved in parenting and their relationship is good, children in blended families can end up with more parental support and guidance than children in traditional families (Amato, 1999; Hetherington, Bridges, & Insabella, 1998; Wallerstein, Lewis, & Blakeslee, 2000).

Of course, blended families face particular challenges, especially when the relationships are new. The rules of engagement are likely to change, and it takes time to establish new routines and responsibilities. Also, there may be some competition among children for parents' attention, or between children and a stepfather for a mother's attention. In some cases, children are worse off than before their parent remarried (Wallerstein et al., 2000). For example, when fathers remarry, they may be more financially stressed than before, trying to support both their biological children and their stepchildren. The result can be a decrease in both financial security and emotional support for their biological children, especially if their children do not live with them. In general, stepfathers are less involved and less emotionally supportive than biological fathers who are continuously involved in their children's lives (Hetherington & Clingempeel, 1992). These examples point to the multiple complex issues influencing children's experiences in blended families.

GAY AND LESBIAN FAMILIES. Estimates of the number of lesbian and gay parents in the United States varied from 1 to 9 million in the sources we consulted. Experts agree these estimates can be conservative because some parents conceal their homosexual orientation in response to lingering prejudice about the appropriateness of children being raised in a gay- or lesbian-headed household. According to Charlotte Patterson (2002), a prominent researcher in this field, approximately 20% of lesbians and 10% of gay men have children. Many of these children were conceived when their parents were in heterosexual relationships, but more and more gay and lesbian couples are using alternate means, such as surrogacy and donor insemination, to have children. Other couples are adopting children or providing foster homes to children in need of families.

In general, children raised by homosexual parents are well adjusted and have good relationships with their parents (AAP Committee on Psychosocial Aspects of Child and Family Health, 2002; Golombok et al., 2003; Patterson, 1992; 2002; Tye, 2003). They are not more likely to suffer crises of gender identity or to be homosexuals themselves. School-age children living in gay and lesbian families demonstrate the same developmental trends as children raised in heterosexual families. For example, they prefer playing with same-sex peers and gender-stereotypic toys and games. Moreover, these children are not significantly different from peers in terms of popularity, sociability, hyperactivity, emotional difficulty, moral maturity, or intelligence. The greatest challenge for children with gay and lesbian parents may be coping with the prejudice directed at their families by various groups in society.

ADOPTIVE AND FOSTER FAMILIES. Many children grow up in adoptive families (approximately 2.5%) and most of these children adjust well and function normally (U.S. Census Bureau, 2005). These children do much better on psychological, educational, social, and emotional measures than children who are cared for in residential and long-term foster care settings, or children who are shuttled between foster care settings and parents who are either unable or unwilling to parent effectively (Morgan, 1998; Triseliotis & Hill, 1990). There are approximately 600,000 children in foster care and around 70% are school age (U.S. Department of Health and Human Services, 2001). As a group, these children suffer severe functional impairment, which manifests itself in poor academic achievement, behavioral and emotional problems, and poor health (Black, 2006; Emerson & Lovitt, 2003; Kools, 1997). Of course, there are foster families who are strongly committed to providing loving and stable environments for children who have experienced much turmoil in their short lives. In general, however, adoptive families provide a more financially and emotionally secure environment. Most adoptive parents are highly motivated and committed to helping their children prosper. Also, adopted children can settle into this new environment, knowing it is permanent. As a result, most children who are adopted develop a strong sense of identity and report feeling emotionally attached to their adoptive parents (Sharma, McGue, & Benson, 1996, 1998; Stams, Juffer, Rispens, & Hoksbergen, 2000).

There are, however, some special challenges associated with adopting children, and there is evidence that these children are more at risk for adjustment problems than their nonadopted peers (Miller, Xitao, Christensen, Grotevant, & van Dulmen, 2000). Adopted children are more likely to receive psychological treatment and are at increased risk for experiencing behavior problems, learning disabilities, and adjustment difficulties in school. This is particularly true of children who were not adopted as infants; this behavior is more likely the result of their early experiences as opposed to their being adopted per se. Often, these problems don't appear until late childhood and adolescence (Goodman, Emery, & Haugaard, 1998; Sharma, McGue, & Benson, 1996). In Chapter 13, we will see that a major task for adolescents is to define and develop their identity. Adolescents who have limited knowledge about their biological history may have difficulty accomplishing this task, and their relationship with their adoptive parents may be stressed during this period of their lives. For these reasons, adoptive parents should try to learn as much as possible about their children's previous family history. Also, they may need to support their adolescents in locating and contacting their biological parents. This is becoming easier with the rise in **open adoption**—an arrangement in which the adults involved share information and, in some cases, interact directly. Not only can this help adoptive parents to prepare for—and proactively work to curtail—psychological problems but also it can be invaluable in preventing or treating genetically determined illnesses.

Challenges Families Face

In our family portraits, we have already alluded to many challenges facing families. In this section, we focus on two challenges that are common to many families in our modern society: experiencing divorce and finding adequate childcare.

DISHARMONY AND DIVORCE. The divorce rate in the United States is the highest in the world. Some analysts estimate that between 40% and 50% of first-time marriages end in divorce (National Center for Health Statistics, 2004). In 1998, 14.4% of children under the age of 18 lived in homes in which parents were either divorced or separated—that's more than 10 million children (U.S. Census Bureau, 1998). Similarly, it is estimated that 36% of marriages in Canada will end in divorce within 30 years of the wedding (Ambert, 2005). As many of us know from experiences in our own families, separation and divorce are stressful events for all participants, even under the best circumstances. The actual separation of the parents may have been preceded by years of tension and conflict in the home, or it may come as a shock to all, including friends and children. During the divorce itself, tensions may increase as property and custody rights are being decided. What do parents and other caregivers need to consider for children experiencing divorce?

Divorce is disruptive. Today, as in the past, the mother is most often the custodial parent, even though the number of households headed by fathers has been increasing to about 15% in the United States (Fields, 2003) and 10–12% in Canada (Ambert, 2005). The parent who has custody may have to move to a less expensive home, find new sources of income, go to work for the first time, or work longer hours. For children, this can mean leaving behind important friendships in the old neighborhood or school, just when support is needed the most. It may mean having just one parent, who has less time than ever to be with the children. Also, about two-thirds of parents remarry and then half of them divorce again, so there may be more adjustments ahead for some children (Ambert, 2005; Nelson, 1993).

The first 2 to 4 years after the divorce are the most difficult for children. During this time, they may have problems in school, lose or gain an unusual amount of weight, develop difficulties sleeping, and experience other problems. Young children may blame themselves for the breakup of their family or hold unrealistic hopes for reconciliation (Hetherington, 1999). Older children are better able to understand why their parents are separated, but can still react strongly to it and may protest by running away or engaging in undesirable or antisocial behaviors (Hetherington & Stanley-Hagan, 1999). In general, boys whose parents are divorced show higher rates of behavioral and interpersonal problems at home and in school than either girls in general or boys from intact families. Girls may have trouble in their dealings with males, and may become more sexually active or have difficulties trusting males.

Children of divorced parents may feel pressured to take on more responsibility or to grow up faster (Hetherington, 1999). This can be positive as long as parents are not drawing too much on their children for help in the house, care for siblings, or emotional support for themselves. When parents lean too much on children, the result can be depression, anxiety, compulsive caretaking, anger, and resentment. Children whose parents are divorced may experience psychological and emotional pain and distress and may have lower self-esteem than children of intact families (Emery, 1999). Children who feel these pressures are more likely to exhibit externalizing problems, such as aggression and juvenile delinquency (Amato, 2001; Wallerstein, Lewis, & Blakeslee, 2000).

We want to emphasize that the outcomes of divorce are not always negative. In one of the most comprehensive studies of divorce to date, Mavis Hetherington (with John Kelly, 2003) studied 1,400 families, with more than 2,500 children, for three decades. In her study, the majority of children from divorced homes (75–80%) coped well with divorce and adapted to their new situations. In particular, women and girls seemed to fare better after divorce than did men and boys. Even though women faced greater economic hardships, they tended to develop competencies they might not have otherwise and, likewise, their daughters increased in confidence and competence. Although Hetherington is not an advocate for divorce, she does see it as a legitimate decision that can serve children better than when adults stay in unhappy and conflictual relationships.

In some divorces there are few conflicts, ample resources, and the continuing support of friends and extended family. Also, some groups of children appear to be less at risk for negative effects from divorce than others. For example, Hispanic or African American children are less likely than non-Hispanic White children to experience the behavioral and academic problems we've listed (Dunifon & Kowaleski-Jones, 2002; McLanahan, 1999). The overall effect of divorce depends on several factors, including mediating events and processes (e.g., the degree of parental effectiveness and conflict, and child-specific vulnerabilities, such as difficult temperament or predisposition to psychological problems), and protective factors (e.g., social factors and coping strategies) (Amato, 2000; Buehler & Gerard, 2002; Hetherington & Elmore, 2003). Living with one fairly content, if harried, parent is better than living in a conflict-filled situation with two unhappy parents. Children benefit when parents can devote themselves to developing positive relationships with their children once the stress and strife that characterized their relationship is over. And, if one parent engages in high levels of antisocial behavior, children are better off spending less time with that parent (Jaffee, Moffitt, Caspi, & Taylor, 2003). See the ***Connecting with Children*** guidelines for ideas about how to help children cope with divorce.

CONNECTING WITH CHILDREN

Guidelines for Families, Teachers, and Other Professionals: Helping Children through Divorce

Minimize conflict.
Examples
1. Place the needs of your children ahead of your own needs when negotiating such things as custody, finances, and schooling.
2. Be careful not to belittle your partner in front of your children.
3. Don't ask children to take sides in a dispute or to assume unreasonable responsibilities around the house or in terms of emotional support for parents and siblings.

Minimize the number of changes children must experience as a consequence of divorce.
Examples
1. If possible, avoid having both partners move to new residences. At least limit the number of moves children need to experience in a short time.
2. Help children to maintain contact with friends, extended family members, teachers, and other positive community contacts.
3. Introduce changes gradually and be sensitive to how children are experiencing them.

Develop consistent rules and routines for children as they navigate across settings.
Examples
1. Try to agree on rules concerning your children's behavior and what the consequences will be when expectations are not met. Be consistent about monitoring behavior and enforcing consequences.
2. Be clear and consistent in communication about schedules, assignments for school, and equipment needed for out of school activities. Otherwise important meetings or activities may be missed.

Whenever possible, help children to maintain consistent contact with both parents.
Examples
1. Schedule regular visits with the non-custodial parent, making adjustments according to the children's needs and interests.
2. Keep connected. Regular telephone or email contact can substitute for regular visits when a parent no longer lives near the children.
3. Make sure birthdays and other important dates are not forgotten, and show interest in your children's interests and activities by attending recitals and sports events.

Take note of sudden changes in behavior that may indicate adjustment problems.
Examples
1. Be aware of physical symptoms, such as headaches or stomach upset, rapid weight gain or loss, and fatigue or excess energy that can signal distress.
2. Be alert to the signs of emotional distress, such as moodiness, temper tantrums, and difficulty paying attention or concentrating.
3. Caregivers, other than parents, should communicate noted changes to parents right away.

Give children opportunities to talk about their feelings.
Examples
1. Let children know you are available to talk.
2. Be a good listener and let children set the agenda.

Seek professional help for children who are experiencing pain and distress.
Examples
1. Provide group support that is designed to reduce the distress they are feeling about the divorce.
2. Teach children coping strategies (e.g., seeking support from adults and friends) and help them develop a belief that they can handle the stresses they are experiencing.
3. Provide opportunity for individual therapies if the problem appears more severe (e.g., suspected depression, conduct disorder).

Source: Woolfolk, A. Educational Psychology *(10th Ed., p. 75). Boston: Pearson and Allyn & Bacon.*

WORKING PARENTS AND CHILDCARE. Finding dependable, good quality care for children is one of the most pressing problems for parents today. However, this problem is not as new as you might think. Non-parental childcare has been a common practice in the majority of cultures throughout most time periods (Lamb, 1998). What has changed in recent decades is the kind of the non-parental care children have received. There has been a dramatic increase in childcare arrangements that are center-based and involve non-relatives (U.S. Census Bureau, 2005). Also, there are large numbers of school-age children who care for themselves on a regular basis. These children are sometimes referred to as **latchkey kids.** Self-care is more common for boys than for girls and, interestingly, for children from upper-income White families than children from poor or ethnic families (Lamb, 1998; Urban Institute, 2000); it is less common for children under the age of 12 in father-only living arrangements (U.S. Census Bureau, 2006). Alarmingly, the self-care arrangement for many children actually fits the legal definition of child neglect.

A number of factors need to be considered when assessing the potential impact of non-parental care on children's social, emotional, and cognitive development, including (a) children's home environment, (b) the nature and quality of the non-parental care received, (c) family SES, (d) the age of children when placed in childcare, (e) the time they spend there, and (f) vulnerabilities that are specific to particular children (Keating & Hertzman, 1999; Lowe, Weisner, Geis, & Huston, 2005). What does the research say about some of these issues? A report of the National Institute of Child Health and Human Development (NICHD) Early Child Care Research Network (2003) indicates the quality of adult–child interactions and overall ambiance in childcare contexts are modestly associated with ratings of children's social and cognitive competence. Specifically, higher quality care is associated with higher levels of cooperation and participation among children, higher ratings of independence and overall social competence, and lower ratings of anxiety. However, quality of care interacts with other factors and appears to be more important for some children than others. For example, the quality of children's home environments and relationships with parents are far more important for predicting their future social and cognitive competence than the quality of the non-parental care they receive (Lowe et al., 2005). Also, researchers found children from low SES communities benefited most from high-quality childcare (Fuller, Kagan, & Loeb, 2002; Keating & Hertzman, 1999; Lamb, 1998), and children who were socially fearful developed positive peer relationships in high quality care settings, but not in lower quality care settings (Volling & Feagans, 1995).

Not all parents can access high quality childcare. As is true of so many services, you get what you pay for, and not all parents can afford to pay for the better programs. Parents who earn incomes just above the poverty level are most disenfranchised in this regard. They cannot afford to pay the full cost of the high quality care, but their income is too high for them to qualify for government childcare assistance (Helburn & Howes, 1996). Another issue for poor families concerns the stability of their childcare arrangements. Although not as much is known about childcare stability, the existing evidence indicates that instability can negatively affect children's development (Lowe et al., 2005). In an ethnographic study of 42 families from low SES communities, Lowe and his colleagues found that the majority of families (84%) experienced at least one change in childcare during their 2-year study. A sizeable minority (29%) experienced a change in childcare 4 or 5 times during the same period. Many parents (62%) indicated that school year cycles or child maturation had something to do with their decision to change. However, 89% of parents also referred to changes in their family routine, social support, and finances, or some type of conflict as causes of the changes they made. Lowe et al. concluded that childcare stability is an important indicator of other things working well within families.

There is some evidence to suggest that children's age at entry to childcare, the time they spend in childcare, and their mothers' attitude toward work and childcare can influence its overall effect on their development. For example, teachers associated more problem behaviors with children who spent more time in childcare during their preschool years and entered childcare early (Belsky, 2002; Belsky, Weinraub, Owen, & Kelly, 2001; Lamb, 1998). However, there is disagreement among researchers about the extent to which increased aggressive behavior demonstrated by children in childcare settings reflects an increased risk from participating in such settings, or normal amounts of aggression and increased opportunities to exercise it (NICHD Early Child Care Research Network, 2003). Regarding mothers' attitudes, researchers have found that children adjust better when mothers are committed to their work and feel satisfied and secure with their childcare arrangement (Harrison & Ungerer, 2002).

What about children who care for themselves? Self-care can have several benefits when it is managed and monitored. Children who are in regular telephone contact with their parents—checking in—or have a trusted adult neighbor who is available if and when needed tend to do better in self-care (Lamb, 1998). It is preferable for children to be home alone with a set of rules and routines to follow than to be hanging out at the mall or entertaining friends without adult supervision (Steinberg, 1986; Steinberg & Silk, 2002). Also, the amount of time children spend alone is important: The more time children spend alone, the more susceptible they are to problem behaviors (Vandell & Posner, 1999; Vandell & Shumow, 1999). Finally, how should parents judge their children's preparedness for staying alone? In general, children under 10 should not stay alone, but parents need to judge their child's level of cognitive and emotional maturity. Also, they need to evaluate the security of the neighborhood in which they live. Some of the authoritative parenting practices that we described earlier will prepare children for self-care. Recall that the children of authoritative parents tend to be more independent and resourceful than other children.

School

Do you remember your first day of school? Were you filled with excitement and ambition, looking forward to meeting your teacher and classmates? Or were you filled with apprehension, needing to be tugged and cajoled by your parents and, perhaps, your teacher to enter the school building and your classroom? Children's experiences in school can vary from the start. In this section, we examine the critical transition from home to school and some of the ways parents and teachers can make children's experiences in school positive.

Starting School

Most children in the majority of countries around the world enter school between the ages of 5 and 7. School is a big adjustment. It requires spending hours every weekday in a new physical and social environment. Children must learn how to behave in classrooms and to trust new adults. This can be especially challenging for children whose family and community life differs greatly from the environment of school. At the same time, the new psychosocial challenge of industry versus inferiority looms large. As we discussed at the start of this chapter, school-age children are typically ready and interested to master new skills, but they also are becoming aware of their strengths and weaknesses in relation to the work that needs to be done (Jacobs et al., 2002; Wigfield et al., 1997). In school, the child must master new skills and work toward new goals, while being compared to others and risking failure. This can be particularly daunting for children who feel inferior in school-related tasks.

Most children in the majority of countries around the world enter school between the ages of 5 and 7. These children are attending school in Sirin Tegav, Afghanistan.

The way children cope with these challenges has implications for the rest of their school experience. Two of the best predictors of dropping out of school are academic difficulties by the third grade and being held back in one of the primary grades (Paris & Cunningham, 1996). Children who do well in first grade are on their way to achievement, whereas those who flounder are on a path toward difficulty (Schaeffer, Petras, Ialongo, Poduska, & Kellam, 2003; Snow, Burns, & Griffin, 1998; Sprague & Walker, 2000). The achievement differences among students from high and low socioeconomic groups in first grade are relatively small, but they quickly become resistant to interventions (Stanovich, 1986; Torgesen et al., 2001), and by the 6th grade, the differences have tripled. "How well students do in the primary grades matters more for their future success than does their school performance at any other time" (Entwisle & Alexander, 1998, p. 354).

What can be done to make children's early years in school positive? Research points to a few answers. First, quality preschool and kindergarten experiences are critical for helping children, especially children from low-income homes, to do well in first grade. When children achieve in first grade, they also tend to do better in later grades. For this reason, early and intensive intervention programs to support young children who are having difficulty in school have been a focus of governments and school districts across North America for a number of years. Parents and caregivers also can help by trying to ensure continuity in children's school experiences. In particular, staying in the same school for kindergarten and first grade, with the same peers and teachers, can be helpful. Finally, relationships with teachers have an important impact on children's adjustment to school.

Teacher–Student Relationships

Who doesn't remember their first teacher? Mrs. Barrow was your text author Nancy's kindergarten teacher. She was a kind and gentle woman. Most primary teachers are wonderful people. Those who establish positive relationships with students are characterized as warm, friendly, and sincere (Davis, 2001, 2003; Wentzel, 1997, 2002). They convey a genuine respect for students and are sympathetic and responsive to their needs. But students also like teachers who are effective managers—teachers who focus on helping students learn what is expected and showing them how to meet those expectations without threatening or punishing children who fail to do so (Brophy, 2004). Students want teachers to be authority figures, to articulate clear standards for behavior, and to care about their success (Askell-Williams & Lawson, 2001; Cothran, Kulinna, & Garrahy, 2003). It appears that authoritative teaching strategies, like authoritative approaches to parenting, lead to positive relationships with students and enhance motivation for learning (Wentzel, 2002). Moreover, teachers' "immediacy behaviors" (e.g., eye contact, relaxed body posture, smiling) are associated with students' liking of teachers, interest in courses, and desire to study thoughtfully and do well on assignments (Kerssen-Griep, 2001; Richmond, 2002).

Baker, Grant, and Morlock (2008) examined the influence of student-teacher relationships on achievement, school adjustment, and work habits in elementary school children. Close relationships were characterized by trust, warmth, and low conflict. In their study, close student-teacher relationships were positively related to achievement and school adjustment and negatively related to conflict. In contrast, teacher-student conflict was negatively related to achievement, school adjustment, and work habits. Baker and her colleagues argued that close teacher-student relationships are part of a positive school climate that leads to positive outcomes for children. Similarly, Wang (2009) included teacher emotional support in her study of how positive school climates are related to children's social competence. Her findings indicate that positive school climates are associated with lower levels of deviant behavior and depression.

Students avoid interacting with teachers who come across as uncaring or uninterested in them and will stop asking such teachers for help if their responses are perceived as nonsupportive (Brophy, 2004; Martin, Myers, & Moffet, 2002; Turner, Meyer, Midgley, & Patrick, 2003). When teachers' interactions with students are verbally abusive (e.g., when teachers consistently engage in negative comparisons, or issue verbal putdowns and threats), targeted students are more likely to experience both academic and behavioral problems in both the short and the long term (Brendgen, Wanner, & Vitaro, 2006; Brendgen, Wanner, Vitaro, Bukowski, & Tremblay, 2007). For example, Brendgen and her colleagues followed a sample of 231 boys and girls over 17 years, beginning in kindergarten, and examined links between teachers' verbal abuse in middle childhood and high school graduation rates and behavioral problems in young adulthood. In their study, students who experienced high levels of conflict and verbal abuse in their relationships with teachers were more likely to experience behavior problems in young adulthood, and girls were at higher risk for dropping out of school before graduation.

Similarly, Bridget Hamre and Robert Pianta (2001) followed 179 children in a small school district from kindergarten through eighth grade. The results of their study suggest that children's relationships with teachers in kindergarten predicted both academic and behavioral outcomes for children through eighth grade, especially for children who had high levels of behavioral problems. Their research indicates that children with significant behavior problems in kindergarten were less likely to have problems later in school when their kindergarten teachers were sensitive to their needs and provided them with frequent and consistent feedback. Moreover, even when gender, ethnicity, cognitive ability, and behavior ratings of students were accounted for in this study, children's relationship with their teachers still predicted aspects of their school success. Other studies have concluded that positive relationships with teachers can offset the negative effects of peer rejection (Wentzel & Asher, 1995).

Teachers are human and relationships are reciprocal, so the ways in which teachers relate and respond to students can be influenced by student characteristics. For example, teachers tend to respond more positively to students who achieve, conform, and are agreeable and compliant (Hughes & Kwok, 2007; Wentzel, 2003; Wentzel & Asher, 1995). They give attention to students whom they perceive make appropriate demands in the classroom, but they may be indifferent to students whom they perceive are silent or withdrawn, and they may reject students who make demands they perceive are illegitimate or who present behavior problems. Some teachers may stereotype children on the basis of gender, race, culture, or social class, interacting more positively with children whom they hold in high esteem. Some evidence, for example, indicates boys are more likely to experience negative relationships with teachers than girls (Brendgen et al., 2007; Hughes & Kwok, 2007), perhaps because, at least in the early grades, they are more active, less conforming, and less self-regulated than girls. There also is evidence that children of minority groups, especially African American children and children in low SES communities, are less likely to experience positive relationships with their teachers than students from Caucasian and higher SES communities (Hamre & Pianta, 2001; Hughes & Kwok, 2007). Moreover, Hughes and Kwok found that parents who were African American had less positive relationships with teachers and less involvement with schools than parents who were either Caucasian or Hispanic.

One reason for this disparity may relate to the ethnic imbalance between teachers and students in North America. By far, the majority of teachers in the United States are Caucasian (82% in 2006-07, according to the Commission on Teacher Credentialing, 2008). Research indicates that teachers rate their relationships with students more positively when they are ethnically matched (Saft & Pianta, 2001), perhaps because they understand these children better and can be more responsive to their needs. Efforts to increase the ethnic diversity of teachers are needed and teachers must accept that it is their responsibility to make all children feel welcome in their classrooms.

Creating Caring Communities

Victor Battistich and colleagues (Battistich, Solomon, Watson, & Schaps, 1997) define **learning communities** as: ". . . places where members care about and support each other, actively participate in and have influence on the group's activities and decisions, feel a sense of belonging and identification with the group, and have common norms, goals, values." (p. 137). In their research, they conceptualize community at both individual and group levels. At the individual level, "students have basic psychological needs for belonging, autonomy, and competence, and their level of engagement or disengagement with school is largely dependent on the degree to which these needs are being fulfilled there" (p. 137). But these needs are given meaning in a group setting. Specifically, at the social level, "students' needs for competence, autonomy, and belonging are met when they are able to participate actively in a cohesive, caring group with a shared purpose; that is, a community" (p. 138). Their research is based on the premise that when these conditions are met and a community of learning is established, students' needs are most likely met and, as a result, they become more inclined to identify with and behave in accordance with the school's expressed goals and values. (Also see Deci & Ryan, 1985; Noddings, 1992; Ryan & Deci, 2000, Wang, 2009, and Wentzel, 1997, 2003 for explanations of how a culture of caring enhances children's cognitive and social emotional development and, hence their adjustment in school.) Of course, positive teacher-student relationships are key in all descriptions of classrooms as caring communities. Teachers in these contexts also are instrumental in promoting positive home-school connections and positive peer relations both in and outside the classroom. The ***Connecting with Children*** guidelines describe what teachers can do to create caring communities in their classrooms.

Blakeburn Elementary School in Port Coquitlam, British Columbia, participated in some research that your author Nancy conducted with student teachers. When the school opened in September 2000, the faculty set a school-wide goal to develop supportive, caring relationships among colleagues, with parents and students, and among students. Another goal was to help students to become socially responsible. This required consistency and modeling at all levels, and the students learned the language of solving problems, respecting diversity, and contributing to the classroom and the school. In interviews, students talked about feeling safe, included, and happy to be at school. Parents said, "There is a

CONNECTING WITH CHILDREN

Guidelines for Teachers: Creating Caring Communities

Be warm and supportive in interactions with students.

Examples

1. Take time to build positive relationships with students. Get to know them as individuals, and find out about their concerns and interests.
2. Find ways to incorporate students' backgrounds and interests into your teaching and tasks in ways that are compatible with curricular goals.
3. Let students know you believe in their abilities and will support them in ways that ensure their success (e.g., teaching strategies that help them cope with difficult tasks).

Promote cooperation and collaboration among students.

Examples

1. Downplay the importance of individual grades and accomplishments that can lead to competition.
2. Set group, classroom, and school goals to encourage students to work with and help one another.
3. Celebrate group accomplishments (e.g., the completion of a class project) and group cohesiveness (e.g., reward teams for working well together and encouraging one another).

Elicit students' thinking and discussion.

Examples

1. Use class meetings and discussions to encourage students to share ideas and consider ideas that are different from their own.
2. Encourage students to follow up on one another's ideas.
3. Engage students in high-level thinking, reasoning, and problem-solving about issues in their classroom, school, and community.

Emphasize prosocial values.

Examples

1. Model concern for others, and praise students when you observe them caring for one another (e.g., "Helping Bruce when he fell off his bike was very kind. I'm sure he appreciated the way you cared for him.").
2. Teach students to resolve conflicts peacefully (e.g., help them to express their feelings and to consider the feelings of their peers).
3. Encourage acceptance of less popular children by highlighting their strengths or putting them in an enviable position (e.g., being in charge of a popular task).

Increase students' perceived autonomy and reduce teacher control.

Examples

1. Give students choices, especially those that enable them to control the level of challenge presented by tasks and activities.
2. Encourage students to "ask three before me"—go to peers for support before the teacher.
3. Establish routines and participation structures (e.g., turn-taking during discussions) early in the year that students can follow without the teacher's constant direction.

Source: Battistich, V., Solomon, D., Watson, M., & Schaps, E. (1996). Caring School Communities. Educational Psychologist, *32, 137-151; Brophy, J. (2004).* Motivating students to learn. *Mahwah, NJ: Lawrence Erlbaum Associates.*

different atmosphere at this school . . . There is a sense of mutual trust. The expectation is that the kids will manage and get along, and they do" (Laidlaw, 2001, p. 1).

Whether you are working as an individual or as part of a school-wide team, creating the kind of community that was visible in the day-to-day routines at Blakeburn Elementary School does not happen automatically (Laidlaw, 2001). It involves input from many different levels to develop a philosophy and participation structures that will foster self-control and social responsibility on the part of students. At Blakeburn, the "leadership team" met first and talked about how to create a caring and socially responsible learning community. Team members used the Ministry of Education's Performance Standards for Social Responsibility as a framework for developing a common language and set of expectations. Then, they involved the children and their families. The first week of school was devoted to the articulation of what it means (for *all* members) to be part of a socially responsible community. Students participated in multi-age, "family" groups on relevant activities. Throughout this process, the staff recognized that this work must be multifaceted and integrated in all the curricula and interactions in their classrooms and at the school. They realized that creating positive classroom and school climates requires more than the implementation of prepackaged programs at a scheduled time in the day. It involves "living the principles of inclusion and responsibility . . . all day, every day" (Laidlaw, 2001, p. 4).

Challenges for Children

This chapter concludes with an examination of some mental health concerns for school-age children: childhood depression, and fear, stress, and phobias.

Childhood Depression

Estimates of the prevalence of childhood depression vary, and some children are more at risk than others (e.g., children who have disabilities and children whose family members have depression). According to the National Mental Health Association (NMHA, 2006) less than 1% of very young children will experience a major depressive episode, but this number increases through childhood to about 8% in adolescence. During middle childhood, the numbers of boys and girls who experience depression are approximately equal; however, by adolescence, girls outnumber boys two to one in reported cases. Caution needs to be used in interpreting this statistic. Whereas girls are more likely to report feeling sad or miserable, depression in boys may be masked by angry and aggressive outbursts. Importantly, the rate of death from suicide is higher for boys than girls, although girls engage in more non-fatal, self-injurious behavior. Suicide is a topic we will return to in Chapter 13.

Children who experience **depression** display persistent negative moods and lack of interest or pleasure in life. It can be difficult to recognize depression in children, especially when they are very young and may not have the language to describe how they are feeling. Older children may not admit to feelings associated with depression. Therefore, parents, teachers, and other caregivers need to be aware of signs and symptoms that may point to depression. These can include psychosomatic symptoms, such as headaches or stomachaches, unexplained boredom or lack of interest in activities, disinterest in school and learning, moodiness, or feeling misunderstood. Table 10.5 provides a list of signs and symptoms of depression in children.

The causes of childhood depression are not well understood, but are believed to fall in three categories relating to biology, temperament, and social factors (NMHA, 2006; Shugart & Lopez, 2002). Some types of depression appear to run in families (e.g., bipolar disorder), suggesting that some children may have a genetic predisposition for the illness. Also, depressive illnesses are shared by approximately 50% of identical twins compared with 25% of fraternal twins. Other evidence indicates that neurochemicals in the brain are involved or that depressive episodes can be triggered by physical changes in the body, such as a serious illness (cancer) or changes in hormones. Still other evidence suggests that some

TABLE 10.5 • **Signs and Symptoms of Depression in Children**

Frequent sadness, tearfulness, or crying
Feelings of hopelessness
Withdrawal from friends and activities
Lack of enthusiasm or motivation
Decreased energy level
Major changes in eating or sleeping habits
Increased irritability, agitation, anger, or hostility
Frequent physical complaints such as headaches or stomachaches
Indecision or inability to concentrate
Feelings of worthlessness or excessive guilt
Extreme sensitivity to rejection or failure
Pattern of dark images or drawings or paintings
Play that involves excessive aggression directed toward oneself or others, or involves persistently sad themes
Recurring thoughts or talk of death, suicide, or self-destructive behavior

Source: National Mental Health Association. (2006). Children's mental health matters: Depression and children. *Copyrighted and published by Mental Health America, no part of this document may be reproduced without written consent.*

children are temperamentally predisposed to depression. They react to stressors more intensely and experience more negative moods than other children. Finally, children who live in stressful circumstances are at risk for depression. For example, children whose parents are emotionally unavailable, perhaps because they are depressed, or critical and rejecting may become depressed. Children who are abused, who have poor social skills and difficulty establishing and maintaining meaningful relationships, or who experience trauma, such as the loss of a parent or war, also are at risk for depression.

Unfortunately, childhood depression often goes undiagnosed. However, when identified, several treatment options can be applied, depending on the age of the child, specific symptoms, and cause of depression. One option is to reduce or remove the stressors feeding the depression. For example, if difficulties in school are causing low self-esteem and feelings of helplessness, a tutor or some other form of individualized instruction may boost a child's self-efficacy in the problem area. Alternatively, highlighting a child's strengths in another area (e.g., music, art, sports) can deflect attention from the source of depression and balance a child's perceptions of overall competence. Another option is to seek help from professionals. Counselors, psychologists, and psychiatrists can help children and their families cope with depression. Finally, medication, a treatment often used with adults who are depressed, is typically reserved for the most severe cases of childhood depression (Wagner & Ambrosini, 2001). Many of these drugs were not developed for children, and there are few studies on their safe use with children. Antidepressant medications need to be taken under the watchful eye of a professional, and more research on drug treatments for childhood depression needs to be conducted (AACAP, 2004; NIMH, 2006).

Fear, Stress, and Phobias

Some fears are common—apparently innate—among people and actually serve to protect us (e.g., fear of loud noises and severe pain; fear of high places, darkness, and being approached suddenly). Other fears are learned (e.g., fear of spiders or snakes), typically from others who are afraid. Whereas very young children have fears of imaginary creatures (e.g., monsters under their beds or in their closets), school-age children tend to fear things that pose a real threat (e.g., being kidnapped, being in a plane crash, being bullied, riding on a roller coaster). Between the ages of 7 and 8, when children come to understand causality, they develop fears of things that might harm them or significant people in their lives. Children this age may become worried about losing a parent or fear death after a grandparent dies.

Children can also experience stress related to moving, school, and parental discord. Some children change homes and enter new schools frequently for a variety of reasons. We have already described that lack of stability in living arrangements can be an indicator of other problems in children's lives (e.g., family discord, financial difficulties) (Lowe et al., 2005). Regardless of what is going on at home, a move to a new neighborhood, even to a better neighborhood, can be stressful if it means making new friends and establishing relationships with new teachers. Also, recall that school-age children recognize the importance of achievement and are able to compare their performance in a number of domains with that of peers (consider the Casebook scenario at the start of this chapter). If they perceive they are not achieving in school or in other aspects of their lives, they may become worried about failing. Such fears can threaten self-concept and lead to feelings of inadequacy (Harter, 2005; Wigfield & Eccles, 2002). Finally, children are sensitive to problems and conflicts in their families, and this can be stressful, especially if children perceive the problems threaten the stability of their family unit (El-Sheikh & Harger, 2001). Importantly, children's appraisal of the level of threat a problem poses and the extent to which they feel responsible are implicated in how well they are able to cope (Jackson & Werner, 2000).

Stress and fear are a part of childhood, and most children learn to cope with them. In fact, some children remain amazingly resilient in the face of very difficult circumstances. These children seem to hold their composure in the face of difficulty, act competently, or bounce back after a traumatic event (Masten, 2001). What accounts for their resiliency? Typically, these children have some good things going for them: protective factors. Key protective factors include, not surprisingly, good family relationships, good cognitive functioning, an easygoing temperament, and compensatory experiences (e.g., good relationships with teachers, involvement in athletics and other community organizations) (Battistich et al., 1997; Masten & Coatsworth, 1998; Wentzel, 2003). However, it is important to be aware that stresses are cumulative (Fergusson & Horwood, 2003; Hammen, 2003) and that when stress and fear become overwhelming, children can experience psychological problems.

David Elkind, author of *The Hurried Child* (2001, first published in 1981) worries that the stresses of modern life can be hazardous to children's psychological well-being. He argues that, increasingly, children are being forced to grow up too fast. Often they are faced with adult problems they are not emotionally prepared to process. This is especially true for children who live in stressful circumstances, such as poverty, violent families or communities, and countries at war. Children in the United States have been living with war for a decade now. The impact parents' involvement in the Iraqi and Afghan wars has on children is described in a recent report from the RAND Corporation (Chandra, 2010). Children in military families whose parents were deployed to war locations reported higher levels of emotional difficulties (e.g., getting into trouble, feeling sad or tearful) and fear than children in the general population, and length of deployment was associated with difficulties at school and home. What about children living in countries where wars are taking place? The ***Relating to Every Child*** discussion describes the experiences of children living with war in Iraq.

In recent years, children in North America have witnessed some very frightening events, either through the media or in real life. Witnessing the devastation of disasters like 9/11 or Hurricane Katrina or Columbine can have a profound emotional impact on children and leave them feeling very insecure. Children who are surrounded by trauma or violence can develop post-traumatic stress symptoms, academic and behavior problems, and feelings of depression and anxiety (RAND Corporation, 2005). They may have trouble sleeping and concentrating, and have difficulty forming relationships or trusting other people, fearing more hurt or loss (Garbarino, 1999).

In addition to these legitimate fears, it is possible for children to develop irrational fears, or **phobias**, that persist and significantly affect their social functioning (APA, 1994). This is the case for approximately 3–5% of children, and girls are more likely to report extreme fears than boys. One of the most common phobias of late childhood is school

RELATING TO

EVERY CHILD

▸ Children Living with War

SINCE THE 2003 INVASION (and even before that), children in Iraq have been living with war. Abdul Kareem Al-Obaidi and colleagues (Al-Obaidi, Budosan, & Jeffrey, 2010) provide a poignant account of what their experiences have been. Many of these children have witnessed family members and friends getting seriously injured, or worse. Many have lost parents or been seriously injured themselves. Some have been kidnapped for ransom or inducted into military or insurgence groups, and an estimated 2 million have been displaced from their homes. These experiences undermine children's fundamental sense of security. In 2005, 14% of children surveyed in Baghdad reported symptoms consistent with post-traumatic stress disorder (PTSD, Razoki, Taha, Taib, Sadik, & Al Gasseer, 2006); the figure was 30% for children surveyed in Mosul. High rates of anxiety and behavior disorders and depression among children also are reported (Al-Obaidi et al., 2010).

What do children with such experiences need? According to Al-Obaidi et al. (2010), mental health services for children and adolescents are not separate from those provided to adults in Iraq. Trained personnel and age appropriate interventions are very limited. The need for professionals who are trained to meet the unique challenges of child and adolescent mental health and age-appropriate, evidence-based services is critical. Al-Obaidi and colleagues advocate an intersectoral approach that would have educators and medical professionals working together as part of multidisciplinary teams. Interventions need to be culturally sensitive and involve families and other key stakeholders. Public education needs to occur to increase awareness and decrease the stigma associated with mental illness in Iraq. Research is needed to understand how children are coping with war, what meaning war has for them, and which factors can protect them from negative outcomes (e.g., families, health resources, extended social networks). Finally, Al-Obaidi et al. call on the government to implement an *Iraqi Child Protection Act* to "ensure children are brought up in a protective and healthy environment focused on [their] best interests" (p. 46). The goal should be to foster resilience, which "does not lie in the avoidance of stress, but rather in encountering stress at a time, and in a way, that allows self-confidence and social competence to increase . . ." (p. 47).

Children sometimes are faced with adult problems that they are not emotionally prepared to process, such as poverty, violent families or communities, and countries at war.

phobia (Elliott, 1999), which is an extreme fear associated with the school environment. Children who have this fear typically refuse to go to school, which causes them to fall behind and lose contact with their peers. The consequences of school phobia for children's academic and social development can be quite severe.

What can adults do to help children cope with stress and fear? The ***Connecting with Children*** guidelines on the next page describe ways adults can help the children in their lives. In addition, some educators and mental health professionals are collaborating to design programs that help particular groups of children cope with anxiety and depression that can result from the stress and violence in their lives. For example, the RAND Center for Domestic and International Health Security, in collaboration with University of California at Los Angeles and the Los Angeles Unified School District, has created a program that teaches children how to relax, cope with negative thoughts, solve real-life problems, approach

CONNECTING WITH CHILDREN

Guidelines for Families, Teachers, and Other Professionals: Helping Children Cope with Frightening Events and Disaster

Help children to feel safe and secure.
Examples

1. Help children to understand when the immediate danger has passed and what steps can be taken to prevent similar events in the future.
2. Help them to put their fears in perspective. When children witness a frightening or stressful event, they may think the same thing can happen to them or someone they love. Reassure them if this is not the case, or not likely the case.
3. Reassure children that you are there to protect and care for them.

Encourage children to talk about the events and express their feelings.
Examples

1. Tolerate children retelling events many times.
2. Encourage them to talk about confusing feelings, worries, dreams, and disruptions of concentration.
3. Help children to know what to say if they are in delicate situations (e.g., what to say at a funeral or what to say to a friend who has experienced a stressful event).

Be honest.
Examples

1. Don't deny the seriousness of the situation.
2. Don't tell children such events can't happen again, but do explain that they are very rare.
3. Don't be afraid to say, "I don't know."

Protect children from re-exposure to the events and reminders of the trauma.
Examples

1. Monitor children's television viewing, as disasters often are replayed over and over again in the news.
2. Monitor your conversations with other adults—be aware of how and how much you are talking about the events in the presence of children, and how it is affecting them.

Involve children in planning what to do to restore their sense of control in the situation.
Examples

1. Design cards and write notes for people who are experiencing stress or trauma.
2. Plant a tree as a memorial for a death.
3. Collect money or other resources for victims of disasters.

Pay special attention to students who are affected more deeply by the events.
Examples

1. Provide "special attention" following the events to children who experience frightening events or disaster first-hand.
2. Contact community resources that can help children and their families with specific support.
3. Watch for signs of more serious distress and access appropriate supports (e.g., medical or mental health professionals).

Source: Gurwitch, R. H., Silovsky, J. F., Schultz, S., Kees, M., & Burlingame, S. (2001). Reactions and guidelines for children following trauma/disaster. *Norman, OK: Department of Pediatrics, University of Oklahoma Health Sciences Center; National Association of School Psychologists.* Children and Responding to National Disaster: Information for teachers. *Retrieved from: www.nasponline .org/neat/terror_eds.html; National Mental Health Association.* Coping with Tragedy: After Hurricane Katrina. *Retrieved from: www.nmha.org/reassurance/hurricane/children.cfm; Waddell, D. & Thomas, A. Disaster: Helping children cope. Retrieved from www.naspcenter.org/safe_schools/coping.html. (Written for NASP).*

anxiety-provoking situations, and cope with violent events by talking, drawing, and writing (RAND, 2005, p. 2). This program is also designed to promote both peer and parental support. Data collected from students participating in the program indicate students were significantly better at coping with the effects of violence after three months of the intervention. Moreover, these effects were maintained after three months, and school-based clinicians were able to deliver the program with high levels of integrity and quality. A similar program titled "Friends for Life" helps children cope with anxiety and depression. The program has been implemented in Australia and Canada, and it helps children to develop skills to deal with difficulties, recognize the signs of anxiety, relax, engage in positive thinking and problem solving, gain emotional resilience, and use peer support and conflict resolution techniques. For more information about the Friends program, go to: www .friendshipinfo.net/canadafriendsindex.html.

▼ SUMMARY AND KEY TERMS

• Moving Beyond Basic Needs

According to Freud's psychoanalytic theory, middle childhood is characterized by a focus on pursuing knowledge and mastering social and intellectual skills, rather than meeting basic biological needs. Erikson referred to this drive for mastery as the period of industry, in which the conflict for children is between industry and inferiority. Children who successfully master valued skills are industrious, and industriousness leads to feelings of competence and self-satisfaction. When children struggle to master valued skills or are unsuccessful, they are at risk for developing feelings of inferiority and low self-worth. Good relationships with parents and teachers and adequate resources at home and school support children to meet the challenges of middle childhood.

• My Peers and Me

During middle childhood, self-perceptions become much more refined and realistic than they were in the early years. Children begin to recognize and acknowledge their strengths and limitations relative to standards of particular tasks and domains of activity, and compared to peers. They describe themselves in more abstract psychological terms (e.g., "I am kind." "I try to be honest."). Cognitive development accounts for some changes, but so does experience. Most research on self-concept has been conducted with North American and European populations. It is important to remember that self-concept does not follow the same developmental path in all societies.

Children's self-esteem also becomes more differentiated as they experience success and failure in a variety of domains and in comparison to peers. Some skills and abilities are valued more highly than others and, therefore, have a greater influence on children's sense of self-worth. Typically, children's self-esteem declines from early to middle childhood, but the declines are small and attributed to their more realistic self-assessments. Self-esteem can be influenced negatively and positively by personal judgments, support from significant others, and values held by families, communities, and cultures. High self-esteem is associated with positive outcomes, so enhancing self-esteem should lead to improvements in other aspects of children's development.

Children are less at the mercy of strong emotions than they were in the early years. Increased emotion regulation enables them to remain focused on their goals, even in the face of difficult and stressful circumstances. At this age, children don't rely on parents and other caregivers to monitor and guide their reactions to emotional events as much as young children do. However, there are individual differences in emotion control and self-regulation that need to be understood in a social and cultural context. Some cultures value emotional restraint and a calm demeanor, whereas others value excitement. Also, children who are mistreated or exposed to violence are more likely to experience problems with emotion regulation.

Children's emotion regulation is linked to their development of perspective-taking abilities. School-age children understand that others may not interpret or respond to a situation in the same way they do. They can imagine what

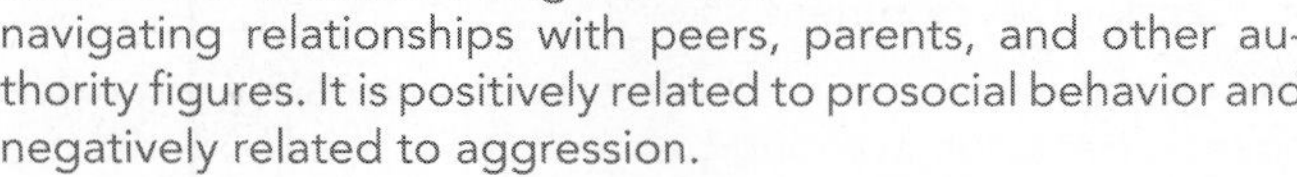

others are thinking and feeling. Developing age-appropriate social perspective-taking skills is fundamental for understanding self and navigating relationships with peers, parents, and other authority figures. It is positively related to prosocial behavior and negatively related to aggression.

• Knowing and Doing the Right Thing

Children's ability to think about moral issues expands tremendously during middle childhood. At age 5 or 6, children believe fair distribution is equal distribution, but by age 6 or 7, they understand that some people should be treated differently on the basis of merit, and at age 8, they realize some people require different treatment because they have exceptional needs. Similarly, when children are 5 or 6, they believe rules are absolute and punishments for breaking rules should reflect how much damage was done, not the intentions of the rule breaker. After age 8, children understand that people can agree to change rules; they also understand that intentions, as well as the damage done, are considerations in determining a just punishment.

Kohlberg's theory of moral development includes three levels: preconventional, where judgment is based solely on a person's own needs and perceptions; conventional, where the expectations of society and law are taken into account; and postconventional, where judgments are based on abstract, more personal principles that are not necessarily based on society's laws. Although many research studies have supported Kohlberg's theory, some scholars argue the theory is biased in favor of Western cultures that value individualism and that it doesn't adequately reflect women's moral development.

Prosocial behavior increases during the elementary school years. In general, children with higher, more other-oriented levels of moral reasoning and higher levels of self-regulation, self-esteem, and perspective-taking engage in more prosocial behavior and are motivated to do so by more altruistic concerns. Research indicates children who lack empathy or who reason ineffectually about moral issues are more likely to engage in immoral or antisocial behavior. Prosocial behavior is influenced by cultural and familial practices. Approaches to discipline that emphasize reasons why behavior is wrong and how it might affect others also promote prosocial behavior. Finally, parents and teachers and characters in television shows and books can be powerful models of moral behavior.

Physical aggression declines in middle childhood, but when it does occur it is more hostile, person-directed, and relational. Boys are more physically aggressive than girls, and girls engage in more relational aggression than physical aggression. Some research points to a biological basis for aggression (e.g., twin studies and studies of pre- and perinatal complications or exposure to toxins), but family, media, social policies, and cultural norms also influence children's aggressive behavior. One form of aggression, bullying, is a serious problem for school-age children, and negative outcomes accrue to bullies, victims, or bystanders. Experts recommend comprehensive, systems-wide approaches to bullying and other forms of school violence, and a reduction in the use of punitive and exclusionary practices. School-wide positive behavior supports and social emotional learning are two approaches that are making a difference.

• Gender Development

During the middle years, children adopt increasingly gender-specific behavior, avoiding behavior associated with the opposite sex. Boys continue to be stronger and more physically active than girls. When interacting with one another, girls are more agreeable than boys (e.g., boys interrupt one another, make demands and compete with one another for attention. Finally, girls and boys have different interests in reading, writing, and drawing. These differences reinforce gender segregation, which also increases during middle childhood.

Parents continue their differential treatment of boys and girls during the middle years, but schools and teachers also are influential. Research indicates teachers interact more with boys than girls (e.g., they ask boys more questions, wait longer for them to respond, and provide them with more detailed feedback), but interactions with boys and girls are equally positive. More cross-cultural research is needed in this area to know if findings generalize to different populations. Also, the impact of the differential treatment has not been studied, so questions remain about the size of the impact and whether some children are more sensitive to differential treatment than others. Research on gender stereotypes indicates they appear earlier and are more rigid in boys than girls, and these findings are robust across cultures.

In general, boys have higher competence beliefs about sports and math than girls, who have higher competence beliefs about reading, English, and social activities. These differences emerge early and remain over time. Beliefs about competence and values are important because they influence the choices children make to participate in particular activities, which subsequently influence the choices available to them as they move through school and out into the workforce. Children's beliefs about which sex is likely to be more talented in a given domain predict the likelihood their competence judgments and expectations will be distorted in a gender stereotypic direction.

Most children begin experiencing feelings of sexual attraction during late childhood, but sexual orientation does not appear with any clarity until adolescence. Research on why people develop a particular sexual orientation or gender identity favors biology, but more research is needed to clarify this very complex picture.

• Peer Relationships

Cliques predominate peer groups in middle childhood, whereas affiliation with larger crowds becomes salient during adolescence. Children's ties to peer groups can be formal, as is the case with after-school clubs, and informal as is the case with friendships. Children can be accepted or rejected by peers for a variety of reasons. Popular children are characterized as cooperative, friendly, sociable, and sensitive, and they have higher perceived social competence and social efficacy. Typically, these children have positive relationships with parents, and their parents scaffold their interactions with peers. When children are unpopular, they can experience academic difficulties as well as problems relating to psychosocial adjustment and functioning.

Friends serve a number of functions in middle childhood, including helping children acquire knowledge of behavioral norms and skills for interacting successfully with peers. Resolving conflicts with friends provides practice for solving conflicts with others later in life. Most children of this age have a mutual best friend, but boys and girls have different expectations for friendship. Both boys and girls depend on friends for company, approval, and support; however, girls focus on what they receive from friends and intimacy, whereas boys emphasize reciprocity and shared interests. Interestingly, boys are more likely to maintain mutual friends than girls. Children who don't have friends report more loneliness and often have low self-esteem as adults. The significance of friendships is evident in research that shows having even one close friend can alleviate the negative effects of being disliked and rejected by peers.

• Families

Middle years children spend less time at home and, when they are at home, less time interacting directly with parents. However, they continue to require a good deal of support from parents to learn appropriate behavior and make good choices. Authoritative parents who give children reasonable amounts of freedom, while setting and enforcing limits, teach children to be responsible and self-regulated. Authoritarian approaches to discipline can also be effective when they are balanced by warm and caring interactions most of the time. Parents in minority groups, and those living in unsafe neighborhoods, often feel they need to use stricter disciplinary practices to protect their children from harm and to ensure their success in and beyond school.

Sibling relationships provide a context for children to learn and practice a wide range of prosocial skills (e.g., perspective-taking, sharing, and caring for others). Older siblings may model and encourage behavior that is harmful or antisocial, but often they comfort, support, and care for younger children. This is particularly true in large families and non-industrialized societies where there is a strong sense of interdependence among family members, and in families where both parents work and are often unavailable. Sibling rivalry increases during middle childhood, but when parent–child relationships are positive and children perceive parents love them equitably, conflicts rarely lead to negative outcomes. Similarly, being an only child or having step-siblings doesn't necessarily lead to negative outcomes. Only children tend to enjoy closer relationships with parents than peers with siblings, and step-siblings tend to get along better than other siblings.

Families come in all shapes and sizes. Some children have no siblings, whereas other children have many siblings. Some children live in blended or extended families, whereas other children live by themselves with one parent. Some children have two moms or two dads, and some children live in foster and adoptive families. Between 33% and 50% of children in North America experience divorce in their family. Divorce is stressful but does not lead to negative outcomes for the majority of children, and it may be the most positive solution when the parents' relationship is full of irreconcilable conflict. Another challenge for contemporary families is finding dependable, good quality childcare. More and more, families rely on care that is center-based and involves non-relatives. Also, a large number of school-age children care for themselves. Children under 10 should not stay alone, but parents need to judge their older children's level of cognitive and emotional maturity, as well as children's safety in the neighborhood in which they live.

• School

The majority of children in most countries around the world enter school between the ages of 5 and 7. Success in the early grades typically sets the stage for future success in school. Quality preschool and kindergarten experiences are critical for helping children to do well in first grade. Early and intensive intervention programs to support young children who are having difficulty also are important. Finally, parents and caregivers can help by ensuring continuity in children's school experiences. Staying in the same school for kindergarten and first grade, with the same peers and teachers can be helpful.

Relationships with teachers have an important impact on children's adjustment to school. Teachers who establish positive relationships with students are characterized as warm, friendly, sincere, respectful of students, and responsive to their needs. Also, they are effective managers who set clear standards for behavior and care about students' success. In contrast, students avoid interacting with teachers who come across as uncaring or uninterested in them and will stop asking for help if their responses are perceived as non-supportive. Positive relationships with teachers have been shown to ameliorate children's behavior problems and the negative effects of peer rejection. Teachers respond more positively to students who achieve, conform, and are agreeable and compliant. They tend to have more positive relationships with girls than with boys, and less positive relationships with children from minority groups and low SES communities.

Some research indicates students' level of engagement or disengagement with school is largely dependent on the degree to which their needs for belonging, autonomy, and competence are being fulfilled. Establishing cohesive, caring learning communities is one way to meet these needs. Teachers are key in establishing such communities and promoting positive home–school connections and positive peer relationships both in and outside classrooms.

• Challenges for Children

Depression can be difficult to recognize in children. Signs include persistent displays of negative moods and lack of interest or pleasure in life, as well as psychosomatic symptoms, such as headaches and stomachaches. The causes of depression can be biological or genetic, temperamental, or social. Sometimes, solutions are a simple change in children's environment (e.g., getting a tutor for school or highlighting areas of strength). Counselors, psychologists, and psychiatrists can help. Medications are typically reserved for the most severe cases of childhood depression and need to be taken under the watchful eye of a professional.

During the middle years, children's fears become more realistic (e.g., they fear things that might harm significant people in their lives). Children also experience stress related to moving, school, and parental discord. Fears can threaten self-concept and lead to feelings of inadequacy. Good family relationships, good cognitive functioning, and an easygoing temperament are protective factors that help children to face fear and stress, even extremely stressful circumstances, such as living in poverty or in countries at war. Some programs have been developed to help children cope with the anxiety and depression that can result from the stress and violence in their lives. These programs teach children how to relax, cope with negative thoughts, solve problems, recognize the signs of anxiety, and think positively. Participants in these programs have demonstrated increased ability to cope with stress and violence, and the effects of the programs have been maintained over time.

▾ KEY TERMS

aggressive behavior (403)
collective self-esteem (392)
controversial children (415)
depression (432)
distributive justice (398)
emotional self-regulation (394)
gender constancy (410)
gender segregation (410)
inductive discipline (403)
industry, or **industriousness** (390)
internalize (403)
latchkey kids (427)
learning communities (430)
moral dilemmas (400)
moral realism (398)
moral reasoning (397)
moral relativism (398)
mutual best friend (417)
neglected children (415)
open adoption (424)
peer groups (415)
perspective-taking (396)
phobias (434)
popular children (415)
prosocial behavior (402)
rejected children (415)
self-concept (390)
self-esteem (391)
sexual orientation (413)

▼ THE CASEBOOK

COACHING CHILDREN—AND PARENTS—ON THE SOCCER FIELD

Jeanie pulled into a parking space at the local soccer field and reached for her latte. It was Saturday morning and she wished she could say she was looking forward to meeting her commitment to the community—she had signed on as director of recreation for children and youth in the small town where she grew up. She had such fond memories of playing baseball and soccer when she was a kid, but things were quite different now. The coaches and parents took the whole thing so seriously. They put so much pressure on the kids to win, yelling at them from the sidelines, reprimanding them when they came off the field. It was becoming difficult to find referees because the parents and coaches harassed them so much about their calls. It was embarrassing to watch; and of greater concern was seeing how it affected the children. Some claimed they were "no good" at soccer. Others were beginning to bully teammates who never scored a goal. "They're only eight years old," thought Jeanie. "Shouldn't the focus be on fun, learning some skills (e.g., being a team player), and doing the best you can?" Jeanie wondered how she should handle this problem. As she walked onto the field, she wondered if anyone had written a book on the etiquette of watching from the sidelines.

WHAT WOULD THEY DO?

Here is how some professionals in several fields responded:

TRACY MACDONALD—School Counselor
Chesapeake Bay Middle School, Pasadena, Maryland

The role of the Director of Recreation is to ensure that the sporting activities are facilitated in a manner that builds character, teamwork, and good sportsmanship. If parents are modeling poor behavior on the sidelines of games, this could have a negative impact on the players' self-esteem and appreciation of sports. There should be a discussion of the rules and expectations for parents and other onlookers to follow while watching the games. Each coach should then be directed to hold a meeting with the parents of the children on their teams. Examples of inappropriate behavior should be given and parents should be asked to sign a rules and policies form at the end of the meeting to show their commitment. Parents should be encouraged to model good sportsmanship etiquette such as cheering for every child who scores regardless of which team they are on and shaking hands at the end of the game with parents of players on both teams. Recreational sports should be an opportunity for children to have fun and get some exercise without having to worry about the stresses that come with serious competition.

AMANDA BOSDECK—8th Grade Math and Science
West De Pere Middle School, De Pere, Wisconsin

When parents and coaches exhibit overly competitive behaviors and put pressure on younger players, the children many times become discouraged, and in extreme cases, a child may no longer want to participate in a sport. These stressful behaviors may affect some of the children and cause them to develop issues with self-confidence that in the future may have a negative effect on them off the courts and fields. The focus of programs at this level should be for the children to develop motor skills and strategic thinking while building social relationships with other children. Unfortunately, overbearing parents and coaches seem to appear with alarming frequency in today's sports environment, which diminishes the gains achieved by participation in sports. If Jeanie had started the season with a meeting that set ground rules and expectations, some of these issues would have been avoided. Letting the parents and coaches know what their roles are at the beginning of the season will generally help create a more positive environment. In addition, creating sportsmanship awards for the events may encourage the majority of spectators, players, and coaches to conduct themselves in a respectful and nurturing manner to facilitate the polishing of young child athletes. Having such an inviting atmosphere would allow children to get the necessary physical exercise, create meaningful relationships, and develop important skills that could be used in the future while having the fun all children deserve to have.

JUDY S. PIEPER—Language Arts, Art, and Religion; Grades 6–8
Holy Trinity Junior High, Newport, Kentucky

The reality is that organized sports for children have become the standard by which many parents "grade" their child. How well they stack up compared to the next girl or boy on the field or court is their "test" for whether he or she is or will be successful in life. They see the fact that their child is on a winning team as him or her having "passed the test." What this more often than not leads to is the demand for a coach who wants to win and parents who see winning as a sign of "giftedness" in their child. It becomes an ego enhancement for the adults. Many parents live vicariously through their child and see any failure on the part of the child or team as a personal failure.

With this mentality comes problems, so the number one priority for any sport-related activity is to make sure the person who coaches has an understanding of the age and psychology of the children he or she is coaching. It matters little if the coach knows the game well, was a standout in college or high school, plays professionally or recreationally, or is even the only person who would step up. The same parents who demand credibility in their child's school or day care often have little to say about the person who coaches the local school, community, or select team. More often than not, parents follow the herd mentality and go with the team that the child's friends and classmates are on without considering the compatibility of the coach, or their child.

It is important for the adults involved to know that each player will be at a different level during the process. Some will be there because they like to bounce a ball, or run, or swing a bat, or swim a length, and some will just enjoy the exercise, social interaction, or personal challenge. If the parents know that the coach is a mentor and will utilize his or her knowledge of the game to encourage and support each individual child, then the parents have made a good match. The coaches must express to the parents that they recognize each child's individual skills and that they will nurture each child no matter where that child is in the process. If parent and coach are on the "same page," then sports and games become enjoyable whether teams win or lose. Unfortunately though, many parents are encouraged by bad coaches to react in ways that embarrass their child or make them feel inferior, and many coaches are faced with parents who do not understand the uniqueness of each child.

LOU DE LAURO—5th Grade Reading, Language Arts, and Social Studies
John P. Faber School, Dunellen, New Jersey

Every parent and every player in the league must sign a code of conduct form before they set foot on the field. The code of conduct form specifically informs players how they should treat their teammates on and off the field and informs parents of how they should behave and how they shouldn't behave on the sidelines. It should also be displayed on posters near the parking area and near the field of play.

If a child ignores the code of conduct form he or she is asked to skip the next game. The child of course is not penalized by his parents' actions, but the parent must skip a game if he or she ignores the form.

The officials will thank all parents and children before and after each game for their sportsmanship. Both teams will also shake hands after each game to congratulate each other on their good sportsmanship. And a good time will be had by all!

PEARSON myeducationlab

Now go to MyEducationLab at *www.myeducationlab.com*, where you can:

- Find the instructional objectives for this chapter in the **Study Plan**.
- Take a quiz as a part of the **Study Plan** to self-assess your mastery of chapter content. The program generates an individualized Study Plan based upon your answers to the quiz.
- Complete **Activities and Applications** to assist you in deepening your understanding of important chapter concepts.
- Apply what you have learned through **Building Teaching Skills**, exercises that guide you in trying out skills and strategies you will use in professional practice.

11

PHYSICAL DEVELOPMENT IN ADOLESCENCE

THE CASEBOOK

WHAT WOULD YOU DO?

ADOLESCENT SMOKING

You are late for a meeting, and to save time, you cut through "the pit" (a courtyard between buildings designated for smoking). Good grief! The second-hand smoke is thick and you try to hold your breath until you get to the door that will let you back into the building. With all the information—the irrefutable evidence—available about the harmful effects of smoking, why are young people still lighting up? You don't understand why this habit hasn't extinguished itself by now! Once you are inside and able to breathe, it crosses your mind that you, as a guidance counselor, might tackle the issue of smoking in some of your classes—but how? What works as a deterrent?

CRITICAL THINKING

- Why do adolescents engage in risky behaviors?
- How do they interpret and internalize evidence concerning things that can harm them?
- Can education make a difference? What kind of a program would you design to address smoking and other risky behaviors adolescents are tempted to try?

Andrea Teresa Kurian, Age 10—Botswana

▶ OVERVIEW AND OBJECTIVES

How tall are you? What grade were you in when you reached that height? Were you one of the tallest or shortest students in your middle or high school, or were you about average? Did you know students who were teased because of something about their physical appearance? In this chapter we examine physical development and the dramatic changes that occur in adolescence—changes that can affect body size and shape, emotions, attractions, sleep patterns, nutritional needs, thinking, and many other dimensions of development. We also examine challenges to well-being, such as risky behaviors like smoking, that are especially prevalent in adolescence. By the time you finish this chapter you should be able to:

Objective 11.1	Discuss the timing and impact of puberty on boys and girls, including ethnic and cultural differences.
Objective 11.2	Connect brain changes for adolescents to other changes in their cognitive development.
Objective 11.3	Explain the consequences of sexual development and sex education for adolescents.
Objective 11.4	Elaborate on the health and nutritional requirements for adolescents, as well as health concerns.
Objective 11.5	Identify threats to adolescent well-being and describe what can be done to prevent them.

Puberty—Ready or Not

Puberty is the process that leads to sexual maturity, the "beginning of the end" of childhood. Puberty is not a single event, but a series of synchronized and interconnected changes involving almost every part of the body, from hormones to height to emotions to body shape. Puberty is orchestrated through biology, but is affected by social and physical contexts. Some of the changes during puberty are welcome, but some create concerns. Let's look first at the biological system that controls all these changes, and then at the physical, often observable changes of puberty.

The Biology of Puberty

To get an overview of the biology of puberty, we need to define a few terms. **Hormones** are chemical substances that affect cells throughout the body. Hormones influence your metabolism, growth, moods, immune system, emotions, sleep, appetite, sexual arousal, and reproductive cycle—to name just a few areas. Hormones are produced by small organs called **glands** that are part of the **endocrine system**. During puberty, the production of sex hormones such as estrogens and testosterone increases dramatically. Both girls and boys produce estrogens and testosterone, but at puberty estrogen production soars in girls and testosterone production escalates in boys. These hormones, and the other hormones they stimulate, regulate many of the changes in puberty. In addition, this rapid increase in hormones is related to sudden emotional changes such as cycles of anger, depression, sexual arousal, and happiness. The mood swings that may be a part of the menstrual cycle for women are regulated in part by hormone changes. In Chapter 13 you will read more about the implications of puberty for adolescents' emotions and sense of self. Here we focus on physical changes.

Physical Development: Changes That Show

Years ago, William Marshall and James Tanner (1986) listed the major physical changes of puberty, still true today:

1. The adolescent growth spurt—rapid then slower growth in bones and many internal organs.
2. The development of the **primary sex characteristics** (called *primary* because they include organs directly involved in reproduction). For example, the testes and penis in boys and the uterus and ovaries in girls grow much larger and mature in their function to make reproduction possible.
3. The development of **secondary sex characteristics** (those not needed for reproduction, but still markers of mature males or females), such as changes in breasts, pubic hair, voice, and facial hair.
4. Changes in body composition—the distribution of fat and growth of muscles.
5. Changes in the respiratory and circulatory systems, leading to greater strength and endurance.

At the end of puberty both girls and boys will have an adult shape—girls will have developed breasts and hips, boys will have a developed penis and broadened shoulders. Both will have lower, more adult voices. They will be at or near their full adult height and shoe size. They will have much greater strength and endurance than they had just a few years earlier.

But theses changes take time. The earliest visible signs of puberty in girls are the growth of nipples and budding of their breasts at around age 10 for European American and Canadian adolescents. About the same time boys' testes and scrotum begin to grow larger. The next step for girls is the growth of pubic hair about age 11; boys develop pubic hair about age 11½. The changes around age 12 for girls are increases in hip width, and for boys the penis begins to grow. Between 12 and 13 is the average

OUTLINE ▼

age for girls to have their first menstrual period (called **menarche**) and for boys to have their first sperm ejaculation (called **spermarche**). Boys develop facial hair over the next several years, beginning in the corners of the upper lip around age 14 to 15 and reaching final beard potential by about age 18 or 19—with some exceptions who take longer to develop their final facial hair. Less welcome changes in puberty are increases in skin oiliness, skin acne, and body odor.

One noticeable difference between boys' and girls' puberty is that girls reach their final height by age 15 or 16, several years ahead of boys, so there is a time in middle school when many girls are taller than their male classmates. Most boys continue growing until about age 19, but both boys and girls can continue to grow slightly until about age 25 (Thomas & Thomas, 2008; Wigfield, Byrnes, & Eccles, 2006). As you will see shortly, the ages for reaching maximum height are a bit younger for African American and Latino/a adolescents and a bit older for Asian Americans.

Physical development is public—everyone sees how tall, short, heavy, thin, muscular, or coordinated you are. You will see in the next chapter that when students move into adolescence, they feel "on stage," as if everyone is evaluating them, with an "imaginary audience" watching everything they do (Elkind, 1985). Physical development is part of what is evaluated (or seems to be) by that audience. Also in Chapter 13 you will learn more about how feeling self-conscious can influence an adolescent's self-concept and self-esteem. So there are psychological consequences to physical development, too (Thomas & Thomas, 2008).

Timing and the Secular Trend

On average, girls begin puberty about two years ahead of boys. Generally, as you saw above, girls begin the physical changes of puberty between ages 10 and 11—although some, particularly African American girls, may begin as early as 8. Around 80% of American girls experience menarche between the ages of 11 and 14, but ages as young as 7 and as old as 26 have been reported in studies. Around the world the range in average age of menarche is amazing—from 12 years old in some modern urban centers to 18-1/2 in the high altitudes of Papua New Guinea and Nepal (Ellis, 2004). What causes these differences?

INDIVIDUAL DIFFERENCES: GENES AND THE ENVIRONMENT. Genetics play a role in the timing of puberty. Correlations between mothers' and daughters' age at menarche and between identical twins' timing of puberty suggest that timing "runs in the family." Some estimates are that around 50% of the variation in timing of puberty is controlled by genes (Ellis, 2004; Palmert & Boepple, 2001). Health and nutrition are major influences on the timing of puberty as well, with healthier adolescents experiencing puberty earlier than unhealthy, poorly nourished adolescents.

Another aspect of biology that may affect the timing of puberty involves the human ability to adapt to different environments. Based on an extensive review of research on the causes of differences in timing of menarche, Bruce Ellis (2004) suggested that puberty, in girls at least, is part of an integrated, complex strategy that allows girls to adapt to the quality of their family developmental environments. Family environment quality includes such things as the warmth and possessiveness of relationships among family members, the amount of conflict in the home, the presence of a step-father or other men in the home not related to the adolescent girl, and the type of discipline and control used by parents. Childhood is lengthened (and puberty delayed) when the family environment is high in quality (warm relationships, little conflict, fewer unrelated men, supportive discipline) and shortened when the environment is of poor quality. In simplistic terms, children exit childhood earlier when their family environments are less supportive and more stressful. However, severe stress, such as living through a war, can delay puberty because stress can suppress the system that regulates hormones (Ellis, 2004). The body is a complex system.

THE SECULAR TREND. A recent survey of over 8,000 young women in Canada reported 12.9 as the average age for menarche (Harris, Prior, & Koehoom, 2008). This study also confirmed a **secular trend**—that is, a trend for menarche and other events in puberty to be experienced earlier with each new generation. For example, girls born before 1933 averaged 13.2 years old at menarche, but those born from 1986 to 1990 experienced menarche at the average age of about 12.5, a decrease of about nine months over the last five decades. Other studies show a full year decrease since the 1960s.

Another reflection of this secular trend is that for both boys and girls, the growth spurt in puberty has been happening earlier. These adolescents also are taller as adults than previous generations. The same trend has been reported in Canada, Mexico, Korea, Italy, Israel, the United States, and most westernized countries.

What has caused the secular trend? There are several theories, including better nutrition and medical care, or more toxins in the environment that act like hormones to stimulate changes. But the trend may be slowing, so the age for girls' first menstrual period may not keep decreasing and the height of the next generation may not keep increasing, at least as much as in previous generations (Harris et al., 2008; Mendle, Turkheimer, & Emery, 2007).

Ethnicity, Geography, and Puberty

We have seen already that there are some universals in the timing and effects of puberty, but there are also some ethnic and geographic differences. In the United States, for example, African American and Latina girls begin breast development about age 9-1/2 compared to almost 10-1/2 for European American girls (Wu, Mendola, & Buck, 2002). In general, Asian adolescents move through puberty later than European, African, or Latino/a adolescents. One large study of almost 84,000 boys found that the average age for spermarche in China was about 14-1/2 years, compared to between 12 and 13 years old for European American boys. For boys in 17 different minority ethnic groups in China, the mean age ranged from about 13 to 16 years (Ji & Ohsawa, 2000).

If we look at the timing of puberty around the world, we see that girls in Africa tend to experience menarche later than American or European girls—as late as 17 for some areas of central Africa. But because the onset of puberty is related to health and nutrition, and because adolescents in poverty may have poorer health and nutrition, it is important to distinguish between ethnic or geographic variations and differences resulting from affluence or poverty. In wealthier parts of Africa, the mean age of menarche is closer to 13 to 14 years old (Eveleth & Tanner 1990). For most of the groups studied around the world, girls in economically advantaged homes experience menarche earlier than girls who live in poverty (Steinberg, 2005).

In most Westernized countries around the world, including Mexico, Korea, Italy, and Israel, adolescents are going through puberty earlier than they did several generations ago. This phenomenon is called *the secular trend.*

The Psychological Impact of Puberty

One source of tension for adolescents is that they are physically and sexually mature years before they are psychologically or financially ready to shoulder the adult responsibilities of caring for children. But there are other psychological effects, based on *when* an individual actually experiences the changes of puberty. With all the anxieties and concerns caused by changing bodies and the new social expectations that follow, it helps if your friends are experiencing the same challenges at the same time. But what if you are all alone—maturing well ahead of or behind your friends? Psychologists have been particularly interested in the academic, social, and emotional differences between adolescents who mature early and those who mature later, summarized in Table 11.1.

TABLE 11.1 • **Possible Advantages and Disadvantages of Early and Later Maturing for Boys and Girls**

	POSSIBLE ADVANTAGES	POSSIBLE DISADVANTAGES
Early maturing boys	Popularity with peers	More symptoms of depression, more delinquent behavior, greater risk for abusing alcohol and cigarettes
Later maturing boys	As adults, more creative, tolerant, and perceptive	Lower self-esteem
Early maturing girls	Few advantages	Depression, anxiety, eating disorders, lower achievement in schools, drug and alcohol abuse, unplanned pregnancy, suicide, and greater risk of breast cancer in later life
Later maturing girls	Fewer problems	May be concerned about being behind in maturity

GIRLS. For girls, maturing way ahead of classmates can be a definite disadvantage. Being larger and more "developed" than everyone else your age is not a valued characteristic for girls in many cultures (Jones, 2004). Early maturation is associated with emotional difficulties such as depression, anxiety, and eating disorders, especially in societies that define thinness as attractive (Steinberg, 2005). Other problems for early maturing girls are lower achievement in school, drug and alcohol abuse, unplanned pregnancy, suicide, and greater risk of breast cancer in later life. Some research indicates that these problems affect both European American and African American girls, but other research points toward greater depression and eating disorders for European American girls compared to African American girls. Around the world, early menarche has been related to bulimia and alcohol use in Finland, suicide and alcohol use in Norway, and depression and anxiety in Australia (Mendle et al., 2007). In addition, researchers have found a correlation between age at menarche and adult **body mass index (BMI,** a measure of body fat); the younger the girl was when she had her first period, the greater her adult BMI, on average (Harris et al., 2008).

What causes these problems? The explanation probably involves biological, psychosocial, and friendship selection factors—all acting together. Very early maturing girls may have hormonal differences that could account for depression. Hormones trigger sexual attractions, so early maturing girls are more likely to be involved in romantic or sexual relationships that can cause emotional upsets and anxiety. Also, early maturing girls may be the focus of uninvited, stress-producing attention from older males. Being different from peers can lead to problems making friends and rejections. Finally, friendship selection can lead to problems. Most people have a tendency to seek friends who are similar. Early maturing girls, especially those who have had behavior problems as children, are more likely to select friends who are involved in drinking, skipping school, shoplifting, dating older boys, or other activities that can create a negative context for development (Mendle et al., 2007).

Later-maturing girls seem to have fewer problems, but they may worry that something is wrong with them, so adult reassurance and support can be important.

BOYS. Much of the work on timing and puberty focuses on girls, but there are some conclusions about boys. Research in the 1960s and 1970s found that early maturation seems to have certain advantages for boys: Their classmates rated them as more good-natured, poised, and athletic. Their taller, broader-shouldered body type fit the cultural stereotype for the male ideal (Jones, 1965). Even today, early maturity in males is associated with popularity; late maturing boys may experience lower self-esteem because they are smaller and less muscular than the "ideal" for men. In fact, there is some evidence that the standards regarding physical appearance have increased (Harter, 2006; Harter et al., 2006).

It is still true that early-maturing boys are more likely to have advantages in sports, but recent research points to more disadvantages than advantages for early maturation (Westling, Andrews, Hampson, & Peterson, 2008). At least one study also found early maturing fifth-grade boys to have more symptoms of depression (Wigfield, Byrnes, & Eccles, 2006). They also tend to engage in more delinquent behavior—and this is true for White, African American,

CONNECTING WITH ADOLESCENTS

Guidelines for Teachers: Dealing with Puberty in the Classroom

Address students' physical differences in ways that do not call unnecessary attention to the variations.

Examples

1. Try to seat smaller students so they can see and participate in class activities, but avoid seating arrangements that are obviously based on height.
2. Don't use or allow students to use nicknames based on physical traits.

Help students obtain factual information on differences in physical development.

Examples

1. Set up science projects on sex differences in growth rates.
2. Have readings available that focus on differences between early and late maturers. Make sure that you present the positives and the negatives of each.
3. Find out the school policy on sex education and on informal guidance for students. Some schools, for example, encourage teachers to talk to girls who are upset about their first menstrual period, while other schools expect teachers to send the girls to talk to the school nurse (if your school still has one—budget cuts have eliminated many).
4. Give the students models in literature or in their community of accomplished and caring individuals who do not fit the culture's ideal physical stereotypes.

Accept that concerns about appearance and the opposite sex will occupy much time and energy for adolescents.

Examples

1. Allow some time at the end of class for socializing.
2. Deal with some of these issues in curriculum-related materials.

For more information about accommodations for physical differences in your classroom, see http://dos.claremontmckenna.edu/PhysicalLearningDiff.asp

and Mexican American boys (Cota-Robles, Neiss, & Rowe, 2002). Early maturing boys also appear to be at greater risk for abusing alcohol and cigarettes (Westling et al., 2008).

Boys who mature late may have a more difficult time initially. However, some studies show that in adulthood, males who matured later tend to be more creative, tolerant, and perceptive. Perhaps the trials and anxieties of maturing late teach some boys to be better problem solvers (Brooks-Gunn, 1988; Steinberg, 2005). All adolescents can benefit from knowing that there is a very wide range for timing and rates in "normal" maturation and that there are advantages for both early and late maturers. The ***Connecting with Adolescents*** suggestions give more ideas for helping adolescents deal with puberty.

Body Image

Body image is an individual's dynamic perception of his or her body—how it looks, feels, and moves. Body image might be an evaluation of the whole body, or of certain parts, such as hair, legs, chest, or face. Because their bodies are changing rapidly and because adolescents tend to feel "on stage," body image is a key concern. In addition, popular culture provides many messages in films, television, magazines, and other media about ideal bodies: thin for girls and muscular for boys. Just watch all the makeover, plastic surgery, and weight loss shows on television to get a sense of the culture's emphasis on appearance. And remember Barbie and Ken? One analysis calculated what they would look like if they were real. Barbie would be 7′2″ tall with a 40-inch chest, 22-inch waist, and a 6-inch neck. Not that we need to tell you, but the average real female is closer to 5′3″ tall, with a 36-inch chest, 32-inch waist, and 3-inch neck. Ken would be 7′ with a 50-inch chest (Croll, 2005)! And current action figures for boys set an even more unrealistic ideal than Ken (Lock, 2009). How about top models? The average female model is 5′10″ and weighs 110 pounds. Miss Americas have gotten thinner over the past 75 years and even girls pictured in textbooks are thinner.

These cultural images prime girls to be dissatisfied as their thinner child bodies become fuller in adolescence. In fact, negative perceptions of body weight increase as girls advance through stages of puberty. This is not true for boys. At all ages, girls are more

Thin is in. Not only would a real-life Barbie be 7′2″ tall and have a 22″ waist, but even Miss Americas have been getting thinner over the years.

dissatisfied with their weight than boys, and the greater their body mass index, the greater their dissatisfaction (Clark & Tiggemann, 2008; Siegel, Yancey, Aneshensel, & Schuler, 1999). Consider these statistics from Croll (2005):

- 50–88% of adolescent girls feel negatively about their body shape or size.
- Only 33% of girls say they are at the "right weight for their body," whereas 58% want to lose weight. Just 9% want to gain weight.
- Over one-third of males think their current size is too small, but only 10% of women consider their size too small.
- 85% of young women worry "a lot" about how they look; twice as many males as females say they are satisfied with their appearance.
- For girls, "the way I look" is the most important indicator of self-worth; for boys, self-worth is based on abilities, rather than looks.

In a careful study that looked at girls and boys in several ethnic groups, Judith Siegel and her colleagues found that compared to boys, adolescent girls generally reported more symptoms of depression and less satisfaction with their bodies. The only exception was for Asian Americans; boys and girls reported no differences in body image (Siegel et al., 1999). In terms of ethnic differences, in general, Hispanic adolescents were the most dissatisfied with their body images and African Americans had the most positive images. And studies in the People's Republic of China indicate that only 45% of boys and girls who had a normal body weight for their age were satisfied with their current body size; rates were even lower for overweight and underweight adolescents (Chen & Jackson, 2008). So even though there may be fewer gender differences for Asian adolescents, almost half appear to be dissatisfied with their bodies.

Maturing earlier or later than your peers can affect body image. For European American adolescents, girls who develop early and boys who develop late tend to have more negative body images. For African American girls and boys, late maturing is related to more negative body image, and for Latina girls, developing either early or late is associated with greater dissatisfaction with their bodies. The timing of puberty does not seem to affect

CONNECTING WITH ADOLESCENTS

Guidelines for Teachers and Other Professionals: Supporting Positive Body Images

Listen to adolescents talk about their health.

Examples

1. If they mention wanting to lose weight, seize the opportunity to talk about healthy weight, body image, and cultural influences on youth.
2. It they mention diets they or friends are trying, seize the opportunity to provide them with nutritionally sound information about myths, misinformation, and dangers related to fad diets.
3. In general, be attentive. An adolescent may make a brief comment that could serve as a terrific entrance into a valuable conversation about body image.

Ask questions.

Examples

1. Are you concerned about your weight (or shape or size) at all? Do you think your friends are concerned about their weight? Do you or your friends talk a lot about your weight?
2. Do you know that diets are the worst way to lose or maintain weight? Have you ever dieted? Why?
3. Do you know that eating only low-fat or fat-free foods is NOT healthy eating? Do you know that you need fat in your diet, and that without it you can have all kinds of health problems?

Have resources for adolescents who do have body image issues.

Examples

1. Have accurate, youth-oriented resources available to read, look up on the Internet, or find in a library.
2. Encourage youth to continue conversations about these issues, either with you, their parents, another health professional, a trusted teacher, or a caring, knowledgeable adult.
3. Deal with some of these issues in curriculum-related materials.

Source: Adapted from Story, M., & Stang, J. (2005). Nutrition needs of adolescents. In J. S. M. Story (Ed.), Guidelines for adolescent nutritional services. *Minneapolis, MN: University of Minnesota, pp. 158-159. For more information about adolescents and body image, see http://www.epi.umn.edu/let/pubs/img/adol_ch13.pdf*

body image for Asian American adolescents. Even with these dissatisfactions, time helps. Adolescents who are unhappy about their bodies at age 13 generally are more satisfied by age 18 (Zuckerman & Abraham, 2008). The ***Connecting with Adolescents*** guidelines give some ideas about supporting positive body images in adolescents.

NEUROBIOLOGY AND ADOLESCENT DEVELOPMENT

Along with the other physical changes in puberty come changes in the brain and neurological system that affect all aspects of development. First, axons (nerves that transmit information) in the frontal lobe continue to be myelinated (coated) during adolescence, so information can move faster in the frontal cortex (Blakemore & Choudhury, 2006).

Second, there is an increase in neural connections followed by a pruning down to fewer, more selective and stronger connections. Each adolescent's experiences and choices affect which connections will get "wired together" for efficiency and which connections will be pruned away. Areas of the brain become more integrated and connected in these networks of associations. Jay Giedd (2008) uses a linguistic analogy: This stage of brain development is *not* like adding new letters, but more like combining earlier formed letters into words, and then words into sentences, and then sentences into paragraphs—interconnections that make meaning. Different areas of the brain "talk to each other" and integrate their functions more thoroughly. The corpus callosum (the connection between the right and left sides of the brain) shows the greatest increases in size during the adolescent years (McAnarney, 2008).

Finally, by the end of adolescence, brain and neurological changes help individuals to avoid risky behaviors, be more purposeful and organized, and inhibit impulsive behavior (Wigfield et al., 2006). But the changes are not complete until early adulthood, so adolescents often have trouble avoiding risks and controlling impulses. Why is this? One explanation looks to differences in the pace of development for two key systems involved in making sound decisions about risky behaviors and controlling impulsive behavior—the

FIGURE 11.1

ADOLESCENT DEVELOPMENT IN THE LIMBIC SYSTEM AND PREFRONTAL CORTEX

The limbic system that influences emotions and responses to rewards (nucleus accumbens) matures before the prefrontal cortex that controls acting impulsively to gain rewards, so there is a time during which adolescents may "leap" to get rewards before they "look" at the risks and long-term consequences.

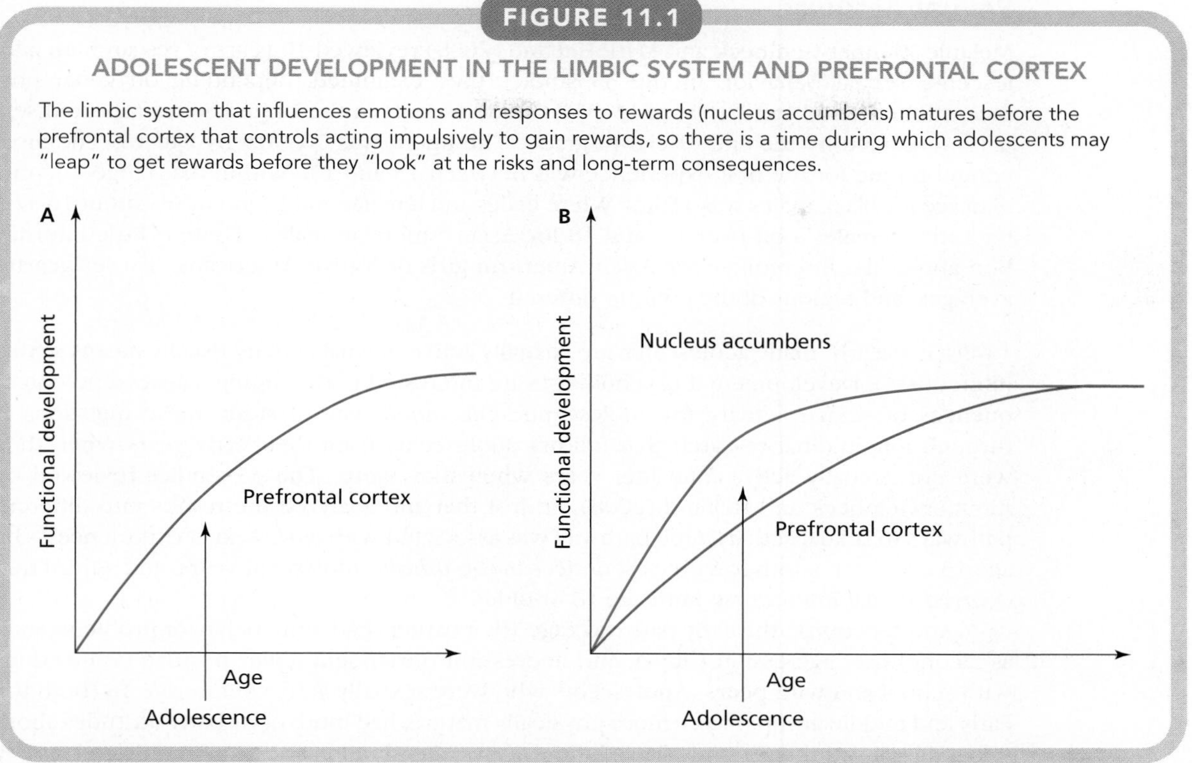

Source: Reprinted from Developmental Review, 28, *Casey, B. J., Getz, S. & Galvan, A. The adolescent brain, p. 64. Copyright 2008 with permission from Elsevier.*

limbic system and the prefrontal cortex of the brain (Casey, Getz, & Galvan, 2008). As you can see in Figure 11.1, the limbic system develops earlier; it is involved with emotions and reward-seeking/novelty/risk-taking/sensation-seeking behaviors. The prefrontal lobe takes more time to develop; it is involved with judgment and decision making.

As the limbic system matures, adolescents become more responsive to pleasure and emotional stimulation. In fact, adolescents appear to need more intense emotional stimulation than either children or adults, so these young people are set up for taking risks and seeking thrills. Risk taking and novelty seeking can be positive factors for adolescent development as young people courageously try new ideas and behaviors—learning is stimulated (McAnarney, 2008). But their less mature prefrontal lobe (see Figure 11.1) is not yet good at saying, "Whoa—that thrill is too risky!" So in emotional situations, thrill seeking wins out over caution, at least until the prefrontal lobe catches up and becomes more integrated with the limbic system toward the end of adolescence. Then risks can be evaluated in terms of long-term consequences, not immediate thrills (Casey et al., 2008; Steinberg, 2008). In addition, there are individual differences; some adolescents are more prone than others to engage in risky behaviors.

What is the effect? Adolescents may "seem" like adults, at least in low-stress situations, but their brains and neurological systems are not fully developed. Teachers can take advantage of their adolescent students' intensity by helping them devote their energy and passion to areas such as politics, the environment, or social causes (Price, 2005) or by guiding them to explore emotional connections with characters in history or literature. Connections to family, school, community, and positive belief systems help adolescents "put the brakes" on reckless and dangerous behaviors (McAnarney, 2008).

People certainly are more than physical bodies and brains. The rest of this chapter addresses other aspects of physical development.

Sexual Development

In this section, we turn to the questions of when and why adolescents become sexually active and the consequences of these decisions.

Sexual Activity

Melanie Zimmer-Gembeck and Mark Helfand (2008) reviewed 10 years of research on adolescents' sexual behavior. In the 35 studies they examined, depending on geography, race/ethnicity, and gender, from 13–35% of adolescents in the United States reported sexual intercourse by the end of eighth grade. The figure was 70–90% by age 18. The most common time for the first experience was between 15 and 17. Within that range, the median age for Black males was 15, for White males and females and Latino males about 16-1/2, for Latina females a bit over 17, and 18 for Asian American males. There is little information about first intercourse for Asian American girls or Native Americans. These ages are averages, and regions of the country differed.

TIMING. Clearly, many adolescents are sexually active (sexual activity usually means sexual intercourse). Developmental psychologists are interested in the timing, causes, and consequences of sexual activity for adolescents. One good way to study these questions is through longitudinal research that follows adolescents from their early years when they were not sexually active into later years when they were. The 35 studies reviewed by Zimmer-Gembeck and Helfand (2008) did just that and analyzed the results into different pathways to sexual activity. One pathway was associated with *early* sexual experiences—by age 15 or earlier, another with experiences in the *middle* adolescent years, and a third that *delayed* sexual intercourse until age 18 or older.

Adolescents on the early pathway (age 15 or earlier) had more behavior problems such as alcohol use, aggression (boys), and depression (girls), and fewer positive connections with school and with peers. Adolescents who were sexually active before age 18 (both the early and middle groups) were more physically mature, had more permissive attitudes about sex and believed their friends shared these views, dated more, and were monitored less by their parents. They were also less likely to live with two biological parents.

The girls who took the delayed pathway, with no sexual activity until 18 or older, were more committed to their religious beliefs and had friends who shared their commitments. The girls' families were clear about their disapproval of sexual activity. Boys who delayed sexual activity shared some of these characteristics, but also were more anxious than boys who were sexually active before age 18. You might be surprised to learn that these studies found little support for a link between age of first sexual intercourse and religious attendance, adolescent self-esteem, family SES, or parents' warmth and involvement.

VIRGINITY PLEDGES. Does making a public commitment to abstinence, a *virginity pledge*, make a difference in when adolescents have their first sexual experience? In the United States, estimates are that about 23% of female and 16% of male adolescents have made such pledges. Steven Martino and his colleagues followed a sample of 12- to 17-year-olds for four years. In the group that already favored abstinence, about 34% who took the pledge went on to have sexual intercourse, but more (about 42%) who had not taken the pledge had intercourse (Martino, Elliot, Collins, Kanouse, & Berry, 2008). So for adolescents already inclined to delay intercourse, making a pledge may increase the chances they will wait.

How do pledgers differ from nonpledgers? They are stronger in their religious commitments, more closely monitored by their parents, participate more in clubs and community activities, and have lower self-efficacy for sexual activities. One related issue is that pledgers are *less* likely than nonpledgers to use a condom the first time they have sexual relations, so their chances of unintended pregnancy are higher. But once pledgers become sexually active, they appear to educate themselves, so they carry and use condoms (Martino et al., 2008).

So should all adolescents be encouraged to make virginity pledges? Based on the research, Martino and his colleagues (2008) say no:

> For youth who want to have sex and whose social environments support doing so, pledging is not likely to be an effective means of delaying sexual initiation (and it is doubtful that sincere pledges could be elicited from such youth). These youth need sex education that helps reduce sexual risk taking and unintended pregnancy, as do the substantial number of pledgers who eventually have sex. (p. 347)

This brings us to our next topic—sex education.

Sex Education

As we have seen, many adolescents are sexually active. Does this cause problems?

NEGATIVE CONSEQUENCES OF SEXUAL ACTIVITY. Some negative consequences of sexual activity can include exposure to HIV/AIDS, sexually transmitted diseases (STDs), unwanted pregnancies, and emotional stress.

In 1990, the teen pregnancy rate in the United States was 117 pregnancies per 1,000 adolescents, ages 15–19. That rate declined dramatically over the next 15 years to 69.5 pregnancies per 1,000 girls in 2005, due to more teens using contraception and using it effectively. During the same time period, adolescent births and abortion rates dropped 35% and 56% respectively. But in 2008, this trend reversed and there were increases in both teen pregnancies and abortions. Heather Boonstra, a researcher at the Alan Guttmacher Institute, which focuses on sexual and reproductive health worldwide, noted, "After more than a decade of progress, this reversal is deeply troubling. It coincides with an increase in rigid abstinence-only-until-marriage programs" (Wind, 2010, p. 1). We examine these programs in the Point/Counterpoint later in this chapter.

Here are some other sobering facts from the Alan Guttmacher Institute (http://www.guttmacher.org/) and from a study by Christopher Trenholm and his colleagues (2008).

- More than one in five students report having had four or more sexual partners by the time they complete high school.
- 10% of young women ages 18–24 who have had sex before age 20 report that their first sex was involuntary. The younger they were at first intercourse, the more likely the sex was forced.
- A sexually active adolescent girl who does not use contraceptives has a 90% chance of becoming pregnant within a year.
- Teen pregnancy rates in the United States are twice as high as in England and Wales or Canada, and eight times as high as in the Netherlands or Japan.
- In 2006, Black and Hispanic adolescent girls had the highest teen pregnancy rate (126 per 1,000 for ages 15–19), followed by non-Hispanic White adolescents (44 per 1,000).
- Teen mothers are now more likely than in the past to complete high school or obtain a GED, but they are still less likely than women who delay childbearing to go on to college.
- Of the 18.9 million new cases of STDs each year, 9.1 million (48%) occur among 15- to 24-year-olds.
- If they are sexually active, adolescents have a one in four chance of contracting an STD—many are lifelong infections with no cure.

Statistics like these suggest that adolescents need to learn about the possible consequences of sexual activity.

APPROACHES TO SEX EDUCATION. What is the best way to educate adolescents about sex? The answers to this question are often fraught with emotions and embedded in beliefs about morality, the role of parents and the schools, and the value of specific programs. Research results cannot say what moral position people should hold or whether parents, schools, or religious organizations should be responsible for sex education. But research can inform educational policy if schools or other institutions decide to offer sex education. The two most widely used approaches to sex education are **abstinence-only (AO) education** and **comprehensive sex education (CSE).** Abstinence-only programs teach that in all cases, sex should be delayed until marriage. The only information provided about birth control typically is that these methods are not very effective. Comprehensive sex education programs also encourage abstinence, but they include information about birth control to prevent pregnancy and condoms to prevent STDs (Kohler, Manhart, & Lafferty, 2008). From 1996 until 2009, only AO programs could receive federal funding. The ***Point/Counterpoint*** on the next page examines these programs.

If abstinence-only programs have not been successful with every age group, what about comprehensive sex education (CSE), which includes teaching about birth control and condom use? After analyzing the responses of 1,700 never-married, heterosexual adolescents

POINT/COUNTERPOINT: Abstinence-Only Sex Education

Some people believe abstinence only is the only way to go. Others disagree, as you can see below.

POINT

▶ **Abstinence-only programs do not work.** The research on the effectiveness of AO programs shows few positive results, but many of these studies were focused on particular groups, not adolescents in general. In 2008, Christopher Trenholm and his colleagues published the results of their experimental study of AO programs. The research question was, "What are the impacts of these four abstinence education programs on teens' sexual abstinence, their risks of pregnancy and STDs, and other behavioral outcomes?" Participants included 2,057 adolescents in four abstinence-only sex education programs, each in a different United States city. The students were from a mix of urban, rural, and suburban communities. The teens' families were poor, working class, or middle class and in single- or two-parent households and varied in race and ethnicity. About half of the adolescents were in middle school and half were in upper elementary school.

Students (who had their parents' permission) were randomly assigned to either the abstinence-only program for their research site or a control group that did not participate in the AO program. Checks of the characteristics of the students in the program and control groups showed that the groups were very similar. Each city offered a different AO sex education program that was supported by federal Title V funds—*My Choice, My Future*; *ReCapturing the Vision*; *Families United to Prevent Teen Pregnancy;* or *Teens in Control.* The first two programs targeted middle school grades and the second two focused on elementary students. All programs offered more than 50 hours of instruction, but two of the programs, one for middle and one for elementary students, met every school day and participants could continue for up to four years. In addition to a focus on abstinence, all four programs taught youth about physical development and reproduction, goal setting, good decision making, healthy relationships, and risk-avoidance skills.

A follow–up survey (82% response rate) was conducted 42 to 78 months after the students began participating in the study. What were the key findings? None of the abstinence-only programs had statistically significant impacts on participants' rate of sexual abstinence compared to students who did not participate in the AO programs. Program participation did not affect the age at which students became sexually active; the number of sexual partners they had; or how likely they were to have unprotected sex, get pregnant, have the baby, or get a STD.

COUNTERPOINT

▶ **Abstinence-Only Programs Can Work for Younger Adolescents.** In a recent study with 662 African American students in grades 6 and 7, John B. Jemmott III and his colleagues (2010) compared an abstinence-only (AO) intervention with three other approaches—a safer sex program that targeted condom use, two comprehensive programs (8 hours or 12 hours) that targeted abstinence and condom use, and a health promotion program that targeted other health issues not related to sex. Each student was randomly assigned to one of the programs. The researchers found that after two years, about 33% of the participants in the AO program had started having sex, whereas the numbers were 50% for those assigned to either the safer sex or the general health programs and 42% for those in the comprehensive programs. When interviewed by the *New York Times* (Lewin, 2010), Sarah Brown of the National Campaign to Prevent Teen and Unplanned Pregnancy said, "This new study is game-changing. For the first time, there is strong evidence that an abstinence-only intervention can help very young teens delay sex and reduce their recent sexual activity as well. Importantly, the study also shows that this particular abstinence-only program did not reduce condom use among the young teens who did have sex."

Beyond Either/Or

How do we reconcile these findings? First, we have to be cautious because the Jemmott et al. (2010) study is the only one so far to demonstrate that AO programs can be effective. But there were some interesting differences between the Jemmott et al. study and previous work. Unlike most AO programs, the AO program in their study did not advocate abstinence until marriage, it did not portray sex negatively or suggest that condoms are ineffective, and it contained only medically accurate information. Also, participants were young—an average of 12 years old. Perhaps AO can be helpful for younger adolescents when they are given accurate information and learn about the value of delaying sex until they are older.

(ages 15–19) from the 2002 National Survey of Family Growth, researchers concluded that formal CSE reduced the risk for teen pregnancy without increasing the likelihood that adolescents will engage in sexual activity. Findings also reconfirmed results from the randomized controlled trials described in the ***Point/Counterpoint*** that abstinence-only programs have a minimal effect on sexual risk behavior for older adolescents (Kohler, Manhart, & Lafferty, 2008). In addition, from 80–90% of parents support CSE. The main exceptions are parents who identify themselves are "very conservative." But even half of this group supports CSE (Constantine, 2008).

It is likely that the debates about sex education will continue. The physical changes of puberty also have implications for nutrition and exercise, as we will see next.

Nutrition and Exercise

During adolescence, we establish patterns and habits in diet, physical activity, lifestyle, and exercise that probably will shape us (literally and metaphorically) well into our adult years. Our bones will reach their peak density and this level helps determine if and when we develop osteoporosis. But adolescents are not cognitively mature as they make decisions about physical activity and eating. Here we look more closely at nutrition and physical activity in adolescents' lives.

Nutrition

The dramatic physical growth and development during puberty requires increases in energy, protein, vitamins, and minerals. In fact, total nutrient needs are higher in adolescence than in any other period of life, and they peak during the period when growth is fastest. Table 11.2 shows the calorie and protein needs for adolescents by age and sex. While their nutritional needs are increasing, adolescents are becoming more independent, both financially and in their daily choices about what and when to eat. They are hungry, but their brains are not yet expert at weighing risks and rewards, and their body image concerns push them to focus on appearances, so they may make poor nutritional choices—skipping breakfast, snacking, eating fast foods, or dieting in dangerous ways. As a consequence, many teens, especially girls, have inadequate diets. On average their diets are low in vitamins A and E, iron, zinc, magnesium, calcium, and fiber. On the other hand, they eat too much total fat and saturated fat, cholesterol, sodium, and sugar. Poor nutrition during adolescence

Why is Jeremy so hungry these days?

Zits, May 9, 2009. Jerry Scott and Jim Borgman. ZITS © 2009 Zits Partnership, King Features Syndicate.

TABLE 11.2 • **Recommended Daily Calorie and Protein Intakes for Adolescents**

During adolescence, needs for energy (calories) and protein increase substantially.

	CALORIES PER DAY		PROTEIN GRAMS PER DAY	
Age	Females	Males	Females	Males
11–14	2,200	2,500	46	49
15–18	2,200	3,000	44	59
19–24	2,200	2,900	46	58

Source: Adapted from Story, M., & Stang, J. (2005). Nutrition needs of adolescents, p. 27. in J. S. M. Story (Ed.), Guidelines for Adolescent Nutritional Services. *Minneapolis, MN: University of Minnesota. Used with permission. For the most recent dietary guidelines, see http://www.health.gov/dietaryguidelines/*

TABLE 11.3 • **The Increase in Adolescent Obesity**

The data below are from the National Health and Nutrition Examination Survey (NHANES) completed by the National Center for Health Statistics.

PREVALENCE OF OVERWEIGHT AMONG U.S. ADOLESCENTS (AGED 12–19 YEARS)				
	SURVEY PERIODS			
	1971–1974	1976–1980	1988–1994	2003–2004
Ages 12 through 19	6.1%	5%	10.5%	17.4%

Source: Used courtesy of Centers for Disease Control and Prevention, www.cdc.gov, http://www.cdc.gov/nccdphp/dnpa/obesity/childhood/prevalence.htm

can contribute to many adult health problems such as diabetes, obesity, coronary artery disease, osteoporosis, and cancer (Stang & Story, 2005; Story & Stang, 2005).

FAST FOOD. Fast food is everywhere in the adolescents' world. Schools, dorms, laundromats, gas stations, convenience stores, bodegas, clinics, and roadside rest stops all have vending machines with high-calorie, high-fat snacks. Theaters offer enormous buckets of popcorn and boxes of candy. Every neighborhood has burger-and-fries, taco, chicken, or ice cream chain restaurants. Malls have huge food courts. Bus stations, train stations, and airports offer fast foods from counters and vending machines. Even hospitals have fast food outlets. These offerings are tasty and convenient, but fast foods and soft drinks replace needed nutrients in teens' diets with sugar, salt, and fat.

What is the appeal of fast food? Well, for one thing, fast food is fast—handy for a quick snack. It also is inexpensive, with the cheaper items often having the most calories. For example, the dollar menus at fast food restaurants have more high-calorie items (e.g., double cheeseburger—480 calories and 27 grams of fat) than low-calorie offerings (e.g., small fruit and yogurt parfait—160 calories and 2 grams of fat).

How much fast food do teens consume? One study followed over 1,600 students as they moved from high school to the world of young adults (from about ages 16 to 21). Researchers found that 21% of girls and 24% of boys in high school reported eating fast food frequently (at least three times a week). As they moved into young adulthood, the number of girls who ate fast food three times a week or more stayed about the same, but the number of boys who were frequent fast food eaters had increased significantly to 33%. African American adolescents were more likely than European Americans to be frequent fast food consumers (Neumark-Sztainer, Story, Wall, Harnack, & Eisenberg, 2008). Many researchers think fast foods may be contributing to the increases in obesity we see among adolescents, shown in Table 11.3.

Unfortunately for the rest of the world, one of America's most successful exports is fast food—and all the health problems that can follow.

Once in a fast food restaurant, what do teens order? Julienne Yamamoto and her colleagues asked adolescents (ages 11 to 18) to order meals at McDonald's, Panda Express, and Denny's. The average calorie content for their chosen meals was 933, 874, and 1,031 calories, respectively. But some participants ordered meals that were 1,200 to 1,500 calories. When these teens ordered from a menu that also listed calorie and fat content next to each item, 80% did not change what they ordered, but 20% did modify their orders based on the nutritional information, so it seems some adolescents might modify their fast food intake if they have the facts when they order (Yamamoto, Yamamoto, Yamamoto, & Yamamoto, 2005).

BREAKFAST. Did you eat breakfast today? We know you have heard it many times: Breakfast is the most important meal of the day. Even a small breakfast provides needed nutrition and helps

TABLE 11.4 • **Recommendations for Teens about Nutrition and Fitness**

Remove televisions from teen's bedrooms and limit the time they spend looking at any screen to 2 hours or fewer per day.
Avoid beverages sweetened with sugar or high fructose corn syrup.
Strive to eat at least 5 servings of fruits and vegetables daily.
Engage in moderate to vigorous physical activity for at least 60 minutes a day.
Actually prepare and eat meals at home as a family at least 5–6 times a week.
Limit eating out, especially at fast food restaurants.
Don't skip breakfast and make sure it is healthy.
Limit portion sizes.
Make lifestyle changes a whole family project.

Source: Based on information from NICH. Expert committee recommendations on the assessment, prevention and treatment of child and adolescent overweight and obesity - *2007. Boston: National Initiative for Children's Healthcare Quality. Available online at http://www.nichq.org/documents/coan-papers-and-publications/ COANImplementationGuide62607FINAL.pdf*

adolescents avoid unhealthy snacking and fast food attacks. But adolescents are more likely to miss breakfast than any other meal. Often the reason is to cut down on calories and lose weight, but young people who skip breakfast actually are more likely to be overweight or obese. In addition, skipping breakfast is associated with poorer performance in school. Eating breakfast, in contrast, may improve cognitive functioning and school achievement (Pearson, Biddle, & Gorley, 2009).

What encourages adolescents to eat breakfast? Studies around the world point to two factors associated with eating breakfast—having parents who eat breakfast too and living in a two-parent family. Nutritional habits are shaped early, so it pays to provide children and adolescents with good role models (Pearson et al., 2009). Table 11.4 lists specific recommendations for teens about nutrition and fitness from the *Focused Understanding of Nutrition and Fitness in Teens* health education curriculum developed by the Cincinnati Children's Hospital (NICH, 2007).

BONE DENSITY. One of the nutrients that adolescents often lack is calcium. The recommended intake of calcium is 1,300 milligrams (mgs) per day between the ages of 9 and 18. Calcium is critical in the growth of bones. About half of your adult bone mass developed during adolescence, and by 18, you had 90% of your skeletal mass. The bone mass you build in adolescence is important for the prevention of osteoporosis in later years. Genetics probably account for 60–80% of the variation among individuals in bone mass, with diet and physical activity helping to determine if you will reach the peak bone mass your genes will allow.

Results of the Berkeley Bone Health Study—which started in 1988 and ended in 1997, following 693 African American and White girls from ages 9 or 10 to 21—indicated that their average calcium intake actually fell to 789 mgs per day during puberty, instead of rising like it should to about 1,300 mgs (Wang et al., 2003). In addition, the researchers found that the middle years of puberty were especially important for developing strong bones. Calcium intake during this time positively predicted bone density at age 21 for both African American and White girls. Activity level, especially before puberty, also was related to bone density. Girls who were more sedentary during the prepuberty years had lower bone density at 21. Calcium intake was lower on average for African American girls, who also were more sedentary and watched more television and videos. Educating all adolescents, but especially African American girls, about the importance of nutrition and physical activity is an important goal for parents, teachers, and other professionals.

Female athletes who have stopped having their normal menstrual cycle, a condition called **amenorrhea**, are another group at risk. Almost one quarter of female high school athletes have reported amenorrhea at some point. These girls are at risk for decreased bone density during the critical period in which they are building bone mass for a lifetime. Perhaps because of the repetitive movements and low impact associated with the activity, long-distance runners seem especially vulnerable. High-impact activities in sports such as gymnastics tend to build bone density. Long-distance runners are even more likely to have decreased bone density if they have a history of eating disorders—described next (Misra, 2008).

Eating Disorders

Adolescents going through the changes of puberty are very concerned about their bodies. This has always been true, but today, the emphasis on fitness and appearance makes adolescents even more likely to worry about how their bodies "measure up." As you saw earlier when we discussed body image, boys and girls can become dissatisfied with their bodies during adolescence because they don't match the cultural ideals in magazines and films (or Barbie!). For girls, it also appears that conversations with friends about appearance can make dissatisfactions worse (Jones, 2004).

For some adolescents, the concern with body image becomes excessive. One consequence is disordered eating such as **binge eating**. The proposed revision of the *Diagnostic and Statistical Manual (DSM-5)* of the American Psychiatric Association has added binge eating as a disorder defined by two indicators: "eating, in a discrete period of time (e.g., within any 2-hour period), an amount of food that is definitely larger than most people would eat in a similar period of time under similar circumstances" and "a sense of lack of control over eating during the episode" (APA, 2010). The two other eating disorders already listed in the current DSM-IV are **bulimia nervosa** (binge eating followed by purging, fasting, or excessive exercise), and **anorexia nervosa** (self-starvation).

Even though anorexia is more common for girls, boys can be affected, too, and anorexia may go undetected in boys. About half of the adolescent boys in one study in Switzerland had serious concerns about eating or had tried unhealthy eating practices such as binging or dangerous weight loss attempts.

Anorexia is more common in females than in males, but current research is showing that anorexia and bulimia in boys often goes undetected. Some estimates now are that 10–20% of anorexia and bulimia cases are boys. About half of the adolescent boys in one study in Switzerland had serious concerns about eating or had tried unhealthy eating practices such as binging or dangerous weight loss attempts (Dominé et al., 2009; Lock, 2009). Risk factors for boys include participation in weight-conscious sports such as body building, wrestling, and being a jockey or using anabolic steroids. Risk factors for both boys and girls include having a history of impulsive behavior, depression, perfectionism, teasing by peers, sexual abuse, and being overweight (McCabe & Vincent, 2003).

Bulimics often binge, eating an entire gallon of ice cream or a whole cake. Then, to avoid gaining weight, they force themselves to vomit or they use strong laxatives to purge themselves of the extra calories. Adolescents with bulimia are hard to detect because they tend to maintain a normal weight, but their digestive systems can be permanently damaged.

Anorexia is an even more dangerous disorder, because anorexics either refuse to eat or eat practically nothing while often exercising obsessively. In the process, they may lose 20–25% of their body weight, and some (about 20%) literally starve themselves to death. Anorexic adolescents become very thin, and may appear pale, have brittle fingernails, and develop fine dark hairs all over their bodies. They are easily chilled because they have so little fat to insulate their bodies. They often are depressed, insecure, moody, and lonely. Girls

CONNECTING WITH ADOLESCENTS

Guidelines for Families, Teachers, and Other Professionals: Encouraging Healthy Eating in Adolescence

Discourage unhealthy dieting; emphasize instead the kinds of eating and physical activity that can be maintained over time.

Examples

1. Explain that dieting, skipping meals, and using food substitutes or diet pills actually can lead to weight gain over the long term and is dangerous over the short term—emphasize healthy eating instead.
2. Don't use dissatisfaction with appearance as a motivator—stress caring for your body instead of making it "look better."
3. Challenge adolescents if they say (and don't say yourself) "I'm starting a diet on Monday, so I am going to splurge this weekend." Or "I've already broken my diet so I might as well keep on eating."

Enlist family support in healthy eating: Give ideas for families to "talk less and do more" about healthy eating.

Examples

1. Have more frequent, and more enjoyable, family meals.
2. Talk less about everyone's weight and appearance. No teasing at all about weight, even as an attempt to "motivate."
3. Have more fruit and vegetables in the home.
4. Take televisions out of children's bedrooms.

Assume that overweight or underweight teens have experienced some mistreatment around weight issues.

Examples

1. Individuals may have been directly teased about weight.
2. Individuals may have been excluded from teams or social groups.

Source: Adapted from Neumark-Sztainer, D. (2009). Preventing obesity and eating disorders in adolescents: What can health care providers do? Journal of Adolescent Health, *44, 206–213.*

may stop having their menstrual period. These eating disorders often begin in adolescence and are becoming more common—about 1% of adolescents become anorexic (Rice & Dolgin, 2002). These individuals usually require professional help—don't ignore the warning signs—few people with eating disorders actually receive treatment (Stice & Shaw, 2004; Stice, Marti, Spoor, Presnell, & Shaw, 2008). A teacher may be the person who begins the chain of help for students with these tragic problems. The ***Connecting with Adolescents*** guidelines for supporting positive body images on page 450 offer some good ideas. In addition, the ***Connecting with Adolescents*** guidelines above list research-based ideas for preventing obesity and eating disorders from project EAT (Eating Among Teens, Neumark-Sztainer, 2009).

Biorhythms and Sleep

Other changes in the neurological system during adolescence affect sleep. Teenagers need about 9 hours of sleep per night, but many adolescents' biological clocks are reset, so it is difficult for them to fall asleep before midnight. If high school begins by 7:30, as it does in many school districts, getting 9 hours of sleep is impossible and students are continually sleep deprived. Then on weekends, adolescents often "sleep in" to catch up; this makes it even more difficult to go to bed earlier on Sunday night, and the whole cycle of late to bed and up too early starts again. At school, classes that keep students in their seats, taking notes for the full period may literally "put the students to sleep." With no time for breakfast, and little for lunch, these students' nutritional needs are often deprived as well (Sprenger, 2005). Read the ***Relating to Every Adolescent*** account on the next page to learn about a school-based intervention designed to address this problem.

About one-quarter to one-half of adolescents report experiencing insomnia for periods from one to four years. Adolescents with insomnia are more depressed, anxious, irritable,

RELATING TO

EVERY ADOLESCENT

▸ Learning about Sleep in Australia

In order to get their required 9 hours of sleep every night, one simple strategy for adolescents would be to resist the temptation to "sleep in" on the weekends and instead go to bed and get up at the same time every day. Researchers in Adelaide, South Australia (Moseley & Gradistar, 2009) designed a school-based intervention—four 50-minute classes taught over a 4-week period—for high school students in two schools. The classes focused on adolescent well-being and healthy lifestyles using a cognitive behavioral approach that included learning about healthy lifestyles, understanding unproductive thinking and beliefs, setting short- and long-term personal goals, monitoring behaviors, and targeting a personal change project. Information about sleep was one of several topics covered. The sleep-related components included instruction about adolescent sleep needs and practices, the consequences of poor sleep practices, strategies for healthy sleep including regularization of sleep/wake schedules and early morning bright light exposure, and ways to deal with insomnia.

What did the researchers find? First, over half of the high school students reported too little sleep on school nights—less than 8 hours—and 78% reported sleeping late more than 2 hours both mornings on weekends. After the classes, there was a statistically significant improvement in all the participants' knowledge of sleep. In addition, for the group that had problems with their sleep cycles (delayed bedtime during the week, sleeping late on weekends), there was a statistically significant improvement in their weekend sleeping in time. Unfortunately, even though they didn't sleep as late on weekends, they still got up about 2 hours later on the weekends than they did on school days. And six weeks later, they had returned to their old habits. It is difficult to give up those weekend morning sleep-ins. The researchers recommend targeting motivation as well as knowledge in future work.

fearful, angry, tense, emotional, and inattentive. They report more conduct problems, drug and alcohol use, fatigue, problems with peers, and health complaints. There likely is a reciprocal relationship between insomnia and all these problems—the insomnia leads to problems and then the problems cause more insomnia (Roberts, Roberts, & Duong, 2008). Good nutrition, exercise, and mental health services all could help adolescents get the sleep they need. The ***Connecting with Adolescents*** guidelines for families, teachers, and students has ideas for how to advocate for later school start times and how to help adolescents deal with changing sleep patterns.

Sports and Exercise

The American Academy of Pediatrics stated, "Play is essential to development because it contributes to the cognitive, physical, social, and emotional well-being of children and youth" (Ginsburg, 2007, p. 182). We saw that the brain develops with stimulation; play, physical activity, and sports provide part of that stimulation at every age. In fact, some neuroscientists suggest that play might help in the important process of pruning brain synapses during childhood (Pellis, 2006). Other psychologists believe play allows young people to experiment safely as they learn about their environment, try out new behaviors, solve problems, and adapt to new situations (Pellegrini, Dupusis, & Smith, 2007). Babies in the sensorimotor stage learn by exploring, sucking, pounding, shaking, throwing—acting on their environments. Preoperational preschoolers love make-believe play and use pretending to form symbols, use language, and interact with others. Elementary school-age children also like fantasy, but are beginning to play more complex games and sports, and thus learn cooperation, fairness, negotiation, and winning and losing as well as developing more sophisticated language. As children grow into adolescents, play and sports continue to be part of their physical and social development.

PHYSICAL ACTIVITY. Physical activity is important in preventing or treating many health problems such as obesity, osteoporosis, heart disease, and diabetes. Children who develop skills kicking, catching, and throwing objects such as balls or Frisbees™ are more likely to

CONNECTING WITH ADOLESCENTS

Guidelines for Families, Teachers, and Students: Dealing with Changing Sleep Needs

For Families and Teachers: Advocate for later school start times for adolescents.

Examples

- Start early to educate the community and all parties involved. Use hard data and testimonials.
- Network with other schools to learn from their experience. Apply what you learn to your school district's particular challenges or concerns. Be prepared with concrete examples of the successes of others.
- Involve parents, students, and teachers, as well as transportation, cafeteria, and extracurricular personnel, coaches, employers, and others in a variety of ways (email, letters, forums, surveys, etc.) and allow all participants the opportunity to express their opinions anonymously.
- Be clear about your goals: the academic performance, health, safety, and quality of life for students. Students' needs are foremost.
- Be flexible as the process proceeds. Consider all of the issues, needs, and agendas of all parties. Identify potential sources of resistance and address their needs. Be prepared with research and the facts.
- Have a clear plan. Gather a coalition and form organized committees. Develop a timetable. Decide on guidelines for the change and create goals to measure your progress.
- Communicate all along the way and especially through the implementation of the changes.

For Adolescents: Develop healthy sleep habits.

Examples

- Work with your internal clock. Most teens' internal body clocks cause them to fall asleep and wake up later. You can't change this, but you can participate in activities and classes to help counteract your sleepiness.
- Make sleep a priority. Decide what you need to change to get enough sleep to stay healthy, happy, and smart!
- Beware of taking too many naps. Naps that are too long or too close to bedtime can interfere with your regular sleep.
- Make your room a sleep haven—cool, quiet, and dark. If you need to, get eyeshades or blackout curtains. Let in bright light in the morning to signal your body to wake up.
- Don't use substitutes for a good night's rest. No pills, vitamins, or drinks can replace good sleep. Avoid caffeine—coffee, tea, soda/pop and chocolate—late in the day. Nicotine and alcohol will also interfere with your sleep.
- Recognize sleep deprivation and call someone else for a ride. Drowsy driving causes over 100,000 auto crashes each year.
- Establish a bed- and wake-time and stick to it, coming as close as you can on the weekends. A consistent sleep schedule allows your body to get in sync with its natural patterns.
- Don't eat, drink, or exercise within a few hours of your bedtime. Don't leave your homework for the last minute. Avoid the TV, computer, and telephone in the hour before you go to bed. Stick to quiet, calm activities.
- Establish a consistent evening schedule. If you do the same things every night before you go to sleep, you teach your body the signals that it's time for bed. Try taking a bath or shower (this will leave you extra time in the morning), or reading a book.
- Try keeping a diary or to-do lists. If you jot notes down before you go to sleep, you'll be less likely to stay awake worrying or stressing.
- Don't follow your friends' bad habits. When you hear your friends talking about their all-nighters, tell them how good you feel after getting enough sleep.

Source: Used with permission of the National Sleep Foundation. For further information, please visit http://www.sleepfoundation.org <http:// www.sleepfoundation.org/>. http://www.sleepfoundation.org/article/hot-topics/general-advocacy-tips-changing-school-start-times http:// www.sleepfoundation.org/article/sleep-topics/teens-and-sleep

be active as adolescents, and adolescents who are physically active are more likely to remain active as adults (Barnett, van Beurden, Morgan, Brooks, & Beard, 2009).

Boys tend to be more active than girls at every age, but when you compare boys and girls based on biological (maturational) age, not chronological age, the gender differences disappear. Girls are more biologically mature compared to boys the same age, and greater biological maturity is related to decreased physical activity and exercise. Studies of adolescents in the United States, Canada, and Great Britain show similar results. Thus when you take biological maturation into account, there are no differences in physical activity and exercise levels between boys and girls. But in schools, boys and girls tend to be grouped by age, so teachers will notice that boys seem more physically active at each grade level. Even so, physical activity tends to decrease for both boys and girls as they mature, about 3–8% per year (Cumming, Standage, Gillison, & Malina, 2008; Pate et al., 2009; Walters, Barr-Anderson, Wall, & Neumark-Sztainer, 2009).

The U.S. Department of Health and Human Services recommends that adolescents engage in at least 60 minutes of physical activity on most, but preferably all days of the week. Even the U.S. federal government has recognized the value of physical activity. In 2004, the U.S. Congress passed a law that requires educational agencies receiving federal aid, which covers most schools, to have a wellness policy that includes a *minimum of 30 minutes per day* of moderate to vigorous physical activity, with 60 minutes recommended (McKenzie & Kahan, 2008). But one nationwide study found that in ninth grade, only about 64% of girls and 73% of boys were getting enough vigorous physical activity. Because physical activity levels tend to decline in adolescence, by twelfth grade, the numbers had dropped to 46% for girls and 64% for boys. The increasingly sedentary lifestyle of adolescents probably is one cause for the recent rise in adolescent obesity (Sirard & Barr-Anderson, 2008; Walters et al., 2009).

As you saw in previous chapters, in the preschool and school years there are some differences in physical activity associated with SES: There is less money for organized sports, but also concern on the part of parents with letting children play outside in unsafe neighborhoods. These early restrictions may shape patterns of activity that are carried into adolescence and adulthood.

ENCOURAGING PHYSICAL ACTIVITY. Both boys and girls are more physically active if they see themselves as capable and also if they value physical activity—an example of the expectancy-value model of motivation as it explains motivation for physical activity and

Carolina Panthers wide receiver Steve Smith challenges a group of adolescents to "play hard" and enjoy physical activity. The NFL sponsors Play 60, a program that encourages 60 minutes of active play every day—see http://www.nflrush.com/play60/ for more information. Used with permission of the Carolina Panthers.

exercise. Briefly, this means that motivation is the product of two main forces: the individual's expectation of reaching a goal and the value of that goal to him or her. In other words, the important questions are: "If I try hard, can I succeed at physical activities?" and "If I succeed, will the outcome be valuable or rewarding to me?" Motivation is a product of these two forces, because if either factor is zero, there is no motivation to work toward the goal (Tollefson, 2000). But boys tend to value physical activity more and feel more competent compared to girls, so they are more motivated. That is one reason why boys are more active than girls of the same age (Sabiston & Crocker, 2008). Given their value, many researchers worry that we are overlooking physical activity and play as important aspects of human development today.

There are cultural differences in motivation for physical activity. Jin Yan and Penny McCullagh (2004) studied boys and girls ages 12 to 16 in the United States (both American born Chinese and Caucasian American adolescents) and in the People's Republic of China. They concluded that Caucasian American male and female participants take part in sports or physical activities primarily for competition and improving skills. However, for the adolescents from the People's Republic of China, social affiliation and wellness are the main participation reasons for both males and females. The American born Chinese adolescents are more likely to participate because of travel, equipment use, and having fun through physical activities and sports than their People's Republic of China and Caucasian American counterparts.

Adolescents spend many of their waking hours in school. Because most teens do not get much physical activity in their daily lives today, schools have a role in promoting active play. This can be especially important for students living in poverty and children with disabilities. Unfortunately, physical education time is being cut to allow for more academic time focused on test preparation (Ginsburg, 2007; Pellegrini & Bohn, 2005).

What sort of activity helps students develop lifelong habits of exercise and physical activity? You would think that participating in sports programs in high school would carry over into being more physically active in early adulthood, but research does not support that idea, especially for adolescents from lower SES families (Walters et al., 2009). More important than just participating in sports seems to be the way the teacher/coach structures the experience for the adolescents. One study found that middle school students were more likely to be physically active during leisure time if their physical education teachers supported the students' sense of self-determination during classes. This meant giving choices and good rationales for PE tasks, acknowledging students' perspectives, fostering students' feelings of competence, and developing caring relationships with the students. Middle school may be an especially important time as students form habits of activity and exercise (Cox, Smith, & Williams, 2008; Sirard & Barr-Anderson, 2008).

Threats to Well-Being in Adolescence

Adolescents take risks. Like the students in "the pit" at the beginning of the chapter, many smoke. Others also may drink, drive too fast, have unprotected sex, use drugs, and get into fights. Why?

Why Do Adolescents Take Risks?

We saw earlier in this chapter that the adolescent brain is not the best at balancing short-term thrills with long-term consequences. You will see in the next chapter that there are two cognitive processes involved in making decisions—and one is faster, simpler, and more intuitive. If you get anxious when you think about flying or are tempted to eat a second big piece of chocolate cake, this system likely is at work. The second system is slower, more effortful, and more analytic. This system reminds you that air travel is safer than driving and that the second piece of chocolate cake will be "minutes on your lips and years on your hips," as some diet coaches have said. Because the teenage brain is more developed in the intuitive reward-seeking system than in the analytic system, risky behaviors may be too attractive to resist. This helps us understand the students puffing away in "the pit."

> Teenage smoking can be understood in this light. The bad consequences of smoking are not much associated with the behavior, and the meaning of smoking—as fun, exciting, and social—is what affects behavior. It should not be surprising in this light that emotional arousal can overwhelm efforts to engage in self-regulation. (Sunstein, 2008, p. 148)

When teenagers smoke, abuse drugs, or drive recklessly, they may do so in part because they are impulsive, lack self-control (especially in groups), or are unrealistically optimistic and feel invulnerable (Sunstein, 2008). But there is another aspect of risk taking besides balancing intuition and analysis: the meaning of the behavior in the adolescent's social group. Is smoking "cool" or "disgusting"? The answer is found in the values and beliefs of the adolescents' social networks—something that often is difficult for adults to control.

Since 2000, *Healthy People 2010*, a joint project of the Centers for Disease Control and the U.S. Department of Health and Human Services, has monitored progress toward 107 national objectives for improving the health and lowering the risks of youth, ages 10 to 24. The objectives are grouped into six areas: mortality, unintentional injury, substance abuse and mental health, violence, reproductive health, and chronic diseases.

In 2008, researchers did a midcourse review to see how we were doing in our efforts to meet the 2010 goals. They concluded that there had been little to no progress on most objectives (Park, Brindis, Chang, & Irwin, 2008). We have already examined reproductive health in the earlier section on sexual activity, so let's look at each of the other areas more closely.

Deaths and Injuries

In terms of mortality, in 2004, young adolescents (ages 10 to 14) died at the rate of 19 out of every 100,000. This represented a decrease from mortality rates in the late 1990s and was on target to meet objectives by 2010. But older adolescents (ages 15 to 19) died at the rate of 66 per 100,000 youth. This was a slight decrease over rates in the late 1990s, but way off target to meet the 2010 objective of 38 per 100,000.

Since the early 1990s, mortality rates for all motor vehicle crashes and for alcohol-related crashes have increased slightly for teens. Of the 13,000 adolescent deaths per year, about 70% result from auto crashes, unintended injuries, homicides, and suicides. Many of these deaths were caused by risky behaviors such as driving under the influence of alcohol, not wearing a seat belt, carrying weapons, or using illegal drugs (Casey, Getz, & Galvan, 2008). There is some good news. The percentage of students in 2005 who reported riding with a driver who had been drinking *decreased* and the percentage who said they use a seat belt *increased*. Both are at or near the target for 2010 (Park et al., 2008).

About one quarter of injuries for adolescents are work related. The risk is greater for males than females and increases with age. In addition, adolescents from lower SES families are more likely to be injured while working (Rauscher & Myers, 2008). These injuries can have implications for the rest of these adolescents' lives. Injuries to the musculoskeletal system, such as back injuries and broken bones, are especially likely to cause continuing problems for adolescent boys (Koehoorn, Breslin, & Xu, 2008).

Drug Abuse and Mental Health

Although drug abuse is not always associated with emotional or behavioral problems and people without these challenges may abuse drugs, many adolescents with emotional problems also abuse drugs. Abusing drugs is especially dangerous for African American males. In one study that followed a sample of adolescents from ages 19 to 27, about 33% of the African American young men who abused drugs died by age 27, compared to 3% for White males. The death rates for both African American and White females who abused drugs were 1% (Clark, Martin, & Cornelius, 2008).

TABLE 11.5 • How Many Adolescents Use Alcohol, Tobacco, and Other Drugs?

Results from the *Monitoring the Future* survey of about 46,000 adolescents conducted in 2008 by the University of Michigan and the National Institute on Drug Abuse. Here are the percentages of the respondents who reported that they had: (a) ever used drugs and (b) used drugs in the past month.

	% WHO EVER USED?			*% WHO USED IN THE PAST MONTH*		
GRADE LEVEL	*ALCOHOL*	*TOBACCO*	*ILLICIT DRUGS*	*ALCOHOL*	*TOBACCO*	*ILLICIT DRUGS*
8th	25	21	20	16	7	8
10th	34	32	34	29	12	16
12th	47	45	47	43	20	22

Source: Johnston, L. D., O'Malley, P. M., Bachman, J. G., & Schulenberg, J. E. (2009). Monitoring the future: National results on adolescent drug use. Overview of key findings, 2008 *(No. NIH Publication No. 09-7401). Bethesda, MD: The University of Michigan Institute for Social Research and the National Institute on Drug Abuse.*

HOW MANY ADOLESCENTS USE DRUGS? Accurate statistics are hard to find, but estimates from the *Monitoring the Future* survey of about 46,000 adolescents conducted by the University of Michigan and the National Institute on Drug Abuse indicated that 14% of eighth graders, 27% of tenth graders, and 37% of twelfth graders had used an illicit drug in the last year, with marijuana being the most popular drug besides alcohol (Johnston, O'Malley, Bachman, & Schulenberg, 2009). Table 11.5 gives some specifics.

Drug use among secondary school students has been gradually declining or holding steady since about 2001, with the exception of OxyContin, which has increased slightly. Alcohol is the most widely used drug, with 13% of eighth graders, 30% of tenth graders, and 66% of twelfth graders indicating on the *Monitoring the Future* survey that they *had been drunk* at least once in the last year. In addition, about 7% of eighth graders, 12% of tenth graders, and 20% of twelfth graders reported smoking cigarettes in the last month. Nearly half of U.S. adolescents have tried cigarettes by the twelfth grade and 1 out of 5 are current smokers (Johnston et al., 2009). Even though the number of younger Americans who smoke has been going down since the late 1990s, the rate of tobacco smoking among teenagers still is higher than the rate for adults.

Remarkably, about 1 in 7 high school boys use some form of spit or other type of smokeless tobacco. More than 2% of high school girls use spit or smokeless tobacco. The use of smokeless tobacco can cause cancers of the mouth, throat, larynx, esophagus, stomach, pancreas; receding gums and gum disease, leading finally to tooth loss, precancerous spots in the mouth, nicotine addiction, and possibly to heart disease and stroke (NCS, 2010).

We should distinguish between experimentation and abuse. Many students try something at a party, but do not become regular users. The best way to help students who have trouble saying no appears to be through peer programs that teach them how to say no assertively. Also, the older students are when they experiment with drugs, the more likely they are to make responsible choices, so helping younger students say no is a clear benefit.

WHY DO ADOLESCENTS USE DRUGS? Modern society makes growing up a very confusing process. Notice the meanings and messages from films and billboards. "Beautiful" popular people drink alcohol and smoke cigarettes, with little concern for their health. We have over-the-counter drugs for almost every common ailment. Coffee wakes us up, and a pill helps us sleep. And then we tell students to "say no!" to drugs. For many reasons, not just because of these contradictory messages, drug use has become a problem for students.

Research by Mark Cleveland and his colleagues surveyed over 90,000 students in grades 6, 8, 9, and 12 in Pennsylvania to study the risk and protective factors that predict use of alcohol, tobacco, and other drugs. They studied three categories of risk factors: individual risk factors such as sensation seeking and rebelliousness; peer factors including friends' use of drugs and gang involvement; family risk factors such as parent attitudes favorable to drug use and antisocial behavior. All three kinds of factors—individual, peer, and family—predicted adolescents' drug use. The researchers also studied the protective factors of family cohesions (e.g., attachment to family, supervision, opportunities for positive social connections), school cohesion (e.g., school commitment, opportunities for positive involvement), and community cohesion (e.g., laws and norms about drug use). These factors did protect adolescents from drug use, but the risk factors were more powerful than these protective factors in predicting drug use. Also, as you might guess, family and community factors were more important for younger adolescents, whereas peer and school factors were more important for older adolescents (Cleveland, Feinberg, Bontempo, & Greenberg, 2008). So schools have a role to play in protecting adolescents from drug abuse. What can they do? We turn to that question next.

PREVENTION. First, what doesn't seem to work? Providing information or "scare" tactics such as the DARE drug prevention program seems to have little positive effect and may even encourage curiosity and experimentation (Dusenbury & Falco, 1995; Tobler & Stratton, 1997).

So what is more effective? Adam Fletcher and his colleagues analyzed research on school programs around the world. One overwhelmingly frequent finding was that after taking into account students' prior drug use and personal characteristics, "disengagement from school and poor teacher–student relations were associated with subsequent drug use and other risky health behaviors" (Fletcher, Bonell, & Hargreaves, 2008, p. 217). For example, the researchers describe one study that found, for young adolescents, that being disconnected with school predicted their drug use 2 to 4 years later. One implication is that engaging adolescents in schools, forming positive relationships, and connecting the students to caring adults and peers is critical in creating a protective environment. The report of the Committee on Increasing High School Students' Engagement and Motivation to Learn (2004) summarizes the importance of positive relationships with family, peers, and teachers in supporting students' engagement and learning:

> The likelihood that students will be motivated and engaged is increased to the extent that their teachers, family, and friends effectively support their purposeful involvement in learning in school. . . . Engaging schools promote a sense of belonging by personalizing instruction, showing an interest in students' lives, and creating a supportive, caring social environment. (p. 3)

The most promising prevention programs use developmentally appropriate language and concepts; teach students to resist social pressure; provide accurate information about rates of behavior (*not* everyone is doing it); use interactive teaching methods such as role-playing or small groups; provide training in skills that help in many situations; give thorough coverage of the topic with follow-up; and practice cultural sensitivity.

Steroids

Anabolic-androgenic steroids—usually called simply **steroids**—are commercially produced drugs related to male sex hormones. The *anabolic* part of the name refers to muscle building and the *androgenic* part refers to increased male characteristics. There are more than 100 kinds of steroids and all are legally available only by prescription. Legitimate uses include treating people who produce too little testosterone or who have certain muscle loss problems that accompany AIDS or other diseases. But most steroids used in the United States are smuggled in illegally from other countries or created in illegal labs (Gober, Klein, Berger, Vindigni, & McCabe, 2006a).

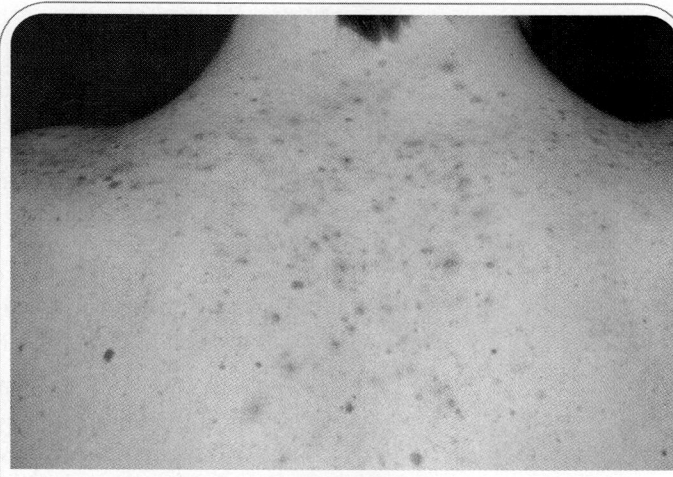
Some of the possible side effects of steriod use are acne on the shoulders and back, breast development in males, persistent bad breath, receding hairline, shrinking of the testicles, and elevated blood pressure, among others.

EFFECTS OF STEROIDS. Unlike alcohol or marijuana, anabolic steroids are not taken for their effects on how they make you feel—they are not recreational. Adolescents, like adults, take steroids for muscle strength and development. Using steroids causes the body to retain nitrogen and this, combined with exercise, builds muscles. But steroids are similar to other drugs and alcohol; they are controlled substances with negative effects for users. Some side effects include irritability, aggression and manic episodes (called "roid rage" in the popular press), mood swings, increased energy, distractibility, forgetfulness, and confusion. In men, other side effects can be decreased sperm count, shrunken testicles, and breast development. For women, side effects can include abnormal hair growth or baldness, acne, and menstrual irregularities. Even more serious side effects for adolescents are heart attacks and strokes, liver tumors, and the premature stopping of bone development. Withdrawing from steroids combined with fluctuations in natural hormones can lead to depression and also can be a factor in adolescent suicides. In addition, risk taking and impulsive behaviors—two concerns for adolescents—may be intensified with steroids (Gober et al., 2006a; Gober, McCabe, & Klein, 2006b).

WHO USES STEROIDS AND WHAT CAN YOU DO? Steroids are used mostly by boys; in 2008, the rates of use for eighth, tenth, and twelfth graders were 1.2%, 1.4%, and 2.5% respectively. For girls, the rates were .5%, .5%, and .4% respectively. These rates were down by about half since their peaks in the early 2000s (Johnston et al., 2009). Rates in other developed countries are about the same. For example, in Sweden, about 3% of 16- and 17-year-old boys were using steroids in 2001 (Nilsson, Baigi, Marklund, & Fridlund, 2001). Girls are less likely than boys to use steroids, but girls with eating disorders may use steroids to lose fat. Feeling pressure from the media or parents to have a "perfect" body or having a distorted body image can lead some adolescents to use steroids to attain the "ideal" (Gober et al., 2006a). Both male and female athletes and individuals with poor body images are more likely to use steroids.

What can professionals and parents do to prevent steroid abuse? Helping adolescents have a positive body image, as we discussed earlier, is a first step. Talking about harmful messages from the media is another possibility. As with other drug prevention programs, scare tactics are not as effective as programs that provide information and focus on positive body image. One program funded by the National Institute on Drug Abuse is called Athletes Training and Learning to Avoid Steroids (ATLAS). The program provides nutrition and weight training alternatives for adolescent athletes and has been effective in reducing steroid use in 31 high schools in the Portland, Oregon area (Gober et al., 2006a, b). See www.ohsu.edu/hpsm/atlas.html for more details.

Violence

Many adolescents live in a violent world. When the Healthy People 2010 objectives were set in 2000, more than 400,000 youth between the ages of 10 and 19 were injured as a result of violence. About 4% of all high school students reported being injured so severely in a physical fight that they needed medical attention—ninth and tenth graders seem to have more fights than eleventh and twelfth graders. About 17% of adolescents said they had carried a weapon and about 7% had carried a weapon on school property. Unfortunately, these numbers have barely changed since 2000, so we are far from meeting the 2010 objectives on adolescent violence (Park et al., 2008; Towey & Fleming, 2003).

Chronic Disease

Many health problems can affect students' learning, in great part because the students miss school, leading to lost instructional time and missed opportunities for friendships. Some adolescents must use special devices such as braces, special shoes, crutches, or wheelchairs to participate in a normal school program. If the school has the necessary architectural features, such as ramps, elevators, and accessible rest rooms, and if teachers allow for the physical limitations of students, little needs to be done to alter the usual educational program. Two health impairments you may encounter in middle and high school are HIV/AIDS and diabetes. We talked about diabetes in previous chapters, so here we focus on HIV/AIDS. Even though some children are born with HIV infections passed on from their mothers, these conditions also can be consequences of increased sexual activity for adolescents or drug use with needles.

WHO HAS HIV/AIDS? You probably have heard quite a bit about Human Immunodeficiency Virus/Acquired Immunodeficiency Syndrome (HIV/AIDS). This is a chronic illness in children and adolescents. The disease begins with HIV and can progress to AIDS, but today the progression can be delayed with appropriate drug therapy.

Around the world, half of the new HIV infections are among young people. In the United States, about 7% of the 35,962 new cases of HIV/AIDS reported to the Centers for Disease Control in 2007 were in adolescents and young adults from 13 to 24 years old. As you can see in Table 11.6, in the United States, by the end of 2007, there were over 54,000 adolescents and young adults (ages 13 to 24) living with AIDS.

Since 1999, the number of males in this group has increased while the number of females has remained steady or declined. Gay and bisexual males are the most at risk. There are great disparities related to race, ethnicity, and HIV/AIDS. About 65% of the new HIV cases in 2006 were African Americans, Latinos/as, Native Americans, or Asians/Pacific Islanders. The rate of new infections for African Americans was 7 times the rate for Whites (CDC, 2008; Rangel, Gavin, Reed, Fowler, & Lee, 2006; Veinot et al., 2006).

For children and young adolescents, the main cause of HIV/AIDS was that their mother had AIDS when they were born and transmitted HIV to them. As this group grows older and becomes sexually active, the number of cases of HIV/AIDS probably will increase. In 2002, HIV/AIDS was among the top 10 causes of death for all youth ages 20 to 24, and for African American young people ages 15 to 24 (Rangel et al., 2006).

LIVING WITH HIV/AIDS. These are grim statistics, but today HIV/AIDS often can be controlled with medication. Current treatments involve combinations of drugs, called **highly active antiretroviral therapy (HAART)**. This is an aggressive treatment package, usually two or three different drugs, that suppresses the replication of the virus, strengthens the immune system, and controls the progression of HIV. In some cases, the treatment reduces the amount of active virus so that it is undetectable in blood tests. Without the drug, 9 out of 10 people infected with HIV progress to AIDS in 5 to 10 years (Wang, Chai, Lin, Yao, & Chen, 2009).

TABLE 11.6 • **Children and Adolescents Living with AIDS in the United States**

AGE (YEARS)	ESTIMATED # OF AIDS CASES IN 2007	CUMULATIVE ESTIMATED # OF AIDS CASES, THROUGH 2007*
Under 13	28	9,209
Ages 13–14	80	1,169
Ages 15–19	455	6,089
Ages 20–24	1,927	38,175

**Includes persons with a diagnosis of AIDS from the beginning of the epidemic through 2007.*
Source: Courtesy of Centers For Disease Control and Prevention, available at: http://www.cdc.gov/hiv/topics/surveillance/basic.htm

Adolescents and young adults face a lifetime of treatment with HAART. With this regimen, the progression from HIV to AIDS can be delayed for years. These therapies require careful procedures, often taking several pills a day at specific times. Tiffany Veinot and her colleagues (2006) stress "high adherence to antiretroviral therapy (>95%) is required to achieve optimal viral suppression and to prevent the development of drug resistance" (p. 265). In other words, if adolescents do not take the medications as prescribed, they not only miss out on the protective power of the treatment, but also they can develop a resistance to the drugs themselves. But adolescents may find it difficult to commit to a lifetime of carefully timed treatment. They may be embarrassed when friends ask, "What's all those pills?" They may fear possible side effects such as nausea, headaches, diarrhea, hepatitis, mouth sores, insomnia, liver failure, or nightmares. Sometimes adolescents' feelings of being invulnerable or of valuing present comfort over long-term benefit interfere with sticking to the treatment. The fact that HAART can't cure HIV, but only manage it, is discouraging to many adolescents. Finally, treatment is costly, but supports for low-income families are available. Adolescents living with HIV/AIDS need developmentally appropriate educational materials and social support, especially the support of caring adults (Veinot et al., 2006). Like everyone, they need to know the myths and facts about HIV/AIDS, as you can see in Table 11.7.

TABLE 11.7 • **Myths and Facts about HIV/AIDS**

MYTHS	FACTS
Only gay men and women get HIV and AIDS.	Worldwide, HIV and AIDS are spread most often through heterosexual contact. Anyone can get HIV and AIDS if they engage in the unsafe practices below.
1. You can get HIV from kissing. 2. You can get HIV by drinking from a glass used by someone who has HIV. 3. You can get HIV from *giving* blood. 4. You can get HIV from a toilet seat. 5. HIV is spread through casual social contact. 6. You can get HIV from sweat or tears, so gyms are places you can be infected. 7. You can get HIV and AIDS from mosquito bites.	HIV is spread only by doing the following: 1. Having unprotected sex with an HIV positive person. 2. Sharing needles or syringes with an HIV positive person. 3. Getting a blood transfusion from an HIV positive person. 4. During pregnancy, birth, or breast-feeding from an infected mother to her baby. 5. Drinking alcohol can increase the risk of getting HIV.
You cannot get HIV and AIDS from oral sex.	You can get HIV by having oral sex with a man or a woman.
You can prevent AIDS and HIV by using birth control such as spermicides, cervical caps, diaphragms, sponges, or the Pill.	Birth control may prevent pregnancy but can't prevent AIDS and HIV. Spermicides with nonoxynol-9 may even increase the chance of getting AIDS and HIV. Using a latex condom during sex can reduce the risk of getting HIV.
You can tell by looking at someone if they have HIV/AIDS.	Someone who has HIV, but looks and feels healthy, can still infect other people.
When you're on HIV therapy you can't transmit the virus to anyone else.	Even if the therapy is working well, you can still transmit HIV to others.
Most people who get infected with HIV become seriously ill within three years.	After a person is infected with HIV, there is usually no change in that person's health for quite a few years.
Vaccination can protect people from HIV infection.	AIDS is a syndrome that has no cure, but can be managed.
The number of new HIV cases is going down.	Actually the number is going up, but better treatments allow people with HIV to stay healthier longer and deaths due to AIDS are going down in the developed countries.

Source: Based on information available online at Medicine.Net (http://www.medicinenet.com/script/main/art.asp?articlekey=); Family Health International (http://www.farmradio.org/english/radio-scripts/62-2script_en.asp.); and Sowadsky (2010) http://www.thebody.com/content/art2293.html.

With all health conditions, teachers need to talk to parents to find out how the problems are handled, what the signs are that a dangerous situation might be developing, and what resources are available for the student. Keep records of any incidents—they may be useful in the student's medical diagnosis and treatment.

Staying Healthy and Safe

What would help protect adolescents from problem behaviors such as delinquency, drug abuse, risky sexual activity, and also encourage positive healthy lifestyles such as a nutritious diet and adequate physical activity? One longitudinal study of over 14,000 adolescents reached three interesting conclusions:

1. Problem behaviors and unhealthy lifestyles are related for adolescents.
2. Low self-control of emotions and behaviors is related to both problem behaviors and unhealthy lifestyles. For example, adolescents who can't control their anger are more likely to get into fights or use weapons and adolescents who cannot delay gratification are more likely to buy a candy bar from a vending machine when they are hungry instead of waiting until they get home to eat a healthy snack.
3. Poor decision making is a much weaker predictor of problem behaviors and unhealthy lifestyles than self-control. In other words, adolescents may know what they should do, but they may not be able to regulate their emotions or behaviors well enough to do it (Kim, Guerra, & Williams, 2008).

The importance for adolescent health of self-regulating emotions and behaviors means that the information in Chapter 13 on social emotional development is also connected to adolescent physical development. And we have seen that decision making affects mental and physical health as well, a topic we discuss in the next chapter on cognitive development.

▼ SUMMARY AND KEY TERMS

• Puberty: Ready or Not

During puberty, the production of sex hormones such as estrogens and testosterone increases dramatically. These hormones, and the other hormones they stimulate, regulate many of the changes in puberty. On average, girls begin puberty about two years ahead of boys and reach their final height by age 15 or 16, several years ahead of boys. Genetics, health, nutrition, stress, and quality of the family developmental environment affect the timing of puberty for girls. Over the past five decades, the age for girls' first menstrual period has decreased by about nine months; this has been termed the *secular trend*. In general, Asian adolescents move through puberty later than European, African, or Latino/a adolescents. Earlier sexual maturity has a number of disadvantages for both boys and girls. One problem today for many boys and girls is dissatisfaction with body image, although there are cultural differences in body image and satisfaction.

• Neurobiology and Adolescent Development

During adolescence, axons in the frontal lobe continue to be myelinated (coated), so information can move faster in the frontal cortex. There is an increase in neural connections followed by a pruning down to fewer, more selective and stronger connections. Areas of the brain become more integrated and connected in these networks of associations. By the end of adolescence, brain and neurological changes help individuals avoid risky behaviors, be more purposeful and organized, and inhibit impulsive behavior. But the changes are not complete until early adulthood. Because the limbic system (which is related to seeking novelty and sensation) matures faster than the prefrontal cortex (which supports judgment), in emotional situations, thrill seeking wins out over caution, at least until the prefrontal lobe catches up and becomes more integrated with the limbic system toward the end of adolescence.

• **Sexual Development**

From 13–35% of adolescents in the United States reported sexual intercourse by the end of eighth grade. The figure was 70–90% by age 18. The most common time for the first experience is between 15 and 17, although these figures differ by geography, culture, and ethnicity. Earlier sexual activity (beginning at age 15 or before) is associated with more behavior problems such as alcohol use, aggression (boys), and depression (girls), and fewer positive connections with school and with peers. Some negative consequences of sexual activity can include exposure to HIV/AIDS, sexually transmitted diseases (STDs), unwanted pregnancies, and emotional stress.

For adolescents already inclined to delay intercourse, making a virginity pledge may increase the chances they will wait. The two most widely used approaches to sex education are abstinence-only (AO) education and comprehensive sex education (CSE). Most research shows that AO is not effective, but recent research suggests that AO that is honest and nonjudgmental can help younger adolescents to delay becoming sexually active.

• **Nutrition and Exercise**

During adolescence, we establish patterns and habits in diet, physical activity, lifestyle, and exercise that probably shape us well into our adult years. Our bones will reach their peak density and this level helps determine if and when we develop osteoporosis, but many adolescents do not get enough calcium. The dramatic physical growth and development during puberty requires increases in energy, protein, vitamins, and minerals. Adolescents are hungry, but their brains are not yet expert at weighing risks and rewards, and their body image concerns focus them on appearances, so they may make poor nutritional choices—skipping breakfast, snacking, eating fast foods, or dieting in dangerous ways.

Eating disorders are a problem for both girls and boys, but they often go undetected in boys. Other changes in the neurological system during adolescence affect sleep. Teenagers need about 9 hours of sleep per night, but many adolescents' biological clocks are reset, so it is difficult for them to fall asleep before midnight; thus they suffer from sleep deprivation.

Boys tend to be more active than girls at every age, but when you compare boys and girls based on biological (maturational) age, not chronological age, the gender differences disappear. The U.S. Department of Health recommends that adolescents engage in at least 60 minutes of physical activity a day, but only about 64% of girls and 73% of boys in the ninth grade are getting enough vigorous physical activity, with percentages decreasing for older students. Unfortunately, physical education time is being cut to allow for more academic time focused on test preparation.

• **Threats to Well-Being in Adolescence**

When teenagers smoke, abuse drugs, or drive recklessly, they may do so in part because they are impulsive, lack self-control (especially in groups), or are unrealistically optimistic and feel invulnerable. But another aspect of risk taking is the meaning of the behavior in the adolescent's social group.

Since the early 1990s, mortality rates for all motor vehicle crashes and for alcohol-related crashes have increased slightly for teens. About one quarter of injuries for adolescents are work related. The risk is greater for males than females and increases with age. In addition, adolescents from lower SES families are more likely to be injured while working.

About 14% of eighth graders, 27% of tenth graders, and 37% of twelfth graders had used an illicit drug in the last year, with marijuana being the most popular drug besides alcohol. Alcohol is the most widely used drug. Providing information or "scare" tactics such as the DARE drug prevention program seems to have little positive effect and may even encourage curiosity and experimentation. Students who are disengaged from school and have poor relationships with their teachers are more likely to use drugs and engage in other risky behaviors. Adolescents, like adults, take steroids for muscle strength and development—both male and female athletes and individuals with poor body images are more likely to use steroids. In 2008 the rates of use for eighth, tenth, and twelfth grade boys were 1.2%, 1.4%, and 2.5% respectively. For girls, the rates were .5%, .5%, and .4% respectively. These rates were down by about half since the peaks in the early 2000s. More than 400,000 youth between the ages of 10 and 19 were injured as a result of violence. About 4% of all high school students reported being injured so severely in a physical fight that they needed medical attention.

Human Immunodeficiency Virus/Acquired Immunodeficiency Syndrome (HIV/AIDS) is a chronic illness in children and adolescents. Around the world, half of the new HIV infections are among young people. In the United States, about 7% of the new cases of HIV/AIDS in 2007 were in adolescents and young adults from 13 to 24 years old. Current treatments involve combinations of drugs that suppress the replication of the virus, strengthen the immune system, and control the progression of HIV.

▼ KEY TERMS

abstinence-only (AO) education (453)
amenorrhea (458)
anorexia nervosa (458)
binge eating (458)
body image (448)
body mass index (BMI) (447)
bulimia nervosa (458)
comprehensive sex education (CSE) (453)
endocrine system (444)
glands (444)
highly active antiretroviral therapy (HAART) (468)
hormones (444)
menarche (445)
primary sex characteristics (444)
puberty (444)
secondary sex characteristics (444)
secular trend (445)
spermarche (445)
steroids (466)

THE CASEBOOK

ADOLESCENT SMOKING

You are late for a meeting, and to save time, you cut through "the pit" (a courtyard between buildings designated for smoking). Good grief! The second-hand smoke is thick and you try to hold your breath until you get to the door that will let you back into the building. With all the information—the irrefutable evidence—available about the harmful effects of smoking, why are young people still lighting up? You don't understand why this habit hasn't extinguished itself by now! Once you are inside and able to breathe, it crosses your mind that you, as a guidance counselor, might tackle the issue of smoking in some of your classes—but how? What works as a deterrent?

WHAT WOULD THEY DO?

Here is how some professionals in several fields responded:

JILL SULLIVAN—Math, Grades 9–11
Northside College Prep High School, Chicago, Ilinois

The first thing to come to mind is a chapter called "Suicide, Smoking, and the Search for the Unsticky Cigarette" from Malcolm Gladwell's book *The Tipping Point*. I would reread it and consider planning a lesson around it. I recall that he relates smoking to coolness in a very powerful way and references studies that show how certain people may be predisposed to smoke while others can try it and quit with minimal consequence. What I like about using his text is that it would be nontraditional and fun reading for adolescents. It presents messages about smoking being unhealthy, but looks at why people still do it. Further, students are increasingly aware of how they're being marketed to and Gladwell exposes this aspect of smoking in an accessible and interesting way. Lastly, when planning any broad program, I'd build in time for feedback from a small group of teenagers likely to be affected. Here, I'd ask a few smokers from "the pit" or ex-smokers to read the chapter and help me plan the program. People tend to support things they help create, and seeking input first could make the program stronger. I also recommend always looking for existing resources first because as a teacher you'll have little time to reinvent the wheel. You might just find something that requires minimal tailoring to meet your needs.

KAMI M. WAGNER—School Counselor, Grades 9–12
Mt. Hebron High School, Ellicott City, Maryland

Young people might engage in risky behaviors for a variety of reasons. Some use it as a stress reliever, to fit in with a group of kids, as a way to rebel, or maybe as an alternative to using other substances. It seems evident that the amount of education provided on the destructive and harmful effects of cigarettes is helpful, but isn't always a main factor in a young person's decision. There are so many outside influences that impact this decision; it's hard to focus on one solution. A multifaceted approach seems to be effective in working with adolescents on decision making. One solution might be to have an honest discussion with the students. By finding out if they recognize the reason(s) they are smoking, one might be able to help find alternatives or more fully understand the underlying reason why they began smoking. Adolescents often make decisions impulsively, and normal brain development at this age often hinders their ability to weigh consequences effectively. Therefore many young people are physically unable to make an educated decision for some behaviors. This is not to say that we should not continue to try to help them navigate those tough decisions, but this is one challenge in working with adolescents.

CATHY BLANCHFIELD—English/Language Arts, Grades 10 and 12
Duncan Polytechnical High School, Fresno, California

Most professionals who work with adolescents understand that risk taking is a common character trait observed in most teens. No amount of "preaching" or disciplinary actions will actually stop a teen from participating in activities that might be harmful. Brain researchers have noted that when peers are present, a teen's social-emotional response of taking part in a risky activity will overrule any logical response concerning the dangers of the activity. This holds true in any number of activities including drinking, taking drugs, driving recklessly, and smoking. It clear that we must do more than just educate about the perils of these types of activities. Most schools and districts have adopted excellent programs that give students all the reasons they need to not engage in smoking. What must also accompany the education is to engage students in peer discussions and social situations where smoking is discouraged. If the peer culture does not engage in smoking, then many fewer teens will do so.

As a classroom teacher, I see my class as a springboard to begin discussions about this type of behavior. Our school has an active advisory program where we might be able to conduct discussions. We might read articles concerning teenage smoking and stage a Socratic seminar regarding why adolescents smoke and what might be done to discourage such behavior. When students are allowed to come to consensus concerning issues, they are much more likely to take their own advice.

HOLLY FITCHETTE—French Teacher, Grades 9–12
Fleming Island High School, Fleming Island, Florida

Smoking has long been a popular way for teens to assert their autonomy by engaging in what appears to them to be "adult behavior." Despite conclusive evidence and campaigns to stop teen smoking, many persist in lighting up. Adolescents are too concerned with the present to worry about what may happen to them in twenty or more years. From my classroom experience, I know full well that many teens rarely worry about the future consequences of their actions. It's a challenge to motivate some students to improve their grades in the course of the nine-week grading period! It is heartbreaking to think that some adolescents will eventually reap the deadly consequences of poor choices in their youth. I think students could benefit from the right kind of education about the consequences of smoking. Sadly, many teen girls may be more inclined to stop smoking when they see the adverse effects smoking has on one's appearance. Teenage boys may be more inclined to kick the habit when they learn of its effect on virility. Some teens may still respond to medical shock information when they are shown the difference in appearance and function between a smoker's and a non-smoker's lungs. Adolescents benefit when all of this information is in tandem with the responsible choices of adults whom they trust.

myeducationlab

Now go to MyEducationLab at ***www.myeducationlab.com***, where you can:

- Find the instructional objectives for this chapter in the **Study Plan.**
- Take a quiz as a part of the **Study Plan** to self-assess your mastery of chapter content. The program generates an individualized Study Plan based upon your answers to the quiz.
- Complete **Activities and Applications** to assist you in deepening your understanding of important chapter concepts.
- Apply what you have learned through **Building Teaching Skills,** exercises that guide you in trying out skills and strategies you will use in professional practice.

12 COGNITIVE DEVELOPMENT IN ADOLESCENCE

THE CASEBOOK

WHAT WOULD YOU DO?
ADOLESCENT DECISION MAKING

"You just don't get it! This is important and I'M GOING TO DO IT!" Danielle slammed the door to make perfectly clear her intention to get her eyebrow pierced.

Her parents stared at each other. They couldn't believe that their seemingly sensible daughter was so insistent about piecing any part of her body. Danielle argued that she was a senior in high school—"an adult"—and should be allowed to make her *own* decisions about her *own* body. She listed the friends who had this or that body part pierced or tattooed, "and their parents were OK with it." She showed them pictures of celebrities and models. She told them how safe it was. Nothing worked.

Her parents had tried reasoning with Danielle, listing the reasons why this was a bad idea. They told her it would interfere with getting a "good job at a respectable place." They warned Danielle that her grandparents would be "horrified and embarrassed." They showed her an article from the newspaper about the dangers of piercing. They tried negotiating/bribing. Nothing worked.

When everything failed, Danielle's parents forbid her from piercing or tattooing anything and threatened severe punishments. She responded by screaming "You just don't understand!" They were "hopeless, out of touch, controlling," and would "ruin her life." Then she left, hurling the proclamation, "I'M GOING TO DO IT."

Ganna Tarapygina, Age 9—Ukraine

CRITICAL THINKING

- Why would Danielle be so determined to pierce her eyebrow?
- How would Freud, Erikson, Skinner, Piaget, Vygotsky, or Lorenz answer that question?
- Is Danielle an "adult," ready to make her own decisions about issues related to her own body?
- Could her parents have approached this discussion differently? How?
- Are there cultural differences in the ways parents might react to this situation?

▶ OVERVIEW AND OBJECTIVES

Beginning in late childhood or early adolescence, differences in children's experiences bring about countless variations in their development. Changes in the brain, learning, increased knowledge, and growing expertise all combine and interact to create a wide range of cognitive skills and abilities for adolescents (Kuhn & Franklin, 2006). Also, adolescents play a greater role in shaping their own unique development through choices about activities, courses in school, friends, goals, and commitments. Along the way, these unique individuals are making some major decisions and choices about schooling and careers that will shape the rest of their lives.

Even though there are few universals in adolescent cognitive development, several themes appear throughout this chapter. As they develop, adolescents become increasingly able to *think about their own thinking*. They can move beyond specific contexts or situations to *form abstractions and generalizations* that apply across situations. They can stand back from what they experience to *question* their own (or others') actions and beliefs. They can use *deductive or inductive reasoning* to move beyond the information given and form conclusions. They can focus on several variables and *direct their attention* back and forth between tasks. They can begin to develop *expert knowledge* in some domains inside or outside school. Notice the word is "*can.*" Adolescents, and adults for that matter, *don't always do what they can*—we are not perfect or expert thinkers all of the time. By the time you finish this chapter you should be able to:

Objective 12.1 Explain developments in the language of adolescents, including bilingual adolescents.

Objective 12.2 Evaluate Piaget's and Vygotsky's analyses of cognitive development in adolescence, including the implications of their theories for teaching and learning.

Objective 12.3 Summarize developments in metacognition, attention, inquiry, argument, and critical thinking in adolescence.

Objective 12.4 Compare and contrast analytic and heuristic thinking, including the dangers and benefits of each in real-world reasoning.

Objective 12.5 Evaluate evidence for differences in cognitive abilities based on gender, ethnicity, and culture, and elaborate on steps teachers can take to reach every student.

Objective 12.6 Describe the family, peers, and schools as contexts for cognitive development in adolescence.

Objective 12.7 Assess how technology can support learning in the adolescent years.

OUTLINE ▼

Adolescent Language Development: Connections

In many ways, language development in adolescents is about connections: connecting events in their own lives to a life story, connecting to each other through shared vocabulary and phrases, and connecting to technology through special codes and shorthand.

Narratives and Life Stories

School-age children are beginning to organize their memories into stories about their own experiences, although children in different cultures may organize these narratives in different ways. In adolescence, we see the emergence of a particular kind of narrative—*a life story*. Eric Erikson (1968) was one of the first psychologists to suggest that developing a personal life story is the hallmark of forming a mature identity—and identity development is a key process for adolescents. In their life stories, adolescents describe themselves as consistent across situations and time, so they have an enduring identity. At least three aspects of cognitive development make life stories possible. The first is an ability to use language and memory to create a coherent story that explains who you are. The second is the ability to be metacognitive—to reflect on situations and behavior and ask, "Why did I do that?" or "Why did that happen?" The third is a theory of mind—an understanding that you and others have thoughts, feelings, and personal histories. In addition, the social demands on adolescents—writing autobiographies in school, interviewing for jobs, keeping diaries, writing college admissions essays, introducing themselves to friends or prospective dates, reading about the lives of others, watching films—encourage them to create coherent life narratives as ways of explaining themselves to others (Habermas & de Silveira, 2008).

Connecting with Peers: A Language of Their Own

Adolescents connect with peers and solidify their identity through their special **registers**—ways of speaking that fit specific social situations. These particular ways of speaking may include different vocabulary, pronunciation, or uses of words. You have heard and said many of these things yourself. In terms of vocabulary, if something is great is it "groovy," "da bomb," "sick," "way cool," "sweet," "awesome," "phat," or "excellent"? That depends in part on your age. If you grew up in the 1960s, then you know "groovy," but today "groovy" is not too sweet. There are also cultural differences—variations by social class, ethnicity, or nationality (Gee, Allen, & Clinton, 2001). Technology has added new "words" to the language of adolescents, too.

THE SPREAD OF "LIKE"ING: MALLSPEAK. Some linguists suggest that adolescents speak two dialects, *mallspeak* and *texting*. Mallspeak is minimal and informal, overusing words such as "like," "ya'know," "OK," and "whatever" (Owens, 2005b). These distinctive ways of speaking may originate in particular groups, but migrate to the entire culture. One example is the use of "like," as in "She isn't, *like*, really crazy or anything, but her and her, *like* five buddies did, *like*, paint their hair a really fake-looking, *like*, purple color" (Siegel, 2002, p. 36, italics added). Linguists trace the use of "like" to 15- to 20-year-old girls in California in the 1980s. Sometimes called the "Valley Girl like," this use has spread across geography and ages. Listen to almost any group of adolescent girls (or maybe to yourself) to hear how "like" has, like, taken over. The word serves several functions—to soften what is said, to move forward in speaking without fully planning what to say, or to speak informally among friends. Girls use *like* more than boys (Siegel, 2002).

We probably don't have to tell you what the "texting" dialect is—a combination of letter and number shorthand to send messages on cell phones: @TEOTD (at the end of the day), 9 (parent watching), 99 (parent not watching anymore), CYO (see you online), EML (email me later). Go to http://www.netlingo.com/emailsh.cfm for many more examples.

TECHNOLOGY AND THE LANGUAGE OF LEADERSHIP. Let's take a look at adolescent leadership language and technology use. One study examined the language of over 3,000 young people from 139 countries who participated in the Junior Summit online community to discuss global issues (Cassell, Huffaker, Tversky, & Ferriman, 2006). The researchers were interested in the language of leadership—how the young people elected to represent the global community talked online. The results showed that these online leaders did not use language in the ways that characterize adult leaders. Adult leaders tend to use powerful language, stick to the task, and contribute many of their own ideas. The young leaders, on the other hand, focused on the goals of the group, synthesized the posts of others, and referred to the group rather than to themselves. Both boys and girls followed the same pattern. So the language of leadership for adolescents may be more engaged and community minded, at least when the community is online.

Diversity in Language Development: Bilingual Education

We have observed many times in this book that the number of people in the United States who speak languages other than English is growing. There are some projections that by 2030, about 40% of the students in pre-kindergarten through high school will speak limited English (Guglielmi, 2008). By 2031, one in three Canadians will belong to a visible minority and one in four will be foreign-born, so it is likely that the number of people who speak languages other than the official English and French will grow in Canada (Freisen, 2010). In the United States, these students sometimes are called **limited-English-proficient** or **LEP.** In the adolescent years, limited proficiency in English often means lower academic achievement and poorer job prospects. So one issue around diversity in language development is how we should teach these students.

Virtually everyone agrees that all citizens should learn the official language of their country. But when and how should instruction in that language begin? There are two basic positions, which have given rise to two contrasting teaching approaches: one that focuses on making the *transition* to English as quickly as possible and the other that attempts to *maintain* or improve the native language and use the native language as the primary teaching language until English skills are more fully developed.

Proponents of the *transition* approach believe that English ought to be introduced as early as possible; they argue that valuable learning time is lost if students are taught in their native language. Most bilingual programs today follow this line of thinking.

Proponents of *native-language maintenance instruction,* however, raise four important issues (Gersten, 1996b; Goldenberg, 1996; Hakuta & Garcia, 1989). First, deep learning in the first language supports second language learning. For example, research on a large national sample that followed eighth graders for 12 years found that for Latino students, proficiency in the first language of Spanish predicted reading ability in English and English reading ability predicted achievement in school and in careers (Guglielmi, 2008). The metacognitive strategies and knowledge developed when students learn to read in their first language are transferred to reading in a second language as well (van Gelderen, Schoonen, Stoel, de Glopper, & Hulstijn, 2007). So maintaining and increasing proficiency in the first language is important. The learning strategies and academic content (math, science, history, etc.) that students learn in their native language are not forgotten when they learn English.

Second, children who are forced to try to learn math or science in an unfamiliar language are bound to have trouble. What if you had been forced to learn fractions or biology in a second language that you had studied for only a semester? Some psychologists believe students taught by this approach may become **semilingual;** that is, they are not proficient in either language. Being semilingual may be one reason the dropout rate is so high for low-SES Latino students (Ovando & Collier, 1998).

Third, if the first language is neglected and the entire emphasis is on English, students may get the message that their home languages (and therefore, their families and cultures) are second class. You can see the seeds of these feelings in the stories of these two students:

> A ninth grade boy, who had recently arrived in California from Mexico: "There is so much discrimination and hate. Even from other kids from Mexico who have been here longer. They don't treat us like brothers. They hate even more. It makes them feel more like natives. They want to be American. They don't want to speak Spanish to us; they already know English and how to act. If they are with us, other people will treat them more like wetbacks, so they try to avoid us." (Olsen, 1988, p. 36)
>
> A tenth grade Chinese American girl who had been in America for several years: "I don't know who I am. Am I the good Chinese daughter? Am I an American teenager? I always feel I am letting my parents down when I am with my friends because I act so American, but I also feel that I will never really be an American. I never feel really comfortable with myself anymore." (Olsen, 1988, p. 30)

Finally, fourth is what Kenji Hakuta years ago called a "paradoxical attitude of admiration and pride for school-attained bilingualism on the one hand and scorn and shame for home-brewed immigrant bilingualism on the other" (1986, p. 229). Ironically, by the time students have mastered academic English and let their home language deteriorate, they reach secondary school and are encouraged to learn a "second" language.

The goal of schools should be balanced bilingualism. One approach to reaching this goal is to create classes that mix students who are learning a second language with students who are native speakers. The objective is for both groups to become fluent in both languages (Sheets, 2005). A daughter of one of your text authors spent a summer in such a program in Quebec and was ahead in every French class after that. For truly effective bilingual education, we will need many bilingual teachers. If you have a competence in another language, you might want to develop it fully for your work.

With this background in language development, we turn to more general questions about the development of thinking and reasoning in adolescence.

PIAGET AND VYGOTSKY

Piaget described the emergence of three qualitatively different modes of thought, from thinking based on actions (sensory-motor), to logical thinking about concrete objects that exist (concrete operations), to abstract scientific thinking about hypothetical situations that may or may not be real (formal operations). For decades, Piaget's theory of formal operational thought was the main explanation of adolescent thinking. Recent research calls some of his ideas into question, but his description of formal operational thinking is a good starting point for our look at adolescent cognitive development.

Piaget: Formal Operations

According to Piaget, around the age of 11 or 12, children develop **formal operations**—a new way of reasoning that involves "thinking about thinking" or "mental operations on mental operations" (Inhelder & Piaget, 1958). For example, the child using concrete operations can categorize animals by their physical characteristics or by their habitats, but a child using formal operations can perform "second-order" operations on these category operations to *infer relationships between* habitat and physical characteristics—such as understanding that the physical characteristic of thick fur on animals is related to their arctic habitats (Kuhn & Franklin, 2006). Even more important, with formal operational thinking, students can apply a complex system of propositions and deductions to abstract ideas, not just to concrete situations. These students can move from reasoning about what is concrete and real to reasoning about what might be. Let's look first at basic types of reasoning.

DEDUCTIVE AND INDUCTIVE REASONING. Quite a bit of research on adolescent and adult thinking focuses on deductive and inductive reasoning. **Deductive reasoning** moves from the general assumption to the specific, as in "All songs on iTunes cost $1.29. 'Born in the USA' by Bruce Springsteen is available on iTunes; therefore, 'Born in the USA' costs $1.29 on iTunes." You can see that if the first two statements are true, then the specific deduction *must* be true. If *all* iTunes songs cost $1.29, then *each* particular iTunes song must cost $1.29. Police use deductive reasoning as they solve crimes, scientists as they test their theories, lawyers as they argue their cases, debate teams as they plan their strategies, and high school students as they set up proofs in algebra or geometry (Byrnes, 2006).

Inductive reasoning goes from specific instances to a general conclusion—something like, "Every song my friends and I have bought on iTunes has cost $1.29, so all songs on iTunes must cost $1.29." Younger children tend to use inductive reasoning—what I see and experience (specifics) tells me what is true (general). "If it has four legs, fur, and barks, it must be a dog" because every four-legged, furry, barking animal I have encountered was a dog. Of course, inductions can be wrong—some four-legged, furry, barking animals might be hyenas or even rabbits.

Older children and adolescents are more likely to understand that *deductions* from a true general premise are always correct, whereas *inductions* from observed specifics are probably, but not certainly, correct (Siegler & Alibali, 2005). For example, economists observe many specific changes in the stock market and attempt to induce general principles about economic cycles, but we have seen that even the best economists have made incorrect inductions about the stock market.

A main characteristic of formal operational thinking is a specific type of *deductive* reasoning called hypothetical-deductive reasoning.

With the development of thinking in the teen years, adolescents can make deductions and inferences about abstract concepts and events never experienced, so science fiction becomes more intriguing.

HYPOTHETICAL-DEDUCTIVE REASONING. At the level of formal operations, the focus of thinking can shift from what *is* to what *might be*. Situations do not have to be experienced to be imagined. You met Jamal in Chapter 1. Even though he is a bright elementary school student, he could not answer the question, "How would life be different if there were no darkness at night?" because he insisted, "It IS DARK at night!" In contrast, the adolescent can consider contrary-to-fact questions. In answering, the adolescent demonstrates the hallmark of formal operations—**hypothetical-deductive reasoning.** The formal thinker can consider a hypothetical situation (it is light 24 hours a day) and reason *deductively* (from the general assumption to specific implications, such as no need for street lights, more products that create darkness for sleeping such as window or eye shades, more sporting events at night, more people having difficulties sleeping, decreasing crime rates, increases in skin cancer, and vampires all die (well, adolescent fans of the vampire movies might say that!). Differences between children and adolescents in deductive thinking become apparent when the information in the premises is *counterfactual,* that is, when the information is not consistent with what the child knows or believes. For example, consider this hypothetical situation:

All wrestlers are police officers.
All police officers are women.

Assume the two statements above are true. Is the following statement true or false?

All wrestlers are women.

Adolescents are better than children at solving this hypothetical deduction, in part because they can distinguish between truth and validity. Ignoring what you know to be true (not all wrestlers are police officers and not all police officers are women) and just reasoning through the problem to a valid conclusion requires **metacognitive skills**—skills that generally improve in the adolescent years. The reasoner has to set aside or inhibit knowledge about *what is* in order to figure out *what could be*. But even though adolescents are better than young children at doing this, both adolescents and adults can make errors when their knowledge conflicts with the information they are reasoning about (Kuhn & Franklin, 2006).

REASONING ABOUT COMBINATIONS. According to Piaget, formal operational thinking allows adolescents to answer questions like this: *You are packing for a long trip, but want to pack light. How many different three-piece outfits (slacks, shirt, jacket) will you have if you include three shirts, three slacks, and three jackets (assuming of course that they all go together in fashion perfection)?* Time yourself to see how long it takes to arrive at the answer.

When a number of variables combine, as in this question or in a laboratory experiment, Piaget believed that working through these possibilities systematically required formal operational thinking. The answer to the different shirt/slacks/jacket outfits problem is 27 possible combinations (did you get it right?). A concrete thinker might name just a few combinations, using each piece of clothing only once. Piaget believed that the younger child could not solve the problem because the underlying system of forming all possible combinations—an aspect of formal operations—was not yet available.

REASONING LIKE A SCIENTIST. The tasks Piaget used to study formal operations looked like scientific experiments or inquiry learning. For example, he asked children to determine which variables affected the *period* of a pendulum (the time it takes for the pendulum to swing back to its starting point). Is it the length of the string? The weight at the end of the string? How high you lift the weight before you drop it? How hard you push the weight? With these 4 variables there are 16 possible combinations (short string, light weight, high drop, hard push; short string, light weight, high drop, soft push; long string, light weight, high drop, hard push; and so on). You can't figure out what matters unless you systematically change one variable at a time, while holding the other three constant. Then you would find out that it is the length of the string that matters.

Another Piagetian task required children to use different distances and weights to balance a scale, as shown in Figure 12.1. Piaget believed that children who can think at a formal level discover the formula that *weight* × *distance* from the center has to be equal on both sides of the center to make the scale balance. This abstract relationship will hold for any concrete balance scale situation.

FIGURE 12.1

BALANCING A SCALE

One of Piaget's tests of formal operational thinking used a balance scale similar to the one below. When the same weight was placed the same distance from the fulcrum on each side, the scale balanced—an ancient idea.

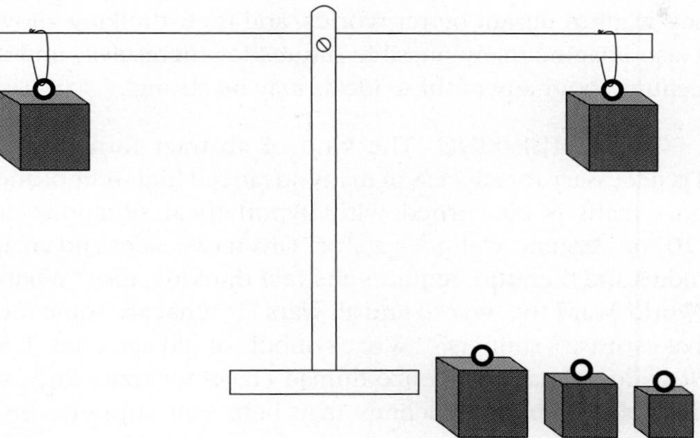

This young girl wonders why the two equal weights aren't in balance—She does not know that distance matters too.

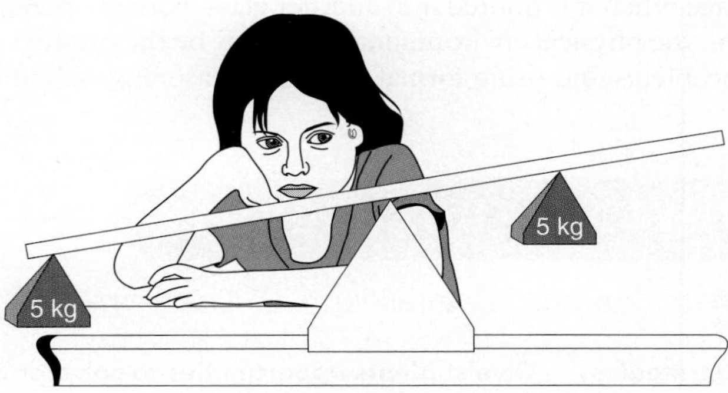

But this adolescent has figured out that the scale will balance if Weight × Distance is the same on both sides of the scale: W × D = W × D. This mathematical relationship holds no matter what the weights and distances are.

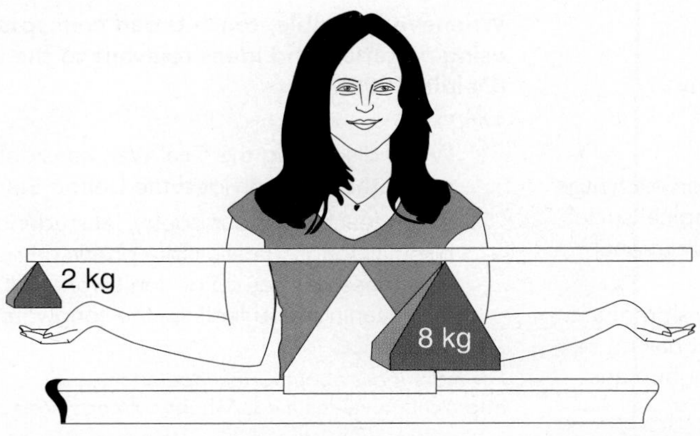

The ability to think hypothetically, identify all possible combinations, and isolate causes has some interesting consequences for adolescents. Because they can think about worlds that do not exist, they often become interested in science fiction. And because they can reason from general principles to specific actions, they often are critical of people whose actions seem to contradict their principles. Adolescents can deduce the set of "best" possibilities and imagine ideal worlds (or ideal parents and teachers, for that matter). This explains why many students at this age develop interests in utopias, political causes, and social issues. They want to design better worlds, and their thinking allows them to do so. Adolescents can also imagine many possible futures for themselves and may try to decide which is best. Feelings about any of these ideals may be strong.

SCHOOLS AND FORMAL THINKING. The kind of abstract formal operational thinking Piaget described is necessary for success in many advanced high school and college courses. For example, most math is concerned with hypothetical situations, assumptions, and givens: "Let $x = 10$," or "Assume $x^2 + y^2 = z^2$," or "Given two sides and an adjacent angle . . ." Work in social studies and literature requires abstract thinking, too: "What did Wilson mean when he called World War I the 'war to end all wars'?" "What are some metaphors for hope and despair in Shakespeare's sonnets?" "What symbols of old age does T. S. Eliot use in *The Waste Land*?" "How do animals symbolize human character traits in Aesop's fables?" The ***Connecting with Adolescents*** guidelines may help you support the development of formal operations with your students.

DO WE ALL REACH THE FOURTH STAGE? There is a debate about how universal formal operational thinking actually is, even among adults. The first three stages of Piaget's theory are forced on most people by physical realities. Objects really are permanent. The amount of water doesn't change when it is poured into another glass. Formal operations, however, are not so closely tied to the physical environment. They may be the product of practice in solving hypothetical problems and using formal scientific reasoning—abilities that are valued

CONNECTING WITH ADOLESCENTS

Guidelines for Teachers: Helping Adolescents to Use Formal Operations

Continue to use concrete operational teaching strategies and materials.
Examples
1. Use visual aids such as charts and illustrations as well as somewhat more sophisticated graphs and diagrams, especially when the material is new.
2. Compare the experiences of characters in stories to students' experiences.

Give students the opportunity to explore many hypothetical questions.
Examples
1. Have students write position papers and then exchange them with the opposing side and debate topical social issues—the environment, the economy, and national health insurance.
2. Ask students to write about their personal vision of a utopia; write a description of a universe that has no sex differences; write a description of Earth after humans are extinct.

Give students opportunities to solve problems and reason scientifically.
Examples
1. Set up group discussions in which students design experiments to answer questions.
2. Ask students to justify two different positions on animal rights, with logical arguments for each position.

Whenever possible, teach broad concepts, not just facts, using materials and ideas relevant to the students' lives (Delpit, 1995).
Examples
1. When discussing the Civil War, consider racism or other issues that have divided the United States since then.
2. When teaching about poetry, let students find lyrics from popular songs that illustrate poetic devices, and talk about how these devices do or don't work well to communicate the meanings and feelings the songwriters intended.

For more ideas about formal operations, see http://chiron.valdosta.edu/whuitt/col/cogsys/piagtuse.html

and taught, particularly in college. So, not all high school students can do Piaget's formal operational tasks (Shayer, 2003). And although taking a college class fosters formal operational abilities in that academic subject, this skill does not necessarily carry over to other subjects (Lehman & Nisbett, 1990). So expect many adolescents in a middle school or high school class to have trouble thinking hypothetically, especially when they are learning something new. Sometimes, students find shortcuts for dealing with problems that are complex; they may memorize formulas or lists of steps. These systems may be helpful for passing tests, but real understanding will take place only if students are able to go beyond this superficial use of memorization.

Evaluating Piaget

No one denies Piaget's central notion about adolescent thinking: As they develop, adolescents become more able to think about their own thinking. You have seen in previous chapters that there are other names for this process: *metacognition* or *executive functions*. With these developing capabilities, adolescents gain increasing control over their thoughts and actions. They can analyze why they believe something or feel a certain way and they can imagine consequences of other thoughts or feelings (Kuhn & Franklin, 2006).

That said, today most psychologists do not agree with Piaget that children's thinking becomes *qualitatively* different in adolescence, even though older children generally are better than younger children at the kind of scientific, hypothetical reasoning described by Piaget. Deanna Kuhn and Sam Franklin say bluntly, "no contemporary reviewer of research evidence endorses the emergence of a discrete new cognitive structure at adolescence that closely resembles Inhelder and Piaget's description of formal operations" (2006, p. 954). The evidence against the emergence of a *new* logical structure for thinking in adolescence comes from three sources.

First, different people are able to solve formal thinking tasks at different ages—some at young ages. A number of studies have shown that younger children can reason by analogy, solve the balance scale problem in Figure 12.1, isolate the cause in a multivariable problem, and think systematically, as long as they are working with familiar materials, context, and language (Goswami, 2008; Schulz & Gopnick, 2004).

Second, the same person might be able to solve some kinds of formal thinking tasks but not others. But if one formal thinking structure were involved in all formal tasks, you would think that experience or interest would not matter; a person who was successful on one type of formal task would be successful on every formal task. Actually, Piaget himself acknowledged that a structure such as formal operational thinking might apply only in particular content areas or domains; most adults use formal operational thought in only a few areas in which they have the greatest experience or interest (Miller, 2011; Piaget, 1974).

Finally, the kind of task, the instructions, the support of the teacher, and the way competence is assessed all can determine if the child seems able to think formally. Children can be more or less cognitively competent, depending on their familiarity with the task and the support they receive in doing it (Goswami, 2008). For example, elementary age children can be successful in scientific reasoning when they develop hypotheses in small groups, reach a consensus about what to do, and then have teacher guidance as they test their hypotheses (Howe & Tolmie, 2003). These contextual factors that support or scaffold competence are very important in another explanation of cognitive development—the theories of Vygotsky.

Vygotsky's Sociocultural Theory

Vygotsky stressed scaffolded or mediated learning in the learner's zone of proximal development—that area where the learner can't succeed independently, but can be successful with the right support. As the learner and a more competent peer solve the problem together, they co-construct an understanding. The teacher supports understanding with just the right scaffolding—cues, examples, questions, demonstrations, hints, and so on. The learner *appropriates* or internalizes that understanding and can now solve similar problems independently or with less support. So Vygotsky believed that learning can lead to cognitive development: "properly organized learning results in mental development and sets in motion a variety of developmental processes that would be impossible apart from learning. Thus learning is a necessary and universal aspect of the process of developing culturally organized, specifically human, psychological functions" (Vygotsky, 1978, p. 90).

SPONTANEOUS AND SCIENTIFIC THINKING. Like Piaget, Vygotsky distinguished between concrete and abstract thought, but Vygotsky called these *spontaneous* concepts and *scientific* concepts respectively. Spontaneous (concrete) concepts are ideas generated based on direct observations and experiences in the world. This is how children learn the Piagetian operations of conservation and classification—by acting on their world. But these spontaneous concepts can be wrong. For example, young children may believe that the moon follows them around because that is what they observe. Even older children and adults may believe temperatures are warmer in the summer because the earth's orbit is closer to the sun (not true!). Scientific (formal) concepts are the more accurate, often more abstract, understandings that are learned mostly in school. These scientific understandings require attention and effort, and sometimes the unlearning of inaccurate spontaneous concepts (Goswami, 2008). For example, students have to overcome spontaneous concepts about standing closer to a fire and being warmer to learn the scientific explanation for why temperatures are warmer in summer: The angle of the earth on its axis means that the earth's hemisphere that is experiencing summer gets more hours of daylight and more direct, concentrated sunlight.

Alexander Luria, one of Vygotsky's students, tested ideas about schooling and scientific thinking by asking unschooled adults in remote villages of Uzbekistan to apply syllogistic reasoning, a form of higher-level scientific thinking. He asked the villagers questions such as "In the Far North, where there is snow, all bears are white. Novaya Zemla is in the Far North. What color are the bears there?" Most of the villagers answered some version of "you would have to ask people who have been there. I can't say. I haven't seen the bears" (Luria, 1976). These people, according to Luria, were focused on their spontaneous concepts based on experience and observation—or in this case, lack of observation. Results like these suggest schooling and culture play important roles in developing some kinds of scientific or formal thinking (Goswami, 2008).

CULTURAL TOOLS. You may recall from previous chapters that Vygotsky emphasized the importance of language and other cultural tools in cognitive development. Different cultural and historical contexts support the development of different cognitive abilities. When the culture provides teaching and support for certain abilities—for example, using a computer or accessing information via search engines—these abilities will develop and shape learning.

The use of material cultural tools such as calculators and spell checkers is somewhat controversial in education. Technology is increasingly "checking up" on us. We (your authors) rely on the spell checkers in our word processing programs to protect us from embarrassment. But we also read papers from students with spelling replacements that must have been made by a spell checker without a "sense check" by the writer. Is student learning harmed or helped by these technology supports?

Speaking on the harm side, when your text author Anita polled her graduate class of experienced teachers and principals, she got various opinions, such as: "When students are given calculators to do math in the early grades, most of them never learn rudimentary mathematical concepts; they only learn to use the calculator" and "To learn math, students need repetition and practice on the concepts to remember the operations—calculators get in the way." In terms of word processing, results of the National Assessment of Educational Progress (NAEP, 1997) indicated that even though the use of word processors by eleventh graders increased from 19% in 1984 to 96% in 1997, the average writing scores of eleventh graders declined during those years.

Rather than deciding that technology is either good or bad, we have to consider each teaching situation on a case-by-case basis to determine if paper-and-pencil procedures or technology or some combination provides the best way to learn. The research on calculators over the past decade has found that using calculators has positive effects on students' problem-solving skills and attitudes toward math (Waits & Demana, 2000).

What about word processors and spelling checkers? Pricilla Norton and Debra Sprague (2001) suggest "no other technology resource has had as great an impact on education as word processing" (p. 78). They list the following effects: Word processing enhances learners' perceptions of themselves as "real" writers, lets students reflect on the thinking that goes on behind the writing, facilitates collaborative writing, and helps students be more critical and creative in their writing. An advisor working with undergraduate engineering students pointed out another plus for technology: "We have many international students who have an average-to-good command of English. In my opinion, they need Spellcheck to catch the errors as well as to 'teach' them the corrected form. Spellcheck is at times a nuisance to us by questioning everything, but I think it's very helpful to ESL students and for general proofreading purposes."

There is a caution about word processing. If students' typing is slower than their longhand writing, then typed compositions may be of lower quality than handwritten ones. Students need to be taught both typing and revising skills before their writing quality can benefit from using word processing tools (MacArthur, 2009).

Applying Vygotsky's Ideas: Cognitive Apprenticeships and Reciprocal Teaching

The kind of adult-mediated learning that Vygotsky described is evident in apprenticeships. By working alongside a master and perhaps other apprentices, young people have learned many skills, trades, and crafts. A knowledgeable guide provides models, demonstrations, and corrections in the apprentice's zone of proximal development. The performances required of the learner are real and important and grow more complex as the learner becomes more competent (Collins, 2006; Hung, 1999; Linn & Eylon, 2006). Along with *guided participation* in real tasks comes *participatory appropriation*—students appropriate the knowledge, skills, and values involved in doing the tasks (Rogoff, 1995, 1998). In addition, both the newcomers to learning and the old-timers contribute to the community of practice by mastering and remastering skills—and sometimes improving these skills in the process (Lave & Wenger, 1991).

COGNITIVE APPRENTICESHIPS. Allan Collins (2006) suggests that knowledge and skills learned in school have become too separated from their use in the world beyond school. To correct this imbalance, some educators recommend that schools adopt many of the features of apprenticeships. But rather than learning to sculpt or dance or build a cabinet, apprenticeships in school would focus on cognitive objectives such as reading comprehension, writing, or mathematical problem solving. There are many **cognitive apprenticeship** models, but most share six features:

- Students observe an expert (usually the teacher) *model* the performance.
- Students get external support through *coaching* or tutoring (including hints, feedback, models, and reminders).
- Students receive conceptual *scaffolding,* which is then gradually faded as the student becomes more competent and proficient.
- Students continually *articulate* their knowledge—putting into words their understanding of the processes and content being learned.

In an apprenticeship, a knowledgeable guide provides models, demonstrations, and corrections in the apprentice's zone of proximal development. The performances required of the learner are real and important and grow more complex as the learner becomes more competent. The relationship provides support and motivation.

- Students *reflect* on their progress, comparing their problem solving to an expert's performance and to their own earlier performances.
- Students are required to *explore* new ways to apply what they are learning—ways that they have not practiced at the master's side.

As students learn, they are challenged to master more complex concepts and skills and to perform them in many different settings (Roth & Bowen, 1995; Shuell, 1996).

RECIPROCAL TEACHING. How can teaching provide cognitive apprenticeships? One example is **reciprocal teaching.** The goal of reciprocal teaching is to help students understand and think deeply about what they read (Palincsar & Brown, 1989; Rosenshine & Meister, 1994). To accomplish this goal, students in small reading groups learn four strategies: *summarizing* the content of a passage, *asking a question* about the central point, *clarifying* the difficult parts of the material, and *predicting* what will come next. These are "thinking about thinking" or metacognitive strategies. Skilled readers apply these higher-level thinking strategies almost automatically, but poor readers seldom do—or they don't know how. To use the strategies effectively, poorer readers need scaffolding: direct instruction, modeling, and practice in actual reading situations.

First, the teacher introduces these strategies, perhaps focusing on one strategy each day. As the expert, the teacher explains and models each strategy and encourages student apprentices to practice. Next, the teacher and the students read a short passage silently. Then, the teacher again provides a model by summarizing, questioning, clarifying, or predicting based on the reading. Everyone reads another passage, and the students gradually begin to assume the teacher's role. The teacher becomes a member of the group, and may finally leave, as the students take over the teaching. Often, the students' first attempts are halting and incorrect. But the teacher gives clues, guidance, encouragement, support doing parts of the task (such as providing question stems), modeling, and other forms of scaffolding to help the students master these strategies. The goal is for students to learn to apply these strategies independently as they read so they can make sense of the text.

Although reciprocal teaching seems to work with almost any age student, most of the research has been done with younger adolescents who can read aloud fairly accurately, but who are far below average in reading comprehension. In contrast to some approaches that try to teach 40 or more strategies, an advantage of reciprocal teaching is that it focuses attention on four powerful strategies. But these strategies must be taught—not all students develop them on their own. One study of reciprocal teaching spanning over three years found that questioning was the strategy used most often, but that students had to be taught how to ask higher-level questions because most student questions were literal or superficial (Hacker & Tenent, 2002). Another advantage of reciprocal teaching is that it emphasizes practicing these four strategies in the context of actual reading—reading literature and reading texts. Finally, the idea of scaffolding and gradually moving the student toward independent and fluid reading comprehension is a critical component in reciprocal teaching and cognitive apprenticeships in general (Rosenshine & Meister, 1994).

Information Processing: Metacognition and Scientific Thinking

Piaget emphasized qualitative changes in thinking—a shift in kind of thinking based on the individual's encounters with the physical and social world. Vygotsky described a more gradual change based on co-constructing knowledge with teachers and peers. There is another explanation of cognitive development that stresses gradual changes—information processing. The consequences of these changes are that adolescents can process information *faster* and more efficiently. Also, processing *capacity* improves, perhaps because changes in the brain actually create more working memory space, and/or because faster speed, improved strategies, and increased knowledge free up working memory to create more operating space. Older children are more able to *inhibit* responses: They can ignore irrelevant information, focus attention, and control their impulses to say or do things that interfere with their information processing goals. All of these capabilities allow adolescents to improve in their metacognitive skills and knowledge—they can be more strategic and "in control" of their own thinking. Not to say that they are perfect—judgment and self-regulation may still have a ways to go to reach mature thinking—but at least these abilities are improving for adolescents (Kuhn & Franklin, 2006).

You may remember from previous chapters that the information processing system is managed and controlled by executive processes such as selective attention and memory strategies. These abilities are sometimes called **executive functioning;** they are the neuropsychological skills that we need to plan, focus, remember, and rethink. A hallmark of adolescence is the *emergence and strengthening of this executive functioning*—"arguably the single most important and consequential intellectual development to occur in the second decade of life" (Kuhn & Franklin, 2006, p. 987). Metacognition is key to executive functioning.

Metacognition

We have seen that adolescents are better than younger children at monitoring and managing their thinking—they can control their attention, use strategies to remember, and inhibit impulses long enough to consider alternatives. But remember, *can* is no guarantee they always *will*. Even though adolescents have developed metacognitive knowledge and skills, they may not be motivated in every situation to use them (Klaczynski, 2006). Let's consider some aspects of metacognition in relation to adolescence.

ATTENTION AND MULTITASKING. We have seen in previous chapters that as children develop, they are better at focusing attention on what is important and ignoring irrelevant information. But we are willing to bet you have seen someone texting, surfing the web, watching TV, listening to an iPod, and doing homework—in other words, multitasking, the modern way of life.

You may be multitasking right now. Adolescents are multitasking more than ever, perhaps because they have access to so much technology. In one survey of 8- to 18-year-olds, about one-third of them reported multitasking with multimedia while they do their homework (Azzam, 2006). These students reported using media about 6 to 7 hours each day on average, but with the multitasking, they were exposed to more like 8 to 9 hours of media. Teens often see no problem with multitasking. For example, Andy, a 17-year-old boy, explained how he does homework:

> "I sit down in my living room, put my cell phone down next to me, and turn on the TV shows I recorded the night before," he says. Then Andy gets online and opens up his e-mail account, instant messenger, and MySpace page. "I switch back and forth between work and the other stuff the whole time," he says. "Otherwise, I find it hard to concentrate. Plus, I hate to be out of touch with my friends." (Paulos, 2007, p. 11)

Is multitasking a good idea? Research by David Meyer and his colleagues at the Brain, Cognition, and Actions Laboratory of Michigan University says it depends. Actually, there are two types of multitasking—*sequential multitasking,* in which you switch back and forth from one task to another, but focus on only one at a time, and *simultaneous multitasking,* in which there is overlapping in focus on several tasks at time. Also, the content of the tasks makes a difference. Some tasks, such as walking and chewing gum, call on different cognitive and physical resources—and both walking and chewing are pretty automatic. But other complex tasks, such as driving and talking on the phone, require some of the same cognitive resources—paying attention to traffic and paying attention to what the caller is saying. The problem with multitasking comes with simultaneous, complex tasks.

> For tasks that are at all complicated, no matter how good you have become at multitasking, you're still going to suffer hits against your performance. You will be worse compared to if you were actually concentrating from start to finish on the task. (David Meyer interviewed by Hamilton, 2009, p. 1)

As soon as you turn your attention to something else, the brain starts to lose connections to what you were thinking about, like the answer to question 4 in your math assignment.

Jeremy—multitasking his way through homework . . .

To find that brain pathway again (to *spread activation* toward the needed information) means repeating what you did to find the path in the first place, so finding the answer to question 4 takes more time. In fact, it can take up to 400% longer to do a homework assignment if you are multitasking (Paulos, 2007). In complicated situations, the brain prioritizes and focuses on one thing. You may be able to listen to quiet instrumental music in the background while you study, but favorite songs with words will steal your attention away and it will take time to get back to what you were doing. See the ***Connecting with Adolescents*** guidelines for ideas about dealing with multitasking.

Some adolescents who have attention deficit-hyperactive disorders (ADHD) experience even more difficulty focusing their attention.

ADHD. ADHD usually is diagnosed in elementary school. Just a few years ago, most psychologists thought that ADHD diminished as children entered adolescence, but now there is evidence that the problems can persist into adulthood (Hallowell & Ratey, 1994; Hinshaw, Carte, Fan, Jassy, & Owens, 2007). Adolescence—with the increased stresses of puberty, transition to middle or high school, more demanding academic work, and more engrossing social relationships—can be an especially difficult time for students with ADHD (Taylor, 1998).

CONNECTING WITH ADOLESCENTS

Guidelines for Teachers (and All Students): Multitasking

Advise students to separate schoolwork from time spent maintaining their social life.

Examples

1. Reward yourself for completing one homework assignment by surfing the Web or texting friends for a set time period.
2. Turn off your Internet connection and cell phone when you are doing homework.

Remind students to control their online life—set priorities.

Examples

1. Don't try to be a BFF to all 140 of your Facebook pals.
2. Don't eat dinner in front of your computer. Swallowing dinner in the time it takes to upload pictures is bad for digestion.

Teach students strategies for minimizing distractions.

Examples

1. If you need music, keep it low and instrumental.
2. Set your cell answering message to ask friends to call after a certain time.

Source: Adapted from Paulos (2007).

What can teachers do? Long assignments may overwhelm students with attention deficits, so give them a few problems or paragraphs at a time, with clear consequences for completion. Another promising approach combines instruction in learning and memory strategies with motivational training. The goal is to help students develop the "skill and will" to improve their achievement. They are also taught to monitor their own behavior and encouraged to be persistent and to see themselves as being "in control" (Pfiffner, Barkley, & DuPaul, 2006). Here are some general strategies for teaching adolescents with ADHD and learning disabilities taken from Smith and Tyler (2010):

- Provide support and guidance for completing assignments, for example, clear goals and timelines, step-by-step directions orally and in writing, clear criteria for evaluations, checklists to monitor progress.
- Directly teach self-monitoring strategies, such as cueing students to ask, "Was I paying attention?"
- Connect new material to knowledge a student already has and take cultural knowledge into account.
- Teach students to use external memory strategies and devices (audio-recording, note taking, to-do lists, etc.).

Adolescents with ADHD also may have trouble with another aspect of executive functioning—inhibiting impulses.

INHIBITING IMPULSES. We saw earlier that being able to inhibit impulses—to step back from what you know or believe to consider alternative hypothetical premises such as "All wrestlers are police officers," is a key in hypothetical-deductive reasoning. Without the ability to control your own thinking and set aside existing beliefs, you would be trapped by the way things appear; new learning, inductive and deductive reasoning, and changes in understanding would be difficult. The ability to inhibit impulses improves during adolescence. So metacognition, including directing attention and inhibiting impulses, is a key element in the higher-level reasoning skills needed for scientific thinking. We look next to an information processing view of scientific reasoning.

Scientific Reasoning about Causes and Evidence: Inquiry and Argument

Much of the research on adolescent cognitive development from Piaget to today is concerned with scientific reasoning—inquiry, analysis, inference, and argument. Specifically, researchers have studied developing and testing hypotheses, designing experiments, coordinating variables in order to isolate a cause, making inferences, and supporting claims with evidence (Zimmerman, 2007). Two key scientific reasoning skills, inquiry and argumentation, are the focus of many courses in high school and college.

INQUIRY. How would you design an experiment to determine which factor made the difference in how fast a pendulum swings: The length of the string? The weight at the end of the string? How high you lift the weight before you drop it? How hard you push the weight? If this question sounds familiar, good; you remember what you read earlier in the chapter. If not, you might review the section on Piaget's ideas about thinking like a scientist. With these 4 variables there are 16 possible combinations. The challenge is to design an experiment that allows you to control the variables one at a time and isolate the cause.

As we saw earlier, younger children have a hard time being systematic. They might change three or four variables at once, then not know which one made the difference (it is the length of the string, remember?). Adolescents are more likely to be systematic, but even younger children can succeed if they get the right scaffolding. For example, without instruction and teacher-guided practice, no fifth graders and only a few eighth graders in one study succeeded on an isolation of variables task. With instruction and practice, most of the fifth and all the eighth graders succeeded (Zimmerman, 2007).

One important factor that leads to success for older adolescents and adults is that they are aware of their memory limitations—a metacognitive skill that starts to develop between the ages of 10 and 13. Knowing memory is limited, adolescents and adults generally don't attempt to remember the results of all the possible combinations they try, so they often use some kind of record keeping, chart, or notes. The bottom line is that with teaching and teacher-guided practice, many younger children and most adolescents can learn to design experiments that keep track of results with good record systems and thus can succeed in making correct inferences about the variable that causes the effect (Zimmerman, 2007).

Much of the research on inquiry has used microgenetic methods. Researchers track actions moment by moment to see what strategies are used and which ones are abandoned. As you saw in Chapter 6, there are few "aha" moments when an effective strategy is discovered and all ineffective strategies are dropped. Adolescents move back and forth between effective and ineffective strategies. Even after they discover the most effective isolation of variables strategy, for example, they do not use it exclusively. But gradually, they let go of less effective strategies and focus on the one that works. This pattern has been called the overlapping wave theory of strategy development, shown in Figure 6.4 on page 225 (Siegler, 2006).

Besides designing experiments that allow the young scientist to inquire, analyze, and make inferences, there is another challenge in scientific thinking—making an argument for your conclusions.

ARGUING. Constructing and supporting a position is central in science, in politics, in persuasive writing, and in critical thinking, to name just a few areas. In fact, one procedure that assesses cognitive development in college-aged students, the *College Learning Assessment* (Hersh, 2005), tests the ability to construct and evaluate arguments. The heart of **argumentation** (the process of debating a claim with someone else) is supporting your position with evidence and understanding, then refuting your opponent's claims and evidence. Children are not good at argumentation, adolescents are a bit better, and adults are better still, but not perfect. Children don't pay very much attention to the claims and evidence of the other person in the debate. Adolescents understand that their opponent in a debate has a different position, but they tend to spend much more time presenting their own position rather than understanding and critiquing their opponent's claims (Kuhn & Dean, 2004). It is as if the adolescents believe "winning an argument" means making a better presentation, but they don't appreciate the need to understand and weaken the opponent's claims. One reason that children and adolescents focus more on their own positions may be because remembering and processing your own and your opponent's claims and evidence at the same time is too cognitively demanding—there is just too much to think about. Whatever the reason, it is clear that few adolescents, even older adolescents, are skilled at argumentation. These skills are not natural. They take both time and instruction to learn (Kuhn, Goh, Iordanou, & Shaenfield, 2008; Udell, 2007).

But what has to be learned? In order to make a case while understanding and refuting the opponent's case, you must be aware of what you are saying, what your opponent is saying, and how to refute your opponent's claims. This takes planning, evaluating how the plan is going, reflecting on what the opponent has said, and changing strategies as needed—in other words, metacognitive knowledge and skills for argumentation. Deanna Kuhn and her colleagues (2008) designed a process for developing metacognitive argumentation skills. They presented a sixth grade class with this dilemma:

> The Costa family has moved to the edge of town from far away Greece with their 11-year-old son Nick. Nick was a good student and soccer player back home in Greece. Nick's parents have decided that in this new place, they want to keep Nick at home with them, and not have him be at the school with the other children. The family speaks only Greek, and they think Nick will do better if he sticks to his family's language and doesn't try to learn English. They say they can teach him everything he needs at home.
>
> What should happen? Is it okay for the Costa family to live in the town but keep Nick at home, or should they be required to send their son to the town school like all the other families do? (p. 1313)

Based on their initial position on the dilemma, the 28 students in the class were divided into two groups—"Nick should go to school" or "Nick should be taught at home." These two groups were divided again into same-gender pairs and all the "Nick should go to school" pairs moved to a room next door to their class. For about 25 minutes, each pair from one side "debated" a pair in the other room using instant messaging (IM). Later in the week the process was repeated, but with different pairs debating. In all, there were seven IM debates, so every "go to school" pair debated every "stay home" pair over several weeks. After four of the seven sessions, the pairs were given a transcript of the dialogue from their last debate, along with worksheets that scaffolded their reflection on their own arguments or the arguments of their opponents. The students evaluated their arguments and tried to improve them, with some adults coaching. These reflective sessions were repeated three times.

Next, there was a "showdown" debate—the entire "go to school" team debated the entire "stay home" team via one computer per team and a smart board. For this debate, half of each team prepared as experts on their position and half as experts on the opponent's arguments. After winter break and again after spring break, the whole process was repeated with new dilemmas.

You can see that there were three techniques in the study, supported by technology, to help students become more metacognitive about argumentation. First, they had to work in pairs to collaborate and agree on each communication with the opposing pair. Second, the researchers provided the pairs with transcripts of parts of their dialogue with the opponents so the partners could reflect on the discussions. Third, the dialogues were conducted via instant messaging, so the pairs had a permanent record of the discussion.

So what happened? Because the researchers had records of the written IMs of all the arguments, they could trace moment-by-moment changes in students' abilities—a microgenetic study of how argumentation skills develop (see Chapter 2 to review microgenetic methods). The pairs, IM, and reflection strategies were successful for most students in helping them take into account the opponent's position and create strategies for rebutting the opponent's arguments. Working in pairs seemed to be especially helpful. When adolescents and even adults work alone, they often are not successful at creating effective counterarguments and rebuttals (Kuhn & Franklin, 2006). In general, it is difficult for children and adults to stop focusing on what they believe and to listen to the opponents' arguments, even as a strategy to make their rebuttals more effective.

Epistemological Beliefs and Critical Thinking: What Does It Take to Know?

In the past few years, developmental researchers have looked at how beliefs about knowledge change as children mature (Hofer, 2005; Kuhn, 2005). One model is shown in Table 12.1 on the next page. Very young children are *realists*—they assume what they see and believe is what everyone else sees and believes because knowledge is just a copy of what is real and everyone experiences what is real the same way—"I can know what I see and you see the same thing." Critical thinking is unnecessary because "everybody knows." Elementary school children tend to be *absolutists*. They believe that facts can be correct or incorrect; some outside authority knows what is true—"The experts know what is right." Critical thinking helps to sort out the right facts from the wrong ones. During adolescence there is a move toward relativist or *multiplist* views. Experts often disagree, so all knowledge is just opinions—"you have your facts, I have mine—whatever." Critical thinking is irrelevant—it's all opinion. Finally, during early adulthood, some people come to an *evaluativist* view of knowledge that asserts ideas and opinions can be judged based on sound arguments and evidence—"the weight of the evidence is on the side of. . . ." Critical thinking evaluates claims against criteria and evidence.

The adolescent's discovery that knowledge is not absolute and external—that experts can disagree—leads to a radical change. Now everyone is right and "whatever" is the appropriate response to, well, whatever. Adolescents fall hard and deep into a well of whatever and not all of them make it back out (Chandler & Lalonde, 2003). The *multiplist* thinking of many adolescents explains in part why argument and inquiry don't come

TABLE 12.1 • **The Stages of Beliefs about Knowing**

LEVEL	ASSERTIONS ARE . . .	KNOWLEDGE IS . . .	CRITICAL THINKING IS . . .
Realist	COPIES of an external reality	from an external source and is certain	unnecessary
Absolutist	FACTS that are correct or incorrect in their representation of reality	from an external source and is certain but not directly accessible—producing false beliefs	a vehicle for comparing assertions to reality and determining their truth or falsehood
Multiplist	OPINIONS freely chosen by and accountable only to their owners	generated by human minds therefore uncertain	irrelevant
Evaluativist	JUDGMENTS that can be evaluated and compared according to criteria of argument and evidence	generated by human minds and is uncertain but susceptible to evaluation	valued as a vehicle that promotes sound assertions and enhances understanding

Source: Reprinted by permission of the publisher from Education for Thinking *by Deanna Kuhn, p. 31, Cambridge, Mass.: Harvard University Press, Copyright © 2005 by the President and Fellows of Harvard College.*

naturally. If experts disagree and all knowledge is just opinions, then why apply criteria to test a hypothesis? Why listen and respond to the opponents' argument? Argument and critical thinking are just irrelevant. If you think about it, the mature stance of the *evaluativist* (there are multiple perspectives, but some fit the evidence better than others) is a combination of the absolutist child's belief that there are right and wrong ideas and the multiplist adolescent's appreciation for multiple perspectives. With the move to a mature evaluativist view of knowledge, some older adolescents and adults realize that everyone has a right to a personal opinion, but some positions are better supported by evidence. Inquiry, argument, and critical thinking become central and valued processes of knowing (Kuhn, 2005).

So far our discussion of adolescent cognitive development has been pretty formal, rational, and logical. We have looked at *thinking like a scientist* for several perspectives—Piaget, Vygotsky, and information processing. We have examined abstract thinking, inductive and deductive reasoning, inquiry, argumentation, critical thinking, and epistemology—cold cognition. Partly because Piaget got the ball rolling that way, quite a bit of the research on adolescents has focused on this kind of "formal" thinking. We have dedicated several pages to scientific reasoning, inquiry, and argumentation, in part because these are not "natural" ways of thinking; teachers play a very important role in developing these ways of knowing. But you know from experience that not all thinking is scientific. What about everyday thinking? We turn to this question next.

Beyond Reason: Thinking in the Real World

For years, psychologists focused on rational processes in everyday thinking and decision making. But these ideas have been challenged. Several theories of how real people make real decisions in real life point to the role of biases, out-of-awareness processes, short cuts, fast and frugal thinking, gut feelings, and intuition (Boyer, 2006; Evans, 2008; Gigerenzer, 2007; Klaczynski, 2001, 2004, 2005). These often are called **dual process theories** because they describe two modes of thinking—conscious, logical, analytic thinking and out-of-awareness, emotional, intuitive thinking. Let's examine the dual process theory of Paul Klaczynski (2001), who has studied how adolescents make everyday decisions.

Analytic and Heuristic Thinking

As we have seen so far, adolescents are better than children at using formal reasoning. But adolescents, and adults for that matter, are not always logical or analytical. They often make quick decisions based on what seems or feels right—they use shortcuts and heuristics.

Heuristics are "rules of thumb" or intuitive guesses that you can apply quickly. For example, if we ask you whether a slim, short stranger who enjoys poetry is more likely to be a truck driver or an Ivy League classics professor, what would you say?

You might be tempted to answer based on your impressions and intuitions about truck drivers or professors. But consider the odds. With about 10 Ivy League schools and 4 or so classics professors per school, we have 40 professors. Say 10 are both short and slim, and half of the 10 like poetry: We are left with 5. But there are at least 400,000 truck drivers in the United States. If only 1 in every 800 of those truck drivers were short, slim poetry lovers, we have 500 truck drivers who fit the description. With 500 truck drivers versus 5 professors, it is 100 times more likely that our stranger is a truck driver (Myers, 2005). But most adolescents and adults would guess he is an Ivy League classics professor, based on what seems intuitively right. Notice if you took the problem out of the context of your stereotypes of truck drivers and professors and just did the probability calculations, you would be more analytical and logical. But if you went with your first impressions based on context and experience, you would be using heuristics and intuition. Table 12.2 contrasts these two kinds of thinking.

So what does this distinction between analytical and heuristic thinking have to do with adolescent thinking? Klaczynski and others have done many studies with questions like the truck driver question above and found that even though adolescents *can* use scientific thinking, they often *don't*. Here is another problem that has been used with adolescents:

> Linda is 31 years old, single, outspoken, and very bright. She majored in philosophy. As a student she was deeply concerned with issues of social justice and participated in antinuclear demonstrations. Which of the following two alternatives is more probable?
>
> 1. Linda is a bank teller.
> 2. Linda is a bank teller and active in the feminist movement. (Gigerenzer, 2007, p. 93)

You may be tempted to use heuristic thinking and choose option 2 because Linda's interest in social justice might include feminist causes, but then you probably stopped and thought, the number of bank tellers who also are feminists has to be smaller than the total number of bank tellers, so the answer has to be option 1. Only about 30% of middle adolescents (average age 16.3) in Klaczynski's study made the right choice in problems like these. With questions like those presented earlier and others, most of the adolescents in the study could use analytical thinking on some problems to make the correct choice, with older adolescents generally doing better than younger ones; verbal intelligence did not make a difference, but age and years of education did. In fact, some research demonstrates that mature decision making does not emerge until the middle twenties (Smetana, Campione-Barr, & Metzger, 2006). Let's look more closely at some of the problems that can arise with heuristic thinking.

TABLE 12.2 • **Two Kinds of Thinking: Analytic and Heuristic**

	DEFINITION	EXAMPLE	USED WHEN	COGNITIVE COSTS
Analytic	Formal, rational, abstract, thinking that separates a problem from the immediate situation to apply general logical rules—scientific	Slim, short stranger who enjoys poetry is more likely to be a truck driver because there are more of them	Required in school; have plenty of time to make decisions; to get the best answer	Effortful; time consuming; difficult
Heuristic/ Intuitive	Informal, based on feelings, biases, appearances, past experiences; relies on the immediate situation to guide gut-feeling responses	Slim, short stranger who enjoys poetry is more likely to be an Ivy League classics professor because that's what they are like	You need a quick decision; to get an OK answer; you have lots of experience in the situation	Effortless; quick; easy

SOME PROBLEMS WITH HEURISTICS. The mind can react automatically and instantaneously, but the price we often pay for this efficiency may be bad problem solving, which can be costly. Making judgments by invoking your stereotypes leads even smart people to make dumb decisions. For example, we might use **representativeness heuristics** to make judgments about possibilities based on our images and stereotypes of what best represents the situation—as in the truck driver problem—slim, short, poetry loving professors fit our stereotypes.

Adolescents and adults are busy people, and they often base their decisions on what they have in their minds at the time. When judgments are based on the availability of information in our memories, we are using the **availability heuristic.** If instances of events come to mind easily, we think they are common occurrences, but that is not necessarily the case; in fact, it is often wrong. People remember vivid stories and quickly come to believe that such events are the norm, but again, they often are wrong. For example, you may be surprised to learn the average family in poverty has only 2.2 children (Children's Defense Fund, 2005) if you have vivid memories from viewing a powerful film about a large, poor family. Data may not support a judgment, but **belief perseverance,** or the tendency to hold on to our beliefs, even in the face of contradictory evidence, may make us resist change.

The **confirmation bias** is the tendency to search for information that confirms our ideas and beliefs: This arises from our eagerness to get a good solution. You have often heard the saying "Don't confuse me with the facts." This aphorism captures the essence of the confirmation bias. Most people seek evidence that supports their ideas more readily than they search for facts that might refute them (Myers, 2005). For example, once you decide to buy a certain car, you are likely to notice reports about the good features of the car you chose, not the good news about the cars you rejected.

Our automatic use of heuristics to make judgments, our eagerness to confirm what we like to believe, and our tendency to explain away failure combine to generate *overconfidence.* Students usually are overconfident about how fast they can get their papers written; it typically takes twice as long as they estimate (Buehler, Griffin, & Ross, 1994). In spite of their underestimation of their completion time, they remain overly confident of their next prediction. Students are not the only ones—this book took twice as long to write as we first estimated.

BENEFITS OF DUAL PROCESSES. The preceding section makes it sound like heuristic thinking always is a problem, but that is not the case. There are too many decisions to be made in a day to be logical and analytical about every one. We often apply heuristics automatically to make quick judgments; that saves us time in everyday problem solving. Heuristics and intuitive thinking often quickly identify a "good enough" decision. You probably know someone who is immobilized by decisions and never has enough information to act. That person would benefit from using heuristics to "just do it."

Luckily, humans can move quickly based on affect and heuristics or more deliberately based on logic and analysis. In fact, there probably are individual differences in tendencies to use more affective or rational approaches. Also, some research shows that with increasing experience and expertise, decisions become quicker and seem intuitive, but that is because the intuition is grounded in years of study and reflection on what works (Gerrand, Gibbons, Houlihan, Stock, & Pomery, 2008).

Dual-process theories of decision making have been helpful in understanding adolescent risk taking.

Risk Taking

Until recently, most research on adolescents' decision making about risky behaviors—such as smoking, drinking, using drugs, or driving recklessly—assumed that these decisions were rational. The theory was that teenagers weighed the risks and rewards and then decided to drink—or not. But if we take dual-processing models seriously, we can see there is more to these decisions than cold cognition. Meg Gerrand and her colleagues (2008) have proposed a dual-process approach to health risk decision making that describes two modes of thinking operating simultaneously—deliberate, systematic, rational thinking and affective, heuristic, experiential thinking. In the rational mode, adolescents consider what they know about risks, how their family will react, and other information. On the affective side, images

RELATING TO

EVERY ADOLESCENT

▸ Cultural Perspectives on Decision Making

THE STRONG AFRICAN AMERICAN FAMILIES Program (SAAF) is designed to help parents support their children in avoiding problem drinking. The program includes both the usual logical information about alcohol and how to better monitor adolescents, but also has a curriculum based on images and heuristics. The goal is to make children's mental images of drinkers more negative and less appealing and also to educate the children about the differences between planned and reactive behavior, so they will be less willing to drink when the social situation is "intoxicating." Results show that the positive effects of the program are caused more by the image components than by the logical, information components (Brody et al., 2006). Table 12.3 shows the protective factors the program targets to increase and the risk factors it seeks to decrease. You can see that both information and images are part of the intervention.

TABLE 12.3 • **The Strong African American Families Program: Intervention Target Areas**

PROTECTIVE FACTORS TO INCREASE	RISK FACTORS TO DECREASE
Caregiver • Age-appropriate expectations of youth • Monitoring skills	Caregiver • Harsh or inconsistent discipline • Harsh or indulgent parenting style
Youth • Positive future orientation • Self-regulation • Strong racial identity • Acceptance of peer influences	Youth • Overestimation of peer substance usage and sexual involvement • Poor image of African Americans • Poor emotion regulation
Family • Family cohesiveness • Family routines • Reinforcement of youth assets • Racial socialization • Empathy between youth and parent • Conflict resolution skills • Supportive parent-child relationship • Supportive family involvement	Family • Parent-youth conflict • Poor communication of family rules • Chaotic family environment • Family conflict
Peer • Prosocial friends • Skills for resisting negative peer pressure	Peer • Negative peer influence

Source: Table based on Brody, G. H., Murry, V. M., Gerrard, M., Gibbons, F. X., Molgaard, V., McNair, L., Brown, A. C., Willis, T. A., Spoth, R. L., Luo, Z., Chen, Y. F. & Neubaum-Carlan, E. (2004). The Strong African American Families Program: Translating research into prevention programming, Child Development, 75, 900–917. *Reprinted with permission from the Center for Family Research, University of Georgia.*

and feelings are central. What are kids my age who drink like—popular and cool or rejects and stupid? If images are more positive, then the adolescent is more willing to drink. When adolescents find themselves in social situations that make drinking easier—a party with alcohol flowing and no adults around—positive images and willingness are more powerful than rational risk assessment and logic.

Using the dual-process approach as a base, researchers have designed interventions that target both logic and images. See the ***Relating to Every Adolescent*** feature for an example.

Adolescent Egocentrism

Another characteristic of adolescent everyday thinking is **adolescent egocentrism.** Unlike egocentric young children, adolescents do not deny that other people may have different perceptions and beliefs; they just become very focused on their own ideas. Adolescents spend much time analyzing their own beliefs and attitudes. This extreme focus on self has some interesting consequences. Adolescents may decide they are unique; no one has ever felt or experienced exactly what they do. Like Danielle at the beginning of this chapter, they may be sure that parents or other adults "just don't understand!" And those dangerous consequences of piercing an eyebrow (or smoking, or going to a party where there will be drinking, or . . .)—those consequences will not happen to me because *I am unique!*

Adolescent egocentrism also leads to what Elkind (1967, 1985) calls the sense of an *imaginary audience* described in Chapter 11—the feeling that everyone is watching. Thus, adolescents believe that others are analyzing them: "Everyone noticed that I wore this shirt twice this week." "The whole class thought my answer was dumb!" You can see that social blunders or imperfections in appearance can be devastating if "everybody is watching." Luckily, this feeling of being "on stage" seems to peak in early adolescence by age 14 or 15, although in unfamiliar situations we all may feel our mistakes are being noticed. And maybe they are. Sometimes the audience is not so imaginary. Adolescents, with their developing abilities to think more abstractly and their interest in ideals, can be harsh critics—of each other and of themselves.

Diversity in Adolescent Cognitive Development and School Achievement

We saw at the beginning of the chapter that cognitive development becomes increasingly diversified as adolescents make choices and have different experiences. In this section we look at two individual characteristics that can influence choices and experiences—gender and ethnicity—and we explore reasons for differences in school achievement for some groups of students.

Cognitive Abilities: Does Gender Matter?

From infancy through the preschool years, most studies find few differences between boys and girls in overall mental and motor development or in specific abilities. During the school years and beyond, psychologists find no differences in general intelligence on the standard measures; these tests have been designed and standardized to minimize sex differences. However, scores on some tests of specific abilities show sex differences (Bruner, Krauss, & Kunter, 2007).

SEX DIFFERENCES IN SPECIFIC ABILITIES. Girls do better on verbal fluency, writing, and arithmetic calculation, for example, whereas boys do better on verbal analogies and math word problems (Spelke, 2005). Girls and boys seem to approach solving problems in different ways. In navigation tasks, for example, boys tend to use geometric solutions (follow a diagonal path, the street is perpendicular, etc.) and girls rely on landmarks (turn at the Starbucks). In comparing two visual objects, boys form a mental image and turn it in their minds, whereas girls tend to compare features of the two objects. In math word problems, girls use verbal computation and boys spatial imagery, which can give the boys an advantage on timed tests like the math section of the SAT (Gallagher & Kaufman, 2005). But with instruction, both girls and boys can learn to use these different strategies. Diane Halpern and her colleagues (2007) summarize the research:

> By the end of grade school and beyond, females perform better on assessments of verbal abilities when assessments are heavily weighted with writing and the language-usage items cover topics with which females are familiar; sex differences favoring females are much larger in these conditions than when assessments of verbal abilities do not include writing. In contrast, males excel on certain visuospatial-ability measures. (p. 40)

These differences, though detectable, are small. There are women, like your text author Anita, who navigate with both geometry and landmarks, whereas her husband is always turned around and has parallel streets running perpendicular in his mind. There are boys whose math calculation skills are excellent. The larger concerns are that at the very top levels of achievement in mathematics, there are more males than females and therefore there are more men than women in high-level careers in science, engineering, and mathematics. So these differences in quantitative abilities have received the most attention (Halpern et al., 2007).

There is a caution, however. The scores of males tend to be more variable in general, so there are more males than females with very high *and* very low scores on tests (Halpern et al., 2007; Johnson, Carothers, & Deary, 2008). There also are more boys diagnosed with learning disabilities, ADHD, and autism. In addition, in most studies of sex differences, race and socioeconomic status are not taken into account. When racial groups are studied separately, African American females outperform African American males in high school mathematics; however, there is little or no difference in the performance of Asian American girls and boys in math or science (Grossman & Grossman, 1994; Yee, 1992). Girls in general tend to get higher grades than boys in mathematics classes (Halpern et al., 2007).

WHY THESE DIFFERENCES? What is the basis for the differences? The answers are complex and contested. One popular explanation is that from the beginning, males are more oriented toward objects and girls are more oriented toward people (Connellan et al., 2000). But Elizabeth Spelke (2005) concluded that thousands of studies of infants over a span of 30 years have found no male advantage for perceiving, learning, or reasoning about objects. In fact, "male and female infants perceive and learn about objects in highly convergent ways" (p. 952). Some researchers argue that evolution has favored spatial and navigational skills in males because they hunted, followed trails, explored, built shelters and used tools, etc. (Buss, 1995; Geary, 1995, 1999), whereas other researchers relate these skills to males' more active play styles and their participation in athletics (Linn & Hyde, 1989; Newcombe & Baenninger, 1990; Stumpf, 1995). Cross-cultural comparisons suggest that much of the difference in visual-spatial and mathematics abilities comes from learning, not biology. Girls in many countries score as well as or better than boys on quantitative tests. For example, international studies of 15-year-olds in 41 countries show no sex differences in mathematics for half of the countries tested (Angier & Chang, 2005). More recently in the 2007 *Trends in International Mathematics and Science Study* (TIMSS), in eighth grade, on average, girls had higher math achievement than boys (Mullis, Martin, & Foy, 2009). However, the International Comparisons in Fourth-Grade Reading Literacy (Mullis, Martin, Gonzalez, & Kennedy, 2003) revealed that in 34 countries, fourth grade boys scored below girls in reading literacy. Elizabeth Spelke (2005) concludes:

> In summary, males and females show somewhat different cognitive profiles when presented with complex tasks that can be solved by multiple strategies, but they show equal performance on tasks that tap the core foundations of mathematical thinking. Moreover, males and females show equal abilities to learn advanced, college-level mathematics. Insofar as mathematical ability is central to students' progress in the sciences, males and females would seem to be equally capable of learning science. (p. 955)

In the 2007 Trends in International Mathematics and Science Study (TIMSS) at the eighth grade, on average, girls had higher math achievement than boys. However, the International Comparisons in Fourth-Grade Reading Literacy revealed that in 34 countries, fourth-grade boys scored below girls in reading literacy.

In spite of the evidence that males and females are equally capable of learning high-level science and mathematics, there are more men than women in high-level science and mathematics jobs, as we saw earlier. The situation has improved. In 1973, only 6% of the Ph.D. scientists in academia and business were women; by 2006, the number was 27%. At the same time, the number of women who were full professors in science had gone from 5% to 20% (Angier, 2009). But men still outnumber women in these jobs. For example, there are from 7 to 14 times more men than women faculty in science and math at the top universities. These numbers may only get worse: In 2005, 70% of female high school graduates went to college, but only 20% of college graduates in engineering were women (Frehill & Di Fabio, 2008).

There is so much interest in preparing students in science, technology, engineering, and mathematics that we now have an acronym for the fields—STEM, short for (you guessed it) science, technology, engineering, and mathematics. Many programs focus on STEM education, getting more women and other underrepresented groups into STEM majors. As you can see in Figure 12.2, there are more women than men in some fields, such as agricultural engineering, but men still dominate in most STEM degrees.

What could explain these disparities? The answers appear to be sex differences in motivation, life priorities, self-confidence, and interests, as well as differences in vulnerability to *stereotype threat,* something that can affect the performance of many groups of students, as we will see later in this chapter (Johnson et al., 2008). Another possibility is gender bias in teaching.

GENDER BIAS IN TEACHING. Studies showing that adults rated a math paper attributed to "John T. McKay" a full point higher on a 5-point scale than the same paper attributed to "Joan T. McKay" suggests that gender discrimination may be a danger in teaching (Angier & Chang, 2005). There has been quite a bit of research on teachers' treatment of male and female

FIGURE 12.2

WOMEN EARNING STEM DEGREES IN THE UNITED STATES IN 2006

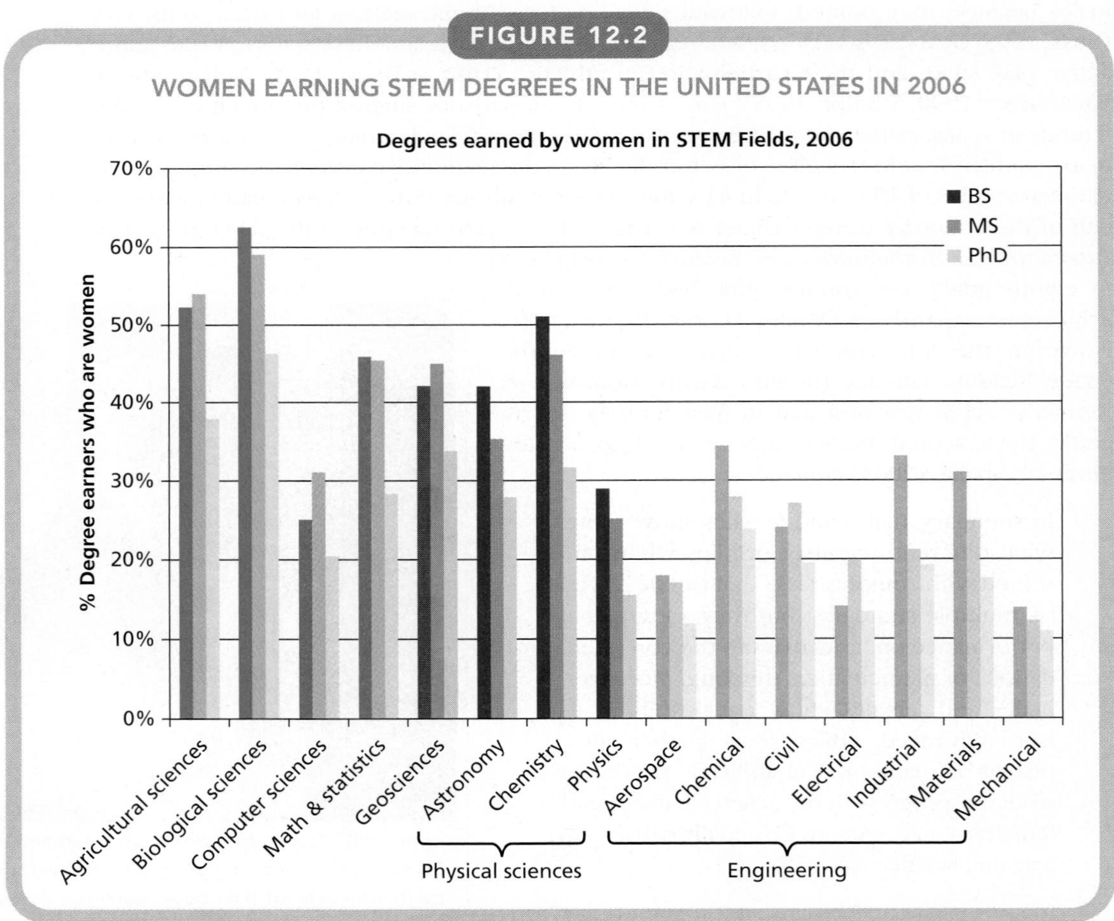

Source: National Science Foundation. (2007a). Women, minorities, and persons with disabilities in science and engineering: *NSF 07-315. Arlington, VA, National Science Foundation, Division of Science Resources Statistics.*

students. You should know, however, that most of these studies have focused on White students, so the results reported in this section hold mostly for White male and female students.

Many studies document what seem to be biases favoring boys. One of the best-documented findings of the past 25 years is that teachers have more overall interactions and more negative interactions, but not more positive interactions, with boys than with girls (Jones & Dindia, 2004). This is true from preschool to college. Teachers ask more questions of males, give males more feedback (praise, criticism, and correction), and give more specific and valuable comments to boys. As girls move through the grades, they have less and less to say. By the time students reach college, men are twice as likely to initiate comments as women (Bailey, 1993; Sadker & Sadker, 1994). The effect of these differences is that from preschool through college, girls, on the average, receive 1,800 fewer hours of attention and instruction than boys (Sadker, Sadker, & Klein, 1991). Of course, these differences are not evenly distributed. Some boys, generally high-achieving White students, receive more than their share, whereas high-achieving girls receive the least teacher attention.

Not all biases in school favor boys. In the past 10 years in North America, Western Europe, Australia, and some Asian countries, there have been questions about whether schools are serving boys well. This concern is fueled by data from many countries that seems to show underachievement in boys. For example, data from a U.S. government survey shows the average twelfth grade boy writes at the level of an average eighth grade girl (Younger & Warrington, 2006). More dramatic accusations include that schools are trying to destroy "boys' culture" and force "feminine, frilly content" on boys (Connell, 1996).

> Discrimination against girls has ended, the argument runs. Indeed, thanks to feminism, girls have special treatment and special programs. Now, what about the boys? It is boys who are slower to learn to read, more likely to drop out of school, more likely to be disciplined, more likely to be in programs for children with special needs. In school it is girls who are doing better, boys who are in trouble—and special programs for boys that are needed. (Connell, 1996, p. 207)

One explanation for why boys struggle in school is that the expectations of schooling do not fit the way boys learn (Gurian & Henley, 2001), particularly African American boys (Stinson, 2006). Another suggestion is that boys sabotage their own learning by resisting school expectations and rules to "display their masculinity and get respect" (Kleinfeld, 2005, p. B6). Critics of the schools suggest that boys need changes such as smaller classes, more discussions, better discipline, mentoring programs, and more men in their schools—90% of elementary teachers are female (Svoboda, 2001).

Would single-sex schools help boys and girls learn more? Research in the late 1980s and early 1990s generally supported the single-sex secondary schools for girls and for African American and Latino/a students regardless of gender (Lee & Bryk, 1986; Lee & Marks, 1990; Riordan, 1998). Girls who attended all-girl high schools made greater achievement gains, had higher educational aspirations, and had more positive attitudes toward academics, and these advantages followed them to college. The results are even more dramatic for African American and Latino/a adolescents. These students in single-sex schools averaged almost a year higher on achievement tests than similar students in coed settings (Riordan, 1990, 1994, 1998).

A current suggestion for making schools more effective for both boys and girls is single-sex classrooms (Weil, 2008). The research today on this approach from around the world suggests that teaching boys and girls in separate classes can be have positive effects on student learning, motivation, and engagement, but only if certain demanding conditions are met. Teachers must realize that there are no boy- or girl-specific teaching strategies: Good teaching is good teaching. Regrouping students by sex does not make teaching easier; in fact, it can make class management more difficult. To succeed, both teachers and students must understand that the goal of single-sex classrooms is better learning for everyone in an atmosphere that supports more open discussions with less concern about making impressions on peers (Younger & Warrington, 2006).

We can consider this research on boys and girls in school in the context of **person-environment fit theory.** According to this theory, development and learning are greatest when the needs and characteristics of the learner fit the characteristics of the learning environment

(Eccles & Roeser, 2006). The needs of the individual might be identified based on their gender, culture, language, learning abilities or disabilities, or developmental level. For example, the research on teaching girls in science and mathematics has led to a picture of girl-friendly classrooms. In these classrooms, learning is cooperative or individualized rather than competitive. The focus is applied and person-centered rather than highly theoretical or "book-centered" (Eccles & Roeser, 2006). We are not convinced that these ideas apply only to girls. The ***Connecting with Adolescents*** guidelines provide additional ideas about avoiding gender bias for all students in your classes. Some are taken from Rop (1997/1998). Another source of concern for all of us involves achievement gaps between some racial and ethnic groups.

Ethnic and Racial Differences in School Achievement

A major concern in schools is that some ethnic groups consistently achieve below the average for all students (Okagaki, 2006; Uline & Johnson, 2005). This pattern of results tends to hold for all standardized achievement tests, but the gaps have been narrowing over the past two to three decades.

CONNECTING WITH ADOLESCENTS

Guidelines for Teachers: Avoiding Gender Bias in Teaching

Check to see if textbooks and other materials you are using present an honest view of the options open to both males and females.

Examples

1. Identify whether both males and females are portrayed in traditional and nontraditional roles at work, at leisure, and at home.
2. Discuss your analyses with students, and ask them to help you find sex-role biases in other materials—magazine advertising, video games, TV programs, and news reporting, for example.

Watch for any unintended biases in your own classroom practices.

Examples

1. Do you group students by sex for certain activities? Is the grouping appropriate?
2. Do you call on one sex or the other for certain answers—boys for math and girls for poetry, for example?
3. Monitor your metaphors. Don't ask students to "tackle the problem."

Look for ways in which your school may be limiting the options open to male or female students.

Examples

1. Find out what advice guidance counselors give to students in course and career decisions.
2. Look into whether there is a good sports program for both girls and boys.
3. See if girls are encouraged to take advanced placement courses in science and mathematics and if boys are encouraged in English and foreign language classes.

Use gender-free language as much as possible.

Examples

1. Make sure you speak of "law-enforcement officer" and "mail carrier" instead of "policeman" and "mailman."
2. Be sure you name a committee "head" instead of a "chairman."

Provide role models.

Examples

1. Assign articles in professional journals written by female research scientists or mathematicians.
2. Have recent female graduates who are majoring in science, math, engineering, or other technical fields come to class to talk about college.
3. Create electronic mentoring programs for both male and female students to connect them with adults working in areas of interest to the students.

Make sure all students have a chance to do complex, technical work.

Examples

1. Experiment with same-sex lab groups so girls do not always end up as the secretaries, boys as the technicians.
2. Rotate jobs in groups or randomly assign responsibilities.

What if you witness gender bias as a student teacher? See this site for ideas: http://www.tolerance.org/teach/magazine/features.jsp?p=0&is=36&ar=563#

Because many students from minority groups are also economically disadvantaged, it is important to separate the effects of these two sets of influences on school achievement. For example, in an analysis of National Assessment of Educational Progress (NAEP) mathematics test results, James Byrnes (2003) found that less than 5% of the variance in math test scores was associated with race, but about 50% of the variance came from differences in SES, motivation, and exposure to learning opportunities (course work, calculator use, homework, etc.). Although there still are consistent differences among ethnic groups on tests of cognitive abilities, most researchers agree that the reasons for these differences are mainly the product of cultural mismatches and language differences, a result of growing up in poverty, or the legacy of discrimination.

THE LEGACY OF DISCRIMINATION. When we considered explanations for why low-SES students have trouble in school in Chapter 9, we listed the low expectations and biases of teachers and fellow students. This has been the experience of many ethnic minority students as well. One suggested solution is desegregation—educating students of different racial and ethnic groups together. But years of research on the effects of desegregation have mostly shown that legally mandated integration is not a quick solution to the detrimental effects of centuries of racial inequality. In part because White students left integrated schools as the number of students of color increased ("white flight"), many urban schools today are more segregated than they were before the Supreme Court ordered busing and other desegregation measures. The schools in Los Angeles, Miami, Baltimore, Chicago, Dallas, Memphis, Houston, and Detroit have fewer than 11% non-Hispanic White students. And in almost 90% of the schools that have mostly African American and Latina/o students, at least half of the students live in poverty, so racial segregation becomes economic segregation as well (Ladson-Billings, 2004; Orfield & Frankenberg, 2005). Too often, even in integrated schools, minority group students are resegregated in low-ability tracks. Simply putting people in the same building does not mean that they will come to respect each other or even that they will experience the same quality of education (Ladson-Billings, 2004; Pettigrew, 1998).

FOCUSING ON STRENGTHS. Rather than focusing on achievement gaps, many educators have called for more research on the successes of African American and Latino/a students. Berry (2005) studied two middle-school-aged African American boys who were successful in mathematics. In the lives of those students, Berry found support and high expectations from family and teachers; positive math experiences in preschool and elementary school; positive identities as math students; and connections to church and athletic extracurricular activities. Unfortunately, these factors are not available for all students. Eric Dearing and his colleagues (2009) studied participation in extracurricular activities for 1,420 predominantly African American children and found that the likelihood of participating in these activities is related to family income, with the poorest children least likely to reap the benefits of participation.

Berry (2005) encouraged educators and researchers "to focus on the success stories of those African American men and boys who are successful to identify the strengths, skills, and other significant factors it takes to foster success" (p. 61). One final theme characterized the successful African American boys: Their families had prepared them to understand and deal with discrimination. Recent research points to an intriguing explanation related to discrimination for the gaps in performance between many groups—males and females, as well as African American, Latino/a, and European American students. The explanation is stereotype threat.

Stereotype Threat

Stereotype threat is "an apprehensiveness about confirming a stereotype" (Aronson, 2002, p. 282). The basic idea is that when individuals are in situations in which a stereotype applies, they bear an extra emotional and cognitive burden. The burden is the possibility of confirming the stereotype, either in the eyes of others or in their own eyes. Thus, when girls are asked to solve complicated mathematics problems, for example, they are at risk of confirming widely held stereotypes that girls are inferior to boys in mathematics. It is not necessary that the individual even believe the stereotype. All that matters is that the person is *aware* of the stereotype and *cares about performing* well enough to disprove its unflattering implications (Aronson et al., 1999; Huguet & Régner, 2007). What are the results of stereotype threat? Recent research provides answers that should interest all parents and teachers.

One review of the research on women, math, and stereotype threat concluded that very subtle clues that might activate anxiety, such as asking test takers to indicate their gender on an answer sheet before taking a math test, tend to lower math scores for women, especially when tests are difficult, the women are moderately identified with the math field, and being female is an important part of their identity. The differences are small on average—something like a female with average math ability scoring 450 instead of the expected average of 500 on an SAT- or GRE-type test. One study estimated that removing stereotype threat might mean an additional 6% of women getting a passing score on a high-stakes calculus test (Nguyen & Ryan, 2008; Wout, Dasco, Jackson, & Spencer, 2008). In other studies, girls in high school and college have scored below boys on a math test when stereotype threats are present, but the same as boys when these threats are not present (Smith & Hung, 2008). Just telling the girls that the math test they are about to take does not reveal gender differences is enough to eliminate any differences.

In a series of experiments, Joshua Aronson, Claude Steele, and their colleagues demonstrated that when African American or Latino college students are put in situations that induce stereotype threat, their performance suffers (Aronson, 2002; Aronson & Steele, 2005; Okagaki, 2006). For example, in an experiment at Stanford University, African American and White undergraduate subjects were told that the test they were about to take would precisely measure their verbal ability. A similar group of subjects was told that the purpose of the test was to understand the psychology of verbal problem solving and not to assess individual ability. As shown in Figure 12.3, the group of African American students who believed their ability was being tested solved about one-half as many problems as the other group of African American students who were not told the test assessed ability. The performance of European American students was not affected by the threat conditions.

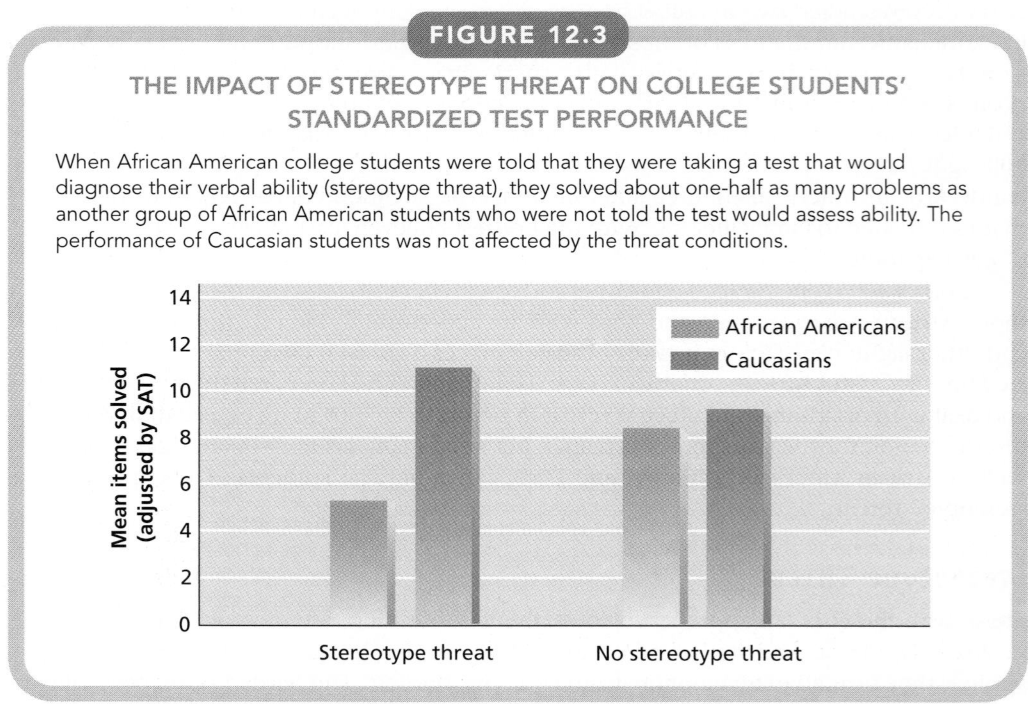

Source: Figure: "The Impact of Stereotype Threat on College Students' Standardized Test Performance," by J. Aronson, M. J. Lustina, M. F. Salinas, and C. M . Steele, in Readings About the Social Animal, 4E, Elliot Aronson (ed.), Worth Pubilshers, © 1973, 1977, 1981, 1992, 1995.

All groups, not just minority group students, can be susceptible to stereotype threat. In another study, the subjects were White male college students who were very strong in mathematics. One group was told that the test they were taking would help experimenters determine why Asian students performed so much better than Whites on that particular test. Another group just took the test. The group that faced the stereotype threat of confirming that "Asians are better in math" scored significantly lower on the test (Aronson et al., 1999). The individuals most vulnerable to stereotype threat are those who care the most and who are most deeply invested in high performance (Ryan & Ryan, 2005). The pressures of No Child Left Behind testing are likely to increase this vulnerability.

WHAT HAPPENS? Why does stereotype threat affect test performance? Self-handicapping and anxiety are part of the problem (Delgado & Prieto, 2008; Ryan & Ryan, 2005). When students are in situations that evoke stereotype threats, such as high-pressure tests, they tend to adopt self-handicapping strategies such as not trying or procrastinating—they just want to survive without looking stupid. But because they put off studying or didn't try, they are anxious and unprepared during the test. Anxiety and worry interfere with thinking about math solutions. Two other related explanations are that by increasing anxiety, stereotype threat reduces working memory capacity—so students can't hold as much in their minds (Okagaki, 2006) and that stereotype threat also decreases interest and engagement in the task: Why get absorbed in something that will make you look incompetent? (Smith, Sansone, & White, 2007).

If students continue to develop self-defeating strategies to avoid looking stupid—they withdraw, claim to not care, exert little effort, or even drop out of school—they psychologically disengage from success and claim "math is for nerds" or "school is for losers." Once students define math and science as "uncool," it is unlikely they will exert the effort needed for real learning. We cannot say that all differences between boys and girls in math performance are due to stereotype threat (Sackett, Hardison, & Cullen, 2005), but the process probably plays a role. The message for teachers is to help all students see mathematics and science achievement as part of their identity.

COMBATING STEREOTYPE THREAT. In one study, teachers in rural Texas randomly divided 138 seventh graders into four groups for a computer class. In the classes that got positive information suggesting intelligence can be improved and everyone can learn math, year-end math achievement scores improved for the girls (Good, Aronson, & Inzlicht, 2003). So, believing that intelligence can be improved might inoculate students against stereotype threat. A book by Carol Dweck (2006) called *Mindset: The New Psychology of Success* discusses how a positive mindset of growth and improvement can be learned and will be an asset throughout life. Other ideas include using role models and emphasizing that if a boy does better than a girl in math, he probably studied harder or persisted longer. The same is true for a girl who does better in writing—stress that she may have worked harder or revised more.

What can teachers do in any school to help close the achievement gap? In many ways this is a question about person-environment fit theory again (Eccles & Roeser, 2006). How can we make the environment of the school fit the culture, language, abilities, and values of the students? How can teachers build on all the cultures in the classroom? Here are three general teaching principles to guide you in finding answers to these questions.

KNOW YOUR STUDENTS. We must learn who our students are and the legacies they bring (Delpit, 2003). Nothing you read in a text will teach you enough to understand the lives of all your students. If you can take other courses in college or read about other cultures, we encourage you to do it. But reading and studying are not enough. You should get to know your students' families and communities. Elba Reyes, a successful bilingual teacher for children with special needs, describes her approach:

> Usually I find that if you really want to know a parent, you get to know them on their own turf. This is key to developing trust and understanding the parents' perspective. First, get to know the community. Learn where the local grocery store is and what the children do after school. Then schedule a home visit at a time that

> is convenient for the parents. The home environment is not usually as ladened with failure. I sometimes observed the child being successful in the home, for example, riding a bicycle or helping with dinner. (Bos & Reyes, 1996, p. 349)

Try to spend time with students and parents on projects outside of school. Ask parents to help in class or to speak to your students about their jobs, their hobbies, or the history and heritage of their ethnic group. In the elementary grades, don't wait until a student is in trouble to have the first meeting with a family member. Watch for and listen to the ways that your students interact in large and small groups. Have students write to you, and write back to them. Eat lunch with one or two students. Spend some nonteaching time with them.

RESPECT YOUR STUDENTS. From knowledge ought to come respect for your students' learning strengths—for the struggles they face and the obstacles they have overcome. We must believe in our students (Delpit, 2003). For a child, genuine acceptance is a necessary condition for developing self-esteem. Sometimes the self-image and occupational aspirations of minority children actually decline in their early years in public school, probably because of the emphasis on majority culture values, accomplishments, and history. By presenting the accomplishments of particular members of an ethnic group or by bringing that group's culture into the classroom (in the form of literature, history, art, music, or any cultural knowledge), teachers can help students maintain a sense of pride in their cultural group. This integration of culture must be more than the "tokenism" of sampling ethnic foods or wearing costumes. Students should learn about the socially and intellectually important contributions of the various groups. There are many excellent references that provide background information, history, and teaching strategies for different groups of students (e.g., Banks, 2009; Bennett, 2011; Milner, 2009; Tiedt & Tiedt, 2009).

TEACH YOUR STUDENTS. The most important thing you can do for your students is teach them to read, write, speak, compute, think, and create—through constant, rigorous, culturally connected instruction (Delpit, 2003). Too often, goals for low SES or minority group students have focused exclusively on basic skills. Students are taught words and sounds, but the meaning of the story is supposed to come later. Years ago, Knapp, Turnbull, and Shields (1990, p. 5) made these suggestions. They are still excellent:

- Focus on meaning and understanding from beginning to end—for example, by orienting instruction toward comprehending reading passages, communicating important ideas in written text, or understanding the concepts underlying number facts.
- Balance routine skill learning with novel and complex tasks from the earliest stages of learning.
- Provide context for skill learning that establishes clear reasons for needing to learn the skills.
- Influence attitudes and beliefs about the academic content areas as well as skills and knowledge.
- Eliminate unnecessary redundancy in the curriculum (e.g., repeating instruction in the same mathematics skills year after year).

And finally, teach students directly about how to be students. In the early grades, this could mean directly teaching the courtesies and conventions of the classroom: how to get a turn to speak, how and when to interrupt the teacher, how to whisper, how to get help in a small group, how to give an explanation that is helpful. In the later grades, it may mean teaching the study skills that fit your subject. You can ask students to learn "how we do it in school" without violating principle number two above—respect your students. Ways of asking questions around the kitchen table at home may be different from ways of asking questions in school, but students can learn both ways, without deciding that either way is superior. And you can expand ways of doing it in school to include more possibilities. The ***Connecting with Adolescents*** guidelines give more ideas for teachers.

CONNECTING WITH ADOLESCENTS

Guidelines for Teachers: Culturally Relevant Teaching

Experiment with different grouping arrangements to encourage social harmony and cooperation.
Examples
1. Try "study buddies" and pairs.
2. Organize heterogeneous groups of four or five.
3. Establish larger teams for older students.

Provide a range of ways to learn material to accommodate a range of learning styles.
Examples
1. Give students verbal materials at different reading levels.
2. Offer visual materials—charts, diagrams, and models.
3. Provide tapes for listening and viewing.
4. Set up activities and projects.

Teach classroom procedures directly, even ways of doing things that you thought everyone would know.
Examples
1. Tell students how to get the teacher's attention.
2. Explain when and how to interrupt the teacher if students need help.
3. Show which materials students can take and which require permission.
4. Demonstrate acceptable ways to disagree with or challenge another student.

Learn the meaning of different behaviors for your students.
Examples
1. Ask students how they feel when you correct or praise them. What gives them this message?
2. Talk to family and community members and other teachers to discover the meaning of expressions, gestures, or other responses that are unfamiliar to you.

Emphasize meaning in teaching.
Examples
1. Make sure students understand what they read.
2. Try storytelling and other modes that don't require written materials.
3. Use examples that relate abstract concepts to everyday experiences; for instance, relate negative numbers to being overdrawn in your checkbook.

Get to know the customs, traditions, and values of your students.
Examples
1. Use holidays as a chance to discuss the origins and meaning of traditions.
2. Analyze different traditions for common themes.
3. Attend community fairs and festivals.

Help students detect racist and sexist messages.
Examples
1. Analyze curriculum materials for biases.
2. Make students "bias detectives," reporting comments from the media.
3. Discuss the ways that students communicate biased messages about each other and what should be done when this happens.
4. Discuss expressions of prejudice such as anti-Semitism.

For ways to use technology for culturally relevant teaching see: http://preservicetech.edreform.net/techindicator/culturallyrelevantpedagogy

Contexts for Cognitive Development

One theme is especially important for all who work with adolescents: The "good enough" intellectual environment that supported basic cognitive development during infancy, early childhood, and the middle childhood years *is not good enough* to fully develop the adolescents' cognitive potentials (Kuhn & Franklin, 2006). The thinking and reasoning abilities and expertise described in this chapter will not happen "naturally" as adolescents grow. Parents, teachers, guides, support, and thoughtfully designed learning experiences are needed.

As in previous chapters, let's examine the child, now an adolescent, in context. European American and European adolescents spend less and less time with parents and more time with peers, but the family remains an important context for child development. Obviously, peers are another increasingly influential context. Finally, schools and jobs are two other contexts that shape cognitive development. For all ages, but particularly in the adolescent years, it is difficult to separate contextual influences on cognitive development from influences on emotional/social development. With this caution in mind, in this chapter we explore families, peers, and the school as contexts for cognitive development; then, Chapter 13 looks again at these contextual factors in relation to social and emotional development.

The Family

As you know by now, quite a bit of research has focused on parenting styles. Diane Baumrind (1991, 1996) and the other researchers who built on her findings identified four parenting styles based on the parents' high or low levels of *warmth* and *control*. We described these styles in earlier chapters, but to review, *authoritative* parents (high warmth, high control) set clear limits, enforce rules, and expect mature behavior. But they are warm with their children and allow more democratic decision making (Hoffman, 2001). *Authoritarian* parents (low warmth, high control) seem cold and controlling in their interactions with their children. The children are expected to be mature and to do what the parent says, "Because I said so!" *Permissive* parents (high warmth, low control) are warm and nurturing, but they have few rules or consequences for their children and expect little in the way of mature behavior. *Rejecting/Neglecting/Uninvolved* parents (low warmth, low control) don't seem to care at all and can't be bothered with controlling, communicating, or teaching their children.

In broad strokes, there are differences in adolescents' social and academic behavior based on their parents' styles. At least in European American, middle-class families, children of *authoritative* parents are more likely to do well in school, be happy with themselves, and relate well to others. Children of *authoritarian* parents are more likely to feel guilty or depressed, and children of *permissive* parents may have trouble interacting with peers—they are used to having their way (Spera, 2005; Steinberg, 2005).

Of course, the extreme of permissiveness is indulgence. Indulgent parents cater to their adolescent's every whim; perhaps it is easier than being the adult who must make unpopular decisions. Both *indulgent* and *rejecting/neglecting/uninvolved* parenting styles can be harmful. For example, when 3,407 ninth through twelfth grade European American students described their parents' styles and their peer-group orientation, those students, especially girls, who characterized their parents as uninvolved were more likely to be oriented toward "partyers" and "druggies" who did not endorse adult values. Boys with indulgent parents were more likely to be oriented toward fun-cultures such as "partyers" (Durbin, Darling, Steinberg, & Brown, 1993). In contrast, adolescents who characterized their parents as *authoritative* (demanding but responsive, rational, and democratic) were more likely to favor well-rounded crowds who did well in school, such as "normals" and "brains" (Collins, Maccoby, Steinberg, Hetherington, & Bornstein, 2000).

You also saw in Chapter 1 that there are cultural differences in parenting styles. Even though the authoritative parenting style seems to benefit adolescents of all ethnicities and SES levels (Steinberg, 2005), some researchers believe that the styles discussed above fit the European American, middle-class culture best. Other cultures should be assessed in ways that fit the meaning and values of the culture (Smetana et al., 2006). For example, Ruth Chao's (2001) research on Chinese parenting style shows that strict parenting fits the Confucian ideal of child-centered training, and is not like the authoritarian adult-centered punitive style described by Baumrind.

Recently, parenting style has been reconceptualized as multidimensional—not just high to low on control, but high to low on what kind of control? Is the parent focused on controlling the adolescent's thoughts and feelings or on controlling his or her behavior? Trying to control thoughts and feelings is more intrusive and is associated with behavior problems for adolescents. But when parents try to influence behaviors by monitoring their teen's activities and friends, the adolescents tend to be better adjusted and higher achieving in school. More parental involvement and monitoring seem productive in early and middle adolescence, but older adolescents need more autonomy to make decisions. One group that may lack adequate parental monitoring at every age is adolescents in very affluent communities where parents are caught up in work and social events and may neglect their adolescents (Smetana et al, 2006).

Peers

Conventional wisdom claims that during adolescence parents have less and less influence, but peer influence grows. Is this right? Well, it depends. To understand the power of peers, we have to look at situations in which the values and interests of parents clash with those of peers, and then see whose influence dominates. In these comparisons, peers usually win in matters of style, socializing, and priorities for spending time—fun versus schoolwork, for example. Parents (and teachers) still are influential in matters of morality, career choice, and religion. Peers and parents affect different aspects of an adolescent's life. Of course, parents often guide their teens in choices of friends, so the parents can have an indirect effect on peer influences (Harris, 1998; Smetana, 2006). Let's focus here on peers and cognitive outcomes such as achievement in school.

CROWDS AND CLIQUES. Think back to high school—did you have friends in any of these groups: normals, populars, brains, jocks, partyers, stoners, others? What were the main "crowds" at your school? How did your friends influence you? Laurence Steinberg and his colleagues have studied the role of parents, peers, and community contexts in school achievement and identified large peer groups or *crowds* such as "jocks," "brains," "populars," and "druggies" that share common behaviors and attitudes (Durbin, Darling, Steinberg, & Brown, 1993; Steinberg, 1998). Based on a three-year study that surveyed 20,000 students in nine high schools in Wisconsin and California, Steinberg found that adolescents' peers provide incentives for certain activities and ridicule others, which creates a school culture that affects the way the teachers behave. One in every five students Steinberg studied said that their friends made fun of people who tried to do well in school. When asked what crowd they would most like to belong to:

> [F]ive times as many students say the "populars" or "jocks" as say the "brains." Three times as many say they would rather be "partyers" or "druggies" than "brains." And of all the crowds, the "brains" were least happy with who they are—nearly half wished they were in a different crowd. (Steinberg, 1998, p. 332)

Steinberg concluded that about 40% of the students were just going through the motions of learning. About 90% had copied someone else's homework and 66% had cheated on a test within the last year. Steinberg claims that this lack of investment is due in part to peer pressure because for many adolescents, "peers—not parents—are the chief determinants of how intensely they are invested in school and how much effort they devote to their education" (1998, p. 331). Let's look more closely at these powerful peer influences.

PEER SUPPORT FOR PEER LEARNING. Today, students often are expected to collaborate in peer learning groups (Johnson & Johnson, 2009). In these groups, peers can support or undermine learning. First, the undermining. Without careful planning and monitoring by the teacher, group interactions can hinder learning and reduce rather than improve social relations in classes. For example, if there is pressure in a group for conformity—perhaps because rewards are being misused or one student dominates the others—interactions can be unproductive and unreflective. Misconceptions might be reinforced, or the worst, not the best, ideas may be combined to construct a superficial understanding. Students who work in groups but arrive at wrong answers may be more confident that they are right—a case of "two heads are worse than one" (Puncochar & Fox, 2004). Also, the ideas

To be a member of a crowd or clique has implications for how you dress, act, and speak; who can be a friend; and what you think about school.

of low-status students may be ignored or even ridiculed while the contributions of high-status students are accepted and reinforced, regardless of the merit of either set of ideas (Anderson, Holland, & Palincsar, 1997).

What about peer support of learning? How can teachers avoid these problems? David and Roger Johnson (1999) list five elements that define true cooperative learning groups:

- Face-to-face interaction
- Positive interdependence
- Individual accountability
- Collaborative skills
- Group processing

Students *interact face-to-face* and close together, not across the room. Group members experience *positive interdependence*—they need each other for support, explanations, and guidance. Even though they work together and help each other, members of the group must ultimately demonstrate learning on their own; they are held *individually accountable* for learning, often through individual tests or other assessments. *Collaborative skills* are necessary for effective group functioning. Often, these skills, such as giving constructive feedback, reaching consensus, and involving every member, must be taught and practiced before the groups begin a learning task. Finally, members monitor *group processes* and relationships to make sure the group is working effectively and to learn about the dynamics of groups. They take time to ask, "How are we doing as a group? Is everyone working together?"

Research in grades 8 through 12 in Australia found that students in cooperative groups that were structured to require positive interdependence and mutual helping learned more in math, science, and English than students in unstructured learning groups (Gillies, 2003). In addition, compared to students in the unstructured groups, students in the structured groups also said learning was more fun.

In practice, the effects of learning in a group vary, depending on what actually happens in the group and who is in it. If only a few people take responsibility for the work, these people will learn, but the nonparticipating members probably will not. Students who ask questions, get answers, and attempt explanations are more likely to learn than students whose questions go unasked or unanswered. In fact, there is evidence that the more a student provides elaborated, thoughtful explanations to other students in a group, the more the *explainer* learns. Giving good explanations appears to be even more important for learning than receiving explanations (O'Donnell, 2006; Webb, Farivar, & Mastergeorge, 2002; Webb & Palincsar, 1996). In order to explain, you have to organize the information, put it into your own words, think of examples and analogies (which connect the information to things you already know), and test your understanding by answering questions. These are excellent learning strategies (King, 1990, 2002).

Good explanations are relevant, timely, correct, and elaborated enough to help the listener correct misunderstandings; the best explanations tell why (Webb et al., 2002; Webb & Mastergeorge, 2003). For example, in a middle-school mathematics class, students worked in groups on the following problem:

> Find the cost of a 30-minute telephone call to the prefix 717 where the first minute costs $0.22 and each additional minute costs $0.13.

The level of explanation and help students received was significantly related to learning; the higher the level, the more learning. Table 12.4 shows the different levels of help. Of course, the students must pay attention to and use the help in order to learn. And the help-receiver also has responsibilities if learning is to go well. For example, if a helper says, "13 times 29," then the receiver should say, "Why is it 29?" Asking good questions and giving clear explanations are critical, and usually these skills must be taught.

Often, cooperative learning strategies include group reports to the entire class. If you have been on the receiving end of these class reports, you know that they can be deadly dull. To make the process more useful for the audience as well as the reporters, Annemarie Palincsar and Leslie Herrenkohl (2002) taught the class members to use intellectual roles as

TABLE 12.4 • **Levels of Help in Cooperative Groups**

Students are more likely to learn if they give and get higher level help.

LEVEL	DESCRIPTION AND EXAMPLE
Highest	
6	Verbally labeled explanation of how to solve part or all of the problem ("Multiply 13 cents by 29, because 29 minutes are left after the first minute.")
5	Numerical rule with no verbal labels for the numbers ("This is 30, so you minus 1.")
4	Numerical expression or equation ("13 times 29.")
3	Numbers to write or copy ("Put 13 on top, 29 on the bottom. Then you times it.")
2	Answer to part or all of the problem ("I got $3.77.")
1	Non-content or non-informational response ("Just do it the way she said.")
0	No response
Lowest	

Source: From "Productive helping in cooperative groups," by N. M. Webb, S. H. Farviar, & A. M. Mastergeorge. Theory in Practice, 41(1), p. 14.

they listened to reports. These roles were based on the scientific strategies of predicting and theorizing, summarizing results, and relating predictions and theories to results. Some audience members were assigned the role of checking the reports for clear relationships between predictions and theories. Other students in the audience listened for clarity in the findings. And the rest of the students were responsible for evaluating how well the group reports linked prediction, theories, and findings. Research shows that using these roles promotes class dialogue, thinking and problem solving, and conceptual understanding (Palincsar & Herrenkohl, 2002).

Schools (and the Teachers in Them)

How do schools serve as contexts for adolescent cognitive development? Because adolescents spend so much time in schools, we could write pages and pages about this topic—but we promise to be selective. In this section we will look at person- and stage-environment fit, how transitions to middle or high school affect students, teachers' relationships with students, and part-time work.

One way to explore schools as contexts for cognitive development is to apply *person-environment fit theory*, discussed earlier in this chapter. When the person's needs are developmental, we talk about **stage-environment fit theory** (Eccles, 2004). This theory describes the possible effects of a match (or mismatch) between the developmental needs of adolescents and the opportunities afforded by their social environments, including schools. But because adolescence is marked by many changes including puberty, the development of abstract thinking abilities, shifts in family relationships, and transitions to new schools—all happening at the same time—what "fits" developmental needs at one point may not fit a few months later. For example, as they mature, adolescents have increasing needs for autonomy—the chance to make choices that affect their lives. Do their families, peers, and schools change in response to the adolescents' needs for increasing autonomy? According to stage-environment fit theory, when adolescents' social environments respond to their changing needs, then positive outcomes are likely. But when parents, schools, or teachers don't change or when they respond in ways that conflict with needs, then the adolescent's development may be harmed and problems will arise (Gutman & Eccles, 2007).

TRANSITIONS IN SCHOOL. After elementary school, in the transition to middle school, students confront an increased focus on grades and performance as well as more competition on all fronts—academic, social, and athletic. Just when they are eager to make decisions and assume more independence, students encounter more rules, required courses, and assignments. They change from a close connection with one teacher all year to more impersonal relations with many teachers in many different subjects across the year. Some researchers have argued that these features of middle school—more rules and regulations but fewer personal connections with adults—are just the opposite of what these developing adolescents need. So the stage-environment fit is weak. These developing adolescents also go from being the most mature and highest status students in a small, familiar elementary school to being the "babies" in a large, impersonal middle school (Murdock, Hale, & Weber, 2001; Rudolph, Lambert, Clark, & Kurlakowsky, 2001).

In a policy brief prepared for the Congressional Children's Caucus, Jacquelynne Eccles (1999) summarizes the mismatches between needs and social contexts that young adolescents encounter when they move to middle school. These mismatches

> . . . seem especially harmful in that they emphasize competition, social comparison, and ability self-assessment at a time of heightened self-focus; they decrease decision-making and choice at a time when the desire for control is growing; they emphasize lower level cognitive strategies at a time when the ability to use higher level strategies is increasing; and they disrupt social networks at a time when adolescents are especially concerned with peer relationships and may be in special need of close adult relationships outside of the home. (p. 2)

In recent years, as educators better understood the developmental needs of young adolescents, they refined a middle school philosophy that contrasts with the junior high school philosophy of treating younger adolescents as "small" high school students. The National Middle School Association published a summary of this philosophy called *This We Believe: Keys to Educating Young Adolescents* (NMSA, 2010). In the publication they listed 16 attributes and characteristics of successful schools, summarized in Figure 12.4. You can see that schools with these characteristics would have a better stage-environment fit for young adolescents.

In the move to high school, students often experience even larger, more bureaucratic structures and rules. There is little opportunity for students to form the relationships with adults that support their development. The chance for positive mentoring relationships, described earlier, is lost (Eccles & Roeser, 2006).

THE STUDENTS' PERSPECTIVE. Of course, some aspects of the transitions to middle or high school are attractive: increased freedom, moving from class to class, different teachers, new friends, and extracurricular options (Akos & Galassi, 2004). But from the students' perspective, the new social demands of middle or high school also can be scary. You may remember the fears and concerns you had. Anita was sure she would get lost in her big, two-story junior high, fumble her locker combination, and be late to class—a fate punishable by something horrible, she was sure. Common fears fall into three categories: social (dealing with older students or bullies, making and keeping friends); procedural (learning school rules, navigating larger buildings, and Anita's dreaded locker issues); and academic (more homework, worries about tough classes—math in particular, pressure to make good grades, and college admission for high school students).

What are the potential effects of mismatches between adolescents' needs and the social environment of middle and high schools? For many adolescents, academic motivation and achievement decline along with self-efficacy for school. Some students respond to the pressure to perform and competition for grades by cheating. For other students, soon after the transition to high school, academic achievement declines again, and they drop out of school. Those who don't drop out fall farther behind (Akos & Galassi, 2004; Anderman & Maehr, 1994; Anderman & Midgley, 2004; Wigfield, Eccles, & Pintrich, 1996).

What can be done to help adolescents make smoother transitions to middle school and high school? The ***Connecting with Adolescents*** guidelines on page 512 have ideas for parents and teachers.

FIGURE 12.4

ESSENTIAL ATTRIBUTES AND CHARACTERISTICS OF SUCCESSFUL SCHOOLS FOR YOUNG ADOLESCENTS

The National Middle School Association identified 16 attributes and characteristics of successful schools for young adolescents.

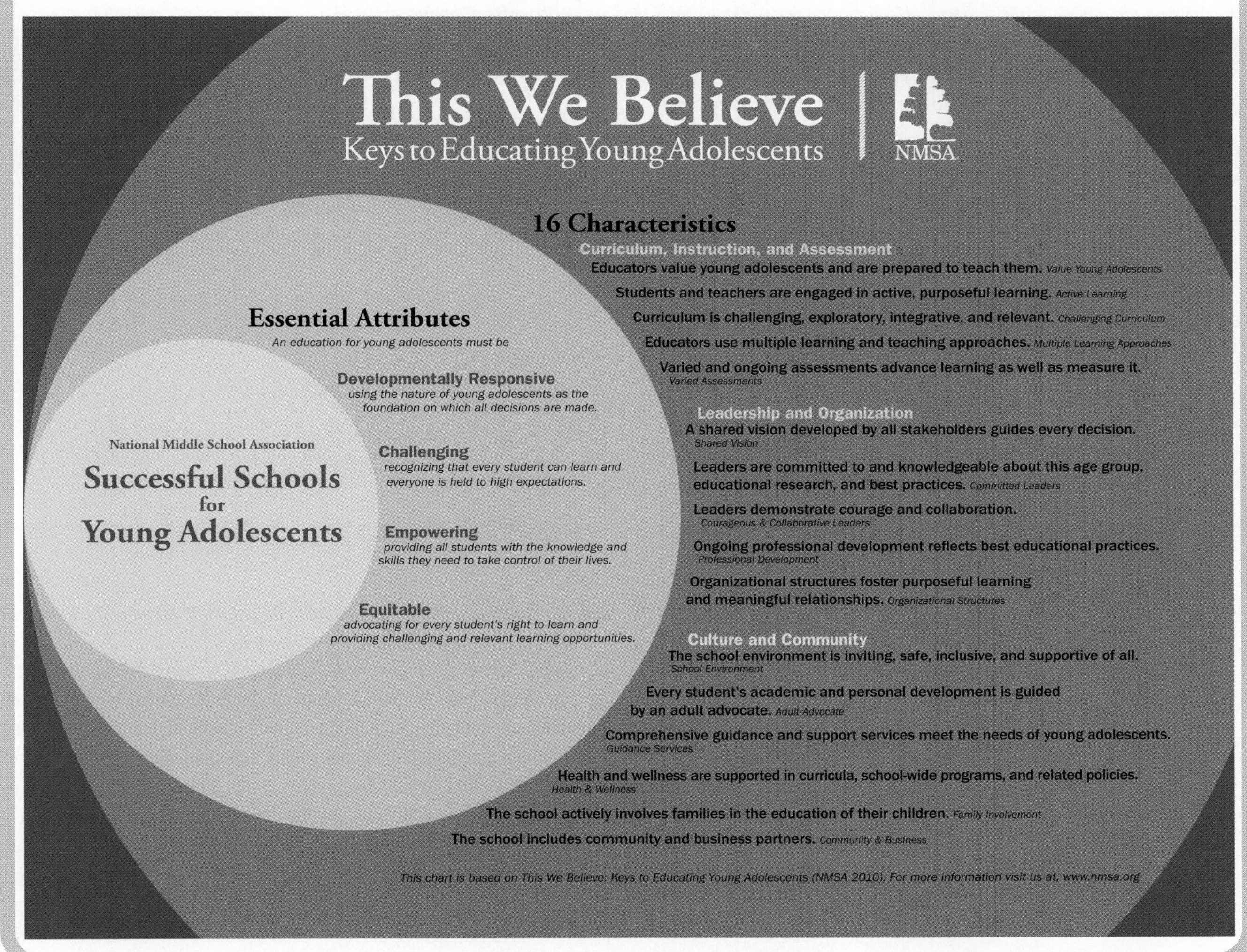

Source: From This We Believe: Keys to Educating Young Adolescents, *© 2010 National Middle School Association. Reprinted with permission from National Middle School Association.*

TEACHERS: ACADEMIC AND PERSONAL CARING. When researchers ask students to describe a "good teacher," three qualities are at the center of their descriptions. Good teachers have positive interpersonal relationships—they care about their students. Second, good teachers keep the classroom organized and maintain authority without being rigid or "mean." Finally, good teachers are good motivators—they can make learning fun by being creative and innovative so students learn something (Noguera, 2005; Woolfolk Hoy & Weinstein, 2006).

For the past 15 years, research has documented the value and importance of positive relationships with teachers for students at every grade level (Davis, 2003). For example, one of Anita's doctoral graduates studied middle-school mathematics classes and found that students' perceptions of their teachers' affective support and caring were related to the effort they invested in learning math (Sakiz, Pape, & Woolfolk Hoy, 2008). Tamera Murdock and Angela Miller (2003) found that eighth-grade students' perceptions that their teachers cared

CONNECTING WITH ADOLESCENTS

Guidelines for Families and Teachers: Supporting School Transitions

Discuss academic expectations with students.
Examples
1. Without panicking students, show examples of texts and assignments for the grade they are moving into.
2. Allow time to discuss "scare stories" students may have heard.

Teach appropriate time management and study skills before and after the transition.
Examples
1. Practice using a simple assignment book or computer calendar.
2. Practice note taking from class or from readings.

Make sure teachers at the sending and receiving schools are in communication.
Examples
1. Get e-mail addresses so you can be in touch with other teachers.
2. Learn about academic expectations and assignments that often prove difficult.

Set up supports for transitioning students.
Examples
1. Establish homework hotlines.
2. Offer tutoring programs for entering students staffed by upperclassmen in their school.
3. Make sure the first weeks allow time for positive "getting to know you" social activities.

Source: Adapted from Akos & Galassi, 2004, available at http://findarticles.com/p/articles/mi_m0KOC/is_4_7/ai_n6033397/pg_11?tag=content;col1

about them were significantly related to the students' academic motivation, even after taking into account the motivational influences of parents and peers.

Students define caring in two ways. One is *academic caring*—setting high, but reasonable expectations and helping students reach those goals. The second is *personal caring*—being patient, respectful, humorous, willing to listen, interested in students' issues and personal problems. For higher-achieving students, academic caring is especially important, but for students who are placed at risk and often alienated from school, personal caring is critical (Cothran & Ennis, 2000; Woolfolk Hoy & Weinstein, 2006). In fact, in one study in a Texas high school, the Mexican and Mexican American students saw teacher caring as a prerequisite for their own caring about school; in other words, they needed to be *cared for* before they could *care about* school (Valenzuela, 1999). Unfortunately, in the same school, the mostly non-Latino teachers expected the students to care about school before they would invest their caring in the students. And for many teachers, caring about school meant behaving in more "middle-class" ways.

These contrasting student and teacher views can lead to a downward spiral of mistrust. Students withhold their cooperation until teachers "earn it" with their authentic caring. Teachers withhold caring until students "earn it" with respect for authority and cooperation. Marginalized students expect unfair treatment and behave defensively when they sense any unfairness. Teachers get tough and punish. Students feel correct in mistrusting, and become more guarded and defiant. Teachers feel correct in mistrusting and become more controlling and punitive, and so it goes (Woolfolk Hoy & Weinstein, 2006).

Of course, students need both academic and personal caring. Katz (1999) interviewed eight Latino immigrant students in a middle school and concluded:

> High expectations without caring can result in setting goals that are impossible for the student to reach without adult support and assistance. On the other hand, caring without high expectations can turn dangerously into paternalism in which teachers feel sorry for "underprivileged" youth but never challenge them academically. High expectations and caring in tandem, however, can make a powerful difference in students' lives. (p. 814)

FIGURE 12.5

HOW MANY HIGH SCHOOL STUDENTS WORK?

From 1997 to 2003, working during school or in the summer steadily increases from freshman to senior year.

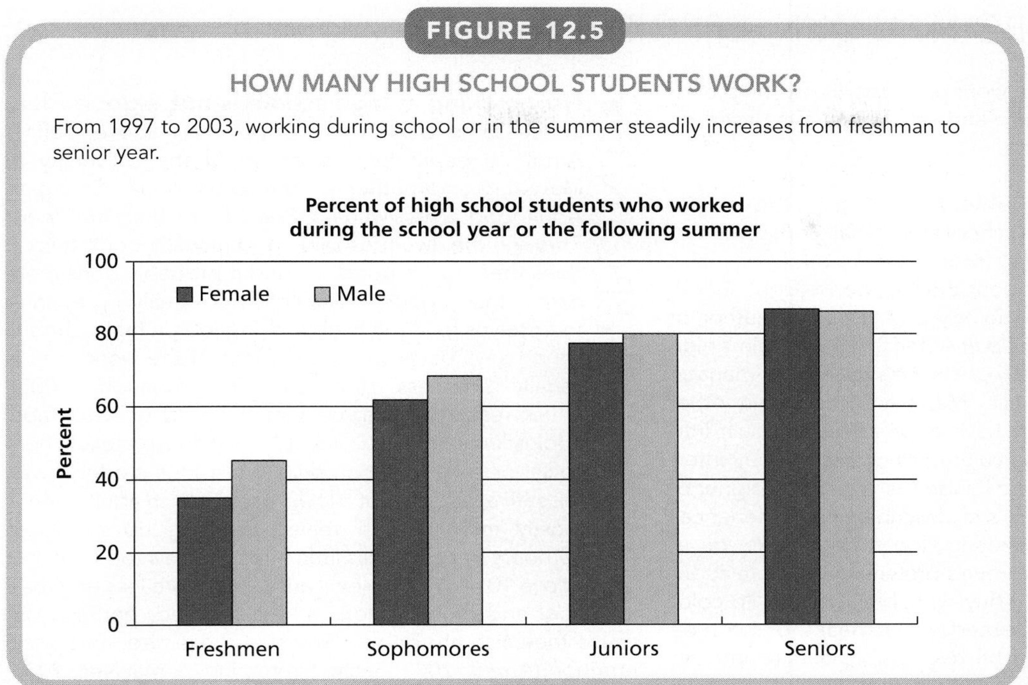

Source: U.S. Department of Labor, Bureau of Labor Statistics http://www.bls.gov/opub/ted/2005/apr/wk4/art04.htm

In short, caring means not giving up on students in addition to demonstrating and teaching kindness in the classroom (Davis, 2003).

PART-TIME WORK IN SCHOOL. Did you work in high school? If so, you were not alone. As you can see in Figure 12.5, by senior year over 80% of students have worked at least part time. Did the job take time away from their education or did the job give them an education—about effort, punctuality, and office politics? These are some of the arguments for and against part-time work for adolescents. Even the research has reached contradictory conclusions, as you can see in the ***Point/Counterpoint*** on the next page.

Staying In and Dropping Out of School

Over their lifetime, people without high school degrees earn substantially less than those who have completed high school, and so they pay less in taxes. They often depend on public assistance for health care or childcare, and they are more likely to end up in prison (Barton, 2009). How many students complete high school? This is a much more complicated question than it first appears. Do we mean in North America, or in the world? If the United States, then in which state or what type of school? Do alterative certifications such as the GED count as graduation? Every one of these questions has a different answer.

Completing secondary education is not necessarily a goal for youth in every country. For example, in many countries of Southern Africa, only about 10–20% of adolescents complete secondary school, whereas in most developed countries about 70–80% complete high school. In some countries such as Japan and Sweden, the graduation rate is closer to 100% (Cuadra & Moreno, 2005).

In the United States, a recent report by the Educational Testing Service (Barton, 2009) used multiple data sources to estimate the trends in graduation rates over the past 40 years. The researchers reached six conclusions:

- The true high school graduation rate is substantially lower than the official rate, reported for example by the United States Census.
- The rate has been declining over the past 40 years.

POINT/COUNTERPOINT: Should Teens Work Part Time?

Many high school students work part time. Is this helpful or harmful? There are both pro and con arguments based on research and common sense.

POINT

Yes, working is valuable. Arguments for the value of part-time work in high school assert that work gives students marketable skills, fosters good work habits, and provides knowledge about the real world (Light, 1995). Jeylan Mortimer, a sociology professor and author of *Working and Growing up in America* (2005), claims high school students learn to deal with supervisors, manage time, and handle stress. Many adolescents in other countries such as Germany have apprenticeships built into their secondary school curriculum. When *USA Today* interviewed Liz Lange, CEO of Liz Lange Maternity, a designer of high-end maternity clothes, she described her experiences working in the beauty marketing department at Revlon at age 16. "I was analyzing women's preferences, and relationships between their beauty-buying habits, such as lip color vs. nail color," she says. "I learned what it means for me to be somewhere every day and be responsible and to interact with others" (Hagenbaugh, 2005).

COUNTERPOINT

No, working in high school is not a good idea. In the same *USA Today* article cited above, Jeffrey Arnett, a psychology professor at the University of Maryland and author of the 2004 book, *Emerging Adulthood: The Winding Road From the Late Teens Through the Twenties* said, "I personally don't think it does them much good . . . and it probably does more harm than good. They're not really preparing themselves for adult life by having jobs in high school," Arnett says because "the content of the work itself is usually mindless drudgery" (Hagenbaugh, 2005). Other researchers agree that the kind of work most adolescents do in high school really doesn't teach them social or self-regulation skills. Most jobs are low level, repetitive, and do not allow close ties with adults. Teens mostly interact with teens. Working up to about 10 hours per week has little effect on development, but above 10 hours problems arise. Teens are less engaged in school and more anxious and depressed, perhaps because they also are getting less sleep, exercise, and good nutrition (Arnett, 2009; Sears, Simmering, & MacNeil, 2006; Steinberg, Fegley, & Dornbush, 1993). In a study of over 12,000 youth from 1979 to 1991, Light (1995) found no effect of high school work, positive or negative, on wages earned after high school.

Beware of Either/Or

In reality, it is difficult to untangle the effects of working in high school from other factors that might affect learning and life after high school. For example, some students do not have part-time jobs because they live in impoverished communities where there are few employment opportunities (Light, 1995). Living in these areas also is associated with going to lower quality schools, so which factor matters most—not working or going to an inferior school? It is clear that what matters is the type of work adolescents actually do on the job and how much time is taken away from other productive activities such as school or extracurricular involvement.

- Graduation rates for minority group students are substantially lower than for the majority group and have not converged with majority group graduation rates over the past 35 years.
- The decline in high school graduation rates is among native populations and is not solely a consequence of increasing proportions of immigrants and minorities in American society.
- The decline in high school graduation rate explains part of the recent slowdown in college attendance.
- The pattern of the decline of high school graduation rates by gender helps to explain the recent increase in male-female college attendance gaps.

These are large trends. Let's look more closely at the discrepancy between ethnic groups. Across all the United States in 2007, about 80% of the White students graduated from high school, compared to 60% of African American students, 62% of Latino/a students, 91% of Asian/Pacific Islanders, and 61% of Native Americans. But again, these are averages

TABLE 12.5 • **Selected State High School Completion Rates (in Percents) 2006–2007, by Race/Ethnicity**

STATE	TOTAL	AMERICAN INDIAN/ ALASKA NATIVE	WHITE NON-HISPANIC	BLACK	HISPANIC	ASIAN/PACIFIC ISLANDER
Alabama	67	61	80	60	62	91
Alaska	69	72	72	59	61	80
Connecticut	82	63	87	71	64	97
Georgia	64	48	69	55	53	95
Iowa	87	59	88	70	71	90
California	71	62	79	58	59	90
Florida	65	65	69	52	62	92
Maine	79	73	78	85	87	100
Nebraska	86	56	90	73	67	98
New Jersey	84	91	88	73	74	100
New Mexico	59	54	69	58	54	84
Ohio	79	68	84	55	66	96
North Dakota	83	53	86	93	62	100
Texas	72	85	99	65	63	99

Source: The total rate is from The Averaged Freshman Graduation Rate for Public High Schools from the Common Core Data: School Years 2002–2005 and 2003–2004, *National Center for Education Statistics, table 3, June 2007. The rates by race and ethnicity are from Tables 2 through 5 of the NCES Common Core Data Base, http://nces.ed.gov/pubs2010/2010313/tables/table_02.asp . Original sources explain reasons for missing data, which include no report from state, missing data in report, or very small populations.*

across all the states. If we look state by state, we see some interesting differences, as you can see in the sample of states in Table 12.5.

Nevada (not in Table 12.5 because there were no data by race for 2007) has the lowest overall completion rate (52%), whereas Iowa, Nebraska, Vermont, and Wisconsin all have rates above 86%. In the other states, completion rates for White students range from 66% in South Carolina to 94% in Wisconsin; for African Americans from 51% in Florida and South Carolina to 100% in New Hampshire; Latino/a students from 44% in South Carolina to over 90% in West Virginia and Vermont; and Asian American students from 77% in Hawaii to 100% in Arkansas, Delaware, Idaho, Illinois, Maine, Missouri, Montana, New Hampshire, New Jersey, North Dakota, Oklahoma, South Dakota, and West Virginia (NCES, 2009). There probably are multiple reasons for these differences. Some states have many more students of all ethnicities than other states. Some states have more families in poverty, more urban schools, less support for education, and other challenges.

What Can Be Done?

So many factors influence students' staying in or dropping out of school that we can't consider all of them. But we can look at three that are under the control of schools and teachers: teacher quality, instructional practices, and zero tolerance approaches to school and classroom management.

TEACHER QUALIFICATIONS. In the last 10 years we have seen quite a bit or research on teacher quality and student learning. Teacher education researcher Linda Darling-Hammond (2000) examined the ways in which teacher qualifications are related to student achievement across states. Her findings indicated that the quality of teachers—as measured by whether the teachers were fully certified and had a major in their teaching field—was related to student performance. In fact, measures of teacher preparation and certification were by far the strongest predictors of student achievement in reading and mathematics, both before and after controlling for student poverty and English language proficiency. Michelle Fine and her colleagues interviewed students in some of California's urban schools and synthesized research from other studies. They concluded:

> The longer students stay in schools with structural problems, high levels of unqualified teachers, inappropriate pedagogy, teacher turnover, and inadequate instructional materials, the wider the academic gaps between White children and children of color or wealthy children and poor children, and the more alienated they become. (Fine, Burns, Payne, & Torre, 2004, p. 2200)

Economists have found similar results (Aaronson, Barrow, & Sander, 2007). But is dropping out of school related directly to teacher qualifications? There are not many studies on this question, but research by Cory Koedel (2008) has identified a clear connection between math teacher qualifications and student graduation rate. So teacher quality, measured in terms of qualifications, may well be related to students staying in school.

INSTRUCTIONAL PRACTICES. High school students who are deeply engaged in their classes and feel a sense of belonging are less likely to drop out. What supports engagement? Relationships with parents, teachers, and peers are critical, as we saw earlier in this chapter (Legault, Green-Demers, & Pelletier, 2006). We can sum up the importance of relationships and belonging in supporting engaged learning by examining a comment in the report of the Committee on Increasing High School Students' Engagement and Motivation to Learn (2004):

> Although learning involves cognitive processes that take place within each individual, motivation to learn also depends on the student's involvement in a web of social relationships that supports learning. The likelihood that students will be motivated and engaged is increased to the extent that their teachers, family, and friends effectively support their purposeful involvement in learning in school. Thus a focus on engagement calls attention to the connection between a learner and the social context in which learning takes place. Engaging schools promote a sense of belonging by personalizing instruction, showing an interest in students' lives, and creating a supportive, caring social environment. (p. 3)

This is the big picture. What about specific practices? Jacquelynne Eccles and Robert Roeser (2006) reviewed the research on high school students' motivation to learn and identified practices that support motivation and engagement, shown in Table 12.6.

All of the strategies and practices we have described so far using person-environment fit theory and stage-environment fit theory will help to create an engaging learning environment for adolescents that should keep them in school. Next we look at one management policy that seems to encourage dropping out: zero tolerance.

ZERO TOLERANCE. The arguments for zero tolerance, which means that school rules are strictly enforced without considering circumstances, focus on school safety and the responsibilities of schools and teachers to protect the students and themselves. An Internet search using keywords [*zero tolerance* and *schools*] will locate a wealth of information about the policy, much of it against it. For example, Oren Dorrell reported this incident in the November 2, 2009 edition of *USA Today*:

> The most recent high-profile case [of zero tolerance] involved Zachary Christie, a 6-year-old who was suspended for five days on Sept. 29 after he brought a camping utensil that was part knife, fork and spoon to Downes Elementary in Newark, Del. School officials considered it a dangerous instrument and suspended the boy, adding that he couldn't return to Downes until he completed at least 45 days at an alternative school.

TABLE 12.6 • **Practices That Support High School Students' Motivation to Learn**

Jacquelynne Eccles and Robert Roeser (2006) reviewed the research on high school students' motivation to learn and identified these practices that support motivation and engagement.

PRACTICE	EXAMPLE
In teaching and grading, stress personal improvement rather than social comparisons and competition.	Have students chart their personal progress. Keep portfolios of first attempts, revisions, best work.
Communicate high expectations to all students.	Show examples of previous students' good work. Return work with ideas for improvement. Give bonus points for careful revisions.
Make sure all students participate. Don't let some students hide.	Develop a system for calling on everyone. Have quick work conferences and set goals with each student.
Include hands-on, minds-on activities such as laboratory exercises and field-based data collections.	In math, conduct surveys, then analyze and graph results. Use Internet databases to research questions of interest to the local community.
Support student autonomy, choices, decision making, and responsibility.	Design several different ways to meet a learning objective (e.g., a paper, a compilation of interviews, a test, a news broadcast) and let students choose one. Encourage them to explain the reasons for their choice. If students choose to work with friends and do not finish a project because too much time was spent socializing, grade the project as it deserves and help the students see the connection between lost time and poor performance.
Makes sure teaching is compatible with students' cultural and home values.	Learn from parents about common occupations and interests of the families in the school—tie academic objectives to these. Know who works best in groups and who is better alone.
Focus on meaning, big ideas, and importance of what students are learning.	Have a good rationale for assignments—focus on value. Teach fewer details and more big ideas and themes.
Create positive and supportive relationships with students.	Find ways to connect with students outside class in clubs or extracurricular activities. Bring in personal interests and learn about student interests.
Create a climate that supports positive peer relationships and classroom community.	Use some cooperative learning activities. Assign popular students as guides for new students.

Source: Based on Eccles, J. S. & Roeser, R. W. (2006). Schools as developmental contexts. In G. A. M. D. Berzonsky (ed.), Blackwell Handbook of Adolescence (pp. 134–135). Blackwell/Wiley Publishing.

But you know by now not to base your judgments solely on news stories or the Internet. What does the research say? In 2006, the American Psychological Association set up a Zero Tolerance Task Force to answer that question (Reynolds et al., 2008). Analyzing a decade of research, they reached the following conclusions:

- Schools are not any safer or more effective in disciplining students now than before they instituted zero tolerance.
- The higher rates of suspension caused by zero tolerance have not led to less racial bias in disciplining students.
- Zero tolerance policies can actually lead to increases in bad behavior that then lead to higher dropout rates.

In addition, zero tolerance policies can discourage students from informing teachers when the students learn that a classmate is "planning to do something dangerous." The zero tolerance rules get in the way of trusting relationships between teachers and students

TABLE 12.7 • **Improvements and Alternatives to Zero-Tolerance Policies in Schools**

IMPROVEMENTS	ALTERNATIVES
Be flexible. Take teacher expertise and social context into account.	Replace one-size-fits-all discipline strategies with graduated consequences.
Let teachers who know the students communicate with families when discipline problems arise.	Focus on prevention and improving school climate and belonging.
Carefully define major and minor infractions so all teachers are on the same page—train everyone in how to handle each type of problem.	Connect with alienated youth and build relationships with teachers.
Reserve zero tolerance for the most serious problems.	Train teachers in culturally relevant discipline strategies.
Require school police officers to have training in adolescent development.	Improve communication between home, school, and community.

Source: Adapted from Reynolds et al. (2008). Are zero-tolerance policies effective in the schools? American Psychologist, *63, 852–862.*

(Syvertsen, Flanagan, & Stout, 2009). Adolescents need both structure and support, but zero tolerance policies can create a highly structured, rigid environment that ignores the need for support. Amy Gregory and Dewey Cornell (2009) suggest that:

> Rather than treat structure and support as opposing ends of a continuum between being tough or soft on students, we recommend that high school safety reform efforts strive to create learning environments that are both structured and supportive, so that students will feel safe, yet treated with respect. (p. 111)

The APA Task Force makes a number of recommendations for schools, as you can see in Table 12.7.

Adolescents in a Digital World

Adolescents spend more time online than adults—they are the defining users of the Internet (Valkenburg & Peter, 2009). When we talked about multitasking, you saw that computers, cell phones, iPods, iPads, video games, DVDs, Wiis, e-mail, texting, and other digital possibilities have changed life for everyone. For adolescents, doing homework often involves exchanging messages with friends via e-mail, instant messaging, or cell phones; searching the Web; and downloading resources—all the time listening to music via an iPod or watching television (Roberts, Foehr, & Rideout, 2005). As you would expect, older children have more encounters with computers; 86% of 8- to 18-year-olds had computers in their homes in 2006 (Roberts, Foehr, & Rideout, 2005). The number probably is larger now.

The most common use of the Internet appears to be searching for information for school projects, followed by communication with friends (girls tend to communicate with friends more than boys), but these numbers generally are based on self-report. We are not sure exactly how students are using the Internet at home (Jackson et al., 2006). In spite of this widespread use, we have to remember that adolescents are individuals and their relationships with technology vary from technophilia (love of technology) to technomania (obsession with technology) to technophobia (fear of technology) (Petrina, Feng, & Kim, 2008).

As with previous technologies such as the radio and television, parents and educators have a fear/hope relationship with current digital interactive technologies. They fear the harm that lurks in violent video games, sedentary Web surfing, online predators, and inappropriate Internet content, but they also have high hopes for the learning possibilities of new technologies (Houston, 2004). Chapter 13 will explore some of the fears about technology. Here let's consider the hopes.

Technology-Rich Learning Environments: TREs

With all this technology, there is growing interest in **technology-rich learning environments** or **TREs.** These environments include virtual worlds, computer simulations that support problem-based learning such as the *River of Life Challenge* described below, intelligent tutoring systems, educational games, audio recordings, hand-held wireless devices, and multimedia environments—to name just a few. There are debates about whether technology-rich learning environments should teach students directly (as in expert tutoring systems) or support the learning of students (as in problem-based learning simulations). These arguments mirror the debates about teachers as "sages on the stage" or "guides by the side." As you can imagine, supporters of Piaget's and Vygotsky's theories favor TREs that scaffold student learning and engagement—giving students more control over their own learning. TREs can situate learning in authentic contexts and support the social construction of knowledge by providing models and coaching as well as support for collaboration. In fact, students can collaborate with peers around the world (Lajoie & Azevedo, 2006; Pea & Maldonado, 2006).

In a computer simulation called the *River of Life Challenge* (Sherwood, 2002), students meet Billy and his lab partner Suzie, who are analyzing the quality of water from a local river. Suzie is concerned that Billy's conclusions are careless and incomplete. The Legacy League, a multiethnic group of characters who raise questions and direct Billy and Suzie to resources so they can research the answers using the STAR Legacy Cycle, challenges Billy to research in more depth. The phases of the cycle are: encounter the challenge, generate ideas, consider multiple perspectives, research and revise your ideas, test your mettle (check your understanding), and go public about your conclusions. Undergraduate science education students who used this simulation improved their graph-reading skills as well as their conceptual understanding of several topics such as the composition of air and classes of organisms in a river ecosystem (Kumar & Sherwood, 2007).

Let's look at these phases more closely as they might take place in an upper-level science class (Klein & Harris, 2007).

1. The cycle begins with an intriguing *challenge* to the whole class. For example, in biomechanics it might be "Assume you are a living cell in a bioreactor. What things will influence how long you live?" or "Your grandmother is recovering from a broken hip. In which hand should she hold the cane to help her balance?" The question is framed in a way that makes students bring to bear their current knowledge and preconceptions.
2. Next, students *generate ideas* to compile what they currently know and believe using individual, small group, or whole group brainstorming or other activities.
3. *Multiple perspectives* are added to the process in the form of outside experts (live, on video, or from texts), Web sites, magazine or journal articles, or a CD on the subject. In the river challenge above, the Legacy League guided Billy and Suzie to explore multiple perspectives.
4. Students go deeper to *research and revise*. They consult more texts or hear class lectures, all the while revising ideas and perhaps journaling about their thinking.
5. Students *test their mettle* by getting feedback from other students or the teacher about their tentative conclusions. Some formative (ungraded) tests might check their understanding at this point.
6. Students *go public* with their final conclusions and solutions in the form of an oral presentation, poster/project, or final exam.

Project-based science is a videodisc-based learning environment similar to problem-based learning that focuses on the middle grades (Krajcik & Czerniak, 2007).

Effects on Learning

There is evidence that using computers—especially games that require multiple activities, visual attention, imagery, and fast action—supports the development of visual skills, as long as the tasks fit the student's level of ability (Subrahmanyam, Greenfield, Kraut, & Gross,

2001). But does computer use support academic learning? The answer is complex and even surprising. After reviewing hundreds of studies, including five other research reviews, Roschelle et al, (2000) concluded that there were no strong conclusions. Using computer tutorial programs appeared to improve achievement test scores for K–12 students, but simulations and enrichment programs had few effects—perhaps another example of the rule is that when you teach and test specific skills, students learn the skills. Computers may be more useful in improving mathematics and science than other subjects. Like any teaching tool, computers can be effective if used well, but just being on a computer will not automatically increase academic achievement. Roschelle and colleagues concluded that computers are more likely to increase achievement if they support the basic processes that lead to learning: active engagement, frequent interaction with feedback, authenticity and real-world connection, and productive group work (Jackson et al., 2006). See the ***Connecting with Adolescents*** guidelines for more ideas.

Assistive Technology

Technology provides tools that change the lives of many people with disabilities. Consider this observation by Dr. Frank Bowe:

> I've been deaf since I was 3. When watching TV, hearing people had to stop and explain to me what was going on. If someone telephoned me, somebody else took the call. . . . Now I have a fax machine . . . I'm on the Internet . . . I have regular communications with people who are blind, people who are both deaf and blind, and it's all completely accessible to me. (Scherer, 2004, p. 147)

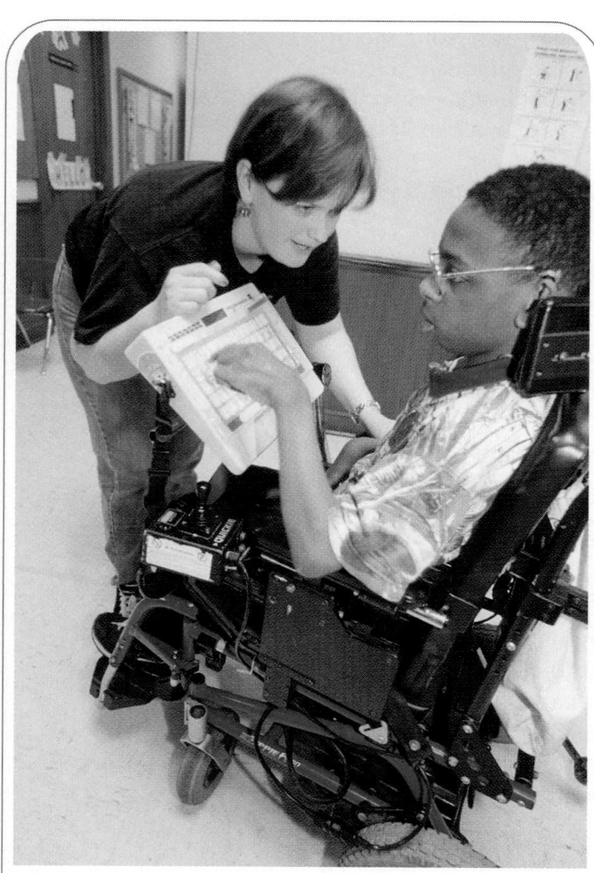

A communication board helps this adolescent with cerebral palsy interact with his therapist. The board is mounted on his wheelchair so it is easily accessible. Through the use of electronic and nonelectronic devices, Alternative and Augmentative Communication (AAC) provides alternate methods for communicating needs, feelings, ideas, and information.

The Individuals with Disabilities Act (2004) requires that all students eligible for special education services must be considered for assistive technology. **Assistive technology** is any product, piece of equipment, or system that is used to increase, maintain, or improve the functional capabilities of individuals with disabilities (Goldman, Lawless, Pellegrino, & Plants, 2006). For students who require small steps and many repetitions to learn a new concept, computers are the perfect patient tutors, repeating steps and lessons as many times as necessary. A well-designed computer instructional program is engaging and interactive—two important qualities for students who have problems paying attention or a history of failure that has eroded motivation. For example, a math or spelling program might use images, sounds, and game-like features to maintain the attention of a student with an attention-deficit disorder. Interactive digital media programs teach hearing people how to use sign language. Many programs do not involve sound, so students with hearing impairments can get the full benefit from the lessons. Students who have trouble reading can use programs that will "speak" a word for them if they touch the unknown word. With this immediate access to help, the students are much more likely to get the reading practice they need to prevent falling farther and farther behind. Other devices actually convert printed pages and typed texts into spoken words for students who are blind or others who benefit from hearing information. For the student with a learning disability and illegible writing, word processors produce perfect penmanship so the ideas can finally get on paper. Once the ideas are recorded, the student can reorganize and improve his or her writing without the agony of rewriting by hand (Hallahan, Kauffman, & Pullen, 2009).

CONNECTING WITH ADOLESCENTS

Guidelines for Teachers and Families: Using Computers

TEACHERS

- ***If you have only one computer in your classroom:***

Provide convenient access.

Examples

1. Find a central location if the computer is used to display material for the class.
2. Find a spot on the side of the room that allows seating and view of the screen, but does not crowd or disturb other students if the computer is used as a workstation for individuals or small groups.

Be prepared.

Examples

1. Check to be sure software needed for a lesson or assignment is installed and working.
2. Make sure instructions for using the software or doing the assignment are in an obvious place and clear.
3. Provide a checklist for completing assignments.

Create "trained experts" to help with computers.

Examples

1. Train student experts, and rotate experts.
2. Use adult volunteers—parents, grandparents, aunts and uncles, older siblings—anyone who cares about the students.

Develop systems for using the computer.

Examples

1. Make up a schedule to insure that all students have access to the computer and no students monopolize the time.
2. Create standard ways of saving student work.

- ***If you have more than one computer in your classroom:***

Plan the arrangement of the computers to fit your instructional goals.

Examples

1. For cooperative groups, arrange so students can cluster around their group's computer.
2. For different projects at different computer stations, allow for easy rotation from station to station.

Experiment with other models for using computers.

Examples

1. *Navigator Model*—4 students per computer: One student is the (mouse and keyboard) driver, another is the "navigator." "Back-seat driver 1" manages the group's progress and "back-seat driver 2" serves as the timekeeper. The navigator attends a 10-minute to 20-minute training session in which the facilitator provides an overview of the basics of particular software. Navigators cannot touch the mouse. Driver roles are rotated.
2. *Facilitator Model*—6 students per computer: the facilitator has more experience, expertise, or training—serves as the guide or teacher.
3. *Collaborative Group Model*—7 students per computer: Each small group is responsible for creating some component of the whole group's final product. For example, one part of the group writes a report, another creates a map, and a third uses the computer to gather and graph census data.

- ***No matter how many computers you have in your classroom:***

Select appropriate programs that encourage learning, creativity, and social interaction.

Examples

1. Encourage two students to work together rather than having children work alone.
2. Check the implicit messages in programs. For example, some drawing programs allow children to "blow up" their projects if they don't like them, so instead of solving a problem, they just destroy it. Tsantis et al. (2003) recommend a recycle metaphor instead of a "blow it up" option.
3. Look for programs that encourage discovery, exploration, problem solving, and multiple responses.

PARENTS AND TEACHERS

Monitor adolescents as they work at computers.

Examples

1. Make sure computers are in areas where an adult can observe them.
2. Discuss why some programs or websites are off limits.

Keep adolescents safe as they work at computers.

Examples

1. Teach adolescents to shield their identity on the Internet and monitor any "friends" they may be communicating with.
2. Install filtering software to protect children from inappropriate content.

For more ideas about older students, see http://www.internet4classrooms.com/one_computer.htm

With these tremendous advances in technology have come new barriers, however. Many computers have graphic interfaces. Manipulating the programs requires precise "mouse movements," as you may remember when you first learned to point and click. These maneuvers are difficult for students with motor problems or visual impairments. The information available on the Internet often is unusable for students with visual impairments. Researchers are working on the problem—trying to devise ways for people to access the information nonvisually, but the adaptations are not perfected yet (Hallahan, Kauffman, & Pullen, 2009). Tools can help, but also pose challenges themselves. Describing assistive tools for writing, Charles MacArthur (2009) sums up the situation:

> For example, word processing removes concerns with handwriting, but requires typing, which may slow text production and take attention away from the content of writing, unless the student has developed fluent typing skills. Dictating to a tape-recorder removes concerns about the mechanics of writing, but imposes a new burden on working memory because the user cannot see the text already written. Search tools on the Internet greatly expand the amount of information available to use in our writing, but impose tremendous challenges for critical evaluation of information. Whether a new tool will increase or decrease the overall cognitive burden depends on the skills of an individual student and the quality of training. (p. 2)

The bottom line? As we saw earlier, word processing can help struggling writers if the writers have good typing skills and have been taught how to revise and improve their writing (MacArthur, 2009).

For gifted students, computers can be a connection with databases and computers in universities, museums, and research labs. Computer networks allow students to work on projects and share information with others across the country. It is also possible to have gifted students write programs for students and teachers. Quite a few principals rely on their students to make the technology in the school work. These are just a few examples of what technology can do. One current trend is **universal design**—considering the needs of all users in creating living and learning environments. The goal of universal design is to create products and environments—buildings, stairs, furniture, fixtures, tools, cooking utensils, learning programs, websites—that are usable by everyone regardless of age or ability (Pisha & Coyne, 2001). The future promises to hold even more possibilities for technology-supported learning.

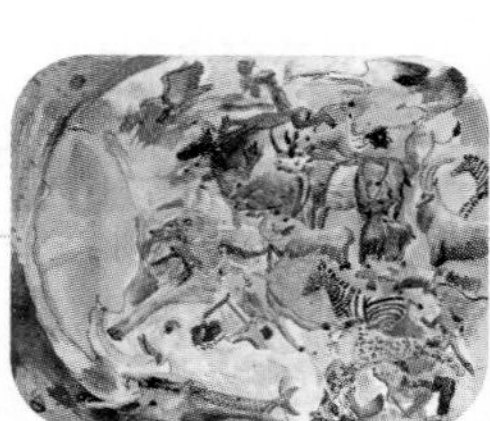

▼ SUMMARY AND KEY TERMS

• Adolescent Language Development: Connections

During adolescence, young people use language and memory, metacognitive abilities, and contextual factors to explain themselves to others and create a coherent life—a part of their identity. They also use special language registers such as "mallspeak" to connect with friends. As the United States and other countries become more diverse, there are increasing numbers of adolescents who speak two languages. For those in the United States who are limited in their English proficiency, there are two approaches to bilingual education—transition programs that introduce English as early as possible and native-language maintenance instruction that seeks to maintain and develop the first language while teaching the second, so that adolescents become balanced bilinguals—proficient in both languages.

Piaget and Vygotsky

According to Piaget, at around the age of 11 or 12, children develop formal operations—a new way of reasoning that involves "thinking about thinking" or "mental operations on mental operations." Quite a bit of research on adolescent and adult thinking focuses on deductive and inductive reasoning. Deductive reasoning moves from the general assumption to the specific, whereas inductive reasoning moves from specific to general. A main characteristic of formal operational thinking is a specific type of deductive reasoning called hypothetical-deductive reasoning in which the focus of thinking can shift from what is to what might be, including reasoning about counterfactual premises. Other cognitive abilities that develop during adolescence are systematic reasoning about combining multiple variables and scientific reasoning using inquiry to identify causes. Schooling is central in developing these kinds of reasoning abilities. Piaget's critics note that people can reason formally only in some areas, but Piaget himself acknowledged that formal operational thinking might apply only in particular content areas or domains.

Vygotsky also identified a level of abstract thinking beyond concrete thought. He distinguished between spontaneous and scientific concepts and noted that schooling is important to develop the latter. Vygotsky also stressed the importance of cultural tools such as language and technology. Educators debate the values of tools such as calculators and spell checkers in developing cognitive abilities. Two current educational applications of Vygotsky's idea of guided participation and scaffolding are cognitive apprenticeships and reciprocal teaching.

- **Information Processing: Metacognition and Scientific Thinking**

Information processing approaches to cognitive development in adolescence emphasize the ability to inhibit responses, focus attention, and control impulses that interfere with information processing goals. All of these capabilities allow adolescents to improve in their metacognitive skills and knowledge—they can be more strategic and "in control" of their own thinking. A hallmark of adolescence is the emergence and strengthening of this executive functioning. One challenge to this functioning is multitasking—something that adolescents often believe they can handle, but that often harms learning and performance. ADHD is another challenge experienced by many adolescents that requires skillful teaching. Teachers also can help students develop inquiry and argumentation skills, by teaching memory support and organization strategies and encouraging collaboration. Even with good support, it is difficult for adolescents to stop focusing on what they believe and listen to their opponents' arguments. Adolescents' beliefs about knowledge—whether they are realists, absolutists, multiplists, or evaluativists—affect their beliefs about the value of critical thinking.

- **Beyond Reason: Thinking in the Real World**

Dual process theories of decision making describe two modes of thinking—conscious, logical, analytic thinking and out-of-awareness, emotional, intuitive thinking. There are advantages and disadvantages for both modes if used exclusively or inappropriately. Analytic decision making takes time and ignores emotions. Heuristic thinking can involve dangers such as using representativeness heuristics to make judgments about possibilities based on images and stereotypes of what best represents the situation. The availability heuristic is based on instances of events that come to mind easily. Belief perseverance (the tendency to hold on to our beliefs), and confirmation bias (the tendency to search for information that confirms our ideas) also can harm good decision making. On the positive side, heuristics thinking can often quickly identify a "good enough" decision. These analytic and heuristic decision-making modes explain some of the risky decisions of adolescents. In the rational mode, adolescents consider what they know about risks, how their family will react, and other information. On the affective side, images and feelings are central. When the context is right—a party with alcohol flowing and no adults around—images and emotions often win the day. Adolescent egocentrism, the extreme focus on self that leads to feelings of uniqueness and the belief in an imaginary audience, plays a role, too.

- **Diversity in Adolescent Cognitive Development and School Achievement**

There appear to be some gender differences in cognitive abilities, but they are small. Women perform better on assessments of verbal abilities when the assessments are heavily weighted with writing and the language-usage items cover topics with which females are familiar; males excel on certain visuospatial-ability measures. Males also are more extreme in their scores—more males than females score at the very high and very low ends of many cognitive tests. Some explanations claim evolution or participation in sports has favored spatial and navigational skills in males. Others point to gender discrimination on schooling. There are cultural differences, however, and research indicates males and females show equal abilities to learn advanced, college-level mathematics and are equally capable of learning science, even though there are fewer women in STEM careers. Single-sex schooling is one suggestion for dealing with biases against both boys and girls, but to be valuable, the teaching in these schools must fit the needs of the students.

There are persistent differences in the achievement of European American, Latino/a, and African American students, mostly due to cultural mismatches and language differences, growing up in poverty, or the legacy of discrimination. Rather than focus on problems, teachers can focus on students' strengths, help them cope with stereotype threat, and engage in culturally relevant practices in order to know, respect, and teach their students well.

- **Contexts for Cognitive Development**

Main contexts for cognitive development in adolescence include the family, peers, and school. In European American, middle-class families, children of authoritative parents are more likely to do well in school, be happy with themselves, and relate well to others. Children of authoritarian parents are more likely to feel guilty or depressed, and children of permissive parents may have trouble interacting with peers. Both indulgent and rejecting/neglecting/uninvolved parenting styles can be harmful. Recently, parenting style has been reconceptualized as multicultural and multidimensional, but for most adolescents, more parental involvement and monitoring seem productive in early and middle adolescence; older adolescents need more autonomy to make decisions. Adolescents often adopt the attitudes toward and investment in schooling of their clique or crowd. In classrooms, peers can be powerful supports for learning in well-designed and carefully implemented cooperative learning strategies.

Stage-environment fit theory helps us understand how schools can meet the developmental needs of adolescents, especially as they make transitions from elementary to middle and middle to high school. The challenge is to provide strong adult support and caring relationships along with increasing opportunities for autonomy. In adolescence, the problem of dropping out becomes a concern. When schools do not meet the needs of developing adolescents, students are more likely to drop out. Qualified teachers who use appropriate instructional and managerial practices are more likely to keep students engaged in school.

- **Adolescents in a Digital World**

The most common use of the Internet appears to be searching for information for school projects, followed by communication with friends (girls tend to communicate with friends more than boys). In learning, technology-rich learning environments or TREs include virtual worlds, computer simulations that support problem-based learning, intelligent tutoring systems, educational games, audio recordings, handheld wireless devices, and multimedia environments. Using computers—especially games that require multiple activities, visual attention, imagery, and fast action—supports the development of visual skills, as long as the tasks fit the student's level of ability. Research so far shows that using computer tutorial programs appears to improve achievement test scores for K–12 students, but simulations and enrichment programs have few effects. In contrast, assistive technologies and universal design provide access and learning support for adolescents with disabilities and learning challenges.

▼ KEY TERMS

adolescent egocentrism (496)
argumentation (490)
assistive technology (520)
availability heuristic (494)
belief perseverance (494)
cognitive apprenticeship (485)
confirmation bias (494)
deductive reasoning (479)
dual process theories (492)
executive functioning (487)
formal operations (479)
heuristics (493)
hypothetical-deductive reasoning (480)
inductive reasoning (479)
limited-English-proficient (LEP) (477)
metacognitive skills (480)
person-environment fit theory (499)
reciprocal teaching (486)
registers (477)
representativeness heuristics (494)
semilingual (478)
stage-environment fit theory (509)
stereotype threat (501)
technology-rich learning environments (TREs) (519)
universal design (522)

▼ THE CASEBOOK

ADOLESCENT DECISION MAKING

"You just don't get it! This is important and I'M GOING TO DO IT!" Danielle slammed the door to make perfectly clear her intention to get her eyebrow pierced.

Her parents stared at each other. They couldn't believe that their seemingly sensible daughter was so insistent about piecing any part of her body. Danielle argued that she was a senior in high school—"an adult"—and should be allowed to make her *own* decisions about her *own* body. She listed the friends who had this or that body part pierced or tattooed, "and their parents were OK with it." She showed them pictures of celebrities and models. She told them how safe it was. Nothing worked.

Her parents had tried reasoning with Danielle, listing the reasons why this was a bad idea. They told her it would interfere with getting a "good job at a respectable place." They warned Danielle that her grandparents would be "horrified and embarrassed." They showed her an article from the newspaper about the dangers of piercing. They tried negotiating/bribing. Nothing worked.

When everything failed, Danielle's parents forbid her from piercing or tattooing anything and threatened severe punishments. She responded by screaming "You just don't understand!" They were "hopeless, out of touch, controlling," and would "ruin her life." Then she left, hurling the proclamation, "I'M GOING TO DO IT."

WHAT WOULD THEY DO?

Here is how some professionals in several fields responded:

JILL SULLIVAN—Math, Grades 9–11
Northside College Prep High School, Chicago, Illinois

After all the preventive tactics that Danielle's parents have tried, I would try *agreement* as it is often effective in stopping arguments. My theory is that if Danielle knows her parents are okay with getting the piercing, she might just lose her desire to do it. Thus, I would ask Danielle to research online or through friends how one *actually* goes about getting her eyebrow pierced and report back. In essence, let her feel ownership and independence by putting her in charge of the adult "next step" of investigating options to make an educated decision. I would also establish a "waiting period" up front—maybe agree she can do it in two months if she's still interested. Instruct her to find 2–3 businesses where she could get her eyebrow pierced, the cost, what's involved in the procedure, if it's painful, and how permanent it is. My hope would be that in learning more, she chooses to not go through with it or finds it prohibitively expensive. I spent less than 2 minutes looking at some results to "eyebrow pierced Chicago" and quickly learned that there are some after-care piercing steps—a possible deterrent and something I'd never thought of and she might not have either. The important thing is to create the opportunity for Danielle to change her mind without losing face. Teenagers crave fairness, so ideally the guidelines you set come across that way and she feels like it was a just process.

ELAINE S. BOOTHBY—AP Literature, Grade 12
South River High School, Edgewater, Maryland

Many states still require written consent for piercing and/or tattooing under state statutes; in most states, 18 is the viable age, not senior status in high school. In some religions it is still considered a form of body mutilation and therefore forbidden. However, in high school, many students, teachers, and staff have some body art. I have seen parents take such a hard line that students will move out to "prove" to the parents that they can be independent. Rather than steps as drastic as this, a conversation to determine just what the piercing may represent to Danielle should take place. Perhaps being recognized in other ways with adult responsibility can assure her that she is being seen by her parents as no longer a child.

In some cases the parent knows the church position on this and may want to discuss this with Danielle, but most likely a small compromise of a piercing can be mutually agreed to, perhaps as an experiment that Danielle may outgrow. Confrontation like this must generate conversation and dialogue to find out the real issue in question.

CATHY BLANCHFIELD—English/Language Arts, Grades 10 and 12
Duncan Polytechnical High School, Fresno, California

It is common knowledge that adolescents, especially 17- to 19-year-olds, are creating their own identities. This is the time when teens make decisions about who they are and what ideologies they want to embrace. No matter what their parents have taught, adolescents want to make their own decisions. Danielle's case is typical, as is her parents' response. In fact, Danielle's parents have managed to appeal to her logic, emotions, and ethics, but all to no avail.

Every generation has this parent–adolescent struggle. In the 60s, if a teenage male wanted to grow his hair to his shoulders, his parents would have made all the arguments about why he shouldn't. In the 80s, if a teenage boy wanted to pierce his ear, his parents would again have made all the arguments about why he shouldn't. In the 90s and 2000s, if a teenage boy or girl wanted a tattoo, the parents would have made more than enough arguments against it. If parents forbid teens from making this type of decision, it might deter them for a short time period; however, they will find a way to express their new-found identity.

The parental role in this identity crisis is to assist their teen in making informed decisions and to lend support in that decision-making. After all, most long-haired, tattooed, and pierced young adults have found a way to reverse the effects of these decisions in later life or have found a place in society where those markings do not deter their progress.

HOLLY FITCHETTE—French Teacher, Grades 9–11
Fleming Island High School, Fleming Island, Florida

Danielle's parents may be fighting a losing battle. Once Danielle turns 18, she will indeed be able to make the decision to pierce or tattoo her body without her parents' consent. I think her parents should try a different tactic. The more they try to control Danielle's behavior, the more she may choose to rebel. By calmly discussing what kind of piercing Danielle wants, Danielle is likely to remain more open to her parents' input and concerns. Even the state acknowledges that Danielle is old enough to have some control over these decisions. Instead of issuing ultimatums, her parents could try reasoning with Danielle about when it may be appropriate for her to remove her brow ring. Her parents could also negotiate with her about the size or location of a potential tattoo. Since Danielle's parents are primarily concerned with her safety, they could help her research to find the safest place in her community to have it done. When Danielle's parents have made it clear to her that it is her safety and well-being that concerns them most, Danielle will likely be more open to their rational input in this decision and others in her future.

PEARSON myeducationlab

Now go to MyEducationLab at ***www.myeducationlab.com,*** where you can:

- Find the instructional objectives for this chapter in the **Study Plan**.
- Take a quiz as a part of the **Study Plan** to self-assess your mastery of chapter content. The program generates an individualized Study Plan based upon your answers to the quiz.
- Complete **Activities and Applications** to assist you in deepening your understanding of important chapter concepts.
- Apply what you have learned through **Building Teaching Skills**, exercises that guide you in trying out skills and strategies you will use in professional practice.

13 SOCIAL EMOTIONAL DEVELOPMENT IN ADOLESCENCE

THE CASEBOOK

WHAT WOULD YOU DO?

PRIVACY VERSUS PROTECTION FOR TEENS

The library at Alder Woods Secondary School has become a popular hangout for students ages 13 to 17. It has a large bank of computers equipped with state-of-the-art software for searching and researching. At the moment, students pretty much have unlimited access to the Internet and *all* it has to offer. This is a bit of a concern for the librarians who can't possibly monitor all the activities of the kids who drop in before, during, and after school hours. Also, they feel torn—even if they could monitor the goings on or limit access in some way to sites that are potentially problematic, should they? Is it their responsibility? Is it an invasion of the right to privacy that teenagers hold very dear? How can concerned adults strike the right balance between granting privacy and protecting youth from harm that can come from using the Internet?

CRITICAL THINKING

- What characteristics of teenagers make them particularly vulnerable to some dangers on the Internet?
- How should adults/caregivers approach this problem? Should they restrict access, or monitor activities, teach coping strategies, and exercise trust?
- How can adults respect the privacy rights of adolescents—their growing need/desire to take care of themselves and make their own decisions—while protecting them from potential harm? And what should teenagers reasonably expect from the adults in their lives concerning privacy?

Soema Abdullaeva, Age 12—Tajikistan

▶ OVERVIEW AND OBJECTIVES

G. Stanley Hall (1904), one of the founders of child and developmental psychology, described adolescence as a time of "storm and stress." This description may resonate with your experience or reflect your apprehensions about teaching and parenting teens. But is adolescence as tumultuous as it is made out to be? Are conflict, mood swings, and risky behavior the exception or the rule for the majority of teens? In Chapters 11 and 12, we discussed the dramatic physical and cognitive changes that take place during adolescence, and it's true these changes are associated with increased conflict with parents and other authority figures, mood disruptions, and increased risk-taking behavior (Arnett, 1999). However, it's also true that most adolescents pass through this period without getting into excessive trouble, and they experience a healthy deepening of self-awareness and friendships, not to mention the excitement (and heartbreak) of romantic relationships. We begin this chapter with a description of the changes in self-concept and search for identity that are strongly associated with this developmental period and often linked to discussions of storm and stress. Next, we examine adolescents' relationships with peers and parents, and observe how these and other factors are implicated in their decisions about how to behave. We look at adolescents' social lives in school as well as some extreme challenges experienced by a small proportion of youth. Finally, we end with a brief discussion of the transition out of adolescence and into adulthood. By the time you finish this chapter you should be able to:

Objective 13.1	Describe processes by which adolescents search for identity and identify factors that support or challenge this search.
Objective 13.2	Identify a set a threats to adolescents' well-being and explain what makes teens vulnerable to them.

Objective 13.3 Describe the range and role of peer relationships in adolescents' lives.
Objective 13.4 Connect qualities of parent–adolescent relationships to low levels of conflict during the teen years.
Objective 13.5 Synthesize the research on secrecy and disclosure in parent–adolescent relationships.
Objective 13.6 Relate qualities of schools to adolescents' school adjustment and attachment.
Objective 13.7 Discuss issues associated with the emergence of serious mental illness during adolescence.
Objective 13.8 Create a portrait of young adults in contemporary, technologically advanced societies.

The Search for Identity

Issues of Identity

According to Erikson (1950), the most important developmental task for adolescents is the search for identity, resulting in a complex answer to the question, "Who am I?" Although children have been developing a sense of self from infancy, adolescents' increased ability to think abstractly about personal characteristics, interests, and the future makes identity issues a central focus for them. Moreover, biological and social pressures to think and behave more like adults (e.g., to become sexually active; to consider occupational goals, social and political values, and religious beliefs) motivate adolescents to consider who they are and who they want to be.

Erikson viewed the crisis for teenagers as one of *identity versus role confusion*. Most adolescents resolve this crisis with a healthy degree of exploration. They try out different roles or "possible selves." They explore the possibilities and consequences of displaying different characteristics in different settings with different groups and reconsider goals their parents, and perhaps, teachers, set for them, typically accepting some and rejecting others. In the end, most adolescents successfully negotiate this crisis and emerge with a secure sense of self. Often, they remain connected to the values they've learned, but not bound by them (Chandler et al., 2003).

Ericson (1968) recognized that many socialization factors influence identify formation, which can make the process more difficult for some groups of adolescents than for others. For example, youth from diverse cultural groups may receive multiple and mixed messages that affect their identity formation. Almost all teens experience some periods of uncertainty about who they are and what they want to do with their lives. However, for some adolescents, lack of direction and self-doubt are extreme and can be associated with personality and behavior problems. For these individuals, unsuccessful resolution of their identity crisis may result in depression, substance abuse, delinquency, and even suicide.

Marcia: Building on Erikson

James Marcia (1966, 1993) expanded on Erikson's theory of identity formation. Specifically, he focused on two processes Erikson deemed essential to achieving a mature identity: exploration and commitment. **Exploration** refers to the process by which adolescents consider and try out alternative beliefs, values, and behaviors in an effort to determine which will give them the most satisfaction. **Commitment** refers to individuals' choices concerning political and religious beliefs, for example, usually as a consequence of exploring the options. Marcia conducted studies of male college students' career choices and beliefs about politics and religion; from this research he identified four categories of identity status that

TABLE 13.1 • **Marcia's Theory of Identity Development**

COMMITMENT STATUS	IDENTITY STATUS			
	IDENTITY ACHIEVED	IDENTITY FORECLOSED	IDENTITY DIFFUSED	MORATORIUM
Exploration/In process	—	—	Not exploring, not committing	Actively exploring alternatives
Committed	Result of healthy exploration and decision making	Result of commitment without exploration	—	—

Source: Based on: J. E. Marcia. (1980). Criteria for identity statuses. In J. Adelson (Ed.), Handbook of Adolescent Psychology *(p. 159). New York: John Wiley & Sons.*

arise from four patterns of exploration and commitment. His theory is represented in Table 13.1 and summarized below.

According to Marcia, **identity achievement** is the result of healthy exploration and decision making regarding identities involved in occupations, political and religious affiliations, and relationships. It is associated with higher levels of achievement, morality, and intimacy than the other statuses in Marcia's framework (Adams, Berzonsky, & Keating, 2006). **Identity foreclosure** occurs when adolescents make commitments without exploring options. Sometimes this happens because commitments are handed down to them (e.g., the expectation that a son or daughter will continue in the family business). It may also be reflected in a youth's decision to join a strict religious cult or radical political cell; in this case, the individual embraces expectations handed down from the cult or cell without exploring options. Foreclosure is characteristic of individuals who have a high need for approval and low levels of autonomy (Adams, Berzonsky, & Keating, 2006). Alternatively, **identity diffusion** refers to a state in which adolescents are not exploring identity alternatives, or making commitments. Teens with this status are often described as apathetic or aimless, lacking motivation to succeed in school, hold down a job, or maintain healthy and lasting relationships. As indicated above, role confusion and identity diffusion are common experiences in most adolescents' lives for brief periods. However, parents and teachers need to attend to the extent and duration of these statuses because prolonged role confusion or identity diffusion can signal more serious social and emotional problems. Finally, adolescents who are actively exploring identity alternatives but have yet to make a commitment are in **moratorium.** In complex modern societies, a moratorium on major life commitments is not only common, but considered healthy. For example, youth are encouraged to delay making important and potentially lifelong commitments and to explore their options by going to college, traveling, or joining the military.

Other researchers have replicated and extended Marcia's studies in different domains of experience (e.g., family life, friendships, and dating). A consistent finding across studies is that from adolescence into adulthood, identity achievement increases and diffusion decreases (Goossens, 2001; Grotevant & Cooper, 1998; Kroger, 2003). In general, identity development is a lifelong process that begins in infancy and continues through old age; for most people, this process is far more gradual and less traumatic than Erikson's term *crisis* implies. Importantly, identity achievement in adolescence does not mean that one's identity will remain stable throughout adulthood. (Consider the likelihood that modern day teens will change careers, homes, communities, and partners at least once during their adult lives.) More typically, identity development happens in segments and is recursive, so people may reconsider and reorganize or completely change aspects of their identity over time. Ideally, a person who develops a healthy identity early on can adapt more easily to changes—voluntary or not—that require identity development across the lifespan.

Because identity achievement is such an important goal in adolescence, much attention has been given to factors that help or hinder its attainment. We examine some of these factors next.

Who Am I, and How Do I Like Myself?

Adolescent Self-Concept

Children's sense of self continues to become more complex and differentiated during adolescence. Likely this is the result of their more advanced thinking abilities and exposure to more diverse social contexts. According to Harter's research (1998, 1999, 2006), there is a proliferation of selves in adolescence: self with mother, father, friends, and romantic partners, as well as self as student, athlete, musician, worker, etc. Whereas children tend to describe themselves in terms of five domains, including cognitive ability, athleticism, behavior, social competence, and physical appearance, adolescents further differentiate their descriptions of cognitive abilities to include scholastic achievements, intellectual abilities, and creativity, and their benchmarks for social competence include close friendships, romantic relationships, and job competence (see Table 13.2).

Along with this increasingly differentiated view of self comes the ability to think about self in conflicting ways, depending on the setting and circumstance. For example, it's not uncommon for adolescents to describe themselves as successful in some contexts (e.g., "At school, I'm pretty intelligent . . . I get better grades than most . . .") and not successful in others (e.g., "Sometimes I'm really stupid . . . I act really dumb and say things that are simply stupid."), or as an extrovert with close friends and as an introvert with people they don't know. (Examples are from Harter, 2006, p. 531.) Many of these self-descriptions represent abstractions that integrate categories of attributes that younger children use to describe themselves (e.g., "I'm pretty intelligent" reflects the integration of labels such as *smart, curious,* and *creative*).

At first, these abstractions are highly compartmentalized—being intelligent at school is quite distinct from being smart in other contexts (Harter, 2006). Therefore, young adolescents may appear unaware of or unconcerned about the seeming contradictions in their self-descriptions across different roles (student, daughter, friend) and settings (school, home, at a party). However, in middle adolescence, such contradictions become a big concern. According to Fischer (1980), once adolescents are able to make comparisons across abstractions, they become aware of and concerned about inconsistencies (e.g., "I don't understand how I can switch so fast from being cheerful with my friends, then coming home and feeling anxious, and then getting frustrated and sarcastic with my parents," from Harter, 2006). The question, "Who is the REAL me?" arises and there is a desire to "bring

TABLE 13.2 • **Self-Concept Differentiation in Adolescence**

SELF-CONCEPT DOMAINS	EXAMPLES OF ADOLESCENTS' SELF-DESCRIPTIONS
Scholastic achievement	I do school work quickly. I do well in school.
Intellectual ability	I'm just as smart as other people.
Athletic competence	I am good at new sports.
Behavioral conduct	I don't get into trouble. I act the way I am supposed to act.
Close friendships	I share things with my close friends.
Romantic appeal	I believe that I am fun and interesting on dates.
Job competence	I have the skills to succeed at a part-time job.
Physical appearance	I like the way I look.

Source: Based on Harter, S. (1999). The Construction of Self. *New York: Guilford. Renick-Thomson, N. & Zand, D. H. (2002). The Harter Self-Perception Profile for Adolescents: Psychometrics for an early adolescent, African American sample.* International Journal of Testing, *2, 297–310. Renick, N. T. & Zand, D. H. (2002). The Harter Self-Perception Profile for Adolescents: Psychometrics for an early adolescent, African American sample.* International Journal of Testing, *2, 297–310.*

self-attributes into harmony with one another" (Harter, 2006, p. 542). But harmony is not always easy or even possible. Especially in modern and technologically advanced societies, where youth can present or re-present themselves in many different, perhaps contradictory, roles to many different audiences (e.g., using technology and a whole host of social networking tools), achieving self-coherence is a difficult task. And for minority youth, the challenges associated with understanding and integrating multiple selves is exacerbated by their need to reconcile multiple selves in multiple worlds—some populated with members of their own ethnic group (family, friends) and others populated with members of the majority culture (teachers, classmates, employers, and co-workers).

Two other characteristics of middle adolescents are associated with considerable distress. Middle adolescents tend to be preoccupied with what others think of them, and contradictory messages from different groups of significant others (e.g., parents, peers, popular culture) can lead to confusion and conflict about which characteristics to adopt (Harter, 2006). Moreover, adolescents can distinguish between what they perceive are characteristics of their "real" versus "ideal" selves. In contrast to young children, who often conflate their actual characteristics with those they'd like to have, adolescents can recognize a discrepancy between their current level of achievement and what they would like to achieve in the future. When the discrepancy between real and ideal states is small, most adolescents maintain good feelings about themselves. They can set goals and identify actions that will lead to improvement. In contrast, when the discrepancy between real and ideal selves appears impossible to bridge, self-esteem can suffer.

Adolescent Self-Esteem

Recall from Chapters 7 and 10 that self-esteem refers to the subjective, evaluative sense of self, and positive self-evaluations (i.e., high self-esteem) are associated with positive outcomes, such as scholastic achievement, popularity, and a general sense of happiness and well-being. In adolescence, positive self-regard is generally thought to protect youth against negative outcomes, such as school failure and dropout, delinquency, early sexual behavior, alcohol and drug abuse, and depression (Harter, 2006; Mann, Hosman, Schaalma, & deVries, 2004; Salazar et al., 2004). However, there are exceptions. Some youth who report high self-esteem engage in bullying and high-risk behavior, and some become gang leaders (Baumeister et al., 2003; Costello & Dunaway, 2003; Damon, 1995). According to Harter (2006), these youth typically have other characteristics, in addition to self-reported self-esteem, that are more closely linked with such behavior (narcissism, low empathy, and high sensitivity to rejection). Therefore, their engagement in aggressive and antisocial behavior may reflect efforts to enhance self-esteem and win the approval of peers.

In Chapter 10, we described how, like self-concept, self-esteem becomes more differentiated as school-age children experience success and failure in a variety of domains and

Jeremy's self-image. In adolescence, social comparisons and the opinions of significant others still influence self-esteem.

in comparison to peers. This differentiation continues during adolescence when youth tend to report differences in self-esteem across relational contexts (e.g., with parents, teachers, classmates). Also, early adolescents (ages 11 to 13) continue to experience a decline in self-esteem as they become increasingly concerned with the opinions of others and social comparison information becomes even more salient in the environments in which they find themselves (Harter, 2006; Shapka & Keating, 2005).

TRANSITIONS AND SELF-ESTEEM. Jackie Eccles and her colleagues (Eccles & Midgley, 1989; Eccles, Midgley, & Adler, 1984; Wigfield & Eccles, 2002) argue that differences in emphases from elementary to middle and junior high schools are in part responsible for the observed decline in students' perceptions of academic competence. For example, compared to elementary school, middle and high schools place far greater emphasis on grades and other results from competitive activities. Moreover, whereas students in elementary schools are encouraged and praised for effort, performance in middle and junior high schools often is attributed to ability, leaving those who perform poorly with the interpretation that they lack ability or intelligence. Eccles and others (e.g., Harter, 2006) point out the mismatch between the school environment and the needs of adolescents; it would seem more prudent to downplay social comparisons at a time in development when individuals are at their most self-conscious. The mission of the National Middle School Association (NMSA, 2010) is to create school environments that better meet the social emotional as well as academic needs of this age group. This organization has identified 16 characteristics of successful middle schools, which emphasize developmentally and individually responsive school organizations, policies, curricula, instruction, and assessments. These characteristics were outlined in Figure 12.4 on page 511 in Chapter 12.

INDIVIDUAL DIFFERENCES IN SELF-ESTEEM. Harter (1999, 2006) cautions that focusing on mean levels of change during transitions to high school and college can mask individual differences in self-esteem. Her research identified three groups: those whose self-esteem increased, decreased, or stayed the same. Increased self-esteem was associated with greater perceived competence in subjects considered important and higher levels of perceived social acceptance in the new setting, whereas decreased self-esteem was associated with perceived declines in performance in valued subjects and reported reductions in social support. Research also indicates that the magnitude of declines may be related to the timing of the school shift and pubertal change (Brooks-Gunn, 1988; Simmons & Blyth, 1987). Apparently, changing schools between sixth and seventh grades is more detrimental to self-esteem than changing schools a year later. Similarly, early transitions coinciding with early maturing are associated with greater declines in self-esteem, especially for girls. Finally, there are inter- and intra-individual differences in the stability of self-evaluations. Individuals who are more sensitive to evaluative events and who rely overmuch on external sources for self-esteem are likely to experience greater fluctuations. Also, the dramatic physical, cognitive, and social changes adolescents experience can be overwhelming and can lead to changes in self-esteem over time and across domains and relationships.

INCREASING SELF-ESTEEM IN ADULTHOOD. Fortunately, both global assessments of self-worth and domain-specific self-evaluations tend to become more positive from middle adolescence into adulthood (Harter, 2006; Shapka & Keating, 2005). Increases are associated with increased autonomy (e.g., having more opportunities to choose courses and activities in which success is likely) and increased role-taking ability, which leads to increased opportunities to present oneself in a positive light in a variety of situations. Moreover, most youth emerge from adolescence understanding that they possess a core set of characteristics that remain fairly consistent across time and settings. They are able to organize qualities that seem inconsistent or incongruent into a set of higher order abstractions. For example, older adolescents can reconcile the fact that they behave differently with friends than they do with strangers or older adults; they might describe this difference as the ability to adapt to varying social situations. In addition, they are less concerned about what others think of them and more realistic about their futures.

Next, we examine some key aspects of identity formation: gender identity, sexual identity and sexual orientation, and ethnic identity.

Gender Identity

In Chapter 7, we defined gender identity as the sense of being male or female, and the beliefs one holds about gender roles and attributes. We also described how gender identity is an important part of children's self-concept and a powerful source of self-esteem. From the time they understand they are a boy or a girl and know what it means to be a boy or girl, most children show preferences for looking like, behaving like, and playing with same-sex peers. Children, especially boys, who do not conform to gender norms often are ostracized by peers and even adults. With age, children's knowledge of gender stereotypes increases, but they think more flexibly about them, recognizing that stereotypes are products of societal values and accepting a wider range of "normal," at least up to adolescence. Some research suggests adolescents again go through a period of **gender intensification,** a decline in flexibility that reflects adolescents' enhanced self-consciousness and increased awareness of social norms and expectations concerning masculinity and femininity (Barnett & Rivers, 2004; Galambos, 2004; Ruble et al., 2006). However, other studies have not found declines in flexibility, except in particular domains, and more so in males than in females (Fredericks & Eccles, 2002; Harter, 2006).

We examine two domains in which gender norms are salient and associated with identity and self-esteem: physical appearance and academic/career aspirations.

PHYSICAL APPEARANCE. Boys consistently give themselves higher ratings in physical domains, such as physical appearance and athletic ability, than girls, who feel most confident about their social competencies (Harter, 2006; Ruble et al., 2006; Shapka & Keating, 2005). Importantly, physical appearance is the strongest predictor of global self-worth, with correlations ranging from .66–.82 (Harter, 2006). Therefore, not surprisingly, adolescent boys rate their global self-concept and self-esteem more positively than adolescent girls. Standards for physical appearance reflect societal and cultural beliefs about what is attractive, and research has clearly shown that these standards have an impact on individuals' identity and self-esteem (Harter, 1999, 2006; Kiang & Harter, 2004). Teenagers, with their heightened self-consciousness and desire for social approval, are particularly aware of and concerned about prevailing standards for physical appearance (Harter, 2006), and physical appearance is a strong predictor of popularity, especially for girls (LaFontana & Cillessen, 2002; Xie, Li, Boucher, Hutchins, & Cairns, 2006).

Standards for physical appearance reflect societal and cultural beliefs about what is attractive, and research has clearly shown that these standards have an impact on individuals' identity and self-esteem.

For many decades, the perceived ideal for females in North America, and in many societies around the world, has been tall, thin, and ample-breasted women who have pretty faces and great hair, and who wear stylish and sexy clothes. For many girls, the goal of meeting such standards is unrealistic, and a significant proportion of adolescent girls express dissatisfaction with their physical appearance (Harter, 2006; Ruble et al., 2006). Recall from Chapter 11 that 85% of young women worry about how they look and 50–88% of adolescent girls are dissatisfied with their body size and shape (Croll, 2005). Unfortunately, the distance between real and ideal physical selves causes many girls considerable emotional distress and is linked to serious mental health concerns, including depression, suicide, and severe eating disorders (Harter, 2006; Ruble et al., 2006; Stice & Bearman, 2001; Stice & Whitenton, 2002). Early-maturing females are particularly at risk for experiencing low self-esteem regarding body image because they tend to be shorter and heavier than girls who mature later. Also, many are unprepared for and cope inappropriately with the attention their developing bodies attract (e.g., becoming sexually active, engaging in extreme forms of dieting).

Historically, males have had more leeway concerning standards for physical appearance, and popularity for boys has been associated more with what they can do (e.g., athletic ability) than with what they look like. Also, judgments about men's attractiveness have been based on money, status, and power, in addition to physical appearance (Harter, 2006). Moreover, most adolescent boys express satisfaction with the changes in their bodies (i.e., changes that signal masculinity), and early maturity in boys is associated with popularity and positive self-regard (Harter, 2006). Some later-maturing boys experience lower self-esteem because they tend to be smaller—less muscular and less able to compete athletically—than their peers. This makes them feel they are not meeting up to the stereotype for their gender (Harter, 2006; Ruble et al., 2006).

The finding that boys rate their physical appearance more highly than girls is very robust; it has been replicated across countries and cultures (Harter, 2006), and it persists through the college years, even among athletes. Crocker and Ellsworth (1990) studied perceptions of appearance and athletic ability in college students majoring in physical education. In their study, female physical education students reported perceptions of greater athletic ability than a normative sample of girls. In fact, their ratings of athletic ability did not differ significantly from those of males in the same program. However, their ratings of physical appearance continued to be significantly lower than those of their male counterparts.

One powerful source of influence about standards for male and female physical appearance is the media. Teenagers are bombarded with images (e.g., via movies, magazines, TV, the Internet) that promote "good" looks reflecting the ideal we described above, and target audiences are becoming younger and younger all the time. Peer pressure, particularly conversations about appearance, and maternal pressure to lose weight also are associated with body dissatisfaction (Carlson Jones, 2004; Ricciardelli & McCabe, 2001). Greater emphasis needs to be placed on developing more realistic standards for physical appearance and setting goals that promote overall health and physical fitness (review the guidelines in Chapter 11 for supporting positive body image).

ACADEMIC AND CAREER ASPIRATIONS. In Chapter 10, we reviewed research concerning boys' and girls' self-concepts and self-esteem in academic domains; we noted that differences emerge early and are fairly consistent over time, especially within gender-stereotyped domains (Wigfield & Eccles, 2001; Wigfield et al., 1997). Popular belief holds that boys do better in math and science than girls, and research consistently indicates boys have higher self-concepts and self-esteem in these domains (Frome, Alfeld, Eccles, & Barber, 2006; Jacobs et al., 2002; Simpkins, Davis-Kean, & Eccles, 2006). However, achievement data in recent years indicates girls' performance in math and science courses is similar to that of boys (and sometimes girls do better), and girls' ratings of the importance of these subject areas also is similar to that of boys. Differences between the sexes do appear in their ratings of intrinsic interest for these subject areas. For example, Simpkins and her colleagues found, on average, that high school boys in their study attached greater personal significance to math and science course work and took more math and science courses than did high school girls. Their findings are consistent with other research indicating girls continue to be underrepresented in academic programs and careers involving math, science, and technology (Eccles, 2007; Frome et al., 2006, 2008), and this is cause for concern, given the increased reliance of the new economy on math, science, and technology.

Frome and her colleagues (2006) examined stability and change in the career aspirations of 104 women participating in the Michigan Study of Adolescent Life Transitions (MSALT). The career aspirations of these women were assessed in grade 12 and again at age 25. In the study, male-dominated occupations had 30% or fewer women in their workforce and included the fields of engineering and architecture and the profession of airline pilot. At age 25, 82% of the women reported changes in their career aspirations, with 55% changing to more neutral occupations (e.g., accounting, pharmacy) and 27% changing to female-dominated occupations (nursing, secretarial). When asked to give reasons for their change in aspirations, women in the study cited a desire for more flexibility in the workplace (e.g., daycare availability, scheduling flexibility) and low intrinsic value for the physical sciences. Women want to be successful in their careers, but they also want to have a family, and many still perceive the need to make a choice between career and family in occupations that continue to be dominated by men. In the Frome et al. study, women who stayed in male-dominated occupations typically held jobs that involved fewer hours of work each year, they expressed higher levels of intrinsic value for their work, and they reported lower desire for a family-flexible job.

Eccles's (2007, 2009) analyses indicate the main source of sex differences in choosing careers in the natural sciences or engineering is a fundamental difference in the intrinsic value boys and girls attach to these occupations as opposed to a difference in aptitude or perceived competence. Many girls want careers that will enable them to fulfill humanistic and helping values, and they believe falsely that careers in the natural sciences or engineering will not support these values. According to Eccles, if we want to increase the number of females entering these fields, we need to provide them with better information about the nature of these occupations, along with a full range of options, so they can make more informed decisions about careers that fit their personal values and identities as well as their short- and long-term goals—and the earlier the better. Along these lines, the ***Connecting with Adolescents*** guidelines offer some ideas about how to encourage young women's participation in the fields of math and science.

CONNECTING WITH ADOLESCENTS

Guidelines for Families and Teachers: Encouraging Young Women to Participate in Math- and Science-Related Courses and Careers

Encourage and build girls' confidence in taking high-level courses in math and sciences.

Examples

1. Help teenage girls develop positive attitudes about math, technology, and science by devising comprehensive evaluation-of-project outcomes that are sensitive to the needs of female students.
2. Design activities around girls' interests, and encourage the use of advanced technology applications that are more relevant to girls.
3. Offer extra support for girls by working systematically through complex math and science problems.
4. Encourage girls to participate in math- and science-related contests and competitions.

Show girls real role models.

Examples

1. Ensure that there are female teachers in the math- and science-related subjects, so that female students have role models to look up to.
2. Ask female students from senior grade levels to mentor younger students and encourage cooperative learning approaches.
3. Show videos that highlight female high flyers in math, science, and technology fields to assure girls that the possibility of success in science, engineering, and math-related careers exists.
4. Allow students to job-shadow female role models in the math, science, and technical fields.

Prove that many male-dominated careers are compatible with family goals.

Examples

1. Hold workshops or presentations that introduce teenage girls to the wide range of employment opportunities in the field of science and information technology.
2. Arrange career-awareness days or fairs that focus on women in technology, math, and science.
3. Invite role models to discuss how they balance career and family.

Look for opportunities for girls to engage in math and science activities outside of school.

Examples

1. Enroll girls in summer camps and extracurricular programs that allow them to become involved in hands-on science-related activities.
2. Have programs in which girls can participate to earn certificates or badges in math, science, and computers.
3. Set up all-girl science and math clubs to raise awareness, and recruit girls to participate in promoting the development of technology skills.
4. Arrange girls' gatherings during lunchtime to let them share their experiences and challenges in math and science classes.

Source: Adapted from Frome, P. M., Alfeld, C. J., Eccles, J. S., & Barber, B. L. (2006). Why don't they want a male-dominated job? An investigation of young women who changed their occupational aspirations. Educational Research and Evaluation, 12(4), 359-372. http://www.miamisci.org/great/ http://www.charityguide.org/volunteer/fifteen/math-science.htm

What about boys? What is their self-concept and self-esteem in domains traditionally thought of as dominated by females? In general, girls report higher ability beliefs and greater interest than boys in subjects involving reading and language arts (Durik, Vida, and Eccles, 2006; Harter, 2006; Ruble et al., 2006). Therefore, it's not surprising that girls report reading more for pleasure than boys. In terms of actual performance, the research findings are mixed. Some studies favor females (e.g., Phillips, Norris, Osmond, & Maynard, 2002), but others report small or no sex differences (e.g., Hyde & Linn, 1988), and still others indicate differences on particular literacy-related tasks and activities (Baker & Wigfield, 1999). Durik and her colleagues (2006) examined such differences in relation to high school boys' ability beliefs and valuing of literacy coursework and activities. In their study, girls valued reading and English more than boys, in terms of both intrinsic interest and importance, and they performed better on reading and writing tasks. Girls also reported reading for pleasure more than boys. Interestingly, the boys' ratings of self-concept were similar to those of the girls, and they reported taking a similar number of courses relating to language arts and literacy in high school. The researchers suggest that similar ratings of self-concept may reflect boys' tendency to overestimate and girls' tendency to underestimate their abilities—the net effect is ratings close together. That boys and girls take similar numbers of language arts courses in high school is likely unavoidable, even if boys value them less, since most academic programs and careers require reading and writing skills.

Sexual Orientation

Sexual orientation reflects a person's preferences for sexual partners. Typically, people who are attracted to members of the opposite sex identify as **heterosexual,** whereas people who are attracted to members of the same sex identify as **homosexual,** gay, or lesbian. Some people are **bisexual**—they are attracted to both sexes. Sexual orientation does not always align with sexual behavior, especially during adolescence when teens engage in many forms of sexual activity, regardless of their sexual orientation (Ruble et al., 2006). For example, it's common for gay and lesbian youth to have heterosexual experiences prior to defining their sexuality, and it's not uncommon for heterosexual youth to engage in homosexual behaviors with same-sex partners (Savin-Williams & Diamond, 1999). Also, sexual orientation does not always align with gender identity or perceived gender roles (Hines, 2004). For example, some women appear quite masculine in the way they dress, and they engage in activities not typically associated with their sex (e.g., they become construction workers or body builders), but still are heterosexual. Similarly, the term *metrosexual* was coined to describe contemporary men, typically city dwellers, who are interested in fashion and "in touch with their feminine side." However, gender atypical behavior is more likely in children who later identify as homosexuals than in children who are heterosexual, and retrospective reports from homosexual adults indicate they had more cross-gendered interests during childhood than their heterosexual peers (Baily & Zucker, 1995; Ruble et al., 2006).

ORIGINS OF ORIENTATIONS. As mentioned in Chapter 10, sexual attractions begin to emerge around age 10, but this varies by sex, culture, and sexual orientation (Herdt & McClintock, 2000; Ruble et al., 2006). Much of the research on the development of sexual orientation has focused on sexual minorities and their progression from awareness of same-sex attractions in late childhood/early adolescence through a period of testing and exploration, and finally to identifying as a homosexual, disclosing this identity to others, and becoming involved in same-sex relationships in late adolescence/early adulthood (Ruble et al., 2007; Troiden, 1993). This progression is more typical in men than in women, and it appears to be more of a process than an event (i.e., most individuals, whether heterosexual or homosexual, don't recall a particular point in time when their sexual orientation crystallized). Also mentioned earlier, there is much debate about the origins of sexual orientation. Is the greater influence nature or nurture? As is true with most forms of development, the evidence points to an interaction between biology and environment. Research examining genetic, hormonal, and brain structural links to sexual orientation offer strong evidence for a biological component (Ruble et al., 2006), but biology can influence temperament, which can influence beliefs and feelings. Also, a search for identity can drive behavioral changes: Children and youth who question their sexuality may engage in gender-atypical behavior and, consequently, develop self-concepts consistent with their developing notions of sexual minorities (Carver, Egan, & Perry, 2004).

Youth become aware of same-sex attractions in late childhood/early adolescence, about the same time all youth develop romantic and sexual attractions.

EXPERIENCES. Researchers estimate that between 5% and 13% of the population is homosexual (Savin-Williams, 2006), but these statistics may not be accurate because many gay and lesbian individuals hide their sexual orientation for fear they will be rejected by their families, friends, and communities. In fact, many gay and lesbian youth are ostracized and victimized at school and in their communities (D'Augelli, 2003; D'Augelli, Pilkington, & Hershberger, 2002), which has led to tragic outcomes for some youth. Such verbal and physical abuse places these youth at higher risk for experiencing serious social and mental health problems (e.g., depression, hopelessness, substance abuse, prostitution, and suicide) than their heterosexual peers (D'Augelli, 2003; Udry & Chantala, 2002). As one example, Jaheem Herrera committed suicide at age 11 after sustained teasing from peers. He told his mother, "They keep telling me this gay word . . . I'm tired of hearing it . . ." (Simon, 2009). Fortunately, having a supportive family, feeling comfortable about their sexual orientation, and participating in gay, lesbian, and bisexual support groups can protect these youth from such negative outcomes.

In general, adolescents with same-sex attractions have the same needs and concerns as all teenagers and although many suffer in their formative years, most emerge from adolescence with positive self-concepts and a sense of optimism about their future (Diamond & Savin-Williams, 2003).

Ethnic Identity

Whereas Erikson's theory of identity formation focused on the development of personal identity ("Who am I? Who will I be in the future?"), social identity theories focus on how individuals identify with social groups and the processes associated with ethnic group membership (Pahl & Way, 2006; Tajfel & Turner, 1986). Along these lines, **ethnic identity** refers to an individual's sense of belonging to an ethnic group and being affiliated with the beliefs and behaviors that reflect ethnic group membership.

A MODEL OF ETHNIC IDENTITY FORMATION. Jean Phinney (1989) proposed a 3-stage model of ethnic identity development, extending from Marcia's model of personal identity formation:

1. *Unexamined.* In early adolescence, individuals may have unexamined positive or negative attitudes toward their ethnic group. They may be unidentified or prematurely identified as a member of an ethnic group. At this point, they are experiencing a kind of ethnic identity diffusion (French, Seidman, Allen, & Aber, 2006).
2. *Moratorium or search.* By middle adolescence, youth are typically exploring aspects of their ethnicity. Advances in cognitive development, exposure to more diverse groups of peers (e.g., high schools often are more ethnically and racially diverse than elementary schools), and/or specific "encounters" (e.g., exposure to prejudice or discrimination) may trigger explorations, which are believed critical for reaching the third stage (Cross, 1995; French et al., 2006; Pahl & Way, 2006).
3. *Achieved or committed.* Older adolescents become more secure in their personal and social identities, and exploration decreases as they identify with and become committed to an ethnic group. Typically, this stage is accompanied by strong feelings of affirmation and belonging (Pahl & Way, 2006).

The search for an ethnic identity can give rise to competing and ambivalent feelings, especially for minority youth who must integrate what can be contrasting viewpoints—those of their their cultural group and those of the majority group—into a unified sense of self. Even adolescents in remote, fairly traditional communities are influenced by dominant, typically Western cultures (e.g., through access to television and the Internet). Lene Arnett-Jensen (2003, citing an anthropological study by Condon, 1988) described changes in Inuit adolescents from the Canadian Arctic that were the result of government interventions and access to Western media. Traditionally, these youth had been socialized by their families and spent much of their time ice fishing and hunting, but now they spend most of their time outside the family environment (e.g., in school and peer groups), and fishing and hunting have become recreational activities. Boys have taken up hockey and have begun to brag about their sports ability. This stands in stark contrast to traditional Inuit culture, which discourages calling attention to personal skills and accomplishments. Often teens are torn between the values of their cultural communities and what they perceive to be advantages in the majority culture. In Jensen's own research (1998), she found that young adults in India were split on the value of arranged versus love marriages, arguing that arranged marriages make sense "within a traditional Indian worldview that emphasizes duty to family, respect for elders, and behaving according to one's station in life," but not within the context of globalization that emphasizes Western values, including freedom of choice and individual rights (p. 192).

How do such identity issues get resolved? Phinney (1996) proposed four outcomes to ethnic identity exploration:

1. *Assimilation.* The individual identifies with the majority culture and rejects his or her ethnic culture.
2. *Marginal.* The individual lives within the majority culture but feels alienated from it.
3. *Separated.* The individual identifies with his or her ethnic culture and rejects the majority culture.
4. *Bicultural.* The individual identifies with both the minority and the majority culture.

Research conducted in the United States indicates resolutions to this commitment issue vary across ethnic groups (Chavous et al., 2003; Phinney, DuPont, Espinosa, Revill, & Sanders, 1994). For example, European American youth typically identify themselves as assimilated, whereas African American and Latino youth more frequently perceive they are separated, and Mexican and Asian American adolescents are the most likely to perceive they are bicultural.

INFLUENCES ON ETHNIC IDENTITY. Parents have an important impact on adolescents' ethnic identity formation. Secure ethnic identities are fostered in families in which parents openly discuss ethnic issues with their adolescents and model and promote a sense of pride in their heritage, participation in their ethnic community, and strategies for coping with discrimination (Hughes et al., 2006). In some cases, ethnic identity issues can be a source of tension between parents and adolescents. For example, Phinney, Kim, Ossorio, and Vilhjalmsdottir (2002) asked adolescents from four ethnic groups to reason about scenarios that described common disagreements between teens and their parents (e.g., disagreements about doing chores and dating) and found differences in the teens' responses were related to culture and development. European American youth shifted from an emphasis on exercising personal autonomy in middle adolescence (ages 14 to 17) to considering the views and feelings of their parents in late adolescence and early adulthood (ages 18 to 22). Armenian and Mexican American youth shifted in the opposite direction; they showed more consideration for parents' values during middle adolescence and asserted more autonomy in late adolescence. Korean American adolescents tended to show consideration for their parents' point of view throughout adolescence. According to Arnett-Jensen (2003), ethnic identity formation is especially complex when adolescents are exposed to multiple cultures and when their heritage culture represents a minority culture. She also argues that a universal path to ethnic identity development cannot be assumed in a world of globalization (p. 194).

The education system also can have a profound influence on ethnic identity formation. Earlier, we alluded to the ways in which government schools have changed the developmental trajectories of Inuit children in the Canadian Arctic. In fact, governments have a long history of creating residential schools that separated First Nations, or Aboriginal children, in Canada from their families, their culture, and their language. Today, many universities are developing teacher education programs and preparing teachers who have a First Nations heritage. The goal is to prepare teachers who will either return to teach in their First Nations communities or provide high-quality, culturally sensitive instruction to First Nations learners in multi-ethnic public schools across the country. Research conducted in the United States supports this goal. For example, one study found Native American youth who attended schools with predominantly Native American student bodies formed a stronger sense of ethnic identity than those who attended schools in which they were in the minority (Lysne & Levy, 1997). Another study showed how complex rituals and rights of passage can connect adolescents (in this case, females) to their culture and lead to optimal ethnic identity formation (Markstrom & Iborra, 2003).

Native American youth who attended schools with predominantly Native American student bodies formed a stronger sense of ethnic identity than those who attended schools where they were in the minority.

DISCRIMINATION AND IDENTITY. Exposure to prejudice and discrimination is another powerful influence on adolescents' ethnic identity formation. In fact, some research indicates that being the recipient of overt acts of discrimination provides a powerful incentive to explore one's ethnic identity, and may contribute to higher levels of affirmation for and belonging to a cultural group (Cross, 1971; French, Seidman, Allen, & Aber, 2006; Pahl & Way, 2006). However, there also is evidence linking perceived discrimination to decreased self-esteem and increased symptoms of depression (Greene, Way, & Pahl, 2006). It appears that discrimination by peer groups has a stronger influence on these outcomes than discrimination by adults, perhaps because discrimination by peers is similar to peer rejection, which has a strong negative association with teens' psychosocial adjustment. Discrimination by adults may be more strongly linked to other kinds of outcomes, such as academic achievement and career aspirations.

Some adolescents who experience discrimination form an **oppositional identity:** they commit to an identity in opposition to what they perceive is the collective identity of the dominant group (Fordham & Ogbu, 1986; Ogbu, 2004). As a way of protecting their self-esteem, they devalue domains in which their ethnic group is expected to do poorly. Much of the research about oppositional identity formation has focused on African American youth and has been used to explain their diminished motivation for school and achievement compared with that of other ethnic groups (e.g., European and Asian American youth), but any minority group who experiences status problems can form a collective identity in opposition to what they perceive is the collective identity of the dominant group (Chavous et al., 2003; Graham & Taylor, 2002; Ogbu, 2004).

Storm and Stress

There is evidence that some degree of storm and stress is typical during adolescence, at least in North America for adolescents in the middle-class majority culture (Arnett, 1999). This is not surprising, given the many personal changes and transitions adolescents are experiencing, and the complex task of forming an identity in the context of all this change. In this section, we focus on two aspects of storm and stress that characterize the teen years: mood disruptions and risky behavior. A third aspect of what characterizes this period of life as stormy and stressful is increased conflict with parents, which is addressed in the section on parenting adolescents. Individual differences as well as differences across cultures will also be discussed.

Mood Disruptions

Is adolescence a time of temperamental volatility? In studies of mood, adolescents do report greater extremes and more changes in mood than either preadolescents or adults (Arnett, 1999). Moreover, in longitudinal studies, negative affect has been found to increase from early to middle adolescence and then decrease during late adolescence and early adulthood (Buchanan, Eccles, & Becker, 1992; Natvig, Albrektsen, & Qvarnstrom, 2003; Seiffge-Krenke & Gelhaar, 2008). Adolescents report feeling self-conscious, embarrassed, awkward, nervous, lonely, and ignored more often than adults do (Arnett, 1999), and they give lower ratings to items that reflect feeling great, proud, and in control, and higher ratings to items associated with depressed mood. According to Arnett, the result is an "overall deflation of childhood happiness as childhood ends and adolescence begins" (p. 321).

Of course, adolescents vary in the extent to which they experience mood disruptions. Girls tend to be more prone to negative mood and mood swings than boys (Arnett, 1999), and some research indicates youth from ethnic minority groups have lower levels of life satisfaction and happiness than other groups of teens (Brown, Wallace, & Williams, 2001). In Brown and his colleagues' study, which included a national sample of American high school students, the majority of adolescents reported they were satisfied with their lives and happy. However, African American youth reported lower levels of life satisfaction and happiness than their European American and Hispanic peers.

What accounts for differences in mood and levels of happiness in adolescents? Research points to a variety of factors, including low popularity with peers, low self-esteem, poor school performance, and school alienation (Arnett, 1999; Furnham & Cheng, 2000; Natvig et al., 2003). With regard to school, Natvig and her colleagues found that perceived support from teachers (i.e., positive ratings of items indicating teachers "treat me fairly" or are "interested in me as a person") increased the odds of feeling happy. This signals the important role of teacher–student relationships in the lives of adolescents, a topic we will return to in the section titled "Life at School." Furnham and Cheng examined the relationship between parenting styles and adolescent happiness. Consistent with our review of research on parenting styles in Chapters 7 and 10, these researchers found authoritative parenting styles were associated with positive outcomes for adolescents, including higher self-esteem and general happiness. In particular, they found authoritative parenting was associated with higher levels of self-esteem in boys, which was related to their self-reported happiness. Interestingly, boys were more likely than girls to characterize the parenting they received as authoritarian, and mothers' self-reports about their parenting concurred with the boys' opinions. Girls who reported authoritarian or permissive parenting styles described lower levels of self-esteem and happiness.

Finally, Olsson, Fahlen, and Janson (2008) asked children and youth (ages 7 to 19) in Sweden to describe in their own words what made them anxious or unhappy. Early adolescents (ages 11 to 13) attributed these feelings to "angry and shouting parents," parents being away from home often, economic hardship in the family, peer problems, and bullying in school. For 14- to 16-year-olds, "feeling deserted and disliked by parents, teachers, and peers" was stressful and, in late adolescence (ages 17 to 19), stress was attributed to absent or uninterested adults, boring weekends, and abundant homework. When asked what adults might do to make teens feel better, adolescents of all ages consistently requested more choice for leisure time activities, more time with parents, increased attention to and respect for their thoughts and opinions, more action against bullying in school, and more attention to youth who are obviously unhappy.

Risky Behavior

As we described in Chapter 11, adolescence is the period in life associated with the highest rates of risky behavior (i.e., behavior that has the potential to harm self or others). According to Ronald Dahl (2004, p. 3):

> Adolescence presents a striking paradox with respect to overall health statistics. This developmental period is marked by rapid increases in physical and mental capabilities . . . Compared to young children, adolescents are stronger, bigger, and

> faster . . . achieving maturational improvements in reaction time, reasoning abilities, immune function, and capacities to withstand cold, heat, injury, and physical stress. In almost every measureable domain, this is a *developmental period of strength and resilience.*

However, Dahl goes on to claim: ". . . despite these robust maturational improvements . . . , overall morbidity and mortality rates *increase* over 200% during the same interval of time" (italics are from the original).

What accounts for this paradox? Recall from Chapter 11 that although teenagers have better reasoning abilities and decision-making skills than children, in situations where emotions flare or peers exert pressure, they may have difficulty thinking and behaving responsibly. Cognitively, they may understand potential consequences of risky behavior, but become overwhelmed by emotions and/or their desire to seek experiences that lead to high-intensity feelings (Dahl, 2004; Sunstein, 2008). Like Arnett (1999), Dahl cautions against characterizing all youth as "impulsive and hot-headed," citing research findings that up to 80% of adolescents go through these "tumultuous" times without major difficulties; in addition, those engaged in high-risk behavior during adolescence typically have a history of problem behaviors and impulsivity during early and middle childhood. However, it is important to focus attention on the significant minority of youth who do get into trouble, because adolescence is a time when one's life course and habits are set. Lifetime problems with nicotine, drugs and alcohol, personal relationships, and failure to acquire knowledge and skills that support productive work and careers may stem from risky adolescent explorations and experimentation.

Smoking, drugs and alcohol, fast driving, and sex have been threats to the well-being of teenagers for many decades. Today, teens also face a number of significant threats through their use of new technologies.

New Media, New Risks

Electronic media is pervasive in the lives of youth. Through access to the Internet, satellite TV, cell phones, iPods, and video game systems, it is estimated that the average American teen spends about 5 hours each day consuming screen media (Carnagey, Anderson, & Bartholow, 2007). A recent report from *Pew Internet & American Life Project* indicates approximately 90% of adolescents can access the Internet in their homes (Lenhart, 2009), and 63% report they go online daily. Internet access also is available to teens in most schools and libraries, and more than 70% of youth own cell phones, many types of which also give them access to the Internet. How are adolescents using the Internet? They are doing research for school assignments; surfing websites to find out about movies, TV shows, and music groups; shopping; and, of course, social networking (Lenhart, 2009; Nielson Company, 2009; Wartella, Caplovitz, & Lee, 2004). Boys are more likely to use the Internet for fun and games, buying and selling things, and making Web pages than girls, who use the Internet for information seeking and communication more than boys.

DANGERS IN SOCIAL NETWORKING. Along with the undeniable benefits of accessible, advanced technologies, it's hard not to also be aware of the threats to safety and overall well-being that are associated with teens' use of new media. Herein lies the conundrum the teachers and librarians were struggling with in this chapter's Casebook. Even though recent research has quashed the myth that Internet use leads to social isolation and loneliness, there is concern that children and youth who already are socially isolated and lonely are more likely to interact with strangers on the Internet than well-adjusted youth, who tend to limit their social networking activities to their everyday peers (Wartella et al., 2004). Moreover, posting photos and personal profiles on social networking sites such as Facebook and Twitter increases the likelihood of being contacted by a stranger online (Lenhart, 2009). Finally, a posting that seems harmless or "hip" during high school or college has the potential to come back to haunt you in your adult life (e.g., former Miss California 2009, Carrie Prejean, was stripped of her crown when topless photos of her hit the Internet), and recall that adolescents, in the thrill of the moment, may not make the best judgments concerning behaviors that can affect their reputation, not to mention job prospects, long term.

ADVERTISING. Another potential threat on the Internet comes from advertisers. According to Wartella et al. (2004), the deluge of advertising in online environments raises two important issues concerning children and youth. First, advertisers often ask for personal information in exchange for merchandise or even gifts and, increasingly, websites contain cookies and other "intelligent agents" that track and catalogue the interests and habits of online visitors. As a result, companies may have elaborate profiles of users without their giving permission or even having knowledge the profiles exist. A survey of parents (Annenberg Public Policy Centre, 2000) found many were not aware that websites could gather personal information without asking permission, and children and youth were much more willing than parents to say it was OK to provide personal and family information to commercial websites in exchange for goods and/or services. Their naïveté in this regard makes them easy prey for Internet scammers who use such information to take advantage of consumers. Second, online advertising often is integrated in the content of a branded environment. The separation between content and commercials that is usually clear on television is not required on the Internet. Advertising can be inconspicuously embedded in websites, or advertisers can blatantly devote entire websites to opportunities for children and youth to interact with the products they're selling. Wartella and her colleagues claim this leads to unfair and deceptive advertising practices.

ADDICTED TO THE INTERNET? Is it possible to become addicted to the Internet? There is evidence indicating some youth use technology and the Internet excessively and display characteristics of Internet "dependence" or addiction (Greenfield, 1999; Kim et al., 2006; Lin & Tsai, 2002). For example, Kim and colleagues administered the *Internet Addiction Scale* (see Young, 1998 for the original English version) to 1,573 high school students in Korea. This assessment indicated 1.6% of their sample, or 25 students, had an Internet addiction (e.g., compulsive use and withdrawal, interference in personal relationships, and effects on commitments for school and work), and a further 38% (almost 600 students) exhibited characteristics that put them at risk for developing an Internet addiction. Similarly, Lin and Tsai identified 88 "dependent" Internet users in a group of 753 high school students in Taiwan. Compared to non-dependent users, these students spent more time online and reported significantly more negative influences on their daily lives and relationships. These students also scored higher on overall sensation seeking and disinhibition than the non-dependent users, suggesting that individuals who are at risk for addictions generally also are at risk for excessive Internet involvement.

VIDEO VIOLENCE. Much of the research concerning the impact of new technologies on the social and emotional development of children and youth focuses on their use of violent video games. In general, the findings indicate statistically significant, but small (e.g., $r = .15$ or $.19$), positive correlations between using violent interactive media and aggressive behavior (Anderson & Bushman, 2001; Carnagey et al., 2007; Wartella et al., 2004). Specifically, use of violent video games has been linked to increases in aggressive cognition, affect, and behavior; physiological arousal; and a decrease in prosocial behavior. One study examined the desensitizing effects of violent media on helping others (Bushman & Anderson, 2009). In this study, college students played either violent or nonviolent video games for 20 minutes and then completed a questionnaire. While they were completing the questionnaire, a fight was staged outside the lab and one person was injured. On average, students who had played the violent game took longer (over 450% longer) to help the injured victim than students who played the nonviolent game. Moreover, students who played the violent game were less likely to notice the fight and rated it less serious than those who played the nonviolent game, which prevented them from helping the victim. Of course, these findings should be kept in perspective. Not all individuals who interact with violent video games become violent themselves (Olson, Kutner, & Warner, 2008), and, as was true about television viewing, some research indicates youth with more overall risk factors are more likely to commit violent acts after playing violent video games (Anderson, Shibuya, & Ihori et al., 2010; Bushman, Rothstein, & Anderson, 2010).

Clearly, adolescents are engaged in numerous activities that have risks associated with them. What can adolescents do to protect themselves, and how can parents, teachers, and other adults help?

Exercising Self-Control

In Chapters 7 and 10, we went into a great deal of detail about the development of self-regulation. Being a responsible adult requires the development and exercise of self-control over thoughts and actions (i.e., emotion and behavior control). During adolescence this often requires the inhibition and modification of behaviors—despite strong emotions—to avoid terrible consequences (Dahl, 2004). Adolescents must learn to navigate and negotiate complex social situations, online and face to face, often without the direct support of parents or another adult caregiver—but recall from Dahl that "adolescence proves to be a difficult time to develop positive abilities to use strategies, make plans, set goals, learn the social rules, and navigate ambiguous situations as the cognitive and emotional systems are integrated" (p. 18).

So how can adults help? One way to support teens is to provide the right balance of monitoring and interest and to scaffold their development of skills and strategies for self-control. Monitoring is one of the most important things parents, teachers, coaches, and other responsible adults can do for teens. According to Ann Masten and colleagues (Masten & Shaffer, 2006; Shaffer, Burt, Obradovic, Herbers, & Masten, 2009), adult monitoring of adolescents' activities is all too frequently and prematurely withdrawn. Effective scaffolding should be gradually faded, so that adolescents are increasingly able to make decisions for themselves, but not put in situations that they are not ready and able to handle. The ***Connecting with Adolescents*** guidelines describe ways to monitor adolescents' interactions with media and offer some solutions for this chapter's Casebook.

Another way to support teens is to provide opportunities for positive "high intensity" experiences. Risky behavior is not the only way to activate the high intensity feelings that are so appealing for adolescents (Dahl, 2004). It also is possible to ignite high levels of

CONNECTING WITH ADOLESCENTS

Guidelines for Families, Teachers, and Other Professionals: Protecting Adolescents from Harm from Media

Set a good example and limit the use of media.
Examples
1. Be critical and discriminating users of media, because your habits and preferences provide powerful role models for adolescents.
2. Share your viewing decisions with teenagers.
3. Limit the time spent on various media at home.
4. Seek out useful websites and other resources, and share information about them with adolescents.

Spend time with teenagers selecting appropriate media offerings.
Examples
1. Locate television programs, video games, and Internet websites that can provide occasions for discussing values, beliefs, and moral issues with teenagers.
2. Treat TV watching, game playing, and Internet browsing as family activities. Find programs that the whole family can enjoy.

Help teenagers seek alternative entertainment.
Examples
1. Help teenagers develop interests in other meaningful activities, such as sports or music.
2. Shop for games with adolescents; steer them away from games that involve violence and toward games that allow them to have fun and learn.

Help teenagers to be critical consumers of the Internet.
Examples
1. Help teenagers understand that not all information on the Internet is reliable and true. Help them to analyze the information they find there.
2. Help teenagers understand the consequences of posting personal information on the Internet.
3. Teach them the steps they must take to protect themselves from bullying, sexual abuse, and offensive language.
4. Monitor the sites that are popular among teenagers in order to understand the trends that are engaging them.

Source: Adapted from http://www.parentstv.org/ptc/parentsguide/main.asp http://www.advocatesforyouth.org/index.php?option=com_content&task=view&id=1293&Itemid=206

passion to pursue goals in academic, sport, music, and social service domains. Therefore, adults should look for ways to support adolescents' engagement in activities that are both healthy and rewarding.

Storm and Stress Across Cultures

Not all cultures experience adolescent storm and stress to the same degree. Schegel and Barry (1991) studied 186 traditional cultures around the world and found less evidence of storm and stress among adolescents in these societies than is reported in Western cultures. According to Schegel and Barry, expectations concerning adolescent autonomy may, in part, account for observed differences between cultures. In Western cultures that value individualism, we take for granted that adolescents will become increasingly independent as they progress through the teen years. However, conflicts arise when adolescents want to gain independence at a quicker pace, or over a wider range of activities, than the adults in their lives are prepared to grant them. Arnett (1999) agrees conflicts often arise when adults try to regulate the pace of adolescents' growing independence. Of course, parents, teachers, and other adult caregivers typically are motivated to "put on the brakes" out of concern that too much autonomy too soon will lead to participation in risky behavior. In traditional cultures, which tend to be more interdependent, adolescents' striving for independence is less likely to be a source of conflict between adolescents and their adult caregivers.

However, there can be other sources of storm and stress in traditional cultures (Arnett, 1999). In ethnographies of traditional cultures, adolescence is often referred to as a challenging time. In particular, problems for adolescent boys are more likely to occur in cultures in which they are excluded from activities with men than in cultures in which boys take part in men's activities (Schegel & Barry, 1991). Also, with increasing globalization, youth in traditional cultures have access to Western media and are influenced by Western culture. This can be a source of conflict between them and the more traditional adults in their lives. Similarly, the degree of storm and stress adolescents from minority cultures in the United States experience appears to increase with the number of generations the adolescent's family has been in America (Arnett, 1999; Steinberg, 1996). Nevertheless, so-called storm and stress among adolescents is more common among youth in Western majority cultures than it is among youth from traditional cultures (Arnett, 1999; Bradford et al., 2004).

Relationships with Peers

Continuing the trend they started in middle childhood, adolescents spend increasing amounts of time with peers, and these relationships become increasingly important sources of social and emotional support. Parents often worry about the influence peers will have on *their* teenagers. Will peers pressure their teenagers to use drugs, skip school, or engage in sexual and delinquent activities? Research has tended to highlight the negative influence of friends during adolescence as well (Crosnoe, Cavanagh, & Elder Jr., 2003). What is the reality? Do peers get a bad rap?

From Peer Groups to Peer Culture

Most adolescents belong to a peer group, and different groups of adolescents identify with different social values and norms for behavior, sometimes referred to as **peer culture.** These groups may identify a set of "rules" concerning how to dress, talk, style hair, and interact with others, and they may determine which activities, music, or other students are in or out of favor. For example, when Jessica, a popular high school student, was asked to explain the rules that her group lives by, she had no trouble:

> OK. No. 1: clothes. You cannot wear jeans any day but Friday, and you cannot wear a ponytail or sneakers more than once a week. Monday is fancy day—like black pants or maybe you bust out with a skirt. You have to remind people how cute you are in case they forgot over the weekend. No. 2: parties. Of course we sit down and discuss which ones we're going to because there is no point in getting all dressed up for a party that's going to be lame. (Talbot, 2002, p. 28)

These peer cultures encourage conformity to the group rules. When another girl in Jessica's group wore jeans on Monday, Jessica confronted her: "Why are you wearing jeans today? Did you forget it was Monday?" (Talbot, 2002, p. 28). Jessica explained that the group had to suspend this "rebel" several times, not allowing her to sit with them at lunch.

Of course, not all aspects of peer cultures are bad or cruel. The norms in some groups are positive and support healthy lifestyles and achievement in school. Two types of groups are especially prominent in adolescent peer culture: cliques and crowds.

CLIQUES. In Chapter 10, we described cliques as relatively small, friendship-based groups ranging in size from 3 to a dozen (Rubin et al., 2005). Cliques exist in childhood and adulthood, but adolescent cliques distinguish themselves in terms of their standards for group membership and degree of "cliquishness" (Collins & Steinberg, 2006). During childhood and early adolescence, cliques typically include peers of the same sex and age who share common interests and engage in similar activities. Cliques serve adolescents' emotional and security needs by providing a stable social context in which group members know each other well and form close friendships (Brown, 2004; Henrich, Brookmeyer, Shrier, & Shahar, 2006). Adolescents can belong to more than one clique. For example, most adolescents belong to a friendship clique, but individuals also may belong to cliques in the clubs and organizations to which they belong (after school clubs, church groups). During adolescence, clique membership helps to establish individuals' status in the social hierarchy of high schools (Collins & Steinberg, 2006).

CROWDS. Associating with crowds occurs during early and middle adolescence (Collins & Steinberg, 2006; Rubin et al., 2005). As the term implies, crowds are larger than cliques, less intimate, and more loosely organized. In fact, members of a crowd may or may not interact directly with one another. However, crowds provide opportunities for adolescents to expand their peer network beyond their clique(s), meet new people, and explore new identities (Tarrant, 2002). Crowds are reputation-based; that is, they are distinguished from one another by the attitudes and activities their members share (Rubin et al., 2005). Members of particular crowds typically share clothing styles, use similar language, smoke or don't smoke, and achieve or don't achieve in school. These choices influence both how others view them (e.g., "jocks," "brains," "partyers") and how they view themselves.

Status and self-esteem are associated with crowd membership. For example, members of high-status crowds—jocks—typically have higher self-esteem than members of relatively lower-status crowds (Prinstein & LaGreca, 2002). Furthermore, the stigma placed on individuals who are associated with particular crowds typically channels their relationship, even dating, patterns such that they may be prevented from making new friends, exploring new identities, or changing crowd membership. Crowds become far less prominent in late adolescence. According to Collins and Steinberg (2006, p. 1022), "crowds may serve as an identity 'way station' or placeholder during the period between individuation from parents and establishment of a coherent personal identity." Interestingly, adolescents who are relatively more confident in their identity tend not to value crowd affiliations as much as those who are still exploring, and by high school, many adolescents believe affiliations with particular crowds stifle their identity and self-expression (Collins & Steinberg, 2006). Crowds begin to dissolve as late adolescents begin to focus more on close friendships and romantic relationships.

Crowds are reputation-based. Members of particular crowds typically share clothing styles, use similar language, smoke or don't smoke, achieve or don't achieve in school.

Peer Pressure

During adolescence, the pressure to conform, or "be like" peers, can be strong (Brown, Bakken, Ameringer, & Mahon, 2008). **Peer pressure** refers to the influence peers have on one's attitudes and behaviors, including attitudes about school, clothing and hairstyles, movies and music. In general, peer pressure has a negative connotation, but peers can pressure for good or bad (Lacourse, Nagin, Trembly, Vitaro, & Claes, 2003). How does peer pressure work? Denise Kandel (1978) identified two key processes in a now seminal study of adolescents' drug use, educational goals, and delinquency. **Selection** is the process by which adolescents choose friends and peer groups. Typically, they target individuals and groups who have traits and characteristics similar to their own, or peers they would like to emulate or be like (e.g., teenagers with academic aspirations seek out other high-achieving teens). Once selections have been made, the process of **socialization** begins. Within peer groups, attitudes and behaviors are modeled and reinforced. The socialization of destructive and deviant behavior is a concern for adults as they observe the power of peer cultures in the lives of adolescents; research has shown how deviancy can be socialized in the context of peer relationships (Blanton & Burkley, 2008; Kandel & Chen, 2000). Thomal Dishion and colleagues (Dishion & Patterson, 2006; Piehler & Dishion, 2007) claim that **deviancy training** occurs when peer groups talk favorably about breaking rules and engaging in delinquent behavior. They observed that "deviant talk" among peers ages 13 and 14 predicted smoking, drug and alcohol use, and violent behavior by age 15 or 16 (Dishion, McCord, & Poulin, 1999). Peer pressure is strongest during early and middle adolescence when teenagers are trying to establish identities separate from their parents. By late adolescence, increased autonomy and the establishment of personal identity makes teenagers depend less on peers and feel more confident to make their own decisions and develop their own style.

Friendships

In Chapters 7 and 10, we established the importance of friendships in children's lives, and they are no less important for adolescents. In fact, adolescents report that friends are their most important resource outside their family, and relationships with friends are consistently implicated in adolescents' overall competence and well-being (Brown, 2004; Collins & Steinberg, 2006). Poor-quality friendships in adolescence are associated with negative outcomes, including loneliness, depression, and decreased productivity in school and work settings. In contrast, high-quality friendships are important protective factors for adolescents with emotional problems and adolescents experiencing problems at home (Collins & Steinberg, 2006; Laible, Carlo, & Raffaelli, 2000). Adolescents who are rejected by peers participate less in school activities, so their achievement suffers; they are more likely to drop out of school and may even evidence more problems as adults. For example, rejected aggressive adolescents are more likely to commit crimes as they grow older (Buhs, Ladd, & Herald, 2006; Coie & Dodge, 1998; Fredricks, Blumenthal, & Paris, 2004). Thus, helping adolescents make and keep friends is a valuable investment.

Friendships continue to deepen during adolescence. Specifically, adolescents continue to regard companionship and shared interests as important in friendships, but they also expect commitment and intimacy (Collins & Steinberg, 2006). This is particularly true for girls. More so than younger children, adolescents share secrets, empathize, and cooperate with their friends (Collins & Steinberg, 2006; Eisenberg, Fabes, & Spinrad, 2006). Also, they understand one another better, and this increased sense of mutuality and reciprocity increases trust, respect, and support in their relationships. Conflicts continue to be more common among friends than acquaintances (Collins & Steinberg, 2006). However, when conflicts occur, adolescents are more skilled at resolving them, and the conflicts are less likely to disrupt the relationship.

Adolescent girls are more interested in close friendships, and they report more intimacy, prosocial support, and esteem support in their friendships than do boys (Collins & Steinberg, 2006). Also, teenage girls are more concerned with loyalty in friendships, more likely to desire exclusivity in relationships, and more anxious about the potential for rejection (Johnson, 2004). Such closeness to friends may also account for some negative features of adolescent girls' friendships (Collins & Steinberg, 2006; Benenson & Christakos, 2003). For example, adolescent girls' friendships tend to be of shorter duration than boys' friendships, and girls are more likely than boys to report actions that have harmed existing friendships and instances of friendships ending. It seems the emotional intensity of girls' friendships creates potential for frustration and disappointment, and this can increase the risk for depression and internalized distress when friendships end (Collins & Steinberg, 2006). Boys, on the other hand, continue to focus on shared activities. These differences also are evident in early dating and romantic relationships.

Romantic Relationships

In the United States, 25% of 12-year-olds report having had a romantic relationship. By age 18, this statistic increases to 70% (Carver, Joyner, & Udry, 2003; Collins & Steinberg, 2006). On average, girls begin dating before boys do (girls at 12 or 13 years of age; boys about a year later). At first, dating and romantic coupling are supported through peer networks—all-girl and all-boy cliques come together, and partners are typically chosen on the basis of membership in what has become a mixed-gender peer group (Connolly, Furman, & Konarski, 2000). Dating at this stage typically occurs as small groups of couples engaging in dating activities (e.g., going to a movie or a school dance). Later, when adolescents can drive and parents ease up on curfews and supervision, adolescents depend less on peer networks and spend more time as separate couples. Increasingly, partners are chosen on the basis of physical attraction, personal qualities, and common interests (Bouchey & Furman, 2003).

Most early romances do not last beyond adolescence, but these relationships can be formative in the lives of teenagers. For example, most adults who survived them would agree their adolescent romances offered important life lessons, and high-quality romantic relationships during adolescence are positively associated with the development of romantic self-concept and general self-worth (Collins & Steinberg, 2006). However, adolescents involved in romantic relationships experience more conflict and more extreme mood swings than other adolescents, and early dating and sexual activity are associated with problem behavior and social and emotional difficulties. In general, it appears extremes of dating—too early, too much, not at all—are associated with problems (Brown, 2004). For example, high rates of dating are associated with depression and lower academic achievement, whereas not dating at all is associated with depression, excessive dependence on parents, and deficient social skills (Quatman, Sampson, Robinson, & Watson, 2001; Seiffge-Krenke, 1997).

BOYS AND GIRLS AND ROMANCE. There is evidence that boys and girls have different attitudes about dating and romantic relationships (Leaper & Anderson, 1997; Underwood & Rosen, 2009). Boys tend to focus on the sexual aspects of dating and the physical attractiveness of their partners, whereas girls look for opportunities for closeness and communication (Furman & Wehner, 1997; Shulman & Seiffge-Krenke, 2001). Similarly, adolescent boys emphasize physical gratification over intimacy in early sexual encounters and view these sexual experiences in terms of conquest, status, and recreation (Hendrick & Hendrick, 1995; Martin, 1996). In contrast, girls are more focused on intimacy and relationship issues and, therefore, more likely to have their first sexual experience in the context of an emotional relationship. Also, girls are more likely to report conflicted feelings about sex: They feel happy and excited about their relationship, but guilty and anxious about its physicality (Brooks-Gunn & Paikoff, 1997). We described current trends in adolescent sexual activity in Chapter 11, including some negative consequences associated with early onset of sexual activity.

SEXUAL MINORITY STATUS AND ROMANCE. Sexual minority adolescents often are slower to begin dating and develop romantic attachments. They may be unsure of their sexual orientation or reluctant to acknowledge it for fear of ridicule (Savin-Williams, 2003). In fact, they may date and have relationships with members of the opposite sex just to fit in. In one study of more than 3,000 adolescents in grades 9 through 12 (Garofalo, Wolf, Wissow, Woods, & Goodman, 1999), only 0.5% self-disclosed their gay or lesbian status. Similarly, recall that in Maguen et al.'s (2002) retrospective study, young adults (age 20) reported

In Middle Eastern cultures, especially those that are heavily influenced by Islamic traditions, adolescents have far fewer opportunities for dating and couples are more closely monitored by parents.

knowing that they were interested in same-sex relationships long before they disclosed their preferences to anyone. Lesbian youth, in particular, are unlikely to have their first same-sex relationship until later in adolescence (Savin-Williams & Diamond, 2004).

CULTURE AND ROMANCE. Culture also influences the onset of dating, romantic relationships, and sexual intercourse. In Western industrialized societies, for example, most adolescents report having had sex by age 18 (Guttmacher Institute, 2006), but some ethnic groups report having sexual intercourse earlier than others. For example, African American youths' first sexual encounters tend to occur earlier than either their Caucasian American or Latino peers. In contrast, in Middle Eastern cultures, especially those that are heavily influenced by Islamic traditions, adolescents have far fewer opportunities for dating and couples are more closely monitored by parents (Mahdi, 2003).

THE INFLUENCE OF PARENTS, PEERS, AND PARTNERS. Finally, parents, peers, and partners can influence the initiation of sexual relationships (Brown, 2004; Collins & Steinberg, 2006). Peers who are sexually active set social norms and may encourage others to engage in sexual relations. However, peers also can be influential in teenagers' decisions to wait for sex. Recall our discussion of virginity pledges in Chapter 11. Partners can exert pressure, too. For example, girls who date early often date older males (Abma, Martinez, Mosher, & Dawson, 2004). In these relationships, they may feel pressured to have sexual intercourse to maintain the relationship. Parents and other adult caregivers have an important role to play in mediating these influences. Adults who communicate permissive attitudes about sex may encourage early sexual activity. However, there is danger in being overly controlling, too—teenagers may rebel. When adolescents enjoy close relationships with parents and can talk openly with them (or other caregivers) about dating and romance, they often postpone sexual activity or at least behave responsibly in their sexual interactions (Doyle, Brendgen, Markiewicz & Kamkar, 2003). Adults sometimes feel awkward talking with teenagers about sex. The ***Connecting with Adolescents*** guidelines offer some strategies for engaging in free and frank discussions about dating, romance, and sex.

Relating to Peers through Technology

One way in which adolescence for today's teenagers is remarkably different than their parents' and teachers' experience is the extent to which they can connect with one another, even when they are not together. Let's look at the ways teenagers are using technology to relate to peers.

SOCIAL NETWORKING. According to a recent Nielsen survey (2009), "member communities," which include social networks and blogs, consistently rank among the top categories for media use by teens. Currently, MySpace and Facebook "are critical elements of the teen experience." Also, the survey indicates teenagers are prolific online publishers, with 67% of teenage responders indicating they update their pages at least once each week. Interestingly, mobile phones are the equipment of choice for much of adolescents' online socializing (see Figure 13.1). Seventy-seven percent of adolescent respondents indicated they own their own phones. Another 11% reported that they borrow one frequently, leaving only 12% of teenagers mobile free. And teenagers use text messaging and MMS/picture messaging at incredible

CONNECTING WITH ADOLESCENTS

Guidelines for Families and Teachers: Discussing Dating, Romance, and Sex

Develop honest and open environments for discussion.
Examples

1. Find a safe and comfortable setting, so both parents and adolescents feel easy about opening a discussion about dating and sexuality.
2. Invite adolescents to participate in the conversations, and be open to their opinions.
3. Communicate in a non-threatening manner, and help adolescents understand the responsibilities associated with certain actions.

Adapt an authoritative style of communication.
Examples

1. Combine warmth with firmness, and be consistent about discipline. Be clear about your standards and expectations concerning dating, romance, and sex.
2. Assure adolescents that you will always support them, no matter what happens.
3. Be sensitive and monitor teens' activities, but never become overly intrusive or invade their privacy.

Take active roles in the lives of teens.
Examples

1. Be proactive about initiating positive conversations with teens about a variety of issues; do not wait until conflicts erupt.
2. Never talk down to them; treat them respectfully.
3. Know their interests, and engage in activities for fun and enjoyment.
4. Have a sense of humor.

Source: Adapted from http://www.camh.net/tips_for_parents_teens .html http://www.sexualityandu.ca/parents/role-3.aspx

FIGURE 13.1

MOBILE COMMUNICATION USE AMONG U.S. TEENS 13–17

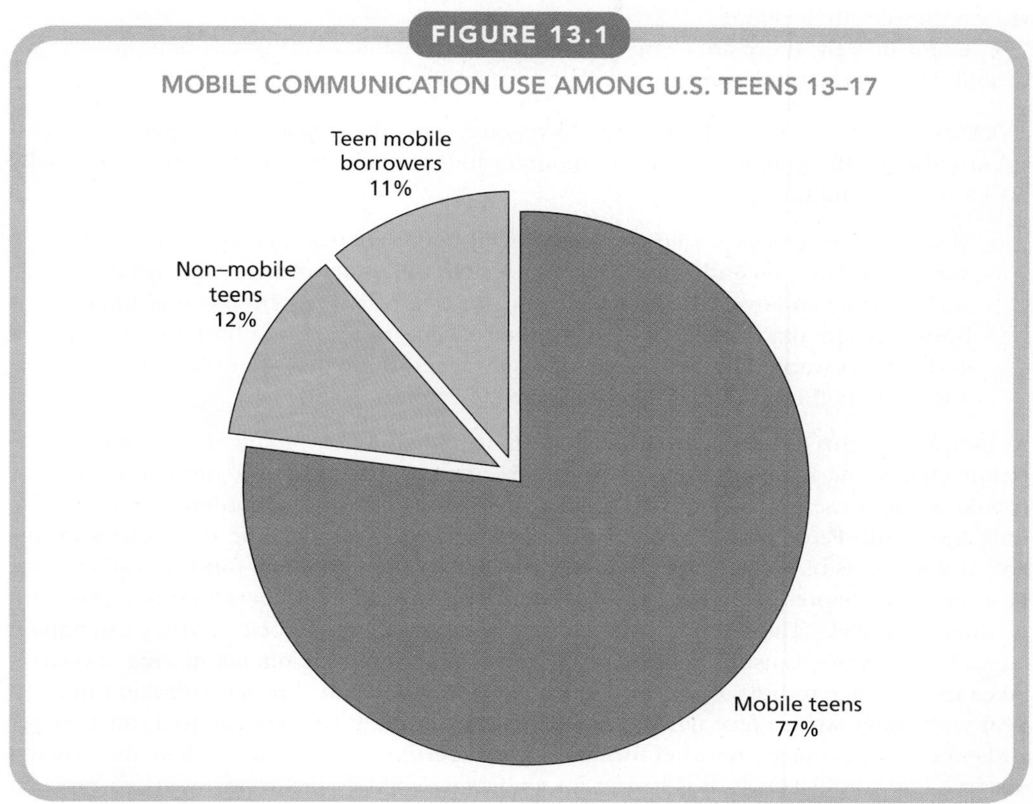

Source: Nielsen Company, (2009). How teens use media. A Nielsen report on the myths and realities of teen media trends. *http://en-us.nielsen.com/main/insights/consumer_insight/August2009/breaking_teen_myths, p. 8. Used with permission.*

FIGURE 13.2

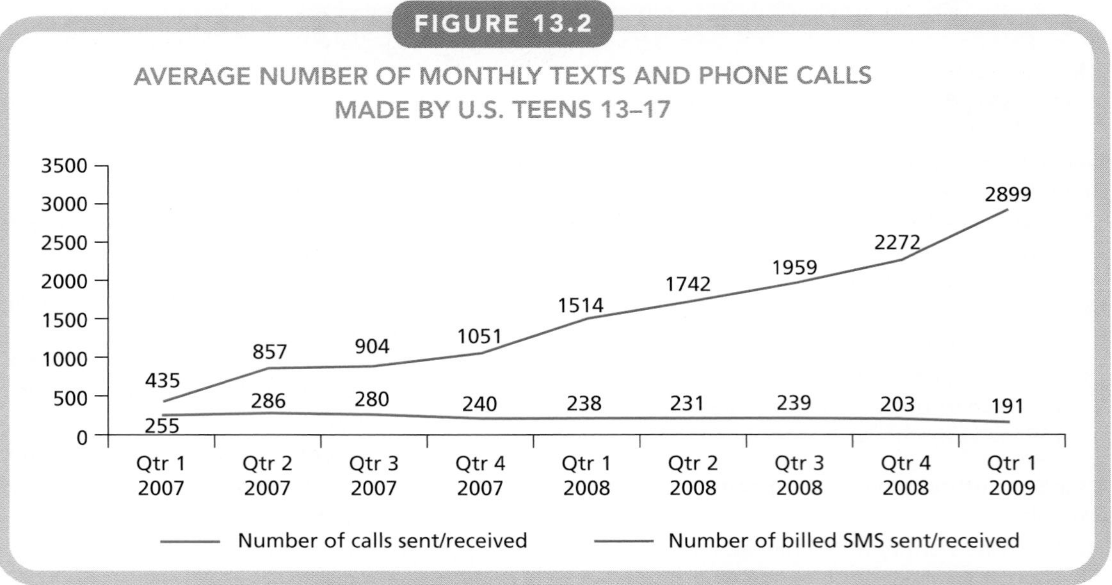

Source: Nielsen Company, (2009). How teens use media. A Nielsen report on the myths and realities of teen media trends. *http://en-us.nielsen.com/main/insights/consumer_insight/August2009/breaking_teen_myths, p. 8. Used with permission.*

rates! Figure 13.2 shows how this trend has been increasing in recent years. According to the survey, the average American mobile phone user sent or received 2,899 text messages each month during the first quarter of 2009. This compares to 191 voice calls. More than half of these users indicated they prefer text messaging to calling and 34% reported it was the reason they got their phone.

Unfortunately, there are some negative trends in adolescents' social networking. We examine two such trends next.

CYBERBULLYING. Here is how one 13-year-old girl described her experience with **cyberbullying**—the practice of using computers and other electronic media to intentionally inflict harm on another person:

> "I was talking to 2 girls who used to be my friends. Then (they) went on a chat I was also talking on and started saying horrible things about me. They used my screen name and everything. They even told one of my guy friends that I liked him since the day we met and he stopped talking to me. I was both depressed and angry. I wanted to die. I wanted to leave everything behind. I blocked them and signed off the Internet" (from Hinduja & Patchin, 2008).

As indicated in this example, cyberbullying can include publicly humiliating someone in an online chat room, harassing someone through email or text messages, or posting content (could be pictures, text, or a movie) about a person on a website. According to Sameer Hinduja and Justin Patchin (2009; Patchin & Hinduja, 2006), two leading researchers in this area, these forms of bullying are about as prevalent as the traditional forms of bullying we described in Chapter 10, and at least as damaging to victims. Cyberspace is a powerful medium for bullies. They may be emboldened by electronic media because they can remain virtually anonymous, using temporary email accounts or pseudonyms in chat rooms: It takes less courage to hurt a peer or damage his or her reputation when you don't need to deal with them face to face. Furthermore, bullies can get their message to a much larger audience; because many Internet forums are unsupervised, bullies worry less about being observed by adults. Finally, it is harder for victims to avoid bullies who now have capabilities to harass them 24-7 with persistent phone calls or text messages.

For victims, the consequences of cyberbullying can be devastating and long lasting. According to Hinduja and Patchin (2007, 2008), these negative experiences can undermine adolescents' freedom to use online resources, ruin their reputations for years to come, and cause serious emotional and psychological harm. They are associated with problems in school and delinquent behavior offline. Therefore, it is not surprising that cyberbullying is at the forefront of behavioral agendas in many schools and communities. Another related behavior is getting the attention of parents, educators, and the legal profession too: "sexting."

SEXTING. Sending sexually explicit content, including photos or text messages, over the Internet is **sexting.** According to a report from the National Campaign to Prevent Teen and Unplanned Pregnancy, 39% of teenagers (ages 13 to 19) have sent sexually suggestive messages via text messages, IM, or email, and 20% have posted nude or semi-nude photos or videos of themselves. Teenagers may be engaging in sexting "as a joke" or as a way of flirting, but for legal authorities, this is serious business. In an article for the *New York Times*, Riva Richmond (March, 2009) explains:

> It is illegal under federal and state child-porn laws to create explicit images of a minor, possess them or distribute them. These laws were drafted to address adult abuse of minors but it turns out they don't exempt minors who create and distribute images, even if the pictures are of them (making them, presumably, the victims).

More than a few teens are finding themselves in trouble with the law as a result of their sexting behavior. For example, three teenage girls in Pennsylvania who allegedly sent nude or semi-nude photos to three of their male classmates were charged with manufacturing, disseminating, or possessing child pornography, and the boys were charged with possession (wpxi.com, January, 2009). Another teenage girl in Florida was convicted of similar offenses. Parents, educators, and child/youth advocates are very concerned. Is punishment by law the right solution? Conversations about the merits of criminalizing this very risky behavior are just beginning among parents, educators, members of the legal profession, and advocacy organizations, such as Family Online Safety. While they deliberate, what can parents and other caregivers do to protect adolescents engaged in sexting? The National Campaign to Prevent Teen and Unplanned Pregnancy suggests adults emphasize the following points with teenagers:

- Don't assume anything you send or post is going to remain private.
- There is no changing your mind in cyberspace—anything you send or post will never truly go away.
- Don't give in to pressure to do something that makes you uncomfortable, even in cyberspace.
- Consider the recipient's reaction. Just because a message is meant to be fun doesn't mean the person who gets it will see it that way.
- Nothing online is truly anonymous. If someone knows you by screen name, online profile, phone number, or email address, they can probably find you if they try hard enough.

After all this, it is easy to see why adolescence is the period of children's lives parents are most nervous and apprehensive about (Pasley & Gecas, 1984; Steinberg & Silk, 2002). Are these fears rational? We examine this topic next.

PARENTING ADOLESCENTS

In part, parents' concern is rational. With the possible exception of toddlerhood, adolescence brings with it more rapid and remarkable physical, cognitive, and social transformations than any other period in development. However, parents' anxiety also is fueled by what Steinberg and Silk (2002) refer to as "widespread and erroneous stereotypes." Specifically, they critique the plethora of popular books and articles suggesting that "surviving," rather than "thriving" adolescence is the goal, and contrasting "cuddly" infants with "spiteful and problem-ridden teenagers." So what's the truth about parent–adolescent relationships?

Although it is true that adolescence is a time of significant change and adjustment in parent–child relationships, the vast majority of adolescents continue to feel close to their parents during this time, enjoy spending time with them, value their opinions, and respect them as authority figures (Arnett, 1999; Holmbeck, Friedman, Abad, & Jandasek, 2006;

Steinberg & Silk, 2002). Moreover, tensions in most parent–adolescent relationships tend to be about mundane issues, such as personal appearance, dating, and curfews, not about core values, work, education, religion, and politics (Arnett, 1999; Smetana, 1988; Steinberg & Silk, 2002). Nevertheless, Steinberg and Silk stress the importance of "establishing a new equilibrium." Typically, this requires a renegotiation of the parent–child relationship and, for parents, adjusting how they relate to, discipline, and guide their children, who are now adolescents.

Redefining the Parent–Child Relationship

We have already discussed the profound physical changes associated with puberty and adolescence and how these changes affect the way adolescents view themselves and how they are treated by others. Also, we know that adolescence is associated with increases in negative affect (i.e., moodiness). These changes may influence the way teenagers behave toward their parents and they may lead parents to over- or underestimate their adolescents' needs and capabilities (Steinberg & Silk, 2002). Similarly, changes in adolescents' cognitive abilities can alter the interpersonal dynamic between parents and teenagers. As we saw in Chapter 12, adolescents think more like adults. They are able to think abstractly, and their reasoning becomes more multidimensional and relativistic. According to Steinberg and Silk, adolescents bring a new cognitive frame to family discussions. They want to be treated more like adults, and they want a greater say in discussions about family affairs and decision-making. They may challenge the way the family currently functions to make decisions, perhaps questioning the rules and reasons for them. Such challenges can be hard for parents to take: They may interpret these challenges as their child rejecting their values and questioning their judgment as parents. They may feel hurt when (not if) their adolescents criticize the things they say and do. These tensions create emotional distance between parents and adolescents, which often is reflected in increased negative and decreased positive interactions (Flanner, Torquati, & Lindemeier, 1994). However, such distancing is a normal feature of the parent–adolescent relationship, even in species other than humans (Steinberg, 1989), and it typically doesn't weaken the parent–child bond established in earlier years.

Adolescence is marked by increased independence and a greater need for privacy. Especially in Western industrialized societies, adolescents expect fewer restrictions and increased opportunities for autonomy and self-management (Arnett, 1999; Steinberg & Silk, 2002). Adolescents spend less time with their families and, as we saw in the previous section, their relationships with peers become more important and influential, and less subject to parental control. Moreover, adolescents have more "free" time, and much of this time is spent in activities that are not supervised by adults. They also have greater mobility than they did as children (e.g., they can take public transit, or drive once they are 16 years old). Although adolescents tend to welcome this newfound freedom, it gives parents cause for concern. In particular, parents worry about their ability to monitor and control their adolescents' behaviors, and fear for their adolescents' safety (e.g., they worry about their involvement in taking drugs, drinking alcohol, engaging in sexual activity, social networking, and surfing the Internet). Parents also may find it difficult to adjust to the fact that their adolescents prefer peers as confidants and choose to spend time with peers over participating in family activities. In particular, parents may find it difficult to cope with their adolescents' first romantic or sexual relationships.

HOW SHOULD PARENTS RESPOND? Steinberg and Silk (2002) acknowledge that adolescence tests the boundaries of trust in the parent–adolescent relationship, but highlight the need for parents to strike a balance between granting autonomy and maintaining control. They argue parents must give teens some freedom to make decisions about how, where, and with whom to spend their unstructured and unsupervised time. However, some concern is warranted, as research demonstrates that antisocial behavior is more common among adolescents who spend large amounts of time in unstructured and unsupervised activities (Masten, 1999; Osgood, Wilson, O'Malley, Bachman, & Johnston, 1996). Research also indicates that well-adjusted youth have parents who know where they are and what they are doing most of the time (Pettit, Bates, Dodge, & Meece, 1999; Steinberg & Silk, 2002). Ideally, parents foster independence and self-control in their adolescents (starting from an early age—see Chapter 7), but also monitor their activities so they know what they are doing and that they are safe. They strike the right balance between respecting their teenagers' right to privacy and protecting them from risks associated with the teenage years.

In general, adolescents raised by authoritative parents are more socially competent and emotionally well adjusted than adolescents whose parents are characterized as authoritarian, permissive, or neglectful (Peterson, 2005; Rubin et al., 2004; Steinberg & Silk, 2002). Recall from Chapters 7 and 10 that authoritative parents are warm and responsive, and nurture autonomy, but they also have high expectations and set and enforce rules for their children. Adolescents who experience this combination of warmth, autonomy support, and structure tend to be more responsible, self-assured, and successful in school than those who do not (Parker & Benson, 2004; Steinberg & Silk, 2004). They also are less likely to experience anxiety and depression, and are less likely to become involved in problem behaviors (Lau, Litrownik, Newton, Black, & Everson, 2006; Rubin et al., 2004). These teenagers are likely to have secure attachments with parents, which increases the probability that parents will continue to have a strong positive influence on their behavior (Ducharme, Doyle, & Markiewicz, 2002; Laible, Carlo, & Raffaelli, 2000), even when peer influence is at its strongest. Evidence linking authoritative parenting to healthy adolescent development has been found in countries all over the world and in studies across a wide range of ethnicities, cultures, social strata, and family structures (Steinberg & Silk, 2002).

Research demonstrates that antisocial behavior is more common among adolescents spending large amounts of time in unstructured and unsupervised activities.

Authoritative parents are likely to use inductive forms of discipline; that is, they use logical reasoning and persuasion to appeal to adolescents' desire to do the right thing. According to Peterson (2005), induction helps adolescents to understand why rules are necessary and why certain behavior is unacceptable. Also, through discussion, parents engaged in inductive discipline help their adolescents to make adjustments and amend wrongdoings. Steinberg and Silk (2002) agree that the verbal give and take that characterizes parent–adolescent interactions in authoritative households fosters reasoning ability and moral judgment, which helps teenagers to make good decisions when they are away from their families. Moreover, the nurturance and involvement that typify authoritative parenting make adolescents more receptive to what adults have to say. Inductive discipline communicates confidence in adolescents' desire and ability to make good choices and legitimizes parents' authority without engendering hostility, which is associated with problem behavior (Buehler, 2006). Finally, inductive discipline is associated with positive social values, high self-esteem, and good school performance (Amato & Fowler, 2002; Aunola, Stattin, & Nurmi, 2000). In contrast, discipline that is harsh and punitive can lead to hostility, open disregard for parents' authority, and involvement in problem behaviors (Benderet al., 2007).

MONITORING AND SUPERVISION. Parental monitoring and supervision are linked to social and emotional adjustment throughout childhood and especially in adolescence (Crouter & Head, 2002). Specifically, low levels of parental monitoring are associated with high levels of problem behavior, including conduct problems and delinquency, substance use, early sexual activity, and problems at school (Crouter & Head, 2002; Masten, 1999; Smetana, 2008; Steinberg & Silk, 2002). According to Crouter and Head, most measures of parental monitoring are actually measures of parents' knowledge about what their adolescents do when not under direct parental supervision, where they do it, and with whom. But how do parents gather this information without engaging in overly intrusive behaviors, such as tracking and surveillance? Mainly, parents rely on what their teenagers tell them. In addition, sensitive parents are good at noticing and listening when their adolescents are around. However, parents cannot become or remain knowledgeable if adolescents are unwilling to share information with them, or if they deliberately omit or lie about crucial information. Therefore, recent research about parental monitoring (parental knowledge) has focused on disclosure and secrecy in parent–adolescent relationships (Jensen, Arnett, Feldman, & Cauffman, 2004; Marshall, Tilton-Weaver, & Bosdet, 2005; Smetana, Villabos, Rogge, & Tasopoulos-Chan, 2010; Tasopoulos-Chan, Smetana, Yau, 2009).

Jensen and her colleagues (2004) studied high school and college students' perceptions about the acceptability of lying to parents under a variety of conditions. They found lying to parents was quite common among the adolescents and emerging adults in their study; it was perceived as an acceptable a way to assert autonomy. Figure 13.3 shows the range of issues about which high school and college students lie to their parents. Boys lied more frequently than girls, and adolescents lied more frequently than emerging adults in this study. In other studies (e.g., Perkins & Turiel, 2007), adolescents have reported views of lying as morally wrong, and lying has been associated with greater tolerance for deviant or delinquent behavior (Engles et al., 2006). Tasopoulos-Chan et al. (2009) extended the research on lying to examine other strategies adolescents might use to "manage information." They studied various methods of nondisclosure used by Chinese, Mexican, and European American adolescents in interactions with parents (e.g., avoiding the topic, omitting information, "only tell if asked"). Also, they examined whether and how disclosure practices varied as a function of the kind of information to be shared (e.g., information about moral issues and social conventions versus information viewed as personal and up to the individual to decide). Their findings indicate that across ethnic groups, adolescents used avoidance and

FIGURE 13.3

COMPARING FREQUENCY FOR HIGH SCHOOL AND COLLEGE STUDENTS LYING TO THEIR PARENTS ABOUT A WIDE RANGE OF ISSUES

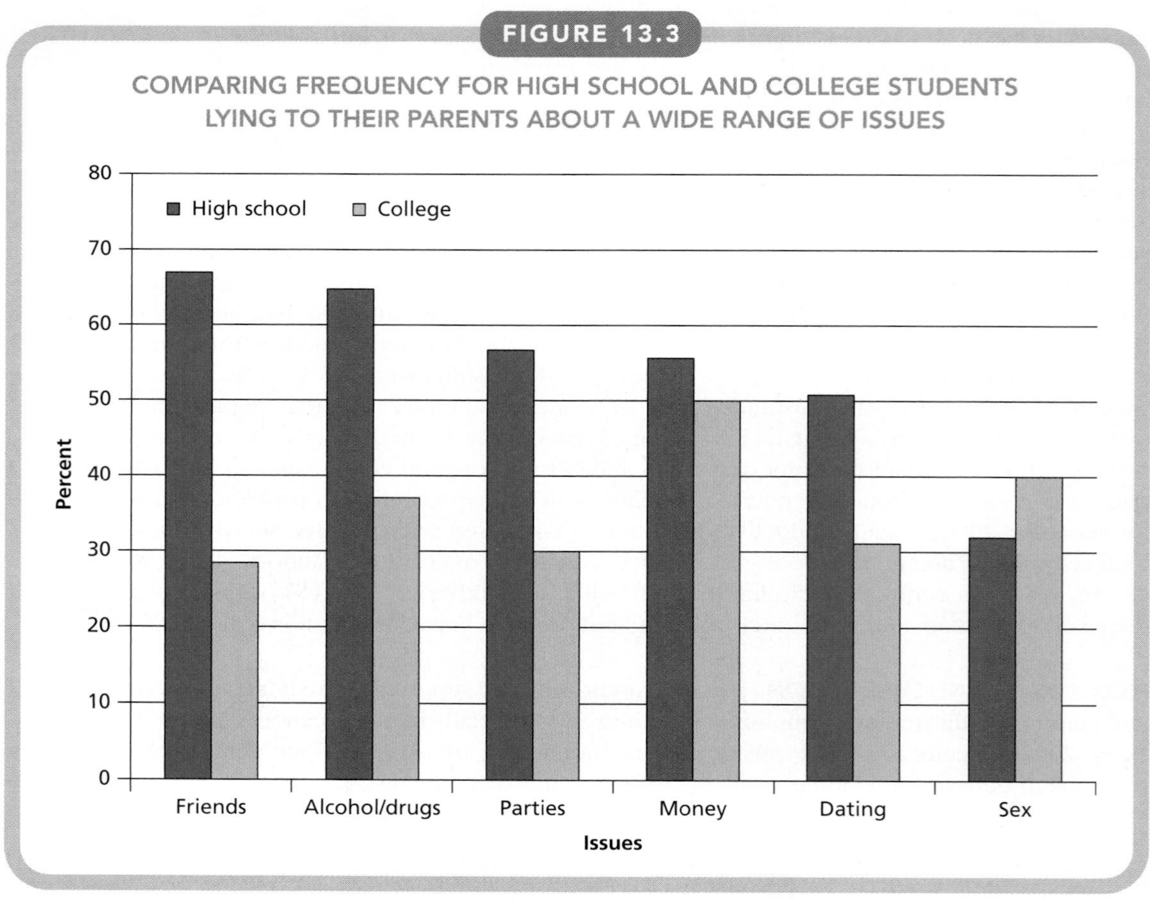

Source: With kind permission from Springer Science + Business Media: Journal of Youth and Adolescence, *33(2), The Right to Do Wrong: Lying to Parents Among Adolescents and Emerging Adults, 2004, p. 106, by Jensen, L. A., Arnett, J. J., Feldman, S. S., & Cauffman, E.*

partial disclosure (only tell if asked) more than either full disclosure or lying. In fact, lying was relatively infrequent, regardless of the information to be shared, when examined in the context of other strategies for nondisclosure. Chinese American youth concealed information by partially disclosing it more than adolescents from other ethnic groups. European and Mexican American youth were more likely to disclose information of a personal nature to mothers than to fathers, perhaps reflecting more distant relationships with fathers than mothers in these groups. Girls disclosed more than boys, and boys were more likely to lie to parents than were girls. Overall, disclosure was associated with adolescents' reports of stronger ties to family, more trust in parents, and less problem behavior. Alternatively, lying was associated with more depressed mood. Table 13.3 shows how adolescents reason about whether and what to disclose to parents.

What predicts adolescent disclosure versus secrecy? Primarily, research indicates parental knowledge develops in the context of a harmonious and trusting parent–adolescent relationship (Crouter & Head, 2002; Smetana, 2008; Smetana et al., 2010; Steinberg & Silk, 2002). Specifically, disclosure is more common among adolescents whose parents are authoritative and who do not engage in activities that would lead to parental disapproval. Moreover, parental acceptance is associated with disclosure, whereas disagreement and conflict is associated with greater secrecy on the part of teenagers. According to Smetana, most adolescents feel obligated to disclose information and activities for which they perceive the parent has legitimate authority to regulate. Both adolescents and parents perceive that teenagers are obligated to disclose behavior that affects one's safety, comfort, or health, but view as discretionary the disclosure of information pertaining to personal issues, such as what they spend their money on or how they spend their time. Adolescents' sense of obligation to disclose information about peers falls somewhere in the middle. Smetana emphasizes that most parents know less than they think they do: "Even in good relationships parents overestimate their adolescents' disclosure, particularly at middle adolescence

TABLE 13.3 • **Adolescent Reasoning about Disclosing Information about Their Whereabouts and Activities**

THEME	DEFINITION	EXAMPLES
Jurisdiction	Decision to inform parent is founded upon whether activities are under the jurisdiction of the adolescent (i.e., nearby, shorter period of time) or parent (i.e., far away, longer period of time)	"When you're within town and visiting friends or going to the library or to a store" "When it's night, when they don't know who I'm going with, when I go somewhere I've never been before"
Social support	Decision to inform parent is associated with support such as protection from safety or assistance with daily tasks. Social support may be from the parent to the adolescent or vice versa	". . . when my mother needed me to babysit my sister I would give the number where I was" "When there is a potential for danger. For example, if I'm going hiking in the woods they should know exactly where I am in case I get hurt or something"
Ask me no questions, tell you no lies	Information is conveyed only if the parent asks; not conveyed if parent doesn't ask	"only if they wanted to know" "if they are going to check [on where I am]"
Sort of tell	Parent is provided with partial information as to the adolescent's whereabouts and activities	"When they won't let me go, we don't explain exactly where I'm going" "For example, if I'm out with friends they don't need to know where. At least they know I'm out and will be back later"
Tell or else	Adolescent conveys whereabouts and activities to avoid consequences of parent not being informed	"If I don't tell them I get into big trouble" "The consequences [of not telling] are too high"

Source: Reprinted from Journal of Adolescence, 28, *Marshall, S. K., Tilton-Weaver, L. C., & Bosdet, L. Information management: Considering adolescents' regulation of parental knowledge, p. 642. Copyright 2005, with permission from Elsevier.*

and with regard to peers" (p. 22). Moreover, according to Masten (1999; Masten & Shaffer, 2006), many parents withdraw monitoring and supervision before adolescents are mature enough to cope with the complex social situations in which they find themselves, leaving youth vulnerable to a wide range of risk factors. For these reasons, parents and other adults need to work hard to build relationships with teenagers that include trust, security, and easy communication.

Coping with Conflict

As indicated previously, tensions between most parents and adolescents are not serious enough to cause a dramatic deterioration in their relationships during the adolescent years. In fact, only 5–10% of parents and adolescents who enjoy positive relationships during childhood develop serious relationship problems during adolescence (Lamb & Lewis, 2005; Steinberg, 1990; Steinberg & Silk, 2002). Therefore, although some emotional distance and minor but persistent squabbling is typical, frequent, high-intensity fighting is not a normal part of adolescence. In general, conflict between parents and adolescents increases in frequency during early adolescence, reaches a peak in intensity during middle adolescence, and then declines in late adolescence as teenagers come to value the restrictions their parents place on them, and parents come to respect the authority and jurisdiction of their maturing youth (Arnett, 1999; Laursen, Coy, & Collins, 1998; Steinberg & Silk, 2002).

Smetana and her colleagues (1996; Yau & Smetana, 2003) have found similar patterns of interaction in both Western and non-Western nations (e.g., Hong Kong and China). For example, in a study of families in the United States and Hong Kong, Smetana (1996) identified three patterns of parent–adolescent conflict. She labeled the largest group of families the "frequent squabblers." Their relationships were typical in that they involved high rates of mildly intense conflict. A second, smaller group of families was characterized as "placid." In these families, conflict was rare, perhaps because they had successfully renegotiated their relationships already. Finally, a third group of families was characterized as "tumultuous." These families reported frequent conflict that was extreme in its affective intensity. According to Smetana, adolescents from these families are most at risk for experiencing problems with adjustment.

Overall, few effects on parent–adolescent conflict have been linked to the sex of teenagers. Sons and daughters report similar amounts of closeness and conflict with parents, and it appears they interact with parents in very similar ways (Hauser et al., 1987; Hill & Holmbeck, 1987; Youniss & Ketterlinus, 1987). However, some research indicates mothers and fathers relate to male and female adolescents differently (Collins & Russell, 1991; Lamb & Lewis, 2005; Steinberg, 1990; Steinberg & Silk, 2002). On average, mothers who spend more time with their teenagers and adolescents report feeling closer to them and more comfortable talking with them about problems and emotional issues. Mother–adolescent relationships are characterized as more intense in general, including not only greater closeness but also more frequent and intense conflict. Fathers are perceived as more distant authority figures. Father–adolescent interactions are more likely to revolve around recreational activities and goal-oriented tasks (e.g., schoolwork). Father–daughter relationships are characterized as particularly distant, which can be hard for fathers who enjoyed a very close relationship with their daughters during childhood. Adolescent boys ask fathers for support more often than do daughters, but father–son relationships are not as intimate as mother–son relationships.

Finally, the effects of conflict on parent–adolescent relationships over the short and long term appear to have less to do with the content of the conflict than how it is managed and resolved. Many conflicts between adolescents and their parents end because one party gives in or walks away (Laursen & Collins, 1994; Smetana & Gaines, 1999; Steinberg & Silk, 2002; Yau & Smetana, 2003), as opposed to both parties engaging in a process of productive problem solving. Steinberg and Silk argue that mild conflict presents an opportunity for parents and adolescents to review their expectations for one another and renegotiate their relationships. In fact, in families in which members are invited to express their points of view and disagreements with one another are tolerated, adolescents are more assertive and have more advanced skills for conflict resolution. Importantly, these benefits are only realized in parent-adolescent relationships that have a high degree of harmony and cohesion (Steinberg & Silk, 2002). Parent-adolescent conflict is associated with negative outcomes for adolescents when it occurs in the context of an already hostile relationship (Buehler, 2006).

Life in School

More and more research is pointing to the importance of adolescents' positive experiences at school for promoting healthy social and emotional development (Eccles & Roeser, 2003; Pittman & Richmond, 2007; Suldo, Shaffer, & Riley, 2008). Specifically, satisfaction in school is associated with good conduct in school, positive relationships with peers and teachers, motivation for learning, self-efficacy for learning, academic achievement, good overall mental health, and global life satisfaction (i.e., positive perceptions of one's quality of life). However, adolescence is a time for school transitions—from elementary to middle school and then to high school—and these transitions can prove challenging for teenagers who already are coping with profound personal (physical, cognitive, and emotional) changes.

Adjusting to Middle and High School

Although school transitions can negatively affect academic performance, behavior, and self-esteem, even in adolescents generally regarded as well adjusted, the disruption is typically temporary (Collins & Steinberg, 2006). Most adolescents adapt to changing schools over time, especially when they have stable and supportive family and peer relationships and the new schools are responsive to their needs (Eccles, 2004; Roeser et al., 2000). The students to worry about are those who have pre-existing problems and vulnerabilities. Adolescents with a history of academic, social, and/or emotional problems have greater difficulty adapting to middle and high school than students whose experiences in school have been primarily positive (Anderman, 1998; Collins & Steinberg, 2006; Murdock, Anderman, & Hodge, 2000). Middle schools and high schools tend to be more impersonal than elementary schools, and this can make adjustment to the new environment particularly difficult for students with few social supports either inside or outside of school. Finally, students in poor, inner city neighborhoods are more likely to experience negative outcomes associated with transitions, including falling grades and declines in motivation and self-esteem.

In the sections on adolescent self-concept and self-esteem, we described the general decline in students' self-evaluations as they advance through school and linked them to failure on the part of middle and high schools to meet the developmental needs of adolescents. In particular, Eccles and her colleagues (Eccles, 2004; Roeser et al., 2000; Wigfield & Eccles, 2002) have criticized schools' increased emphasis on grades and social comparisons at a period in life when individuals are most self-conscious and self-critical. Also, they argue that middle and high school teachers often trust students less and want to control them more. This creates a mismatch between what adolescents want (greater autonomy) and what schools provide (control).

Collins and Steinberg (2006) argue that the same factors that influence positive adolescent adjustment at home also influence adjustment at school. Specifically, they assert that schools need to be both responsive and demanding (i.e., authoritative contexts), and teachers need to be supportive and firm, maintaining high, well-defined standards for behavior and academic work. In these contexts, students are more satisfied in school and have stronger bonds to school. They are more motivated for learning, have higher rates of achievement, and are less likely to engage in problem behavior (Collins & Steinberg, 2006; Eccles, 2004; Ryan & Patrick, 2001; Way & Pahl, 2001). In contrast, students in classrooms that emphasize grades, social comparisons, and teacher control tend to be less motivated for learning and more anxious about school.

School Attachment

School attachment, also referred to as school connectedness and school belonging, describes the extent to which students feel accepted, valued, respected, supported, and included in their schools (Goodenow, 1993; Shochet, Dadds, Ham, & Montague, 2006).

A common measure of school attachment first appeared in the National Longitudinal Study of Adolescent Health (Bearman, Jones, Udry, 1997). Items such as "I feel close to people at this school" and "I feel like I am part of this school" provide a "school connectedness score" for adolescents who complete the survey. Researchers then correlate this score with other information they have about the adolescents (e.g., age, sex, ethnicity, SES) and their schools (e.g., urban, ethnically diverse), and a wide range of positive and negative outcomes (e.g., academic achievement, motivation for learning, social and emotional functioning). Although qualities of specific relationships (e.g., teacher–student, student–student) are associated with school attachment, this construct implies something beyond relationships and includes feelings of commitment to an institution and a sense of belonging to a larger community (Pittman & Richmond, 2007). Ideally, all students, from preschool through college should feel "attached" to their schools, but Goodenow stressed the importance of school attachment during adolescence, when teenagers are relying less on their families for support and more on extra-familial connections for individuation.

School attachment was originally studied as a critical factor relating to school retention and dropout (Wehlage, Rutter, Smith, Lesko, & Fernandez, 1989), but has been subsequently positively linked to school performance and adjustment, motivation for learning, self-esteem, self-regulation, expectations for future success, general well-being, and global life satisfaction (L. H. Anderman & Freeman, 2004; Shochet et al., 2006; Suldo et al., 2008). In addition, low levels of school attachment have been linked to low self-esteem, higher rates of delinquency, and engagement in behavior that poses a significant health risk, including smoking, alcohol and drug use, and early sexual activity (Bond et al., 2007; Dornbusch, Erickson, Laird, & Wong, 2001; Henry & Slater, 2007). In one study (Wilson, 2004), school connectedness was considered alongside school size, ethnic makeup, performance, and climate as a predictor of violent behavior and aggressive victimization. Relative to all these influences, disconnection from school was the greatest predictor of these violent outcomes. Similarly, Mulvey and Cauffman (2001) linked school attachment to a belief in the fairness of school rules and discipline, and found these beliefs were more powerful in lowering school violence than zero-tolerance policies. Finally, research investigating the relationship between school attachment and mental health has demonstrated a strong correlation between poor school attachment and mental health concerns, such as depression, anxiety, and deficits in overall functioning. Thus, research demonstrates a clear and important role for school attachment in the lives of adolescents.

Research also indicates that students who are members of ethnic minority groups, sexual minority groups, low SES groups, disability groups, and low-achievement groups are particularly at risk for school "disconnectedness" (Bonny, Britto, Klostermann, Hornung, & Slap, 2000; Galliher, Rostosky, & Hughes, 2004; Pittman & Richmond, 2007). Attending urban schools, not being involved in extracurricular activities, having "declining health status" (judged by the number visits to the school nurse), and being younger or older than classmates also are risks for feeling less connected to schools (Bonny et al., 2000). Conversely, school attachment appears to buffer "at risk" youth from many of the negative outcomes listed here. Sanchez, Colon, and Esparza (2005) examined relationships between school attachment and academic outcomes in 143 Latino adolescents in grade 12. For these youth, school attachment was positively correlated with effort, motivation for learning, and attendance in school. Similarly, Kia-Keating and Ellis (2007) found that school belonging was associated with lower levels of depression and higher levels of self-efficacy in a group of adolescent refugees from Somalia. Finally, school attachment is associated with lower rates of internalizing and externalizing problems, better GPA, and more positive attitudes toward school in adolescents from low SES communities (Pittman & Richmond, 2007).

Not surprisingly, students form positive attachments to schools they perceive are supportive and caring environments with professionals who are interested in their learning progress and general well-being (L. H. Anderman, 2003; Gomez & Ang, 2007; Vieno, Santinello, Pastore, & Perkins, 2007). Much of what we described in Chapter 10 concerning teacher–student relationships and creating caring communities applies here as

CONNECTING WITH ADOLESCENTS

Guidelines for Schools: What Schools Can Do to Foster Students' School Attachment

Involve students in planning.
Examples

1. Involve students in developing classroom rules, devising suitable table and seating arrangements in classrooms, assemblies, and concerts, and so on.
2. Invite ideas and perspectives from all cultural and social groups.
3. Make time for negotiating tasks and evaluation standards.
4. Encourage students to speak up for themselves and be assertive.

Foster close relationships with students.
Examples

1. Engage in ongoing communication with parents, teachers, and students. Such relationships build rapport and collaboration.
2. Accept the values of all youths, and be sure to treat everyone fairly.
3. Help adolescents to identify a reliable and close relationship with at least one adult in school.

Be supportive to meet students' needs.
Examples

1. Be sensitive to students' needs, and provide extra resources and assistance to ensure academic success.
2. Provide support to students grappling with challenges, and assure them that they can meet their high hopes for school performance.
3. Set up after-school sports clubs or musical instrument practice sessions to support students with different interests.

Source: Adapted from http://www.heretohelp.bc.ca/publications/schools/alt/1

well. Gomez and Ang identify several contextual factors that are key for "positive youth development" in school, including the presence of positive adults, positive places, and positive opportunities for social and emotional development. According to Gomez and Ang, positive adults recognize and support adolescents' need for ongoing support and connectedness to others. They make themselves available and cheer students on, celebrating successes and offering encouragement in the face of failures, while setting healthy boundaries and realistic expectations. Positive places have clearly articulated sets of rules and regulations that members of the community need to follow, and they place a priority on managing bullying and aggression. Also, positive places allow for age-appropriate levels of autonomy and self-regulation, so students are involved in decision-making and governance. They share responsibility for ensuring their school is a safe and caring environment for everyone in it. Finally, positive opportunities for social and emotional development include activities and programs that promote what Gomez and Ang refer to as the "six Cs" of positive youth development: competence, confidence, connections, character, caring, and contribution to society. The ***Connecting with Adolescents*** guidelines offer specific ideas about what schools can do to foster students' school attachment.

CHALLENGES FOR ADOLESCENTS

We have seen throughout this chapter that adolescence poses some significant challenges for most individuals. In this section, we examine some less common, more extreme challenges that are associated with the emergence of mental illness in adolescents. Research indicates that half of all lifetime cases of mental illness appear by age 14 (NIMH, 2009; NCCP, 2009). Table 13.4 lists factors that put adolescents at risk for experiencing mental illness, alongside factors that are associated with mental health. In Chapter 10, we discussed childhood depression and fears and phobias. Depression and anxiety disorders continue to be the most common forms of mental illness in adolescence, and they place youth at risk for attempting or completing suicide.

TABLE 13.4 • **Risk and Protective Factors for Experiencing Mental Illness**

	RISK FACTORS	PROTECTIVE FACTORS
Biological		
	Exposure to toxins (e.g., tobacco, alcohol) in pregnancy Genetic tendency to psychiatric disorder Head trauma Hypoxia at birth and other birth complications HIV infection Malnutrition Substance abuse Other illnesses	Age-appropriate physical development Good physical health Good intellectual functioning
Psychological		
	Learning disorders Maladaptive personality traits Sexual, physical, emotional abuse and neglect Difficult temperament	Ability to learn from experiences Good self-esteem High level of problem-solving ability Social skills
Social		
Family	Inconsistent care-giving Family conflict Poor family discipline Poor family management Death of a family member	Family attachment Opportunities for positive involvement in family Rewards for involvement in family
School	Academic failure Failure of schools to provide appropriate environment to support attendance and learning Inadequate or inappropriate provision of education Bullying	Opportunities for involvement in school life Positive reinforcement from academic achievement Identity with school or need for education attainment
Community	Transitions (e.g., urbanisation) Community disorganisation Discrimination and marginalisation Exposure to violence	Connectedness to community Opportunities for leisure Positive cultural experiences Positive role models Rewards for community involvement Connection with community organisations

Source: Reprinted from The Lancet, *369, Patel, V., Fisher, A., & McGorry, P. Mental health of young people: A global public-health challenge, p. 642. Copyright 2005, with permission from Elsevier.*

Suicide

Suicide is the third leading cause of death among older adolescents, accounting for 12.3% of all adolescent deaths each year (CDC, 2008; NCCP, 2009; Thompson, Kuruwita, & Foster, 2009). Figure 13.4 shows the rates of adolescent suicide by age, gender, and ethnicity. You can see that the rate of suicide death is higher for boys than for girls. However, it is important to note that non-fatal, self-inflicted injuries, many of which are suicide attempts, are more common in girls. In general, the rate of suicide in youth from minority groups is lower than it is in White/non-Hispanic populations. However, some minority groups, including youth with disabilities and youth who are gay or lesbian are more vulnerable than others (Galliher et al., 2004; Wilson, Deri Armstrong, Furrie, & Walcot, 2009). Suicide among Aboriginal youth is alarmingly high compared with that of other groups, and this finding is true in other countries around the world, including Australia and Canada. In 2006, Health Canada estimated the rates of suicide for First Nations youth were five to seven times that for non-Aboriginal youth, and among the highest in the world for Inuit youth (11 times the national average).

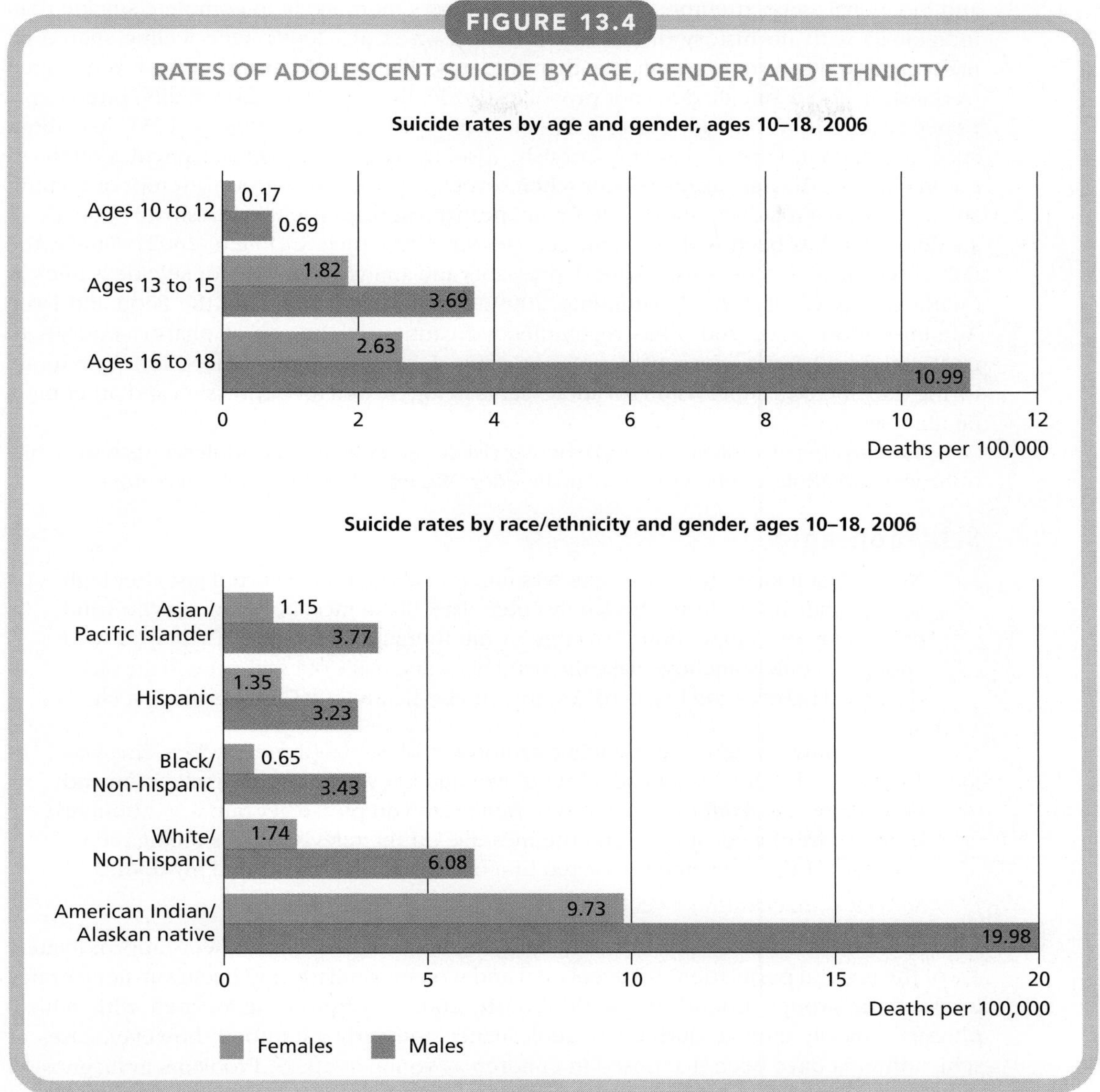

Source: National Center for Children in Poverty. (2009). Adolescent mental health in the United States. *New York: NY: Schwarz, S. W.*

Suicide typically is a response to life problems—problems that parents and teachers may dismiss. Therefore, it is important to watch for warning signs, such as changes in eating or sleeping habits, weight, grades, disposition, activity level, or interest in friends. Adolescents at risk sometimes suddenly give away prized possessions such as electronic gadgets, CDs, clothing, or pets. They may seem depressed or hyperactive and may say things like "Nothing matters any more," "You won't have to worry about me any more," or "I wonder what dying is like." They may start missing school or quit doing work. Thoughts of suicide, referred to as **suicidal ideation,** are not uncommon during adolescence, but any thoughts or actions that could result in harm to self should be taken seriously and addressed immediately.

Adult caregivers who suspect a potential for suicide should talk to the adolescent directly. It is a myth that people who talk about suicide do not complete suicide. In fact, approximately 80% of suicide completions are preceded by one or more suicide attempts, and individuals who attempt suicide are 38–40 times more likely to complete suicide than individuals with no history of attempts (Thompson et al., 2009). One feeling shared by many people who attempt suicide is that no one really takes them seriously, so remember, "A question about suicide does not provoke suicide. Indeed, teens (and adults) often experience relief when someone finally cares enough to ask" (Range, 1993, p. 145). Ask about specifics, and take the adolescent seriously. Also, be aware that teenage suicides often occur in clusters. **Cluster suicides** occur when several members of a group attempt or commit suicide within a relatively short time frame, perhaps in response to a classmate's suicide or a suicide that has been widely publicized (Joiner, 1999; Rice & Dolgin, 2002). Finally, the link between adolescents' use of antidepressants and an increased risk for suicide is unclear (Markowitz & Cuellar, 2007; Sammons, 2009), but hotly debated, and the Food and Drug Administration (FDA, 2004) has recommended caution in the use of pharmaceuticals to treat childhood and adolescent depression. This debate highlights a need for close monitoring (i.e., medical supervision) of adolescents being treated for depression and other mental illnesses.

Two groups of adolescents at particular risk for suicide include adolescents with schizophrenia and adolescents with bipolar disorder. We examine these disorders next.

Schizophrenia

> Nigel's first inkling that something was different about him occurred just after high school graduation. He and his family entered a sailboat race, but there was no wind on the day of competition. "An urge in me thought that maybe if I prayed hard enough, I could somehow make the wind blow and make our sailboat win the race." He closed his eyes and began to gesture with his hands . . . "That was the first clue."
>
> Tammy started experiencing symptoms of schizophrenia when she was 14 years old. "One time I had a friend over and we were watching television and I got a message from the TV. I said to him, 'Can you please get out.' . . . I thought he was part of a conspiracy and the message on the television was telling me he was part of the conspiracy. I kicked him out and then I barricaded my doors."
>
> *Source:* Canadian Press. (2008).

Schizophrenia is a chronic and severely disabling brain disorder that affects approximately 1% of the general population. It affects men and women similarly and occurs at similar rates in all ethnic groups around the world (NIMH, 2006). Symptoms associated with schizophrenia typically emerge during late adolescence and early adulthood; however, cases of schizophrenia have been diagnosed in children as young as age 5. Problems in diagnosing child and adolescent onset schizophrenia often occur because early symptoms are confused with normal development in childhood (e.g., a rich fantasy life) or other mental illnesses in adolescents (e.g., depression), or because the symptoms are attributed to other factors, such as alcohol and drug abuse (Findling, 2008; Hollis, 2000).

The symptoms of schizophrenia fall into three broad categories (Children, Youth, and Women's Health Service, 2009; NIMH, 2006; Wozniak, et al., 2008):

- **Positive symptoms** are easy to spot because they include behaviors and changes in thought processes not seen in healthy people, including hallucinations, delusions (e.g., paranoia or delusions of grandeur), thought disorders, and disorders of movement. Positive symptoms can come and go, and can be severe or hardly noticeable, depending on whether a person is receiving treatment. When individuals are experiencing these changes in thought processes, they are said to be experiencing "acute psychosis."
- **Negative symptoms** include reductions in normal emotional and behavioral states. For example, individuals with schizophrenia often are described as having flat affect (e.g., they don't show happiness or sadness when these emotions seem appropriate) and loss of drive (e.g., they are not motivated to complete day-to-day tasks, such as cooking and cleaning, or even taking a shower and changing their clothes). Sometimes these symptoms make the individuals appear lazy, but these behaviors are part of the

illness. In addition, these individuals may become socially withdrawn because they are afraid someone will harm them or they worry they will not be able to interact well with others because of their disease.

- **Cognitive symptoms** include problems with executive functions, such as planning, organizing, and evaluating, difficulties sustaining attention, slower processing speed and problems with working memory (e.g., individuals with schizophrenia may have difficulty holding relevant information in mind as they complete a task or make a decision).

As you can imagine, these symptoms make it difficult for people with schizophrenia to lead a normal life—to work and go to school, to cultivate and maintain relationships—and they are the cause of a great deal of emotional distress. The rates of depression and substance abuse are higher among adolescents with schizophrenia than they are for the general population, and adolescents who have schizophrenia are at higher risk for suicide (NIMH, 2006; Stenager & Qin, 2008). The cause of schizophrenia is believed to be a combination of genetic, biochemical, and environmental factors (Children, Youth, and Women's Health Service, 2009; NIMH, 2006). Whereas the risk of developing schizophrenia is 1 in 100 for members of the general population, the risk is increased to 1 in 10 for people with a parent or sibling with the disorder; having a twin with schizophrenia increases the risk to between 40% and 65%. Research also links schizophrenia to an imbalance of chemical reactions in the brain. Specifically, neurotransmitters that enable brain cells to communicate with one another are thought to be involved. Finally, stress may trigger symptoms of the illness in vulnerable people. Stressful events (e.g., tensions in the family, anxiety about school) are often associated with the first signs of the illness; however, it can be difficult to discern whether the tensions precede or supersede the illness (Children, Youth, and Women's Health Service, 2009).

Schizophrenia is a chronic illness (like diabetes or high blood pressure), so there is no cure. However, many people with schizophrenia find their illness responds well to treatment; with appropriate treatment, they are able to resume independent, productive, and satisfying lives. Primarily, schizophrenia is treated with antipsychotic medications. In addition, counseling and family support can be invaluable in helping individuals to manage and cope with their disease. Because schizophrenia is a chronic disorder, it requires constant management (NIMH, 2006), and it is very important for people with schizophrenia to take their medication regularly for as long as their doctors prescribe, so they experience fewer "positive" symptoms. This is where a support network (i.e., parents, medical professionals, professional case workers, teachers, and friends) can help.

Sometimes people with schizophrenia do not take their medication because they believe they no longer need it (the medication makes them feel well), or they don't like the side effects. Also, disordered thought processes and the use of other substances can interfere with treatment regimes (e.g., they may forget to take their medication). Medical professionals can help by seeing these patients regularly, asking them how their treatment regime is working, being sensitive to their complaints about side effects, and changing or modifying medications to increase their quality of life. Other caregivers can help by monitoring the manifestation of symptoms and helping their loved ones and friends to develop strategies to ensure they take their medications regularly (e.g., initiate a calendar routine or use pill boxes labeled with the days of the week). Finally, working hard to maintain positive relationships is crucial. For example, one group of researchers studied interactions between parents and adolescents with schizophrenia and found positive interactions, characterized by warmth and positive remarks from parents, decreased negative symptoms and enhanced social functioning in youth with the disease (O'Brien et al., 2008). The ***Connecting with Adolescents*** guidelines at the end of this section offer ideas about how adults can support adolescents with serious mental illnesses, such as schizophrenia and bipolar disorder.

Bipolar Disorder

Sometimes Sophie finds even brushing her teeth too much of an effort. At times like these, she locks herself away, telling everyone she's busy, so they won't know she hasn't gotten out of bed all day. "I never used to worry about it; I thought,

> 'That's just me.' . . . And other people, when they saw me up—excited and exuberant, partying all night, never sleeping—thought, 'That's just Sophie.'"
>
> (*Source:* MailOnline, 2009)

Now she knows those extreme emotional highs and lows occur because she has a manic-depressive illness, also known as **bipolar disorder.** Like schizophrenia, bipolar disorder typically develops during adolescence or early adulthood (more than half of all cases begin before age 25), although it can develop during childhood or even late in life (NIMH, 2008). It is a serious brain disorder that causes unusual and extreme shifts in mood, energy, and activity levels, and, as we saw in Sophie's case, it can affect people's ability to carry out their daily tasks. Bipolar disorder can be difficult to spot when its symptoms first emerge; the symptoms may seem like separate problems as opposed to parts of one large problem. Also, people are more likely to seek treatment when they feel depressed, so bipolar disorder may first be diagnosed as depressive disorder. For these reasons, people may suffer with bipolar disorder for several (or many) years before it is accurately diagnosed and effectively treated. This is unfortunate because bipolar disorder usually becomes worse if not treated (i.e., episodes become more frequent and severe), and, untreated, it can cause serious personal, social, and school/work-related problems, including impulsive acts of aggression, self-injury, substance abuse, and suicide (Child & Adolescent Bipolar Foundation (CABF), 2007; NIMH, 2008). One of the most formidable barriers to adolescents seeking help or mental health care is the stigma associated with mental illness. We discuss this topic further in the ***Relating to Every Adolescent*** feature.

Table 13.5 lists symptoms associated with bipolar disorder. These symptoms can be more severe in children and youth than in adults (CABF, 2007; NIMH, 2008). For example, young people tend to have symptoms and switch moods more often than adults with the disease. Mood changes, or "mood episodes," refer to periods of mania—an overly joyful or excited state, depression, or mixed mania and depression. Children and teenagers with bipolar disorder are more likely to experience mixed mood episodes than adults with the illness (NIMH, 2008).

As was the case for schizophrenia, researchers agree bipolar disorder likely is the result of both biological and environmental factors. The illness tends to run in families—children whose parents or siblings have bipolar disorder are 4 to 6 times more likely to develop the illness than children with no family history of the disease (NIMH, 2008; Nurnberger &

TABLE 13.5 • **Symptoms of Bipolar Disorder in Children and Teens**

SYMPTOMS OF MANIA OR A MANIC EPISODE INCLUDE:	SYMPTOMS OF DEPRESSION OR A DEPRESSIVE EPISODE INCLUDE:
Mood Changes • A long period of feeling overly happy or acting silly in a way that's unusual. • Extremely irritable mood, agitation, or "wired."	**Mood Changes** • A long period of feeling worried, sad, and empty. • Loss of interest in activities once enjoyed. • Feel guilty and worthless.
Behavioral Changes • Talking very fast about lots of different things. • Having a very short temper and being easily distracted. • Having trouble sleeping and being restless. • Having an unrealistic belief in one's abilities. • Behaving impulsively and taking part in a lot of pleasurable and risky behaviors (such as impulsive sex and spending sprees).	**Behavioral Changes** • Changing eating, sleeping, or other habits. • Thinking of death or suicide, or attempting suicide. • Feeling tired, having little energy and no interest in fun activities. • Complaining about pain a lot, like stomachaches and headaches. • Being restless and irritable. • Having problems concentrating, remembering, and making decisions.

Source: National Institutes of Mental Health. *(2008). Bipolar disorder.*

RELATING TO

EVERY ADOLESCENT

▸ The Stigma Associated with Mental Illness and Mental Health Care

ANITA CHANDRA AND CYNTHIA MINKOVITZ (2007) studied youths' perceptions of mental health, how these views are shaped, and how they affect adolescents' willingness to seek mental health services when needed. Specifically, they interviewed 57 eighth grade students attending two public middle schools in a mid-Atlantic state. The topics addressed in the interviews included youths' personal experiences with mental illness and mental health services; experiences of family members or other people in their social networks; knowledge and attitudes about mental illness; and willingness to seek mental health care when needed.

Almost 90% of the students reported an experience with a mental health issue that affected their attitudes about confronting mental health problems. Some adolescents reported a positive and beneficial experience, but the majority described negative experiences in which either they or someone they knew had been dissatisfied with the services received. They described feeling "offended" or "dismissed" (Chandra & Minkovitz, p. 767). The researchers also noted that the students who had limited or inaccurate knowledge about mental illness voiced more negative attitudes toward individuals with mental health disorders and the use of mental health services. They talked more about negative stereotypes and a lack of hope or options for individuals with serious mental illnesses. Many students did not feel comfortable talking about mental health issues with peers—"these revelations were rare and minimally discussed" (p. 774). The majority perceived friends would react negatively if they learned that someone their age was seeking or receiving mental health services; they indicated the individual likely would be teased or avoided.

This is an area where adults can make a difference. Students in the Chandra and Minkovitz study who felt comfortable talking to parents about mental health issues held more positive views about seeking help for such issues. Unfortunately, many of these adolescents reported their parents' belief that mental health concerns should not be discussed outside their homes. Similarly, teachers' concern for students' mental health informed more positive attitudes about mental illness and seeking mental health care.

The British Columbia Schizophrenia Society (2010, p. 32) offers the following suggestions for addressing the stigma associated with mental health concerns:

- learn as much as you can about mental illness and mental health care;
- share your knowledge with your children/students;
- dispel the myths;
- be sensitive to the challenges children and families face when someone they love has a mental illness; and
- listen to youth with mental illness who say don't just tolerate me, don't be afraid of me, and don't expect less of me just because I have an illness you don't understand.

Foroud, 2000). Also, studies using MRI technology indicate the brains of children with bipolar disorder may develop differently than other brains. For example, Gogtay and colleagues (2007) found similar patterns of brain activity and development in children with bipolar disorder and children with multidimensional impairment—a disorder causing symptoms that overlap with bipolar disorder and schizophrenia. Linking patterns of brain development to risks for developing mood disorders may help scientists to predict who is at risk for developing them and to design better treatments for managing, and perhaps preventing, the disease (NIMH, 2008).

Currently, the most effective treatment plans combine medication and psychotherapy. In particular, it is important for medications to be monitored and maintained. Children respond differently to medications, and the dosage and type of medications may need to be changed as children grow and develop, or experience side effects—it is not a one size fits all solution forever. In therapy, children can learn about their illness and learn to manage their behavior. One study taught adolescents to reshape negative thinking to shield themselves from depression (Garber et al., 2009). Therapy that includes family members builds

CONNECTING WITH ADOLESCENTS

Guidelines for Families, Teachers, and Other Professionals: Creating Multifaceted Approaches to Working with Adolescents with Mental Illnesses

Establish networks of support.
Examples

1. Find community workshops and seminars for families to help them learn about treatments available for teenagers suffering from mental illness.
2. Educate students in school about the meaning of illnesses and the importance of acceptance and tolerance.
3. Develop coping skills for families, teachers, and adolescents, both at home and in school. Take action together to solve problems.
4. Develop realistic expectations of adolescents with mental illnesses.

Strengthen support networks.
Examples

1. Identify the needs of the different sectors, and be flexible about the treatments and services that meet those needs.
2. Always keep in mind that work with adolescents with mental illness must be constructive and collaborative.
3. Create supportive environments for the adolescents by maintaining a hopeful attitude.
4. Encourage families and teachers to seek help.
5. Ensure that help and information are easily accessible.

Source: Adapted from http://www.acf.hhs.gov/programs/fysb/content/aboutfysb/yes_mentalhealth.htm http://www.aamft.org/families/Consumer_Updates/Schizophrenia.asp

stronger bonds among family members and improves coping strategies, communication, and problem solving (NIMH, 2008). Schools and teachers also can help. Bipolar disorder can affect school attendance; alertness and concentration; sensitivity to light, noise, and stress; and motivation and energy for learning (CABF, 2007). Transitioning to new schools and teachers or returning from prolonged absences, even vacations, can increase symptoms. Teachers and parents need to collaborate to address the needs of children and youth with bipolar disorder. Like any other disability or chronic illness, mental illness entitles students to accommodations that address their exceptional learning needs.

Depression and anxiety disorders, schizophrenia, and bipolar disorder present serious threats to some adolescents' health and well-being. With treatment, however, these adolescents can lead healthy, happy, and productive lives. It really helps when adults and adolescents work together, and when solutions are multifaceted and family, school, and community based. The ***Connecting with Adolescents*** guidelines offer some ideas for accomplishing this.

EMERGING ADULTHOOD

Adolescence is a time of profound changes—physical, cognitive, social, and emotional—that can be accompanied by conflict and uncertainty. However, for most young people, adolescence also is an wonderfully exciting time of life: Their bodies grow taller and stronger and awaken sexually; their minds develop in ways that allow them to think more deeply and quickly than before; and they feel satisfied with most of their relationships most of the time. But what's on the other side of adolescence? What's in store for teenagers emerging from adolescence into adulthood?

Issues of Identity

According to Erikson (1950), the primary psychosocial task for early adults is one of developing intimate relationships. This includes finding a life partner and forming a family apart from the one in which we grew up. However, Salkind (2004) argues that it also includes striving for intimacy in non-romantic relationships. In essence, intimacy in adulthood refers to the development and maintenance of deep, meaningful relationships in a variety of forms.

In Erikson's theory, the crisis of early adulthood is one of *intimacy versus isolation*. Establishing intimate relationships requires the ability to trust others and share feelings, beliefs, values, and goals. Adults who don't achieve intimacy in their relationships are likely to feel left out and lonely (Salkind, 2004). If they are unable to communicate or share feelings with others, they may be ostracized and isolated throughout the remainder of their lives. In addition, intimacy requires a degree of autonomy and a clear sense of identity. Teenagers who don't resolve their crisis of identity during adolescence may enter adulthood with a sense of role diffusion. They may be unprepared for intimacy and, as a consequence, experience only superficial and primarily unsuccessful relationships.

Traditionally, early adulthood has been perceived as a time for taking on more responsibility and gaining independence from parents. In contemporary technologically advanced societies, however, this is becoming less the norm (Arnett, 2007; Eccles et al., 2003). In these societies, success in adulthood typically requires advanced education. As a result, young adults are delaying marriage and childbearing, living with parents longer, and relying on them for financial support. Perhaps this is why they have been referred to as the "Peter Pan" generation in the popular media. More commonly, today's adolescents and emerging adults are referred to as "Generation Y" or "Millennials." We conclude this chapter with a look at some of their unique characteristics and how they differ from previous teenage cohorts.

Who Is Generation Y?

The timelines for Generation Y vary, but range from the early 1980s through to 2003 (Bibby, 2009; Howe & Radner, 2009; Strauss & Howe, 2000; 2003). They are today's teenagers and early adults. Popular culture portrays them as sheltered, perhaps too much, by their parents (late "Boomers" and "Generation Xers"), giving them unrealistic expectations and making them overly demanding at school and in the workplace. Stephanie Armour, a columnist for *USA Today*, characterized Millennials as "young, smart, brash . . . wear[ing] flip-flops to the office and listen[ing] to iPods at their desks . . . want[ing] to work, but [not wanting] work to be their lives" (2005, June). Is this a fair assessment? The ***Point/Counterpoint*** addresses this issue.

One characteristic that makes the Millennials unique among other generations of teenagers is their relationship with technology. Also dubbed "Net Gen," teenagers today have been immersed in technology throughout their lives. Recall from earlier in this chapter how prevalent computers and other technologies are in adolescents' homes, schools, and communities (Lenhart, 2009; Nielsen, 2009), as well as the wide range of uses to which they are put (e.g., Net Gen uses computers, cell phones, and other media to read and study, stay in touch with parents, socialize with friends, and entertain themselves). The popular perception is that teenagers today are constantly "connected"—that technology is integrated in all aspects of their lives. They have been characterized as experiential learners and proficient multitaskers whose technological skill far outstrips that of many of today's teachers and employers (Bennett, Maton, & Kervin, 2008). Writing about his 10-year-old son, the VP of Sony Pictures Television, had this to say: "Our 'Chief Technology Officer' can play an online game while seamlessly chatting in a forum, downloading music, watching TV, and talking on the telephone. He doesn't have a short attention span, he has a 'shared' attention span" (p. 11-11). He goes on to say, "Technology is a huge force shaping the way Millennials consume as well as 'commune' with media." His advice to employers, "Get a Millennial makeover."

Bennett et al. (2008) are more cautious. Their review of research about how adolescents and young adults access and use technology offers a more diverse view of its role in their lives. They conclude that access, interest, and skills vary within Generation Y, perhaps as much they do across generations. Also, it is important to note that much of the research on the generations refers to findings in Western and/or technologically advanced societies; young people's experiences with technology may be very different in various parts of the world. However, one thing is certain: Technology is not going anywhere, and the teenagers

POINT/COUNTERPOINT: What's the Truth about Generation Y?

Some people perceive that members of Generation Y have had the most child-centered upbringing ever (Armour, 2005) and, as a result, have been pampered and programmed since toddlerhood. These young people have high self-esteem, which is sometimes perceived as a sense of entitlement. Other people admire Gen Yers' "speak-your-mind" philosophy and believe their values are just what they should be. Which view is closest to reality?

POINT

▶ **Gen Yers exude a sense of entitlement that can seem disrespectful.** Armour (2005) offers insights from the perspective of employers as well as more mature employees, some of whom perceive that this new generation of workers is both high performance and high maintenance. This is a generation that grew up questioning their parents, so they are not afraid to question their employers. According to Armour, this can be irritating for the 50-year-old employer who wants to say, "Do it and do it now." Generation Y is used to receiving constant feedback from parents, teachers, and coaches—they expect to be told how they are doing, and regularly. Many have lived a privileged existence, relative to previous generations—they seem surprised they have to work for money, or to get the corner office. And, for colleagues who have spent 20, 30, 40 years doing the same tasks in the same occupation and who have organized personal and family life around work schedules, Generation Y's preference for "flexible" employment in which tasks vary and opportunities for telecommuting and working part time are available seems like a lack of commitment.

COUNTERPOINT

▶ **Gen Yers exude confidence and their assertiveness is refreshing.** Neil Howe and Reena Nadler's (2009) research debunks many popular myths about today's teenagers and young adults, and puts a more positive spin on adjectives used to describe them. They characterize Generation Y as confident and productively goal oriented. "This generation exudes a 'yes we can' optimism about their futures" (p. 11), but they also believe reaching their goals is dependent on their hard work. Generation Y wants to excel in school and in the workplace. As students, they support standardized testing and high standards, believing the best cure for boredom is a tougher curriculum. They look for measureable achievements and advancement in the workplace, but they are group-oriented, team players. They have more traditional values than the generations immediately preceding them. They are more civic minded, more involved in politics, and more committed to monogamy, marriage, and parenthood. They listen to their parents' advice and share their tastes in music and clothing.

Another survey of Canadian teenagers (ages 15 to 19) yielded findings consistent with Howe and Nadler's research. Reginald Bibby, a sociologist at the University of Lethbridge, recently surveyed adolescents about their beliefs, values, and behavior as part of Project Teen Canada (Bibby, Russell, & Rolheiser, 2009), which has surveyed Canadian youth in 1984, 1992, 2000, and 2008. The latest findings indicate teenagers today are drinking, smoking, and using illegal drugs less than previous generations, and they are more likely to be virgins and hold traditional views on commitment, love, and long-term relationships. In an interview with *Maclean's* magazine (2009), Bibby attributed these findings to increased efforts to educate parents and teens about health and safety and increases in secular morality, but he also emphasized the role of the family.

Certainly, Generation Y is different than any that have come before. However, it appears that despite adult angst over their attitudes and behavior, these young adults may be more independent and productive, and may balance idealism and pragmatism better than their Generation X and Baby Boomer parents (Brownstein, 2009). According to Brownstein, "This generation, like all others, will have its failures and blind spots. It is emerging at a grim moment. But it is arriving with an invigorating ethic of responsibility and a refreshingly practical bent" (p. 3–3).

of tomorrow (aka "digital natives") are likely to be even more vested in new technologies (whatever they may be) than the teenagers of today. Born between 1995 and 2009, they will always have lived in a world in which computers are commonplace, and they will be the first generation whose parents embrace new technologies with them. Educators and employers, make way for Generation Z.

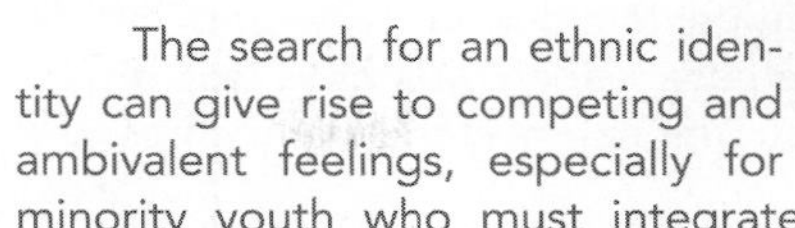

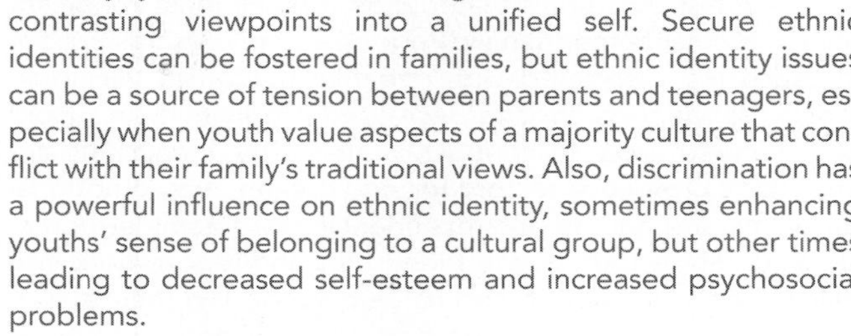

▼ SUMMARY AND KEY TERMS

• **The Search for Identity**

Erikson believed the most important developmental task for adolescents is the search for identity. Most adolescents try out different roles and most emerge with a secure sense of self, although the process is more difficult for some than for others (e.g., especially adolescents from diverse cultural groups who receive mixed messages concerning identity). Some adolescents' lack of direction and self-doubt is extreme, which can lead to serious problems, including depression, substance abuse, even suicide.

Marcia focused on exploration and commitment, and identified four categories of identity status that result from these activities: identity achievement, identity foreclosure, identity diffusion, and moratorium. In general, identity achievement increases and diffusion decreases from adolescence to adulthood, but identity development is a lifelong process. For most individuals, this process is more gradual and less traumatic than the term "crisis" implies.

• **Who Am I, and How Do I Like Myself?**

Adolescents may describe themselves in conflicting ways, depending on the setting and circumstances, and these contradictions can be a source of concern for them: "Who is the REAL me?" Adolescents also are concerned with what others think of them, and mixed messages from different groups of significant others can leave them confused about which characteristics to adopt. Adolescents recognize the discrepancy between their real and their ideal selves and, if this discrepancy is large, self-esteem can suffer. In general, positive self-esteem protects youth against negative outcomes; however, some adolescents report high self-esteem, but engage in high-risk and antisocial behaviors. Self-esteem tends to decline in early adolescence, but increases again from middle adolescence to adulthood, as adolescents become less concerned about what others think of them and more realistic about their future.

Boys consistently rate themselves higher in physical domains than girls do. This finding is robust across countries and cultures and persists through the college years, even among athletes. Also, boys continue to have higher self-concepts and self-esteem in math and science than do girls. Girls have lower interest and career aspirations in these domains. They want careers that fulfill humanistic and helping values and perceive that careers in science and engineering do not address these goals. Girls report higher ability beliefs and greater interest in subjects involving language arts than do boys. Findings concerning sex differences in actual performance in these domains are mixed.

Sexual orientation does not always align with sexual behavior, or with gender identity or perceived gender roles. Many sexual minority youth hide their sexual orientation, fearing rejection from family, friends, and communities. These youth have been ostracized and victimized at school and in the community, putting them at higher risk than their heterosexual peers for experiencing serious social and mental health problems.

The search for an ethnic identity can give rise to competing and ambivalent feelings, especially for minority youth who must integrate contrasting viewpoints into a unified self. Secure ethnic identities can be fostered in families, but ethnic identity issues can be a source of tension between parents and teenagers, especially when youth value aspects of a majority culture that conflict with their family's traditional views. Also, discrimination has a powerful influence on ethnic identity, sometimes enhancing youths' sense of belonging to a cultural group, but other times leading to decreased self-esteem and increased psychosocial problems.

• **Storm and Stress**

Some degree of storm and stress is typical during adolescence. For example, adolescents report greater extremes and more changes in mood than preadolescents and adults do. They report more negative affect and give lower ratings to questionnaire items that reflect feeling great, proud, and in control. Girls are more prone to negative moods and mood swings than boys, and ethnic minority youth report lower levels of life satisfaction and happiness than other groups of teenagers. Popularity with peers, self-esteem, school performance, and school alienation are associated with adolescents' moods. Perceived support from teachers is associated with happiness, as are authoritative parenting styles.

Adolescence also is the period in life associated with the highest rates of risky behavior. Risky behaviors, such as smoking, using drugs and alcohol, driving dangerously, and engaging in unsafe sex, have long been threats to the well-being of adolescents. Today, new technologies create new threats. Teenagers may interact with strangers through social networking sites, post or give away information that should remain private, form an unhealthy dependence on technological tools, or be negatively influenced by their exposure to violence in video games. Experiences during the teen years offer opportunities for developing self-regulation. Adults can help by providing the right balance of monitoring and interest plus scaffolding skills and strategies for self-control. Also, adults can encourage adolescents to get involved in activities that ignite high intensity feelings, but are healthy and rewarding (e.g., involvement in sports, music, or social service). Importantly, storm and stress is not extreme for most teenagers, and is more common in Western majority cultures that emphasize independence than in traditional cultures that value interdependence.

• **Relationships with Peers**

Peer relationships become increasingly important sources of social and emotional support during adolescence. Most adolescents belong to a peer group, and different groups have different peer cultures, which can promote positive or negative behavior. Cliques are small, friendship-based groups with common interests, and adolescents can belong to more than one clique. Crowds are larger than cliques, less intimate and organized, and more reputation-based. Status and self-esteem are associated with crowd membership, and crowds are most influential during early and middle adolescence. In late adolescence, crowds hold less prominence as teenagers focus more on close friendships and romantic relationships.

Adolescents report that friends are their most important resource outside their family. Poor quality friendships in adolescence are associated with negative outcomes, including loneliness, depression, and decreased productivity in school and work settings. In contrast, high-quality friendships are important protective factors for adolescents with emotional problems and adolescents experiencing problems at home. Girls are interested in close friendships and report more intimacy, prosocial support, and esteem support in their friendships than do boys. However, girls' friendships tend to be of shorter duration than boys' friendships, and more likely to involve conflict.

High-quality romantic relationships are positively associated with romantic self-concept and general self-worth, but adolescents involved in romantic relationships experience more conflict and more extreme mood swings than other adolescents. Dating early, too much, or not at all are associated with problems. Boys tend to focus on sexual aspects of dating, whereas girls are more focused on intimacy and relationship issues and are more conflicted about sex. Sexual minority youth often are slower to begin dating and develop romantic relationships, perhaps reflecting uncertainty or fear of being ridiculed. Cultural and family values also influence the onset of dating, romantic relationships, and sexual intercourse, as do peers and partners.

Today, teenagers connect with one another through social software and other media. Unfortunately, there are some negative trends in adolescents' social networking, including cyberbullying and sexting. Bullies may be emboldened by electronic media because they can remain anonymous and get their message to a much larger audience. The consequences for victims can be devastating and long lasting, undermining their freedom to use online resources, ruining their reputations, and causing serious emotional and psychological harm. Similarly, sexting—sending sexually explicit material over the Internet—can have serious consequences for both perpetrators and victims, and it's illegal.

• Parenting Adolescents

Most adolescents continue to feel close to their parents, but some distancing is a normal feature of the parent–adolescent relationship. Adolescents want to be treated more like adults. They also want more independence and privacy, especially in Western societies. Parents worry about their ability to monitor and control their adolescents' behavior, and fear for their safety. Authoritative parenting and inductive discipline continue to be effective approaches to parenting. Adolescents who experience warmth, autonomy support, and structure tend to be responsible, self-assured, and successful in school, and less likely to experience anxiety and depression, or become involved in problem behavior. When attachment between parents and teenagers is strong and secure, parents continue to influence adolescents' behavior. Similarly, inductive discipline communicates confidence in adolescents' desire and ability to make good choices. In contrast, harsh discipline can lead to hostility and open disregard for parents' authority.

Low levels of parental monitoring are associated with high levels of problem behavior, including conduct problems, delinquency, substance use, early sexual activity, and problems at school. Parents who monitor effectively gather information about what their adolescents do without engaging in overly intrusive behaviors. Mainly, they rely on what teenagers tell them. Adolescents' willingness to disclose information to parents has been linked to harmonious and trusting parent–adolescent relationships as well as to the kind of information to be shared. Teenagers feel obliged to reveal information that threatens their health or safety, but not information about personal issues or their peers. Most parents know less than they think they do, and many withdraw monitoring and supervision before adolescents are ready to cope with the complex situations in which they find themselves.

Conflict between parents and adolescents tends to increase in frequency during early adolescence, reach a peak in intensity during middle adolescence, and then decline in late adolescence. Sons and daughters report similar amounts of closeness and conflict with parents, but relationships with mothers are characterized as closer and more intense than relationships with fathers, who often are perceived as distant authority figures. Father–daughter relationships during adolescence are characterized as particularly distant. The long-term effects of conflict on parent–adolescent relationships appear to have less to do with the content of the conflict than how it is managed and resolved. When parent–adolescent relationships are positive, mild conflict presents an opportunity to review expectations with one another and renegotiate the relationship.

• Life in School

Adolescence involves transitions from elementary to middle and middle to high school. Most adolescents adjust to these new environments, especially when family and friends are supportive and schools are responsive to their needs. Students with histories of academic, social and/or emotional problems, and students in poor neighborhoods have a more difficult time. Middle and high schools tend to emphasize grades and social comparisons more than elementary schools. Often these schools are less personal, and teachers trust students less and want to control them more, which creates a mismatch between what adolescents want and schools provide. Experts argue that schools should be authoritative contexts in which teachers are supportive but maintain high, well-defined standards for behavior and academic work. In these contexts, students have stronger bonds with school, and high levels of school attachment are associated with positive outcomes, including higher rates of achievement, greater motivation for learning, and fewer problem behaviors.

Students who are low achieving or members of ethnic or sexual minority groups are at risk for school "disconnectedness." Attending urban schools, not being involved in extracurricular activities, experiencing health problems, and being younger or older than classmates also make youth feel less connected to school. Conversely, school attachment appears to buffer youth from negative outcomes, such as low self-esteem and risky and delinquent behavior. Students form positive attachments to schools they perceive care about their learning and general well-being, so fostering positive teacher–student relationships and creating caring communities continue to be important. Characteristics of caring schools include positive adults, positive places, and positive opportunities.

• Challenges for Adolescents

Half of all lifetime cases of mental illness appear by age 14. Suicide and anxiety disorders continue to be the most common forms of mental illness in adolescence. Suicidal ideation is not uncommon during adolescence, but thoughts or actions that could result in self-harm should be taken seriously and addressed immediately. Some groups of adolescents are at higher risk for suicide, including Aboriginal youth and youth with other forms of mental illness, such as schizophrenia and bipolar disorder.

Schizophrenia is a chronic brain disorder that typically emerges during late adolescence or early adulthood. Symptoms fall into three broad categories—positive, negative, and cognitive—and may be difficult to recognize in young children or confused with other illnesses and behaviors in adolescence. Schizophrenia has been linked to genetic, biochemical, and environmental factors. It is a chronic illness, so there is no cure, although treatment with antipsychotic medications and counseling can be effective. Sticking to the treatment regime is important, and this can be challenging. People with schizophrenia may perceive that they do not need their medication, or they may not like its side effects. Medical professionals and caregivers need to work collaboratively to support individuals with this illness, and positive relationships with friends and family members are crucial.

Like schizophrenia, bipolar disorder typically emerges during adolescence or early adulthood. It can be difficult to spot when it first emerges because symptoms may be perceived as separate problems as opposed to different aspects of one problem. Also, people are more likely to seek treatment when they are depressed, so the disorder may be misdiagnosed as depression. Children with the disorder tend to have symptoms and switch moods more often than adults, and they are more likely to experience mixed mood episodes than adults. As was true with schizophrenia, sources of the illness are believed to be both biological and environmental. The most effective treatments combine medication and psychotherapy, and the use of medications needs to be closely monitored. Moreover, strong family bonds and support from friends, schools, and the community improve outcomes for individuals with this illness.

• Emerging Adulthood

Traditionally, early adulthood has been perceived as a time for taking on more responsibility and gaining independence from parents. In contemporary, technologically advanced societies, however, young adults are putting off marriage and childbearing and living with parents longer. Popular culture portrays "Millennials" as sheltered and overly demanding, but survey research characterizes them as confident and productively oriented. Surveys also indicate they are more conservative than the generations immediately preceding them. Their access to and uses of technology also set them apart from preceding generations.

▼ KEY TERMS

bipolar disorder (564)
bisexual (536)
cluster suicides (562)
cognitive symptoms (563)
commitment (528)
cyberbullying (550)
deviancy training (546)
ethnic identity (537)
exploration (528)
gender intensification (533)
heterosexual (536)
homosexual (536)
identity achievement (529)
identity diffusion (529)
identity foreclosure (529)
moratorium (529)
negative symptoms (562)
oppositional identity (539)
peer culture (544)
peer pressure (546)
positive symptoms (562)
schizophrenia (562)
school attachment (557)
selection (546)
sexting (551)
sexual orientation (536)
socialization (546)
suicidal ideation (561)

▼ THE CASEBOOK

PRIVACY VERSUS PROTECTION FOR TEENS

The library at Alder Woods Secondary School has become a popular hangout for students ages 13 to 17. It has a large bank of computers equipped with state-of-the-art software for searching and researching. At the moment, students pretty much have unlimited access to the Internet and *all* it has to offer. This is a bit of a concern for the librarians who can't possibly monitor all the activities of the kids who drop in before, during, and after school hours. Also, they feel torn—even if they could monitor the goings on or limit access in some way to sites that are potentially problematic, should they? Is it their responsibility? Is it an invasion of the right to privacy that teenagers hold very dear? How can concerned adults strike the right balance between granting privacy and protecting youth from harm that can come from using the Internet?

WHAT WOULD THEY DO?

Here's how some professionals in several fields responded:

JILL SULLIVAN—Math, Grades 9–11

Northside College Prep High School, Chicago, Illinois

At my high school, we have to abide by district-level controls. Both students and teachers alike know that if you try to visit certain sites such as Facebook or YouTube, you will instead get a pop-up blocker with both an audible and a written warning. It seems to work pretty well, although sometimes an ad on a page of legitimate educational content will set it off. The largest controversy is over educational videos that happen to be on YouTube since the whole site is blocked. Not surprisingly, many students have figured out workarounds. I think it's fine for schools to limit some of the content just as they do with books. In other words, the library already has chosen a subset of printed educational material to make available. so the Internet is not necessarily different. And, many students have Internet access at home and can get to all content there. I imagine that elementary schools will have to start teaching Internet usage guidelines since by the time students get to high school (ages 13–17 in this scenario), they will have already spent considerable time online.

CATHY BLANCHFIELD—English/Language Arts, Grades 10 and 12

Duncan Polytechnical High School, Fresno, California

For sure, teenagers can access almost any site they wish in a non-school setting. However, I don't know of a school that has not purchased a filter of some sort to limit access to Internet sites for a variety of reasons: sexual content, illegal content, and predator access to underage students, to name a few. As adults in the lives of adolescents, we must protect them from their own vulnerabilities.

As a public school, we must make sure that students cannot put themselves into harmful situations where they might have few or no defenses. Teenagers make split-second decisions on the computer that might result in an unwanted, harmful situation. That said, I believe that as adults in their lives we must teach them about both the advantages and dangers of the Internet. We can and must instruct them in decision processes that involve which sites should be used in various situations, why some may not be appropriate, and why revealing too much about themselves can have dangerous results.

Students need to be able to make informed decisions, and where better can they learn this information but in high school? At the same time, it is our responsibility to keep them safe by monitoring their activities and restricting potentially dangerous decisions. Social websites are not private, so personal information should remain limited. We can still encourage private emails and activities, but with the caveat that in any work place, including school, those emails can be accessed, so all activity should remain legal and appropriate. I have witnessed adolescents learning these principles and becoming informed Internet users.

ELAINE S. BOOTHBY—AP Literature, Grade 12

South River High School, Edgewater, Maryland

The technical ability of adults to monitor computer use through an overseeing program is standard operating procedure in most high schools. This ability assures that students are not in jeopardy by exposing too much information about themselves or by accessing materials not appropriate in school or library sector use. Since taxpayers are affording computer services, it is inherent that adults actively and carefully scrutinize use.

Students' natural curiosity makes them easy prey to predators. This monitoring of web use is not a breech of trust, as the public has a right to have its young people protected by public servants. In the home, parents should also monitor Facebook and other public sites because college entrance offices and future employers are doing just that and parents should be aware of the public face that their children are presenting to the world.

HOLLY FITCHETTE—French Teacher, Grades 9–11

Fleming Island High School, Fleming Island, Florida

Teens are especially susceptible to dangers found on the Internet because they believe they are too mature to require the input and protection of the adults around them. In my opinion, the Internet is not a safe place for teens without adult supervision. There are laws in place that protect minors from purchasing pornography, tobacco, alcohol, firearms, etc.

Unfortunately, when teenagers have unrestricted Internet access, they are unprotected minors who have access to material and individuals from whom they require protection. If I were a school librarian in such a situation, I would raise the red flag in my school and district. I think the school or school district should make the joint determination of what kinds of materials should be unavailable to students in a school setting. I feel that it is the job of parents to make the decision whether to allow access to those sites that may be controversial. In the meantime, I think the school should make sure it is providing a safe education for students and not allowing them to get into dangerous situations on the Internet. I think the school district should filter these sites so that parents can make the call on their own.

PEARSON myeducationlab

Now go to MyEducationLab at ***www.myeducationlab.com,*** where you can:

- Find the instructional objectives for this chapter in the **Study Plan**.
- Take a quiz as a part of the **Study Plan** to self-assess your mastery of chapter content. The program generates an individualized Study Plan based upon your answers to the quiz.
- Complete **Activities and Applications** to assist you in deepening your understanding of important chapter concepts.
- Apply what you have learned through **Building Teaching Skills**, exercises that guide you in trying out skills and strategies you will use in professional practice.

GLOSSARY

abstinence-only (AO) education: A form of sex education that teaches that in all cases, sex should be delayed until marriage. The only information provided about birth control typically is that these methods are not very effective.

accommodation: The process of altering existing schemes or creating new ones in response to new information.

action research: Systematic observations or tests of methods conducted by teachers or schools to improve teaching and learning for their students.

adolescent egocentrism: The assumption that everyone else shares one's thoughts, feelings, and concerns; adolescents become very focused on their own ideas.

aggressive behavior: Behavior that is intended to hurt others or damage property.

altruistic empathy: Empathy that occurs when a child stops her own activity to help a distressed child who is farther away.

amenorrhea: The cessation of a woman's normal menstrual cycle.

anorexia nervosa: Self-starvation.

anoxia: A lack of oxygen to the fetus that, depending on its severity, may or may not lead to brain damage.

APGAR: A rating system that determines the level of intervention that an infant might need and the infant's response to intervention.

appropriating: Taking in and using ways of acting and thinking provided by the culture and by the more capable members of the group.

argumentation: The process of debating a claim with someone else, supporting your position with evidence and understanding, and then refuting your opponent's claims and evidence.

assessment bias: The qualities of an assessment instrument that offend or unfairly penalize a group of students because of the students' gender, SES, race, ethnicity, etc.

assimilation: Fitting new information into existing schemes.

assisted learning/guided participation: Providing strategic help in the initial stages of learning, gradually diminishing as students gain independence.

assistive technology: Devices, systems, and services that support and improve the capabilities of individuals with disabilities.

asthma: An inflammation of the airways—the tubes that carry air in and out of lungs—that interferes with breathing.

ataxic CP: A type of cerebral palsy that affects balance and coordination.

athetotic CP: A type of cerebral palsy that causes uncontrolled, slow body movements and affects the entire body.

attachment: A term that describes the emotional bond between infants/toddlers and the adults who care for them.

attention: Focus on a stimulus; also, the awareness of and interest in phenomena.

attention-deficit hyperactivity disorder (ADHD): The current term for disruptive behavior disorders marked by overactivity, excessive difficulty sustaining attention, or impulsiveness.

authoritarian parents: Parents who are high in control and low in warmth and responsiveness. They set firm limits and expect children will follow orders because they say so, often without an explanation or negotiation.

authoritative parents: Parents who are high in warmth, but also exert firm control. They monitor their children closely, set clear standards, and have high expectations for behavior.

autism: A developmental disorder of communication and perception identified before age 3.

autism spectrum disorders: A range of disorders in social communication and interactions from mild to major, accompanied by restricted, repetitive patterns of behavior, interests, and activities.

automaticity: The ability to perform thoroughly learned tasks without much mental effort.

autonomy: Independence.

availability heuristic: Judging the likelihood of an event based on what is available in your memory, assuming those easily remembered events are common.

aversive: Irritating or unpleasant.

balanced bilingualism: People who are equally fluent in two languages.

behavioral genetics: A field that seeks to understand the extent to which characteristics that vary from individual to individual are the result of genetic versus environmental variation.

behaviorism: Explanations of learning that focus on external events as the cause of changes in observable behaviors.

belief perseverance: The tendency to hold on to beliefs, even in the face of contradictory evidence.

bilingualism: Speaking two languages.

binge eating: Eating an amount of food that is definitely larger than most people would consume in a similar period of time, with a lack of control over eating.

bioecological model: Bronfenbrenner's theory describing the nested social and cultural contexts that shape development. Every person develops within a *microsystem*, inside a *mesosystem*, embedded in an *exosystem*, all of which are a part of the *macrosystem* of the culture. All development occurs in and is influenced by the time period—the *chronosystem*.

bipolar disorder: A manic-depressive illness characterized by extreme emotional highs and lows.

bisexual: Individuals who are attracted to both sexes.

blastocyst: The ball of cells that results after cell divisions in the zygote.

blended families: Parents, children, and stepchildren merged into families through remarriages.

body image: An individual's dynamic perception of his or her body—how it looks, feels, and moves.

body mass index (BMI): A measure of body fat that evaluates weight in relation to height and can be calculated using either English or metric units.

bulimia nervosa: Binge eating followed by purging, fasting, or excessive exercise.

caesarean section: The surgical removal of the infant from the uterus.

case study: The intensive study of one person or one situation.

central executive: The part of working memory that is responsible for monitoring and directing attention and other mental resources.

cerebral palsy (CP): A disorder that affects muscle tone, movement, and motor skills.

child development: The study of human growth and change in the physical, cognitive, emotional, social, and personality realms from conception through adolescence—about to age 20.

childcare/day care: The care of children outside the home for a large portion of the day, generally arranged for working parents.

chromosomes: Chemical segments that exist within the nucleus of cells and consist of 23 pairs of elongated bodies, each comprising thousands of segments.

circumcision: A medical procedure that removes the foreskin on the penis.

classical conditioning: The association of automatic responses with new stimuli.

classification: Grouping objects into categories.

clinical interview: A research approach that uses open-ended questioning to probe responses and follow up on answers.

cluster suicides: A situation in which several members of a group attempt or commit suicide within a relatively short time frame, perhaps in response to a classmate's suicide or a suicide that has been widely publicized.

co-constructed process: A social process in which people interact and negotiate (usually verbally) to create an understanding or to solve a problem. All participants shape the final product.

co-dominance: Occurs when the alleles of the gene (the members of a pair or series of genes that occupy a specific position on a specific chromosome) are expressed equally, or when one is stronger, yet does not mask the effects of the other.

coactions: Joint actions of nature and nurture, or heredity and environment, working together in interactions to produce growth and development.

cochlear implant: A surgically implanted electronic device that provides a sense of sound.

code-switching: Moving between two languages or language forms.

cognitive apprenticeship: A relationship in which a less experienced learner acquires knowledge and skills under the guidance of an expert.

cognitive development: Changes in problem solving, memory, language, reasoning, and other aspects of thinking.

cognitive symptoms: Problems associated with schizophrenia that involve executive functions, such as planning, organizing, and evaluating; difficulties sustaining attention; slower processing speed; and problems with working memory.

cohort: A group of people who share the same historical context because they were born during the same time period.

collective monologue: A form of speech in which children in a group talk, but do not really interact or communicate.

collective self-esteem: Self-esteem that is influenced by the qualities of the groups to which an individual belongs.

commitment: Individuals' choices concerning political and religious beliefs, for example, usually as a consequence of exploring the options.

community-based research: Research that is conducted by, with, and for communities.

compensation: The principle that changes in one dimension can be offset by changes in another dimension.

comprehensive sex education (CSE): Sex education programs that encourage abstinence, but also include information about birth control to prevent pregnancy and condoms to prevent STDs.

concrete operations: Mental tasks that are tied to concrete objects and situations.

concussion: A trauma-induced alteration in mental status that may or may not involve a loss of consciousness.

confirmation bias: Seeking information that confirms our choices and beliefs, while ignoring disconfirming evidence.

conjunctives: Words followed by information that is consistent with the overall message.

consequences: Events that follow an action.

conservation: The principle that some characteristics of an object remain the same despite changes in appearance.

constructive play: A type of play that is more goal oriented than functional play; it emerges after children figure out how things work and understand the effects of their actions.

context: The total setting or situation that surrounds and interacts with a person or event.

continuous development: A gradual, continuing process of increase (or decrease) in abilities, knowledge, skills, strength, or other aspects of physical, cognitive, and social development—"more of the same."

controversial children: Children who have mixed reviews from peers because they display a combination of positive and negative social behaviors.

correlations: Statistical descriptions of how closely two variables are related; indicates both the strength and the direction of a relationship between two events or measurements.

critical periods: A time during which certain types of learning or development must take place or they will not happen at all.

cross-modal abilities: The ability to coordinate two or more senses.

cross-sectional studies: Studies in which different age groups are compared at the same time.

crystallized intelligence: The ability to apply the problem-solving methods appropriate in your cultural context.

cultural tools: The real tools (computers, scales, etc.) and symbol systems (numbers, language, graphs) that allow people in a society to communicate, think, solve problems, and create knowledge.

culturally relevant pedagogy: Excellent teaching for students of color that includes academic success, developing/maintaining cultural competence, and developing a critical consciousness to challenge the status quo.

culture: The knowledge, values, attitudes, and traditions that guide the behavior of a group of people and allow them to solve the problems of living in their environment.

culture-fair/culture-free test: A test without cultural bias.

curvilinear: A relationship between two variables that changes at different points.

cyberbullying: The practice of using computers and other electronic media to intentionally inflict harm on another person.

debrief: The process of explaining to research participants what was done and why.

decentering: Focusing on more than one aspect at a time.

deductive reasoning: Drawing conclusions by applying rules or principles; logically moving from a general rule or principle to a specific solution.

deferred imitation: The ability to remember and imitate after a period of time.

dependent variable: The factor in the experiment you are trying to predict; the one that might change when you apply the treatment (manipulate the independent variable).

depression: A condition characterized by persistent negative moods and lack of interest or pleasure in life.

development: Orderly, adaptive changes we go through from conception to death.

developmental crisis: A specific conflict whose resolution prepares the way for the next stage.

developmental science: The multidisciplinary study of human growth and change from conception until death, often called *lifespan development*.

developmental systems theories: Explanations of development and human diversity that focus on understanding change by studying interactions in the different ecological systems of human life.

developmentally appropriate practices (DAP): Educational materials and practices that are adapted to fit the emotional, physical, and cognitive characteristics and needs of children at different stages.

deviancy training: Learning that occurs in peer groups when members talk favorably about breaking rules and engaging in delinquent behavior.

deviation IQ: Score based on a statistical comparison of an individual's performance with the average performance of others in that age group.

dialect: A variation of language spoken in a particular region that is characterized by its own distinct grammar, vocabulary, and pronunciation.

differentiation: The process of specialization of embryonic cells to perform particular functions.

digital divide: The disparities in access to technology between poor and more affluent students and families.

dilation: The first stage of the birth process in which the mother experiences uterine contractions at 10- to 15-minute intervals, and ends when the cervix is fully dilated (10 cm or about 4 inches) so that the fetus's head can pass through it.

discipline: Any attempts parents make to change the behavior or attitudes of their children to conform to what they and society deem appropriate.

discontinuous development: Leaps and changes resulting in qualitatively different stages of development.

disequilibrium: In Piaget's theory, the "out-of-balance" state that occurs when a person realizes that his or her current ways of thinking are not working to solve a problem or understand a situation.

disjunctives: Words (such as *but*) that prepare the listener for information that is inconsistent or out of keeping with previous statements.

display rules: Standards for conduct and the appropriate expression of emotions.

distributive justice: A concern with distributing or sharing materials fairly.

DNA: Deoxyribonucleic acid; a self-replicating material that is present in nearly all living organisms. It is the main constituent of chromosomes and carries genetic information.

domain-specific knowledge: Information that is useful in a particular situation or that applies mainly to one specific topic.

dominant-recessive inheritance: The inheritance of one gene for each trait from each parent.

doula: A person trained in supporting women through labor and delivery.

Down syndrome (trisomy 21): A condition that results when a child inherits all or part of an extra 21st chromosome.

dual process theories: Theories that describe two modes of thinking—conscious, logical, analytic thinking and out-of-awareness, emotional, intuitive thinking.

ecological validity: The extent to which the situations, methods, settings, and procedures in an experiment are consistent with real life.

ectoderm: The embryonic layer of cells that will become the major organs and the nervous system, skin, and hair.

educationally blind: Individuals who have 20/200 vision.

egocentric: The assumption that others experience the world the way you do.

elaborative rehearsal: Keeping information in working memory by associating it with something else you already know.

embryo: The implanted blastocyst up through the eighth week after conception.

embryonic stem cells: Cells derived from embryos developed during *in vitro* fertilization that were not implanted, and donated to research.

emergent literacy: The skills and knowledge, usually developed in the preschool years, that are the foundation for the development of reading and writing.

emotional self-regulation: The quality that enables individuals to remain focused on goals, even in the face of difficult and stressful circumstances. It involves effortful, voluntary control of emotions, attention, and behavior.

emotional/social development: Changes over time in an individual's feelings, personality, self-concept, and relations with other people.

empathy: The ability to understand what another person is feeling, and, as a consequence, experience the same or similar emotions.

empirical: Based on data.

endocrine system: A system of glands that each secrete a type of hormone to regulate the body.

endoderm: The embryonic layer of cells that will become the internal glands, digestive tract, lungs, urinary tract, pancreas, and liver.

English language learners (ELLs): Students whose primary or heritage language is not English.

entity view of ability: The belief that ability is a fixed characteristic that cannot be changed.

epigenesis: A molecular mechanism that describes how the environment affects the way genes express themselves.

equilibration: The search for mental balance between cognitive schemes and information from the environment.

ethnic identity: An individual's sense of belonging to an ethnic group and the beliefs and behaviors that reflect ethnic group membership.

ethnicity: A cultural heritage shared by a group of people.

ethnographic methods: A descriptive approach to research that focuses on life within a group and tries to understand the meaning of events to the people involved.

ethology: The study of how behaviors adapt to support the survival of animals, including humans.

executive functioning: The neuro-psychological skills that we need to plan, focus, remember, and rethink.

expanded core curriculum: A body of knowledge and skills that addresses the unique disability-specific needs of children with visual impairments.

experimentation: A research method in which variables are manipulated and the effects are recorded.

explicit memory: Long-term memories that involve deliberate or conscious recall.

exploration: The process by which adolescents consider and try out alternative beliefs, values, and behaviors in an effort to determine which will give them the most satisfaction.

expressive vocabulary: The words a person can use appropriately in speaking or writing.

expulsion: The second stage of the birth process that begins as the fetus's head passes through the cervix into the vagina and ends when the baby emerges from the mother's body.

extended families: Family members such as grandparents, aunts, uncles, and cousins living in the same household, or at least in daily contact with each other, cooperating to take care of children.

external validity: The extent to which the results found in a study might generalize to groups or settings not studied.

fast-mapping: A strategy toddlers use for learning words in which they connect a word to its meaning after just one exposure.

fetal alcohol spectrum disorder (FASD): The child's symptoms of poor motor skills, attention problems, and below normal intellectual performance due to the mother's alcohol consumption during pregnancy.

fetal alcohol syndrome (FAS): The most severe type of FASD, in which babies are likely to display excessive irritability, hyperactivity, seizures, and tremors.

fetus: Name given to the embryo after all of the body's structures have begun to form; the fetal period lasts from the ninth week to the fortieth week.

fine motor skills: Small muscle movements that are more limited and controlled (e.g., eating with a fork or spoon, tying shoelaces, cutting with a pair of scissors).

fluid cognition: All-purpose cognitive processing that involves holding and working with verbal and visual information in working memory in order to plan and move toward goals.

fluid intelligence: Mental efficiency and reasoning ability.

Flynn effect: Because of better health, smaller families, the need to deal with increased complexity in the environment, and more and better schooling, IQ test scores are steadily rising.

food security: Consistent access to sufficient quantities of food.

formal operations: Reasoning that involves thinking about thinking or mental operations on mental operations, e.g., mental tasks involving abstract thinking and coordination of a number of variables.

fraternal twins (dizygotic twins): Occur when two sperm fertilize two ova.

full-term: Refers to a fetus that is born about 40 weeks after the mother's last menstrual period.

functional magnetic resonance imaging (fMRI): A procedure that uses radio waves in a strong magnetic field to measure the small metabolic changes that take place in areas of the brain that are active.

functional play: A description of how infants and toddlers are drawn to toys on the basis of how they look or what noises they make and play with them to find out what they do and how they work. Also referred to as *sensorimotor play*.

funds of knowledge: The understandings and skills developed over generations that families need to function.

***g*:** General intelligence; mental energy.

gender: The social and psychological dimensions of being male or female.

gender constancy: Children's understanding of the biologically based permanence of gender.

gender identity: The sense of self as male or female as well as the beliefs one has about gender roles and attributes.

gender intensification: Adolescents' decline in flexibility, which reflects their enhanced self-consciousness and increased awareness of social norms and expectations concerning masculinity and femininity.

gender schema theory: The assumption that as children interact with the world, they form organized cognitive structures, or *schemas* that include gender-related information, which influences how children think and behave.

gender segregation: Children's preference for playing with same-sex peers.

genderlects: Different way of talking for males and females.

generalizing: Applying findings to a wider group than those studied.

generativity: A sense of concern for future generations.

genes: The parts of DNA that tell cells which proteins to make.

genetic counseling: A forum for helping prospective parents assess the likelihood of their children developing hereditary defects.

genetics: The study of heredity—how human beings inherit traits from their ancestors.

germ cells: Cells involved in reproduction (i.e., ova, sperm, or their precursors).

gestation: The period of pregnancy.

gifted children: Very bright, creative, and talented children.

glands: Small organs, part of the endocrine system, that produce hormones.

goodness of fit: A term used to describe how well the caregiver's temperament matches the child's temperament or how caregivers understand, accept, and work with the child's temperament.

graduated extinction: Extinction with parental presence. Parents can remain in children's bedrooms until they fall asleep, but still ignore their bedtime-resistant behavior.

gross motor skills: The movement of the large muscle groups.

habituation: The tendency for the infants to diminish their attention and reduce their responses to stimuli over time with repeated exposure.

handedness: Individuals' preference for using one hand or another to perform one-handed tasks.

heritability: A statistical calculation that is used to estimate the proportion of observed variance of a behavior that can be ascribed to genetic differences within a particular population.

heritage language: The language spoken in a student's home or by older members of the family.

heteronomous: The fairly rigid moral reasoning of young children—the perception that rules are unchangeable and should be adhered to strictly.

heterosexual: Individuals who are attracted to members of the opposite sex.

heuristics: A general strategy used in attempting to solve problems; "rules of thumb" or intuitive guesses that you can apply quickly.

highly active antiretroviral therapy (HAART): An aggressive treatment package, usually two or three different drugs, that suppresses the replication of the virus, strengthens the immune system, and controls the progression of HIV.

homosexual: Individuals who are attracted to members of the same sex.

hormones: Chemical substances that affect cells throughout the body.

hostile aggression: Behaviors that are intended to harm another person, including physical or verbal assaults and direct or indirect confrontation.

hypothesis/hypotheses: A prediction about the relationship between variables.

hypothetical-deductive reasoning: A formal operations problem-solving strategy in which an individual begins by identifying all the factors that might affect a problem and then deduces and systematically evaluates specific solutions.

id, ego, and superego: Freud's terms for the three elements of personality—the childlike *id* that demands immediate satisfaction, the *superego* that is the conscience telling what should be done, and the reality-minded *ego* that navigates how to satisfy the id without offending the superego.

identical twins (monozygotic twins): Occur when a single fertilized ovum splits during the first two weeks after conception, resulting in two zygotes.

identity achievement: The result of healthy exploration and decision-making regarding identities involved in occupations, political and religious affiliations, and relationships.

identity diffusion: A state in which adolescents are not exploring identity alternatives or making commitments.

identity foreclosure: Occurs when adolescents make commitments without exploring options.

identity principle (Piaget): Principle that a person or object remains the same over time. Also, the complex answer to the question: "Who am I?"

implantation: The process of the blastocyst attaching to the endometrial tissue lining of the uterus.

implicit memory: Knowledge that we are not conscious of recalling, but that influences behavior or thought without our awareness.

imprinting: The tendency of some animals to attach to the first nurturing figure they observe after they are born.

incremental view of ability: The belief that ability is a set of skills that can be changed; ability is controllable and potentially always expanding.

independent variable: The variable in an experiment that is altered or manipulated; the treatment.

Individualized Family Service Plan (IFSP): A document the family and professionals develop together. This plan includes the goals for the child's development and the supports/services that the child and family need to achieve them.

inductive discipline: Emphasizes positive, prosocial behavior and involves strategies such as reasoning, negotiating, explaining, and even eliciting input from children.

inductive reasoning: Formulating general principles based on knowledge of examples and details.

industry, or industriousness: A characteristic associated with children's drive for mastery. Children who successfully master valued skills feel competent and satisfied. Industry is reflected in individuals' eagerness to engage in productive work.

infant-directed speech: A type of speech used with young infants that has more intonation, repeated words, shorter sentences, and a higher pitch than adult-directed speech.

information processing: The human mind's activity of taking in, storing, and using information.

initiative: The willingness to begin new activities and explore new directions.

inside-out skills: The emergent literacy skills of knowledge of graphemes, phonological awareness, syntactic awareness, phoneme-grapheme correspondence, and emergent writing.

insight: The sudden realization of a solution; in Sternberg's triarchic theory of intelligence, the ability to deal effectively with novel situations.

Institutional Review Boards, or IRBs: Individuals who evaluate every study involving human subjects conducted at universities and other research institutions such as hospitals or mental health agencies.

instructional conversation: A situation in which students learn through interactions with teachers and/or other students.

instrumental aggression: Aggression that is inadvertent—more likely the result of having a specific goal and poor self-control than having malicious intent—and may not target a particular person.

integrity: A sense of self-acceptance and fulfillment.

intellectual disabilities: Significantly below-average intellectual and adaptive social behavior, evident before age18.

intelligence: The ability or abilities to acquire and use knowledge to solve problems and adapt to the world.

internalize: The behavior that occurs when children adopt external standards as their own.

intimacy: In Erikson's theory, intimacy refers to a willingness to relate to another person on a deep level, to have a relationship based on more than mutual need.

intrauterine growth restriction: Poor growth of the fetus in the uterus.

iron deficiency anemia: A decrease in the number of red blood cells due to lack of iron.

keyword method: A system of associating new words or concepts with similar-sounding cue words and images.

Klinefelter's syndrome: A condition in which a male is conceived with more than one X chromosome in addition to his Y chromosome (1 in 750 male births are XXY).

laboratory/structured observation: Setting up a structured, somewhat controlled environment in a laboratory or other situation so that the research participants encounter tasks or situations the researcher wants to study.

language explosion: Toddlers' rapid learning of words between 12 and 18 months.

latchkey kids: A term used to refer to children who care for themselves on a regular basis.

late effects: Treatment effects that may not show up until months or even years after treatment; they range from mild to severe.

late-preterm babies: Infants who are born between 34 and 36 weeks gestation.

lateralization: The specialization of the two hemispheres of the brain.

learned helplessness: The expectation, based on previous experiences with a lack of control, that all of one's efforts will lead to failure.

learning communities: Groups of teachers and students who care about and support one another to learn. They share goals and values and have a group identity.

learning disability: Disorders that involve central processing problems and affect the ability to understand or use spoken or written language, do mathematical calculations, coordinate movements, or direct attention.

leukemias: Blood cell cancers, and brain and central nervous system tumors.

limited English proficient (LEP): Students who are learning English and are not currently proficient in using the language in school.

long-term memory: The component of memory where all that we know is permanently stored.

longitudinal studies: Research that collects information on the same participants over time, often over many years.

low birth weight: Babies who are born weighing below 5-1/2 pounds.

low vision: Individuals who have some useful vision between 20/70 and 20/200.

maintenance rehearsal: Keeping information in working memory by repeating it to yourself.

male gametes: Male sperm cells.

maturation: Genetically influenced, naturally occurring changes over time.

meiosis: A form of cell production in which the new cells receive only half of the original chromosomal material of the parent cell.

menarche: The first menstrual period in girls.

mesoderm: The embryonic layer of cells that will become the muscles, bones, circulatory system, heart, blood, gonads, muscles, and skeleton.

metacognition: Knowing about how your own cognitive processes work and using that knowledge to reach your goals.

metacognitive skills: Skills to self-regulate based on knowledge about our own thinking processes.

metalinguistic awareness: An understanding about one's own use of language.

microgenetic approach: The detailed observation and analysis of changes in a cognitive process as the process unfolds over a several day or week period of time.

minority group: A group of people who have been socially disadvantaged—not always a minority in actual numbers.

mitosis: A process in which two identical cells are produced by one cell that has divided.

mnemonics: Systematic procedures for improving memory; also, the art of memory.

mobility: People's ability to move safely and efficiently in their environment.

moral dilemmas: Hypothetical situations that ask people to make difficult decisions and then justify them.

moral imperatives: Universally accepted rules of conduct that apply even when authority figures aren't present to punish those who break them and laws don't exist to prohibit behavior that goes against them.

moral realism: Young children's belief that rules are absolute and cannot be changed.

moral reasoning: Reasoning that involves making judgments about the rightness or wrongness of certain acts.

moral relativism: Children's advanced understanding that people can agree to change rules if they want to and that what is important is that all participants in an activity understand and operate according to the same set of rules.

moratorium: The process by which adolescents actively explore identity alternatives, without committing to one identity.

multiples: The term used to refer to more than one developing fetus in a given pregnancy.

mutations: Random changes in the chemical structure of one or more genes that lead to the production of a different phenotype and may or may not be harmful.

mutual best friend: A child who reciprocates a "best" friend nomination.

mutual exclusivity: The assumption that each object in the world belongs in just one category, so it has just one label.

mutualism: A theory that suggests in the beginning of cognitive development, humans have many unrelated cognitive processes such as short-term memory or reaction time. Over time, these processes work together to the mutual benefit of each other and the problem-solving capabilities of the developing individual.

myelination: The growth of neural fibers and the coating of the fibers with fatty myelin that increases brain efficiency, particularly in the parts of the brain involved with memory.

naturalistic observation: The observation of children or adults in their natural setting as they go about their lives.

negative correlation: A relationship between two variables in which a high value on one variable is associated with a low value on the other. An example is height and the distance from the top of the head to the ceiling.

negative reinforcement: Strengthening behavior by removing an aversive stimulus when the behavior occurs.

negative symptoms: Symptoms associated with schizophrenia that reflect reductions in normal emotional and behavioral states (e.g., flat affect and loss of drive).

neglected children: Children who have few peer nominations of any kind.

neo-Piagetian theories: More recent theories that integrate findings about attention, memory, and strategy use with Piaget's insights about children's thinking and the construction of knowledge.

Neonatal Behavioral Assessment Scale (NBAS): A subtle and specific measure of the neonate's health, neurological well-being, and behavior.

neural tube: The precursor to the brain and spinal cord that forms at about 21 days after conception.

neuromotor impairments: A type of disability that involves the central nervous system.

night terrors: Partial arousal from the deepest phase of non-REM sleep. Children are not fully awake during night terrors.

nightmares: Scary dreams that occur during REM sleep.

non-embryonic adult stem cells: Cells that are not embryonic that can grow into different types of cells.

nuclear family: A mother and father (or a single parent) along with biological, adopted, or stepchildren living in the same household.

object permanence: The belief that an object continues to exist when it is out of sight.

open adoption: An arrangement in which the biological and adoptive parents share information and, in some cases, interact directly.

operant conditioning: Learning in which voluntary behavior is strengthened or weakened by consequences or antecedents.

operations: Actions a person carries out by thinking them through instead of literally performing the actions.

oppositional identity: A commitment to an identity in opposition to what an individual perceives is the collective identity of the dominant group.

orientation: People's ability to establish their position in relation to their environment.

orthopedic impairment: A type of disability that involves the skeletal system (bones, joints, and associated muscles).

osteoporosis: A disease that involves serious loss of bone density and leaves bones fragile and at risk for breaking.

other race effect: The ability of infants to distinguish only faces of races that are in their own visual environment.

outside-in skills: The emergent literacy skills of language, narrative, conventions of print, and emergent reading.

ova: Female egg cells.

overlapping wave theory: A model of how children move from less to more adaptive strategies, by trying, discarding, retrying, and adapting strategies over time.

overregularize: The application of a rule of syntax or grammar in situations where the rule does not apply, e.g., "the bike was broked."

oxytocin: A powerful smooth muscle stimulant hormone that causes receptors in the uterus to respond and contract.

parental warmth: A description of how responsive parents are to the needs of their children (i.e., how supportive, nurturing, compassionate, and caring they are and to what extent they put the needs of their children ahead of their own).

parenting styles: Different combinations of high and low parental warmth and high and low parental control.

peer culture: The social values and norms for behavior that different groups of adolescents share.

peer groups: Social groups formed on the basis of shared interests and values; they are typically composed of children of the same age, sex, race/ethnicity, as well as other commonalities (e.g., achievement levels, popularity, athleticism).

peer pressure: The influence peers have on each other's attitudes and behaviors.

peer review: The evaluation and screening of a research report or other scholarly work by carefully chosen reviewers who are experts in the area. To be published in refereed journals, a manuscript must pass peer review.

permissive parents: Parents who are warm, but have little control. They fail to set standards or enforce rules for their children and avoid conflict and confrontation.

person-environment fit theory: According to this theory, development and learning are greatest when the needs and characteristics of the learner fit the characteristics of the learning environment.

person-first language: Referring to people "with a disability" because they are individuals first and the disability is just a part of who they are.

perspective-taking ability: The ability to imagine what other people are thinking or feeling.

phenotypic characteristics: Observable traits that are influenced by conditions present in the environment, both before and after birth, which influence cell division and activation.

phenylketonuria: A genetic disorder characterized by a lack of ability to produce the enzyme that allows metabolism of phenylalanine (which is found in many foods, including milk), resulting in microencephaly (abnormal smallness of the brain), congenital heart disease, and severe mental retardation.

phobias: Irrational fears that persist and significantly affect functioning.

phonemic awareness: The knowledge that words are made up of sounds in a sequence.

phonological loop: Part of working memory; a holding system for verbal/sound information.

phonology: The study of how sounds function in a language system.

physical development: Changes in body structure and function over time.

placenta: The sac that nourishes and protects the embryo.

plasticity: A term that refers to the way the brain can reorganize in response to environmental stimuli and experience.

Poly-X syndrome: Condition in which a female is conceived with more than two X chromosomes (1 in 1,000 births).

Polycystic Ovary syndrome (PCOS): Condition in which women have high levels of certain hormones, may be infertile, and have cysts on their ovaries.

polygenetic: Characteristics caused by multiple gene actions (e.g., height, weight, and skin color).

popular children: Children who are well liked by their peers. They may achieve their social status by engaging in either prosocial or antisocial behavior.

population: The total group of interest in a research study; the group to which the investigator hopes the results will apply (e.g., parents of twins, low-birth-weight infants, etc.).

positive bedtime routine: A routine that includes familiar and relaxing activities that children come to associate with bedtime.

positive correlation: A relationship between two variables in which the two increase or decrease together. An example is calorie intake and weight gain.

positive reinforcement: The strengthening of behavior by presenting a desired stimulus after the behavior.

positive symptoms: Behaviors and changes in thought processes not seen in healthy people, including hallucinations, delusions, thought disorders, and disorders of movement.

positron emission tomography (PET): A method of localizing and measuring brain activity using computer-assisted motion pictures of the brain.

post-industrial: Societies in which most people make a living in the service sector or using information technologies, not in manufacturing or farming.

power assertion: Parents' attempts to stop behavior by making demands or threats, or by withdrawing privileges.

pragmatics: The rules for when and how to use language to be an effective communicator in a particular context or culture.

premature: A fetus that is born before 37 weeks' gestational age.

prenatal: Literally, "before birth." The time period between conception and birth, typically 38 weeks.

preoperational: The stage before a child masters logical mental operations.

presentation punishment: Decreasing the chances that a behavior will occur again by presenting an aversive stimulus following the behavior; also called *Type I punishment*.

pretend play: Children's use of objects and toys symbolically and integrating them in imaginary scenarios; promotes abstract and creative thinking.

primary sex characteristics: Physical characteristics that are directly involved with reproductive organs.

primitive reflexes: Reflexes that have developed in humans over many thousands of years and include the grasping, moro, babinski, and tonic-neck reflexes.

private speech: Children's self-talk, which guides their thinking and action. Eventually these verbalizations are internalized as silent inner speech.

production deficiency: Failing to produce a strategy when it would be useful, even though you know the strategy.

prosocial: A term that is used to describe helping, being cooperative, comforting, responding to peer cries, and displaying empathy behaviors; voluntary behavior that is intended to benefit other people.

proximal empathy: Empathy that includes those times when a child does not cause a second child's distress, but chooses to help the peer.

pruning: The mechanisms by which the brain becomes more finely tuned and functional.

psychoanalysis: The approach to therapy that Freud developed to help patients discover, talk about, and understand emotional conflicts from childhood, buried in their unconscious.

psychosocial: A description of the relation of the individual's emotional needs to the social environment.

puberty: All the processes involved that make a person capable of reproduction.

punishment: A process that weakens or suppresses behavior.

race: A social category that is defined on the basis of physical characteristics such as skin color or hair texture.

rapid eye movement (REM) sleep: The stage of sleep during which dreams take place.

readiness testing: Assessment procedures used to determine if children have the knowledge and skills necessary to move to the next level of schooling—usually administered in preschool or kindergarten.

receptive vocabulary: The words a person can understand in spoken or written words.

reciprocal teaching: A method of supporting reading comprehension that involves four strategies: questioning, summarizing, clarifying, and predicting.

reflexes: Involuntary movements of infants that support their survival.

registers: Ways of speaking that fit specific social situations.

reinforcer: Any event that follows a behavior and increases the chances that the behavior will occur again.

rejected children: Children who are actively disliked by peers; they may be aggressive, immature, socially unskilled, or socially wary and withdrawn.

relational aggression: Behavior whose goal is to damage a peer's social status and/or relationships.

reliability: The consistency of test results.

removal punishment: Decreasing the chances that a behavior will occur again by removing a pleasant stimulus following the behavior; also called *Type II punishment*.

representativeness heuristics: Judging the likelihood of an event based on how well the event matches your prototypes—what you think is representative of the category.

reversibility: A characteristic of Piagetian logical operations—the ability to think through a series of steps, then mentally reverse the steps and return to the starting point; also called *reversible thinking*.

reversible thinking: Thinking backward, from the end to the beginning.

sample: A selected portion of the entire population of interest. The sample is used to estimate likely relationships among variables in the population.

scaffolding: Support for learning and problem solving. The support could be clues, reminders, encouragement, breaking the problem down into steps, providing an example, or anything else that allows the student to grow in independence as a learner.

schemas: Ideas and actions that infants develop through exploring and learning.

schemes: Mental systems or categories of perception through exploring and learning.

schizophrenia: A chronic and severely disabling brain disorder that affects approximately 1% of the general population.

school attachment: The extent to which students feel accepted, valued, respected, supported, and included in their schools.

script: A schema or expected plan for the sequence of steps in a common event such as buying groceries or ordering take-out pizza.

secondary sex characteristics: Physical characteristics that are not needed for reproduction, but are still markers of mature males or females.

secular trend: The trend for menarche and other events in puberty to be experienced earlier with each new generation.

selection: The process by which adolescents choose friends and peer groups.

self-concept: Our integrated view of the attributes, abilities, and attitudes that define us.

self-conscious emotions: Feelings such as pride, envy, guilt, and shame that are linked to other and self-evaluations.

self-corrective empathy: Empathy that occurs when one child causes another child distress and then tries to help, seemingly to make amends, or at least to comfort the other child.

self-efficacy: A person's sense of being able to deal effectively with a particular task.

self-esteem: The self-evaluative part of the self-concept; the judgments children make about their overall self-worth.

self-organization: Patterns and orders that emerge from the interactions of the components in a complex system.

self-regulation: Our ability to voluntarily control our thoughts and actions to achieve personal goals and cope with environmental contingencies.

semilingual: A lack of proficiency in any language; speaking one or more languages inadequately.

semiotic function: The ability to use symbols—language, pictures, signs, or gestures—to represent actions or objects mentally.

sensitive periods: A time during which certain types of plasticity are dominant in the brain and certain types of learning or development are most likely to occur or occur most easily.

sensory memory: The system that holds sensory information very briefly.

sequential studies: Studies that combine longitudinal and cross-sectional research by examining different age groups and then following those groups as they develop across time.

seriation: The arranging of objects in sequential order according to one aspect, such as size, weight, or volume; he process of making an orderly arrangement from large to small or vice versa.

sex: The biological differences between boys and girls, men and women.

sex-linked inheritance: Certain genetic effects that are linked to particular genes located on the sex chromosomes.

sexting: The practice of sending sexually explicit content, including photos or text messages, over the Internet.

sexual orientation: Individuals' attractions to members of the same sex, the opposite sex, or both sexes.

short-term memory: A component of the memory system that holds information for about 20 seconds.

sickle cell anemia: A severe blood disorder in which there is a chronic deficiency in distribution of oxygen in the blood.

sign language and signed English: Visual languages; manual approaches to communication.

sleep associations: Any conditions children have come to connect with falling asleep (e.g., rocking or nursing until they fall asleep).

small-for-gestational-age (SGA): Babies that are born too small (under 5-1/2 pounds) because of slow growth as fetuses, even though they are delivered close to their due date.

social cognitive theory: A theory that adds concern with cognitive factors such as beliefs, self-perceptions, and expectations to social learning theory.

social construction: An idea or concept that has been invented and/or accepted by a group of people.

social conventions: Generally understood rules about how one should act; often they reflect cultural norms.

social learning theory: A theory that emphasizes learning through observation and the interaction of person (beliefs, cognitions, emotions, etc.), environment, and behavior in determining human thoughts and actions.

socialization: The process by which attitudes and behaviors are modeled and reinforced.

sociobiology: The multidisciplinary study of human and animal social behaviors that considers the survival value of the behaviors as explanations for development.

sociocultural theory: A theory that emphasizes the role in development and learning of society, culture, context, interpersonal interaction, and time period.

socioeconomic status (SES): An individual's relative standing in the society based on income, power, background, and prestige.

somatic cells: Cells in the body other than germ cells.

source monitoring: Remembering the source of information, and where you encountered the information.

spastic CP: A type of cerebral palsy that causes muscles to stiffen and makes movement difficult. It can affect just one side of the body, both legs, or both arms and legs.

speech reading: An oral approach to communication and education, also called *lip reading.*

sperm: A male gamete cell that is composed of a head, a flagellum, and a cap containing enzymes that facilitate infiltration into the egg.

spermarche: The first sperm ejaculation for boys.

spermatogenesis: The process of maturation of sperm cells.

stage-environment fit theory: A theory that describes the possible effects of a match (or mismatch) between the developmental needs of the individual and the opportunities afforded by social environments, including schools.

standard extinction: The process of putting children to bed and then ignoring disruptions (e.g., not attending to their crying, tantrums, calls to parents) until eventually, they fall asleep on their own.

states: Cyclic periods of infant arousal, activity, and sleep.

Statistically significant: Something that is not likely to be a chance occurrence.

stereotype threat: The extra emotional and cognitive burden that your performance in an academic situation might confirm a stereotype that others hold about you; apprehensiveness about confirming a stereotype.

steroids: Commercially produced drugs related to male sex hormones that are used legally to treat some diseases, but more often illegally to build muscle mass and strength.

strategy: A general plan or set of plans to achieve a goal.

suicidal ideation: Thoughts of suicide.

surfactin: A substance that normally coats the lungs of the fetus during the last three to four weeks of pregnancy to prevent them from collapsing.

survival reflexes: Reflexes such as the breathing, rooting, sucking and swallowing, and eye blink reflexes that ensure neonates will be able to breathe, find the nipple, eat by sucking, and protect their eyes.

sympathy: Feeling sorry or concerned for another person because he or she is experiencing negative emotions.

syntagmatic-paradigmatic shift: In language development, the change from organizing words by what might come next (syntagmatic associations such as "beach—ball") to organizing by meaning (paradigmatic associations such as "beach, sand, ocean").

syntax: The order of words in phrases or sentences.

tabula rasa: Latin for "blank slate"; Locke's idea that children are blank slates and their development is molded by experience, education, training, etc.

technology-rich learning environments (TREs): Digital environments created to support learning, including virtual worlds, computer simulations that support problem-based learning, intelligent tutoring systems, educational games, audio recordings, hand-held wireless devices, and multimedia environments.

temperament: Unique characteristics of children that influence how they react to environmental stimuli. Temperament includes the dimensions of emotionality, sociability, and activity level.

teratogen: Any disease, drug, or other environmental agent that can harm a developing embryo or fetus.

theory: In science—concepts and relations that explain and predict phenomena in the world.

theory of mind: Children's understandings about the nature of thinking and mental states—their knowledge that other people have minds, thoughts, feelings, beliefs, and desires that may be different than their own.

theory of multiple intelligences: In Gardner's theory of intelligence, a person's eight separate abilities: logical-mathematical, linguistic, musical, spatial, bodily-kinesthetic, interpersonal, intrapersonal, and naturalist.

transition and functional skills: The skills needed to prepare a student to live and work in the community.

triangulation: The seeking of multiple perspectives, for example, by gathering data from multiple sources (observation, interviews, diaries, etc.) or using multiple investigators to make interpretations.

triarchic theory of successful intelligence: A three-part description of the mental abilities (utilizing thinking processes, coping with new experiences, and adapting to context) that lead to more or less intelligent behavior.

Turner's syndrome: A condition in which a female is conceived with only one X chromosome rather than two (occurs approximately 1 in 2,500 female births).

Type 2 Diabetes: A chronic condition that affects the way the body metabolizes sugar (glucose).

umbilical cord: A cord that connects the embryo to the placenta and delivers oxygen and nutrients into the embryo's bloodstream from the mother.

uninvolved parents: Parents who are neither warm nor in control. They put little effort into parenting and often are more focused on their own needs than the needs of their children.

universal design: Considering the needs of all users in the creation of living and learning environments, such as architectural features, new tools, learning programs, or websites.

universal language learner: Infants' ability at birth to learn any language.

validity: The degree to which a test measures what it is intended to measure.

variable: Any factor, characteristic, or event that can change or vary.

vernix: A white cheesy substance that covers the fetus, which protects the skin from chapping during the time the fetus lives in fluid.

very low birth weight: Babies who are born weighing below 1,500 grams or approximately 3.3 pounds.

visual acuity: Refers to the sharpness of vision.

visual perception: Includes attention to and processing of visual information.

visual sketchpad: A part of working memory; a holding system for visual and spatial information.

well-being: A sense of happiness, health, comfort, and security.

withdrawal of love: A situation that occurs when parents attempt to gain compliance from children by withholding affection or ignoring or rejecting them.

working memory: The information that you are focusing on at a given moment.

X-linked diseases: Single gene disorders that reflect the presence of defective genes on the X chromosome.

zone of proximal development (ZPD): The phase at which a child can master a task if given appropriate help and support; the area between his or her current development level—where the child can solve problems independently—and the level of development that the child could achieve with support from others.

zygote: A diploid cell with 46 chromosomes created by the fusion of male and female cell nuclei.

REFERENCES

AAIDD. (2010). *Definition of intellectual disability*. Retrieved from http://www.aamr.org/content_100.cfm?navID=21

AAN Report of the Quality Standards Subcommittee. (1997). *Neurology, 10*, 350–357.

AAP Committee on Injury, Violence, and Poison Prevention. (2003). Poison treatment in the home. *Pediatrics, 112*, 1182–1185.

Aaronson, D., Barrow, L., & Sander, W. (2007). Teachers and student achievement in the Chicago public high schools. *Journal of Labor Economics, 25*, 95–135.

Abma, J. C., Martinez, G. M., Mosher, W. D., & Dawson, B. S. (2004). Teenagers in the United States: Sexual activity, contraceptive use, and childbearing. *National Survey of Family Growth, 24*, 1–48.

Abramowicz, J. S., Barnett, S. B., Duck, F. A., Edmonds, P. D., Hynynen, K., & Ziskin, M. (2008). Fetal thermal effects of diagnostic ultrasound. *Journal Ultrasound Medicine, 27*, 541–559.

Ackerman, B. P., & Brown, E. D. (2006). Income poverty, poverty co-factors, and the adjustment of children in elementary school. In R. V. Kail (Ed.), *Advances in child development and behavior* (Vol. 34, pp. 91–129). New York, NY: Elsevier.

Ackerman, B. P., Brown, E. D., & Izard, C. E. (2004). The relations between contextual risk, earned income, and the school adjustment of children from economically disadvantaged families. *Developmental Psychology, 40*, 204–216.

ADA. It's' about eating right: Balanced meals. Retrieved from http://www.eatright.org/Public/content.aspx?id=6745

Adams, G. R., Berzonsky, M. D., & Keating, L. (2006). Psychosocial resources in first-year university students: The role of identity processes and social relationships. *Journal of Youth and Adolescence, 35*(1), 78–88.

Adolph, K. E. (2009). Perceptual learning. Retrieved from http://www.psych.nyu.edu/adolph/research1.php

Adolph, K. E., & Avolio, A. M. (2000). Walking infants adapt locomotion to changing body dimensions. *Journal of Experimental Psychology: Human Perception & Performance, 26*(3), 1148–1166.

Adolph, K. E., & Eppler, M. A. (2002). Flexibility and specificity in infant motor skill acquisition. In J. W. Fagen & H. Hayne, *Progress in infancy research* (Vol. 2, pp. 121–169). Hillsdale, NJ: Erlbaum.

Adoph, K. E., Karasik, L. B., & Tamis-LeMonda, S. (2010). Motor skill. In M. Bornstein (Ed.), *Handbook of cross-cultural developmental science, Vol. 1, Domains of development across cultures* (pp. 61–88). New York, NY: Taylor & Francis.

Adzick, N. S., & Kitano Y. (2003). Fetal surgery for lung lesions, congenital diaphragmatic hernia, and sacrococcygeal teratoma. *Seminars in Pediatric Surgery, 12*, 154–167.

AGI. (2002). *Teenagers' sexual and reproductive health: Developed countries*. Retrieved from http://www.guttmacher.org/pubs/fb_teens.html

AGI. (2006). *Facts on American teens' sexual and reproductive health*. Retrieved from http://www.guttmacher.org/pubs/fb_ATSRH.html

Ainsworth, M. D. S. (1989). Attachments beyond infancy. *American Psychologist, 44*, 709–716.

Ainsworth, M. D. S., Blehar, M. C., Waters, E., & Wall, S. (1978). *Patterns of attachment: A psychological study of the strange situation*. Hillsdale, NJ: Erlbaum.

Akos, P., & Galassi, J. P. (2004). Middle and high school transitions as viewed by students, parents, and teachers, *Professional School Counseling, 7*(4), 212–221.

Alasker, F. D., & Olweus, D. (1992). Stability of global self-evaluations in early adolescence: A cohort longitudinal study. *Journal of Research on Adolescence, 2*, 123–145.

Albee, G. W. (2002). Interactions among scientists and policymakers: Challenges and opportunities. *American Psychologist [Special Issue], 57*, 161–122.

Alberto, P., & Troutman, A. C. (2006). *Applied behavior analysis for teachers: Influencing student performance* (7th ed.). Upper Saddle River, NJ: Prentice-Hall/Merrill.

Alessandri, S. M., & Lewis, M. (1993). Parental evaluation and its relation to shame and pride in young children. *Sex roles, 29*, 335–343.

Alexander, K., & Entwistle, D. (1998). Achievement in the first two years of school: Patterns and processes. *Monographs of the Society for Research in Child* Development, *53* (Serial No. 218).

Alexander, P. A. (1996). The past, present, and future of knowledge research: A reexamination of the role of knowledge in learning and instruction. *Educational Psychologist, 31*, 89–92.

All About Vision. (2010). *General vision and eye news*. Retrieved from http://www.allaboutvision.com/conditions/eye-news.htm#earlyscreening

Allen, K. L., Byrne, S. M., Blair, E. M., & Davis, E. A. (2006). Why do some overweight children experience psychological problems? The role of weight and shape concern. *International Journal of Pediatric Obesity, 1*, 239–247.

Alliance for Children. (September 12, 2000). *Children and computers: A call for action*.

Alloway, T. P., Gathercole, S. E., & Pickering, S. J. (2006). Verbal and visuo-spatial short-term and working memory in children: Are they separable? *Child Development, 77*, 1698–1716.

Al-Obaidi, A. K., Budosan, B., & Jeffrey, L. (2010). Child and adolescent mental health in Iraq: Current situation and scope for promotion of child and adolescent mental health policy. *Intervention, 8*(1), 40–51.

Amartya, S. (2003). Missing women—revisited: Reduction in female mortality has been counterbalanced by sex selective abortions. *British Medical Journal, 327*, 1297–1299.

Amato, P. R. (1999). Children of divorced parents as young adults. In E. M. Hetherington (Ed.), *Coping with divorce, single parenting, and remarriage: A risk and resiliency perspective* (pp. 147–163). Mahwah, NJ: Erlbaum.

Amato, P. R. (2000). The consequences of divorce for adults and children. *Journal of Marriage and the Family, 62*, 1269–1287.

Amato, P. R. (2001). Children of divorce in the 1990s: An update of the Amato and Keith (1991) meta-analysis. *Journal of Family Psychology, 15*, 355–370.

Amato, P. R., & Fowler, F. (2002). Parenting practices, child adjustment, and family diversity. *Journal of Marriage & Family, 64*(3), 703–716.

Amato, P. R., & Gilbreth, J. G. (1999). Nonresident fathers and children's well being: A meta-analysis. *Journal of Family Psychology, 15*, 355–373.

Ambert, A. M. (2005). *Divorce: Facts, causes and consequences*. Retrieved from http://www.vifamily.ca/library/cft/divorce_05.html# Canadian

American Academy of Child & Adolescent Psychiatry. (2004). AACAP recommends monitoring research and access in antidepressant use: Workforce Support Critical. Retrieved from http://www.aacap.org/press_releases/2004/0915.htm

American Academy of Family Physicians. (2009). *Cerebral palsy in children*. Retrieved from http://familydoctor.org/online/famdocen/home/children/parents/special/birth/901.html

American Academy of Pediatrics. (1999). Trampolines at home, school, and recreational centers. *Pediatrics, 103*(5), 1053–1056.

American Academy of Pediatrics. (2005). *Policy statement. Breastfeeding and the use of human milk*. Retrieved from http://aappolicy.aappublications.org/cgi/content/full/pediatrics;115/2/496

American Academy of Pediatrics. (2006). *The Apgar score*. Retrieved from http://aappolicy.aappublications.org/cgi/content/full/pediatrics;117/4/1444

American Academy of Pediatrics, Council on Sports Medicine and Fitness and Council on School Health. (2006). Active healthy living: Prevention of childhood obesity through increased physical activity. *Pediatrics, 117*, 1834–1842.

American Academy of Pediatrics, Task Force on Infant Positioning and SIDS. (1992). Positioning and SIDS [published correction appears in *Pediatrics, 90*(2):264 and *Pediatrics, 89*(6), 1120–1126.

American Academy of Pediatrics, Task Force on Sudden Infant Death Syndrome. (2005). The changing concept of sudden infant death syndrome: Diagnostic coding shifts, controversies regarding the sleeping environment, and new variables to consider in reducing risk. *Pediatrics, 116*(5), 1245–1255.

American Cancer Society. (2009). *Childhood cancer: Late effects of cancer treatment*. Retrieved from http://ww3.cancer.org/docroot/CRI/content/CRI_2_6x_Late_Effects_of_Childhood_Cancer.asp

American Dietetic Association [ADA]. (nd). *It's' about eating right: Balanced meals*. Retrieved from http://www.eatright.org/Public/content.aspx?id=6745

American Dietetic Association. (2008, June). Position of the American Dietetic Association: Nutrition guidance for healthy children ages 2 to 11 years. *Journal of the American Dietetic Association, 108*, 1038–1047.

American Federation for the Blind. (2010). *The expanded core curriculum for blind and VI children and youths*. Retrieved from http://www.afb.org/Section.asp?SectionID=44&TopicID=189&SubTopicID=4&DocumentID=2117

American Heart Association. (2010). *Table: Dietary recommendations for children*. Retrieved from http://www.americanheart.org/presenter.jhtml?identifier=3033999

American Printing House for the Blind. (2009). *Distribution of eligible students*. Retrieved from http://www.aph.org/fedquotpgm/dist09.html.

American Psychiatric Association. (2010). *DSM-5 development*. Available online at http://www.dsm5.org/Pages/Default.aspx.

American Psychological Association. (2000). *Diagnostic and statistical manual of mental disorders* (4th ed., text revision). Washington, DC: Author.

Anderman, E. M. (1998). The middle school experience: Effects on math and science achievement of adolescents with LD. *Journal of Learning Disabilities, 31*, 128–139.

Anderman, E. M., & Maehr, M. L. (1994). Motivation and schooling in the middle grades. *Review of Educational Research, 64*, 287–310.

Anderman, E. M., & Midgley, C. (2004). Changes in self-reported academic cheating across the transition from middle school to high school. *Contemporary Educational* Psychology, *29*, 499–517.

Anderman, L. H. (2003). Academic and social perceptions as predictors of change in middle school students' sense of school belonging. *Journal of Experimental Education, 72*, 5–23.

Anderman, L. H., & Freeman, T. M. (2004). Students' sense of belonging in school. In M. L. Maehr & P. R. Pintrich (Eds.), *Motivating students, improving schools, vol. 13: The legacy of Carol Midgley (advances in motivation and achievement)* (pp. 26–64). New York, NY: Elsevier.

Anderson, C. A., Berkowitz, L., Donnerstein, E., Huesmann, L. R., Johnson, J. D., Linz, D., . . . Wartella, E. (2003). The influence of media violence on youth. *Psychological Science in the Public Interest, 4*, 81–110.

Anderson, C. A., & Bushman, B. J. (2001). Media violence and the American public: Scientific facts versus media misinformation. *American Psychologist, 56*(6–7), 477–489.

Anderson, C. A., Shibuya, A., Ihori, N., Swing, E. L., Bushman, B. J., Sakamoto, A., & Saleem, M. (2010). Violent video game effects on aggression, empathy, and prosocial behavior in Eastern and Western countries. *Psychological Bulletin, 136*, 151–173. doi:10.1037/a0018251

Anderson, C. W., Holland, J. D., & Palincsar, A. S. (1997). Canonical and sociocultural approaches to research and reform in science education: The story of Juan and his group. *Elementary School Journal, 97*, 359–384.

Anderson, E. R. (1999). Sibling, half-sibling, and step-sibling relationships in remarried families. *Monographs of the Society for Research in Child Development, 64*(4), 101–126.

Anderson, J. R. (1995). *Cognitive psychology and its implications* (4th ed.). New York, NY: Freeman.

Anderson, P. J., & Graham, S. M. (1994). Issues in second-language phonological acquisition among children and adults. *Topics in Language Disorders, 14*, 84–100.

Anderson, S. W., Bechara, A., Damasio, H., Tranel, T., & Damasio, A. R. (1999). Impairment in social and moral behaviour and early damage in the prefrontal cortex. *Nature Neuroscience, 2*, 1032–1037.

Angier, N. (2009, January 20). In 'Geek Chic' and Obama, new hope for lifting women in science. *The New York Times*, p. D1.

Angier, N., & Chang, K. (2005, January 24). Gray matter and the sexes: Still a scientific gray area. *The New York Times*, p. A1.

Anglin, J. M. (1993). Vocabulary development. *Monographs of the Society for Research in Child Development, 58*(165).

APA. (2009). *Sexual orientation and homosexuality*. Retrieved from http://www.apahelpcenter.org/articles/article.php?id=31

APA. (2010). *American Psychiatric Association DSM-5 development: Eating disorders*. Retrieved from http://www.dsm5.org/ProposedRevisions/Pages/EatingDisorders.aspx

Apgar, V. (1953). A proposal for a new method of evaluation of the newborn infant. *Anesth Analg, 32*, 260–267.

Armour, S. (2005, June 11). Generation Y: They've arrived at work with a new attitude. *USA Today*. Retrieved from http://www.usatoday.com/money/workplace/2005-11-06-gen-y_x.htm

Arnett, J. J. (1999). Adolescent storm and stress, reconsidered. *American Psychologist, 54*, 317–326.

Arnett, J. J. (2007). Emerging adulthood: What is it, and what is it good for? *Child Development Perspectives, 1*, 68–73.

Arnett, J. J. (2009). Adolescence and emerging adulthood: A cultural approach (4th ed.). Upper Saddle River, NJ: Prentice-Hall/Pearson.

Aronson, J. (2002). Stereotype threat: Contending and coping with unnerving expectations. In J. A. D. Cordova (Ed.), *Improving education: Classic and contemporary lessons from psychology* (pp. 279–301). New York, NY: Academic Press.

Aronson, J., Lustina, M. J., Good, C., Keough, K., Steele, C. M., & Brown, J. (1999). When White men can't do math: Necessary and sufficient factors in stereotype threat. *Journal of Experimental Social Psychology, 35*, 29–46.

Aronson, J., & Steele, C. M. (2005). Stereotypes and the fragility of human competence, motivation, and self-concept. In E. E. C. Dweck (Ed.), *Handbook of competence and motivation* (pp. 436–456). New York, NY: Guilford.

Arseneault, L., Moffitt, T. E., Caspi, A., Taylor, A., Rijsdijk, F. V., Jaffee, S. R., Ablow, J. C., & Measelle, J. R. (2003). Strong genetic effects on cross-situational antisocial behaviour among 5-year-old children according to mothers, teachers, examiner-observers, and twins' self-reports. *Journal of Child Psychology and Psychiatry, 44*, 832–848.

Arsenio, W. F., & Fleiss, K. (1996). Typical and behaviorally disruptive children's understanding of the emotional consequences of sociomoral events. *British Journal* of *Developmental Psychology, 14*, 173–186.

Arsenio, W. F., & Lemerise, E. A. (2004). Aggression and moral development: Integrating social information processing and moral domain models. *Child Development, 75*, 987–1002.

ASHA [The American Speech-Language-Hearing Association]. (2010). *Hearing screening*. Retrieved from www.asha.org

Ashcraft, M. H. (2006). *Cognition* (3rd ed.). Upper Saddle River, NJ: Prentice-Hall.

Ashcraft, M. H., & Radvansky, G. A. (2009). *Cognition* (4th ed.). Upper Saddle River, NJ: Prentice-Hall.

Askell-Williams, H., & Lawson, M. (2001). Mapping students' perceptions of interesting class lessons. *Social Psychology of Education, 5*, 127–147.

Aslin, R. N., & McMurray, B. (2004). Where babies look: An overview of methods for assessing visual fixations and eye movements in young infants. *Infancy, 6*(2), 155–163.

ASRM [American Society of Reproductive Medicine]. (2009). *Frequently asked questions about infertility*. Retrieved from http://www.asrm.org/Patients/faqs.html#Q6

Astington, J. W., & Dack, L. A. (2008). Theory of mind. In M. M. Haith & J. B. Benson (Eds.), *Encyclopedia of infant and early childhood development* (Vol. 3, pp. 343–356). San Diego, CA: Academic Press.

Astington, J. W., & Gopnik, A. (1988). Knowing you've changed your mind: Children's understanding of representational change. In J. W. Astington, P. L. Harris, & D. R. Olson (Eds.), *Developing theories of mind* (pp. 193–206). New York, NY: Cambridge University Press.

Atkinson, R. C., & Shiffrin, R. M. (1968). Human memory: A proposed system and its control processes. In K. Spence & J. Spence (Eds.), *The psychology of learning and motivation* (Vol. 2, pp. 89–195). New York, NY: Academic Press.

Atkinson, R. K., Levin, J. R., Kiewra, K. A., Meyers, T., Atkinson, L. A., Renandya, W. A., & Hwang, Y. (1999). Matrix and mnemonic text-processing adjuncts: Comparing and combining their components. *Journal of Educational Psychology, 91*, 242–257.

Atwell, P. (2000). *Beyond the digital divide [Working paper No. 164]*. New York, NY: Russell Sage Foundation.

Au, K. H. (1980). Participation structures in a reading lesson with Hawaiian children: Analysis of a culturally appropriate instructional event. *Anthropology and Education Quarterly, 11*, 91–115.

Au, T. K., Knightly, L. M., Jun, S., & Oh, J. S. (2002). Overhearing a language during childhood. *Psychological Science, 13*, 238–243.

Aunola, K., Stattin, H., & Nurmi, J. (2000). Adolescents' achievement strategies, school adjustment, and externalizing and internalizing problem behaviors. *Journal of Youth and Adolescence, 29*(3), 289–306.

Ausubel, D. P. (1963). *The psychology of meaningful verbal learning*. New York, NY: Grune and Stratton.

Ausubel, D. P. (1977). The facilitation of meaningful verbal learning in the classroom. *Educational Psychologist, 12*, 162–178.

Avgitidou, S. (2001). Peer culture and friendship relationships as contexts for the development of young children's pro-social behavior. *International Journal of Early Years Education, 9*(2), 145–152.

Aviezar, O., Sagi, A., Joels, T., & Ziv, Y. (1999). Emotional availability and attachment representations in kibbutz infants and their mothers. *Developmental Psychology, 35,* 811–821.

Aydt, H., & Corsaro, W. A. (2003). Differences in children's construction of gender across culture: An interpretive approach. *The American Behavioral Scientist, 46,* 1306–1325.

Azzam, A. M. (2006, April). A generation immersed in media. *Educational Leadership,* 92–93.

Baddeley, A. (2006). Working memory: An overview. In S. J. Pickering (Ed.), *Working memory and education.* New York, NY: Elsevier.

Baek, H. J. (2002). A comparative study of moral development of Korean and British children. *Journal of Moral Education, 31,* 374–391.

Baghurst, P. A., McMichael, A. J., Wigg, N. R., Vimpani, G. V., Robertson, E. F., Roberts, R. J., & Tong, S.-L. (1992). Environmental exposure to lead and children's intelligence at age of seven years: The Port Pirie cohort study. *New England Journal of Medicine, 327,* 1279–1284.

Bagnato, S., Grom, R., & Haynes, L. (2003). Alternative designs for community-based research: Pittsburgh's Early Childhood Initiative. *The Evaluation Exchange, 9*(3), 6–7.

Bailey, J. M., & Pillard, R. C. (1991). A genetic study of male sexual orientation. *Archives of General Psychology, 48*(12), 1089–1096.

Bailey, J. M., & Zucker, K. J. (1995). Childhood sex-typed behavior and sexual orientation: A conceptual and quantitative review. *Developmental Psychology, 31,* 43–55.

Bailey, S. M. (1993). The current status of gender equity research in American schools. *Educational Psychologist, 28,* 321–339.

Bailey, U. L., Lorch, E. P., Milich, R., & Charnigo, R. (2009). Developmental changes in attention and comprehension among children with attention deficit hyperactivity disorder. *Child Development, 80,* 1842–1855.

Baker, C. (1993). *Foundations of bilingual education and bilingualism.* Clevedon, England: Multilingual Matters.

Baker, J., Grant, S., & Morlock, L. (2008). The teacher-student relationship as a developmental context for children with internalizing or externalizing behaviour problems. *School Psychology Quarterly, 23,* 3–15.

Baker, L., & Wigfield, A. (1999). Dimensions of children's motivation for reading and their relations to reading activity and reading. *Reading Research Quarterly, 34*(4), 452–477.

Bakerman, R., Adamson, L. B., Koner, M., & Barr, R. G. (1990). !Kung infancy: The social context of object exploration. *Child Development, 61,* 794–809.

Bakermans-Kraneburg, M. J., van Ijzendoorn, M. H., & Bradley, R. H. (2005). Those who have, receive: The Matthew effect in early childhood intervention in the home environment. *Review of Educational Research, 75,* 1–26.

Baldwin, A. L., Baldwin, C., & Cole, R. E. (1990). Stress-resistant families and stress-resistant children. In J. Rolf, A. S. Masten, D. Cicchetti, K. H. Nuechterlein, & S. Weintraum (Eds.), *Risk and protective factors in the development of psychopathology* (pp. 257–280). New York, NY: Cambridge University Press.

Baldwin, J. M. (1895). *Mental development in the race and the child: Methods and processes.* London, England: MacMillan.

Ball, D. L. (1997). What do students know? Facing challenges of distance, context, and desire in trying to hear children. In B. J. Biddle, T. L. Good, & I. F. Goodson (Eds.), *The international handbook of teachers and teaching* (pp. 769–818). Dordrecht, the Netherlands: Kluwer.

Ball, H. L. (2002). Reasons to share: Why parents sleep with their infants. *Journal of Repro & Infant Psychology, 20*(4), 207–221.

Balleyguier, G. (1991). The development of attachment according to the temperament of the newborn. *Psychiatric Enfant, 34*(2), 641–647.

Bandstra, E. S., Vogel, A. L., Morrow, C. E., Xue, L., & Anthony, J. (2004). Severity of prenatal cocaine exposure and child language functioning through age seven years: A longitudinal latent growth curve analysis. *Substance Use and Abuse, 39*(1), 25–59.

Bandura, A. (1965). Influence of models' reinforcement contingencies on the acquisition of imitative responses. *Journal of Personality and Social Psychology, 1,* 589–595.

Bandura, A. (1977). *Social learning theory.* Englewood Cliffs, NJ: Prentice-Hall.

Bandura, A. (1986). *Social foundations of thought and action.* Englewood Cliffs, NJ: Prentice-Hall.

Bandura, A. (1997). *Self-efficacy: The exercise of control.* New York, NY: Freeman.

Bandura, A. (2006a). Towards a theory of human agency. *Perspectives on Psychological Science, 1,* 164–180.

Bandura, A. (2006b). Autobiography. M. G. Lindzey & W. M. Runyan (Eds.) *A history of psychology in autobiography* (Vol. IX, pp. 42–75). Washington, DC: American Psychological Association.

Bandura, A., Ross, D., & Ross, S. A. (1963). Imitation of film-mediated aggressive models. *Journal of Abnormal and Social Psychology, 66,* 3–11.

Bandura, A., Ross, D., & Ross, S. A. (1963). Vicarious reinforcement and imitative learning. *Journal of Abnormal and Social Psychology, 67,* 601–607.

Banerjee, N. (2000, April 14). Rodniki journal: Bloodsuckers of old are poised for a comeback. *The New York Times on the web.*

Banks, J. A. (1993). Multicultural education: Characteristics and goals. In J. Banks & C. M. Banks (Eds.), *Multicultural education: Issues and perspectives* (2nd ed., pp. 2–26). Boston, MA: Allyn & Bacon.

Banks, J. A. (2002). *An introduction to multicultural education* (3rd ed.). Boston, MA: Allyn & Bacon.

Banks, J. A. (2008). *Introduction to multicultural education* (4th ed.). Boston: Allyn & Bacon/Merrill.

Banks, J. A. (2009). *Teaching strategies for ethnic studies* (8th ed.). Boston: Allyn & Bacon.

Banks, J. A., & McGee Banks, C. A. (Eds.). (2009). *Multicultural education: Issues and perspectives.* San Francisco, CA: John Wiley & Sons.

Barber, B. K. (2002). Reintroducing parental psychological control. In B. K. Barber (Ed.), *Intrusive parenting: How psychological control affects children and adolescents* (pp. 3–13). Washington, DC: American Psychological Association.

Bargh, J. A., & Chartrand, T. L. (1999). The unbearable automaticity of being. *American Psychologist, 54,* 462–479.

Barkin, S., Scheindlin, B., Edward, H., Richardson, I., & Finch, S. (2007). Determinants of parental discipline practices: A national sample from primary care practices. *Clinical Pediatrics, 46,* 64–69.

Barkley, R. A. (2006). *Attention-deficit hyperactive disorder: A handbook for diagnosis and treatment.* (3rd ed.). New York, NY: Guilford.

Barnard-Brak, L. (2008). Academic red-shirting among children with learning disabilities. *Learning Disabilities: A Contemporary Journal, 6,* 43–54.

Barnett, L. M., van Beurden, E., Morgan, P. J., Brooks, L. O., & Beard, J. R. (2009). Childhood motor skill proficiency as a predictor of adolescent physical activity. *Journal of Adolescent Health, 44,* 252–259.

Barnett, R., & Rivers, C. (2004). *Same difference: How gender myths are hurting our relationships, our children, and our jobs.* New York, NY: Basic Books.

Baron, L. J. (2007). *Contemporary issues in youth sport.* New York, NY: Nova Science.

Baron, R. A. (1998). *Psychology* (4th ed.). Boston, MA: Allyn & Bacon.

Barr, R. G., Rivara, F. P., Barr, M., Cummings, P., Taylor, J., Lengua, L. J., & Meredith-Benitz, E. (2009). Effectiveness of educational materials designed to change knowledge and behaviors regarding crying and Shaken-Baby Syndrome in mothers of newborns: A randomized, controlled trial. *Pediatrics, 123*(3), 972–980.

Barrash, J., Tranel, D., & Anderson, S. W. (2000). Acquired personality disturbances associated with bilateral damage to the ventromedial prefrontal region. *Developmental Neuropsychology, 18,* 355–381.

Barros, R. M., Silver, E. J., & Stein, R. E. K. (2009). School recess and group classroom behavior. *Pediatrics, 123*(2), 431–436.

Barrouillet, P., Bernardin, S., & Camos, V. (2004). Time constraints and resource sharing in adults' working memory spans. *Journal of Experimental Psychology: General, 133,* 83–100.

Barton, P. E. (2009). *Chasing the high school graduation rate: Getting the data we need and using it right* (Policy Report). Princeton, NJ: Educational Testing Service.

Bartsch, K., & Wellman, H. M. (1995). *Children talk about the mind.* New York, NY: Oxford University Press.

Battistich, V., Solomon, D., & Delucci, K. (1993). Interaction processes and student outcomes in cooperative groups. *Elementary School Journal, 94*(1), 19–32.

Battistich, V., Solomon, D., Watson, M., & Schaps, E. (1997). Caring school communities. *Educational Psychologist, 32,* 137–151.

Battle, J. (2002). Longitudinal analysis of academic achievement among a nationwide sample of Hispanic students in one- versus dual-parent households. *Hispanic Journal of Behavioral Sciences, 24,* 430–447.

Bauer, P. J. (2006). Event memory. In D. Kuhn & R. S. Siegler (Eds.), *Cognition, perception, and language* (6th ed., Vol. 2, pp. 373–425). New York, NY: John Wiley & Sons.

Bauman, A., Schoeppe, S., & Lewicka, M. (2005). *Review of best practice in interventions to promote physical activity in developing countries.* Geneva, Switzerland: World Health Organization.

Baumeister, R. F. (1998). Inducing guilt. In J. Bybee (Ed.), *Guilt and children* (pp. 127–138). San Diego, CA: Academic Press.

Baumeister, R. F., Campbell, J. D., Krueger, J. I., & Vohs, K. D. (2003). Does high self-esteem cause better performance, interpersonal success, happiness, or healthier lifestyles? *Psychological Science in the Public Interest, 4,* 1–44.

Baumrind, D. (1966). Effects of authoritative parental control on child behavior. *Child Development, 37,* 887–907.

Baumrind, D. (1971). Current patterns of parental authority. *Developmental Psychology, 4,* 1–103.

Baumrind, D. (1972). An exploratory study of socialization effects on black children: Some black-white comparisons. *Child Development, 43,* 261–267.

Baumrind, D. (1973). The development of instrumental competence through socialization. In A. D. Pick (Ed.), *Minnesota Symposium on Child Psychology* (Vol. 7, pp. 3–46). Minneapolis, MN: University of Minnesota Press.

Baumrind, D. (1991). Effective parenting during early adolescent transitions. In P. Cowan & E. Hetherington (Eds.), *Family transitions* (pp. 111–164). Mahwah, NJ: Erlbaum.

Baumrind, D. (1991). The influences of parenting style on adolescent competence and substance use. *Journal of Early Adolescence, 11,* 56–95.

Baumrind, D. (1996). The discipline controversy revisited. *Family Relations, 45,* 405–414.

Baumrind, D. (2005). Patterns of parental authority and adolescent authority. *New Directions for Child and Adolescent Development,* doi:10.1002/cd.128

Baumrind, D., Larzelere, R. E., & Cowan, P. A. (2002). Ordinary physical punishment: Is it harmful? Comment on Gershoff (2002). *Psychological Bulletin, 128,* 580–589.

Bayliss, D. M., Jarrold, C., Baddeley, A. D., Gunn, D., & Leigh, E. (2005). Mapping the developmental constraints on working memory span performance. *Developmental Psychology, 41,* 579–597.

BBC. (2008). *Premature babies "need cuddles."* Retrieved from http://news.bbc.co.uk/2/hi/health/7417316.stm

BBC News World Edition. (28 June, 2004). *Scans uncover secrets of the womb.*

BC Early Hearing Program. (2008). *Report on program start-up and implementation 2005–2008: A sound start for BC babies.* Retrieved from http://www.phsa.ca/NR/rdonlyres/8705F38C-7EA6-4320-B1AC-2B2E4F399023/0/BCEHPProgressReport2.pdf

Bearman, P., Jones, J., & Udry, J. R. (1997). *The National Longitudinal Study on Adolescent Health: Research design.* Chapel Hill, NC: Carolina Population Center.

Beaton, A. A. (2003). The nature and determinants of handedness. In K. Hugdahl & R. J. Davidson (Eds.), *The asymmetrical brain* (pp. 105–158). Cambridge, MA: MIT Press.

Beauchamp, G. K., & Mennella, J. A. (2009). Early flavor learning and its impact on later feeding behavior. *Journal of Pediatric Gastroenterology and Nutrition, 48*(1), S25–30.

Bech, B. H., Nohr, E. A., Vaeth, M., Henriksen, T. B., & Olsen, J. (2005). Coffee and fetal death: A cohort study with prospective data. *American Journal of Epidemiology, 162*(10), 983–990.

Beck, I. L., & McKeown, M. G. (2007). Increasing young low-income children's oral vocabulary through rich and focused instruction. *Elementary School Journal, 107,* 251–271.

Beckung, E., Carlsson, G., Carlsdotter, S., & Uvebrant, P. (2007). The natural history of gross motor development in children with cerebral palsy aged 1 to 15 years. *Developmental Medicine and Child Neurology, 49,* 751–756.

Bee, H. (1981). *The developing child* (3rd ed.). New York, NY: Harper & Row.

Beebe-Frankenberger, M., Bocian, K. L., MacMillan, D. L., & Gresham, F. M. (2004). Sorting second grade students with academic deficiencies: Characteristics differentiating those retained in grade from those promoted to third grade. *Journal of Educational Psychology, 96,* 204–215.

Behne, T., Carpenter, M., Call, J., & Tomasello, M. (2005). Unwilling versus unable: Infants' understanding of intentional action. *Developmental Psychology, 41*(2), 328–337.

Behrman, R. E., & Kliegman, R. M. (2002). *Nelson essentials of pediatrics* (4th ed.). Orlando, FL: W.B. Saunders.

Bell, L. A. (1989). Something's wrong here and it's not me: Challenging the dilemmas that block girls' success. *Journal of the Education of the Gifted, 12,* 118–130.

Bell, S. M., & Ainsworth, M. D. (1972). Infant crying and maternal responsiveness. *Child Development, 43*(4), 1171–1190.

Belluck, P. (2010, February 16). Wanted: Volunteers, all pregnant. *The New York Times,* p. D1+.

Belsky, J. (2002). Quantity counts: Amount of childcare and children's socioemotional development. *Journal of Developmental and Behavioral Pediatrics, 23,* 167–170.

Belsky, J., Weinraub, M., Owen, M., & Kelly, J. F. (2001, April). Quantity of childcare and problem behavior. *Society for Research in Child Development,* Minneapolis, MN.

Bender, H. L., Allen, J. P., McElhaney, K. B., Antonishak, J., Moore, C. M., Kelly, H. B., & Davis, S. M. (2007). Use of harsh physical discipline and developmental outcomes in adolescence. *Development and Psychopathology, 19*(1), 227–242.

Benderly, L. (2000). Book review of *Are We Hardwired?: The role of genes in human behavior. Genome Network News.*

Benenson, J. F., & Christakos, A. (2003). The greater fragility of females' versus males' closet same-sex friendships. *Child Development, 74*(4), 1123–1129.

Bennett, C. I. (2011). *Comprehensive multicultural education: Theory and practice* (7th ed.). Boston, MA: Allyn & Bacon.

Bennett, S., Maton, K., & Kervin, L. (2008). The "digital natives" debate: A critical review of the evidence. *British Journal of Educational Technology, 39*(5), 775–786.

Berger, S. E., Adolph, K. E., & Lobo, S. A. (2005). Out of the toolbox: Toddlers differentiate wobbly and wooden handrails. *Child Development, 76*(6), 1294–1307.

Berger, S. E., Theuring, C., & Adolph, K. E. (2007). How and when infants learn to climb stairs. *Infant Behavior and Development, 30,* 36-49.

Berk, L. E., & Spuhl, S. T. (1995). Maternal interaction, private speech, and task performance in preschool children. *Early Childhood Research Quarterly, 10,* 145–169.

Berko, J. (1958). The child's learning of English morphology. *Word, 14,* 150–177.

Berliner, D. C. (2002). Educational research: The hardest science of all. *Educational Researcher, 31*(8), 18–20.

Berndt, T. J. (2004). Children's friendships: Shifts over a half-century in perspectives on their development and effects. *Merrill-Palmer Quarterly, 50,* 206–223.

Berndt, T. J, Hawkins, J. S., & Jiao, Z. (1999). Influences of friends and friendships on adjustment to junior high school. *Merrill-Palmer Quarterly, 45,* 13–41.

Berrueta-Clements, J. R., Schweinhart, L. J., Barnett, W. S., & Weikart, D. P. (1987). Effects of early educational intervention on crime & delinquency in adolescence & early adulthood. In J. D. Burchard & S. N. Burchard (Eds.), *Prevention of delinquent behavior* (pp. 220–240). Newbury Park, CA: Sage.

Berry, R. Q., III. (2005). Voices of success: Descriptive portraits of two successful African American male middle school mathematics students. *Journal of African American Studies, 8*(4), 46–62.

Best, J. R., Miller, P. H., & Jones, L. L. (2009). Executive functions after age 5: Changes and correlates. *Developmental Review, 29,* 180–200.

Betancourt, H., & Lopez, S. R. (1993). The study of culture, ethnicity, and race in American psychology. *American Psychologist, 48,* 629–637.

Bethell, C., Reuland, C. H. P., Halfon, N., & Schor, E. L. (2004). Measuring the quality of preventive and developmental services for young children: National estimates and patterns of clinicians' performance. *Pediatrics, 113,* 1973–1983.

Better Brains for Babies (BBB). (2007). Retrieved from http://www.bbbgeorgia.org/

Bhatia, T. K., & Richie, W. C. (1999). The bilingual child: Some issues and perspectives. In *Handbook of child language acquisition.* San Diego, CA: Academic Press.

Bialystok, E. (1999). Cognitive complexity and attentional control in the bilingual child. *Child Development, 70,* 636-644.

Bialystok, E. (2001). *Bilingualism in development: Language, literacy, and* cognition. New York, NY: Cambridge University Press.

Bialystok, E., Majumder, S., & Martin, M. M. (2003). Developing phonological awareness: Is there a bilingual advantage? *Applied Linguistics, 24,* 27–44.

Bibby, R. W. (2009). The most sensible generation in years. *Maclean's, 122* (13), 4-4.

Bibby, R. W. (2009, May). *Restless gods and restless youth: An update on the religious situation in Canada.* Presented at the Annual Meeting for the Canadian Sociological Association, Ottawa, Ontario.

Bibby, R. W., Russell, S., & Rolheiser, R. (2009). *The emerging millennials: How Canada's newest generation is responding to change and choice.* Lethbridge, Canada: Project Canada Books.

Bigler, R. S., & Liben, L. S. (1992). Cognitive mechanisms in children's gender stereotyping: Theoretical and educational implications of a cognitive-based intervention. *Child Development, 63*(6), 1351–1363.

Binfet, T. (1995, Winter). Sixth and seventh grade students' reactions to moral dilemma discussions. *Moral Development and Education SIG Newsletter, 3*(1), 4.

Binfet, T. (2004). It's all in their heads: Reflective abstraction as an alternative to the moral discussion group. *Merrill-Palmer Quarterly, 50,* 181–201.

Biringen, Z. (2000). Emotional availability: Conceptualization and research findings. *American Journal of Orthopsychiatry, 70,* 104–114.

Bjorklund, D. F. (2004). Special issue: Memory development in the new millennium. *Developmental Review, 24,* 343–346.

Bjorklund, D. F. (2005). *Children's thinking: Cognitive development and individual differences* (4th ed.). Belmont, CA: Thompson-Wadsworth.

Bjorklund, D. F., Brown, R. D., & Bjorklund, B. R. (2002). Children's eyewitness memory: Changing reports and changing representations. In P. G. N. Ohta (Ed.), *Lifespan development of human memory.* Cambridge, MA: MIT Press.

Bjorklund, D. F., & Rosenblum, K. E. (2002). Context effects in children's selection and use of simple arithmetic strategies. *Journal of Cognition and Development, 3,* 225–242.

Black, J. E. (1998). How a child builds a brain: Some lessons from animal studies of neural plasticity. *Preventive Medicine, 27,* 168–171.

Black, S. (2006). Fostering the right relationships. *American School Board Journal, 193*(12), 50–52.

Blair, C. (2002). School readiness: Integrating cognition and emotion in a neurobiological conceptualization of children's functioning at school entry. *American Psychologist, 57,* 111–127.

Blair, C. (2006). How similar are fluid cognition and general intelligence? A developmental neuroscience perspective on fluid cognition as an aspect of human cognition. Main article with commentaries. *Behavioral and Brain Sciences, 29,* 109–160.

Blake, J. (1989). *Family size and achievement.* Berkeley, CA: University of California Press.

Blakemore, J. E. O. (2003). Children's belief about violating gender norms: Boys shouldn't look like girls, and girls shouldn't act like boys. *Sex Roles, 48,* 411–419.

Blakemore, S., & Firth, U. (Eds.). (2005). *The learning brain: Lessons for education.* Malden, MA: Blackwell Publishing.

Blakemore, S.-J., & Choudhury, S. (2006). Brain development during puberty: State of the science. *Developmental Science, 9*(1), 11–14.

Blakemore, S.-J., & Frith, U. (2005). The learning brain: Lessons for education: A précis. *Developmental Science, 8,* 459–461.

Blanton, H., & Burkley, M. (2008). Deviance regulation theory: Applications to adolescent social influence. In M. J. Prinstein & K. A. Dodge (Eds.), *Understanding peer influence in children and adolescents* (pp. 94–123). New York, NY: Guilford.

Blatchford, P., Baines, E., & Pellegrini, A. (2003). The social context of school playground games: Sex and ethnic differences and changes over time after entry to junior high. *British Journal of Developmental Psychology, 21,* 481–505.

Block, J., & Robins, R. W. (1993). A longitudinal study of consistency and change in self-esteem from early adolescence to early adulthood. *Child Development, 64,* 909–923.

Bloom, B. S. (1985). *Developing talent in young people.* New York, NY: Ballantine Books.

Bloom, B. S., Sosniak, L. A., Sloane, K. D., Kalinowski, A. G., Gustin, W. C., & Monsaas, J. A. (1985). *Developing talent in young people.* New York, NY: Ballantine Books.

Bloom, L. (1998). Language acquisition in its developmental context. In W. Damon (Ed.), *Handbook of child psychology* (Vol. 2, pp. 309–370). New York, NY: Wiley.

Bloom, P. (2002). *How children learn the meanings of words.* Cambridge, MA: MIT Press.

Blotner, R., & Bearison, D. J. (1984). Developmental consistencies in socio-moral knowledge: Justice reasoning and altruistic behavior. *Merrill-Palmer Quarterly, 30,* 349–367.

Bogartz, R. S., Shinskey, J. L., & Speaker, C. J. (1997). Interpreting infant looking: The event set × event set design. *Developmental Psychology, 33,* 408–422.

Bogin, B. (2001). *The growth of humanity.* New York, NY: Wiley-Liss.

Boldizar, J. P., Perry, D. G., & Perry, L. C. (1989). Outcome values and aggression. *Child Development, 60,* 571–579.

Bond, L., Butler, H., Thomas, L., Carlin, J., Glover, S., Bowes, G., & Patton, G. (2007). Social and school connectedness in early secondary school as predictors of late teenage substance use, mental health, and academic outcomes. *Journal of Adolescent Health, 40,* 9–18.

Bond, M. H. (1993). Emotions and their expression in Chinese culture. *Journal of Nonverbal Behavior, 17,* 245–262.

Bonnano, R. A., & Hymel, S. (2006, May). Witnessing bullying: Assessing exposure and negative consequences. *The Annual International Conference on Promoting Relationships and Eliminating Violence*, Ottawa, Ontario.

Bonny, A. E., Britto, M. T., Klostermann, B. K., Hornung, R. W., & Slap, G. B. (2000). School disconnectedness: Identifying adolescents at risk. *Pediatrics, 106*(5), 1017–1021.

Bono, M., & Stifter, C. (2003). Maternal attention-directing strategies and infant-focused attention during problem solving. *Infancy, 4,* 235–250.

Borg, M. G. (1998). Secondary school teachers' perception of pupils' undesirable behaviors. *British Journal of Educational Psychology, 68,* 67–79.

Borse, N. N., Gilchrist, J., Dellinger, A. M., Rudd, R. A., Ballesteros, M. F., & Sleet, D. A. (2008). *CDC childhood injury report: Patterns of unintentional injuries among 0–19 year olds in the United States, 2000–2006.* Atlanta (GA): Centers for Disease Control and Prevention, National Center for Injury Prevention and Control.

Bortfeld, H., Morgan, J. L., Golinkoff, R. M., & Rathbun, K. (2005). Mommy and me: Familiar names help launch babies into speech stream segmentation. *Psychological Science, 16,* 298–304.

Bos, C. S., & Reyes, E. I. (1993). Conversations with a Latina teacher about education for language-minority students with special needs. *Elementary School* Journal, *96,* 344–351.

Bouchard, T. J., Jr., Lykken, D. T., McGue, M., Segal, N. L., & Tellegen, A. (1990). Sources of human psychological differences: The Minnesota Study of Twins Reared Apart. *Science, 250,* 223–228.

Bouchard, T. J., Jr., & McGue, M. (2003) Genetic and environmental influences on human psychological differences. *Journal of Neurobiology, 54,* 4–45.

Bouchey, H. A., & Furman, W. (2003). Dating and romantic experiences in adolescence. In G. R. Adams & M. Berzonsky (Eds.), *The Blackwell handbook of adolescence.* Oxford, UK: Blackwell Publishers.

Bouchey, H. A., & Harter, S. (2005). Reflected appraisals, academic self-perceptions, and math/science performance during early adolescence. *Journal of Educational Psychology, 97,* 673–686.

Boutin, D., Lassonde, M., Robert, M., Vanassing, P., & Ellemberg, D. (2008). Neurophysiological assessment prior to and following sports-related concussion during childhood: A case study. *Neurocase, 14*(3), 239–248.

Bowkers, A., Gabdois, S., & Cornock, B. (2003). Sports participation and self-esteem: Variations as a function of gender and gender role orientation. *Sex Roles, 49,* 47–58.

Bowlby, J. (1960a.) Grief and mourning in infancy and early childhood. *The Psychoanalytic Study of the Child, 15,* 9–52.

Bowlby, J. (1960b.). Separation anxiety. *International Journal of Psycho-Analysis, 41*(2–3), 89–113.

Bowlby, J. (1961). Separation anxiety: A critical review of the literature. *Journal of Child Psychology and Psychiatry, 1*(16), 251–269.

Bowlby, J. (1969/1982). *Attachment and loss, Vol. 1: Attachment.* New York, NY: Basic Books.

Bowlby, J. (1979). *The making and breaking of affectional bonds.* London, England: Tavistock.

Bowlby, J. (1988). *Clinical applications of attachment theory. A secure base.* London, England: Routledge.

Boyer, T. W. (2006). The development of risk-taking: A multi-perspective review. *Developmental Review, 26,* 291–348.

Boyle, M. H., Georgiades, K., Mustard, C., & Racine, Y. (2007). Neighborhood and family influences on educational attainment: Results from the Ontario Child Health Study Follow-Up 2001. *Child Development, 78,* 168–189.

Bradford, K., Barber, B. K., Olsen, J. A., Maughan, S. L., Erickson, L. D., Ward, D., & Stolz, H. E. (2004). A multi-national study of interparental conflict, parenting, and adolescent functioning. *Marriage & Family Review, 35*(3), 107–137.

Brandone, A. C., & Wellman, H. M. (2009). You can't aways get what you want: Infants understand failed goal-directed actions. *Psychological Science, 20*(1), 85–91.

Brannon, L. (2002). *Gender: Psychological perspectives* (3rd ed.). Boston, MA: Allyn & Bacon.

Bransford, J. D., Brown, A. L., & Cocking, R. R. (2000). *How people learn: Brain, mind, experience, and school.* Washington, DC: National Academy Press.

Braungart-Rieker, J. M., Garwood, M. M., Powers, B. P., & Wang, X. (2001). Parental sensitivity, infant affect, and affect regulation: Predictors of later attachment. *Child Development, 72,* 252–270.

Brayden, R. (2008, February 1). *Trampoline safety.* Retrieved from Pediatric Advisor website: http://www.med.umich.edu/1libr/pa/pa_trampinj_pep.htm

Brazelton, B., & Nugent, J. K. (1995). *The Neonatal Behavioral Assessment Scale.* Cambridge, MA: Mac Keith Press.

Brazelton Institute. (2008). *Understanding the baby's language.* Retrieved from http://www.brazelton-institute.com/intro.html

Brehaut, J. C., Miller, A., Raina, P., & McGrail, K. M. (2003). Childhood behavior disorders and injuries among children and youth: A population-based study. *Pediatrics, 111*(2), 262–269.

Brendgen, M., Wanner, B., & Vitaro, F. (2006). Verbal abuse by the teacher and child adjustment from kindergarten through grade 6. *Pediatrics, 117,* 1585–1598.

Brendgen, M., Wanner, B., Vitaro, F., Bukowski, W. M., & Tremblay, R. E. (2007). Verbal abuse by the teacher during childhood and academic, behavioral, and emotional adjustment in young adulthood. *Journal of Educational Psychology, 99*, 26–38.

Brenner, J. S., & Council on Sports Medicine and Fitness. (2007). Overuse injuries, overtraining, and burnout in child and adolescent athletes. *Pediatrics, 119*(6), 1242–1245.

Brice, A. E. (2002). *The Hispanic child: Speech, language, culture, and education.* Boston, MA: Allyn & Bacon.

Brice, A. E., & Brice, R. G. (2009). *Language development: Monolingual and* bilingual *acquisitions.* Boston, MA: Allyn & Bacon.

British Columbia Schizophrenia Society. (2010). *How you can help: A toolkit for families.* Retrieved from http://www.bcss.org/2010/03/resources/family-friends/family-toolkit/.

Britner, P. A., Balczar, F. E., Bechman, E. A., Blinn-Pike, L., & Larose, S. (2006). Mentoring special youth populations. *Journal of Community Psychology, 34*, 747–763.

Brody, G. H. (2004). Siblings' direct and indirect contributions to child development. *American Psychological Society, 13*, 124–126.

Brody, G. H., Murray, V. M., Gerrard, M., Gibbons, F. X., McNair, L., Brown, A. C., Wills, T. A., . . . Chen, Y. (2006). The Strong African American Families Program: Prevention of youths' high-risk behavior and a test of a model of change. *Journal of Family Psychology, 20*(1), 1–11.

Brody, L. (1999). *Gender, emotion and the family.* Cambridge, MA: Harvard University Press.

Broidy, L. M., Nagin, D. S., Tremblay, R. E., Brame, B., Dodge, K. A., Fergusson, D., Horwood, J. L, . . . Vitaro, F. (2003). Developmental trajectories of childhood disruptive behaviors and adolescent delinquency: A six-site, cross-national study. *Developmental Psychology,* 39, 222–245.

Bronfenbrenner, U. (1970, November). *Who cares for America's children?* Keynote address delivered at the Annual Conference of the National Association for the Education of Young Children, Boston, Massachusetts.

Bronfenbrenner, U. (1979). *The ecology of human development: Experiments by nature and design.* Cambridge, MA: Harvard University Press.

Bronfenbrenner, U., & Evans, G. W. (2000). Developmental science in the 21st century: Emerging theoretical models, research designs, and empirical findings. *Social Development, 9*, 115–125.

Bronfenbrenner, U., McClelland, P., Wethington, E., Moen, P., & Ceci, S. (1996). *The state of Americans: This generation and the next.* New York, NY: Free Press.

Bronfenbrenner, U., & Morris, P. A. (2006). The bioecological model of human development. In W. Damon & R. M. Lerner (Eds.), *Handbook of child psychology: Theoretical models of human development* (6th ed., Vol. 1, pp. 793–827). Hoboken, NJ: Wiley.

Bronson, M. (2000). *Self-regulation in early childhood: Nature and nurture.* New York, NY: Guilford.

Brook, J. S., Zheng, L., Whiteman, M., & Brook, D. (2001). Aggression in toddlers: Associations with parenting and marital relations. *Journal of Genetic Psychology, 162*(2), 228–241.

Brooks, R., & Meltzoff, A. N. (2005). The development of gaze following and its relation to language. *Developmental Science, 8*(6), 535–543.

Brooks-Gunn, J. (1988). Antecedents and consequences of variations in girls' maturational timing. In Melvin D. Levine & E. R. McAnarney (Eds.), *Early adolescent transitions* (pp. 101–121). Lexington, MA: Lexington Books.

Brooks-Gunn, J. (1989). Adolescent sexual behavior. *American Psychologist, 44*(2), 249–257.

Brooks-Gunn, J. (2003). Do you believe in magic? What can we expect from early childhood intervention programs? *Society for Research in Child Development Social Policy Report, 17*(1).

Brooks-Gunn, J., & Paikoff, R. (1997). Sexuality and developmental transitions during adolescence. In J. Schulengerg & J. L. Maggs (Eds.), *Health risks and developmental transition during adolescence* (pp. 190–129). New York, NY: Cambridge University Press.

Brophy, J. (2004). *Motivating students to learn* (2nd ed.). Mahwah, NJ: Erlbaum.

Brown, B. B. (2004). Adolescents' relationships with peers. In R. M. Lerner & L. Steinberg (Eds.), *Handbook of adolescent psychology* (2nd ed., pp. 363–394). Hoboken, NJ: Wiley.

Brown, B. B., Bakken, J. P., Ameringer, S. W., & Mahon, S. D. (2008). A comprehensive conceptualization of the peer influence process in adolescence. In. M. J. Prinstein & K. A. Dodge (Eds.), *Understanding peer influence in children and adolescents* (pp. 17–44). New York, NY: Guilford.

Brown, T. N., Wallace, J. M., & Williams, D. R. (2001). Race-related correlates of young adults' subjective well-being. *Social Indicators Research, 53*, 97–116. doi:10.1023/A:1007190226538

Brownstein, R. (2009, February). Millennial tremors. *National Journal*, p. 3-3. Retrieved from http://web.ebscohost.com/ehost/detail?vid=2&hid=12&sid=ab476cc6-0fa5-4ea5-ba93-e2c646f6e052%40sessionmgr4&bdata=JnNpdGU9ZWhvc3QtbGl2ZQ%3d%3d#db=a9h&AN=36557459.

Bruck, M., Ceci, S. J., & Hembrooke, H. (2002). The nature of children's true and false narratives. *Developmental Review, 22*, 520–554.

Bruder, C. E., Piotrowski, A., Gijsbers, A. A., Andersson, R., Erickson, S., de Ståhl, T. D., Menzel, U., . . . Dumanski, J. (2008). Phenotypically concordant and discordant monozygotic twins display different DNA copy-number-variation profiles. *American Journal of Human Genetics. 82*(3), 763–771.

Bruner, J. S., Goodnow, J. J., & Austin, G. A. (1956). *A study of thinking.* New York, NY: Wiley.

Brunner, M., Krauss, S., & Kunter, M. (2008). Gender differences in mathematics: Does the story need to be rewritten? *Intelligence, 36*(5), 403–421.

Bryant, B. K. (1982). Sibling relationships in middle childhood. In M. E. Lamb & B. Sutton-Smith (Eds.), *Sibling relationships* (pp. 87–122). Hillsdale, NJ: Erlbaum.

Bryant, B. K. (1985). The neighbourhood walk: Sources of support in middle childhood. *Monographs of the Society for Research in Child Development, 50*(Serial no. 210), 1–116.

Bryant, B. K. (1992). Sibling caretaking: Providing emotional support during middle childhood. In F. Boer & J. Dunn (Eds.), *Children's sibling relationships: Developmental and clinical issues* (pp. 55–70). Hillsdale, NJ: Erlbaum.

Bryant, P., & Nunes, T. (2004). Children's under-standing of mathematics. In U. Goswami (Ed.), *Blackwell handbook of childhood cognitive development* (pp. 412–439). Malden, MA: Blackwell.

Buchanan, C. M., Eccles, J. S., & Becker, J. B. (1992). Are adolescents the victims of raging hormones? Evidence for activational effects of hormones on moods and behavior at adolescence. *Psychological Bulletin, 111*(1), 62–107.

Buckhalt, J. A., Wolfson, A. R., & El-Sheikh, M. (2009). Children's sleep and school psychology practice. *School Psychology Quarterly, 24*, 60–69. doi:10.1037/a0014497

Budd, K., Carson, E., Garelick, B., Klein, D., Milgram, R. J., Raimi, R. A., Schwartz, M., . . . Wilson W. S. (2005). *10 Myths about math education and why you shouldn't believe them.* Retrieved from http://nychold.com/myths-050504.html

Buehler, C. (2006). Parents and peers in relation to early adolescent problem behavior. *Journal of Marriage & Family, 68*(1), 109–124.

Buehler, C., & Gerard, J. M. (2002). Marital conflict, ineffective parenting, and children's and adolescents' maladjustment. *Journal of Marriage & Family, 64*, 78–92.

Buehler, R., Griffin, D., & Ross, M. (1994). Exploring the "planning fallacy": Why people underestimate their task completion times. *Journal of Personality and Social* Psychology, *67*, 366–381.

Bugental, D. B., Ellerson, P. C., Lin, E. K., Rainey, B., Kokotovic, A., & O'Hara, N. (2002). A cognitive approach to child abuse prevention. *Journal of Family Psychology, 16*, 243–258.

Buhs, E. S., Ladd, G. W., & Herald, S. L. (2006). Peer exclusion and victimization: Processes that mediate the relation between peer group rejection and children's classroom engagement and achievement? *Journal of Educational Psychology, 98*(1), 1–13.

Bupa Health Information Team. (2009). *Caring for your child's teeth.* Retrieved from http:// hcd2.bupa.co.uk/fact_sheets/html/child _dental.html

Burack, J. A., Flanagan, T., Peled, T., Sutton, H. M., Zygmuntowicz, C., & Manly, J. T. (2006). Social perspective-taking skills in maltreated children and adolescents. *Developmental Psychology, 42*, 207–217.

Burgess, S., Hecht, S., & Lonigan, C. (2002). Relations of the home literacy environment (HLE) to the development of reading-related abilities: A one-year longitudinal study. *Reading Research Quarterly, 37*, 408–426.

Bushman, B. J., & Anderson, C. A. (2009). Effects of violent video games on aggressive behavior, aggressive cognition, aggressive affect, physiological arousal, and prosocial behavior: A meta-analytic review of the scientific literature. *Psychological Science, 12*(5), 353–359.

Bushman, B. J., Rothstein, H. R., & Anderson, C. A. (2010). Much ado about something: Violent video game effects and a school of red herring: Reply to Ferguson and Kilburn (2010). *American Psychological Association, 136*, 182–187. doi:10.1037/a0018718

Buss, D. M. (1995). Psychological sex differences: Origin through sexual selection. *American Psychologist, 50*(164–168).

Butler, R. (1998). Age trends in the use of social and temporal comparison for self-evaluation: Examination of a novel developmental hypothesis. *Child Development, 69*, 1054–1073.

Butler, R. W., & Haser, J. K. (2006). Neurocognitive effects of treatment for childhood cancer. *Mental Retardation and Developmental Disabilities Research Reviews, 12*, 184–191.

Bynner, J. (2005). Rethinking the youth phase of the life course: The case for emerging adulthood? *Journal of Youth Studies, 8*, 367–384.

Byrnes, D. A. (1989). Attitudes of students, parents, and educators toward repeating a grade. In L. A. Shepard & M. L. Smith (Eds.), *Flunking grades: Research and policies on retention* (pp. 108–131). Philadelphia, PA: Falmer Press.

Byrnes, J. P. (2001). *Minds, brains, and education: Understanding the psychological and educational relevance of neuroscientific research.* New York, NY: Guilford.

Byrnes, J. P. (2003). Factors predictive of mathematics achievement in White, Black, and Hispanic 12th graders. *Journal of Educational Psychology, 95*, 316–326.

Byrnes, J. P. (2006). Cognitive development during adolescence. In G. Adams & M. D. Berzonsky (Eds.), *Blackwell handbook of adolescence* (pp. 227–246). Malden, MA: Blackwell Publishing.

Byrnes, J. P., & Fox, N. A. (1998). The educational relevance of research in cognitive neuroscience. *Educational Psychology Review, 10*, 297–342.

Cahill, L. (2005). His brain, her brain. *Scientific American Magazine, 292*(5), 40–47.

Cairns, R. B., & Cairns, B. D. (2006). The making of developmental psychology. In R. M. Lerner (Ed.), *Theoretical models of human development* (6th ed., Vol. 1, pp. 89–165). New York, NY: Wiley.

Caldwell, B. M., & Bradley, R. H. (1984). *Home observation for measurement of the environment.* Little Rock, AR: The University of Arkansas.

Caldwell, B. M., & Bradley, R. H. (1994). Environmental issues in developmental follow-up research. In S. L. Friedman & H. C. Haywood (Eds.), *Developmental follow-up* (pp. 235–256). San Diego, CA: Academic Press.

Calkins, S. D., & Johnson, M. C. (1998). Toddler regulation of distress to frustrating events: Temperamental and maternal correlates. *Infant Behavior and Development, 21*, 379–395.

Cameron, C. E., & Hagen, J. W. (2005). Women in child development: Themes from the SRCD Oral History Project. *History of Psychology, 8*, 289–316.

Campbell, A., Shirley, L., & Caygill, L. (2002). Sex-typed preferences in three domains: Do two-year-olds need cognitive variables? *British Journal of Psychology, 93*, 203–217.

Campbell, F. A., Pungello, E. P., Miller-Johnson, S., Burchinal, M., & Ramey, C. T. (2001). The development of cognitive and academic abilities: Growth curves from an early childhood education experiment. *Developmental Psychology, 37*, 231–242.

Canadian Association of the Deaf. (2007). *Position statement on cochlear implants.* Retrieved from http://www.cad.ca/en/issues/cochlear_implants.asp

Canadian Fitness and Lifestyle Research Institute. (2008). Kids CAN PLAY! Encouraging children to be active at home, at school, and in their communities. Retrieved from http://www.cflri.ca/eng/statistics/surveys/documents/CANPLAY_2008_b1.pdf

Canadian Lung Association. (2007). *Smoking and tobacco: Second-hand smoke.* Retrieved from http://www.lung.ca/protect-protegez/tobacco-tabagisme/second-secondaire/children-enfants_e.php

Canadian Press. (2008, May 23). More education needed about schizophrenia in teen years: Experts. *CBC News.* Retrieved from http://www.cbc.ca/health/story/2008/05/23/schizophrenia-teens.html

Cannon, M. (2009). Contrasting effects of maternal and paternal age on offspring intelligence. *PLoS Med 6*(3): e1000042.

Canter, L., & Canter, M. (1992). *Lee Canter's Assertive Discipline: Positive behavior management for today's classroom.* Santa Monica, CA: Lee Canter and Associates.

Capatides, J., Collins, C. C., & Bennett, L. (1996). *Peer interaction in toddlers: Parallel play revisited.* Paper presented at the conference Ask the child: Why, when, and how? Teacher's College, Columbia University, New York.

Cappuccio, F. P., Taggart, F. M., Kandala, N. B., Currie, A., Peile, E., Stranges, S., & Miller, M. A. (2008). Meta-analysis of short sleep duration and obesity in children and adults. *Sleep, 31*, 619–626.

Carey, S. (1985). Are children fundamentally different thinkers and learners from adults? In J. W. Segal & R. Glasser (Eds.), *Thinking and learning skills* (Vol. 2, pp. 485–517). Hillsdale, NJ: Erlbaum.

Carey, S. (1999). Sources of conceptual change. In E. K. Scholnick, K. Nelson, S. A. Gelman, & P. H. Miller (Eds.), *Conceptual development: Piaget's legacy* (pp. 293–308). Oxford, England: Clarendon Press.

Carlson, E. A., & Sroufe, L. A. (1995). Contribution of attachment theory to developmental psychopathology. In D. Cicchetti & D. Cohen (Eds.), *Developmental psychopathology: Vol. 1. Theory and methods* (pp. 581–617). Oxford, England: Wiley.

Carlson, S. M., & Taylor, M. (2005). Imaginary companions and impersonated characters: Sex differences in children's fantasy play. *Merrill-Palmer Quarterly, 51*, 93–118.

Carlson Jones, D. (2004). Body image among adolescent girls and boys: A longitudinal study. *Developmental Psychology, 40*, 823–835.

Carnagey, N. L., Anderson, C. A., & Bartholow, B. D. (2007). Media violence and social neuroscience: New questions and new opportunities. *Current Directions in Psychological Science, 16*, 178–182.

Carnegie Corporation. (1996). *Report on education for young children 3–10 years of age.* New York, NY: The Carnegie Corporation.

Carney, R. N., & Levin, J. R. (2000). Mnemonic instruction, with a focus on transfer. *Journal of Educational Psychology, 92*, 783–790.

Carpenter, M., Akhtar, N., & Tomasello, M. (1998). Fourteen- through 18-month-old infants differentially imitate intentional and accidental actions. *Infant Behavior & Development, 21*, 315–330.

Carpenter, S. (2000). In the digital age, experts pause to examine the effects on kids. *Monitor on Psychology, 31*(11), 48–49.

Carr, M., Kurtz, B. E., Schneider, W., Turner, L. A., & Borkowski, J. G. (1989). Strategy acquisition and transfer among American and German children: Environmental influences on metacognitive development. *Developmental Psychology, 25*, 765–771.

Carroll, J. B. (1997). The three-stratum theory of cognitive abilities. In D. P. Flanagan, J. L. Genshaft, & P. L. Harrison (Eds.), *Contemporary intellectual assessment: Theories, tests, and issues* (pp. 122–130). New York, NY: Guilford.

Carson, D. K., Klee, T., Perry, C. K., Muskina, G., & Donaghy, T. (1998). Comparisons of children with delayed and normal language at 24 months of age on measures of behavioral difficulties, social and cognitive development. *Infant Mental Health Journal, 19*, 59–75.

Carver, K., Joyner, K., & Udry, J. R. (2003). National estimates of adolescent romantic relationships. In P. Florsheim (Ed.), *Adolescent romantic relations and sexual behavior* (pp. 23–56). Mahwah, NJ: Erlbaum.

Carver, P. R., Egan, S. K., & Perry, D. G. (2004). Children who question their heterosexuality. *Developmental Psychology, 40*(1), 43–53.

Carver, P. R., Yunger, J. L., & Perry, D. G. (2003). Gender identity and adjustment in middle childhood. *Sex Roles, 49*, 95–109.

Case, R. (1985). *Intellectual development: Birth to adulthood.* New York, NY: Academic Press.

Case, R. (1992). *The mind's staircase: Exploring the conceptual underpinnings of children's thought and knowledge.* Mahwah, NJ: Erlbaum.

Case, R. (1992). The role of the frontal lobes in the regulation of cognitive development. *Brain and Cognition, 20*, 51–73.

Case, R. (1998). The development of conceptual structures. In D. Kuhn & R. S. Siegler (Eds.), *Handbook of child psychology: Vol. 2: Cognition, perception, and language* (pp. 745–800). New York, NY: Wiley.

Casenhiser, D., & Goldberg, A. E. (2005). Fast mapping between a phrasal form and meaning. *Developmental Science, 8.*

Casey, B. J., Getz, S., & Galvan, A. (2008). The adolescent brain. *Developmental Review, 28*, 62–77.

Casey, B. M., McIntire, D. D., & Leveno, K. J. (2001). The continuing value of the Apgar score for the assessment of newborn infants. *The New England Journal of Medicine, 7*(344), 467–471.

Cassell, J., Huffaker, D., Tversky, D., & Ferriman, K. (2006). The language of online leadership: Gender and youth engagement on the Internet. *Developmental Psychology, 42*, 436–449.

Castek, J., & Bevans, J. (in press). Reading adventures online: Five ways to introduce the new literacies of the Internet through children's literature. *The Reading Teacher.*

Cattell, R. B. (1963). Theory of fluid and crystallized intelligence: A critical experiment. *Journal of Educational Psychology, 54*, 1–22.

Cattell, R. B. (1998). Where is intelligence? Some answers from the triadic theory. In J. J. McArdle & R. W. Woodcock (Eds.), *Human cognitive abilities in theory and practice* (pp. 29–38). Mahwah, NJ: Erlbaum.

Caughy, M. O. (1996). Health and environmental effects on the academic readiness of school-age children. *Developmental Psychology, 32*, 515–522.

Cavanaugh, M., & Walsh, N. (2009). *How the deaf community is dealing with cochlear implants.* Retrieved from the KPBS website: http://www.kpbs.org/news/2009/nov/03/how-deaf-community-dealing-cochlear-implants/

Cavill, S., & Bryden, P. (2003). Development of handedness: Comparison of questionnaire and performance-based measures of preference. *Brain Cognition, 53*, 149–151.

Cazden, C. B. (1988). *Classroom discourse: The language of teaching and learning.* Portsmouth, NH: Heinemann.

CBC Segment A. (2006, March). On *Morning Show.*

CBC Segment B. (2006, March). On *As It Happens.*

CBS News. (2002 November 8). *Choosing your baby's gender.*

CDC [Centers for Disease Control and Prevention]. (2003). *Physical activity levels among children aged 9–13 years—United States, 2002.* Retrieved from http://www.cdc.gov/mmwr/preview/mmwrhtml/mm5233a1.htm

CDC. (2005). *Births, marriages, divorces, and deaths: Provisional data for 2004.* Retrieved from http://www.cdc.gov/nchs/fastats/divorce.htm

CDC. (2006). *Revised recommendations for HIV testing of adults, adolescents, and pregnant women in health-care settings.* Retrieved from http://www.cdc.gov/mmwr/preview/mmwrhtml/rr5514a1.htm

CDC. (2007). *Children and secondhand smoke exposure.* Retrieved from http://www.cdc.gov/features/childrenandsmoke/.

CDC. (2008). *CDC childhood injury report: Patterns of unintentional injuries among 0–19 year olds in the United States, 2000–2006.*

CDC. (2008). *Estimates of new HIV infections in the United States.* Retrieved from http://www.cdc.gov/hiv/topics/surveillance/resources/factsheets/incidence.htm

CDC. (2008). *Suicide facts at a glance.* Retrieved from http://www.cdc.gov/ViolencePrevention/pdf/Suicide-DataSheet-a.pdf

CDC. (2008). *Toxoplasmosis Fact Sheet.* Retrieved from http://www.cdc.gov/toxoplasmosis/factsheet.html

CDC. (2009a). *Assisted reproductive technology.* Retrieved from http://www.cdc.gov/ART/

CDC. (2009b). *Sexually transmitted diseases. Treatment guidelines 2006.* Retrieved from http://www.cdc.gov/STD/treatment/

CDC. (2009c). *Prevention tips.* Retrieved from http://www.cdc.gov/nceh/lead/tips.htm

CDC. (2009d). *Possible side-effects from vaccines.* Retrieved from http://www.cdc.gov/vaccines/vac-gen/side-effects.htm

CDC. (2009e). *Infants & toddlers (ages 0–3)—diseases & conditions.* Retrieved from http://www.cdc.gov/

CDC. (2009f). *Lead.* Retrieved from http://www.cdc.gov/nceh/lead/

CDC. (2009g).*Defining childhood overweight and obesity.* Retrieved from http://www.cdc.gov/obesity/childhood/defining.html

CDF. (2008, March 7). *The minimum wage will not support a family of four.* Retrieved from http://www.childrensdefense.org/site/DocServer/min_wage_fam4.pdf? doc ID=752.

Ceci, S. J., & Bruck, M. (1993). Suggestibility of the child witness: A historical review and synthesis. *Psychological Bulletin, 113,* 403–439.

Ceci, S. J., & Roazzi, A. (1994). The effects of context on cognition: Postcards from Brazil. In R. J. Sternberg (Ed.), *Mind in context* (pp. 74–101). New York, NY: Cambridge University Press.

Ceci, S. J., & Williams, W. M. (1997). Schooling, intelligence, and income. *American Psychologist, 52,* 1051–1058.

CERHR [Center for the Evaluation of Risks to Human Reproduction]. (2010). *Multiple births—Carrying to term.* Retrieved from http://cerhr.niehs.nih.gov/healthtopics/multbirths.html

Chandler, M., & Lalonde, C. (2003). Representational diversity redux. *Society for Research in Child Development*, Tampa, Florida.

Chandler, M. J., Lalonde, C. E., Sokol, B. W., & Hallett, D. (with Marcia, J. E.). (2003). Personal persistence, identity development, and suicide: A study of Native and Non-Native North American adolescents. *Monographs of the Society for Research in Child Development, 68*(2, Serial No. 273).

Chandra, A. (2010). *Children on the home front: The experiences of children from military families.* RAND Corporation. Retrieved from http://www.rand.org/pubs/testimonies/2010/RAND_CT341.pdf.

Chandra, A., & Mikovitz, C. S. (2007). Factors that influence mental health stigma among 8th grade adolescents. *Journal of Youth Adolescence, 36,* 763–774.

Chang, L., Schwartz, D., Dodge, K. K., & McBride, C. A. (2003). Harsh parenting in relation to child emotion regulation and aggression. *Journal of Family Psychology, 17,* 598–606.

Chao, R. K. (1994). Beyond parental control and authoritarian parenting style: Understanding Chinese parenting through the cultural notion of training. *Child Development, 65,* 1111–1119.

Chao, R. K. (2001). Extending research on the consequences of parenting style for Chinese Americans and European Americans. *Child Development, 72,* 1832–1843.

Chao, R. K., & Sue, S. (1996). Chinese parental influence and their children's success: A paradox in the literature on parenting styles. In S. Lau (Ed.), *Youth and child development in Chinese societies.* Hong Kong: Chinese University of Hong Kong.

Chao, R. K., & Tseng, V. (2002). Parenting of Asians. In M. H. Bornstein (Ed.), *Handbook of parenting: Social conditions and applied parenting* (2nd ed., Vol. 4, pp. 59–93). Mahwah, NJ: Erlbaum.

Charach, A., Pepler, D. J., & Ziegler, S. (1995). Bullying at school: A Canadian perspective. *Education Canada, 35,* 12–18.

Chavous, T. M., Bernat, D. H., Schmeelk-Cone, K., Caldwell, C. H., Kohn-Wood, L., & Zimmerman, M. A. (2003). Racial identity and academic attainment among African American Adolescents. *Child Development, 74*(4), 1076–1090.

Chen, H., & Jackson, T. (2008). Prevalence and sociodemographic correlates of eating disorder endorsements among adolescents and young adults. *European Eating Disorder Review, 16*(5), 375–385.

Chen, X., Rubin, K. H., Li, B., & Li, Z. (1999). Adolescent outcomes of social functioning in Chinese children. *International Journal of Behavior Development, 23,* 199–223.

Cheng, M-F., & Johnson, J. E. (2010). Research on children's play: Analysis of developmental and early education journals from 2005 to 2007. *Early Childhood Education Journal, 37,* 249–259. doi:1007/s10643-009-0347-7

Cheour-Luhtanen, M., Alho, K., Sainio, K., Rinne, T., Reinikainen, K., Pohjavuori, M., . . . Naatanen, R. (1996). The ontogenetically earliest discriminative response of the human brain. *Psychophysiology, 33*(4), 478–481.

Child and Adolescent Bipolar Foundation. (2010). *About pediatric bipolar disorder: A guide for families.* Retrieved from http://www.bpkids.org/learn/library/about-pediatric-bipolar-disorder#pro

Children's Bureau. (2004). *Child maltreatment 2004.* Retrieved from http://www.acf.hhs.gov/programs/cb/pubs/cm04/index.htm.

Children's Defense Fund. (2005). *Child poverty.* Retrieved from http://www.childrensdefense.org/familyincome/childpoverty/default.aspx

Children's Defense Fund. (2008). *Data.* Retrieved from http://www.childrensdefense.org/child-research-data-publications/data/state-data-repository/cits/children-in-the-states-2008-unitedstates.pdf

Children's Hospital Boston. (2005–2009). *Birth defects and congenital abnormalities.* Retrieved from http://www.childrenshospital.org/az/Site479/mainpageS479P0.html

Children's Hospital Boston. (2005–2010). *Sports injury statistics.* Retrieved from http://www.childrenshospital.org/az/Site1112/mainpageS1112P0.html

Choi, J. K., & Kim, S. C. (2007). Environmental effects on gene expression have regional biases in the human genome. *Genetics, 175*(4), 1607–1613.

Chomitz, V. R., Slining, M. M., McGowan, R. J., Mitchell, S. E., Dawson, G. F., & Hacker, K. A. (2009). Is there a relationship between physical fitness and academic achievement? Positive results from public school children in the northeastern United States. *Journal of School Health, 79,* 30–37.

Chomsky, C. (1969). *The acquisition of syntax in children from five to ten.* Cambridge, MA: MIT Press.

CHS. (2007). *News Release: Children's Hospital Boston. A first glimpse at healthy brain and behavioral development: First report from large-scale study establishes norms for 6- to 18-year-olds* (Vol. 2008). Boston, MA: Children's Hospital Boston.

Church, R. M. (1959). Emotional reactions of rats to the pain of others. *Journal of Comparative and Physiological Psychology, 52*(2), 132–134. doi:10.1037/h0043531

Clark, D. B., Martin, C. S., & Cornelius, J. R. (2008). Adolescent-onset substance use disorders predict young adult mortality. *Journal of Adolescent Health, 42,* 637–639.

Clark, J. M., & Paivio, A. (1991). Dual coding theory and education. *Educational Psychology Review, 3,* 149–210.

Clark, L., & Tiggemann, M. (2008). Sociocultural and individual psychological predictors of body image in young girls: A prospective study. *Developmental Psychology, 44,* 1124–1134.

Clarke-Stewart, K. A. (1998). Historical shifts and underlying themes in ideas about rearing young children in the United States: Where have we been? Where are we going? *Early Development & Parenting, 7,* 101–117.

Clarke-Stewart, K. A., Vandell, D. L., Burchinal, M., O'Brien, M., & McCartney, K. (2002). Do regulable features of child-care homes affect children's development? *Early Child Research Quarterly, 17,* 52-86.

Claxton, L. J., Keen, R., McCarty, M. E., & Adolph, K. E. (2003). Evidence of motor planning in infant reaching behavior. *Psychological Science, 14*(4), 354–356.

Clearfield, M. W., & Mix, K. S. (1999). Number versus contour length in infants' discrimination of small visual sets. *Psychological Science, 10,* 408–411.

Clements, D. H. (1994). The uniqueness of the computer as a learning tool: Insights from research and practice. In J. L. Wright & D. D. Shade (Eds.), *Young children: Active learners in a technological age.* Washington, DC: NAEYC.

Cleveland, M. J., Feinberg, M. E., Bontempo, D. E., & Greenberg, M. T. (2008). The role of risk and protective factors in substance use across adolescence. *Journal of Adolescence Health, 43*, 157–164.

CMCE. (2009). *PCAP-13 2007: Contextual report on student achievement in reading.* Council of Ministers of Education, Canada.

Coatsworth, J. D., & Conroy, D. E. (2009). The effects of autonomy-supportive coaching, need satisfaction, and self-perceptions on initiative and identity in youth swimmers. *Developmental Psychology, 45*(2), 320–328.

Coe, D. P, Pivarnik, J. M., Womack, C., Reeves, M. J., & Malina, R. M. (2006). Effect of physical education and activity levels on academic achievement in children. *Medicine & Science in Sports & Exercise, 38*(8), 1515–1519.

Cohen, D. (2006). Pretending. In D. Cohen (Ed.), *The development of play* (pp. 84–105). New York, NY: Routledge.

Cohen, E. G. (1994). *Designing group work* (2nd ed.). New York, NY: Teachers College Press.

Cohen, G. L., & Steele, C. M. (2003). A barrier of mistrust: How negative stereotypes affect cross-race mentoring. In J. Aronson (Ed.), *Improving academic achievement: Impact of psychological factors on education* (pp. 303–328). San Diego, CA: Academic Press.

Cohen, M. R. (1997). Individual and sex differences in speed of handwriting among high school students. *Perceptual and motor skills, 84*(3, Pt. 2), 1428–1430.

Coie, J. D., & Dodge, K. A. (1998). Aggression and antisocial behavior. In W. Damon & N. Eisenberg (Eds.), *Handbook of child psychology: Vol. 3. Social, emotional, and personality development* (pp. 779–862). New York, NY: Wiley.

Coie, J. D., & Krehbiehl, G. (1984). Effects of academic tutoring on the social status of low-achieving, socially rejected children. *Child Development, 55*, 1465–1478.

Colapinto, J. (2000). *As nature made him: The boy who was raised as a girl.* New York, NY: Harper Collins.

Colby, A., Kohlberg, L., Gibbs, J. C., & Lieberman, M. (1983). A longitudinal study of moral judgment. *Monographs of the Society for Research in Child Development, 48*, (1–2, Serial No. 200).

Cole, C., Binney, G., Casey, P., Fiascone, J., Hagadorn J., & Kim C. (2002). *Criteria for determining disability in infants and children: Low birth weight.* Evidence Report/Technology Assessment No. 70 (Prepared by Tufts New England Medical Center Evidence-based Practice Center under Contract No. 290-97-0019). AHRQ Publication No. 03-E010. Rockville, MD: Agency for Healthcare Research and Quality. Retrieved from http://www.ncbi.nlm.nih.gov/books/bv.fcgi?rid=hstat1a.chapter.31157

Cole, D. A., Maxwell, S. E., Martin, J. M., Peeke, L. G., Seroczynski, A. D., Tram, J. M., . . . Maschman, T. (2001). The development of multiple domains of child and adolescent self-concept: A cohort sequential longitudinal design. *Child Development, 72*, 1723–1746. doi:10.1111/1467-8624.00375

Cole, P. M., Bruschi, C. J., & Tamang, B. L. (2002). Cultural differences in children's emotional reactions to difficult situations. *Child Development, 73*, 983–996.

Cole, P. M., & Tamang, B. L. (1998). Nepali children's ideas about emotional displays in hypothetical challenges. *Developmental Psychology, 34*, 640–646.

Cole, P. M., Tamang, B., L., & Shrestha, S. (2006). Cultural variations in the socialization of young children's anger and shame. *Child Development, 77*, 1237–1251.

Coles, J., & Hall, C. (2002). Gendered readings: Learning from children's reading choices. *Journal of Research on Reading, 25*, 96–108.

Colledge, E., Bishop, D. V. M., Koeppen-Schomerus, G., Price, T. S., Happe, F., Eley, T., . . . Plomin, R. (2002). The structure of language abilities at 4 Years: A twin study. *Developmental Psychology, 38*, 749–757.

Colletti, L. (2009). Long-term follow-up of infants (4–11 months) fitted with cochlear implants. *Acta Otolaryngol, 129*(4), 361–366.

Collins, A. (2006). Cognitive apprenticeship. In R. K. Sawyer (Ed.), *The Cambridge handbook of the learning sciences* (pp. 47–77). New York, NY: Cambridge University Press.

Collins, W. A., Maccoby, E. E., Steinberg, L., Hetherington, E. M., & Bornstein, M. H. (2000). Contemporary research on parenting: The case for nature and nurture. *American Psychologist, 55*, 218–232.

Collins, W. A., & Russell, G. (1991). Mother-child and father-child relationships in middle childhood and adolescence: A developmental analysis. *Developmental Review, 11*(2), 99–136.

Collins, W. A., & Steinberg, L. (2006). Adolescent development in interpersonal context. In W. Damon & R. Lerner (Series Eds.) & N. Eisenberg (Vol. Ed.), *Handbook of child psychology: Vol. 3. Social, emotional, and personality development* (5th ed.). New York, NY: Wiley.

Commission on Teacher Credentialing. (2008). *Racial and ethnic distribution of teachers.* Retrieved from http://www.ctc.ca.gov/educator-prep/statistics/2008-01-stat.pdf

Committee on Assessment in Support of Learning. (2004). *Assessment in support of instruction and learning: Bridging the gap* between *large-scale and classroom assessment.* Washington. DC: The National Academies Press.

Committee on Increasing High School Students' Engagement and Motivation to Learn. (2004). *Engaging schools: Fostering high school students' motivation to learn.* Washington, DC: The National Academies Press.

Committee on Nutrition. (2001). The use and misuse of fruit juice in pediatrics. *Pediatrics, 107*, 1210–1213. doi:10.1542/peds.107.5.1210

Committee on Nutrition. (2003). Prevention of pediatric overweight and obesity. *Pediatrics, 112*, 424–430. doi:10.1542/peds.112.2.424

Committee on Sports Medicine and Fitness. (2000). Climatic heat stress and the exercising child and adolescent. *Pediatrics, 106*, 158–159. doi:10.1542/peds.106.1.158

Condon, R. G. (1988). *Inuit youth: Growth and change in the Canadian Arctic.* New Brunswick, NJ: Rutgers University Press.

Conklin, H. M., Salorio, C. F., & Slomine, B. S. (2008). Working memory performance following paediatric traumatic brain injury. *Brain Injury, 22*(11), 847–857.

Connell, R. W. (1996). Teaching the boys: New research on masculinity, and gender strategies for schools. *Teachers College Record, 98*, 206–235.

Connellan, J., Baron-Cohen, S., Wheelwright, S., Batki, A., & Ahluwalia, J. (2000). Sex differences in human neonatal social perception. *Infant Behavior and Development, 23*, 113–118.

Connolly, J., Furman, W., & Konarski, R. (2000). The role of peers in the emergence of heterosexual romantic relationships in adolescence. *Child Development, 71*(5), 1395–1408.

Connor, P. D., Sampson, P. D., Bookstein, F. L., Barr, H. M., & Streissguth, A. (2001). Direct and indirect effects of prenatal alcohol damage on executive function. *Developmental Neuropsychology, 18*, 331–333.

Constantine, N. A. (2008). Editorial: Converging evidence leaves policy behind: Sex education in the United States. *Journal of Adolescent Health, 42*, 324–326.

Cooper, R. P. (1997). An ecological approach to infants' perception of intonation contours as meaningful aspects of speech. In C. Dent-Read & P. Zukow-Goldring (Eds.), *Evolving explanations of development: Ecological approaches to organism-environment systems* (pp. 55–85). Washington, DC: American Psychological Association.

Coplan, R. J., Prakash, K., O'Neil, K., & Armer, M. (2004). Do you "want" to play? Distinguishing between conflicted shyness and social disinterest in early childhood. *Developmental Psychology, 40*, 244–258.

Copple, C., & Bredekamp, S. (Ed.). (2009). *Developmentally appropriate practice in early childhood programs serving children from birth through age 8* (3rd ed.). Washington, DC: National Association for the Education of Young Children.

Coren, S. (1993). The Lateral Preference Inventory for measurement of handedness, footedness, eyedness and earedness: Norms for young adults. *Bulletin of the Psychonomic Society, 31*, 1–3.

Coren, S. (1993). *The left-hander syndrome.* New York, NY: Vintage Books.

Cortes, R. A., & Farmer D. L. (2004). Recent advances in fetal surgery. *Seminars in Perinatology, 28*, 199–211.

Costello, B. J., & Dunaway, R. G. (2003). Egotism and delinquent behavior. *Journal of Interpersonal Violence, 18*(5), 572–590.

Cota-Robles, S., Neiss, M., & Rowe, D. C. (2002). The role of puberty in violent and nonviolent delinquency among Anglo American, Mexican American and African American boys. *Journal of Adolescent Research, 17*, 364–376.

Cothran, D., Kulinna, P., & Garrahy, D. (2003). "This is kind of giving a secret away . . .": Students' perspectives on effective classroom management. *Teaching and Teacher Education, 19*, 435–444.

Cothran, D. J., & Ennis, C. D. (2000). Building bridges to student engagement: Communicating respect and care for students in urban high school. *Journal of Research and Development in Education, 33*(2), 106–117.

Council on Sports Medicine and Fitness and Council on School Health. (2006). Active healthy living: Prevention of childhood obesity through increased physical activity. *Pediatrics, 117*, 1834-1842. Retrieved from http://www.pediatrics.org/cgi/doi/10.1542/peds.2006-0472

Cox, A. E., Smith, A. L., & Williams, L. (2008). Change in physical education motivation and physical activity behavior during middle schools. *Journal of Adolescent Health, 43*, 506–513.

Coyle, T. R., & Bjorklund, D. F. (1997). Age differences in, and consequences of, multiple-variable-strategy use on multitrial sort-recall task. *Developmental Psychology, 33*, 372–380.

Craft, A. (1994). Five and six year olds' views of friendship. *Educational Studies, 20*, 181–194.

Craig, W., & Harel, Y. (2004). Bullying, physical fighting and victimization. In C. Currie et al. (Eds.), *Young people's health in context: Health behaviour in school-aged children (HBSC) study: International report from the 2001/2002 survey* (pp. 133–144). Retrieved from http://www.euro.who.int/__data/assets/pdf_file/0008/110231/e82923.pdf

Craig, W. M., & Pepler, D. J. (1998). Observations of aggressive and non-aggressive children on the school playground. *Merrill-Palmer Quarterly, 44*, 55–76.

Craig, W. M., & Pepler, D. J. (2003). Identifying and targeting risk for involvement in bullying and victimization. *Canadian Journal of Psychiatry, 48*, 577–582.

Craig, W. M., Peters, R. D., & Konarski, R. (1998, October). *Bullying and victimization among Canadian School Children.* Hull, QC: Applied Research Branch of Strategic Policy, Human Resources and Development Canada.

Craik, F. I. M., & Lockhart, R. S. (1972). Levels of processing: A framework for memory research. *Journal of Verbal Learning and Verbal Behavior, 11*, 671–684.

Cratty, J. B. (1986). Acquiring skill: Development perspectives. In J. B. Cratty (Ed.), *Perceptual and motor development in infants and children* (pp. 146–157). Englewood Cliffs, NJ: Prentice Hall.

Crick, N. R., & Grotpeter, J. K. (1995). Relational aggression, gender, and social-psychological adjustment. *Child Development, 66*, 710–722.

Crick, N. R., Grotpeter, J. K., & Bigbee, M. A. (2002). Relationally and physically aggressive children's intent attributions and feelings of distress for relational and instrumental peer provocations. *Child Development*, 73, 1134–1142.

Crick, N. R., Nelson, D. A., Morales, J. R., Cullerton-Sen, C., Casas, J. F., & Hickman, S. E. (2001). Relational victimization in childhood and adolescence. In J. Juvonen & S. Graham (Eds.), *Peer harassment in school: The plight of the vulnerable and victimized* (pp. 196–214). New York, NY: Guilford.

Crick, N. R., & Zahn-Waxler, C. (2003). The development of psychopathology in females and males: Current progress and future challenges. *Development and psychopathology, 15*, 719–742.

Crocker, P. R., & Ellsworth, J. P. (1990). Perceptions of competence in physical education students. *Canadian Journal of Sport Sciences, 15*(4), 262–266.

Croll, J. (2005). Body image and adolescents. In J. Stang & M. Story (Eds.), *Guidelines for adolescent nutrition services* (pp. 155–166). Minneapolis, MN: Center for Leadership, Education and Training in Maternal and Child Nutrition, Division of Epidemiology and Community Health, School of Public Health, University of Minnesota. Retrieved from http://www.epi.umn.edu/let/pubs/img/adol_ch13.pdf

Crosnoe, R., Cavanagh, S., & Elder, G. H., Jr. (2003). Adolescent friendships as academic resource: The intersection of friendship, race, and school disadvantage. *Sociological Perspectives, 46*(3), 331–352.

Cross, W. E., Jr. (1971). Toward a psychology of Black liberation: The Negro-to-Black convergence experience. *Black World, 20*(9), 13–27.

Cross, W. E., Jr. (1987). A two-factor theory of Black identity: Implications for the study of identity development in minority children. In J. S. Phinney & M. J. Rotherham (Eds.), *Children's ethnic socialization: Pluralism and development* (pp. 117–133). Newbury Park, CA: Sage.

Cross, W. E., Jr. (1995). The psychology of Nigrecence. In J. G. Ponterotto, J. M. Casas, L. A. Suzuki, & C. M. Alexander (Eds.), *Handbook of multicultural counseling* (pp. 93–122). Thousand Oaks, CA: Sage.

Crouter, A. C., & Head, M. R. (2002). Parental monitoring and knowledge of children. In M. H. Bornstein (Ed.), *Handbook of parenting: Being and becoming a parent* (Vol. 3, pp. 461–483). Mahwah, NJ: Erlbaum.

Crouter, A. C., Manke, B. A., & McHale, S. M. (1995). The family context of gender intensification in early adolescence. *Child Development, 66*, 317–329.

Csikszentmihalyi, M., & Larson, R. (1984). *Being adolescent: Conflict and growth in the teenage years.* New York, NY: Basic Books.

Cuadra, E., & Moreno, J. M. (2005). *Expanding opportunities and building competencies for young people: A new agenda for secondary education.* New York, NY: World Bank.

Cumming, S. P., Standage, M., Gillison, F., & Malina, R. M. (2008). Sex differences in exercise behavior during adolescence: Is biological maturation a confounding factor? *Journal of Adolescent Health, 42*, 480–485.

Cummins, J. (1994). The acquisition of English as a second language. In K. Spangenberg-Urbschat & R. Prichard (Eds.), *Kids come in all languages: Reading instruction for ESL students.* Newark, DE: International Reading Association.

Dahl, R. E. (2004). Adolescent development and the regulation of behavior and emotion. *New York Academy of Sciences, 1021*, 294–295.

Daley, T. C., Whaley, S. E., Sigman, M. D., Espinosa, M. P., & Neumann, C. (2003). IQ on the rise: The Flynn Effect in rural Kenyan children. *Psychological Science, 14*(3), 215–219.

Dalman, C. (2009). Advanced paternal age and increased risk of bipolar disorder in offspring. *Evidence Based Mental Health, 12*(59). doi:10.1136/ebmh.12.2.59

Daly, B. P., Kral, M. C., & Brown, R. T. (2008). Cognitive and academic problems associated with childhood cancers and sickle cell disease. *School Psychology Quarterly, 23*, 230–242. doi:10.1037/1045 3830.23.2.230

D'Amico, A., & Guarnera, M. (2005). Exploring working memory in children with low arithmetical achievement. *Learning and Individual Differences, 15*, 294–321.

Damon, W. (1977). *The social world of the child.* San Francisco, CA: Jossey-Bass.

Damon, W. (1988). *The moral child.* New York, NY: Free Press.

Damon, W. (1994). Fair distribution and sharing: The development of positive justice. In B. Puka (Ed.), *Fundamental research in moral development. Moral development: A compendium* (Vol. 2, pp. 189–254). New York, NY: Garland Publishing.

Damon, W. (1995). *Greater expectations: Overcoming the culture of indulgence in America's homes and schools.* New York, NY: Free Press.

Damon, W. (2006). Preface to Handbook of child psychology, 6th edition. In W. Damon & R. M. Lerner (Eds.), *Handbook of child psychology* (6th ed., Vol. 1, pp. ix–xvi). New York, NY: Wiley.

Damon, W., & Hart, D. (1988). *Self-understanding in childhood and adolescence.* New York, NY: Cambridge University Press.

Darling-Hammond, L. (2000). Teacher quality and student achievement: A review of state policy evidence. *Educational Policy Analysis Archives, 8*, 1–458. Retrieved from http://epaa.asu.edu/epaa/v2008n2001/.

Darling-Hammond, L., & Youngs, P. (2002). Defining "Highly Qualified Teachers": What does "Scientifically-Based Research" actually tell us? *Educational Researcher*, 13–25.

Darnovsky, M. (2003). Sex selection moves to consumer culture–ads for "family balancing" in *The New York Times. Genetic Crossroads, 33*, 1.

Darwin, C. (1877). A biographical sketch of an infant. *Mind, 2*, 285–294.

Das, J. P. (1995). Some thoughts on two aspects of Vygotsky's work. *Educational Psychologist, 30*, 93–97.

D'Augelli, A. R. (2003). Coming out in community psychology: Personal narrative and disciplinary change. *American Journal of Community Psychology, 41*(3–4), 343–354.

D'Augelli, A. R., Pilkington, N. W., & Hershberger, S. L. (2002). Incidence and mental health impact of sexual orientation victimization of lesbian, gay, and bisexual youths in high school. *School Psychology Quarterly, 17*(2), 148–167.

Davies, D. (2004). *Child development: A practitioner's guide* (2nd ed.). New York, NY: Guilford.

Davis, H. A. (2001). The quality and impact of relationships between elementary school children and teachers. *Contemporary Educational Psychology, 26*, 431–453.

Davis, H. A. (2003). Conceptualizing the role and influence of student-teacher relationships on children's social and cognitive development. *Educational Psychologist, 38*, 207–234.

Davis-Kean, P. (2005). The influence of parent education and family income on child achievement: The indirect role of parental expectations and the home environment. *Journal of Family Psychology, 19*, 294–304.

Dawson, D. A. (1991). Family structure and children's mental health and well-being. *Journal of Marriage and the Family, 60*, 79–94.

DeAngelis, T. (2008). A fresh look at race and ethnicity. *Monitor on Psychology, 39*(9), 30.

Dearing, E., Wimer, C., Simpkins, S. D., Lund, T., Bouffard, S. M., Caronongan, P., Kreider, H., & Weiss, H. (2009). Do neighborhood and home contexts help explain why low-income children miss opportunities to participate in activities outside of school? *Developmental Psychology, 45*, 1545–1562.

DeCasper, A., & Fifer, W. P. (1980). On human bonding: Newborns prefer their mothers' voices. *Science, 208*, 1174–1176.

DeCasper, A., & Spence, M. J. (1986). Prenatal maternal speech influences newborns' perception of speech sounds. *Infant Behavior and Development, 9*, 133–150.

Deci, E., & Ryan, R. (1985). *Intrinsic motivation and self-determination in human behavior.* New York, NY: Plenum.

Deci, E. L., & Ryan, R. M. (Eds.). (2002). *Handbook of self-determination research.* Rochester, NY: University of Rochester Press.

Deci, E. L., Vallerand, R. J., Pelletier, L. G., & Ryan, R. M. (1991). Motivation and education: The self-determination perspective. *The Educational Psychologist, 26*, 323–346.

Deforche, B. I., Bourdeaudhuij, I. M. D., & Tanghe, A. P. (2006). Attitude toward physical activity in normal-weight, overweight and obese adolescents. *Journal of Adolescent Health, 38*, 560–568.

Dehaene-Lambertz, G., Dehaene, S., & Hertz-Pannier, L. (2002). Functional neuroimaging of speech perception in infants. *Science, 6*(5600), 2013–2015.

DeHann, L. (1997). *Bullies.* Retrieved from http://www.ext.nodak.edu.extpubs/yf/famsci/fs570w.htm

Delgado, A. R., & Prieto, G. (2008). Stereotype threat as validity threat: The anxiety–sex–threat interaction. *Intelligence, 36*, 635–640.

De Lisi, R., & Gallagher, A. M. (1991). Understanding of gender stability and constancy in Argentinean children. *Merrill Palmer Quarterly, 37*, 483–502.

DeLoache, J. S., Uttal, D. H., Rosengren, K. S. (2004). Scale errors offer evidence for a perception-action dissociation early in life. *Science, 14* (304, no. 5673), 1027–1029.

Delpit, L. (1995). *Other people's children: Cultural conflict in the classroom.* New York, NY: New York Press.

Delpit, L. (2003). Educators as "Seed People": Growing a new future. *Educational Researcher, 7*(32), 14–21.

Demetriou, A., Christou, C., Spanoudis, G., & Platsidou, M. (2002). The development of mental processing: Efficiency, working memory and thinking. *Monographs of the Society for Research in Child Development, 67*(1).

De Michele, A. M., & Ruth, R. A. (2010). Newborn hearing screening. Retrieved from http://emedicine.medscape.com/article/836646-overview

Demon, W. (2004). What is positive youth development? *The Annals of the American Academy of Political and Social Science, 591*(1), 13–24.

Demuth, K. (1990). Subject, topic, and Sesotho passive. *Journal of Child Language, 17*, 67–84.

Denham, S., & Kochanoff, A. T. (2002). Parental contributions to preschoolers' understanding of emotion. *Marriage & Family Review, 34*, 311–343.

Denham, S. A., Blair, K., Schmidt, M., & DeMulder, E. (2002). Compromised emotional competence: Seeds of violence sown early? *American Journal of Orthopsychiatry, 72*, 70–82.

Dennis, T. A., Cole, P. M., Zahn-Waxler, C., & Mizuta, I. (2002). Self in context: Autonomy and relatedness in Japanese and U.S. mother-preschooler dyads. *Child Development, 73*, 1803–1817.

Derry, S. J. (1989). Putting learning strategies to work. *Educational Leadership, 47*(5), 4–10.

DeSouza, A., & Chen, X. (2002, July). *Social initiative and responses of shy and non-shy children in China and Canada.* Paper presented at the Biennial Conference of the international Society for the Study of Behavioral Development (ISSBD), Ottawa, Canada.

de Waal, F. B. (2007/2008). Do animals feel empathy? *Scientific American Mind, 18*, 28–35.

de Waal, F. B. M., & Johanowicz, D. L. (1993). Modification of reconciliation behavior through social experience: An experiment with two macaque species. *Child Development, 64*, 897–908. doi:10.1111/j.1467-8624.1993.tb02950.x

Dewan, S. (2010, January 10). Southern schools mark two minorities. *The New York Times*, p. A19+.

Deynoot-Schaub, M. G., & Riksen-Walraven, M. (2006). Peer interaction in child care centres at 15 and 23 months: Stability and links with children's socio-emotional adjustment. *Infant Behavior and Development, 29*(2), 276–288.

Diamond, A. (2000). Close interrelation of motor development and cognitive development and of the cerebellum and prefrontal cortex. *Child Development, 71*(1), 44–56.

Diamond, A. (2009). The interplay of biology and the environment broadly defined. *Developmental Psychology, 45*, 1–8.

Diamond, A., & Kirkham, N. Z. (2005). Not quite as grown-up as we like to think: Parallels between cognition in childhood and adulthood. *Psychological Science, 16*, 291–297.

Diamond, L. M., & Savin-Williams, R. C. (2003). The intimate relationships of sexual-minority youths. In G. R. Adams & M. D. Berzonsky (Eds.), *The Blackwell handbook of adolescence* (pp. 393–412). Oxford, UK: Blackwell.

Diamond, M., & Sigmundson, H. K. (1997). Sex reassignment at birth: Long-term review and clinical implications. *Archives of Pediatric and Adolescent Medicine, 151*, 298–304.

Diaz-Rico, L. T., & Weed, K. Z. (2002). *The crosscultural, language, and academic development handbook* (2nd ed.). Boston, MA: Allyn & Bacon.

Dickinson, D., McCabe, A., Anastopoulos, L., Peisner-Feinberg, E., & Poe, M. (2003). The comprehensive language approach to early literacy: The interrelationships among vocabulary, phonological sensitivity, and print knowledge among preschool-aged children. *Journal of Educational Psychology, 95*, 465–481.

Dick-Read, G. (1972). *Childbirth without fear: The original approach to natural childbirth.* New York, NY: Harper & Row. (Original work published 1933).

Diego, M., Field, T., & Hernandez-Reif, M. (2005). Vagal activity, gastric motility, and weight gain in massaged preterm neonates. *Journal of Pediatrics, 147*(1), 50–55.

Dieter, J. N. I., Field, T., Hernandez-Reif, M., Emory, E. K., & Redzepi, M. (2003). Stable preterm infants gain more weight and sleep less after five days of massage therapy. *Journal of Pediatric Psychology, 28*, 403–411.

DiPaula, A., & Campbell, J. D. (2002). Self-esteem and persistence in the face of failure. *Journal of Personality and Social Psychology, 83*, 711–724.

Dirix, C. E. H., Nijhuis, J. G., Jongsma, H. W., & Hornstra, G. (2009). Aspects of fetal learning and memory. *Child Development, 80*(4), 1251–1258.

Dishion, T. J., McCord, J., & Poulin, F. (1999). When interventions harms: Peer groups and problem behavior. *American Psychologist, 54*(9), 755–764.

Dishion, T. J., & Patterson, G. R. (2006). The development and ecology of antisocial behavior. In D. Cicchetti & D. J. Cohen (Eds.), *Developmental psychopathology. Vol. 3: Risk, disorder, and adaptation* (pp. 503–541). New York, NY: Wiley.

Dnsari, D. (2005). Paving the way toward meaningful interactions between neuroscience and education. *Developmental Science, 8*, 466–467.

Dodge, K. A., Coie, J. D., & Lynam, D. (2006). Aggression and antisocial behavior in youth. In W. Damon & R. M. Lerner (Series Ed.) and N. Eisenberg (Vol. Ed.), *Handbook of child psychology. Vol. 3: Social, emotional, and personality development* (6th ed., pp. 719–788). New York, NY: Wiley.

Dodge, K. A., McLoyd, V. C., & Lansford, J. E. (2005). The cultural context of physically disciplining children. In V. C. McLoyd, N. E. Hill, & K. A. Dodge (Eds.), *African American family life: Ecological and cultural diversity.* New York, NY: Guilford.

Dodge, K. A., & Pettit, G. S. (2003). A biopsychosocial model of the development of chronic conduct problems in adolescence. *Developmental Psychology, 39*, 180–190.

Doggett, A. M. (2004). ADHD and drug therapy: Is it still a valid treatment? *Child Health Care, 8*, 69–81.

Domenech Rodgriguez, M. M., Donovick, M. R., & Crowley, S. L. (2009). Parenting styles in a cultural context: Observations of protective parenting in first-generation Latinos. *Family Process, 48*(2), 195–210.

Dominé, F., Berchtold, A., Akré, C., Michaud, P-A., & Suris, J-C. (2009). Disordered eating behaviors: What about boys? *Journal of Adolescent Health, 44*, 111–117.

Donnerstein, E., Slaby, R. G., & Eron, L. D. (1994). The mass media and youth aggression. In L. D. Eron, J. H. Gentry, & P. Schlegel (Eds.), *Reason to hope: A psychosocial perspective on violence and youth* (pp. 219–250). Washington, DC: American Psychological Association.

Donnez, J., Martinez-Madrid, B., Jadoul, P., Langendonckt, A. V., Demylle, D., & Dolmans, M. (2006). Ovarian tissue cryopreservation and transplantation: A review. (2006). *Human Reproduction Update, 12*(5), 519–535.

Dornbusch, S. M., Erickson, K. G., Laird, J., & Wong, C. A. (2001). The relation of family and school attachment to adolescent deviance in diverse groups and communities. *Journal of Adolescent Research, 16*(4), 396–422.

Doyle, A. B., Brendgen, M., Markiewicz, D., & Kamkar, K. (2003). Family relationships as moderators of the association between romantic relationships and adjustment in early adolescence. *The Journal of Early Adolescence, 23*(3), 316–340.

Drexler, P. (2005). *Raising boys without men: How maverick moms are creating the next generation of exceptional men.* Emmaus, PA: Rodale Press.

Driscoll, M. P. (2005). *Psychology of learning for instruction* (3rd ed.). Boston, MA: Allyn & Bacon.

DuBois, D. L., Holloway, B. E., Valentine, J. C., & Cooper, H. Effectiveness of mentoring programs for youth: A meta-analytic review. *American Journal of Community Psychology, 30*, 157–197.

DuBois, D. L., & Silverthorn, N. (2005). Natural mentoring relationships and adolescent health: Evidence from a national study. *American Journal of Public Health, 95*, 518–524.

Dubois L., Girard M., & Kent M. (2006). Breakfast eating and overweight in a pre-school population: Is there a link? *Public Health Nutrition, 9*, 436–442.

Ducharme, J., Doyle, A. B., & Markiewicz, D. (2002). Attachment security with mother and father: Associations with adolescents' reports of interpersonal behavior with parents and peers. *Journal of Social and Personal Relationships, 19*(2), 203–231.

Duffy, J., Warren, K., & Walsh, M. (2002). Classroom interactions: Gender of teacher, gender of student, and classroom subject. *Sex Roles, 45*, 579–593.

Duncan, G. J., & Brooks-Gunn, J. (2000). Family poverty, welfare reform, and child development. *Child Development, 71*, 188–196.

Duncan, R. M., & Cheyne, J. A. (1999). Incidence and functions of self-reported private speech in young adults: A self-verbalization questionnaire. *Canadian Journal of Behavioural Sciences, 31*, 133–136.

Dunifon, R., & Kowaleski-Jones, L. (2002). Who is in the house? Race differences in cohabitation, single parenthood, and child development. *Child Development, 73*, 1249–1264.

Dunn, J., & Cutting, A. L. (1999). Understanding others, and individual differences in friendship interactions in young children. *Social Development, 8*, 201–219.

Dunn, J., Cutting, A. L., & Fisher, N. (2002). Old friends, new friends: Predictors of children's perspective on their friends at school. *Child Development, 73*, 621–635.

Durbin, D. L., Darling, N., Steinberg, L., & Brown, B. B. (1993). Parenting style and peer group membership among European-American adolescents. *Journal of Research on Adolescence, 3*, 87–100.

Durik, A. M., Vida, M., & Eccles, J. S. (2006). Task values and ability beliefs as predictors of high school literacy choices: A developmental analysis. *Journal of Educational Psychology, 98*(2), 382–393.

Dusenbury, L., & Falco, M. (1995). Eleven components of effective drug abuse prevention curricula. *Journal of School Health, 65*, 420–425.

Dwairy, M., Achoui, M., Abouserie, R., & Farah, A. (2006). Parenting styles, individuation, and mental health of Arab adolescents. *Journal of Cross-Cultural Psychology, 37*, 262–272. doi:10.1177/0022022106286924

Dweck, C. S. (2000). *Self-theories: Their role in motivation, personality, and development.* Philadelphia: Routledge Press.

Dweck, C. S. (2002). The development of ability conceptions. In A. Wigfield & J. Eccles (Eds.), *The development of achievement motivation.* San Diego, CA: Academic Press.

Dweck, C. S. (2006). *Mindset: The new psychology of success.* New York, NY: Random House.

Dykens, E. M., Rosner, B. A., & Butterbaugh, G. (1998). Exercise and sports in children and adolescents with developmental disabilities. Positive physical and psychosocial effects. *Child and Adolescent Psychiatric Clinics of North America, 7*(4), 757–771.

Eaton, W. O., & Enns, L. R. (1986). Sex differences in human motor activity level. *Psychological Bulletin, 100*, 19–28.

Eccles, J. S. (1999, June 18). *Making school transitions a positive experience: The middle graders school transition.* Retrieved from http://www.apa.org/ppo/issues/peccles.html

Eccles, J. S. (2004). Schools, academic motivation, and stage-environment fit. In R. M. Lerner & L. Steinberg (Eds.), *Handbook of adolescent psychology* (2nd ed., pp. 125–153). Hoboken, NJ: Wiley.

Eccles, J. S. (2007). Where are all the women? Gender differences in participation in physical science and engineering. In S. J. Ceci & W. M. Williams (Eds.), *Why aren't more women in science? Top researchers debate the evidence.* Washington, DC: American Psychological Association.

Eccles, J. S., Barber, B. L., Stone, M., & Hunt, J. (2003). Extracurricular activities and adolescent development. *Journal of Social Issues, 59*(4), 865–889.

Eccles, J. S., & Midgley, C. (1989). Stage/environment fit: Developmentally appropriate classrooms for early adolescents. In R. Ames & C. Ames (Eds.), *Research on motivation in education* (Vol. 3, pp. 138–181). New York, NY: Academic Press.

Eccles, J. S., Midgley, C., & Adler, T. F. (1984). Grade-related changes in school environment: Effects on achievement motivation. In J. G. Nicholls (Ed.), *Advances in motivation and achievement* (pp. 283–331). Greenwich, CT: JAI Press.

Eccles, J. S. & Roeser, R. W. (2003). Schools as developmental contexts. In G. Adams & M. D. Berzonsky (Eds.), *Blackwell handbook of adolescence* (pp. 129–148). Malden, MA: Blackwell Publishing.

Eccles, J. S., & Roeser, R. W. (2006). Schools as developmental contexts. In G. A. M. D. Berzonsky (Ed.), *Blackwell handbook of adolescence* (pp. 129–148). Malden, MA: Blackwell Publishing.

Eckerman, C., & Whitehead, H. (1999). How toddler peers generate coordinated action: A cross-cultural exploration. *Early Education & Development, 10*(3) 241–266.

Eckerman, C. O., & Didow, S. M. (1996). Nonverbal imitation and toddlers' mastery of verbal means of achieving coordinated action. *Developmental Psychology, 32*, 141–152.

ECS. (2010). *No Child Left Behind: NCLB reauthorization database.* Retrieved from http://www.ecs.org/ecsmain.asp?page=/html/educationIssues/NCLBreauthorization/NCLB_parapro_DB_intro.asp

Eder, R. A. (1989). The emergent personologist: The structure and content of 3 ½, 5 ½, and 7 ½ year-olds' concepts of themselves and other persons. *Child Development, 60*, 1218–1228.

Education Commission of the States. (2006). *Quick facts: What research shows about the brain.* Retrieved from http://ecs.org/html/IssueSection.asp?issueid=17&s=Quick+Facts

Edwards, M. E. (2002). Attachment, mastery, and interdependence: A model of parenting processes. *Family Process, 41*(3), 389–404.

Edwards, P. A. (2002). Three approaches from Europe: Waldorf, Montessori, and Reggio Emilia. *Early Childhood Practice and Research, 4*, 36–40.

Egan, S. K., Monson, T. C., & Perry, D. G. (1998). Social-cognitive influences on change in aggression over time. *Developmental Psychology, 34*, 996–1006.

Eiden, D. (2009). Infants exposed to cocaine in utero react more emotionally to stress. *DATA: The Brown University Digest of Addiction Theory & Application, 28*(3), 8.

Eiden, R. D., Foote, A., & Schuetze, P. (2007). Maternal cocaine use and caregiving status: Group differences in caregiver and infant risk variables. *Addictive Behaviors, 32*, 465–476.

Eimas, P. D., Sigueland, E. R., Jusczyk, P., & Vigorito, J. (1971). Speech perception in infants. *Science, 171*, 303–306.

Einarson, A., Selby, P., & Koren, G. (2001). Abrupt discontinuation of psychotropic drugs during pregnancy: Fear of teratogenic risk and impact of counselling. *Journal of Psychiatric Neuroscience, 26*(1), 44–48.

Eisenberg, N. (2003). Prosocial behaviour, empathy, and sympathy. In M. H. Bornstein, L. Davidson, C. L. M. Keyes, & K. A. Moore (Eds.), *Well-being: Positive development across the life course* (pp. 253–267). Mahwah, NJ: Erlbaum.

Eisenberg, N., & Fabes, R. A. (1998). Prosocial development. In W. Damon & N. Eisenberg (Eds.), *Handbook of child psychology: Vol. 3. Social, emotional, and personality development* (pp. 701–778). New York, NY: Wiley.

Eisenberg, N., Fabes, R. A., Shepard, S. A., Gurthrie, I., Murphy, B. C., & Reiser, M. (1999). Parental reactions to children's negative emotions: Longitudinal relations to quality of children's social functioning. *Child Development, 70*, 513–534.

Eisenberg, N., Fabes, R. A., & Spinrad, T. L. (2006). Prosocial development. In N. Eisenberg (Ed.), *Handbook of child psychology, Vol. 3. Social, emotional, and personality development* (pp. 646–718), New York, NY: Wiley.

Eisenberg, N., Gershoff, E. T., Fabes, R. A., Shepard, S. A., Cumberland, A. J., Losoya, S. H., . . . Murphy, B. C. (2001). Mothers' emotional expressivity and children's behavior problems and social competence: Mediation through children's regulation. *Developmental Psychology, 37*, 475–490.

Eisenberg, N., Liew, J., & Pidada, S. (2001). The relations of parental emotional expressivity with the quality of Indonesian children's social functioning. *Emotion, 1*, 107–115.

Eisenberg, N., Martin, C., & Fabes, R. A. (1996). Gender-related development and gender differences. In D. C. Berliner & R. C. Calfee (Eds.), *The handbook of educational psychology.* New York, NY: Macmillan.

Eisenberg, N., & McNally, S. (1993). Socialization and mothers' and adolescents' empathy-related characteristics. *Journal of Research on Adolescence, 3*, 171–191.

Eisenberg, N., Michalik, N., Spinrad, T. L., Hofer, C., Kupfer, A., Valiente, C., . . . Reiser, M. (2007). The relations of effortful control and impulsivity to children's sympathy: A longitudinal study. *Cognitive Development, 22*(4), 544–567. doi:10.1016/j.cogdev.2007.08.003

Eisenberg, N., & Morris, A. S. (2004). Moral cognitions and prosocial responding in adolescence. In R. Lerner & L. Steinberg (Eds.), *Handbook of adolescent psychology.* New York, NY: Wiley.

Eisenberg, N., & Spinrad, T. L. (2004). Emotion-related regulation: Sharpening the definition. *Child Development, 75*, 334–339.

Eisenberg, N., Spinrad, T. L., Fabes, R. A., Reiser, M., Cumberland, A., Shepard, S. A., Valiente, C., . . . Murphy, B. (2004). The relations of effortful control and impulsivity to children's resiliency and adjustment. *Child Development* (75), 25–46.

Eisenberg, N., & Zhou, Q. (2000). Regulation from a developmental perspective. *Psychological Inquiry, 11*, 166–171.

Eisenberg, N., Zhou, Q., & Koller, S. (2001). Brazilian adolescents' prosocial moral judgment and behavior: Relations to sympathy, perspective taking, gender-role orientation, and demographic characteristics. *Child Development, 72*, 518–534.

El-Sheikh, M., & Harger, J. (2001). Appraisals of marital conflict and children's adjustment, health, and physiological reactivity. *Developmental Psychology, 37*, 875–885.

Elkind, D. (1967). Egocentrism in adolescence, *Child Development, 38*, 1025–1034.

Elkind, D. (1985). Egocentrism redux. *Developmental Review, 5*, 127–134.

Elkind, D. (2001). *The hurried child* (3rd ed.). Reading, MA: Addison-Wesley.

Elkind, D. (2007). *The power of play: How spontaneous imaginative activities lead to happier, healthier children.* Cambridge, MA: Da Capo Press.

Elliot, A. J., & Thrash, T. M. (2004). The intergenerational transmission of fear of failure. *Personality & Social Psychology Bulletin, 30*, 957–971.

Elliot, J. G. (1999). School refusal: Issues of conceptualization, assessment, and treatment. *Journal of Child Psychology and Psychiatry and Allied Disciplines, 40*, 1001–1012.

Ellis, B. J. (2004). Timing of pubertal maturation in girls: An integrated life history approach. *Psychological Bulletin, 130*, 920–958.

Ely, R. (1997). Language and literacy in the school years. In J. B. Gleason (Ed.), *The development of language* (pp. 398–439). Boston, MA: Allyn & Bacon.

Ely, R., & McCabe, A. (1994). The language play of kindergarten children. *First Language, 14*, 19–35.

Emde, R. N. (1988). The effect of relationships on relationships: A developmental approach to clinical intervention. In R. Hinde & J. Stevenson-Hinde (Eds.), *Relationships within families: Mutual influences* (pp. 354–364). Oxford, England: Clarendon Press.

Emde, R. N. (1998). Early emotional development: New modes of thinking for research and intervention. *Pediatrics, 102*, 1236–1243. Retrieved from http://www.pediatrics.org/cgi/content/full/102/5/SEI/1236

Emde, R. N., & Clyman, R. B. (1997). "We hold these truths to be self-evident": The origins of moral motives in individual activity and shared experience. In J. D. Noshpitz (Series Ed.) & S. Greenspan, S. Wieder, & J. Osofsky (Vol. Eds.), *Handbook of child and adolescent psychiatry: Vol. I. Infants and preschoolers: Development and syndromes* (pp. 320–339). New York, NY: Wiley.

Emde, R. N., & Robinson, J. (2000). Guiding principles for a theory of early intervention: A developmental-psychoanalytic perspective. In J. Shonkoff & S. Meisels (Eds.), *Handbook of early childhood intervention.* Cambridge, England: Cambridge University Press.

Emerson, J., & Lovitt, T. (2003). The educational plight of foster children in schools and what can be done about it. *Remedial and Special Education, 24*, 199–203.

Emerson, M. J., & Miyake, A. (2003). The role of inner speech in task switching: A dual-task investigation. *Journal of Memory and Language, 48*, 148–168.

Emery, R. E. (1999). *Marriage, divorce, and children's adjustment* (2nd ed.). Thousand Oaks, CA: Sage.

Engel, P. (1991). Tracking progress toward the school readiness goal. *Educational Leadership, 48*(5), 39–42.

Engle, R. W., Tuholski, S. W., Laughlin, J. E., & Conway, A. R. A. (1999). Working memory, short-term memory, and general fluid intelligence: A latent-variable approach. *Journal of Experimental Psychology: General, 128*, 309–331.

Engles, K. L., Bown, J. D., & Kenneavy, K. (2006). The mass media are an important context for adolescents' sexual behavior. *Journal of Adolescent Health, 38*(3), 186–192.

Entenman, J., Murnen, T. J., & Hendricks, C. (2005). Victims, bullies, and bystanders in K–3 literature. *The Reading Teacher, 59*, 352–364.

Entwisle, D. R., & Alexander, K. L. (1998). Facilitating the transition to first grade: The nature of transition and research on factors affecting it. *The Elementary School Journal, 98*, 351–364.

Entwisle, D. R., Alexander, K. L., & Olson, L. (1997). *Children, schools, and inequality.* Boulder, CO: Westview Press.

Epps, S. R., & Huston, A. C. (2007). Effects of a poverty intervention policy demonstration on parenting and child behavior: A test of the direction of effects. *Social Science Quarterly, 88*, 344–365.

Epstein, A. S., Schweinhart, L. J., & McAdoo, L. (1996). *Models of early childhood education.* Ypsilanti, MI: High/Scope Press.

Erikson, E. H. (1950). *Childhood and society.* New York, NY: Norton.

Erikson, E. H. (1963). *Childhood and society* (2nd ed.). New York, NY: Norton.

Erikson, E. H. (1968). *Identity, youth, and crisis* (2nd ed.). New York, NY: Norton.

Erikson, E. H. (1980). *Identity and the life cycle* (2nd ed.). New York, NY: Norton.

Ernst, M., Moolchan, E. T., & Robinson, M. L. (2001). Behavioral and neural consequences of prenatal exposure to nicotine. *Journal of the American Academy of Child & Adolescent Psychiatry, 40*(6), 630–641.

Eron, L. D. (1987). The development of aggressive behavior from the perspective of a developing behaviorism. *American Psychologist, 42*, 435–442.

Essex, M. J., Klein, M. H., Cho, E., & Kalin, N. H. (2002). Maternal stress beginning in infancy may sensitize children to later stress exposure: Effects on cortisol and behavior. *Biological Psychiatry, 52*(8), 776–784.

Evans, G. W. (2004). The environment of childhood poverty. *American Psychologist, 569*(77–92).

Evans, J. St. B. T. (2008). Dual-process accounts of reasoning, judgment, and social cognition. *Annual Review of Psychology, 59*, 255–278.

Evans, L., & Davies, K. (2000). No sissy boys here: A content analysis of the representation of masculinity in elementary school reading texts. *Sex Roles, 42*, 255–270.

Eveleth, P. B., & Tanner, J. M. (1990). *Worldwide variation in human growth.* Cambridge, England: Cambridge University Press.

Fabes, R. A., Eisenberg, N., Jones, S., Smith, M., Guthrie, I., Poulin, R., . . . Friedman, J. (1999). Regulation, emotionality, and preschoolers' socially competent peer interactions. *Child Development, 70*, 432–442.

Fabes, R. A., Hanish, L. D., & Martin, C. L. (2003). Children at play: The role of peers in understanding the effects of child care. *Child Development, 74*, 1039–1043. doi:10.1111/1467-8624.00586

Fabes, R. A., Leonard, S. A., Kupanoff, K., & Martin, C. L. (2001). Parental coping with children's negative emotions: Relations with children's emotional and social responding. *Child Development, 72*, 902–920.

Fabes, R. A., Martin, C. L., & Hanish, L. D. (2004). The next 50 years: Considering gender as a context for understanding young children's peer relationships. *Merrill-Palmer Quarterly, 50*, 260–273.

Fabiano, C. A., Pelham, W. E., Coles, E. K., Gnagy, E. M., Chronis-Tuscano, A., & O'Connor, B. C. (2009). A meta-analysis of behavioral treatments for attention deficit/hyperactivity disorder. *Clinical Psychology Review, 29*, 129–140.

Fagan, J. (2000). African American and Puerto Rican American parenting styles, parental involvement, and Head Start children's social competence. *Merrill-Palmer Quarterly, 46*, 592–612.

Fagot, B. I., & Leinbach, M. D. (1989). The young child's gender schema: Environmental input, internal organization. *Child Development, 60*, 663–672.

Falbo, T., & Polit, D. E. (1986). A quantitative review of the only child literature: Research evidence and theory development. *Psychological Bulletin, 100*, 176–189.

Falbo, T., Poston, D. L., Jr., Triscari, R. S., & Zhang, X. (1997). Self-enhancing illusions among Chinese schoolchildren. *Journal of Cross-Cultural Psychology, 28*, 172–191.

Fallone, G., Owens, J. A., & Deane, J. (2002). Sleepiness in children and adolescents: Clinical implications. *Sleep Medicine Reviews, 6*, 287–306.

Fang, G., Fang, F., Keller, M., Edelstein, W., Kehle, T. J., & Bray, M. A. (2003). Social and moral reasoning in Chinese children: A developmental study. *Psychology in the Schools, 40*, 125–138.

Farver, J. A. (2007, April). *Family environments and Latino preschoolers' emergent literacy skills.* Paper presented at the Society for Research in Child Development, Boston, Massachusetts.

Farver, J. A., Lonigan, C. J., & Eppe, S. (2009). Effective early literacy skill development for young Spanish-speaking English language learners: an experimental study of two methods. *Child Development, 80*, 703–719.

Fay, T. B., Yeates, K. O., Wade, S. L., Drotar, D., Stancin, T., & Taylor, H. G. (2009). Predicting longitudinal patterns of functional deficits in children with traumatic brain injury. *Neuropsychology, 23*, 271–282.

Fazzi, E., Lanners, J., Ferrari-Ginevra, O., Achille, C., Luparia, A., Signorini, S., & Lanzi, G. (2002). Gross motor development and reach on sound as critical tools for the development of the blind child. *Brain Development, 24*, 269–275.

Ferber, R. (2006). *Solve your child's sleep problems.* New York, NY: Simon & Schuster.

Fergusson, D. M., & Horwood, L. J. (2003). Resilience to childhood adversity: Results of a 12-year study. In S. Luthar (Ed.), *Resilience and vulnerability: Adaptation in the context of childhood adversities* (pp. 130–155). New York, NY: Cambridge University Press.

Ferrer, E., & McArdle, J. J. (2004). An experimental analysis of dynamic hypotheses about cognitive abilities and achievement from childhood to early adulthood. *Developmental Psychology, 40*, 935–952.

Fetal Behaviour Research Center. (2009). *Research.* Retrieved from http://www.psych.qub.ac.uk/Research/Centres/FetalBehaviourResearchCentre/Research/#perception

Fields, J. (2003). *Children's living arrangements and characteristics: March 2002.* Current population Reports (P20-547). Washington, DC: U.S. Census Bureau.

Fifer, W. P., & Moon, C. (1994). The role of mother's voice in the organization of brain function in the newborn. *Acta Paediatrica Supplement, 397*, 86–93.

Filmore, L. W., & Snow, C. (2000). *What teachers need to know about language.* Retrieved from http://www.cal.org/resources/digest/0006fillmore.html

Findlay, L. C., & Coplan, R. J. (2008). Come out and play: Shyness in childhood and the benefits of organized sports participation. *Canadian Journal of Behavioural Science, 40*(3), 154–161.

Findling, R. L. (2008). Evolution of the treatment of attention-deficit/hyperactivity disorder in children: A review. *Clinical Therapeutics, 30*(5), 942–957.

Fine, G. A. (1987). *With little boys: Little league baseball and preadolescent culture.* Chicago, IL: University of Chicago Press.

Fine, M., Burns, A., Payne, Y. A., & Torre, M. E. (2004). Civic lessons: The color and class of betrayal. *Teachers College Record, 106*, 2193–2223.

Finkel, D., Reynolds, C. A., McArdle, J. J., Gatz, M., & Pedersen, N. L. (2003). Latent growth curve analyses of accelerating decline in cognitive abilities in adulthood. *Developmental Psychology, 39*, 535–550.

Finnila, K., Mahlberga, N., Santtilaa, P., & Niemib, P. (2003). Validity of a test of Page: Children's suggestibility for predicting responses to two interview situations differing in degree of suggestiveness. *Journal of Experimental Child Psychology, 85*, 32–49.

Fisch, H., Hyun, G., Golden, R., Hensle, T. W., Olsson, C. A., & Liberson, G. L. (2003). The influence of paternal age on Down Syndrome. *Journal of Urology, 169*(6), 2275–2278.

Fischer, K. W. (1980). A theory of cognitive development: The control and construction of hierarchies of skills. *Psychological Review, 87*(6), 477–531.

Fischer, K. W., & Bidell, T. R. (2006). Dynamic development of action and thought. In R. M. Lerner (Ed.), *Theoretical models of human development* (6th ed., Vol. 4, pp. 313–399). New York, NY: Wiley.

Fischer, K. W., & Silvern, L. (1985). Stages and individual differences in cognitive development. *Annual Review Psychology, 36*, 613–648.

Fischer, M. A., & Gillespie, C. S. (2003). Computers and young children's development. *Young Children, 58*(4), 85–91.

Fisher, C. B., Hoagwoood, K., Boyce, C., Duster, Frank, D. A., Grisso, T., Levine, R. J., . . . Zayas, L. H. (2002). Research ethics for mental health science involving ethnic minority children and youths. *American Psychologist, 57*, 1024–1040.

Fisher, J. O., & Birch, L. L. (1999). Restricting access to palatable foods affects children's behavioral response, food selection, and intake. *American Journal of Clinical Nutrition, 69*, 1264–1272.

Fisher, K. W., & Pare-Blagoev, J. (2000). From individual differences to dynamic pathways of development. *Child Development, 71*, 850–851.

Fiske, E. B. (1998, April, 10). America's test mania. *The New York Times*, pp. 16–20.

Fitzgerald, D. P., & White, K. J. (2003). Linking children's social worlds: Perspective-taking in parent-child and peer contexts. *Social Behavior and Personality, 31*, 509–522.

Fivush, R., & Haden, C. (1997). Narrating and representing experience: Preschoolers' developing autobiographical recounts. In P. van den Broek, P. J., Bauer, & T. Bourg (Eds.). *Event comprehension and representation* (pp. 169–198). Hillsdale, NJ: Erlbaum.

Fivush, R., & Hamond, N. R. (1990). Autobiographical memory across the preschool years: Toward reconceptualizing childhood amnesia. In R. Fivush & J. A. Hudson (Eds.), *Knowing and remembering in young children* (pp. 223–248). New York, NY: Cambridge University Press.

Fivush, R., Hazzard, A., Sales, J. M., Sarfati, D., & Brown, T. (2003). Creating coherence out of chaos: Children's narratives of emotionally positive and negative events. *Applied Cognitive Psychology, 17*(1–19).

Fivush, R., & Nelson, K. (2004). Culture and language in the emergence of autobiographical memory. *Psychological Science, 15*, 573–577.

Flanner, D. J., Torquati, J. C., & Lindemeier, L. (1994). The method and meaning of emotional expression and experience during adolescence. *Journal of Adolescent Research, 9*(1), 8–27.

Flavell, J. H. (1985). *Cognitive development* (2nd ed.). Englewood Cliffs, NJ: Prentice-Hall.

Flavell, J. H. (2004). Theory-of-Mind development: Retrospect and prospect. *Merrill-Palmer Quarterly, 50*, 274–290.

Flavell, J. H., Green, F. L., & Flavell, E. R. (1995). Young children's knowledge about thinking. *Monographs of the Society for Research in Child Development, 60*(1) (Serial No. 243).

Flavell, J. H., Miller, P. H., & Miller, S. A. (2002). *Cognitive development* (4th ed.). Upper Saddle River, NJ: Prentice-Hall.

Fleming, M., Towey, K., & Jarosik, J. (2003). *Healthy youth 2010: Supporting 21 critical adolescent objectives.* Washington DC: American Medical Association.

Fletcher, A., Bonell, C., & Hargreaves, J. (2008). School effects on young people's drug use: A systematic review of intervention and observational studies. *Journal of Adolescent Health, 42*, 209–220.

Fletcher, J. L., & Jolly, V. (2009). *'Sexting': Self-destructive of simple rebellion.* Retrieved from http://www.ocregister.com/news/teens-140903-sexting-kids.html

Floor, P., & Akhtar, N. (2006). Can 18-month-old infants learn words by listening in on conversations. *Infancy, 9*(13), 327–339.

Flynn, J. R. (1984). The mean IQ of Americans: Massive gains 1932–1978. *Psychological Bulletin, 95*, 29–51.

Folic Acid. (2010). Retrieved from http://www.marchofdimes.com/professionals/19695_1151.asp

Food and Drug Administration. (2004). *Antidepressant use in children, adolescents, and adults.* Retrieved from http://www.fda.gov/Drugs/DrugSafety/InformationbyDrugClass/UCM096273

Foote, T. (2003). *My potty reward stickers for boys: 126 boy stickers and chart to motivate toilet training*, from Tracytrends.com.

Ford, D. Y. (2000). *Infusing multicultural content into the curriculum for gifted students.* (ERIC EC Digest #E601). Arlington, VA: The ERIC Clearinghouse on Disabilities and Gifted Education.

Fordham, S., & Ogbu, J. U. (1986). Black students' school success: Coping with the "burden of 'acting white.'" *The Urban Review, 18*(3), 176–206.

Foster, G. D., Sherman, S., Borradaile, K. E., Grundy, K. M., Vander Veur, S. S., Nachmani, J., . . . Shults, J. (2008). A policy-based school intervention to prevent overweight and obesity. *Pediatrics, 121*, e794-802. doi:10.1542/peds .2007-1365.

Fowles, D. C., & Kochanska, G. (2000). Temperament as a moderator of pathways to conscience in children: The contribution of electrodermal activity. *Psychophysiology, 37*, 788–795.

Fowles-Mates, B., & Strommen, L. (1996). Why Ernie can't read: Sesame Street and literacy. *The Reading Teacher, 49*, 300–306.

Fox, H. E. (1993). APGAR: A commentary. *P & S Medical Review, 1*(1). Retrieved from http://www.cumc.columbia.edu/news/review/archives/medrev_v1n1_0013.html#top

Fox, M. (2005, September 27). Urie Bronfenbrenner, 88, an authority on child development. *The New York Times*, p. 7.

Franklin, J. (2007). Achieving with autism: Dispelling common misconceptions is essential for success. *Education Update, 49*(7), 1–9.

Frans, E. M., Sandin, S., Reichenberg, A., Lichtenstein, P., Långström, N., & Hultman, C. M. (2008). Advancing paternal age and bipolar disorder. *Archives of General Psychiatry, 65*(9), 1034.

Fredericks, J., Blumenfeld, P., & Paris, A. (2004). School engagement: Potential of the concept, and state of the evidence. *Review of Educational Research, 74*, 59–109.

Fredericks, J. A., & Eccles, J. S. (2002). Children's competence and value beliefs from childhood through adolescence. *Developmental Psychology, 38*(4), 519–533.

Frehill, L., & Di Fabio, N. (2008). *Professional women and minorities: A total human resources data compendium* (17 ed.). New York, NY: Commission on Professionals in Science and Technology.

Freisen, J. (2010, March 10). The hanging face of Canada: Booming minority populations by 2031. *The Globe and Mail: National.*

French, S. E., Seidman, E., Allen, L., & Aber, J. L. (2006). The development of ethnic identity during adolescence. *Developmental Psychology, 42*(1), 1–10.

Frey, K. S., & Ruble, D. N. (1990). Strategies for comparative evaluation: Maintaining a sense of competence across the lifespan. In R. J. Stemberg & J. Kolligan, Jr. (Eds.), *Competence considered* (pp. 167–189). New Haven, CT: Yale University Press.

Fried, P. A., Watkinson, B., & Gray, R. (2003). Differential effects on cognitive functioning in 13- to 16-year olds prenatally exposed to cigarettes and marijuana. *Neurotoxicology & Teratology, 25*(4), 427–436.

Friedlander, S. L., Larkin, E. K., Rosen, C. L., Palermo, T. M., & Reline S. (2003). Decreased quality of life associated with obesity in school-aged children. *Archives of Pediatric and Adolescent Medicine, 157*, 1206–1211.

Friedman, D. (2005). *Interaction and the architecture of the brain*. Retrieved from http://www.developingchild.net

Friend, M. (2006). *Special education: Contemporary perspectives for school professionals*. Boston, MA: Allyn & Bacon.

Friend, M. (2011). *Special education: Contemporary perspectives for school professionals* (3rd ed.). Boston, MA: Allyn & Bacon.

Friend, M., & Bursuck, W. D. (2002). *Including students with special needs: A practical guide for classroom teachers* (3rd ed.) Boston, MA: Allyn & Bacon.

Friend, M., & Bursuck, W. D. (2009). *Including students with special needs: A practical guide for classroom teachers* (5th ed.). Upper Saddle River, NJ: Prentice Hall.

Frome, P. M., Alfeld, C. J., Eccles, J. S., & Barber, B. L. (2006). Why don't they want a male-dominated job? An investigation of young women who changed their occupational aspirations. *Educational Research & Evaluation, 12*(4), 259–372.

Frome, P. M., Alfeld, C. J., Eccles, J. S., & Barber, B. L. (2008). Is the desire for a family flexible job keeping young women out of male-dominated occupations? In H. M. G. Watt & J. S. Eccles (Eds.), *Gender and occupational outcomes: Longitudinal assessments of individual, social, and cultural influences* (pp. 195–214). Washington, DC: American Psychological Association.

Frost, J. L., Wortham, S. C., & Reifel, S. (2005). *Play and child development* (2nd ed.). Upper Saddle River, NJ: Prentice-Hall.

Fuchs, L. S., Fuchs, D., Compton, D. L., Powell, S. R., Seethaler, P. M., Capizzi, A. M., Schatschneider, C., & Fletcher, J. M. (2006). The cognitive correlates of third-grade skill in arithmetic, algorithmic computation, and arithmetic work problems. *Journal of Educational Psychology, 98*, 29–43.

Fujisawa, K. K., Kutsukake, N., & Hasegawa, T. (2008). Reciprocity of prosocial behavior in Japanese preschool children. *International Journal of Behavioral Development*, 32, 89–97.

Fuller, B., Kagan, S. L., & Loeb, S. (2002). *New lives for poor families? Mother and young children move through welfare reform*. Berkley, CA: University of California.

Furman, W., & Wehner, E. A., (1997). Adolescent romantic relationships: A developmental perspective. *New Directions for Child and Adolescent Development, 78*, 21–36.

Furnham, A., & Cheng, H. (2000). Lay theories of happiness. *Journal of Happiness Studies, 1*(2), 227–246.

Furstenberg, F. F., Jr., Cook, T. D., Eccles, J., Elder, G. H. Jr., & Sameroff, A. (1999). *Managing to make it: Urban families and adolescent success*. Chicago, IL: University of Chicago Press.

Gagne, R. M. (1985). *The conditions of learning and theory of instruction* (4th ed.). New York, NY: Holt, Rinehart & Winston.

Galambos, N. L. (2004). Gender and gender role development in adolescence. In R. M. Lerner & L. Steinberg (Eds.), *Handbook of adolescent psychology* (2nd ed., pp. 233–262). Hoboken, NJ: John Wiley & Sons.

Galambos, N. L., Barker, E. T., & Almeida, D. M. (2003). Parents *do* matter: Trajectories of change in externalizing and internalizing problems in early adolescence. *Child Development, 74*, 578–594.

Galambos, S. J., & Goldin-Meadow, S. (1990). The effects of learning two languages on metalinguistic development. *Cognitions, 34*, 1–56.

Galardini, A., & Giovannini, D. (2001). Pistoia: Creating a dynamic, open system to serve children, families, and communities. In L. Gandini & C. P. Edwards (Eds.), *Bambini: The Italian approach to infant/toddler care* (pp. 89–108). New York, NY: Teachers College Press.

Gallagher, A. M., & Kaufman, J. C. (2005). *Gender differences in mathematics*. New York, NY: Cambridge University Press.

Gallahue, D. L, & Ozmun, J. C. (1995). *Understanding motor development: Infants, children, adolescents, adults* (3rd ed.). Madison, WI: Brown & Benchmark.

Galliher, R. V., Rostosky, S. S., & Hughes, H. K. (2004). School belonging, self-esteem, and depressive symptoms in adolescents: An examination of sex, sexual attraction status, and urbanicity. *Journal of Youth and Adolescence, 33*(3), 235–245.

Gallistel, C. R., & Gelman, S. A. (1992). Preverbal and verbal counting and computation. *Cognition, 44*, 43–74.

Gano-Overway, L. A., Newton, M., Magyar, T. M., Fry, M. D., Kim, M., & Guivernau, M. R. (2009). Influence of caring youth sport contexts on efficacy-related beliefs. *Developmental Psychology, 45*(2), 329–340.

Gantz, B. J., & Tyler, R. S. (2010). Special issue: Cochlear implant research from the University of Iowa. *Journal of the American Academy of Audiology, 21*, 4.

Garbarino, J. (1999). The effects of community violence on children. In L. Balter & C. S. Tamis-LeMonda (Eds.), *Child psychology: A handbook of contemporary issues* (pp. 412–425). Philadelphia, PA: Psychology Press.

Garber, J., Clarke, G. N., Weersing, R., Beardslee, W. R., Brent, D. A., Gladstone, T. R., DeBar, L. L, . . . Iyengar, S. (2009). Prevention of depression in at-risk adolescents. *The Journal of the American Medical Association, 301*(21), 2215–2224.

Garcia, E. (2002). *Student cultural diversity: Understanding the meaning and meeting the challenge*. Boston, MA: Houghton Mifflin.

Garcia, E., & Jensen, B. (2009). Early educational opportunities for children of Hispanic origins. *SRCD Social Policy Report, 23*(2), 3–12.

Gardner, H. (1980). *Artful scribbles: The significance of children's drawings*. New York, NY: Basic Books.

Gardner, H. (1983). *Frames of mind: The theory of multiple intelligences*. New York, NY: Basic Books.

Gardner, H. (1998). Reflections on multiple intelligences: Myths and messages. In A. Woolfolk (Ed.), *Readings in educational psychology* (2nd ed., pp. 61–67). Boston, MA: Allyn & Bacon.

Gardner, H. (2003, April 21). *Multiple intelligence after twenty years*. Paper presented at the American Educational Research Association, Chicago, Illinois.

Gardner, H. (2009). Birth and the spreading of a "Meme." In S.-Q. Chen, S. Moran, & H. Gardner (Eds.), *Multiple intelligences around the world* (pp. 3–16). San Francisco, CA: Jossey-Bass.

Garmon, L. C., Basinger, K. S., Gregg, V. R., & Gibbs, J. C. (1996). Gender differences in stage and expression of moral judgment. *Merrill-Palmer Quarterly, 42*, 418–437.

Garner, P. W., Curenton, S. M., & Taylor, K. (2005). Predictors of mental state understandings in preschoolers of varying socioeconomic backgrounds. *International Journal of Behavioral Development, 29*, 271–281.

Garner, P. W., & Spears, F. M. (2000). Emotion regulation in low-income preschool children. *Social Development, 9*, 246–264.

Garner, R. (1990). When children and adults do not use learning strategies: Toward a theory of settings. *Review of Educational Psychology, 60*, 517–530.

Garnets, L. (2002). Sexual orientations in perspective. *Cultural Diversity and Ethnic Minority Psychology, 8*, 115–129.

Garofalo, R., Wolf, R. C., Wissow, L. S., Woods, E. R., & Goodman, E. (1999). Sexual orientation and risk of suicide attempts among a representative sample of youth. *Archives of Pediatrics & Adolescent Medicine, 153*(5), 487–493.

Gaskins, S. (1996). How Mayan parental theories come into play. In S. Harkness & C. Super (Eds.), *Parents' cultural belief systems: Their origins, expressions, and consequences* (pp. 345–363). New York, NY: Guilford.

Gaskins, S. (2000). Children's daily activities in a Mayan village: A culturally grounded description. *Cross-Cultural Research, 34*, 375–389.

Gathercole, S. E., Pickering, S. J., Ambridge, B., & Wearing, H. (2004). The structure of working memory from 4 to 15 years of age. *Developmental Psychology, 40*, 177–190.

Gauvain, M. (2004). Bringing culture into relief: Cultural contributions to the development of children's planning skills. In R. Kail (Ed.), *Advances in child development and behavior* (Vol. 32, pp. 37–71). Amsterdam, The Netherlands: Elsevier.

Gay, G. (2000). *Culturally responsive teaching: Theory, research, and practice*. New York, NY: Teachers College Press.

Geary, D. C. (1995). Sexual selection and sex differences in spatial cognition. *Learning and Individual Differences, 7*, 289–303.

Geary, D. C. (1998). *Male, female: The evolution of human sex differences*. Washington, DC: American Psychological Association.

Geary, D. C. (1998). What is the function of mind and brain? *Educational Psychologist, 10*, 377–388.

Geary, D. C. (1999). Evolution and developmental sex differences. *Current Directions in Psychological Science, 8*, 115–120.

Geary, D. C. (2005). Evolution and cognitive development. In R. L. Burgess & K. MacDonald (Eds.), *Evolutionary perspectives on human development* (2nd ed., pp. 99–134). Thousand Oaks, CA: Sage Publications.

Geary, D. C. (2006). Development of mathematical understanding. In D. Kuhn & R. S. Siegler (Eds.), *Handbook of child psychology* (Vol. 2, Cognition, perception, and language, pp. 777–810). New York, NY: Wiley.

Geary, D. C., & Bjorklund, D. F. (2000). Evolutionary developmental psychology. *Child Development, 7*, 57–65.

Geary, D. C., Bow-Thomas, C. C., Liu, F., & Siegler, R. S. (1996). Development of arithmetical competence in Chinese and American children: Influence of age, language, and schooling. *Child Development, 67*, 2022–2044.

Gee, J. P., Allen, A.-R., & Clinton, K. (2001). Language, class, and identity: Teenagers fashioning themselves through language. *Linguistics and Education, 12*, 175–194.

Gehlbach, H. (2004). A new perspective on perspective taking: A multidimensional approach to conceptualizing an aptitude. *Educational Psychology Review, 16*, 207–234. doi:10.1023/B:EDPR.0000034021.12899.11

Gelman, R. (2000). The epigenesis of mathematical thinking. *Journal of Applied Developmental Psychology, 21*, 27–35.

Gelman, R., & Cordes, S. A. (2001). Counting in animals and humans In E. Dupoux (Ed.), *Cognition*. Cambridge, MA: MIT Press.

Gelman, R., & Gallistel, C. R. (1978). *The child's understanding of number*. Cambridge, MA: Harvard University Press.

Genetic Engineering. (2002–2010). *Arguments against embryonic stem-cell research*. Retrieved from http://www.bootstrike.com/Genetics/StemCells/arguments_against.html

Gerber, J. S., & Offit, P. A. (2009). Vaccines and autism: a tale of shifting hypotheses. *Vaccines, 48*, 4, 456–461. Retrieved from http://www.journals.uchicago.edu/doi/pdf/10.1086/596476

Gergen, K. J. (1996). The language-minority students in transition: Contemporary instructional research. *The Elementary School Journal, 96*, 217–220.

Gerhardt, S. (2004). *Why love matters: How affection shapes a baby's brain*. Hove: Bruner Routledge.

Gerrand, M., Gibbons, F. X., Houlihan, A. E., Stock, M. L., & Pomery, E. A. (2008). A dual-process approach to health risk decision making: The prototype willingness model. *Developmental Review, 28*, 29–61.

Gershkoff-Stowe, L., & Hahn, E. R. (2007). Fast mapping skills in the developing lexicon. *Journal of Speech, Language, and Hearing Research*, 50, 682–697.

Gershoff, E. T. (2002). Corporal punishment by parents and associated child behaviors and experiences: A meta-analytic and theoretical review. *Psychological Bulletin, 128*, 539–579.

Gershoff, E. T., Aber, J. L., Raver, C. C., & Lennon, M. C. (2007). Income is not enough: Incorporating material hardship into models of income associations with parenting and child development. *Child Development, 78*, 70–95.

Gershoff, E. T., & Bitensky, S. H. (2007). The case against corporal punishment of children: Converging evidence from social science research and international human rights law and implications for U.S. public policy. *Psychology, Public Policy, and Law, 13*, 231–272.

Gersten, R. (1996). Literacy instruction for language-minority students: The transition years. *Elementary School Journal, 96*(3), 227–244.

Gerwe, M., Stollhoff, K., Mossakowski, J., Kuehle, H-J., Goertz, U., Schaefer, C. M., & Heger, S. (2009). Tolerability and effects of OROS_ MPH (Concerta) on functioning, severity of disease and quality of life in children and adolescents with ADHD: Results from a prospective, non-interventional trial. *ADHD Attention Deficit Hyperactivity Disorder, 1*, 175–186.

Giedd, J. N. (2008). The teen brain: Insights from neuroimaging. *Journal of Adolescent Health, 42*, 335–343.

Gigerenzer, G. (2007). *Gut feelings: The intelligence of the unconscious*. New York, NY: Penguin Publishers.

Gillies, R. (2003). The behaviors, interactions, and perceptions of junior high school students during small-group learning. *Journal of Educational Psychology, 96*, 15–22.

Gilligan, C. (1982). *In a different voice: Psychological theory and women's development*. Cambridge, MA: Harvard University Press.

Gilligan, C., & Attanucci, J. (1988). Two moral orientations: Gender differences and similarities. *Merrill-Palmer Quarterly, 34*, 223–237.

Gilliom, M., Shaw, D. S., Beck, J. E., Schonberg, M. A., & Lukon, J. L. (2002). Anger regulation in disadvantaged preschool boys: Strategies, antecedents, and the development of self-control. *Developmental Psychology, 38*, 222–235.

Gilmore, A. (2005). *The impact of PIRLS (2001) and TIMSS (2003) in low- and middle-income countries: An evaluation of the value of World Bank support for international surveys of reading literacy (PIRLS) and mathematics and science (TIMSS)*. The Hague, The Netherlands: International Association for the Evaluation of Educational Achievement. Retrieved from http://www.iea.nl/fileadmin/user_upload/docs/WB_report.pdf

Gilstrap, L. L. (2004). A missing link in suggestibility research: What is known about the behavior of field interviewers in unstructured interviews with young children? *Journal of Experimental Psychology: Applied, 10*, 13–24.

Gingras, J. L., Mitchell, E. A., & Grattan, K. E. (2005). Fetal homologue of infant crying. *Archives of Disease in Childhood Fetal and Neonatal Edition, 90(5)*, F415–F418.

Ginsburg, A., Leinwand, S., Anstrom, T., & Pollock, E. (2005). *What the United States can learn for Singapore's world-class mathematics system (and what Singapore can learn from the United States): An exploratory study*. Washington, DC: American Institutes for Research.

Ginsburg, K. R. (2007). The importance of play in promoting healthy child development and maintaining strong parent-child bonds. *Pediatrics, 119*, 182–191.

Glasgow, K. L., Dornbusch, S. M., Troyer, L., Steinberg, L., & Ritter, P. L. (1997). Parenting styles, adolescents' attributions, and educational outcomes in nine heterogeneous high schools. *Child Development, 68*, 507–523.

Glassman, M. (1994). All things being equal: The two roads of Piaget and Vygotsky. *Developmental Review, 14*, 186–214.

Glassman, M. (2001). Dewey and Vygotsky: Society, experience, and inquiry in educational practice. *Educational Researcher, 30*(4), 3–14.

Gleason, J. B., & Ely, R. (2002). Gender differences in language development. In A. McGillicuddy-De Lisi & R. De Lisi (Eds.), *Biology, society and behavior: The development of sex differences in cognition* (pp. 127–154). Westport, CT: Greenwood Publishing Group.

Gleason, T. R. (2005). Mothers' and fathers' attitudes regarding pretend play in the context of imaginary companions and of child gender. *Merrill-Palmer Quarterly, 51*, 412–436.

Gleason, T. R., Gower, A. L., Hohmann, L. M., & Gleason, T. C. (2005). Temperament and friendship in preschool-aged children. *International Journal of Behavioral Development, 29*, 336–344.

Gleason, T. R., & Hohmann, L. M. (2006). Concepts of real and imaginary friendships in early childhood. *Social Development, 15*, 128–144.

Gleason, T. R., Sebanc, A. M., & Hartup, W. W. (2000). Imaginary companions of preschool children. *Developmental Psychology, 36*, 419–428.

Glick, P. (1997). Demographic pictures of African American families. In H. McAdoo (Ed.), Black families (3rd ed., pp. 118–138). Thousand Oaks, CA: Sage.

Gmitrova, V., Podhajecká, M., & Gmitrov, J. (2007). Children's play preferences: Implications for the preschool education. *Early Child Development and Care*, 1–14.

Gober, S., Klein, M., Berger, T., Vindigni, C., & McCabe, P. C. (2006a). Steroids in adolescence: The cost of achieving a physical ideal. *NASP Communiqué, 34*(7), 1–8.

Gober, S., McCabe, P. C., & Klein, M. (2006b). Adolescents and steroids: What principals should know. *Student Services, November*, 11–15.

Gogtay, N., Ordonez, A., Herman, D. H., Hayashi, K. M., Greenstein, D., Vaituzis, C., Lenane, M., . . . Rapoport, J. L. (2007). Dynamic mapping of cortical development before and after the onset of pediatric bipolar illness. *Journal of Child Psychology and Psychiatry, 48*(9), 852–862.

Goldenberg, C. (1996). The education of language-minority students: Where are we, and where do we need to go? *Elementary School Journal, 96*, 353–361.

Goldman, S. R., Lawless, K., Pellegrino, J. W., & Plants, R. (2006). Technology for teaching and learning with understanding. In J. Cooper (Ed.), *Classroom teaching skills* (8th ed., pp. 104–150). Boston: Houghton-Mifflin.

Golomb, C. (2003). *The child's creation of a pictorial world*. Mahwah, NJ: Erlbaum.

Golombok, G., Perry, B., Burston, A., Murray, C., Mooney-Somers, J., Stevens, M., & Golding, J. (2003). Children with lesbian parents: A community study. *Developmental Psychology, 39*, 20–33.

Golombok, S., & Fivush, R. (1994). *Gender development*. Cambridge, England: Cambridge University Press.

Golombok, S., Rust, J., Zervoulis, K., Croudace, T., Golding, J., & Hines, M. (2008). Developmental trajectories of sex-typed behavior in boys and girls: A longitudinal general population study of children aged 2.5–8 years. *Child Development, 79*, 1583–1593.

Gomez, B. J., & Ang, P. M. (2007). Promoting positive youth development in schools. *Theory Into Practice, 46*(2), 97–104.

Gonzalez, V. (1999). *Language and cognitive development in second language learning: Educational implications for children and adults*. Boston, MA: Allyn & Bacon.

Good, C., Aronson, J., & Inzlicht, M. (2003). Improving adolescents' standardized test performance: An intervention to reduce the effects of stereotype threat. *Journal of Applied Developmental Psychology, 24*, 645–662.

Good, W. V. (2007). The spectrum of vision impairment caused by pediatric neurological injury. *J AAPOS, 11*(5), 424–425.

Good, W. V. (2007). An eye on vision screening for children with developmental disabilities. *Developmental Medicine & Child Neurology, 49*, 485.

Goodenow, C. (1993). Classroom belonging among early adolescent students: Relationships to motivation and achievement. *The Journal of Early Adolescence, 13*(1), 21–43.

Goodman, G. S., Emery, R. E., & Haugaard, J. J. (1998). Developmental psychology and law: Divorce, child maltreatment, foster care, and adoption. In D. William, I. E. Sigel, & K. A. Renninger (Eds.), *Handbook of child psychology: Vol. 4. Child psychology in practice* (pp. 775–874). New York, NY: Wiley.

Goodnow, C. (2004, December 7). Researchers take on imaginary playmates—for real. *Seattle Post-Intelligencer Reporter.*

Goodwyn, S., Acredolo, L., & Brown, C. (2000). Impact of symbolic gesturing on early language development. *Journal of Nonverbal Behavior, 24*(2), 81–103.

Goossens, L. (2001). Global versus domain-specific statuses in identity research: A comparison of two self-report measures. *Journal of Adolescence, 24*(6), 681–699. doi: 10.1006/jado.2001.0438

Gonzalez, N., Greenberg, J., & Velez, C. (1994). *Funds of knowledge: A look at Luis Moll's research into hidden family resources.* CITYSCHOOLS. North Central Regional Educational Laboratory. Retrieved from http://www.ncrel.org/sdrs/cityschl/city1_1c.htn.

Gopnik, A., Meltzoff, A., & Kuhl, P. (1999). *The scientist in the crib: What early learning tells us about the mind.* New York, NY: HarperCollins.

Gordon, B. N., Baker-Ward, L., & Ornstein, P. A. (2001). Children's testimony: A review of research for past experiences. *Clincal Child and Family Psychology Review, 4*, 157–181.

Gordon, M. (2005). *Roots of empathy: Changing the world child by child.* Markham, ON: Thomas & Allen.

Goswami, U. (2005). The brain in the classroom? The state of the art. *Developmental Science, 8*, 468–469.

Goswami, U. (2008). *Cognitive development: The learning brain.* London, England: Psychology Press.

Gottlieb, G. (1997). *Synthesizing nature and nurture.* Mahwah, NJ: Erlbaum.

Gottlieb, G. (2003). On making behavioral genetics truly behavioral. *Human Development, 46*, 337–355.

Gottlieb, G., Wahlsten, D., & Lickliter, R. (2006). The significance of biology for human development: A developmental psychobiological systems view. In R. M. Lerner (Ed.), *Theoretical models of human development* (6th ed., Vol. 1, pp. 210–257). New York, NY: Wiley.

Gould, D., & Carson, S. (2004). Myths surrounding the role of youth sports in developing Olympic champions. *Youth Studies Australia, 23*(1), 19–26.

Graber, K. C., Locke, L. F., Lambdin, D., & Solmon, M. A. (2008). The landscape of elementary school physical education. *The Elementary School Journal, 108* (3), 151–159.

Graham, C. (2008). *Teaching physical education: Becoming a master teacher* (3rd ed.). Champaign, IL: Human Kinetics.

Graham, G. (2008). Children's and adults' perceptions of elementary school physical education. *The Elementary School Journal, 108*, 241–249.

Graham, S., & Taylor, A. Z. (2002). Ethnicity, gender, and the development of achievement values. In A. Wigfield & J. S. Eccles (Eds.), *Development of achievement motivation* (pp. 121–146). San Diego, CA: Academic Press.

Granot, D., & Mayseless, D. (2001). Attachment security and adjustment to school in middle childhood. *International Journal of Behavioral Development, 25*, 530–541.

Gredler, M. E. (2005). *Learning and instruction: Theory into practice* (5th ed.). Boston, MA: Allyn & Bacon.

Green, M., & Piel, J. A. (2010). *Theories of human development: A comparative approach* (2nd ed.). Boston, MA: Allyn & Bacon.

Greene, M. L., Way, N., & Pahl, K. (2006). Trajectories of perceived adult and peer discrimination among Black, Latino, and Asian American adolescents: Patterns and psychological correlates. *Developmental Psychology, 42*(2), 218–238.

Greenfield, D. N. (1999). Psychological characteristics of compulsive Internet use: A preliminary analysis. *CyberPsychology and Behavior, 2*, 403–412. doi:10.1089/cpb.1999.2.403

Gregg, V., Gibbs, J. C., & Basinger, K. S. (1994). Patterns of developmental delay in moral judgment by male and female delinquents. *Merrill-Palmer Quarterly, 40*, 538–553.

Gregory, A., & Cornell, D. (2009). "Tolerating" adolescent needs: Moving beyond zero tolerance policies in high school. *Theory Into Practice, 48*(2), 106–113.

Griesenbach, U., Geddes, D. M., & Alton, E. W. (2004). Advances in cystic fibrosis gene therapy. *Current Opinions in Pulmonary Medicine, 10*(6), 542–546.

Griffins, P. E., & Gray, R. D. (2005). Discussion: Three ways to misunderstand developmental systems theory. *Biology and Philosophy, 20*, 417–425.

Grimes, C. L., Klein, T. P., & Putallaz, M. (2004). Parents' relationships with their parents and peers: Influences on children's social development. In J. B. Kupersmidt & K. A. Dodge (Eds.), *Children's peer relations: From development to intervention* (pp. 141–158). Washington, DC: American Psychological Association.

Groark, C. J., & McCall, R. B. (2005). Integrating developmental scholarship into practice and policy. In M. H. Bornstein & M. E. Lamb (Eds.), *Developmental science: An advanced textbook* (5th ed., pp. 557–601). Mahwah, NJ: Erlbaum.

Gron, G., Wunderlich, A. P., Spitzer, M., Tomczak, R., & Riepe, M. W. (2000). Brain activation during human navigation: Gender-different neural networks as substrate of performance. *Nature Neuroscience, 3*, 404–408.

Grossman, H., & Grossman, S. H. (1994). *Gender issues in education.* Boston, MA: Allyn & Bacon.

Grossman, K., Grossman, K. E., Fremmer-Bombik, E., Kindler, H., Scheuerer-Englisch, H., & Zimmermann, P. (2002). The uniqueness of the child-father attachment relationship: Father's sensitive and challenging play as a pivotal variable in a 16-year longitudinal study. *Social Development, 11*, 307–331.

Grotevant, H. D. (1978). Sibling constellations and sex typing of interests in adolescence. *Child Development, 49*, 540–542.

Grotevant, H. D., & Cooper, C. R. (1998). Individuality and connectedness in adolescent development: Review and prospects for research on identity, relationships, and context. In E. Skoe & A. von der Lippe (Eds.), *Personality development in adolescence: A cross national and life span perspective* (pp. 3–37). London, England: Routledge.

Guglielmi, R. S. (2008). Native language proficiency, English literacy, academic achievement, and occupational attainment in limited-English-proficient students: A latent growth modeling perspective. *Journal of Educational Psychology, 100*(2), 322–342.

Guilford, J. P. (1988). Some changes in the Structure-of-Intellect model. *Educational and Psychological Measurement, 48*, 1–4.

Guillaume, M., & Lissau, I. (2002). Epidemiology. In W. Burniat, T. Cole, I. Lissau, & E. Poskitt (Eds.), *Child and adolescent obesity: Causes and consequences, prevention and treatment* (pp. 28–49). Cambridge, England: Cambridge University Press.

Gulson, B. L., Mizon, K. J., Davis, J. D., Palmer, J. M., & Vimpani, G. (2004). Identification of sources of lead in children in a primary Zn–Pb smelter environment. *Environmental Health Perspective, 112*, 52–60.

Gulson, B. L., Mizon, K. J., Palmer, J. M., Korsch, M. J., Taylor, A. J., & Mahaffey, K. R. (2004). Blood lead changes during pregnancy and postpartum with calcium supplementation. *Environmental Health Perspective, 112*, 1499–1507.

Gur, R. C., Turetsky, B. I., Matsui, M., Yan, M., Bilker, W., Hughett, P., & Gur, R. E. (1999). Sex differences in brain gray and white matter in healthy young adults: Correlations with cognitive performance. *Journal of Neuroscience, 19*, 4065–4072.

Gurian, M., & Henley, P. (2001). *Boys and girls learn differently: A guide for teachers and parents.* San Francisco, CA: Jossey-Bass.

Gutman, L. M., & Eccles, J. S. (2007). Stage–environment fit during adolescence: Trajectories of family relations and adolescent outcomes. *Developmental Psychology, 43*(2), 522–537.

Gutman, L. M., Sameroff, A., & Cole, R. (2003). Academic growth curve trajectories from 1st grade to 12th grade: Effects of multiple social risk factors and preschool child factors. *Developmental Psychology, 39*, 777–790.

Guttmacher Institute. (2006). Facts on sex education in the United States. Retrieved from http://www.guttmacher.org/pubs/fb_sexEd2006.html

Habermas, T., & de Silveira, C. (2008). The development of global coherence in life narratives across adolescence: Temporal, causal, and thematic aspects. *Developmental Psychology, 44*(3), 707–721.

Hacker, D. J., & Tenent, A. (2002). Implementing reciprocal teaching in the classroom: Overcoming obstacles and making modifications. *Journal of Educational Psychology, 94*, 699–718.

Hagenbaugh, B. (2005, April 6). Full activity, study schedules have many teens just saying no to jobs. *USA Today.*

Hair, E., Halle, T., Terry-Humen, E., Lavelle, B., & Calkins, J. (2006). Children's school readiness in the ECLS-K: Predictions to academic, health, and social outcomes in first grade. *Early Childhood Research Quarterly, 221*, 431–454.

Hakuta, K. (1986). *Mirror of language: The debate on bilingualism.* New York, NY: Basic Books.

Hakuta, K., & Garcia, E. E. (1989). Bilingualism and education. *American Psychologist, 44,* 374–379.

Halberda, J. (2003a). *Two-year-olds fast-mapping of novel labels: How fast is fast?* Paper presented at the biannual meeting of the Society for Research in Child Development, Tampa, Florida.

Halberda, J. (2003b). The development of a word-learning strategy. *Cognition, 87,* B23–B34.

Halfon, N., Shulman, E., & Hochstein, M. (2001). *Brain development in early childhood.* Retrieved from http://www.healthychild.ucla.edu/Publications/Documents/halfon.health.dev.pdf

Halford, J. M. (1999). A different mirror: A conversation with Ronald Takaki. *Educational Leadership, 56*(7), 8–13.

Hall, G. S. (1904). *Adolescence: Its psychology and its relations to physiology, anthropology, sociology, sex, crime, religion, and education.* New York, NY: D. Appleton.

Hallahan, D. P., & Kauffman, J. M. (2006). *Exceptional learners: Introduction to special education* (10th ed.). Boston, MA: Allyn & Bacon.

Hallahan, D. P., Kauffman, J. M., & Pullen, P. C. (2008). *Exceptional learners: Introduction to special education* (11th ed.). Boston, MA: Allyn & Bacon.

Hallahan, D. P., Lloyd, J. W., Kauffman, J. M., Weiss, M. P., & Martinez, E. A. (2005). *Introduction to learning disabilities* (5th ed.). Boston, MA: Allyn & Bacon.

Hallowell, E. M., & Ratey, J. J. (1994). *Driven to distraction.* New York, NY: Pantheon Books.

Halpern, D. F., Benbow, C. P., Geary. D. C., Gur, R. C., Hyde, J. S., & Gernsbacher, M. A. (2007). The science of sex differences in science and mathematics. *Psychological Science in the Public Interest, 8,* 1–51.

Hamamy, H., & Dahoun, S. (2004). Prenatal decisions following the prenatal diagnosis of sex chromosome abnormalities. *European Journal of Obstetrics & Reproductive Biology, 116,* 58–62.

Hamers, J. F., & Blanc, M. H. A. (2000). *Bilinguality and bilingualism* (2nd ed.). Cambridge, England: Cambridge University Press.

Hamilton, B. E., Martin, J. A., & Ventura, S. J. (2009). Births: Preliminary data for 2007. *National Vital Statistics Reports, 57*(12). Retrieved from http://www.cdc.gov/nchs/data/nvsr/nvsr57/nvsr57_12.pdf

Hamilton, J. (2009). *Multitasking teens may be muddling their brains.* Retrieved from http://www.npr.org/templates/story/story.php?storyId=95524385

Hammen, C. (2003). Risk and protective factors for children of depressed parents. In S. Luthar (Ed.), *Resilience and vulnerability: Adaptation in the context of childhood adversities* (pp. 50–75). New York, NY: Cambridge University Press.

Hammer, C. S., Farkas, G., & Maczuga, S. (2010). The language and literacy development of Head Start children: A study using the Family and Child Experiences Survey database. *Language, Speech, and Hearing Services In Schools, 41,* 70–83.

Hammer, C. S., Lawrence, F. R., & Miccio, A. W. (2007). Bilingual children's language abilities and reading outcomes in Head Start and kindergarten. *Language, Speech and Hearing Services in Schools, 38,* 237–248.

Hampton, T. (2007). Food insecurity harms health, well-being of millions in the United States. *Journal of the American Medical Association, 298,* 1851–1853.

Hamre, B. K., & Pianta, R. C. (2001). Early teacher-child relationships and the trajectory of children's school outcomes through eighth grade. *Child Development, 72,* 625–638.

Hanawalt, B. (1993). *Growing up in medieval London: The experience of childhood in history.* New York, NY: Oxford University Press.

Hara, H. (2002). Justifications for bullying among Japanese school children. *Asian Journal of Social Psychology, 5,* 197–204.

Hardman, M. L., Drew, C. J., & Egan, M. W. (2005). *Human exceptionality: Society, school, and family* (8th ed.). Boston, MA: Allyn & Bacon.

Hardy, C. L., Bukowski, W. M., & Sippola, L. K. (2002). Stability and change in peer relationships during the transition to middle-level school. *Journal of Early Adolescence, 22,* 117–142.

Harel, J., & Scher, A. (2003). Insufficient responsiveness in ambivalent mother-infant relationships: Contextual and affective aspects. *Infant Behavior and Development, 26*(3), 371–383.

Harmer, C. S., Farkas, G., & Maczuga, S. (2010). The language and literacy development of Head Start children: A study using the family and child experiences survey database. *Language, Speech, and Hearing Services in Schools, 41,* 70–83.

Harms, T., Clifford, R. M., & Cryer, D. (1998). *Early Childhood Environment Rating Scale-Revised.* New York, NY: Teachers College Press.

Harris, J. R. (1998). *The nurture assumption: Why children turn out the way they do: Parents matter less than you think and peers matter more.* New York, NY: Free Press.

Harris, M. A., Prior, J. C., & Koehoom, M. (2008). Age at menarche in the Canadian population: Secular trends and relationship to adulthood BMI. *Journal of Adolescent Health, 43,* 548–554.

Harris, P. L. (2006). Social cognition. In D. Kuhn & R. Siegler (Eds.), *Handbook of child psychology* (6th ed., Vol. 2). New York, NY: Wiley.

Harrison, L., & Belcher, D. (2006). Race and ethnicity in physical education. In D. Kirk, D. Macdonald, & M. O'Sullvian (Eds.), *Handbook of physical education* (pp. 740–751). London, England: Sage.

Harrison, L. J., & Ungerer, J. A. (2002). Maternal employment and infant-mother attachment security at 12 months postpartum. *Developmental Psychology, 38,* 758–773.

Harrower, J. K., & Dunlap, G. (2001). Including children with autism in general classrooms. *Behavior Modification, 25,* 762–784.

Harry, J. (1983). Parasuicide, gender, and gender deviance. *Journal of Health and Social Behavior, 24,* 350–361.

Hart, B., & Risley, T. R. (1995). *Meaningful differences in the everyday experiences of young American children.* Baltimore, MD: Paul H. Brookes.

Hart, B., & Risley, T. R. (1999). *The social world of children learning to talk.* Baltimore, MD: Paul H. Brookes Publishing.

Hart, C. (2004). What toddlers talk about. *First Language, 24,* 91–106.

Hart, C., & Risley, T. R. (1992). American parenting of language-learning children: Persisting differences in family-child interactions observed in natural home environments. *Developmental Psychology, 28,* 1096–1105.

Hart, D., & Damon, W. (1988). Self-understanding and social cognitive development. *Early Child Development and Care, 40*(1), 5–23. doi:10.1080/0300443880400102

Harter, S. (1982). The perceived competence scale for children. *Child Development, 53,* 87–97.

Harter, S. (1987). The determinations and meditational role of global self-worth in children. In N. Eisenberg (Ed.), *Contemporary topics in developmental psychology* (pp. 219–242). New York, NY: Wiley-Interscience.

Harter, S. (1990). Processes underlying adolescent self-concept formation. In R. Montemayor, G. R. Adams, & T. P. Gullotta (Eds.), *From childhood to adolescence: A transitional period* (pp. 205–239). Newbury Park, CA: Sage.

Harter, S. (1998). The development of self-representations. In W. Damon & N. Eisenberg (Eds.), *Handbook of child psychology* (5th ed., Vol. 3. Social, emotional, and personality development, pp. 553–618). New York, NY: Wiley.

Harter, S. (1999). Symbolic interactionism revisited: Potential liabilities for the self constructed in the crucible of interpersonal relationships. *Merrill Palmer Quarterly,* 45: 677–703.

Harter, S. (1999). *The construction of self: A developmental perspective.* New York, NY: Guilford.

Harter, S. (2005). Self-concepts and self-esteem, children and adolescents. In C. B. Fisher & R. M. Lerner (Eds.), *Encyclopedia of applied development science* (pp. 972–977). Thousand Oaks, CA: Sage Publications.

Harter, S. (2006). The self. In W. Damon & R. M. Lerner (Series Eds.) *Social, emotional and personality development* (6th ed., pp. 646–718). New York, NY: Wiley.

Hartshore, J. K., & Ullman, M. T. (2006). Why girls say "holded" more than boys. *Developmental Science, 9,* 21–32.

Hartup, W. W. (1981). The peer system. In P. Mussen (Ed.), *Handbook of child psychology,* 4th ed. New York, NY: Wiley.

Hartup, W. W. (1992). Friendships and their developmental significance. In H. McGurk (Ed.), *Childhood social development: Contemporary perspectives* (pp. 175–205). Hillsdale, NJ: Erlbaum.

Hartup, W. W. (2002). Growing points in developmental science: A summing up. In W. W. Hartup & R. K. Siebereisen (Eds.), *Growing points in developmental science: An introduction* (pp. 329–344). New York, NY: Psychology Press.

Haselager, G. J. T., Cillessen, A. H. N., Lieshout, C. F. M., Riksen-Walraven, J. M. A., & Hartup, W. W. (2002). Heterogeneity among peer-rejected boys across middle childhood: developmental pathways of social behavior. *Developmental Psychology, 38,* 446–456.

Haugland, S. W., & Wright, J. L. (1997). *Young children and technology: A world of discovery.* Boston, MA: Allyn & Bacon.

Hauser, S. T., Book, B. K., Houlihan, J., Powers, S., Weiss-Perry, B., Follansbee, D., Jacobson, A. M., & Noam, G. G. (1987). Sex differences within the family: Studies of adolescent and parent family interactions. *Journal of Youth and Adolescence, 16*(3), 199–220.

Hawkins, D. L., Pepler, D. J., & Craig, W. M. (2001). Naturalistic observations of peer interventions in bullying. *Social Development, 10*, 512–527.

Hawkins, J. N. (1994). Issues of motivation in Asian education. In J. H. F O'Neil & M. Drillings (Eds.), *Motivation: Theory and research* (pp. 101–115). Hillsdale, NJ: Erlbaum.

Hay, D. F., Caplan, M., Castle, J., & Stimson, C. A. (1991). Does sharing become increasingly "rational" in the second year of life? *Developmental Psychology, 27*, 987–993.

Hay, D. F., Payne, A., & Chadwick, A. (2004). Peer relations in childhood. *Journal of Child Psychology and Psychiatry, 45*, 84–108.

Hay, D. F., Pedersen, J., & Nash, A. (1982). Dyadic interaction in the first year of life. In K. Rubin & H. S. Ross (Eds.), *Peer relationships and social skills in childhood.* New York, NY: Springer-Verlag.

Head Start Bureau. (2001). *Building their futures: How Early Head Start programs are enhancing the lives of infants and toddlers in low-income families.* Washington, DC: Author, Department of Health and Human Services.

Heath, S. B. (1989). Oral and literate traditions among Black Americans living in poverty. *American Psychologist, 44*, 367–373.

Heine, S. J., & Lehman, D. R. (1995). Cultural variation in unrealistic optimism: Does the West feel more invulnerable than the East? *Journal of Personality and Social Psychology, 68*, 595–607.

Heinrich, C. C., Brookmeyer, K. A., Shrier, L. A., & Shahar, G. (2006). Supportive relationships and sexual risk behavior in adolescence: An ecological-transactional approach. *Journal of Pediatric Psychology, 31*, 286–297.

Helburn, S. W., & Howes, C. (1996). Child care cost and quality. *The Future of Children, 6*, 62–82.

Henderson, H. A., Marshall, P. J., Fox, N. A., & Rubin, K. H. (2004). Psychophysiological and behavioral evidence for varying forms and functions of nonsocial behavior in preschoolers. *Child Development, 75*, 251–263.

Hendrick, C., Hendrick, S., & Bettor, L. (1995). Gender and sexual standards in dating relationships. *Personal Relationships, 2*(4), 359–369.

Hendrick, S. S., & Hendrick, C. (1995). Gender differences and similarities in sex and love. *Personal Relationship, 2*, 55–65.

Hendry, L. B., & Kloep, M. (2007). Conceptualizing emerging adulthood: Inspecting the emperor's new clothes? *Child Development Perspectives, 1*(2), 74–79.

Henrich, C. C., Brookmeyer, K. A., Shrier, L. A., & Shahar, G. Supportive relationships and sexual risk behavior in adolescence: An ecological-transactional approach. *Journal of Pediatric Psychology, 31*, 286–297.

Henrich, J., & Henrich, N. (2006). Culture, evolution and the puzzle of human cooperation. *Cognitive Systems Research, 7*, 221–245.

Henry, K. L., & Slater, M. D. (2007). The contextual effect of school attachment on young adolescents' alcohol use. *Journal of School Health, 77*(2), 67–74.

Henry, L. A. (2006). SEARCHing for an answer: The critical role of new literacies while reading on the Internet. *The Reading Teacher, 59*, 614–627.

Herdt, G., & McClintock, M. (2000). The magical age of 10. *Archives of Sexual Behavior, 29*(6), 587–606.

Hernandez-Reif, M., Diego, M., & Field, T. (2007). Preterm infants show reduced stress behaviors and activity after 5 days of massage therapy. *Infant Behavior and Development, 30*(4), 557–561.

Hersh, R. (2005, November). What does college teach? *Atlantic Monthly*, 140–143.

Hetherington, E. M. (1999). Should we stay together for the sake of the children? In E. M. Hetherington (Ed.), *Coping with divorce, single parenting, and remarriage: A risk and resiliency perspective* (pp. 93–116). Mahwah, NJ: Erlbaum.

Hetherington, E. M., Bridges, M., & Insabella, G. M. (1998). What matters? What does not? *American Psychologist, 53*, 167–184.

Hetherington, E. M., & Clingempeel, W. G. (1992). Coping with marital transitions. *Monographs of the Society for Research in Child Development, 57* (No. 2-3). Chicago, IL: University of Chicago Press.

Hetherington, E. M., & Elmore, A. M. (2003). Risk and resilience in children coping with their parents' divorce and remarriage. In S. Luthar (Ed.), *Resilience and vulnerability: Adaptation in the context of childhood adversities* (pp. 182–212). New York, NY: Cambridge University Press.

Hetherington, E. M., & Kelly, J. (2003). *For better or for worse: Divorce reconsidered.* New York, NY: Norton.

Hetherington, E. M., & Stanley-Hagan, M. M. (1999). Parenting in divorced and remarried families. In M. H. Bornstein (Ed.), *Handbook of parenting: Vol. 3. Status and social conditions of parenting* (pp. 233–254). Mahwah, NJ: Erlbaum.

Herrnstein, R., & Murray, C. (1994). *The bell curve.* New York, NY: Simon & Schuster.

Herrnstein, R. J., Nickerson, R. S., de Se Sanchez, M., & Swets, J. A. (1986). Teaching thinking skills. *American Psychologist, 41*, 1279–1289.

Hertz, R. (2006). *Single by chance, mothers by choice: How women are choosing parenthood without marriage and creating the new American family.* New York, NY: Oxford University Press.

Hewson, P. W., Beeth, M. E., & Thorley, N. R. (1998). Teaching for conceptual change. In B. J. Fraserr & K. G. Tobin (Eds.), *International handbook of science education* (pp. 199–218). New York, NY: Kluwer.

Hickling, A. K., & Wellman, H. M. (2001). The emergence of children's casual explanations. *Developmental Psychology, 37*, 668–683.

Hill, A. J., & Lissau, I. (2002). Psychosocial factors. In W. Burniat, T. Cole, I. Lissau, & E. Poskitt (Eds.), *Child and adolescent obesity: Causes and consequences, prevention and treatment* (pp. 109–128). Cambridge, England: Cambridge University Press.

Hill, E. L., & Khanem, F. (2009). The development of hand preference in children: The effect of task demands and links with manual dexterity. *Brain and Cognition, 71*, 99–107. doi:10.1016/j.bandc.2009.04.006

Hill, J. P., & Holmbeck, G. N. (1987). Disagreements about rules in families with seventh-grade girls and boys. *Journal of Youth and Adolescence, 16*(3), 221–246.

Hill, W. F. (2002). *Learning: A survey of psychological interpretations* (7th ed.). Boston, MA: Allyn & Bacon.

Hinduja, S., & Patchin, J. W. (2007). Offline consequences of online victimization: School violence and delinquency. *Journal of School Violence, 6*(3), 89–112.

Hinduja, S., & Patchin, J. W. (2008). Cyberbullying: An exploratory analysis of factors related to offending and victimization. *Deviant Behavior, 29*(2), 129–156.

Hinduja, S., & Patchin, J. W. (2009). *Bullying beyond the schoolyard: Preventing and responding to cyberbullying.* Thousand Oaks, CA: Corwin Press.

Hines, M. (2004). *Brain gender.* New York, NY: Oxford University Press.

Hines, M., Ahmed, F., & Hughes, I. A. (2003). Psychological outcomes and gender-related development in complete androgen insensitivity syndrome. *Archives of Sexual Behavior, 32*, 93–101.

Hines, M., Brook, C., & Conway, G. S. (2004). Androgen and psychosexual development: Core gender identity, sexual orientation, and recalled childhood gender role behavior in women and men with congenital adrenal hyperplasia (CAH). *Journal of Sex Research, 41*, 75–81. doi:10.1080/00224490409552215

Hinshaw, S. P., Carte, E. T., Fan, C., Jassy, J. S., & Owens, E. B. (2007). Neuropsychological functioning of girls with attention-deficit/hyperactivity disorder followed prospectively into adolescence: Evidence for continuing deficits? *Neuropsychology, 21*(2), 263–273.

Hirsh, K. W., Morrison, C. M., Gaset, S., & Carnicer, E. (2003). Age of acquisition and speech production in L2. *Bilingualism, Language, and Cognition, 6*, 117–128.

Hobbs, R. (2004). A review of school-based initiatives in media literacy education. *American Behavioral Scientist, 48*, 42–59.

Hodges, E. V. E., Boivin, M., Vitario, F., & Bukowski, W. M. (1999). The power of friendship protection against an escalating cycle of peer victimization. *Developmental Psychology, 35*, 94–101.

Hodnett, E. D., Gates, S., Hofmeyr, G. J., & Sakala, C. (2003). Continuous support for women during childbirth. *Cochrane Database System Review, 3.*

Hoehl, S., Wiese, L., & Striano, T. (2008). Young infants' neural processing of objects is affected by eye gaze direction and emotional expression. *PLoS ONE, 3*(6), e 2389.

Hofer, B. K. (2005). The legacy and the challenges: Paul Pintrich's contributions to personal epistemology research. *Educational Psychologist, 40*, 95–105.

Hoff, E. (2003). The specificity of environmental influence: Socioeconomic status affects early vocabulary development via maternal speech. *Child Development, 74*, 1368–1378.

Hoff, E. (2006). How social contexts support and shape language development. *Developmental Review, 26*, 55–88.

Hoffman, M. L. (2000). *Empathy and moral development.* New York, NY: Cambridge University Press.

Hoffman, M. L. (2001). A comprehensive theory of prosocial moral development. In A. C. Bohart & D. J. Stipek (Eds.), *Constructive and destructive behavior: Implications for family, school and society* (pp. 61–86). Washington, DC: American Psychological Association.

Hoffrage, U., Weber, A., Hertwig, R., & Chase, V. M. (2003). How to keep children safe in traffic: Find the daredevils early. *Journal of Experimental Psychology: Applied, 9*(4), 249–260.

Hohman, C. (1998). Evaluating and selecting software for children. *Child Care Information Exchange, 123*, 60–62.

Holahan, C., & Sears, R. (1995). *The gifted group in later maturity*. Stanford, CA: Stanford University Press.

Hollis, C. (2000). Adult outcomes of child- and adolescent-onset schizophrenia: Diagnostic stability and predictive validity. *The American Journal of Psychiatry, 157*, 1652–1659.

Holmbeck, G. N., Friedman, D., Abad, M., & Jandasek, B. (2006). Development and psychopathology in adolescence. In D. A. Wolfe & E. J. Mash (Eds.), *Behavioral and emotional disorders in adolescents* (pp. 21–55). New York, NY: Guilford.

Holmes, R. M, & Procaccino, J. K. (2008). Preschool children's outdoor play area preferences. *Early Child Development and Care*, 1–10.

Holt, R. F., & Svirsky, M. A. (2008). An exploratory look at pediatric cochlear implantation: Is earliest always best? *Ear and Hearing, 29*(4), 492–511.

Honein, M. A., Kirby, R. S., Meyer, R. E., Xing, J., Skerrette, N. I., Yuskiv, N., Marengo, L., . . . Sever, L. E. (2009). The association between major birth defects and preterm birth. *Maternal and Child Health Journal, 13*(2), 1573–6628.

Hong, C., & Jackson, T. (2008). Prevalence and sociodemographic correlates of eating disorder endorsements among adolescents and young adults from China. *European Eating Disorders Review, 16*, 375–385.

Hong, G., & Raudenbush, S. W. (2005). Effects of kindergarten retention policy on children's cognitive growth in reading and mathematics. *Educational Evaluation and Policy Analysis, 27*, 205–224.

Honig, A. S. (2002). *Secure relationships. Nurturing infant/toddler attachment in early care settings*. Washington, DC: NAEYC.

Hood, B. M. (1995). Shifts of visual attention in the human infant: A neuroscientific approach. In C. Rovee-Collier & L. Lipsett (Eds.), *Advances in infancy research* (Vol. 9, pp. 163–216). Norwood, NJ: Ablex.

Hooper, S. R., Schwartz, C. W., Wakely, M. B., DeKruif, R. E. L., & Montgomery, J. W. (2002). Executive functions in elementary school children with and without problems in written expression. *Journal of Learning Disabilities, 35*(1), 57–68.

Hopkins, B., & Westra, T. (1990), Motor development, maternal expectations, and the role of handling. *Infant Behavior and Development, 13*, 117–122.

Horn, J. L. (1998). A basis for research on age differences in cognitive capabilities. In J. J. McArdle & R. W. Woodcock (Eds.), *Human cognitive theories in theory and practice* (pp. 57–87). Mahwah, NJ: Erlbaum.

Horovitz, B. (2002, April 22). Gen Y: A tough crowd to sell. *USA Today*, pp. B1–2.

Houston, A. (2004). In new media as in old, content matters most. *Social Policy Report, 18*(4), 4.

Howard-Jones, P. (2005). An invaluable foundation for better bridges. *Developmental Science, 8*, 470–471.

Howe, C. J., & Tolmie, A. (2003). Group work in primary school science: Discussion, consensus, and guidance from experts. *International Journal of Educational Research, 39*, 51–72.

Howe, N., & Nadler, R. (2009). *Yes we can. The emergence of millennials as a political generation*. Washington, DC: New America Foundation. Retrieved from http://www.newamerica.net/publications/policy/yes_we_can

Howe, N., & Strauss, W. (2000). *Millennials rising: The next great generation*. New York, NY: Vintage Books.

Howes, C. (2000). Social-emotional classroom climate in child care, child-teacher relationships and children's second grade peer relations. *Social Development, 9*, 191–204.

Howes, C., & Phillipsen, L. (1998). Continuity in children's relationships with peers. *Social Development, 7*(3), 340–349.

Hrdlicka, A. (1928). Children running on all fours. *American Journal of Physical Anthropology, XI*, 149–185.

Huesmann, L. R., Eron, L. D., Lefkowitz, M. M., & Walder, L. O. (1984). Stability of aggression over time and generations. *Developmental Psychology, 20*, 1120–1134.

Huesmann, L. R., & Miller, L. S. (1994). Long-term effects of repeated exposure to media violence in childhood. In L. R. Huesmann (Ed.), *Aggressive behavior: Current perspectives* (pp. 153–186). New York, NY: Plenum Press.

Huesmann, L. R., Moise, J. F., & Podolski, C. (1997). The effects of media violence on the development of antisocial behavior. In D. M. Stoff & J. D. Maser (Eds.), *Handbook of antisocial behavior* Hoboken, NJ: Wiley.

Huesmann, L. R., Moise-Titus, J., Podolski, C., & Eron, L. D. (2003). Longitudinal relations between children's exposure to TV violence and their aggressive and violent behavior in young adulthood: 1977–1992. *Developmental Psychology, 39*, 201–221.

Hughes, D., Rodriguez, J., Smith, E. P., Johnson, D. J., Stevenson, H. C., & Spicer, P. (2006). Parents' ethnic-racial socialization practices: A review of research and directions for future study. *Developmental Psychology, 42*(5), 747–770.

Hughes, F. P. (1995). *Children, play and development* (2nd ed.). Boston, MA: Allyn & Bacon.

Hughes, J., & Kwok, O. (2007). Influence of student–teacher and parent–teacher relationships on lower achieving readers' engagement and achievement in the primary grades. *Journal of Educational Psychology, 99*, 39–51.

Huguet, P., & Régner, I. (2007). Stereotype threat among school girls in quasi-ordinary classroom circumstances. *Journal of Educational Psychology, 88*, 545–560.

Hulit, L., & Howard, M. (2006). *Born to talk: An introduction to speech and language development* (4th ed.). Boston, MA: Allyn & Bacon.

Hulit, L. M., Howard, M. R., & Fahey, K. R. (2011). *Born to talk: An introduction to speech and language development* (5th ed.). Boston, MA: Allyn & Bacon.

Human Early Learning Partnership. (2008). StrongStart BC: A family drop-in program. Evaluation Report. Retrieved from http://www.frpbc.ca/news-and-events/documents/StrongStartBC_Evaluation_Report.pdf.

Human Genome Project Information. (2001). *Human genome project information*. Retrieved from www.ornl.gov/hgmis

Human Genome Project Information. (2008a.). *About the Human Genome Project*. Retrieved from http://www.ornl.gov/sci/techresources/Human_Genome/home.shtml

Human Genome Project Information. (2008b.). *Behavioral genetics*. Retrieved from http://www.ornl.gov/sci/techresources/Human_Genome/elsi/behavior.shtml).

Human Genome Project Information. (2008c.) *How many genes are in the human genome?* Retrieved from http://www.ornl.gov/sci/techresources/Human_Genome/faq/genenumber.shtml

Human Genome Project Information. (2008d.). *Genetic anthropology, ancestry, and ancient human migration*. Retrieved from http://www.ornl.gov/sci/techresources/Human_Genome/elsi/humanmigration.shtml#4Information

Hung, D. W. L. (1999). Activity, apprenticeship, and epistemological appropriation: Implications from the writings of Michael Polanyi. *Educational Psychologist, 34*, 193–205.

Hunt, E. (2000). Let's hear it for crystallized intelligence. *Learning and Individual Differences, 12*, 123–129.

Hunt, J. McV. (1961). *Intelligence and experience*. New York, NY: Ronald.

Hunt, N., & Marshall, K. (2002). *Exceptional children and youth* (3rd ed.). Boston, MA: Houghton Miffin.

Hunt, R. R., & Ellis, H. C. (1999). *Fundamentals of cognitive psychology* (6th ed.). New York, NY: McGraw-Hill.

Hunter, S. K., & Yankowitz, J. (1996). Medical fetal therapy. In J. A. Kuller, N. C. Cheschier, & R. C. Cefalo (Eds.), *Prenatal diagnosis and reproductive genetics*. St. Louis, MO: Mosby.

Hutchinson, N. L. (2007). Inclusion of exceptional learners in Canadian classrooms: A practical handbook for teachers (3rd ed.). Toronto, Canada: Prentice Hall.

Hyde, J. S., & Linn, M. C. (1988). Gender differences in verbal ability: A meta-analysis. *Psychological Bulletin, 104*(1), 53–69.

Hyman, M. (2009, April). American's obsession with youth sports and how it harms our kids. *Sports Illustrated*. Retrieved from http://sportsillustrated.cnn.com/2009/more/04/06/youthsports.untilithurts/index.html

IDEA. (2006). Who are children with disabilities? Coming to an agreed definition. Retrieved from http://makingendsmeet.idea.gov.uk/idk/core/page.do?pageId=5111113

Iannelli, V. (2008). Weight loss goals for kids: Childhood obesity basics. Retrieved from http://pediatrics.about.com/od/obesity/a/0707_wt_loss_gl.htm.

Iglowstein I., Jenni, O. G., Molinari L., & Largo R. H. (2003). Sleep duration from infancy to adolescence: Reference values and generational trends. *Pediatrics, 111*(2), 302–307.

Information, National Clearinghouse on Child Abuse and Neglect (2005, May 11, 2006). *Long-term consequences of child abuse and neglect*. Retrieved from http://nccanch.acf.hhs.gov/pubs/factsheets/long_term_consequences.cfm

Inhelder, B., & Piaget, J. (1958). *The growth of logical thinking from childhood to adolescence: An essay on the construction of formal operational structures*. New York, NY: Basic Books.

Irvine, J. J., & Armento, B. J. (2001). *Culturally responsive teaching: Lesson planning for elementary and middle grades*. New York, NY: McGraw-Hill.

Irwin, L. G., Siddiqi, A., & Hertzman, C. (2007). *Early child development: A powerful equalizer*. Geneva, Switzerland: World Health Organization.

Isabella, R., & Belsky, J. (1991). Interactional synchrony and the origins of infant–mother attachment: A replication study. *Child Development, 62*, 373–384.

Jablonka, E., & Raz, G. (2009). Transgenerational epigenetic inheritance: Prevalence, mechanisms, and implications for the study of heredity and evolution. *The Quarterly Review of Biology, 84*(2), 131–176.

Jackson, L. A., von Eye, A., Biocca, F. A., Barbatsis, G., Zhao, Y., & Fitzgerald, H. E. (2006). Does home Internet use influence the academic performance of low-income children? *Developmental Psychology, 42*, 429–435.

Jackson, Y., & Werner, J. S. (2000). Appraisal, social support, and life events: Predicting outcome behavior in school-age children. *Child Development, 71*, 1441–1457.

Jacobs, J. E., Lanza, S., Osgood, D. W., Eccles, J. S., & Wigfield, A. (2002). Changes in children's self-competence and values: Gender and domain differences across grades one through twelve. *Child Development, 73*, 509–527.

Jacoby, J. (2004). Gene therapy: Cornerstone of modern medicine in the new millennium? *Gene Therapy, 11*, 427–428.

Jaenisch, R., & Bird, A. (2003). Epigenetic regulation of gene expression: How the genome integrates intrinsic and environmental signals. *Nat Genet 33*(suppl), 245–254.

Jaffe, E. (2008). Mirror neurons: How we reflect on behavior. *Observer, 20*(5), 2–25.

Jaffe, M. L. (1997). *Understanding parenting.* Boston, MA: Allyn & Bacon.

Jaffee, S., & Hyde, J. S. (2000). Gender differences in moral orientation. *Psychological Bulletin, 126*, 703–726.

Jaffee, S. R., Moffitt, T. E., Caspi, A., & Taylor, A. (2003). Life with (or without) father: The benefits of living with two biological parents depend on the father's antisocial behavior. *Child Development, 74*, 109–126.

Jahromi, L. B., & Stifter, C. A. (2007). Individual differences in the contribution of maternal soothing to Infant distress reduction. *Infancy, 11*(3), 255–269. Retrieved from http://www.informaworld.com/smpp/title~db=all~content=t775653654~tab=issueslist~ branches=11 - v11

Jalongo, M. R., Dragich, D., Conrad, N. K., & Zhang, A. (2002). Using wordless picture books to support emergent literacy. *Early Childhood Education Journal, 29*(3), 167–177.

James, D. K., Spencer, C. J., & Stepsis, B. W. (2002). Fetal learning: a prospective randomized controlled study. *Ultrasound Obstet Gynecol 20*, 431–438.

James, S. J., Pogribna, M., Pogribna, I. P., Melnyk, S., Hine, R. J., Gibson, J. B., Vi, P., . . . Gaylor, D. W. (2000). Abnormal folate metabolism and mutation in the methylene tetrahydrofolate reductase gene may be maternal risk factors for Down Syndrome. *American Journal of Clinical Nutrition, 70*, 495–501.

James, W. (1890). *Principles of psychology.* New York, NY: Holt.

Jarrett, R. L. (1995). Growing up poor: The family experiences of socially mobile youth in low-income African American neighborhoods. *Journal of Adolescent Research, 10*, 111–135.

Jaswal, V. K., & Hansen, M. B. (2006). Learning words: Children disregard some pragmatic information that conflicts with mutual exclusivity. *Developmental Science, 9*, 158–165.

Jaswal, V. K., & Markman, E. M. (2001). Learning proper and common names in inferential versus obstensive contexts. *Child Development, 72*, 787–802.

Jemmott, J. B. I., Jemmott, L. S., & Fong, G. T. (2010). Efficacy of a theory-based abstinence-only intervention over 24 months: A randomized controlled trial with young adolescents. *Archives of Pediatric & Adolescent Medicine, 164*, 152–159.

Jensen, A. R. (1969). How much can we boost IQ and scholastic achievement? *Harvard Educational Review, 39*, 1–123.

Jensen, A. R. (1998). *The g factor : The science of mental ability.* New York, NY: Prager.

Jensen, J. J. (1998). Learning to stand alone: The contemporary American transition to adulthood in cultural and historical context. *Human Development, 41*, 295–315.

Jensen, L. A. (2003). Coming of age in a multicultural world: Globalization and adolescent cultural identity formation. *Applied Developmental Science, 7*(3), 189–196.

Jensen, L. A., Arnett, J. J., Feldman, S. S., & Cauffman, E. (2004). The right to do wrong: Lying to parents among adolescents and emerging adults. *Journal of Youth and Adolescence, 33*(2), 101–112.

Ji, C-Y., & Ohsawa, S. (2000). Onset of the release of spermatozoa (spermarche) in Chinese male youth. *American Journal of Human Biology, 12*, 577–587.

Jie, L., & Desheng, G. (2004). New directions in the moral education curriculum in Chinese schools. *Journal of Moral Education, 33*, 495–510.

Jimerson, S. R. (1999). On the failure of failure: Examining the association between early grade retention and education and employment outcomes during late adolescence. *Journal of School Psychology, 37*, 243–272.

Jimerson, S. R., Anderson, G. E., & Whipple, A. D. (2002). Winning the battle and losing the war: Examining the relation between grade retention and dropping out of high school. *Psychology in the Schools, 39*, 441–457.

John-Steiner, V., & Mahn, H. (1996). Sociocultural approaches to learning and development: A Vygotskian framework. *Educational Psychologist, 31*, 191–206.

Johnson, A. (2003). Procedural memory and skill acquisition. In A. F. Healy & R. W. Proctor (Eds.), *Experimental psychology* (Vol. 4, pp. 499–523). New York, NY: Wiley.

Johnson, C., & Anglin, J. M. (1995). Qualitative developments in the content and form of children's definitions. *Journal of Speech and Hearing Research, 38*, 612–629.

Johnson, D. W., & Johnson, R. T. (1999). *Learning together and alone: Cooperation, competition, and individualization* (5th ed.). Boston, MA: Allyn & Bacon.

Johnson, D. W., & Johnson, R. T. (2009). *Joining together: Group theory and group skills* (10th ed.). Columbus, OH: Merrill.

Johnson, H. D. (2004). Gender, grade and relationship differences in emotional closeness within adolescent friendships. *Adolescence, 39*, 243–255.

Johnson, S. C., Booth, A., & O'Hearn, K. (2001). Inferring the unseen goals of a non-human agent. *Cognitive Development, 16*, 637–656.

Johnson, S. P., Bremner, J. G., Slater, A., Mason, U., Foster, K., & Cheshire, A. (2003). Infants' perception of object trajectories. *Child Development, 74*, 94–108.

Johnson, W., Carothers, A., & Deary, I. J. (2008). Sex differences in variability in general intelligence: A new look at the old question. *Perspectives on Psychological Science, 3*, 518–531.

Johnston, L. D., O'Malley, P. M., Bachman, J. G., & Schulenberg, J. E. (2009). *Monitoring the future: National results on adolescent drug use. Overview of key findings, 2008* (NIH Publication No. 09-7401). Bethesda, MD: National Institute on Drug Abuse.

Joiner, T. E. (1999). The clustering and contagion of suicide. *Current Directions in Psychological Science, 8*, 89–92.

Jonassen, D. H. (2003). Designing research-based instruction for story problems. *Educational Psychology Review, 15*, 267–296.

Jones, D. C. (2004). Body image among adolescent girls and boys: A longitudinal study. *Developmental Psychology* (40), 823–835.

Jones, M. C. (1965). Psychological correlates of somatic development. *Child Development, 36*, 899–911.

Jones, M. S., Levin, M. E., Levin, J. R., & Beitzel, B. D. (2000). Can vocabulary-learning strategies and pair-learning formats be profitably combined? *Journal of Educational Psychology, 92*, 256–262.

Jones, S., Eisenberg, N., Fabes, R. A., & MacKinnnon, D. P. (2002). Parents' reactions to elementary school children's negative emotions: Relations to social and emotional functioning at school. *Merrill-Palmer Quarterly, 48*, 133–159.

Jones, S. M., & Dindia, K. (2004). A meta-analytic perspective on sex equity in the classroom. *Review of Educational Research, 74*, 443–471.

Joyner, B. L., Gill-Bailey, C., & Moon, R. Y. (2009). Infant sleep environments depicted in magazines targeted to women of childbearing age, *Pediatrics, 124*(3), e416–e422 appears in the September issue of *Pediatrics.* Retrieved from http://pediatrics.aappublications.org/cgi/content/full/124/3/e416

Justice, L. M., Bowles, R. P., Turnbull, K. L. P., & Skibbe, L. E. (2009). School readiness among children with varying histories of language difficulties. *Developmental Psychology, 45*, 460–476.

Juvonen, J., Graham, S., & Schuster, M. A. (2003). Bullying among young adolescents: The strong, the weak, and the troubled. *Pediatrics, 112*, 1231–1237.

Kaestner, R., & Xu, X. (2010). Title IX, girls' sports participation, and adult female physical activity and weight. *Evaluation Review, 34*(1), 52–78.

Kagan, J. (2004). The limitations of concepts in developmental psychology. *Merrill-Palmer Quarterly, 50*, 291–298.

Kagan, J., & Herschkowitz, N. (2005). *A young mind in a growing brain.* Mahwah, NJ: Erlbaum.

Kagan, J., & Scott-Little, C. (2004). Early learning standards. *Phi Delta Kappan, 82*, 388–395.

Kail, R. (2000). Speed of processing: Developmental change and links to intelligence. *Journal of School Psychology, 38*, 51–61.

Kail, R., & Park, Y. (1994). Processing time, articulation time, and memory span. *Journal of Experimental Child Psychology, 57*, 281–291.

Kail, R. V. (2004). Cognitive development includes global and domain-specific processes. *Merrill-Palmer Quarterly, 50*, 445–455.

Kaiser, L. L., Melgar-Quinonez, H. R., Lamp, C. L., Johns, M. C., Sutherlin, J. M., & Harwood, J. O.

(2002). Food security and nutritional outcomes of preschool-age Mexican-American children. *Journal of the American Dietetic Association, 102*, 924–929.

Kalb, C. (2004, January 26). Brave new babies: Parents now have the power to choose the sex of their children. But as technology answers prayers, it also raises some troubling questions. *Newsweek.*

Kalyuga, S., Chandler, P., Tuovinen, J., & Sweller, J. (2001). When problem solving is superior to studying worked examples. *Journal of Educational Psychology, 93*, 579–588.

Kamawar, D., LeFevre, J-A., Bisanz, J., Fast, L., Skwarchuk, S-L., Smith-Cahnt, B., & Penner-Wilger, M. (2010). Knowledge of counting principles: How relevant is order irrelevance? *Journal of Experimental Child Psychology, 105*, 138–145.

Kamm K., Thelen E., & Jensen J. L. (1990). Dynamical systems approach to motor development. *Physical Therapy, 70*, 763–775.

Kanaya, T., Scullin, M. H., & Ceci, S. J. (2003). The Flynn effect and U.S. policies: The impact of rising IQ scores on American society via mental retardation diagnoses. *American Psychologist, 58*, 1–13.

Kandel, D. B. (1978). Homophily, selection, and socialization in adolescent friendships. *American Journal of Sociology, 84*(2), 427–436.

Kandel, D. B., & Chen, K. (2000). Extent of smoking and nicotine dependence in the United States: 1991–1993. *Nicotine & Tobacco Research, 2*, 263–274.

Kane, E. (2000). Racial and ethnic variations in gender-related attitudes. *Annual Review of Sociology, 26*, 419–439.

Kane, E. W. (2006). "No way my boys are going to be like that!": Parents' responses to children's gender nonconformity. *Gender & Society, 20*, 149–176.

Kaneshiro, N. K. (2010). Lead poisoning. Retrieved from http://www.nlm.nih.gov/medlineplus/ency/article/002473.htm

Kanetsuna, T., & Smith, P. K. (2002). Pupil insight into bullying and coping with bullying: A bi-national study in Japan and England. *Journal of School Violence, 1*, 5–29.

Kanters, M. A., & Casper, J. (2008). Supported or pressured? An examination of agreement among parents and children on parents' role in youth sports. *Journal of Sport Behavior, 31*(1), 64–80.

Karpov, Y. V. (2006). *The neo-Vygotskian approach to child development.* New York, NY: Cambridge University Press.

Karpov, Y. V., & Bransford, J. D. (1995). L. S. Vygotsky and the doctrine of empirical and theoretical learning. *Educational Psychologist, 30*, 61–66.

Karpov, Y. V., & Hawood, H. C. (1998). Two ways to elaborate Vygotsky's concept of mediation implications for instruction. *American Psychologist, 53*, 27–36.

Katz, J. R. (2001). Playing at home: The talk of pretend play. In D. K. Dickinson & P. O. Tabors (Eds.), *Beginning literacy with language: Young children learning at home and school* (pp. 53–73). Baltimore, MD: P. H. Brookes.

Katz, R. B. (2000). *Recreating motherhood.* New Brunswick, NJ: Rutgers University Press.

Katz, S. R. (1999). Teaching in tensions: Latino immigrant youth, their teachers, and the structures of schooling. *Teachers College Record, 100*(4), 809–840.

Katzmarzyk, P. T., Baur, L. A., Blair, S. N., Lambert, E. V., Oppert, J-M., & Riddoch, C. (2008). International conference on physical activity and obesity in children: Summary statement and recommendations. *International Journal of Pediatric Obesity, 3*, 3–21.

Kauerz, K. (2002). *No Child Left Behind policy brief: Literacy.* Denver, CO: Education Commission of the States.

Kaufman, A. S., & Kaufman, N. L. (1983). *Kaufman Assessment Battery for Children: Interpretive manual.* Circle Pines, MN: American Guidance Service.

Kaufman, A. S., & Kaufman, N. L. (2003). *Kaufman Assessment Battery for Children* (2nd ed.). Circle Pines, MN: American Guidance Service.

Keating, D. P., & Hertzman, C. (1999). *Developmental heath and the wealth of nations: Social, biological, and educational dynamics.* New York, NY: Guilford.

Kelley, S., & Brownell, C. (2000). Mastery motivation and self-evaluative affect in toddlers: Longitudinal relations with maternal behavior. *Child Development, 71*, 1061.

Kellogg, R. (1970). *Analyzing children's art.* Palo Alto: CA: Mayfield.

Kelly, D., Liu, S., Lee, K., Quinn, P., Pascalis, O., Slater, A., & Ge, L. (2009). Development of the other-race effect during infancy. Evidence toward universality? *Journal of Experimental Child Psychology, 104*(1), 105–114.

Kelly, K. (1999). Retention vs. social promotion: Schools search for alternatives. *Harvard Education Letter, 15*(1), 1–3.

Kennedy Institute of Ethics Georgetown University. (2006). Case 4 *Genie, The Wild Child Research or Exploitation?* Washington, DC: Author.

Kerr, D. C. R., Lopez, N. L., Olson, S. L., & Sameroff, A. J. (2004). Parental discipline and externalizing behavior problems in early childhood: The roles of moral regulation and child gender. *Journal of Abnormal Child Psychology, 32*, 369–383.

Kerssen-Griep, J. (2001). Teacher communication activities relevant to student motivation: Classroom framework and instructional communication competence. *Communication Education, 50*, 256–273.

Kerssmakers, S. P., Fotiadou, A. N., de Jonge, M. C., Karantanas, A. H., & Maas, M. (2009). Sport injuries in the paediatric and adolescent patient: A growing problem. *Pediatric Radiology, 39*(5), 471–484.

Kia-Keating, M., & Ellis, B. H. (2007). Belonging and connection to school in resettlement: Young refugees, school belonging, and psychosocial adjustment. *Clinical Child Psychology and Psychiatry, 12*(1), 29–43.

Kiang, L., & Harter, S. (2008). Do pieces of the self-puzzle fit? Integrated/fragmented selves in biculturally-identified Chinese Americans. *Journal of Research in Personality, 42*, 1657–1662.

Kibby, J. E., Mersch, J., Bredenkamp, J. K., & Shiel, W. C. (2009). Newborn infant hearing screening. Retrieved from http://www.medicinenet.com

KidsHealth. (2009). *Cerebral palsy.* Retrieved from http://kidshealth.org/parent/medical/brain/cerebral_palsy.html

KidsHealth. (2009). *Kids and exercise.* Retrieved from http://kidshealth.org/parent/nutrition_fit/fitness/exercise.html#

KidsHealth. (2010). *Iron-deficiency anemia.* Retrieved from http://kidshealth.org/parent/medical/heart/ida.html#a_What_Is_Iron_Deficiency_Anemia_

Kim, K., Ryu, E., Chon, M., Yeun, E., Choi, S., Seo, J., & Nam, B. (2006). Internet addiction in Korean adolescents and its relation to depression and suicidal ideation: A questionnaire survey. *International Journal of Nursing Studies, 43*(2), 185–192.

Kim, L. S., Jeong, S. W., Lee, Y. M., & Kim, J. S. (2010). Cochlear implantation in children. *Auris, Nasus, Larynx, 37*, 6–17.

Kim, T. E., Guerra, N. G., & Williams, K. R. (2008). Preventing youth problem behaviors and enhancing physical health by promoting core competencies. *Journal of Adolescent Health, 43*, 401–407.

King, A. (1990). Enhancing peer interaction and learning in the classroom through reciprocal questioning. *American Educational Research Journal, 27*, 664–687.

King, A. (2002). Structuring peer interactions to promote high-level cognitive processing. *Theory Into Practice, 41*, 31–39.

King, G., Law, M., King, S., Rosenbaum, P., Kertoy, M. K., & Young, N. L. (2003). A conceptual model of the factors affecting the recreation and leisure participation of children with disabilities. *Physical and Occupational Therapy in Pediatrics, 23*(1), 63–90.

Kirk, S., Gallagher, J., & Anastasiow, N. (1993). *Educating exceptional children* (7th ed.). Boston, MA: Houghton Mifflin.

Kirst, M. (1991). Interview on assessment issues with Lorrie Shepard. *Educational Researcher, 20*(2), 21–33.

Kisilevsky, B. S., Hains, S. M. J., Lee, K., Xie, X., Huang, H., Ye, H. H., Zhang, K., & Wang, Z. (2003). Effects of experience on fetal voice recognition. *Psychological Science, 14*(3), 220–224.

Klaczynski, P. A. (2001). The influence of analytic and heuristic processing on adolescent reasoning and decision making. *Child Development, 72*, 844–861.

Klaczynski, P. A. (2004). A dual-process model of adolescent development: Implications for decision making, reasoning, and identity. In R. V. Kail (Ed.), *Advances in child development and behavior, Vol. 31* (pp. 73–123). San Diego, CA: Academic Press.

Klaczynski, P. A. (2005). Metacognition and cognitive variability: A two-process model of decision making and its development. In J. E. Jacobs & P. A. Klaczynski (Eds.), *The development of judgment and decision making in children and adolescents* (pp. 39–76). Mahwah, NJ: Erlbaum.

Klaczynski, P. A. (2006). Learning, belief biases, and metacognition. *Journal of Cognition and Development, 7*(3), 295–300.

Klaczynski, P. A., Schuneman, M. J., & Daniel, D. B. (2004). Theories of conditional reasoning: A developmental examination of competing hypotheses. *Developmental Psychology, 40*, 559–571.

Klein, P. J., & Meltzoff, A. N. (1999). Long-term memory, forgetting, and deferred imitation in 12-month-old infants. *Developmental Science, 2*, 102–113.

Klein, S. S., & Harris, A. H. (2007). *A user's guide to the Legacy Cycle.* Retrieved from http://www.scientificjournals.org/journals2007/articles/1088.pdf

Kleinfeld, J. (2005). Culture fuels boys' learning problems. *Alaska Daily News*, p. B6.

Klibanoff, R. S., Levine, S. C., Huttenlocher, J., Vasilyeva, M., & Hedges, L. V. (2006). Preschool children's mathematical knowledge: The effect of teacher "math talk." *Developmental Psychology, 42*, 59–69.

Klinefelter's syndrome. (2008). Retrieved from http://ghr.nlm.nih.gov/condition=klinefelter syndrome

Kmietowicz, Z. (2003). Fertilization authority recommends a ban on sex selection. *British Medical Journal, 327*, 1123.

Knafo, A., Iervolino, A. C., & Plomin, R. (2005). Masculine girls and feminine boys: Genetic and environmental contributions to atypical gender development in early childhood. *Journal of Personality and Social Psychology, 88*, 400–412.

Knafo, A., & Schwartz, S. H. (2003). Parenting and adolescents' accuracy in perceiving parental values. *Child Development*, 74, 595–611.

Knapp, M., Turnbull, B. J., & Shields, P. M. (1990). New directions for educating children of poverty. *Educational Leadership, 48*(1), 4–9.

Knoph, M., & Schneider, W. (2007, April). *The development of episodic memory from preschool to young adulthood.* Paper presented at the Society for Research in Child Development, Boston, Massachusetts.

Knox, M. (2010). On hitting children: A review of corporal punishment in the United States. *Journal of Pediatric Health Care, 24*, 103–107.

Kobiella, A., Grossmann, T., Reid, V. M., & Striano, T. (2008). The discrimination of angry and fearful facial expressions in 7-month-old infants: An event-related potential study. *Cognition and Emotion 22*(1): 134–146.

Kochanska, G. (2002). Mutually responsive orientation between mothers and their young children: A context for the early development of conscience. *Current Directions in Psychological Science, 11*, 191–195.

Kochanska, G., Aksan, N., & Nichols, K. E. (2003). Maternal power assertion in discipline and moral discourse contexts: Commonalities, differences, and implications for children's moral conduct and cognition. *Developmental Psychology, 39*, 949–963.

Kochanska, G., Coy, K. C., & Murray, K. T. (2001). The development of self-regulation in the first four years of life. *Child Development, 72*, 1091–1111.

Kochanska, G., Gross, J. N., Lin, M.-H., & Nichols, K. E. (2002). Guilt in young children: Development, determinants, and relations with a broader system of standards. *Child Development, 73*, 461–482.

Koedel, C. (2008). Teacher quality and dropout outcomes in a large, urban school district. *Journal of Urban Economics, 64*, 560–572.

Koehoorn, M., Breslin, F. C., & Xu, F. (2008). Investigating the longer-term health consequences of work-related injuries among youth. *Journal of Adolescent Health, 43*, 466–473.

Kohlberg, L. (1963). The development of children's orientations toward moral order: Sequence in the development of moral thought. *Vita Humana, 6*, 11–33.

Kohlberg, L. (1966). A cognitive-developmental analysis of children's sex-role concepts and attitudes. In E. E. Maccoby (Ed.), *The development of sex differences* (pp. 82–173). Palo Alto, CA: Stanford University Press.

Kohlberg, L. (1975). The cognitive developmental approach to moral education. *Phi Delta Kappan, 56*, 670–677.

Kohlberg, L. (1981). *The philosophy of moral development.* New York, NY: Harper & Row.

Kohlberg, L., & Power, C. (1981). Moral development, religious thinking, and the question of a seventh stage. In L. Kohlberg (Ed.), *Essays on moral development: Vol. 1. The philosophy of moral development: Moral stages and the idea of justice* (pp. 311–372). New York, NY: Harper & Row.

Kohler, P. K., Manhart, L. E., & Lafferty, M. E. (2008). Abstinence-only and comprehensive sex education and the initiation of sexual activity and teen pregnancy. *Journal of Adolescent Health, 42*, 433–351.

Kools, S. M. (1997). Adolescent identity development in foster care. *Family Relations, 46*, 263–271.

Korenman, S., Miller, J., & Sjaastad, J. (1995). Long-term poverty and child development in the United States: Results from the NLSY. *Children and Youth Services Review, 17*, 127–155.

Kozulin, A. (2003). Psychological tools and mediated learning. In A. Kozulin, B. Gindid, V. S. Ageyev, & S. M. Miller (Eds.), *Vygotsky's educational theory in cultural context* Cambridge, England: Cambridge University Press.

Kozulin, A., & Presseisen, B. Z. (1995). Mediated learning experience and psychological tools: Vygotsky's and Feuerstein's perspective in a study of student learning. *Educational Psychologist, 30*, 67–75.

Krajcik, J. S., & Czerniak, C. (2007). *Teaching science in elementary and middle school classrooms: A project-based approach* (3rd ed.). Mahwah, NJ: Erlbaum.

Krakow, E. (2007). Why do babies cry? *Bulletin of the Centre of Excellence for Early Childhood Development, 6*(2), 2–3.

Kramer, L., & Bank, L. (2005). Sibling relationship contributions to individual and family well-being: Introduction to the special issue. *Journal of Family Psychology, 19*, 483–485.

Kramer, M. R., & Hogue, C. R. (2009). What causes racial disparity in very preterm birth? A biosocial perspective. *Epidemiological Reviews, 31*, 84–98.

Kramer, M. S. (2009). Late preterm birth: Appreciable risks, rising incidence. *The Journal of Pediatrics, 154*(2), 159–160.

Kramer, M. S., Petrini, J. R., Dias, T., McCormick, M. C., Massolo, M. L., Green, N. S., & Escobar, G. J. (2009). Increased risk of adverse neurological development for late preterm infants. *Journal of Pediatrics, 154*(2), 169–176.

Kratochvil C. J. (2009). Current pharmacotherapy for ADHD. 2nd International Congress on ADHD. From Childhood to Adult Disease, May 21–24, 2009, Vienna, Austria. *ADHD Attention Deficit and Hyperactivity disorders* 1:61.

Krauss, M. (1992). Statement of Michael Krauss, representing the Linguistic Society of America. In U.S. Senate, *Native American Languages Act of 1991: Hearing before the Select Committee on Indian Affairs* (pp. 18–22). Washington, DC: U.S. Government Printing Office.

Kreutzer, M. A., Leonard, C., & Flavell, J. H. (1975). *An interview study of children's knowledge about memory.* Chicago, IL: University of Chicago Press.

Krevans, J., & Gibbs, J. C. (1996). Parents' use of inductive discipline: Relations to children's empathy and prosocial behaviour. *Child Development, 67*, 3263–3277. doi:10.1111/1467-8624.ep9706244859

Kriedler, W. (1996). Smart ways to handle kids who pick on others. *Instructor, 106*, 70–77.

Kroger, J. (2003). Identity development during adolescence. In G. R. Adams & M. D. Berzonsky (Eds.), *Blackwell handbook of adolescence.* Oxford, England, Blackwell Publishing Ltd.

Kuhl, P. (2000). A new view of language acquisition. *PNAS, 97*(2), 11850–11857.

Kuhl, P. K., Stevens, E., Hayashi, A., Deguchi, T., Kiritani, S., & Iverson, P. (2006). Infants show facilitation for native language phonetic perception between 6 and 12 months. *Developmental Science, 9*, 13–21.

Kuhl, P. K., Tsao, F. M., & Liu, H. M. (2003). Foreign-language experience in infancy: Effects of short-term exposure and social interaction on phonetic learning. *Proceedings of the National Academy of Sciences*, 100, 9096–9101.

Kuhn, D. (2005). *Education for thinking.* Cambridge, MA: Harvard University Press.

Kuhn, D., & Dean, D. (2004). Connecting scientific reasoning with casual inference. *Journal of Cognition and Development, 5*, 261–288.

Kuhn, D., & Franklin, S. (2006). The second decade: What develops (and how). In D. Kuhn & R. S. Siegler (Eds.), *Cognition, perception, and language* (6th ed., Vol. 2, pp. 953–993). New York, NY: Wiley.

Kuhn, D., Goh, W., Kalypso, I., & Shaenfield, D. (2008). Arguing on the computer: A microgenetic study of developing argument skills in a computer-supported environment. *Child Development, 79*, 1310–1328.

Kujawski, J. H., & Bower, T. G. R. (2003). Same-sex preferential looking during infancy as a function of abstract representation. *British Journal of Developmental Psychology, 11*(2), 201–209.

Kumar, D. D., & Sherwood, R. D. (2007). Effect of problem-based simulation on the conceptual understanding of undergraduate science educational majors. *Journal of Science Education and Technology, 16*, 239–246.

Kupersmidt, J. B., & Coie, J. D. (1990). Preadolescent peer status, aggression, and school adjustment as predictors of externalizing problems in adolescence. *Child Development, 61*, 1350–1362.

Kurtz, B. E., Schneider, W., Carr, M., Borkowski, J. G., & Rellinger, E. (1990). Strategy instruction and attributional beliefs in West Germany and the United States: Do teachers foster metacognitive development? *Contemporary Educational Psychology, 15*, 268–283.

Lacourse, E., Nagin, D., Trembly, R. E., Vitaro, F., & Claes, M. (2003). Development trajectories of boys' delinquent group membership and facilitation of violent behaviors during adolescence. *Development and Psychopathology, 15*(1), 183–197.

Ladd, G. W. (1999). Peer relationships and social competence during early and middle childhood. *Annual Review of Psychology, 50*, 333–359.

Ladd, G. W., & Troop-Gordon, W. (2003). The role of chronic peer difficulties in the development of children's psychological adjustment problems. *Child Development*, 74, 1344–1367.

Ladson-Billings, G. (1992). Culturally relevant teaching: The key to making multicultural education work. In C. A. Grant (Ed.), *Research and multicultural education* (pp. 106–121). London, England: Falmer Press.

Ladson-Billings, G. (1994). *The dream keepers.* San Francisco, CA: Jossey-Bass.

Ladson-Billings, G. (1995). But that is just good teaching! The case for culturally relevant pedagogy. *Theory Into Practice, 34,* 161–165.

Ladson-Billings, G. (2004). Landing on the wrong note: The price we paid for Brown. *Educational Researcher, 33*(7), 3–13.

LaFontana, K. M., & Cillessen, A. H. N. (2002). Children's perceptions of popular and unpopular peers: A multimethod assessment. *Developmental Psychology, 38*(5), 635–647.

Laible, D. J., Carlo, G., & Raffaelli, M. (2000). The differential relations of parent and peer attachment to adolescent adjustment. *Journal of Youth and Adolescence, 29*(1), 45–59.

Laidlaw, L. (2001, March). I can be happy at this school: Creating a socially responsible learning community. *Teacher: Newsmagazine of the BC Teachers' Federation,* 1–4.

Lajoie, S. P., & Azevedo, R. (2006). Teaching and learning in technology-rich environments. In P. A. Alexander & P. H. Winne (Eds.), *Handbook of educational psychology* (2nd ed., pp. 803–823). Mahwah, NJ: Erlbaum.

Lally, J. R. (2006). Metatheories of childrearing. In J. R. Lally, P. L. Mangione, & D. Greenwald (Eds.), *Concepts of care* (pp. 7–14). Sausalito, CA: PITC.

Lally, J. R, Lurie-Hurvitz, E., & Cohen, J. (2006). Good health, strong families, and positive early learning experiences: Promoting better public policies for America's infants and toddlers. *ZERO TO THREE, 26*(6), 6–9.

Lamarche, V., & Brendgen, M. (2006). Do friendships and sibling relationships provide protection against peer victimization in a similar way? *Social Development, 15,* 373–393.

Lamaze, F. (1958). *Painless childbirth: Psychoprophylactic method.* London, England: Burke.

Lamb, M. E. (1998). Non-parental childcare: Context, quality, correlates, and consequences. In W. Damon, I. E. Sigel, & K. A. Renninger (Eds.), *Handbook of child psychology: Vol. 4. Child psychology in practice* (pp. 73–133). New York, NY: Wiley.

Lamb, M. E. (1999). Noncustodial fathers and their impact on the children of divorce. In R. A. Thompson & P. R. Amato (Eds.), *The postdivorce family: Children, parenting, and society* (pp. 105–125). Thousand Oaks, CA: Sage.

Lamb, M. E. (2005). Attachments, social networks, and developmental contexts. *Human Development, 48* (1/2), 108–112.

Lamb, M. E., Bornstein, M. H., & Teti, D. M. (2002). *Development in Infancy* (4th ed.). Mahwah, NJ: Erlbaum.

Lamb, M. E., & Lewis, C. (2005). The role of parent-child relationships in child development. In M. H. Bornstein & M. E. Lamb (Eds.), *Developmental science: An advanced textbook* (5th ed., pp. 429–468). Mahwah, NJ: Erlbaum.

Lamborn, S. D., Mounts, N. S., Steinberg, L., & Dornbusch, S. M. (1991). Patterns of competence and adjustment among adolescents from authoritative, authoritarian, indulgent, and neglectful families. *Child Development, 63,* 1049–1065.

Lampl, M., Veldhuis, J. D., & Johnson, M. L. (1992). Saltation and stasis: A model of human growth. *Science, 258,* 801–803.

Lander, E. S., Linton, L. M., Birren, B., Nusbaum, C., Zody, M. C., & Baldwin, J. (2001). Initial sequencing and analysis of the human genome. *Nature, 409,* 860–921.

Landrum, T. J., & Kauffman, J. M. (2006). Behavioral approaches to classroom management. In C. M. Evertson & C. S. Weinstein (Eds.), *Handbook of classroom management: Research, practice, and contemporary issues.* Mahwah, NJ: Erlbaum.

Lane, K., Falk, K., & Wehby, J. (2006). Classroom management in special education classrooms and resource rooms. In C. M. Evertson & C. S. Weinstein (Eds.), *Handbook of classroom management: Research, practice, and contemporary issues.* Mahwah, NJ: Erlbaum.

Langlois, C. (2006). *Child nutrition.* Retrieved from http://www.nationalchildrensalliance.com/nca/pubs/2006/Child%20Nutrition%20Policy%20Brief.pdf

Langlois, J. A., Rutland-Brown, W., & Thomas, K. E. (2004). Traumatic brain injury in the United States: Emergency department visits, hospitalizations, and deaths. doi:10.1016/j.jsr.2008.05.001

Langlois, J. H., & Stephan, C. W. (1981). Beauty and the beast: The role of physical attraction in peer relationships and social behavior. In S. S. Brehm, S. M. Kassin, & S. X. Gibbans (Eds.), *Developmental social psychology: Theory and research* (pp. 152–168). New York, NY: Oxford.

Larose, S., & Tarabulsy, G. M. (2005). Mentoring academically at-risk students: Processes, outcomes, and conditions for success. In D. L. DuBois & M. J. Karcher (Eds.), *Handbook of youth mentoring* (pp. 440–453). Thousand Oaks, CA: Sage.

Larson, R., Hansen, D. M., & Moneta, G. B. (2006). Differing profiles of developmental experiences across types of organized youth activities. *Developmental Psychology, 42,* 849–863.

Larson, R. W., & Richards, M. H. (1994). Family emotion: Do young adolescents and their parents experience the same states? *Journal of Research on Adolescence, 4*(4), 567–583.

Larzelere, R. E. (2000). Child outcomes of non-abusive and customary physical punishment by parents: An updated literature review. *Clinical Child and Family Psychology Review, 3,* 199–221.

Lau, A. S., Litrownik, A. J., Newton, R. R., Black, M. M., & Everson, M. D. (2006). Factors affecting the link between physical discipline and child externalizing problems in Black and White families. *Journal of Community Psychology, 34*(1), 89–103.

Laursen, B., & Collins, W. A. (1994). Interpersonal conflict during adolescence. *Psychological Bulletin, 115*(2), 197–209.

Laursen, B., Coy, K. C., & Collins, W. A. (1998). Reconsidering changes in parent-child conflict across adolescence: A meta-analysis. *Child Development, 69*(3), 817–832.

Lave, J., & Wenger, E. (1991). *Situated learning: Legitimate peripheral participation.* Cambridge, England: Cambridge University Press.

Leaper, C. (1994). Exploring the consequences of gender segregation on social relationships. *New Directions for Child and Adolescent Development, 65,* 67–86.

Leaper, C. (2002). Parenting girls and boys. In M. H. Bornstein (Ed.), *Handbook of parenting: Vol. 1. Children and parenting* (2nd ed., pp. 127–152). Mahwah, NJ: Erlbaum.

Leaper, C., & Anderson, K. J. (1997). Gender development and heterosexual romantic relationships during adolescence. *New Directions of Child and Adolescent Development, 78,* 85–103.

Leaper, C., & Smith, T. S. (2004). A meta-analytic review of gender variations in children's language use: Talkativeness, affiliative speech, and assertive speech. *Developmental Psychology, 40,* 993–1027.

Learn.Genetics. (2010). Retrieved from http://learn.genetics.utah.edu/

Learning about sickle cell disease. (2009). Retrieved from http://www.genome.gov/10001219

Leathers, H. D., & Foster, P. (2004). *The world food problem: Tackling the causes of undernutrition in the Third World.* Boulder, CO: Lynne Rienner Publishers.

Lecanuet, J., & Schaal, B. (2002). Sensory performances in the human foetus: A brief summary of research. *Intellectica, 1*(34), 29–56.

Lee, C. D. (2003). Why we need to re-think race and ethnicity in educational research. *Educational Researcher, 32*(5), 3–5.

Lee, K. (n.d.). *Best ways to build healthy food habits.* Retrieved from http://childparenting .about.com/od/nutrition/tp/healthyfoodhabits .htm

Lee, K. T., Mattson, S. N., & Riley, E. P. (2004). Classifying children with heavy prenatal alcohol exposure using measures of attention. *Journal of the International Neuropsychological Society, 10,* 271–277.

Lee, M., Liu, Y., & Newell, K. M. (2006). Longitudinal expressions of infant's prehension as a function of object properties. *Infant Behavior and Development, 29*(4), 481–493.

Lee, V. E., & Bryk, A. S. (1986). Effects of single-sex secondary schools on student achievement and attitudes. *Journal of Educational Psychology, 78,* 381–395.

Lee, V. E., & Marks, H. M. (1990). Sustained effects of the single-sex secondary school experience on attitudes, behaviors, and values in college. *Journal of Educational Psychology, 82,* 578–592.

Leeb, R. T., Paulozzi, L., Melanson, C., Simon, T., & Arias, I. (2007). Child maltreatment surveillance: Uniform definitions for public health and recommended data elements, Version 1.0. Atlanta (GA): Centers for Disease Control and Prevention, National Center for Injury Prevention and Control. Retrieved from http://www.cdc.gov/ncipc/dvp/CMP/CMP-Surveillance.htm

Leeds, Grenville, & Lanark District Health Unit. (n.d.). *Oral hygiene for children.* Retrieved from http://www.healthunit.org/dental/children_oral/hygienechild.htm

Leeman, L., Fontaine, P., King, V., Klein, M., & Ratcliffe, S., (2003a.). The nature and management of labor pain: Part I. Nonpharmacologic pain relief. *American Family Physician, 68,* 1109–1112.

Leeman, L., Fontaine, P., King, V., Klein, M., & Ratcliffe, S. (2003b). The nature and management of labor pain: Part II. Pharmacologic pain relief. *American Family Physician, 68,* 1115–1120.

Leets, L., & SunWolf. (2005). Adolescent rules for social exclusion: When is it fair to exclude someone else? *Journal of Moral Education, 34,* 343–362.

Legault, L., Green-Demers, I., & Pelletier, L. (2006). Why do high school students lack motivation in the classroom? Toward an understanding of academic amotivation and the role of social support. *Journal of Educational Psychology, 98,* 567–582.

Lehman, D. R., & Nisbett, R. E. (1990). A longitudinal study of the effects of undergraduate training on reasoning. *Developmental Psychology, 26,* 952–960.

Leitner, R. K. (1991). Comparing the effects on reading comprehension of educational video, direct experience, and print. Unpublished doctoral thesis, University of San Francisco, CA.

Lemelson, R. (2003). Obsessive-compulsive disorder in Bali. *Transcultural Psychiatry, 40,* 377–408.

Lemke, M., Sen, A., Pahlke, E., Partelow, L., Miller, D., Williams, T., Kastberg, D., & Jocelyn, L. (2004). *International outcomes of learning in mathematics literacy and problem solving: PISA 2003 results from the U.S. perspective.* Washington DC: National Center for Educational Statistics.

Lenhart, A. (2009). *Teens and social media: An overview.* Retrieved from http://pewinternet.com/Presentations/2009/17-Teens-and-Social-Media-An-Overview.aspx

Lenneberg, E. H. (1969). On explaining language. *Science, 164,* 635–643.

Leo, I., & Simion, F. (2009). Face processing at birth: A Thatcher Illusion study. *Developmental Science, 12*(3), 492–498.

Lerner, R. M. (2002). *Concepts and theories of human development.* Mahwah, NJ: Erlbaum.

Lerner, R. M. (2006). Developmental science, developmental systems, and contemporary theories of human development. In R. M. Lerner (Ed.), *Theoretical models of human development* (6th ed., Vol. 1, pp. 1–17). New York, NY: Wiley.

Lerner, R. M., Theokas, C., & Bobek, D. L. (2005). Concepts and theories of human development: Historical and contemporary dimensions. In M. H. Bornstein & M. E. Lamb (Eds.), *Developmental Science: An advanced textbook* (5th ed., pp. 3–43). Mahwah, NJ: Erlbaum.

Leveno, K. J., McIntire, D. D., Bloom, S. L., Sibley, M. R., & Anderson, R. J. (2009). Decreased preterm births in an inner-city public hospital. *Obstetrics & Gynecology, 113*(3), 578–584.

Leventhal, T., & Brooks-Gunn, J. (2004). A randomized study of neighborhood effects on low-income children's educational outcomes. *Developmental Psychology, 40,* 488–507.

Leventhal, T., Martin, A., & Brooks-Gunn, J. (2004). The EC- HOME across five national datasets in the third to fifth year of life. *Parenting: Science and Practice, 4*(2–3), 161–188.

Levin, J. R. (1994). Mnemonic strategies and classroom learning: A twenty-year report card. *Elementary School Journal, 94,* 235–254.

Levin, T. (2006, September 13). Report urges changes in the teaching of math in U.S. schools. *The New York Times,* p. 20.

Lewin, T. (2010). Quick response to study of abstinence education. *The New York Times,* p. A18.

Lewis, M. (2005). The child and its family: The social network model. *Human Development, 48,* 8–27.

Lewis, M., & Sullivan, M. W. (1996). The role of situation and child status on emotional learning. In M. Lewis & M. W. Sullivan (Eds.), *Emotional development in atypical children* (pp. 43–64). Mahwah, NJ: Erlbaum.

Lewit, E. M., & Baker, L. S. (1995). School readiness. *The Future of Children, 5,* 128–139.

Leyendecker, B., Harwood, R. L., Lamb, M. E., & Scholmerich, A. (2002). Mothers' socialization goals and evaluations of desirable and undesirable everyday situations in two diverse cultural groups. *International Journal of Behavioral Development, 26,* 248–258.

Liang, B., Spencer, R., Brogan, D., & Corral, M. (2008). Mentoring relationships from early adolescence through emerging adulthood: A qualitative analysis. *Journal of Vocational Behavior, 72,* 168–182.

Liben, L. S., & Bigler, R. S. (1987). Reformulating children's gender schemata. *New Directions for Child and Adolescent Development, 38,* 89–105.

Liben, L. S., & Bigler, R. S. (2002). The developmental course of gender differentiation: Conceptualizing, measuring, and evaluating constructs and pathways. *Monographs of the Society for Research in Child Development, 67*(2), 1–187.

Liben, L. S., & Signorella, M. L. (1993). Gender-schematic processing in children: The role of initial interpretations of stimuli. *Developmental Psychology, 29,* 141–149.

Lichten, W. (2004). On the law of intelligence. *Developmental Review, 24,* 252–258.

Light, A. (1995). *High school employment* (No. NLS 95-27): U.S. Department of Labor, Bureau of Labor Statistics.

Lillard, A. (2004). Pretend play and cognitive development. In U. Goswami (Ed.), *Blackwell handbook of childhood cognitive development* (pp. 188–205). Malden, MA: Blackwell.

Lillard, A. (2005). *Montessori: The science behind the genius.* New York, NY: Oxford.

Liller, K. D. (2007). Unintentional injuries in children. Retrieved from http://cme.medscape.com/viewarticle/553273

Lim, S., & Lim, B. K. (2004). Parenting style and child outcomes in Chinese and immigrant Chinese families: Current findings and cross-cultural considerations in conceptualization and research. *Marriage and Family Review, 35*(3), 21–43.

Lin, S. S. J., & Tsai, C. (2002). Sensation seeking and Internet dependence of Taiwanese high school adolescents, *Computers in Human Behavior, 18*(4), 411–426.

Lindsey, E. W., & Colwell, M. J. (2003). Preschoolers' emotional competence: Links to pretend and physical play. *Child Study Journal, 33,* 39–52.

Linebarger, D. L., Kosanic, A., Greenwood, C. R., & Doku, N. S. (2004). Effects of viewing the television program *Between the Lions* on the emergent literacy skills of young children. *Journal of Educational Psychology, 96,* 297–308.

Linebargar, D. L., & Wainwright, D. K. (2007). Learning while viewing: Urban myth or dream come true? In S. R. Mazzarella (Ed.), *20 Questions about youth and the media* (pp. 179–196). New York, NY: Peter Lang.

Lingren, H. (1997) *"Bullying"—How to stop it.* Retrieved from http//:www.ianr.unl.edu/pubs/family/nf309.htm

Linn, M. C., & Eylon, B. S. (2006). Science education: Integrating views of learning and instruction. In P. A. Alexander. & P. H. Winne (Ed.), *Handbook of educational psychology* (2nd ed., pp. 511–544). Mahwah, NJ: Erlbaum.

Linn, M. C., & Hyde, J. S. (1989). Gender, mathematics, and science. *Educational Researcher, 18,* 17–27.

Linn, R. L. (1986). Educational testing and assessment: Research needs and policy issues. *American Psychologist, 41,* 1153–1160.

Linn, R. L., & Gronlund, N. E. (2000). *Measurement and assessment in education* (8th ed.). Columbus, OH: Merrill.

Linnenbrink, E. A., & Pintrich, P. R. (2003). The role of self-efficacy beliefs in student engagement and learning in the classroom. *Reading & Writing Quarterly, 19,* 119–137.

Linton, B. (2009). Men and fatherhood: Pregnancy and birth. FATHERS' FORUM ONLINE. Retrieved from http://www.fathersforum.com/

Linver, M. R., Brooks-Gunn, J., & Cabrera, N. (2004). The Home Observation for Measurement of the Environment (HOME) inventory: The derivation of conceptually designed subscales. *Parenting: Science and Practice, 4,* 99–114.

Littlefield, T. R., Kelly, K. M., Reiff, J. L., & Pomatto, J. K. (2003). Car seats, infant carriers, and swings: Their role in deformational plagiocephaly. *Journal of Prosthetics and Orthodics, 15*(3), 102–106.

Liu, W. M., Ali, S. R., Soleck, G., Hopps, J., Dunston, K., & Pickett, T., Jr. (2004). Using social class in counseling psychology research. *Journal of Counseling Psychology, 51,* 3–18.

Lobo, I. (2008). Environment influences on gene expression. *Nature, 1*(1). Retrieved from http://www.nature.com/scitable/topicpage/Environmental-Influences-on-Gene-Expression-536

Lock, J. D. (2009). Trying to fit square pegs in round holes: Eating disorders in males. *Journal of Adolescent Health, 44,* 99–100.

Locke, J. (1690/1892). Some thoughts concerning education. In R. H. Quick (Ed.), *Locke on education* (pp. 1–236). Cambridge, England: Cambridge University Press.

Locke, J. L. (1993). *The child's path to spoken language.* Cambridge, MA: Harvard University Press.

Locke, L. F., & Graber, K. C. (2008). Elementary school physical education: Expectations and possibilities. *The Elementary School Journal, 108,* 265–273.

Lockl, K., & Schneider, W. (2007). Knowledge about the mind: Links between theory of mind and later metamemory. *Child Development, 78,* 148–167.

Lokken, G. (2000a). The playful quality of the toddling style. *International Journal of Qualitative Education, 13*(5), 531–542.

Lokken, G. (2000b). Tracing the social style of toddler peers. *Scandinavian Journal of Educational Research, 44*(2), 163–176.

Lorenz, K. Z. (1973/1977). *Behind the mirror: A search for a natural history of human knowledge.* New York, NY: Harcourt Brace Jovanovich.

Lovett, M. W., Lacerenza, L., Borden, S. L., Frijters, J. C., Steinback, K. A., & DePalma, M. (2000). Components of effective remediation for developmental disabilities: Combining phonological and strategy-based instruction to improve outcomes. *Journal of Educational Psychology, 92,* 263–283.

Lovett, S. B., & Flavell, J. H. (1990). Understanding and remembering: Children's knowledge about the differential effects of strategy and task variables on comprehension and memorization. *Child Development, 61,* 1842–1858.

Lowe, E. D., Weisner, T. S., Geis, S., & Huston, A. (2005). Childcare instability and the effort to sustain a working daily routine: Evidence from the New Hope Ethnographic Study of low-income families. In C. R. Cooper, C. T. Garcia-Coll, W. T. Bartko, H. Davis, & C. Chatman (Eds.), *Developmental pathways through middle childhood: Rethinking contexts and diversity as resources* (pp. 121–144). Mahwah, NJ: Erlbaum.

Lucyshyn, J. M., Albin, R. W., Horner, R. H., Mann, J. C., Mann, J. A., & Wadsworth, G. (2007). Family implementation of positive behavior support for a child with autism: Longitudinal, single-case, experimental, and descriptive replication and extension. *Journal of Positive Behavior Interventions, 9,* 131–150.

Lupart, J., & Barva, C. (1998). Promoting female achievement in the sciences: Research and implications. *International Journal for the Advancement of Counselling, 20,* 319–338.

Luria, A. R. (1976). *Cognitive development: Its cultural and social foundations.* Cambridge, MA: Harvard University Press.

Luster, T., & McAdoo, H. P. (1995). Factors related to self-esteem among African-American youths: A secondary analysis of the High/Scope Perry Preschool data. *Journal of Research on Adolescence, 5,* 451–467.

Lysne, M., & Levy, G. D. (1997). Differences in ethnic identity in Native American adolescents as a function of school context. *Journal of Adolescent Research, 12,* 372–388. doi:10.1177/0743554897123007

MacArthur, C. A. (1998). From illegible to understandable: How word prediction and speech synthesis can help, *Teaching Exceptional Children, 30*(6), 66–71.

MacArthur, C. A. (2009). Technology and struggling writers: A review of research. *British Journal of Educational Psychology, 79,* 1–8.

Maccoby, E. E. (1980). *Social development: Psychological growth and the parent-child relationship.* New York, NY: Harcourt Brace Jovanovich.

Maccoby, E. E. (1998). *The two sexes: Growing up apart, coming together.* Cambridge, MA: Harvard University Press.

Maccoby, E. E., & Jacklin, C. N. (1987). Gender segregation in childhood. In H. W. Reese (Ed.), *Advances in child development* (Vol. 20, pp. 239–288). New York, NY: Academic Press.

Maccoby, E. E., & Martin, J. A. (1983). Socialization in the context of the family: Parent-child interaction. In E. M. Hetherington (Vol. Ed.), *Handbook of child psychology: Vol. 4. Socialization, personality, and social development* (4th ed., pp. 1–101). New York, NY: Wiley.

MacDonald, S. C., Pertowski, C. A., & Jackson, R. J. (1996). Environmental public health surveillance. *Journal of Public Health Management and Practice, 2,* 45–49.

Madsen, C. H., Becker, W. C., & Thomas, D. R. (1968). Rules, praise, and ignoring: Elements of elementary classroom control. *Journal of Applied Behavior Analysis, 1,* 139–150.

Magai, C., Hunziker, J., Mesias, W., & Culver, L. C. (2000). Adult attachment styles and emotional biases. *International Journal of Behavioral Development, 24,* 301–309.

Magnuson, K. A., & Duncan, G. J. (2004). Parent- versus child-based intervention strategies for promoting children's well-being. In A. Kalil & T. DeLeire (Eds.), *Family investments in children's potential: Resources and parenting behaviors that promote success. Monographs in Parenting* (pp. 209–235). Mahwah, NJ: Erlbaum.

Maguen, S., Floyd, F. J., Bakeman, R., & Armistead, L. (2002). Developmental milestones and disclosure of sexual orientation among gay, lesbian, and bisexual youths. *Journal of Applied Developmental Psychology, 23*(2), 219–233.

Maguire, E. A., Gadian, D. G., Johnsrude, I. S., Good, C. D., Ashburner, J., Frackowiak, R. S., & Frith, C. D. (2000). Navigation-related structural change in the hippocampi of taxi drivers. *Proceedings of the National Academy of Science, USA, 97*(8), 4398–4403.

Mahdi, A. A. (2003). Introduction: Teens, Islam, and the Middle East. In A. A. Mahdi (Ed.), *Teen life in the Middle East* (pp. 1–12). Westport, CT: Greenwood Press.

Mahoney, G., Boyce, G., Fewell, R., Spiker, D., & Wheeden, A. C. (1998). The relationship of parent-child interaction to the effectiveness of early intervention services for at-risk children and children with disabilities. *TECSE, 18*(1), 5–17.

Main, M., & Solomon, J. (1990). In M. T. Greenberg, D. Cicchetti, & M. Cummings (Eds.), *Attachment in the preschool years: Theory, research, and intervention* (pp. 121–160). Chicago, IL: University of Chicago Press.

Malone, F. D., Canick, J. A., Ball, R. H., Nyberg, D. A., Comstock, C. H., Bukowsky, R., Berkowitz, R., . . . D'Alton, M. E. (2005). First-trimester or second-trimester screening, or both, for Down's syndrome. *New England Journal of Medicine, 353*(19), 2001–2011.

Malone, T. W., & Lepper, M. (1987). Making learning fun: A taxonomy of intrinsic motivations for learning. In R. E. Snow & M. J. Farr (Eds.), *Aptitude, learning and instruction, Volume 3: Cognitive and affective process analysis* (pp. 223–253). Mahwah, NJ: Erlbaum.

Mandler, J. M., & McDonough, L. (1996). Drinking and driving don't mix: Inductive generalizations in one-year-olds. *Cognition, 59,* 307–335.

Mann, M. M., Hosman, C. M. H., Schaalma, H. P., & deVries, N. K. (2004). Self-esteem in a broad-spectrum approach for mental health promotion. *Health Education Research, 19*(4), 357–372.

Mantzicopolos, P., & Morrison, D. (1992). Kindergarten retention: Academic and behavioral outcomes through the end of second grade. *American Educational Research Journal, 29,* 182–198.

March of Dimes. (2009a). *Newborn screening tests.* Retrieved from www.marchofdimes.com

March of Dimes. (2009b). *Premature births.* Retrieved from http://www.marchofdimes.com/prematurity/21326_1157.asp#head1

March of Dimes. (2010a). *Amniocentesis.* Retrieved from http://www.marchofdimes.com/professionals/14332_1164.asp#head5

March of Dimes. (2010b) *Chromosomal abnormalities.* Retrieved from www.marchofdimes.com

March of Dimes. (2010c). *Maternal blood screening for birth defects.* Retrieved from http://www.marchofdimes.com/professionals/14332_1166.asp

Marchbank, T., Weaver, G., Nilsen-Hamilton, M., & Playford, R. J. (2009). Pancreatic secretory trypsin inhibitor us a major motogenic and protective factor in human breast milk. *American Journal of Physiol Gastrointest Liver Physiol, 296,* G697–G703.

Marcia, J. E. (1966). Development and validation of ego-identity status. *Journal of Personality Psychology, 3,* 551–558.

Marcia, J. E. (1993). The relational roots of identity. In J. Kroger (Ed.), *Discussions on ego identity* (pp. 101–120). Mahwah, NJ: Erlbaum.

Marcia, J. E. (1999). Representational thought in ego identity, psychotherapy, and psychosocial development. In I. E. Sigel (Ed.), *Development of mental representation: Theories and applications.* Mahwah, NJ: Erlbaum.

Marinova-Todd, S., Marshall, D., & Snow, C. (2000). Three misconceptions abut age and L2 learning. *TESOL Quarterly, 34*(1), 9–34.

Markman, E. M. (1992). Constraints on word learning: Speculations about their nature, origins, and domain specificity. In M. R. Gunnar & M. P. Maratsos (Eds.), *Modularity and constraints in language and cognition* (Vol. 25, pp. 59–101). Mahwah, NJ: Erlbaum.

Markman, E. M., Wasow, J. L., & Hansen, M. B. (2003). Use of the mutual exclusivity assumption by young word learners. *Cognitive Psychology, 47,* 241–275.

Markowitz, S., & Cuellar, A. (2007). Antidepressants and youth: Healing or harmful? *Social Science and Medicine, 64,* 2138–2151. doi:10.1016/j.socscimed.2007.02.025

Markstrom, C. A., & Iborra, A. (2003). Adolescent identity formation and rites of passage: The Navajo Kinaaldá ceremony for girls. *Journal of Research on Adolescence, 13*(4), 399–425.

Markus, H. R., & Kityayama, S. (1991). Culture and the self: Implications for cognition, emotion, and motivation. *Psychological Review, 98,* 224–253.

Markus, H. R., & Nurius, P. (1987). Possible selves. *American Psychology, 41,* 954–969.

Marsh, H. W., Smith, I. D., & Barnes, J. (1985). Multidimensional self-concepts: Relations with sex and academic achievement. *Journal of Educational Psychology, 77,* 581–596.

Marshall, S. K., Tilton-Weaver, L. C., & Bosdet, L. (2005). Information management: Considering adolescents' regulation of parental knowledge. *Journal of Adolescence, 28*(5), 633–647.

Marshall, W. A., & Tanner, J. M. (1986). Puberty. In F. Faulkmer & J. M. Tanner (Eds.), *Human growth: A comprehensive treatise* (Vol. 2: Postnatal growth, neurobiology, pp. 171–210). New York, NY: Springer.

Martens, P. J., & Romphf, L. (2007). Factors associated with newborn in-hospital weight loss: Comparisons by feeding methods, demographics, and birthing procedures. *Journal of Human Lactation, 23,* 233–241.

Martin, C. L., & Fabes, R. A. (2001). The stability and consequences of young children's same-sex peer interactions. *Developmental Psychology, 37,* 431–446.

Martin, C. L., & Halverson, C. F., Jr. (1981). A schematic-processing model of sex typing and stereotyping in children. *Child Development, 52,* 1119–1134.

Martin, C. L., & Ruble, D. (2004). Children's search for gender cues cognitive perspectives on gender development. *Current Directions in Psychological Science, 13,* 67–70.

Martin, K. A. (1996). *Puberty, sexuality, and the self: Boys and girls at adolescence.* New York, NY: Routledge.

Martin, M., Myers, S., & Moffet, T. (2002). Students' motives for communicating with their instructors. In J. Cheesebro & J. McCroskey (Eds.), *Communication for teachers* (pp. 35–46). Boston, MA: Allyn & Bacon.

Martino, S. C., Elliot, M. N., Collins, R. L., Kanouse, D. E., & Berry, S. H. (2008). Virginity pledges among the willing: Delays in first intercourse and consistency of condom use. *Journal of Adolescent Health, 43*, 341–348.

Martorell, G. A., & Bugental, D. B. (2006). Maternal variations in stress reactivity: Implications for harsh parenting practices with very young children. *Journal of Family Psychology, 20*, 641–647.

Masten, A. S. (1999). Resilience comes of age: Reflections on the past and outlook for the next generation of research. In M. D. Glantz & J. Johnson (Eds.), *Resilience and development: Positive life adaptations* (pp. 281–296). New York, NY: Plenum.

Masten, A. S. (2001). Ordinary magic: Resilience processes in development. *American Psychologist, 56*, 227–238.

Masten, A. S. (2004). Regulatory processes, risk and resilience in adolescent development. *New York Academy of Sciences, 1021*, 310–319.

Masten, A. S., & Coatsworth, J. D. (1998). The development of competence in favorable and unfavorable environments: Lessons on research from successful children. *American Psychologist, 53*, 205–220.

Masten, A. S., Shaffer, A. (2006). How families matter in child development: Reflections from research on risk and resilience. In A. Clarke-Stewart & J. Dunn (Eds.), *Families count: Effects on child and adolescent development* (pp. 5–25). New York, NY: Cambridge University Press.

Matalon, K. M., Acosta, P. B., & Azen, C. (2003). Role of nutrition in pregnancy with phenylketonuria and birth defects. *Pediatrics, 112*, 1534–1536.

Matatyaho, D. J., & Gogate, L. J. (2008). Type of maternal object motion during synchronous naming predicts preverbal infants' learning of word-object relations. *Infancy, 13*(2), 172–184.

Matson, J. L., Matson, M. L., & Rivet, T. T. (2007). Social–skills treatments for children with autism spectrum disorders. *Behavior Modification, 31*, 682–707.

Mattanah, J. F., Pratt, M. W., Cowan, P. A., & Cowan, C. P. (2005). Authoritative parenting, parental scaffolding of long-division mathematics, and children's academic competence in fourth grade. *Journal of Applied Developmental Psychology, 26*, 85–106.

Mayer, R. E. (1992). *Thinking, problem solving, cognition* (2nd ed.). New York, NY: Freeman.

Maynard, A. E. (2002). Cultural teaching: The development of teaching skills in Maya sibling interactions. *Child Development, 73*, 969–982.

Mayo Clinic. (2009). *Type 2 diabetes: Complications*. Retrieved from http://www.mayoclinic.com/health/type-2-diabetes/DS00585/DSECTION=complications

Mayo Clinic. (2010). Chorionic villus sampling. Retrieved from http://www.mayoclinic.com/health/chorionic-villus-sampling/MY00154/DSECTION=risks

McAdoo, H. P. (2001). Parent and child relationships in African American families. In N. B. Webb (Ed.), *Culturally diverse parent-child and family relationships: A guide for social workers and other practitioners* (pp. 89–106). New York, NY: Columbia University Press.

McAnarney, E. R. (2008). Adolescent brain development: Forging new links. *Journal of Adolescent Health, 42*, 321–323.

McCabe, A. (1996). *Chameleon readers: Teaching children to enjoy all kinds of good stories*. New York, NY: McGraw-Hill.

McCabe, M. P., & Vincent, M. A. (2003). The role of biodevelopmental and psychological factors in disordered eating among adolescent males and females. *European Eating Disorders Review, 11*, 315–328.

McCafferty, S. G. (2004). Introduction. *International Journal of Applied Linguistics, 14*(1), 1–6.

McCall, R. B. (1987). The media, society, and child development research. In J. D. Osofsky (Ed.), *Handbook of infant development* (2nd ed., pp. 1199–1255). New York, NY: Wiley.

McCall, R. B., Groark, C. J., & Nelkin, R. P. (2004). Integrating developmental scholarship and society: From dissemination and accountability to evidence-based programming and policies. *Merrill-Palmer Quarterly, 50*, 326–340.

McCann, J. C., & Ames, B. N. (2007). An overview of evidence for a causal relation between iron deficiency during development and deficits in cognitive or behavioral function. *Journal of Clinical Nutrition, 85*(4), 931–945.

McCaslin, M., & Hickey, D. T. (2001). Self-regulated learning and academic achievement: A Vygotskian view. In B. Zimmerman & D. Schunk (Eds.), *Self-regulated learning and academic achievement: Theoretical perspectives* (2nd ed., pp. 227–252). Mahwah, NJ: Erlbaum.

McCoach, D. B., Kehle, T. J., Bray, M. L., & Siegle, D. (2001). Best practices in the identification of gifted students with learning disabilities. *Psychology in the Schools, 38*, 403–411.

McCormack, T. D., & Hoeri, C. (2005). Children's reasoning about the causal significance of the temporal order of events. *Developmental Psychology, 41*, 54–63.

McCoy, A. R., & Reynolds, A. J. (1999). Grade retention and school performance: An extended investigation. *Journal of School Psychology, 37*, 273–298.

McCrory, E. J., Mechelli, A., Frith, U., & Price, C. J. (2005). More than words: A common neural basis for reading and naming deficits in developmental dyslexia? *Brain, 128*(2), 261–267.

McCurdy, C. E., Bishop, J. M., Williams, S. M., Grayson, B. E., Smith, S. M., Friedman, J., & Grove, K. L. (2009). Maternal high-fat diet triggers lipotoxicity in the fetal livers of nonhuman primates. *Journal of Clinical Investigation, 119*(2), 323–335.

McDevitt, T. M., & Ormrod, J. E. (2010).*Child development and education*. Columbus, OH: Merrill.

McDougall, P., Hymel, S., Vaillancourt, T., & Mercer, L. (2001). The consequences of childhood peer rejection. In M. R. Leary (Ed.), *Interpersonal Rejection*. New York, NY: Oxford.

McDowell, D. J., Parke, R. D., & Wang, S. (2003). Differences between mothers' and fathers' advice-giving style and content: Relations with social competence and psychological functioning in middle childhood. *Merrill-Palmer Quarterly, 49*, 55–76.

McElrath, T. F., Hecht, J. L., Dammann, O., Boggess, K., Onderdonk, A., Markenson, G., Harper, M., . . . Leviton, A. (2008). Pregnancy disorders that lead to delivery before the 28th week of gestation: An epidemiologic approach to classification. *American Journal of Epidemiology, 168*(9),990–992. Retrieved from http://aje.oxfordjournals.org/cgi/content/abstract/kwn202v1

McElwain, N. L., & Booth-LaForce, C. (2006). Maternal sensitivity to infant distress and non-distress as predictors of infant-mother attachment security. *Journal of Family Psychology, 20*(2), 247–255.

McElwain, N. L., Booth-LaForce, C., Lansford, J. E., Wu, X., & Dyer, W. J. (2008). A process model of attachment-friend linkages: Hostile attribution biases, language ability, and mother-child affective mutuality as intervening mechanisms. *Child Development, 79*(6), 1891–1906.

McElwain, N. L., Cox, M. J., Burchinal, M. R., & Macfie, J. (2003). Differentiating among insecure mother-infant attachment classifications: A focus on child-friend interaction and exploration during solitary play at 36 months. *Attachment & Human Development, 5*(2), 136–164.

McHale, J., Lauretti, A., Talbot, J. A., & Pouquette, C. (2002). Retrospect and prospect in the psychological study of coparenting and family group process. In J. McHale & W. Grolnick (Eds.), *Retrospect and prospect in the psychological study of families* (pp. 127–165). Mahwah, NJ: Erlbaum.

McHale, J. P., & Rasmussen, J. L. (1998). Coparental and family group-level dynamics during infancy: Early family precursors of child and family functioning during preschool. *Development and Psychopathology, 10*, 39–59.

McHale, S. M., Crouter, A. C., & Whiteman, S. D. (2003). The family contexts of gender development in childhood and adolescence. *Social development, 12*, 125–148.

McKenna J. J., & McDade T. (2005). Why babies should never sleep alone: A review of the co-sleeping controversy in relation to SIDS, bedsharing, and breast feeding. *Paediatric Respiratory Reviews, 6*, 134–152.

McKenzie, T. L., & Kahan, D. (2008). Physical activity, public health, and elementary schools. *Elementary School Journal, 108*, 171–180.

McLanahan, S. S. (1997). Parent absence or poverty: Which matters more? . In G. J. Duncan & J. Brooks-Gunn (Eds.), *Consequences of growing up poor* (pp. 25–48). New York, NY: Russell Sage Foundation.

McLanahan, S. S. (1999). Father absence and the welfare of children. In E. M. Hetherington (Ed.), *Coping with divorce, single parenting, and remarriage: A risk and resiliency perspective* (pp. 117–145). Mahwah, NJ: Erlbaum.

McLaughlin, T., Humphries, O., Jr., Nguyen, T., Maljanian, R., & McCormack, K. (2004). "Getting the lead out" in Hartford, Connecticut: A multifaceted lead-poisoning awareness campaign. Environmental Health Perspective, 112, 1–5. doi:10.1289/ehp.6391

McLoyd, V. C. (1998). Economic disadvantage and child development. *American Psychologist, 53*, 185–204.

McLoyd, V. C., Aikens, N. L., & Burton, L. M. (2006). Childhood poverty, policy, and practice. In W. Damon & R. M. Lerner (Series Eds.) & K. A. Renninger & I. Sigel (Vol. Eds.), *Handbook of child psychology: Vol. 4. Child psychology in practice* (6th ed., pp. 700–775). New York, NY: Wiley.

McNamee, S., & Peterson, J. (1986). Young children's distributive justice reasoning, behavior, and role taking: Their consistency and relationship. *Journal of Genetic Psychology, 146*, 399–404.

McWayne, C. M., Fantuzzo, J. W., & McDermott, P. A. (2004). Preschool competency in context: An investigation of the unique contribution of child competencies to early academic success. *Developmental Psychology, 40*, 633–645.

McWayne, C. M., Owsianik, M., Green, L. E., & Fantuzzo, J. W. (2008). Parenting behaviors and preschool children's social and emotional skills: A question of the consequential validity of traditional parenting constructs for low-income African Americans. *Early Childhood Research Quarterly, 23*, 173–192.

Mead, G. H. (1934). *Mind, self, and society.* Chicago, IL: University of Chicago Press.

Meadows, S. (2006). *The child as a thinker* (2nd ed.). New York, NY: Routledge.

Meaney, M. J., Stewart, J., & Beatty, W. W. (1985). Sex differences in social play: The socialization of sex roles. In J. S. Rosenblatt (Ed.), *Advances in the study of behaviour: Vol. 15.* (pp. 2–58). Orlando, FL: Academic Press.

Mears, T. (1998, April 12). Saying "Si" to Spanish. *Boston Globe.*

Mediascope. (1996). *National television violence study: Executive summary 1994–1995.* Studio City, CA: Author.

Medina, J. A. M., Lozano V. M., & Goudena P. P. (2001). Conflict management in preschoolers: a crosscultural perspective. *International Journal of Early Years Education, 9*, 153–60.

MedlinePlus. (2010). *Asthma.* Retrieved from http://www.nlm.nih.gov/medlineplus/ency/article/000141.htm

MedlinePlus. (2010). *Iron deficiency anemia—children.* Retrieved from http://www.nlm.nih.gov/medlineplus/ency/article/007134.htm

Meece, J. L. (2002). *Child and adolescent development for educators* (2nd ed.). New York, NY: McGraw-Hill.

Meece, J. L., & Kurtz-Costes, B. (2001). Introduction: The schooling of ethnic minority children and youth. *Educational Psychologist, 36*, 1–7.

Mehler, J., Dupoux, E., Nazzi, T., & Dehaene-Lambertz, G. (1996). Coping with linguistic diversity: The infant's point of view. In J. L. Morgan & K. Demuth (Eds.), *Signal to syntax.* Mahwah, NJ: Erlbaum.

Mehler, J., Jusczyk, P. W., Lambertz, G., Halsted, N., Bertoncini, J., & Amiel-Tison, C. (1988). A precursor of language acquisition in young infants. *Cognition, 29*, 144–178.

Mei, Z., Scanlon, K. S., Grummer-Strawn, L. M., Freedman, D. S., Yip, R., & Trowbridge, F. L. (1998). Increasing prevalence of overweight among US low-income preschool children: the Centers for Disease Control and Prevention, Pediatric Nutrition Surveillance, 1983 to 1995. *Pediatrics, 101*(1), e12.

Meichenbaum, D., Burland, S., Gruson, L., & Cameron, R. (1985). Metacognitive assessment. In S. Yussen (Ed.), *The growth of reflection in children* (pp. 1–30). Orlando, FL: Academic Press.

Meisels, S. J. (1989). High-stakes testing in kindergarten. *Educational Leadership, 46*(7), 16–22.

Meltzoff, A. N. (1985). Immediate and deferred imitation in fourteen- and twenty-four-month-old infants. *Child Development, 56*, 62–72.

Meltzoff, A. N. (1995). Understanding the intentions of others: Re-enactment of intended acts by 18-month-old children. *Developmental Psychology, 31*, 1–16.

Meltzoff, A. N. (1999). Born to learn: What infants learn from watching us. In N. Fox & J. G. Worhol (Eds.), *The role of early experiences in infant development* (pp. 1–10). Skillman, NJ: Pediatric Institute Publicaitons.

Meltzoff, A. N. (2005). Imitation and other minds: The "Like Me" hypothesis. In S. Hurley & N. Chater (Eds.), *Perspectives on imitation: From neuroscience to social science* (Vol. 2, pp. 55–77). Cambridge, MA: MIT Press.

Meltzoff, A. N., & Brooks, R. (2007). Eyes wide shut: The importance of eyes in infant gaze following and understanding other minds. In R. Flom, K. Lee, & D. Muir (Eds.), *Gaze following: Its development and significance* (pp. 217–241). Mahwah, NJ: Erlbaum.

Meltzoff, A. N., & Kuhl, P. K. (1989). Infants' perception of faces and speech sounds: Challenges to developmental theory. In P. R. Zelazo & R. G. Barr (Eds.), *Challenges to developmental paradigms: Implications for theory, assessment and treatment* (pp. 67–91). Hillsdale, NJ: Erlbaum.

Meltzoff, A. N., & Moore, M. K. (1977). Imitation of facial and manual gestures by human neonates. *Science 7*(198).

Meltzoff, A. N., & Moore, M. K. (1983). Newborn infants imitate adult facial gestures. *Child Development, 54*, 702–709.

Mendle, J., Turkheimer, E., & Emery, R. E. (2007). Detrimental psychological outcomes associated with early pubertal timing in adolescent girls. *Developmental Review, 27*, 151–171.

Merewood, A. (2000). Sperm under siege. In K. L. Freiberg (Ed.), *Human development* 00/01 (28th ed., pp. 41–45). Guilford, CT: Dushkin/McGraw-Hill.

Merrell, K. W., & Gimpel, G. A. (1998). *Social skills of children and adolescents: Conceptualization, assessment, and treatment.* Mahwah, NJ: Erlbaum.

Merrell, K. W., Gueldner, B., Ross, S. W., & Isava, D. (2008). How effective are school bullying intervention programs? A meta-analysis of intervention research. *School Psychology Quarterly, 23*, 26–42.

Mertler, C. A., & Charles, C. M. (2005). *Introduction to educational research* (5th ed.). Boston, MA: Allyn & Bacon.

Meyer, D. R. (1999). Compliance with child support orders in paternity and divorce cases. In A. Thompson & P. R. Amato (Eds.), *The postdivorce family: Children, parenting, and society* (pp. 127–157). Thousand Oaks, CA: Sage.

Miller, B. C., Xitao, F., Christensen, M., Grotevant, H. D., & van Dulmen, M. (2000). Comparisons of adopted and nonadopted adolescents in a large, nationally representative sample. *Child Development, 71*, 1458–1473.

Miller, G. A. (1969). Psychology as a means of promoting human welfare. *American Psychologist, 24*, 1063–1075.

Miller, G. A., Galanter, E., & Pribram, K. H. (1960). *Plans and the structure of behavior.* New York, NY: Holt, Rinehart & Winston.

Miller, L. C., Putcha-Bhagavatula, A. D., & Pedersen, W. C. (2002). Men's and women's mating preferences: Distinct evolutionary mechanisms? *Current Directions in Psychological Science, 11*, 88–93.

Miller, P. H. (2011). *Theories of developmental psychology* (5th ed.). New York, NY: Worth.

Miller, P. H., & Seier, W. (1994). Strategy utilization deficiencies in children: When, where, and why. In H. Reese (Ed.), *Advances in child evelopment and behavior* (Vol. 25, pp. 107–156). New York, NY: Academic Press.

Miller, S. P., & Mercer, C. D. (1997). Educational aspects of mathematics disabilities. *Journal of Learning Disabilities, 30*, 47–56.

Mills, R. S. L., & Grusec, J. E. (1989). Cognitive, affective, and behavioral consequences of praising altruism. *Merrill-Palmer Quarterly, 35*, 299–326.

Mills-Koonce, W. R., Gariepy, J-L., Propper, C., Sutton, K., Calkins, S., Moore, G., & Cox, M. (2007). Infant and parent factors associated with early maternal sensitivity: A caregiver-attachment systems approach. *Infant Behavior & Development, 30*(1), 114–126.

Milner, H. R. (Ed.). (2009). *Diversity and education: Teachers, teaching, and teacher education.* Springfield, IL: Charles C. Thomas.

Milunsky, A. (1992). *Genetic disorders and the fetus: Diagnosis, prevention, and treatment* (3rd ed.). Baltimore, MD: Johns Hopkins University Press.

Minami, M. (2001). Maternal styles of narrative elicitation and the development of children's narrative skill: A study on parental scaffolding. *Narrative Inquiry, 11*, 55–80.

Mindell, J. A. (2005). *Sleeping through the night: How infants, toddlers, and their parents can get a good night's sleep* (Rev. ed.). New York, NY: Harper Paperbacks.

Minnesota Department of Health. (nd). Hearing and vision screening. Retrieved from http://www.health.state.mn.us/divs/fh/mch/hlth-vis/index.html

Minton, C., Kagan, J., & Levine, J. A. (1971). Maternal control and obedience in the two-year-old. *Child Development, 42*, 1873–1894.

Mintz, T. H. (2005). Linguistic and conceptual influences on adjective acquisition in 24- and 36-month olds. *Developmental Psychology, 41*, 17–29.

Mischel, W., & Leibert, R. M. (1966). Effects of discrepancies between observed and imposed reward criteria on their acquisition and transmission. *Journal of Personality and Social Psychology, 3*, 45–53.

Misra, M. (2008). Bone density in the adolescent athlete. *Reviews in Endocrine and Metabolic Disorders, 9*, 139–144.

Mitchell, J. A. (2005). *Sleeping through the night: How infants, toddlers, and their parents can get a good night's sleep.* New York, NY: Harper Collins.

Mitomo, K., Griesenbach, U., Inoue, M., Somerton, L., Meng, C., Akiba, E., Tabata, T., . . . Alton, E. W. F. W. (March 23, 2010). Toward gene therapy for cystic fibrosis: Using a lentivirus pseudotyped with sendai virus envelopes. *Molecular Therapy 18*, 1173–1182. doi:10.1038/mt.2010.13.

Miyamoto, R. T., Houston, D. M., & Bergeson, T. (2005). Cochlear implantation in deaf infants. *Laryngoscope, 115*(8), 1376–1380.

Mize, J., & Pettit, G. S. (1997). Mother's social coaching, mother-child relationship style, and children's peer competence: Is the medium the message? *Child Development, 68*, 312–332.

Moffitt, T. E. (2005). The new look of behavioral genetics in developmental psychopathology: Gene-environment interplay in antisocial behaviors. *Psychological Bulletin, 131*, 533–554.

Molenaar, P. C. M, Huizinga, H. M., & Nesselroade, J. R. (2003). The relationship between the structure of inter-individual and intra-individual variability: A theoretical and empirical vindication of developmental systems theory. In U. M. Staudinger and U. Lindenberger (Eds.), *Understanding human development* (pp. 339–360). Boston, MA: Kluwer.

Molina, B. S. G., & Chassin, L. (1996). The parent-adolescent relationship at puberty: Hispanic ethnicity and parent alcoholism as moderators. *Developmental Psychology, 32*, 675–686.

Moll, L. C., Amanti, C., Neff, D., & Gonzalez, N. (1992). Funds of knowledge for teaching: Using a qualitative approach to connect homes and classrooms. *Theory Into Practice, 31*, 132–141.

Moll, L. C., & Whitmore, K. F. (1993). Vygotsky in classroom practice: Moving from individual transmission to social transaction. In E. Forman, N. Minick, & C. A. Stone (Eds.), *Contexts for learning: Sociocultural dynamics in children's development* (pp. 19–42). New York, NY: Oxford.

Money, J., & Ehrhardt, A. A. (1972). *Man and woman: Boy and girl*. Baltimore, MD: Johns Hopkins University Press.

Montgomery, M. J., & Cote, J. E. (2006). College as a transition to adulthood. In G. R. Adams & M. D. Berzonsky (Ed.), *Blackwell handbook of adolescence* (pp. 149–172). Malden, MA: Blackwell Publishing.

Moon, C., Cooper, R. P., & Fifer, W. P. (1993). Two-day old infants prefer their native language. *Infant Behavior and Development, 16*, 495–500.

Moore, D. S. (2001). *The dependent gene: The fallacy of "nature vs. nurture."* New York, NY: Freeman.

Moore, K. L., & Persaud, T. V. N. (2003). *Before we are born: Essentials of embryology and birth defects* (6th ed.). Philadelphia, PA: Saunders.

Moore, R. S. (2002). Influence of multicultural singing games on primary school children's attentiveness and song preferences in music classes. *International Journal of Music Education, 39*, 31–39.

Morgan, P. (1998). *Adoption and the care of children*. London, England: IEA Health and Welfare Unit.

Morgane, P. J., Mokler, D. J., & Galler, J. R. (2002). Effects of prenatal protein malnutrition on the hippocampal formation. *Neuroscience and Biobehavioral Reviews, 26*, 471–483.

Morrison, G. S. (2011). *Fundamentals of early childhood education* (6th ed.). Upper Saddle River, NJ: Prentice-Hall.

Morrow, L. M. (1983). Home and school correlates of early interest in literature. *Journal of Educational Research, 76*, 221–230.

Morrow, V. (2006). Understanding gender differences in context: Implications for young children's everyday lives. *Children & Society, 20*, 92–104.

Mortimer, J. (2005). *Working and growing up in America*. Cambridge, MA: Harvard University Press.

Moseley, L., & Gradisar, M. (2009). Evaluation of a school-based intervention for adolescent sleep problems. *Sleep, 32*, 334–341.

Moshman, D. (1997). Pluralist rational constructivism. *Issues in Education: Contributions from Educational Psychology, 3*, 229–234.

MPI. (2010). *2008 American Community Survey and census data on the foreign born by state.* Washington DC: Migration Policy Institute National Center on Immigration Integration Policy.

Muir, D. A. (2002). Adult communications with infants through touch: The forgotten sense. *Human Development*, 45, 95–99.

Mulder, E. J. H., Robles de Medina, P. G., Huizink, A. C., Van den Bergh, B. R. H., Buitelaar, J. K., & Visser, G. H. A. (2002). Prenatal maternal stress: Effects on pregnancy and the (unborn) child. *Early Human Development, 70*, 3–14.

Mullis, I. V. S., Martin, M. O., & Foy, P. (2005). *A developmental project to report TIMSS 2003 mathematics achievement in cognitive domains.* Chestnut Hill, MA: TIMSS & PIRLS International Study Center, Boston College.

Mullis, I. V. S., Martin, M. O., & Foy, P. (2009). *TIMSS 2007 International Mathematics Report: Findings from IEA's Trends in International Mathematics and Science Study at the fourth and eighth Grades.* Chestnut Hill, MA: TIMSS & PIRLS International Study Center, Boston College.

Mullis, I. V. S., Martin, M. O., Gonzalez, E., & Kennedy, A. M. (2003). *PIRLS 2001 International report: IEA's study of reading literacy achievement in primary schools.* Chestnut Hill, MA: Boston College.

Mulvey, E. P., & Cauffman, E. (2001). The inherent limits of predicting school violence. *American Psychologist, 56*(10), 797–802.

Munakata, Y. (2006). Information processing approaches to development. In D. Kuhn & R. S. Siegler (Eds.), *Cognition, perception, and language* (6th ed., Vol. 2, pp. 426–463). New York, NY: Wiley.

Munroe, R. L., & Romney, A. K. (2006). Gender and age differences in same-sex aggregation and social behavior: A four-culture study. *Journal of Cross-Cultural Psychology*, 37, 3–19.

Murdock, T. B., Anderman, L. H., & Hodge, S. A. (2000). Middle-grade predictors of students' motivation and behavior in high school. *Journal of Adolescent Research, 15*(3), 327–351.

Murdock, T. B., Hale, N. M., & Weber, M. J. (2001). Predictors of cheating among early adolescents: Academic and social motivations. *Contemporary Educational Psychology, 26*, 96–115.

Murdock, T. B., & Miller, A. (2003). Teachers as sources of middle school students' motivational identity: Variable-centered and person-centered analytic approaches. *Elementary School Journal, 103*, 383–399.

Murphy, N. A., Carbone, P. S., & the Council on Children with Disabilities. (2008). Promoting the participation of children with disabilities in sports, recreation, and physical activities. *Pediatrics, 121*(5), 1057–1061. doi:10.1542/peds.2008–0566

Murray, J. P. (1980). *Television and youth: 25 years of research and controversy.* Boys Town, NB: The Boys Town Center for Study of Youth Development.

Mustillo, S., Worthman, C., Erkanli, A., Keeler, G., Angold, A., & Costello, E. J. (2003). Obesity and psychiatric disorder: Developmental trajectories. *Pediatrics, 111*, 851–859. doi:10.1542/peds.111.4.851

Muter, V., Hulme, C., Snowling, M. J., & Stevenson, J. (2004). Phonemes, rimes, vocabulary, and grammatical skills as foundation of early reading development: Evidence from a longitudinal study. *Developmental Psychology, 40*, 665–681.

Myers, D. G. (2005). *Exploring psychology* (6th ed.). New York, NY: Worth.

Nachmias, M., & Gunnar, M. (1996). Behavioral inhibition and stress reactivity: The moderating role of attachment security. *Child Development, 67*(2), 508–523.

NAEP. (1997). *National Assessment of Educational Progress.* Washington, DC: National Center for Educational Statistics.

NAGC. (2010). *Is there a definition of "gifted"?* Retrieved from http://www.nagc.org/index2.aspx?id=548.

Nansel, T. R., Overpeck, M., Pilla, R. S., Ruan, W., Simons-Morton, B., & Scheidt, P. (2001). Bullying behaviors among US youth: Prevalence and association with psychosocial adjustment. *Journal of the American Medical Association, 285*, 2094–2100.

National Association of the Deaf. (2000). *Position statement on cochlear implants.* Retrieved from http://www.nad.org/issues/technology/assistive-listening/cochlear-implants

National Association for Sport and Physical Education (NASPE). (2000). *Public attitudes toward physical education.* Reston, VA: Author.

National Association for Sport and Physical Education and American Heart Association (NASPE). (2006). *2006 shape of the nation report: Status of physical education in the USA.* Reston, VA: Author.

National Campaign to Prevent Teen and Unplanned Pregnancy. (n.d.). *Sex and tech: Results from a survey of teens and young adults.* Retrieved from http://www.thenationalcampaign.org/sextech/PDF/SexTech_Summary.pdf

National Cancer Institute. (2009). *A snapshot of pediatric cancers.* Retrieved from http://www.cancer.gov/aboutnci/servingpeople/snapshots/pediatric.pdf

National Center for Children Exposed to Violence. (2003). *Violence in the media.* Retrieved from http://www.nccev.org/violence/statistics/statistics-media.html.

National Center on Shaken Baby Syndrome. (nd). Retrieved from http://www.dontshake.org/

National Clearinghouse on Child Abuse and Neglect Information. (2005). *Long-term consequences of child abuse and neglect.* Retrieved from http://www.childprotectionoffice.org/pdf/long_term_consequences.pdf

National Institute on Deafness and Communication Disorders. (2001). *Has your baby's hearing been screened?* Retrieved from http://www.nidcd.nih.gov/health/hearing/screened.asp.

National Institute of Health Stem Cell Institute. (2009). *Stem cell basics.* Retrieved from http:// stemcells.nih.gov/info/basics/

National Institutes of Mental Health. (2006). *Schizophrenia.* Retrieved from http://www.nimh.nih.gov/health/publications/schizophrenia/schizophrenia-booket-2009.pdf

National Institutes of Mental Health. (2008). *Bipolar disorder.* Retrieved from http://www.nimh.nih.gov/health/publications/bipolar-disorder/complete-index.shtml

National Program for Playground Safety. (n.d.). Safety tips. Retrieved from http://www.playgroundsafety.org

National Scientific Council on the Developing Child. (2004) *Young children develop in an environment of relationships* (Working Paper No. 1). Retrieved from http://www.developingchild.net/papers/environment_of_relationships.pdf

National Scientific Council on the Developing Child. (2006). *Perspectives: Iron deficiency's long-term effects.* Retrieved from http://www.developingchild.net

Natvig, G. K., Albrektsen, G., & Qvarnstrom, U. (2003). Associations between psychosocial factors and happiness among school adolescents. *International Journal of Nursing Practice, 9*(3), 166–175.

NCEE. (1983). *A nation at risk: The imperative for educational reform.* Washington, D.C.: National Commission on Excellence in Education.

NCES. (2004, February 27, 2007). *Comparing NAEP, TIMSS, and PISA in Mathematics and Science.*

NCES. (2009). *Public school graduates and dropouts form the Common Core of Data: School year 2006–2007.* Retrieved from http://nces.ed.gov/pubs2010/2010313/tables.asp

NCREL. (1994). Funds of Knowledge: A look at Luis Moll's research into hidden family resources. *CitySchools, 1*(1), 10–21.

NCS. (2010). *Child teen and tobacco use.* Retrieved from http://www.cancer.org/docroot/PED/content/PED_10_2X_Child_and_Teen_Tobacco_Use.asp

NCTI, & CITE. (2006). Boosting inclusion in after school activities with AT and supplemental services. *Tech Works.* Retrieved from http://www.ldonline.org/article/Boosting_Inclusion_in_After_School_Activities_with_AT_and_Supplemental_Services

NCTM. (2006). *Curriculum focal points for prekindergarten through grade 8 mathematics: A quest for coherence.* Reston, VA: National Council of Teachers of Mathematics.

NECTAC (The National Early Childhood Technical Assistance Center). (2009). NECTAC list of Part C Lead Agencies. Retrieved from http://www.nectac.org

Neisser, U. (1976). *Cognition and reality.* San Francisco, CA: Freeman.

Neisser, U., Boodoo, G., Bouchard, A., Boykin, W., Brody, N., Ceci, S. J., Halpern, D. F., . . . Urbina, S. (1996). Intelligence: Knowns and unknowns. *American Psychologist, 51,* 77–101.

Nelson, C. A. (1995). Basic and applied perspectives on learning, cognition, and development. *Minnesota Symposia on Child Psychology (Vol. 28).* Mahwah, NJ: Erlbaum.

Nelson, C. A. (2001). The development and neural bases of face recognition. *Infant and Child Development, 10,* 3–18.

Nelson, G. (1993). Risk, resistance, and self-esteem: A longitudinal study of elementary school-aged children from mother-custody and two-parent families. *Journal of Divorce and Remarriage, 19,* 99–119.

Nelson, K. (2004). Evolution and the development of human memory systems. In B. J. Ellis & D. Bjorklund (Eds.), *Origins of the social mind: Evolutionary psychology and child development.* New York, NY: Guilford.

Nelson, K., & Fivush, R. (2004). The emergence of autobiographical memory: A social cultural developmental theory. *Psychological Review, 111,* 486–511.

Neuman, S. B., & Koskinen, P. (1992). Captioned television as comprehensible input: Effects of incidental word learning from context for language minority students. *Reading Research Quarterly, 27*(1), 94–106.

Neumark-Sztainer, D. R. (2009). Preventing obesity and eating disorders in adolescents: What can health care providers do? *Journal of Adolescent Health, 44,* 206–213.

Neumark-Sztainer, D. R., Story, M. T., Wall, M. M., Harnack, L. J., & Eisenberg, M. E. (2008). Fast food intake: Longitudinal trends during the transition to young adulthood and correlates of intake. *Journal of Adolescent Health, 43,* 79–86.

Neville, H. (2007, March). *Experience shapes human brain development and function.* Paper presented at the biennial meeting of the Society for Research in Child Development, Boston, Massachusetts.

Newcombe, N., & Baenninger, M. (1990). The role of expectations in spatial test performance: A meta-analysis. *Sex Roles, 16,* 25–37.

Newcombe, N., & Huttenlocher, J. (1993). *Making space: The development of spatial representation and reasoning.* Cambridge, MA: MIT Press.

Newman, R. S., & Hussain, I. (2006). Changes in preference for infant-directed speech in low and moderate noise by 4.5- to 13-month-olds. *Infancy,* 10(1), 61–76.

Nguyen, H.-H. D., & Ryan, A. M. (2008). Does stereotype threat affect test performance of minorities and women? A meta-analysis of experimental evidence. *Journal of Applied Psychology, 93,* 1314–1334.

NICH. (2007). Expert committee recommendations on the assessment, prevention and treatment of child and adolescent overweight and obesity—2007. Boston, MA: National Initiative for Children's Healthcare Quality.

NICHD Early Child Care Research Network. (2003). Childcare structure, process, and outcome: Direct and indirect effects of childcare quality on young children's development. *Psychological Science, 13,* 199–206.

NICHD Early Child Care Research Network. (2003). Do children's attention processes mediate the link between family predictors and school readiness? *Developmental Psychology, 39,* 581–593.

NICHD Early Child Care Research Network. (2004a). Affect dysregulation in the mother-child relationship in the toddler years: Antecedents and consequences. *Development and Psychopathology, 16,* 43–68.

NICHD Early Child Care Research Network. (2004b). Fathers' and mothers' parenting behavior and beliefs as predictors of children's social adjustment in the transition to school. *Journal of Family Psychology, 18,* 628–638.

NICHD Early Child Care Research Network. (2005). *Child care and child development.* New York, NY: Guilford.

NICHD Early Child Care Research Network. (2005a). Pathways to reading: The role of oral language in the transition to reading. *Developmental Psychology, 41*(2), 428–442.

NICHD Early Child Care Research Network. (2005b). Predicting individual differences in attention, memory, and planning in first graders from experiences at home, child care, and school. *Developmental Psychology, 41*(2), 99–114.

NICHD Early Child Care Research Network. (2006). Infant–mother attachment classification: Risk and protection to changing maternal caregiving quality. *Developmental Psychology, 42*(1), 38–58.

NICHD. (2008). *Beyond infertility: Polycystic ovary syndrome (PCOS).* Retrieved from www.nichd.nih.gov

Nicholas, J. G., & Geers, A. E. (2006). Effects of early auditory experience on the spoken language of deaf children at 3 years of age. *Ear and Hearing, 27,* 286–298.

Nichter, M., Adrian, S., Goldade, K., Tesler, L., & Muramato, M. (2008). Smoking and harm-reduction efforts among postpartum women. *Qualitative Health Research, 18*(9), 1184–1194.

NIDCD (National Institute on Deafness and other Communication Disorders). (2009). *Cochlear implants.* Retrieved from http://www.nidcd.nih.gov/health/hearing/coch.asp

Nielson. (2009). *How teens use media.* Retrieved from http://blog.nielsen.com/nielsenwire/reports/nielsen_howteensusemedia_june09.pdf

Nielsenwire (2009, August). *Breaking teen myths.* Retrieved from http://blog.nielsen.com/nielsenwire/online_mobile/breaking-teen-myths/

NIL. (2008). *Developing early literacy: A scientific synthesis of early literacy development and implications for intervention. Report of the National Early Literacy Panel.* Washington, DC: National Institute for Literacy (NIL), available online at http://www.nifl.gov/publications/pdf/NELPReport09.pdf.

Nilsson, S., Baigi, A., Marklund, B., & Fridlund, B. (2001). The prevalence of the use of androgenic anabolic steroids by adolescents in a county of Sweden. *European Journal of Public Health, 11,* 195–197.

NINDS. (2009). *NINDS learning disabilities information page.* Retrieved from http://www.ninds.nih.gov/disorders/learningdisabilities/learningdisabilities.htm#What_is

Nippold, M., Hegel, S., Sohlberg, M., & Schwarz, I. (1999). Defining abstract entities: Development in preadolescents, adolescents, and young adults. *Journal of Speech and Hearing Research, 42,* 473–481.

Nippold, M., Moran, C., & Schwarz, I. E. (2001). Idiom understanding in preadolescents: Synergy in action. *American Journal of Speech Language Pathology and Audiology, 10*(2), 169–179.

Nissani, M., & Hoefler-Nissani, D. M. (1992). Experimental studies of belief dependence of observations and of resistance to conceptual change. *Cognition and Instruction, 9,* 97–111.

NMSA. (2010). *This we believe: Keys to educating young adolescents.* Westerville, OH: National Middle School Association.

Noddings, N. (1992). *The challenge to care in schools: An alternative approach to education.* New York, NY: Teachers College Press.

Noël, M.-P. (2009). Counting on working memory when learning to count and to add: A preschool study. *Developmental Psychology, 45,* 1630–1643.

Noguera, P. (2005). The racial achievement gap: How can we assume an equity of outcomes. In L. Johnson, M. E. Finn, & R. Lewis (Eds.), *Urban education with an attitude.* Albany, NY: SUNY Press.

Noon, D. H. (2004). Situating gender and professional identity in American child study 1880–1910. *History of Psychology, 7,* 107–129.

Noonan, K. J., Farnum, C. E., Leiferman, E. M., Lampl, M., Markel, M. D., & Wilsman, N. J. (2004). Growing Pains: Are they due to increased growth during recumbency as documented in a lamb model? *Journal of Pediatric Orthopedics, 24,* 726–731.

Norbert, F. (2005). Research findings on early first language attrition: Implications for the discussion of critical periods in language acquisition. *Language Learning, 55*(3), 491–531.

Norton, P., & Sprague, D. (2001). *Technology for teaching.* Boston, MA: Allyn & Bacon.

NSF. (2007). *Women, minorities, and persons with disabilities in science and engineering* (No. NSF 07-315). Arlington, VA: National Science Foundation: Division of Science Resources Statistics.

Nucci, L. P. (2001). *Education in the moral domain.* New York, NY: Cambridge Press.

Nugent, J. K., Petrauskas, B., & Brazelton, T. B. (Eds.). (2008). *The newborn as a person: Enabling healthy infant development worldwide.* Hoboken, NJ: Wiley.

Nunes, T., & Roazzi, A. (1999). Education, social identity, and occupational aspirations in Brazil: Reasons for (not) learning. In F. E. Leach & A. W. Litle (Eds.), *Education, culture and economics: Dilemmas for development* (pp. 27–343). New York, NY: Falmer Press.

Nurnberger, J. I., & Foroud, T. (2000). Genetics of bipolar affective disorder. *Current Psychiatry Reports, 2*(2), 147–157.

Nylund, D. (2000). *Treating Huckleberry Finn: A new narrative approach to working with kids diagnosed ADD/ADHD.* San Francisco, CA: Jossey-Bass.

O'Boyle, M. W., & Gill, H. S. (1998). On the relevance of research findings in cognitive neuroscience to educational practice. *Educational Psychology Review, 10,* 397–409. doi:10.1023/A:1022889317826

O'Brien, M. (1992). Gender identity and sex roles. In V. B. Hasselt & M. Hersen (Eds.), *Handbook of social development: A lifespan perspective* (pp. 325–345). New York, NY: Plenum.

O'Brien, M. P., Zinberg, J. L., Bearden, C. E., Lopez, S. R., Kopelowicz, A., Daley, M., & Cannon, T. D. (2008). Parent attitudes and parent adolescent interaction in families of youth at risk for psychosis and with recent-onset psychotic symptoms. *Early Intervention in Psychiatry, 2*(4), 268–276.

O'Donnell, A. M. (2006). The role of peers and group learning. In P. A. Alexander & P. H. Winne (Eds.), *Handbook of educational psychology* (2nd ed., pp. 781–802). Mahwah, NJ: Erlbaum.

O'Donnell, A. M., & O'Kelly, J. (1994). Learning from peers: Beyond the rhetoric of positive results. *Educational Psychology Review, 6,* 321–350.

Oakes, J. (1999). Promotion or retention: Which one is social? *Harvard Education Letter, 15*(1), 8.

Oakes, L. M., Messenger, I. M., Ross-Sheehy, S., & Luck, S. J. (2009). New evidence for rapid development of colour-location binding in infants' visual short-term memory. *Visual cognition, 17*(1/2), 67–82.

Odegard, T. N., Cooper, C. M., Lampinen, J. M., Reyna, V. F., & Brainerd, C. J. (2009). Children's eyewitness memory for multiple real-life events. *Child Development, 80,* 1877–1890.

OECD. (2009). *Highlights from Education at a Glance 2009.* Paris, France: Organisation for Economic Co-Operation and Development.

Ogbu, J. U. (2004). Collective identity and the burden of "acting white" in Black history, community, and education. *The Urban Review, 36*(1), 1–35.

Ogden, J. E., Brophy, J. E., & Evertson, C. M. (1997). *An experimental investigation of organization and management techniques in first-grade reading groups.* Paper presented at the annual meeting of the American Educational Research Association, New York, NY.

Okagaki, L. (2006). Ethnicity, learning. In P. A. Alexander & P. H. Winne (Eds.), *Handbook of educational psychology* (2nd ed., pp. 615–634). Mahwah, NJ: Lawrence Erlbaum.

Oller, D. K., Eilers, R. E., Neal, A. R., & Cobo-Lewis, A. B. (1998). Late onset canonical babbling: A possible early marker of abnormal development. *American Journal of Mental Retardation, 103*(3), 249–263.

Olsen, L. (1988). *Crossing the schoolhouse border: Immigrant students and the California public schools.* San Francisco, CA: California Tomorrow.

Olson, C. K., Kutner, L. A., & Warner, D. E. (2008). The role of violent video game content in adolescent development. *Journal of Adolescent Research, 23*(1), 55–75.

Olson, D. R. (2004). The triumph of hope over experience in the search for "what works": A response to Slavin. *Educational Researcher, 33*(1), 24–26.

Olsson, A., Fahlen, I., & Janson, S. (2008). Health behaviours, risk-taking and conceptual changes among schoolchildren aged 7 to 19 years in semi-rural Sweden. *Child: Care, Health & Development, 34*(3), 302–309.

Olweus, D. (1991). Bully/victim problems among school-children: Basic facts and effects of a school-based intervention program. In D. Pepler & K. Rubin (Eds.), *The development and treatment of childhood aggression* (pp. 411–448). Mahwah, NJ: Erlbaum.

Omi, M., & Winant, H. (1994). *Racial formation in the United States: From the 1960s to the 1990s* (2nd ed.). New York, NY: Routledge.

Optum Health. (2008). Accidental poisoning in children. Retrieved from http://www.myoptumhealth.com/portal/Information/item/Accidental+Poisoning+in+Children?archiveChannel=Home%2FArticle&clicked=true

Orfield, G., & Frankenberg, E. (2005). Where are we now? In F. Shultz (Ed.), *Annual editions: Multicultural education* (pp. 10–12). Dubuque, IA: McGraw-Hill/Dushkin.

Orlando, L., & Machado, A. (1996). In defense of Piaget's theory: A reply to 10 common criticisms. *Psychological Review, 103,* 143–164.

Orme, N. (2001). *Medieval children.* New Haven, CT: Yale University Press.

Ornstein, P. A., & Haden, C. A. (2001). Memory development or the development of memory? *Current Directions in Psychological Science, 10,* 202–206.

Osgood, D. W., Wilson, J. K., O'Malley, P. M., Bachman, J. G., & Johnston, L. D. (1996). Routine activities and individual deviant behavior. *American Sociological Review, 61*(4), 635–655.

Osher, D., Bear, G. G., Sprague, J. R., & Doyle, W. (2010). How can we improve school discipline? *Educational Researcher, 39*(1), 48–58. doi:10.3102/0013189X09357618

Oskar, J. G., & O'Connor, B. B. (2005). Children's sleep: An interplay between culture and biology. *Pediatrics 115*(1), (Supplement) 204–216.

Otto, B. (2010). *Language development in early childhood* (5th ed.). Columbus, OH: Merrill.

Ovando, C. J., & Collier, V. P. (1998). *Bilingual and ESL classrooms: Teaching in multicultural contexts* (2nd ed.). New York, NY: McGraw-Hill.

Overton, W. F. (1998). Developmental psychology: Philosophy, concepts, and methodology. In R. M. Lerner (Ed.), *Handbook of child psychology: Volume 1. Theoretical models of human development* (5th ed., pp. 107–188). New York, NY: Wiley.

Overton, W. F. (2003). Development across the life span: Philosophy, concepts, theory. In: R. M. Lerner, M. A. Easterbrooks, & J. Mistry (Eds.), *Comprehensive handbook of psychology: Developmental psychology* (Vol. 6, pp. 13–42). New York, NY: Wiley.

Overton, W. F. (2006). Developmental psychology: Philosophy, concepts, and methodology. In R. M. Lerner (Ed.), *Handbook of child psychology* (6th ed., Vol. 1: Theoretical models of human development, pp. 18–88). New York, NY: Wiley.

Owens, J. A., Palermo, T. M., & Rosen, C. L. (2002). Overview of current management of sleep disturbances in children: II—Behavioral interventions. *Current Therapeutic Research, 63,* 38–52.

Owens, R. E. (2005a). *Language disorders: A functional approach to assessment and intervention* Boston, MA: Allyn & Bacon.

Owens, R. E. (2005b). *Language development: An introduction* (6th ed.). Boston, MA: Allyn & Bacon.

Owens, R. E. (2008). *Language development: An introduction* (7th ed.). Boston, MA: Allyn & Bacon.

Owusu-Bempah, J., & Howitt, D. (2000). *Psychology beyond Western perspectives.* Leicester, England: BPS Books.

Oyama, S. (2000). *The ontogeny of information: Developmental systems and evolution.* Durham, NC: Duke University Press.

Ozonoff, S., Young, G. S., Goldring, S., Greiss-Hess, L., Herrera, A. M., Steele, J., . . . Rogers, S. J. (2008). Gross motor development, movement abnormalities, and early identification of autism. *Journal of Autism and Developmental Disorders, 38,* 644–656.

Ozturk, A., Mazicioglu, M. M., Poyrazoglu, S., Cicek, B., Gunay, O., & Kurtoglu, S. (2009). The relationship between sleep duration and obesity in Turkish children and adolescents. *Acta Paediatrica, 98,* 699–702.

Pahl, K., & Way, N. (2006). Longitudinal trajectories of ethnic identity among urban Black and Latino adolescents. *Child Development, 77*(5), 1403–1415.

Pai, Y., & Adler, S. A. (2001). *Cultural foundations of education* (3rd ed.). Upper Saddle River, NJ: Merrill.

Paik, H., & Comstock, G. (1994). The effects of television violence on antisocial behavior: A meta-analysis. *Communication Research, 21,* 516–546.

Palinscar, A. S. (1998). Social constructivist perspectives on teaching and learning. *Annual Review of Psychology, 49,* 345–375.

Palincsar, A. S., & Brown, A. L. (1989). Classroom dialogues to promote self-regulated comprehension. In J. Brophy (Ed.), *Advances in research on teaching* (Vol. 1, pp. 35–67). Greenwich, CT: JAI Press.

Palincsar, A. S., & Herrenkohl, L. R. (2002). Designing collaborative learning contexts. *Theory Into Practice, 61,* 26–32.

Palmert, M. R., & Boepple, P. A. (2001). Variation in the timing of puberty: Clinical spectrum and genetic investigation. *Journal of Clinical Endocrinology & Metabolism, 86,* 2634–2668.

Panneton, R. K. (1985). Prenatal experience with melodies: Effect on postnatal auditory preference in human newborns. *Unpublished doctoral dissertation,* University of North Carolina at Greensboro.

Parasad, B. & Lewis, L. (2006). Calories in, calories out: Food and exercise in public elementary schools, 2005 (NCES 2006-057). U.S. Department of Education. Washington, DC: National Center for Education Statistics.

Paris, S. G., & Cunningham, A. E. (1996). Children becoming students. In D. Berliner & R. Calfee (Eds.), *Handbook of educational psychology* (pp. 117–146). New York, NY: Macmillan.

Park, M. J., Brindis, C. D., Chang, F., & Irwin, C. E. (2008). A midcourse review of the healthy people 2010: 21 critical health objectives for adolescents and young adults. *Journal of Adolescent Health, 42*, 329–334.

Parke, R. D. (2004). Development in the family. *Annual Review of Psychology, 55*, 365–399.

Parke, R. D., & Buriel, R. (1998). Socialization in the family: Ethnic and ecological perspectives. In W. Damon & N. Eisenberg (Eds.), *Handbook of child psychology* (5th ed., Vol. 3. Social, emotional, and personality development, pp. 553–618). New York, NY: Wiley.

Parke, R. D., & Buriel, R. (2006). Socialization in the family: Ethnic and ecological perspectives. In W. Damon, R. M. Lerner, & N. Eisenberg (Eds.), *Handbook of Child Psychology Vol. 3:* (pp. 429–504). New York, NY: Wiley.

Parker, J. G., & Gottman, J. M. (1989). Social and emotional development in a relational context: Friendship interaction from early childhood to adolescence. In T. J. Berndt & G. W. Ladd (Eds.), *Peer relationships in child development*. New York, NY: Wiley.

Parker, J. S., & Benson, M. J. (2004). Parent-adolescent relations and adolescent functioning: Self-esteem, substance abuse, and delinquency. *Adolescence, 38*(155), 519–530.

Parker-Pope, T. (2009, February 23). *The 3 r's? A fourth is crucial, too: Recess*. Retrieved from http://www.nytimes.com/2009/02/24/health/24well.html

Parker-Pope, T. (2010, February 16). As girls become women, sports pay dividends. *The New York Times*, p. D5.

Parten, M. B. (1932). Social participation among preschool children. *Journal of Abnormal and Social Psychology, 27*, 243–269.

Pasley, K., & Gecas, V. (1984). Stresses and satisfactions of the parental role. *Personnel and Guidance Journal, 62*(7), 400–404.

Pasterski, V. L., Geffner, M. E., Brain, C., Hindmarsh, P., Brook, C., & Hines, M. (2005). Prenatal hormones and postnatal socialization by parents as determinants of male-typical toy play in girls with congenital adrenal hyperplasia. *Child Development, 76*, 264–278.

Patchin, J. W., & Hinduja, J. (2006). Bullies move beyond the schoolyard: A preliminary look at cyberbullying. *Youth Violence and Juvenile Justice, 4*, 148–169.

Pate, R. R., Stevens, J., Webber, L. S., Dowda, M., Murray, D. M., Young, D. R., & Going, S. (2009). Age-related change in physical activity in adolescent girls. *Journal of Adolescent Health, 44*, 275–282.

Patel, V., Flisher, A. J., Hetrick, S., & McGorry, P. (2007). *Mental health of young people: A global public-health challenge, 369*. Retrieved from http://www.thelancet.com/search/results?searchTerm=patel&fieldName=Authors&year=2007&volume=369&page=&journalFromWhichSearchStarted=

Patterson, C. J. (1992). Children of lesbian and gay parents. *Child Development, 63*, 1025–1042.

Patterson, C. J. (2002). Lesbian and gay parenthood. In M. C. Bornstein (Ed.), *Handbook of parenting* (Vol. 3, pp. 317–338). Hillsdale, NJ: Erlbaum.

Patterson, G. R. (1982). Self-control and self-regulation in childhood. In T. Field & A. Huston-Stein (Eds.), *Review of human development* (pp. 222–241). New York, NY: Wiley.

Patterson, G. R., & Forgatch, M. S. (2005). *Parents and adolescents living together: The basics* (2nd ed.). Champaign, IL: Research Press.

Pauen, S., & Träuble, B. (2009). How 7-month-olds interpret ambiguous motion events: Category-based reasoning in infancy. *Cognitive Psychology, 59*(3), 275–295.

Paulos, L. (2007). Multitasking madness. *Scholastic Choices, 23*(1), 10–13.

Payne, K. J., & Biddle, B. J. (1999). Poor school funding, child poverty, and mathematics achievement. *Educational Researcher, 28*, 4–12.

Pea, R. D., & Maldonado, H. (2006). WILD for learning: Interacting through new computing devices anywhere, anytime. In R. K. Sawyer (Ed.), *The Cambridge handbook of the learning sciences* (pp. 427–441). New York, NY: Cambridge University Press.

Pearson, B. Z., Fernandez, S. C., Lewedeg, V., & Oller, D. K. (1997). The relation of input factors to lexical learning by bilingual infants. *Applied Linguistics, 18*, 41–58.

Pearson, N., Biddle, S. J. H., & Gorley, T. (2009). Family correlates of breakfast consumption among children and adolescents: A systematic review. *Appetite, 52*, 1–7.

Pelham, S. (2009, March 14) Actress Sophie Pelham: "My brain is like a filing cabinet organized by really bad secretary." *MailOnline*. Retrieved from http://www.dailymail.co.uk/home/you/article-1161180/Actress-Sophie-Pelham—8216-My-brain-like-filing-cabinet-organised-really-bad-secretary-8217.html

Pelham, W. E. (1981). Attention deficits in hyperactive and learning-disabled children. *Exceptional Education Quarterly, 2*, 13–23.

Pellegrini, A. D., & Bohn, C. M. (2005). The role of recess in children's cognitive performance and school adjustment. *Educational Researcher, 34*, 13–19.

Pellegrini, A. D., Dupuis, D., & Smith, P. K. (2007). Play in evolution and development. *Developmental Review, 27*, 261–276.

Pellegrini, A. D., & Smith, P. K. (1998). Physical activity play: The nature and function of a neglected aspect of play. *Child Development, 69*, 577–598.

Pellis, S. (2006). The effects of orbital frontal cortex damage on the modulation of defensive responses by rats in playful and nonplayful social contexts. *Behavioral Neuroscience, 120*, 72–84.

Peltola, M. J., Leppänen, J. M., Palokangas, T., & Hietanen, J. K. (2009). Fearful faces modulate looking duration and attention disengagement in 7-month-old infants. *Developmental Science, 11*(1), 60–68.

Peng, S., & Lee, R. (1992, April). *Home variables, parent–child activities, and academic achievement: A study of 1988 eighth graders*. Paper presented at the annual meeting of the American Educational Research Association, San Francisco, CA.

Penuel, W. R., & Wertsch, J. V. (1995). Vygotsky and identity formation: A sociocultural approach. *Educational Psychologist, 30*, 83–92.

Pepler, D. J., & Sedighdeilami, F. (1998, October). *Aggressive girls in Canada*. Hull, QC: Applied Research Branch of Strategic Policy, Human Resources and Development Canada.

Perkins, S. A., & Turiel, E. (2007). To lie or not to lie: To whom and under what circumstances. *Child Development, 78*(2), 609–621.

Perlman, M., & Ross, H. S. (1997). The benefits of parent intervention in children's disputes: An examination of concurrent changes in children's fighting styles. *Child Development*, 68, 690–700.

Perner, J. (2000). About + belief + counterfactual. In P. Mitchell & K. J. Riggs (Eds.), *Children's reasoning and the mind*. Hove, East Sussex: Psychology Press.

Perry, N. E., Phillips, L., & Dowler, J. (2004). Examining features of tasks and their potential to promote self-regulated learning. *Teachers College Record, 106*, 1854–1878.

Perry, N. E., VandeKamp, K. O., Mercer, L. K., & Nordby, C. J. (2002). Investigating teacher–student interactions that foster self-regulated learning. *Educational Psychologist, 37*, 5–15.

Petersen, S. H., & Wittmer, D. S. (2009). *Endless opportunities for infant and toddler curriculum. A relationship-based approach*. Upper Saddle River, NJ: Pearson.

Peterson, C. (2002). Children's long-term memory for autobiographical events. *Developmental Review, 22*.

Peterson, C., & McCabe, A. (1983). *Developmental psycholinguists: Three ways of looking at a child's narrative*. New York, NY: Plenum Press.

Peterson, G. W. (2005). Family influences on adolescent development. In T. P. Gullotta & G. R. Adams (Eds.), *Handbook of adolescent behavioral problems: Evidence-based approaches to prevention and treatment* (pp. 27–55). New York, NY: Springer.

Peterson, G. W., Cobas, J. A., Bush, J. R., Supple, A., & Wilson, S. M. (2004). Parent-youth relationships and the self-esteem of Chinese adolescents: Collectivism versus individualism. *Marriage & Family Review, 36*, 173–200.

Peterson, J. T. (1993). Generalized extended family exchange: A case from the Philippines. *Journal of Marriage and the Family, 55*, 570–584.

Petitclerc, A., Boivin, M., Dionne, G., Zoccolillo, M., & Tremblay, R. E. (2009). Disregard for rules: The early development and predictors of a specific dimension of disruptive behavior disorders. *Journal of Child Psychology and Psychiatry, 50*, 1477–1484.

Petitto, L. A., & Kovelman, I. (2003). The bilingual paradox: How signing-speaking bilingual children help us resolve bilingual issues and teach us about the brain's mechanisms underlying all language acquisition. *Language Learning, 8*(3), 5–18.

Petitto, L. A., & Marentette, P. (1991). Babbling in the manual mode: Evidence for the ontogeny of language. *Science, 251*, 1483–1496.

Petrill, S. A., Lipton, P. A., Hewitt, J. K., Plomin, R., Cherny, S. S., Corley, R., & DeFries, J. C. (2004). Genetic and environmental contributions to general cognitive ability through the first 16 years of life. *Developmental Psychology, 40*, 805–812.

Petrill, S. A., & Wilkerson, B. (2000). Intelligence and achievement: A behavioral genetic perspective. *Educational Psychology Review, 12*, 185–199.

Petrina, S., Feng, F., & Kim, J. (2008). Researching cognition and technology: How we learn across the lifespan. *International Journal of Technology and Design Education, 18*, 375–396.

Petrini, J. R., Dias, T., McCormick, M. C., Massolo, M. L., Green, N. S., & Escobar, G. J. (2009). Increased risk of adverse neurological development for late preterm infants. *Journal of Pediatrics, 154*, 169–176.

Pettigrew, T. (1998). Intergroup contact theory. *Annual review of psychology* (pp. 65–85). Palo Alto: CA: Annual Reviews.

Pettit, G. S., Bates, J. E., Dodge, K. A., & Meece, D. W. (1999). The impact of after-school peer contact on early adolescent externalizing problems is moderated by parental monitoring, perceived neighborhood safety, and prior adjustment. *Child Development, 70*(3), 768–778.

Pfiffner, L., Barkley, R. A., & DuPaul, G. J. (2006). Treatment of ADHD in school settings. In R. A. Barkley (Ed.), *Attention-deficit hyperactivity disorder: A handbook for diagnosis and treatment* (3rd ed., pp. 547–588). New York, NY: Guilford.

Phelan, K. J., Khoury, J., Kalkwarf, H., & Lanphear, B. (2001). Trends and patterns of playground injuries in United States children and adolescents. *Ambulatory Pediatrics, 1*(4), 227–233.

Philippot P., & Feldman, R. S. (Eds.). (2004). *The regulation of emotion*. Mahwah, NJ: Erlbaum.

Phillips, L. M., Norris, S. P., Osmond, W. C., & Maynard, A. M. (2002). Relative reading achievement: A longitudinal study of 187 children from first through sixth grades. *Journal of Educational Psychology, 94*(1), 3–13.

Phinney, J. S. (1989). Stages of ethnic identity development in minority group adolescents. *Journal of Early Adolescence, 9*, 34–49.

Phinney, J. S. (1996). When we talk about American ethnic groups, what do we mean? *American Psychologist, 51*(9), 918–927.

Phinney, J. S., DuPont, S., Espinosa, C., Revill, J., & Sanders, K. (1994). Ethnic identity and American identification among ethnic minority youths. In A. Bouvy, F. van de Vijver, P. Boski, & P. Schmitz (Eds.), *Journeys into Cross-Cultural Psychology*. Amsterdam, Netherlands: Swets & Zeitlinger.

Phinney, J. S., Kim, T., Ossorio, S., & Vilhjalmsdottir, P. (2002). *Self- and other-orientation in the resolutions of adolescent-parents disagreements: Cultural and developmental differences*. Unpublished manuscript. Los Angeles, CA: California State University, Los Angeles.

Piaget, J. (1932). *The moral judgment of the child*. New York, NY: Macmillan.

Piaget, J. (1951). *Play, dreams and imitation in childhood*. New York, NY: W. W. Norton.

Piaget, J. (1952). *The origins of intelligence in children*. New York, NY: International Universities Press.

Piaget, J. (1954). *The construction of reality in the child* (M. Cook, Trans.). New York, NY: Basic Books.

Piaget, J. (1962). *Play, dreams and imitation in childhood*. New York, NY: Norton.

Piaget, J. (1963). *Origins of intelligence in children*. New York, NY: Norton.

Piaget, J. (1964). Development and learning. In R. Ripple & V. Rockcastle (Eds.), *Piaget rediscovered* (pp. 7–20). Ithaca, NY: Cornell University Press.

Piaget, J. (1965). *The moral judgment of the child*. New York, NY: Free Press.

Piaget, J. (1965/1995). *Sociological studies*. New York, NY: Routledge.

Piaget, J. (1969). *Science of education and the psychology of the child*. New York, NY: Viking.

Piaget, J. (1970a). Piaget's theory. In P. Mussen (Ed.), *Handbook of child psychology* (3rd ed., Vol. 1, pp. 703–732). New York, NY: Wiley.

Piaget, J. (1970b). *The science of education and the psychology of the child*. New York, NY: Orion Press.

Piaget, J. (1971). The theory of stages in cognitive development. In D. R. Green, M. P. Ford, & G. B. Flamer (Eds.), *Measurement and Piaget*. New York, NY: McGraw-Hill.

Piaget, J. (1974). *Understanding causality* (D. Miles & M. Miles, Trans.). New York, NY: Norton.

Piaget, J. (1975/1985). *The equilibration of cognitive structures*, Chicago, IL: University of Chicago Press.

Piaget, J. (1978). *Success and understanding*. London, England: Routledge & Kegan Paul.

Piehler, T. F., & Dishion, T. J. (2007). Interpersonal dynamics within adolescent friendships: Dyadic mutuality, deviant talk, and patterns of antisocial behavior. *Child Development, 78*(5), 1611–1624.

Pipe, M., Lamb, M. E., Orbach, Y., & Esplin, P. W. (2004). Recent research on children. *Developmental Review, 24*, 440–468.

Pisha, B., & Coyne, P. (2001). Smart for the start: The promise of universal design for learning. *Remedial and Special Education* (22), 197–203.

Piske, T., MacKay, I. R. A., & Flege, J. E. (2001). Factors affecting degree of foreign accent in an L2: A review. *Journal of Phonetics, 29*, 191–215.

Pittman, L. D., & Richmond, A. (2007). Academic and psychological functioning in late adolescence: The importance of school belonging. *The Journal of Experimental Education, 75*(4), 270–290.

Plomin, R. (1990). *Nature and nurture: An introduction to behavior genetics*. Pacific Grove, CA: Brooks/Cole.

Plomin, R. (1990). The role of inheritance in behavior. *Science, 248*(4952), 183–188.

Plomin, R. (1997). Identifying genes for cognitive abilities and disabilities. In R. J. Sternberg & E. L. Grigorenko (Eds.), *Intelligence, heredity, and environment* (pp. 89–104). New York, NY: Cambridge University Press.

Plomin, R. (2004). Genetics and developmental psychology. *Merrill-Palmer Quarterly, 50*, 341–352.

Plomin, R., & Koeppen-Schomerus, G. (2002). Beyond heritability. *Psychosomatic Medicine, 64*, 204–205.

Plomin, R., & Spinath, F. M. (2004). Intelligence: Genetics, genes, and genomics. *Journal of Personality and Social Psychology, 86*, 112–129.

Plummer D. L., & Graziano W. G. (1987). Impact of grade retention on the social development of elementary school children. *Developmental Psychology, 23*, 267–275.

Polit, D. E., & Falbo, T. (1987). Only children and personality development: A quantitative review. *Journal of Marriage and the Family, 49*, 309–325.

Pomares, C. G., Schirrer, J., & Abadie, V. (2002). Anaysis of the olfactory capacity of healthy children before language acquisition. *Journal of Developmental Behavior and Pediatrics, 23*, 203–207.

Popham, W. J. (2005). *Classroom assessment: What teachers need to know* (4th ed.). Boston, MA: Allyn & Bacon.

Porac, C., Coren, S., & Searlman, A. (1986). Environmental factors in hand preference formation: Evidence from attempts to switch the preferred hand. *Behavioral Genetics, 16*, 250–261.

Portes, A., & Hao, L. (1998). E pluribus unum: Bilingualism and loss of language in the second generation. *Sociology of Education, 71*, 269–294.

Posada, G., Jacobs, A., Richmond, M., Carbonell, O. A., Alzate, G., Bustamante, M. R., & Quiceno, J. (2002). Maternal care giving and infant security in two cultures. *Developmental Psychology, 38*, 67–78.

Powlishta, K. K. (2004). Gender as a social category: Intergroup processes and gender-role development. In M. Bennet & F. Sani (Eds.), *The development of the social self* (pp. 103–134). New York, NY: Psychology Press.

Prather, R. W., & Alibali, M. W. (2009). The development of arithmetic principle knowledge: How do we know what learners know? *Developmental Review, 29*, 21–248.

Pressley, M. (1996 August). *Getting beyond whole language: Elementary reading instruction that makes sense in light of recent psychological research*. Paper presented at the Annual meeting of the American Psychological Association, Toronto, ON.

Pressley, M., & Hilden, K. (2006). Cognitive strategies. In D. Kuhn & R. S. Siegler (Eds.), *Cognition, perception, and language* (6th ed., Vol. 2, pp. 511–556). New York, NY: Wiley.

Pressley, M., Raphael, L. M., Gallagher, D., & DiBella, J. (2004). Providence-St. Mel School: How a school that works for African-American students works. *Journal of Educational Psychology, 96*, 216–235.

Price, L. F. (2005). The biology of risk taking. *Educational Leadership, 62*(7), 22–27.

Price, W. F., & Crapo, R. H. (2002). *Cross-cultural perspectives in introductory psychology* (4th ed.). Pacific Grove, CA: Wadsworth.

Prinstein, M. J., & La Greca, A. M. (1999). Links between mothers' and children's social competence and associations with maternal adjustment. *Journal of Clinical Child Psychology, 28*, 197–210.

Prinstein, M. J., & LaGreca, A. M. (2002). Peer crowd affiliation and internalizing distress in childhood and adolescence: A longitudinal follow-back study. *Journal of Research on Adolescence, 12*(3), 325–351.

Project Zero, Reggio Emilia, & Children (Eds.). (2001). *Making learning visible: Children as individual and group learners*. Cambridge, MA: Project Zero Publications.

Pruden, S. M., Hirsh-Pasek, K., Golinkoff, R. M., & Hennon, E. A. (2006). The birth of words: Ten-month-olds learn words through perceptual salience. *Child Development, 77*(2), 266–280.

Puckett, M. B., Black, J. K., Wittmer, D. S., & Petersen, S. H. (2009) *The young child: Development from prebirth through age eight* (5th ed). Columbus, OH: Pearson/Merrill.

Puncochar, J., & Fox, P. W. (2004). Confidence in individual and group decision-making: When "Two Heads" are worse than one. *Journal of Educational Psychology, 96*, 582–591.

Purcell-Gates, V. (2001). Emergent literacy is emerging knowledge of written, not oral, language. *New Directions for Child and Adolescent Development, 92*, 7–22.

Purdie, N., Hattie, J., & Carroll, A. (2002). A review of the research on interventions for Attention

Deficit Hyperactivity Disorder: What works best? *Review of Educational Research, 72,* 61–99.

Quann, V., & Wien, C. A. (2006). The visible empathy of infants and toddlers. *Young Children, 61*(4): 22–29.

Quatman, T., Sampson, K., Robinson, C., & Watson, C. M. (2001). Academic, motivational, and emotional correlates of adolescent dating. *Genetic, Social, and General Psychology Monographs, 127*(1), 211–234.

Queensland University of Technology. (2006, October 28). For crying out loud—Pick up your baby. *ScienceDaily*. Retrieved from http://www.sciencedaily.com

Quinn, P. C. (2002). Category representation in infants. *Current Directions in Psychological Science, 11,* 66–70.

Quinn, P. C., Yahr, J., Kuhn, A., Sater, A. M., & Pascalis, O. (2002). Representation of the gender of human faces by infants: A preference for female. *Perception, 31,*1109–1121.

Rachlin, H. (1991). *Introduction to modern behaviorism* (3rd ed.). New York, NY: W.H. Freeman.

Raffaelli. M., & Ontai, L. L. (2004). Gender socialization in Latino/a families: Results from two retrospective studies. *Sex Roles, 50,* 287–299.

Rahi, J. S., & Dezateux, C. (1999). National cross sectional study of detection of congenital and infantile cataract in the United Kingdom: Role of childhood screening and surveillance. *BMJ, 318*, 362–365.

Raikes, H. A., Robinson, J. L., Bradley, R. H., Raikes, H. H., & Ayoub, C. C. (2007). Developmental trends in self-regulation among low-income toddlers. *Social Development, 16*(1), 128–149.

Raikes, H. A., & Thompson, R. A. (2005). Efficacy and social support as predictors of parenting stress among families in poverty. *Infant Mental Health Journal, 26,* 177–190.

Rakoczy, H., Tomasello, M., & Striano, T. (2004). Young children know that trying is not pretending: A test of the "Behaving-As-If" construal of children's early concept of pretense. *Developmental Psychology, 40,* 388–399.

Ralston, A., & Shaw, K. (2008). Gene expression regulates cell differentiation. *Nature Education, 1*(1). Retrieved from http://www.nature.com/scitable/topicpage/gene-expression-regulates-cell-differentiation-931

RAND Center for Domestic and International Health Security. (2005). *Helping children cope with violence: A school-based program that works.* Retrieved from http://www.rand.org/pubs/research_briefs/RB4557-2/index1.html

Range, L. M. (1993). Suicide prevention: Guidelines for schools. *Educational Psychology Review, 5,* 135–154.

Rangel, M. C., Gavin, L., Reed, C., Fowler, M. G., & Lee, L. M. (2006). Epidemiology of HIV and AIDS among adolescents and young adults in the United States. *Journal of Adolescent Health, 39,* 156–163.

Rao, M. R., Brenner, R. A., Schisterman, E. F., Vik, T., & Mills, J. L. (2004). Long term cognitive development in children with prolonged crying. *Archives of Disease in Childhood, 89,* 989–992.

Rao, M. R., Hediger, M. L., Levine, R. J., Naficy, A. B., & Vik, T. (2002). Effect of breastfeeding on cognitive development of infants born small for gestational age. *Acta Paediatr,* 91, 267–274.

Rao, N., & Stewart, S. M. (1999). Cultural influences on sharer and recipient behavior: Sharing in Chinese and Indian preschool children. *Journal of Cross-Cultural Psychology, 30,* 219–241.

Rathus, S. A. (1988). *Understanding child development.* New York, NY: Holt, Rinehart & Winston.

Rauscher, K. J., & Myers, D. J. (2008). Socioeconomic disparities in the prevalence of work-related injuries among adolescents in the United States. *Journal of Adolescent Health, 42,* 50–57.

Raver, C. C. (2004). Placing emotional self-regulation in sociocultural and socioeconomic contexts. *Child Development, 75*, 346–353.

Razoki, A. H., Taha, I. K., Taib, N. I., Sadik, S., & Al Gasseer, N. (2006). Mental health of Iraqi children. *Lancet, 368,* 838–839.

Reder, L. M. (1996). Different research programs on metacognition: Are the boundaries imaginary? *Learning and Individual Differences, 8,* 383–390.

Reich, P. A. (1986). *Language development.* Englewood Cliffs, NJ: Prentice-Hall.

Reichman, N. E., & Teitler, J. O. (2003). Effects of psychosocial risk factors and prenatal interventions on birth weight: Evidence from New Jersey's HealthStart Program. *Perspectives on Sexual and Reproductive Health*, 35(3), 130–137.

Reiner, W. G., & Gearhart, J. P. (2004). Discordant sexual identity in some genetic males with cloacal exstrophy assigned to female sex at birth. *The New England Journal of Medicine, 350,* 333–341.

Reis, S. M., Kaplan, S. N., Tomlinson, C. A., Westberg, K. L., Callahan, C. M., & Cooper, C. R. (2002). Equal does not mean identical. In L. Abbeduto (Ed.), *Taking sides: Clashing on controversial issues in educational psychology* (pp. 31–35). Guilford, CT: McGraw-Hill/Duskin.

Reiss, D., Neiderhiser, J. M., Hetherington, E. M., & Plomin, R. (2000). *The relationship code: Deciphering genetic and social influences on adolescent development.* Cambridge, MA: Harvard University Press.

Rennie, L. J., & Parker, L. H. (1987). Detecting and accounting for gender differences in mixed-sex and single-sex groupings in science lessons. *Educational Review, 39,* 65–73.

Renouf, A. G., & Harter, S. (1990). Low self-worth and anger as components of the depressive experience in young adolescents. *Development and Psychopathology, 2,* 293–310.

Renzulli, J. S., & Reis, S. M. (2003). The schoolwide enrichment model: Developing creative and productive giftedness. In N. Colangelo & G. A. Davis (Eds.). *Handbook of gifted education* (pp. 184–203). Boston, MA: Allyn & Bacon.

Report of the Quality Standards Subcommittee, (1997). *Neurology, 10,* 350–357.

Reuters (June 25, 2009). Few sexually active teens in US get HIV test-CDC. Retrieved from http://www.reuters.com/article/idUSN25284459

Reynolds, A. J. (2000). *Success in early intervention: The Chicago Child-Parent Centers.* Lincoln, NE: University of Nebraska Press.

Reynolds, A. J., Temple, J. A., Robertson, D. L., & Mann, E. A. (2001). Long-term effects of an early childhood intervention on educational achievement and juvenile arrest: A 15-year follow-up of low-income children in public schools. *Journal of the American Medical Association, 285*(18), 2339–2346.

Reynolds, C. R., Skiba, R., Graham, S., Sheras, P., Conoley, J. C., & Garcia-Vazquez, E. (2008). Are zero tolerance policies effective in school: An evidentiary review and recommendations. *American Psychologist, 63,* 852–862.

Rhee, S. H., & Waldman, I. D. (2002). Genetic and environmental influences on antisocial behavior: A meta-analysis of twin and adoption studies. *Psychological Bulletin, 128,* 490–529.

Rhodes, J. (2002). *Stand by me: The risks and rewards of mentoring today's youth.* Cambridge, MA: Harvard University Press.

Rhodes, J., Spencer, R., Keller, T., & Liang, B. (2006). A model for the influence of mentoring relationships on youth development. *Journal of Community Psychology, 34,* 691–701.

Ricciardelli, L. A. (1992). Bilingualism and cognitive development: Relation to threshold theory. *Journal of Psycholinguistic Research, 21,* 301–316.

Ricciardelli, L. A., & McCabe, M. P. (2001). Children's body image concerns and eating disturbance: A review of the literature. *Clinical Psychology Review, 21*(3), 325–344.

Rice, M. L. (1989). Children's language acquisition. *American Psychologist, 44,* 149–156.

Rice, P., & Dolgin, K. G. (2002). *The adolescent: Development, relationships, and culture* (12th ed.). Upper Saddle River, NJ: Allyn & Bacon/Longman.

Richmond, R. (2009, March 26). Sexting may place teens at legal risk. *The New York Times.* Retrieved from http://gadgetwise.blogs.nytimes.com/2009/03/26/sexting-may-place-teens-at-legal-risk/

Richmond, V. (2002). Teacher nonverbal immediacy: Uses and outcomes. In J. Cheesebro & J. McCroskey (Eds.), *Communication for teachers* (pp. 35–46). Boston, MA: Allyn & Bacon.

Rideout, V. J., Foehr, U. G., & Roberts, D. F. (2010). Generation M^2: Media in the lives of 8- to 18-year-olds. Retrieved from http://www.kff.org/entmedia/upload/8010.pdf

Rideout, V. J., Vandewater, E. A., & Wartella, E. A. (2003). *Zero to Six: Electronic media in the lives of infants, toddlers, and preschoolers* (No. 3378). Menlo Park, CA: Henry J. Kaiser Family Foundation and the Children's Digital Media Centers (CDMC).

Rine, R. M., Cornwall, G., Gan, K., LoCascio, C., O'Hare, T., Robinson, E., & Rice, M. (2000). Evidence of progressive delay of motor development in children with sensorineural hearing loss and concurrent vestibular dysfunction. *Perceptual and Motor Skills, 90,* 1101–1112.

Riordan, C. (1990). *Girls and boys in school: Together or separate.* New York, NY: Teachers College Press.

Riordan, C. (1994). Single-gender schools: Outcomes for African and Hispanic Americans. *Research in Sociology of Education and Socialization, 18,* 177–205.

Riordan, C. (1998). The future of single-sex schools. In S. Morse (Ed.), *Separated by sex: A critical look at single-sex education for girls* (pp. 53–62). Washington, DC: American Association of University Women Educational Foundation.

Rittle-Johnson, B., & Kmicikewycz, A. O. (2008). When generating answers benefits arithmetic skill: The importance of prior knowledge. *Journal of Experimental Child Psychology, 101,* 75–81.

Rivera-Gaxiola, M., Silva-Pereyra, J., & Kuhl, P. K. (2008). Brain potentials to native and non-native speech contrasts in 7- and 11-month-old American infants. *Developmental Science, 8(2)*:162–172.

Rivers, I., Poteat, P., Noret, N., & Ashurst, N. (2009). Observing bullying at school: The mental health implications of witness status. *School Psychology Quarterly, 24*, 211–223.

Rivkin, S. G., Hanushek, E. A., & Kain, J. F. (2001). *Teachers, schools, and academic achievement.* Amherst, MA: Amherst College.

Roazzi, A., & Bryant, A. (1997). Explicitness and conservation: Social class differences. *International Journal of Behavioral Development, 21*, 51–70.

Roberson, D., Davidoff, J., Davies, I. R. L., & Shapiro, L. R. (2004). The development of color categories in two languages: A longitudinal study. *Journal of Experimental Psychology: General, 133*, 554–571.

Roberts, D. F., Foehr, U. G., & Rideout, V. (2005). *Generation M: Media in the lives of 8–18 year-olds. Technical Reports 7250/7251*. Retrieved 2008 from http://www.kff.org/entmedia/7251.cfm.

Roberts, R. E., Roberts, C. R., & Duong, H. T. (2008). Chronic insomnia and its negative consequences for health and functioning of adolescents: A 12-month prospective study. *Journal of Adolescent Health, 42*, 294–302.

Robins, R. W., & Trzesniewski, K. H. (2005). Self-esteem development across the lifespan. *Directions in Psychological Science, 14*, 158–162.

Robinson, A. M. (2009). The SLP and early intervention with infants and toddlers with hearing loss. *The ASHA Leader, 14*(4), 16–17.

Robinson, B. L., & Lieberman, L. J. (2004). Effects of visual impairment, gender, and age on self-determination. *Journal of Visual Impairment & Blindness, 6*, 351–366.

Robinson, J. L., & Acevedo, M. C. (2001). Infant reactivity and reliance on mother during emotion challenges: Prediction of cognition and language skills in a low-income sample. *Child Development, 72*(2), 402–416.

Robson, P. (1984). Prewalking locomotor movements and their use in predicting standing and walking. *Child: Care, Health, and Development, 10*, 317–330.

Rocha, N. A. C. F., Silva, F. P. D. S. S., & Tudella, E. (2006). The impact of object size and rigidity on infant reaching. *Infant Behavior and Development, 29*(2), 251–261.

Rochat, P. (2001). *The infant's world.* Cambridge, MA: Harvard University Press.

Rochat, P. (2007). Intentional action arises from early reciprocal exchanges. *Acta Psychology, 124*(1), 8–25.

Rodgers, J. L., & Bard, D. E. (2006). Behavior genetics and adolescent development: A review of recent literature. In G. A. M. D. Berzonsky (Ed.), *Blackwell handbook of adolescence* (pp. 3–23). Malden, MA: Blackwell Publishing.

Rodrigo, M., Janssen, T., & Ceballos, E. (1999). Do children's perceptions and attributions mediate the effects of mothers' child rearing actions? *Journal of Family Psychology, 13*, 508–522.

Roebers, C. M., Bjorklund, D. F., & Schneider, W. (2002). Differences and similarities in event recall and suggestibility between children and adults in Germany and the United States. *Experimental Psychology, 49*, 132–140.

Roeser, R. W., Eccles, J. S., & Sameroff, A. J. (2000). School as a context of early adolescents' academic and social-emotional development: A summary of research findings. *The Elementary School Journal*, 100, 443–471.

Rogers, E. E., & Piecuch, R. E. (2009). Neurodevelopmental outcomes of infants who experience intrauterine growth restriction. *NeoReviews, 10*(3), 100–112.

Rogoff, B. (1990). *Apprenticeship in thinking: Cognitive development in social context.* New York, NY: Oxford University Press.

Rogoff, B. (1995). Observing sociocultural activity on three planes: Participatory appropriation, guided participation, and apprenticeship. In J. V. Wertsch, P. del Rio, & A. Alverez (Eds.), *Sociocultural studies of mind* (pp. 139–164). Cambridge, England: Cambridge University Press.

Rogoff, B. (1998). Cognition as a collaborative process. In W. Damon, D. Kuhn, & R. S. Siegler (Eds.), *Handbook of child psychology* (5th ed., Vol. 2: Cognition, perception, and language, pp. 553–618). New York, NY: Wiley.

Rogoff, B. (2003). *The cultural nature of human development.* New York, NY: Oxford University Press.

Rogoff, B., & Morelii, G. (1989). Perspectives on children's development from cultural psychology. *American Psychologist, 44*, 343–348.

Roid, G. H. (2003). *Stanford-Binet intelligence scales* (5th ed.). Itasca, IL: Riverside Publishing.

Roid, G. H., Shaughnessy, M. F., & Greathouse, D. (2005). An interview with Gale Roid about the Stanford-Binet 5. *North American Journal of Psychology, 7*.

Rop, C. (1997/1998). Breaking the gender barrier in the physical sciences. *Educational Leadership, 55*(4), 58–60.

Rosales, F., Reznick, J., & Zeisel, S. (2009, October). Understanding the role of nutrition in the brain and behavioral development of toddlers and preschool children: Identifying and addressing methodological barriers. *Nutritional Neuroscience,12*(5), 190–202. doi:10.1179/147683009X423454

Roschelle, J. M., Pea, R. D., Hoadley, C. M., Gordon, D. N., & Means, B. M. (2000). Changing how and what children learn in school with computer-based technologies. *Children and Computer Technology, 10*(2), 76–101.

Rose-Krasnor, L., Rubin, K. H., Booth, C. L., & Coplan, R. (1996). Maternal directiveness and child attachment security as predictors of social competence in preschoolers. *International Journal of Behavior Development, 19*, 309–325.

Rosen, L. (2010). *Rewired: Understanding the iGeneration and the way they learn.* New York, NY: Palgrave Macmillan.

Rosenberg, M. S., Westling, D. L., & McLeskey, J. (2008). *Special education for today's teachers: An introduction.* Boston, MA: Allyn & Bacon.

Rosenshine, B., & Meister, C. (1992, April). *The uses of scaffolds for teaching less structured academic tasks.* Paper presented at the annual meeting of the American Educational Research Association, San Francisco.

Rosenshine, B., & Meister, C. (1994). Reciprocal teaching: A review of the research. *Review of Educational Research, 64*, 479–530.

Rosenstein, D., & Oster, H. (1988). Differential facial responses to four basic tastes in newborns. *Child Development, 59*(6), 1555–1568.

Roser, R. W., Eccles, J. S., & Sameroff, A. J. (2000). School as a context of early adolescents' academic and social-emotional development: A summary of research findings. *The Elementary School Journal, 100*(5), 443–471.

Roskos, K. A., & Christie, J. F. (2007). Play in the context of the new preschool basic. In K. A. Roskos & J. F. Christie (Eds.), *Play and literacy in early childhood: Research from multiple perspectives* (2nd ed., pp. 83–100). Mahwah, NJ: Erlbaum.

Roskos, K. A., & Neuman, S. B. (1998). Play as an opportunity for literacy. In O. N. Saracho & B. Spodek (Eds.), *Multiple perspectives on play in early childhood education* (pp. 100–115). Albany, NY: University of New York Press.

Roslow, P. (2005). *The future use of the Spanish language in the USA—Projected to 2015 & 2025.* Miami, FL: Hispanic U.S.A.

Roth, W.-M., & Bowen, G. M. (1995). Knowing and interacting: A study of culture, practices, and resources in a grade 8 open-inquiry science guided by an apprenticeship metaphor. *Cognition and Instruction, 13*, 73–128.

Rothbart, M. K., Ahadi, S. A., & Evans, D. E. (2000). Temperament and personality: Origins and outcomes. *Journal of Personality and Social Psychology, 78*, 122–135.

Rothbaum, F., Pott, M., Azuma, H., Miyake, K., & Weisz, J. (2000). The development of close relationships in Japan and the US: Pathways of symbiotic harmony and generative tension. *Child Development, 71*, 1121–1142. doi:10.1111/1467-8624.00214

Rousseau, J. J. (1762/1979). *Emile, or on education.* New York, NY: Basic Books.

Rubin, K. (2002). *The friendship factor.* New York, NY: Penguin Books.

Rubin, K. H., Bukowski, W. M., & Parker, J. (1998). Peer interactions, relationships, and groups. In W. Damon & N. Eisenberg (Eds.), *Handbook of child psychology: Vol. 3. Social, emotional, and personality development* (pp. 619–700). New York, NY: Wiley.

Rubin, K. H., & Coplan, R. (2004). Paying attention to and not neglecting social withdrawal and social isolation. *Merrill-Palmer Quarterly, 50*(4), 506–535.

Rubin, K. H., Coplan, R., Chen, X., Buskirk, A. A., & Wojslawowicz, J. C. (2005). Peer relationships in childhood. In M. H. Bornstein & M. E. Lamb (Eds.), *Developmental science: An advanced textbook* (pp. 469–512). Mahwah, NJ: Erlbaum.

Rubin, K. H., Dwyer, K. M., Booth-LaForce, C., Kim, A. H., Burgess, K. B., & Rose-Krasnor, L. (2004). Attachment, friendship, and psychosocial functioning in early adolescence. *The Journal of Early Adolescence, 24*(4), 326–356.

Rubin, K. H., Fein, G., & Vandenberg, B. (1983). Play. In E. M. Hetherington (Ed.), P. H. Mussen (Series Ed.), *Handbook of child psychology: Vol. 4. Socialization, personality, and social development* (pp. 693–774). New York, NY: Wiley.

Ruble, D. N., & Dweck, C. S. (1995). Self-conceptions, person conceptions and their development. In N. Eisenberg (Ed.), *Review of Personality and Social Psychology: Vol. 15. Social development* (pp. 109–139). Thousand Oaks, CA: Sage.

Ruble, D. N., & Martin, C. L. (1998). Gender development. In W. Damon & N. Eisenberg (Eds.), *Handbook of child psychology: Vol. 3.*

Social, emotional, and personality development (pp. 933–1016). New York, NY: Wiley.

Ruble, D. N., Martin, C. L., & Berenbaum, S. (2006). *Gender development.* In W. Damon & R. M. Lerner (Series. Eds.) & N. Eisenberg (Vol. Ed.), *Handbook of child psychology: Vol. 3. Social, emotional, and personality development* (6th ed., pp. 858–932). New York, NY: Wiley.

Ruble, D. N., Taylor, L. J., Cyphers, L., Greulich, F. K., Lurye, L. E., & Shrout, P. E. (2007). The role of gender constancy in early gender development. *Child Development, 78,* 1121–1136.

Rudolph, K. D., Lambert, S. F., Clark, A. G., & Kurlakowsky, K. D. (2001). Negotiating the transition to middle school: The role of self-regulatory processes. *Child Development, 72,* 926–946.

Rudy, D., & Grusec, J. (2006). Authoritarian parenting in individualist and collectivist groups: Associations with maternal emotion and cognition and children's self-esteem. *Journal of Family Psychology, 20,* 68–78.

Ruff, H. A., & Capozzoli, M. C. (2003). Development of attention and distractibility in the first 4 years of life. *Developmental Psychology, 39,* 877–890.

Ruffman, T., Slade, L., & Crowe, E. (2002). The relation between children's and mothers' mental state language and theory of mind understanding. *Child Development, 73,* 734–751.

Rummel, N., Levin, J. R., & Woodward, M. M. (2003). Do pictorial mnemonic text-learning aids give students something worth writing about? *Journal of Educational Psychology, 95,* 327–334.

Russ, S. W. (2006). Pretend play, affect, and creativity. In P. Locher, C. Martindale, & L. Dorfman (Eds.), *New directions in aesthetics, creativity, and the arts* (pp. 239–250). Amityville, NY: Baywood.

Russell, A., Pettit, G. S., & Mize, J. (1998). Horizontal qualities in parent-child relationships: Parallels with and possible consequences for children's peer relationships. *Developmental Review, 18,* 313–352.

Rust, J., Golombok, S., Hines, M., Johnston, K., Golding, J., & the ALSPAC Study Team. (2000). The role of brothers and sisters in the gender development of preschool children. *Journal of Experimental Child Psychology, 77,* 292–303.

Ryalls, B. O., Gul, R. E., & Ryalls, K. R. (2000). Infant imitation of peer and adult models: Evidence for a peer model advantage. *Merrill-Palmer Quarterly, 46*(1), 188–202.

Ryan, A. M., & Patrick, H. (2001). The classroom social environment and changes in adolescents' motivation and engagement during middle school. *American Educational Research Journal, 38*(2), 437–460.

Ryan, K. E., & Ryan, A. M. (2005). Psychological processes underlying stereotype threat and standardized math test performance. *Educational Psychologist, 40,* 53–63.

Ryan, R. M., & Deci, E. L. (2000). Self-determination theory and the facilitation of intrinsic motivation, social development, and well-being. *American Psychologist, 55,* 68–78.

Saarni, C. (1984). An observational study of children's attempts to monitor their expressive behavior. *Child Development, 55,* 1504–1513.

Saarni, C. (1999). *The development of emotional competence.* New York, NY: Guilford.

Sabiston, C. M., & Crocker, P. R. E. (2008). Examining an integrative model of physical activity and healthy eating self-perceptions and behaviors among adolescents. *Journal of Adolescent Health, 42,* 64–72.

Sabiston, C. M., & Crocker, P. R. E. (2008). Exploring self-perceptions and social influences as correlates of adolescent leisure-time physical activity. *Journal of Adolescent Health, 42,* 64–72.

Sackett, P. R., Hardison, C. M., & Cullen, M. J. (2005). On interpreting research on stereotype threat and test performance. *American Psychologist, 60,* 271–272.

Sadeh, A. (2007). Consequences of sleep loss or sleep disruption in children. *Sleep Medicine Reviews, 2,* 513–520.

Sadeh, A., Gruber, R., & Raviv, A. (2002). Sleep, neurobehavioral functioning, and behavior problems in school-age children. *Child Development, 73,* 405–417.

Sadker, M., & Sadker, D. (1994). *Failing at fairness: How America's schools cheat girls.* New York, NY: Scribner.

Sadker, M., Sadker, D., & Klein, S. (1991). The issue of gender in elementary and secondary education. *Review of Research in Education, 17,* 269–334.

Safe Kids. (n.d.). Preventing injuries at home, at play, and on the way. Retrieved from http://www.safekids.org

Saffran, J. R., & Estes, K. G. (2006). Mapping sound to meaning: Connections between learning about sounds and learning about words. In R. V. Kail (Ed.), *Advances in child development and behavior* (Vol. 34, pp. 1–38). San Diego, CA: Academic Press.

Saft, E. W., & Pianta, R. C. (2001). Teachers' perceptions of their relationships with students: Effects of child age, gender, and ethnicity of children and teachers. *School Psychology Quarterly, 16,* 125–141.

Saha, S., Barnett, A. G., Foldi, C., Burne, T. H., Eyles, D. W., Buka, S. L., & McGrath, J. J. (2009). Advanced paternal age is associated with impaired neurocognitive outcomes during infancy and childhood. *PloS Medicine, 6*(3). E40.

Sakiz, G., Pape, S., & Woolfolk Hoy, A. (2008, March). Does teacher affective support matter? The role of affective support in middle school mathematics classrooms. New York, NY: American Educational Research Association.

Salazar, L. F., DiClemente, R. J., Wingood, G. M., Crosby, R. A., Harrington, K., Davis, S., . . . Oh, M. K. (2004). Self-concept and adolescents' refusal of unprotected sex: A test of mediating mechanisms among African American girls. *Prevention Science, 5*(3), 137–149.

Salkind, N. J. (2004). *An introduction to theories of human development.* Thousand Oaks, CA: Sage.

Salmivalli, C., Ojanen, T., Haanapaa, J., & Peets, K. (2005). "I'm OK but you're not" and other peer-relational schemas: Explaining individual differences in children's social goals. *Developmental Psychology, 41,* 363–375.

Sameroff, A. J., & Feise, B. H. (2000). Transactional regulation: The development ecology of early intervention. In J. P. Shonkoff & S. J. Meisels (Eds.), *Handbook of early childhood intervention* (2nd ed., 135–159). New York, NY: Cambridge University Press.

Sammons, M. T. (2009). Writing a wrong: Factors influencing the overprescription of antidepressants to youth. *Professional Psychology: Research and Practice, 40,* 327–329.

Sampaio, R. C., & Truwit, C. L. (2001). Myelination in the developing human brain. In C. A. Nelson & M. Luciana (Eds.), *Handbook of developmental cognitive neuroscience* (pp. 35–44). Cambridge, MA: MIT Press.

Sanchez, B., Colon, Y., & Esparza, P. (2005). The role of sense of school belonging and gender in the academic adjustment of Latino adolescents. *Journal of Youth and Adolescence, 34*(6), 619–628.

Sánchez Medina, J. A., Martínez Lozano, V., & Goudena, P. P. (2001). Gestión de Conflictos en los Preescolares: Una perspectiva inter-cultural. *International Journal of Early Years Education, 9,* 153–160.

Sanders, W. L., & Rivers, J. C. (1996). *Cumulative and residual effects of teachers on student academic achievement.* Knoxville, TN: University of Tennessee Value-Added Research and Assessment Center.

Sandnabba, N. K., & Ahlberg, C. (1999). Parents'attitudes and expectations about children's cross-gender behavior. *Sex Roles, 40,* 249–264.

Sanefuji, W., Ohgami, H., & Hashiya, K. (2006). Preference for peers in infancy. *Infant Behavior and Development, 29*(4), 584–593.

Sangrigoli, S., & de Schonen, S. (2004a). Effects of visual experience on face processing: A developmental study of inversion and non-native effects. *Developmental Science, 7,* 74–87.

Sangrioli, S., & de Schonen, S. (2004b). Recognition of own-race and other-race faces by three-month-old infants. *Journal of Child Psychology and Psychiatry, 45,* 1–9.

Sasaki, K., Sasaki, S., Takahashi, S., Nakajo, Y., & Kyono, K. (2004). Neonatal outcome and congenital malformations after *in vitro* fertilization and embryo transfer. *Fertility & Sterility,* S203.

Sattler, J. M. (2008). *Assessment of children: Cognitive foundations* (5th ed.). La Mesa, CA: Jerome M. Sattler, Publisher.

Savage, W. (2000). The cesarean section epidemic. *Journal of Obstetrics and Gynecology, 20,* 223–225.

Savin-Williams, R. C. (2003) Lesbian, gay, and bisexual youths' relationships with their parents. In L. D. Carnets & D. C. Kimmel (2nd ed.), *Psychological perspectives on lesbian, gay, and bisexual experiences.* New York, NY: Columbia University Press.

Savin-Williams, R. C. (2006). Who's gay? Does it matter? *Current Directions in Psychological Science, 15*(1), 40–44.

Savin-Williams, R. C., & Diamond, L. M. (1999). Sexual orientation. In W. K. Silverman & T. H. Ollendick (Eds.), *Developmental issues in the clinical treatment of children* (pp. 241–258). Boston, MA: Allyn & Bacon.

Savin-Williams, R. C., & Diamond, L. M. (2004). Sex. In R. M. Lerner & L. Steinberg (Eds.), *Handbook of adolescent psychology* (2nd ed., pp. 189–231). New York, NY: John Wiley & Sons.

Savitz, D. A., Chan, R. L., Herring, A. H., Howards, P. P., & Hartmann, K. E. (2008). Caffeine and miscarriage risk. *Epidemiology, 19*(1), 55–62.

Saxe, G. B. (1999). Source of concepts: A cross cultural-developmental perspective. In

E. K. Scholnick, K. Nelson, S. A. Gelman, & P. H. Miller (Eds.), *Conceptual development: Piaget's legacy* (pp. 253–267). Mahwah, NJ: Erlbaum.

Schaal, B., Marlier, B., & Soussignan, R. (2000). Human foetuses learn odours from their pregnant mother's diet. *Chem Senses, 25*, 729–737. Retrieved from http://chemse.oxfordjournals.org/cgi/ijlink?linkType=ABST&journalCode=chemse&resid=25/6/729

Schaeffer, C. M., Petras, H., Ialongo, N., Poduska, J., & Sheppard, K. (2003). Modeling growth in boys' aggressive behavior across elementary school: Links to later criminal involvement, conduct disorder, and antisocial personality disorder. *Developmental Psychology, 39*, 1020–1035.

Schegel, A., & Barry, H. (1991). *Adolescence: An anthropological inquiry.* New York, NY: Free Press.

Scheibe, C., & Rogow, F. (2004). *12 basic principles for incorporating media literacy and critical thinking into any curriculum* (2nd ed.). Ithaca, NY: Project Look Sharp—Ithaca College.

Scheibe, C. L. (2004). A deeper sense of literacy: Curriculum-driven approaches to media literacy in the K–12 classroom. *American Behavioral Scientist, 48*, 60–68.

Scher, A., & Mayseless, O. (2000). Mothers of anxious/ambivalent infants: Maternal characteristics and child-care context. *Child Development, 71*(6), 1629–1639.

Scherer, M. (2004). *Connecting to learn: Educational and assistive technology for people with disabilities.* Washington, DC: American Psychological Association.

Schmitt, K. L. (2009). *Public policy, family rules and children's media use in the home.* Retrieved from http://www.annenbergpublicpolicycenter.org/Downloads/Media_and_Developing_Child/20000626_public_policy_Vchip_report.pdf

Schneider, W. (1998). The development of procedural metamemory in childhood and adolescence. In G. Mazzoni & T. O. Nelson (Eds.), *Metacognition and cognitive neuropsychology: Monitoring and control processes* (pp. 1–21). Mahwah, NJ: Erlbaum.

Schneider, W. (2004). Memory development in childhood. In U. Goswami (Ed.), *Blackwell handbook of childhood cognitive development* (pp. 236–256). Malden, MA: Blackwell.

Schneider, W., & Bjorklund, D. F. (1998). Memory. In W. Damon (Series Ed.) & D. Kuhn & R. S. Siegler (Vol. Eds.), *Handbook of child psychology: Vol. 2. Cognitive, language, and perceptual development* (5th ed., pp. 467–521). New York, NY: Wiley.

Schneider, W., & Bjorklund, D. F. (2003). Memory and knowledge development. In J. Valsiner & K. Connolly (Eds.), *Handbook of developmental psychology* (pp. 370–403). London, England: Sage.

Schneider, W., Korkel, J., & Weinert, F. E. (1989). Domain-specific knowledge and memory performance: A comparison of high- and low-aptitude children. *Journal of Educational Psychology, 81*, 306–312.

Schneider, W., & Lockl, K. (2002). The development of metacognitive knowledge in children and adolescents. In T. Perfect & B. Schwartz (Eds.), *Applied metacognition* (pp. 224–260). Cambridge, England: Cambridge University Press.

Schneider, W., Schlagmüller, M., & Visé, M. (1998). The impact of metamemory and domain-specific knowledge on memory performance. *European Journal of Psychology of Education, 13*, 91–103.

Schonert-Reichl, K. A., & Scott, F. (2009). Effectiveness of "The Roots of Empathy" program in promoting children's emotional and social competence: A summary of research findings. In M. Gordon, *The roots of empathy: Changing the world child by child* (pp. 239–252). Toronto, Ontario: Thomas Allen Publishers.

Schuetze, P., & Zeskind, P. S. (1997). Relation between reported maternal caffeine consumption during pregnancy and neonatal state and heart rate. *Infant Behavior and Development, 20*, 559–562.

Schulz, L., & Gopnik, A. (2004). Causal learning across domains. *Developmental Psychology, 40*, 162–176.

Schunk, D. H. (2004). *Learning theories: An educational perspective* (4th ed.). Columbus, OH: Merrill/Prentice-Hall.

Schunk, D. H., & Zimmerman, B. J. (1997). Social origins of self-regulatory competence. *Educational Psychologist, 32*(4), 195–208. doi:10.1207/s15326985ep3204_1

Schwarz, S. W. (2009). *Adolescent mental health in the United States.* New York, NY: National Center for Children in Poverty, Mailman School of Public Health, Columbia University. Retrieved from http://www.nccp.org/publications/pub_878.html

Schweinhart, L. J. (2004). *The High/Scope Perry Preschool Study through age 40: Summary, conclusions, and frequently asked questions.* Yipsilanti, MI: High/Scope Educational Research Foundation.

Schweinhart, L. J., Barnes, H. V., & Weikart, D. P. (1993). Significant benefits: The High/Scope Perry Preschool Study through age 27. (Monographs of the High/Scope Educational Research Foundation, 10). Ypsilanti, MI: High/Scope Press.

Schweinhart, L. J., & Weikart, D. P. (1997). Lasting differences: The High/Scope preschool curriculum comparison study through age 23. Ypsilanti, MI: High/Scope Education Foundation.

Schwenck, C., Bjorklund, D. F., & Schneider, W. (2009). Developmental and individual differences in young children's use and maintenance of a selective memory strategy. *Developmental Psychology, 45*, 1034–1050.

Scolove, R. E., Scammell, M. L., & Holland, B. (1998). *Community-based research in the United States: An introductory reconnaissance, including twelve organizational case studies and comparison with the Dutch science shops and the mainstream American research system.* Amherst, MA: The Loka Institute.

Scott, J. (2006). Cesarean delivery on request: Where do we go from here. *Obstetrics & Gynecology, 107*(6), 1222–1223.

Sears, H. A., Simmering, M. G., & MacNeil, B. A. (2006). Canada. In J. J. Arnett (Ed.), *Routledge international encyclopedia of adolescence* (Vol. 1, pp. 140–156). New York, NY: Routledge.

Sebanc, A. M., Kearns, K. T., Hernandez, M. D., & Galvin, K. B. (2007). Predicting having a best friend in young children: Individual characteristics and friendship features. *The Journal of Genetic Psychology, 168*, 81–95.

Segal, N. L. (2005). Twins reared apart design. In B. Everitt & D. C. Howell (Eds.) *Encyclopedia of statistics in behavioral science* (Vol. 4, pp. 2072–2076). Chichester, UK: John Wiley & Sons.

Seiffge-Krenke, I. (1997). Imaginary companions in adolescence: Sign of a deficient or positive development? *Journal of Adolescence, 20*(2), 137–154.

Seiffge-Krenke, I., & Gelhaar, T. (2008). Does successful attainment of developmental tasks lead to happiness and success in later developmental tasks? A test of Havighurst's (1948) Theses. *Journal of Adolescence, 31*(1), 33–52.

Seligman, M. E. P. (1975). *Helplessness: On depression, development, and death.* San Francisco, CA: Freeman.

Selman, R. L. (1980). *The growth of interpersonal understanding.* New York, NY: Academic Press.

Sénéchal, M., & LeFevre, J. (2002). Parental involvement in the development of children's reading skill: A five-year longitudinal study. *Child Development, 73*, 445–460.

Senghas, A., & Coppola, M. (2001). Children creating language: How Nicaraguan Sign Language acquired a spatial grammar. *Psychological Review, 96*, 323–328.

Serbin, L. A., Poulin-Dubois, D., Colburne, K. A., Sen, M. G., & Eichstedt, J. A. (2001). Gender stereotyping in infancy: Visual preferences for and knowledge of gender-stereotyped toys in the second year. *International Journal of Behavioral Development, 25*, 7–15.

Serpell, R. (1997). Literacy connection between school and home: How should we evaluate them? *Journal of Literacy Research, 29*, 587–616.

Shaffer, A., Burt, K. B., Obradovic, J., Herbers, J. E., & Masten, A. S. (2009). Intergenerational continuity in parenting quality: The mediating role of social competence. *Developmental Psychology, 45*, 1227–1240.

Shapka, J. D., & Keating, D. P. (2005). Structure and change in self-concept during adolescence. *Canadian Journal of Behavioural Science, 37*(2), 83–96.

Share Our Strength. Plan to end childhood hunger in America. Retrieved from http://strength.org/childhood_hunger/our_plan/

Sharma, A. R., McGue, M. K., & Benson, P. L. (1996). The emotional and behavioral adjustment of United States adopted adolescents: I. A comparison study. *Children and Youth Services Review, 18*, 77–94.

Sharma, A. R., McGue, M. K., & Benson, P. L. (1998). The psychological adjustment of United States adopted adolescents and their nonadopted siblings. *Child Development, 69*, 791–802.

Sharma, D. C. (2003). Widespread concern over India's missing girl: Selective abortion and female infanticide cause girl-to-boy ratios to plummet. *The Lancet, 362*, 1553.

Shaw, D. S., Gilliom, M., Ingoldsby, E. M., & Nagin, D. S. (2003). Trajectories leading to school-age conduct problems. *Developmental Psychology, 39*, 189–200.

Shaw, D. S., & Vondra, J. I. (1995). Infant attachment security and maternal predictors of early behavior problems: A longitudinal study of low-income families. *Journal of Abnormal Child Psychology, 23*(3), 335–357.

Shaw, G. M., Carmichael, S. L., Vollset, S. E., Yang, W., Finnell, R. H., Blom, H., Midttun, O., & Ueland, P. M. (2009). Mid-pregnancy cotinine and risks of orofacial clefts and neural tube defects. *Journal of Pediatrics, 154*(1), 17–19.

Shayer, M. (2003). Not just Piaget; not just Vygotsky, and certainly not Vygotsky as alternative to Piaget. *Learning and Instruction, 13*, 465–485.

Shaywitz, S. E., & Shaywitz, B. A. (2005). Dyslexia (specific reading disability). *Biological Psychiatry, 7*, 1301–1309.

Shaywitz, B. A., Shaywitz, S. E., Pugh, K. R., Constable, R. T., Skudlarski, P., Fulbright, R. K., . . . Gore, J. C. (1995). Sex differences in the functional organization of the brain for language. *Nature, 373*, 607–609. doi:10.1038/373607a0

Sheets, R. H. (2005). *Diversity pedagogy: Examining the role of culture in the teaching-learning process.* Boston, MA: Allyn & Bacon.

Shepard, L. A. (1989). A review of research on kindergarten retention. In L. A. Shepard & M. L. Smith (Eds.), *Flunking grades: Research and policies on retention* London, UK: The Falmer Press.

Shepard, L. A., & Smith, M. L. (1988). Escalating academic demand in kindergarten: Counterproductive policies. *The Elementary School Journal, 89*(2), 135–145.

Shephard, R. J., & Trudeau, F. (2008). Physical education, school physical activity, school sports and academic performance. *International Journal of Behavioral Nutrition and Physical Activity, 5*(10), doi:10.1186/1479.

Sherman, A. (1994). *Wasting America's future: The Children's Defense Fund report on the costs of child poverty.* Boston, MA: Beacon Press.

Sherwood, R. D. (2002). Problem-based multimedia software for middle grades science: Development issues and an initial field study. *Journal of Computers in Mathematics and Science Teaching, 21*, 147–165.

Shields, A., Dickstein, S., Siefer, R., Giusti, L., Magee, K. D., & Spritz, B. (2001). Emotional competence and early school adjustment: A study of preschoolers at risk. *Early Education & Development, 12*, 73–96.

Shields, P., Gordon, J., & Dupree, D. (1983). Influence of parent practices upon the reading achievement of good and poor readers. *Journal of Negro Education, 52*, 436–445.

Shochet, I. M., Dadds, M. R., Ham, D., & Montague, R. (2006). School connectedness is an underemphasized parameter in adolescent mental health: Results of a community prediction study. *Journal of Clinical Child and Adolescent Psychology, 35*(2), 170–179.

Shonkoff, J. P., & Phillips, D. A. (Eds.). (2000). *From neurons to neighborhoods: The science of early childhood development.* Retrieved from http://books.nap.edu/books/0309069882/html/index.html

Shrager, J., & Siegler, R. S. (1998). SCADS: A model of children's strategy choices and strategy discoveries. *Psychological Science, 9*, 405–410.

Shuell, T. J. (1996). Teaching and learning in a classroom context. In D. Berliner & R. Calfee (Eds.), *Handbook of educational psychology* (pp. 726–764). New York, NY: Macmillan.

Shugart, M. A., & Lopez, E. M. (2002). Depression in children and adolescents: When "moodiness" merits special attention. *Postgraduate Medicine Online, 112*(3). Retrieved from http://www.postgradmed.com/issues/2002/09_02/shugart3.htm

Shulman, S., & Seiffge-Krenke, I. (2001). Adolescent romance: Between experience and relationships. *Journal of Adolescence, 24*(3), 417–428.

Shweder, R. A., Much, N. C., Mahapatra, M., & Park, L. (1997). The "big three" of morality (autonomy, community, and divinity) and the "big three" explanations of suffering. In A. Brandt & P. Rozin (Eds.), *Morality and health* (pp. 119–169). Palo Alto, CA: Stanford University Press.

Siddle Walker, V. (2001). African American teaching in the South: 1940–1960. *Review of Educational Research, 38*, 751–779.

Siegel, J. M., Yancey, A. K., Aneshensel, C. S., & Schuler, R. (1999). Body image, perceived pubertal timing, and adolescent mental health. *Journal of Adolescent Health, 25*, 155–165.

Siegel, L. S. (1999). Issues in the definition and diagnosis of learning disabilities. *Journal of Learning Disabilities, 32*(4), 304–319. doi:10.1177/002221949903200405

Siegel, L. S. (2003). Basic cognitive processes and reading disabilities. In H. L. Swanson, K. R. Harris, & S. Graham (Eds.), *Handbook of learning disabilities* (pp. 158–181). New York, NY: Guilford.

Siegel, M. E. A. (2002). *Like*: The discourse particle and semantics. *Journal of Semantics, 19*, 35–71.

Siegler, R. S. (1987). The perils of averaging data over strategies: An example from children's addition. *Journal of Experimental Psychology: General, 116*, 250–264.

Siegler, R. S. (1998). *Children's thinking* (3rd ed.). Upper Saddle River, NJ: Prentice-Hall.

Siegler, R. S. (2000). The rebirth of children's learning. *Child Development, 71*, 26–35.

Siegler, R. S. (2004). Turning memory development inside out. *Developmental Review, 24*, 469–475.

Siegler, R. S. (2006). Microgenetic analyses of learning. In D. Kuhn & R. S. Siegler (Eds.), *Cognition, perception, and language* (6th ed., Vol. 2, pp. 464–510). New York, NY: Wiley.

Siegler, R. S., & Alibali, M. W. (2005). *Children's thinking* (4th ed.). Upper Saddle River, NJ: Prentice-Hall.

Siegler, R. S., & Crowley, K. (1991). The microgenetic method: A direct means for studying cognitive development. *American Psychologist, 56*, 606–620.

Signorella, M. L., Bigler, R. S., & Liben, L. S. (1997). A meta-analysis of children's memories for own-sex and other-sex information. *Journal of Applied Developmental Psychology, 18*, 429–445.

Signorielli, N. (2001). Television's gender role images and contribution to stereotyping: Past, present, future. In D. Singer & J. Singer (Eds.), *Handbook of children and the media* (pp. 341–358). Thousand Oaks, CA: Sage.

Simkin, P. P., & O'Hara, M. (2002). Nonpharmacologic relief of pain during labor: Systematic reviews of five methods. *American Journal of Obstetric Gynecologic, 186*(Suppl 5), S131–159.

Simmons, R. G., & Blyth, D. A. (1987). *Moving into adolescence.* Hawthorne, NY: de Gruyter.

Simon, M. (2009, April 24). My bullied son's last day on Earth. *CNN.* Retrieved from http://www.cnn.com/2009/US/04/23/bullying.suicide/

Simpkins, S. D., Davis-Kean, P. E., & Eccles, J. S. (2006). Parents' socializing behavior and children's participation in math, science, and computer out-of-school activities. *Applied Developmental Science, 9*(1), 14–30.

Singer, D. G., & Singer, J. L. (1990). *The house of make-believe: Play and the developing imagination.* Cambridge, MA: Harvard University Press.

Singer, E., & Hannikainen, M. (2002). The teacher's role in territorial conflicts of 2- to 3-year-old children. *Journal of Research in Early Childhood Education, 17*(1), 5–18.

Singer, J. L. (1994). Imaginative play and adaptive development. In J. H. Goldstein (Ed.), *Toys, play, and child development* (pp. 6–26). Cambridge, England: Cambridge University Press.

Sirard, J. R., & Barr-Anderson, D. J. (2008). Physical activity in adolescents: From associations to interventions. *Journal of Adolescent Health, 42*, 327–328.

Sirin, S. R. (2005). Socioeconomic status and academic achievement: A meta-analytic review of research. *Review of Educational Research, 75*, 417–453.

Skinner, B. F. (1953). *Science and human behavior.* New York, NY: Macmillan.

Skinner, B. F. (1989). The origins of cognitive thought. *American Psychologist, 44.*

Slaby, R. G., Roedell, W. C., Arezzo, D., & Hendrix, K. (1995). *Early violence prevention.* Washington, DC: National Association for the Education of Young Children.

Slater, A., Field, T., & Hernandez-Reif, M. (2007). The development of the senses. In A. Slater & M. Lewis (Eds.), *Introduction to infant development* (pp. 81–99). London, United Kingdom: Oxford University Press.

Slavin, R. E. (2002). Evidence-based education policies: Transforming education practice and research. *Educational Researcher, 31*(7), 15–21.

Slomkowski, C., & Manke, B. (2004). Sibling relationships during childhood: Multiple perceptions from multiple perspectives. In R. D. Conger, F. O. Lorenz, & K. A. S. Wickrama (Eds.), *Continuity and change in family relations: Theory, methods, and empirical findings* (pp. 293–318). Mahwah, NJ: Erlbaum.

Slykerman, R. F., Thompson, J. M., Becroft, D. M., Robinson, E., Pryor, J. E., Clark, P. M., . . . Mitchell, E. A. (2005). Breastfeeding and intelligence of preschool children. *Acta Paediatric, 94*(7), 832–837.

Small, M. F. (1998). *Our babies, ourselves: How biology and culture shape the way we parent.* New York, NY: Anchor.

Smedley, A., & Smedley, B. D. (2005). Race as biology is fiction: Racism as a social problem is real. *American Psychologist, 60*, 16–26.

Smetana, J. G. (1988). Adolescents' and parents' conceptions of parental authority. *Child Development, 59*(2), 321–335.

Smetana, J. G. (1996). Adolescent–parent conflict: Implications for adaptive and maladaptive development. In D. Cicchetti & S. L. Toth (Eds.), *Adolescence: Opportunities and challenges* (pp. 1–46). Rochester, NY: University of Rochester Press.

Smetana, J. G. (2000). Middle-class African American adolescents' and parents' conceptions of parental authority and parenting practices: A longitudinal investigation. *Child Development, 71*, 1672–1686.

Smetana, J. G. (2008). "It's 10 o'clock: Do you know where your children are?" Recent advances in understanding parental monitoring and adolescents' information management.

Child Development Perspectives, 2, 19–25. doi:10.1111/j.1750-8606.2008.00036.x

Smetana, J. G., Campione-Barr, N., & Metzger, A. (2006). Adolescent development in interpersonal and societal contexts. *Annual Review of Psychology, 57,* 255–284.

Smetana, J. G., & Gaines, C. (1999). Adolescent-parent conflict in middle-class African American families. *Child Development, 70,* 1447–1463.

Smetana, J. G., Villalobos, M., Rogge, R. D., & Tasopoulos-Chan, M. (2010). Keeping secrets from parents: Daily variations among poor, urban adolescents. *Journal of Adolescence, 33,* 321–331. doi:10.1016/j.adolescence .2009.04.00

Smith, C. S., & Hung, L-C. (2008). Stereotype threat: Effects on education. *Social Psychology of Education, 11,* 243–257.

Smith, D. D., & Tyler, N. C. (2010). *Introduction to special education: Making a difference* (7th ed.). Columbus, OH: Merrill.

Smith, J. L., Sansone, C., & White, P. H. (2007). The stereotyped task engagement process: The role of interest and achievement motivation. *Journal of Educational Psychology, 99,* 99–114.

Snarey, J. R. (1995). In a communitarian voice: The sociobiological expansion of Kohlbergian theory, research, and practice. In W. M. Kurtines & J. L. Gerqirtz (Eds.), *Moral development: An introduction* (pp. 109–134). Boston, MA: Allyn & Bacon.

Snow, C. E. (1991). The theoretical basis for relationships between language and literacy development. *Journal of Research in Childhood Education 6,* 5–10.

Snow, C. E. (1993). Families as social contexts for literacy development. New Directions for Child and Adolescent Development, 1993: 11–24. doi:10.1002/cd.23219936103

Snow, C. E., Burns, S. M., & Griffin, P. (Eds.). (1998). *Preventing reading difficulties in young children.* Washington, DC: National Academy Press.

Spong, C. Y. (2006). Protection against prenatal alcohol-induced damage. *PLoS Med 3*(4), e196.

Society for Neuroscience (SFN). (2009). Brain facts. A primer on the brain and nervous system. Retrieved from http://www.sfn.org/skins/main/pdf/brainfacts/2008/brain_facts.pdf http://www.sfn.org/index.aspx?pagename=brainfacts

Sodian, B., & Schneider, W. (1999). Memory strategy development: Gradual increase, sudden insight, or roller coaster? In F. E. Weinert & W. Schneider (Eds.), *The Munich Longitudinal Study on the Genesis of Individual Competencies (LOGIC).* Cambridge, England: Cambridge University Press.

Solmon, M. A., & Lee, A. M. (2008). Research on social issues in elementary school physical education. *The Elementary School Journal, 108*(3), 229–239.

Sonuga-Barke, E., Auerbach, J., Campbell, S. B., Daley, D., & Thompson, M. (2005). Varieties of preschool hyperactivity: Multiple pathways from risk to disorder. *Developmental Science, 8,* 141–150.

Spearman, C. (1927). *The abilities of man: Their nature and measurement.* New York, NY: Macmillan.

Spelke, E. S. (2002). These years are critical for brain development. A developmental psychologist looks ahead. *Developmental Science, 5*(3), 392–396.

Spelke, E. S. (2005). Sex differences in intrinsic aptitude for mathematics and science?: A critical review. *American Psychologist, 60,* 950–958.

Spelke, E. S., & Newport, E. L. (1998). Nativism, empiricism, and the development of knowledge. In W. Damon & R. M. Lerner (Eds.), *Handbook of child psychology* (5th ed., Vol. 1: Theoretical models of human development, pp. 275–340). New York, NY: John Wiley & Sons.

Spencer, J. P., Vereijken, B., Diedrich, F. J., & Thelen, E. (2000). Posture and the emergence of manual skills. *Developmental Science, 3*(2), 216–233.

Spencer, R. (2006). Understanding the mentoring process between adolescents and adults. *Youth and Society, 37,* 287–315.

Spencer, R. (2007). "I just feel safe with him": Emotional closeness in male youth mentoring relationships. *Psychology of Men & Masculinity, 8,* 185–198.

Spera, C. (2005). A review of the relationship among parenting practices, parenting styles, and adolescent school achievement. *Educational Psychology Review, 17,* 125–146.

Spinrad, T. L., Eisenberg, N., Cumberland, A., Fabes, R. A., Valiente, C., Shepard, S. A., . . . Guthrie, I. K. (2006). Relation of emotion-related regulation to children's social competence: A longitudinal study. *Emotion, 6,* 498–510. doi:10.1037/1528-3542.6.3.498

Spinrad, T. L., Eisenberg, N., & Gaertner, B. M. (2007). Measures of effortful regulation for young children. *Infant Mental Health Journal,* 28, 606–626.

Spitz, R. (1945). Hospitalism: An inquiry into the genesis of psychiatric conditions in early childhood. *Psychoanalytic Study of the Child, 1,* 53–74.

Spitz, R. (1946). Anaclitic depression. *Psychoanalytic Study of the Child, 2,* 313–342.

Spong, C. Y. (2006). Protection against prenatal alcohol-induced damage. *Public Library of Science Medicine.* Published online 2006 April 18. doi:10.1371/journal.pmed.0030196.

Sprague, J. R., & Walker, H. (2000). Early identification and intervention for youth with antisocial and vihyolent behavior. *Exceptional Children, 66,* 367–379.

Sprenger, M. (2005). Inside Amy's brain. *Educational Leadership, 62*(7), 28–32.

SRCD. (2009). Young Hispanic children: Boosting opportunities for learning. *Society for Research in Child Development Social Policy Report Brief, 23*(2).

Stahl, S. A., McKenna, M. C., & Pagnucco, J. R. (1994). The effects of whole-language instruction: An update and a reappraisal. *Educational Psychologist, 29,* 275–285.

Stallings, J. A. (1975). Implementations and child effects of teaching practices in Follow Through classrooms. *Monographs of the Society for Research in Child Development* (Vol. 40, Nos. 7–8).

Stams, L. E., Juffer, F., Rispens, J., & Hoksbergen, R. A. C. (2000). The development and adjustment of 7-year-old children adopted in infancy. *Journal of Child Psychology and Psychiatry, 41,* 1025–1037.

Stang, J., & Story, M. (2005). Adolescent growth and development. In J. S. M. Story (Ed.), *Guidelines for adolescent nutritional services.* Minneapolis, MN: University of Minnesota.

Stanger, C., Achenbach, T. M., & Verhulst, F. C. (1997). Accelerated longitudinal comparisons of aggressive versus delinquent syndromes. *Developmental Psychopathology, 9,* 43–58.

Stanovich, K. (1986). Matthew effects in reading: Some consequences of individual differences in the acquisition of literacy. *Reading Research Quarterly, 21,* 360–407.

Stanovich, K. E. (1992). *How to think straight about psychology* (3rd ed.). Glenview, IL: Scott, Foresman.

Stanovich, K. E. (1994). Constructivism in reading. *Journal of Special Education, 28,* 259–274.

Starkey, P., Spelke, E. S., & Gelman, R. (1990). Numerical abstraction by human infants. *Cognition, 36,* 97–128.

Starr, R. H., Jr. (1979). Child abuse. *American Psychologist, 34,* 872–878.

Steinberg, L. (1986). Latchkey children and susceptibility to peer pressure: An ecological analysis. *Developmental Psychology, 10,* 433–439.

Steinberg, L. D. (1989). Pubertal maturation and parent-adolescent distance: An evolutionary perspective. In G. R. Adams, R. Montemayor, and T. P. Gullotta (Eds.), *Advances in adolescent development. Vol. 1: Biology of adolescent behavior and development.* Newbury Park, CA: Sage.

Steinberg, L. (1990). Autonomy, conflict, and harmony in the family relationship. In S. S. Feldman & G. R. Elliot (Eds.), *At the threshold: The developing adolescent* (pp. 255–276). Cambridge, MA: Harvard University Press.

Steinberg, L. (1996). *Beyond the classroom: Why school reform has failed and what parents need to do.* New York, NY: Simon & Schuster.

Steinberg, L. (1998). Standards outside the classroom. In D. Ravitch (Ed.), *Brookings papers on educational policy* (pp. 319–358). Washington, DC: Brookings Institute.

Steinberg, L. (2005). *Adolescence.* New York, NY: McGraw-Hill.

Steinberg, L. (2008). A social neuroscience perspective on adolescent risk-taking. *Developmental Review, 28,* 78–106.

Steinberg, L., Brown, B. B., & Dornbusch, S. M. (1997). *Beyond the classroom: Why schools are failing and what parents need to do.* New York, NY: Simon & Schuster.

Steinberg, L., Fegley, S., & Dornbush, S. M. (1993). Negative impact of part-time work on adolescent adjustment: Evidence from a longitudinal study. *Child Development, 29,* 171–180.

Steinberg, L., & Silk, J. S. (2002). Parenting adolescents. In M. H. Bornstein (Ed.), *Handbook of parenting: Vol. 1. Children and parenting* (2nd ed., pp. 103–133). Mahwah, NJ: Erlbaum.

Stenager, K., & Qin, P. (2008). Individual and parental psychiatric history and risk for suicide among adolescents and young adults in Denmark. *Social Psychiatry and Psychiatric Epidemiology, 43*(11), 920–926.

Sternberg, R. J. (1997). *Successful intelligence.* New York, NY: Plume.

Sternberg, R. J. (1999). *Cognitive psychology* (2nd ed.). Ft. Worth, TX: Harcourt Brace.

Sternberg, R. J. (2004). Culture and intelligence. *American Psychologist, 59,* 383–393.

Sternberg, R. J., & Grigorenko, E. L. (1999). Myths in psychology and education regarding the gene environment debate. *Teachers College Record, 100,* 536–553.

Sternberg, R. J., Grigorenko, E. L., & Kidd, K. K. (2005). Intelligence, race, and genetics. *American Psychologist, 60,* 45–59.

Stevenson, B. (2010). *Beyond the classroom: Using Title IX to measure the return to high school sports.* Cambridge, MA: National Bureau of Economic Research.

Stevenson, H. W., & Stigler, J. (1992). *The learning gap.* New York, NY: Summit Books.

Stewart, C. (2007). *Physical activity in children: Tips to help parents encourage exercise in kids.* Retrieved from http://earlychildhood.suite101.com/article.cfm/your_childs_fitness

Stewart, L., Henson, R., Kampe, K., Walsh, V., Turner, R., & Frith, U. (2003). Brain changes after learning to read and play music. *NeuroImage, 20*(1), 71–83.

Stewart, S. M., & Bond, M. H. (2002). A critical look at parenting from the mainstream: Problems uncovered while adapting Western research to non-Western cultures. *British Journal of Developmental Psychology, 20*, 379–392.

Stewart, S. M., & McBride-Chang, C. (2000). Influences on children's sharing in a multicultural setting. *Journal of Cross-Cultural Psychology, 31*, 333–348.

Stice, E., & Bearman, S. K. (2001). Body image and eating disturbances prospectively predict increases in depressive symptoms in adolescent girls: A growth curve analysis. *Developmental Psychology, 37*(5), 597–607.

Stice, E., Marti, C. N., Spoor, S., Presnell, K., & Shaw, H. (2008). Dissonance and healthy weight eating disorder prevention programs: Long-term effects from a randomized efficacy trial. *Journal of Consulting and Clinical Psychology, 76.*

Stice, E., & Shaw, H. (2004). Eating disorder prevention programs: A meta-analytic review. *Psychological Bulletin, 130.*

Stice, E., & Whitenton, K. (2002). Risk factors for body dissatisfaction in adolescent girls: A longitudinal investigation. *Developmental Psychology, 38*(5), 669–678.

Stifter, C. A., Spinrad, T. L, & Braungart-Rieker, J. M. (1999). Toward a developmental model of child compliance: The role of emotion regulation in infancy. *Child Development*, 70, 21–32.

Stiles, J., Reilly, J., Paul, B., & Moses, P. (2005). Cognitive development following early brain injury: Evidence for neural adaptation. *Trends in Cognitive Science, 9*, 136–143.

Stinson, D. W. (2006). African American male adolescents, schooling, (and mathematics): Deficiency, rejection, and achievement. *Review of Educational Research, 76*, 477–506.

Stipek, D. J. (1995). The development of pride and shame in toddlers. In: J. P. Tangney & K. W. Fischer (Eds.), *Self conscious emotions: The psychology of shame, guilt, embarrassment, and pride* (pp. 237–253). New York, NY: Guilford.

Stipek, D. J. (2002). *Motivation to learn: Integrating theory and practice* (4th ed.). Boston, MA: Allyn & Bacon.

Stipek, D. J., & Ryan, R. H. (1997). Economically disadvantaged preschoolers: Ready to learn but further to go. *Developmental Psychology, 33*, 711–723.

Stone, M. R., Barber, B. L., & Eccles, J. S. (2008). We knew them when: Sixth grade characteristics that predict adolescent high school social identities. *Journal of Early Adolescence, 28*, 304–328.

Storch, S., & Whitehurst, G. (2002). Oral language and code-related precursors to reading: Evidence from a longitudinal structural model. *Developmental Psychology, 38*, 934–947.

Stork, S., & Sanders, S. W. (2008). Physical education in early childhood. *The Elementary School Journal, 108*(3), 197–206.

Stormont, M., Stebbins, M. S., & Holliday, G. (2001). Characteristics and educational support needs of underrepresented gifted adolescents. *Psychology in the Schools, 38*, 413–423.

Story, M., & Stang, J. (2005). Nutrition needs of adolescents. In J. S. M. Story (Ed.), *Guidelines for adolescent nutritional services.* Minneapolis, MN: University of Minnesota.

Strachan, T., & Read, A. P. (1996). *Human molecular genetics.* New York, NY: Wiley.

Stratmeyer, M. E., Greenleaf, J. F., Dalecki, D., & Salvesen, K. A. (2008). Fetal ultrasound mechanical effects. *Journal of Ultrasound Medicine, 27*, 597–605.

Straus, M. A., & Field, C. J. (2003). Psychological aggression by American parents: National data on prevalence, chronicity, and severity. *Journal of Marriage and the Family*, 65, 795–808.

Strauss, W., & Howe, N. (2000). *Millennials rising the next great generation.* New York, NY: Vintage. Retrieved from http://club.fom.ru/books/Millennials_Rising_bkreview.pdf

Strauss, W., & Howe, N. (2003). *Millennials go to college: Strategies for a new generation on campus.* Washington: DC: American Association of Collegiate Registrars and Admissions Officers. Retrieved from http://eubie.com/millennials.pdf

Strayer, J., & Roberts, W. (2004). Empathy and observed anger and aggression in five-year-olds. *Social Development, 13*, 1–13.

Strickland, C. (1990, June 17). Preventive medicine, Soviet style. *The New York Times.*

Strickling, L. E., & Gomez, A. (2010). Digital Nation: 21st century America's progress toward universal broadband Internet access. Washington, DC: U.S. Department of Commerce National Telecommunications and Information Administration.

Strong, S. M., Singh, D., & Randall, P. K. (2000). Childhood gender nonconformity and body dissatisfaction in gay and heterosexual men. *Sex Roles, 43*, 427–439.

Strough, J., & Covatto, A. M. (2002). Context and age differences in same and other-gender peer preferences. *Social Development, 11*, 346–361.

Stumpf, H. (1995). Gender differences on tests of cognitive abilities: Experimental design issues and empirical results. *Learning and Individual Differences, 7*, 275–288.

Subrahmanyam, K., Greenfield, P., Kraut, R., & Gross, E. (2001). The impact of computer use on children's and adolescents' development. *Applied Developmental Psychology, 22*, 7–30.

Suizzo, M., Chen, W., Cheng, C., Liang, A. S., Contreras, H., Zanger, D., . . . Robinson, C. (2008). Parental beliefs about young children's socialization across US ethnic groups: Coexistence of independence and interdependence. *Early Child Development and Care, 178*, 467–486. doi:10.1080/03004430600823917

Suldo, S. M., & Shaffer, E. J. (2008). Looking beyond psychopathology: The dual-factor model of mental health in youth. *School Psychology Review, 37*(1), 52–68.

Suldo, S. M., Shaffer, E. S., & Riley, K. (2008). A social-cognitive-behavioral model of academic predictors of adolescents' life satisfaction. *School Psychology Quarterly, 23*, 56–69.

Sullivan, K. (2000). *The anti-bullying handbook.* New York, NY: Oxford University Press.

Sulzby, E., & Teale, W. (1991). Emergent literacy. In R. Barr, M. L. Kamil, P. B. Mosenthal, & P. D. Pearson (Eds.), *Handbook of reading research, Vol. II* (pp. 727–758). New York, NY: Longman.

Suman, R. P., Udani, R., & Nanavati, R. (2008). Kangaroo mother care for low birth weight infants: A randomized controlled trial. *Indian Journal of Pediatrics, 45*(1), 17–23.

Sunstein, C. R. (2008). Adolescent risk-taking and social meaning: A commentary. *Developmental Review, 28*, 145–152.

Sunstein, C. R. (2008). Illusory losses. *The Journal of Legal Studies, 37*, 157–194.

Susman, E. J., Inoff-Germain, G., Nottelmann, E. D., Loriaux, D. L., Cutler, G. B. J., & Chrousos, G. P. (1987). Hormones, emotional dispositions, and aggressive attributes in young adolescents. *Child Development, 58*, 1114–1134.

Sutfin, E. L., Fulcher, M., Bowles, R. P., & Patterson, C. J. (2008). How lesbian and heterosexual parents convey attitudes about gender to their children: The role of gendered environments. *Sex Roles, 58*, 501–513.

Svoboda, J. S. (2001). *Review of Boys and Girls Learn Differently.* Retrieved from http://www.themenscenter.com/mensight/reviews/Svoboda/boysandgirls.htm

Swaab, D. R., Gooren, L. J. G., & Hofman, M. A. (1995). Brain research, gender, and sexual orientation. *Journal of Homosexuality, 28*, 283–301.

Swanson, H. L., & Sachse-Lee, C. (2001). Mathematical problem solving and working memory in children with learning disabilities: Both executive and phonological processes are important. *Journal of Experimental Child Psychology, 79*, 294–321.

Swanson H. L., & Saez, L. (2003). Memory difficulties in children and adults with learning disabilities. In H. L. Swanson, S. Graham, & K. R. Harris (Eds.). *Handbook of learning disabilities* (pp. 182–198). New York, NY: Guilford.

Swearer, S., Espelage, D. L., Vaillancourt, T., & Hymel, S. (2010). What can be done about school bullying?: Linking research to educational practice. *Educational Researcher, 39*, 38–47.

Symons, D. K. (2004). Mental state discourse, theory of mind, and the internalization of self-other understanding. *Developmental Review, 24*, 159–188.

Syvertsen, A. K., Flanagan, C. A., & Stout, M. D. (2009). Code of silence: Students' perceptions of school climate and willingness to intervene in a peer's dangerous plan. *Journal of Educational Psychology, 101*, 219–232.

Szagun, G. (1992). Children's understanding of the feeling experience and causes of sympathy. *Journal of Child Psychology and Psychiatry, 33*, 1183–1191. doi:10.1111/j.1469–7610.1992.tb00937.x

Tajfel, H., & Turner, J. (1986). The social identity theory of intergroup behavior. In S. Worchel & W. Austin (Eds.), *Psychology of intergroup behavior* (2nd ed., pp. 7–24). Chicago, IL: Nelson-Hall.

Talbot, M. (2002, February 24). Girls just want to be mean. *The New York Times.* Retrieved from http://www.nytimes.com/2002/02/24/magazine/24GIRLS.html?pagewanted=1

Tarrant, M. (2002). Adolescent peer groups and social identity. *Social Development, 11*(1), 110–123.

Tasopoulos-Chan, M., Smetana, J. G., & Yau, J. P. (2009). How much do I tell thee? Strategies for managing information to parents among American adolescents from Chinese, Mexican, and European backgrounds. *Journal of Family Psychology, 23*(3), 364–374.

Taylor, E. (1998). Clinical foundation of hyperactivity research. *Behavioural Brain Research, 94*, 11–24.

Taylor, M., & Carlson, S. M. (1997). The relation between individual differences in fantasy and theory of mind. *Child Development, 68*, 436–455.

Taylor, M., Carlson, S. M., Maring, B. L., Gerow, L., & Charley, C. M. (2004). The characteristics and correlates of fantasy in school-age children: Imaginary companions, impersonation, and social understanding. *Developmental Psychology, 40*, 1173–1187.

Teachman, J. D., Paasch, K., & Carver, K. (1996). Social capital and dropping out of school. *Journal of Marriage and the Family, 58*, 773–783.

Teicher, M. D. (2000). Wounds that time won't heal: The neurobiology of child abuse. *Cerebrum: The Dana Forum on Brain Science, 2*(4), 50–67.

Terman, L. S. (1925). *Genetic studies of genius* (Vol. 1). Stanford, CA: Stanford University Press.

Terman, L. S. (1947). *Genetic studies of genius* (Vol. 4). Stanford, CA: Stanford University Press.

Terman, L. S. (1959). *Genetic studies of genius* (Vol. 5). Stanford, CA: Stanford University Press.

Thach, B. T, Rutherford, G. W, & Harris, K. (2007). Deaths and injuries attributed to infant crib bumper pads. *Journal of Pediatric, 151*(3), 271–274.

Thackeray, E., & Richdale, A. (2002). The behavioural treatment of sleep difficulties in children with an intellectual disability. *Behavioral Intervention, 17*, 211–231. doi:10.1002/bin.123

Tharp, R. G. (1989). Psychocultural variables and constants: Effects on teaching and learning in schools. *American Psychologist, 44*, 349–359.

Tharp, R. G., & Gallimore, R. (1988). *Rousing minds to life: Teaching, learning, and schooling in social context.* New York, NY: Cambridge University Press.

Thelen, E. (1995). Motor development: A new synthesis. *American Psychologist*, 50(2), 79–95. doi:10.1037/0003-066X.50.2.79.

Thelen, E. (1995) Time scale dynamics and the development of an embodied cognition. In R. Port & T. van Gelder (Eds.), *Mind as motion: Explorations in the dynamics of cognition* (pp. 69–100). Cambridge, MA: MIT Press.

Thelen, E., & Corbetta, D. (1996). The development origins of bimanual coordination: A dynamic perspective. *Journal of Experimental Psychology: Human Perception & Performance, 22*(2), 502–522.

Thelen, E., & Corbetta, D. (2009). Microdevelopmental and dynamic systems: Applications in infant motor development. In N. Granott & J. Parziale (Ed.), *Microdevelopment: Transition processes in development and learning* (pp. 59–79). New York, NY: Cambridge University Press.

Thelen, E., & Smith, L. B. (1998). Dynamic systems theories. In W. Damon & R. M. Lerner (Eds.), Handbook of child psychology: Vol. 1. *Theoretical models of human development* (pp. 563–634). New York, NY: Wiley.

Thelen, E., & Smith, L. B. (2006). Dynamic systems theories. In W. Damon & R. M. Lerner (Ed.), *Handbook of child psychology: Theoretical models of human development* (6th ed., Vol. 1, pp. 258–312). New York, NY: Wiley.

Theokas, C. (2009). Youth sport participation—a view of the issues: Introduction to the special section. *Developmental Psychology, 45*(2), 303–306. doi:10.1037/a0015042.

Thiedke, C. (2001). Sleep disorders and sleep problems in childhood. *American Family Physician, 63*, 277–284.

Thiessen, E. D., Hill, E. A., & Saffran, J. R. (2005). Infant-directed speech facilitates word segmentation. *Infancy, 7*(1), 53–71.

Thomas, A., Chess, S., & Birch, H. G. (1970). The origin of personality. *Scientific American*, 102–109.

Thomas, A., Chess, S., Birch, H., Hetzig, M., & Korn, S. (1963). *Behavioral individuality in early childhood.* New York, NY: New York University Press.

Thomas, K. T., & Thomas, J. R. (2008). Principles of motor development for elementary school physical education. *The Elementary School Journal, 108*, 181–195.

Thomas, M. S. C., & Johnson, M. H. (2008). New advances in understanding sensitive periods in brain development. *Association for Psychological Science, 17*(1), 1–5.

Thome, J., & Reddt, D. P. (2009). The current status of research into attention deficit hyperactivity disorder: Proceedings of the 2nd International Congress on ADHD: Proceedings from childhood to adult disease. *ADHD Attention Deficit Hyperactivity Disorder, 1*, 165–174.

Thompson, A., Hollis, C., & Richards, D. (2003). Authoritarian parenting attitudes as a risk for conduct problems. *European Child & Adolescent Psychiatry, 12*, 84.

Thompson, M., Kuruwita, C., & Foster, E. M. (2009). Transitions in suicide risk in a nationally representative sample of adolescents. *Journal of Adolescent Health, 44*(5), 458–463.

Thompson, R. A. (1994). Emotion regulation: A theme in search of definition. In N. A. Fox (Ed.), The development of emotion regulation: Biological and behavioral considerations (pp. 25–52). *Monographs of the Society for Research in Child Development*, 59(2–3, Serial No. 240).

Thompson, R. A., & Goodvin, R. (2005). The individual child: Temper, emotion, self, and personality. In M. H. Bornstein & M. E. Lamb (Eds.), *Developmental science: An advanced textbook* (pp. 391–428). Mahwah, NJ: Erlbaum.

Thompson, R. A., Laible, D. J., & Ontai, L. L. (2003). Early understandings of emotion, morality, and self: Developing a working model. *Advances in Child Development and Behavior, 31*, 137–171.

Thompson, R. A., Meyer, S., & McGinley, M. (2006). *Understanding values in relationships: The development of conscience.* In M. Killen & J. Smetana (Eds.), *Handbook of moral development* (pp. 267–298). Mahwah, NJ: Erlbaum Associates.

Thompson, R. A., & Wyatt, J. M. (1999). Current research on child maltreatment: Implications for educators. *Educational Psychology Review, 11*, 173–202.

Thorndike, E. (1933). A proof of the law of effect. *Science, 77*, 173–175.

Tice, D. M., Baumeister, R. F., & Zhang, L. (2004). The role of emotion in self-regulation: Differing roles of positive and negative emotion. In P. Philippot & R. S. Feldman (Eds.), *The regulation of* emotion (pp. 215–230). Mahwah, NJ: Erlbaum.

Tiedt, P. L., & Tiedt, I. M. (2009). *Multicultural teaching: A handbook of activities, information, and resources* (8th ed.). Boston, MA: Allyn & Bacon.

TIMSS. (2008). *Fourth International Mathematics and Science Study*. Retrieved from http://nces.ed.gov/timss/

Tobler, N., & Stratton, H. (1997). Effectiveness of school-based drug prevention programs: A metaanalysis of the research. *Journal of Primary Prevention, 18*, 71–128.

Tollefson, N. (2000). Classroom applications of cognitive theories of motivation. *Educational Psychology Review, 12*, 63–83.

Tomasello, M. (1998). Having intentions, understanding intentions, and understanding communicative intent. In P. D. Zelazo, J. W. Astington, & D. R. Olson (Eds.) *Developing theories of intention: Social understanding and self control* (pp. 63–75). Mahwah, NJ, Erlbaum.

Tomasello, M. (2002). Acquiring linguistic constructions. In D. Kuhn & R. S. Siegler (Eds.), *Handbook of child psychology* (6th ed., Vol. 2, Cognition, language, and perception, pp. 255–298). New York, NY: Wiley.

Tomasello, M. (2006). Acquiring linguistic constructions. In D. Kuhn & R. S. Siegler (Eds.), *Handbook of child psychology* (6th ed., Vol. 2, Cognition, language, and perception, pp. 255–298). New York, NY: Wiley.

Tomasello, M., Kruger, A. C., & Ratner, H. H. (1993). Cultural learning. *Behavioral and Brain Sciences, 16*, 495–552.

Tomlinson-Keasey, C. (1990). Developing our intellectual resources for the 21st century: Educating the gifted. *Journal of Educational Psychology, 82*, 399–403.

Torgesen, J. K., Alexander, A. W., Wagner, R. K., Rashotte, C. A., Voeller, K., & Conway, T. (2001). Intensive remedial instruction for children with severe reading disabilities. *Journal of Learning Disabilities, 34*, 33–58.

Touchette, E., Petit, D., Tremblay, R. E., Boivin, M., Falissard, B., Genolini, C., & Montplaisir, J. Y. (2008). Associations between sleep duration patterns and overweight/obesity at age 6. *Sleep, 31*, 1507–1514.

Towey, K., & Fleming, M. (2003). *Healthy youth 2010: Supporting the 21 critical adolescent objectives.* Washington, DC: American Medical Association.

Trachtenberg, J. (nd). Weight management: 7 ways to help your child lose weight. Retrieved from http://parenting.ivillage.com/gs/gshealth/0,,n9k5,00.html.

Trautner, H. M., Gervai, J., & Nemeth, R. (2003). Appearance–reality distinction and development of gender constancy understanding in children. *International Journal of Behavioral Development, 27*, 275–283.

Trautner, H. M., Ruble, D. N., Cyphers, L., Kirsten, B., Behrendt, R., & Hartmann, P. (2005). Rigidity and flexibility of gender stereotypes in children: Developmental or differential? *Infant and Child Development, 14*, 365–381.

Trebaticka J., Paduchova Z., Suba J. et al. (2009) Markers of oxidative stress in ADHD and their modulation by Polyhenolic extract, Pycnogenal. 2nd International Congress on ADHD. From Childhood to Adult Disease, May 21–24, 2009, Vienna, Austria. *ADHD Attention Deficit Hyperactivity Disorder* 1:33.

Tremblay, R. E. (2000). The development of aggressive behavior during childhood: What have we learned in the past century? *International Journal of Behavioral Development, 24*, 129–141.

Tremblay, R. E., Boulerice, B., Harden, P. W., McDuff, P., Perusse, D., Pihl, R. O., & Zoccolillo, M. (1996). Do children in Canada become more aggressive as they approach adolescence? In *Growing up in Canada: National Longitudinal Study of Children and Youth.* Ottawa, Canada: Statistics Canada, Human Resources and Development.

Tremblay, R. E., Nagin, D. S., Seguin, J. R., Zoccolillo, M., Zelazo, P. D., Boivin, M., . . . Japel, C. (2004). Physical aggression during early childhood: Trajectories and predictors. *Pediatrics, 113*, 43–50.

Trenholm, C., Deveney, B., Fortson, K., Clark, M., Quay, L., & Wheeler, J. (2008). Impacts of abstinence education on teen sexual activity, risk of pregnancy, and risk of sexually transmitted diseases. *Journal of Policy Analysis and Management, 27*, 255–276.

Trettien, A. W. (1900). Creeping and walking. *The American Journal of Psychology, 12*, 1–57.

Triandis, H. C. (1989). The self and social behavior in differing cultural contexts. *Psychological Review, 96*, 506–520.

Triseliotis, J., & Hill, M. (1990). Contrasting adoption, foster care, and residential rearing. In M. Brodzinsky & M. D. Schechter (Eds.), *The psychology of adoption* (pp. 107–120). New York, NY: Oxford University Press.

Troiden, R. R. (1993). The formation of homosexual identities. In L. Garnets & D. Kimmel (Eds.), *Psychological perspectives on lesbian and gay male experiences* (pp. 191–217). New York, NY: Columbia University Press.

Trost, S. G., Owen, N., Bauman, A. E., James, F., & Brown, W. (2002). Correlates of adults' participation in physical activity: Review and update. *Medicine & Science in Sports & Exercise, 34*(12). 1996–2001.

Tryon, R. C. (1940). Genetic differences in maze learning in rats. *Yearbook of the National Society for Studies in Education, 39*, 111–119.

Tsantis, L. A., Bewick, C. J., & Thouvenelle, S. (2003). Examining some common myths about computer use in the early years, *Beyond the Journal: Young Children on the Web* (pp. 1–9).

Tsiaras, A., & Werth, B. (2002). *From conception to birth.* New York, NY: Doubleday.

Tsuang, M. T., Bar, J. L., Harley, R. M., & Lyons, M. J. (2001). The Harvard Twin Study of Substance Abuse: What we have learned. *Harvard Rev Psychiatry, 9*(6), 267–279.

Tucker-Drob, E. M. (2009). Differentiation of cognitive abilities across the life span. *Developmental Psychology, 45*, 1097–1118.

Turiel, E. (1998). The development of morality. In W. Damon (Series Ed.) & N. Eisenberg (Vol. Ed.), *Handbook of child psychology: Vol. 3. Social, emotional, and personality development* (5th ed., pp. 863–932). New York, NY: Wiley.

Turiel, E. (2002). *The culture of morality: Social development, context, and conflict.* Cambridge, England: Cambridge University Press.

Turiel, E. (2006). The development of morality. In W. Damon, R. M. Lerner, & N. Eisenberg (Eds.), *Handbook of child psychology: Vol. 3. Social, emotional, and personality development* (6th ed., pp. 789–857). Hoboken, NJ: Wiley.

Turnbull, A. P., Taylor, R. L., Erwin, E. J., & Soodak, L. C. (2005). Families, professionals and exceptionality: Positive outcomes through partnership and trust (5th ed.). Mahwah, NJ: Merrill.

Turner, J. C., Meyer, D. K., Midgley, C., & Patrick, H. (2003). Teacher discourse and sixth graders' reported affect and achievement behaviors in two high mastery/high performance mathematics classrooms. *Elementary School Journal, 103*, 357–382.

Tye, M. C. (2003). Lesbian, gay, bisexual, and transgender parents: Special considerations for the custody and adoption evaluator. *Family Court Review, 41*, 92–103.

Udell, W. (2007). Enhancing adolescent girls' argument skills in reasoning about personal and non-personal decisions. *Cognitive Development, 22*, 341–352.

Udry, J. R., & Chantala, K. (2002). Risk assessment of adolescents with same-sex relationships. *Journal of Adolescent Health, 31*(1), 84–92.

Uline, C. L., & Johnson, J. F. (2005). Closing the achievement gap: What will it take? *Special Issue: Theory Into Practice, 44*(1).

Ulrich, D. A., Ulrich, B. D., Angulo-Kinzler, R. M., & Yun, J. (2001). Treadmill training of infants with Down Syndrome: Evidence-based developmental outcomes. *Pediatrics, 108*(5), e84.

Underwood, M. K. (2003). *Social aggression among girls.* New York, NY: Guilford.

Underwood, M. K., Galen, B. R., & Paquette, J. A. (2001). Top ten challenges for understanding aggression and gender: Why can't we all just get along. *Social development, 10*, 248–266.

Underwood, M. K., & Rosen, L. H. (2009). Gender, peer relations, and challenges for girlfriends and boyfriends coming together in adolescence. *Psychology of Women Quarterly, 33*(1), 16–20.

United Nations Educational, Scientific, and Cultural Organization (UNESCO). (2007). *Strong foundations: Early childhood care and education.* Retrieved from http://www.unesco .org/education/GMR/2007/Full_report.pdf.

University of Maryland Medical Center. (2009). Iron deficiency anemia—children. Retrieved from http://www.umm.edu/ency/article/ 007134.htm

Updegraff, K. A., & Obeidallah, D. A. (1999). Young adolescents' patterns of involvement with siblings and friends. *Social Development, 8*, 52–69.

USAID. (2009). *Child blindness.* Retrieved from http://www.usaid.gov/our_work/global_health/ mch/ch/techareas/child_blindness.html

U.S. Bureau of the Census. (2004). *National population projections* Retrieved from http:// www.census.gov/Press-Release/www/releases/ archives/population/001720.html.

U.S. Bureau of the Census. (2009). *Facts for Hispanic Heritage Month 2009: September 15 to October 15.* Retrieved from http://www .census.gov/Press-Release/www/releases/ archives/facts_for_features_special_editions/ 013984.html

U.S. Bureau of the Census (2010a). *State and country quick facts.* Retrieved from http://quickfacts .census.gov/qfd/states/00000. html

U.S. Bureau of the Census. (2010b). *Hispanic population of the United States: Projections.* Retrived from http://www.census.gov/ population/www/socdemo/hispanic/ hispanic_pop_presentation.html

U.S. Bureau of Labor. (2009). Labor force statistics from the current population survey. Retrieved from http://www.bls.gov/cps/ wlftable5.htm.

U.S. Census Bureau, Housing and Household Economic Statistics Division, Fertility & Family Statistics Branch. (2006). *Children in self-care, by age of child, employment status of mother, and selected characteristics for children living with mother: Summer 2006.* Retrieved from http://www.census.gov/population/socdemo/ child/table-2006/tab04.xls

U.S. Consumer Product Safety Commission, Office of Compliance. (2001). *Requirements for full size baby cribs.* Bethesda, MD: Author.

U.S. Department of Agriculture, U.S. Department of Education, and U.S. Department of Health and Human Services. (2002). *Healthy start, grow smart, your newborn.* Retrieved from http:// www.ed.gov/parents/earlychild/ready/ healthystart/newborn.pdf

U.S Department of Health and Human Services. (2001). Adoption and foster care analysis and reporting system. Rockville, MD: Author.

U.S. Department of Health and Human Services. (2005). *Dietary guidelines for Americans.* Rockville, MD: Author.

U.S. Department of Health and Human Services. (2006). *Child maltreatment 2006.* Retrieved from http://www.acf.hhs.gov/programs/cb/ pubs/cm06/cm06.pdf

U.S. Department of Health and Human Services. (2010). *Trends in foster care and adoption—FY 2002–2009.* Retrieved from http://www.acf.hhs .gov/programs/cb/stats_research/afcars/trends .htm

U.S. Department of Health and Human Services, Administration on Children, Youth and Families. (2009). *Child Maltreatment 2007.* Retrieved from http://www.childwelfare .gov.2).

U.S. Department of Health and Human Services, National Institute of Health. (2008). *What is asthma?* Retrieved from http://www.nhlbi.nih .gov/health/dci/Diseases/Asthma/Asthma_ WhatIs.html

Vaillancourt, T., Hymel, S., & McDougall, P. (2003). Bullying is power. *Journal of Applied School Psychology, 19*, 157–176

Valent, F., Brusaferro, S., & Barbone, F. (2001). A case-crossover study of sleep and childhood injury. *Pediatrics, 107*, 1–7.

Valenzuela, A. (1999). *Subtractive schooling: U.S.–Mexican youth and the politics of caring.* Albany, NY: SUNY Press.

Valkenburg, P. M., & Peter, J. (2009). Social consequences of the Internet for adolescents: A decade of research. *Current Directions in Psychological Science, 18*, 1–5.

Vandell, D. L. (2004). Early child care: The known and the unknown. *Merrill-Palmer Quarterly, 50*, 387–414.

Vandell, D. L., & Posner, J. (1999). Conceptualization and measurement of children's after-school environments. In S. L. Friedman & T. D. Wachs (Eds.), *Assessment of the environment across the lifespan* (pp. 167–197). Washington, DC: American Psychological Association.

Vandell, D. L., & Shumow, L. (1999). After school care programs. *The Future of Children, 9,* 64–80.

van der Kolk, B. A., & Fisler, R. E. (1994). Childhood abuse and neglect and loss of self-regulation. *Bulletin of the Menninger Clinic, 58*(2),145–168.

van der Mass, H. L. J., Dolan, C. V., Grasman, R. P. P. P., Wicherts, J. M., Huizenga, H. M., & Raijmakers, M. E. J. (2006). A dynamic model of general intelligence: The positive manifold of intelligence by mutualism. *Psychological Review, 113,* 842–861.

Vandermass-Peler, M. (2002). Cultural variations in parental support of children's play. In W. J. Lonner, D. L. Dinnel, S. A. Hayes, & D. N. Sattler (Ed.), *Online Readings in psychology and* culture (Unit 11, Chapter 3; Vol. 2007). Bellingham, WA: Center for Cross-Cultural Research, Western Washington University.

Vandewater, E. A., Bickham, D. S., Lee, J. H., Cummings, H. M., Wartella, E. A., & Rideout, V. J. (2005). When the television is always on: Heavy television exposure and young children's development. *American Behavioral Scientist, 48,* 562–557.

Vandivere, S., Malm, K., & Radel, L. (2009). *Adoption USA: A chartbook based on the 2007 National Survey of Adoptive Parents.* Washington, DC: The U.S. Department of Health and Human Services, Office of the Assistant Secretary for Planning and Evaluation.

van Geert, P., & Steenbeek, H. (2005). Explaining after by before: Basic aspects of a dynamic systems approach to the study of development. *Developmental Review, 25,* 408–442.

van Gelderen, A., Schoonen, R., Stoel, R. D., de Glopper, K., & Hulstijn, J. (2007). Development of adolescent reading comprehension in language 1 and language 2: A longitudinal analysis of constituent components. *Journal of Educational Psychology, 99*(3), 477–491.

van Kraayenoord, C. E., Rice, D., Carroll, A., Fritz, E., Dillon, L., & Hill, A. (2001). *Attention Deficit Hyperactivity Disorder: Impact and implications for Queensland.* Queensland, Australia: Queensland Disability Services. Retrieved from www.families.qld.gov.au.

Varela, R. E., Vernberg, E. M., Sanchez-Sosa, J. J., Riveros, A., Mitchell, M., & Mashunkashey, J. (2004). Parenting style of Mexican, Mexican American, and Caucasian–non-Hispanic families: Social context and cultural influences. *Journal of Family Psychology, 18,* 651–657.

Vartanian, L. R., Schwartz, M. B., & Brownell, K. D. (2007). Effects of soft drink consumption on nutrition and health: A systematic review and meta-analysis. *American Journal of Public Health, 97,* 667–675.

Vaughn, B. E. (2001). A hierarchical model of social competence for preschool-age children: Cross-sectional and longitudinal analyses. *Revue Internationale de Psychologie Sociale, 14,* 13–40.

Veinot, T. C., Flicker, S. E., Skinner, H. A., McClellend, A., Saulnier, P. Read, S. E., & Goldberg, E. (2006). "Supposed to make you better but it doesn't really": HIV-positive youths' perceptions of HIV treatment. *Journal of Adolescent Health, 38,* 261–267.

Venter, J. C., Adams, M. D., Myers, E. W., Li, P. W., Mural, R. J., Sutton, G. G., . . . Zhu, X. (2001). The sequence of the human genome. *Science, 291,* 1304–1351.

Ventura, S. J., Peters, K. D., Martin, J. A., & Maurer, J. D. (1997). Births and deaths: United States, 1996. *Monthly Vital Statistics Report, 46*(1), supp. 2. Hyattsville, MD: National Center for Health Statistics.

Verhallen, M. J. A. J., Bus, A. G., & de Jong, M. T. (2006). The promise of multimedia stories for kindergarten children at risk. *Journal of Educational Psychology, 98,* 410–419.

Verkuyten, M., & Thijs, J. (2001). Ethnic and gender bias among Dutch and Turkish children in late childhood: The role of social context. *Infant and Child Development, 10,* 203–217.

Vieno, A., Santinello, M., Pastore, M., & Perkins, D. D. (2007). Social support, sense of community in school, and self-efficacy as resources during early adolescence: An integrative, developmentally oriented model. *American Journal of Community Psychology, 39,* 177–190.

Volkow, N. D., Wang, G. J., Newcorn, J., Fowler, J. S., Telang, F., Solanto, M. V., . . . Pradhan, K. (2007). Brain dopamine transporter levels in treatment and drug naïve adults with ADHD. *NeuroImage,* 34, 1182–1190

Volling, B. L., & Feagans, L. V. (1995). Infant day care and children's social competence. *Infant Behavior and Development, 18,* 177–188.

Vondracek, F. W., & Porfeli, E. J. (2006). The world of work and careers. In G. A. M. D. Berzonsky (Ed.), *Blackwell handbook of adolescence* (pp. 109–128). Malden, MA: Blackwell Publishing.

Vygotsky, L. S. (1978). *Mind in society: The development of higher mental process.* Cambridge, MA: Harvard University Press.

Vygotsky, L. S. (1986). *Thought and language.* Cambridge, MA: MIT Press.

Vygotsky, L. S. (1987). *Problems of general psychology.* New York, NY: Plenum.

Vygotsky, L. S. (1987). Thinking and speech (N. Minick, Trans.). (Orig. 1934) In R. W. Rieber & A. S. Carton (Eds.), *The collected works of L. S. Vygotsky. Volume 1: Problems of general psychology* (pp. 37–285). New York, NY: Plenum Press.

Vygotsky, L. S. (1993). *The collected works of L. S. Vygotsky: Vol. 2* (J. Knox & C. Stevens, Trans.). New York, NY: Plenum.

Vygotsky, L. S. (1997). *Educational psychology* (R. Silverman, Trans.). Boca Raton, FL: St. Lucie.

Waber, D. P., De Moor, C., Forbes, P. W., Almli, C. R., Botteron, K. N., Leonard, G., . . . Brain Development Cooperative Group. (2007). The NIH MRI study of normal brain development: Performance of a population based sample of healthy children aged 6 to 18 years on a neuropsychological battery. *Journal of the International Neuropsychological Society, 13,* 1–18.

Wadsworth, B. (2004). *Piaget's theory of cognitive and affective development: Foundations of constructivism* (5th ed.). Boston, MA: Allyn & Bacon.

Wagner, K. D., & Ambrosini, P. J. (2001). Childhood depression: Pharmacological therapy/treatment. *Journal of Clinical Child Psychology, 30,* 88–97.

Wagner, N., Meusel, D., & Kirch. W. (2005). Nutritional education for children: Results and perspectives. *Journal of Public Health, 13,* 102–110. doi:10.1007/s10389-004-0091-9

Waits, B. K., & Demana, F. (2000). Calculators in mathematics teaching and learning: Past, present, future. In M. J. Burke & F. R. Curcio (Eds.), *Learning mathematics for a new century: NCTM 2000 Yearbook* (pp. 51–66). Reston, VA: National Council of Teachers of Mathematics.

Wald, J. (2001, August 29). *The failure of zero tolerance.* Retrieved from http://www.salon.com/mwt/feature/2001/08/29/zero_tolerance/index.html?sid=1046257

Walker, L. J., & Hennig, K. H. (1997). Moral development in the broader context of personality. In S. Hala (Ed.), *The development of social cognition* (pp. 297–327). Hove, England: Psychology Press.

Walker, L. J., Hennig, K. H., & Krettenauer, T. (2000). Parent and peer contexts for children's moral reasoning development. *Child Development, 71,* 1033–1048.

Walker, L. J., Pitts, R., Hennig, K., & Matsuba, M. K. (1995). Reasoning about morality and real-life moral problems. In M. Killen & D. Hart (Eds.), *Morality in everyday life: Development perspectives* (pp. 371–407). New York, NY: Cambridge University Press.

Wallerstein, J. S., Lewis, J. M., & Blakeslee, S. (2000). *The unexpected legacy of divorce: A 25-year landmark study.* New York, NY: Hyperion.

Walters, S., Barr-Anderson, D., Wall, M., & Neumark-Sztainer, D. (2009). Does participation in organized sports predict future physical activity for adolescents from diverse economic backgrounds? *Journal of Adolescent Health, 44,* 268–274.

Wang, A. Y., & Thomas, M. H. (1995). Effects of keywords on long-term retention: Help or hindrance? *Journal of Educational Psychology, 87,* 468–475.

Wang, A. Y., Thomas, M. H., & Ouellette, J. A. (1992). Keyword mnemonic and retention of second-language vocabulary words. *Journal of Educational Psychology, 84,* 520–528.

Wang, M.-C., Crawford, P. B., Hudes, M., Loan, M. V., Siemering, K., & Bachrach, L. K. (2003). Diet in midpuberty and sedentary activity in prepuberty predict peak bone mass. *American Journal of Clinical Nutrition, 77,* 495–503.

Wang, M. T. (2009). School climate support for behavioral and psychological adjustment: Testing the mediating effect of social competence. *School Psychology Quarterly, 24,* 240–251.

Wang, Q. (2004). The emergence of cultural self-constructs: Autobiographical memory and self-description in European American and Chinese children. *Developmental Psychology, 40*(1), 3–15. doi:10.1037/0012-1649.40.1.3

Wang, X., Chai, H., Lin, P. H., Yao, Q., & Chen, C. (2009). Roles and mechanisms of HIV protease inhibitor Ritonavir and other anti-HIV drugs in endothelial dysfunction of porcine pulmonary arteries and human pulmonary artery endothelial cells. *American Journal of Pathology, 174,* 771–781.

Wang, Y., & Beydoun, M. A. (2007). The obesity epidemic in the United States—gender, age, socioeconomic, racial/ethnic, and geographic characteristics: A systematic review and meta-regression analysis. *Epidemiology, 29,* 6–28.

Warden, D., & MacKinnon, S. (2003). Prosocial children, bullies, and victims: An investigation of their sociometric status, empathy, and social problem-solving. *British Journal of Developmental Psychology, 21,* 367–385.

Warren, S. L., & Simmens, S. J. (2005). Predicting toddler anxiety/depressive symptoms: Effects of caregiver sensitivity on temperamentally vulnerable children. *Infant Mental Health Journal, 26*(1), 40–55.

Wartella, E., Caplovitz, A. G., & Lee, J. H. (2004). From baby Einstein to Leapfrog, from Doom to the Sims, from instant messaging to Internet chat rooms: Public interest in the role of interactive media in children's lives. *Social Policy Report, 18*(4), 1–20.

Waters, H. F. (1993, July 12). Networks under the gun. *Newsweek*, 64–66.

Waters, H. S. (2000). Memory strategy development: Do we need yet another deficiency? *Child Development, 71*, 1004–1012.

Watson, J. B. (1924). *Behaviorism*. New York, NY: Norton.

Watters, E. (2010). *Crazy like us: The globalization of the American psyche*. New York, NY: Free Press.

Waxman, S. R., & Lidz, J. L. (2006). Early word learning. In D. Kuhn & R. S. Siegler (Eds.), *Handbook of child psychology* (6th ed., Vol. 2, Cognition, perception, and language, pp. 299–335). New York, NY: Wiley.

Way, N., & Pahl, K. (2001). Individual and contextual predictors of perceived friendship quality among ethnic minority, low-income adolescents. *Journal of Research on Adolescence, 11*(4), 325–349.

Webb, N. M., Farivar, S. H., & Mastergeorge, A. M. (2002). Productive helping in cooperative groups. *Theory Into Practice, 41*, 13–20.

Webb, N. M., & Mastergeorge, A. M. (2003). The development of students' helping behavior and learning in peer-directed small groups. *Cognition and Instruction, 21*, 361–428.

Webb, N. M., & Palincsar, A. (1996). Group processes in the classroom. In D. C. Berliner & R. C. Calfee (Eds.), *Handbook of educational psychology* (pp. 841–876). New York, NY: Macmillan.

Weber, R. (2009). Protection of children in competitive sport. *International Review for the Sociology of Sport, 44*(1), 55–69. doi:10.1177/1012690208101485

Wechsler, P. (2010, November 12). ADHD diagnoses soar in 4 years. *Columbus Dispatch*, p. A3.

Wehlage, G. G., Rutter, R. A., Smith, G. A., Lesko, N., & Fernandez, R. R. (1989). *Reducing the risk: Schools as communities of support*. New York, NY: Falmer Press.

Weil, E. (2008, March 2). Should boys and girls be taught separately? *The New York Times Magazine*, 33–45+.

Weil, J. L. (1992). *Early deprivation of empathic care*. Madison, CT: International University Press.

Weinberg, J., Sliwowska, J. H., Lan, N., & Hellemans, K. G. (2008). Prenatal alcohol exposure: Fetal progamming, the hypothalamic-pituitary-adrenal axis and sex differences in outcome. *Journal of Neuroendocrinology, 20*(4), 470–488.

Weinberg, R. A. (1989). Intelligence and IQ. *American Psychologist, 44*, 98–104.

Weinberger, D. (2001, March 10). A brain too young for good judgment. *The New York Times*, p. A13.

Weisner, T. S. (1993). Overview: Sibling similarity and difference in different cultures. In C. W. Nuckolls (Ed.), *Siblings in South Asia: Brothers and sisters in cultural context* (pp. 1–17). New York, NY: Guilford.

Weiss, M. R. (2004). *Developmental sport and exercise psychology: A lifespan perspective*. Morgantown, NV: Fitness Information Technology.

Wellman, H. M. (2004). Understanding the psychological world: Developing a theory of mind. In U. Goswami (Ed.), *Blackwell handbook of childhood cognitive development* (pp. 167–187). Malden, MA: Blackwell.

Wells, G. L., Memon, A., & Penrod, S. D. (2006). Eyewitness evidence: Improving its probative value. *Psychological Science in the Public Interest, 7*(2), 45–75.

Welsh, M. C. (2002). Developmental and clinical variations in executive functions. In D. L. Molfese & V. J. Molfese (Eds.), *Developmental variations in learning: Applications to social, executive function, language, and reading skills* (pp. 139–185). Mahwah, NJ: Erlbaum.

Wen, S., Demissie, K., Yang, Q., & Walker, M. (2004). Maternal morbidity and obstetric complications in triplet pregnancies and quadruplet and higher-order multiple pregnancies. *American Journal of Obstetrics and Gynecology, 191*, 254–258.

Wentzel, K. R. (1997). Student motivation in middle school: The role of perceived pedagogical caring. *Journal of Educational Psychology, 89*, 411–419.

Wentzel, K. R. (2002). Are effective teachers like good parents? Teaching styles and student adjustment in early adolescence. *Child Development, 73*, 287–301.

Wentzel, K. R. (2003). School adjustment. In W. M. Reynolds & G. E. Miller (Eds.), *Handbook of psychology: Educational psychology, Vol. 7*. Hoboken, NJ: John Wiley & Sons.

Wentzel, K. R., & Asher, S. R. (1995). Academic lives of neglected, rejected, popular, and controversial children. *Child Development, 66*, 754–763.

Werner, E. E. (1989). Children of the garden island. *Scientific American, 260*, 107–111.

Werner, N. E., & Crick, N. R. (2004). Maladaptive peer relationships and the development of relational and physical aggression during middle childhood. *Social Development, 13*, 495–514.

Werts, M. C., Culatta, A., & Tompkins, J. R. (2007). *Fundamentals of special education: What every teacher should know* (3rd ed.). Columbus, OH: Pearson/Allyn & Bacon/Merrill.

Wertsch, J. V. (1991). *Voices of the mind: A sociocultural approach to mediated action*. Cambridge, MA: Harvard University Press.

Wertsch, J. V., & Tulviste, P. (1992). L. S. Vygotsky and contemporary developmental psychology. *Developmental Psychology, 28*, 548–557.

Westby, C. E. (2000). *Play diagnosis and assessment*. New York, NY: John Wiley & Sons, Inc.

Westling, E., Andrews, J. A., Hampson, S. E., & Peterson, M. (2008). Pubertal timing and substance use: The effects of gender, parental monitoring and deviant peers. *Journal of Adolescent Health, 42*, 555–563.

Wheeler, V. A., & Ladd, G. W. (1982). Assessment of children's self-efficacy for social interaction with peers. *Developmental Psychology, 18*, 795–805.

White, T. G., Graves, M. F., & Slater, W. H. (1990). Growth of reading vocabulary in diverse schools: Decoding and word meaning. *Journal of Educational Psychology, 82*, 281–290.

Whitehurst, G. J., Epstein, J. N., Angell, A. L., Payne, A. C., Crone, D. A., & Fischel, J. E. (1994). Outcomes of an emergent literacy program in Headstart. *Journal of Educational Psychology, 86*, 542–555.

Whitehurst, G. J., & Lonigan, C. J. (1998). Child development and emergent literacy. *Child Development, 69*, 848–872.

Whiting, B. B., & Edwards, C. P. (1988) *Children of different worlds: The formation of social behaviour*. Cambridge, England: Cambridge University Press.

Wigfield, A., Byrnes, J. P., & Eccles, J. S. (2006). Development during early and middle adolescence. In P. A. Alexander & P. H. Winne (Eds.), *Handbook of educational psychology* (2nd ed., pp. 87–113). Mahwah, NJ: Erlbaum.

Wigfield, A., & Eccles, J. S. (2001). Introduction. In A. Wigfield & J. S. Eccles (Eds.), *Development of achievement motivation* (pp. 1–11). San Diego, CA: Academic Press.

Wigfield, A., & Eccles, J. S. (2001). The development of competence beliefs, expectancies for success, and achievement values from childhood through adolescence. In A. Wigfield & J. S. Eccles (Eds.), *Development of achievement motivation* (pp. 92–115). San Diego, CA: Academic Press.

Wigfield, A., & Eccles, J. S. (2002). Motivation beliefs, values, and goals. *Annual Review of Psychology, 53*, 109–132.

Wigfield, A., Ecces, J. S., & Pintrich, P. R. (1996). Development between the ages of 11 and 25. In D. Berliner & R. Calfee (Eds.), *Handbook of educational psychology* (pp. 148–185). New York, NY: Macmillan.

Wigfield, A., Eccles, J. S., Yoon, K. S., Harold, R. D., Arbreton, A., Freedman-Doan, C., & Blumenfeld, P. C. (1997). Change in children's competence beliefs and subjective task values across the elementary school years: A three-year study. *Journal of Educational Psychology, 89*, 451–469.

Wiley, A. R., Rose, A. J., Burger, L. K., & Miller, P. J. (1998). Constructing autonomous self through narrative practices: A comparative study of working-class and middle-class families. *Child Development, 69*, 833–847.

Wilkening, F., & Huber, S. (2004). Children's intuitive physics. In U. Goswami (Ed.), *Blackwell handbook of childhood cognitive development* (pp. 349–370). Malden, MA: Blackwell.

Willicutt, E. G., Pennington, B. F., Boada, R., Ogline, J. S., Tunick, R. A., Chabildas, N. A., & Olson, R. K. (2001). A comparison of the cognitive deficits in reading disability and attention-deficit/hyperactivity disorder. *Journal of Abnormal Psychology, 110*, 157–172.

Willoughby, M., Kupersmidt, J., & Bryant, D. (2001). Overt and covert dimensions of antisocial behavior in early childhood. *Journal of Abnormal Child Psychology, 29*, 177–187.

Wilson, A. M., Deri Armstrong, C., Furrie, A., & Walcot, E. (2009). The mental health of Canadians with self-reported learning disabilities. *Journal of Learning Disabilities, 42*, 24–40. doi:10.1177/0022219408326216

Wilson, D. (2004). The interface of school climate and school connectedness and relationships with aggression and victimization. *Journal of School Health, 74*, 293–299.

Wilson, E. O. (1975). *Sociobiology: The new synthesis*. Cambridge, MA: Belknap Press of Harvard Univ. Press.

Wilson, E. O. (2006). *Nature revealed*. Baltimore, MD: The Johns Hopkins University Press.

Wilson, N. L., Robinson, L. J., Donnet, A., Bovetto, L., Packer, N. H., & Karlsson, N. G. (2008). Glycoproteomics of milk: Differences in sugar epitopes on human and bovine milk fat globule membranes. *Journal of Proteome Research, 7*(9), 3687–3696.

Wimmer, H., & Perner, J. (1983). Beliefs about beliefs: Representation and constraining function of wrong beliefs in young children's understanding of deception. *Cognition, 13*, 41–68.

Wind, R. (2010). *Following decade-long decline, U.S. teen pregnancy rate increases as both births and abortions rise* (pp. 1–2). New York, NY: Guttmacher Institute.

Wind, W. M., Schwend, R. M., & Larson, J. (2004). Sports for the physically challenged child. *Journal of the American Academy of Orthopaedic Surgeons. 12*(2), 126–137.

Wink, J., & Putney, L. (2002). *A vision of Vygotsky*. Boston, MA: Allyn & Bacon.

Winner, E. (2000). The origins and ends of giftedness. *American Psychologist, 55*, 159–169.

Winsler, A., Carlton, M. P., & Barry, M. J. (2000). Age-related changes in preschool children's systematic use of private speech in a natural setting. *Journal of Child Language, 27*, 665–687.

Winsler, A., Diaz, R. M., Espinosa, L., & Rodriquez, J. L. (1999). When learning a second language does not mean losing the first: Bilingual language development in low-income, Spanish-speaking children attending bilingual preschool. *Child Development, 70*, 349–362.

Winsler, A., & Naglieri, J. A. (2003). Overt and covert verbal problem-solving strategies: Developmental trends in use, awareness, and relations with task performance in children age 5 to 17. *Child Development, 74*, 659–678.

Witelson, S. F., Glezer, I. I., & Kigar, D. L. (1995). Women have greater density of neurons in posterior temporal cortex. *Journal of Neuroscience, 15*, 3418–3428.

Wittmer, D. S. (2008).*Focusing on peers in the early years. The importance of relationships.* Washington, DC: ZERO TO THREE Press.

Wittmer, D. S., & Petersen, S. H. (2009). *Infant and toddler development and responsive program planning. A relationship-based approach.* Upper Saddle River, NJ: Pearson.

Wood, D., Bruner, J., & Ross, S. (1976). The role of tutoring in problem solving. *British Journal of Psychology, 66*, 181–191.

Woodward, A. L., & Guajardo, J. J. (2002). Infants' understanding of the point gesture as an object-directed action. *Cognitive Development, 17*, 1061–1084.

Woodward, A. L., Markman, E. M., & Fitzsimmons, C. M. (1994). Rapid word learning in 13- and 18-month-olds. *Developmental Psychology, 30*, 553–566.

Woolfolk, A. (2010). *Educational psychology* (11th ed.). Columbus, OH: Pearson/Allyn & Bacon.

Woolfolk Hoy, A., Davis, H., & Pape, S. (2007). Teachers' knowledge, beliefs, and thinking. In P. A. Alexander & P. H. Winne (Eds.), *Handbook of educational psychology* (2nd ed., pp. 715–737). Mahwah, NJ: Erlbaum.

Woolfolk Hoy, A., & Weinstein, C. S. (2006). Students' and teachers' perspectives about classroom management. In C. M. Evertson & C. S. Weinstein (Eds.), *Handbook for classroom management: Research, practice, and contemporary issues* (pp. 181–220). Mahwah, NJ: Erlbaum.

Wong, A. H. C., Gottesman, I. I., & Petronis, A. (2005). Phenotypic differences in genetically identical organisms: The epigenetic perspective. *Human Molecular Genetics, 14*(Review Issue 1), R11–R-18. (chart, p. R 12) Retrieved from http://hmg.oxfordjournals.org/cgi/reprint/14/suppl_1/R11

Worku, B., & Kassie, A. (2005). Kangaroo mother care: A randomized controlled trial on effectiveness of early kangaroo mother care for the low birthweight infants in Addis Ababa, Ethiopia. *Journal of Tropical Pediatrics, 51*(2), 93–97.

World Food Program. (2006). *Ending child hunger and undernutrition initiative: Global framework for action–Summary Note.* Retrieved from http://documents.wfp.org/stellent/groups/public/documents/resources/wfp111813.pdf

World Health Organization (WHO). (2004). *Global strategy on diet, physical activity, and health.* Geneva, Switzerland: Author.

World Health Organization. (2008). *Early child development: A powerful equalizer* (final report). Vancouver, BC: Author.

Wout, D., Dasco, H., Jackson, J., & Spencer, S. (2008). The many faces of stereotype threat: Group- and self-threat. *Journal of Experimental Social Psychology, 44*, 792–799.

Wozniak, J. R., Block, E. E., White, T., Jensen, J. B., & Scultz, S. C. (2008). Clinical and neurocognitive course in early-onset psychosis: A longitudinal study of adolescents with schizophrenia-spectrum disorders. *Early Intervention in Psychiatry, 2*, 169–177. doi:10.1111/j.1751-7893.2008.00075.x

Wright, S. C., & Taylor, D. M. (1995). Identity and the language of the classroom: Investigating the impact of heritage versus second language instruction on personal and collective self-esteem. *Journal of Educational Psychology, 87*, 241–252.

Wu, T., Mendola, P., & Buck, G. M. (2002). When do milestones of puberty occur? *Pediatrics, 110*, 752–757.

Xie, H., Li, Y., Boucher, S. M., Hutchins, B. C., & Cairns, B. D. (2006). What makes a girl (or a boy) popular (or unpopular)? African American children's perceptions and developmental differences. *Developmental Psychology, 42*(4), 599–612.

Yamamoto, J. A., Yamamoto, J. B., Yamamoto, B. E., & Yamamoto, L. G. (2005). Adolescent fast food and restaurant ordering behavior with and without calorie and fat content menu information. *Journal of Adolescent Health, 37*, 397–402.

Yan, J. H., & McCullagh, P. (2004). Cultural influence on youth's motivation of participation in physical activity. *Journal of Sport Behavior, 27*, 378–390.

Yan, Z. (2006). What influences children's and adolescents' understanding of the Internet? *Developmental Psychology, 42*, 418–428.

Yang L., Shuai L., Du, Q., et al. (2009). Atomoxetine and executive function in Chinese ADHD children. 2nd International Congress on ADHD. From Childhood to Adult Disease, May 21–24, 2009, Vienna, Austria. *ADHD Attention Deficit Hyperactivity Disorder* 1:135.

Yankowitz, J. (1996). Surgical fetal therapy. In J. A. Kuller, N. C. Cheschier, & R. C. Cefalo (Eds.), *Prenatal diagnosis and reproductive genetics* (pp. 181–187). St. Louis, MO: Mosby.

Yard, E. E., & Comstock, R. D. (2009). Effects of field location, time in competition, and phase of play on injury severity in high school football. *Research in Sports Medicine, 17*(1), 35–49.

Yarhouse, M. A. (2001). Sexual identity development: The influence of valuative frameworks on identity synthesis. *Psychotherapy, 38*(3), 331–341.

Yarrow, M. R., Scott, P. M., & Waxler, C. Z. (1973). Learning concern for others. *Developmental Psychology, 8*, 240–260.

Yau, J., & Smetana, J. G. (2003). Conceptions or moral, social-conventional, and personal events among Chinese preschoolers in Hong Kong. *Child Development, 74*(3), 647–658.

Yeates, K. O., & Enrile, B. G. (2005). Implicit and explicit memory in children with congenital and acquired brain disorder. *Neuropsychology, 19*, 618–628.

Yee, A. H. (1992). Asians as stereotypes and students: Misperceptions that persist. *Educational Psychology Review, 4*, 95–132.

Yee, L. (2007, December). Sports-related injuries in children and adolescents. *Emergency Medicine, 12*(11), 1–15.

Yee, M., & Brown, R. (1994). The development of gender differentiation in young children. *British Journal of Social Psychology, 33*, 183–196.

Yetman, N. R. (1999). *Majority and minority: The dynamics of race and ethnicity in American life* (6th ed.). Boston, MA: Allyn & Bacon.

Yoshinaga-Itano C., & Apuzzo, M. L. (1998) Identification of hearing loss after age 18 months is not early enough. *American Annals of the Deaf, 143*(5), 380–387.

Yoshinaga-Itano, C., Sedey, A. L., Coulter, D. K., & Mehl, A. L. (1998). Language of early- and later-identified children with hearing loss. *Pediatrics, 102*(5), 1161–1171.

Young, K. S. (1998). Internet addiction: The emergence of a new clinical disorder. *CyberPsychology and Behavior, 1*, 237–244. doi:10.1089/cpb.1998.1.237

Younger, M. R., & Warrington, M. (2006). Would Harry and Hermione have done better in single-sex teaching in coeducational secondary schools in the United Kingdom? *American Educational Research Journal, 43*, 579–620.

Youniss, J., & Ketterlinus, R. D. (1987). Communication and connectedness in mother- and father-adolescent relationships. *Journal of Youth and Adolescence, 16*(3), 265–280.

Yu, M., Lombe, M., & Nebbitt, V. E. (2010). Food stamp program participation, informal supports, household food security and child food security: A comparison of African American and Caucasian households in poverty. *Children and Youth Services Review, 32*, 767–773.

Yuill, N., & Perner, J. (1988). Internationality and knowledge in children. *Developmental Psychology, 24*, 358–365.

Zach, T., Arun, K., Pramanik, A. K., & Ford, S. P. (2007). *Multiple births.* Retrieved from http,://emedicine.medscape.com/article/977234-overview

Zahn-Waxler, C. (2000). The development of empathy, guilt, and internalization of distress: Implications of gender differences in internalizing and externalizing problems. In R. J. Davidson (Ed.), *Anxiety, depression, and emotion* (pp. 222–265). New York, NY: Oxford University Press.

Zahn-Waxler, C., Friedman, R. J., Cole, P. M., Mizuta, I., & Hiruma, N. (1996). Japanese and United States preschool children's responses to conflict and distress. *Child Development, 67*, 2462–2476.

Zahn-Waxler, C., & Robinson, J. (1995). Empathy and guilt: Early origins of feelings of responsibility. In J. P. Tangne (Ed.), *Self-conscious emotions* (pp. 143–173). New York, NY: Guilford.

Zeanah, C. H., & Fox, N. A. (2004). Temperament and attachment disorders. *Journal of Clinical Child and Adolescent Psychology, 33* (1), 32–41.

Zeanah, C. H., & Smyke, A. T. (2005). Building attachment relationships following maltreatment and severe deprivation. In L. Berlin, Y. Ziv, L. Amaya-Jackson, & M. Greenberg (Eds.), *Interventions to enhance early attachments* (pp. 195–216). New York, NY: Guilford.

Zeece, P. D. (2008). Linking life and literature in early childhood settings. *Early Childhood Education Journal, 35*, 565–569.

Zelazo, P. D., Frye, D., & Rapus, T. (1996). An age-related dissociation between knowing rules and using them. *Cognitive Development, 11*, 37–63.

ZERO TO THREE. (2009). Brain development. Retrieved from http://zttcfn.convio.net/site/PageServer?pagename=key_brain

Zhang, J., Hamilton, B., Martin, J., & Trumble, A. (2004). Delayed interval delivery and infant survival: A population-based study. *American Journal of Obstetrics and Gynecology, 191*, 470–476.

Zhang, X., Sliwowska, J. H., & Weinberg, J. (2005). Prenatal alcohol exposure and fetal programming: Effects on neuroendocrine and immune function. *Experimental Biology and Medicine, 230*(6), 376–388.

Zhou, Z., Peverly, S. T., Beohm, A. E., & Chongde, L. (2001). American and Chinese children's understanding of distance, time, and speed interrelations. *Cognitive Development, 15*, 215–240.

Zhu, W. X., Lu, L., & Hesketh, T. (2009). China's excess males, sex selective abortion, and one child policy: Analysis of data from the 2005 national intercensus survey. *British Medical Journal*, doi:10.1136/bmj.b1211

Zimmer-Gembeck, M. J., & Helfand, M. (2008). Ten years of longitudinal research on U.S. adolescent sexual behavior: Developmental correlates of sexual intercourse, and the importance of age, gender and ethnic background. *Developmental Review, 28*, 153–224.

Zimmerman, B. J. (2008). Investigating self-regulation and motivation: Historical background, methodological developments, and future prospects. *American Educational Research Journal, 45*, 166–183. doi:10.3102/0002831207312909

Zimmerman, B. J., & Schunk, D. H. (2003). *Educational psychology: A century of contributions* (A Project of Division 15 (Educational Psychology) of the American Psychological Association ed.). Mahwah, NJ: Erlbaum.

Zimmerman, C. (2007). The development of scientific thinking skills in elementary and middle school. *Developmental Review, 27*, 172–223.

Zucker, K. J., & Bradley, S. J. (1995). *Gender identity disorder and psychosexual problems in children and adolescents*. New York, NY: Guilford.

Zuckerman, D., & Abraham, A. (2008). Teenagers and cosmetic surgery: Focus on breast augmentation and liposuction. *Journal of Adolescent Health, 43*, 318–324.

NAME INDEX

SUBJECT INDEX

Note: **Bold-face type** indicates key terms.

PHOTO CREDITS

Blair Seitz/Photo Researchers, Inc., p. 6; © Frédéric Soltan/CORBIS All Rights Reserved, pp. 7, 252; Jupiterimages, p. 9; © Janet Jarman/Corbis, p. 15 (left); Fotolia, LLC – Royalty Free, pp. 15 (right), 80, 188, 374; John Eder/Getty Images, Inc./Riser, p. 21 (center); © Henry Diltz/CORBIS All Rights Reserved, p. 21 (left); Shutterstock, pp. 21 (right), 84, 107 (left), 125, 149, 422 (top left, middle left, top right), 507, 545; Courtesy of Ruth Chao, p. 17; Victor Ruiz Caballero/AP Wide World Photos, p. 32 (left); Dreamstime LLC – Royalty Free, p. 32 (right); www.operationmigration.org, p. 34; George Dodson/PH College, p. 39; Jon Brenneis/Getty Images/Time Life Pictures, p. 43; © Pixelhouse/CORBIS All Rights Reserved, p. 52; Bill Anderson/Photo Researchers, Inc., p. 60; Thinkstock, p. 82; APTV/AP Wide World Photos, p. 94; © PHOTOTAKE Inc./Alamy, pp. 98, 377; Claude Edelmann/Photo Researchers, Inc., p. 99; John Watney/Photo Researchers, Inc., p. 100; © Robert W. Ginn/PhotoEdit, pp. 107 (right), 479; © brt PHOTO/Alamy, p. 111; © Catchlight Visual Services/Alamy, p. 119; Meltzoff, A.N., Kuhl, P.K., Movellan, J. & Sejnowski, T.J. (2009). Foundations for a new science of learning. *Science*, 325, 284–288, p. 141; © David Young-Wolff/PhotoEdit, pp. 155, 199 (right); © PVstock.com/Alamy, p. 158; Paul Harrison/Photolibrary/Peter Arnold, Inc., p. 171; Gillian Craven, p. 174; © Kayte Deioma/PhotoEdit, p. 179; RAPHO Agence/Photo Researchers, Inc., p. 184; © Tony Freeman/PhotoEdit, p. 191; © Eastcott/Momatiuk/The Image Works, p. 199 (left); © Ellen B. Senisi/The Image Works, pp. 208, 219, 251, 403; © Laura Dwight/PhotoEdit, p. 210; © Inspirestock Inc./Alamy, p. 213; © Richard Lord/PhotoEdit, p. 223; Photo of Cuisenaire Rods® courtesy of ETA/Cuisenaire® © ETA/Cuisenaire, p. 233; © Rolf Bruderer/CORBIS All Rights Reserved, p. 256; © Corbis Super RF/Alamy, p. 260; Albert Bandura, Stanford University, p. 266; © Yan Liao/Alamy, p. 280; © David Halbakken/Alamy, p. 301; © Nik Wheeler/CORBIS All Rights Reserved, p. 306; © Jim West/Alamy, p. 307 (left); © Dennis MacDonald/Alamy, p. 307 (right); Bob Bird/AP Wide World Photos, p. 310; © Lin Yiguang/CORBIS All Rights Reserved, p. 311; Katelyn Metzger/Merrill, p. 324; Robert Daemmrich/Getty Images Inc. – Stone Allstock, p. 334; © Spencer Grant/PhotoEdit, p. 337 (left); Kyle Rothenborg/PacificStock.com, p. 337 (right); © Oswaldo Rivas/CORBIS All Rights Reserved, p. 341; © Jeff Greenberg/PhotoEdit, p. 353; PhotoDisc/Getty Images, p. 391; SW Productions/Getty Images, Inc. – Photodisc/Royalty Free, p. 408; Geri Engberg/Geri Engberg Photography, p. 420; Rachel Epstein/The Image Works, p. 422 (bottom left); © Images & Stories/Alamy, p. 428; Karim Kadim/AP Wide World Photos, p. 435; © Alexandre Silva/Alamy, p. 446; Getty Images Inc. – Hulton Archive Photos, p. 449 (left); Getty Images, Inc., p. 449 (right); © Blue Jeans Images/Alamy, p. 456; © KAKIMAGE/Alamy, p. 458; Science Photo Library/Custom Medical Stock Photo, Inc., p. 467; © Sean Sprague/The Image Works, p. 485; Ron Nickel/Corbis RF, p. 497; © Directphoto.org/Alamy, p. 514; © Jeff Greenberg/Alamy, p. 520; © Marco Secchi/Alamy, p. 533; © Image Source/Alamy, p. 537; © Ed Kashi/CORBIS All Rights Reserved, p. 539; Superstock Royalty Free, p. 548; © Adrian Sherratt/Alamy, p. 553; iStockphoto.com, p. 568.